W9-AHK-337

lonely planet

California
& Nevada

Andrea Schulte-Peevers
David Peevers
Nancy Keller
Marisa Gierlich
Scott McNeely
James Lyon
Tony Wheeler

LONELY PLANET PUBLICATIONS
Melbourne · Oakland · London · Paris

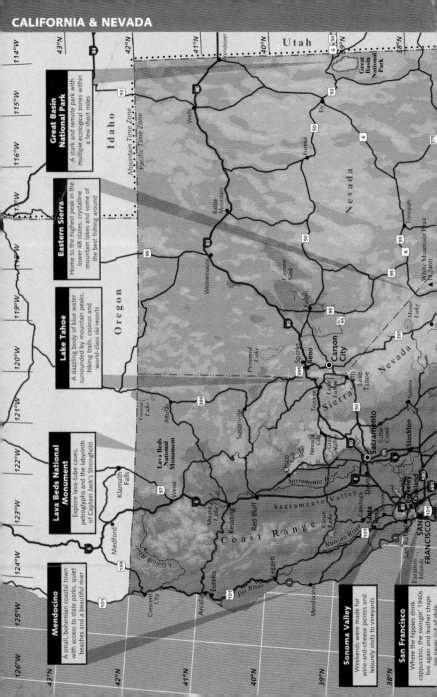

CALIFORNIA & NEVADA

Big Sur
Nature at its most breathtaking, evocative and elemental

Death Valley
A desert to die for

Las Vegas
A desert oasis of casinos, kitsch and commerce

Los Angeles
Eccentric, twisted Tinseltown and world-class art, history, architecture, museums, beaches, fine dining – you name it

La Jolla
Two miles of superior surfing, an underwater ecological preserve and superb architecture

Valley of Fire State Park
A fantasy of shapes carved in psychedelic sandstone by the elements, and well-preserved Anazasi petroglyphs

Elevation
12,000 ft
10,000 ft
8000 ft
6000 ft
4000 ft
2000 ft
Sea Level

California & Nevada
2nd edition – January 2000
First published – May 1996

Published by
Lonely Planet Publications Pty Ltd A.C.N. 005 607 983
192 Burwood Rd, Hawthorn, Victoria 3122, Australia

Lonely Planet Offices
Australia PO Box 617, Hawthorn, Victoria 3122
USA 150 Linden St, Oakland, CA 94607
UK 10a Spring Place, London NW5 3BH
France 1 rue du Dahomey, 75011 Paris

Photographs
Bancroft Library, Tom Bean, John Elk III, Lee Foster, Rick Gerharter, Mary Lou Janson, Nancy Keller, James Lyon, Scott McNeely, David Peevers

Some of the images in this guide are available for licensing from Lonely Planet Images.
email: lpi@lonelyplanet.com.au

Front cover photograph
Mission Santa Barbara (Macduff Everton/The Image Bank)

ISBN 0 86442 644 5

text & maps © Lonely Planet 2000
photos © photographers as indicated 2000
climate charts compiled from information supplied by Patrick J Tyson, © Patrick J Tyson, 2000

Printed by SNP Printing Pte Ltd, Singapore

All rights reserved. No part of this publication may be reproduced, stored in a retrieval system or transmitted in any form by any means, electronic, mechanical, photocopying, recording or otherwise, except brief extracts for the purpose of review, without the written permission of the publisher and copyright owner.

Although the authors and Lonely Planet try to make the information as accurate as possible, we accept no responsibility for any loss, injury or inconvenience sustained by anyone using this book.

Contents

1

2   Contents

NORTH COAST

CENTRAL COAST

SAN JOAQUIN VALLEY

SIERRA NEVADA   538

LOS ANGELES   601

ORANGE COUNTY   684

SAN DIEGO AREA   704

CALIFORNIA DESERTS 773

FACTS ABOUT NEVADA 818

GAMBLING 829

LAS VEGAS & CANYON COUNTRY 834

WESTERN NEVADA 872

NEVADA GREAT BASIN 891

GLOSSARY 911

TOLL-FREE NUMBERS 914

CLIMATE CHARTS 916

INDEX 920

CHAPTERS MAP INDEX

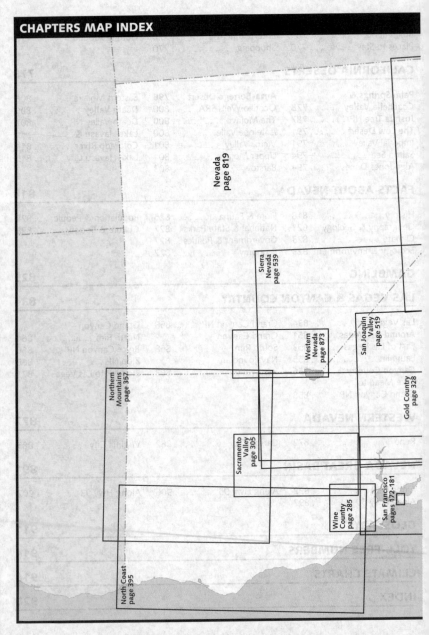

Nevada
page 819

Sierra
Nevada
page 539

Western
Nevada
page 873

San Joaquin
Valley
page 519

Northern
Mountains
page 357

Gold Country
page 328

Sacramento
Valley
page 305

North Coast
page 395

Wine
Country
page 285

San Francisco
pages 172–181

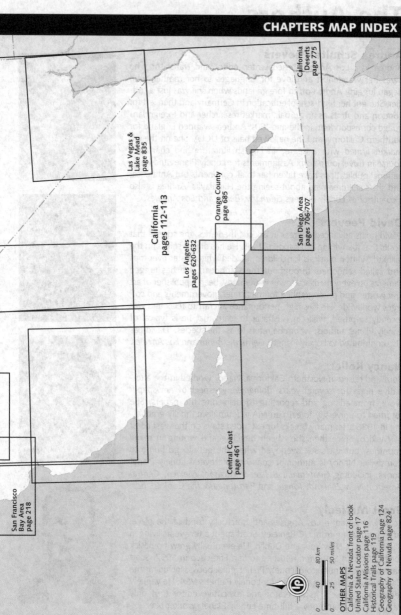

CHAPTERS MAP INDEX

California
pages 112–113

California
Deserts
page 775

Las Vegas &
Lake Mead
page 835

Orange County
page 685

San Diego Area
pages 706–707

Los Angeles
pages 620–632

San Francisco
Bay Area
page 218

Central Coast
page 461

0   40   80 km

0   25   50 miles

The Authors

Andrea Schulte-Peevers

Andrea is a Los Angeles-based writer, editor and translator who owes her wanderlust and love for languages to her mother, who began lugging Andrea off to foreign lands when she was just a toddler. She got her high-school education in Germany and then left for London and stints as an au pair, market researcher and foreign language correspondent. In the mid-'80s, Andrea swapped England for Southern California and the hallowed halls of UCLA. She hit the job market armed with a degree in English literature and charted a course in travel journalism. Assignments for Lonely Planet and international publications have taken her to all continents but Antarctica, and she's still dreaming of seeing the Himalayas. Andrea is also a coauthor of Lonely Planet's *Germany*, *Berlin* and *Los Angeles*.

David Peevers

David holds advanced degrees in eclectic theoretics, the science that posits that if anything can happen, it will. He has driven spikes on the railroad, written musicals for children, guided white-water river trips and sailed schooners throughout the Caribbean. He has lugged cameras up every medieval tower in Germany, been a publisher of art and written and photographed for magazines, governments and colleges worldwide. He flies high-performance aircraft to relax and was recently surprised, while in Australia, to learn that he is typical of Lonely Planet authors, whom he refers to as 'the species.' David has also contributed to Lonely Planet's *Germany*, *Berlin* and *Los Angeles*.

Nancy Keller

Born and raised in Northern California, Nancy worked in the alternative press for several years, doing every aspect of newspaper work, from editing and reporting to delivering the papers. She returned to university to earn an MA in journalism, finally graduating in 1986 after many breaks for extended stays on the west coast of Mexico. Since then she's been traveling and writing in many countries, but she's still overjoyed when she gets to go home to Forestville. Nancy is author or coauthor of several Lonely Planet books, including *Guatemala, Belize & Yucatán*; *Mexico*; *Central America*; *New Zealand*; *Tonga*; and *Rarotonga & the Cook Islands*.

Scott McNeely

Scott was raised in Los Angeles and is actually fond of the place. After graduating from UC Berkeley, Scott spent a few years living in San Francisco, New York and Dublin. He eventually grew homesick for the Golden State and returned to San Francisco in 1997. Scott has written for numerous Lonely Planet guidebooks, including the California and Nevada chapters for Lonely Planet's *USA*. He vaguely remembers careers as an editor and executive editor (but only vaguely) and is currently a full-time Lonely Planet worker bee.

Marisa Gierlich

Born in Hermosa Beach, California, Marisa grew up with the beach as her backyard and the Pacific Ocean as her playground. Thanks to adventurous parents, she started traveling at age six. While getting her degree in English from UC Berkeley, she wrote guides to France, Sweden, Sicily, Rome and Alaska for the Berkeley Guides, then headed 'out west' to write the Montana chapter of Lonely Planet's *Rocky Mountains*. Her ultimate goals in life are to surf the perfect wave and attain unsurpassed complete perfect enlightenment.

James Lyon

A skeptic by nature and a social scientist by training, James worked as an editor at Lonely Planet's Melbourne office before he 'jumped the fence' to become a researcher and writer. He's worked on Lonely Planet's *Mexico*, *Maldives* and *South America* guides.

Tony Wheeler

Tony Wheeler was born in England, but grew up in Pakistan, the Bahamas and the United States. He returned to England to do a degree in engineering at Warwick University, worked as an automotive design engineer, returned to London Business School to complete an MBA, then set out on an Asian overland trip with his wife, Maureen. That trip led Tony and Maureen to found Lonely Planet Publications in Australia in 1973, and they've been traveling, writing and publishing guidebooks ever since.

FROM THE AUTHORS

David Peevers & Andrea Schulte-Peevers Books like these would not be done without the help, encouragement and professionalism of a wide range of people. The following deserve special mention: Carol Martinez and Stacy Litz of the LACVB for their unstinting support, good meals and help in contacting all the right people; their colleague Marcus Bastida for opening the doors to LA's seamier sides; Jack Kyser of the LA Economic Development Corporation for sharing economic and culinary insights; and Al and Vi Peevers for their hospitality and enormous insight into Nevada lore.

We are also grateful to all the tourist office people who assisted in our research, including Tere Frank Stamoulis (Long Beach), Ann-Marie Rogers (Santa Barbara), Julien Foreman (Catalina Island), Kathleen Spalione (Laguna Beach), Connie Baker (Big Bear Lake), Amy Herzog (Monterey), DeRoy Hurst Jensen (Hearst Castle), Carol Tanis (Reno), Kay Ogden (Mono Lake Committee), Rosalind Williams (Newport Beach) and Susan Carvalho (San Luis Obispo). Heaps of thanks also to our fellow authors: Marisa Gierlich for sharing her firsthand knowledge of bars and restaurants in the South Bay cities and Rob Rachowiecki for use of his research and information on the Canyon Country.

Finally, a heartfelt thank-you to all the folks at Lonely Planet Oakland who worked so hard to make this guide a great one, including Kate Hoffman, Jacqueline Volin, Wade Fox, Elaine Merrill and the team of cartographers and designers.

Nancy Keller Innumerable people throughout Northern California were helpful with my chapters for this edition. Staff in every little chamber of commerce, visitor center and ranger station generously shared their ideas, knowledge and expertise about their areas. They are too numerous to mention each by name here, but collectively they are a great resource for travelers, and I send a heartfelt thanks to them all.

Special thanks for enthusiasm and helpfulness above and beyond the call of duty must go to Suzi Brakken of the Plumas County Visitors Bureau in Quincy, Kathleen Gordon-Burke of the Eureka-Humboldt County Convention & Visitors Bureau in Eureka, and Jody Hansen of the Arcata Chamber of Commerce & Visitor Information Center in Arcata.

Thanks also to Scott Stampfli of the Lonely Planet office in Oakland for ecological material and general enthusiasm, and to Ray Lingel of the Mattole Salmon Group, which works for restoration of salmon in Northern California's Mattole River, for information on his favorite animal.

Thanks to Forestville. (It's a poor frog that won't praise its own pond – hurrah for my hometown!) Thanks to Roon, Trish, Jerry, Azza, the Schraters, Rudy Edwards, and especially to Greater Power House COGIC and Papa Tuti, all of whom made the job brighter.

I would like to dedicate my portion of this book to my church mother, Evangelist FM Holloway, a spiritual giant and a very kind mother.

Scott McNeely Scott would like to thank Mr Bing, Kelly Green, Kurt & Emily Hobson, Amy Iannone, Ray Klinke, Peter Morris, Jane Rawson, Lisa Reile, Brett Remy, Heidi Schlegel, Tony Smiroldo, Jim Stanley, Karen Stock, John Turco. Special thanks to Teal Lewsadder. Extra-special thanks to Tom Downs, who did a superb job laying the groundwork with Lonely Planet's San Francisco city guide.

Marisa Gierlich First off, many thanks to my colleagues: David Peevers and Andrea Schulte-Peevers are a joy to work with, always upbeat and full of enthusiasm (especially regarding our beloved and too often slandered Los Angeles); Nancy Keller, besides providing a good example of how to be a kind person, is always supportive and relaxed when it comes to our shared projects – you're awesome Nancy (wherever you are); Jacqueline Volin, the senior editor, is, as always, the best lead for any task that involves lots of people and organization; Elaine Merrill and Wade Fox are a patient and strong editorial team who've been simultaneously anal and laissez-faire – a perfect combo in the world of travel writing. Thanks to all of you.

My mom, Jane, was the primary road companion this time around and is, as always, the best traveling companion anyone could ask for. Thanks for the fun research help, Mom. The Gold Country awaits our return. As do the Gaslamp Quarter and Tijuana and Catalina and Lake Tahoe and…

Jim and Carroll Terrazas provided comfortable accommodations and plenty of cynical commentary in their town they love to hate – Fresno. Ann and Stephen were troopers in Death Valley, laughing as we hid from 103°F temperatures in the pathetic shade of a Jeep.

The Burgins were great fun to explore the backcountry ski trails of Sequoia National Park with and, as always, supergenerous in their gift of food and lodging. They've also provided the best office and best rent (not to mention being the best landlords) possible. Thanks so much. Thanks also to the naturalists and rangers of Yosemite, Sequoia and Kings Canyon national parks who labored over small details to ensure accuracy. Our tax dollars at work!

Thanks to Donna and George Lee for accommodations, information, laughs and shelter from the serious storm encountered at Lake Tahoe. Jill Haky was also a great help in piecing together the best places to eat and drink in the Tahoe area, and Kim Haky was kind enough to provide accommodations and plenty of recommendations in Davis – the town she never thought she could love so much. Thanks, bra.

My San Diego brethren – Kristen, Ashley, Kate and Ian, Todd, Eric, David Singer, John and Gidon – made good suggestions and helped fill in the blanks for the San Diego chapter. Lee, at Old Town State Historic Park, was a great help in exploring the history of that place. The Lands deserve a big thanks for being themselves, as does my dad, Jim.

And last but not least, thanks to my dear husband, Paul, who puts up with my long absences and, when he can, makes my research trips more fun. Half Dome in the snow wouldn't have been the same without you, my love.

This Book

The first edition of *California & Nevada* was researched and written by James Lyon, Tony Wheeler, Marisa Gierlich, Nancy Keller and John Gottberg. This second edition was updated by Andrea Schulte-Peevers, David Peevers, Nancy Keller, Marisa Gierlich and Scott McNeely. Andrea and David worked together as the coordinating authors and wrote the introductory chapters and the Central Coast, Eastern Sierra, Los Angeles, Orange County and Nevada chapters. Nancy Keller wrote the North Coast and Northern Mountain chapters. Marisa wrote the Gold Country, San Joaquin Valley, Sierra Nevada, San Diego and California Deserts chapters, and Marisa and Nancy co-wrote the Sacramento Valley chapter. Scott wrote the San Francisco, Bay Area and Wine Country chapters.

FROM THE PUBLISHER

This second edition of *California & Nevada* is a product of Lonely Planet's US office, in Oakland, California. Many people contributed their time, energy and talent to this book. Thanks to everyone for your good work. Jacqueline Volin, as the senior editor, was an indispensible guide for the editorial team. Wade Fox and Elaine Merrill edited this book, as did freelancers Roxane Buck-Ezcurra, Susan Charles Bush and Andrew Nystrom, who helped with the copyediting. Kevin Anglin, Roxane, Susan, Shea Dean and Tullan Spitz proofread the book and the maps. Sandra Bao checked facts, phone numbers and addresses. Ken DellaPenta indexed this book.

Rini Keagy designed the cover, and Ruth Askevold, Shelley Firth and Larry Hermsen laid out the book, with guidance from senior designer Margaret Livingston. Illustrations were drawn by Hayden Foell, Wendy Yanagihara, Jennifer Steffey, Shelley Firth, Alex Guilbert, Jim Swanson, Hugh D'Andrade, John Fadeff and Lara Sox Harris.

A slew of people worked on the many maps necessary for this book. Eric Thomsen was the lead cartographer. Colin Bishop, Patrick Bock, Sean Brandt, Tracey Croom, Ivy Feibelman, Chris Gillis, Dion Good, Guphy, Mary Hagemann, Monica Lepe, Connie Lock, Kimra McAfee, Roisin O'Dwyer, Andy Rebold, John Spelman and Bart Wright drew and edited maps, supervised by Alex Guilbert and senior cartographer Amy Dennis.

THANKS
Many thanks to the travelers who used the last edition and wrote to us with helpful hints, advice and interesting anecdotes. Your names appear in the back of this book.

Foreword

ABOUT LONELY PLANET GUIDEBOOKS

The story begins with a classic travel adventure: Tony and Maureen Wheeler's 1972 journey across Europe and Asia to Australia. Useful information about the overland trail did not exist at that time, so Tony and Maureen published the first Lonely Planet guidebook to meet a growing need.

From a kitchen table, then from a tiny office in Melbourne (Australia), Lonely Planet has become the largest independent travel publisher in the world, an international company with offices in Melbourne, Oakland (USA), London (UK) and Paris (France).

Today Lonely Planet guidebooks cover the globe. There is an ever-growing list of books, and there's information in a variety of forms and media. Some things haven't changed. The main aim is still to help make it possible for adventurous travelers to get out there – to explore and better understand the world.

At Lonely Planet we believe travelers can make a positive contribution to the countries they visit – if they respect their host communities and spend their money wisely. Since 1986 a percentage of the income from each book has been donated to aid projects and human-rights campaigns.

Updates Lonely Planet thoroughly updates each guidebook as often as possible. This usually means there are around two years between editions, although for more unusual or more stable destinations the gap can be longer. Check the imprint page (following the color gap at the beginning of the book) for publication dates.

Between editions, up-to-date information is available in two free newsletters – the paper *Planet Talk* and email *Comet* (to subscribe, contact any Lonely Planet office) – and on our website at www.lonelyplanet.com. The *Upgrades* section of the website covers a number of important and volatile destinations and is regularly updated by Lonely Planet authors. *Scoop* covers news and current affairs relevant to travelers. And, lastly, the *Thorn Tree* bulletin board and *Postcards* section of the site carry unverified, but fascinating, reports from travelers.

Correspondence The process of creating new editions begins with the letters, postcards and emails received from travelers. This correspondence often includes suggestions, criticisms and comments about the current editions. Interesting excerpts are immediately passed on via newsletters and the website, and everything goes to our authors to be verified when they're researching on the road. We're keen to get more feedback from organizations or individuals who represent communities visited by travelers.

Lonely Planet gathers information for everyone who's curious about the planet – and especially for those who explore it firsthand. Through guidebooks, phrasebooks, activity guides, maps, literature, newsletters, image library, TV series and website, we act as an information exchange for a worldwide community of travelers.

Research Authors aim to gather sufficient practical information to enable travelers to make informed choices and to make the mechanics of a journey run smoothly. They also research historical and cultural background to help enrich the travel experience and allow travelers to understand and respond appropriately to cultural and environmental issues.

Authors don't stay in every hotel because that would mean spending a couple of months in each medium-size city and, no, they don't eat at every restaurant because that would mean stretching belts beyond capacity. They do visit hotels and restaurants to check standards and prices, but feedback based on readers' direct experiences can be very helpful.

Many of our authors work undercover; others aren't so secretive. None of them accept freebies in exchange for positive write-ups. And none of our guidebooks contain any advertising.

Production Authors submit their raw manuscripts and maps to offices in Australia, the USA, the UK or France. Editors and cartographers – all experienced travelers themselves – then begin the process of assembling the pieces. When the book finally hits the shops, some things are already out of date, we start getting feedback from readers and the process begins again....

WARNING & REQUEST

Things change – prices go up, schedules change, good places go bad and bad places go bankrupt – nothing stays the same. So, if you find things better or worse, recently opened or long since closed, please tell us and help make the next edition even more accurate and useful. We genuinely value all the feedback we receive. Julie Young coordinates a well-traveled team that reads and acknowledges every letter, postcard and email and ensures that every morsel of information finds its way to the appropriate authors, editors and cartographers for verification.

Everyone who writes to us will find their name in the next edition of the appropriate guidebook. They will also receive the latest issue of *Planet Talk*, our quarterly printed newsletter, or *Comet*, our monthly email newsletter. Subscriptions to both newsletters are free. The very best contributions will be rewarded with a free guidebook.

Excerpts from your correspondence may appear in new editions of Lonely Planet guidebooks, the Lonely Planet website, *Planet Talk* or *Comet*, so please let us know if you *don't* want your letter published or your name acknowledged.

Send all correspondence to the Lonely Planet office closest to you:

Australia: PO Box 617, Hawthorn, Victoria 3122
USA: 150 Linden St, Oakland, CA 94607
UK: 10A Spring Place, London NW5 3BH
France: 1 rue du Dahomey, 75011 Paris

Or email us at: talk2us@lonelyplanet.com.au

For news, views and updates, see our website: www.lonelyplanet.com

HOW TO USE A LONELY PLANET GUIDEBOOK

The best way to use a Lonely Planet guidebook is any way you choose. At Lonely Planet, we believe the most memorable travel experiences are often those that are unexpected, and the finest discoveries are those you make yourself. Guidebooks are not intended to be used as if they provided a detailed set of infallible instructions!

Contents All Lonely Planet guidebooks follow the same format. The Facts about the Country chapters or sections give background information ranging from history to weather. Facts for the Visitor gives practical information on issues like visas and health. Getting There & Away gives a brief starting point for researching travel to and from the destination. Getting Around gives an overview of the transport options available when you arrive.

The peculiar demands of each destination determine how subsequent chapters are broken up, but some things remain constant. We always start with background, then proceed to sights, places to stay, places to eat, entertainment, getting there and away, and getting around information – in that order.

Heading Hierarchy Lonely Planet headings are used in a strict hierarchical structure that can be visualized as a set of Russian dolls. Each heading (and its following text) is encompassed by any preceding heading that is higher on the hierarchical ladder.

Entry Points We do not assume guidebooks will be read from beginning to end, but that people will dip into them. The traditional entry points are the list of contents and the index. In addition, however, some books have a complete list of maps and an index map illustrating map coverage.

There may also be a color map that shows highlights. These highlights are dealt with in greater detail later in the book, along with planning questions. Each chapter covering a geographical region usually begins with a locator map and another list of highlights. Once you find something of interest in a list of highlights, turn to the index.

Maps Maps play a crucial role in Lonely Planet guidebooks and include a huge amount of information. A legend is printed on the back page. We seek to have complete consistency between maps and text, and to have every important place in the text captured on a map. Map key numbers usually start in the top left corner.

Although inclusion in a guidebook usually implies a recommendation, we cannot list every good place. Exclusion does not necessarily imply criticism. In fact, there are a number of reasons why we might exclude a place – sometimes it is simply inappropriate to encourage an influx of travelers.

Introduction

In 1510, the Spanish novelist Garci Rodriguez de Montalvo described a mythical golden island, rich beyond all dreams, ruled by the beautiful virgin Queen Calafia, giving California its name and its image some 30 years before Europeans discovered it. At that time, half of North America's indigenous population was living peacefully along the West Coast and the inland hills, finding all they needed in the sea and the forests. The early Spanish explorers, who visited the California coast in 1542, were unimpressed and did not stay. It was 200 years before the first Spanish missions gave California its architectural motif, and another 100 years before wealthy Californio cattle barons pioneered California's leisurely outdoor lifestyle.

California's frenetic energy dates from the 1849 gold rush and the state's admission to the Union in 1851. From those days up to the present, people have brought their dreams to California, where optimism is a religion, opportunity is an article of faith and reality can be made to order. The movie industry found that California had every location it wanted, from sand dunes to snow fields. Entertainment became an industry; Hollywood became the dream factory of the world; and the image of the California lifestyle became Hollywood's most successful product. However, California is also a place where problems emerge, and where solutions are tested – Los Angeles may have been the first city to experience serious air pollution from motor vehicles, but it has also been a pioneer in emission controls.

Nowadays visitors come to California not so much for its history as to gain a glimpse of the future. National trends may not all start here, but this is where they catch on first and

fastest – from supermarkets to snowboards, personal computers to health-food pizzas, vanity license plates to plastic credit cards. California is where the world discovers which way-out fad will be next year's mainstream fashion.

For the traveler, California has everything. Accommodations range from free campsites to luxury suites, and dining options range from fast food to gourmet restaurants with celebrity chefs. The cities have music, art, nightlife and every luxury and frivolity imaginable. In the suburbs, where shopping is a major leisure activity, life centers on the shopping mall. Beaches, forests, mountains, deserts, rivers and islands cater to every conceivable outdoor pursuit, from scuba diving to ice climbing, from bird watching to running triathlons. And because every pastime is an industry in California, it is the best place to see the very latest trends and equipment in windsurfing, mountain biking, bungee jumping, in-line skating, or whatever else you're into.

In California nobody needs to feel like a tourist, because here no race, accent or national origin is out of place. Californians may not distinguish between a visitor and an immigrant – they assume that anyone who visits for more than a few days will want to stay for life. Every visitor will find California at least somewhat familiar – it's just like on TV, only more so. Meanwhile, it's the Californians who act like tourists: from the surf at Mission Beach to the ski slopes of Squaw Valley, they're here to enjoy themselves, seriously.

Nevada is a state of its own, with a long historical tie with California and a long history of entertaining Californians – but it's more Wild West than West Coast. When you've had enough of the hype and commercialism of California, travel across the border and see hype and commercialism reach their ultimate conclusions in the glitter of Las Vegas. Then get back to nature in a vast expanse of uncrowded mountain ranges, deserts and lakes, and take a detour to Arizona's Grand Canyon and the national parks of southern Utah.

Only 150 years ago, California was the last outpost of European settlement, on the very edge of the known world, much less accessible than Africa or the Amazon. Now, travelers will find it's one of the most accessible places on the earth. It's also surprisingly economical if you can restrict your spending to the necessities. It has a scale, a diversity and a richness that are reflected in its landscapes, its people, its food and its mythology – it's the place where everything is possible. There may be other visions of the future, but at the moment, California is the most user-friendly, and the most fun.

Facts for the Visitor

PLANNING
When to Go
Any time is a good time to visit California, depending on what you want to do. You can enjoy hiking, canoeing, white-water rafting and other warm-weather outdoor activities in the summer, spring and fall; and skiing is good in the winter and early spring. Beaches are scenic all year, but the water tends to be cold in Northern California, where swimming is only comfortable for a month or so. In Southern California, swimming is comfortable from around May to October, though surfers and divers hit the waters year round in wet suits. Winter is whale-watching season, when gray whales migrate down the coast from Alaska.

Wildflowers bloom everywhere in spring and summer; trees, orchards and vineyards change colors in fall; and winter weather is beautiful and temperate in the desert areas. Many of the most scenic mountain areas, national forests and parks are, however, inaccessible in winter because of heavy snow. Urban attractions – museums, music and cultural performances, cafes and restaurants, zoos and aquariums – are enjoyable year round.

California has a wide variety of climatic zones, so you should consider individual towns and regions, rather than the state as a whole.

Nevada has a higher mean elevation than California, and its weather tends to be more extreme. If you're just hitting the casinos in Las Vegas and Reno, any time is fine, but the Great Basin can be bitterly cold in winter, when some of the most scenic areas are closed or inaccessible. Summers are hot but bearable, and late spring and early fall are probably the best times to explore the outdoors in Nevada. Check the Climate sections in the Facts about California and Facts about Nevada chapters.

School holidays are from early June to early September, and around Christmas and Easter. Memorial Day weekend and Labor Day weekend mark the beginning and end of the 'official' summer tourist season – the busiest season for tourism, when prices are highest. Visiting California just before or just after the summer school holidays enables you to take advantage of some brilliant weather, while avoiding the tourist rush.

Maps
If you're a member of the American Automobile Association (AAA) or one of its foreign affiliates, you can obtain superb free maps from any AAA office upon presenting your membership card (for contact information, see American Automobile Association in the Getting Around chapter). Besides folding maps of California and Nevada, AAA also produces more detailed maps covering specific regions and major metropolitan and recreation areas. Tell them where you're going, and they will give you the maps they think you'll need. Maps are available to nonmembers for around $3 to $4. AAA also produces entire tour books on individual states, including one of California and Nevada, listing all AAA-certified lodgings. These books are free to members and about $12 for nonmembers.

Visitor centers and chambers of commerce often have quite good local maps, free or at low cost. In Nevada, visitor centers give out a good color map of the state produced by the Department of Transportation. National park entrance stations or visitor centers will give you a free color map after you pay the entrance fee. US Forest Service (USFS) ranger stations sell topographical maps of the various national forests for around $4 each.

Hikers and backpackers can purchase topographic maps from the US Geological Survey (USGS) Map & Book Sales. The headquarters is in Denver, Colorado, but the store (☎ 650-853-8300) is at 345 Middlefield Rd, Menlo Park, CA 94025. A list of maps is available upon request. Many camping stores, travel bookstores, national park visitor centers and USFS ranger stations sell USGS topographic maps of their immediate area. The maps most useful for hikers are the 1:62,500 scale (approximately 1 inch to 1 mile).

Many convenience stores and gas stations sell detailed folding maps of the local area that include street name indexes. Map publishers include Rand McNally, Gousha and USA Maps Inc. They all charge around $2.50 for a big color map.

Atlases Those spending a great deal of time in California or Nevada, or those planning to do a lot of traveling off the main highways, might want to acquire the appropriate volume of the DeLorme Atlas & Gazetteer series (about $17 each). These atlases contain detailed topographic and highway maps at a scale of 1:150,000, as well as very helpful listings of campgrounds, historic sites, parks, natural features and even scenic drives. Check for these atlases in good bookstores.

The basic Rand McNally Road Atlas covers all of the US and Canada and is convenient to use in the car. For the most detailed coverage of urban areas, get the appropriate Thomas Brothers Guide, in a handy spiral-bound book format, for around $20.

What to Bring

Anything you can think of, you can buy in California or Nevada, from an alarm clock to a global positioning system that can be mounted on the handlebars of your bike. Don't bring too much, because you'll probably want to buy more things when you arrive. An old travel adage is excellent advice for California – bring half the things you think you'll need, and twice the money. The same is true of Nevada, but if you'll be gambling, you might want to leave some of your money at home.

Dress is generally casual in public places. Men will only need a jacket and tie for the fanciest restaurants or for business. Pantsuits are acceptable business attire for women, except in the most conservative industries, like banking, where a skirt is often required. When packing, be sure to choose clothes that will enable you to dress in layers. The climate varies throughout the region, and any one day can present many climatic changes; even hot days can be followed by chilly nights.

You'll need warm clothes in winter. Although winters are much warmer in the south than in the north, cold, rainy weather can still catch you anywhere, at any time. Be prepared for snow and below-freezing temperatures in the mountains.

For very hot weather, you'll need a hat, sunscreen and some light, loose clothing and pants. A water bottle and sunglasses are also essential. In the desert, long-sleeved light clothing and long pants will aid in protection from sun- and windburn and help retain moisture.

A sleeping bag is a good idea if you'll be using hostels. You can bring a tent, but rentals are usually available near parks and camping areas. Basic utensils like a cup, bowl and spoon allow you to have cereal and a drink for a light breakfast, and they're useful for kids. Some travelers bring a small immersion heater and a cup to heat up water for instant coffee or soup in their room. American coffee is sadly anemic. Those who want a decent 'jolt' should carry a small jar of instant coffee into restaurants and then 'season to taste.'

Many of these items are easily and cheaply bought after your arrival, so if you have forgotten something or don't want to weigh down your luggage, don't worry about it.

RESPONSIBLE TOURISM

The consumer society generates vast amounts of packaging, but the waste disposal industry is very efficient, too. Littering is loathed throughout California and Nevada, and travelers should show respect for the places they visit. Both states have antilittering laws and can impose hefty fines on offenders. Trash bins are everywhere you're likely to need them, and they are cleared regularly. Some neighborhoods are dirty, but in general, highways, parks and urban areas in California and Nevada are remarkably clean and free of rubbish.

You'll find recycling centers in the larger towns. Materials accepted are plastic and glass bottles, aluminum and tin cans and newspapers. Some campgrounds and a few roadside rest areas also have recycling bins next to the trash bins, so look for those. Perhaps better than recycling is to reduce your use of throwaway products. Many gas stations and convenience stores sell large plastic insulated cups with lids, which are inexpensive and ideal for hot and cold drinks. You can usually save a few cents by using your own cup to buy drinks.

When hiking and camping in the wilderness, take out everything you bring in – this includes *any* kind of garbage you may create. See the Activities chapter for more on low-impact camping.

TOURIST OFFICES
Local Tourist Offices

The California Division of Tourism (☎ 916-322-2881, 800-862-2543, www.gocalif.ca.gov), PO Box 1499, Sacramento, CA 95812-1499, mails out a useful free information packet for visitors and can answer most questions about travel in California.

The Nevada Commission on Tourism (☎ 702-687-4322, www.travelnevada.com) is also helpful in providing information. Tourism is a big part of the Nevada economy, and the commission will send you free brochures and maps that cover the whole state and provide an overview of attractions, events and lodging options.

Many towns have a visitor center, which will typically have tons of brochures and local information. The staff is usually helpful and well informed. In some places, the visitor center function is performed by the local chamber of commerce. Their offices are typically closed on weekends, and information may be limited to member establishments, often excluding worthwhile – or inexpensive – places to stay and eat.

Tourist Offices Abroad

The US has no government-affiliated tourist offices in other countries. Contact a travel agent for tourist information.

VISAS & DOCUMENTS
Passports & Visas

Canadians must have proper proof of Canadian citizenship, such as a citizenship card with photo ID or a passport. Visitors from other countries must have a valid passport, and many will also require a US visa.

However, there is a reciprocal visa-waiver program in which citizens of certain countries may enter the US for stays of 90 days or less with a passport and without first obtaining a US visa. Currently these countries are Andorra, Argentina, Australia, Austria, Belgium, Brunei, Denmark, Finland, France, Germany, Iceland, Ireland, Italy, Japan, Liechtenstein, Luxembourg, Monaco, The Netherlands, New Zealand, Norway, San Marino, Slovenia, Spain, Sweden, Switzerland and the UK. Under this program you must have a roundtrip ticket that is nonrefundable in the US, and you will not be allowed to extend your stay beyond 90 days.

Other travelers will need to obtain a visa from a US consulate or embassy. In most countries the process can be done by mail.

Your passport should be valid for at least six months longer than your intended stay in the US. You'll need to submit a recent photo 1½ inches square (37mm x 37mm) with the visa application. Documents of financial stability and/or guarantees from a US resident are sometimes required, particularly for those from developing countries. In addition, it may be necessary to 'demonstrate binding obligations' that will ensure a traveler's return to his or her home country. Because of this requirement, those planning to travel through other countries before arriving in the US are generally better off applying for their US visa while they are still in their home country – rather than while on the road.

The most common visa is a Nonimmigrant Visitors Visa: B1 for business purposes, B2 for tourism or visiting friends and relatives. A visitor's visa is good for one or five years with multiple entries, and it specifically prohibits the visitor from taking paid employment in the US. The validity period for a US visitor's visa depends on your home country. The

HIV & Entering the USA

Everyone entering the US who is not a US citizen is subject to the authority of the Immigration and Naturalization Service (INS). The INS can keep someone from entering or staying in the US by excluding or deporting them. This is especially relevant to travelers with HIV (human immunodeficiency virus). Though being HIV-positive is not grounds for deportation, it is a 'ground of exclusion,' and the INS can invoke this rule and refuse to admit visitors to the country.

Although the INS doesn't test people for HIV at the point of entry into the US, they may try to exclude anyone who answers 'yes' to the following question on the nonimmigrant visa application form: 'Have you ever been afflicted with a communicable disease of public health significance?' INS officials may also stop people if they seem sick, are carrying AIDS/HIV medicine or, sadly, if the officer happens to think the person looks gay, though sexual orientation is not legally a ground of exclusion. A visitor may be deported if the INS later finds that they have HIV but did not declare it. Being HIV-positive is not a 'ground for deportation,' but failing to provide correct information on the visa application is.

If you do have HIV but can prove to consular officials you are the spouse, parent or child of a US citizen or legal permanent resident (green-card holder), you are exempt from the exclusionary law.

It is imperative that visitors know and assert their rights. Immigrants and visitors who may face exclusion should discuss their rights and options with a trained immigration advocate within the US before applying for a visa. For legal immigration information and referrals to immigration advocates, contact the National Immigration Project of the National Lawyers Guild (☎ 617-227-9727), 14 Beacon St, Suite 506, Boston, MA 02108; or Immigrant HIV Assistance Project, Bar Association of San Francisco (☎ 415-982-1600), 465 California St, Suite 1100, San Francisco, CA 94104.

length of time you'll be allowed to stay in the US is ultimately determined by US immigration authorities at the port of entry.

If you're coming to the US to work or study, you will need a different type of visa. In the case of work, the company you're going to work with should make the arrangements. Allow six months in advance for processing the application. For information on work visas and employment in the US, see the Work section later in this chapter.

You'll need a picture ID to show that you are over 21 to buy alcohol or gain admission to bars or clubs (make sure your driver's license has a photo on it, or else get some other form of picture ID).

Visa Extensions & Reentry

If you want, need or hope to stay in the US longer than the date stamped on your pass-port, go to the local office of the Immigration and Naturalization Service (INS) *before* the stamped date to apply for an extension. Any time after that will usually lead to a not-very-amusing conversation with an INS official who will assume you want to work illegally. If you find yourself in that situation, it's a good idea to bring a US citizen with you to vouch for your character. It's also a good idea to have some verification that you have enough money to support yourself. In theory, it's also possible to call the INS at ☎ 800-755-0777 (or at the local office number found in the white pages of the telephone directory under 'US Government'), though this is usually an exercise in frustration.

Travel Insurance

No matter how you're traveling, be sure you take out travel insurance. This should cover you not only for medical expenses and luggage theft or loss, but also for cancellations or delays in your travel arrangements. Everyone should be covered for the worst possible case, such as an accident that requires hospital treatment or a flight home (see Health Insurance in the Health section of this chapter). Coverage depends on your insurance and type of ticket, so ask both your insurer and your ticket-issuing agency to explain the finer points. STA Travel (☎ 800-777-0112, www.sta-travel.com) and Council Travel (☎ 800-226-8624, www.council travel.com) offer travel insurance options at reasonable prices. Ticket loss is also covered by travel insurance. Make sure you have a separate record of all your ticket details – or better still, a photocopy of your ticket. Also make a copy of your policy, in case the original is lost.

Buy travel insurance as early as possible. If you buy it the week before you fly, you may find, for instance, that you're not covered for delays to your flight caused by strikes or other industrial action in force before you took out the insurance.

Insurance may seem very expensive, but it's nowhere near the cost of a medical emergency in the US.

Driver's License & Permits

Visitors to California and Nevada over 18 years of age can drive using their driver's license from their home state or country, as long as that license remains valid. Visitors 16 to 18 years old can drive using their home driver's license provided they obtain a Nonresident Minor's Certificate from the Department of Motor Vehicles (DMV) within 10 days of arrival in California. Nevada does not require the certificate.

If you're a foreign visitor, an International Driving Permit is a useful, though not mandatory, accessory. Local traffic police are more likely to accept it as valid identification than an unfamiliar document from another country. Permits are usually available for a small fee from your national automobile association and valid for one year. Make sure to also bring your valid national license, since you will need to present it along with the international one. Driver's licenses are also a useful form of identification when seeking access to bars, shows or other age-restricted facilities.

Hostel Card

Most hostels in the US are members of Hostelling International-American Youth Hostel (HI-AYH), which is affiliated with the International Youth Hostel Federation (IYHF). You can purchase membership on the spot when checking in, although it's probably advisable to purchase it before you leave home. Most hostels allow nonmembers to stay for a few dollars more.

Student & Youth Cards

If you're a student, get an international student identity card (ISIC) or bring along a school or university ID card to take advantage of the discounts available to students. The 1999 version of ISIC comes with a free Internet-based email account and worldwide voice and fax mail message service. Contact Council Travel (☎ 800-226-8624, www.counciltravel.com) or STA Travel (☎ 800-777-0112, www.sta-travel.com) for details.

Seniors' Cards

All people over the age of 65 get discounts throughout the US. Sometimes benefits are extended to people aged 55, 60 or 62. All you need is an ID with proof of age should you be carded. Organizations such as the American Association of Retired Persons (see Senior Travelers) offer membership cards for further discounts and extend coverage to citizens over 50 and to citizens of other countries.

Automobile Association Membership Cards

Even if you'll only be driving a little in the US, it's worth being a member of the AAA or one of its foreign affiliates in order to qualify for countless lodging and other discounts. More information is provided under Useful Organizations later in this chapter and American Automobile Association in the Getting Around chapter.

Photocopies

All important documents (passport data page and visa page, credit cards, travel insurance policy, air/bus/train tickets, driver's license) should be photocopied before you leave home. Leave one copy with someone at home and keep another with you, separate from the originals. If a document is lost or stolen, having photocopies will make replacing it much easier.

Embassies & Consulates

US Embassies & Consulates Abroad

US diplomatic offices abroad include the following:

Australia
(☎ 2-6270-5000)
21 Moonah Place
Yarralumla, ACT 2600
(☎ 2-9373-9200)
Level 59 MLC Center
19-29 Martin Place
Sydney, NSW 2000
(☎ 3-9526-5900)
553 St Kilda Rd
Melbourne, Victoria
Canada
(☎ 613-238-5335)
100 Wellington St
Ottawa, Ontario K1P 5T1
(☎ 604-685-1930)
1095 W Pender St
Vancouver, BC V6E 2M6
(☎ 514-398-9695)
1155 rue St-Alexandre
Montreal, Quebec

France
(☎ 01 42 96 12 02)
2 rue Saint Florentin
75001 Paris
Germany
(☎ 0228-33-91)
Deichmanns Aue 29
53179 Bonn
(☎ 030-238 51 74)
Neustädtische
Kirchstrasse 4-5
10117 Berlin
Ireland
(☎ 1-688-7122)
42 Elgin Rd
Ballsbridge, Dublin
Japan
(☎ 3-224-5000)
1-10-5 Akasaka Chome
Minato-ku, Tokyo
Mexico
(☎ 5-211-0042)
Paseo de la Reforma 305
06500 Mexico City

Netherlands
(☎ 70-310-9209)
Lange Voorhout 102
2514 EJ The Hague
(☎ 20-310-9209)
Museumplein 19
1071 DJ Amsterdam
New Zealand
(☎ 4-722-068)
29 Fitzherbert Terrace
Thorndon, Wellington
UK
(☎ 0171-499-9000)
5 Upper Grosvenor St
London W1
(☎ 31-556-8315)
3 Regent Terrace
Edinburgh EH7 5BW
(☎ 232-328-239)
Queens House
14 Queen St
Belfast BT1 6EQ

Foreign Consulates

Most foreign embassies in the US are located in Washington, DC, but many countries, including the following, have consular offices in Los Angeles, San Francisco and San Diego. For addresses and telephone numbers of other consulates, please consult the Yellow Pages under 'Consulates & Other Foreign Government Representatives.' For telephone numbers of embassies in Washington, DC, call that city's directory assistance (☎ 202-555-1212).

Australia
(☎ 415-362-6160)
1 Bush St
San Francisco, CA

(☎ 310-229-4800)
2049 Century Park E,
19th Floor
Los Angeles, CA

Canada
(☎ 213-346-2700)
550 S Hope St, 9th Floor
Los Angeles, CA

CUSTOMS

US customs allows each person over the age of 21 to bring 1 liter of liquor and 200 cigarettes duty-free into the country. US citizens are allowed to import, duty-free, $400 worth of gifts from abroad, while non-US citizens are allowed to bring in $100 worth. Should you be carrying more than $10,000 in cash, traveler's checks, money orders and the like, you need to declare the excess amount.

Embassies & Consulates

France
(☎ 310-235-3200)
10990 Wilshire Blvd,
Suite 300
Los Angeles, CA
(☎ 415-397-4330)
540 Bush St
San Francisco, CA
(☎ 619-239-4814)
1477 La Playa Ave
San Diego, CA
Germany
(☎ 323-930-2703)
6222 Wilshire Blvd,
Suite 500
Los Angeles, CA
(☎ 415-775-1061)
1960 Jackson St
San Francisco, CA
(☎ 619-551-5162)
2223 Av de La Playa
San Diego, CA

Ireland
(☎ 415-392-4214)
655 Montgomery St
San Francisco, CA
Japan
(☎ 213-617-6700)
350 S Grand Ave,
Suite 1700
Los Angeles, CA
(☎ 415-777-3533)
50 Fremont St
San Francisco, CA
New Zealand
(☎ 310-207-1605)
12400 Wilshire Blvd,
Suite 1150
Los Angeles, CA
(☎ 415-399-1455)
1 Maritime Plaza,
Suite 700
San Francisco, CA

(☎ 619-677-1485)
4365 Executive Drive
San Diego, CA
South Africa
(☎ 310-657-9200)
50 N La Cienega Blvd
Beverly Hills, CA
UK
(☎ 310-477-3322)
11766 Wilshire Blvd,
Suite 400
Los Angeles, CA
(☎ 415-981-3030)
1 Sansome St
San Francisco, CA
(☎ 619-459-8232)
7979 Ivanhoe St
San Diego, CA

Your Own Embassy

As a tourist, it's important to realize that your own embassy – the embassy of the country of which you are a citizen – can and can't do.

Generally speaking, your embassy won't be much help in emergencies if the trouble you're in is remotely your own fault. Remember that you are bound by the laws of the country you're visiting. Your embassy will not be sympathetic if you end up in jail after committing a crime locally, even if such actions are legal in your own country.

In genuine emergencies you might get some assistance, but only if other channels have been exhausted. For example, if you need to get home urgently, a free ticket home is exceedingly unlikely – the embassy would expect you to have insurance. If you have all your money and documents stolen, it might assist you in getting a new passport, but a loan for onward travel is out of the question.

Embassies used to keep letters for travelers or have small reading rooms with home newspapers, but these days the mail holding service has been stopped and even newspapers tend to be out of date.

There is no legal restriction on the amount of currency that may be imported, but undeclared sums in excess of $10,000 may be subject to confiscation.

California is an important agricultural state. To prevent the spread of pests, fungi and other diseases, most food products – especially fresh, dried and canned meat, fruit, vegetables and plants – may not be brought into the state. Don't bring any such items with you or, if you arrive by air, leave them on the plane or discard before going through customs. Bakery items or cured cheeses are admissible. There's the threat of potential fines and jail time if you break this law, though in reality the items in question are more likely to be simply confiscated (the fate of a wonderful Westphalian ham we once brought back from Germany).

If you drive into California across the border from Mexico or the neighboring states of Oregon, Nevada or Arizona, you may have to stop for a quick inspection and questioning by officials of the California Department of Food and Agriculture.

MONEY
Currency
The US dollar is divided into 100 cents (¢). Coins come in denominations of 1¢ (penny), 5¢ (nickel), 10¢ (dime), 25¢ (quarter) and the seldom seen 50¢ (half dollar). Quarters are the most commonly used coins in vending machines and parking meters, so have a stash of them. Notes, commonly called 'bills,' come in $1, $2, $5, $10, $20, $50 and $100 denominations – $2 bills are rare, but perfectly legal. The government has tried unsuccessfully to bring a $1 coin in mass circulation; you may get one as change from ticket and stamp machines. Be aware that they look similar to quarters.

Exchange Rates
Most banks will exchange cash or traveler's checks in major foreign currencies, though banks in outlying areas don't do so very often, and it may take them some time. It's probably less of a hassle to exchange foreign currency in larger cities. Additionally, Thomas Cook, American Express and exchange windows in international airports offer exchange (although you'll get a better rate at a bank).

At press time, exchange rates were:

country	unit		dollars
Australia	A$1	=	US$0.63
Canada	C$1	=	US$0.67
euro	€1	=	US$1.05
France	FF1	=	US$0.16
Germany	DM1	=	US$0.54
Hong Kong	HK$10	=	US$1.29
Japan	¥100	=	US$0.90
New Zealand	NZ$1	=	US$0.53
UK	£1	=	US$1.59

Exchanging Money
Cash Though carrying cash is more risky, it's still a good idea to travel with some for the convenience; it's useful to help pay all those tips, and some smaller, more remote places may not accept credit cards or traveler's checks.

Traveler's Checks Traveler's checks offer greater protection from theft or loss than cash and in many places can be used as cash. American Express and Thomas Cook are widely accepted and have efficient replacement policies.

Keeping a record of check numbers and the checks you have used is vital when replacing lost checks. Keep this record separate from the checks themselves.

You'll save yourself trouble and expense if you buy traveler's checks in US dollars. The savings you *might* make on exchange rates by carrying traveler's checks in a foreign currency don't make up for the hassle of exchanging them at banks and other facilities. Restaurants, hotels and most stores accept US-dollar traveler's checks as if they were cash, so if you're carrying these, the odds are you'll rarely have to use a bank or pay an exchange fee.

Take most of the checks in large denominations. It's only toward the end of a stay that you may want to change a small check to make sure you aren't left with too much local currency.

ATMs Automated teller machines (ATMs) are a convenient way of obtaining cash from a bank account back home (within the US or from abroad). Even small-town banks in the middle of nowhere have ATMs, and they're common at airports, supermarkets, shopping malls and in a growing number of convenience stores. Most ATMs are accessible around the clock and are affiliated with several networks, the most prevalent being Cirrus, Plus, Star and Interlink.

For a small charge, you can withdraw cash from an ATM using a credit card or a charge card. Credit cards usually have a 2% fee with a $2 minimum, and you must first have established a personal identification number (PIN). Using bank cards linked to a personal checking account is usually far cheaper. Check with your bank or credit card company for exact information.

Credit & Debit Cards Major credit cards are accepted at hotels, restaurants, gas stations, shops and car rental agencies throughout the US. In fact, you'll find it hard to perform certain transactions – such as renting a car or purchasing tickets to events – without one.

Even if you loathe credit cards and prefer to rely on traveler's checks and ATMs, it's a good idea to carry one for emergencies. If you're planning to rely primarily upon credit cards, it would be wise to have a Visa or MasterCard in your deck, since other cards aren't as widely accepted.

Places that accept Visa and MasterCard are also likely to accept debit cards. Unlike a credit card, a debit card deducts payment directly from the user's checking account. Instead of an interest rate, users are charged a minimal fee for the transaction. Be sure to check with your bank to confirm that your debit card will be accepted in other states – debit cards from large commercial banks can often be used worldwide.

Carry copies of your credit card numbers separately from the cards. If you lose your credit cards or they get stolen, contact the credit card company immediately. Following are toll-free numbers for the main credit card companies.

American Express	☎ 800-528-4800
Diners Club	☎ 800-234-6377
Discover	☎ 800-347-2683
MasterCard	☎ 800-826-2181
Visa	☎ 800-336-8472

International Transfers You can instruct your bank back home to send you a draft. Specify the city, bank and branch to which you want your money directed, or ask your home bank to tell you where a suitable bank is, and make sure you get the details right. The procedure is easier if you've authorized someone back home to access your account.

Money sent by telegraphic transfer should reach you within a week; by mail, allow at least two weeks. When the transfer arrives it will most likely be converted into local currency – you can take it as cash or buy traveler's checks.

You can also transfer money by American Express, Thomas Cook or Western Union, though the latter has fewer international offices.

Security

Be cautious – but not paranoid – about carrying money. If your hotel or hostel has a safe, keep your valuables and excess cash in it. Don't display large amounts of cash in public. A money belt worn under your clothes is a good place to carry excess currency when you're on the move or otherwise unable to stash it in a safe. Avoid carrying your wallet in a back pocket of your pants. This is a prime target for pickpockets, as are handbags and the outside pockets of day packs and fanny packs (bum bags). See Dangers & Annoyances later in this chapter.

Costs

The cost of travel in California and Nevada depends a great deal on the degree of comfort you require. Generally it's more expensive to travel alone, and moving around a lot costs more than having longer stays in fewer places. The main expenses are transportation, accommodations, food and drink, and sightseeing and entertainment.

Transportation The best way to get around is by car, except in a few central city areas, like downtown San Francisco or the Strip in Las Vegas. Car rental is available in most towns of any size. Rates can be as cheap as $100 a week for a compact or subcompact at off-peak rates. More often, though, rentals begin around $130 for a week. Liability insurance, if you are not already covered by a credit card or personal insurance policy, is usually another $7 a day, and collision insurance for the car itself may be another $9. Gas (gasoline, petrol) can be expensive in California, ranging from about $1.75 to $1.80 in the San Francisco Bay Area for a US gallon, depending on the location and grade of fuel. Remote places charge the highest prices – often higher than $2 for a gallon – so fill up in towns.

If you'll be in California more than three months, it may be worth buying a car, which will change your cost structure a little. For more information on rentals and purchasing a car, see the Getting Around chapter.

Intercity buses are inexpensive – Los Angeles to San Francisco can be as little as $30 on a special Greyhound fare. Trains are more expensive than buses, though there may be cheap roundtrip deals. The cost of flying varies greatly, but cheap tickets are available, and the prices can be competitive with bus fares (see the Getting There & Away and Getting Around chapters).

Accommodations Lodging costs vary seasonally, with prices usually the highest between Memorial Day and Labor Day and around Thanksgiving and Christmas. At ski resorts, prices naturally skyrocket during the winter months.

The cheapest option is camping, which will usually cost a minimum of around $5 for a basic site in campgrounds on public land. Developed campgrounds, public or private, charge around $12 for a tent site if there are hot showers and other facilities available. An RV site, with power and water hookups, will cost up to around $20. Camping is not really an option unless you have a car, which offsets some of the savings.

Youth hostels affiliated with HI-AYH cost around $12 for a bunk bed in a dorm room.

Independent hostels are becoming more common and charge about the same. Cheap and basic motels are also a good deal if there's more than one of you traveling. Doubles can cost as little as $30 (single rooms are not much cheaper), and a room for a family or two couples won't cost much more.

Travelers looking for more than a basic room can find very comfortable mid-range accommodations for $50 to $70 a double in most places; some towns have luxury hotels with rooms for more than $100. Any place near a beach, national park or major attraction will be relatively expensive, especially in the tourist season. Even in cheap hotels, beware of grossly inflated charges for some services, especially telephones and laundry. To avoid unpleasant surprises, ask about these before you incur any expenses.

B&Bs are not for budget travelers; they start at about $50 for a double, but most are in the $80 to $150 range. There is more information about accommodations later on in this chapter.

Food & Drink Basic food items and prepackaged meals are cheap, so if you're staying in one place for more than a few days and you have minimal kitchen facilities, you can prepare your own meals for as little as $5 for two. At the cheapest fast-food restaurants, you can get a large hamburger, soft drink and french fries for about $3 or $4. Many towns have all-you-can-eat restaurants where the starving budget traveler can fill up for about $5. Mexican or Chinese restaurants offer great meals for around $6 to $8, and a large pizza – enough for two – can be had for $10 and up. Tax and tips add to the cost of eating out, so budget a minimum of around $5 for breakfast, $7 for lunch and $12 for dinner. At better restaurants, you can eat very well for under $25 per person, including a beer or a glass of wine. At first-class restaurants, you can easily spend $100 on dinner for two. Also see the Food and Drinks section later in this chapter.

A 12oz bottle of domestic beer can range from $1.50 to $4 in a bar or restaurant. A six-pack of domestic beers costs $3 to $6 in the supermarket, while a six-pack of soft drinks is around $2, depending on the brand. A cup of coffee is usually $1.

Sightseeing & Entertainment Many of the best and most interesting things to see and do cost nothing – like walking across the Golden Gate Bridge, enjoying the coastal views from Big Sur, checking the scene at Venice Beach or browsing in a big shopping mall. But California is consumer country, and most things will cost money sooner or later. Small museums may charge as little as $1 or $2, but $3 to $6 is more common. Bigger or more commercial attractions cost more – $16 for the San Diego Zoo, $35 for SeaWorld and $38 for Disneyland and Universal Studios. Entrance into national parks and historic sites costs $3 to $20 per vehicle (irrespective of whether there are six people or just a driver) and is usually good for multiple entries over seven days. First-run movies are usually $7, but you can sometimes pay as little as $2 in budget theaters showing second-run movies.

It's easy to spend lots of money in California – there are just so many tempting shops, restaurants, attractions and activities. Venice Beach may be free, but if you rent a bike or in-line skates, buy a hot dog and a soft drink and see some irresistible souvenir, your cheap afternoon can easily cost $50. Traveling on a super-tight budget can be frustrating, even depressing, if you just can't afford to enjoy the place.

Tipping
Tipping is expected in restaurants and better hotels, and by taxi drivers, hairdressers and baggage carriers. Servers in restaurants are often paid minimum wage and rely upon tips for their livelihoods. Tip 15% unless the service is terrible (in which case a complaint to the manager is warranted) or 20% if the service is great. A quick rule of thumb for tipping in restaurants: simply double the sales tax. Never tip in fast-food, take-out or buffet-style restaurants where you serve yourself.

Taxi drivers expect a 10% tip, and hairdressers get 15% if their service is satisfactory. Baggage carriers (skycaps in airports, bellhops in hotels) receive $1 for the first bag and 50¢ for each additional bag carried. In luxury hotels, tipping can reach irritating proportions – door attendants, bellhops, parking attendants and chambermaids are all tipped. However, simply saying 'thank you' to an attendant who merely opens the door when you could just as easily have done it yourself is OK.

Special Deals
The US is probably the most promotion-oriented society on the earth. Though the bargaining common in many other countries is not widespread, you can work angles to cut costs. For example, at hotels in the off-season, casually and respectfully mentioning a competitor's rate may prompt a manager to lower the quoted price. Be confident, but don't be rude. Indicate the amount you would be prepared to pay – 'Do you have any rooms under $30?' is a good way to ask.

Visitor centers and chambers of commerce usually have lots of brochures, often with discount coupons for local attractions, restaurants and accommodations. You'll find similar brochures in motel lobbies. Free tourist information publications often have discount coupons. Sunday newspapers typically have discount coupons for local supermarkets.

Don't get too excited about all these coupons – there's usually a catch. 'Free Pizza' can mean a free version of their smallest, cheapest pizza, for a party of four, with purchase of another pizza of equal or greater value; offer not valid after 5 pm or on weekends; tax and gratuity not included. But $2 off the admission price of an attraction you wanted to see anyway is not to be sneezed at.

Taxes
Almost everything you pay for in the US is taxed. Occasionally, the tax is included in the advertised price (for example, plane tickets, gas, drinks in a bar and tickets for museums or theaters). Restaurant meals and drinks, accommodations and most other purchases are taxed, and this is added to the advertised cost.

Basic state sales taxes are 7.25% in California and 6.75% in Nevada (7% in Clark County). For meals, rooms and other purchases, there are state plus local (city or county) taxes added on to lodging, restaurant and car rental bills. As you move around California and Nevada, you'll pay different taxes in every town. The prices given in this book do not include taxes.

POST & COMMUNICATIONS
Postal Rates
Postage rates increase every few years. At this writing, rates for 1st-class mail within the US are 33¢ for letters up to 1oz (22¢ for each additional ounce) and 20¢ for postcards.

International airmail rates (except to Canada and Mexico) are 60¢ for a ½oz letter, $1 for a 1oz letter and 40¢ for each additional ½oz. International postcard rates are 50¢. Letters to Canada are 46¢ for a ½oz letter, 52¢ for a 1oz letter and 40¢ for a postcard. Letters to Mexico are 40¢ for a ½oz letter, 46¢ for a 1oz letter and 35¢ for a postcard. Aerogrammes are 50¢.

The cost for heavier letters and small parcels – sent as Priority Mail (1st-class) – airmailed anywhere within the US is $3.20 for 2lbs or less, increasing by $1.10 per pound up to $6.50 for 5lbs. For heavier items, rates differ according to the distance mailed. Books, periodicals and computer disks can be sent by a cheaper 4th-class rate. The US Postal Service (USPS) has a website at www.usps.gov.

Sending Mail
If you have the correct postage, you can drop your mail into any blue mailbox. However, to send a package 16oz or larger, you must bring it to a post office. If you need to buy stamps or weigh your mail, go to the nearest post office. Larger towns have branch post offices and post office centers in some supermarkets and drugstores. For the address of the nearest, call the main post office listed under 'Postal Service' in the US Government section of the white pages telephone directory.

Usually, post offices in main towns are open 8 am to 5 pm weekdays and 8 am to 3 pm Saturday, but it all depends on the branch.

Receiving Mail
You can have mail sent to you care of (c/o) General Delivery at any post office that has its own zip (postal) code. Mail is usually held for 10 days before it's returned to sender; you might request your correspondents to write 'Hold for Arrival' on their letters. You'll need a picture ID to collect general delivery mail. Mail should be addressed like this:

Lucy Chang
c/o General Delivery
Santa Monica, CA 90408

If you have an American Express Card or traveler's checks, you may have mail sent to any Amex (American Express) office; most major cities have branches (check the local phone book). In order for the service to be free, you must present your card or checks upon pickup. The sender should make sure that the words 'Client's Mail' appear somewhere on the envelope. American Express will hold mail for 30 days but won't accept registered post or parcels.

Telephone
All phone numbers within the US consist of a three-digit area code followed by a seven-digit local number. If you are calling locally, just dial the seven-digit number. If you are calling long distance, dial 1 + the three-digit area code + the seven-digit number. If you're calling from abroad, the international country code for the US is 1.

For local directory assistance, dial ☎ 411. For directory assistance outside your area code, dial 1 + the three-digit area code of the place you want to call + 555-1212 (for example, ☎ 415-555-1212 for a number in San Francisco). To obtain directory assistance for a toll-free number, dial ☎ 1-800-555-1212. Area codes for places outside the region are listed in telephone directories.

Be aware that, due to skyrocketing demand for phone numbers (for faxes, cellular phones, etc), some metropolitan areas are being divided into multiple new area codes. Some areas are also receiving new area code 'overlays,' in which a new area code number is added to an area with a pre-existing area code. Local calls within these areas must be made as if they were long distance calls, dial 1 + the three-digit area code + the seven-digit number.

At this writing, the 415 (San Francisco and Marin counties), 310 (in the LA metropolitan area) and 408 (along the Central Coast) areas have or will soon have overlays. None of these changes are reflected in older phone books. When in doubt, ask the operator (☎ 0). Directory assistance (☎ 411) and the emergency number (☎ 911) are still dialed with three numbers.

The 800, 888 and 877 area codes are designated for toll-free numbers within the US and sometimes from Canada as well. The 900 area code is designated for calls for which the caller pays a premium rate – phone sex, horoscopes, jokes, etc.

Many businesses use letters instead of numbers for their telephone numbers in an attempt to make it snappy and memorable. Sometimes it works, but sometimes it is difficult to read the letters on the keyboard. If you can't read the letters, here they are: 1 – doesn't get a letter, 2 – ABC, 3 – DEF, 4 – GHI, 5 – JKL, 6 – MNO, 7 – PRS, 8 – TUV, 9 – WXY. Sorry no Qs or Zs.

Pay Phones Most local calls cost 35¢. Long-distance rates vary depending on the destination and which telephone company you use – call the operator (☎ 0) for rate information. Be sure to decline the operator's offer to put your call through, though, because operator-assisted calls are exorbitant compared to direct-dial calls.

Making long-distance or international calls with cash from pay phones is expensive and frustrating, because phones are only equipped to take quarters and dimes. You will be required to deposit sufficient coins to pay for the first three minutes (after you've dialed the number, a robot voice will tell you the minimum amount that must be deposited).

Some pay phones allow the use of credits cards, but be sure to read the small print

about rates before punching in your number. You can save if the person you're calling is willing to call you back. Simply place a brief call to provide the direct number listed on the pay phone itself. Some pay phones, however, do not accept incoming calls. Usually a sign on the phone will state if this is the case.

International Calls To make a direct international call, dial 011 + the country code + the area code and phone number. (To find the country code, check a local phone book or call the operator.) International rates depend on the time of day, the destination and the telephone company used. The lowest international rates available are for calls made from phones in private homes. So if you're staying with someone, find out what they pay, then reimburse them.

Hotel Phones If you're staying at expensive hotels, resist making calls from your room. Most hotels add a service charge of 50¢ to $1.50 per call, even for local and toll-free calls, and have especially hefty surcharges for long-distance calls. Just as with pay phones, it may be cheaper to ask the person you want to contact for a callback, so you just need to relay your hotel and room number. Ironically, the cheaper the hotel, the more likely they are to levy no surcharges at all; sometimes local calls are even free.

Prepaid Calling Cards A new long-distance alternative is prepaid calling cards, which allow purchasers to pay in advance, with access through a toll-free 800 number. In amounts of $5, $10, $20 and $50, these cards are available from Western Union, machines in some supermarkets, convenience stores, tourist offices and other sources. They may be used from any phone by dialing the 800 number followed by the card code (both listed on the card itself) before entering the number you are calling. The company's computer keeps track of how much value you have left. These cards are often a good deal and are definitely a superior alternative to using coins at pay phones. Be cautious of people watching you dial in the card code – thieves memorize numbers and use them to make costly calls.

Lonely Planet's eKno Communication Card (see the insert at the back of this book) is aimed specifically at travelers and provides cheap international calls, a range of messaging services and free email; for local calls, you're usually better off with a local card. To access the eKno service from California or Nevada, dial ☎ 800-706-7333 or ☎ 213-927-0100 in Los Angeles. For further information, visit the eKno website at www.ekno.lonelyplanet.com.

Fax

Shops that specialize in office services are the best and most reasonably priced locations from which to send and receive faxes. Mail Boxes Etc and the 24-hour Kinko's Copies have franchises throughout California and Nevada. Hotel business service centers are more costly and may charge as much as $1.50 per page within the US and up to $10 per page overseas. Most hotels don't charge for receiving faxes.

Email & Internet Access

Traveling with a portable computer is a great way to stay in touch with life back home, but unless you know what you're doing it's fraught with potential problems. You may also need a US plug adapter – often it's easiest to buy these before you leave home, though they are also available at stores like Radio Shack and Circuit City, with branches throughout California and Nevada.

Another potential problem is that your PC-card modem may or may not work in the US – and you won't know for sure until you try. The safest option is to buy a reputable 'global' modem before you leave home, or buy a local PC-card modem. Keep in mind that the US uses a telephone socket different from other countries, so ensure that you have an adapter that works with your modem. For more information on traveling with a portable computer, visit www.teleadapt.com or www.warrior.com.

Major Internet service providers (ISPs) such as AOL (www.aol.com), CompuServe (www.compuserve.com) and IBM Net (www.ibm.net) have dial-in nodes throughout the US. If you access your Internet email account at home through a smaller ISP or your office or school network, your best option is either to open an account with a global ISP, like those mentioned above, or to rely on cybercafes and other public access points (like public libraries) to collect your mail.

If you do intend to rely on cybercafes, you'll need to carry three pieces of information with you to enable you to access your Internet mail account: your incoming (POP or IMAP) mail server name, your account name and your password. Your ISP or network supervisor will be able to give you these. Armed with this information, you should be able to access your Internet mail account from any net-connected machine in the US, provided it runs some kind of email software (remember that Netscape and Internet Explorer both have mail modules). A final option to collect mail through cybercafes is to open a free Web-based email account such as HotMail (www.hotmail.com) or Yahoo! Mail (mail.yahoo.com). You can then access your mail from anywhere in the world from any net-connected machine running a standard Web browser.

INTERNET RESOURCES

The World Wide Web is a rich resource for travelers. You can research your trip, hunt down bargain airfares, book hotels, check on weather conditions or chat with locals and other travelers about the best places to visit (or avoid!).

There's no better place to start your Web explorations than the Lonely Planet website (www.lonelyplanet.com). You'll find succinct summaries on traveling to most places on the earth, postcards from other travelers and the Thorn Tree bulletin board, where you can ask questions before you go or dispense advice when you get back. You can also find travel news and updates to many of our most popular guidebooks, and the sub-WWWay section links you to many of the most useful travel resources elsewhere on the Web.

Here are a few other helpful resources for travelers visiting California and Nevada:

California Division of Tourism
www.gocalif.ca.gov
(lots of travel-related information)

Nevada Commission on Tourism
www.travelnevada.com
(same thing for Nevada)

Golden State Reservations
goldenstate.worldres.com/help/
(extensive reservation network for hotels, B&Bs and resorts; membership-based, but membership is free)

California State Parks
www.cal-parks.ca.gov
(information about all California state parks and links to online campground reservations)

California Government Home Page
www.ca.gov
(general information, with topics like history, culture, doing business and environmental protection)

Eureka!
eureka.cahwnet.gov/
(amazing search engine for California state, county and city agencies; government documents in 25 languages)

Caltrans
www.dot.ca.gov
(packed with tourist assistance, route planning, mapping assistance, highway and weather conditions)

AAA Travel Services
www.csaa.com/travel
(gives members access to information from AAA tour books, reservations service and travel articles)

Travel.org
www.travel.org/na.html#usa
(comprehensive travel site with lots of links)

Hostels.com
www.hostels.com/us.html
(state-by-state list of every hostel and backpackers' place)

BOOKS

There are a vast number of books on just about every aspect of California and Nevada, and guides to the most esoteric activities. If you want to find out about art deco architecture, killer roller coasters, how to win in casinos or the gay rodeo circuit,

one of the many excellent bookstores or libraries in California or Nevada will be able to help you. Many national park offices and museums have excellent selections of specialized books and maps.

Most books are published in different editions by different publishers in different countries. As a result, a book might be a hardcover rarity in one country while it's readily available in paperback in another. Fortunately, bookstores and libraries can search by title or author, so your local bookstore or library is the best place to find out about the availability of the following recommended titles.

Lonely Planet

Lonely Planet publishes several titles that visitors to California and Nevada should find useful. Both the *San Francisco* city guide, by Tom Downs, and the *Los Angeles* city guide, by Andrea Schulte-Peevers and David Peevers, who also worked on the update of this book, are chock-full of in-the-know sightseeing, entertainment, restaurant and lodging tips. The *Las Vegas* city guide by Scott Doggett is perfect for those wanting to make an in-depth study of that city. Those with a deep interest in the Arizona and Utah Canyon Country will find Rob Rachowiecki's *Southwest USA* a fascinating read. Adventurous forays south of the border to Baja California are best accompanied by a copy of *Baja California* by Wayne Bernhardson.

Lonely Planet also publishes a series of books on the world's best diving and snorkeling areas. Called Pisces Books, the series includes the following titles: *Northern California & the Monterey Peninsula* by Steve Rosenberg, *California Central Coast* and *Southern California* by Darren Douglas, and *Baja California* by Walt Peterson. All books are available at good bookstores or may be ordered from the Lonely Planet website at www.lonelyplanet.com.

Guidebooks

Most of the main guidebook publishers have guides to California or to Californian cities. Nevada is not covered as well – guides are usually limited to Las Vegas or Reno. The

AAA tour books, free to members and affiliates, have good editions on California and Nevada and specific parts of the states, like the desert areas or Lake Tahoe, as well as guides to the main cities. Some specialized guidebooks for specific activities, like hiking and skiing, are listed in the Activities chapter. Other guides to local areas may be mentioned in the sections under those places.

Field Guides

A variety of books will help you identify Californian and Nevadan plants and animals, tell you where you can see them and give you insight into their biology.

The Peterson Field Guide series has almost 40 excellent books, including *Mammals* by William H Burt and Richard P Grossenheider; *Western Birds* by Roger Tory Peterson; *Western Reptiles & Amphibians* by Robert C Stebbins; *Western Butterflies* by Tilden & Smith; and *Southwestern & Texas Wildflowers* by Niehaus, Ripper & Savage.

There are numerous other field guides. The series of Audubon Society field guides covers birds, plants and animals, arranged by color using photos – a departure from the standard field guides, which are arranged by biological type. The Audubon Society Nature Guide *Deserts*, by James A MacMahon, gives a fine overview of the Southwestern deserts and the most important plants and animals of these regions. The Golden Field Guide series is known for its simple approach and is often preferred by beginners. The National Geographic Society's *Field Guide to the Birds of North America* is well done and one of the most detailed.

History & Politics

For an overall history of California, try *California: an Interpretive History*, by Walton Bean and James Rawls. A history of the US will help you get an understanding of California in context, because the state has a particular place in the national history and the national psyche. For a more social history, read some of the fictional works set in California at various periods (see Literature in the Facts about California chapter). To get a picture of the first European settle-

ments, read some of the works by early visitors and residents.

One of the first travelers to record his impressions of California was Richard Henry Dana, whose visits to California in 1835, during the Mexican rancho period, are recounted in *Two Years Before the Mast*. It's a good read and is widely available. Dana Point, south of LA, is named for the author.

Nevada: A Bicentennial History, by Robert Laxalt, is a somewhat idiosyncratic but entertaining history of the silver state. Another easy-to-follow history is *The Nevada Adventure: A History*, by James Hulse.

Several well-known writers have aimed their pens at Las Vegas. The infamous *Fear & Loathing in Las Vegas* is mostly about Hunter S Thompson's reactions to a wide variety of drugs, but you may have similar reactions to the city itself.

Environment

Cadillac Desert: The American West and Its Disappearing Water, by Marc Reisner, is a thorough account of how the exploding populations of Western states have exploited and argued over every drop of available water. It's relevant to both California and Nevada.

A combination travel book and geological text, *Basin and Range*, by John McPhee, is based around a drive across Nevada and Utah on I-80, and is a recommended read.

Native Americans

The best introduction to Native Americans for the serious student is the 20-volume *Handbook of North American Indians*. The areas covered in this book are found in volume eight, *California*, edited by Robert Heizer, and volume 11, *Great Basin*, edited by Warren L D'Azevedo. Another authoritative text is *The California Indians: A Source Book* by Robert Heizer and M A Whipple. With a price tag around $150, it's for the dedicated only.

NEWSPAPERS & MAGAZINES

Over 1500 daily newspapers are published in the US. The newspaper with the highest circulation is the *Wall Street Journal*, followed by *USA Today*, the *New York Times* and the *Los Angeles Times*, which are all available in major cities. Besides the *Los Angeles Times*, California's most widely read newspapers are the *San Francisco Chronicle* and the *San Diego Union-Tribune*. These newspapers' Sunday editions have supplements listing the coming week's events in arts and entertainment. The *Las Vegas Review-Journal* is the largest paper in Nevada. Other large papers are the *Las Vegas Sun* and the *Reno Gazette-Journal*.

Most other cities have a local daily newspaper. These papers are worth looking at to get an idea of the local issues in the areas you visit – bridge congestion in the Bay Area, salination in the Imperial Valley, or gambling revenues in Reno.

Newspapers such as the *SF Weekly*, the *San Francisco Bay Guardian*, the *LA Weekly* and the *San Diego Reader* are independent and have well-written stories concerning local and national news and current entertainment listings including restaurant and theater reviews.

RADIO

All rental cars have car radios. Most stations have a range of less than 100 miles, so you'll have to keep changing stations as you drive. In the southern parts of California, Mexican stations can easily be picked up, but they're hard to distinguish from the US stations broadcasting in Spanish. In and near major cities, there's a wide variety of music and entertainment. In rural areas, be prepared for a predominance of country & western music, Christian programming, local news and 'talk radio.'

National Public Radio (NPR) features a more level-headed approach to news, discussion and music. NPR normally broadcasts on the lower end of the FM band.

TV

Even the cheapest motel rooms have a color TV, though sometimes the set won't work very well. Most motel TVs receive the local affiliates of the five networks that dominate American broadcast television – ABC, CBS, NBC, FOX and PBS. PBS, the Public Broadcasting System, is not commercial, and has a quite good news service and some thoughtful current affairs programming, including the *NewsHour with Jim Lehrer*. Other PBS programs feature educational shows, classical music and theater and quite a few BBC productions.

Better motels have TV with access to cable stations, usually ESPN (all sports), CNN (all news), the Weather Channel (you guessed it) and HBO (movies). Pay-per-view events or movies are going to cost you and usually only better hotels carry the service. Check with the front desk if you're unsure.

PHOTOGRAPHY & VIDEO
Film & Equipment

Print film is widely available at supermarkets and discount drugstores. In general, buy film for the purpose you intend to use it. For general shooting – either prints or slides – 100 ASA film is just about the most useful and versatile, as it gives you good color and enough speed to capture most situations on film. If you plan to shoot in dark areas or in brightly lit night scenes without a tripod, switch to 400 ASA.

The best and most widely available films are made by Fuji and Kodak. Fuji Velvia and Kodak Elite are easy to process and provide good slide images. Stay away from Kodachrome: it's difficult to process quickly and generates lots of headaches if not handled properly. For print film, you can't beat Kodak Gold, though Fuji is comparable and Agfa is coming along.

Film can be damaged by excessive heat, so avoid leaving your camera and film in the car or placing them on the dash while you're driving.

Carry a spare battery for your camera to avoid disappointment when your camera dies in the middle of nowhere. If you're buying a new camera for your trip, do so several weeks before you leave and practice using it.

Drugstores are good places to get your film processed cheaply. If you drop it off by noon, you can usually pick it up the next day. A roll of 100 ASA 35mm color film with 24 exposures will cost about $6 to get processed. Many places offer double sets of prints for much less than double the cost. One-hour processing services, though, charge up to $11 per 24-exposure roll.

Technical Tips

Proverbially sunny California offers plenty of light for photography, especially in the southern and desert areas. When sunlight is strong and the sun is high in the sky, photographs of people tend to have harsh shadows. It's best to shoot during early morning and late afternoon.

A polarizing filter is a most useful piece of gear as it deepens the blue of the sky and water, can eliminate many reflections and makes clouds appear quite dramatic. It's best used to photograph scenes in nature, but using a filter at high altitudes where the sky is already deep blue can result in pictures with a nearly black and unrealistic sky. The effect of a polarizer is strongest when you point your camera 90° away from the sun. By spinning the filter around, you'll see a pretty fair approximation of what the effect will be.

In forests, you'll find that light levels are surprisingly low, and fast film or using your camera's fill-flash function may be helpful. A monopod or lightweight tripod is an invaluable piece of gear for 'steadying up' your camera for slow exposure times or when using a telephoto lens, also allowing you to take those great night shots of neon, theater marquees and 'streaking taillights' shots of cars rushing along city streets.

Video Systems

The US uses the National Television System Committee (NTSC) color TV standard. Unless converted it is not compatible with other standards – Phase Alternative Line (PAL), Système Electronique Couleur avec Memoire (SECAM) – used in Africa, Europe, Asia and Australia.

Photographing People

Californians tend to be deferential around photographers and will make a point of not walking in front of your camera, even if you want them to. No one seems to mind being

photographed in the context of an overall scene, but if you want a close-up shot, you should ask for permission first. Then the problem is making the subject look natural. Native Americans on reservations may prefer not to be photographed, or they may ask for payment.

Airport Security

All flight passengers have to pass their luggage through X-ray machines. In general, airport X-ray technology isn't supposed to jeopardize lower-speed film (under 1600 ASA). Recently, however, new high-powered machines designed to inspect *checked* luggage have been installed at major airports around the world. These machines are capable of conducting high-energy scans that may destroy unprocessed film. Be sure to carry film and loaded cameras in your hand luggage and ask airport security people to inspect it manually. Pack all your film into a clear plastic bag that you can quickly whip out of your luggage. This saves time at the inspection points and helps minimize confrontations with security staff. In this age of terrorism, their job is tough, but they can also add to your preflight hell if not treated with respect.

TIME

California and Nevada are on Pacific Standard Time, which is Greenwich Mean Time minus eight hours. Thus when it is noon in Los Angeles, it is 8 pm in London, 9 am in Honolulu, 3 pm in New York, 4 am (the next day) in Singapore and 6 am (the next day) in Sydney or Auckland.

Daylight saving time is in effect from the first Sunday in April to the last Sunday in October. Clocks are set ahead one hour in the spring ('spring forward'), and set back one hour in the fall ('fall back'), meaning that sunset is an hour later during the long days of summer. Since most US states (exceptions include Hawaii and Arizona) do this, the time differences remain constant within the country, but they may create an hour of difference in relation to other countries (who may also observe their own daylight saving hours).

ELECTRICITY

Electric current in the US is 110V, and outlets are suited for flat two-prong or three-prong (two flat, one round) plugs. If your appliance is made for another electrical system, you will need a transformer or adapter; if you didn't bring one along, check drugstores, hardware or consumer electronics stores.

WEIGHTS & MEASURES

When it comes to measurement, California and Nevada are no different from the rest of the US, which clings stubbornly to its system based on the British imperial system. Distances are in inches, feet, yards and miles. Three feet equals one yard (.914 meters); 1760 yards, or 5280 feet, are 1 mile (1.6km).

Dry weights are in ounces (oz), pounds (lb) and tons (16oz equal 1lb; 2000lb equal 1 ton). There are 454 grams in 1lb.

Liquid measures differ from dry measures in that 1 pint equals 16 fluid oz; 2 pints equal 1 quart, 4 quarts make a US gallon – or 3.8 liters. Gasoline is also dispensed by the US gallon.

Temperature is given in degrees Fahrenheit, whereby 32° is the freezing point (0° Celsius); it's virtually impossible it will drop below that level during your stay in California. More commonly, the temperature will hover between 70° and 90°F (21° and 32°C).

For information at a glance, see the conversion chart on the inside back cover of this book.

LAUNDRY

Most towns of any size and better campgrounds have self-service coin-operated laundry facilities. Washing a load costs about $1, and drying it another $1. Coin-operated vending machines sell single-wash packages of detergent, but it's usually cheaper to pick up a small box at the supermarket. Some laundries have attendants who will wash, dry and fold your clothes for you for an additional charge. To find a laundry, look under 'Laundries' or 'Laundries – Self-Service' in the Yellow Pages of the telephone directory. Dry cleaners are also listed under 'Laundries' or 'Cleaners.'

TOILETS

Foreign visitors will soon realize that a certain prudery is common in the US concerning this most basic human need. Toilets are never called 'toilets' but a slew of euphemisms such as 'rest room,' 'bathroom,' 'powder room,' 'men's room,' 'ladies' room,' 'washroom' and 'little boys' room' or 'little girls' room.'

Public toilets are hard to come by, so you have to get a little more assertive and creative in finding facilities. Shopping malls and department stores, hotel lobbies, museums and other public places are your best bets. Ducking into a bar is an OK alternative, though keep in mind that you have to be over 21 to even enter and may be carded at the entrance. Casual restaurants, like diners or cafes, are usually an option, but in fancy restaurants a host or hostess may stop you.

Except in emergencies, don't even bother with places posting signs saying something like 'No public rest room' or 'No public facilities.' Though ubiquitous, gas station toilets can be dirty, and you often have to ask the cashier for the key. Many public beaches have decent facilities.

HEALTH

For most foreign visitors, no immunizations are required for entry, though cholera and yellow fever vaccinations may be required of travelers from areas with a history of those diseases.

Generally speaking, the US is a healthy place to visit. No prevalent diseases or risks are associated with traveling here, and the country is well served by hospitals. However, because of the high cost of health care, international travelers should take out comprehensive travel insurance before they leave home (see Health Insurance in this section).

Should you fall ill, avoid going to emergency rooms. Although these are often the easiest places to go for treatment, they are also incredibly expensive. Many city hospitals have 'urgent care clinics,' which are designed to deal with walk-in clients with less than catastrophic injuries and illnesses.

You'll pay a lot less for treatment at these clinics. If you know someone in the area, consider asking them to call their doctor: often private doctors are willing to examine foreign visitors as a courtesy to their regular patients, but a fee, often around $100, may still be applied.

In a serious emergency, call ☎ 911 for an ambulance to take you to the nearest hospital's emergency room.

Predeparture Preparations

Make sure you're healthy before you start traveling. If you are embarking on a long trip, make sure your teeth are in good shape. If you wear glasses, take a spare pair and your prescription. You can get new eyeglasses made up quickly and competently for as little as $50 to $100, depending on the prescription and frame you choose. Cheap reading glasses are available for as little as $10 at many large pharmacies. If you require a particular medication, take an adequate supply and bring a prescription in case you lose your supply. Diabetics should contact their physician before traveling.

Health Insurance

Health care is excellent in most of California and Nevada, but it's also very expensive. Without insurance even minor health concerns can easily bust your entire travel budget. Unless your health plan at home provides worldwide coverage, definitely take out travel health insurance (see Travel Insurance in the Visas & Documents section earlier in this chapter). Without evidence of insurance, some hospitals may refuse care in all but life-threatening emergencies and refer you to a public or county hospital where you may be faced with long waits and possibly inferior care.

Wide varieties of policies are available and your travel agent should have recommendations. International student travel policies handled by STA Travel and other organizations are usually good value. Highly regarded insurers are Access America (☎ 800-284-8300) and Travel Guard (☎ 800-826-1300). Some policies specifically exclude 'dangerous activities' like scuba diving, motorcycling and even trekking. If these activities are on your agenda, search for policies that include them.

While you may find a policy that pays doctors or hospitals directly, be aware that many private doctors and clinics will still demand payment at the time of service if you're not a local resident. Unless you need acute treatment, it's best to call around and choose a doctor willing to accept your insurance.

Medical Kit

If you're going off the beaten path, it's wise to take a small, straightforward medical kit with you. This should include at least the following:

- ☐ **Aspirin, acetaminophen** or **Panadol** – for pain or fever
- ☐ **Antihistamine** (such as Benadryl) – which is useful as a decongestant for colds; to ease the itch from allergies, insect bites or stings; or to help prevent motion sickness
- ☐ **Bismuth subsalicylate** preparation (Pepto-Bismol), **Imodium** or **Lomotil** – for stomach upsets
- ☐ **Rehydration mixture** – to treat severe diarrhea, which is particularly important if you're traveling with children
- ☐ **Antiseptic, mercurochrome** and **antibiotic powder** or similar 'dry' spray – for cuts and grazes
- ☐ **Calamine lotion** – to ease irritation from bites or stings
- ☐ **Cold and flu tablets** and **throat lozenges** – pseudoephedrine hydrochloride (Sudafed) may be useful if you are flying with a cold, to avoid ear damage
- ☐ **Bandages** and **Band-Aids** – for minor injuries
- ☐ **Scissors, tweezers** and a **thermometer** (note that airlines prohibit mercury thermometers)
- ☐ **Insect repellent, sunscreen lotion, lip balm** and **water purification tablets**

No matter what the circumstances, be sure to keep all receipts and documentation. Some policies ask you to call back (reverse charges) to a center in your home country for an immediate assessment of your problem. Also check whether the policy covers ambulance fees or an emergency flight home.

Food & Water

Care in what you eat and drink is the most important health rule; stomach upsets are the most common travel health problem (between 30% and 50% of travelers in a two-week stay experience them), but the majority of these upsets will be relatively minor. US standards of cleanliness in places serving food and drink are very high.

Bottled drinking water, both carbonated and noncarbonated, is widely available in the US. Tap water is always OK to drink, though not always very tasty.

In hot climates, make sure you drink enough water – don't rely on feeling thirsty to indicate when you should drink. Not needing to urinate or very dark yellow urine is a danger sign. Always carry a water bottle with you on long trips and *never* drink directly from any stream or river, regardless how fresh the water might look. They *all* may have a giardia or 'beaver fever' – a most unpleasant little bugger that makes being seasick seem pleasant by comparison. *Always* thoroughly purify any water taken from rivers and streams.

Travel- & Climate-Related Problems

Motion Sickness Eating lightly before and during a trip will reduce the chances of motion sickness. If you are prone to motion sickness, try to find a place that minimizes disturbance – for example, near the wing on aircraft or near the center on buses and boats. Fresh air usually helps. Commercial anti-motion-sickness preparations, which can cause drowsiness, have to be taken before the trip commences; once you feel sick, it's too late. Ginger, a natural preventative, is available in capsule form from health-food stores. Acupressure wrist straps are also quite effective for many people.

Jet Lag Jet lag is experienced when a person travels by air across more than three time zones (each time zone usually represents a one-hour time difference). It occurs because many of the functions of the human body are regulated by internal 24-hour cycles called circadian rhythms. When we travel long distances rapidly, our bodies take time to adjust to the 'new' time of our destination, and we may experience fatigue, disorientation, insomnia, anxiety, impaired concentration and loss of appetite. These effects will usually be gone within three days of arrival, but there are ways of minimizing the impact of jet lag:

- Rest for a couple of days prior to departure; try to avoid late nights and last-minute dashes for traveler's checks or your passport.

- Try to select flight schedules that minimize sleep deprivation; arriving in the early evening means you can go to sleep soon after you arrive. For very long flights, try to organize a stopover.

- Avoid excessive eating (which bloats the stomach) and alcohol (which causes dehydration) during the flight. Instead, drink plenty of noncarbonated, nonalcoholic drinks such as fruit juice or water.

- Make yourself comfortable by wearing loose-fitting clothes and perhaps bringing an eye mask and earplugs to help you sleep.

Sunburn Most doctors recommend sunscreen with a high protection factor for easily burned areas like your shoulders and, if you'll be on nude beaches, areas not normally exposed to sun.

Heat Exhaustion Dehydration or salt deficiency can cause heat exhaustion. Take time to acclimatize to high temperatures and make sure that you get enough liquids. Salt deficiency is characterized by fatigue, lethargy, headaches, giddiness and muscle cramps. Salt tablets may help. Vomiting or diarrhea can also deplete your liquid and salt levels. Anhydrous heat exhaustion, caused by the inability to sweat, is quite rare, but unlike the other forms of heat exhaustion, it is likely to strike people who have been in a hot climate for some time, rather than newcomers. Again, always carry – and use – a water bottle on long trips.

Heatstroke Long, continuous periods of exposure to high temperatures can leave you vulnerable to this serious, sometimes fatal, condition, which occurs when the body's heat-regulating mechanism breaks down and body temperature rises to dangerous levels. Avoid excessive alcohol intake or strenuous activity when you first arrive in a hot climate.

Symptoms include feeling unwell, lack of perspiration and a high body temperature of 102° to 105°F (39° to 41°C). Hospitalization is essential for extreme cases, but meanwhile get out of the sun, remove clothing, cover with a wet sheet or towel and fan continually.

Hypothermia Changeable weather at high altitudes can leave you vulnerable to exposure: after dark, temperatures in the mountains or desert can drop from balmy to below freezing, while a sudden soaking and high winds can lower your body temperature too rapidly. If possible, avoid traveling alone; partners are more likely to avoid hypothermia successfully. If you must travel alone, especially when hiking, be sure someone knows your route and when you expect to return.

Seek shelter when bad weather is unavoidable. Woolen clothing and synthetics, which retain warmth even when wet, are superior to cottons. A quality sleeping bag is a worthwhile investment, although goose down loses much of its insulating qualities when wet. Carry high-energy, easily digestible snacks like chocolate or dried fruit.

Get hypothermia victims out of the wind or rain, remove their clothing if it's wet and replace it with dry, warm clothing. Give them hot liquids – not alcohol – and high-calorie, easily digestible food. In advanced stages, it may be necessary to place victims in warm sleeping bags and get in with them. Do not rub victims, but place them near a fire or, if possible, in a warm (not hot) bath.

Fungal Infections Fungal infections, which occur with greater frequency in hot weather, are most likely to occur on the scalp, between the toes or fingers (athlete's foot),

Everyday Health

Normal body temperature is 98.6°F (37°C); more than 4°F (2°C) higher indicates a high fever. The normal adult pulse rate is 60 to 100 beats per minute (children 80 to 100, babies 100 to 140). As a general rule, the pulse increases about 20 beats per minute for each 2°F (1°C) rise in fever.

Respiration (breathing) rate is also an indicator of illness. Count the number of breaths per minute (count once for a cycle of inhalation and exhalation): between 12 and 20 is normal for adults and older children (up to 30 for younger children, 40 for babies). People with a high fever or serious respiratory illness breathe more quickly than normal. More than 40 shallow breaths a minute may indicate pneumonia.

in the groin (jock itch or crotch rot) and on the body (ringworm). You get ringworm (which is a fungal infection, not a worm) from infected animals or by walking on damp areas, like shower floors.

To prevent fungal infections, wear loose, comfortable clothes, avoid artificial fibers, wash frequently and dry carefully. If you do get an infection, wash the infected area daily with a disinfectant or medicated soap and water, and rinse and dry well. Apply an antifungal powder and try to expose the infected area to air or sunlight as much as possible. Change underwear and towels frequently and wash them often in hot water.

Altitude Sickness Acute mountain sickness (AMS) occurs at high altitude and can be fatal. In the thinner atmosphere of the high mountains, lack of oxygen causes many individuals to suffer headaches, nausea, nosebleeds, shortness of breath, physical weakness and other symptoms that can lead to very serious consequences, especially if combined with heat exhaustion, sunburn or hypothermia. Most people recover within a few hours or days. If the symptoms persist, it's imperative to quickly descend to lower elevations. For mild cases, everyday painkillers such as aspirin will relieve symptoms until the body adapts. Avoid smoking, drinking alcohol, eating heavily or exercising strenuously.

There is no hard and fast rule as to how high is too high: AMS has been fatal at altitudes of 10,000 feet, although it is much more common above 11,500 feet. It is always wise to sleep at a lower altitude than the greatest height reached during the day. A number of other measures can prevent or minimize AMS:

• Ascend slowly. Take frequent rest days, spending two to three nights at each rise of 3000 feet. If you reach a high altitude by trekking, acclimatization takes place gradually and you are less likely to be affected than if you fly directly to a high altitude.

• Drink extra fluids. Mountain air is dry and cold and you lose moisture as you breathe.

• Eat light, high-carbohydrate meals for more energy.

• Avoid alcohol, which may increase the risk of dehydration.

• Avoid sedatives.

Infectious Diseases

Diarrhea A change of water, food or climate can cause the runs; diarrhea caused by contaminated food or water is more serious, but it's unlikely in the US. Despite all your precautions you may still have a mild bout of traveler's diarrhea from exotic food or drink. Dehydration is the main danger with any diarrhea, particularly for children, in whom dehydration can occur quite quickly. Fluid replacement remains the mainstay of management. Weak black tea with a little sugar, soda water or soft drinks diluted 50% with water are all good. With severe diarrhea, a rehydrating solution is necessary to replace minerals and salts. Such solutions, like Pedialyte, are available at pharmacies.

Giardiasis Commonly known as giardia, and sometimes 'beaver fever,' this intestinal parasite is present in contaminated water. Giardiasis has even contaminated apparently pristine rushing streams in the back-country.

Symptoms are stomach cramps, nausea, a bloated stomach, watery, foul-smelling diarrhea and frequent gas. Giardia can appear several weeks after exposure; symptoms may disappear for a few days and then return, a pattern which may continue. If you think you have it, see a doctor: antibiotics are useless.

Hepatitis Hepatitis is a general term for inflammation of the liver. There are many causes of this condition: poor sanitation, contact with infected blood products, drugs, alcohol and contact with an infected person are but a few. The symptoms are fever, chills, headache, fatigue and feelings of weakness and aches and pains, followed by loss of appetite, nausea, vomiting, abdominal pain, dark urine, light-colored feces and jaundiced skin. The whites of the eyes may also turn yellow. Hepatitis A is the most common strain. You should seek medical advice, but there is not much you can do apart from resting, drinking lots of fluids, eating lightly and avoiding fatty foods. People who have had hepatitis should avoid alcohol for some time after the illness, as the liver needs time to recover. Viral hepatitis is an infection of the liver, which can have several unpleasant symptoms, or no symptoms at all, and infected people may not know that they have the disease.

Sexually Transmitted Diseases Sexual contact with an infected partner spreads these diseases, called STDs. While only abstinence is 100% preventative, using condoms is also effective. Gonorrhea and syphilis are the most common STDs; sores, blisters or rashes around the genitals, discharges or pain when urinating are common symptoms. Symptoms may be less marked or not observed at all in women. The treatment of gonorrhea and syphilis is by antibiotics. Herpes, however, has no known cure. Don't be shy about going to the hospital to get any symptoms checked.

HIV/AIDS HIV, the human immunodeficiency virus, develops into AIDS, acquired immune deficiency syndrome, which is a fatal disease. Any exposure to blood, blood products or body fluids may put an individual at risk. The disease is often transmitted through sexual contact or dirty needles – vaccinations, acupuncture, tattooing and body piercing can be potentially as dangerous as intravenous drug use. Fear of HIV infection, however, should never preclude treatment for serious medical conditions.

A good resource for help and information is the US Center for Disease Control AIDS hotline (☎ 800-342-2437, 800-344-7432 in Spanish). AIDS support groups are listed in the front of phone books.

Cuts, Bites & Stings

Cuts & Scratches Skin punctures can easily become infected in hot climates and heal slowly. Treat any cut with an antiseptic such as Betadine. Where possible avoid bandages and Band-Aids, which can keep wounds wet.

Bites & Stings Bee and wasp stings and nonpoisonous spider bites are usually painful rather than dangerous. Calamine lotion will give relief, and ice packs will reduce the pain and swelling. You can best avoid bites by not using your bare hands to turn over rocks or large pieces of wood.

First Aid In the case of a snakebite, avoid slashing and sucking the wound, avoid tight tourniquets (a light constricting band above the bite can help), avoid ice, keep the affected area below the level of the heart and move it as little as possible. Do not ingest alcohol or any drugs. Stay calm and get to a medical facility as soon as possible.

In the case of spiders and scorpions, there are no special first-aid techniques, but you should call Poison Control (in the front of the phone book or ask the operator) for advice. Use ice on minor bites, but visit a doctor if an unusual reaction develops.

If you are hiking a long way from the nearest phone or other help, and you are bitten or stung, you should hike out and get help, particularly in the case of a snakebite or spider bite. Often, reactions are delayed

for up to 12 hours and you can hike out before then. For more information on some of these bugs and reptiles, see Dangers & Annoyances later in this chapter.

Ticks Ticks are parasitic arachnids that may be present in brush, forest and grasslands, where hikers often get them on their legs or in their boots. The adults suck blood from hosts by burying their head into skin, but they are often found unattached and can simply be brushed off. To remove an attached tick, use a pair of tweezers, grab it by the head and gently pull it straight out – do not twist it. (If no tweezers are available, use your fingers, but protect them from contamination with a piece of tissue or paper.) Do not touch the tick with a hot object like a match or a cigarette – this can cause it to regurgitate noxious gut substances or saliva into the wound. And do not rub oil, alcohol or petroleum jelly on it. If you get sick in the next couple of weeks, consult a doctor.

WOMEN TRAVELERS
Safety Precautions

Women often face different situations when traveling than men do. If you are a woman traveler, especially a woman traveling alone, it's not a bad idea to get in the habit of traveling with a little extra awareness of your surroundings.

In general, you must exercise more vigilance in large cities than in rural areas. Try to avoid the 'bad' or unsafe neighborhoods or districts; if you must go into or through these areas, it's best to go in a private vehicle (car or taxi). It's more dangerous at night, but in the worst areas crime can occur even in the daytime. If you are unsure which areas are considered unsafe, ask at your hotel or telephone the tourist office for advice. Tourist maps can sometimes be deceiving, compressing areas that are not tourist attractions and making the distances look shorter than they are.

While there is less to watch out for in rural areas, women may still be harassed by men unaccustomed to seeing women traveling solo. Try to avoid hiking or camping alone, especially in unfamiliar places. Hikers all over the world use the 'buddy system,' not only for protection from other humans, but also for aid in case of unexpected falls or other injuries, or encounters with rattlesnakes, bears or other potentially dangerous wildlife.

Women must recognize the extra threat of rape, which is a problem not only in urban but also in rural areas, albeit to a lesser degree. Avoiding vulnerable situations and conducting yourself in a commonsense manner will help you to avoid most problems. You're more vulnerable if you've been drinking or using drugs than if you're sober; you're more vulnerable alone than if you're with company; and you're more vulnerable in a high-crime urban area than in a 'better' district.

If you are assaulted, call the police (☎ 911). In some rural areas where 911 is not active, just dial ☎ 0 for the operator. The cities and larger towns have rape crisis centers and women's shelters that provide help and support; they are listed in the telephone directory, or if not, the police should be able to refer you to them.

Given strict US anti-sexual harassment laws, getting hassled by men is a much rarer occurrence here than in other parts of the world. Some men may interpret a woman drinking alone in a bar as a bid for male company, whether you intend it that way or not. If you don't want the company, most men will respect a firm but polite 'no thank you.' If someone continues to harass you, protesting loudly will often will make the offender slink away with embarrassment – or will at least draw attention to your predicament.

Don't hitchhike alone, and don't pick up hitchhikers when you're driving alone. If you get stuck on a road and need help, it's a good idea to have a premade sign to signal for help. At night, avoid getting out of your car to flag down help; turn on your hazard lights and wait for the police to arrive. Be extra-careful at night on public transit, and remember to check the times of the last bus or train before you go out at night.

To deal with potential dangers, many women protect themselves with a whistle, mace, pepper spray or some karate training. If you do decide to purchase a spray, contact a police station to find out about regulations and training classes. Laws regarding sprays vary from state to state and town to town, so be informed based on your destination. It is a federal offense to carry defensive sprays on airplanes.

Organizations & Resources

Check the Yellow Pages phone directory under 'Women's Organizations and Services' for local resources. Women's bookstores, found in the Yellow Pages under 'Bookstores,' are good places to find out about gatherings, readings and meetings. Sometimes these also have bulletin boards where you can find or place travel and short-term housing notices. Here are two organizations with affiliates nationwide:

National Organization for Women (NOW) (☎ 202-331-0066, fax 202-785-8576) 1000 16th St NW, Suite 700, Washington, DC 20036. A good resource for any women-related information – can refer you to state and local chapters.

Planned Parenthood (☎ 212-541-7800, fax 212-245-1845) 810 7th Ave, 12th Floor, New York, NY 10019. Can refer you to clinics throughout the country and offer advice on medical issues.

GAY & LESBIAN TRAVELERS

By far the most established gay communities are in the major cities of California, where gay men and women can live their lives openly. With the nation's largest gay population residing in San Francisco, Californians tend to be tolerant (although there have been cases of 'gay bashing' even in metropolitan areas, and away from major cities 'tolerance' is sometimes more of a 'don't ask, don't tell' policy). In Nevada, being open about sexual preferences is much harder, and gays can be prosecuted for open displays of affection. Gay travelers should be *especially* careful in rural areas – holding hands might get you bashed.

Apart from the Castro District in San Francisco, the Hillcrest suburb of San Diego, West Hollywood in LA, and Palm Springs/Cathedral City have established gay communities. All these places have gay and alternative newspapers that list what's happening and provide phone numbers of local organizations.

With AIDS as a constant and harsh reality, California's gay communities are becoming strong advocates of safe sex and anti-AIDS campaigns. Single-sex marriages are also increasingly popular, though not yet recognized by the state of California.

Organizations & Resources

A couple of good national guidebooks are *The Women's Traveler*, providing listings for lesbians, and *Damron's Address Book* for men, both published by the Damron Company (☎ 415-255-0404, 800-462-6654), PO Box 422458, San Francisco, CA 94142-2458. Ferrari's *Places for Women* and *Places for Men* are also useful, as are guides to specific cities like *Betty & Pansy's Severe Queer Reviews* to San Francisco, New York City and Washington, DC. These can be found at any good bookstore.

Another good resource is the Gay & Lesbian Yellow Pages series (☎ 212-674-0120, www.glyp.com), PO Box 533, Village Station, NY 10014-0533, which has national as well as regional editions. Also available is the *Gay Guide to Los Angeles & Southern California* by Andrew Collins.

For people with online capabilities, America Online (AOL) hosts the Gay & Lesbian Community Forum. Several national and worldwide organizations also have a Web presence. These include the National Gay/Lesbian Task Force (NGLTF) at www.ngltf.org, the Gay and Lesbian Alliance Against Defamation (GLAAD) at www.gladd.org, and Parents, Families and Friends of Lesbians and Gays (P-FLAG) at www.pflag.org.

National resource numbers include the National AIDS/HIV Hotline (☎ 800-342-2437), the National Gay/Lesbian Task Force (☎ 202-332-6483 in Washington, DC) and the Lambda Legal Defense Fund (☎ 212-995-8585 in New York City, 213-937-2727 in Los Angeles).

DISABLED TRAVELERS

Travel within the US is becoming easier for people with disabilities, and California is as good as its gets. The more populous the area, the greater the likelihood of facilities for the disabled, so it's important to call ahead to see what is available. The biggest favor you can do yourself is to plan ahead.

The Americans with Disabilities Act (ADA) requires that all public buildings (including hotels, restaurants, theaters and museums) be wheelchair accessible. Buses and trains must have wheelchair lifts and telephone companies are required to provide relay operators (available via TTY numbers) for the hearing impaired. Many banks now provide ATM instructions in Braille, and you'll find dropped curbs at most intersections and occasionally audible crossing signals as well.

Larger private and chain hotels have suites for disabled guests. Major car rental agencies offer hand-controlled vehicles and vans with wheelchair lifts at no extra charge, but you must reserve them well in advance.

All major airlines, Greyhound buses and Amtrak trains will allow service animals like guide dogs to accompany passengers and will frequently sell two-for-one packages when attendants of disabled passengers are required. Airlines must accept wheelchairs as checked baggage and have an onboard chair available, though some advance notice may be required on smaller aircraft. Airlines will also provide assistance for connecting, boarding and deplaning flights – just ask for assistance when making your reservation. American Airlines is said to have an especially well-trained staff.

Most national and state parks and recreation areas have paved or boardwalk-style nature trails. Blind or permanently disabled US residents can get a Golden Access Passport for free admission to all national parks (available at park entrances). Contact the Outdoors Disabled Foundation (☎ 312-927-6834) for recommended destinations and stores where you can find adventurous attendants and travel partners.

Books worth checking out include *California Parks Access*, by Linda and Allen Mitchell, and *Easy Access to National Parks* by Wendy Roth and Michael Tompane.

Organizations & Resources

A number of organizations and tour providers specialize in the needs of disabled travelers:

Access-Able Travel Source
(☎ 303-232-2979, fax 303-239-8486, www.access able.com) PO Box 1796, Wheat Ridge, CO 80034. Has an excellent website with many links.

Access
(☎ 516-887-5798) PO Box 356, Malverne, NY 11565. The Foundation for Accessibility by the Disabled.

Mobility International USA
(☎ 541-343-1284, fax 541-343-6812, info@miusa .org) PO Box 10767, Eugene, OR 97440. Advises disabled travelers on mobility issues. It primarily runs an educational exchange program.

Moss Rehabilitation Hospital's Travel Information Service
(☎ 215-456-9600, TTY 456-9602) 1200 W Tabor Rd, Philadelphia, PA 19141-3099

SATH (Society for the Advancement of Travel for the Handicapped)
(☎ 212-447-7284, sathtravel@aol.com) 347 Fifth Ave, No 610, New York, NY 10016.

Travelin' Talk
(☎ 615-552-6670, fax 615-552-1182, trvlntlk@aol .com) PO Box 3534, Clarksville, TN 37047. An international network of people providing assistance to disabled travelers.

Twin Peaks Press
(☎ 360-694-2462, 800-637-2256) PO Box 129, Vancouver, WA 98666. A quarterly newsletter; also publishes directories and access guides.

Handicapped Travel Newsletter
(☎/fax 903-677-1260) PO Box 269, Athens, TX 75751. This nonprofit publication has good information on US government legislation and traveling around the world. Subscriptions are $10 annually.

The Center for Independent Living
(☎ 510-841-4776) 2539 Telegraph Ave, Berkeley, CA 94705. Has counseling and information services.

SENIOR TRAVELERS

Though the age when the benefits begin varies with the attraction, travelers from 50 years and up can expect to receive cut rates and benefits. Be sure to inquire about such seniors' rates at hotels, museums and restaurants.

Visitors to national parks and camp-grounds can cut costs greatly by using the Golden Age Passport ($10), a card that allows permanent US residents over 62 (and everyone else traveling in the same car) unlimited free admission to all national park sites nationwide and a 50% reduction on camping and other fees. These are available in person at any national park.

Organizations

Some national seniors' advocacy groups that can help in planning your travels include the following:

American Association of Retired Persons (AARP)
(☎ 800-424-3410, www.aarp.org) 3200 E Carson St, Lakewood, CA 90712 (membership). AARP is an advocacy group for Americans 50 years and older and is a good resource for travel bargains. US residents can get one-year/three-year memberships for $8/20. Citizens of other countries can get the same memberships for $10/24.

Elderhostel
(☎ 877-426-8056), 75 Federal St, Boston, MA 02110-1941. This is a nonprofit organization that offers those over 55 the opportunity to attend academic college courses throughout the US and Canada. The programs last one to three weeks and include meals and accommodations.

Grand Circle Travel
(☎ 617-350-7500) 347 Congress St, Boston, MA 02210. This group offers escorted tours and travel information in a variety of formats and distributes a free useful booklet, *Going Abroad: 101 Tips for Mature Travelers*.

TRAVEL WITH CHILDREN

Successful travel with young children requires planning and effort. Don't try to overdo things; even for adults, packing too much into the time available can cause prob-lems. And make sure the activities include the kids as well – balance that morning at the art museum with a visit to the zoo or the beach. Include the kids in the trip planning; if they've helped to work out where you are going, they will be much more interested when they get there. Various children's activ-ities are mentioned in appropriate places in the text. For information on enjoying travel with the young ones, read *Travel with*

Children by Lonely Planet cofounder Maureen Wheeler.

Children's discounts are widely available for everything from museum admissions to bus fares and motel stays. The definition of a child varies – some places count anyone under 18 eligible for children's discounts, while others only include children under six. Unless specified, prices quoted for children in this book refer to those ages three to 12.

Many hotels and motels allow children to share a room with their parents for free or for a modest fee, though B&Bs rarely do and some don't allow children at all. Larger hotels often have a baby-sitting service, and other hotels may be able to help you make arrangements. Alternatively, look in the Yellow Pages for local agencies. Be sure to ask whether sitters are licensed and bonded, what they charge per hour, whether there's a minimum fee and whether they charge extra for meals and transportation.

Most car rental firms have children's safety seats for hire at a nominal cost, but be sure to book them in advance. The same goes for highchairs and cribs; they're common in many restaurants and hotels, but numbers are limited. The choice of baby food, infant formulas, soy and cow's milk, disposable diapers and other necessities is great in supermarkets throughout California and Nevada. Diaper changing stations can be found in many public toilets in malls, department stores and even in many restaurants.

It's perfectly acceptable to bring your kids, even toddlers, along to casual restaurants (though not to many upscale ones at dinnertime), cafes and daytime events.

USEFUL ORGANIZATIONS
American Automobile Association

The AAA has offices throughout California and Nevada and provides useful information, free maps and routine road services like tire repair and towing and other services to its members. For more, see American Automobile Association in the Getting Around chapter.

National Park Service

National parks surround spectacular natural features and cover hundreds of square miles. The National Park Service (NPS), part of the Department of the Interior, administers national parks, monuments, historic sites and a few other areas. Visitors can often camp and hike in the bigger areas, but hunting and commercial activities like logging are prohibited in these protected sites. All national parks have visitor centers with information (exhibits, films, park ranger talks) about why that particular site has been preserved for posterity.

Most NPS areas charge entrance fees, valid for multiple entries during a seven-day period, of $4 to $20 per vehicle (usually half price or less for walk-in or biking visitors). A few sites are free, and some don't collect entrance fees during periods of low visitation (usually late fall to early spring). Additional fees are charged for camping and some other activities, depending on each park.

For details on how to obtain camping information and reservations, please see Camping under Accommodations later in this chapter.

Golden Eagle Passports Golden Eagle Passports cost $50 annually and offer unlimited one-year entry into all national parks to the holder (and anyone in the holder's car). You can buy one at any NPS fee area, and it is valid immediately, so you can use it for your first visit to any national park and all visits to all NPS sites for the next year – a great deal!

Golden Age Passports cost $10 and allow permanent US residents 62 years and older unlimited free entry to all NPS sites, plus 50% discounts on camping and other fees.

Golden Access Passports are free and give free admission to US residents who are medically blind or permanently disabled.

US Forest Service

The US Forest Service (USFS) is part of the Department of Agriculture. National forests are less protected than parks, allowing commercial exploitation in some areas (usually logging or privately owned recreational facilities). Forests are multiuse, with recreational activities such as hunting, fishing, snowmobiling, 4WD use and mountain biking permitted in many areas, unlike the NPS parks where these activities are infrequently permitted.

Entrance into national forests is usually free, although in 1997 Congress introduced a new experimental program by which several forests now require the purchase of a permit of $5 per day or $20 to $30 per year (per vehicle) to make use of forest facilities. Golden Passports are accepted in some, but not all, cases. Details are given in the respective geographic chapters. See also the 'National Forest Adventure Pass' boxed text in the Activities chapter.

For details on how to make campground reservations, see Camping under Accommodations later in this chapter.

Bureau of Land Management

The BLM, as it is commonly called, manages public use of federal lands. They offer nofrills camping, often in remote settings. The California regional office (☎ 916-978-4400, www.ca.blm.gov) is at 2135 Butano Drive, Sacramento, CA 95825. The Nevada branch (☎ 775-861-6586) is at PO Box 12000, Reno, NV 89520.

State Parks

State parks are usually small and protect a specific natural or historical feature. California has 270 state parks, managed by the Department of Parks & Recreation (☎ 916-653-6995), Box 942896, Sacramento, CA 94296. The department's excellent website is at cal-parks.ca.gov. For campground reservations, see Camping under Accommodations later in this chapter.

Nevada has 14 state parks and recreation areas but there's no central administrative body. A good source of information is on the Web at www.publiclands-usa.com/html/explore/nv_splash.asp.

Fish & Wildlife Service

Each state has a few regional Fish & Wildlife Service (FWS) offices that can provide information about viewing local wildlife and about fishing and hunting seasons, licenses and other regulations.

California Department of Fish & Game
(☎ 916-653-7664, www.dfg.ca.gov) 1416 9th St, Sacramento, CA 95814

Nevada Department of Wildlife
(☎ 775-688-1500) 1100 Valley Rd, Reno, NV 89512

DANGERS & ANNOYANCES

Road accidents are probably the greatest single risk of injury – see the Getting Around chapter for more information on driving.

Otherwise, California and Nevada are not dangerous places. There are, however, some things to be aware of. There is some risk of violent crime, but it is mostly confined to particular areas. Wildlife presents some potential dangers, though not a big threat. Then there are the earthquakes (see the boxed text 'Shake, Rattle & Roll').

See the California Deserts chapter for advice on minimizing the risks of desert travel, as well as the boxed text 'Outdoor Dangers & Annoyances' in the Sierra Nevada chapter for advice on wilderness safety.

Crime

The good news is that tourists will rarely get tricked, cheated or conned simply because they're tourists. The bad news is that violent crime is a problem for tourists as well as locals, especially in the cities. Gang violence is a serious inner-city issue, notably in areas of Oakland, South San Francisco, parts of Bakersfield, Modesto and Stockton, and parts of LA like Compton, East LA and Watts. Avoid these neighborhoods, especially after dark.

If you find yourself in a neighborhood where you'd rather not be, do your best to look confident; don't stop every few minutes to look at your map. Hail a taxi and get out of there if you can. Don't abandon a bright street for a darker one. If you're accosted by a mugger, there's no 100% recommended policy, but handing over whatever the

Shake, Rattle & Roll: What to Do in an Earthquake

San Francisco had the Big One in 1906, followed 83 years later by the not-quite-so-Big One in 1989. In 1994, it was Los Angeles' turn, when a 6.6-magnitude quake damaged buildings, collapsed freeways and caused a dozen deaths.

Earthquakes occur in greater number than most visitors realize – dozens a week. Most are of a magnitude that makes them detectable only by sensitive seismological instruments. Occasionally a tremor of 4.5 or 5.0 on the Richter scale may give you a start and rattle a few glasses; it will pass in a moment, leaving only heart palpitations.

Many Californians are prepared with an emergency kit for major earthquakes (although many are so blasé about earthquakes that they make no preparations at all). Ideally, the emergency kit includes a first-aid kit, portable radio, flashlights and extra batteries, blankets, essential medications, three days' worth of food, three gallons of water per person and various other items.

Here are some things to remember in the unlikely event that the earth shakes seriously during your stay:

If you are indoors, stay indoors. Immediately take cover under a desk or table, or failing that, a doorway. Stay clear of windows, mirrors or anything with a danger of falling, like bookshelves or file cabinets. Don't use the elevators. If you're in a shopping mall or large public building, expect the alarm or sprinkler systems to come on.

If you are outdoors, get into an open area away from buildings, trees and power lines. If you are driving, pull over to the side of the road away from bridges, overpasses and power lines. Stay inside the car until the shaking stops.

If you are on a sidewalk near buildings, duck into a doorway to protect yourself from falling bricks, glass and debris.

Prepare for aftershocks.

Afterwards, check first for personal injuries, then for fire hazards (such as gas leaks or electrical-line damage) and spilled chemicals or medicines. As the city water supply may become polluted, you should boil any tap water before you drink it, until notified otherwise. Use the telephone only if absolutely necessary. Turn on the radio and listen for bulletins.

mugger wants is much better than getting knifed or shot. Have something to hand over: it's a good idea not to carry too much cash or too many valuables, but it can be a very bad idea to carry nothing. Muggers are not too happy to find their victims penniless.

Carry your money (and only the money you'll need for that day) somewhere inside your clothing (in a money belt, a bra or your socks) rather than in a handbag or an outside pocket. Stash the money in several places. Most hotels and hostels provide safe-keeping, so you can leave your money, passport and other valuables with them. Hide, or don't wear, any valuable jewelry.

Always lock cars and put valuables out of sight, whether leaving the car for a few

minutes or longer, and whether you are in a town or in the remote backcountry. Rent a car with a lockable trunk. If your car is bumped from behind by another vehicle in a remote area, try to keep going to a well-lit area, service station or even a police station.

Be aware of your surroundings and who may be watching you. Avoid walking dimly lit streets at night, particularly if you are alone. Walk purposefully. Exercise particular caution in large parking lots or parking structures at night. Try to use ATM machines only in well-trafficked areas.

In hotels, don't leave valuables lying around your room. Use safety deposit boxes, or at least place valuables in a locked bag. Don't open your door to strangers – check the peephole or call the front desk if unexpected people are trying to enter.

Street People

The US has a lamentable record in dealing with its most unfortunate citizens, who often roam the streets of large cities in the daytime and sleep in storefronts, under freeways or in alleyways and abandoned buildings.

This problem is less acute in rural areas than urban areas of California, but it is certainly not absent. Street people and panhandlers may approach visitors in the larger cities and towns; nearly all of them are harmless. Many are very polite, and suggest you have a nice day even if you don't give them money. Often they have witty signs like: 'residentially challenged,' 'nonaggressive panhandler' and 'Let's be honest, I need a beer.'

It's an individual judgment call whether it's appropriate to offer them money or anything else – you might just offer food if you have it. If you are truly concerned about the problem, you might consider a donation to a charity that cares for the urban poor.

Wildlife

Drivers should watch for stock or deer on highways, especially in the deserts, mountains and Nevada's range country. Areas are signed as Open Range or with the silhouette of a cow, deer or something to that effect. Hitting a large mammal at 55 mph will total your car, kill the animal and might kill you as well.

There are snakes, spiders, scorpions and other venomous creatures in the region, but fatalities are very rare; partly because these animals tend to avoid humans, and partly because their venom is designed to kill small animals rather than big ones. The descriptions below are largely for interest, but note that most of these venomous animals are found in urban as well as rural areas. If you are bitten or stung by one of these small critters, refer to the Health section under Cuts, Bites & Stings. Some larger animals could cause serious injury or death, but you would have to be foolish and unlucky to be attacked.

Bears Bears are attracted to campgrounds where they may find accessible food in bags, tents, cars or picnic baskets. For details on how to prevent bears from damaging your property or attacking you, see the boxed text 'Bears, Your Food & You' in the Activities chapter.

Mountain Lions These beautiful creatures, also called 'cougars' or 'pumas,' have been known to attack humans. Though there was one fatal attack in 1994 that received much publicity, attacks are rare. Mountain lions are most common in the lower western Sierra, and the mountains and forests east of Los Angeles and San Diego, especially in areas with lots of deer. Rangers recommend staying calm if you meet a lion. Hold your ground, try to appear large by raising your arms or grabbing a stick. If the lion gets aggressive or attacks, fight back, shout and throw objects at it.

Gila Monsters One of only two venomous lizards in the world, the Gila monster is found in the deserts of California and Nevada. It's large and slow with a bizarre, multicolored, beaded appearance, and it can reach 2 feet in length. Although a bite could be fatal, it's very hard to get bitten: you pretty much have to pick the monster up and force-feed it your finger. There have been no fatalities in the last several years. Gila monsters are legally protected and should not be handled.

Snakes When hiking, watch where you step, particularly on hot summer afternoons and evenings when rattlesnakes like to bask in the middle of the trail. They are also often active at night. There are many species of rattler, most easily identified by the 'rattle' of dried segments of skin at the tip of the tail, which emit a rapid rattling sound when the snake is disturbed. Most rattlesnakes have roughly diamond-shaped patterns along their backs and vary in length from 2 to 6 feet. If you are bitten, you will experience rapid swelling, very severe pain and possible temporary paralysis, but victims rarely die. Antivenin is available in most hospitals. See Cuts, Bites & Stings in the Health section of this chapter and seek medical help; if the snake is dead, bring it in for identification, but don't attempt to catch the snake if there is even a remote possibility of being bitten again.

Scorpions Scorpions spend their days under rocks or woodpiles, so use caution when around these. The long stinger curving up and around the back is characteristic of these animals. The stings can be very painful but are almost never fatal; small children are at highest risk.

Spiders The most dangerous spider in the area is the black widow, a species that has gained notoriety because the venomous female eats her mate after sex. The female has a small, round body marked with a red hourglass shape under its abdomen. She makes very messy webs, so avoid these, as the widow will bite if harassed. Bites are very painful but rarely fatal, except in young children. Antivenin is available.

The large (up to 6 inches in diameter) and hairy tarantula looks much worse than it is – it bites very rarely and then usually when it is roughly handled. The bite is not very serious, although it is temporarily quite painful.

Other Creatures Centipedes bite occasionally, resulting in a painfully inflamed wound that lasts for about a day. Some local ants may also give painful stings. Conenose bugs (also called 'kissing' or 'assassin' bugs) are from ½ to 1 inch long and have elongated heads. The winged bodies are oval and brown or black with lighter markings (sometimes orange) around the edges. Bites are painful and can result in severe allergic reactions.

EMERGENCY

Throughout most of the US, dial ☎ 911 for emergency service of any sort; in large cities or areas with substantial Latino populations, Spanish-speaking emergency operators may be available, but other languages are less likely. This is a free call from any phone. A few rural phones might not have this service,

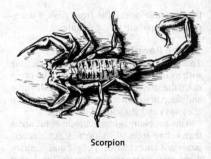

Scorpion

in which case dial ☎ 0 for the operator and ask for emergency assistance – it's still free. Each state also maintains toll-free numbers for traffic information and emergencies.

LEGAL MATTERS

If you are stopped by the police for any reason, bear in mind that there is no system of paying fines on the spot. For traffic offenses, the police officer will explain your options to you. Attempting to pay the fine to the officer is frowned upon at best and may lead to a charge of bribery to compound your troubles. If the officer decides that you should pay up front, he or she can take you directly to the judge instead of allowing the usual 30-day period to pay the fine.

If you are arrested for more serious offenses, you are allowed to remain silent and are presumed innocent until proven guilty. There is no legal reason to speak to a police officer if you don't wish. All persons who are arrested are legally allowed (and given) the right to make one phone call. If you don't have a lawyer or family member to help you, call your embassy. The police will give you the number upon request.

Driving & Drinking Laws

Speed limits are 65mph, sometimes 70mph, on interstates, freeways and some highways, unless otherwise posted. Speed limits on other highways are 55mph or less, and in cities can vary from 25 to 45mph. Seat belts must be worn; children must have proper seats and restraints; and motorcyclists must wear helmets.

The legal drinking age is 21, and you can be asked for a photo ID to prove your age. Being 'carded' is standard practice in many places – it may be a pain if you're in your 20s, but it's nice to be carded after you turn 30. Stiff fines, jail time and other penalties can be incurred for driving under the influence of alcohol or drugs. A blood alcohol content of 0.08% is illegal, even if you're still able to drive. During festive holidays and special events, roadblocks are sometimes set up to deter drunk drivers. For further details, see Car & Motorcycle in the Getting Around chapter.

Drugs

In California, possession of under 1 ounce of marijuana is a misdemeanor, and though it is punishable by up to one year in jail, a fine is more likely. Possession of any other drug, including cocaine, ecstasy, LSD, heroin, hashish or more than an ounce of weed is a felony, punishable by lengthy jail sentences, depending on the circumstances. Conviction of any drug offense is grounds for deportation of a foreigner. Drug laws in Nevada are generally harsher on soft drugs, and more strictly enforced.

BUSINESS HOURS

In any large city, a few supermarkets, restaurants and the main post office are open 24 hours. Shops are usually open from 9 or 10 am to 5 or 6 pm (often until 9 pm in shopping malls), except Sunday when hours are noon to 5 pm (often later in malls). Post offices are open weekdays 8 am to 4 or 5:30 pm, and some are open 8 am to noon on Saturday. Banks are usually open from 9 or 10 am to 5 or 6 pm weekdays; a few banks are also open until 1 or 2 pm on Saturday. Check with an individual branch for precise hours.

PUBLIC HOLIDAYS

National public holidays are celebrated throughout the US. Banks, schools and government offices (including post offices) are closed and transportation, museums and other services are on a Sunday schedule.

Holidays falling on a weekend are usually observed the following Monday.

New Year's Day	January 1
Martin Luther King Jr Day	3rd Monday in January
Presidents' Day	3rd Monday in February
Memorial Day	last Monday in May
Independence Day (Fourth of July)	July 4
Labor Day	1st Monday in September
Columbus Day	2nd Monday in October
Veterans' Day	November 11
Thanksgiving Day	4th Thursday in November
Christmas Day	December 25

CULTURAL EVENTS

The US is always ready to call a day an event. Retailers remind the masses of coming events with huge advertising binges running for months before the actual day. Some of these are also public holidays, and banks, schools and government buildings are closed.

California's rich mixture of cultures means there's plenty of variety in its events. In the urban centers, there are celebrations for everything from Chinese New Year to St Patrick's Day to Mexico's Cinco de Mayo.

January

Chinese New Year begins at the end of January or the beginning of February and lasts two weeks. The first day is celebrated with parades, firecrackers, fireworks and lots of food. The biggest celebrations are in San Francisco and Los Angeles.

Vietnamese New Year, or Tet, at about the same time as Chinese New Year, is a big celebration in San Jose, California.

February

Valentine's Day is on February 14. No one knows why St Valentine is associated with romance in the US, but this is the day of roses, sappy greeting cards and packed restaurants. Some people wear red and give out 'Be My Valentine' candies.

March

St Patrick's Day is March 17. The patron saint of Ireland is honored by all those who feel the Irish in their blood. Everyone wears green (or you can get pinched), stores sell green bread, bars serve green beer, and towns and cities put on frolicking parades of marching bands and community groups.

April

Easter is observed by going to church, painting eggs, eating chocolate eggs or any mixture of the above. Travel during this weekend is usually expensive and crowded. Good Friday is usually not observed as a holiday.

Passover is celebrated either in March or April, depending on the Jewish calendar. Families get together to partake in the symbolic *seder* dinner, which celebrates the exodus of the Jews from slavery.

May

Cinco de Mayo, on May 5, celebrates the day the Mexicans wiped out the French army in 1862. Big celebrations are in San Diego, San Jose, Los Angeles, Oceanside, Calexico, San Francisco and anywhere else with a Mexican population.

Mother's Day is held on the second Sunday of the month. Moms receive lots of cards and flowers, and restaurants are busy.

June

Father's Day is the third Sunday. Same idea as Mother's Day, different parent.

Juneteenth, on June 17, celebrates the emancipation of African-American slaves on this day. Large celebrations are held in Oakland, Berkeley and other communities with large African-American populations.

July

Independence Day is more commonly called the 4th of July. American flags are flown, parades storm the streets of many towns and barbecues and fireworks shows abound.

October

Halloween is on October 31. Kids and adults dress in costumes. In safer neighborhoods, children go 'trick-or-treating' for candy. San Francisco has many events: an official Halloween party at the Civic Center, the gala Exotic-Erotic Halloween Ball, and the Castro District's well-known evening street festival. Come in costume.

November

Day of the Dead is observed in areas with Mexican communities on November 2. This is a day for families to honor dead relatives, and make breads and sweets resembling skeletons, skulls and such.

Thanksgiving is held on the last Thursday of the month. This important family gathering is celebrated with a bounty of food, football games on TV and a big parade in New York City. The following day is the busiest shopping day of the year.

December

Christmas, on December 25, is preceded by a dizzying commercial frenzy of shopping for food and gifts. The holiday is celebrated with church masses, dinners, parties and gift giving. Christmas Eve is as much of an event as the day itself, with church services, caroling in the streets, people cruising neighborhoods looking for the best light displays and stores full of procrastinators.

Kwanza is held from December 26 to 31. This seven-day African-American celebration is based on African harvest festivals and celebrates family, heritage and community.

Hanukkah is usually in December (the date varies from year to year, as it's tied to the Hebrew calendar). It's an eight-day Jewish holiday celebrating the rededication of the Temple of Jerusalem.

New Year's Eve is on December 31. People celebrate with little tradition other than dressing up, going to parties and drinking champagne. The following day people stay home to nurse their hangovers and watch college football on TV.

SPECIAL EVENTS

Apart from national holidays and cultural events, many local celebrations, sporting events, art festivals, county fairs, car shows, Native-American powwows and so on, are common in California and Nevada. Most of these are annual, usually scheduled for a weekend at about the same time every year.

Rural events usually include all the amusements of small town life. Each county has an annual fair, where competitions are held for everything from prize pigs to apple pie, and they also put forth music, arts and crafts, rodeos and carnival rides.

Only a small selection of such events is given here – for more information, see the geographical entries or contact the state tourism commissions.

California

For a complete, current list, with exact dates and a year's worth of events, contact the California Division of Tourism (☎ 800-862-2543), PO Box 1499, Sacramento, CA 95812-1499, and ask for their special events booklet. Information on special events is also available on their website at www.gocalif.ca.gov.

January

Tournament of Roses is the famous New Year's Day parade of flower-coated floats, marching bands and equestrians held in the Los Angeles suburb of Pasadena (☎ 818-795-4171).

Whalefest, held in Monterey each year, is a celebration of the gray whales' annual migration, with music, exhibits and art (☎ 831-649-2836).

February

Riverside County Fair & National Date Festival (mid-February) combines a county fair with a celebration of the date industry in Indio, plus pig, camel and ostrich races (☎ 800-811-3247).

Tower District Mardi Gras, in Fresno, is California's largest Mardi Gras, with a parade, food, floats and beer gardens (☎ 559-497-8362).

March

Great Western Livestock Show and Exposition is a huge exhibition with Western dance, a rodeo, a chili cook-off and then some, in Tulare (☎ 559-686-4707).

San Diego Latino Film Festival screens films from throughout Latin America and the US (☎ 619-230-1938).

April

I Madonnari Italian Street Painting Festival lends some color to San Luis Obispo, as artists decorate the streets with colorful chalk paintings (☎ 805-569-3873).

Sacramento Valley Scottish Games & Gathering, in Woodland, is a celebration of Scottish culture, with bagpipes, dancing, Scottish athletics and more (☎ 916-557-0764).

Toyota Grand Prix, the largest Indy street race in North America, races through the streets of Long Beach (☎ 800-452-7829).

Red Bluff Round-Up is the largest three-day rodeo in the country (☎ 530-527-1000).

San Francisco International Film Festival, in late April to early May, is the country's oldest film festival.

May

Stanford Powwow is a big intertribal gathering in Palo Alto.

Calaveras County Fair & Jumping Frog Jubilee is a classic county fair, with a famous frog jumping contest, in Angels Camp (☎ 209-736-2561).

San Francisco Examiner Bay to Breakers, the largest and craziest footrace in the world, is a mob of costumed runners, world-class athletes and weekend warriors.

June

West Coast Antique Fly-In, in Merced, is an air show with old and home-built aircraft (☎ 800-446-5353).

Tour of Nevada City Bicycle Classic is a race through the streets of historic Nevada City (☎ 530-265-2692).

Lesbian, Gay, Bisexual and Transgender Pride Parade, in late June, attracts thousands of people to San Francisco.

July

Festival of the Arts and Pageant of the Masters features exhibits by hundreds of artists and a pageant of art masterpieces 're-created' with real people, in Laguna Beach (☎ 800-487-3378).

Gilroy Garlic Festival celebrates the stinking rose with lots of garlic food and jokes (☎ 408-842-6436).

US Open Sandcastle Contest turns the sandcastle into art, as sand sculptures compete on Imperial Beach in San Diego (☎ 619-424-6669).

August

Steinbeck Festival celebrates California's Nobel laureate with films, theater, lectures on John Steinbeck in Salinas (☎ 831-796-3833).

Old Spanish Days Fiesta, in early August, is the biggest of several ethnic festivals in Santa Barbara (☎ 800-927-4688).

Nisei Week Japanese Festival is a week of Japanese parades, dancing and martial arts, in Los Angeles (☎ 213-687-7193).

Monterey Historic Automobile Races, in late August, is a combination vintage vehicle race and car show, in Monterey.

African Marketplace and Cultural Faire, three weekends in late August and early September, celebrates African-American culture with African food, art and entertainment, in Los Angeles (☎ 323-734-1164).

September

Fringe Festival theater marathon brings performers from around the world to San Francisco (☎ 415-931-1094).

Monterey Jazz Festival, in mid-September, is a long-running, big-name festival of traditional and modern styles (☎ 800-307-3378).

Simon Rodia Watts Towers Jazz Festival, in late September, features jazz, gospel, R&B, and other African-American sounds, in the shadow of the Watts Towers on the edge of downtown LA (☎ 213-485-1795).

Oktoberfest, throughout September and October, is a celebration of German heritage held in many cities throughout the state with music, dancing, costumes and lots of beer.

Kern County Fair has arts and crafts, antiques, livestock, carnival rides and rodeo events, in Bakersfield (☎ 805-833-4900).

October

San Francisco Jazz Festival features live music from established and new artists throughout the city (☎ 415-398-5655, sfjazzfst@sirius.com).

Halloween, October 31, is a popular night of celebration throughout the state, with all sorts of costume parades and parties, the most outrageous in San Francisco and West Hollywood.

Great Pumpkin Weigh-Off, in Half Moon Bay, is a competition of West Coast pumpkin growers (☎ 650-726-4485).

November

49er Art and Music Festival, in Death Valley National Park, features fiddlers, barbecues, and backcountry caravans recalling the history of early immigrants to California.

Christmas Tree Lighting is in the end of November. Many communities kick off the Christmas season by lighting up a large tree in a public place.

Hollywood Christmas Parade features celebrities waving at fans lining Hollywood Boulevard (☎ 213-469-2337).

Doo Dah Parade is an irreverent spoof of the parade tradition, in Pasadena.

December

Christmas festivities occur all month across the state – some of the more unusual include the following:

Truckers Christmas Convoy, in early December, is a memorable parade and display of big rigs decked out with lively Christmas decorations. Put a manger on your Mack truck and bring it on up to Eureka (☎ 707-442-5744).

Christmas Boat Parade, in mid-December, is a parade of hundreds of brightly lit boats that float past Newport Beach (☎ 949-729-4400).

First Night Santa Cruz is a street festival with dance, theater and music but no alcohol. Santa Rosa, Stockton and Monterey also have First Night celebrations.

Nevada

Las Vegas has more special events than the rest of the state put together. Apart from the many gaming tournaments, there are lots of trade fairs and industry expositions using the city's extensive conference facilities. Reno also has some big events, and towns throughout Nevada have county fairs, rodeos, powwows and off-road car and motorbike races. Contact the Nevada Commission on Tourism (☎ 702-687-4322, www.travelnevada.com) for a complete list with exact dates.

January

Cowboy Poetry Gathering, in late January, features poetry, music, art, yodeling, drinking and other manifestations of cowboy culture, in Elko (☎ 775-738-7508).

February

Las Vegas International Marathon & Half-Marathon is a traditional race with 6000 runners from around the world (www.lvmarathon.com).

Annual Snowfest winter carnival has a torchlight ski parade, races and arts and crafts, in North Lake Tahoe.

March

Mother Earth Awakening Pow Wow is a Native-American celebration of the spring equinox, with dancers, drummers and singers, in Carson City (☎ 775-882-6929).

April

Laughlin River Run/Harley Days is the largest motorcycle event in the western US, with tens of thousands of Harley-Davidson fans descending on Laughlin for a spirited celebration (☎ 909-340-0094).

Las Vegas City of Lights Jazz Festival presents 10 hours of jazz with renowned performers (☎ 800-969-8342).

May

Helldorado Days & Rodeo brings the Wild West to Las Vegas (☎ 702-870-1221).

Snow Mountain Paiute Pow Wow is celebrated in late May in Las Vegas.

June

Gridley Days brings the state fiddling championship, a motorcycle poker run, mining games and other silliness to Austin (☎ 775-964-2200).

Winnemucca Basque Festival includes a parade, wood chopping, weight carrying and a mass yelling contest, in Winnemucca (☎ 800-962-2638).

Reno Rodeo in mid-June, is one of the biggest rodeos in the country (☎ 775-329-3877).

Summerfest Powwow is held at the Stewart Indian Cultural Center in Carson City (☎ 775-882-1808).

July

National Basque Festival, July 4th weekend, is a big Basque festival featuring lots of food and dance, in Elko.

All Indian Rodeo & Stampede Indian Days Powwow is a big intertribal gathering in Fallon (☎ 702-423-3634).

August

Hot August Nights features parades of '50s cars and concerts of '50s music, in Reno (☎ 775-356-1956).

Nevada State Fair, in late August, has rides, games and livestock events at the Reno Fairgrounds (☎ 702-688-5767).

Shakespeare Festival, at Sand Harbor, presents the Bard near Lake Tahoe (☎ 800-468-2463).

September

Burning Man is a wildly popular weeklong participatory arts and performance festival that culminates in the burning of a gigantic wooden and neon man, in the Black Rock Desert (☎ 415-863-5263, www.burningman.com).

International Camel Races are held by the International Order of Camel Jockeys in Virginia City each year (☎ 775-847-0311).

October

Vegas to Reno is a 534-mile off-road race with drivers from around the world.

Las Vegas Balloon Classic is an annual event in which 100 hot-air balloons take to the sky (☎ 702-452-8066).

December

National Finals Rodeo, early December, draws wranglers from across the country to Las Vegas to compete (☎ 888-637-7633).

WORK

Seasonal work is possible in national parks and other tourist sites, especially ski areas; for information, contact park concessionaires or local chambers of commerce. However, if you're not a US citizen or legal resident (with a 'green card'), there's a lot of red tape involved in getting work in the US, and rather severe penalties (a heavy fine for your employer, deportation for yourself) if you're caught working illegally. If you have particular skills, as well as a sponsoring employer or close relative living in the US, you have a reasonable chance of getting a special working visa from an American embassy before you leave your own country.

The type of visa varies depending on how long you're staying and the kind of work you plan to do. Generally, you need either a J1 visa, which you can obtain by joining a visitor-exchange program, or a H2B visa, which you get when sponsored by a US employer. The latter is not easy to obtain (since the employer has to prove that no US citizen or permanent resident is available to do the job); the former is issued mostly to students for work in summer camps. If you lack connections, it's unlikely you'll be granted a working visa.

Information on legal student employment opportunities is best obtained from a university, either in your own country or in the US.

ACCOMMODATIONS

California's accommodations cover the full spectrum from primitive campsites to luxurious resorts. Seasonal price fluctuations are quite common, with rates leaping up in summer in most places, except in ski resorts where premium rates apply in winter. Rates are also high – and availability low – around major holidays like Labor Day, Thanksgiving and Christmas. On weekends year round, hotels catering primarily to business travelers often have special deals.

Room rates vary by type of room and even by type of bed. While price differences between single and double occupancy are nonexistent or small, it does matter whether you're staying in a room with two queen-size beds or a king-size bed. The location of the room may also affect the price; larger hotels spread over different buildings may charge more for rooms in recently renovated structures. Rooms with a view naturally cost more than those without. Hotels facing a noisy street may charge slightly more for quieter rooms. Also see Costs in the Money section earlier in this chapter.

Whenever possible, we have provided the range of rates a hotel may charge, though changes may occur frequently and spontaneously. Rooms get renovated, managers change and hotels are taken over by chains. Thus, the rates quoted in this book should serve merely as guidelines.

Discounts

Discounts of 10% or more off published rates are frequently available. Are you a member of the AAA or one of its foreign affiliates? Are you a senior citizen? (This usually means age 65, but could also mean 62 or 60 or even 55, depending upon the hotel. Best yet, bring your AARP card – see Senior Travelers earlier in this chapter.) You might also cash in on discounts for university students, military personnel and travel-industry members. Also look out for magazines with hotel discount vouchers, often available at gas stations and tourist offices. In general, ask about discounts when booking a room.

Reservations

Where available, we have listed a property's toll-free 800 telephone number in this book.

Note that these numbers are for information or to make a reservation; for private calls to your room, use the direct hotel number. If you're having trouble finding accommodations, consider using one of several free hotel reservation services. They include Hotel Reservations Network (☎ 800-964-6835) and Central Reservation Service (☎ 800-548-3311).

Budget hotels and motels may not accept reservations, but at least phone from the road to see what's available; even if they don't take reservations, they'll often hold a room for an hour or two.

Chain hotels will take reservations days or months ahead. Normally, you must give a credit-card number to hold the room. If you don't show up and don't call to cancel, you will be charged the first night's rental. Cancellation policies vary, so find out the hotel's policies when you book.

Also make sure to let the hotel know if you plan on a late arrival. Many motels will give your room away if you haven't arrived or called by 6 pm. Chains have toll-free numbers, but their central reservation system might not be aware of local special discounts. Booking ahead, however, gives you the peace of mind of a guaranteed room when you arrive.

Camping

While you'll find loads of campgrounds in California (over 800 at last count), not all provide a back-to-nature experience. And unless you travel in spring or fall, plenty of other people will be sharing the campgrounds with you.

Tenters will find the best camping on the North Coast, in the Sierra and in the deserts. The higher and more northerly areas are often too cold for winter camping, and the deserts may be too hot in summer. Facilities at backcountry campgrounds range from pit toilets, pumped water and fire grates to a flat spot with a sign telling you that this is indeed a campground. State park campgrounds cost $7 to $11 and include potable water, picnic tables and fire pits, though not always flush toilets and electricity. A state park campground price schedule is available free from

California Department of Parks & Recreation, PO Box 942896, Sacramento, CA 94296-0001.

California's private campgrounds often offer hot showers, laundry facilities, a store, and sometimes a pool or volleyball courts. These places usually cater to the RV crowd, with dump stations and spacious RV sites with hookups for electricity and water for about $25. Tenters are usually herded together on a strip of grass that may or may not be shaded and is usually not secluded. Tent sites normally have a picnic table and fire pit and cost $11 to $18 per night for two people; pets and extra people cost around $2 each. For information on California's private campgrounds, contact the California Travel Parks Association (☎ 916-885-1624, 888-782-9872, www.campgrounds.com).

Kampgrounds of America (KOA) is the largest and most visible chain of private campgrounds, perched at many a freeway exit near the outskirts of town. In addition to the above-mentioned amenities, KOAs have Kamping Kabins that sleep up to four people and cost around $40. You provide your own blanket or sleeping bag and share the campground bathrooms. Regular campsites are around $28 with hookups, $22 for tents. For the free KOA directory, contact KOA (☎ 406-248-7444, 800-548-7239, www .koakampgrounds.com), PO Box 30558, Billings, MT 59114. Free campsite reservations can be made by calling ☎ 800-562 plus the four digit campground number listed in their directory.

National Parks National park campgrounds are generally rather spiffy, with flush toilets and access to hot showers. Prices are usually $10 to $15, with walk-in sites (for backpackers and cyclists) for around $3. Dispersed camping in undeveloped sites is allowed on BLM land with a fire permit (available free at ranger stations).

Camping information and site reservations for most national parks are handled by the National Park Reservation Service (NPRS) at ☎ 800-365-2267, daily 7 am to 7 pm Pacific time (from outside the US call ☎ 301-722-1257). A few parks, including Yosemite, Death Valley and the Grand Canyon, are handled by ☎ 800-436-7275. Reservations are free and may be made up to five months ahead.

In winter 1999, the National Park Service also began offering online reservations (http://reservations.nps.gov) for 26 of its parks, including Yosemite, Channel Islands, Death Valley, Grand Canyon, Joshua Tree, Sequoia, Kings Canyon, Whiskeytown National Recreation Area and Zion, all of which are covered in this book. Lodges within parks, and motels and campgrounds near them, are privately owned. Details are given in the text.

National Forests National forests have many campgrounds, which vary from simple sites with a fire ring and a pit toilet, but no water, to campgrounds with showers and sometimes limited RV hookups. Most sites are $6 to $12; a few without water are free. Campground reservations in national forests may be made up to eight months ahead by calling the National Recreation Reservation Service (☎ 800-280-2267, 877-444-6777) between 7 am and 4 pm or via their website at www.reserve.usa. Each reservation costs $8.65.

State Parks California campground information and reservations are handled by Parknet (☎ 800-444-7275) 8 am to 5 pm daily, though it's often impossible to get through. For online reservations, log on to www.park-net.com. Reservations cost $7.50.

Nevada does not have a central reservation agency. Reservations must be made directly with the campground.

Hostels
Hostelling International The 'official' youth hostels in the US are affiliated with Hostelling International-American Youth Hostels (HI-AYH), which is a member of the International Youth Hostel Federation. California has about 25 HI-AYH hostels, well located in the large cities or in remote picturesque settings. All of them are covered in detail in their respective geographic chapters throughout this book.

HI-AYH, whose website is at www.hiayh.org, publishes an annual guide listing all their hostels in North America. It's available for $7 from hostels, most bookstores and from the regional offices. There are three regional HI-AYH offices in California:

Golden Gate Council (☎ 415-863-1444, fax 415-863-3865), 425 Divisadero St, No 307, San Francisco, CA 94117; Travel Center (☎ 415-701-1320), 425 Divisadero St, Suite 307, San Francisco, CA 94117

Los Angeles Council (☎ 310-393-6263, fax 310-393-1769), 1434 2nd St, Santa Monica, CA 90401; Travel Center (☎ 310-393-3413), same location

San Diego Council (☎ 619-339-9981, fax 619-525-1533), 655 4th Ave, Suite 46, San Diego, CA 92101

Beds are $7 to $24 per person for HI-AYH members, and usually $3 more for nonmembers. Membership costs $25 per year, free for those under 18 and $15 for those over 55. Memberships are available at most hostels, Council Travel agencies and the hostel regional offices.

Basic facilities include dormitory-style, gender-segregated rooms (though more expensive private rooms are sometimes available), shared single-sex bathrooms, equipped kitchens and usually a common room with TV, games and magazines and books. Most hostels close during the day, and some have a curfew, though these rules vary from place to place.

Reservations are advised during peak season. They can be made with a credit card by calling the hostel directly during office hours (these vary but are usually between 7 and 10 am or 5 and 10 pm). If you don't show up, you are still charged for one night's stay. Most hostels also accept fax reservations, though you must provide your credit card number and expiration date to guarantee your booking. A toll-free number (☎ 800-909-4776) is available for reservations at about 60 hostels. (You need the access code for the hostels to use this service, available from any HI-AYH office or listed in their handbook).

Places in California with HI-AYH hostels include the following:

San Francisco Bay Area
   San Francisco (2)
   Point Reyes National Seashore
   Marin Headlands
   Los Altos
   San Jose
   Santa Cruz
   Pigeon Point
   Point Montara
Sacramento Valley
   Sacramento
Northern Mountains
   Mt Shasta
North Coast
   Klamath
Central Coast
   San Luis Obispo
San Joaquin Valley
   Merced
Sierra Nevada
   Independence
   Midpines (near Yosemite)
Southern California
   Los Angeles (3)
   Fullerton (in Orange County)
   San Diego (2)

Independent Hostels A growing number of independent hostels provide basic dormitory accommodations to low-budget travelers and the occasional private double room for couples. The quality of these hostels varies quite a bit, but bathrooms are usually shared and most hostels have a kitchen, laundry, notice board and TV. Sometimes a light breakfast is included. Some of these hostels put on a cheap evening meal, throw regular parties for the guests, arrange local tours and pick up guests at transportation hubs. They don't usually have curfews, and dorms are not gender-segregated. Dormitory beds cost about $10 to $16 a night. A private room starts at about $20 for two people. *The Hostel Handbook* by Jim Williams is a 66-page listing of hostels and is available for $5 payable to the author; write to 722 St Nicholas Ave, New York, NY 10031 (☎ 212-926-7030, infohostel@aol.com). The Internet Guide to Hostelling website at www.hostels.com lists hostels throughout the world.

Often these hostels say they accept only international travelers, basically to keep out destitute locals. In fact, they will usually also take Americans who look like they will fit in with the other guests. A passport, HI-AYH card or international plane ticket will help establish your traveler credentials.

B&Bs

While California's bed and breakfasts range from restored mansions in the middle of town to rustic cabins surrounded by nothing but trees, they all offer the same sort of deal – a private room (bathrooms may or may not be private), a hot breakfast and a personal atmosphere. Rooms with private TV and phones are the exception rather than the rule.

European visitors should be aware that North American B&Bs are much less the casual, inexpensive sort of accommodations found on the Continent or in Britain. Many if not most B&Bs require advance reservations, though some will be happy to oblige the occasional drop-in. Most B&Bs prohibit smoking.

Prices range from $55 to $185 per night for a double room, so B&Bs are not a low-budget option. Sometimes proprietors charge per person rather than per room, so be sure you know the correct rate before getting settled.

B&Bs tend to be frequented by the well-heeled rather than hard-core traveling types. If a substantial breakfast holds you through the day, consider the price of a B&B to include some of your food expenses for the next day. Sometimes the price is not much higher than a motel plus a big breakfast, and the B&B might serve tea and cookies in the afternoon.

For a list of California's B&Bs, contact B&B International (☎ 408-867-9662, 800-872-4500, fax 408-867-0907, www.bbinto .com), 12711 McCartisville Place, Saratoga, CA 95070. This organization also makes reservations at any of their 400 member B&Bs for $10 per booking.

Motels

Motel rooms are often priced by the number of beds in a room, rather than the number of occupants. A room with a double or queen-size bed will often cost the same for one or two people, while a room with two beds will cost more. Many rooms have two double beds, which are good for families if your kids will share a bed. Many motels advertise that 'kids stay free,' but sometimes you will have to pay extra for a crib or a 'rollaway' (portable bed).

Chain Motels The majority of California's motels are affiliated with well-publicized national chains, and clusters of these establishments huddle together around freeway exits. Most have a central phone number, answering 24 hours, but it is only for reservations and may not have any detailed information about an individual property. Each chain has a booklet which lists all of their locations, including the address, facilities and phone number of each place. The reservation numbers of some of the best-known chains are Best Western, Choice Hotels (Econo Lodge, Rodeway Inn, Quality Inn, Sleep Inn, Comfort Inn, Clarion Inn), Days Inn, Howard Johnson, Motel 6, Super 8 Motel, Travelodge (see the Toll-Free Numbers Directory for phone numbers).

Some chains are cheaper than others, and the price also depends on the location and the season. Motel 6 is usually the cheapest of the chains in a given area, while Best Western and Howard Johnson are on the high end. The price of a Motel 6 is a fair index of the cost of accommodations in a

Gas, Food, Lodging

When coming into a city on the highway you will notice signs that say 'Gas Food Lodging,' followed by something like 'Next Three Exits.' Don't assume these exits will lead you directly into the city center – they won't. You'll end up amid strips of chain motels, fast-food restaurants and gas stations with small grocery stores. If you have no intention of staying in town, but want to catch a few hours' sleep and head out early on the road, these establishments provide cheap accommodations, food and a bit of true Americana.

town. For more information on price, see Costs in the Money section earlier in this chapter.

While chain motels are not too exciting, they are reliably clean, and the rooms will have a private bathroom, heating, air-conditioning and usually cable TV. Other amenities might include a swimming pool, coin laundry and phones with free local calls.

Independent Motels Independently owned motels are usually found in the same areas as chain motels and are a bit less standardized in their prices and facilities. The cheapest will cost a few dollars less than the

Motel 6 (ask for discounts when paying cash), though they tend to be more worn than their spiffy corporate counterparts. But many independent motels are well run and friendly, and the rooms will always have a private bathroom, TV and usually a telephone. Often they are owned by families who take pride in their business and keep the facilities especially clean.

Hotels

These differ from motels in that they do not surround a parking lot and usually have some sort of a lobby. The good ones have amenities like in-house restaurants and bars,

---

Houseboating

An alternative to land-based accommodations are the fully equipped, fully operational houseboats that tour the lakes and rivers of California and Nevada. You'll have all the necessities, including hot water, linens and cooking facilities. And thanks to the states' climate, you can usually count on sunny skies, calm waters and warm weather to enhance fishing, sunning, swimming and lake touring.

Renting a boat for a weekend or a week is typically cost-effective for groups of more than three. Most houseboats sleep 10, though eight are more comfortable. Peak season is June to September, with rates plunging during low and shoulder seasons. Most companies have a minimum rental of three days/two nights. Weeklong rentals are a significantly better deal, and discounts of around 20% for accompanying smaller boats are frequent.

For a 10-person houseboat, low-season/high-season rates average $900/1900 for two nights and $1200/2900 for a weekly rental. The only way to get the best deal is to be thorough when inquiring about amenities (ice chests/refrigerators, air-conditioning, stereo, TV, water slide), exactly how many nights are counted in a 'weekend' and a 'week' (it varies) and what accompanying discounts or packages are offered. The following rent houseboats:

Forever Resorts Houseboat Rentals (☎ 800-255-5561, www.foreverresorts .com) operates on Lake Mojave and Lake Mead, both on the Arizona/Nevada border, and on the Sacramento River Delta, in California. PO Box 52038, Phoenix, AZ 85072

Funtime-Fulltime/Bidwell Marina (☎ 530-589-3165) rents on Lake Oroville, California. 801 Bidwell Canyon Rd, Oroville, CA 95966

Herman and Helen's Marina (☎ 800-676-4841) rents on the Sacramento River Delta, California. Venice Island Ferry, Stockton, CA 95219

Lake Powell Reservations (☎ 800-528-6154) operates on Lake Powell, between Arizona and Utah.

Seven Crown Resorts (☎ 800-752-9669) rents on Lake Mead and Lake Mojave, and Lake Shasta, California. PO Box 16247, Irvine, CA 92713-0068

swimming pools, fitness centers and room service. In California – especially in the Wine Country, the North Coast and around LA and Palm Springs – look for the fabled 'spa' feature, which could include mineral baths, mud baths and hot springs or may simply be a beauty outpost that provides facials and foot rubs. When you see or hear 'spa,' ask the hotel exactly what is meant and what services are included in the price of a room.

Most hotels are national chains with central 24-hour reservation numbers. Prices at these places range from $90 to $150 per night for a double room. National hotel chains include Holiday Inn, Hyatt, Marriott, Radisson, and Sheraton (see the Toll-Free Numbers Directory for phone numbers).

At the opposite end of the spectrum are old hotels that double as transient rooming houses. Though these hotels are not usually dangerous, they are often near train and bus stations, downtown areas or in the less-than-desirable parts of large cities. The cheapest of these hotels will have shared bathroom and toilet facilities. Watch out for dishonest desk clerks who may try to convince you that their hotel is the only place to stay for miles around. This is rarely the case. So don't pay more than $30 for a scummy looking hotel just because it's near the train station.

In historic towns or districts in cities, old hotels are sometimes restored to their original period decor and outfitted with modern plumbing, TV and telephones. These hotels can be nice, atmospheric places to stay, but they will cost more than a motel with equivalent standards.

Resorts & Lodges

Luxury resorts give their guests so many things to do that often they are destinations in themselves. They are very expensive and only a few are mentioned in the text.

Ski resorts usually have a central reservations hotline to fill their full range of accommodations, from motel rooms to condos. They might charge up to $200 or so per night/per bed in midwinter and drop prices to less than half that in summer.

Lodges are often in touristy rural areas and are rustic-looking but usually quite

comfortable inside. Restaurants are on the premises, and tour services are often available. National park lodges are not cheap, with most rooms going for $100 or more for a double during the high season, but they can be your only option if you want to stay inside a park without camping. Therefore, many lodges are fully booked months in advance during the summer.

FOOD

California's dining scene is as diverse as the state's population. It is possible to eat Mexican *huevos rancheros* for breakfast, a Thai curry for lunch and fish and chips for dinner – without venturing out of one neighborhood. Of course this is primarily true in big cities, but even small towns are likely to have at least one Mexican and one Chinese restaurant. For those with tame tastes, the standard American fare is served at diners, coffee shops and fast-food chains, and is never too far away. Pizza is ubiquitous.

Whenever you eat at a restaurant, remember that your final tab will be inflated by 25% over prices quoted on the menu because of the addition of 7% or 8% sales tax and a 15% or so tip. Tipping is, of course, left to your discretion and should reflect the quality of service given, but 15% is considered normal. It is not expected at fast-food restaurants with counter service. For more on this, see Costs in the Money section earlier in this chapter.

Breakfast

Big breakfasts are an affordable way to fill yourself up, provided you can stomach large quantities of food before noon. A breakfast of pancakes, eggs and sausage or a hearty omelet costs around $4.50. Breakfast often includes home fries (diced potatoes fried with onions, bell peppers or spices) or hash browns (shredded or sliced potatoes fried to a golden brown), toast and 'bottomless cups' (unlimited refills) of coffee. You get a choice of how your eggs are cooked – scrambled, sunny-side up, over easy (flipped, but with a runny yolk), or over hard (flipped with a hard yolk). Typically, the low-price breakfast special is available from about 6 to 11 am.

Denny's and IHOP (International House of Pancakes) are restaurant chains that serve good breakfasts, sometimes 24 hours a day.

Lunch

Usually served from 11:30 am to 2 pm, lunch is another inexpensive meal. Prices may be more than one third less expensive than the dinner menu, though the food and portions are identical. For a bustling, energetic lunch scene, head to the business district of any city – like San Francisco's Financial District – where the number of suit-clad business-people is an indication of the best or cheapest places to eat. Many ethnic eateries – Indian, Thai, Chinese – usually have set three-course lunches for around $5.

Dinner

In large cities, many restaurants offer 'early-bird specials,' which feature a complete meal (usually the menu is limited) for around $7, between 4 and 6 pm. Spending a few dollars on drinks during 'happy hour' (usually between 4 and 7 pm) will often get you free appetizers, which can be anything from a bowl of peanuts to a full hot buffet. Sports bars and bars in large hotel chains such as Hyatt, Red Lion and Holiday Inn have the best deals. People tend to eat early, and many restaurants are closed or deserted by 10 pm.

California Cuisine

A gourmet movement in the mid-1980s, led by Alice Waters of Berkeley's Chez Panisse restaurant, Wolfgang Puck of LA's Spago and Nancy Waters of San Francisco's Boulevard, established a definable California cuisine that revolves around fresh, seasonal ingredients, unusual combinations and artistic presentation. Low-fat recipes and cooking methods are a big part of California cuisine, but by no means define it. Typical entrées might include angel-hair pasta with sun-dried tomatoes, garlic and fresh basil, or braised chicken with sesame-ginger soy sauce on a bed of wilted greens, accompanied by a California Chardonnay, of course. The main problem with this kind of food is that, although it's often a feast for the eyes, it may leave you $20 poorer and still hungry.

Seafood

Fish and shellfish are great in California, especially along the coast. In Northern California, Dungeness crab is in season from November to March. Seafood restaurants serve traditional dishes like clam chowder and *cioppino* (a tomato-based stew of crab, clams and whitefish seasoned with wine and herbs), and usually have fresh salmon. South of San Francisco, seafood takes on a Mexican flair and may be served as fish tacos or Vera Cruz style (cooked with tomatoes, peppers and onions and served over rice). And most seafood restaurants still serve plain old grilled, sautéed or fried fish served with rice or potatoes and a salad. Prices are typically in the $7 to $20 range, depending on how fancy the restaurant is. For the best prices, and often the best quality (though choices might be limited to fish and chips or fried clams), hunt out fish markets with a deli counter or look for small stands on the ends of piers.

Ethnic Food

You'll find just about every type of international food in California – Italian, Peruvian, Cambodian, Cuban – you name it, but the two most common types are Mexican and Chinese.

Mexican Food from south of the border is a staple of many a Californian's diet, and until you've eaten *carnitas* (pork) or fish tacos washed down by a Pacífico, you have not experienced California culture. Chain restaurants like Taco Bell serve American-ized Mexican food – good for the faint of stomach. *Taquerías* are, strictly speaking, little places serving tacos, but they are cheap, good and usually have other fare as well. The farther south you travel in California, the better and more frequent Mexican restaurants become.

For the real thing, you have to find a place with red vinyl booths, Mexican music blaring on the radio and fake flowers hung on the wall. Here you will get authentic *enchiladas* (chicken, beef or cheese wrapped in a corn tortilla and smothered with red or green sauce and cheese), *tacos* (a soft or deep-fried corn tortilla filled with beef or chicken, cheese, lettuce and salsa), *tamales* (usually ground meat rolled in cornmeal, wrapped in corn husks and steamed) and *huevos rancheros* (a corn tortilla topped with fried eggs and red ranchero sauce), all of which come with chips, salsa, rice and beans. A burrito is a flour tortilla filled with beans, rice and meat or vegetables. A California staple, burritos are tasty, filling and cheap.

Most Mexican food contains substantial amounts of cheese or lard, though healthier versions have lately become more prevalent.

Chinese With the largest Chinese population outside of China, San Francisco's Chinatown has Chinese restaurants ranging from hole-in-the-wall joints where the menu is scribbled (sometimes in Chinese characters) on a paper place mat to posh restaurants with live lobster tanks and pink tablecloths: this range is repeated all over the state. Most Chinese restaurants offer the standard sweet-and-sour, moo shu (eaten with little rice pancakes), and kung pao (made with peanuts and spicy chiles) dishes and can easily accommodate vegetarians. As a rule, Hunan and Szechwan food tends to be spicier than Mandarin food. Dim sum is a Chinese brunch. The waiter brings small dishes of meat- or bean-filled buns, pot stickers (fried, filled dumplings), rice balls and other sweet and savory pastries around on carts. You point to what you want then pay according to the number of plates you've accumulated at the end – a really fun way to eat.

Pacific Rim The newest trend in upscale California restaurants (especially in Los Angeles and San Francisco) is Pacific Rim or Cal-Asian cooking. The focus of Pacific Rim cooking is on the use of local ingredients and seasonings and cooking methods traditional in Chinese and Japanese cuisine. Meats and fish are seasoned with unlikely combinations of turmeric, cilantro (fresh coriander), ginger, garlic, chile paste and fresh fruit juices (usually citrus) and served with Asian staples like rice, sweet potatoes or buckwheat *udon* noodles. Appetizers are often the most interesting things on the menu, ranging from grilled portobello mushrooms to pounded rice wrapped in seaweed to mustard-spiked crab cakes. Don't hesitate to order several appetizers and make them your entire meal.

Wolfgang Puck, the father of the movement, dominates the scene with his Chinois on Main in Santa Monica and Postrio in San Francisco. Röckenwagner, in Santa Monica, and California Fats in Sacramento are also recommended. All of these restaurants are quite expensive.

Fast Food
Though not particularly exciting or healthy, fast-food chains are cheap, reliable standbys for just about any meal and will usually have clean bathrooms. In many ways they are characteristically Californian – efficient, convenient, colorful and close to the freeway.

For hamburgers, the main choices are McDonald's, Burger King, Carl's Jr (only in California) and Wendy's. Unique to California is the venerable In-N-Out Burger, which has a brief menu, but die-hards will travel 50 miles out of the way to find one.

Jack in the Box, also unique to the Western states, ventures beyond burgers with tacos and burritos. Taco Bell has really cheap and fairly decent quasi-Mexican food. A meal at Del Taco, another Western chain and Taco Bell's main rival, costs a dollar or two more and has a larger selection of non-Mexican items and more dishes with vegetables.

Pizza Hut, Shakey's, Straw Hat and Round Table are the most common pizza parlor chains and require a bit more time and money than other fast-food places. Domino's Pizza has delivery or pickup only; they don't have tables. Crispy thin-crust pizza with unique ingredients and less grease is available at California Pizza Kitchen, a chain started in California and usually found in malls.

Markets
California's climate is very conducive to picnicking, and you'll find many delis, markets and cafes that stock all the necessary items, from premade salads to single-serving bottles

of wine. In the Central Valley, roadside fruit stands sell locally grown, seasonal produce and a variety of dried fruits and nuts.

Health food stores and natural foods markets usually have organic produce, bulk food and a deli section with sandwiches, burritos and beverages. Prices are higher than at supermarkets because of the cost of organic ingredients often farmed on a small scale.

Real shoestringers will want to stick to supermarkets like Ralphs, Safeway, Vons, Lucky or Albertson's, which have very competitive prices and are found everywhere. These stores are often open 24 hours, and some have salad bars, delis and bakeries. Each supermarket has different specials every week. To qualify for some heavily discounted items, you may have to become a 'club' member, a free formality that's instantly accomplished by filling out a short form. In return, you'll receive a 'club card' that must be presented at the cash register to get a discount. The Sunday edition of metropolitan newspapers often has coupon books that that can be clipped to help you cut costs further. Another option are '99 cent' stores, where everything costs just that, though their food items are usually limited to cans and candy.

One of the most popular food markets throughout California (more prevalent in coastal communities and not at all represented in Nevada) is Trader Joe's, which packs its bare-bones, warehouselike stores with gourmet foods at discount prices. Their cheese offerings are legendary, as are their wine and beer selections. They also have delicious breads, frozen foods, dairy and ready-made salads and wraps. Branches are not as ubiquitous as the major supermarket chains, but to find the nearest, you can call ☎ 800-746-7857. Then punch in your zip code, and the machine will tell you where to go. And then...go there.

DRINKS
Nonalcoholic

Most restaurants provide customers with free ice water; it's tap water and safe to drink. All the usual soft drinks are available, although you may be asked if you'll drink Coke instead of Pepsi and vice versa.

Lemonade is a lemon-sugar-ice water mix: if you want the clear, fizzy stuff that the British call lemonade, ask for Sprite or 7-Up.

For the ultimate low-calorie, caffeine-free soft drink, ask for club soda (soda water) or mineral water. Fancy French and Italian brands – like Vittel, Evian and Pelegrino – are popular with yuppies, but the local product, Calistoga, from the small spa town in Northern California, is also trendy and just as good.

Many restaurants offer milk, including low-fat varieties. You can often get fresh-squeezed orange juice at better restaurants, but packaged juices are more common.

Coffee is served much more often than tea, usually with a choice of regular or 'decaf.' Drinkers of English-style tea will be infuriated: tea is usually a cup or pot of hot water with a tea bag next to it. Milk is almost never added, but a slice of lemon often is. Iced tea, along with almost every imaginable drink under the sun, is available at most roadside gas stations or convenience stores.

Alcoholic

Persons under the age of 21 (minors) are prohibited from consuming alcohol in the US. Carry a driver's license or passport as proof of age to enter a bar, to order alcohol at a restaurant or buy alcohol at a supermarket. Servers have the right to ask to see your ID and may refuse service without it. Minors are not allowed in bars and pubs, even to order nonalcoholic beverages. This means that most dance clubs are also off-limits to minors, although a few clubs have solved the under-age problem with a segregated drinking area. Minors are, however, welcome in the dining areas of restaurants where alcohol may be served.

Beer The big name brands of domestic beer are available everywhere, though some locals as well as visitors find them lacking in taste. To order beer, you must specify the type you want. If you just ask for a beer, you'll get whatever they pour – usually a Budweiser. Many California restaurants are only licensed to serve wine and beer and not 'hard liquor' like cognac and whisky.

Microbreweries, or 'brewpubs,' are very popular. These brew various beers on the premises, and you can get up to a dozen different types on tap. Supermarkets and big liquor stores can stock a bewildering variety of imported beers – more expensive but, perhaps, more to your taste.

Beer sold in the US has a lower alcohol content than that in most other countries, which may be why many visitors find it bland. Imported beers must conform to the same restriction on alcohol content and are often specially made for export to the US. If you're particularly fond of Foster's, Heineken or Moosehead at home, you *will* be disappointed to find that it's been wimped down for the American market. For example, the Foster's Lager sold in the US is actually made in Canada and doesn't taste much like the Foster's sold in Australia at all.

Note that 'lite' beer means lower in calories (90 instead of 180), but not necessarily lower in alcohol. But it brings up the question: is there such a thing as 'light' beer?

Wine California produces excellent varietal wines and some very affordable generic wines that are an excellent value for the tippler on a tight budget. The first California wine growing dates from the Spanish mission period, when grapes were grown to make sacramental wines. The industry is now very sophisticated, and its best wines are respected the world over.

While grapes are grown in most of the fertile areas of the state, the Napa and Sonoma valleys – north of San Francisco – produce the very best wine (see the Wine Country chapter). Californian white wines include Sauvignon Blanc, Fumé Blanc, Riesling, Gewürztraminer, Chenin Blanc, Zinfandel and – the most popular – Chardonnay. Reds include Pinot Noir, Merlot, Beaujolais, Cabernet Sauvignon and Zinfandel. A reasonable bottle of red or white from the Central Valley or Southern California vineyards can be bought for $6 to $10. At a good discount liquor store or supermarket, you can get something quite drinkable for $3 to $6.

If you want to taste the best California wines, look for those that are labeled as 'pro-

duced and bottled by' a Sonoma or Napa Valley winery. This means that at least 85% of the grapes were grown in that area and 75% were fermented by the vintner who bottled the wine. The Sonoma Valley Chardonnay is among the best California white wines, while Napa Valley Cabernet Sauvignon is among the best reds. Zinfandel is a varietal unique to California and is available as both a red and a white. Sparkling wines of the region easily measure up to French champagne, though at much more reasonable prices.

Spirits All bars have a wide range of 'hard liquor': gin, brandy, rum, vodka and whiskey – invariably served with lots of ice ('on the rocks') unless you ask for it 'straight up.' If you ask for whiskey, you'll get American whiskey. If you want Scotch whiskey, ask for Scotch. And if you have a particular allegiance, specify.

Other typically local types of firewater come from south of the border. Tequila, from Mexico, is popular in such drinks as a margarita or tequila sunrise. The American taste for cocktails originated during Prohibition, when lots of flavorful mixers were used to disguise the taste of bathtub gin. These days there are thousands of named cocktail recipes, and many bars will have their own special concoction, usually with a fancy or a funny name, like the 'screaming orgasm' or the 'slow easy screw up against the wall.'

ENTERTAINMENT
Cinemas

Nearly every town – and just about every shopping mall – in California has a movie theater. Movie listings can be found in the entertainment section of local papers. The average ticket price is $7, with discounts usually offered for films showing before 6 pm. Look for two-for-one or half-price tickets on Monday or Tuesday night.

In larger cities, you'll find small, independent theaters that show alternative, classic and foreign films. In any theater, popcorn, candy and soda concessions can end up costing twice as much as your ticket, if you're not careful.

Clubs

Nightclubs have long been popular in California. In the 1950s, many dance styles originated on Hollywood stages, at beach parties, and in Los Angeles nightclubs. The 'shag' and 'swim,' both Gidget-type teenybopper dances that involve profuse arm and hip swinging, are said to have come from the surf scene on beaches southwest of Los Angeles. In the early '90s, 'line dancing' (where people stand shoulder to shoulder executing choreographed moves in unison) became popular in funk and hip-hop clubs and country-&-western bars.

Since the mid-'90s, swing music has swept urban areas, and we're not talking about the surviving members of the Glen Miller Orchestra; we're talking about serious swingers who can really hi-di-ho, and make you feel that hepcat jive. This isn't a straight retro-scene, either. Anything goes in the swing revival. So what you get is a cross between big band, jazz, blues and rockabilly. Cab Calloway, Louis Jordan, Elvis Presley and Bob Wills all exert a certain amount of influence. Figure *that* one out!

Santa Monica, Hollywood and San Francisco have the greatest concentration of dance clubs, with a few good spots in San Diego and Fresno's Tower District. The club scene ranges from polished Hollywood spots like House of Blues and the Key Club to grunt-sweat-don't-care-what-you-look-like places such as the Garage in Hollywood and the Stork Club in Oakland. A cover charge (what you must pay to enter) can be free to $20, with higher prices on weekends. Some places have free entrance but a two drink minimum, or charge half price before 9 pm (most clubs don't 'happen' until after 10 pm). Each club has its own musical style, but hip-hop, house and techno are still popular. Dancing alone or in groups is quite acceptable.

San Francisco and Los Angeles have some good Latino nightclubs that have nightly salsa dancing. Usually about half the crowd is Latino, and dance skills vary from nearly professional to 'how in the heck do you do this?' Some clubs are strictly salsa, but most have a good mix throughout the week, then concentrate on salsa on the weekend.

Concerts

Big-name performers from Madonna to Tom Jones usually make the same California route: the San Diego Sports Arena; Los Angeles Coliseum, Hollywood Bowl or Greek Theater; Shoreline Theater in the Bay Area or Oakland's Coliseum; and Cal Expo in Sacramento. Anything at the Hollywood Bowl, on a warm summer night with a picnic and bottle of wine, is bound to be memorable. Los Angeles and San Francisco have many other venues where you can hear anything from Ukrainian folk music to punk rock every night of the week.

San Francisco also has some good medium-size venues like the Fillmore, the Warfield and the Great American Music Hall. Oakland has the best jazz and blues spots, namely Kimball's East and Yoshi's. Tickets to big-name shows cost around $30 to $60, while those at smaller venues range from $2 to $20.

In Nevada, concerts by big-name artists are mostly limited to Las Vegas venues, where most performers appear at the 'big rooms' in the splashy casinos. Reno also attracts its fair share of performers, though not always the top acts.

Theater

Los Angeles is California's undisputed theater capital, launching many plays and musicals that go on to gain international acclaim. A big reason for this is the abundance of talent hanging around Hollywood, waiting for a big break. Actors and actresses who have already 'made it' also like to perform live theater to hone their skills. Most mainstream musicals are performed at the Shubert Theater, Ahmanson Theatre or Dorothy Chandler Pavilion (see the Los Angeles chapter).

San Diego, partly because it's close enough to LA to be accessible to the Hollywood pool of actors, directors and designers, has an excellent reputation for theater.

Venues include the Repertory Theater, La Jolla Playhouse and Old Globe Theater.

While San Francisco doesn't share the same talent pool as Southern California, its theater productions are conceptually strong. The many small theater fringe and avant-garde adaptations are often excellent, though not always for the fainthearted. The nearby Berkeley Repertory Theatre has a national reputation for its productions and has won numerous awards.

Throughout the state, ticket prices vary according to the size and notoriety of a production. Many theaters offer 'rush' or 'student rush' tickets, available for reduced prices a few hours before the performance; there are no reservations or guarantees with these tickets, but they are generally excellent seats. Times Arts Tix in San Diego (☎ 619-497-5000) and Los Angeles (☎ 310-659-3678) and TIX Bay Area (☎ 415-433-7827) in San Francisco sell half-price tickets on the day of performance.

Nevada is definitely not nirvana for theater lovers. An exception here is the Pioneer Center for the Performing Arts in Reno, which does put on quality shows. Las Vegas, though, has mostly hokey musical revues playing at the large casinos.

Classical Music & Opera

San Francisco and Los Angeles both have outstanding symphonies. LA Philharmonic director Esa Peka Salonen, a dashing young Fin, is currently considered one of the finest conductors in the world and enjoys strong public support. Performances are at the Dorothy Chandler Pavilion during the season and at the Hollywood Bowl in summer. San Francisco performances are at Davies Symphony Hall, where even bad seats are pretty good.

The Berkeley Symphony, conducted by Kent Nagano – who also directs the opera in Lyon, France – is said to be world class, but their performances are very sporadic (only about four per year). They perform at Zellerbach Hall on the UC Berkeley campus. The San Diego and San Jose symphonies are also very good, but in a totally different class.

In Los Angeles, the Los Angeles Music Center Opera came under the stewardship of Placido Domingo in 1999 and enjoys a fine reputation. San Francisco Opera's performances range from mediocre to quite good. Unless you spend at least $75 on a ticket (or have good luck getting a last-minute rush seat), you're basically guaranteed a bad seat. The San Diego Opera has a season from January to May, in the Civic Theater, and reasonable seats are affordable.

SPECTATOR SPORTS

Including preseason, the National Football League (NFL) season runs from August to mid-January, Major League Baseball (MLB) from March to October, National Basketball Association (NBA) from November to April, National Hockey League (NHL) ice hockey from October to April and Major League Soccer (MLS) from March to November.

If you're into sports, California is the perfect place in the US to visit: it has more professional teams than any other state. California has three NFL teams (the San Diego Chargers, the San Francisco 49ers and the Oakland Raiders); five MLB teams (the LA Dodgers, California Angels, in Anaheim, San Diego Padres, San Francisco Giants and Oakland A's); three NBA teams (the Sacramento Kings, LA Lakers and Golden State Warriors, in Oakland); three NHL teams (the LA Kings, Mighty Ducks, in Anaheim, and San Jose Sharks); and two MLS teams (the San Jose Clash and LA Galaxy). Games can be sold out – especially 49ers, Lakers and Kings games – so it's best to call ahead.

College sports events are also fun, especially if there is a strong rivalry between schools (for example UCLA versus USC or Stanford versus UC Berkeley). This goes for just about any sport from soccer to ultimate Frisbee.

Beach volleyball is becoming more popular each year. Beach towns in Los Angeles host several professional tournaments each summer, with the Hermosa Open and Manhattan Open being the most important.

SHOPPING

California is a major agricultural producer, so some distinctively Californian purchases are almonds, dried fruit, dates and wine. Fruit and nuts are often sold at roadside stands in the San Joaquin Valley (along I-5, I-80 or small side roads), around Palm Springs and in North County San Diego. The Napa and Sonoma valleys produce the best wines, and you can enjoy tasting and buying directly from the winery, though most well-known wines are actually less expensive at liquor stores.

The sheer variety and quantity of consumer goods – in the US, generally, and in California, particularly – is staggering to many visitors. If you come around Halloween, look at the huge selection of masks and costumes. At Christmas, the decorations and Yuletide junk can be overwhelming. California has many highly specialized shops, with incredible stocks of such esoteric items as high-performance kites, reproduction road signs, hunting knives and Harley-Davidson belt buckles. At a Disney store or a Warner Brothers shop, you can get all sorts of fun stuff emblazoned with your favorite cartoon character. If you're into movie memorabilia, old posters or books about movies, you'll find plenty in LA.

California's diverse communities also offer some interesting things to buy. The Chinatowns in San Francisco and LA have Chinese bookstores and apothecaries that carry ginger and ginseng products said to promote long life and vitality. You can also find interesting green and black teas for very good prices. Los Angeles' Olvera St and Old Town in San Diego have traditional Mexican crafts such as leather, shoes and belts, candles and embroidered fabrics. For better prices – and a glimpse into Mexico – you should visit the border town of Tijuana for the day. For an array of imported goods – from Guatemalan jackets to Indian temple incense – head to Berkeley's Telegraph Ave or to Venice Beach in LA.

Not only is there variety, but prices of most consumer goods are lower in the US than just about anywhere else. If you're really looking for bargains, check out the following.

Outlet Malls Outlet malls, where famous and mainstream stores purportedly sell off their stock at reduced prices, have become all the rage with many visitors who insist on including at least one outlet collection in their shopping. While bargains in these stores are possible, items are often damaged, irregular or leftover from the previous season and are – thus – rejects from regular department stores. That lime-green shirt that was popular last year may get you ticketed by the fashion police this summer. Service in these stores is also kept to a minimum; there are generally fewer employees, dressing rooms and mirrors.

Thrift Shops Thrift shops are stores, usually operated by charities, such as Goodwill, Junior League or the Salvation Army, which sell donated used clothing, housewares, books, furniture and other items, often at ridiculously low prices. Most of the proceeds go back to the charity.

If you've spilled red wine on your only pair of shorts or weren't prepared for that sudden dinner invitation, you're bound to find amazing bargains for just a tiny fraction of what you'd pay in department stores. Designer items and brand-name clothing are especially abundant at stores in fashion-conscious neighborhoods like Beverly Hills and Santa Monica, where – in some circles – nice clothes are donated rather than worn twice.

A derivation of the thrift shop is the vintage clothing stores that sell used clothing, but also specialize in earlier periods. If you want a flared '50s skirt or '40s zoot suit, this is where you'd look. Not surprisingly, these types of stores abound in trendy Hollywood and Silver Lake, though some are in North Hollywood, especially along Melrose Avenue. In San Francisco, the Haight is the center for vintage clothing stores.

Garage Sales As you're driving through neighborhoods on Friday and Saturday, you'll probably notice signs attached to traffic signals and telephone poles announcing 'Moving Sale,' 'Estate Sale,' 'Multi-Family Sale,' 'Garage Sale' and so on. For those holding the sale, it's a way to clean out

the closets and make a buck on the side. For treasure hunters, a garage sale can yield everything from vintage earrings to furniture at rock-bottom prices. Haggling, of course, is just part of the fun.

Activities

California is the only place in the USA where you can surf in the morning and ski in the afternoon, or go from the lowest to the highest point in the lower 48 states in one weekend. This chapter explores some of the many alternatives, ranging from near universals like hiking and backpacking to more esoteric activities like surfing and hot-air ballooning. Though each pursuit has specialized gear shops (usually the best source for local information), Recreational Equipment Incorporated (REI) coop stores are excellent for all-around outdoor needs. The knowledgeable staff sells everything from carabiners to wool socks to stoves to kayak paddles, and rents out tents, skis, stoves, bikes and kayaks. REI stores can be found in Los Angeles, Berkeley and elsewhere. Call ☎ 800-426-4840 to find the branch nearest to you.

HIKING & BACKPACKING

There is perhaps no better way to appreciate the beauty of California – its secluded beaches, rugged coast, lofty glacial peaks and peaceful dense forests – than on foot along the trail. Taking a few days' (or even a few hours') break from the highway to explore the great outdoors can refresh road-weary travelers and give them a heightened appreciation of the scenery that goes whizzing past day after day. Some travelers will experience one good hike and decide to plan the rest of their trip around wilderness or hiking areas.

With California's and Nevada's diverse landscapes, it's possible to experience coastal, desert, mountain and foothill scenery in a pristine state, protected as part of national forest, national or state park, or as wilderness land.

State Parks

California has 270 state parks crisscrossed by about 2000 miles of trails. Most of them are kept in fairly good shape by a league of volunteers and conservation organizations. Parks near urban centers often function as

year-round recreational getaways for locals and may get crowded on weekends. Mt Tamalpais in San Francisco and Will Rogers

Pacific Crest Trail

A truly amazing thing about the West Coast of the USA is that you can walk from Mexico to Canada, across the entire expanse of California, Oregon and Washington, almost without leaving national park or national forest lands. Simply follow the Pacific Crest Trail (PCT).

This 2638-mile trail passes through 24 national forests, seven national parks, 33 designated wilderness areas, and six state parks, following the crest of the Sierra Nevada in California and the Cascade Range in Oregon and Washington, at an average elevation of 5000 feet.

To hike the trail in its entirety, at a good clip of 15 miles a day, would take nearly six months, the California portion about four months. But you don't have to undertake such a dramatic, cross-state trek to take advantage of the PCT. Day or weekend hikers can plan short trips on many accessible segments of the trail.

Some of California's most spectacular wilderness areas are traversed by the PCT, from Anza-Borrego Desert State Park in the very south, through Sequoia and Yosemite National Parks, Lake Tahoe and Lassen National Volcanic Park.

The Pacific Crest Trail Association (☎ 916-349-2109, 888-728-7245, fax 916-349-1268, www.gorp.com/pcta), headquartered at 5325 Elkhorn Blvd, Box 256, Sacramento, CA 95842, can provide detailed information on the trail, as well as addresses for regional USFS and wilderness area offices, tips on long and short backpacking trips, weather conditions and which areas require wilderness permits.

State Park in Los Angeles fall into this category. There's a day-use fee from $2 to $7 for most parks.

National Parks

Unless you have a few days to get into the backcountry of a national park or are visiting during nonpeak season (before Memorial Day and after Labor Day), expect hiking in national parks to be crowded.

Travelers who have little hiking experience will appreciate the well-marked and well-maintained trails in national parks, often with restroom facilities at either end of the trail and interpretive displays along the way. The trails give access to the parks' natural features, and usually show up on NPS maps as nature trails or self-guided interpretive trails. These hikes are usually no longer than 2 miles.

Hikers seeking true wilderness away from heavy foot traffic should avoid national parks and try less-celebrated national forests, especially wilderness areas. Most national parks require overnight hikers to carry backcountry permits, available from visitor centers or ranger stations. This system reduces the chance of people getting lost in the backcountry and limits the number of people using one area at any given time.

Yosemite National Park has a route of High Sierra Camps for people who enjoy backpacking without carrying a heavy load.

Wilderness Areas

About 49% of California land is public, managed by the National Park Service (NPS), United States Forest Service (USFS) and the Bureau of Land Management (BLM). Most designated wilderness areas are on USFS land; the BLM wilderness areas can be among the best in terms of sheer solitude.

The 1964 Wilderness Act, the first major act of Congress to set aside large, federally administered areas, defines wilderness as

An area where the earth and its community of life are untrammeled by man, where man himself is a visitor who does not remain…It is a region which contains no permanent human inhabitants, no possibility for motorized travel, and is spacious enough so that a traveler crossing it by foot or horse must have the experience of sleeping out of doors.

National Forest Adventure Pass

Day-use fees at state and national parks have been commonplace in California and Nevada for several years now. In 1996, however, Congress authorized a controversial pilot project requiring anyone visiting certain national forests by car to purchase a National Forest Adventure Pass (NFAP). The list includes four forests in Southern California: San Bernardino, Cleveland, Angeles and Los Padres. Passes cost $5 per day or $30 per year and must be displayed on the windshield. They are transferable and available from any USFS ranger station in Southern California.

About 80% of the revenue collected is supposed to flow right back into the budgets of the national forests, which will use the money to improve sites and facilities and to protect resources and habitats.

Passes are not needed if you're just driving through the forest without stopping, if you're stopping at a ranger station or visitor center, or if you are already paying another forest-use fee (for example, camping or cabin fees). There's a penalty of $100 if you're caught without the NFAP. Golden Age and Golden Access passports will be honored according to the terms on the back of the cards. They entitle you to 50% off the cost of any use fee. To obtain the discount, you'll need to purchase your National Forest Adventure Pass at Forest Service offices rather than one of the independent vendors. Since this is a recreation use fee, Golden Eagle Passports will not be honored, as they are entrance passes. The Adventure Pass is not an entrance pass.

Wilderness areas in California and Nevada offer excellent hiking and backpacking opportunities. Most wilderness areas do not require permits for hiking and backpacking and often have no developed campsites. Some of the best hiking is found in the USFS wilderness areas of Desolation, Ansel Adams and John Muir (all in the Sierra Nevada).

Responsible Hiking & Backpacking

The popularity of hiking and backpacking is placing great pressure on the natural environment. Consider the following tips and help preserve the ecology and beauty of California's and Nevada's natural areas.

Trash Carry out all your trash, including those easily forgotten items, such as foil, orange peels, cigarette butts and plastic wrappers. Empty packaging weighs very little anyway and should be stored in a dedicated trash bag. Make an effort to carry out trash left by others.

Never bury your trash: Digging disturbs soil and ground cover and encourages erosion. Buried trash will more than likely be dug up by animals, who may be injured or poisoned by it. It may also take years to decompose, especially at high altitudes.

Minimize the waste you must carry out by taking minimal packaging and taking no more food than you will need. If you can't buy in bulk, unpack small packages and combine their contents in one container before your trip. Take reusable containers or stuff sacks.

Rather than bringing bottled water, use iodine drops or purification tablets instead. Sanitary napkins, tampons and condoms should also be carried out, despite the inconvenience. They burn and decompose poorly.

Human Waste Disposal Contamination of water sources by human feces can lead to the transmission of hepatitis, typhoid and intestinal parasites such as giardia, amoebas and roundworms, causing severe health risks not only to members of your party, but also to local residents and wildlife.

Use toilets where available or bury your waste, including toilet paper, by digging a small hole 5 inches (15cm) deep and at least 100 yards or meters from any body of water. Consider carrying a lightweight trowel for this purpose. Cover the waste with soil and a rock.

Washing Don't use detergents or toothpaste, even if they are biodegradable, in or near bodies of water. Use biodegradable soap and a water container (or even a lightweight, portable basin) at least 50 yards or meters away from the body of water. Wash cooking utensils 50 yards or meters from bodies of water, using a scouring brush, sand or snow instead of detergent.

Erosion Hillsides and mountain slopes, especially at high altitudes, are prone to erosion. Stick to existing tracks and avoid shortcuts that bypass switchbacks. If you blaze a new trail straight down a slope, it will turn into a watercourse with the next heavy rainfall and eventually cause soil loss and deep scarring.

If a well-used track passes through a mud patch, walk through the mud; walking around the edge will increase the size of the patch. Avoid removing the plant life that keeps topsoil in place.

Fires & Low-Impact Cooking Don't depend on open fires for cooking. To cut down on deforestation, cook on a lightweight kerosene, alcohol or Shellite (white gas) stove and avoid stoves powered by disposable butane gas canisters. Fires may be acceptable below the tree line in areas that get very few visitors. If you light a fire, use an existing fireplace rather than creating a new one. Use only dead, fallen wood and only as much as needed for cooking. Ensure that you fully extinguish a fire after use. Spread the embers and douse them with water. Then stir them and douse again. A fire is only truly safe to leave when you can comfortably place your hand in it.

Safety

The major forces to be reckoned with while hiking and camping are the weather (which

Bears, Your Food & You

Stories about black bears causing hundreds of thousands of dollars in damage by ripping tents and breaking into cars (even RVs) in search of food have recently been big news. While these incidents always make good headlines, they are a real concern to visitors and administrators of national parks like Yosemite and Sequoia-Kings Canyon, and to visitors in other Sierra Nevada forests.

Black bears, which can in fact be golden to dark brown to black, are not generally aggressive but may attack when startled, and mother bears may charge to protect their cubs. With humans increasingly encroaching upon their natural habitat, though, many have ditched their traditional diet of berries, nuts, roots, grasses and other vegetation in favor of all that they consider 'people food'; this includes everything from toothpaste and suntan lotion to cough syrup.

Bears have an extraordinary ability to recognize food and food containers by sight and smell, and they've developed uncanny proficiency in getting at what they want. A locked car, zipped tent or garbage can does not present a serious obstacle and is easily accessed with cleverly honed techniques. Mother bears have even been observed passing along these thieving skills to their cubs.

This is bad news for you, but also for the bears. As they get more habituated to human food, bears also become more aggressive in getting at it and eventually may have to be killed. The forest service is in the process of retrofitting Dumpsters in all campgrounds, to make them bear-resistant, but in the meantime there are a few things you must do to keep yourself – and the bears – safe.

- If you are at a developed campground with bear-resistant metal food lockers, store food products, toiletries and other smelly things in the lockers.
- If there isn't a locker, the next best thing is to lock everything in the trunk of your car. *Never* store anything inside your tent.
- If you don't have a trunk, cover up all items with bear appeal with a towel or blanket inside the locked car, so bears can't see the items. Then roll up the windows and hope for the best.
- If you don't have a car or are camping in the backcountry, bring a bear-resistant food canister. These weigh 2½lb and fit inside your backpack or may be strapped to its outside. Put all your food and toiletries inside the canister and place it 50 feet from your camp. Hanging your food in a tree no longer works, because most bears have figured out how to get at it anyway.
- While bears usually won't bother you when you're cooking or eating, be sure to clean the camp of food and trash before leaving or going to sleep. Be paranoid about this.
- If you have sex while camping, clean up very well after yourself, as bears associate the attendant smells with food. Seriously, folks.
- Never, ever feed bears (yes, people actually do this).

is uncontrollable) and your own frame of mind. Be prepared for unpredictable weather. In some places, you may go to bed under a clear sky and wake up in two feet of snow, even in mid-August. Afternoon thunderstorms are very common in the Sierra Nevada. Carry a rain jacket and a light pair of long underwear at all times; in spring and fall, take this precaution even on short afternoon hikes. Backpackers should have a pack liner (heavy-duty garbage bags work well), a full set of rain gear and food that does not require cooking.

A positive attitude is helpful in any situation. If a hot shower, comfortable mattress and clean clothes are essential to your well-being, don't head out into the wilderness for five days – stick to day hikes.

Highest safety measures suggest never hiking alone, but solo travelers should not be discouraged, especially if they value solitude. The important thing is to always let someone know where you are going and how long you plan to be gone. Use sign-in boards at trailheads or ranger stations. Increasingly, hikers and campers are finding that a cellular phone is a useful – if not essential – piece of gear. And travelers looking for hiking companions can inquire or post notices at ranger stations, outdoors stores, campgrounds and hostels.

Fording rivers and streams is another potentially dangerous but often necessary part of being on the trail. In national parks and along maintained trails in national forests, bridges usually cross large bodies of water (this is not the case in designated wilderness areas, where bridges are taboo).

Upon reaching a river, unclip all of your pack straps (your pack is expendable, you are not). Avoid crossing barefoot. River cobbles will suck body heat right out of your feet, numbing them and making it impossible to navigate. Bring a pair of lightweight canvas sneakers to avoid sloshing around in wet boots for the rest of your hike.

Although cold water will make you want to cross as quickly as possible, don't rush things: take small steps, watch where you are stepping and keep your balance. Using a staff for balance is helpful, but don't rely on it to support all your weight. Don't enter water higher than midthigh; once higher than that your body gives the current a large mass to work against.

If you get wet, wring your clothes out immediately, wipe off all the excess water on your body and hair and put on any dry clothes you (or your partner) might have. Synthetic fabrics and wool retain heat when they get wet, but cotton does not.

People with little hiking and backpacking experience should not attempt to do too much, too soon, or they might end up being nonhikers for the wrong reasons. Know your limitations, know the route you are going to take and pace yourself accordingly.

Remember, turning back or not going as far as you originally planned is OK.

What to Bring

Equipment The following is meant to be a general guideline for backpackers, not an 'if I have everything here I'll be fine' checklist. And it is not adequate for snow country. Know yourself and what special things you may need; consider the area and climate you will be traveling in.

Boots – light to medium boots are recommended for day hikes; sturdy boots are necessary for extended trips with a heavy pack. Most importantly, they should be well broken in and have a good heel. Waterproof boots are preferable.

Alternative footwear – thongs, sandals or running shoes are ideal for wearing around camp, and canvas sneakers for crossing streams.

Socks – heavy polypropylene or wool will stay warm even when wet. Frequent changes during the day reduce the chance of blisters, but are usually impractical.

Blaze orange – subdued colors are recommended for most of the year, but if hiking during hunting season, blaze orange clothing is a necessity.

Shorts, light shirt – these are good for everyday wear; remember that heavy cotton takes a long time to dry and is very cold when wet.

Long-sleeve shirt – light cotton, wool or polypropylene is best. A button-down front makes layering easy and can be left open when the weather is hot. Long sleeves protect your arms from the sun.

Long pants – heavy denim jeans take forever to dry. Sturdy cotton or canvas pants are good for trekking through brush, and cotton or nylon sweats are comfortable to wear around camp. Long underwear under shorts is the perfect combo – warm but not cumbersome – for trail hiking where there is not much brush.

Wool or polypropylene or polar fleece sweater or pullover – For another layer that can be added and removed easily, this is essential in chilly or cold weather.

Rain gear – light, breathable and waterproof is the ideal combination. If nothing else is available, use heavy-duty trash bags to cover you and your packs.

Hat – wool or polypropylene is best for cold weather, while a cotton hat with a brim is good for sun protection. About 80% of body heat escapes through the top of the head. Keep your head (and neck) warm to reduce the chances of hypothermia.

Bandanna or handkerchief – good for a runny nose, dirty face, unmanageable hair, picnic lunch tablecloth and flag for emergencies (especially a red one).

Small towel – one which is indestructible and will dry quickly is ideal.

First-aid Kit – this should include self-adhesive bandages, disinfectant, antibiotic salve or cream, gauze, small scissors and tweezers.

Knife, fork, spoon and mug – a double-layer plastic mug with a lid is best. A mug acts as eating and drinking receptacle, mixing bowl and wash basin. An extra cup allows you to eat and drink simultaneously.

Pots and pans – aluminum cook sets are best, but any sturdy one-quart pot is sufficient. Trail gourmets who want more than pasta, soup and freeze-dried food will need a skillet or frying pan. A pot scrubber is helpful for removing stubborn food, especially when using cold water and no soap.

Stove – a lightweight and easy to operate stove is ideal. Most outdoor equipment stores rent propane, butane or white gas stoves. White gas cooks the fastest. Test the stove before you head out, even cook a meal on it, to familiarize yourself with any quirks it may have.

Water purifier – this is optional but really nice to have. Water can also be purified by boiling it for at least 10 minutes.

Matches or lighter – waterproof matches are good and having several lighters on hand is smart.

Candle or lantern – candles are easy to operate, but do not stay lit when they are dropped or wet and can be hazardous inside a tent. Outdoor equipment stores rent out lanterns; test it before you hit the trail.

Flashlight – each person should have his or her own flashlight and be sure its batteries have plenty of life left in them.

Sleeping bag – goose-down bags are warm and lightweight, but worthless if they get wet; most outdoor equipment stores rent synthetic bags.

Sleeping pad – this is strictly a personal preference. Use a sweater or sleeping bag sack stuffed with clothes as a pillow.

Tent – make sure it is waterproof, or has a waterproof cover, and know how to put it up *before* you reach camp. Remember that your packs will be sharing the tent with you.

Camera and binoculars – be sure to bring extra film and waterproof film canisters (sealable plastic bags work well).

Compass and maps – each person should have his or her own map.

Eyeglasses – bring a spare pair, and contact-lens wearers should also bring a backup set.

Sundries – biodegradable toilet paper, small plastic bags that can be sealed, insect repellent, sunscreen, lip balm, unscented moisturizing cream, moleskin for foot blisters, dental floss (burnable and good when there is no water for brushing your teeth), sunglasses, a deck of cards, pen or pencil and paper or notebook, books and nature guides are all useful.

Food Keeping your energy up is important, but so is keeping your pack light. Backpackers tend to eat a substantial breakfast and dinner and snack heavily in between. There is no need to be excessive. If you pack loads of food you'll probably use it, but if you have just enough you will probably not miss anything.

Some basic staples are packaged instant oatmeal, bread (the denser the better), rice or pasta, instant soup or ramen noodles, jerky (dehydrated meat), dried fruit, energy bars, chocolate, trail mix, and peanut butter or honey or jam (in plastic jars or squeeze bottles).

Books

The best California-specific guides are those available from Wilderness Press in Berkeley, CA, which publishes *The John Muir Trail*, *The Pacific Crest Trail*, *Sierra North*, *Lassen Volcanic National Park* and *Yosemite*, and The Mountaineers in Seattle, WA, whose books include *California's Central Sierra & Coast Range*, *Best Day Hikes of the California Northwest* and *The West Coast Trail*.

Also consider *LA Times* columnist John McKinney's excellent series of hiking guides published by Olympic Press. These include *Day Hiker's Guide to Southern California*, *Day Hiker's Guide to California State Parks*, *Walking California's Coast Walking the East Mojave Desert* and *Walking Los Angeles: Adventures on the Urban Edge*.

Maps

A good map is essential for any hiking trip. NPS and USFS ranger stations usually stock topographical maps that cost $2 to $6. In the absence of a ranger station, try the local stationery store, gas station or hardware store.

Often just getting to the backcountry can be a trying tangle of switchback roads and unmarked forest service roads. You'll need two types of maps: US Geological Survey (USGS) Quadrangles and US Department of Agriculture-Forest Service maps. To order a map index and price list, contact the USGS, PO Box 25286, Denver, CO 80225, or the Western Region office at 345 Middlefield Rd, Menlo Park, CA 94025 (☎ 650-853-8300).

For general information on maps, also see the Facts for the Visitor chapter; for information regarding maps of specific forests, wilderness areas, or national parks, see the appropriate geographic entry.

BICYCLING & MOUNTAIN BIKING

Bike-friendly cities where you can ditch the car and ride to museums and other attractions on a network of routes include Santa Barbara, Santa Cruz, Davis, Berkeley, and parts of San Diego and Los Angeles. San Francisco also has many ardent cyclists; though its hills and traffic might be daunting, the city's compact size makes the bicycle an ideal form of transportation.

Marin County (specifically Mt Tamalpais) is the birthplace of mountain biking (see 'The Mountain, the Bike, the Story' in the San Francisco Bay Area chapter). Just across the Golden Gate Bridge from San Francisco, the Marin Headlands are filled with wonderful biking trails (and also full of cyclists on weekends). California's current MTB mecca, however, is Mammoth Mountain, home to the annual Kamikaze World Cup Downhill Race – one of the fastest races on the circuit (held in early July). Mammoth's mountain bike park has a slalom course and obstacle area, plus miles of steep dirt just begging for fat tires.

Multiday bike tours – from Death Valley blossom rides to Napa Valley wine tasting trips – are available through Backroads (☎ 510-527-1555, 800-245-3874, www.backroads.com), 1516 5th St, Berkeley, CA 94710.

Information

Bike shops are the best places to find out about the local cycle scene. *California Bicyclist* magazine, available free at most bike shops, is the definitive resource. They publish monthly Northern California and Southern California editions, with a regional calendar of events, and the annual *Pedalers' Guide*, which lists California's cycling clubs.

Members of the national League of American Bicyclists (LAB; ☎ 202-822-1333, fax 202-822-1334, www.bikeleague.org), 1612 K St NW, Suite 401, Washington, DC 20006, may transport their bikes free on five major airlines and obtain a list of hospitality

Biking by the San Francisco Bay

homes in each state that offer simple accommodations to touring cyclists. LAB also publishes the bimonthly *Bicycle USA* magazine, including the annual Almanac and Tourfinders editions, which list contacts in each state, along with information about bicycle routes and special events. Their California representative is Jim Baross (☎ 619-280-6908, Jbaross@cts.com).

Bicycle tourists will also want to get a copy of *Adventure Cyclist* and *The Cyclist's Yellow Pages*, trip-planning resources, both published by Adventure Cycling Association (☎ 406-721-1776, fax 406-721-8754, acabike@aol.com), 150 E Pine St, Missoula, MT 59802.

Kimberly Grob's *Best Bike Rides in California* is a concise, user-friendly guide to mountain bike trails and touring routes. Also by Grob is *Best Bike Rides in Northern California*.

An excellent and comprehensive website is Bicyclopedia at www.pwp.starnetinc.com/olderr/bcwebsite. DeLorme publishes a topographic *Atlas & Gazetteer* for each state – good tools for planning trail rides.

Laws and Regulations

Throughout California, bikes are restricted from entering designated wilderness areas and national park trails, but may otherwise be ridden on national forest and BLM single-track trails. Trail etiquette requires that cyclists yield to other users. Helmets should always be worn to reduce the risk of head injury, but they are not mandated by law. National parks require that all riders under 18 years wear a helmet.

SKIING

The Sierra Nevada – Lake Tahoe and Mammoth Lakes in particular – is home to California's most popular ski destinations. High mountains and reliable snow conditions have attracted investors and multimillion-dollar ski resorts equipped with the latest in chairlift technology, snow-grooming systems, and facilities. Along with the big-name places like Squaw Valley USA, you'll find small operations with a handful of lifts and cheaper ticket prices good for beginners and

families. Another pocket of ski slopes is in the San Bernardino Forest around Big Bear, in the mountains east of Los Angeles.

In addition to downhill skiing and snowboarding, there are ample opportunities for cross-country and backcountry skiing, especially in the Eastern Sierra. The USFS often maintains summer hiking trails as cross-country ski trails during the winter. Some resorts specialize in cross-country skiing and offer weekend or weeklong packages that include lodging, meals and equipment rentals. Some downhill areas (for example Kirkwood and Northstar-at-Tahoe) also have cross-country areas, and in the winter golf courses often have terrain suited to beginners.

Ski areas are often well-equipped with places to stay, places to eat, shops, entertainment venues, child-care facilities (both on and off the mountain) and transportation. In fact, it is possible to stay a week at some of the bigger places without ever leaving the slopes.

Usually ski areas have at least one comfortable base lodge with a rental office, ski shop and lockers. They also have cafeterias and lounges or bars, where nonskiers or those tired or cold can relax in warmth in front of a bay window looking out over the scene. You do not have to buy a lift ticket or trail pass or pay to enjoy the base lodge. One thing is guaranteed – you can save at least $5 a day by buying food at a grocery store and packing your own lunch. Use lockers and you won't have to tote your food around and worry about falling on your sandwich.

Downhill

Downhill – or alpine – skiing is a way of life for some people. In many places in the Sierra Nevada, you will find genuine ski bums, who do what they can to survive and pass the time during the summer while they wait for the first flakes to fall. Then when the lifts open, usually around Thanksgiving weekend, they either get jobs on the slopes, which provide them with free season passes, or jobs in restaurants, which free the daylight hours for skiing.

Slanging Through the Outdoors

après ski – the after-ski social scene at lodges, restaurants, bars and clubs

backcountry skiing – either walk-in extreme alpine skiing or cross-country skiing beyond marked trails; carries risks of avalanche and getting lost

bumps – moguls

buy it – or 'bite it' or 'biff' – to crash, as in: 'He bought it,' 'He bit it,' 'He totally biffed.'

catch air – also 'get air' – on any jump, from a mogul to a skateboard halfpipe, to put a lot of space (air) between the ground and yourself

chopped up – soft powder snow that is no longer pristine

chute – a narrow ski run sided by rock or trees

cross-country – also known as 'Nordic skiing' or 'ski touring'

demos – high-end rental skis; one often 'demos' a pair of skis before buying them

double – two-person chairlift

dumping – a heavy snow: 'Squaw really got a dumping last night.'

extreme skiing – expert skiing over very steep, varied terrain, often out of bounds of the regular ski area

halfpipe – for skateboarders, a concrete pipe used by boarders for stunts along the inside curve and rim; for snowboarders, the pipe is made of snow

heli-skiing – extreme skiing in which skiers are helicoptered to the top of a mountain and ski their way back to base

hot dog – to perform dangerous acts: 'She was hot-dogging down the hill'; or the performer: 'The dude taking those moguls is such a hot dog.'

peak bagger – one who climbs a mountain only to be able to claim he or she has reached the summit or peak

performance – a higher quality rental ski or mountain bike than the shop's basic package; in the case of skis they're not as high quality as demos.

portage – to carry a kayak or canoe over land to avoid an impassable stretch of river,

or to carry from one body of water to another. Sometimes refers to the foot path or trail used for those purposes

put-in – riverside where rafters or canoers can put in their boats

quad – four-person chairlift

schuss – to ski straight down the fall line, without turns

shredder – a person who cuts up the mountain with his or her expert snowboarding technique

self-register – an important safety precaution, this is a sheet at the head of a backcountry hiking trail where you sign in your destination and how long you plan to be in the wilderness.

Sierra cement – heavy, wet snow common in the Sierra Nevada

ski bums – die-hard skiers who would sell their mothers for lift tickets, often working at resorts, hotels, restaurants in ski towns throughout the West

slalom – smoothly carved parallel turns

snowcat skiing – extreme skiing in which skiers are driven by snowcat to a remote area to ski their way back to base

soaring – an air tour given by specialists in gliders (engine-less aircraft)

suspension bike – a mountain bike with shocks to ease bumps and jarring

telemarking – a downhill turn performed on cross-country skis in which the skier's heel is not attached to the ski and the outside ski slides forward of the inside ski

walking the dog – a slow mountain biker: 'Joe was holding up the rest of us; he was really walking the dog.'

white-water rafting – also known as 'river rafting,' 'river running' or 'shooting the rapids'

x-c skiing – usually a written abbreviation of 'cross-country skiing'

yard sale – when a person leaves a trail of clothing behind after a devastating downhill ski fall, such as hat, gloves, skis and poles scattered along the face of the run

Around Lake Tahoe you can schuss all day on the slopes and spend the evening watching casino shows, drinking free cocktails and trying to win back the price of that expensive lift ticket. Mammoth has a rollicking après-ski scene where people party as hard as they ski. The areas near Los Angeles are popular with day-trippers, which means traffic to and from the slopes (especially Friday and Sunday evenings) is often horrendous.

At major ski areas, lift tickets cost $35 to $49 for a full day and $17 to $37 for a half-day, which usually starts at 1 pm. Three-day or weeklong lift passes are usually more economical and especially useful if they can be used on nonconsecutive days. Equipment rentals are available at or near even the smallest ski areas, though renting equipment in a nearby town can be cheaper if you can transport it to the slopes; basic rentals, including skis, boots, and poles, start at $12 per day.

Visitors planning on taking lessons should rent equipment on the mountain, since the price of a lesson, around $48/30 day/half-day, usually includes equipment rentals, with no discount for having your own gear. Children's ski schools are popular places to stash the kids for a day, offering lessons, day-care facilities and providing lunch for around $35 per child.

Cross-Country

Cross-country or Nordic skiing offers a chance to get exercise, experience natural beauty at close quarters and save a few dollars by not buying a downhill lift ticket. Trail passes at cross-country resorts, where the tracks and trails are groomed, usually cost $12 to $17; skiing in the backcountry is free.

Royal Gorge, near Lake Tahoe, is North America's largest cross-country ski resort and a mecca for enthusiasts. National parks, notably Yosemite and Kings Canyon,

close their roads during the winter and maintain cross-country trails into the parks' interiors. Possibly the most delightful cross-country experience is staying at a remote lodge where you wake up to a hearty breakfast, ski all day and return to a homemade dinner, hot tub and roaring fire. Tioga Pass Resort (near Yosemite National Park) and Montecito-Sequoia Lodge (at Sequoia-Kings Canyon National Park) are favorite cross-country lodges.

Snowboarding

This sport has swept the nation's ski culture and taken on a huge following of its own. Growing legions of snowboarders are seen on California slopes, eschewing the difficult-to-master art of downhill skiing for the more natural maneuvering by standing sideways, strapped to a four-foot board with outside edges. Baggy pants and funky hats have replaced more traditional ski garb, and as a rule, snowboarders love powder snow, hate moguls and ice, and need an older sibling's ID to get into bars at night. Still, the sport is becoming vastly more popular among a more mature crowd.

While no ski mountain has yet declared itself a snowboard-only area, more and more ski mountains are developing half-pipes and renting the necessary equipment in ski shops.

Shreddin' on the slopes, dude!

For comprehensive, up-to-date trends, general information and product evaluations, check out www.snowboards.com.

Books & Magazines

In *Skiing America*, Charles Leocha has compiled facts and figures about all of America's big ski resorts. *Ski* and *Skiing* are both year-round, widely available magazines, featuring travel articles, how-to advice, and equipment tests; try to get a copy of the October or November issues for general information. *Snow Country* magazine ranks ski areas throughout the USA on the basis of categories including terrain, ski school, nightlife, lodging and dining.

Useful books on snowboarding include *Let It Rip – The Ultimate Guide to Snowboarding* by Greg Daniels, *The Complete Snowboarder* by Jeff Bennett & Scott Downey, and *The Snowboard Book* by Lowell Hart.

Popular magazines include Powder Magazine, Mountain Zone, Boarder Line, Snowboarder Magazine and Heckler Magazine.

ROCK CLIMBING & MOUNTAINEERING

People don't just come to California to surf. The granite monoliths and glacial peaks of the Sierra Nevada and singular volcanic domes of the Cascades entice the world's best climbers and mountaineers. El Capitan and Half Dome in Yosemite National Park are both legendary climbs up the face of sheer granite walls. Joshua Tree National Monument is also popular with rock climbers, especially for those who value technique and finesse more than magnitude. The peaks of Mt Shasta, Lassen Peak and Mt Ritter (all above 13,000 feet) are impressive mountaineering destinations, and Mt Whitney, the highest peak in the lower 48 states at 14,497 feet, has a mountaineers' route that is a 'perfect balance of fun and challenge' according to the owner of the Whitney Portal store, who has made the ascent over 50 times.

Recently, rock climbers have subordinated the idea of reaching summits to testing their skills on varied routes on difficult terrain, with the achievement of a summit either secondary or unimportant; the technique of climbing is the important matter.

Climbing and mountaineering are demanding activities requiring top physical condition, an understanding of the composition of various rock types and their hazards, other hazards of the high country and familiarity with a variety of equipment, including ropes, chocks, bolts, carabiners and harnesses. Many climbers prefer granite, like that found in the Sierra, because of its strength and frequent handholds, but some climbers like limestone for a challenge. Some sedimentary rock is suitable for climbing, but crumbling volcanic rock, common at Pinnacles National Monument, can be very difficult, though it's popular too.

Climbers and mountaineers categorize routes on a scale of one to five; Class I is hiking, while Class II involves climbing on unstable materials like talus and may require use of the hands for keeping balance, especially with a heavy pack. Class III places the climber in dangerous situations involving exposed terrain (the Sierra Club uses the example of a staircase on a high building without handholds – scary but not difficult), with the likely consequences of a fall being a broken limb.

Class IV involves steep rock, smaller holds and great exposure, with obligatory use of ropes and knowledge of knots and techniques like belaying and rappelling; the consequences of falling are death rather than injury. Class V divides into a dozen or more subcategories based on degree of difficulty and requires advanced techniques, including proficiency with rope.

Safety

Climbing is a potentially hazardous activity, though serious accidents are more spectacular than frequent; sometimes driving to the climbing site can be more dangerous than the climb itself. Nevertheless, climbers should be aware of hazards that can cause falls and very serious injury or death.

Weather is an important factor, as rain makes rock slippery and lightning can strike an exposed climber; hypothermia is an

NANCY KELLER

JOHN ELK III

JOHN ELK III

JOHN ELK III

LEE FOSTER

California up close and from a distance

Giant sequoias

Lady Bird Johnson Grove, Redwood National Park

Elephant seals, Año Nuevo State Reserve

Death Valley National Park

Barrel cactus, Anza Borrego SP

Canoeing in the Tahoe area

Hang gliding at Mt Tamalpais State Park, Marin County

Golden Gate National Recreation Area coastal trail, San Francisco

Cross-country skiing in Yosemite National Park

LEE FOSTER

Biking in Napa Valley

DAVID PEEVERS

Swinging at the Derby in Los Angeles

JAMES LYON

Relaxing in San Diego

LEE FOSTER

Horseback riding on the beach in San Francisco

additional concern. In dry weather, lack of water can lead to dehydration. Also see the Health section in the Facts for the Visitor chapter for information on hazardous situations and how to avoid them.

Minimum Impact

Many climbers are now following guidelines similar to those established for hikers to preserve the resource on which their sport relies: concentrating impact in high-use areas by using established roads, trails and routes for access; dispersing use in pristine areas and avoiding the creation of new trails; refraining from creating or enhancing handholds; and eschewing the placement of bolts wherever possible. Climbers should also take special caution to respect archaeological and cultural resources, such as rock art, and refrain from climbing in such areas.

Climbing Schools

Travelers wishing to acquire climbing skills can do so at several schools and guide services throughout the region. For the most comprehensive instruction available in any type of outdoor skills – backpacking to mountaineering to sea kayaking – contact the nonprofit National Outdoor Leadership School (NOLS; ☎ 307-332-5300, fax 307-332-1220, www.nols.edu), 288 Main St, Lander, WY 82520. Courses, some of which may even get you academic credit, last 10 to 95 days and cost $80 to $90 per day.

Alpine Skills International (☎ 530-426-9108), PO Box 8, Lake Norden, CA 95724, whose base camp is on Donner Pass near Lake Tahoe, conducts seminars in rock climbing, mountaineering, snow and ice climbing, backcountry skiing and avalanche survival. Their trips are a great way to break into the mountaineering scene. Seminars, for all skill levels, are conducted from the hut, a bunkhouse from which you do a series of day trips, and on the trail. Less of a commitment are classes available through the University of California's recreation department, Cal Adventures (☎ 510-642-4000). These classes are taught on a simulated rock wall on the Berkeley campus,

with the option of a second class on real rock.

The Yosemite Mountaineering School (☎ 209-372-8344 September to May, ☎ 209-372-8435 June to August), headquartered in Yosemite National Park, has daily beginner and intermediate classes ($65) and world-class guides that lead instructional trips up some of the park's star routes.

Books

A good summary of general introductory material on climbing is available in Steve Roper's *The Climbing Guide to the High Sierra*. *The Climbers Guide to Tahoe Rock*, by Mike Carville, is a technical climber's sourcebook for the Lake Tahoe area.

For historical background on climbing and mountaineering in the USA, consult Chris Jones' *Climbing in North America*.

HORSEBACK RIDING

You may rent a horse for a short ride in many areas in California – in parks, on beaches, and in most rural areas. Casual riders will find rides expensive, as visitors during the short summer tourist season end up paying for the cost of feeding these hay burners over the winter. Rates for recreational riding start around $15 per hour or $25 for two hours, though the hourly rate falls rapidly thereafter and full-day trips usually cost around $75 with a guide. Experienced riders may want to let the horse's owners know, or else you may be saddled with an excessively docile stable nag.

Pack Trips

Horseback riding is especially popular in the mountains, where it allows access to high alpine scenery with relatively little effort. On 'spot trips' an outfitter carries your gear (and you, if desired) to a chosen destination and leaves you to hike out or picks you up days or weeks later. Most outfitters also offer full-service trips, where they provide everything from meals to tents to naturalist guides. Spot trips cost about $125 per person, while full-service trips usually cost that much per day. Some of the best outfitters are in the Eastern Sierra. These include Reds Meadow Pack

Station (☎ 760-934-2345) at Devil's Postpile National Monument and Bishop Pack Outfitters (☎ 760-873-4785, 800-316-4252) in Bishop.

RIVER RUNNING

California offers myriad alternatives for one of the most exhilarating outdoor activities: white-water rafting. Commercial outfitters provide white-water experiences ranging from short, inexpensive morning or afternoon trips to overnights and multiday expeditions; outfitters on NPS, USFS and BLM lands operate under permits from the appropriate agency, but individuals and groups with their own equipment do not need permits. People not ready for white-water excitement can try more sedate float or tube trips.

White-water trips take place in either large rafts seating a dozen or more people, or smaller rafts seating half a dozen; the latter are more interesting and exciting because the ride over the rapids can be rougher and because everyone participates in paddling. Most outfitters also rent white-water kayaks and canoes, which require more skill and maneuvering; instruction is usually provided.

While white-water trips are not without danger, and it's not unusual for participants to fall out of the raft in rough water, serious injuries are rare and a huge majority of trips are without incident. All participants must wear US Coast Guard-approved life jackets, and even nonswimmers are welcome. All trips have at least one river guide trained in lifesaving techniques.

River Rankings

Class I – easy
The river ranges from flatwater to occasional series of mild rapids.

Class II – medium
The river has frequent stretches of rapids with waves up to three feet high and easy chutes, ledges and falls. The best route is easy to identify, and the entire river can be run in open canoes.

Class III – difficult
The river features numerous rapids with high, irregular waves and difficult chutes and falls that often require scouting. These rivers are for experienced paddlers who either use kayaks and rafts or have spray covers for their canoes.

Class IV – very difficult
Rivers with long stretches of irregular waves, powerful back eddies and even constricted canyons. Scouting is mandatory, and rescues can be difficult in many places. Rafts or white-water kayaks in which paddlers are equipped with helmets are suitable for these rivers.

Class V – extremely difficult
Rivers with continuous violent rapids, powerful rollers, and high, unavoidable waves and haystacks. These rivers are only for professional rafters and white-water kayakers who are proficient in the Eskimo roll.

Class VI – highest level of difficulty
These rivers are rarely run except by highly experienced kayakers under ideal conditions. The likelihood of serious injury is high.

Wild & Scenic Rivers

Congressional legislation establishes certain criteria for the preservation of rivers with outstanding natural qualities; many of these rivers are the best places for white-water rafting and canoeing. Wild rivers are, simply speaking, free-flowing and remote. Scenic rivers enjoy relatively natural surroundings and are free of impoundment, but have better access by road than wild rivers. Recreational rivers are more developed, and usually have roads close by.

Organized Trips

The most popular destination for river running is the South Fork of the American River. Operators, concentrated in the small town of Coloma (see the Gold Country chapter), run half-day trips and multiday adventures that include meals and camp accommodations. Half-day options are usually more action-packed and economical than full-day trips, though overnighters are the most fun. Half-day trips cost $50 to $90, full-day trips around $100, and two-day trips usually start at $200.

OARS (☎ 209-736-4677, 800-346-6277, www.oars.com), PO Box 67, Angels Camp, CA 95222, runs white-water rafting and kayak trips on the American, Kern, Tuolumne and Mokulumne rivers. Another excellent outfitter is Whitewater Voyages (☎ 800-488-7238, www.whitewatervoyages.com), 5225 San Pablo Dam Rd, El Sobrante,

CA 94803, which offers rafting trips on such rivers as the Rogue, Klamath, California Salmon, American and Kern. (See boxed text 'A River Roars Through It' in the San Joaquin chapter for a personal account of a river trip by one of the authors.)

Through the University of California recreation department, Cal Adventures (☎ 510-642-4000) offers economical raft and kayak trips on the American and Klamath rivers.

SEA KAYAKING

This quiet, unobtrusive sport allows you to visit unexplored islands and stretches of coast and view marine life at close range. Sea kayaks, which hold one or two people, are larger and more stable than white-water boats, making them safer and easier to navigate. They also have storage capacity, so you can take them on overnight or even week-long trips. Imagine paddling to a secluded beach on one of the Channel Islands and setting up camp for a week.

The most popular destinations for sea kayaking are the Channel Islands, off the Central Coast, and Catalina Island further south. These places are good overnight destinations for experienced kayakers. Day trips are also rewarding, especially in areas where you are likely to see seals and sea lions, such as Tomales Bay, Monterey Bay and San Luis Obispo Bay (north of Cayucos).

Island Packers (☎ 805-642-1393, 805-642-7688 for recorded information), 1867 Spinnaker Drive, Ventura, CA 93001, rents equipment and guides trips to several Channel Islands. For instruction, equipment rental, and a list of regional guides, contact California Canoe & Kayak (☎ 510-893-7833), 409 Water St, Oakland, CA 94607. Average prices are $50 to $60 per day, $350 to $450 for a week, including food.

SURFING & WINDSURFING

Surfing is California's signature sport. Invented by the Pacific Islanders, surfing was made popular by Duke Kahanamoku in Hawaii in the 1920s but actually arrived in California in 1907. It has imbued a look, language and way of life that is 'typically' Californian: laid-back, easy-going and totally dedicated to sun and sea.

California's 'big three' surf spots are Rincon, Malibu and Trestles, all point breaks (where swells peak up into steep waves as they encounter a shelf-like point) known for consistently clean, glassy, big waves. Beginner and intermediate surfers should be content to watch the action at these places (which also get very crowded). The best places to learn surfing are at beach breaks or long, shallow bays where waves are small and rolling. San Onofre and San Diego's Tourmaline are good beginner spots. And although long boards are heavy and unwieldy compared to the short boards most commonly used, they are easier to balance on and less likely to 'pearl' (when the tip of the board takes a dive). Morey Doyle boards, made of spongy foam, are the ultimate beginner's tool.

You'll find surfboard rental stands on just about every beach from San Diego to Santa Barbara. Rentals cost around $10 per hour, and lessons, which are much less common, cost about $15.

Northern California has its own surf scene, with colder water, bigger waves and an abundance of sharks. Made popular when professional surfer Mark Foo died there in 1994, Mavericks (near Half Moon Bay) has waves that rival Hawaii's. Humboldt County grows its own crop of big-wave surfers, right along with its marijuana plants.

Windsurfing

Though you can put in with your windsurfing board at any beach or public boat launch, few places rent windsurfing equipment, making it necessary for serious boarders to have their own. Beginners and casual boarders will find rental facilities and relatively calm conditions at San Diego's Mission Bay, Marina Del Rey in Los Angeles and the Berkeley Marina. California's premiere windsurfing locales include the San Francisco Bay, Rio Vista in the Sacramento River Delta, and Lopez Lake, just east of San Luis Obispo. Lake Tahoe also gets decent wind, though the water is quite cold from October to June.

Surfspeak

Much of the general California slang comes from Southern California surfer speak. And a lot of surfspeak goes way beyond the act of surfing. Here's a very small sample. See the book *Surfinary* (from Ten Speed Press) for more in-depth coverage.

all over – really excited about something: 'I'm all over that party tonight, dude.'

ankle slappers – tiny waves that aren't worth surfing

beached – so stuffed with grunts one is unable to surf

beard – a veteran surfer

boardhead – an ardent surfer

body womp – riding waves on one's stomach; 'boogie boarding' or 'body surfing'

burly – very cold outside

butter – women; also 'biddies'

Casper – person without a suntan; from 'Casper the Friendly Ghost'

channel – a relatively deep spot where the waves don't normally break

clean peeler – the ideal wave

da kine – the best kind of wave: 'I just caught da kine, man.'

decoy – a nonsurfer

free it up – come on and tell me

gel – calm down; similar to 'chill'

green room – inside the tube

grommet – disciple of a soul surfer; surfing novice ('gremlin'); or surf groupie ('dismo')

grunts – food: 'Let's grab some grunts.'

hair ball – a big wave that is surfable; also 'grinder'

hollow wave – a wave with a steep face and small barrel

hondo – tourist

insane – totally great: 'Look at those insane waves.'

kneebangers – long baggy shorts worn by surfers

latronic – adios, see ya later: 'Latronic, dude.'

log – long board

macker – a huge wave that is often too big to handle; also 'green monster'

meat wave – a vehicle filled with surfers

nip factor – how cold it is outside

nipple rash – when body boarding rubs your nipples raw

nuch – short for 'not much': 'Hey, wussup?' 'Nuch.'

quimby – jerk, loser

raw – excellent: 'Hey, you've got some raw moves, man.'

schmeg – the crap of the world

scrut – eat maximum quantities of grunts; also 'haken,' 'pig out'

sharking – surfing

skank – raunchy girl

stoked – totally intense feeling you did something awesome

soul surfer – a surfer who surfs for the feel, not the look. A soul surfer wouldn't explain to a nonsurfer why he surfs, because he knows you wouldn't understand. 'Those who understand cannot explain. Those who explain do not understand.'

sponge – body board

styling – surfing really well; also 'killing it'

tubular – literally, surfing in a tube; alternately, anything that is most excellent

veg – to sit around and do nothing; to 'veg out'

wall – when the entire wave breaks at the same time; one can't ride walls without getting 'worked.'

wag – an idiotic male personage; also a 'Gilligan' (from the TV show *Gilligan's Island*) or a 'Barney' (from Barney Rubble on *The Flintstones*)

weeded – crushed by a wave; also 'worked,' 'biffed,' 'toaded,' 'lunched,' 'pounded,' or 'prosecuted'

wicked – very cool

Yar! – way cool: 'Yar! Excellent ride, dude.'

zipper – a fast-breaking wave

DIVING & SNORKELING

To get into the depths of California's waters, you must be certified. This requires 28 hours of classroom and pool experience and one open-water dive – usually an investment of several months and several hundred dollars. For a list of instructors and dive schools, contact the National Association for Underwater Instruction (NAUI; ☎ 714-621-5801, 800-553-6284), PO Box 14650, Montclair, CA 91763. Or contact the Professional Association of Diving Instructors (PADI; ☎ 714-540-7234, 800-729-7234), 1251 East Dyer Road No 100, Santa Ana, CA 92705.

Quick one- to three-day courses can get you into shallow waters to see the under-water world. This is especially satisfying in places like La Jolla, Monterey Bay and Catalina Island, where kelp beds house a rich marine environment close to the surface. Local dive shops are the best resources for equipment, guides and instructors. *Scuba Diving* and *Sport Diver* are widely available magazines dedicated entirely to underwater pursuits.

If you don't have the time, money or desire to dive deep, you can often rent a snorkel, mask and fins for around $5 to $7 per hour or $10 to $12 per day. In touristy spots such as Avalon (on Catalina Island), Morro Bay and Santa Barbara, people rent equipment from the back of vans or trucks parked along the beach.

George Freeth: King of the Surfer Dudes

The Beach Boys, *Beach Blanket Bingo*, Frankie and Annette, 'Surfin' USA' – surfing mythology and California have long been synonymous, and we may owe it all to land baron and railroad tycoon Henry Huntington and his genius for promotion. Having developed Redondo Beach and brought the railroad there, Huntington planned to sell off his parcels of oceanfront property to the well-heeled.

In 1907, to lure prospective buyers to the area, Huntington hired George Freeth, an Irish-Hawaiian athlete, to perform his miracle of 'walking on the water' for visitors to Redondo. The crowds came and Huntington sold a *lot* of real estate.

As a child in Hawaii, Freeth had seen an old painting of his mother's ancestors riding the waves and decided to revive the ancient art. When the gargantuan, traditional 16-foot hardwood boards proved too hard to handle, Freeth cut one in half – thus creating the first 'long board' – and modern surfing was born. Until 1915, Freeth held the beach crowds in thrall with daily performances. Eventually he became the first lifeguard in Southern California. He received a Congressional Medal for bravely rescuing a boatload of stranded fishermen and fathered the surfing revolution that would become an enormous industry and a way of life in California. A bronze memorial to him on the Redondo Pier is frequently draped with leis from surfers from all over the world who come to pay their respects.

Freeth died at only 36, in the great influenza epidemic of 1919, but the mark he left on world culture far surpassed even the legacy of Huntington himself. Freeth's short sweet life was the original 'Endless Summer.' He was *awesome*, dude.

FISHING

California's native fish populations have been devastated by indiscriminate planting of introduced species, overfishing and water pollution. Logging and overgrazing on the North Coast have caused stream banks to erode and temperatures to rise above habitable levels. Overfishing by commercial fishermen, a long-time threat to California's salmon population, is extreme along the North Coast, though valiant efforts have been made in curbing the devastation. Don't eat fish from water near urban areas like Santa Monica and the San Francisco Bay. Despite improvements, the water in these areas still shows fairly high levels of pollution, including sediment deposits of DDT. It is not wise to eat fish caught in these areas.

The *good* news is that some fish are alive and well and waiting to be caught. The Klamath, Eel, Trinity and Pit rivers are excellent for trout, as are Lake Shasta and Whiskeytown Reservoir. The lakes and rivers of the Eastern Sierra – including Virginia Lakes, the East Walker River, Twin Lakes, June, Grant and Silver lakes – are also prime fishing territory.

Deep-sea fishing for salmon, halibut, yellowfin tuna and marlin is popular along the Central Coast (for example Monterey and Morro Bay) and around San Diego.

A California State fishing license costs $27.55 for fresh water only, $16.30 for salt water only and $30.20 for both, including a 5% handling fee; it is valid for a calendar year. One-day ($6.55) and two-day licenses ($10) are available too. Big sporting goods stores like Big 5 or Sports Chalet issue these licenses, as do Department of Fish and Game offices.

CAVING

Experienced spelunkers can explore caves in several areas of limestone bedrock, mostly but not exclusively in the Sierra Nevada foothills. Several cave areas are open to casual visitors for guided tours, without need of equipment or experience: California Caverns and Mercer Caverns in the Gold Country, Boyden Cavern and Crystal Cave in Kings Canyon-Sequoia National Park and Lehman Caves in Great Basin National Park, eastern Nevada.

Because of the delicate and tightly circumscribed subterranean environments, cavers must make special efforts to respect the ecosystem and its inhabitants by leaving no trace of human presence, avoiding contact with sensitive formations and refraining from disturbing bats and other animals. Cavers should also travel in groups, with a minimum of three persons. Hazards associated with caving include poisonous gases and dangerous spores.

The National Speleological Society (☎ 256-852-1300, www.caves.org), 2813 Cave Ave, Huntsville, AL 35810, offers a comprehensive list of caves organized by state.

GOLF

Recent decades have seen a proliferation of golf courses throughout California – in many ways an unfortunate development that wastes colossal amounts of water for irrigation in a very arid region. Even many small towns have nine- or 18-hole courses open to the public at reasonable prices, while the more established resorts have deluxe courses with very high greens fees. California's concentration of courses is ironically greatest where there is the least water: Palm Springs, Palm Desert and San Diego. Other areas, in an attempt to capitalize on the sport's ever-increasing popularity, have also jumped on the bandwagon. These include San Luis Obispo County and Monterey/Salinas on the Central Coast, near the state's premiere courses of Pebble Beach and Spyglass Hill.

HOT-AIR BALLOONING

Floating above California in a wicker gondola has its attractions, given the scenery, but it's not cheap at the relatively few locations that offer it commercially. Most flights leave at dawn and go 1000 to 2000 feet above ground. The most popular spot is the Wine Country, where most operators offer fancy gondola treats like champagne, local wine and cheese. One-hour flights cost around $140 to $180. Other popular ballooning spots are San Diego's North County and around Palm Springs.

SKYDIVING

If jumping out of a plane and falling at 150 miles an hour before opening your chute 3000 feet above the ground sounds fun, then you should head to Perris Valley in southeastern California. At the Perris Valley Skydiving School (☎ 909-657-1664, 800-832-8818), 2091 Goetz Rd, Perris, CA 92570, you can go from the classroom to the sky in half an hour with an instructor, or in six hours if you want to go solo. You must be over 18 years of age, under 215 pounds, and watch the instructional video that includes a lawyer telling you that the skydiving school is not responsible for any accidents.

Jumps over Nevada are offered by the Las Vegas Skydiving Center (☎ 702-877-1010) at the airport in Jean (see the Las Vegas chapter). Accelerated freefall jumps are $300, with static-line jumps going for $195.

Jumps at either location are more for the adrenaline rush than the scenery, since the desert setting isn't particular noted for its prettiness.

Getting There & Away

The fastest way to get to California and Nevada, whether coming from elsewhere in the US or from overseas, is by plane. California's main gateway airports, for domestic and international flights, are Los Angeles (LAX) and San Francisco (SFO). Domestic flights also go to other cities, of which the busiest are San Diego, California, and Las Vegas, Nevada. Excellent highways connect California with the rest of North America, and quite good train and bus services, though distances to major population centers outside these states are fairly vast.

AIR

US domestic airfares vary tremendously depending on the season you travel, the day of the week you fly, the length of your stay and the flexibility the ticket allows for flight changes and refunds. Still, nothing determines fares more than demand, and when things are slow, regardless of the season, airlines will lower their fares to fill empty seats. Airlines are very competitive, and at any given time any one of them could have the cheapest fare. However, expect less fluctuation in airfares with international fares.

Airports

Los Angeles International Airport (LAX; 310-646-5252, www.lawa.org) has eight terminals. Some of the larger US airlines, like United and TWA, have their own terminal from which they operate both domestic and international flights. Most international carriers land at the Tom Bradley International Terminal. Midsize LA area airports, mostly for domestic travel, are in Burbank (☎ 818-840-8847), Ontario/San Bernardino County (☎ 909-983-8282), Long Beach (☎ 562-421-8293) and Irvine/Orange County (☎ 949-252-5200).

Most international flights to the Bay Area land at San Francisco International Airport (SFO; ☎ 650-876-7809), on the west side of the bay. Most international airlines, as well as the international services of several US carriers, are based at the International Terminal. The airports in Oakland (☎ 510-577-4000) and San Jose (☎ 408-501-7600) are important domestic gateways.

McCarran International Airport (☎ 702-261-5743) in Las Vegas has direct flights to and from most US cities, but just a few from Canada and Europe.

International Airlines Some of the more popular airlines servicing US airports are Air Canada, Air France, Air New Zealand, British Airways, Canadian Airlines, Continental, Japan Air Lines, KLM, Northwest Airlines, Qantas Airways and Virgin Atlantic. See the Toll-Free Directory for phone numbers.

WARNING

The information in this chapter is particularly vulnerable to change: prices for international travel are volatile, routes are introduced and canceled, schedules change, special deals come and go, and rules and visa requirements are amended. Airlines and governments seem to take a perverse pleasure in making price structures and regulations as complicated as possible. You should check directly with the airline or a travel agent to make sure you understand how a fare (and ticket you may buy) works. In addition, the travel industry is highly competitive and there are many hidden costs and benefits.

The upshot of this is that you should get opinions, quotes and advice from as many airlines and travel agents as possible before you part with your hard-earned cash. The details given in this chapter should be regarded as pointers and are not a substitute for your own careful, up-to-date research.

Domestic Airlines For information on flights within the US, check out the services of Alaska Airlines, American Airlines, America West, Continental, Delta, Northwest, Southwest, TWA or United. See the Toll-Free Directory for phone numbers.

Buying Tickets

Rather than just walking into the nearest travel agent or airline office, it pays to do a bit of research and shop around. If you're buying tickets within the US, the *New York Times*, *Los Angeles Times*, *Chicago Tribune*, *San Francisco Examiner* and other major newspapers all produce weekly travel sections with numerous travel agents' ads. Council Travel (☎ 800-226-8624, www.council travel.com) and STA (☎ 800-777-0112, www .sta-travel.com) have offices in major cities nationwide. The magazine *Travel Unlimited*, PO Box 1058, Allston, MA 02134, publishes details of the cheapest airfares and courier possibilities.

For those coming from outside the US, you might start by perusing travel sections of magazines like *Time Out* and *TNT* in the UK, or the Saturday editions of newspapers like the *Sydney Morning Herald* and *The Age* in Australia. Ads in these publications offer cheap fares, but don't be surprised if they happen to be sold out when you contact the agents: they're usually low-season fares on obscure airlines with conditions attached.

The plane ticket will probably be the single most expensive item in your budget, and buying it can be intimidating. It is always worth putting aside a few hours to research the current state of the market. Start early – some of the cheapest tickets must be bought months in advance, and popular flights sell out early.

Note that high season in the USA is mid-June to mid-September (summer) and the weeks around the Thanksgiving and Christmas holidays. The best rates for travel to and within the USA are found November through March.

Phone travel agents for bargains (airlines can supply information on routes and timetables; however, except at times of fare wars they do not supply the cheapest tickets). Airlines often have competitive low-season, student and senior citizens fares. Find out the fare, the route, for how long the ticket is valid and any restrictions that might apply.

Cheap tickets are available in two distinct categories: official and unofficial. Official ones have a variety of names including advance-purchase fares, budget fares, Apex and super-Apex.

Unofficial tickets are released by the airlines through selected travel agents (not through airline offices). The cheapest tickets are often nonrefundable, and many cannot be exchanged or may require you to pay a heavy penalty for changing your flight. Many insurance policies will cover this loss if you have to change your flight for emergency reasons.

Return (roundtrip) tickets are usually cheaper than two one-way fares – often *much* cheaper.

Use the fares quoted in this book as a guide only. They are approximate and based on the rates advertised by travel agents and airlines at press time. Quoted airfares do not necessarily constitute a recommendation for the carrier.

If traveling from the UK, you will probably find that the cheapest flights are being advertised by obscure bucket shops whose names haven't yet reached the telephone directory. Many such firms are honest and solvent, but a few rogues will take your money and disappear, only to reopen elsewhere a month or two later under a new name. If you feel suspicious about a firm, don't give them all the money at once. Leave a deposit of 20% or so and pay the balance on receiving the ticket. If they insist on cash in advance, go elsewhere. And once you have the ticket, ring the airline to confirm that you are actually booked on the flight.

You may decide to pay more than the rock-bottom fare by opting for the safety of a better-known travel agent. Established firms like STA Travel and Council Travel, with offices worldwide, Travel CUTS in Canada and Flight Centre in Australia are valid alternatives, and they offer good prices to most destinations.

Once you have your ticket, write down its number, together with the flight number and other details, and keep the information somewhere separate. If the ticket is lost or stolen, this will help you get a replacement.

Remember to buy travel insurance as early as possible (see the introduction to this chapter for details).

Visit USA Passes Almost all domestic carriers offer Visit USA passes to non-US citizens. The passes are actually books of

Air Travel Glossary

Baggage Allowance This will be written on your ticket and usually includes one 20kg item to go in the hold, plus one item of hand luggage.

Bucket Shops These are unbonded travel agencies specializing in discounted airline tickets.

Bumped Just because you have a confirmed seat doesn't mean you're going to get on the plane (see Overbooking).

Cancellation Penalties Canceling or changing a discounted ticket often involves heavy penalties; insurance can sometimes be taken out against these penalties. Some airlines impose penalties on regular tickets as well, particularly against 'no-show' passengers.

Check-In Airlines ask you to check in a certain time ahead of the flight departure (usually one to two hours on international flights). If you fail to check in on time and the flight is overbooked, the airline may cancel your booking and assign your seat to somebody else.

Confirmation Having a ticket written out with the flight and date you want doesn't mean you have a seat until the agent has checked with the airline that your status is 'OK' or confirmed. Meanwhile you could just be 'on request.'

Courier Fares Businesses often need to send urgent documents or freight securely and quickly. Courier companies hire people to accompany the package through customs and, in return, offer a discount ticket that is sometimes a phenomenal bargain. In effect, what the companies do is ship their freight as your luggage on regular commercial flights. This is a legitimate operation, but there are two shortcomings – the short turnaround time of the ticket (usually not longer than a month) and the limitation on your luggage allowance. You may have to surrender all your allowance and take only carry-on luggage.

ITX An ITX, or 'independent inclusive tour excursion,' is often available on tickets to popular holiday destinations. Officially it's a package deal combined with hotel accommodation, but many agents will sell you one of these for the flight only and give you phony hotel vouchers in the unlikely event that you're challenged at the airport.

Lost Tickets If you lose your airline ticket, an airline will usually treat it like a traveler's check and, after inquiries, issue you another one. Legally, however, an airline is entitled to treat it like cash; if you lose it, it's gone forever. Take good care of your tickets.

MCO An MCO, or 'miscellaneous charge order,' is a voucher that looks like an airline ticket but carries no destination or date. It can be exchanged through any International Association

coupons – each coupon equals a flight. Typically, the minimum number of coupons is three or four and the maximum is eight or 10. The passes must be purchased in conjunction with an international airline ticket anywhere outside the USA except Canada and Mexico. Flight coupons cost anywhere

from $100 to $160, depending on how many you choose to buy.

Most airlines require you to plan your itinerary in advance and to complete your flights within 60 days of arrival in the US, but rules may vary between airlines. A few airlines may allow you to use coupons on

Air Travel Glossary

of Travel Agents (IATA) airline for a ticket on a specific flight. It's a useful alternative to an onward ticket in those countries that demand one and is more flexible than an ordinary ticket if you're unsure of your route.

No-Shows No-shows are passengers who fail to show up for their flight. Full-fare passengers who fail to turn up are sometimes entitled to travel on a later flight. The rest are penalized (see Cancellation Penalties).

On Request This is an unconfirmed booking for a flight.

Onward Tickets An entry requirement for many countries is that you have a ticket out of the country. If you're unsure of your next move, the easiest solution is to buy the cheapest onward ticket to a neighboring country or a ticket from a reliable airline that can later be refunded if you do not use it.

Open Jaw Tickets These are return tickets with which you fly out to one place but return from another. If available, these tickets can save you from backtracking to your arrival point.

Overbooking Airlines hate to fly with empty seats, and since every flight has some passengers who fail to show up, airlines often book more passengers than they have seats. Usually excess passengers make up for the no-shows, but occasionally somebody gets bumped. Guess who it is most likely to be? The passengers who check in late.

Point-to-Point Tickets These are discount tickets that can be bought on some routes in return for passengers waiving their rights to a stopover.

Reconfirmation At least 72 hours prior to departure time of an onward or return flight, you must contact the airline and 'reconfirm' that you intend to be on the flight. If you don't do this, the airline can delete your name from the passenger list and you could lose your seat.

Restrictions Discounted tickets often have various restrictions on them – such as advance payment, minimum and maximum periods you must be away (eg, a minimum of two weeks or a maximum of one year), and penalties for changing the tickets.

Standby This is a discounted ticket on which you only fly if there is a seat free at the last moment. Standby fares are usually available only on domestic routes.

Travel Periods Ticket prices vary with the time of year. There is a low (off-peak) season and a high (peak) season, and often a low-shoulder season and a high-shoulder season as well. Usually the fare depends on your outward flight – if you depart in the high season and return in the low season, you pay the high-season fare.

standby, in which case call the airline a day or two before the flight and make a 'standby reservation.' Such a reservation gives you priority over all other standby travelers.

Round-the-World Tickets Airline RTW tickets are often real bargains and can work out to be no more expensive – and possibly even cheaper – than an ordinary roundtrip ticket. Prices start at about UK£850, A$1800 or US$1300 for 'short' routes such as Los Angeles-New York-London-Bangkok-Honolulu-Los Angeles. As soon as you start adding stops south of the equator, fares can go up to the US$2000 to $3000 range.

All the major airlines offer RTW tickets in conjunction with other international airlines, allowing you to fly anywhere you want on their route systems as long as you do not backtrack. You may have to book the first sector in advance; cancellation penalties apply. Tickets are usually valid from 90 days up to a year. An alternative type of RTW ticket can be put together by a travel agent using a combination of discounted tickets.

Most airlines restrict the number of sectors that can be flown within the USA and Canada to four, and some airlines black out a few heavily traveled routes (like Honolulu to Tokyo), though stopovers are otherwise generally unlimited. In most cases a 14-day advance purchase is required. After the ticket is purchased, dates can be changed without penalty and tickets can be rewritten to add or delete stops for $50 each.

The majority of RTW tickets restrict you to just two airlines. For example, Qantas flies in conjunction with either American Airlines, British Airways, Delta, Northwest, Canadian, Air France or KLM. Canadian Airlines links up with either Philippine Airlines, KLM, South African Airways or others. Continental Airlines flies with either Malaysia Airlines, Singapore Airlines or Thai Airways. The possibilities go on and on. Your best bet is to find a travel agent that advertises or specializes in RTW tickets.

Circle Pacific Tickets Circle Pacific tickets use several airlines to circle the Pacific – combining Australia, New Zealand, North America and Asia. These tickets allow you to swing through a variety of destinations, as long as you don't backtrack. Fares, generally about 15% cheaper than RTW tickets, include four stopovers, with the option of adding stops at US$50 each. There's a 14-day advance purchase requirement, a 25% cancellation penalty and a maximum stay of six months.

Getting Bumped

Airlines routinely overbook and count on some passengers canceling or not showing up. Occasionally, almost everybody does show up for a flight, and then some passengers must be 'bumped' onto another flight. Getting bumped can be a nuisance because you have to wait around for the next flight, but if you have a day's leeway, you can turn this to your advantage.

When you check in at the airline counter, ask if the flight is full and if there may be a need for volunteers; if yes, get your name on the list. Depending on how oversold the flight is, compensation may range from a discount voucher toward your next flight to a fully paid roundtrip ticket or even cash. Be sure to try and confirm a later flight so you don't get stuck in the airport on standby. If you have to spend the night, airlines frequently foot the hotel bill for their bumpees. You don't have to accept the airline's first offer and can haggle for a better deal.

However, be aware that being just a little late for boarding could get you bumped with none of these benefits.

Travelers with Special Needs

If you have special needs of any sort – a broken leg, dietary restrictions, dependence on a wheelchair, responsibility for a baby, fear of flying – you should let the airline know as soon as possible so they can make arrangements accordingly. You should remind them when you reconfirm your booking (at least 72 hours before departure) and again when you check in at the airport. It may also be worth calling different airlines before you make your booking, to find out how they can handle your particular needs.

With advance warning, airports and airlines can be surprisingly helpful. Most international airports can provide escorts from the check-in desk to the plane, and should have ramps, lifts, accessible toilets and reachable phones. Aircraft toilets, on the other hand, are likely to present a problem; travelers should discuss this early with the airline and, if necessary, with a doctor.

Guide dogs for the blind often must travel in a specially pressurized baggage compartment with other animals, away from their owners, though smaller guide dogs may be admitted to the cabin. Guide dogs are not subject to quarantine as long as they have proof of being vaccinated against rabies.

Deaf travelers can ask for airport and in-flight announcements to be written down for them.

Children under two travel for 10% of the standard fare (or free, on some airlines), as long as they don't occupy a seat. (They don't get a baggage allowance either.) 'Skycots' should be provided by the airline if requested in advance; these will take a child weighing up to about 22lb. Children between two and 12 can usually occupy a seat for half to two-thirds of the full fare and do get a baggage allowance. Strollers can often be taken on as hand luggage.

Baggage & Other Restrictions

On most domestic and international flights, the checked bag limit is two, or three if you don't have a carry-on. A charge may be levied if a bag exceeds the airline's size limits. On some international flights the luggage allowance is based on weight, not size. If you're worried about either size or weight restrictions, check with the airline.

If your luggage is delayed upon arrival, some airlines will give a cash advance to purchase necessities. If sporting equipment is misplaced, the airline may pay for rentals. Should the luggage be lost, it is important to submit a claim. The airline doesn't have to pay the full amount of the claim. Rather, they can estimate the value of your lost items. It may take them anywhere from six weeks to three months to process the claim and pay you.

Smoking Smoking is prohibited on all domestic flights within the USA and on many international flights as well. Most airports in the USA also restrict smoking.

Illegal Items Items illegal to take on a plane, either checked or as carry-on, include aerosols of polishes, waxes, etc; tear gas and pepper spray; camp stoves with fuel; and full divers' tanks.

Departure Taxes

A $6 airport departure tax is charged to all passengers bound for a destination outside the US. However, this fee, as well as a $6.50 North American Free Trade Agreement (NAFTA) tax charged to passengers entering the USA from a foreign country, is a hidden tax added to the purchase price of your airline ticket.

Routes Within the USA

Although the hundreds of air routes make it possible to fly almost anywhere within the US, ticket prices are usually lowest on the major 'air highways,' especially between San Francisco or LA and major East Coast cities like New York and Washington, DC. Flights to Chicago and Miami are also fairly competitive, but those to smaller cities, in the South or Midwest, are usually expensive and frequently require stops. Flights from LA are usually a few dollars cheaper than those from San Francisco.

Nonstop flights between the coasts take about 4½ hours eastbound and 5½ hours westbound, because of prevailing winds. Round-trip ticket prices can be as low as $300 to Boston, New York and Washington, DC; $200 to Chicago, Houston and Miami; and $100 or less to San Francisco, Las Vegas and Phoenix. Southwest Airlines often has some of the best fares, especially to places west of the Mississippi, like Seattle, San Francisco, Phoenix and Dallas.

Estimated Airfares

Airfares naturally fluctuate constantly, but these figures should provide you with an approximation of the price of a ticket from major gateways around the world. Except where indicated, prices for flights to San Francisco or Los Angeles are about the same.

gateway	low season	high season
London	£220	£320 to 430
Glasgow	£250	£330 to 430
Paris	2800 FF	5400 FF
Frankfurt	DM1100	DM1800
Sydney		
LA	A$1350	A$1800
SF	A$1300	A$1600
Auckland	NZ$1730	NZ$1880

Canada
Travel CUTS (☎ 888-838-2887, 416-977-2185 in Toronto) has offices in all major cities. The Toronto *Globe and Mail* and *Vancouver Sun* carry travel agents' ads.

There are daily flights to San Francisco and Los Angeles from Vancouver and Toronto, and other Canadian cities have connections as well. Flights between Los Angeles and Vancouver cost about $250 to $300 roundtrip.

The UK
Check the ads in *Time Out*, the *Evening Standard*, *TNT* and other publications, including the freebies usually available outside railway and major tube stations in London.

Most British travel agents are registered with the ABTA (Association of British Travel Agents). If you have paid an ABTA-registered agent for your flight, and the agent then goes out of business, ABTA will guarantee a refund or an alternative.

London is arguably the world's headquarters for bucket shops, which are well advertised and can usually beat published airline fares. Good, reliable agents for cheap tickets in the UK are Trailfinders (☎ 0171-937 5400), 194 Kensington High St, London, W8 7RG; Council Travel (☎ 0171-437 7767) 28a Poland St, London, W1, and STA Travel (☎ 0171-581 4132), 86 Old Brompton Rd, London SW7 3LQ.

Continental Europe
Many airlines, including KLM (from Amsterdam), Air France (Paris), Swissair

(Zurich), Lufthansa (Frankfurt) and Iberia (Madrid), have direct flights to Los Angeles or San Francisco. Many other international and US airlines arrive via a stop in a gateway city (usually Chicago or Miami) and continue on domestic flights. The direct flight takes about 11 hours westbound (London to LA), and nine or 10 hours eastbound because of the prevailing winds.

In Amsterdam, NBBS (☎ 020-624 09 89) with several branches around town, is a popular travel agent. In Paris, contact USIT Voyages (☎ 01 42 34 56 90) at 6, rue de Vaugirard, 75006 Paris, for great student fares. Council Travel (☎ 01 44 41 89 80) is at 1, place de l'Odéon, 75006. Council Travel also has two offices in Germany: in Düsseldorf at Graf-Adolph-Strasse 18 (☎ 211-36 30 30) and in Munich at Adalbertstrasse 32 (☎ 089-39 50 22). STA Travel has several offices in Germany, including one in Frankfurt at Bergerstrasse 118 (☎ 069-43 01 91) and two in Berlin at Dorotheenstrasse 30 (☎ 030-20 16 50 63) and at Goethestrasse 73 (☎ 030-311 09 50).

Australia & New Zealand
Qantas flies to Los Angeles from Sydney, Melbourne (via Sydney or Auckland) and Cairns. United flies to San Francisco from Sydney and Melbourne (via Sydney), and also flies to Los Angeles.

In both Australia and New Zealand, STA Travel and Flight Centres International are major dealers in cheap airfares, with special deals for students and travelers under 30. Check the travel agents' ads in the phone directory and ring around. The cheapest tickets have a 21-day advance-purchase requirement, a minimum stay of seven days and a maximum stay of 60 days. Flying with Air New Zealand is slightly cheaper, and both Qantas and Air New Zealand offer more expensive tickets with longer stays or stopovers.

Asia
Hong Kong is the discount plane ticket capital of the region, but its bucket shops can be unreliable. Ask the advice of other travelers before buying a ticket. STA Travel,

which is dependable, has branches in Hong Kong, Tokyo, Singapore, Bangkok and Kuala Lumpur. Many, if not most, flights to the USA go via Honolulu, Hawaii.

United Airlines has three flights a day to Honolulu from Tokyo, with connections to West Coast cities. Northwest and Japan Air Lines also have daily flights to the West Coast from Tokyo; Japan Air Lines also flies to Honolulu from Osaka, Nagoya, Fukuoka and Sapporo.

Central & South America
Most flights from Central and South America go via Miami, Houston or Los Angeles, though some fly via New York. Most countries' international flag carriers (like Aerolíneas Argentinas and LAN-Chile), as well as US airlines like United and American, serve these destinations, with onward connections. Continental has flights from about 20 cities in Mexico and Central America, including San José, Guatemala City, Cancún and Mérida.

Mexico
There are regular flights from San Francisco and Los Angeles to the major cities and tourist destinations in Mexico. At times (depending on prices and exchange rates), it can be substantially cheaper to fly to major Mexican cities from Tijuana than from Los Angeles or even San Diego. Tijuana is the northernmost Mexican city, just across the border from San Diego and only three hours by car or bus from Los Angeles.

Arriving in the USA
Even if you are continuing immediately to another city, the first US airport you land in is where you must carry out immigration and customs formalities. If you are, say, checked in from London to Los Angeles, you will still have to take yourself through immigration – and your luggage through customs – if you first land in Chicago.

If you have a non-US passport and are not a permanent US resident (green card holder), you must complete an Arrival/Departure Record (form I-94) before you front up to the immigration desk. This is usually handed out on the plane, along with the customs declaration, which must be filled out by all arriving passengers.

Although most visitors to the US ultimately have no problem entering the country, immigration and customs officials are not famous for their people skills. Their main concern is to ferret out those likely to work illegally or overstay. You may be subjected to a barrage of questions concerning your length of stay and itinerary, whether you have relatives in the US, whether you have sufficient funds, etc.

Be prepared to show your return flight ticket and that you have $300 or $400 for every week of your intended stay. These days, a couple of major credit cards will go a long way towards establishing 'sufficient funds.' Don't make too much of having friends, relatives or business contacts in the USA – the INS official may decide that this will make you more likely to overstay. Try to remain as calm as possible and answer all questions politely. Be aware that until you have passed through the last formality, you have few rights.

If you feel you've been harassed by an INS or customs officer (sexist comments have been among the unpleasantness experienced by at least one of this author team), demand to speak with a supervisor immediately. They are generally better qualified, and you can state your complaint to them directly or they will give you a complaint form to fill out.

BUS
Greyhound Bus Lines
Greyhound Bus Lines(☎ 800-231-2222, www.greyhound.com), the only nationwide bus company, has reduced local services considerably, but still runs cross-country and to smaller rural communities not served by train or other public transport.

Buses are air-conditioned, and most are decently maintained (though the same may not always be true of your fellow passengers). Dealing with Greyhound on the telephone is often a major investment in time and patience, *especially* once you get through to an operator.

Because buses are so few, schedules are often inconvenient and fares are relatively high. Greyhound's prices are reasonable, though bargain airfares can occasionally match or undercut its fares on long-distance routes. In some cases, on shorter routes, it may be cheaper to rent a car than to ride the bus, especially if you have a group of two or more people.

For fares and further details, see the Getting Around chapter.

USbus

The USbus (☎ 818-721-6000, theusbus@ att.net; in the UK: ☎ 01892-532060, amaduk @attmail.com) covers the country on a flexipass system primarily geared toward young, independent travelers (those under 18 must be accompanied by an adult). USbuses travel in the daytime along nine predetermined routes, picking up and dropping off at HI-accredited youth hostels or other budget accommodations. You may travel on as many routes as you wish while your flexipass is valid.

Los Angeles is the gateway for five routes headed for such destinations as San Diego, San Francisco, Seattle, Las Vegas, Flagstaff (near the Grand Canyon) and Yosemite National Park.

Summer 1999 flexipass fares were $199 for five days of travel within a 15-day period; $299 for 10 days of travel in a 25-day period, $399 for 15 days over a 40-day period, $639 for 30 days over a 60-day period and $799 for 45 days over a 90-day period.

Green Tortoise

Another alternative for West Coast travelers is a throwback to Ken Kesey's Merry Pranksters of the late '60s and the nearest thing in America to the 'Magic Bus.' When you hit the road with San Francisco-based Green Tortoise Adventure Travel (☎ 415-956-7500, 800-867-8647, www.greentortoise .com), 494 Broadway, San Francisco, CA 94133, your journey may be more memorable than your destination.

Green Tortoise operates like a mobile commune. You'll travel in converted sleeper coaches outfitted with mattresses on raised platforms and bunk beds, couches, tables, kitchen appliances and stereos, but no restrooms (the bus will make stops 'as necessary'). No smoking or alcohol is allowed on the bus. Weekly service up and down the West Coast between Seattle and Los Angeles costs $79 each way.

TRAIN

Amtrak (☎ 800-872-7245, 800-USA-RAIL, www.amtrak.com) has a rail system with service to major US cities. The trains are comfortable, with dining and lounge cars on long-distance routes. Reservations can be made any time from 11 months in advance to the day of departure; reserve as early as possible, because space is limited and this gives you the best chance at getting a discount fare.

Three routes operate within California: The *San Joaquin* travels from Oakland/ Emeryville to Los Angeles; the *San Diegan* goes from San Luis Obispo to San Diego; and the *Capitol* connects Sacramento with San Jose.

Four cross-country trains pass through California: The *Southwest Chief* has daily service between Chicago and Los Angeles via Kansas City, Missouri; Albuquerque, New Mexico; Flagstaff, Arizona; and Kingman, Arizona. The *California Zephyr* runs daily between Chicago and Emeryville, near San Francisco, via Omaha, Nebraska; Denver, Colorado; and Salt Lake City, Utah. The *Sunset Limited* train runs three times a week on the southern route from Los Angeles through Tucson, Arizona; El Paso, Texas; New Orleans, Louisiana to Orlando, Florida. The *Coast Starlight* goes up the West Coast, from Los Angeles to Oakland, Sacramento; Portland, Oregon and Seattle, Washington. Los Angeles to Oakland costs up to $75 one way, more than most flights.

Fares

Rail travel in the US is not cheap, but you can cut costs by purchasing special fares in advance. A variety of one-way, roundtrip and promotional fares are available, with discounts for seniors age 62 and over, children ages two to 15, military personnel and disabled travelers. Fares vary according to type of seating; you can travel in coach seats or in various types of sleeping compartments. Children ages two to 15 ride for half price when accompanied by an adult paying full fare, and anyone over age 62 qualifies for a 15% discount. Special fares are available year round but are more likely between mid-October and May.

Passes The best overall value is the Explore America Pass, available to US visitors and North Americans alike, that permits three stops within 45 days of travel. This pass divides the country into three zones, with travel in one zone (western, central or eastern) costing $239/209 peak/off-peak season. Two adjacent zones cost $339/279; all zones cost $399/339. You must book your itinerary in advance, however, specifying traveling dates and destinations.

Non-US citizens also have the option of the USA Rail Pass, which must be purchased from a travel agent outside the US or from an Amtrak office within the country (you must show a foreign passport). While valid, the pass allows you to get on and off wherever you wish. Comfort seats or sleeping accommodations are extra. Prices vary from high to low season:

duration	route	high/low season
15 day	national	$425/285
	West Coast	$315/195
	East Coast	$250/205
30 day	national	$535/375
	West Coast	$310/260
	East Coast	$395/255

Advanced booking is recommended, especially during the peak season.

Note that most small train stations don't sell tickets; you must book them with a travel agent or Amtrak directly. Trains may only stop at certain small stations if you have bought a ticket in advance.

CAR & MOTORCYCLE
Much of the advice on driving in the Getting Around chapter also applies to driving longer distances to and from other parts of the USA; see that chapter for further details.

Drivers of cars and riders of motorcycles will need the vehicle's registration papers and liability insurance, as well as their valid driver's license from their home state or country.

For information on buying or renting a car, see the Getting Around chapter.

Drive-Aways
Drive-aways are cars that belong to owners who can't drive them to a specific destination but are willing to allow someone else to drive for them. For example, if somebody moves from Los Angeles to Chicago, they may elect to fly and leave the car with a drive-away agency. The agency will find a driver and take care of all necessary insurance and permits. If you want to drive from Los Angeles to Chicago, have a valid driver's license and a clean driving record, you can apply to drive the car. Normally, you must pay a small refundable deposit. You pay for the gas (though sometimes a gas allowance is given). You are allowed a set number of days to deliver the car – usually based on driving eight hours a day. You are also allowed a limited number of miles, based on the best route and allowing for reasonable side trips, so you can't just zigzag all over the country. However, this is a cheap way to get around if you like long-distance driving and meet eligibility requirements.

Drive-away companies often advertise in the classified sections of newspapers under the heading 'Travel' and are also listed in the Yellow Pages of telephone directories under 'Automobile Transporters & Drive-away Companies.'

You need to be flexible about dates and destinations when you call. If you are going to a popular area, you may be able to leave within two days or less, or you may have to wait over a week before a car becomes available. The routes most easily available are coast to coast.

ORGANIZED TOURS
Package tours, which may include airfare, accommodations and other features such as

ground transport, tickets to major attractions, sightseeing tours and so on, can work out to be more economical – and more convenient – than if you purchased each element separately. They are often a good way to travel for those with limited time and those otherwise traveling alone.

Tours of California and Southwestern states are so numerous that it would be impossible to attempt any kind of comprehensive listing; for overseas visitors, the most reliable sources of information on what's available are major international travel agents like Thomas Cook and American Express.

Green Tortoise (☎ 415-956-7500, 800-867-8647, www.greentortoise.com), 494 Broadway, San Francisco, CA 94133, offers alternative bus transportation with stops at places like hot springs and national parks. This is not luxury travel, but it can be fun. The National Parks Loop from San Francisco takes 16 days. The cost is $499 plus $121 toward the food fund. They also have three-day trips to Death Valley ($119) and two-day ($69) and three-day ($119) trips to Yosemite.

TrekAmerica (☎ 973-983-1144, 800-221-0596, fax 973-983-8551, www.trekamerica.com), PO Box 189, Rockaway, NJ 07866, offers roundtrip camping tours to different areas of the country. In England, they are at 4 Water Perry Court, Banbury, Oxon OX16 8QG (☎ 01295-256777, fax 01295-257399); in Australia contact Adventure World 75 Walker St, North Sydney, NSW 2060 (☎ 9955-5000, fax 9954-5817). These tours last one to nine weeks and are designed for small, international groups (13 people maximum) of 18 to 38-year-olds. They also offer open-age trips for those 18 to 80 that are very similar. Tour prices vary by season and peak between July and September. Tours including food and occasional hotel nights cost about $800 for a 10-day tour to $3000 for a 64-day tour of the entire country. Some side trips and cultural events are included in the price, and participants help with cooking and camp chores.

Similar deals are available from Suntrek (☎ 707-523-1800, 800-786-8735, fax 707-523-1911), Sun Plaza, 77 West Third St, Santa Rosa, CA 95401. Suntrek also has offices in Germany (☎ 089-480 28 31, fax 089-480 24 11), Sedanstrasse 21, 81667 Munich; and Switzerland (☎ 41-1-387 78 78, fax 41-1-387 78 00), Birmensdorferstr 107, PO Box 8371, CH-8036 Zurich. Their tours are for the 'young at heart' and attract predominantly young international travelers, although there is no age limit. Prices range from about $847 for the three-week trek to about $3194 for their 13-week around America treks.

Road Runner USA/Canada (☎ 800-873-5872), a big Massachusetts-based company, leads small group tours in conjunction with Hostelling International all over the world, including California and the Southwest. Their 10-day 'California Cooler' tour covers Lake Havasu, the Grand Canyon, Las Vegas, Yosemite National Park, San Francisco and the Pacific coast and costs $549 to $689. They also have offices in England (☎ 1892-512700), 64 Mt Pleasant Ave, Tunbridge Wells, Kent TN1 1QY.

Specialized Tours

Elderhostel (☎ 877-426-8056), 75 Federal St, Boston, MA 02110, is a nonprofit organization offering educational programs for those 60 and over with programs throughout the US. Bicycling, hiking and walking, cross-country skiing, running and multisport tours are another possibility, offered by companies like Backroads (☎ 510-527-1555, 800-462-2848), 801 Cedar St, Berkeley, CA 94710.

Getting Around

AIR

Flying is a convenient way of getting around California and Nevada, especially if the amount of time you have to spend in a region is limited. Depending on where you're flying to or from, how far in advance you buy your ticket and a few other factors, air travel can sometimes actually be less expensive than making the same trip by bus, train or rental car.

Besides the major international airports in San Francisco and Los Angeles, a number of smaller airports serve the region. These include Sacramento, Oakland, San Jose, Burbank, Ontario, Orange County, San Diego, Las Vegas and Reno. Even smaller airports include Eureka, Chico, Santa Rosa, Santa Barbara, Long Beach and Palm Springs. Additional tiny airports – often only suitable for small private planes – are mentioned in the regional chapters. See the Getting There & Away chapter for contact information on the major airports.

A number of routes have especially frequent and convenient service, with airplanes taking off every 45 to 90 minutes; these routes include San Francisco-Los Angeles (SF-LA), SF-Burbank, SF-Orange County, SF-San Diego, SF-Reno, Oakland-LA and LA-Las Vegas. It's possible to just show up at the airport, buy your ticket and hop on, though only when buying your ticket in advance will you be guaranteed a seat (and fares are lower when purchasing in advance). See the Getting There & Away chapter for more about advance purchase and other types of discount fares – much of the same advice applies, whether you're flying a route within California and Nevada, within the rest of the United States or internationally.

Some of the main airlines serving California and Nevada include America West, American, Continental, Delta, Northwest, Reno Air, Southwest, United and US Airways (see the Toll-Free Numbers directory for phone numbers).

BUS
Greyhound

Since Americans rely so much on their cars and usually fly for longer distances, bus transport has become rather limited, though some good deals are still available. Greyhound (☎ 800-231-2222, www.greyhound.com) has extensive scheduled routes and its own terminal in most cities, though often in undesirable parts of town. However, the buses are comfortable, the company has an exceptional safety record and buses are more or less on time.

But even Greyhound has reduced or eliminated services to smaller rural communities it once served efficiently. In many small towns Greyhound no longer maintains terminals, but merely stops at a given location, such as fast-food restaurants like McDonald's. In these unlikely terminals, boarding passengers usually pay the driver with exact change.

Tickets may be bought over the phone or on the website with a credit card (MasterCard, Visa or Discover) and mailed to you if purchased 10 days in advance. Otherwise, simply pick up your tickets at the terminal any time before departure (bring proper identification). Greyhound terminals also accept American Express, traveler's checks and cash. Note that all buses are nonsmoking.

Fares Steep discounts are usually available to people making advance reservations. Greyhound frequently changes specific fares, but at the time of research, a 21-day advance purchase, roundtrip ticket to any destination in the US was just $99, with those bought at least 14 days in advance costing just $118 roundtrip and seven days early $158. Other discounts apply to children, college students, military personnel and seniors.

Greyhound's unlimited travel pass, called the Ameripass, is available at any Greyhound depot. Good for seven, 15, 30 or 60 days, at the time of writing, the passes cost

$199/299/409/599, respectively, though these are always subject to change. Children under 11 are half price and students and seniors pay $189/279/379/549.

International Ameripass This pass can be purchased only by foreign tourists and foreign students and lecturers (with their families) staying less than one year in the United States. They come in lengths of seven, 10, 15 and 30 days and cost $179/229/269/369, respectively. Kids' tickets are half price. The pass must be bought at a travel agency abroad, by sending an email to greyhound@crystalholidays.co.uk, or in person from the Greyhound International depot in New York City (☎ 212-971-0492), 625 8th Ave at the Port Authority Subway level, open Monday to Thursday 8am to 4pm, Friday from 8am to 7pm and Saturday from 8am to 3pm. New York Greyhound International accepts MasterCard and Visa, traveler's checks and cash.

To contact Greyhound International to inquire about regular fares and routes, call ☎ 800-246-8572. Those buying an International Ameripass must complete an affidavit and present a passport or visa (or waiver) to the appropriate Greyhound officials.

USbus

The USbus (☎ 818-721-6000, theusbus@att.net; in the UK: ☎ 01892-532060, amaduk@attmail.com) operates nine scheduled routes throughout the US on a flexipass system. Five routes start in Los Angeles and cover destinations of interest in California, Nevada and the Canyon Country, including San Francisco, Las Vegas, Kanab and Yosemite. The number of departures per week varies by route and month, though it's usually two to four times a week. For fares and details, see the Getting There & Away chapter.

Ant

'Ant' stands for Adventure Network for Travelers (☎ 415-399-0880, 800-336-6049, fax 415-399-0949; anttrips@theant.com, www.theant.com), a San Francisco-based company that operates a hop-on, hop-off system service similar to the USbus but limited to California, Nevada and Arizona.

Both of their loop routes pass through Los Angeles, with at least three, and up to five (in peak season), departures a week for each route. The Northern Loop ($239) travels via Las Vegas, Death Valley, Lake Tahoe, Yosemite and San Francisco; the Southern Loop ($199) hits San Diego, Mexicali (Mexico), Phoenix, Grand Canyon, Bryce and Zion national parks and Las Vegas. The combined cost for both loops is $329. There's also the Coastal Cruiser shuttle bus between LA and San Francisco ($89 one way, $169 roundtrip).

You have six months in which to complete the loop(s). Each night, the Ant bus stops at inexpensive hostels, motels or campgrounds for which the guide can make free reservations. If you don't want to do an entire loop, you can also buy individual segments. A one-way trip from LA to Las Vegas, for example, costs $39, and it's $19 to San Diego.

Green Tortoise

This is a truly alternative bus line and tour company (☎ 415-956-7500, 800-867-8647, www.greentortoise.com). The buses, with seats knocked out and replaced by bunks with foam mattresses, cover several regular routes in California, as well as trips further afield. See the Getting There & Away chapter for more information.

TRAIN

Amtrak (☎ 800-872-7245, www.amtrak.com) has an extensive rail-and-bus system throughout California, with buses providing connections to and from rural towns, Yosemite National Park, and a couple of routes crossing Nevada. Reservations (the sooner made, the better the fare) can be held under your surname only; tickets can be purchased by credit card over the phone or online, from a travel agent or at an Amtrak depot. Trains serving California include the *Southwest Chief*, *California Zephyr*, *Sunset Limited* and *Coast Starlight*. See the Getting There & Away chapter for details on reservations, fares and more.

CAR & MOTORCYCLE

Driving is probably the easiest, cheapest and best way to get around California and Nevada; having your own wheels enables you to go wherever you want, whenever you want, giving you the freedom to explore many places that are hard or impossible to reach by public transport.

With a car it's feasible to carry camping and cooking gear and a cooler, enabling you to offset some of the cost of the car by saving on lodging and food. For road conditions anywhere in California, call the California Department of Transportation at ☎ 800-427-7623.

Three north-south routes traverse California. Hwy 1, known as the Pacific Coast Hwy, is the slowest and curviest, but also most scenic, hugging the coast, passing by sandy beaches and clinging to rugged cliffs that drop steeply into the ocean. Hwy 101, hugging the coast together with Hwy 1 for some sections and running the lengths of lovely valleys just inland from the Coastal Range for much of its distance, is also scenic, though not as spectacular as the Pacific Coast Hwy. I-5, the fastest but least scenic and most boring route, traverses the flat San Joaquin Valley and heads up the center of the state into Oregon.

Major east-west highways include I-80, heading northeast from San Francisco through Reno and on to Salt Lake City; I-15, traveling northeast out of Los Angeles through Las Vegas and on to Salt Lake City; I-40, heading east from Barstow to Flagstaff, Arizona and on to Albuquerque, New Mexico; I-10, heading east from Los Angeles to Phoenix, Arizona; and I-8, heading east from San Diego to Tucson, Arizona.

Rules of the Road

The *California Driver Handbook* explains everything you need to know about driving in California; it's available free at any DMV office or you can access it and the motorcycle handbook on the Internet at www.dmv.ca .gov. This easy, illustrated booklet contains all the rules of the road, and it's a good idea to read it. Nevada's driving rules are basically the same as California's.

Seatbelts must be worn at all times. Children under four years old, or those weighing less than 40 pounds, must ride in approved child safety seats.

During winter months, especially at the higher elevations, tire chains may be required on snowy or icy roads. Keep a set of chains in the trunk, since icy or snowy roads are sometimes closed to cars without chains or four-wheel drive. (Note that rental car companies specifically prohibit the use of chains on their vehicles. You are responsible for any damage due to chains.) Roadside services might be available to attach chains to your tires for a fee (around $20). Other cold-weather precautions include keeping a wool blanket, a windshield ice scraper, a spade or snow shovel, flares and an extra set of gloves and boots in the trunk for emergencies.

A few hints for first-time drivers in California and Nevada: Unless a sign indicates otherwise, you can turn right at a red light, as long as you don't impede intersecting traffic, which has the right of way. At intersections with four-way stop signs, cars proceed in the order in which they arrived. If two cars arrive simultaneously, the one on the right has the right of way. This can be an iffy situation, as opinions may differ over who arrived first, so don't insist on going first, even if it's your right.

On freeways, you may pass slower cars on either the left or the right lane; if two cars are trying to get into the same central lane, the one further to the right has priority. Some freeways and highways have lanes marked with a diamond symbol and the words 'car pool.' These lanes are reserved for cars with three or more passengers. Fines for driving in this lane without the minimum number of people are prohibitively stiff (up to $271).

Speed Limits Speed limits, unless posted otherwise, are 35 miles per hour (56km per hour) on city streets and 65 mph (104 kph) on freeways. Most drivers exceed these limits by a few miles per hour, however. But be aware that California has a 'Basic Speed Law' that says you may never drive faster than is safe for the present conditions, regardless of the posted speed limit, and tickets can be given for driving too slow as well as for speeding, based on the police officer's assessment of the safe speed.

In cities and residential areas, watch for school zones, where limits can be as low as 15 mph during school hours. These speeds are strictly enforced. *Never* pass a school bus when its rear red lights are flashing: children are getting off the bus at these times. If you encounter ambulances with their sirens wailing going in your direction, do everything you safely can to steer over to the right curb and halt until they've passed.

Littering California has an aggressive campaign against littering. If you are seen throwing anything from a vehicle onto the roadway – bottles, cans, trash, a lighted cigarette, or anything else – the law states that you must be fined $1000. Littering convictions are shown on your driving record the same as other driving violations. Keep any trash with you inside the vehicle until you get to a place to discard it.

Parking Beware colored curbs (red = no parking or stopping, yellow = loading zone, white = five-minute parking for adjacent businesses, green = 10-minute limit from 9 am to 6 pm, blue = disabled parking), since parking patrols issue tickets relentlessly. If you're parked at a meter, be sure to feed it enough coins: fines may be as much as $30 for simply being 30 seconds late in returning to your vehicle. Always study signposts for restrictions. Parking on residential streets – especially those near nightlife areas – is often reserved for residents. Be sure to keep your vehicle off the road during street cleaning hours – usually early on a weekday morning – which are posted as well. And of course, don't block driveways or park too close to fire hydrants or bus stops.

Driving Under the Influence Penalties are severe for DUI – driving under the influence of alcohol or drugs. If police have any reason to suspect you may have been drinking, they will demand that you take a test to determine the level of alcohol in your body. You have the right to choose a breath test, a

urine test or a blood test, but you do not have the right to refuse to be tested. Refusing to be tested is treated the same as taking and failing the test, and carries the same penalties and a one-year suspension of your driver's license.

The legal limits of alcohol in your body for driving are well below the level of 'drunkenness'; you don't have to be drunk to be breaking the law. If you are found to have a blood alcohol concentration of 0.08% or more (0.01% if you are under 21 years old), you can be required to serve 48 hours to six months in jail, pay $390 to $1000 in fines and have your driver's license suspended for four months to a year. If you own the car in which you were driving, the state can impound it for 30 days – and make you pay for the storage. All of these are for a first offense. Penalties for subsequent offenses are even more severe.

DUIs are completely avoidable when a 'designated driver' is decided upon at the beginning of the evening. One person in a group agrees not to consume alcohol or drugs and to be responsible for transporting the entire group safely. Bars and restaurants sometimes offer free nonalcoholic drinks or other incentives to the designated driver.

It is also illegal to carry open containers of alcohol in a vehicle, even in the passenger section, even if they are empty. Containers that are full and sealed may be carried, but if they have ever been opened they must be stored in the trunk.

Rental

Renting a car is a good value if you want to get around California and Nevada, especially with more than one person to share the costs. Rental companies require that you have a major credit card, that you be at least 25 years old (21 in some cases), and that you have a valid driver's license (your home license will do).

Prices vary widely, so shop around. Be sure to ask for the best rate. Discounts may be offered for renting on weekends, for three days, a week, a month, or even for renting in one place and returning the car to another, if the company needs to move cars in that direction. Car rental is cheaper in big cities, especially Los Angeles. It often makes sense to rent a car there, rather than taking buses or trains to a rural center and then paying a higher rate for a car for a shorter period.

When shopping for a rental, compare the total cost of rates offered by different companies, including insurance and mileage; one company may charge a little less for the car, but a little more for the insurance. Also estimate the distance you'll be driving; an 'unlimited mileage' plan will work out more economically than a 'cost-per-mile' plan if you'll be driving long distances. Increasingly, unlimited mileage is found only in urban areas. For long distances, you might be interested in a drive-away car. See the Getting There & Away chapter for more information.

Basic liability insurance, which will cover damage you may cause to another vehicle, is required by law and comes with the price of renting the car. Liability insurance is also called 'third-party coverage.'

Collision insurance, also called the 'liability damage waiver,' is optional; it covers the full value of the vehicle in case of an accident, except when caused by acts of nature or fire. The average for this kind of insurance is $9 to $12 a day. You don't need to buy this waiver to rent the car.

Some credit cards, such as the Master-Card Gold Card, will cover collision insurance if you rent for 15 days or less and charge the full cost of the rental to your card. If you opt to do that, you'll need to sign the waiver, declining the coverage. If you already have collision insurance on your personal policy, the credit card will cover the large deductible. To find out if your credit card offers such a service, and the extent of the coverage, contact the credit card company.

Some agencies may also tack on a daily fee for each additional driver, though not usually if the other driver is the renter's spouse.

Think about whether you want to rent a car and return it to the same place you got it, or get a one-way rental and return it to a different place. While local rental car companies may have only one or two offices, the larger companies have many offices throughout California, Nevada, and the rest of the USA. Be sure to ask if there is a drop-off charge and if the price of the car is different for a one-way rental. Sometimes hefty drop-off charges make one-way rentals impractical, but there may also be no charge at all.

The major nationwide rental car companies are Alamo, Avis, Budget, Dollar, Enterprise, Hertz, National and Thrifty (see Toll-Free Numbers directory for phone numbers).

Rent-A-Wreck offers older vehicles at cheaper prices, and smaller local companies are sometimes even less expensive. RVs can also be rented; look in the Yellow Pages under 'Recreational Vehicles – Renting & Leasing.'

Purchase

If you're spending several months in the USA, purchasing a car is worth considering; a car is more flexible than public transport and likely to be cheaper than rentals if you're planning on doing a lot of traveling, but buying one can be complicated and require some research.

It's possible to purchase a viable car for about $1500, but you can't expect to go too far before you'll need some repair that could cost several hundred dollars or more. Cars bought at a dealer cost more than cars purchased from individuals, but may come with warranties or financing options. Buying from an individual is usually cheaper; look in the newspaper classified ads or special ad publications for used vehicles.

Check out the official value of a used car in the *Kelley Blue Book*, a listing of cars by make, model, year issued and the average resale price. Local public libraries have copies of the *Blue Book*, as well as back issues of *Consumer Reports*, a magazine that annually tallies the repair records of common makes of cars. It's also worth spending $50 or so to have a mechanic check a car for defects before putting down your money. Many mechanics and some AAA offices have diagnostic centers where they can check a car on the spot for its members and those of foreign affiliates. Bargaining when buying a used car is standard practice.

If you buy from a dealer, the dealer will submit the required forms to the Department of Motor Vehicles (DMV) for the car's registration to be transferred into your name. If you buy from an individual, you (the buyer) must register the vehicle with the DMV within 10 days of purchase. To register the vehicle you will need the bill of sale, the title to the car (the 'pink slip'), proof of insurance or other financial responsibility, and a state smog certificate. Non-US citizens also need an International Driving Permit. Registration fees range from about $100 to $300, depending on the make and age of the car.

Inspect the title carefully before purchasing the car; the owner's name that appears on the title must match the identification of the person selling you the car. If you're not a US citizen, you may find it useful to obtain a notarized document authorizing your use of the car, since the motor vehicle bureau in the state where you buy the car may take several weeks or more to process the change in title.

Insurance California law specifies a fixed minimum amount of liability insurance to protect the health and property of others in case of an accident. If you are involved in any type of accident, regardless of fault – if someone bumps into your car in a parking lot, for example – and you don't have insurance, penalties are severe; in addition to financial penalties, your driver's license will be suspended for one year.

Obtaining insurance, however, is not as simple as walking into an agency, filling out a form and paying for it.

Most large agencies like AAA (see below) require that you have a valid US driver's license. Some, however, (including Solo Insurance at ☎ 800-551-2378) can arrange short-term car insurance for holders of non-US licenses, provided they also have an International Driving Permit.

Many agencies refuse to insure drivers who have no car insurance (a classic catch-22); companies that will do so often charge much higher rates because they presume a higher risk. Male drivers under the age of 25 will pay astronomical rates. The minimum term for a policy is usually six months, but some insurance companies will refund the difference on a prorated basis if the car is sold and the policy voluntarily terminated. It is advisable to shop around.

Insurance rates range from $300 to $1200 a year, depending on the state, the make and age of the car, and where the car is registered. Rates are generally lower if you register it at an address in the suburbs or in a rural area, rather than in a central city. Collision coverage has become very expensive, with high deductibles, and is generally not worthwhile unless the car is somewhat valuable.

American Automobile Association

If you'll be doing much driving, whether in your own vehicle, someone else's or in a rental car, membership in the American Automobile Association (AAA, called 'triple A'; ☎ 800-874-7532) is an excellent thing to have. Having a AAA card entitles you to free 24-hour roadside emergency service anywhere in the US (☎ 800-222-4357), including a few gallons of gas to get you going again if you run out, basic mechanical help and free towing to the nearest mechanic. They also offer free maps and travel planning advice, free tour books and travel literature, advice on how to buy a used car, reasonable car insurance, travel agency services and many other benefits. AAA offices are found throughout California, Nevada, and the rest of the USA; membership varies slightly by city and costs around $60 the first year, $40 per year thereafter; additional members are $20 each. Members of foreign AAA affiliates, like the Automobile Association in the UK or the ADAC in Germany, are entitled to the same services as US AAA members, if they bring along their membership cards.

Car Sharing

If you're looking for someone to ride along to share the cost of fuel, ask around or post a notice in hostels, check the ride boards at universities or the newspaper classified ads.

Hostels can be especially good places to find riders, not only for long trips but also for sharing the cost to rent a car for local day trips. Expenses that would be monumental for one person suddenly become manageable if you can find three or four other people to split the cost.

Motorcycles

To operate a motorcycle or moped you must have a special motorcycle license; separate licenses are issued for driving a motorcycle or moped with an engine size of 149cc or less, a motorcycle with an engine size of 150cc or more, and a motorcycle with three wheels or one with an attached sidecar.

The *Motorcycle Driver Supplement* booklet, a supplement to the *California Driver Handbook*, which gives all the rules of the road for motorcyclists, may be picked up free from any DMV office. The law specifies that all drivers and passengers of motorcycles and mopeds, including children, must wear a securely fastened safety helmet. Motorcycles of less than 150cc engine size may not be driven on freeways.

Recreational Vehicles

You'll see many RVs in California, in sizes up to giant models that are like houses on wheels. Campgrounds with full hookups are found almost everywhere. RVs are more expensive than cars to rent or buy, and they're bulky and not as economical to drive, but they solve all your transport, accommodation and cooking needs.

BICYCLE

Bicycling makes it possible to see the countryside at a slower, more intimate pace than is possible with motorized transport; it's nonpolluting, inexpensive, and you'll get some great exercise in the bargain, as well as having your own transport for getting around once you reach your destination.

Bicycles can be rented by the hour, day week or month. They can be bought new at sporting goods stores, discount warehouse stores and bicycle shops, or used at flea markets and from notice boards at hostels; you could also check the newspaper classi-

fied ads. Prices vary drastically depending on what you get.

A number of books and other publications are available on cycling and route planning in California and Nevada, suggesting local rides, routes for long-distance trips and places for off-road biking. Some of these books are mentioned in the Activities chapter; many others, including those specializing in local areas, can be found in local bookstores or bicycle shops.

You can bicycle anywhere except on freeways, where signs at on-ramps specify that no bicycles, motorized cycles (mopeds with less than 150cc engines) or pedestrians may pass beyond a certain point. You can cycle on parts of the coastal Hwy 1, but beware of treacherous curves and narrow roadways. Cycling is more enjoyable on the less-traveled roads; sometimes parallel or frontage roads enable you to follow the major highways without actually being on them.

If you plan a long bicycling trip and get tired of pedaling, or if you want to avoid the hilliest spots or bad weather, you can always take your bike along on public transport. Greyhound will carry bicycles as luggage for $15, provided the bicycle is disassembled and boxed; boxes are available for sale at some Greyhound stations.

Amtrak will carry bicycles on its long-distance trains (say, the *Coast Starlight* and the *Southwest Chief*) as checked baggage for $5, as long as they are in a special reusable box, sold for $10 at railway stations. The *San Joaquin* (San Francisco to LA), *San Diegan* (San Luis Obispo to San Diego) and *Capitol* (Sacramento to San Jose) routes have cars with bicycle storage areas. Reservations are not necessary and the fee is just $5.

Some airlines will carry boxed bicycles as 'sporting equipment' for no additional cost. You *can* disassemble your bicycle and put it in a bike bag or box, but it's much easier simply to wheel your bike to the check-in desk, where it should be treated as a piece of baggage. You may have to remove the pedals and front tire so your bike takes up less space in the aircraft's hold; check all this with the airline well in advance, preferably before you pay for your ticket. Some airlines welcome bicycles, while others treat them as undesirable nuisances and do everything possible to discourage them.

Safety At the time of writing, state law requires only bicyclists under 18 to wear a safety helmet. Regardless of the law, it's not a bad idea to get in the habit of wearing a helmet to avoid serious injury. A headlight and reflectors are requirements everywhere for riding at night, and reflective or bright clothing is a good idea, too. Carry water with you, and a repair kit in case of a flat tire or other problem.

Using a heavy-duty bicycle lock is essential in California, as bicycle theft is a big business. Some locks come with insurance against bicycle theft – Citadel and Kryptonite are two such companies – and it's worth the investment. Etch your driver's license number or other ID onto the frame of your bike. It takes only a few minutes to do, and most police stations have etching equipment available. Then register bicycle with the police.

HITCHHIKING

Hitchhiking is never entirely safe, and we don't recommend it. Travelers undeterred by the potential risk should be aware that, on the whole, hitchhiking is uncommon in modern-day America, and hitchhikers are generally viewed with suspicion: few motorists are willing to let a thumb stop them. Use extreme caution, both when hitchhiking and picking up hitchhikers.

Women should never hitchhike alone or even with another woman. Drivers are often reluctant to pick up men traveling alone, so most likely a man and a woman together have the best chance of getting a ride and of being safe while hitching. You can hitchhike on roads and highways; on freeways you must stand at the on-ramp. The best method for hitching a ride may be to ask someone at a gas station near a freeway; this also allows you to check out the person (and vice versa), though be prepared for more refusals than offers.

Be alert and cautious when accepting a ride, and discern which rides not to take. Avoid not only crazy or intoxicated drivers, but also rides that will drop you at a terrible spot to continue your journey. Use your instincts and don't get into a car if it seems suspicious for any reason, or even for no reason. You can always wait for another ride, but once you're in a car it might not be so easy to get out again.

BOAT

Boating is a way to get around in a few parts of California, notably to Catalina Island in Southern California. On San Francisco Bay, ferry routes operate between San Francisco and Sausalito, Tiburon, Larkspur, Oakland, Alameda and Vallejo. Details are given in the appropriate sections. Some small ferries and water taxis operate on San Diego Bay and Mission Bay.

LOCAL TRANSPORT
Bus

Most cities and larger towns have local bus systems, sometimes providing service only within the town or city, sometimes ranging farther afield to connect several towns in a regional area. These services are discussed in the geographical chapters.

Train

Bay Area Rapid Transit (BART) is an underground (and underwater) train network around the San Francisco Bay Area. North County Transit District's *Coaster* commuter trains operate along the coast from Oceanside to downtown San Diego.

Other local trains, some of them historic, operate primarily as tourist attractions. Notable among these are the *Skunk Train* between Willits and Fort Bragg, the *Northcoast Daylight* between Willits and Eureka, the *Blue Goose* from Yreka to Montague, the *Napa Valley Wine Train* between Napa and St Helena, the Roaring Camp and Big Trees Narrow-Gauge Railroad from Felton up to the summit of Bear Mountain or into Santa Cruz, the *Mother Lode Cannon Ball* operating from Jamestown, the Sacramento Southern Railroad from Sacramento to Hood, and the Campo Railroad Museum's 16-mile excursion in rugged country near the Mexican border. In Nevada, there are short tourist railway rides in Carson City, Virginia City and Ely.

Taxi

Taxis are metered. While taxis are a comparatively expensive form of transport, they are great for certain occasions, such as coming home late at night in a major city. If you don't spot a taxi cruising, you can phone for one; look under 'Taxi' in the Yellow Pages.

ORGANIZED TOURS

Tours run the gamut from white-water rafting through remote wilderness areas to sightseeing tours of major attractions in the urban centers. Whether you go on a long-distance tour lasting several days, a local sightseeing tour of a few hours or a theme tour – wine tasting, horseback riding, bird watching and nature, rafting, or what have you – tours can often make an easy way to get around and do things, especially if time is limited. Travel agents and tourist offices have bundles of information and brochures about tours; specific tours are also mentioned throughout this book.

For tours departing from specific cities, see the respective geographical chapters. Longer tours are mentioned in the Getting There & Away chapter.

California

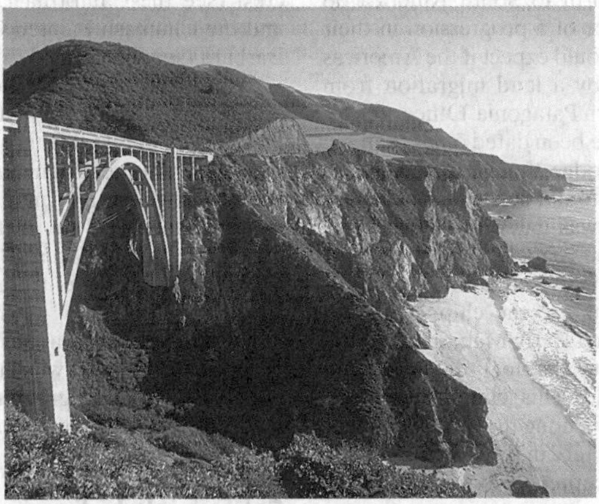

JOHN ELK III

Facts about California

HISTORY

It's generally accepted that the first people to inhabit America came from eastern Asia, over a land bridge to Alaska across what is now the Bering Strait. This land bridge was created by recurrent ice ages during which the sea level was lower. Experts disagree about the time at which migrations took place – the estimates range from as early as 35,000 years ago to somewhere between 12,000 and 13,000 years ago. The oldest undisputed evidence of human occupation in any part of the Americas, chipped flint points and other stone tools found at Clovis, New Mexico, is from about 12,000 years ago.

Some evidence, however, calls the land bridge theory into question. Artifacts and remains from North to South America do not show evidence of a progression in their ages, which one would expect if the Americas were populated by a land migration from Alaska to southern Patagonia. Other archaeological finds have been dated older than the date of the land bridge, though these ages are disputed. A skull found in Southern California, at Del Mar, was dated at 48,000 years old – about 13,000 years before the earliest estimates for the land bridge. The most controversial artifacts are the chipped stones found at the Calico Early Man Site (see the California Deserts chapter), dated around 200,000 years old. This claim, if correct, would place them among the oldest archaeological finds anywhere in the world, forcing a revision of the accepted ideas of human evolution and distribution.

Prehistory

Undisputed Californian archaeological sites indicate the state was inhabited very early. Stone tools found at sites in the Bakersfield area have been dated to around 8000 to 12,000 years ago – about the same period as the early stone points discovered in Clovis, New Mexico. Many other sites across the state have yielded evidence, from large middens of sea shells along the coast to campfire sites in the mountains, of people from around 4000 to 8000 years ago.

Some of the most interesting archaeological remains are the numerous rock art sites, over 1000 dating from 500 to 3000 years ago. They give some idea of the cultural diversity of the indigenous populations, with five identifiable styles of pictographs (designs painted on with one or more colors) and five styles of petroglyphs (designs pecked, chipped or abraded onto the rock). Many of the sites are closed to the public, or access is restricted in the interests of preservation. Three areas where rock art can be seen are Indian Grinding Rock State Historic Park in the Gold Country (see the Gold Country chapter); Little Petroglyph Canyon, north of Ridgecrest (see the California Deserts chapter); and the Chumash Painted Cave, near Santa Barbara (see the Central Coast chapter).

Where rock art depicts identifiable animal and human forms, it gives clues to the lifestyles of the various groups. Petroglyphs from the southeastern part of the state portray the hunting of animals like deer and bighorn sheep and are in the same style as rock art from the Great Basin in Nevada. Chumash pictographs from the coast, near Santa Barbara, show marine animals and indicate that the sea was an important source of food. *Morteros*, bowl-shaped depressions in flat rocks used to grind acorns and other seeds into flour, are often found at the same sites as rock art.

California's Indians

The archaeological evidence, combined with accounts from early European visitors and later ethnographic research, gives quite a clear picture of the Indians at the time of European contact. Several major language families, over 20 language groups with more than 100 dialects, were spread throughout the state. The total population of Native Americans was probably between 150,000 and 300,000, though some recent estimates run considerably higher. This doesn't sound like many, but it is estimated that over half of the Native American population of what is now the continental US lived in the area of modern California when the Spanish arrived. The Indians lived in small groups and villages, often migrating with the seasons from the valleys and the coast up to the mountains. The largest villages of which there are traces, in the Central Valley, are reckoned to have had 1500 to 2000 residents.

Acorn meal was the dietary staple, supplemented by small game, such as rabbits and deer, and fish and shellfish along the coast. Many other plants were used for food and fiber for baskets and clothing. California Indians used earthenware pots, fish nets, bows, arrows and spears with chipped stone points, but their most developed craft was basket making. The Indians wove baskets with local grasses and plant fibers and decorated them with attractive geometric designs. Many baskets were so tightly woven that they would hold water. Examples can be seen in many museums.

There was some trade between the groups, especially between coastal and inland people, but generally they did not interact much. Often, even neighboring villages spoke different languages. Conflict between the groups was almost nonexistent. California Indians did not have a class of warriors or a tradition of warfare, at least until the Europeans arrived.

Several museums have good exhibits on Native American archaeology and anthropology, like the Hearst Museum at UC Berkeley, the Museum of Man in San Diego and the Southwest Museum in Los Angeles..

European Discovery

Following the conquest of Mexico, the Spanish were exploring the limits of their new empire. There was much fanciful speculation about a golden island beyond the West Coast, and California was actually named before it was discovered, after a mythical island in a Spanish novel. The Spanish settled the southern tip of California in 1535, but it was not until 1539 that Francisco de Ulloa established that their settlement was on a peninsula rather than an island. The peninsula became known as Baja (lower) California (today a part of Mexico), and the coast to the north was called Alta (upper) California.

In 1542, the Spanish government engaged Juan Rodríguez Cabrillo, a Portuguese explorer and retired conquistador, to lead an expedition up the West Coast to find the fabled land of gold and spices that many still hoped for. He was also charged to find the equally mythical Strait of Anian, an imagined sea route between the Pacific and the Atlantic – the Spanish version of the Northwest Passage.

Cabrillo's ships sailed into San Diego Harbor (which Cabrillo named San Miguel), and his crew became the first Europeans to see mainland California. The ships sat out a storm in the harbor, then followed the coast north, pausing to check out some of the Channel Islands, where, in 1543, Cabrillo fell ill, died and was buried. The expedition continued north as far as Oregon, then returned to Mexico with charts and descriptions of the coast, but no evidence of a sea route to the Atlantic, no cities of gold and no islands of spice. The Spanish authorities were unimpressed and showed no further interest in California for the next 50 years.

Around 1545, Spanish ships began to ply the Pacific, carrying Mexican silver to the Philippines to trade for the exotic goods of Asia. These Manila galleons often took a northerly route back to the Americas to catch the westerly winds, and they sometimes struck land on the California coast. The galleons were harassed by English pirates, including Sir Francis Drake, who sailed up the California coast in 1579. He missed the entrance to San Francisco Bay, but pulled in near Point Reyes (at what is now Drakes Bay), to repair his ship, which was literally bursting with the weight of plundered Spanish silver. He claimed the land for Queen Elizabeth, named it Nova Albion (New England), then left for other adventures. (He wrote that he left a brass plate nailed to a post to record his visit. A plate was supposedly found there in 1937 – probably a fake – and is now in the Bancroft Library at UC Berkeley.)

CALIFORNIA

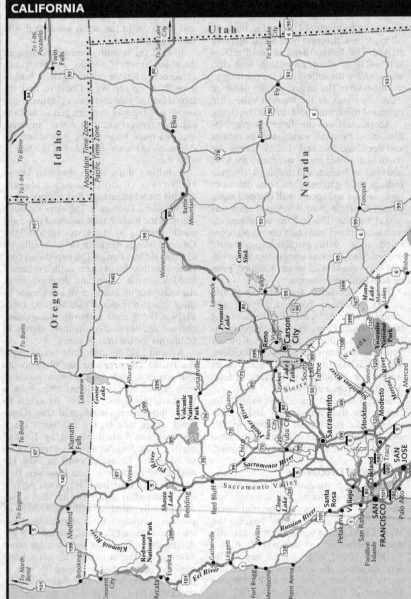

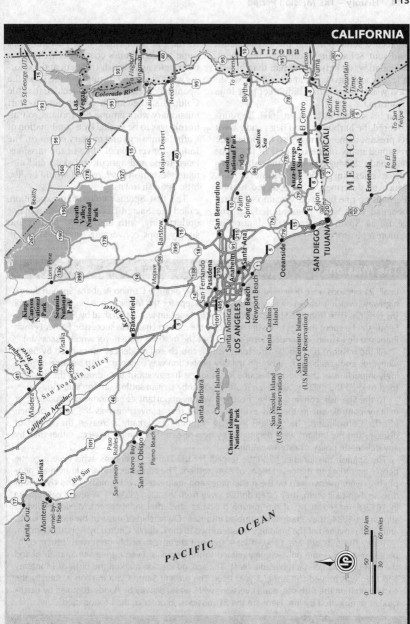

CALIFORNIA

In 1596, the Spanish decided they needed to secure some ports on the Pacific coast, and sent Sebastián Vizcaíno to find them. Vizcaíno was a better salesman than he was a leader and navigator, and his first expedition was a disaster that didn't get past Baja California.

In his second attempt, in 1602, he rediscovered the harbor at San Diego and gave it its present name. Contrary to his orders, he renamed many of the features of the coast and made glowing reports of the value of his 'discoveries,' in particular Monterey Bay, which he described as a protected harbor. Perhaps no one believed Vizcaíno's reports, because they were pigeonholed for 160 years, as Spain continued to ignore its remotest territory.

The Mission Period

In the mid-18th century, as Russian ships came to California's coast in search of sea otter pelts and British trappers and explorers were spreading throughout the West, the Spanish government finally decided to settle California. The church was anxious to start missionary work among the Indians, so California was to be settled by a combination of Catholic missions and military *presidios*. The Indian converts would live in the missions, learn trade and agricultural skills and ultimately establish *pueblos* that would be like little Spanish towns.

The first Spanish colonizing expedition, called the 'Sacred Expedition,' was a major undertaking, with land-based parties and supply ships converging on San Diego in

---

The Missions

In all, 21 missions were built in Alta California, mostly along El Camino Real, the Spanish 'king's highway,' which is traced by today's Hwy 101. Except for the Mexican mission at Sonoma, all the missions date from the Spanish period. The first mission was established by Father Junípero Serra, and he spent the rest of his life nurturing the mission chain. His successor, Father Fermin Francisco de Lasuen, continued Serra's work, but the missions were never wholly successful.

All the missions had similar structures, with a church and residences surrounded by fields, vineyards and ranch land. Although military protection was necessary, and became increasingly important as the Indians became less and less happy about the intruders, the missions tried to keep the military, and even more importantly civilian settlers, at arm's length.

To the Spanish, converting the 'heathen' was as important as economic development or military control, but in the end extinction rather than conversion was the result of their efforts. Consolidating the Indians in small communities greatly increased the spread of disease, and the Indians were decimated by new diseases and simple neglect, rather than by any deliberate policy of extermination.

The Spanish missionaries had little respect for the Native Americans, who were a gentle people according to the descriptions of early settlers. The converted Indians, known as 'neophytes,' were overworked by the missionaries and maltreated by the military and civilians. If disease didn't kill them, they often drifted away from the alien missions. A severe earthquake in 1812 damaged many of the mission buildings, and after independent Mexico ended its support in 1834, they gradually crumbled into ruin. Ownership of most of the mission lands, and what remained of the buildings, was returned to the Catholic Church by Abraham Lincoln.

Today the missions are a mixed lot – some of them remarkably preserved, others completely restored, some only vaguely related to the originals. Even during the Spanish period the missions had been a moveable feast. The second mission marked the birth of Monterey and then was moved to Carmel a year later. The present Santa Clara mission is actually the sixth church on the fifth site; earlier versions were washed away by floods, tumbled by earthquakes or engulfed by fire. Here are the 21 missions, in order of their foundation.

1769. But only half of the original 300 settlers made it that far. Father Junípero Serra stayed in San Diego to set up the first mission, while Gaspar de Portolá continued north with instructions to establish a second Spanish outpost at Monterey.

Portolá went right past Monterey, as he didn't see anything like the fine protected harbor that Vizcaíno had described. His party continued north until they were stopped by a large bay, later named San Francisco. Returning disappointed to San Diego, Portolá found Serra's party desperately awaiting an overdue supply ship, and without a single Indian convert after eight months of missionary activity. They were on the point of abandoning the expedition, but after a day of prayer, the supply ship arrived just in time. Portolá returned north to the unpromising site at Monterey, and though he realized the lack of a good harbor made the site less than ideal, he dutifully followed his orders and established the second presidio and mission.

Four presidios were established, at San Diego (1769), Monterey (1770), Santa Barbara (1782) and San Francisco (1776), to protect the missions and deter foreign intruders. In fact, these garrisons created more threats than they deterred, as the soldiers aroused hostility by raiding the Indian camps to rape and kidnap women. Not only were the presidios militarily weak, but their weakness was well known to Russia and Britain and did nothing to strengthen Spain's claims to California

The Missions

mission	location	date founded
San Diego de Alcalá	San Diego	July 16, 1769
San Carlos Borromeo de Carmelo	Carmel	June 3, 1770
San Antonio de Padua	near King City	July 14 1771
San Gabriel Arcángel	Los Angeles	September 8, 1771
San Luis Obispo de Tolosa	San Luis Obispo	September 1, 1772
San Francisco de Asís	San Francisco	June 29, 1776
San Juan Capistrano	San Juan Capistrano	November 1 1776
Santa Clara de Asís	Santa Clara	January 12, 1777
San Buenaventura	Ventura	March 31, 1782
Santa Barbara	Santa Barbara	December 4, 1786
La Purísima Concepción	near Lompoc	December 8, 1787
Santa Cruz	Santa Cruz	August 28, 1791
Nuestra Señora de la Soledad	near Soledad	October 9, 1791
San José	near Fremont	June 11, 1797
San Juan Bautista	San Juan Bautista	June 24, 1797
San Miguel Arcángel	near Paso Robles	June 25, 1797
San Fernando Rey de España	near San Fernando	September 8, 1797
San Luis Rey de Francia	Oceanside	June 13, 1798
Santa Inés	Solvang	September 17, 1804
San Rafael Arcángel	San Rafael	December 14, 1817
San Francisco de Solano	Sonoma	July 4, 1823

With the Indians decimated by disease, the Spanish attempted to build up the pueblos in California with the families of soldiers and with civilians from Mexico. The first group came overland from Sonora, led by Juan Bautista de Anza on a route across the southern desert. They settled on the San Francisco peninsula in 1776. They named the place *Yerba Buena* (good herb), for the *Satureja douglasi* that grew wild in the area. The Spanish established other civilian pueblos at San Jose (1777) and Los Angeles (1781), but they attracted few settlers from Mexico, and those that came were neither farmers who could cultivate the land nor soldiers who could defend it.

The missions were more successful at agriculture, and by 1800 they were growing grapes, fruit trees, and wheat, raising cattle and supplying enough food for themselves and the presidios. During the Mexican war for independence from Spain, from 1810 to 1821, supplies from Mexico were cut off completely, and Alta California was, of necessity, self-sufficient.

As a way of colonizing the wilds of California and converting the natives to Christianity, the mission period was an abject failure. The Spanish population remained small; the missions achieved little better than mere survival; foreign intruders were not greatly deterred; and more Indians died than were converted. Conflict between the Spanish and Indians persisted, with a major revolt in Santa Barbara as late as 1824.

The Rancho Period

When Mexico became independent of Spain in 1821, the new government regarded the church with mistrust and sought new ways to make California a profitable possession. In 1833 the missions were secularized. Mission lands were appropriated, and divided between the mission Indians and new settlers, who were encouraged to come to California with the promise of land grants. Within two years, some 12 million acres of land were given out in over 700 land grants. Few Indians held on to their land, falling victim to conniving landholders and corrupt administrators, and *ranchos* – huge tracts of

CALIFORNIA MISSIONS

San Francisco de Solano (1823)

San Rafael Arcángel (1817)

San Francisco de Asís (Mission Dolores - 1776)

Santa Clara de Asís (1777)

San José de Guadalupe (1797)

Santa Cruz (1791)

San Carlos Borromeo de Carmelo (1770)

San Juan Bautista (1797)

Nuestra Señora de la Soledad (1791)

San Antonio de Padua (1771)

El Camino Real

San Miguel Arcángel (1797)

San Luis Obispo de Tolosa (1772)

La Purísima Concepción (1787)

Santa Inés (1804)

0   40   80 km
0   25   50 miles

Santa Barbara (1786)

San Buenaventura (1782)

San Fernando Rey de España (1797)

San Gabriel Arcángel (1771)

San Juan Capistrano (1776)

El Camino Real

San Luis Rey de Francia (1798)

San Diego de Alcalá (1769)

PACIFIC OCEAN

land ranging in size from 1000 to 48,000 acres – were acquired by a small number of powerful *rancheros*.

The ranchos were the focal points of a pastoral society that produced huge numbers of cattle, but little else. Though the rancheros made money selling tallow and hide to the ships that plied this trade, they spent most of it importing all manner of goods from outside. There was no diversification of agriculture and no development of industry, infrastructure or commerce. Trade with outsiders had been prohibited by the Spanish, but grew out of control during Mexican rule, with American traders buying the hides and selling every necessity and luxury that could be produced on the East Coast and shipped around Cape Horn.

The society itself was almost feudal. The landholding elite, called *Californios*, dressed in fine clothes, rode fine horses and entertained lavishly, but were basically uneducated and lived in ranch houses without running water, sewerage or wooden floors. Most of the work was done by *mestizos* born of European and Indian parents, and the Indians were almost totally marginalized.

American interest in California increased on two levels. At the official level, driven by a belief in the 'manifest destiny' of the US to control the entire continent across to the Pacific, various offers were made to purchase Alta California from the Mexican government. At the unofficial level, American explorers, trappers, traders, whalers, settlers and opportunists entered California and seized on many of the prospects for profit that the Californios ignored in favor of ranching. Some of the Americans who started businesses became Catholics, married locals, and assimilated into Californio society. One American, Richard Henry Dana, author of *Two Years Before the Mast* (1840), worked on a ship in the hide trade in the 1830s and wrote disparagingly of Californians as 'an idle and thriftless people who can make nothing for themselves.'

Other intruders were Russian hunters of sea otter pelts, who had actually established a fort just north of San Francisco in 1812 (the area is still known as the Russian River). Trappers from the Hudson's Bay Company had reached the Sacramento Valley in the 1820s, and the British government had offered to buy California in exchange for unpaid debts.

When frontiersman Jedediah Smith turned up in San Diego in 1827, the Mexican authorities were alarmed to discover that the route from the east was not impassable. Another frontiersman, Kit Carson, pioneered an emigrant route across the Sierra Nevada to Los Angeles. One interloper whose name was linked to California's destiny was John Sutter, an expatriate Swiss who, in 1839, persuaded the California governor to grant him 50,000 acres in the Sacramento Valley. It happened that his ranch was at the western end of another trail, over the Truckee Pass, on which the first American wagon trundled into California in 1841 and which the ill-fated Donner Party (see 'The Donner Party' in the Sierra Nevada chapter) followed in 1846.

The Bear Flag Republic

American settlers in California became increasingly discontented with the ineffectual and remote government from Mexico City. While the US made proposals to buy the territory from Mexico, some settlers in Northern California plotted a more direct approach, thinking that if they revolted, the US would surely send troops to assist them. When the US annexed Texas, in 1845, the Mexican government ordered all foreigners to leave California. Though the authorities didn't, and probably couldn't, enforce this decree, it certainly increased the discontent of the American settlers.

A few months later, Captain John Frémont, the explorer and map maker, arrived in California with 68 soldiers from the Corps of Topographical Engineers. Emboldened by Frémont's presence, the rebels seized the town of Sonoma, hoisted an improvised flag with a crudely drawn bear and proclaimed California the 'Bear Flag Republic.' It was one of the shortest lived republics in history, but the bear, and the words 'California Republic,' still survive on the state flag.

The Mexican War

In May 1846, the US declared war on Mexico, and US forces quickly occupied all the presidios and imposed martial law. Some Californios took to the hills, but those who remained in the towns experienced an oppressive occupation. In September the Californios revolted. The Californio lancers, with their knowledge of the countryside and their skills on horseback, actually defeated the Americans in small battles near Los Angeles, in the Salinas Valley and at San Pasqual. Their victories were short-lived – the Americans had reinforcements arriving by ship, but the Californios were on their own.

In any case, California was a sideshow. The war was really won and lost in mainland Mexico, where Americans took the important cities of Monterrey, Veracruz, and ultimately, in 1847, Mexico City itself. The Mexicans had little choice but to cede much of their northern territory to the US. The Treaty of Guadalupe Hidalgo, signed on February 2, 1848, turned over California to the US, along with most of New Mexico and Arizona.

An interesting feature of this treaty was that it guaranteed the rights of Mexican citizens living in areas taken over by the US. Many Mexicans feel that this provision still entitles them to live and work in those states, regardless of their country of birth. They joke that Mexicans are now reoccupying the 'stolen lands', one person at a time.

The Gold Rush

By an amazing coincidence, gold was discovered in Northern California within days of the treaty with Mexico being signed. The owner of the land where it was found, John Sutter (remember him?), managed to keep the discovery quiet for a few months, without realizing that Mexico was in the process of signing away a gold mine. Though gold deposits had been found earlier in California, neither the Mexican government nor the rancheros had shown much interest in mining ventures.

With a characteristically Californian blend of hype and enthusiasm, the gold discovery transformed the new American outpost. When Mexican rule ended, the population was about 14,000 (including 6000 Indians). In 1848 and '49, over 90,000 people from other parts of the US, and all over the world, rushed to California and the state population increased by 565%.

The growth and wealth stimulated every aspect of life, from agriculture and banking to construction and journalism. As a result of mining, hills were stripped bare, erosion wiped out vegetation, streams silted up and mercury washed down to San Francisco Bay. San Francisco became a hotbed of gambling, prostitution, drink and chicanery.

Ostensibly under military rule, California had little effective government at all. The currency was a mixture of gold slugs, debased coinage and foreign cash; the main law was 'miners' law' (see 'Miners' Law' in the Gold Country chapter); and land ownership was uncertain. The rancheros still claimed title to most of California's usable lands, but thousands of new immigrants were squatting as homesteaders on untitled lands, in the expectation that they would be able to claim a 160-acre lot for $200.

In 1850, California was admitted to the union as a non-slave state – as part of a political compromise that balanced the slave and nonslave states in the Senate. Locally, there were thoughts of making two states, with slavery in Southern California – but the first task was to sort out the ownership of land.

A congressional commission was sent to California to adjudicate the land claims. Landholders were required to prove their claims with documents and witnesses, and many could not do so. Their lands were then available for settlement or purchase by new arrivals. It was hardly fair to the rancheros, whose land rights had been guaranteed in the Treaty of Guadalupe Hidalgo, but it permitted an explosive growth of agriculture, industry and commerce, not to mention real estate speculation, which has been a major 'sport' in California ever since.

By 1860 California's population reached 380,000, and the easy gold had all been taken. The Indians suffered badly from this growth. Despite armed resistance that con-

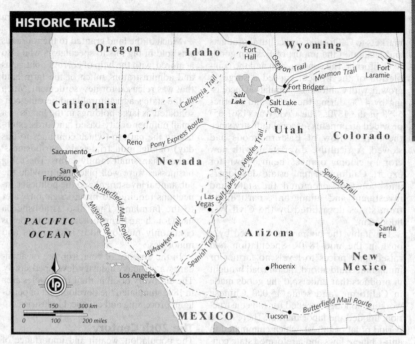

HISTORIC TRAILS

Oregon   *Idaho*   Fort Hall   *Wyoming*

Oregon Trail   Mormon Trail   Fort Laramie

California   California Trail   *Salt Lake*   Fort Bridger   Salt Lake City   *Utah*   *Colorado*

Pony Express Route   Reno   Sacramento   *Nevada*   Spanish Trail

San Francisco   Butterfield Mail Route   Salt Lake-Los Angeles Trail   Las Vegas   Santa Fe

PACIFIC OCEAN   Mission Road   Jayhawkers Trail   Spanish Trail   *Arizona*   *New Mexico*

Los Angeles   Phoenix

LP

0   150   300 km
0   100   200 miles

MEXICO   Tucson   Butterfield Mail Route

tinued into the 1870s, their numbers greatly diminished, and they were displaced from most of their traditional lands and confined to reservations.

A second boom for California came with the discovery of the Comstock silver lode in 1860, though the lode was actually over the border in what would soon become Nevada. Exploiting the lode required deep-mining techniques, which meant companies, stocks, trading and speculation. San Francisco made more money out of stocks than Nevada did out of mining – mansions sprouted on Nob Hill, and Californian businessmen became renowned for their audacity – *not* their scruples.

The Transcontinental Railroad

Railroad building was a mania in mid-19th-century America and was made extra profitable by capitalizing on real estate deals along the route. Though essentially private

projects, railroads were often subsidized with cash and land grants by governments, and towns offered inducements to the railroad companies, to ensure that they would be connected to the new line.

The transcontinental railroad was simple in conception, vast in scale and revolutionary in its impact. The tracks were laid simultaneously from the east and the west, meeting in the middle of Utah in 1869. The track going east from Sacramento was the work of the Central Pacific Railroad and thousands of Chinese laborers. Central Pacific had great political influence and gained substantial subsidies and land grants along the route. One of the railroad's principals, Leland Stanford, became state governor in 1863, and it was all legal because the company lawyer was also a judge of the state supreme court.

The new railroad meant that the trip from New York to San Francisco could be done in four or five comfortable days, rather than two arduous months. It also opened eastern markets to Californian agricultural products and facilitated the import of Eastern goods to California. The construction and the completion of the project caused a surge in growth, with California's population increasing by 47% during the 1860s and another 54% in the 1870s. The Civil War (1861-65) provided an impetus for local industry, since the normal flow of Eastern goods had slowed. Agriculture diversified, with new crops, including oranges, being grown for export. Californian real estate developers and 'boosters' promoted the state, and investment and immigrants, particularly from states devastated by the Civil War flooded in,

Inevitably the boom was followed by a bust in the mid-1870s. Speculation had raised land prices to levels no farmer or immigrant could afford, the railroad brought in products that undersold the goods made in California, and some 15,000 Chinese workers, no longer needed for rail construction, flooded the labor market. There was a period of labor unrest, which culminated in anti-Chinese laws and a reformed state constitution in 1879.

Industry & Agriculture

Los Angeles was not connected to the transcontinental railroad until 1876, when the Southern Pacific Railroad laid tracks from San Francisco to the fledgling city in Southern California. The SP monopoly was broken in 1887, when the Atchinson, Topeka, and Santa Fe Railroad Company also laid tracks into the LA Basin, thereby providing a direct link across the Arizona desert to the East Coast and the Midwest. The competition between the railroads greatly reduced the cost of transport and led to more diverse development across the state, particularly in Southern California and the San Joaquin Valley. The lower fares spurred the so-called 'boom of the eighties,' a major real estate boom lasting from 1886 to 1888. More than 120,000 migrants, mostly from the Midwest, came to Southern California in those years. Many settled in the 25

new towns laid out by AT&SF in the eastern part of Los Angeles County.

Much of the land granted to the railroads was sold in big lots to speculators who also acquired, with the help of corrupt politicians and administrators, much of the farm land that was released for new settlement. Much of the state's agricultural land became consolidated as large holdings in the hands of a small number of city-based landlords, establishing the pattern (which continues to this day) of big, industrial-scale 'agribusiness' rather than small family farms. These big businesses were well placed to provide the substantial investment and the political connections required to bring irrigation water to the farmland. They also established a need for cheap farmworkers, a need which is commonly met by poor immigrants and minorities.

In the absence of coal, iron ore or abundant water, heavy industry developed slowly. The discovery of oil in the Los Angeles area in 1892 stimulated the development of petroleum processing and chemical industries.

The 20th Century

The population, wealth and importance of California have increased dramatically throughout the 20th century. The big San Francisco earthquake and fire of 1906 destroyed most of the city, but it was barely a hiccup in the state's development – the state's population increased by 60% in the decade to 1910. The revolutionary years in Mexico, from 1910 to 1921, caused a huge influx of emigrants from south of the border, reestablishing the Latino heritage that had been almost totally extinguished by American dominance. The Panama Canal, completed in 1914, made bulk shipping feasible between the East Coast and West Coast.

During the 1920s, California's population grew by a mammoth 66%, the highest growth rate since the gold rush. The Great Depression saw another wave of emigrants, this time from the impoverished prairie states of the Dust Bowl. Outbreaks of social and labor unrest led to a rapid growth of the Democratic party in California. Some of the depression-era public works projects had lasting benefits, great and small, from San Francisco's Bay Bridge to the restoration of mission buildings.

WWII had a major impact on California, and not just from the influx of military and defense workers and the development of new industries. Women were co-opted into war work and proved themselves in a range of traditionally male jobs. Anti-Asian sentiments resurfaced at this time, and many Japanese-Americans were interned, and more Mexicans crossed the border to fill labor shortages. Many of the service people who passed through California actually liked the place so much that they returned to settle after the war. In the 1940s the population grew by 53%, and in the 1950s by 49%.

Throughout this century, a number of aspects of Californian life have emerged as recurring themes.

Water California's development, especially Southern California's cities and the agricultural industry throughout the state, has always been heavily dependent on the supply of water. In the early 1900s, the Los Angeles Aqueduct was built, taking water from the Owens Valley in the Eastern Sierra and channeling it hundreds of miles to Southern California. (Also see 'Quenching LA's Thirst' in the Los Angeles chapter.)

California also claims a large share of water from the Colorado River, which is dammed in several places and its waters diverted to the agricultural areas of the Imperial Valley, Coachella Valley and the cities of Southern California. The capacity of these schemes has been expanded throughout the 20th century; they're now close to extracting the maximum available water from all of them.

All these projects have major environmental and political implications, from the drying up of wetlands and habitats in the Sacramento Delta to salination in the Imperial Valley. The channeling of water from north to south causes some resentment in Northern California – 75% of California's water comes from Northern California, but 75% of it is used in the south, much of it in areas that are natural deserts. Conservation-

ists have taken Los Angeles water authorities to court over the depletion of lakes and streams in the Eastern Sierra and won significant concessions. (Also see 'Mono Lake' in the Sierra Nevada chapter.) California's share of the Colorado River water is being contested by the burgeoning states of the Southwest, whose own needs are increasing rapidly.

Growth, Migration & Minorities California has been in a state of demographic and economic growth ever since it was admitted to the union, and much of the growth has been contributed by immigration. The result is a richly multicultural society, but one in which race relations have often been strained.

Immigrants from racial minorities are typically welcomed in times of rapid growth, but have often been rejected when times get tough. Thus, Chinese railway workers were sought after in the 1860s but victimized in the 1870s. The Webb Alien Land Law of 1913 prevented some Asian minorities from owning land. During WWII, 93,000 people of Japanese extraction were interned. African Americans came in large numbers to take jobs in the postwar boom, but often became unemployed when the economy took a downturn. Because of social injustices, predominantly black suburbs of Los Angeles were the scene of violent outbursts, notably in 1965, 1979, and 1992 (see 'The LA Riots' in the Los Angeles chapter). Mexican and Latin American workers do most of the farm labor and domestic work in the state, but in 1994, in the face of increasing unemployment and state government deficits, California voted for Proposition 187, which would deny illegal immigrants access to state government services, including schools and hospitals.

Quite apart from any question of racism, the wisdom of further immigration and growth is now a pertinent question. The urban areas of California are reaching their limits in terms of traffic congestion, air pollution, water supply and available land for housing. Excessive growth may destroy the very features that make the state so

FACTS ABOUT CALIFORNIA

attractive. Many Californians are genuinely concerned that beaches are becoming too crowded, national parks are being damaged by the sheer number of visitors, and the enjoyment of outdoor activities is being diminished by their popularity. California's growth seems to be both unstoppable and unsustainable.

The Military Although California has never been the scene of a major conflict, it must be one of the most militarized places on Earth. During and after WWI, Douglas and the Lockheed brothers in Los Angeles, and Curtiss in San Diego, established aircraft industries.

Following the Japanese bombing of Pearl Harbor, the headquarters of the US Pacific fleet moved to San Diego and has remained there ever since. Camp Pendleton, a big Marine Corps base, was established south of Orange County, and the Colorado Desert, in Southern California, temporarily became one of the biggest military training grounds in history. Shipbuilding started in San Francisco; aircraft plants in Los Angeles turned out planes by the thousands; and the movie industry turned to producing propaganda films.

After WWII, the state retained a sophisticated slice of the military-industrial complex, with some very high-tech Cold War industries, from avionics and missile manufacturing to helicopter and nuclear submarine maintenance. Military activities include recruit training for the Marine Corps, advanced training for navy fighter pilots, submarine bases, aircraft testing facilities, several air force bases, weapons and gunnery ranges, and home ports for the US Navy.

The military has been a source of jobs, and cutbacks in military spending in the 1990s have hit the state hard. While the military played a big part in establishing the manufacturing industry in California and bringing in much of its research & development base, converting military industries to the production of goods for export or domestic consumption has not been easy.

'The Industry' The establishment of the movie industry in California started around 1910, as producers sought conditions for year-round filming. Not only has 'The Industry' become a major employer in Los Angeles, but it has done a lot to promote California's image throughout the country and the world. As film, and later TV, became the predominant entertainment medium of the 20th century, California moved to center stage in the world of popular culture.

Social Change Unconstrained by the burden of traditions, bankrolled by affluence and promoted by film and television, California has become a leader in new attitudes and social movements. As early as the 1930s, Hollywood was promoting fashions and fads for the middle classes, even as strikes and social unrest rocked San Francisco and author John Steinbeck articulated a new concern for the welfare and worth of common people.

With 1950s affluence, the 'Beat' movement in San Francisco reacted against the banality and conformism of suburban life, turning to coffeehouses for jazz, philosophy, poetry and pot. When the postwar baby boomers hit their late teens, many took up where the Beat Generation left off, rejecting their parents' values, doing drugs, dropping out and screwing around in a mass display of adolescent rebellion that climaxed, but didn't conclude, with the San Francisco 'Summer of Love' in 1967. Though the hippie 'counterculture' was an international phenomenon, California was at the leading edge of its music, its psychedelic art and its new libertarianism. Sex, drugs and rock & roll were big on the West Coast.

In the late '60s and early '70s, New Left politics, the anti-Vietnam War movement and Black Liberation were forced onto the political agenda, and flower power and give-peace-a-chance politics seemed instantly naive. The 1968 assassination of Robert Kennedy in Los Angeles, the sometimes violent repression of demonstrations, as at Berkeley in 1968, and the death of a spectator at a Rolling Stones concert at the hands of their security guards (Hell's Angels they had hired for the occasion) all served to strip the era of its innocence.

California has spawned a number of social movements. The Gay Pride movement exploded in San Francisco in the '70s, and San Francisco is still the most openly, exuberantly gay city in the world.

California was way ahead in environmentalism, too. The Sierra Club was founded here in 1892 by John Muir, and is still an active and effective environmental lobby group. Though California has a serious air-pollution problem, it leads the world in vehicle emission controls and environmental legislation.

As a contribution to the yuppie values of the 1980s, Southern California gave the world Ronald Reagan and Reaganomics, and Northern California contributed Michael Milken, the junk-bond king. In the late '80s and '90s, California catapulted right to the forefront of the healthy lifestyle, with more aerobic classes and actualization workshops than you can shake your totem at. Leisure activities like in-line skating, snowboarding and mountain biking are industries in California. Be careful what you laugh at. From hot tubs to soy burgers, California's flavor of the month will probably be next year's world trend.

GEOGRAPHY

The third-largest state after Alaska and Texas, California is roughly the size of Sweden, covering about 157,000 sq miles. It is bordered by Oregon in the north, Mexico in the south, Nevada and Arizona in the east, and the 700-mile Pacific coast to the west. The northern edge of California is at the same latitude as New York or Rome, and the southern edge is at the same latitude as Savannah, Georgia, or Tel Aviv. Mountain ranges and water, or lack of it, determine the state's prominent geographic regions.

Coast The Coast Range runs along most of the coast, with gentle foothills in the east and rocky cliffs that plunge straight into the Pacific on the west. San Francisco Bay divides the range roughly in half: the North Coast, famous for its coast redwoods, is sparsely populated and very foggy; the Central Coast, from San Francisco to

Ventura, has a milder climate, more sandy beaches and many more inhabitants, mostly around Monterey and Santa Barbara, its northern and southern terminus.

Three quarters of the way down the state, the Coast Range is joined to the Sierra by a series of mountains called the Transverse Ranges. These mountains, mostly around 5000 feet high, divide the state into Southern and Northern California. To the south, the Los Angeles Basin directly fronts the ocean, bordered by a series of mountains that extend into Mexico. These mountains, once consistently visible from sea, are often shrouded by a thick layer of smog from the state's most densely populated region. San Diego, on the edge of this plateau, is about 120 miles south, next to the Mexican border.

Sierra Nevada & Northern Mountains

The prominent Sierra Nevada stretches 400 miles along California's eastern border and joins the southern end of the Cascade Range just north of Lake Tahoe. Although the two ranges appear to form an almost continuous line, they contain very different geology: the Sierra Nevada is a westward-tilted fault block with glacier-carved valleys, but the Cascade Range is a chain of distinct volcanic peaks.

Peaks in the Sierra Nevada are higher at the southern end, culminating with 14,497-foot Mt Whitney – the highest in the continental US. The Cascade Range, which extends to Oregon and Washington, is dominated by Mt Lassen (10,457 feet) and Mt Shasta (14,162 feet). East of the Cascades, on the Oregon border, sits the sparsely populated Modoc Plateau. West of the Cascades, the rugged Klamath Mountains have been carved by the unruly Klamath and Trinity Rivers.

The Sierra's western foothills, from 2000 to 5000 feet, were the site of the 1849 gold rush and the destination of California's famous '49ers.

Central Valley Between the Sierra Nevada and the Coast Range lies California's Central Valley, a fertile 430-mile-long region that leads the country in production of

FACTS ABOUT CALIFORNIA

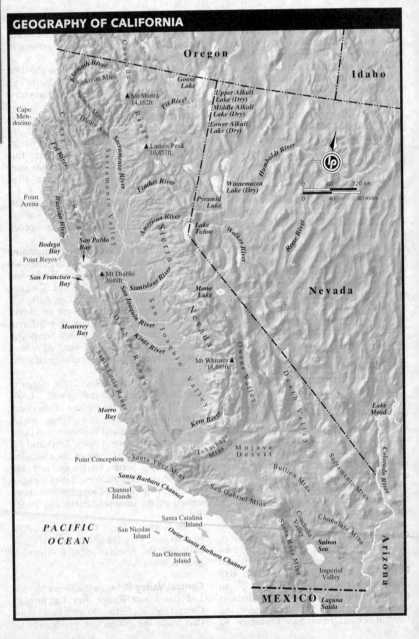

GEOGRAPHY OF CALIFORNIA

cotton, peaches, almonds, walnuts, grapes, apricots, plums, oranges, olives, tomatoes and other crops.

The Central Valley comprises two river valley systems – the Sacramento Valley in the north, and the San Joaquin Valley in the south. The two meet at the Sacramento Delta and flow west to the Pacific via San Francisco Bay.

Deserts The Mojave Desert spreads east and north of Los Angeles, south of the Sierra and east into Nevada. East of the Coast Range, and south of the Mojave, the low desert includes the Imperial and Coachella valleys, now heavily irrigated farmland, and the Salton Sea. East of the Sierra Nevada, Owens Valley and Death Valley are on the edge of the Great Basin of Nevada and Utah.

CLIMATE

California has a great diversity of climates. San Francisco is famous for its fog. 'The morning fog may chill the air, I don't care, my heart waits there…,' sang Tony Bennett, and it's true. A typical weather forecast for San Francisco, at any time of year, as indeed for most of the North Coast, is 'fog night and morning, burning off by midday.' Fog along the coast is especially noticeable in summer, when hot inland temperatures cause a mist to rise from the cooler ocean waters offshore. In the south, the coast is warmer year round, mild in winter, not too hot in summer, but still subject to marine fogs.

The mountainous eastern part of the state, at a much higher elevation, is pleasant in summer and gets snow at higher elevations in winter.

The San Joaquin and Sacramento river valleys are extremely hot in summer. In the winter, these valleys tend to be cool and foggy, with a type of fog known as 'tule fog,' which hugs the ground and is so thick that you can't see through it. For more on tule fog, see the boxed text in the San Joaquin Valley chapter.

The deserts, especially the low desert and Death Valley, are extremely hot in summer, often recording the highest temperatures in the country, but warm, dry and extremely pleasant in winter. The Mojave is higher than Death Valley and not quite so hot in summer, and cool to cold in the winter.

Nights can be chilly in most of the state nearly year round. See the Climate Charts appendix.

ECOLOGY & ENVIRONMENT

According to the *1991-1992 Green Index*, California is ranked number one among states for environmental policies but 19th for its overall environmental conditions. Though conditions are on a general upswing due to the cooperation of environmentalists with farmers and irrigators, and the work of politicians, California still faces complex and catastrophic problems, most caused by people. It's not just the number of people or the rate of growth, it's the level of consumption and affluence.

California's population grew by about 2.5 million between 1990 and 1997, at a rate of 8.3%, which is considerably lower than the 26% posted between 1980 to 1990. Roughly half of all California residents live in the southern fifth of the state, in a desert environment that does not naturally support human life. Water is 'imported' from mountains in the north; fossil fuels are tapped for energy; wetlands and deserts are paved and built upon; freeways connect residential communities to work areas (often an hour's drive apart); and people rely heavily on automobiles. Projections put the state population at 50 million by 2025.

Overgrazing and logging on the North Coast threaten fish populations (namely coho salmon and steelhead trout), which, because these fish are at the base of the food chain, affects all wildlife. Sulfur dioxide and nitrogen oxides creep high into the Sierra, making its seemingly pristine lakes vulnerable to acid rain and snowmelt and damaging over 60% of its pine trees. Housing developments in the Central Valley are causing farmland to vanish and wildlife habitats to dwindle so much that deer and mountain lions are becoming part of the urban landscape. Farming brings up a whole different set of issues dealing with pesticides, water rights (80% of California's water goes to farmers) and, because most farmworkers are Latinos, social justice.

Air Pollution Travelers will probably notice poor air quality more than any other problem. In 1996, federal air pollution standards were exceeded on 115 days at one or more locations in the Los Angeles Basin, most commonly in the eastern San Gabriel Valley. Breathing can become difficult by late afternoon (especially if you're involved in athletic activity), and people often complain of stinging or runny eyes (it's especially bad if you wear contact lenses). The air is considerably cleaner in the coastal communities where offshore breezes provide some relief.

Auto exhaust and industrial emissions are the chief culprits in generating such pollutants as carbon monoxide, nitrogen oxides and particulate matter (PM). The greatest health hazard though – especially for people with respiratory problems – is ozone, which forms when sunshine causes nitrogen oxides and organic gases to react.

The concentration of pollutants varies throughout the year, as weather conditions shift. While carbon monoxide and PM levels are highest in fall and winter, ozone levels reach their peak during sun-intensive summer days. Summer also brings the greatest number of inversion days, when a warm air layer traps the noxious fumes near the ground.

Despite this grim picture, there are reasons to be hopeful. The Air Resources Board, created in 1968, oversees 14 air quality control regions that must meet ever-more-stringent Environmental Protection Agency (EPA) standards. Since the mid-'70s, the South Coast Air Quality Management District (SCAQMD) has been charged with regulating emissions from cars and factories and with enforcing federal, state and local air pollution laws. A far-reaching cleanup plan, adopted in 1989, has already produced tangible improvements: while there were 120 Stage I pollution alerts in 1979, that number dropped to just seven incidents in 1996. Despite such marked progress, there's no denying that air quality in much of Southern California still leaves much to be desired.

Wilderness Preservation Monterey Bay and the Channel Islands are now national marine sanctuaries and many of the state's desert regions, including Death Valley and the Mojave Desert, are protected under the California Desert Protection Act. The more land is placed under National Park Service jurisdiction (whose main goal is to protect and preserve) instead of the National Forest Service (which allows timber and farm industry use of the land) or Bureau of Land Management (often called the Bureau of Logging and Mining) jurisdiction, the better.

Environmental organizations such as the Sierra Club, Friends of the Rivers, the Nature Conservancy, Save San Francisco Bay Association, Klamath Forest Alliance, Santa Monica's Heal the Bay and Monterey's Save Our Shores have made great efforts on behalf of California's environment.

Water From 1987 to 1993, California experienced one of its worst droughts in history, with precipitation ranging between 61% and 90% below normal. As a result, the state has made revolutionary progress in cutting back on water use. Water suppliers signed a conservation agreement with environmental groups requiring water utilities to adopt 16 'best management practices' for conservation, including offering rebates on low-flush toilets and providing free water audits to those who implement the practices with the most force. The Department of Water Resources set up a water bank that bought surplus water and sold it to those with shortages. Meanwhile, some cities began to reuse wastewater, and several coastal communities developed desalinization systems to remove salt from seawater.

California's most controversial water issue deals with the transfer of water from the northern to southern part of the state. The Bureau of Reclamation's Central Valley Project, built in the 1930s, dams most of California's major rivers to provide irrigation and hydroelectric power to the Los Angeles area, which, though basically a desert, supports over half the state's population. See the boxed text on Mono Lake in the Sierra Nevada chapter for more information.

Toxic discharge, primarily from pesticides used in agriculture, is also a serious water issue. With the San Joaquin and Sacramento valleys being the most fertile in the US, crop revenues have long been considered more important than environmental protection.

Waste California produces the most solid waste, per capita, in the US. Its 365 municipal landfills are pushing capacity, causing environmental planners to become increasingly worried about what to do with the phenomenal amount of waste produced each year. Much of the problem lies with the state's burgeoning population, which undermines ever more efficient waste management systems. In 1995, a state law was passed requiring California communities to reduce waste production by at least 25% by 2000. Despite recycling programs instituted in many cities, including Los Angeles, this target has not been met.

Another problem are corporate offenders who often choose to pay exorbitant fines rather than clean up their acts (though fines have risen enough in the past few years that this is becoming less common).

Also, corporate offenders often choose to pay exorbitant fines rather than clean up their acts (though fines have risen enough in the past few years that this is becoming less common).

Energy On the flip side of the waste problem, California gets continually high marks on its 'environmental report card' for Integrated Resource Planning (IRP) practices. Southern California Edison, California's largest utility company, began a positive trend in 1978, when it offered incentives to industrial and residential customers for installing more efficient equipment. The program has proved to be very effective in reducing emissions. Unfortunately, California still produces the second-largest amount of toxic gas emissions in the US, largely due to the population's automobile dependence.

FLORA & FAUNA

California has just about every type of ecosystem in existence, from deserts to forests to wetlands to high alpine zones. Flora and fauna varies accordingly, though some things are common throughout the state, namely oak trees, mule and black-tailed deer, squirrels, Steller's jays and LBBs (little brown birds). Of special note are the superlative trees in the state, including the world's tallest (coast redwood), largest (sequoia) and oldest (bristlecone pine).

Coast

Flora Coastal ecosystems range from very wet in the north to very dry in the south. The Coast Range runs along most of California's coastline, its west side plunging straight into the sea and its eastern side rolling gently toward the Central Valley. The north end of the range has stands of coast redwoods *(Sequoia sempervirens)*, giant beauties with spongy red bark, flat needles and olive-size cones. The lush forest floor surrounding these trees supports sword ferns, redwood sorrel and other plants. (For more on redwood trees, see the boxed text in the North Coast chapter.)

South of Humboldt County, where annual precipitation declines considerably, plant life is less specialized. Along the Central Coast, you'll find Monterey cypress and Monterey pine, which look like they are being blown over even when it's not windy. They both have thick, rough, grayish bark, long, reaching branches clustered at their tops and long needles. Inland, extending from the east side of the Coast Range to the western foothills of the Sierra Nevada, you'll find California black oak, with broad fingery leaves (bristly at the ends) and gray-black bark. The smooth, shiny acorns from these trees were a dietary staple for California Indians.

Further south, past Santa Barbara, is a much more arid region. In the mountains surrounding the Los Angeles Basin you'll find canyon live oak, with holly-like evergreen leaves and fuzzy acorns; aromatic California laurel, with long slender leaves that turn purple; and Eastwood and Cuyamaca manzanita, treelike shrubs with intensely red bark and small berries. The Torrey pine, a species adapted to sparse rainfall and sandy, stony soils, is another rare tree; the last mainland stands are near San Diego.

Fauna The coast offers many chances to see California's Pinnipedia (feather feet), including northern elephant and harbor seals, California sea lions and sea otters. The best place to see these friendly creatures, which like to bask in the sun, is between Point Lobos State Reserve to Santa Barbara (see the Central Coast chapter) and at the La Jolla children's pool (see San Diego chapter). San Miguel, one of the Channel Islands, has the largest pinniped population in the world. Año Nuevo State Reserve on the San Francisco Peninsula is a major elephant seal breeding ground (also see 'Elephant Seals' in the San Francisco Bay Area chapter).

California gray whales are often visible off the coast from December to March, when they head to warm waters in Mexico. Once in a while you'll see a whale breaching (leaping out of a water), but usually you can just spot spray from a blowhole and part of a back or tail. Good whale-watching points are Point Reyes, Eureka, Fort Bragg, Bodega Bay (north of San Francisco), Davenport Landing (near Santa Cruz), Point Loma and Dana Point. Companies all along the coast, including many in Monterey, Santa Barbara, Morro Bay and San Diego, offer whale-watching excursions.

Bottle-nosed dolphins and porpoise swim quite close to shore in groups called 'pods.' They can be seen year round from Morro Bay to Mexico. One of the oddest creatures off the coast are flying fish, often seen between the southern coast and Catalina Island.

California brown pelicans, indigenous to the Channel Islands, were threatened with extinction because the insecticide DDT from Ventura County farms was contaminating the fish on which the pelicans fed. Eating the poisoned fish caused thinning in the pelicans' eggshells, causing few eggs to survive long enough to hatch. DDT was banned more than a decade ago, and the pelican population is on the rise.

Other coastal birds include gulls and grebes, terns, cormorants, sandpipers, and cute little sanderlings that like to chase waves from the shore. The California condor, a black and white bird with a 9- to 10-foot wingspan, has long been one of the state's most endangered animals. Currently there

California Condors: Giants of the Skies

The California condor (*Gymnogyps californianus*) is one of the largest flying birds in the world. It weighs up to 20lb and has a life span of 40 years. Even more impressive is its wingspan, which averages 9 feet and allows the condor to soar and glide for hours without beating its wings. In the wild, carrion is the main diet of these giant vultures.

Until a few years ago, however, not a single condor remained in the wild; they were a species brought to the brink of extinction by human intrusion. Although killing condors has been illegal for about a century, their numbers declined steadily as a result of contamination and pollution, as well as accidents such as collisions with power lines. In 1971, the depleted condor species limped onto the federal endangered species list.

To turn things around, a team of scientists launched extensive conservation efforts, but these came largely too late. In the mid-'80s, the world's 27 surviving condors were captured and taken to breeding programs in the San Diego and LA zoos. It was a risky gamble, but the consensus was that there was nothing to lose.

Fortunately, this tale has a happy ending – at least for now. The first condor chick was hatched in captivity in 1988, and in 1992 the first captive-bred birds soared back into the wild. By 1997, their population had climbed back up to 134, including 27 in the wild. So far, the condors are doing well, but only the future will tell whether the they are truly back in full swing.

are three pairs living in the wild in the San Rafael Mountains near Santa Barbara

Sierra Nevada

Flora The Sierra Nevada has three distinct zones: dry western foothills covered with oak and chaparral; conifer forests from about 2000 to 8000 feet; and a high-alpine zone above 8000 feet, where a lack of humus and alluvial deposit means there's sparse support for tundralike expanses of moss and lichen. Wildflowers such as bright red Indian paintbrush, purplish-blue broadleaf lupine, yellow-orange common monkeyflower and deep purple bowl-tubed iris bloom in alpine meadows between April and June. The *Sierra Club Naturalist's Guide*, by Stephen Whitney, is recommended reading. Ranger stations and visitor centers also provide good information (usually displays and brochures) pertaining to specific areas.

The diversity of plant and animal life within the Sierra's conifer forests (on its western side) make them extremely interesting. This is where the giant sequoias, unique to California, stand in isolated groves in Yosemite, Kings Canyon and Sequoia national parks. With their enormous trunks, red shaggy bark and small, tight pinecones, sequoias are an absolute 'must-see.' Also within the conifer forests are incense cedar, with bark like a sequoia and leaves like a juniper bush; lodgepole and ponderosa pines, both with medium-size pinecones, golden-brown bark that resembles a jigsaw puzzle and long, spindly needles; sugar pine, with large oblong cones and branches that cluster toward the top of the tree; and red and white fir, noticeable for their dense cylindrical cones, short needles and branches that start quite close to the ground.

Broad-leafed trees in the Sierra, found mostly near water, include Pacific dogwood, whose greenish-white flowers bloom in late May; shimmery quaking aspen, with large circular leaves that turn butter-yellow in the fall; black cottonwood, which has small white flowers that shed a fibrous fluff in the wind (enough of this on the ground makes it look like snow); and white alder, whose round, pointed leaves resemble a cotton-wood's, but has reddish bark and small cones instead of flowers.

Fauna Environmental factors that vary according to elevation – notably precipitation (snowfall) and food availability – essentially determine where animals live in the Sierra. For example, gray squirrels, common throughout the lower ranges, can't survive the winters above 7000 feet. Valley pocket gophers and Swainson's thrushes are also found below 7000 feet, though their ecological counterparts, mountain pocket gophers and hermit thrushes, can survive at higher elevations.

Some creatures, however, survive by migrating within the Sierra according to season. These include mule deer, with sharp hooves and large mulelike ears (bucks grow antlers each year), bighorn sheep, and birds such as Steller's jays, hummingbirds and woodpeckers. High in the Sierra you'll find yellow-bellied marmots (essentially large ground squirrels) and several kinds of chipmunks that look like tiny squirrels with slender tails and stripes running down their backs.

Black bears are plentiful from 3000 to about 8000 feet. They are small for bears, weighing around 300 pounds or more, and are omnivorous, eating berries, nuts, roots, grasses, insects, eggs, small mammals, fish and carrion.

Central Valley

Flora Called the 'most fertile valley in the world,' the heavily irrigated Central Valley supports domesticated crops such as apricots, grapes, peaches, almonds, walnuts and cotton. North of Sacramento, wetlands irrigated by the Sacramento River are used to grow rice.

Fauna Mountain lions have become more aggressive recently, as housing developments have encroached on their habitat. Their presence is especially an issue where they threaten livestock and (in one fatal incident in 1994) people.

Also threatened by Central Valley development are ducks, geese, and osprey, pintails,

The Life of a Threatened Fish

Examining the life of a steelhead trout or coho salmon, both 'indicator' fish whose survival or decline tell of the environment's health, gives a good overall picture of California's environmental challenges. A fish's natural life cycle is to hatch in a river, swim out to sea, and return to its home waters to spawn and die. Sounds simple, right? Not for a California fish.

First of all, to get downstream they must pass over dams built in the 1930s as part of the Bureau of Reclamation's Central Valley Project (all of California's major rivers are dammed at least once). If the fish makes it past the dam into the San Joaquin-Sacramento Delta, it then faces the danger of being sucked southward by massive pumps that transport delta waters to farmers in the Central Valley and urban populations. If the fish makes it past the pumps into San Francisco Bay, it has to deal with pollution caused by pesticides, industry and urban runoff. With the bay now a fraction of its original size, pollution's impact is magnified.

Say the fish finally makes it out through the Golden Gate. Now it must be smart enough to avoid the nets of commercial fishermen, who have long overfished the waters off the North Coast, and strong enough to withstand underwater noise pollution caused by tankers and military flights. Apparently this type of pollution, which disrupts mating procedures, is one of the major threats to California's whale population.

When it's time to head back upstream, the fish must contend with dams; logging that may have stripped the stream of its shade, causing river temperatures to rise to a lethal level; and grazing that may have eroded the riverbanks and blocked the way home. The final triumph is if the fish's redd (like a crib) is still intact (undisturbed by logging, mining or grazing) and can hold future generations.

egrets and other waterfowl that depend on the Pacific Flyway for their annual migration. One of four major bird freeways in North America, the Pacific Flyway extends north-south through most of the valley, with the main layover points in the delta and north of Sacramento.

Deserts

Flora Though the word 'desert' conjures up images of vast expanses of nothingness, there is a subtle beauty to California's deserts that intensifies the longer you're there. Most plants have adapted to the arid climate with thin, spiny leaves that resist moisture loss (and deter grazing animals) and seed and flowering mechanisms that kick into full gear during the brief moisture period.

Perhaps the most conspicuous and familiar desert flower is the bright orange California poppy, the state flower, which blooms in March and April. There's a fantastic display of these in the California Poppy Reserve in Antelope Valley, directly north of LA.

More cactuslike are the creosote, a small bush that has small, hard leaves with a waxy feel and a distinctive smell; the spiky ocotillo shrub, with its extended canelike branches (which may seem dead) that sprout leaves after a rainfall and produce bright red-orange flowers in spring; and catclaw, an acacia species with small, sharp, hooked spikes that scratch you or grab your clothing if you brush past – hence the nickname, 'wait-a-minute bush.'

Desert cacti are probably the most intriguing forms of life out here. At first glance the cholla cactus appears so furry and soft that one variety is actually known as 'teddy-bear cactus.' But the fur actually consists of extremely sharp, barbed spines that can bury themselves in skin at the slightest touch. Viewed from a safe distance, chollas show a delightful variety of shapes and a delicate pale-gold color, especially when the light is behind them and each branch is surrounded by a luminous halo. They produce a bright yellow flower in the spring.

Like something from a Dr Seuss book, Joshua trees are a type of yucca and are related to the lily. They're found in much of the Mojave Desert, not just in Joshua Tree National Park, and were named by immigrant Mormons, who saw them as Joshua welcoming them to the promised land. Almost as widespread are prickly pears, flat cacti that produce showy flowers ranging in color from pink and magenta to yellow and orange. The smoke tree, a small, fine-leafed tree with a smoky blue color, is said to indicate the presence of underground water.

Known widely from its presence in Western movies, tumbleweed is actually an import from Eastern Europe. These annuals, which grow quickly to become a ball of tough branches attached to the ground by a single stem, uproot and tumble across the desert in the summer wind. The Washingtonia palm is the only native variety of the trees that are almost emblematic of Southern California. They grow naturally in desert oases and produce stalks of small black berries that are quite tasty.

Irrigated by Colorado River water, the Coachella Valley supports date, citrus, and grape crops. The Imperial Valley has winter vegetables, cotton and fruit.

Fauna Most desert wildlife is nocturnal, rarely visible during the day. Roadrunners, little gray birds with long, straight tails and a poof of feathers on top of their heads, are quite visible on the side of the road. So are desert tortoises, whose slow pace has landed them on the endangered species list because they're often victim to car tires. Other desert inhabitants, all extremely shy, are the

Joshua tree

reddish kit fox, bobcat (which has no tail), coyote (which walks with its hind legs slightly to the left of his front legs), jackrabbit, kangaroo rat, and a variety of snakes, lizards and spiders.

The Salton Sea, a stopover for migratory birds, is an excellent place for bird watching.

NATIONAL & STATE PARKS
With 75% of California's population inhabiting only 1% of the state's land, there is plenty of terrain not yet under concrete or asphalt. Some of California's more famous 'wilderness' areas, notably Yosemite National Park and the Lake Tahoe area, are no longer wild, but their scenery remains awe inspiring. Lesser-known areas, especially in the northern part of the state, contain mountains, rivers and canyons that go relatively unvisited for most of the year.

California has 17 areas that are part of the National Park system, administered by the National Park Service (NPS) under the US Department of the Interior, and 270 units designated as State Parks and run by the California Park System. California's 18 National Forests are run by the United States Forest Service (USFS), which is part of the United States Department of Agriculture (USDA). While all of these designations tend to make one's head spin, they are really only important at an administrative level.

National Parks & Monuments
California's national parks contain some of the most spectacular scenery in the state. In 1994 Death Valley and Joshua Tree were 'upgraded' from national monument to national park status. Although in practice a national monument is equivalent to a national park, the term 'national park' is more widely recognized and accepted as an important region, so the government often changes a national monument to a national park to symbolize an area's importance or need for protection. For additional information, also see Useful Organizations and Accommodations in the Facts for the Visitor chapter.

Yosemite This is California's, and one of America's, most famous and visited parks, known for its solid granite monoliths and numerous waterfalls (see the Sierra Nevada chapter).

Kings Canyon & Sequoia Run as one unit, these parks are famous for giant sequoia trees (found nowhere else in the world), the deepest canyon in North America and excellent hiking (see the Sierra Nevada chapter).

Death Valley This park is an enigmatically beautiful landscape of salt pillars and sun-cracked flats rimmed by dramatic peaks (see the California Deserts chapter).

Joshua Tree Known for its Joshua trees and Mojave yuccas, this park is a mecca for rock climbers (see the California Deserts chapter).

Channel Islands The northern five of an eight-island chain, these islands off the coast of Santa Barbara are prized for their underwater life and populations of seals, sea lions and sea otters (see the Central Coast chapter).

Point Reyes This is a birder's paradise, famous for its many species of shorebirds, and often shrouded in fog (see the San Francisco Bay chapter).

Redwood Here stand the giant coast redwoods, in the same family as giant sequoias, the tallest trees in the world (see the North Coast chapter).

Lava Beds Just below the Oregon border, this area is full of volcanic formations (see the Northern Mountains chapter).

Mt Lassen Shaped by the same igneous intrusion that formed Lava Beds, Mt Lassen is considered an active volcano, though it has been quiet since 1916 (see the Northern Mountains chapter).

The parks are open year round and offer a totally different experience in the off-season, especially Yosemite, Sequoia-Kings Canyon and Mt Lassen, which get snow.

Death Valley and Joshua Tree are best visited October to April, before the thermostat starts soaring above the 100°F (37°C) mark.

Many people feel that Yosemite is best between September and May, when crowds are at a minimum and when, in deep winter, it is blanketed with snow. Of course, hiking and camping are reduced during those months. Information for all the parks is available from the Western Region Information Center (☎ 415-556-0560, www.nps .gov), NPS, Fort Mason Bldg 201, San Francisco, CA 94123.

National Forests

Many of the forests contain designated wilderness areas in which motorized vehicles and bicycles are prohibited, and hikers are required to obtain a permit for any overnight stay. Most of these areas are concentrated along the Sierra Crest, accessible via the Eastern Sierra, Yosemite and Kings Canyon-Sequoia National Parks.

Maps ($3 each) and information are available from the US Department of Agriculture Forest Service (USFS; ☎ 415-705-2874, www.r5.pswfs.gov), 630 Sansome St, San Francisco, CA 94111.

State Parks

California's state park system divides its land into separate categories: state parks (SP), state beaches (SB), state recreation areas (SRA), state historic parks (SHP), state reserves (SR) and state wilderness (SW).

The priority in a state park is protecting valuable resources; many state parks include reserves or preserves set aside to protect threatened or endangered plants, animals and habitats.

In a state recreation area – often around a lake, reservoir or river – recreation is considered the primary resource. While both offer camping and have access roads, state parks have fewer roads open to vehicular traffic and are more strict about campfires and water use.

State beaches are basically state parks by the sea; they usually have campgrounds and day-use areas.

State historic parks protect buildings and land of historical importance. Monterey SHP or Jack London SHP in the Sonoma Valley are good examples.

The land in state wilderness areas is basically left untouched and free of roads or other infrastructure.

Hearst San Simeon State Historical Monument (Hearst Castle) is a historical site in the state park system. The majority of California state parks are concentrated along Hwy 1, on the North and Central coasts.

GOVERNMENT & POLITICS

The United States has a republican form of government, which is popularly defined as government 'of the people, by the people and for the people.' The US Constitution, passed in 1789 and amended 26 times since, provides the fundamental laws for the running of the national government and the relations between the national and state governments.

US citizens over the age of 18 are eligible to vote (criminals may lose this right, depending on the crime). Elections are hotly contested and politicians and parties spend many millions of dollars on political campaigns that can become acrimonious. Despite this, barely half of the eligible voters cast a ballot in most state and federal elections.

The US has two main political parties – the Republicans (called the GOP for Grand Old Party) and the Democrats. Independent politicians occasionally provide a third choice. Other parties do exist, but they are too small to play a significant part in the government. Traditionally, Republicans are conservative and Democrats are liberal, though there is a range of positions in each party – some Southern Democrats can be very conservative. In recent years, the Republican party has increasingly come to be in thrall to right-wing and religious fundamentalist factions. Often, the president and his cabinet are of one party, while either or both chambers of Congress (the Senate and the House of Representatives) may have a majority of the opposing party.

As far as generalizations can be made, Republicans favor cutting taxes, shrinking

nationally funded (federal) programs of health care, education and welfare, and minimizing or eliminating national funding for items such as arts programs and abortion. Republicans believe such programs are better handled at the state level. Democrats prefer higher taxation and more federal funding of these programs. Republicans support spending a larger proportion of the federal budget on the military than do Democrats.

US Government

The national legislature is made up of the bicameral Congress – the Senate and the House of Representatives. The Senate has two senators from each of the 50 states, and the 435-member House is composed of several members from each state, depending on the state's population. Senators are elected for six years and representatives are elected for two.

The judicial branch is headed by the Supreme Court, which consists of nine justices who are appointed for life by the president and approved by the Senate.

The executive branch consists of the president, elected for a four-year term, the cabinet and various assistants. The 14 members of the president's cabinet are each appointed by the president but must be approved by the Senate. The president has the power to veto laws passed by Congress, although a law can still be passed if two thirds of the members vote for it the second time, overriding the president's veto.

The president is chosen by an electoral college consisting of a number of individual electors from each state equivalent to its number of senators and representatives combined. These electors vote in accordance with the popular vote within their state. To be elected, the president must obtain a majority of 270 of the total 538 electoral votes (the District of Columbia has no voting representatives in Congress, but nevertheless has three electoral votes). The president may serve only two terms. The 106th Congress (1999 to 2001), has a Republican majority in both chambers. Both California senators are Democratic women.

FACTS ABOUT CALIFORNIA

California Government

Each of the 50 states has its own government, run along similar lines to the national government. The head of the executive branch of state government is the governor. California's bicameral legislature consists of a 40-member senate and an 80-member general assembly, elected for four-year terms.

National (federal) laws apply to all states, although there are often conflicts between federal and state interests. States can have different laws about driving, drugs, alcohol use and taxes, which are discussed in Facts for the Visitor.

Traditionally, Northern California and most urban areas, especially Los Angeles, are predominantly Democrat, while the state's rural heartland and affluent Orange and San Diego counties are Republican, in some cases conservative Republican. In the 1998 election, the state elected Gray Davis, the first Democratic governor since the late '70s.

There are 58 counties in the state, many of which include one or more incorporated cities.

ECONOMY
US Economy

The US has a GNP of $6,350 billion, making it the largest national economy on Earth. However, the national debt – mostly accumulated by lowering income and capital gains tax rates and by overspending on such abortive programs as the Star Wars antimissile program during the Reagan-era '80s – still stood at $5,605 billion in January 1999. Despite a budget surplus in 1997 and 1998 and a stunning decline in the trade deficit (down to $15.5 billion in November 1998 from $254 billion in 1994), the national debt actually keeps growing at an approximate rate of $316 million a day because of interest payments.

The distribution of income is unequal, with the lowest 20% of income earners receiving 4.4% of national income, while the top 5% receive 17.6%. Whole areas of the US are wealthier than others, and within a city the standard of living can vary considerably from neighborhood to neighborhood. In fact, income in the US is much more equally distributed than in most countries particularly developing countries, because o the large and affluent middle class. Inequality looks bad in the US because many of the poor are highly visible and the general standard of living is so high, but statistics show that countries like France, Argentina, Thailand and Mexico have much higher levels o inequality.

The US has a progressive income tax scale, with the poorest paying around 15% of personal earnings and the richest fifth paying around 40%. A median income earner would pay around 20% of earnings but a sales tax of around 8% is added to the cost of most products.

California Economy

With an extremely large and diverse economy, California has the largest state income in the US. An interesting statistic comparing the gross product ranking of California with that of major nations puts the state's rank at number seven, just ahead o China and Brazil.

California's agricultural output is the highest of any state, with around 7.5 million acres of irrigated farmland producing cattle cotton, dairy products, wine grapes, fruit vegetables, grain and more. Farming is a highly mechanized corporate industry, aptly described as 'agribusiness,' with huge investment in land and a workforce of poorly paid mostly Latino, laborers. Forestry is still big despite conservationists' efforts to preserve more of the state's 17 million acres of public and private forests. Fishing has declined a boats have had to go farther and work harder for fewer fish.

A good deal of secondary industry is based on the processing of primary products including fish packing, fruit and vegetable canning and packaging, wine making, petroleum processing and timber milling. Not well endowed with resources for heavy industry California has successfully concentrated on the manufacture of aircraft, aerospace components, electronics, computers and hi-tech consumer goods. The construction industry civil engineering and military hardware are all huge and highly developed industries.

Nevertheless, California is postindustrial in the range of its tertiary industries – banking, finance, education, research & development, computer software, TV, movies, tourism, corporate services, and so on. Real estate remains a big business – in some places it seems like every second property is on the market. California has always made a big industry out of selling itself.

Though mining was at one time California's greatest industry, it now has a minor place in the economy, with most of the gold gone and the oil reserves depleted. Today's mining is of more prosaic minerals, like sand, cement, gravel, borates and natural gas.

California's economic problems include its share of the national debt, quite a high level of inequality, increasing dependence on imported oil and the loss of many valuable defense contracts and bases. Nonetheless, it remains one of the wealthiest economies anywhere, with a GNP per head of over $22,000 per year and a material standard of living that is the envy of much of the world. Most visitors will be impressed by the evidence of public prosperity – the road system, parks, museums and public buildings.

POPULATION & PEOPLE

California is the most populous state in the US with a population of 32,268,300 in 1997, up from 29,558,000 counted in the 1990 census. Projections estimate that there will be about 50 million people in the state by 2025. If it were a separate nation, it would be the 30th most populous nation in the world. With 190.4 people per sq mile, it ranks 11th in population density out of the 50 states. About 97% of the population lives in metropolitan areas, though, so there are plenty of wide-open spaces. In 1997, the median age was 33 years.

In 1997, California's largest cities were Los Angeles (3,553,638), San Diego (1,171,121), San Jose (838,744), San Francisco (735,315), Long Beach (421,904), Fresno (396,011), Sacramento (376,243) and Oakland (367,230).

If you consider not only the populations within the city limits, but the greater metropolitan areas (including the suburbs), the populations of the cities are much larger. In terms of metropolitan areas, Los Angeles, with a population of 15.8 million ranks second in the US only to New York (population is 18,053,800); the San Francisco metropolitan area (population 5,953,100) comes in fourth in the US (after Chicago), while San Diego's metropolitan population of 2,285,000 ranks 19th in the US; Sacramento, with 1,336,500 people, ranks 28th.

California's racial mixture is rapidly changing. Hispanic and Asian communities are gaining while Whites are the only group actually posting a decline.

White (non-Hispanic) – 49.9% (15.88 million people, down by 0.5 million since 1990)

Latino – 30.8% (9.41 million, up 2.25 million since 1990)

Black – 7.4% (2.39 million, up 92,500)

Asian/Pacific Islander – 11.7% (3.78 million, up 800,000)

Native American – 1% (306,700, up 21,000)

Source: US Bureau of the Census

Foreign-born people make up 15% of the state's population; about 30% of the US's immigrants live in California. Of these, immigrants from Mexico are the largest group, followed by immigrants from the Philippines, China, Vietnam, Korea, Iran, El Salvador, India, Taiwan, Hong Kong, Laos, Cambodia, Thailand, Guatemala, UK, Canada, Japan, Nicaragua, Peru, Afghanistan, Germany, Pakistan (in that order) and many other countries as well. This makes for a lot of diversity in language, religion and every other element of culture, especially in the urban areas where most immigrants live.

California's population figures tell an interesting story of continual increase, starting right off with the gold rush in 1848-49, when the '49ers caused a 565% increase in the recorded population in just two years (see the table on the next page).

EDUCATION

Public elementary and secondary education in all but affluent suburban areas is commonly underfunded in California, and parents with sufficient income increasingly

FACTS ABOUT CALIFORNIA

California Population

year	est population	% of increase	% of US population
1848	14,000	N/A	
1850	93,000	565%	0.4%
1860	380,000	309%	1.2%
1870	560,000	47%	1.4%
1880	865,000	54%	1.7%
1890	1,213,000	40%	1.9%
1900	1,485,000	22%	2.0%
1910	2,378,000	60%	2.6%
1920	3,427,000	44%	3.2%
1930	5,677,000	66%	4.6%
1940	6,950,000	22%	5.2%
1950	10,643,000	53%	7.0%
1960	15,863,000	49%	8.8%
1970	20,039,000	26%	9.8%
1980	23,780,000	19%	10.5%
1990	29,558,000	24%	11.6%
1991	30,321,000	2.6%	12.1%
1992	30,982,000	2.2%	12.2%
1993	31,552,000	1.8%	12.3%

source: 1993 California Almanac

opt out of the system altogether in favor of private or home schooling. Given that far fewer minority families are able to treat their offspring to private education, the gap between the haves and have-nots continues to widen dramatically. In a way, underfunding of schools exacerbates de facto segregation as well.

In recent years, there's been an increase in schools funded by Christian fundamentalists; these schools are often criticized for a lack of tolerance, diversity and academic accuracy (many insist on teaching creationism instead of evolution).

Students who thrive despite these pitfalls face a great many options in higher education throughout the state. The public system is divided into three tiers, the lowest being the state's 107 community colleges. These provide not only vocational education (for auto mechanics, cosmetologists, nurses and the like) but also the academic background for transfer to four-year universities. Public universities in California include the 22 campuses of the California State University system and the nine campuses of the University of California system. UCLA, UC Berkeley and UC San Diego are the top schools of the latter, boasting international teaching and research reputations and numerous nobel laureates on their faculties.

Private top universities include Stanford University in Palo Alto, California Institute of Technology and Arts Center College of Design in Pasadena (Los Angeles).

Despite such choices, according to the 1997 US Census, only about one in two Californians choose to go to college and only 23% of the population are college graduates.

ARTS

California is blessed (or cursed, depending on who you talk to) with two cities that both have as dynamic cultural scenes as you could hope to find anywhere. San Francisco's liberalism and humanistic tradition have made it a publishing center second only to New York, and writers have been flocking there for inspiration for years. Jazz, opera, public theater and splendid museums make San Francisco a very livable city

To the south lies the city that entertainment built, Los Angeles. Actors, and those who would like to think of themselves as such, have given the restaurants of Los Angeles a formidable army of hopeful – and attractive – service staff, always waiting for the big break. Los Angelenos enjoy the spoils of all the wealth generated by 'The Industry' in the form of several world-class museums and a cinema scene whose variety is unparalleled anywhere.

Music

Throughout the 20th century, California has been a mecca for musical talent, whether native or imported.

Ranchero When driving through the Central Valley, turn on your radio and flip through the stations for a while. When you hear something like a polka, except with lyrics in Spanish, you've hit a ranchero station. Ranchero is a music popular in the rural agricultural areas throughout California – indeed throughout the West all the way to Texas (anywhere there's a sizable Mexican-American rural population). German settlers brought polka with them to the Southwest, where it merged with the indigenous Spanish-influenced dance music. It can be a fun alternative to the usual Top 40 blather.

Jazz In the 1940s, jazz arrived in California. It was while holding a nightly gig in Hollywood that Charlie Parker was offered a seven-month engagement in Camarillo State Hospital's drug rehabilitation ward. Looking back on that experience, he later recorded 'Relaxing at Camarillo' for LA's Dial label. Many great jazzmen were born in Los Angeles: Dexter Gordon, Charles Mingus and Art Pepper among them.

In the '50s, cool jazz was born with artists such as Pepper, Dave Brubeck, Vince Guaraldi, Buddy Collette, Gerry Mulligan, Chet Baker, and Shelly Manne performing under the Pacific's relaxing influence. At clubs such as Shelly's Manne-Hole in Hollywood, the Lighthouse at Hermosa Beach, and Bimbo's 365 Club and the Blackhawk in San Francisco's North Beach, they created a soothing, harmonically sophisticated style of jazz that took the edge off the East Coast-oriented bop scene.

Jazz is appealing to a new generation with groove-heavy acid jazz and acts such as the bop-edged Charlie Hunter Trio and Spearhead, who combine activist-inspired verse with a backdrop of free jazz. Swing has also made a huge comeback, complete with athletic jitterbugging and zoot suits.

Rhythm & Blues From the '40s through the '60s, South Central LA was home to a number of outstanding nightclubs presenting blues, R&B, jazz, and soul. Watts churned out vocal groups in the doo-wop tradition, including the Penguins, who first recorded 'Earth Angel' for LA's Doo-Tone records. A juke joint crawl in the mid-'50s would likely have included T-Bone Walker, Amos Milburn or Charles Brown.

At the hub of a thriving Watts musical scene, Johnny Otis brought many forms of music to the public's attention with his popular Johnny Otis Orchestra – featuring Little Esther Phillips – and his record label, DIG. (Johnny Otis still plays in the Bay Area and can be heard on his Saturday morning R&B radio show on KPFA 94.1 FM in Berkeley and KPFK 90.7 FM in LA.) Starting in the early '60s, Sam Cooke performed hit after hit and ran his SAR record label, attracting soul and gospel talent from around the country to Los Angeles.

Rock & Roll Though rock & roll was recorded in California from the beginning, the first homegrown talent to make it big in the '50s was Richie Valens, whose 'La Bamba' was a rockified traditional Mexican folk song. In the early '60s, LA's beaches and suburbs were treated to a highly popular style of rock & roll called 'surf music.' The Beach Boys are the best-known performers of surf music, a combination of lifted Chuck Berry riffs, easy-to-enjoy rock & roll rhythms, innovative use of harmonies and young California themes – cars, girls and surf. They played down the beach themes in the late '60s and pioneered the use of advanced studio recording techniques, especially for their big 1966 hit 'Good Vibrations.' Dick Dale and Jan & Dean were also local talents. In the mid-'60s, a group of UCLA students – among them the 'lizard king,' Jim Morrison – formed the Doors, who grooved the Sunset Strip for half a decade.

Meanwhile, San Francisco had begun a heady ferment that was the beginning of the psychedelic revolution. Apart from big-name acts like the Grateful Dead and the Jefferson Airplane, Bay Area bands like Janis Joplin's Big Brother & the Holding Company, Sly & the Family Stone, and Creedence Clearwater Revival were key players in defining the era's sound. Carlos Santana formed the band Santana during the late '60s and succeeded in blending Latin American rhythm with rock & roll. Master-promoter Bill Graham, often referred to as the 'godfather of San Francisco rock,' used these groups to revolutionize the

Carlos Santana

way popular music is presented and by doing so set the stage for a new era of world-class entertainers.

In direct revolt against the love-bead status quo, the singular Frank Zappa, with his band the Mothers of Invention, began his career with the album *Freak Out* in the mid-'60s. The Mothers' satire took on all comers, from conservative war hawks to mind-numbed hippies. In 1969 at the Altamont Speedway, about 60 miles from San Francisco, security men (actually Hell's Angels) murdered a concertgoer at a Rolling Stones concert. Some claim that this incident marked the end of the hippie era.

About this time, Tom Waits began haunting the smaller clubs of LA. Waits, with a voice rusted over from bottom-shelf bourbon and filterless cigarettes, brought to the world music built on sounds dragged out from a tin pan alley junkyard, influenced by the varied likes of Louis Armstrong, Kurt Weill and Harry Partch.

The late '70's and early '80's brought the young and sick out to hear California's brand of punk. California punk grew up around (of all things) skateboard culture. Early on, LA punks were listening to the punkabilly stylings of X. Though not strictly punk, X's combination of Exene Cervenka and John Doe's vocals over the rockabilly guitar licks of Billy Zoom created an original, decidedly Angeleno sound that simply blew the doors off the local punk scene. With a more pronounced punk sound, Black Flag led the way with the rants of singer Henry Rollins.

In the mid-'80s, Los Lobos emerged from East LA with a Mexican-influenced rock sound and tremendous musicianship that crossed racial boundaries. Also bred locally the Red Hot Chili Peppers exploded on the national scene in the late '80s with a highly charged, funk-punk sound.

San Francisco (whose now-defunct Winterland Ballroom was the scene of the Sex Pistols' final concert) produced the Avengers and the Dead Kennedys. Jello Biafra, the lead singer of the DKs, ran for mayor of San Francisco in the mid-'80s. One of his better remembered campaign promises was to require San Francisco's police force to dress in clown suits while patrolling the city streets.

Rap The area stretching from South Central LA on down to Long Beach is the local rap hotbed, producing such artists as Snoop Doggy Dog and NWA, whose album *Straight Outta Compton* might best represent LA's rap scene, as well as offer insight from some of the city's most popular artists. Successful local record labels are Ruthless and Death Row Records. The northern state also produced some noteworthy acts with less edge, such as Digital Underground, the ribald Too Short, and the brooding Disposable Heroes of Hiphoprisy.

Classical The big cities all have symphony orchestras and opera and concert venues. See the relevant chapters for details. Open air concerts are a pleasant feature of music performances in Southern California, with the Los Angeles Philharmonic Orchestra performing its 'symphonies under the stars' in summer at the Hollywood Bowl.

Dance

The San Francisco Bay Area is one of the best areas in the US for dance. The San Francisco Ballet, the oldest resident ballet company in the US, has an international reputation and draws dancers and commissions works from all over the world. The city is also a center for modern dance, with many modern dance companies – including ODC San Francisco, Lines Contemporary Ballet and Joe Goode Performance Group – and independent choreographers. Many talented dancers make their homes in San Francisco, and there is a constant flow of talent back and forth between San Francisco and New York.

Oakland also has a ballet, and a lively ethnic dance scene. The Oakland Ballet is more community based than the San Francisco Ballet. It relies heavily on local dancers for talent, and is generally more traditional in its repertoire and less expensive than the San Francisco Ballet.

Zellerbach Hall (tel 510-642-9988), on the UC Berkeley campus, frequently gets international ballet and contemporary dance companies.

Performers like Martha Graham, Alvin Ailey and Bella Lewitzky all got their starts in Los Angeles, but dance has never been a major art form in Los Angeles. In the 1980s, the Joffrey Ballet had a brief residency here, but since then LA hasn't had its own ballet company. Over the past 30 years, the trend has been towards the experimental and the avant-garde. One of the oldest local companies, the American Repertory Company (1969) is dedicated to keeping alive the legacy of early 20th-century modern dance pioneers, including Martha Graham and Isadora Duncan. LA Contemporary Dance Theater is an African American troupe founded by Lula Washington that enjoys a dedicated following.

Fascinating, if slightly bizarre, is the critically-acclaimed Diavolo Dance Theatre, which practices a cutting-edge dance form called hyperdance. It involves dancers performing in custom-built spaces by literally slamming their bodies into walls, doors or objects. Another LA jewel is Loretta Livingston & Dancers, a modern dance company led by Loretta who used to dance with the now-retired Bella Lewitzky for 10 years.

Art

The earliest California artists were of course the Indians who used pigment to make pictographs on rocks and caves, often as part of shamanistic rituals intended to ensure successful hunting. While most tribes had their own decorative styles, the Chumash are considered among the most artistic because of the whimsical designs and bright colors they used. Chumash Painted Cave, near Santa Barbara, is a good example (see the Central Coast chapter).

Early Landscape Artists California's first landscape painters were essentially tourists who recorded California's gentle light and natural landscape in their works. Many such artists were trained cartographers accompanying Spanish explorers to record images of Alta California. An impressive reproduction of a scene painted by the artist who accompanied Sebastián Vizcaíno adorns the walls of the Santa Barbara Courthouse.

In the 1850s, California's population increased with Easterners coming west to seek fortune in the gold mines. Gold rush pursuits often proved futile, so artists fell back on painting skills to make a living. Thomas Hill and German immigrant Albert Bierstadt were the two most famous gold rush-era artists.

Travels to Yosemite, Death Valley and the giant sequoia groves supplied most of their subject matter. Bierstadt voiced the general sentiment of early painters in writing that California 'holds land and light that can not be found in such quality nor quantity anywhere else.' As California's popularity grew, Currier & Ives sent landscape artists such as Thomas A Ayers and Charles Nahl to do lithographs of California scenes, which they sold in mail-order catalogs. While most of this work is in the Library of Congress in Washington, DC, a few pieces are in the Haggin Museum in Stockton and at the Oakland Museum.

The High Provincials As California's population grew, artists with East Coast and European training came to California specifically to paint. Known as 'high provincials' (referring to their 'high-brow' training and conviction that California was *the* place to paint), these artists centered themselves in San Francisco, Los Angeles, Carmel, Santa Barbara and Laguna Beach. They were also known as the Southern Californians for geographic reasons. William Chase, often regarded as the finest American art teacher of the late 19th century, paid a visit to California in 1896 and praised California's light and landscape, thus fortifying the state's popularity.

Guy Rose was the first California native to gain international recognition as an artist. He lived in Giverny for one year, studying with Claude Monet, and upon returning in 1914, introduced impressionism to California artists. This ushered in the era of painting out-of-doors, to which California was already conducive. Desert scenes and seascapes were favorite subject matter and eucalyptus trees appeared in so many paintings that California artists were often called the 'eucalyptus school.'

The best places to see these works are in the galleries of Carmel and Laguna Beach, which still survive as artist communities, though they've been overrun with tourism. Laguna Beach's annual Festival of Art and Sawdust Festival are two of California's largest arts festivals.

Modern Art California debuted on the national art scene, previously confined to New York and Chicago, in 1940, when Man Ray moved to Los Angeles. Man Ray brought surrealism and dadaism, both well suited to California's off-the-wall, rebellious lifestyle, to the West Coast and spurred artists to venture away from traditionalism. Artists began to explore texture and shadow, intensified by California's light.

In the '40s and '50s, California art reflected the strong abstract expressionist movement in New York. Then in 1951, San Francisco artist David Park submitted a painting of a woman's figure to a competition, signifying the first move away from abstract expressionism. Elmer Bischoff soon followed Park's lead, and together they revitalized the exploration of painting figures that came to be known as the 'Bay Area figurative art movement.' The large following included Richard Diebenkorn, who eventually took his interpretation of space and light to a more abstract level.

This is also when Asian art began influencing California artists, especially in Los Angeles, where Asian and Californian artists shared work and ideas. Sam Francis, famous for his abstract landscapes, multicolored spatterings and Zen-influenced paintings in which bands of color surround a large blank canvas, played a key part in this Cal-Asian movement with an open-door gallery in Santa Monica. His Japanese wife, an accomplished artist herself, helped connect Japanese art dealers and aspiring California artists. A Japanese Pavilion at the LA County Museum of Art (LACMA) brings California and Japanese movements together according to genre.

Pop Art In the Bay Area, as artists rejected the rigid, contrived categories of stylized art, an art that could not be defined as art according to previous movements emerged. This 'funk art,' as it came to be known, incorporated everyday objects – lampshades, seashells, cigarettes – into elaborate sculptures and pieces of bricolage. At the same time, Los Angeles saw the development of the 'light and space' movement, which also resisted the overcommodification of art, in the work of James Turrell and Robert Irwin.

In the 1960s, California artists were caught up in the nation's growing chaos and confusion. With Vietnam and California's uncontrolled growth, California art turned remarkably disillusioned and dark. Romantic landscapes portraying California as the land of opportunity turned to 'freeway scapes' showing smog and overcrowding.

with much allusion to the lost or tempered American dream. Wayne Thiebaud's pop interpretations of freeways and city streets are strong examples.

San Francisco, with Haight-Ashbury as a focal point, saw a huge output of psychedelic work by poster and album cover artists such as Rick Griffin, Stanley Mouse and Allen Kelley. R Crumb and his art in *Zap Comix* (remember 'Keep on truckin'?) was also very influential in this movement.

Museums The best places to see early California landscapes are the Oakland Museum, the Haggin Museum in Stockton, the Crocker Art Museum in Sacramento and the Laguna Art Museum in Orange County.

California's most progressive art comes out of Los Angeles, with the Museum of Contemporary Art (MOCA) and the Geffen Contemporary, in a converted warehouse in Little Tokyo, producing the most avant-garde shows in the state. The San Francisco Museum of Modern Art (SFMOMA), housed in a controversial modern structure by Swiss architect Mario Botta, has a substantial if conservative permanent collection. Across the bay, the UC Berkeley Art Museum is a bit hit or miss, but it often has excellent contemporary exhibits. The San Diego Museum of Contemporary Art (one downtown and one in La Jolla) shows mostly European works.

For fine art, the Los Angeles County Museum of Art (LACMA) and the Asian Art Museum and the MH de Young Museum in San Francisco have large and varied permanent collections and get world-class traveling exhibits. San Francisco's Palace of the Legion of Honor, in Lincoln Park, has an important collection of European work, as does the Getty Center in Los Angeles.

Funk and pop art pieces grace many a poster shop in San Francisco, mostly on Haight St. Los Angeles' Watts Towers are perhaps the most famous and accessible pieces of folkloric art.

Architecture

California's architecture is a jumble of styles, uses a hodgepodge of materials and reflects various degrees of quality and care. It is as diverse as the state's population.

Spanish-Mexican Period When Spain launched exploratory expeditions to Alta California in the 1770s, the 'Laws of the Indies' served as a blueprint for mission development. The missions, in addition to being near rancherias, waterways and the sea, had to be built around a courtyard where a garden and kitchen could be kept, with buildings for livestock and horses nearby. Building materials reflected what the natives and padres found on hand: adobe, limestone and grass.

Though the missions themselves crumbled into disrepair as the padres' influence waned, the building style was practical for California's climate. Patrons of California's ranchos adopted the style, eventually known as 'California rancho' or 'rancho adobe,' and used it when building headquarters for their enormous properties. There are outstanding examples of adobes in Old Town in San

Tower on a California mission

Diego, in Monterey State Historic Park and in Santa Barbara.

Victorians With the 1849 gold rush and California's statehood, architecture became Americanized almost immediately. As people arrived and accrued great fortunes, they built in a style familiar to them. With few trained architects on the scene and a general labor shortage, new buildings were often constructed using prefabricated structures ordered by mail from England, China and Australia. Victorian buildings became popular, especially in San Francisco and on the North Coast. California's upper class built grand Victorian mansions (such as the Carson Mansion in Eureka, Governor's Mansion in Sacramento and Meux Home in Fresno) to keep up with East Coast fashion that reflected the style popular during the reign of Queen Victoria. Soon smaller, less detailed versions were being produced in great quantities. Their bulging bay windows were good for San Francisco's hills, as they allowed views of more than the neighbors' walls, and prefabricated construction made them cheap.

Mission & Spanish Revival After rejection of its Hispanic heritage during the Victorian period, romantic enthusiasm for California missions was revived thanks to writings by Helen Hunt Jackson. Construction of Leland Stanford, Jr University in Palo Alto, and the arrival of William Templeton Johnson and Irving Gill on the architectural scene, fortified this trend. Architects began to build in mission revival style, using courtyards, arched entryways, long covered porches and fountains. At the same time, architects built in the Spanish colonial revival style, with two-story structures and open balconies. The two styles were frequently intertwined.

Former Santa Fe (now Amtrak) railroad stations throughout the state reflect this style, with outstanding examples in Stockton, Davis, Los Angeles San Juan Capistrano, and San Diego.

California Bungalow In the 1890s, Willis Polk, Bernard Maybeck and John Galen Howard arrived in California – the most influential group in what could be considered California architecture. Working mostly in the Bay Area, these architects consciously responded to California's climate and developing lifestyle. The typical California bungalow, a one-story wood structure with overhanging gables and a large porch, allowed indoor-outdoor living and quick, inexpensive construction. Whole neighborhoods of bungalows sprang up at the end of WWI, during LA's oil boom. The Gamble House in Pasadena is considered a supreme example of the style.

Arts & Crafts The Arts and Crafts movement, started and raised to an art form by Bernard Maybeck, Charles and Henry Greene and Julia Morgan, was a decorative style incorporated into both California bungalows and mission revival styles. Buildings from this movement combined various indigenous styles – Japanese, Spanish, English – with handcrafted details – carved wood, stained glass, sculpted tile – to make some of California's most beautiful buildings, including Bernard Maybeck's First Church of Christ Science (1906) in Berkeley; the Greenes' Gamble House (1908) in Pasadena; the Hollyhock House (1921), a collaboration of Frank Lloyd Wright and Rudolph Schindler, in Los Angeles; and Irving Gill's Marston House (1905) in San Diego. William Wurster, who started with rigid classical buildings and softened under the Arts and Crafts influence, is one of California's most prolific architects, whose work is mostly in Stockton and the Bay Area.

Classical Revival & Eclectic During the rise of Arts and Crafts, big-name architects also felt compelled to prove themselves in established architectural realms – courthouses, civic auditoriums, museums and exposition spaces – which were built in the classical revival style. Thus most of California's monumental buildings reflect stylized European and East Coast training. Examples of the classical revival style include San Francisco's Civic Center and Palace of Fine Arts, and the California Quadrangle in San

Diego's Balboa Park, all of which were built for Panama-Pacific Expositions celebrating the opening of the Panama Canal in 1915.

The best example of California eclectic style, in which basically anything goes, is William Randolph Hearst's estate at San Simeon (Hearst Castle) – a mixture of Gothic, Moorish and Spanish Romanesque – which Julia Morgan described as 'giving the client what he wants.'

Art Deco & Streamline Moderne The favorite styles in the 1920s and '30, especially for public and office buildings, were art deco and streamline moderne. Art deco is characterized by vertical lines and symmetry that create a soaring effect often mitigated by a stepped pattern towards the top. Ornamentation is heavy, especially above doors and windows, and may consist of floral motifs, sunbursts or zigzags. Excellent examples are the Wiltern Theater and the former Bullocks-Wilshire department store in Los Angeles. Downtown Oakland also has many fine examples of art deco buildings. Related to art deco, streamline moderne sought to incorporate the machine aesthetic and, in particular, the aerodynamic aspects of airplanes and ocean liners. Horizontal bands of smallish, circular windows – like ship portholes – and smooth, curved facades were typical, as were simulated railings and the use of aluminum and stainless steel. Look for this style in the Coca-Coca Bottling Plant in downtown LA, in the Crossroads of the World building on Sunset Blvd in Hollywood and in the Maritime Museum in San Francisco.

Modernism Also called the 'International style,' modern architecture had its origins in Europe (mostly in 1920s Germany) with Bauhaus architects Walter Gropius and Mies van der Rohe, and later Le Corbusier. In LA, Rudolph Schindler and Richard Neutra, both of whom had come to Southern California from their native Austria, were its early practitioners. They sowed the seeds for much of the architecture that's still with us today, both in its residential as well as 'corporate' forms. Characteristics include a boxlike shape, open floor plans, flat roofs, plain and unadorned facades and interior walls and the abundant use of glass.

Postwar Architecture After WWII, a large and comfortable middle class demanded 'modern' affordable family housing en masse. Freeways and parking lots influenced public planning, and suburban neighborhoods grew to facilitate the commuters' lifestyles. Inexpensive materials, prefabricated walls, cabinets and fixtures, and standardized floor plans allowed preplanned neighborhoods to be built quickly and cheaply. Tract housing developments, still spreading like wildfire over southeastern California, now surround most major cities. Shopping malls and strip malls have taken the life out of most downtown areas and spread it over miles of boulevards. Fresno is probably the best example of this decentralization.

Postmodernism In response to the bland, mass-produced postwar architecture (which does, however, meet people's needs), important architects have created more reactive and distinctive styles. In LA, where Frank Gehry is reigning guru, contemporary structures still respond to California's climate and light, but with minimalist tendencies and an emphasis on space and color. Aaron Betsky (architectural curator of the San Francisco Museum of Modern Art) says of Los Angeles' and California's postmodern architecture that 'at its best [it] does not look like a building, but is an abstract interruption of the city, a piece of technology honed for living, or a self-consciously vivid set for modern living.' Concentrations of this avant-garde are in the Oakland Hills, which were almost completely leveled by fire in 1989, and in various pockets of Los Angeles (especially Santa Monica and Venice Beach). Richard Meier's monumental Getty Center is another good example.

Mimetic Architecture Of course, California's free and easy style has allowed for zany structures influenced by nothing but whim and imagination. Often dubbed 'California roadside vernacular,' these buildings usually have an imitative character: a hot-dog stand shaped like a hot dog, a donut shop that *is* a huge donut, a production studio shaped like a pair of binoculars, an Orange Julius stand in the form of (what else?) a giant navel orange. Southern California, LA in particular, is a global center for these whacky expressions.

Literature

The name 'California' came into being as a literary device, coming from an imaginary kingdom featured in one of 1510's best-sellers, *Las Sergas de Esplandían*. Perhaps California's 20th century took its cue from this auspicious beginning, because some of the brightest lights in 20th century American literature have made California their home.

Gold Rush to the 1920s Mark Twain came west to work in Carson City, Nevada, but was almost immediately enticed to Virginia City, where he worked on a newspaper there during the frenzied rush to the Comstock Lode. He penned mine company promotional pieces as a lucrative sideline and wrote about pioneering life at the silver mines in *Roughing It* (1872). It covers his stagecoach journey to the West, mining days and his experience of an earthquake. More of Twain's tales from the gold rush are recounted in *The Celebrated Jumping Frog of Calaveras County & Other Stories*.

Another pioneering visitor to the Bay Area, Scottish-born Robert Louis Stevenson, lived briefly in Monterey and San Francisco and honeymooned by an abandoned silver mine in nearby Calistoga. The stay led to his book *The Silverado Squatters* (1872). Professional hell-raiser Jack London was San Francisco-born and Oakland-bred. London turned out a massive volume of writings, including his own suitably fictionalized biography under the title *Martin Eden* (1909).

California increasingly received attention from writers with its rise to prominence in the early part of this century. One of the first novels to look at California's prosperity critically was Upton Sinclair's *Oil!* (1927), a work of muckraking historical fiction with socialist overtones.

The Modern Era Arguably the most influential author to emerge from California was John Steinbeck. Steinbeck turned attention from the two metropolises to the farms of the Central Valley and the down and out of Monterey County. The first of his California novels was *Tortilla Flat* (1935), which dealt with the Mexican-American community of Monterey. His most overtly political novel, *In Dubious Battle* (1936), told a grim story of a violent fruit pickers' strike. *Grapes of Wrath* (1939), considered by many his greatest novel, tells of the struggles of migrant farmworkers in California's Central Valley. The classic portrayal of Monterey is his *Cannery Row* (1945), a humorous description of the working class in and around Monterey's cannery district. For more on Steinbeck, see the Salinas section in the Central Coast chapter.

Another writer who tried to capture life in rural California was William Saroyan, who wrote extensively of the Armenian immigrant community of Fresno where he grew up.

Eugene O'Neill took his 1936 Nobel prize money and transplanted to the sleepy suburban village of Danville on the cusp of the Central Valley near San Francisco, where he wrote the plays *The Ice Man Cometh* (1946) and *Long Day's Journey into Night* (produced posthumously in 1956).

LA's image as a tough, vulgar town emerged in the '30s and the '40s with John Fante's *Ask the Dust* (1939), a tour of Depression-era Los Angeles. The fame and fortune fantasies of struggling writer Arturo Bandini jar violently against the grim reality of LA's dusty downtown streets, where 'the smell of gasoline makes the sight of palm trees seem sad.' Aldous Huxley's novel *After Many a Summer Dies the Swan* (1939) is a fine and ironic work based on the life of newspaper magnate William Randolph Hearst (as was Orson Welles' film *Citizen Kane*).

Nathanael West's *Day of the Locust* (1939) is one of the best – and most cynical – novels about Hollywood ever written. He made one shrewd observation of Hollywood after another, which strangely, for this city that so steadfastly insists on revising itself, still hold true more than a half century later. Two other novels that make sharply critical observations about the early years of Hollywood are F Scott Fitzgerald's final work, *The Last Tycoon* (1940), and Budd Schulberg's *What Makes Sammy Run?* (1941). Evelyn Waugh's *The Loved One* (1948), on the other hand, takes a viciously humorous look at the funeral trade in Hollywood.

Poet-playwright Kenneth Rexroth began his San Francisco tenure of literary domination with his first collection entitled *In What Hour* (1940). Rexroth, also an influential critic, was instrumental in advancing the careers of several Bay Area artists, notably those of the Beat Generation.

The Pulps In the '30s, San Francisco and Los Angeles became the twin capitals of the pulp detective novel. Dashiell Hammett's Sam Spade (*The Maltese Falcon*, 1930) and Nick and Nora Charles (*The Thin Man*, 1932) plied their trade in San Francisco, and Raymond Chandler's Philip Marlowe (*The Big Sleep*, 1939) found trouble in the hills of Los Angeles. Both authors' books are populated with troubled characters riding the tide of evil forces that seem to govern the metropolis – before they sink to the bottom. Hammett made San Francisco's fog a sinister side character in his books; Chandler played on differences between the haves and the have-nots in sunny LA. Latter-day practitioners of the art include Jim Thompson (*The Grifters*, 1963), Elmore Leonard *(Get Shorty*, 1990) and Walter Mosley *(Devil in a Blue Dress,* 1990, and *White Butterfly,* 1992).

The Beats After the chaos of WWII, the Beat Generation brought about a new style of writing: short, sharp and alive. Based in San Francisco, the scene revolved around Jack Kerouac, Allen Ginsberg and Lawrence Ferlinghetti, the Beats' patron and publisher. (For more on the Beats, see the boxed text 'The Beat Generation' in the San Francisco chapter.)

With the Beats came a sort of *glasnost* that spread to other art forms, notably standup comedy. This was the first time in the US that comedians began to ruthlessly explore the underbelly of the American experience. Lenny Bruce, Lord Buckley, Mort Sahl, Bob Newhart and Jonathan Winters were in the vanguard of the new comedy.

The '60s San Francisco dominated the literary scene in California during the '60s. Essayist Joan Didion captures a '60s sense of upheaval in *Slouching Towards Bethlehem* (1968), giving a caustic look at flower power and the Haight-Ashbury. Tom Wolfe also puts '60s San Francisco in perspective with *The Kandy-Kolored Tangerine Flake Streamlined Baby* (1965) and *The Electric Kool-Aid Acid Test* (1968). The latter blends the Grateful Dead, the Hell's Angels and Ken Kesey's band of Merry Pranksters, who began their acid-laced 'magic bus' journey in Santa Cruz. A precursor to the spirit of the era, Kesey's own *One Flew Over the Cuckoo's Nest* (1962) pits a free-thinking individual against stifling authority, drawing from Kesey's experiences working at a local psychiatric ward for its setting.

Richard Brautigan's curious novels haven't aged too well but had a cult following in their time. *Trout Fishing in America* (1967) is one of the best. East Bay writer Philip K Dick is chiefly remembered for his science fiction, notably *Do Androids Dream of Electric Sheep?* (1968), which under the title *Blade Runner* became a classic sci-fi film. Dick's *Man in the High Castle* (1962) envisions a Japanese-dominated San Francisco after Japan and Germany have won WWII, dividing the US between them. Frank Herbert of *Dune* fame was also a local during these years, as was Thomas Pynchon, whose *Crying of Lot 49* (1966) takes place in 1960s Berkeley.

Charles Bukowski's idiosyncratic and drunken poetry and prose depicts the seamier side of working class life in LA, especially rusty old San Pedro: the man could write, drunk or sober.

The '70s & Beyond The bloated excess of '70s California became a favorite target for writers. Hunter S Thompson began his savage exploration of the collapse of the hippie dream with *Hell's Angels* (1970) and

FACTS ABOUT CALIFORNIA

went on to chronicle its death throes throughout the decade. His masterwork remains *Fear and Loathing in Las Vegas* (1971). *The Great Shark Hunt* (1974) is a collection of some of his more acidic (pharmaceutical and otherwise) essays. *Generation of Swine* (1990) is a collection of columns Thompson wrote during a stint at the *San Francisco Examiner*.

For novels about LA, 1970 was a bumper year. Terry Southern's *Blue Movie* concerns the decadent side of Hollywood; Joan Didion's *Play It As It Lays* looks at Los Angelenos with a dry, not-too-kind wit; and *Post Office*, by poet-novelist Charles Bukowski, captures the down-and-out side of downtown. Later works continued to look at LA with a critical eye. *Chicano*(1970), by Richard Vasquez, takes a dramatic look at the Latino barrio of East LA, and LA's cocaine-addled '80s got the treatment in Bret Easton Ellis' *Less than Zero* (1985).

No writer watched San Francisco's gay fraternity emerge from the closet with clearer vision than Armistead Maupin with his Tales of the City series. Starting, like the best Victorian potboilers, as newspaper serials in 1979, they became a smash hit collection of literary soap operas, light as a feather but great to read and a clear-as-day re-creation of the heady days of pre-AIDS excess. *Tales of the City, Further Tales of the City, More Tales of the City, Babycakes*, and *Significant Others* bring that period back to life, and the TV series was equally delightful. The late Randy Shilts, local author of *And the Band Played On* (1987), a moving account of the early years of AIDS awareness, also wrote for the *Examiner* and *Chronicle*.

The West Coast has always attracted artists and writers, and today the California literary community is stronger than ever. Alice Walker, Pulitzer Prize-winning author of *The Color Purple*; Amy Tan, author of *The Joy Luck Club*; Chilean novelist Isabel Allende, author of *The House of Spirits*; romance novelist Danielle Steele (with a new novel appearing, seemingly, every other month); Anne Lamott; Dorothy Allison; Maxine Hong Kingston; Elmore Leonard;

Walter Mosley; Pico Iyer and James Ellroy all make their homes there.

The list of California writers would not be complete without Wallace Stegner, whose prize-winning novels and nonfiction qualify him as one of the great writers of the American West. Stegner died in 1993, but his legacy lives on at the prestigious Stanford University, whose creative writing program is named after him.

Film

California culture is unique in that the state's primary art form, film, is also a major export. It's a medium with a powerful presence in the lives of Americans and people throughout the world. Images of California are distributed far beyond the state's boundaries. Hardly anyone can come to California without having some cinematic reference to the place, and many who have settled here make every effort to live up to the hype.

LA in particular has turned the camera incessantly on itself, and as a result, it's probably the most self-aware city in the world. Billy Wilder's *Sunset Boulevard* (1950), starring Gloria Swanson and William Holden, is a fascinating study of the way in which Hollywood discards its aged stars.

Perhaps the greatest film about Los Angeles is *Chinatown* (1974). Directed by Roman Polanski and starring Jack Nicholson and Faye Dunaway, this is the story of LA's early-20th-century water wars. Robert Towne's brilliant screenplay deftly deals with the shrewd deceptions that helped make Los Angeles what it is today.

Blade Runner (1982) is a sci-fi thriller directed by Ridley Scott and starring Harrison Ford, Rutger Hauer and Sean Young. The film projects modern Los Angeles into the 21st century, with newer buildings reaching further into the sky – icy fortresses contrasting starkly with chaotic, neglected streets.

John Singleton's *Boyz N the Hood* (1991), starring Cuba Gooding Jr, offers a major reality check: maybe this is what it's really like to come of age as a black teen in today's inner city. Meanwhile, Lawrence Kazdan's *Grand Canyon* (1991), starring Danny

Glover and Kevin Kline, presents a glimmer of hope as black and white families cope with the sobering realities of racial tensions in modern LA. *My Family – Mi Familia* (1994) is a multi-generational epic that explores the trials and tribulations of a Mexican-American family in East LA during the first half of the 20th century.

In *LA Story* (1991), comedian Steve Martin parodies the city that he calls home. Just about every aspect of LA life – from traffic to earthquakes to enemas – gets the irreverent Martin treatment.

The Player, released in 1992, is Robert Altman's contemporary comment on Hollywood. Starring Tim Robbins and Fred Ward, this is a classic satire on the movie-making machinery, featuring dozens of cameos by the very actors and actresses being spoofed.

The films of Hollywood's latest auteur, Quentin Tarantino, are self-consciously influenced by noir classics, Westerns and Hong Kong thrillers and prominently feature modern-day Los Angeles. *True Romance* (1993), written by Tarantino, stars Christian Slater as a naive and unbelievably lucky fugitive who deflects his trouble towards greedy film tycoons. *Pulp Fiction* (1994), both written and directed by Tarantino, is a humorous and ironic view of LA from the bottom up. In very Chandleresque fashion, Tarantino creates a surreal Los Angeles through convincingly original dialogue. For all of its action, the film is quite realistically stuck much of the time in cars cruising LA's streets.

But the most recent contender for 'Best LA Movie' this side of *Chinatown* would have to be the visceral and brilliant *LA Confidential* (1997), starring Kevin Spacey, Kim Basinger and the wonderfully slimy Danny DeVito. 'Hard-hitting' doesn't begin to describe the violent world of deals, sexual betrayal and double-crosses that drives both good and bad cops to hubristic destinies – and deaths – in the LA of the crime-ridden '40s. Basinger won the Academy Award for her supporting role as a sensitive whore. But it's a lesson in film acting to watch Russell Crowe – as a victimized and manipulated brute cop – as he dismantles entire buildings

in pursuit of something finer within himself. Tarantino, take note.

San Francisco has made a great backdrop for an amazing number of movies. Almost everything in the Hollywood lexicon, from comedies to sci-fi, has used the 'City by the Bay' as a stage. A number of big production companies are based in the Bay Area, including Francis Ford Coppola's Zoetrope and – most famously, in Marin County – George Lucas' LucasFilm and Industrial Light & Magic, the high-tech company that produces the computer-generated special effects for Hollywood's biggest releases.

The first big San Francisco movie was, of course, Clark Gable's *San Francisco* (1936), which relives the 1906 quake. *The Joy Luck Club* (1993), the film of Amy Tan's best-selling book, explores China old and China new, anchored in the city's Chinatown. Remarkably, no American film company or TV network had the nerve to make a movie out of Armistead Maupin's long-running soap opera *Tales of the City*; it took Britain's Channel 4 to bring it to the small screen in 1993.

The hit film *The Graduate* (1967), set in status-hungry middle-class California, is notable for Dustin Hoffman's unique ability to get to Berkeley by crossing the Bay Bridge in the San Francisco direction – his red Alfa Romeo simply looks better on the top deck.

We've all hurtled up and down San Francisco's streets with Steve McQueen in *Bullit*, the 1968 thriller that served as the benchmark for good car chases ever since, but Clint Eastwood's 'Dirty Harry' character also found San Francisco familiar territory. The highly questionable cop started his film career there in the 1971 *Dirty Harry*.

Alfred Hitchcock's movies often made use of San Francisco locales. 1958's *Vertigo* starred Kim Novak and James Stewart and wandered all over San Francisco, with lengthy pauses at the Palace of the Legion of Honor and at Fort Point. Pesky feathered fiends made nuisances of themselves just north of San Francisco in 1963's *The Birds*.

Of course, the classic San Francisco private eye was Dashiell Hammett's Sam Spade. His screen double, Humphrey Bogart, appeared in *The Maltese Falcon* (1941), a classic murder mystery directed by John Huston.

The Wild One (1954) was one of the first movies to exploit the 'rebellious youth' theme: Marlon Brando leads a motorcycle gang that invades a town in rural California.

For a taste of life in a small Central Valley town (Modesto to be exact) on a June night in '62, check George Lucas' tribute to cruising, *American Graffiti* (1973). For a glimpse of the Malibu surf scene at about the same time, *Big Wednesday* (1978) is worth a rental (although it was actually filmed in Santa Barbara). Santa Cruz became the haunt of Generation X vampires in the *Lost Boys* (1978).

Billy Wilder's classic Marilyn Monroe comedy *Some Like It Hot* (1959) elegantly captures in black & white all the splendor of San Diego's Hotel del Coronado. The schmaltzy *Pretty Woman* (1990) stars Julie Roberts as the luckiest hooker in LA – but it's filmed partly in San Diego.

Martin Mull's *The Serial* is a cutting satire of the feel-good New Age ethos of '70s Marin County (1980). The gold rush is portrayed from very different perspectives in two films. *Paint Your Wagon* (1969) is a bloated musical featuring the chilling vocal talents of Clint Eastwood and Lee Marvin as prospectors in the Mother Lode. Rent this film at your own peril. *1000 Pieces of Gold* (1992) is a small, subdued, independently produced film telling the story of a Chinese woman sold into servitude to a Mother Lode brothel, who manages to become a woman of independent means.

RELIGION

Like the rest of the US, California is primarily Christian; 45% of Californians are Protestant, 25% are Roman Catholic, 5% are Jewish and 7% are of other faiths; 18% express no sectarian preference. Still, only 9% say they are not at all religious; 22% describe themselves as very religious, 47% as fairly religious and 22% as slightly religious.

Within the ranks of Protestants are many different sects, ranging from staid conservative denominations to evangelical 'born-again' Pentecostals. Though they are claimed by only 7% of the population, the 'other' religions probably represent every other religion on Earth. The large numbers of Californians with roots in countries around the world means that California has sizable numbers of Muslims, Hindus, Buddhists, Sikhs, Baha'is, and members of every other religion you can think of. Mosques, temples, synagogues and religious centers of all stripes are found throughout California, especially in the larger population centers where most of the immigrants or people with foreign backgrounds live.

Of course, as 'the land of the fruits and the nuts,' California is also home to a number of unusual religious persuasions, from satanic churches to faith healers. And California, from its earliest days, has had utopian religious communities tucked away in isolated places.

LANGUAGE

According US Bureau of the Census 1997 figures, about 42% of Californians over five years old speak a language other than English at home. Of those, Spanish is by far the most prevalent, spoken by about 5.5 million people, or 17%. Still, American English predominates on the streets and in places of business. You're most likely to hear foreign languages in the ethnic communities of the big cities. Los Angeles, San Francisco and most San Joaquin Valley towns have neighborhoods where Spanish, Chinese, Japanese, Vietnamese, Korean or Cambodian is the dominant language.

Street signs, billboards and menus in San Francisco's Chinatown are mostly in Chinese characters without English translation. In Southern California, geographical features and towns have Spanish names – Santa Barbara, San Diego, La Mesa, El Cajon – but these reflect early history rather than current demography (though rural areas in Southern California and the Central Valley are increasingly Latino). The many Spanish names of suburban streets reflect the desire of developers to come up with something more exotic than Main St or 5th Ave. Wouldn't you rather live on Via de la Valle than Valley Road?

Visitors to the major national parks will often find introductory brochures printed in Spanish, German, French or Japanese.

Pronunciation

Californians tend to speak casually, leaving the endings off words, skipping syllables, and running words together. *Yeah, mmmhmm,* and *uh-huh* mean 'yes'; *uh-uh* and *hmmhm* mean 'no.' Look for a nod or shake of the head to confirm: nod is 'yes'; a shake is 'no.' Dirty is pronounced 'dirdy'; 'Do you want to?' is 'd'yawana'; 'I don't know' is 'Idunno'; 'all right' is 'awright' and 'what is up?' (as in

Human Potential, Self-Realization & Actualization

Rivaling religion in California is the 'human potential' industry, with adherents who put big stock in deep, long, loving looks, and demand 'integrity' and 'space' in their 'primary relationships.' Their vocabulary, let's call it psychobabble, is an amalgam of jargon from humanistic psychology to religion and has started to become part of mainstream language – a lot of people now 'need their space,' and say 'I hear you.'

If you want to get 'deep' and 'meaningful' in your travel experience on the West Coast, plug into the fascinating network of 'facilitators,' 'seminars,' 'trainings,' and 'multilevel marketing schemes' that will bring you closer to your 'inner child,' 'true self,' and your 'soul purpose.' Just remember to act earnest, take everything at face value and keep your wallet close to your side – you may be asked to display your 'prosperity consciousness.' You might find the following phrases useful and 'validating':

actualize – to manifest one's infinite potential

affirmations – lies you tell yourself until you believe them

Are you okay with that? – Does that mesh with your higher purpose and the rantings of your inner child?

channeling – 1. wisdom from people with incredible imaginations and a penchant for Elizabethan theatrics 2. the New Age's answer to speaking in tongues

EST – Erhard Seminar Training. Also known as 'Zen for the Masses.' A human potential process named after former used-car salesman Werner Erhard. Features long-winded lectures and a major league sales spiel. Now known as 'The Forum' or 'Landmark Education'

higher self – your in-tune, in-touch, spiritually together self just waiting to be accessed if you only buy the speaker's book

I honor that – 'I respect what you're saying.' Probably the most annoying of all psychobabble. The key here, as with most psychobabble, is to have an air of earnest authenticity and seriousness about your delivery

I need my space – room to think, breathe or cheat on your spouse

I have problems with that – your action or point of view violates a carefully worked out, ironclad, and rather PC view I have of the world

issues – 1. deep psychological difficulties best resolved through hugely overpriced workshops or therapy, eg, 'It appears you have issues with your father.' 2. a very effective come-on used by facilitators and therapists across the US

male bonding – homoerotic drumming sessions for straight men, easily replaced by smoking cigars or comparing tool collections

newage – the derogatory pronunciation of 'New Age'; rhymes with 'sewage'

past life regression – you and 10,000 other people were Cleopatra in a past life

share – a psychobabbler speaks: 'I'd like to share something with the group.'

Thank you for sharing – a way for a facilitator to get the last word in after someone's sharing.

victim – all psychobabblers have been victims – of something – at one time or another. This is the deepest purpose of their lives.

'what is going on?') sometimes comes out as simply 'sup?'

Greetings & Civilities

Greetings are fairly uncomplicated, with the standard 'hello,' 'hi,' 'good morning,' 'good afternoon,' 'how are you?' and the more colloquial 'hey,' 'hey there,' and 'howdy' among the options. There's more variety with a farewell, including 'bye,' 'goodbye,' 'bye-bye,' 'see ya,' 'take it easy,' 'later,' 'take care,' 'don't work too hard,' and the loathsome 'have a nice day.'

While Americans run short on 'please,' they say 'thank you' after almost anything. You'll hear 'excuse me' instead of 'sorry.' In a conversation, the listener will interject 'mm-hmmm' or 'uh-huh' frequently to let the speaker know they're paying attention and want them to go on. It's a much more enthusiastic style than the judgment-reserving 'mmm.' For some talkers, the enthusiastic 'uh-huhs' aren't enough, and they will pepper their speech with 'y'know' or 'you hear what I'm saying?' – which is not a strictly literal question.

So-Cal Speak

California's most recognized dialect, the style presented in songs and movies, comes from the beaches and shopping malls of Southern California (also called 'So-Cal'). This casual manner of speaking – which is forever evolving – is usually called 'surfer' or 'valley' talk (as in San Fernando Valley), though the two unofficial dialects are very similar. While it may be difficult to believe that people actually talk this way...it's like totally true. Check it out, dude.

The most common zones (places) to scope out (observe) this lingo (language) are on So-Cal (Southern California) beaches, especially where there is killer (good) wave action (surf) and a mellow scene (ambience). This kind of rap (talk) doesn't necessarily reflect the speaker's intelligence or level of education as much as where he or she has been hangin' (as in hanging around).

Killer, *bitchin'*, *awesome*, *sweet*, *stylin'* and *stellar* basically mean 'really good.' *Bunk*, *nappy*, *shitty*, and *slack* mean 'really bad,' and *hairy* means 'scary.' *Gnarly* and *insane* can mean anything extreme, just like *totally* or *hella* put before a word makes its meaning more significant (for example, gnarly or insane waves might be totally killer or totally hairy). *Vibes* are feelings or indications you get from a person or place, and can be good, bad or *weird* (strange).

A *dude* can be male or female and is often precluded by *hey*, the common term for 'hi.' To *cruise* means 'to go,' by foot, car, bike or skateboard. *All right* and *right on* are confirmations that you and whoever you're speaking with are *on the same wavelength* (have similar understanding).

Lots of subcommunities based on common work and leisure interests generate new words and usages at an incredible rate. Californian language is not constrained by tradition. And the catch-all *cool* can be used in almost any situation to indicate agreement, disagreement or anything else the heart desires: Ketchup with that, ma'am? Cool!

San Francisco

Head up to San Francisco's Twin Peaks on a clear summer evening, and you'll see a postcard-perfect view: rows of Victorian houses stretching over more than 40 hills, a curvaceous bay speckled with sailboats, two of the world's best-loved bridges and perhaps a few harmless shreds of the city's famous fog colored in shades of red and pink by the setting sun. It's easy to see why San Francisco consistently tops the polls as America's favorite city. No other city in the US can offer such a seductive sight.

Like all great cities, San Francisco is an amalgam of distinct neighborhoods – vital urban pockets hidden among the hills, compressed into the 7-by-7-mile thumbnail of a peninsula. Colorful, crowded and frenetic Chinatown jostles up against ritzy Union Square and quickly fades to the bars, cafes and Italian restaurants of North Beach, the Beat center of the 1950s. North Beach blends into Fisherman's Wharf, an unapologetic tourist center and jumping-off point for Alcatraz. A hike up hoity-toity Nob Hill segues down to the troubled Tenderloin, the swank department stores of Union Square and the sleek towers of the Financial District. South of Market (the SoMa) offers its own contrasts – a busy warehouse district during the day, nightclub central after dark. The Mission District, a Latino enclave interspersed with hip bars and restaurants, also embodies several personalities. The nearby Castro was claimed by gays in the 1970s, and it remains predominantly gay today, though projecting an assured, almost mainstream, air.

The city abounds with creative energy fed by the richness of its diverse cultures and lifestyles. No aspect of San Francisco life better reflects this cultural exchange than its cuisine. The city is one of the world's great dining centers, with everything from Mexican and Asian cheap eats to stylish restaurants that liberally mix traditions from every continent on the planet.

These are good times for San Francisco. The city has rebounded from recent financial slumps and earthquakes, and though there will no doubt be more setbacks and quakes down the line, for now the city is enjoying itself. San Franciscans are jamming into restaurants, cafes, bars and nightclubs, and more of these establishments are opening all over town all the time to satisfy the demands of a city hell-bent on having a good time.

Highlights

- A perfect Sunday – world-class art at SFMOMA, live music and a picnic at Yerba Buena Gardens
- That taco can run – 100,000 costumed runners in the zany Bay to Breakers in late May
- The (colorful) streets of San Francisco – Haight St, Mission St, Castro St, Grant Ave and Columbus Ave
- Folsom St Fair – leather, whips and naked parading
- Movie palaces – the Castro Theatre, the Metro and the Balboa

HISTORY

San Francisco is a new city. Though Miwok and Ohlone Indians settled the area around 1100 BC, it was less than 250 years ago that San Francisco Bay was 'discovered' by Gaspar de Portolá. In 1769, Portolá and his party had been sent north from San Diego to establish a Spanish mission at Monterey Bay, which Sebastián Vizcaíno, an earlier Spanish explorer, had described as a 'fine, enclosed harbor.' Portolá actually found Monterey Bay, but because the bay did not match Vizcaíno's description, Portola's party continued north. In early November 1769, a detachment of the expedition led by Sergeant José Ortega first set eyes on San Francisco Bay. Realizing they had gone too far, Portolá turned back.

In 1772, a second party led by Don Pedro Fages and Father Juan Crespi set off from the recently built mission in Monterey to have a better look at the bay Ortega had discovered. They were understandably impressed with what they saw; as Crespi noted, 'It is a harbor such that not only the navy of our most Catholic Majesty but those of all Europe could take shelter in it.' The Spanish returned in 1775, when Juan Manuel de Ayala sailed into the bay and became the first European to enter what was later nicknamed the 'Golden Gate.' The following year the presidio was built just above the Golden Gate, and the Misión San Francisco de Asís (Mission Dolores) was established 3 miles south, at a site that today is in the heart of the Mission District.

The mission settlement never really prospered: the soil was sandy and difficult to farm; the presidio rarely exceeded 20 soldiers; and the harbor saw little trade. Not until Mexico gained its independence from Spain did the local economy, based on the hide and tallow trade, begin to show some life. Trading posts, houses, grocery stores and grog shops appeared on the slopes that rose from the bay.

In 1846, war broke out between the US and Mexico. With the American victory in the Mexican War, Mexico ceded the land to the US – excellent timing, because gold was discovered in 1848 in the nearby Sierra Nevada foothills. Almost overnight the sleepy Mexican village of Yerba Buena, newly renamed San Francisco, grew into a full-fledged city. By 1850, the year California was admitted as the 31st state in the union, San Francisco's population had exploded from 800 to 25,000. The newcomers, called '49ers, were mostly men under the age of 40. To keep them entertained, some 500 saloons and 20 theaters opened in the space of five years, not to mention casinos and bordellos, opium dens and distilleries. Certain sin-loving streets in the vicinity of the port (now the northeastern edge of the Financial District) were well on their way to earning the sobriquet 'Barbary Coast' (see 'Legends of the Barbary Coast' boxed text in this section).

San Francisco remained a world-class hotbed of murder and mayhem until April 18, 1906, when the 'Big One' – an earthquake estimated at 8.3 on the yet-to-be-invented Richter scale – and dozens of ensuing fires leveled more than half of the city and killed upwards of 3000 people. The Big One destroyed much of the red-light district, giving the city an opportunity to rebuild itself. San Francisco rapidly reconstructed itself, developing into a bustling modern city. In 1915, San Francisco hosted the Panama-Pacific Exposition, allowing the city to flaunt its stylish new image.

San Francisco still suffered through the Great Depression and, like other cities, gigantic public works projects were one of the attempts to yank the economy out of the doldrums. The Bay Area certainly got its money's worth from these 1930s projects; the Bay Bridge, built in 1936, and the Golden Gate Bridge, built the following year, are still magnificent symbols of the city.

During WWII, the Bay Area became a major launching pad for military operations in the Pacific and huge shipyards soon sprang up around the bay, boosting the population to the highest it's ever been (more than 795,000).

The decades that follow are marked by the prominence of colorful subcultures: the Beats spearheaded the '50s counterculture, and the hippies followed in the '60s. If marijuana was the drug of choice for the 1950s, then LSD was the '60s trip, along with guitar-driven rock music, long hair and 'flower power.' In January 1967, an estimated 20,000 'hippies' – the term was originally a put-down coined by the now-older beatniks who didn't dig these younger hipsters – congregated in Golden Gate Park for a free concert, kicking off the 'Summer of Love.' Across the bay, however, peace and love were not the order of the day. While hippies in the Haight were dropping LSD and wearing flowers in their hair, Berkeley revolutionaries were leading the worldwide student upheavals of the late '60s, slugging it out with the cops and the university administration over civil rights. Meanwhile, in Oakland, Huey Newton and Bobby Seale

SAN FRANCISCO

founded the Black Panther Party for Self-Defense, the most militant of the groups involved in the black-power movement of that era.

After the realignments and upheavals of the '60s, the '70s were comparatively relaxed. The hippies had led a sexual revolution but it was a predominantly heterosexual one; a homosexual revolution followed in the '70s, as San Francisco's gays stepped decisively out of the closet. Gay Pride became a rallying call, and the previously underground homosexual community 'came out' in all its glory.

The 1980s were not especially kind to San Francisco. The first cases of AIDS – at the time known as GRID, Gay-Related Immune Deficiency – were reported in 1981; by the end of the '80s, AIDS had claimed thousands of lives. The late 1980s witnessed yet another startling catastrophe – the Loma Prieta earthquake, which struck on October 17, 1989. It measured 7.1 on the Richter scale, and its damage was far reaching. A section of the Bay Bridge was damaged, the Marina District burned and, in the quake's worst disaster, a double-decker section of I-880 in Oakland collapsed, killing 42 people.

The 1990s ushered in one of the city's great periods of growth. Throughout the decade, the get-rich-quick delirium of Reaganomics helped boost the city's restaurant industry, and San Francisco established

Legends of the Barbary Coast

By the mid-1860s, the notoriety of San Francisco's Barbary Coast, an area of the city roughly defined by Pacific Ave and Stockton, Jackson and Montgomery Sts, had spread round the globe. Its name was decided on more or less by a worldwide consensus that it bore some resemblance to the pirate-plagued coast of North Africa, home of the Berbers.

The heart of the district – described in 1869 as a 'cesspool of rottenness' by a *San Francisco Chronicle* reporter – was Devil's Acre. (Other features on the neighborhood map were Deadman's Alley and Murder Point.) The reporter went on to say: 'Ribald song and bawdy jest float through the polluted atmosphere with the squeal of fiddles and tumming of banjoes. Sometimes in the midst of the noise there is a shot, a curse, a shriek, a groan, and another hulk whirls down the dark whirlpool of death.'

At the time, women were so scarce in California that they could attract a crowd merely by walking down the street. Female singers and dancers of minimal training were therefore prime attractions at the city's first burlesque dance halls, which early San Franciscans called 'melodeons.' Prostitutes were equally in demand, and brothels, called 'cribs' in those early days, did a brisk business.

Another feature of the Barbary Coast was its 'crimps,' proprietors of boardinghouses who did a lucrative business providing crews to ships through highly nefarious means. Boarders would be allowed to run up exorbitant tabs on wine, women and song until they were indebted to the crimp. Through arrangements with ship captains, the crimps would sell their boarders' debts in exchange for advances on the boarders' wages; when a vessel set sail from San Francisco, it was often with a crew of indentured servants.

The most notorious practice of the crimps was that of 'shanghaiing,' in which saloon keepers treated a sailor fresh in town to free drinks containing 'knockout drops.' The sailor was then relieved of his money and possessions and eventually awoke with an unwanted job aboard a ship already on its way to China.

In 1917, California invoked its Red-Light Abatement Act and police blockaded the Barbary Coast, effectively shutting down 83 brothels and 40 saloons all at once, marking the end of the Barbary Coast's most colorful chapter.

itself as an internationally recognized culinary force. San Francisco has continued this remarkable growth trend and has cemented its reputation as the cultural and economic focal point of Northern California.

ORIENTATION

San Francisco is a compact city, covering the tip of a 30-mile-long peninsula, with the Pacific Ocean on one side and San Francisco Bay on the other. The city can be neatly divided into three sections. The central part resembles a slice of pie, with Van Ness Ave and Market St marking the two sides and the Embarcadero the rounded edge of the pie. Squeezed into this compact slice are the Union Square area, the Financial District, the Civic Center area, Chinatown, North Beach, Nob Hill, Russian Hill and Fisherman's Wharf.

To the south of Market St lies the South of Market (SoMa) area, an upwardly mobile warehouse zone. SoMa fades into the Mission, the city's Latino quarter, and then the Castro, the city's gay quarter.

The third and final part of the city is physically the largest – the long sweep from Van Ness Ave all the way to the Pacific Ocean. It's a varied area encompassing upscale neighborhoods such as the Marina and Pacific Heights, less pricey zones such as the Richmond and Sunset districts and areas with flavors all their own, such as Japantown and the Haight. The city's three great parks –

Scenic 49 Mile Drive

Make some stops along the way, and the 49 Mile Scenic Drive could take you all day. Devised for the 1939-40 Treasure Island Exposition, the drive covers almost all the city's highlights, from Coit Tower to the Golden Gate Bridge. Although the route is well signposted with instantly recognizable seagull signs, a map and an alert navigator are still helpful. Pick up a map at the San Francisco Visitors Information Center (see Information).

the Presidio, Lincoln Park and Golden Gate Park – are also in this area.

See Getting Around at the end of this chapter for public transportation options within San Francisco.

Maps

Quality maps of San Francisco are available from bookstores, but giveaway maps from a variety of sources are generally adequate for most visitors. The best of the free maps is the *San Francisco Street Map & Visitor Guide*, available at many of the city's hotels. If you're going to explore the city by public transportation, the Muni *Street & Transit Map* is a smart $2 investment. Get a copy at the Visitors Information Center or any large bookstore. The Rand McNally Map Store (Map 2; ☎ 415-777-3131), 595 Market St at 2nd St, is a good place to pick up maps.

For convenience, nothing beats the *Streetwise San Francisco* map. It's close to pocket size yet still legible, and laminated for durability. Several detailed street atlases to the Bay Area are put out by Thomas Bros Maps; you can pick one up at their store (☎ 415-981-7520), 550 Jackson St at Columbus Ave, or at most bookstores.

INFORMATION
Tourist Offices

In the heart of the city, a stone's throw from Union Square and right by the most popular cable car turnaround, the San Francisco Visitors Information Center (☎ 415-391-2000) is at the lower level of Hallidie Plaza at Market and Powell Sts. It's open 9 am to 5:30 pm weekdays, 9 am to 3 pm Saturday and 10 am to 2 pm Sunday.

The center has a 24-hour phone service offering recorded 'what's on' information in English (☎ 415-391-2001), French (☎ 415-391-2003), German (☎ 415-391-2004), Spanish (☎ 415-391-2122) and Japanese (☎ 415-391-2101).

Money

Banks are ubiquitous in San Francisco and usually offer the best rates for currency exchange. San Francisco International Airport has a currency exchange office at the

Bank of America International Terminal branch (☎ 650-742-8080) and in Boarding Area D; hours are 7 am to 11 pm daily.

If you have a credit card or traveler's checks issued by American Express, you can exchange most foreign currencies at American Express offices (☎ 415-398-8578) at 124 Geary St between Grant Ave and Stockton St and near Fisherman's Wharf at 333 Jefferson St (☎ 415-775-0240).

Post & Communications

The main San Francisco post office (Map 2; ☎ 800-725-2161) is the Civic Center Post Office, 101 Hyde St. Mail can be sent to you here marked c/o General Delivery, San Francisco, CA 94142, USA. Post offices are generally open 9 am to 5 pm weekdays, 9 am to 1 pm Saturday. There's also a post office (☎ 800-275-8777) in the basement of Macy's department store on Union Square, open 10 am to 5:30 pm Monday to Saturday, 11 am to 5 pm Sunday.

Public phones usually cost 35¢ for local calls, more if you're calling to Marin County, the East Bay or the Peninsula.

Starting in October 1999, San Francisco and Marin counties received an area code overlay – a new area code added within the same area. Local calls within the 415 area must be made as if calling long distance, dial 1 + the three-digit area code + the seven-digit number. Directory assistance (☎ 411) and the emergency number (☎ 911) are still dialed with three numbers.

Email & Internet Access

Most of the city's public libraries are equipped to allow Web browsing and access to chat groups, though not to send or receive email. The main branch (☎ 415-557-4400), at Larkin and Grove Sts, near the Civic Center BART/Muni station, has 160 terminals. Staff also can provide information on Internet access throughout the city.

For easy access to all the online services, a group called CafeNet has placed coin-operated (25¢ per five minutes) computer stations in cafes throughout the city. Among the most convenient are Yakety Yak (Map 2; ☎ 415-885-6908), 679 Sutter St, and Muddy

Waters Coffeehouse (☎ 415-621-2233), 260 Church St near Market St.

Travel Agencies

Good travel agents include STA Travel (☎ 415-391-8407) at 51 Grant Ave, and Council Travel at 530 Bush St near Grant Ave (☎ 415-421-3473) or at 919 Irving St (☎ 415-566-6222) in the Sunset District.

Bookstores

Many city bookstores are open late, often every night of the week. Try the ever-popular A Clean Well-Lighted Place for Books (☎ 415-441-6670), 601 Van Ness Ave in Opera Plaza, near the Civic Center. Borders Books and Music (☎ 415-399-1633), a huge bookstore with a cafe, is on the northwest corner of Union Square at Post and Powell Sts.

San Francisco's most famous bookstore, City Lights (Map 3; ☎ 415-362-8193), 261 Columbus Ave in North Beach, was the first paperbacks-only bookstore in the US. It was also the center of the Beat scene in the '50s and is still owned by its founder, poet Lawrence Ferlinghetti.

The Rizzoli Bookstore (☎ 415-984-0225), downtown at 117 Post St, is a pleasant place to browse. Booksmith (☎ 415-863-8688), 1644 Haight St, is a general bookstore in the most ungeneral of neighborhoods. Green Apple Books (☎ 415-387-2272), 506 Clement St between 6th and 7th Aves in the Richmond District, is one of the best bookstores in the city.

In Noe Valley, Phoenix Books (☎ 415-821-3477), 3850 24th St, has a decent collection of new and used books. Its sister shop in the Mission, Dog Eared Books (Map 5; ☎ 415-282-1901), 900 Valencia St, has a strong section on queer studies. A Different Light Bookstore (Map 5; ☎ 415-431-0891), 489 Castro St in the Castro, is one of the city's largest gay and lesbian booksellers.

Newspapers

The Bay Area's number-one daily, the *San Francisco Chronicle*, is definitely not one of the great newspapers in the US. It's supplemented by the evening *San Francisco*

SAN FRANCISCO

Examiner. On Sundays they get together to produce the *San Francisco Examiner-Chronicle*, which includes the helpful Datebook, called the 'Pink Section' by locals, an entertainment supplement printed on pink pages.

Two free weekly papers, the *San Francisco Bay Guardian* and the *SF Weekly*, have intelligent coverage of local events and politics, plus superb restaurant, film and arts reviews. They also have colorful personal ads.

Harold's International Newsstand (☎ 415-441-2665), at 524 Geary St near Union Square, has a good selection of out-of-town newspapers. Café de la Presse (Map 2; ☎ 415-398-2680), 352 Grant Ave at Bush St, opposite the Chinatown gate, sells European newspapers and magazines. Both places are open 7 am to 11 pm daily.

Laundry

Self-service laundries are easy to find in most residential parts of the city; typical costs are $1.25 to $1.50 for washing and 25¢ per 10-minute drying cycle. Be warned that theft is not unheard of in Laundromats – keep an eye on your dryers.

To liven up the drudgery of wash day, try Brain Wash (Map 2; ☎ 415-255-4866), 1122 Folsom St in SoMa, where you can hang out in the cafe and listen to live music while waiting for your clothes.

Medical Services

Check the Yellow Pages under 'Physicians & Surgeons' or 'Clinics' to find a doctor. For a dentist, call the Dental Information Service (☎ 415-398-0618). In real emergencies, call ☎ 911 for an ambulance.

If you are looking for an emergency room under your own power, head to San Francisco General Hospital (☎ 415-206-8000), 1001 Potrero Ave. Be aware that the base fee is $125 for an emergency-room visit.

For nonemergency situations, call the Haight Ashbury Free Clinic (☎ 415-487-5632), 558 Clayton St just off Haight St. Appointments are required, but once you're in, a doctor will see you free of charge.

For women's health issues, contact Planned Parenthood (☎ 415-441-5454), 815 Eddy St, Suite 200, or the St Luke's Women's Center (☎ 415-285-7788), 1650 Valencia St.

Dangers & Annoyances

Like most big US cities, San Francisco has its share of crime, but prudent travelers are not at any undue risk. Certain neighborhoods are seedier than others and considered relatively 'unsafe,' especially at night and for those walking alone; these include the Tenderloin, parts of the Mission, the Western Addition and 6th and 7th Sts south of Market. However, these areas are not always sharply defined, and travelers should be aware of their surroundings whenever they walk in the city.

After dark, some of the city's parks, particularly Dolores Park and Buena Vista Park, become havens for drug dealing and sleazy sex. Bayview-Hunters Point, a poor and largely black neighborhood north of 3Com (Candlestick) Park, where the 49ers play, is not a place for wandering tourists.

If you find yourself somewhere you would rather not be, act confident and sure of yourself; then go into a store and call a taxi.

UNION SQUARE (MAP 2)

Union Square, which gets its name from the pro-Union rallies that took place there during the Civil War, is San Francisco's downtown tourist center. The square is surrounded on all sides by pricey hotels, airline offices and classy shops (including the city's main department stores). The center of the square is dominated by the 97-foot-high **Dewey Monument**, built in 1903 to commemorate Admiral George Dewey's 1898 defeat of the Spanish fleet at Manila Bay, paving the way for the Philippines to become a US territory. Among the buildings flanking the square is the 1904 **Westin St Francis Hotel**, which features in many Dashiell Hammett novels, most notably *The Maltese Falcon*.

In the Grand Hyatt plaza, on Stockton St just off the square, sculptor Ruth Asawa's bronze **Children's Fountain** portrays San Francisco's history in intricate and playful detail. It's worth stepping into the 1982 **Neiman-Marcus Building**, 150 Stockton St, to look up at its stained-glass dome, a hallmark feature of the 1909 City of Paris store that once occupied the site.

On the east side of the square, **Maiden Lane** is crowded with pricey salons and boutiques. This lane had a previous incarnation very much at odds with its present upscale image. Before the 1906 earthquake, Maiden Lane, known then as Morton St, was lined with bordellos and known as one of the bawdiest dives in a city renowned for racy living. During the rebuilding, the city fathers endowed it with its hopeful new name and cleaned up its image to match. The 1949 **Folk Art International Building** (☎ 415-392-9999), 140 Maiden Lane, is the city's only Frank Lloyd Wright building. Have a look at its interior – the spiral walkway marks it as Wright's practice run for the Guggenheim Museum in New York.

The city's famous cable cars groan along Powell St, on the west side of Union Square, to and from the Hallidie Plaza **cable car terminus**, named after the cable car's inventor. This is the most popular and crowded spot to catch a cable car.

San Francisco's dense **theater district** lies immediately southwest of the square, crumbling from there into the dismal Tenderloin.

CIVIC CENTER (MAP 2)

The compact Civic Center area is a study in contrasts, where the city's architectural and cultural aspirations collide head-on with its human problems. Separating City Hall and the Opera House from downtown are the grubby blocks of the **Tenderloin**, an area plagued by gangs, prostitution and porn. If you proceed south down Jones St, you will notice that each block, from Post to Geary to O'Farrell, is slightly more dicey than the previous one. Ellis St, one block below O'Farrell, is even more dangerous, with considerable gang activity.

Long dragged down by its proximity to the Tenderloin, Civic Center appears to be priming itself for a rebirth, partly thanks to the impressively restored **City Hall** (☎ 415-554-4000) at 400 Van Ness Ave. The 1906 disaster razed the earlier city hall, which was replaced in 1915 with the present beaux arts-style structure modeled after St Peter's Basilica in Vatican City. City Hall was badly damaged in the 1989 earthquake; it reopened in 1999 after a $300 million renovation program, and San Franciscans seem pleased with its new light-filled rotunda and gilt dome.

Facing City Hall across the plaza is the currently closed **Old Main Library**, slated to reopen as the new Asian Art Museum by 2000. Down the street is the **New Main Library** (☎ 415-557-4400), which opened in 1996 and cost $134 million. Even if you hate books, the library is worth visiting for its architecture – five stories built around a naturally lit, semicircular atrium – and its newspaper and magazine reading room (free and stocked with many international titles).

Across Hyde St beyond the two library buildings is **United Nations Plaza**, built to commemorate the signing of the UN Charter in San Francisco in 1945. A farmers' market is held at the plaza on Wednesday and Sunday.

Across from City Hall, the **War Memorial Opera House** (☎ 415-864-3330), 301 Van Ness Ave, built in 1932, is the venue for performances by the city's acclaimed opera and ballet companies. Adjacent to the Opera House is the **Veterans Building**, housing the **Herbst Theatre** (☎ 415-392-4400), where the UN Charter was signed in 1945. One block south is the **Louise M Davies Symphony Hall** (☎ 415-431-5400).

The three blocks of Hayes St between Franklin and Laguna Sts, just west of the opera house, constitute a small neighborhood of galleries, coffeehouses and restaurants known as **Hayes Valley**.

SOUTH OF MARKET (MAP 2)

South of Market (or SoMa) is a combination of office buildings spilling out of the Financial District, fancy condominiums popping up along the Embarcadero near the Bay Bridge, a busy tourist and convention precinct around **Yerba Buena Gardens**, and the late-night entertainment scene along Folsom St. The SoMa is a center for recent development that combines high art and low culture. It has many attractions, but parking is in short supply; public transportation is recommended.

The **Yerba Buena Gardens** (☎ 415-541-0312) is the open-air public center of SoMa. The complex includes the **Yerba Buena Center for the Arts** (☎ 415-978-2787), with galleries, short-term exhibits and a theater for performances. The center is open 11 am to 6 pm Tuesday to Sunday; $5 ($3 for students and free the first Thursday of the month). Linked to the gardens by a bridge across Howard St is the **George R Moscone Convention Center** (☎ 415-267-6400), the city's main exhibition hall.

In 1998 and 1999, several additional attractions were added to the Yerba Buena Gardens area. The **Sony Metreon Entertainment Complex** (☎ 415-369-6000), at 101 4th St, is a 350,000-sq-foot high-tech mall combining stores, restaurants, 15 movie screens, an IMAX theater and three theme-park attractions: **Airtight Garage**, an interactive computer game center and arcade designed by and based on the works of French graphic novelist Jean 'Moebius' Giraud; **The Way Things Work**, a 3-D multimedia look at the workings of common items like aerosol and zippers, based on David Macaulay's book by the same name; and **Where the Wild Things Are**, an indoor playground filled with artificial forests, sound effects, giant puppets and oversized creatures from Maurice Sendak's books.

The Metreon is open 10 am to 10 pm daily. Entry to the Metreon is free, but nearly everything in the complex is designed to separate you from your money (particularly the Airtight Garage, which like any arcade, can be a major money drain). Admission to each of the theme areas is $7/5/5 adults/seniors/children, or you can buy a Metreon All Access pass that allows entry to all three areas for $17/13/13.

Across Howard St from the Metreon on the roof of the Moscone Convention Center, the **Zeum** (☎ 415-777-2800) is a hands-on art and tech museum that encourages young people to create and produce their own works with audio, video, computer animation and more. Many of the exhibits and installations are collaborations between Bay Area teenagers and local artists. The Zeum also has a restored **carousel** ($1) originally from Playland at the Beach, an amusement park at San Francisco's Ocean Beach from 1921 to 1972. The Zeum is open noon to 6 pm Wednesday, Thursday and Friday, 11 am to 5 pm Saturday and Sunday; $7/6/5 (children 5 to 18).

Also on the rooftop of the Moscone Center is a more prosaic attraction, the **Yerba Buena Ice Skating and Bowling Center** (☎ 415-777-3727). The bowling center is open 9 am to 10 pm Sunday to Thursday, 9 am to midnight Friday and Saturday; games cost $3.50/2/2 per game, $18/12/12 per hour. Admission to the skate center is $6/4.50/4.50, and skate rental costs $2. The center is open daily for public skating; call for the schedule.

The excellent **San Francisco Museum of Modern Art** (SFMOMA; ☎ 415-357-4000), 151 3rd St, is directly across from the Yerba Buena Gardens. In 1995 the SFMOMA moved into its new home, a striking modernist design by Swiss architect Mario Botta. The permanent collection is particularly strong in American abstract expressionism, with major works by Clyfford Still, Jackson Pollock and Philip Guston. The SFMOMA's photography collection is also world class, with works by Ansel Adams, Edward Weston, Robert Frank, Dorothea Lange and William Klein. The SFMOMA is open 11 am to 6 pm daily except Wednesday (11 am to 9 pm Thursday); $8/5/4 adults/seniors/students (free first Tuesday of the month).

The **Ansel Adams Center for Photography** (☎ 415-495-7000), 250 4th St, is dedicated to photography as an art form, with particular reference to Ansel Adams; it's open 11 am to 5 pm Tuesday to Sunday; $5/2/3 adults/seniors/students (admission is free for children). The worthwhile **Cartoon Art Museum** (☎ 415-227-8666), 814 Mission St, features constantly changing exhibits of cartoon art. It's open 11 am to 5 pm Wednesday to Friday, 10 am to 5 pm Saturday, 1 to 5 pm Sunday; $4/3/2.

The **Jewish Museum of San Francisco** (☎ 415-543-8880), 121 Steuart St near the Ferry Building, has changing exhibits on Jewish life. It's open 11 am to 5 pm Sunday to Wednesday, 11 am to 8 pm Thursday; $5/2.50 adults/seniors (free for children).

Close to the waterfront, the **Rincon Center** occupies the entire block bounded by Mission, Howard, Steuart and Spear Sts. The building – with a shopping center and office buildings – is itself a treasure: look for the dolphin friezes on the facade and the massive murals inside depicting California's history. The latter were completed in 1948 by Anton Refregier. Viewing the murals is free.

The USS *Jeremiah O'Brien* (☎ 415-441-3101), the sole surviving WWII Liberty ship in complete working order, is on display at Pier 32, just south of the Bay Bridge. It had an illustrious history, including 11 voyages as part of the D-Day landings at Normandy.

The ship is open 9 am to 3 pm weekdays, 9 am to 4 pm weekends; $5/3/2 adults/seniors/children.

FINANCIAL DISTRICT (MAP 2)

The city's tall buildings are densely concentrated in the blocks from Union Square to the bay. This is the city's banking center, San Francisco's core business since banks started to appear in the 1850s to handle the state's gold rush fortunes. It's a frantically busy area during the day, with taxis, power-dressing business people and suicidal bike messengers all competing for street space. Come dark it's a different animal; apart from a handful of restaurants and bars, the district is nearly deserted.

Emperor Norton

Emperor Norton I, born Joshua Abraham Norton in 1819, came to San Francisco as a young man and made a fortune off the city's boomtown economy. In 1852, he lost everything in a business gamble and never recovered. After eight years of increasing poverty he seemed to have snapped. He declared himself Emperor of the United States, and within a month added the title Protector of Mexico.

Norton spent the next 20 years of his life as a local icon and widely loved mascot of San Francisco, living an oddly dignified life and causing no one any harm. He never appeared without his uniform, with bulky epaulets, a plumed hat and a sword at his hip. He issued his own scrip in 50¢, $5 and $10 denominations, and though it became mainly a collector's item, it was good-naturedly accepted by many shopkeepers. Thousands of people attended Norton's funeral in 1880; he now rests in Woodlawn Cemetery.

Among the many decrees Norton made as emperor, such as that to dissolve the republican form of government in the US, was his famous injunction against the use of the word 'Frisco':

Courtesy of the Bancroft Library

Whoever after due and proper warning shall be heard to utter the abominable word 'Frisco,' which has no linguistic or other warrant, shall be deemed guilty of a High Misdemeanor, and shall pay into the Imperial Treasury as penalty the sum of $25.

– Chris Carlsson

Visiting the Financial District is essentially an architectural experience. The completion of the **Bank of America Building** in 1969 ushered in a new era for San Francisco's previously low-rise skyline. Not only was the 52-story, 761-foot building at 555 California St much higher than any earlier building, but its red South Dakota granite construction looked very different from the city's consistent pale coloring.

San Francisco's highest building, the 853-foot **Transamerica Pyramid**, 600 Montgomery St, was completed in 1972, and though it was initially reviled, it quickly became a modern symbol of the city. The Transamerica Center includes a half-acre stand of redwood trees in **Redwood Plaza**, where lunchtime concerts take place on Fridays mid-May through September.

After the Transamerica Pyramid, the cylindrical tower at **101 California St** is probably the most instantly recognizable of the city's tall buildings. The Gothic 1928 **Russ Building**, 253 Montgomery St, was the tallest in the city from its creation until 1964.

Other buildings of note in the district include the 1930 **Pacific Stock Exchange** at 301 Pine St and the 1908 **Bank of California Building** at 400 California St, fronted by Corinthian columns and housing the **Museum of Money of the American West** (☎ 415-765-0400) in its basement. The free museum is open 9 am to 5 pm weekdays.

The small but interesting **Wells Fargo History Museum** (☎ 415-396-2619), 420 Montgomery St, tells the story of Wells Fargo Bank, the company founded in 1852 to provide banking and stagecoach delivery services to miners and businesses throughout the West Coast. The museum is free and open 9 am to 5 pm weekdays. At the corner of Market and New Montgomery Sts, the luxurious **Palace Hotel** (☎ 415-512-1111), now the Sheraton Palace Hotel, opened in 1875 as the most opulent hotel in the city. Along the way, it killed its creator, William Ralston, who was driven to bankruptcy and a heart attack by financial pressures. Take an afternoon tea in the leafy Garden Court and contemplate the 1991 renovation, which cost more than $100 million.

The waterfront **Embarcadero**, once the cities busiest area, was killed first by the two bridges across the bay, which ended the ferry boat era, and then by the death of the old-style wharves, superseded by the container ship era. Completed in 1898, the **Ferry Building**, at the bottom of California and Market Sts, had its heyday in the 1920s and '30s, up until the completion of the bridges.

Four skyscrapers mark the huge **Embarcadero Center** between Sacramento and Clay Sts, starting on Embarcadero at the Park Hyatt and Justin Herman Plaza, a popular lunch spot for Financial District workers. At the base of the four buildings (Embarcadero 1 to 4) is a mix of shops and restaurants and a post office.

NOB HILL (MAP 2)

Nob Hill is a classy district perched atop one of the city's famous hills. When the cable cars arrived in the 1870s and made the 338-foot summit accessible, the elite moved in and promptly built the most opulent mansions in the city. Mark Hopkins and Collis P Huntington were the builders who, with financiers Charles Crocker and Leland Stanford, made fortunes from the Central Pacific Railroad. Stanford, Huntington and Hopkins have given their names to Nob Hill hotels – The Huntington, Mark Hopkins and Stanford Court. Crocker's name is applied to a bank, and Stanford went on to become governor of California and to found Stanford University.

Besides hotels and their top-floor bars, Nob Hill has **Grace Cathedral** (☎ 415-749-6300), 1100 California St. The bronze doors are casts of Ghiberti's *Gates of Paradise* in the Cathedral Baptistry of St John in Florence, Italy, and the magnificent rose window was made in Chartres, France, in 1964. Also of note is the Keith Haring altarpiece, *The Life of Christ*, dedicated in 1995 by the AIDS Memorial Chapel Project.

The **Cable Car Barn & Museum** (☎ 415-474-1887), 1201 Mason St, dates from 1910 and is the power plant that tows all the cable cars, the garage where the cable cars park at night, and a museum displaying, among other things, inventor Andrew Hallidie's

Cable Cars

The Transamerica Pyramid and the Golden Gate Bridge make fine city symbols, but San Francisco has another, older icon, the beloved cable car. Cable cars were conceived by English mining engineer Andrew Hallidie as a replacement for the horse-pulled trams that found the city's steep streets difficult and dangerous.

From Hallidie's first experimental line on Clay St in 1873, cable cars quickly caught on, and by 1890 the cable car system had eight operators, 500 cable cars and a route network of more than 100 miles. By the turn of the century, the system was already past its heyday and shrinking in the face of newfangled electric streetcars. The 1906 earthquake was a disaster for the cable car system, but the death knell sounded in January 1947, when the mayor announced the last lines would be replaced by bus services. He hadn't reckoned with Friedel Klussmann's Citizens Committee to Save the Cable Cars and a groundswell of public support that reprieved the Powell St lines.

San Franciscans may have saved the system from politicians and accountants, but saving it from old age became a new problem as derailments and runaways became increasingly frequent. A six-month shutdown in 1979 for a million dollars' worth of repairs was just a Band-Aid solution, and in 1982 the system was finally closed for a $60 million complete overhaul. The rebuilt system, which reopened in 1984, consists of 40 cars on three lines covering a total of 12 miles.

🚲 🚲 🚲 🚲 🚲 🚲

original Clay St cable car. The museum is open 10 am to 5 pm daily (10 am to 6 pm in summer); free.

CHINATOWN (MAP 3)

Chinatown is the most densely packed pocket of the city, and perhaps the most colorful. There are no essential sights, and no single place in Chinatown that a visitor absolutely *must* see. However, it's a great place for casual wandering, soaking up the hectic atmosphere and stumbling across interesting little corners and alleys.

Packed with shops and restaurants, **Grant Ave** has had a colorful history from its inception as Calle de la Fundación, the main street of the Mexican village of Yerba Buena. Renamed Dupont St, or *Du Pon Gai* to the Chinese, the street became known for brothels, gambling dives, opium dens and brawling *tongs* (Chinese gangs). Dupont St was renamed for president and Civil War general Ulysses S Grant when he died in 1885. Get off touristy Grant Ave for a more authentic Chinatown experience – scruffy apothecary shops, multicolored overhanging balconies and backstreet restaurants with glazed ducks dangling in the windows. The most colorful time to visit is during the Chinese New Year in late January/early February, with a parade and fireworks and other festivities, though the day-to-day bustle of Chinatown is reason enough to visit.

Chinatown visits usually begin at the dragon-studded **Chinatown Gate** at the Bush St entrance to Grant Ave. The Taoist **Ching Chung Temple** (☎ 415-433-2623), at 532 Grant Ave, is open daily. It isn't a spectacular sight, but this is as good a look at behind-the-scenes Chinatown as you're likely to get. (Though no one is likely to tell you so, bear in mind that shorts and T-shirts are not considered respectful attire in a temple, and photography is generally frowned upon.) At the intersection with California St is **Old St Mary's Church** (☎ 415-986-4388); its 90-foot tower was the tallest building in the city when it was completed in 1854. **St Mary's Square**, off California St, is one of few large open spaces in Chinatown. When Chinatown was cleaned up in the late 19th century, the brothels, gambling dens and bars from all over the area were concentrated here, only to burn down in the aftermath of the 1906 earthquake.

Visitors are welcome in the **Kong Chow Temple** (☎ 415-434-2513), on the 4th floor at 55 Stockton St, above the post office. The **Chinese Consolidated Benevolent Building,**

843 Stockton St, houses its namesake organization, also known as the 'Six Companies,' which during the 19th century fought for Chinese legal rights and served as an arbitrator in disputes between Chinese people.

For a good idea of off-the-main-street Chinatown, duck into colorful **Waverly Place**, between Grant Ave and Stockton St, with its many open balconies and upstairs temples. Just to the right, when you emerge onto Washington St, is Sam Wo's, a hole-in-the-wall Chinese restaurant renowned for its gruff waiters. Beat writer Jack Kerouac supposedly learned how to use chopsticks here.

A few steps in the opposite direction along Washington St, take a right turn into narrow **Ross Alley**, another picturesque lane. Known at one time as *Gau Leuie Sung Hong* or 'Old Spanish Alley,' this small street was wall-to-wall gambling dens and brothels in the late 1870s. This is a favorite location for filmmakers, featured in films like *Big Trouble in Little China*. At 56 Ross Alley the **Golden Gate Cookie Company** (☎ 415-781-3956) turns out fortune cookies ('sexy' fortunes are a specialty). Incidentally, fortune cookies are a San Francisco invention, not a Chinese one; they were dreamed up for the Japanese Tea Garden in Golden Gate Park.

Portsmouth Square, at Kearny and Washington Sts, almost always has a crowd of young and old people talking or playing checkers, chess or mah-jongg. It was originally the plaza for the Mexican settlement of Yerba Buena, and its name comes from John B Montgomery's sloop, the *Portsmouth*. Montgomery arrived in 1846 to claim the city for the US, and a plaque commemorates the spot where the Stars and Stripes was first raised in San Francisco.

A pedestrian bridge crosses from Portsmouth Square to the **Chinese Culture Center** (☎ 415-986-1822) in the Holiday Inn at 750 Kearny St. It has free changing exhibits on Chinese art and culture and is open 10 am to 4 pm Tuesday to Saturday, noon to 4 pm Sunday.

Turn down Kearny St and left onto Commercial St to the **Chinese Historical Society Museum** (☎ 415-391-1188), 650 Commercial St. It recounts the story of the city's Chinese community and is open noon to 4 pm Tuesday to Saturday; free. The **Pacific Heritage Museum** (☎ 415-399-1124), 608 Commercial St, has exhibits on the city's Asian and Pacific connections. It's open 10 am to 4 pm Monday to Thursday, 10 am to 5 pm Friday; free.

NORTH BEACH (MAP 3)
North Beach started as the city's Italian quarter, and its Italian heritage lives on in the area's restaurants and bars. The Beats took over in the '50s and added cafes, jazz clubs and City Lights Bookstore to the mix. Today, despite gentrification and an onslaught of tourists, North Beach is one of the liveliest parts of the city and a great place for a cheap meal, a cold beer or a strong cup of coffee.

At the corner of Kearny St, the 1905 **Columbus Tower**, with its green copper cupola, has been the property of filmmaker Francis Ford Coppola since 1970. Offices for Coppola's film company, Zoetrope, are in the building.

The block of Columbus Ave from Pacific Ave to Broadway can lay claim to being the literary heart of the city. A drink at **Vesuvio Cafe**, where Dylan Thomas and Jack Kerouac are known to have pissed away a few evenings, is a fine segue to a visit to **City Lights Bookstore** (☎ 415-362-8193), just across Jack Kerouac Alley. City Lights was founded in 1953 by poet Lawrence Ferlinghetti, who still owns it. City Lights Publishers, with offices upstairs from the bookstore, became famous in 1957 when it published Ginsberg's poem 'Howl,' which was promptly banned for obscenity; a highly publicized court ruling finally allowed distribution of the poem.

At the junction of Broadway and Columbus and Grant Aves, there's another historic San Francisco cultural site. The **Condor Bistro** is a very bland replacement for the old Condor Club where, as a plaque solemnly announces, silicon-enhanced Carol Doda first went topless on June 19, 1964, and bottomless on September 3, 1969.

The **Museum of North Beach** (☎ 415-391-6210), 1435 Stockton St, in the Bay View

Bank mezzanine, has photographs and memorabilia tracing the history of this colorful area in the late 19th and early 20th centuries.

The 1924 **Saints Peter & Paul Church**, 666 Filbert St, overlooks **Washington Square**, North Beach's cultural focal point and its only open public space. The church is the largest Catholic church in San Francisco; each October the Santa Maria del Lume (patron saint of fishermen) procession makes its way down Columbus Ave to Fisherman's Wharf to bless the fishing fleet.

Atop Telegraph Hill, the 210-foot **Coit Tower** (☎ 415-362-0808) is one of San Francisco's prime landmarks. It was built in 1934, financed by San Francisco eccentric Lillie Hitchcock Coit, who often dressed as a man to gamble in North Beach, wore short skirts to go ice skating and harbored a lifelong passion for a good fire. In 1863, the 15-year-old Lillie was adopted as the mascot of the Knickerbocker Hose Company No 5, and it's said she 'rarely missed a blaze.'

Inside the tower is a superb series of Diego Rivera-style murals of San Franciscans at work, painted by 25 local artists as part of a '30s WPA project. The tower is open 10 am to 7:30 pm daily. The ride to the top costs $3. If you're on foot, take the wooden Filbert St Steps that lead down past the picturesque cottages of Darrell Place and Napier Lane to Levi's Plaza and the Embarcadero.

The Beat Generation

From the days of the gold rush, San Francisco has been a freewheeling city. Artists, musicians and writers often sang its praises in their works, but it wasn't until the mid-1950s that national attention was first focused on 'the City' as the birthplace of a scene of its own. When Jack Kerouac and Allen Ginsberg, upstart students at Columbia University, fled the indifference of New York City and joined forces with the San Francisco Renaissance, a poets' movement begun by poet and literary critic Kenneth Rexroth, the Beat Generation was given a voice.

They engaged in a new style of writing – short, sharp and alive. Their bible was Kerouac's *On the Road* (1957); Ginsberg's 'Howl' (1956) was their angry anthem. A writer himself, Lawrence Ferlinghetti became the Beats' patron and publisher, and today their era lives on at his City Lights Bookstore, still churning out the hipsters after 40 years in North Beach.

The Beats spoke of a life unbound by social conventions, motivated by spontaneous creativity rather than greed and ambition. Kerouac is widely credited with creating the term 'Beat Generation' after hearing poet Herbert Huncke say, 'Man, I'm beat.' The phrase echoed Hemingway's 'Lost Generation' and alluded to the supreme happiness preached in the Beatitudes of Jesus. The term 'beatnik' came along later, created, it is claimed, by *San Francisco Chronicle* columnist Herb Caen, fusing the 'far out' Beats with the just-launched Sputnik satellite.

RUSSIAN HILL (MAP 4)

West of North Beach are the roller-coaster streets of Russian Hill, with some of the city's prime real estate and the famous **Lombard St** switchback. This stretch of Lombard, at the 1000 block, touted as 'the world's crookedest street,' wiggles down the hillside, notching up 10 turns as it goes. At one time, the crooked block was just as straight as any other, but its 27% incline was too steep for cars to manage, so in 1922 the curves were added.

The top of Russian Hill is so steep that not all the roads manage to surmount it, making way for pocket-size patches of green – affording some incredible views of the city below – like **Ina Coolbrith Park** (Vallejo St), and steep stairways like **Macondray Lane** (between Leavenworth and Taylor Sts). The latter was the model for Barbary Lane in Armistead Maupin's *Tales of the City*. Another lane of literary interest is Russell St where, at No 29, Jack Kerouac drafted *On the Road* and several other works in 1952, while living with Neal and Carolyn Cassady.

The **San Francisco Art Institute** (☎ 415-771-7020), 800 Chestnut St, is renowned for its fine **Diego Rivera Gallery**. The institute's cloisters and courtyards date from 1926, with a 1970 addition. The school has an excellent cafe and fine views over the bay from the terraces. The galleries are free and open 10 am to 5 pm Tuesday to Saturday.

For Russian Hill hangouts and stores, head to **Polk St**, which slopes down to Ghirardelli Square.

FISHERMAN'S WHARF (MAP 4)

Most San Franciscans view Fisherman's Wharf as a necessary evil. On the plus side, it brings in tourist dollars and concentrates all the tackiest tourist traps in a single part of town. On the minus side, the area has been developed almost entirely with tourism in mind – the waterfront's greatest shortcoming is that most 'attractions' are nothing more than thinly disguised shopping malls.

At one time the wharf was alive with the hustle and bustle of honest fishermen, and the city's maritime history is celebrated on Fisherman's Wharf with a distinguished museum and a collection of historic boats. Overlooking Aquatic Park at the waterfront end of Polk St, the **San Francisco National Maritime Museum** (☎ 415-556-8177) recounts the Bay Area's nautical history with a fine collection of ship models. It's free and open 10 am to 5 pm daily. Five classic ships are moored at the **Hyde St Pier** (☎ 415-556-3002), including the *Balclutha*, an iron-hull square-rigger from 1886. The collection is open 9:30 am to 5:30 pm daily May to mid-September; admission is $4 for adults, $3 for kids 12 to 17, free for children under 12 and seniors.

At Pier 45, the USS *Pampanito* (☎ 415-775-1943) is a WWII US Navy submarine that made six Pacific patrols during the last years of the war and sank six Japanese ships, including two carrying British and Australian POWs. It's open 9 am to 6 pm daily (9 am to 8 pm June to October); $6/4/4.

If there's a single focus for the Fisherman's Wharf tourist crush, it's undoubtedly **Pier 39**, a remodeled working pier with a host of restaurants and a huge collection of shops. Other attractions include a **Venetian carousel** ($2) for the kids; the 70mm **Cinemax Theatre** (☎ 415-956-3456) that screens short films about San Francisco and the world's oceans ($7.50/6/4.50); and **Underwater World** (☎ 415-705-5555), an enormous marine aquarium through which a clear pedestrian tunnel passes. It's open 9 am to 8 pm; $13/10/6.50.

Another attraction turned up around 1990, when California sea lions began to haul out on a section of the walkways beside Pier 39. Today, the takeover is complete, and hundreds of sea lions bask in the sun, barking noisily.

The Fisherman's Wharf area includes two shopping centers recycled from factories and industrial zones: **Ghirardelli Square**, 900 North Point St, once home to the namesake San Francisco chocolatier (there are still two GEAR-ar-DELI shops in the square); and the **Cannery**, occupying the old Del Monte fruit canning factory at 2801 Leavenworth St. Upstairs at the Cannery, the free **Museum of the City of San Francisco**

(☎ 415-928-0289) tells the story of the city with, hardly surprisingly, particular emphasis on the earthquakes of 1906 and 1989. It's open 10 am to 4 pm Wednesday to Sunday.

If hokey attractions are your thing, savor the delights of the **Wax Museum** (☎ 800-439-4305) or the **Ripley's Believe It or Not! Museum** (☎ 415-771-6188), both on Jefferson St. Admission to these fine institutions is absurdly high – $12/10 for the Wax Museum, $8.50/5.50 for Ripley's.

Note that Fisherman's Wharf is the jumping-off point for Alcatraz (see The Bay later in this chapter).

THE MARINA & COW HOLLOW (MAP 4)

The Marina, with its pick-up bars and high-priced rental units, is where grown-up frat boys and sorority girls live after they've landed high-paying jobs downtown. Chestnut St is the main commercial strip of the Marina; a few blocks south, Union St is the spine of the **Cow Hollow** neighborhood, so named for a local dairy farm that once occupied the area. In between the Marina and Cow Hollow is motel-lined Lombard St.

The Marina itself only popped up for the 1915 Panama-Pacific International Exposition, when the waterfront marshland was reclaimed to create the grounds for the exhibition commemorating San Francisco's post-earthquake rebirth. One of the few surviving structures from the Exposition is the stunning **Palace of Fine Arts**, on Baker St at Bay St, bordering the Presidio. Bernard Maybeck's artificial classical ruin was so popular that it was spared from its intended demolition when the exhibition closed. In the early '60s, the decaying stucco building was resurrected in durable concrete.

Behind Maybeck's ruin, the **Exploratorium** (☎ 415-561-0360), 3601 Lyon St at Bay St, was established in 1969 as a museum of art, science and human perception; it's enormously popular with children. A highlight is the Tactile Dome, a pitch-black dome that you can crawl, climb and slide through (advance reservations required). The Exploratorium is open 10 am to 5 pm Tuesday to Sunday (10 am to 9:30 pm Wednesday); $9/5 (free the first Wednesday of the month).

Cyclists, in-line skaters, joggers and kite fliers all enjoy the waterfront strip of **Marina Green**. The curious **Wave Organ** is at the tip of the breakwater; incoming and outgoing tides were meant to produce music in the organ's pipes, but if it ever actually worked, it doesn't anymore.

Between Aquatic Park and the Marina lies **Fort Mason** (☎ 415-979-3010), a Spanish and then US military fort. Most of the buildings were handed over for civilian use in the 1970s and now house a mix of galleries and museums – including the **San Francisco Craft & Folk Art Museum** (☎ 415-775-0990), the **Mexican Museum** (☎ 415-441-0445), the **Museo Italo-American** (☎ 415-673-2200) and the **African-American Cultural Society** (☎ 415-441-0640) – theaters and one of the city's finest vegetarian restaurants, **Greens** (see Places to Eat). Hostelling International's popular San Francisco International Hostel is also here (see Places to Stay).

The 1861 **Octagon House** (☎ 415-441-7512), 2645 Gough St at Union St, is one of the two survivors of the city's craze for octagonal houses. They were designed with eight sides to catch direct sunlight from eight angles. It's open the second and fourth Thursday and the second Sunday of each month from noon to 3 pm; $3 suggested donation.

PACIFIC HEIGHTS

This wealthy hilltop area has many of the city's finest residences because Van Ness Ave was where the fire stopped after the 1906 quake. Inspecting the beautiful old houses of Pacific Heights is principally a wander-and-look operation – only a few houses are open to the public. Fillmore St, climbing uphill from Union St and sloping down to Japantown, is the main drag for restaurants and shops.

The **Haas-Lilienthal House** (☎ 415-441-3004), 2007 Franklin St between Jackson and Washington Sts, was built in Queen Anne style between 1882 and '86. The house is externally impressive, but the hour-long tour is tediously slow. Tours are offered noon to 3:15 pm Wednesday and 11 am to 4:15 pm Sunday; $5/3.

The huge baroque **Spreckels Mansion**, at 2080 Washington St, was built in 1912 by George Applegarth (who also created the Palace of the Legion of Honor) for mega-wealthy sugar magnate Adolph Spreckels. It was purchased by novelist Danielle Steele in 1990.

JAPANTOWN

Japanese people have lived in San Francisco since the 1860s, and today only a tiny portion of them live in the compact Japantown area, just to the south of Fillmore St. Known as *Nihonjinmachi* in Japanese, the area was populated by Japanese after the 1906 earthquake. The WWII internment of Japanese and Japanese Americans devastated the community, and many of the former residents were unable to reclaim their homes after the war.

Today, Japantown is primarily a commercial district – it isn't really a neighborhood in the sense that Chinatown is. Japantown does come alive, though, during the two-weekend Cherry Blossom Festival in April, and during the two-day Nihonmachi Street Fair on the first weekend in August.

The neighborhood's focal point is **Japan Center** on Geary Blvd at Fillmore St. The center opened in 1968 around windswept (and surprisingly decrepit) **Peace Plaza**, with its plain five-story Peace Pagoda. The center's three malls are packed with excellent Japanese restaurants and shops.

For a Japanese-style communal bath, try **Kabuki Hot Springs** (☎ 415-922-6000), 1750 Geary Blvd, open noon to 8 pm Wednesday to Saturday, 10 am to 6 pm Sunday. The Kabuki Plan ($45) includes a steam bath, sauna and 25-minute Shiatsu massage; call for massage appointments.

THE HAIGHT

Just east of Golden Gate Park, the Haight-Ashbury area, locally known as 'the Haight,' is roughly divided into two sections: the **Upper Haight**, from Golden Gate Park to Masonic Ave; and the **Lower Haight**, a color-ful few blocks of grungy clubs and bars from Scott St east down to Webster St. South of the Upper Haight, quiet **Cole Valley** is a more upscale area with cafes, restaurants and shops centered around the intersection of Carl and Cole Sts.

Though Haight-Ashbury was the epicenter of the Summer of Love and flower power during the heady years of 1965, '66 and '67, the seminal events of San Francisco's hippie scene actually occurred in other parts of town: Ken Kesey's Trips Festival, in which thousands of people grooved to live music and dropped acid, took place in 1965 at the Longshoremen's Hall, near Fisherman's Wharf; the Gathering of the Tribes-Human Be-In, which ushered in 1967 and the Summer of Love, was held at the Polo Fields in Golden Gate Park. But it was to the somewhat run-down, Victorian Haight-Ashbury that the idealistic 'hippies' gravitated. They were drawn by low rents, proximity to the park and a preexisting bohemian community that had grown out of North Beach's Beat scene.

The 'San Francisco sound' – the LSD-inspired psychedelic rock typified by groups such as the Charlatans and the Grateful Dead – gestated in Haight St clubs like the Straight Theater. The neighborhood was populated with musicians who would become the legends of the '60s: the Dead, Jefferson Airplane, Janis Joplin, Big Brother and the Holding Company, and Country Joe and the Fish were all neighbors as the Haight-Ashbury reached its full flowering.

It proved to be a brief, if glowing, heyday. By late '67 drug overdoses had become commonplace, and incidences of violence were increasing among the hippies, gawkers, media and police. By the early '70s, Haight St was skid row for burnt-out hippies, and as the '60s hippie scene faded the street became a hub of gay nightlife.

Today, despite the throngs of tie-dyed stragglers, the Summer of Love is just a dreamlike memory on Haight St. About all that remains unchanged from the era is the street sign at the corner of Haight and Ashbury Sts. Still, the Haight is a great place to wander: start at the Golden Gate Park end, mosey east down Haight St, dive into a few shops, stop for a cheap meal and a cup of strong coffee – that's what it's all about. Deadheads should pass by **710 Ashbury St**, the onetime communal home of the Grateful Dead (now a private residence).

THE CASTRO (MAP 5)

The compact Castro is the gay center of San Francisco and is one of the city's best neighborhoods for strolling, watching streetlife, stopping for a coffee, shopping, getting a body piercing or having a leisurely lunch. The magnificent **Castro Theatre** (see Entertainment) is the highlight of Castro St and the center for the annual Gay and Lesbian Film Festival. **Harvey Milk Plaza**, at the Muni station at the intersection of Market and Castro Sts, is dedicated to the unofficial

'mayor of Castro St,' and the first openly gay man elected to public office in San Francisco. He was murdered along with Mayor Moscone in 1978.

The Castro's magnificent memorial to the swath AIDS has cut through the gay community is the AIDS Memorial Quilt. Each of the over 50,000 individually crafted, 6-foot-by-3-foot panels commemorates an AIDS victim. The **Names Project Gallery** (☎ 415-863-1966), 2362 Market St, recounts the quilt's ongoing creation and its travels, most remarkably a display of panels in Washington, DC, seen by more than 500,000 people.

Continue south along Castro or Noe Sts, and you'll come to **Noe Valley**, another of San Francisco's colorful small neighborhoods. The mix of Victorian homes, upscale restaurants and coffeehouses and eclectic

Gay San Francisco

In the early 1950s, a chapter of the Mattachine Society, the first serious homosexual rights organization in the US, sprang up in San Francisco, and in 1955 the Daughters of Bilitis (DOB), the nation's first lesbian organization, was founded in San Francisco.

During the 1959 mayoral campaign, challenger Russell Wolden accused incumbent mayor George Christopher of turning San Francisco into 'the national headquarters of the organized homosexuals in the United States.' Christopher was reelected, but was not about to be accused of being soft on queers. He responded with a massive police crackdown on gay male cruising areas, raids which resulted in a public blacklist of gay citizens.

Resistance to this persecution did not come out of the homophile movement but out of bars, and one in particular: the Black Cat, dubbed by Allen Ginsberg as 'the greatest gay bar in America.' (José Sarria, a drag performer at the Black Cat, ran for city supervisor in 1961, becoming the first openly gay person to run for public office in the US.)

The age of tolerance had not yet arrived, however. In 1965, a dance sponsored by the Council on Religion and the Homosexual was raided by the police, and everyone in attendance was arrested and photographed. The city was outraged and even the media denounced the police behavior. This event helped to turn the tide in the city's perception of the gay community. The crackdown on gay bars stopped, and a gay person was appointed to sit on the police community relations board.

With the 1977 election of gay activist Harvey Milk to the Board of Supervisors, recognition of the gay rights movement reached a new peak, but the euphoria was to be short-lived. The following year, Milk and Mayor George Moscone were assassinated by Dan White, an avowedly antigay former police officer.

Their deaths marked the beginning of the end of the heyday, the opulence of which further faded when the first cases of AIDS – at the time known as GRID (Gay-Related Immune Deficiency) – were reported in San Francisco in 1981.

– Heather Harrison

shops gives it a villagey feel; the main drag is the stretch of 24th St between Church and Castro Sts.

THE MISSION (MAP 5)

The Mission, one of the oldest parts of the city, is a largely Spanish-speaking enclave, a center for bohemian and alternative living and a great place for a cheap meal. The heart of the district stretches east-west, between Dolores St and South Van Ness Ave, and north-south, between 16th and 25th Sts. Valencia and Mission Sts are the two main streets for shops and restaurants.

In the last few years, the western half of the Mission – west of Mission St – seems to have hit a new stride. New bars and restaurants reflect a modern sensibility that aims a little higher than the old bohemia in terms of quality and atmosphere. The evolution is undeniably toward gentrification, though alternative lifestyles are still the rule. To sample the Mission's neighborly Latino charm, stroll down shaded 24th St, the neighborhood's true heart.

The area takes its name from the **Mission Dolores** (☎ 415-621-8203) at Dolores and 16th Sts. Originally Misión San Francisco de Asís, it was the sixth mission founded by Father Junípero Serra for the Spanish. Its site was consecrated on June 29, 1776, so this oldest building in San Francisco can claim to be five days older than the US. A more sturdy structure was built in 1782 by Franciscan monks, with Native-American labor. Today, the humble mission building is overshadowed by the adjoining basilica, built in 1913. The mission is open 9 am to 4:30 pm daily; $2.

A few blocks south, **Mission Dolores Park** (called simply Dolores Park by locals) is a popular spot on sunny days, especially with gay sunbathers, who have given it the sobriquet 'Dolores Beach.' After dark, Dolores Park is taken over by drug dealers.

The other prime Mission attraction is its hundreds of colorful **murals**, depicting everything from San Francisco's labor history to Central American independence struggles, the women's movement and local streetlife. One of the most amazing examples of mural art is on the **Women's Build-ing**, 3543 18th St between Valencia and Guerrero Sts. Narrow **Balmy Alley**, between Folsom and Harrison Sts and 24th and 25th Sts, is lined end-to-end with murals.

If you're especially interested in murals stop by the **Precita Eyes Mural Arts Center** (☎ 415-285-2287), 348 Precita Ave, just off Folsom St on the south side of Cesar Chavez St. The center conducts walking tours led by muralists (see Organized Walking Tours later in this chapter) and sells a walking tour map ($1.50) and mural postcards.

THE PRESIDIO

The northwest corner of the San Francisco peninsula was for many decades occupied by a rather low-key army base. As a result the area has not been developed, and most of it remains green and parklike, despite the fact that Hwys 1 and 101 meet in the middle of the Presidio and lead to the Golden Gate Bridge.

The Presidio has a long military history. It was established in 1776 by the Spanish as the site of their first fort, or presidio. The Presidio's military role ended in 1996, with the completion of a three-year changeover to a national park.

Under American rule, **Fort Point** was built at the start of the 1861-65 Civil War, to guard the entrance to the bay, but it never saw a battle or cannon fire and was abandoned in 1900. Today, Fort Point offers some of the most spectacular views of the Golden Gate Bridge and of the brave (crazy?) surfers riding the incoming swells along the rocky shore; the triple-tiered brick fortress is off Marine Drive, just below the Golden Gate Bridge (see The Bay section later in this chapter).

Housed in a Civil War-era hospital building, the **Presidio Museum** (☎ 415-561-4331), at Funston Ave and Lincoln Blvd, documents the history of California and the West Coast, with a military emphasis. It's open noon to 4 pm Wednesday to Sunday; free.

Along the ocean side of the peninsula is **Baker Beach**, the most picturesque of the city's beaches, with craggy rock formations backed up against cliffs. Due to the cold water and currents, it's not much of a swimming beach, but it is popular with sunbathers, with or without swimsuits.

San Francisco Bay Bridge from Yerba Buena Island

Cable car on Washington St, San Francisco

Transamerica Pyramid and Columbus Tower, SF

MAP 1 SAN FRANCISCO

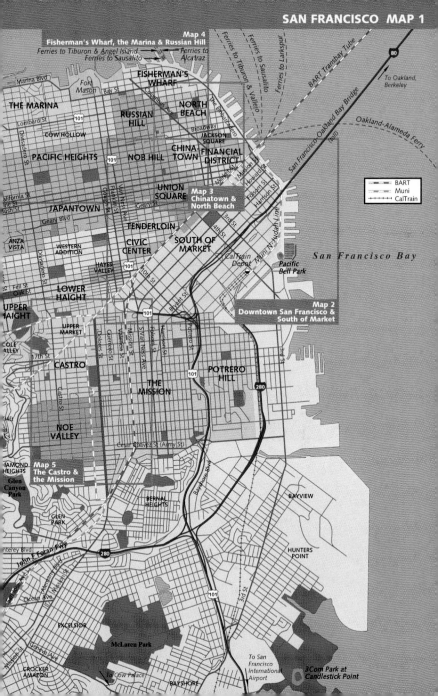

Golden Gate Bridge

Palace of Fine Arts, San Francisco

Lesbian, Gay, Bisexual and Transgender Pride Parade on Market St, San Francisco

MAP 2 DOWNTOWN SAN FRANCISCO & SOUTH OF MARKET

San Francisco Map Section

SAN FRANCISCO

MAP 2 DOWNTOWN SAN FRANCISCO & SOUTH OF MARKET

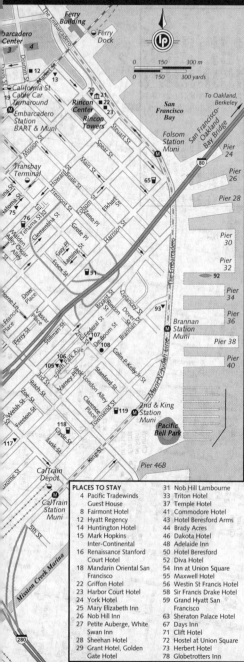

Ferry Building

Ferry Dock

Embarcadero Center

3 4

California St Cable Car Turnaround

Embarcadero Station BART & Muni

Rincon Center

Rincon Towers

San Francisco Bay

Folsom Station Muni

To Oakland, Berkeley

Transbay Terminal

Pier 24

Pier 26

Pier 28

Pier 30

Pier 32

Pier 34

Brannan Station Muni

Pier 36

Pier 38

Pier 40

Pier 46B

Pacific Bell Park

2nd & King Station Muni

CalTrain Depot

CalTrain Station Muni

Mission Creek Marina

0   150   300 m
0   150   300 yards

79 Hotel Bijou
83 Mosser's Victorian Hotel
84 Marriott Hotel
94 Phoenix Motel
95 Embassy Hotel
97 Abigail Hotel
99 Central YMCA Hotel
100 Aida Hotel
112 Best Western Hotel Britton
113 Best Western Carriage Inn
114 Best Western Americana
120 Grand Central Hostel
125 San Francisco International Student Center
128 Globe Hostel
129 Pensione San Francisco

PLACES TO EAT
1 Hyde Street Bistro
3 Yank Sing, Il Massimo del Panino
5 Palio Paninoteca
6 Rubicon
7 Swan Oyster Depot
11 Aqua
13 One Market
20 Boulevard
30 Masa's
32 Oritalia
34 Café Claude
35 360° Gourmet Burritos
36 Café Bastille, Sam's Grill & Seafood Restaurant
40 Brother Juniper's
42 Burma's House, Borobudur
48 Fleur de Lys
51 Postrio
54 Farallon
57 Sears Fine Foods
58 Scala's Bistro
61 San Francisco Health Food Store
69 Dottie's True Blue Cafe
70 Grand Cafe
75 Caribbean Zone
82 John's Grill
89 Hawthorne Lane
90 Max's Diner
93 Delancey Street Restaurant
96 Stars
97 Millennium
101 Tu Lan
104 LuLu
105 South Park Cafe
106 Caffe Centro
107 Infusion
109 Jardinière
110 Hayes St Grill
117 Fringale, Bizou
126 Julie's Supper Club
131 Toledo Lounge
134 Hamburger Mary's

CAFES
33 Café de la Presse
49 Yakety Yak

BARS & CLUBS
8 Crown Room, Tonga Room, New Orleans Bar
12 Equinox
15 Top of the Mark

17 Carnelian Room
41 Red Room
47 C Bobby's Owl Tree
53 Biscuits & Blues
56 Compass Rose
58 Harry Denton's Starlight Room
63 Pied Piper Bar
65 Gordon Biersch Brewery
66 Edinburgh Castle
68 Blue Lamp
71 Redwood Room
74 111 Minna
76 Kate O'Brien's
80 Club 181
91 Sound Factory
94 Backflip
111 Hayes & Vine
115 Covered Wagon Saloon
116 Hotel Utah Saloon
118 330 Ritch
119 Club Townsend
121 CoCo Club
122 1015 Folsom
123 Endup
125 Cat's Grill & Alley Club
127 Up & Down Club
132 Stud
133 V/sf
135 Paradise Lounge, Transmission Theater
136 Slim's
137 El Bobo
138 20 Tank Brewery
139 DNA Lounge
140 The Eagle

OTHER
2 Cable Car Barn & Museum
9 Wells Fargo History Museum
10 Bank of California Building, Museum of Money of the American West
17 Bank of America Building
19 101 California St Building
21 Jewish Museum of San Francisco
38 Russ Building
39 Pacific Stock Exchange
60 Children's Fountain
62 Folk Art International Building
64 Rand McNally Map Store
77 Glide Memorial United Methodist Church
81 San Francisco Visitors Information Center
85 Cartoon Art Museum
86 Sony Metreon Entertainment Complex
87 Yerba Buena Center for the Arts
88 San Francisco Museum of Modern Art (SFMOMA)
92 USS Jeremiah O'Brien
98 Civic Center Post Office
102 Ansel Adams Center for Photography
103 Zeum, Yerba Buena Ice Skating & Bowling Center
108 Start to Finish (Bike Shop)
124 Brain Wash

PLACES TO STAY
4 Pacific Tradewinds Guest House
8 Fairmont Hotel
12 Hyatt Regency
14 Huntington Hotel
15 Mark Hopkins Inter-Continental
16 Renaissance Stanford Court Hotel
18 Mandarin Oriental San Francisco
22 Griffon Hotel
23 Harbor Court Hotel
24 York Hotel
25 Mary Elizabeth Inn
26 Nob Hill Inn
27 Petite Auberge, White Swan Inn
28 Sheehan Hotel
29 Grant Hotel, Golden Gate Hotel
31 Nob Hill Lambourne
33 Triton Hotel
37 Temple Hotel
41 Commodore Hotel
43 Hotel Beresford Arms
44 Brady Acres
46 Dakota Hotel
48 Adelaide Inn
50 Hotel Beresford
52 Diva Hotel
54 Inn at Union Square
55 Maxwell Hotel
56 Westin St Francis Hotel
58 Sir Francis Drake Hotel
59 Grand Hyatt San Francisco
63 Sheraton Palace Hotel
70 Days Inn
71 Clift Hotel
72 Hostel at Union Square
73 Herbert Hotel
78 Globetrotters Inn

PLACES TO STAY
3 Washington Square Inn
15 Hotel Bohème
27 Basque Hotel
30 Green Tortoise Hostel
39 Obrero Hotel
45 Gum Moon Women's Residence
55 YMCA Chinatown
58 Grant Plaza

PLACES TO EAT
2 Liguria
6 Mario's Bohemian Cigar Store
7 Fior d'Italia
8 Rose Pistola
9 L'Osteria del Forno
14 Stella Pastry
19 Ideale
21 Molinari
24 Stinking Rose
25 Gold Mountain
29 Enrico's
31 Helmand
38 Dol Ho
40 House of Nanking
41 DPD
42 Macaroni Express
43 Caffè Macaroni
46 Lucky Creation
47 Sam Wo's
48 Empress of China
52 R&G Lounge
56 Far East Cafe
57 Lotus Garden

CAFES
5 Caffè Malvina
16 Caffè Greco
17 Caffè Puccini
20 Imperial Tea Court
22 Caffe Trieste
23 Steps of Rome

BARS & CLUBS
10 Savoy Tivoli
11 North End Caffe
12 Club Fugazi
18 Gathering Caffe
28 Finocchio
33 Vesuvio Cafe
34 Specs
35 Tosca Cafe
36 Hi-Ball Lounge
37 Broadway Studios

OTHER
1 Lyle Tuttle Tattooing
4 Post Office
13 Museum of North Beach
26 Condor Bistro
32 City Lights Bookstore
44 Golden Gate Cookie Company
49 Chinese Culture Center
50 Kong Chow Temple
51 Chinese Consolidated Benevolent Building
53 Chinese Historical Society Museum
54 Pacific Heritage Museum
57 Ching Chung Temple

P Parking

MAP 4 FISHERMAN'S WHARF, THE MARINA & RUSSIAN HILL

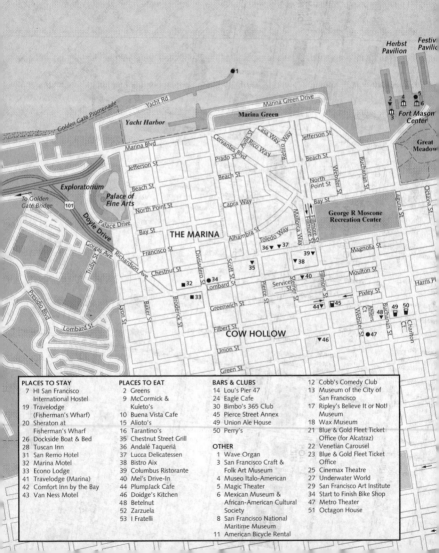

San Francisco Bay

Herbst Pavilion

Festiv Pavilio

Fort Mason Center

Great Meadow

Marina Green Drive

Yacht Rd

Golden Gate Promenade

Yacht Harbor

Marina Green

Marina Blvd

Casa Way

Cervantes Blvd

Rico Way

Retiro Way

Jefferson St

Beach St

Jefferson St

Prado St

Beach St

North Point St

Buchanan St

Exploratorium

Palace of Fine Arts

Beach St

North Point St

Capra Way

Bay St

George R Moscone Recreation Center

Laguna St

Octavia St

To Golden Gate Bridge

101

Palace Drive

Bay St

Doyle Drive

THE MARINA

Alhambra St

Toledo Way

Magnolia St

Gorgas Ave

Richardson Ave

Francisco St

Divisadero St

Scott St

36 ▼ ▼ 37

Fillmore St

Mallorca Way

39 ▼

Chestnut St

35 ▼

▼ 38

Moulton St

Harris P

Lombard St

■ 32

● 34

Pierce St

▼ 40

Pixley St

Baker St

Broderick St

■ 33

Lombard St

Steiner St

Service

Fillmore St

44 ▼ ▼ 45

49 50

Lyon St

Greenwich St

48 ▼

Webster St

Buchanan St

Charlton Ct

Lombard St

Filbert St

COW HOLLOW

▼ 46

● 47

Presidio Blvd

Union St

Green St

PLACES TO STAY
7 HI San Francisco International Hostel
19 Travelodge (Fisherman's Wharf)
20 Sheraton at Fisherman's Wharf
26 Dockside Boat & Bed
28 Tuscan Inn
31 San Remo Hotel
32 Marina Motel
33 Econo Lodge
41 Travelodge (Marina)
42 Comfort Inn by the Bay
43 Van Ness Motel

PLACES TO EAT
2 Greens
9 McCormick & Kuleto's
10 Buena Vista Cafe
15 Alioto's
16 Tarantino's
35 Chestnut Street Grill
36 Andalé Taquería
37 Lucca Delicatessen
39 Columbus Ristorante
40 Mel's Drive-In
44 PlumpJack Cafe
46 Doidge's Kitchen
48 Betelnut
52 Zarzuela
53 I Fratelli

BARS & CLUBS
14 Lou's Pier 47
24 Eagle Cafe
30 Bimbo's 365 Club
45 Pierce Street Annex
49 Union Ale House
50 Perry's

OTHER
1 Wave Organ
3 San Francisco Craft & Folk Art Museum
4 Museo Italo-American
5 Magic Theater
6 Mexican Museum & African-American Cultural Society
8 San Francisco National Maritime Museum
11 American Bicycle Rental
12 Cobb's Comedy Club
13 Museum of the City of San Francisco
17 Ripley's Believe It or Not! Museum
18 Wax Museum
21 Blue & Gold Fleet Ticket Office (for Alcatraz)
22 Venetian Carousel
23 Blue & Gold Fleet Ticket Office
25 Cinemax Theatre
27 Underwater World
29 San Francisco Art Institute
34 Start to Finish Bike Shop
47 Metro Theater
51 Octagon House

San Francisco Bay

Ferries to Alcatraz, Angel Island, Sausalito, Tiburon

Ferries to Vallejo, Six Flags Marine World

Breakwater

Pier 45

USS Pampanito

Pier 43

Pier 41

Municipal Pier

Hyde St Pier

Alma

Pier 43 1/2 (Vista Pier)

Pier 39

22

Pier 35

Balclutha
Eppleton Hall
CA Thayer

Eureka

Ferry Dock

21

24

Ferry Dock

Pier 33

Aquatic Park

Fisherman's Wharf

15

The Embarcadero

23

25

26

27

16

The Embarcadero

Powell-Hyde Cable Car Turnaround

Jefferson St

14

17

18

19

Victoria Park

13

The Cannery

12

20

Beach St

10

28

Ghirardelli Square

11

North Point St

Powell-Mason Cable Car Turnaround

Russian Hill Park Reservoir

Columbus Ave

NORTH BEACH

Francisco St

Houston St

31

Chestnut St

Bay St

29

30

Francisco St

North Beach Playground

Saints Peter & Paul Church

Pioneer Park

Chestnut St

43

Lombard St

Greenwich St

Coit Tower

41

Lombard St

Alice Marble Tennis Courts

Washington Square

Union St

42

Grenard Ter

Greenwich St

Filbert St

Filbert St

Church of Saint Francis of Assisi

Green St

Lurmont Terrace

Montclair Terrace

Union St

Filbert St

Allen St

Hastings Ter

52

Union St

Warner Pl

Russell St

Delgado Pl

RUSSIAN HILL

53

Glover St

Broadway

Green St

Cyrus Pl

Robert Levy Tunnel

Vallejo St

Lynch St

Bernard St

Broadway

Pacific Ave

NOB HILL

Jackson St

Portsmouth Square

Washington St

Clay St

CHINATOWN

Lafayette Park

Sacramento St

St Mary's Square

California St Cable Car Line

California St

California St Cable Car Turnaround

Grace Cathedral

Pine St

Austin St

see Downtown San Francisco & South of Market map

Union Square

Bush St

MAP 5 THE CASTRO & T

PLACES TO STAY
3 Zeitgeist Guest House
5 Perramont Hotel
6 Twin Peaks Hotel
11 Beck's Motor Lodge
33 Dolores Park Inn
40 Black Stallion B&B
44 Andora Inn
46 Inn San Francisco

PLACES TO EAT
7 Chow
8 Café Cuvée
9 Mecca
12 Cafe Flore
13 2223 Market
14 California Harvest Ranch
   Market
18 Pozole
25 Taqueria Zapata
28 Patio Cafe
29 Hot 'n' Hunky
39 Taqueria Can-Cun
42 La Rondalla
43 Herbivore
47 Elysium Cafe
47 Firecracker
52 Flying Saucer
52 Esperpento
56 La Taqueria
58 Bitter Root
59 Ti Couz & Cafe Picaro
63 Truly Mediterranean &
   Sunflower
66 La Cumbre Taqueria
66 Puerto Alegre
68 Slanted Door

CAFES
2 Orbit Room Cafe
10 Red Dora's Bearded Lady
   Cafe & Gallery

55 Muddy's
60 Cafe Macondo

BARS & CLUBS
1 The Mint
3 Zeitgeist
4 Cafe du Nord
15 Metro
18 Detour
19 The Café
21 Twin Peaks Tavern
24 The Bar on Castro
27 Badlands
34 Liquid
37 Elbo Room
38 Lexington Club
45 Bruno's
49 Lone Palm
50 Latin America Club
53 Make-Out Room
53 Kilowatt
61 Dalva
64 Esta Noche
67 Casanova Lounge

OTHER
17 Names Project Gallery
20 The Gauntlet
22 Harvey Milk Plaza
23 Castro Theatre
26 A Different Light Bookstore
30 Body Manipulations
31 Mission Dolores Basilica
32 Mission Dolores
35 ODC Theater
36 Women's Building
41 Dog Eared Books
48 Aquarius Records
54 Good Vibrations
62 Roxie Cinema
57 ?

LEE FOSTER

MAP 6 GOLDEN GATE PARK

PLACES TO STAY
18 Stanyan Park Hotel

PLACES TO EAT
2 Beach Chalet Brewery &
   Restaurant
20 Ganges
21 House
22 Ebisu
23 PJ's Oyster Bed
24 Pluto's

OTHER
1 Dutch Windmill
3 Murphy Windmill
4 Golden Gate Park Stables
5 Redwood Memorial Grove
6 Rose Garden
7 MH de Young Memorial
  Museum
8 Asian Art Museum
9 Japanese Tea Garden

10 Music Concourse
11 California Academy of
   Sciences
12 Shakespeare Garden
13 Conservatory of Flowers
14 AIDS Memorial Grove
15 Children's Playground
16 McLaren Lodge
17 Start to Finish Bike Shop
19 Avenue Cyclery

THE RICHMOND

Bordered by the green Presidio to the north and Golden Gate Park to the south, the uniform rectangular blocks of the Richmond District stretch from Arguello Ave all the way to the ocean. The restaurants and shops along busy Clement St make up the heart of the area, and also the heart of New Chinatown.

The **Cliff House** (☎ 415-386-3330), on the Great Hwy, overlooking the Pacific from the north end of Ocean Beach, was originally built in 1863 as an escape from the crowds. The most impressive of the myriad of Cliff Houses was the elegant eight-story gingerbread resort built by Adolph Sutro in 1896, which contained art galleries, dining rooms and an observation deck. It survived the 1906 earthquake but was destroyed by fire the following year. The 1909 replacement is nowhere near as grand, but it's still a popular restaurant with great views, though unexciting food.

On the deck below the restaurant is a giant **Camera Obscura** (☎ 415-750-0415), an invention that projects the view from outside the building onto a parabolic screen inside. It was built in 1946 by a local engineer, based on diagrams originally drawn by Leonardo da Vinci. At this writing, the Camera Obscura is open 10 or 11 am to sunset daily; $1. However, its future is uncertain. The park service is planning to close it at the end of 1999, but fans of the Camera Obscura have mobilized to save this unique and noble San Francisco landmark from an ignoble end.

Underneath the Cliff House is the superb **Musée Mécanique** (☎ 415-386-1170), with a collection of early-20th-century arcade games, risqué Mutoscope motion pictures ('See what the belly dancer does on her day off!') and player pianos. You are free to pump your quarters into the machines. The museum is open 10 or 11 am to 7 or 8 pm daily; free.

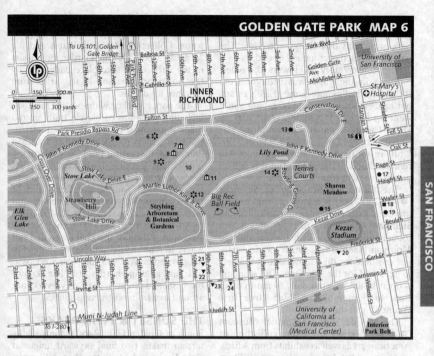

GOLDEN GATE PARK   MAP 6

The ruins in the cove just north of the Cliff House are all that remain of the **Sutro Baths**, the magnificent six-pool, 3-acre indoor swimming pool palace Sutro built in 1896. The baths never made money, however, and the building burned down in 1966, amid rumors of insurance fraud.

There's a fine walking path along this surprisingly rugged stretch of coast from the Cliff House to **Lands End** where there are terrific views across the Golden Gate. It starts by the remains of Sutro Baths and passes through **Lincoln Park**, which was established by Golden Gate park keeper John McLaren.

Off 34th Ave, within Lincoln Park, is the **California Palace of the Legion of Honor** (☎ 415-863-3330), one of San Francisco's premier art museums, with a world-class collection of medieval to 20th-century European art. The museum is open 9:30 am to 5 pm Tuesday to Sunday; $7/4 (free second Wednesday of the month).

GOLDEN GATE PARK (MAP 6)
San Francisco's biggest park stretches almost halfway across the 6-mile-wide peninsula. An 1870 competition to design the park was won by 24-year-old William Hammond Hall; in 1871, he commenced the task of turning 1017 acres of dunes into the largest developed park in the world, and by the 1880s the park had become the city's most popular attraction. John McLaren took over the park's management in 1887 and stayed on as administrator for the next 56 years, until his death at age 97.

Apart from gardens, lakes, sporting facilities and trails, the park also hosts museums and other indoor attractions. Park information, including a detailed map ($2.25), is available from McLaren Lodge (☎ 415-831-2700) at the park entrance at Fell and Stanyan Sts. A $10 'Culture Pass' gives admission to all park attractions that charge entry fees. The pass can be used over a number of days.

The **Conservatory of Flowers**, the oldest building in the park, was brought from Ireland for millionaire James Lick's estate, but he died before it could be rebuilt and it went up instead in Golden Gate Park in 1878. The glass-paned conservatory was heavily damaged by storms in 1996 and '97. Until restoration funds are raised, it will remain closed to the public, but it is still an impressive sight from the outside.

The **California Academy of Sciences** (☎ 415-750-7145) is a large natural history museum with child-pleasing exhibits: the **Steinhart Aquarium**, which features a 'fish roundabout' 180 feet in diameter, and the **Morrison Planetarium**, which has an earthquake simulator that allows out-of-towners to get a feel for the 'Big One.' The academy is open 10 am to 5 pm daily (9 am to 6 pm June to September); $8.50/5 (free first Wednesday of the month).

The **MH de Young Memorial Museum** (☎ 415-863-3330) has a fine collection of American art as well as exhibits from Africa, Oceania and the Americas. It's open 9:30 am to 5 pm Tuesday to Sunday; $7/4.

The adjacent **Asian Art Museum** (☎ 415-668-8921) houses the Avery Brundage Collection and other superb art from the Middle East, the Indian subcontinent, Southeast Asia, Tibet, China, Korea and Japan. The museum is scheduled to move in 2000 to a new site in the Civic Center's Old Main Library. Until then, its hours are the same as for the de Young, and one ticket buys admission to both museums.

The popular **Japanese Tea Garden** (☎ 415-831-2700) features a pagoda, gates, bridges, statues and a pleasant teahouse where you can enjoy green tea and fortune cookies for $2. It's claimed fortune cookies were actually invented here, back in 1909. The gardens are open 9 am to 6:30 pm daily in summer, 8:30 am to 6 pm in winter; $2/1 adults/children.

The **Strybing Arboretum & Botanical Gardens** (☎ 415-661-1316) encompasses a number of smaller gardens within its 70 acres, including the Garden of Fragrance, the California Collection of Native Plants and the Japanese Moon-Viewing Garden. Free tours of the Arboretum take place daily; stop by the bookstore just inside the arboretum entrance for details.

The park is packed with sporting facilities, including 7½ miles of bicycle trails, untold miles of jogging trails, 12 miles of equestrian trails, an archery range, baseball and softball diamonds, fly-casting pools, a challenging nine-hole golf course, lawn bowling greens, *pétanque* courts (a French game similar to lawn bowling), four soccer fields and 21 tennis courts. Rowboats, pedal boats and electric boats can be rented (☎ 415-752-0347) on Stow Lake for $10 to $13 an hour. See the Activities section of this chapter to find out where to rent bicycles and in-line skates. On Sundays some roads in the park are closed to traffic, allowing hordes of in-line skaters, bicyclists and street hockey players to buzz around free from obstructing autos.

THE SUNSET & TWIN PEAKS

South of Golden Gate Park, the city's hilly terrain makes two final skyward lunges at Twin Peaks and Mt Sutro, then rolls westward in block after uniform block to the ocean. Originally known as *El Pecho de la Chola* (the Breasts of the Indian Girl), the two summits of the appropriately named Twin Peaks (922 feet and 904 feet) offer a superb view of the Bay Area, especially at night. You can drive to Twin Peaks by heading southwest on Market St as it climbs steeply uphill (it eventually becomes Portola Ave) and then turning right on Twin Peaks Blvd.

The area south of Golden Gate Park down to Sloat Blvd and from about 16th Ave to the ocean is known as the Sunset District, a mostly residential area filled with pastel-colored stucco homes built between the 1930s and 1950s. The Inner Sunset, centered around 9th Ave at Irving and Judah Sts, has the most to offer visitors, with restaurants and student-filled cafes only a block or two from Golden Gate Park.

Ocean Beach stretches for miles along the coast, from the Cliff House to the cliffs of Fort Funston. On sunny days, you'll find a classic California beach scene: sunbathers, surfers and picnickers. Unfortunately, sunny days are few and far between.

The mediocre San Francisco Zoo (☎ 415-753-7061), Sloat Blvd and 45th Ave, is open 10 am to 5 pm daily; $9/6. One mile south, Fort Funston is a beautiful windswept area of cliffs, trails and beach – a great place to spend an afternoon watching the hang gliders float above the cliffs.

THE BAY

San Francisco Bay is the largest on the California coast, stretching about 60 miles in length and up to 12 miles in width. It's fed by the Sacramento and San Joaquin rivers, mingling with the sea through the Golden Gate. The bay is, however, very shallow, averaging only six to 10 feet deep at low tide.

Golden Gate Bridge

Commenced in January 1933 and opened in May 1937, the beautiful Golden Gate Bridge links San Francisco with Marin County and, despite competition from modern constructions like the Transamerica Pyramid, remains the symbol of the city. The bridge, designed by Joseph B Strauss, is nearly 2 miles in length, with a main span of 4200 feet. When the bridge was completed, it was the longest suspension bridge in the world. Its name comes from the Golden Gate entrance to the harbor, but could just as easily have come from the 'international orange' paint scheme. Painting the bridge is a never-ending job – a team of 25 painters add 1000 golden gallons every week.

A prime starting point for bridge appreciation is the Fort Point Lookout (☎ 415-556-1693) on Marine Drive at the southern end of the bridge. The lookout offers excellent views and has a gift center, a statue of Strauss and a sample of the 3-foot-thick suspension cable. Muni bus No 29 runs to the lookout and the toll plaza, bus No 28 just to the toll plaza. There are even better views from the lookout at Vista Point, on the north side of the bridge. From there, San Francisco forms part of the backdrop.

On weekends, pedestrians can walk across the bridge on the city side, while bicyclists can zoom along on the ocean side. During the week, all merge on the city side. Cars pay a $3 toll for southbound travel (Marin to San Francisco).

Bay Bridge

The vehicle-only Bay Bridge is considerably longer than the Golden Gate Bridge, carries far more traffic and predates it by six months, but it has never enjoyed the same iconic fame. The Bay Bridge actually consists of three separate parts: a double suspension bridge leads from San Francisco to the mid-bay Yerba Buena Island; a tunnel that cuts straight through the rocky island; and a series of latticework spans that connect Yerba Buena Island to Oakland. There's a $2 toll westbound.

The 1989 earthquake caused a 50-foot section of the Yerba Buena-Oakland span to collapse, killing a motorist. This stretch of bridge will be replaced eventually, supposedly by 2005.

Alcatraz

From 1933 to 1963 the rocky island in the middle of San Francisco Bay was the most famous prison in the United States. The 12-acre Alcatraz became the prison of choice for serious offenders for a simple reason – 'the Rock' was believed to be escape-proof, until the Anglin brothers and coconspirator Frank Morris floated away in a self-made raft in 1962 and were never seen again. That enigmatic escape was made famous by the 1979 movie *Escape from Alcatraz*, starring Clint Eastwood. Though Alcatraz is only 1½ miles from the mainland, they are 1½ very cold miles swept by the bay's often ferocious currents, not to mention the occasional shark.

After the prison's closure, the island was more or less forgotten for six years and then taken over by Native Americans who conducted a protest sit-in from 1969 to 1971.

The Anglin brothers and Frank Morris escaped from Alcatraz in 1962.

The Blue & Gold Fleet (Map 4; ☎ 415-773-1188 for information, 415-705-5555 for tickets) runs ferries to the island from Pier 41 at Fisherman's Wharf. It's wise to book or pick up tickets well in advance, especially in summer. Departures to the island are from 9:30 am to 2:45 pm on weekdays and until 2:15 pm on weekends. The roundtrip fare is $11, plus $2 for phone orders. This price includes an excellent audio tour that features firsthand narratives by former guards and inmates. The park ranger station (☎ 415-705-1042) has information on the island and its history.

ACTIVITIES
Bicycling

The mountain bike *was* invented in Marin County, and Golden Gate Park and the Presidio have great cycling potential (but be aware, cyclists must obey traffic laws in the Presidio – the Presidio police are sticklers for giving tickets to bicyclists who don't stop at stop signs, etc). You can bike across the Golden Gate Bridge to the Headlands or

transport your bike up to Mt Tam, the Bay Area's supreme mountain biking challenge (see the San Francisco Bay Area chapter).

Bike route signs around the city point the way to different parks. The routes usually manage to avoid the most suicidal of hills. A free map in the front of the San Francisco phone book lists all the routes. If you're under 18, California law says you must wear a helmet, and every cyclist must have a light when pedaling at night. And of course, always carry a good lock; bike theft is all too common in the city.

For rentals, try Avenue Cyclery (Map 6; ☎ 415-387-3155), 756 Stanyan St at Waller St, right by Golden Gate Park in the Upper Haight. There are three Start to Finish shops: at 672 Stanyan St at Haight St (Map 6; ☎ 415-750-4760) in the Upper Haight, at 2530 Lombard St (Map 4; ☎ 415-202-9830) in the Marina District, and at 599 2nd St at Brannan St (Map 2; ☎ 415-243-8812) in the SoMa. American Bicycle Rental (Map 4; ☎ 415-931-0234), 2715 Hyde St near Beach St, is at Fisherman's Wharf.

Golf

San Francisco has three 18-hole public golf courses: Harding Park (☎ 415-664-4690) at Harding and Skyline Blvds near Lake Merced; Lincoln Park (☎ 415-221-9911), 34th Ave and Clement St; and the stunning Presidio Golf Course (☎ 415-561-4653), near the Presidio's Arguello Gate. There's also a challenging nine-hole course in Golden Gate Park (Map 6; ☎ 415-751-8987), near the beach at the Fulton St and 47th Ave entrance.

Running & Skating

Marina Green has a 2½-mile jogging track and fitness course, and there are many running paths through Golden Gate Park. The Presidio is another great park for running, with plenty of routes from the Marina right past the Golden Gate Bridge to Baker Beach.

In-line skating is very popular in Golden Gate Park; you can rent skates at Skates on Haight (☎ 415-752-8375), 1818 Haight St at Stanyan St, and cruise directly into the park.

Sailing & Windsurfing

Any view of the bay, dotted with sails, shows this is prime sailing country. The bay is tricky territory, though, and only for experienced sailors. Spinnaker Sailing (☎ 415-543-7333), at Pier 40, offers lessons and charters boats. In Marin County, Sausalito's Cass's Marina (☎ 415-332-6789), 1702 Bridgeway, is one of many places that offers lessons and rentals.

The bay also has great windsurfing, but it is not kind to beginners. The San Francisco School of Windsurfing (☎ 415-753-3235) offers lessons on Lake Merced and at Candlestick Point. For more experienced board sailors, the beach off Crissy Field, in the shadow of the Golden Gate Bridge, is a world-class sailing spot. A good place to watch sailboarders is Fort Point, right under the Golden Gate Bridge.

Surfing

Ocean Beach is one of the most challenging and exhausting places to surf in California, especially in winter when the powerful, cold swells can reach 12 feet or more. There are no lifeguards, and you should never surf alone or without at least a 3mm full-length wetsuit. For a recorded message of the latest surfing conditions at Ocean Beach, call Wise Surfing at ☎ 415-665-9473. Go to Fort Point to watch surfers battle the waves under the Golden Gate Bridge.

Tennis

There are free public tennis courts all over San Francisco. The courts at Mission Dolores Park (Map 5) are popular; for others, call San Francisco Recreation & Park Department (☎ 415-753-7001). The 21 courts in Golden Gate Park (Map 6) cost $4 per court for 90 minutes on weekdays, $6 on weekends.

Whale Watching

Mid-October through December is the peak season for whale watching in the Bay Area, as gray whales make their annual migration south from the Bering Sea to Baja California. Five-Star Charters (☎ 415-332-6811) runs all-day, naturalist-led whale-watching expeditions on weekends. They depart from Sausalito (see the Bay Area chapter) for the Farallon Islands, 28 miles outside the Golden Gate. It's $59 per person (15% discount for three or more), and reservations are required.

WALKING TOURS

San Francisco lays out a rich feast for those keen on doing their sightseeing on foot. The visitor information center caters to walkers with an excellent line of walking tour leaflets to Chinatown, Fisherman's Wharf, North Beach, Pacific Heights and Union Square.

Helen's Walk Tours (☎ 510-524-4544) offers a variety of walks from two hours for $20 to a 3-1/2-hour grand tour for $40. San Francisco Strolls (☎ 415-282-7924) also offers lots of possibilities, including a Brothel Stroll and a Barbary Coast Stroll; these 2½ hour perambulations cost $20 each. Friends of the San Francisco Public Library (☎ 415-557-4266) offers an eclectic variety of free (donations accepted) walking tours led by savvy local historians. To join an architectural walk around Pacific Heights, call ☎ 415-441-3004.

Chinatown is a walker's favorite; you can tag along on a Chinese Heritage Walk (Saturday afternoon, $15) or a Chinese Culinary Walk & Luncheon (Friday morning, $30) from the Chinese Culture Center (☎ 415-986-1822) in the Holiday Inn at 750 Kearny St.

The Mission is great for walking, especially for seeking out the district's many superb murals. Precita Eyes Mural Arts Center (☎ 415-285-2287), 348 Precita Ave, conducts a two-hour Mission District Mural Walk ($4) on Saturday afternoons. For the inside line on San Francisco's gay mecca, try Cruisin' the Castro (by reservation only, ☎ 415-550-8110); the four-hour walk ($35), held on mornings Tuesday through Saturday, includes brunch. The Flower Power Haight-Ashbury Walking Tour (☎ 415-221-8442) points out the sites of the Human Be-In and the Grateful Dead's former house. The two-hour walk ($15) is offered Tuesday and Saturday mornings.

One of San Francisco's best-known walks is the Dashiell Hammett tour, led by author Don Herron (☎ 510-287-9540). The summer-only, four-hour tour ($10) gumshoes up and down the streets of the Tenderloin and Union Square.

SPECIAL EVENTS

Chinese New Year
The Golden Dragon Parade, led by a 75-foot-long dragon, is the highlight of the Chinese New Year festivities, in late January and early February. Check with the Chinatown Chamber of Commerce (☎ 415-982-3000), 730 Sacramento St, for details.

SF International Film Festival
The country's oldest film festival – two weeks in April – is concentrated at the Kabuki Theater in Japantown, with films also at other Bay Area cinemas. Phone ☎ 415-929-5000 for details.

Cinco de Mayo
Two days of music, dancing and parades in the Mission on the weekend closest to May 5 mark the Mexican victory over the French at the Battle of Puebla in 1862. Phone ☎ 415-826-1401 for details.

Bay to Breakers
On the third Sunday in May, more than 100,000 joggers (many in crazy costumes) make their way from the Bay (the Embarcadero) to the Breakers (the Pacific Ocean), a distance of about 7 miles. Phone ☎ 415-808-5000 ext 2222 or contact the San Francisco Examiner (☎ 415-777-2424) for details and entry forms.

Carnaval
If Rio and New Orleans can have a Carnaval, why not San Francisco? Held on Memorial Day weekend, Carnaval is celebrated with lots of music and dancing in the streets of the Mission. Phone ☎ 415-826-1401 for details.

Pride Week
June is a celebratory month for San Francisco's gay community, with the Gay and Lesbian Film Festival playing at the Castro Theatre and Pride Week leading up to the last Sunday in June, when the often outrageous Lesbian, Gay, Bisexual and Transgender Pride Parade is held. The evening before the parade is the Pink Saturday party on Castro St. On Sunday, up to a half-million people congregate along Market St for the city's biggest annual parade. Call ☎ 415-864-3733 for parade details.

Cable Car Bell-Ringing Championship
In late June or early July, the cable car drivers compete to be the loudest or most tuneful bell ringer. Phone ☎ 415-923-6202 for details.

Shakespeare Festival
This festival presents free performances of a different play each year, starting Labor Day weekend in Golden Gate Park and other Bay Area parks (see the 'Free & Outdoors' boxed text in the Entertainment section). Phone ☎ 415-422-2221 for details.

Blues Festival
For two days in late September, bands and blues legends jam out the blues on Fort Mason's Great Meadow. Phone ☎ 415-979-5588 for details.

Jazz Festival

In mid to late October and into November, you can catch jazz performances by legendary and up-and-coming artists throughout the city. For schedule and locations, phone ☎ 415-788-7353.

Halloween

With hundreds of thousands of costumed revelers taking to the streets, particularly Castro St and around Civic Center, October 31 is the most crazed night of the year. The Exotic-Erotic Halloween Ball (☎ 415-567-2255) at the Concourse Exhibition Center is one of the highlights. Halloween is also the time for the annual Pumpkin Festival at Half Moon Bay (see the San Francisco Bay Area chapter).

Street Fairs

Pretty much every neighborhood in San Francisco hosts a street fair on its main 'strip' during the year, with most fairs landing in summer. Two of the most popular are the Folsom St Fair in late September (the most 'alternative' fair, with lots of leather, whips and naked people), and the massive Castro St Fair in early October. For arts and crafts mixed with blues or jazz, try the Polk St Fair and the Fillmore St Fair, both in the summer months. North Beach hosts a Columbus Day Fair, and Haight St goes all out in early June for its fair.

PLACES TO STAY

Deciding where you're going to stay in San Francisco requires two decisions: where do you want to stay and what do you want to stay in? The decisions are interrelated: if you want a romantic B&B, you won't end up in the Financial District, and if you want a luxury hotel, you'll probably wind up on Nob Hill or around Union Square. Most backpacker hostels are in SoMa and along the downtown fringes.

Apart from the hostel listings, the recommendations in this chapter are categorized by neighborhood. Some of these neighborhood sectons are then subdivided according to price range. No matter where you stay, reservations are a good idea on summer

weekends, over holiday periods (for example, Christmas to New Year's) and during the city's bigger festivals (especially on Halloween and, in the Castro, on the weekend of the Gay Pride Parade in June).

Hostels

San Francisco's numerous hostels are predominantly used by overseas visitors – in fact, some hostels actively discourage US users. Hostels usually offer kitchen and laundry facilities, a meeting room, a TV lounge and other useful conveniences.

Hostelling International (HI), the long-term survivor of the hostel business, has two San Francisco locations (downtown and at Fort Mason). The other hostels are privately operated.

Union Square HI's large, well-equipped *Hostel at Union Square* (Map 2; ☎ 415-788-5604, 312 Mason St), a stone's throw from Union Square, has 230 beds divided between dorms and double rooms. The cost is $16 for HI-AYH members, $19 for nonmembers. The closest BART station is Powell St.

Globetrotters Inn (Map 2; ☎ 415-346-5786, 225 Ellis St), at Mason St in the Union Square/Tenderloin area, is just around the corner from the HI hostel. Accommodations in this smaller hostel are either in four-bed dorms (beds $12/75 per night/week) or in private rooms ($24).

Financial District In the fuzzy zone where Chinatown descends into the Financial District, the friendly *Pacific Tradewinds Guest House* (Map 2; ☎ 415-433-7970, 680 Sacramento St) is a well-maintained 4th-floor hostel with dorm beds (no private rooms) and a fully equipped kitchen. It's a great place to meet other travelers. Beds are $16, and the maximum stay is two weeks. The nearest BART station is Embarcadero.

Civic Center The *Grand Central Hostel* (Map 2; ☎ 415-703-9988, 1412 Market St) is one of the city's largest hostels, with more than 200 dorm beds ($15) and a few private singles/doubles ($25/35). The location is convenient – take any BART or Muni train to

Civic Center Station, or take the F-Market streetcar up Market St.

The Tenderloin's **Central YMCA Hotel** *(Map 2; ☎ 415-885-0460, 220 Golden Gate Ave)*, at Leavenworth St, is not the best address in town, but it offers simple, clean rooms with shared bathrooms for $40/50 single/double (men and women welcome). Dorm beds are $21. There are discounts for students with ISIC cards.

South of Market The well-run and friendly **Globe Hostel** *(Map 2; ☎ 415-431-0540, 10 Hallam St)*, off Folsom St between 7th and 8th Sts,, is set in a surprisingly quiet location. US citizens need a passport to stay. Dorm rooms sleep five, and each room has an attached bathroom; the nightly charge is $14. Private doubles ($38) are available only in the off-season. The hostel has a laundry and TV room, but no kitchen. There is, however, a cafe and an Irish bar at the corner.

The nearby **San Francisco International Student Center** *(Map 2; ☎ 415-487-1463, 1188 Folsom St)* is an aging hostel with small dorms that sleep three to five people. The nightly cost is $15, a bit more in summer. It has kitchen facilities and clean showers.

North Beach On a slightly seedy but safe stretch of Broadway, the medium-size **Green Tortoise Hostel** *(Map 3; ☎ 415-834-1000, 494 Broadway)* is run by the same people who operate the funky Green Tortoise buses (see Getting There & Away chapter). The hostel has beds in dorms for two to six people at $17, and a few single/double rooms at $39. They provide a free breakfast, and kitchen and laundry facilities are available. Bus No 15 from the Transbay Terminal will get you there.

Fort Mason The second HI hostel, the **San Francisco International Hostel** *(Map 4; ☎ 415-771-7277)*, trades downtown convenience for a quiet setting in Building 240 at Fort Mason, near Fisherman's Wharf. To get there, take Muni bus No 42 from the Transbay Terminal to the stop at Bay St and Van Ness Ave. Bus Nos 30 and 47 also stop there. Beds are $15, and there's a 1 am curfew.

The Haight The Lower Haight's **Easy Goin' Hostel** *(☎ 415-552-8452, 555 Haight St)*, near Fillmore St, is close to bars and cheap restaurants. The drawbacks are street noise and, after dark, the weirdos lurking on Haight St. Dorm beds are $14, private doubles $30.

Union Square (Map 2)

Parking can get pricey in this area, so if the hotel you are staying in doesn't provide parking, try the parking garages at 123 O'Farrell St (☎ 415-986-4800; $5 for 6 pm to 6 am) or the Yerba Buena Garage between 4th and 5th Sts on Mission St (☎ 415-982-8522; $13 for 24 hours).

Budget The area to the west of Union Square has San Francisco's greatest density of hotels. The cheapest of the decent places, ranging from $35 to $65 a night, include: the friendly 18-room **Adelaide Inn** *(☎ 415-441-2261, 5 Isadora Duncan Lane)*, off Taylor St between Post and Geary Sts, and the more basic **Herbert Hotel** *(☎ 415-362-1600, 161 Powell St)*, a block or so south of Union Square. The **Grant Hotel** *(☎ 415-421-7540, 800-522-0979, 753 Bush St)* is on the way up Nob Hill and not far from Chinatown. It's a basic low-priced hotel, offering clean and simple rooms, all with private bathroom.

A step up in price, at $65 to $95, is the snug 42-room **Dakota Hotel** *(☎ 415-931-7475, 606 Post St)* at Taylor St. The Dakota has undergone recent renovations, and some street-facing rooms afford impressive city views. The sprightly 25-room **Brady Acres** *(☎ 415-929-8033, 800-627-2396, 649 Jones St)*, just off Geary St, has reasonable weekly rates, and each room is equipped with a bathroom and small kitchen. Other hotels in this price range include the 64-room **Sheehan Hotel** *(☎ 415-775-6500, 800-848-1529, 620 Sutter St)*, which has fitness facilities and an indoor swimming pool, and the **Golden Gate Hotel** *(☎ 415-392-3702, 775 Bush St)*.

The **Mary Elizabeth Inn** *(☎ 415-673-6768, 1040 Bush St)*, between Jones and Leavenworth Sts, is a women-only establishment run by the United Methodist Church.

Rooms with shared bathrooms are $49, including two meals; the weekly rate is $155.

Mid-Range You'll find some charismatic mid-priced hotels in the $95 to $135 range. The *Maxwell Hotel* (☎ 415-986-2000, 888-734-6299, 386 Geary St), at Mason St, is a smartly restored 1908 hotel, part of the hip Joie de Vivre chain.

The *Hotel Beresford Arms* (☎ 415-673-2600, 800-533-6533, 701 Post St) is a well-kept older hotel with a few spacious rooms, many with kitchens. It's a great value, with 90 rooms starting at $99/109 single/double. Its sister hotel, the 114-room *Hotel Beresford* (☎ 415-673-9900, 800-533-6533, 635 Sutter St), is a few blocks away and is similarly priced. The *Commodore Hotel* (☎ 415-923-6800, 825 Sutter St) is a strikingly hip property that plays on the theme of steamship travel. The rooms, from $99 to $159, are custom furnished and comfortable.

The following hotels are a bit pricier, ranging from $120 to $175 per night. The 108-room *Diva Hotel* (☎ 415-885-0200, 800-553-1900, 440 Geary St) is cleanly modern in the glass, chrome and black-enamel style. The rooms are all comfortable, though some are quite small. Just a few steps from Union Square, the *Inn at Union Square* (☎ 415-397-3510, 800-288-4346, 440 Post St) has 30 elegantly old-fashioned rooms and suites, all nonsmoking. The *York Hotel* (☎ 415-885-6800, 800-808-9675, 940 Sutter St) is a rather elegant hotel that appeared in the stairway scenes of Alfred Hitchcock's *Vertigo*. A short block from Hallidie Plaza, *Hotel Bijou* (☎ 415-771-1200, 111 Mason St) stands out among the area's strip joints and peep-show parlors. Videos of films set in San Francisco screen nightly in a small art deco-style theater just off the lobby.

Another step up in price, the *White Swan Inn* (☎ 415-775-1755, 845 Bush St) and the *Petite Auberge* (☎ 415-928-6000, 863 Bush St) are somewhere between hotel and B&B, with romantic decor and rooms at $150 to $185. The *Triton Hotel* (☎ 415-394-0500, 800-433-6611, 342 Grant Ave) is notable for its 140 exotically designed guest rooms, including the Carlos Santana and Jerry

Garcia suites. For nonrockers, the basic Zen Den starts at $159 a night.

Top End Rooms at the luxury hotels typically start out at $175 to $195 and rise to $275 and more; suites cost significantly more. The *Westin St Francis Hotel* (☎ 415-397-7000, 800-228-3000, 335 Powell St) occupies the entire west side of Union Square and is one of the city's most famous hotels. The *Grand Hyatt San Francisco* (☎ 415-398-1234, 800-233-1234, 345 Stockton St) is on the north side of the square.

The *Clift Hotel* (☎ 415-775-4700, 800-437-4824, 495 Geary St), at Taylor St, is known for its standout service.

The *Sir Francis Drake Hotel* (☎ 415-392-7755, 800-227-5480, 450 Powell St) at Sutter St, is an opulently decorated luxury hotel with beefeater-costumed doormen. The lowest rates for standard rooms are $170 to $250, depending on the season. Package deals can bring these prices down considerably.

Civic Center (Map 2)
Budget The *Aida Hotel* (☎ 415-863-4141, 800-863-2432, 1087 Market St), between 6th and 7th Sts, is neat and tidy and an excellent value, with 174 singles/doubles at $46/56. Rates are $15 higher in summer. On the edge of the Tenderloin, the *Embassy Hotel* (☎ 415-673-1404, 610 Polk St), at Turk St, offers plain but clean rooms for as little as $49/59.

Days Inn (☎ 415-441-8220, 895 Geary St), at Larkin St, is a basic motel with rooms for $89 to $99 (free parking).

Mid-Range The *Abigail Hotel* (☎ 415-861-9728, 800-243-6510, 246 McAllister St), between Larkin and Hyde Sts, adds a little hipness to the Civic Center. The 61 guest rooms, furnished with antiques, are reasonably priced at $79 to $94, and the lobby opens up to Millennium, one of the city's most renowned vegetarian restaurants.

The *Phoenix Motel* (☎ 415-776-1380, 800-248-9466, 601 Eddy St) is in the Tenderloin, but it's just a few blocks from the relative safety of Van Ness Ave. This recycled 1950s motor lodge has boxy rooms that face an arty swimming pool. The ultrahip restaurant Backflip (see Places to Eat) occupies the hotel's former coffee shop. Free parking and a continental breakfast make the rooms, at $109 to $119, a better value.

Pensione San Francisco (☎ *415-864-1271, 1668 Market St*) is a presentable little place, but you must call for current rates – they refuse to publish their prices.

South of Market (Map 2)
Budget & Mid-Range *Mosser's Victorian Hotel* (☎ *415-986-4400, 800-227-3804, 54 4th St*), off Market St, has simple rooms for one or two people starting at $79 in the low season, $109 or $119 in the high season.

The three Best Western hotels on 7th St between Mission and Howard Sts offer standard motel rooms, free parking and shuttle service to Union Square. The cheapest is the *Hotel Britton* (☎ *415-621-7001, 800-444-5817, 112 7th St*), with 79 rooms for $84 to $109. The *Americania* (☎ *415-626-0200, 121 7th St*) and the *Carriage Inn* (☎ *415-552-8600, 140 7th St*) are mid-range hotels – priced from $129 to $214 – with swimming pools and saunas.

Top End The *Griffon Hotel* (☎ *415-495-2100, 800-321-2201, 155 Steuart St*) has a great location at the waterfront, close to Embarcadero Center and the Ferry Building. The 59 rooms are modern and comfortable and cost $190 to $350, including a light breakfast. The adjacent *Harbor Court Hotel* (☎ *415-882-1300, 800-346-0555, 165 Steuart St*) is a larger establishment, with 130 rooms costing $195 to $245. Health club facilities are available to guests at the adjacent YMCA.

The enormous 1500-room *San Francisco Marriott* (☎ *415-896-1600, 55 4th St*) looks across Yerba Buena Gardens and – more to the point – the Moscone Convention Center. It often offers specials that cut into its steep published rates of $275.

Financial District (Map 2)
The *Temple Hotel* (☎ *415-781-2565, 469 Pine St*) is about the only affordable hotel in the district. Rooms are $35 to $45 without bathroom, $45 to $55 with bathroom.

On the other end of the scale, the *Mandarin Oriental San Francisco* (☎ *415-885-0999, 800-622-0404, 222 Sansome St*) has 158 rooms on the 38th to 48th floors of the third-highest building in the city. The views are spectacular, and the rooms cost $325 to $500 (rates drop by $100 or more on weekends). The 800-room *Hyatt Regency* (☎ *415-788-1234, 800-233-1234, 5 Embarcadero Center*) is probably San Francisco's most architecturally memorable hotel, with its backward leaning 20-story atrium. Rates start at $195.

Nob Hill (Map 2)
At the *Nob Hill Lambourne* (☎ *415-433-2287, 800-275-8466, 725 Pine St*) rooms are equipped with computer, fax and voice mail facilities and cost $180 to $280. The *Nob Hill Inn* (☎ *415-673-6080, 1000 Pine St*), at Taylor St, is a pleasant 21-room hotel priced from $99 to $249. Some rooms have kitchen facilities.

Nob Hill is topped by four of the city's oldest and classiest hotels: the *Fairmont Hotel* (☎ *415-772-5000, 800-527-4727, 950 Mason St*); the *Huntington Hotel* (☎ *415-474-5400, 1075 California St*); the *Renaissance Stanford Court Hotel* (☎ *415-989-3500, 800-622-0957, 905 California St*) and the *Mark Hopkins Inter-Continental* (☎ *415-392-3434, 800-327-0200, 999 California St*). Rooms typically cost $170 to $350. Even if you can't afford to stay in one of these hotels, their cocktail lounges are worth a stop: the Mark Hopkins' Top of the Mark lounge is renowned for its views.

Chinatown (Map 3)
The *YMCA Chinatown* (☎ *415-982-4412, 855 Sacramento St*) only takes men and requires reservations; rooms are $30/38 single/double, with the seventh night free. The female alternative is the *Gum Moon Women's Residence* (☎ *415-421-8827, 940 Washington St*), between Powell and Stockton Sts. Gum Moon has a fully equipped kitchen, a charmingly dated parlor and

rooms with shared bathroom for $22 to $27. Reservations are not accepted.

The *Obrero Hotel* (☎ *415-989-3960, 1208 Stockton St)*, between Pacific St and Broadway, has just 12 rooms with shared bathrooms and rock-bottom prices of $40 to $50. The *Grant Plaza* (☎ *415-434-3883, 800-472-6899, 465 Grant Ave)* is just a block from the Chinatown gateway and the California St cable car. The rooms are neat and tidy, all with attached bathroom. Singles are $45 to $52, doubles $55 to $85.

North Beach (Map 3)

Absolutely the best deal in the neighborhood is the 26-room *Basque Hotel* (☎ *415-398-1359, 17 Romolo Place)*. The rooms are small but clean, and the bathrooms are shared. From May to October singles/doubles are $45/60; the rest of the year rooms are only available on a weekly basis ($120/180).

The quaint *Washington Square Inn* (☎ *415-981-4220, 800-388-0220, 1660 Stockton St)* has 15 rooms priced from $125 to $200. Right in the heart of North Beach is the small and very stylish *Hotel Bohème* (☎ *415-433-9111, 444 Columbus Ave)*. Doubles, all with private bathroom, are $125.

Fisherman's Wharf (Map 4)

Fisherman's Wharf is overrun with standard tourist motels such as *Travelodge* (☎ *415-392-6700, 250 Beach St)* and *Sheraton at Fisherman's Wharf* (☎ *415-362-5500, 2500 Mason St)*, both with doubles from $85 to $110, depending on the season.

Some places break out of the cookie-cutter mold, like the pleasantly old-fashioned *San Remo Hotel* (☎ *415-776-8688, 800-352-7366, 2237 Mason St)*, between Chestnut and Water Sts. Singles are $45 to $60, doubles $55 to $70. The 220-room *Tuscan Inn* (☎ *415-561-1100, 800-648-4246, 425 North Point St)* is a luxurious hotel with complimentary wine in the afternoon and prices from $138 (low season) to $190 (high season).

Instead of a room, guests get their own boat at the *Dockside Boat & Bed* (☎ *415-392-5526)*. Rates fluctuate depending on the boat, the season and the night of the week, but range from $140 to $290. The office is at the C Dock on Pier 39.

The Marina & Cow Hollow (Map 4)

This is the real motel quarter of San Francisco. Lombard St (Hwy 101) is packed wall-to-wall with motels and mid-range chain hotels, gas stations and several fast-food outlets. Try the pleasant 1930s *Marina Motel* (☎ *415-921-9406, 800-346-6118, 2576 Lombard St)*; the *Econo Lodge* (☎ *415-921-2505, 2505 Lombard St)*, with a swimming pool, or the *Travelodge* (☎ *415-673-0691, 1450 Lombard St)*, near the corner of Van Ness Ave. The 42-room *Van Ness Motel* (☎ *415-776-3220, 2850 Van Ness Ave)*, between Lombard and Chestnut Sts, has a quieter location than the motels right on the highway. Rates range from $65 to $110 at all of the above.

Head south down Van Ness Ave to find more motels, generally at slightly higher prices. They include the *Comfort Inn by the Bay* (☎ *415-928-5000, 800-228-5150, 2775 Van Ness Ave)*, which has rooms ranging from $90 to $175.

Pacific Heights

Pacific Heights has a scattering of pleasant places. The *Mansions Hotel* (☎ *415-929-9444, 2220 Sacramento St)* is resolutely, almost mustily, old-fashioned, with a resident ghost and pricey rooms ($130 to $350). The breakfast is excellent. Recent renovation has turned the 1903 Edwardian *El Drisco Hotel* (☎ *415-346-2880, 2901 Pacific Ave)* into a drastically overpriced spot (doubles $210 to $310).

Japantown

The *Best Western Miyako Inn* (☎ *415-921-4000, 800-528-1234, 1800 Sutter St)*, at Buchanan St, adds Japanese trimmings to the Best Western formula. Rooms range from $83 to $123. At the eastern end of the Japan Center complex, the larger and more expensive *Radisson Miyako Hotel* (☎ *415-922-3200, 800-533-4567, 1625 Post St)* is a deluxe hotel with shoji screens on the windows and deep Japanese bathtubs in the bathrooms. Doubles are $189 to $199.

The Haight

The **Metro Hotel** (☎ 415-861-5364, 319 Divisadero St), between Oak and Page Sts, is on the edge of the scruffy Lower Haight. The Metro offers cheap and clean rooms with private bathroom ($55 to $66), a private garden patio and overnight parking. The **Stanyan Park Hotel** (Map 6; ☎ 415-751-1000, 750 Stanyan St), near Haight St, is right by Golden Gate Park in a fine old Victorian building. Rooms cost $99 to $145.

The trippy **Red Victorian B&B** (☎ 415-864-1978, 1665 Haight St), between Cole and Clayton Sts, offers a wonderful opportunity to relive the Summer of Love. Choose from the Flower Child Room, the Sunshine Room or even the Summer of Love Room. Rates for two people are $86 to $200. Other B&Bs in the area include the **Victorian Inn on the Park** (☎ 415-931-1830, 800-435-1967, 301 Lyon St), at Fell St, and **Spencer House** (☎ 415-626-9205, 1080 Haight St), a superb 1887 Queen Anne Victorian mansion just east of Buena Vista Park. Rooms in both go for about $120 to $170.

Alamo Square, north of Lower Haight towards Japantown, is famous for its Victorians. The **Alamo Square Inn** (☎ 415-922-2055, 719 Scott St), occupying a pair of Victorian mansions, has rooms for $85 to $195. The **Archbishop's Mansion** (☎ 415-563-7872, 800-543-5820, 1000 Fulton St), on Alamo Square, was built in 1904 for the city's archbishop. Rooms with private bathroom are $129 to $200.

The Castro (Map 5)

The **Twin Peaks Hotel** (☎ 415-621-9467, 2160 Market St) and the adjacent **Perramont Hotel** (☎ 415-863-3222, 2162 Market St) are basic and cheap, with doubles for $35 (shared bathroom) to $55 (private bathroom). **Beck's Motor Lodge** (☎ 415-621-8212, 800-227-4360, 2222 Market St) is a bland 57-room motel priced from $75 to $125.

A couple of places cater to same-sex couples. The **Black Stallion B&B** (☎ 415-863-1031, 635 Castro St), between 19th and 20th Sts, is a black-painted Victorian offering clothing-optional accommodations to gay men; singles/doubles are around $80/95. **House o' Chicks** (☎ 415-861-9849) offers cozy accommodations for lesbians. Since there are only two rooms ($50 to $75), they've asked us not to list their address; reservations are required.

The Mission (Map 5)

In general, cheap hotels in the Mission are places you'd rather not know about. That said, one very inexpensive place worth considering is the **Zeitgeist Guest House** (☎ 415-255-7505, 199 Valencia St) at Duboce St. It's upstairs from the *very* noisy bar of the same name. Basic rooms with shared bathroom are $30/40 single/double. The more upscale **Andora Inn** (☎ 415-282-0337, 2434 Mission St), above the Elysium Cafe, has 12 rooms with shared/private bathroom starting at $69/99 and peaking at $129/169, including breakfast. The **Inn San Francisco** (☎ 415-615-0188, 800-359-0913, 943 South Van Ness Ave), a grand Victorian B&B, has rooms with shared/private bathroom starting at $85/115. Deluxe rooms with hot tub, spa or fireplace are $175 to $225.

The **Dolores Park Inn** (☎ 415-861-9335, 3641 17th St) is a six-room B&B between the Mission Dolores and Dolores Park. It's a relaxed spot with a garden and reasonable doubles ($75 to $160).

Airport

There are more than 20 hotels around the airport, many with free direct-dial phones at the airport's baggage-claim area and free shuttle buses that pick up and drop off guests outside the terminals.

There are a half-dozen places in Millbrae, just south of the airport. Many have rooms in the $80 to $110 range, including the **Clarion Hotel** (☎ 650-692-6363, 800-391-9644, 401 E Millbrae Ave).

PLACES TO EAT

San Francisco has more restaurants per capita than any other city in the US, but the city's culinary distinction is by no means based on sheer quantity. San Francisco's true strength is the diversity of its influences – Afghan, Burmese, Cambodian, Cajun, Ethiopian, Filipino, Greek, Indian, Korean, Lebanese, Moroccan, Spanish, Thai, Turkish and more, including the Bay Area's own invention: California cuisine, where 'fresh,' 'light' and 'creative' are the key words.

The city's culinary landscape is quickly shedding its boundaries: don't think you must go to North Beach for Italian food, Chinatown for Chinese food or the Mission for Mexican food. Otherwise you are likely to miss out on excellent restaurants elsewhere in the city – and ignore some surprising gems in each of those parts of town.

At most mid-range and top-end restaurants, reservations are recommended on weekdays and are nearly mandatory on Friday and Saturday nights.

Union Square (Map 2)

Budget A popular breakfast joint right off the square is **Sears Fine Foods** (☎ 415-986-1160, 439 Powell St), where Swedish pancakes or French toast with coffee comes to about $6. Sears is open 6:30 am to 2:30 pm Thursday to Monday. Right across from the Chinatown Gate, **Cafe de la Presse** (☎ 415-398-2680, 352 Grant Ave) sells an international selection of newspapers and magazines, along with breakfast dishes, sandwiches and burgers in the $7.50 to $9 range.

The **San Francisco Health Food Store** (☎ 415-392-8477, 333 Sutter St) is an old-fashioned soda fountain that also serves health-food dishes (closed Sunday). **Brother Juniper's** (☎ 415-771-8929, 1065 Sutter St), near Larkin St, is a good breakfast spot, with homemade breads and hearty organic food. It's open for lunch and dinner but closed on Sunday.

Named after a famous Javanese Buddhist temple, **Borobudur** (☎ 415-775-1512, 700 Post St) has reasonable lunch specials ($5 to $7) and serves a variety of Indonesian specialties. **Burma's House** (☎ 415-775-1156, 720 Post St) has cheap and tasty Burmese dishes.

Mid-Range **Café Claude** (☎ 415-392-3505, 7 Claude Lane), between Sutter and Bush Sts, is a busy and justly popular French bistro, open for breakfast, lunch and dinner (closed Sunday). **Scala's Bistro** (☎ 415-395-8555, 432 Powell St), at the Sir Francis Drake Hotel, serves up great California-Italian cuisine at a moderate cost ($6 to $10 for appetizers, $11 to $15 for main courses). Reservations are recommended.

John's Grill (☎ 415-986-3274, 63 Ellis St) has served traditional grilled food since 1908. Fish is a safe bet, but the food takes second billing to the atmosphere.

In a former ballroom at the Hotel Monaco, **Grand Cafe** (☎ 415-292-0101, 501 Geary St) is dazzling to look at, and such grandeur makes for an elegant dining experience. The menu is thick with grilled and roasted meats.

Oritalia (☎ 415-346-1333, 590 Bush St), above the Stockton tunnel, is a unique Asian-Italian fusion restaurant. Small plates cost $9 to $12, main courses $16 to $20.

Top End Three of the city's most renowned (and expensive) restaurants are around Union Square. **Postrio** (☎ 415-776-7825, 545 Post St) is one of the city's prime exponents of California cuisine. Appetizers cost about $15, and an entrée costs about $25, but for the quality of the food and service, this place is an absolute bargain. **Masa's** (☎ 415-989-7154, 648 Bush St) and **Fleur de Lys** (☎ 415-673-7779, 777 Sutter St) are both internationally known French restaurants run by celebrity chefs (Julian Serrano and Hubert Kelly, respectively). Entrées at both places range from $15 to $30.

Restaurant designer Pat Kuleto plumbed the deep sea for **Farallon** (☎ 415-956-6969, 450 Post St). The 'coastal cuisine' is outstanding (around $12 for appetizers, $25 for main courses), as is the underwater decor.

Civic Center (Map 2)

Budget There is no better place for breakfast than the Tenderloin's **Dottie's True Blue Cafe** (☎ 415-885-2767, 522 Jones St). On weekends there's a line out the door for solid standards such as eggs, pancake and chicken sausages, all for less than $10. On one of the less savory blocks just south of Market St, *Tu Lan* (☎ 415-626-0927, 8 6th St) has a bustling counter facing the grill cooks, and two cramped dining rooms. The ridiculously low prices – you can eat yourself silly for less than $10 – make food this tasty an unbelievable bargain (closed Sunday).

Mid-Range Hayes Valley, the neighborhood west of Van Ness Ave, is packed with cafes and some good restaurants. The *Hayes St Grill* (☎ 415-863-5545, 324 Hayes St) is a great place for fresh fish, including some upscale fish-and-chips combos. Entrées range from $10 to $18. Down-home Southern cooking draws a steady stream of customers to *Powell's Place* (☎ 415-863-1404, 511 Hayes St). Order fried chicken, corn muffins, red beans and rice and a can of Budweiser (all for just $10.50) and you won't be disappointed. Stay away from the mashed potatoes (instant) and the green beans (from a can). *Suppenküche* (☎ 415-252-9289, 601 Hayes St), at Laguna St, serves Germanic comfort foods such as sautéed venison with spaetzle and smoked pork chops with sauerkraut – food that goes well with frothy glasses of beer. Entrées are $8 to $15. The restaurant is open 5 to 10 pm.

Top End *Stars* (☎ 415-861-7827, 555 Golden Gate Ave) was one of San Francisco's most highly celebrated dining establishments, when owned by chef Jeremiah Tower (an innovator in California cuisine). Despite the prices (main courses from $20), this is a fun and lively – rather than formal – place.

French-California cuisine is at its best at *Jardinière* (☎ 415-861-5555, 300 Grove St), at Franklin St, where chef Traci Des Jardins offers a creative seasonal menu. Main courses start at $20 and appetizers range from $8 to $15. Jardinière features a circular bar downstairs and intimate, velvet-upholstered booths upstairs.

Off the lobby of the Abigail Hotel, *Millennium* (☎ 415-487-9800, 246 McAllister St) is one of the city's best-known vegetarian restaurants; the vegan menu features creative tempeh-, seitan- and tofu-based dishes ($11 to $15) that blend Asian, North African and Mediterranean flavors.

The hottest restaurant in town a decade ago, *Zuni Cafe* (☎ 415-552-2522, 1658 Market St) is now merely a good choice for mesquite-grilled meats and brick-oven pizzas (entrées $15 to $25). The raw oyster bar and the zinc cocktail bar are also popular.

South of Market (Map 2)

Budget *Caffe Centro* (☎ 415-882-1500, 102 South Park) is a popular cafe, with inexpensive sandwiches served at outdoor tables. *Max's Diner* (☎ 415-546-6297, 311 3rd St), at Folsom St, delivers '50s atmosphere and contemporary diner food (entrées $5 to $10).

On the edge of the 11th St nightclub district, *Hamburger Mary's* (☎ 415-626-5767, 1582 Folsom St) is a traditional, noisy, busy bar-and-diner with hefty burgers and sandwiches ($5 to $8). At the *Toledo Lounge* (☎ 415-558-9640, 299 9th St), clubbers fuel up on burgers, fish-and-chips and organic salads for less than $10. Lunch is served on weekdays, and at night the place functions more as a bar where good food is available.

Mid-Range The *South Park Cafe* (☎ 415-495-7275, 108 South Park) has a French flavor and reasonable prices; brunch, lunch and dinner are served. Just east of South Park, *Infusion* (☎ 415-543-2282, 555 2nd St) serves up stylized, moderately priced comfort foods such as roast chicken with mashed potatoes; the signature drink is vodka infused with fresh fruit juices.

The bay-side *Delancey Street Restaurant* (☎ 415-512-5179, 600 The Embarcadero), commendably hires and trains people who are down on their luck, without compromising the quality of the food or service. The reasonably priced menu makes forays into Mexican, Thai, Caribbean and Cajun cuisines.

A stylish converted auto-repair shop, *LuLu* (☎ 415-495-5775, 816 Folsom St) has an open kitchen with several flaming ovens dedicated to cooking rotisserie meats and pizzas. Entrées in the main dining room rarely exceed $15. In the connected rooms, called LuLu Bis and LuLu Cafe, you can assemble an inexpensive meal of antipasti or oysters from the bar.

An old-timer on the SoMa scene (since 1987), *Julie's Supper Club* (☎ 415-861-0707, 1123 Folsom St) is a swinging, kitschy restaurant-bar with an interesting menu that borrows freely from Californian, Asian, Italian and Cajun cuisines.

At *Caribbean Zone* (☎ 415-541-9465, 55 Natoma St), tables are tucked amid lagoons and trickling waterfalls. Lunches are inexpensive and dinner entrées are moderate, but those fancy tropical drinks go for about $6 each.

Fringale (☎ 415-543-0573, 570 4th St) is a crowded and noisy spot with very French waiters and a French-Basque chef who has built his reputation on dishes such as the mashed-potato cake studded with shredded duck confit; closed Monday. A few doors down, *Bizou* (☎ 415-543-2222, 598 4th St) is more of a California-Mediterranean bistro, where rustic French foods are joined by rigatoni and thin-crusted pizzas.

Top End *Boulevard* (☎ 415-543-6084, 1 Mission St), in the prequake Audiffred Building, was designed by Pat Kuleto to look like a belle epoque Parisian salon. Chef Nancy Oakes has a fine way with pork loins, buttery mashed potatoes and crab cakes.

Expect to pay around $50 per person for dinner, not including wine, at *Hawthorne Lane* (☎ 415-777-9779, 22 Hawthorne Lane), housed in a stylishly converted warehouse. Chefs Annie and David Greengrass offer a carefully prepared, seamless blend of Mediterranean, Asian and Californian cuisines. Hawthorne Lane is open for dinner nightly and for lunch on weekdays.

Financial District (Map 2)
Although the Financial District is deathly quiet at night, there are a few interesting restaurants along its borders with the waterfront and North Beach. Many of these places are closed on Sunday.

Budget *Palio Paninoteca* (☎ 415-362-6900, 505 Montgomery St), at Commercial St, is a cafe that makes excellent coffee and focaccia sandwiches. *360° Gourmet Burritos* (☎ 415-989-8077, 359 Kearny St) does nontraditional burritos with ingredients such as Cajun chicken, prawns or roasted duck. *Il Massimo del Panino* (☎ 415-834-0290, 441 Washington St), off Battery St, is a great place for an Italian sandwich.

Many San Franciscans feel *Yank Sing* (☎ 415-781-1111, 427 Battery St) has the best dim sum this side of Hong Kong. It's open 11 am to 3 pm weekdays, 10 am to 4 pm weekends.

Harbor Village (☎ 415-781-8833, 4 Embarcadero Center) also gets a few votes on the 'best dim sum' ballot. At night it metamorphoses into a more upscale establishment.

Mid-Range The most popular spot on restaurant-filled Belden St is *Café Bastille* (☎ 415-986-5673, 22 Belden St), the focal point of the French Ghetto's annual Bastille Day celebration. Standard bistro fare (steak frites, etc), along with savory crepes and live jazz, make Bastille a lively joint most nights of the week.

Sam's Grill and Seafood Restaurant (☎ 415-421-0594, 374 Bush St), at Belden St, is one of the city's oldest restaurants. It dates from 1867 and hasn't changed a bit since moving to its present location in 1946. Stick to the fresh fish offerings. Sam's is open 11 am to 9 pm weekdays only.

Top End With its emphasis squarely on seafood, elegant and expensive *Aqua* (☎ 415-956-9662, 252 California St) is by many accounts San Francisco's best restaurant. French traditions (with subtle California twists) underlie many of the entrées ($28 to $35). Aqua is open weekdays for lunch and every night but Sunday for dinner; make reservations four to six weeks ahead of time.

Chef Bradley Ogden's *One Market* (☎ 415-777-5577, 1 Market St) offers a fresh, seasonal California menu, a fine wine list and an array of creative side dishes. Although devotees of departed chef Traci Des Jardins insist that *Rubicon* (☎ 415-434-4100, 558 Sacramento St) is no longer up to snuff, the restaurant hasn't yet forfeited its national reputation for serving up delicious New American gourmet cuisine.

Nob Hill (Map 2)

Between California and Sacramento Sts, the **Swan Oyster Depot** (☎ 415-673-1101, 1517 Polk St) serves beer, clam chowder, shrimp cocktails and sourdough bread for one of the city's best moderately priced seafood meals (entrées are $9 to $15). They close at 5:30 pm and are closed all day Sunday. Getting a bit fancier, right in the heart of Nob Hill, **Hyde Street Bistro** (☎ 415-441-7778, 1521 Hyde St) has a seasonal menu based on Austrian and northern Italian cuisine at decent prices (entrées are $8 to $15).

Chinatown (Map 3)

Not surprisingly, Chinatown is packed with Chinese restaurants – from tiny hole-in-the-wall places with cheap eats to cavernous but equally economical dim sum houses to pricey restaurants serving the latest Chinese haute cuisine.

Budget **Dol Ho** (☎ 415-392-2828, 808 Pacific Ave) is smaller than most dim sum houses, and the dishes are fresh to the core. **Lucky Creation** (☎ 415-989-0818, 854 Washington St) is one of the city's lesser-known, but excellent, vegetarian restaurants. The little dive called **DPD** (☎ 415-982-0471, 901 Kearny St), at Jackson St, surpasses all expectation with delicious noodle soups and thick Shanghai noodles. Other Chinatown restaurants are more highly acclaimed, but this place is the real deal.

If the streets of Chinatown seem a hustle and bustle, **House of Nanking** (☎ 415-421-1429, 919 Kearny St) is even more of one. The line stretching outside (reservations are not accepted) is a genuine reflection of the good food coming out of the busy kitchen.

You have to make your way through the kitchen and proceed upstairs to feast at the legendary **Sam Wo's** (☎ 415-982-0596, 813 Washington St). It has always been the tongue-in-cheek rudeness of the waiters (rather than the greasy food) that has made

Dim Sum

San Francisco rivals Hong Kong in the popularity and quality of its dim sum restaurants. In the Canton province of China, where dim sum originated, the act of eating dim sum is called *yum cha*, or 'drink tea,' because the snacklike dishes first appeared in teahouses.

Typically, dim sum consists of pastrylike items filled with pork, shrimp, taro root or vegetables and then steamed, fried or baked. Steamed vegetables and hearty congee soups (rice porridge with ingredients such as shrimp, fish and peanuts) are commonly offered as well. The best way to enjoy as many different dishes as possible is to dine with a group of people.

In a typical dim sum parlor, waiters roll carts between crowded tables that are crammed from wall to wall in a cavernous dining room. Some of the flashier waiters have a distinctive call that rises above the steady cacophony to advertise the contents of their cart (for non-Cantonese speakers, they lift the lids of their containers to reveal what's inside). Patrons simply select the plates they'd like from the passing carts. Dishes usually cost less than $2 but sometimes rise to around $3 for specialty items. A running tab is kept at your table.

In San Francisco, you can find good dim sum in many parts of town, but for a real experience go to Chinatown. Dim sum is popular every day; on weekends, Chinatown restaurants become noisy circus tents filled with a constant murmur (to some ears it's a roar) of Cantonese voices.

Sam Wo's so popular. It's open until 3 am (closed Sunday).

Chinatown's most historic restaurant is the **Far East Cafe** (☎ 415-982-3245, 631 Grant Ave). The carved cherry-wood booths in this dark cavern are the main attraction, although $5 lunch specials mean you aren't getting reamed for the atmosphere.

Mid-Range The *Lotus Garden* (☎ 415-397-0707, 532 Grant Ave), which shares space with the Ching Chung Temple, is a kosher Chinese vegetarian restaurant – the only one in town under rabbinical supervision. The fare is simple and cheap. *Gold Mountain* (☎ 415-296-7733, 644 Broadway) is an enormous multilevel dining hall where convoys of fresh dim sum carts file through the aisles during the day. Dinners shine; it's always worth asking what seafood items are fresh.

One of Chinatown's most celebrated eateries, *R&G Lounge* (☎ 415-982-7877, 631 Kearny St) serves capably prepared Cantonese food at reasonable prices – you can easily eat for $15 or less.

Top End *Empress of China* (☎ 415-434-1345, 838 Grant Ave) is a complete contrast to Chinatown's cheap dives, with its displays of Han Dynasty art, superb food and prices to match (full meals are $15 to $25).

North Beach (Map 3)
North Beach is *the* neighborhood for choice Italian food and drinks, from an espresso to kick-start your morning to a plate of pasta to satisfy late-night hunger pangs. Even as North Beach's Italian population has dwindled, the neighborhood has maintained a reasonably authentic European atmosphere, largely thanks to its sidewalk cafes and neighborhood eateries.

Budget *Molinari* (☎ 415-421-2337, 373 Columbus Ave) is a traditional neighborhood delicatessen that turns out some of the best sandwiches in North Beach. It has no tables, but Washington Square is just a few blocks away. *Liguria* (☎ 415-421-3786, 1700 Stockton St) is a no-frills bakery that produces one thing and one thing only: focaccia (with tomato sauce or without). Start your day with a cappuccino and Italian pastry at *Stella Pastry* (☎ 415-986-2914, 446 Columbus Ave), a nice little cafe for breakfast or a snack later in the day.

Mario's Bohemian Cigar Store (☎ 415-362-0536, 566 Columbus Ave) no longer sells cigars. Instead this relaxed cafe-bar serves tasty focaccia sandwiches, strong espresso and rich tiramisu.

Mid-Range *L'Osteria del Forno* (☎ 415-982-1124, 519 Columbus Ave) is a real gem – it's romantic, small (10 tables) and run by two pleasant Italian women who craft tasty thin-crust pizzas and sophisticated antipasti (closed Tuesday).

The *Stinking Rose* (☎ 415-781-7673, 325 Columbus Ave) is L'Osteria's direct opposite – a themed 'garlic restaurant' that projects a touristy party atmosphere.

Go to *Ideale* (☎ 415-391-4129, 1309 Grant Ave) for traditional Italian fare that's superior to the food in most places in the neighborhood.

Caffè Macaroni (☎ 415-956-9737, 59 Columbus Ave) may not look like much, but this tiny cafe with sidewalk tables is a lively spot that churns out some of the neighborhood's best Italian food (entrées $9 to $17). A second branch called *Macaroni Express* (☎ 415-217-8400, 124 Columbus Ave), across the intersection, features cheaper a la carte items. Credit cards and reservations are not accepted at either Macaroni.

Helmand (☎ 415-362-0641, 430 Broadway) serves excellent Afghani food – try the *kaddo borawni* (baked pumpkin with a light yogurt sauce) and the *aushak* (ravioli filled with leeks in a minty yogurt sauce). The vegetarian special ($12), a sampler of several vegetarian dishes, is a good deal.

Top End The ever popular *Rose Pistola* (☎ 415-399-0499, 532 Columbus Ave) fuses updated Beat-pop style (jazz combos play in the evening) with creative regional Italian dishes. Most entrées are under $20. Dinner reservations are recommended.

Enrico's (☎ 415-982-6223, 504 Broadway) is the city's oldest sidewalk cafe, offering delicate pizzas, unique antipasti and traditional seafood and meat dishes (entrées $12 to $20). Evening jazz combos add spice to the dining.

On Washington Square, *Fior d'Italia* (☎ 415-986-1886, 601 Union St) claims to be the oldest Italian restaurant in the entire country (it was founded in 1886). The extensive menu requires careful decision making: order conservatively and you'll make out all right, but expect to drop at least $25 per person.

Zax (☎ 415-563-6266, 2330 Taylor St), near the corner of Columbus Ave and Chestnut St, is a well-kept secret. This Californian-Mediterranean bistro serves its cosmopolitan crowd stupendous food from a small menu that changes weekly.

Russian Hill (Map 4)

I Fratelli (☎ 415-474-8240, 1896 Hyde St), at Green St, has wonderful Italian fare (entrées $10 to $15) and glasses of Chianti in a friendly atmosphere (open for dinner only). *Zarzuela* (☎ 415-346-0800, 2000 Hyde St), at Union St, is an authentic Spanish tapas place where the prices are reasonable but the dishes a bit skimpy. Tapas are $4 to $7, meals $10 to $15. It's open for dinner only and closed Sunday and Monday.

Fisherman's Wharf (Map 4)

Fresh seafood is a Fisherman's Wharf specialty, from the take-out food stalls to expensive waterfront restaurants – although better quality can be found in other parts of the city. If you're here during the mid-November to June crab season, enjoy Dungeness crab and sourdough bread – about as San Franciscan as you can get. Try *Alioto's* (☎ 415-673-0183, 8 Fisherman's Wharf) or *Tarantino's* (☎ 415-775-5600, 206 Jefferson St), both with great views and entrées from $13 to $20. Overlooking the water, *McCormick & Kuleto's* (☎ 415-929-1730) is your best bet for good, inexpensive seafood at Ghirardelli Square. Its informal, busy Crab Cake Lounge offers the best value; the downstairs dining room is more formal but has a more extensive seafood menu.

Near the Hyde St cable car turnaround, the historic *Buena Vista Cafe* (☎ 415-474-5044, 2765 Hyde St) is primarily a classic bar with a few tables and a menu offering breakfast and burgers (under $10). This establishment introduced Irish coffee to the US, so naturally it would be wise to partake of that tradition while you're there.

The Marina & Cow Hollow (Map 4)

In the Marina, Lombard St has a few fast-food eateries, including an old San Francisco standby, *Mel's Drive-In* (☎ 415-921-3039, 2165 Lombard St). This is an authentic '50s diner that played a significant supporting role in the George Lucas film *American Graffiti*.

Chestnut St is the restaurant locus of the Marina. For a hefty Italian hero (around $5) that you can take to the Marina Green, stop by *Lucca Delicatessen* (☎ 415-921-7873, 2120 Chestnut St). The pleasant *Chestnut Street Grill* (☎ 415-922-5558, 2231 Chestnut St) is an old bar and grill that has been expanded to include a lounge area and a heated patio. Its basic American food is reasonably priced. *Andalé Taquería* (☎ 415-749-0506, 2150 Chestnut St) offers health-conscious Mexican dishes for around $5.

Bistro Aix (☎ 415-202-0100, 3340 Steiner St) has a reasonable prix fixe dinner on weeknights ($12). Crispy roasted chicken and buttery mashed potatoes are the kind of down-home fare that makes this a popular neighborhood place. Chef May Ditano of *Columbus Ristorante* (☎ 415-474-4180, 3347 Fillmore St) has long been recognized for her outstanding homemade pastas. After three courses and wine, you'll probably have dropped $35 or more.

A few blocks south, up the hill, is the Cow Hollow neighborhood, with dozens of restaurants along Union St, from Fillmore St east to Laguna St. *Doidge's Kitchen* (☎ 415-921-2149, 2217 Union St) is a Cow Hollow institution for breakfast and lunch; it's not cheap, but the food is great. *Betelnut* (☎ 415-929-8855, 2030 Union St), near Buchanan St, dishes up a kaleidoscope of southeast Asian cuisines (entrées $9 to $15). Reservations are a must. Its streetside bar, the Dragonfly Lounge, is jammed most nights with the young, toned and tanned. The elegant and simple *PlumpJack Cafe* (☎ 415-563-4755, 3127 Fillmore St) has reasonably priced burgers, sandwiches and pastas at lunchtime. At night reservations are recommended.

Over at Fort Mason, **Greens** (☎ 415-771-6222), in Building A, is one of the city's best-known vegetarian restaurants (entrées $9 to $18). It's open for lunch Tuesday to Saturday, brunch on Sunday, and dinner Tuesday to Saturday.

Pacific Heights

The restaurant stretch of Fillmore St between Sutter and Jackson Sts, just north of Japantown, blends Japanese restaurants with other cuisines. The popular **Jackson Fillmore** (☎ 415-346-5288, 2506 Fillmore St) is set in an old-fashioned diner and serves fine southern Italian food at reasonable prices. The **Elite Cafe** (☎ 415-346-8668, 2049 Fillmore St) is a remarkably well-preserved 1920s restaurant. The Cajun and Creole seafood is good but expensive (entrées $15 to $20).

Japantown

The three interconnected shopping centers of Japan Center – the Tasamak Plaza, Kintetsu Restaurant Mall and the Kinokuniya Building – are packed with restaurants. Floating sushi bars like **Isobune** (☎ 415-563-1030, 1737 Post St), in the Kintetsu Mall, are very popular in Japan. The sushi chef stands in the center of the bar, and selections float past the patrons on wooden boats. It's fun and cheap, and the sushi is delicious. Also in the Kintetsu Mall, **Mifune** (☎ 415-922-0337) offers popular Japanese dishes, particularly noodles, at moderate prices.

Sanppo (☎ 415-346-3486, 1702 Post St), across from the Japan Center, is a down-home, inexpensive Japanese restaurant with a communal dining room. In the Kinokuniya Building, **Isuzu** (☎ 415-922-2290, 1582 Webster St) is a slightly more upscale restaurant where fish is prepared in a variety of styles with consistent expertise.

The Haight

The '60s may be long gone but the Haight is still a young slacker zone, and the emphasis here is definitely on cheap eats in a decidedly hip setting.

Budget Breakfast, especially weekend brunch, is a big deal in the Haight. Near the intersection of Haight and Ashbury Sts, fill up on spicy Cajun and Creole vittles at the **Crescent City Cafe** (☎ 415-863-1374, 1418 Haight St) or satisfy carnivorous instincts at the **Pork Store Cafe** (☎ 415-864-6981, 1451 Haight St). For lunch or dinner, the sleek **Citrus Club** (☎ 415-387-6366, 1790 Haight St) serves simple but tasty noodle soups and wok-tossed noodles for less than $8.

In the Lower Haight, popular brunch spots include **Spaghetti Western** (☎ 415-864-8461, 576 Haight St); **Kate's Kitchen** (☎ 415-626-3984, 471 Haight St); and the **Squat & Gobble Cafe** (☎ 415-487-0551, 237 Fillmore St) – all in the blocks between Steiner and Webster Sts.

Mid-Range Kan Zaman (☎ 415-751-9656, 1793 Haight St), near Shrader St, features decent and reasonably priced Middle Eastern food, funky Arabian-nights decor and the opportunity to smoke from a hookah; on some weekend nights there's a belly dancing performance.

The lively, loud and extremely popular **Cha Cha Cha** (☎ 415-386-5758, 1801 Haight St), at Shrader St, offers spicy Caribbean tapas ($4 to $7) and main dishes (under $15). They don't take reservations, so most nights you'll have to wait up to an hour for a table.

Massawa (☎ 415-621-4129, 1538 Haight St), near Ashbury St, serves East African, Eritrean and Ethiopian food (closed Monday).

Hama-Ko (☎ 415-753-6808, 108-B Carl St), near Cole St, is a little hole in the wall that dishes out some of the best sushi in town at remarkably reasonable prices.

The Lower Haight's **Thep Phanom** (☎ 415-431-2526, 400 Waller St), near Haight St, is one of San Francisco's best Thai restaurants. Most entrées cost less than $10.

Top End Eos (☎ 415-566-3063, 901 Cole St), at Carl St, is one of the city's most highly regarded East-West fusion restaurants. Impressively designed starters ($7 to $14) get the palate warmed up for the inventive main courses ($16 to $25), such as quail stuffed with steamed lotus rice and roast Alaskan halibut.

The Castro (Map 5)

The most popular pastime in the Castro is people watching, so naturally, the most popular restaurants tend to be ones with good vantage points. Heading the list is *Cafe Flore* (☎ 415-621-8579, 2298 Market St), at Noe St, a popular coffeehouse with a large outside patio that is packed on sunny days. *California Harvest Ranch Market* (☎ 415-626-0805, 2285 Market St), a gourmet grocery store and deli near 16th St, does not have tables, but the outdoor benches provide a perfect resting spot while you indulge in the market's amazing assortment of edibles.

The *Patio Cafe* (☎ 415-621-4640, 531 Castro St), between 18th and 19th Sts, has a big, noisy, covered patio tucked away in the back. *Hot 'n' Hunky* (☎ 415-621-6365, 4039 18th St), a block off Castro, is a strong contender in the 'best burger in San Francisco' contest. A burger, fries and a shake will cost less than $8.

Pozole (☎ 415-626-2666, 2337 Market St) offers a campy Día de los Muertos environment and Mexican platters. This isn't a taquería, so expect to pay a little more for your food. For a more traditional taquería experience, try *Taquería Zapata* (☎ 415-861-4470, 4150 18th St), a block west of Castro St.

Like a cat that spends its life being called 'kitty,' *2223 Market* (☎ 415-431-0692, 2223 Market St) sits in the lap of the Castro District, loved and cherished, but nameless. The ever-changing menu is small but interesting (entrées $15 to $25). Dress is casual, and reservations are recommended.

A few doors off Market St, *Chow* (☎ 415-552-2469, 215 Church St) is a remarkably affordable place that serves tasty pizzas, pastas and grilled and roasted meats. They also offer a smattering of Asian noodle dishes. Chow is a popular late-night hangout.

At lunchtime, *Café Cuvée* (☎ 415-621-7488, 2073 Market St) is a casual cafe serving salads and sandwiches over the counter. In the evening, it dims the lights and puts Cali-

fornia and New American cuisine on the table (entrées $11 to $16).

When *Mecca* (☎ 415-621-7000, 2029 Market St) opened in 1996, it instantly became the city's hottest restaurant – and reservations are still essential. This place is as much a nightclub as it is a restaurant, but the kitchen turns out respectable entrées (all under $25). The meat-heavy menu ranges from fish to quail to grilled pork, all served in classic Californian style, with plenty of exotic greens and fresh veggies.

The Mission (Map 5)

Italian, Vietnamese, East-West fusion and tapas have all established a presence in the Mission, but the neighborhood's signature food remains the burrito. Every San Franciscan has a favorite taquería – often a source of debate – but several Mission taquerías receive consistently high ratings. *La Cumbre Taquería* (☎ 415-863-8205, 515 Valencia St) and *Puerto Alegre* (☎ 415-626-2922, 546 Valencia St) are cheap, excellent Mexican eateries. The latter is popular more for its margaritas than for its food.

La Rondalla (☎ 415-647-7474, 901 Valencia St) is brave enough to escape from the standard tacos and enchiladas to tackle more adventurous Mexican fare, along with potent pitchers of margaritas.

Taquería Can-Cun (☎ 415-252-9560, 2288 Mission St), at 19th St, is one of the most popular purveyors of burritos in the city, largely on the strength of its superior tortillas, which practically melt in the mouth, and a highly lauded vegetarian burrito.

La Taquería (☎ 415-285-7117, 2889 Mission St), just south of the 24th St BART station, claims to be the Mission's original taquería. The restaurant's menu has no surprises, but it's a popular neighborhood standby. A dozen blocks east on 24th St, the *Roosevelt Tamale Parlor* (☎ 415-550-9213, 2817 24th St) has cheap tasty tamales and is popular with gringos.

If you don't want a burrito, head to the restaurant-packed block of 16th St at Valencia St and simply start walking. *Truly Mediterranean* (☎ 415-252-7482, 3109 16th St) is a small place that serves take-out falafel and shawerma for less than $5. Next door, **Sunflower** (☎ 415-626-5023, 3111 16th St) is one of a handful of Vietnamese restaurants that now flourish in the Mission. Around the corner, Sunflower has a space that serves sushi in addition to Vietnamese fare.

Across the street, **Ti Couz** (☎ 415-252-7373, 3108 16th St) is an authentic Breton creperie that turns out a huge variety of sweet and savory crepes ($3 to $7) and delicious salads. **Cafe Picaro** (☎ 415-431-4089, 3120 16th St) is a colorful Spanish tapas bar decorated with lively Miró-esque murals. **Bitter Root** (☎ 415-626-5523, 3122 16th St), offers hearty traditional American meals that are well made and cheap (fried chicken with mashed potatoes goes for $7.50). They serve three meals a day Tuesday to Saturday and are open for brunch and lunch on Sunday and Monday.

The **Slanted Door** (☎ 415-861-8032, 584 Valencia St), near 17th St, is a Vietnamese restaurant that helped ignite the neighborhood's current culinary boom. Come for a simple and affordable lunch (under $10) or a more elaborate but still reasonably priced dinner (main courses are generally under $15). Expect to wait.

The efficient architectural lines of the interior at **Herbivore** (☎ 415-826-5657, 983 Valencia St), near 21st St, appropriately reflect the clean, healthful vegan dishes on the menu. Regulars recommend the ravioli and lasagna (both under $13; sandwiches cost around $6).

At the southeast corner of Valencia and 21st Sts, **Firecracker** (☎ 415-642-3470, 1007½ Valencia St) combines northern Chinese cuisine with funky Mission District digs. Do you like cabbage? The chef here is cabbage-happy. Most entrées are under $10.

Flying Saucer (☎ 415-641-9955, 1000 Guerrero St), at 22nd St, looks like a gimmicky retro diner, but the chef has created a surprisingly original – and highly lauded – cuisine that plays on California tastes (entrées $9 to $18). It is open 5:30 to 10 pm Tuesday through Saturday. Dinner reservations are advised.

Esperpento (☎ 415-282-8867, 3295 22nd St) is a lively tapas bar that also specializes in Spanish paellas. It's open for lunch and dinner daily except Sunday. Many items cost just a few dollars, but they add up.

Elysium Cafe (☎ 415-282-2447, 2434 Mission St), downstairs from the Andora

SAN FRANCISCO

A Burrito Primer

San Francisco's Mission District is famous for its distinctive burritos. The Mission-style burrito is a perfect rolled-up package: rice, beans, grilled meat, salsa, guacamole and sour cream contained in a flour tortilla and wrapped in aluminum foil. The meat, guacamole and sour cream are optional ingredients, but a burrito without rice is *not* a Mission-style burrito. One burrito, costing $3 to $5, is often more food than a single person can chow down in a sitting.

The flour tortilla originated in Sonora, Mexico (where maize was scarce), and its purpose evolved as it spread north. California's 19th-century agricultural laborers, most of whom were Mexican, began utilizing its glutinous flexibility to create self-contained, easily transported rice-and-bean lunches. Burrito historians trace the burrito's San Francisco roots to the early 1960s, when retailers first began selling the fortifying foodstuff for take-out consumption.

If the Mission District can't claim to have invented the burrito, it should certainly be credited with perfecting and popularizing it. Incredible local competition – there are about 100 taquerías in the Mission – has forced cooks to perfect their grilling techniques, select quality ingredients, create original salsas and develop efficient systems of assembly to ensure a consistently fresh and tasty product. As the burrito's popularity extends across the nation, some of the smarter East Coast restaurants have tried to claim authenticity by boasting they serve 'San Francisco' or 'Mission-style' burritos, but they're mostly pale imitations.

Inn, is a dimly lit, romantic spot that serves a wide range of appetizers ($5 to $9) daily except Sunday from 6 to 10 pm or so.

The Richmond

When you're looking for great food in San Francisco, do not overlook the Richmond. Clement St east of Park Presidio Blvd is the cultural axis of New Chinatown. There's a slew of Chinese restaurants, but you'll also find Korean, Thai, Vietnamese and other Asian restaurants here.

Minh's Garden (☎ 415-751-8211, 208 Clement St), near 3rd Ave, is a neighborhood favorite for inexpensive Vietnamese food in a small dining room decorated with beer advertisements and old calendars. A delicious clay-pot chicken goes for around $5. *Mai's Authentic Vietnamese Kitchen* (☎ 415-221-3046, 316 Clement St), in the next block, is another good, inexpensive Vietnamese restaurant. *Tawain Restaurant* (☎ 415-387-1789, 445 Clement St), at 6th Ave, has the cheapest lunch special around ($3.25 for rice plates) and handcrafted noodles and dumplings made in the restaurant's glassed-in kitchen.

Coriya Hot Pot City (☎ 415-387-7888, 852 Clement St), at 10th Ave, is a do-it-yourself buffet. Each table comes equipped with its own hot pot, and diners select from a generous variety of meats, seafoods, vegetables and spices. This is communal eating, so bring friends and an appetite large enough to eat your money's worth: seatings cost $9 and $12, depending on when you arrive. It's open daily for lunch and dinner (closed Wednesday).

Red Crane (☎ 415-751-7226, 1115 Clement St), just down the street, is an all-vegetarian Chinese restaurant with lunch specials for around $3.50.

Geary Blvd, which runs parallel to Clement St, also has a variety of good restaurants. *Angkor Wat* (☎ 415-221-7887, 4217 Geary Blvd), at 6th Ave, has terrific Cambodian food at inexpensive prices. More than a few sushi enthusiasts have proclaimed *Kabuto* (☎ 415-752-5652, 5116 Geary Blvd), near 15th Ave, the best sushi bar in the city. It's closed Monday and can be

crowded on weekends. *Tommy's Mexican Restaurant* (☎ 415-387-4747, 5929 Geary Blvd), between 23rd and 24th Aves, specializes in Yucatán cuisine and fresh-squeezed lime margaritas.

In the same block, *Khan Toke Thai House* (☎ 415-668-6654, 5937 Geary Blvd), the best-known Thai restaurant in the area, has a romantic but casual atmosphere; you'll be asked to remove your shoes and sit at low tables. One of the city's best Vietnamese restaurants is *La Vie* (☎ 415-668-8080, 5830 Geary Blvd). You can't order pho here, but the catfish in pineapple and tamarind broth more than makes up for it. Prices are remarkable – two can eat well for $25.

The *Pacific Cafe* (☎ 415-387-7091, 7000 Geary Blvd), between 34th and 35th Aves, is a popular restaurant for fresh seafood. It's open for dinner every night, and each diner gets a complimentary glass of wine. Reservations are not accepted, so bring a jacket, as you might find yourself waiting in the Richmond District fog.

Keep heading east on Geary Blvd and it becomes Point Lobos Ave. Right at the end, the *Cliff House* (☎ 415-386-3330, 1090 Point Lobos Ave) is known for its colorful history and great views (if you can snag a window seat) but not for its food, which consists of ordinary sandwiches and burgers starting at $8.

At the western end of Golden Gate Park, across from Ocean Beach, the bustling *Beach Chalet Brewery & Restaurant* (Map 6; ☎ 415-386-8439, 1000 Great Highway) offers great bistro food (moderate in price), house-brewed beers, live jazz and blues, plus spectacular sunsets. Reservations are recommended.

The Sunset

The Sunset District, south of Golden Gate Park, has a large collection of budget ethnic restaurants, particularly along Irving St from 5th Ave all the way to 25th Ave. The up-and-coming Inner Sunset, concentrated around the intersection of 9th Ave and Irving St, has a healthy mix of traditional neighborhood establishments and fashionable new eateries.

PJ's Oyster Bed (Map 6; ☎ 415-566-7775, 737 Irving St), at 9th Ave, is of the traditional variety. It's a Cajun-Creole seafood restaurant that prepares tapas both exotic and ordinary (around $9), such as alligator fillets and crab cakes. Lines of people wait to get into *Ebisu (Map 6; ☎ 415-566-1770, 1283 9th Ave)*, near Irving, a Japanese restaurant and sushi bar that constantly earns rave reviews. *House (Map 6; ☎ 415-682-3898, 1269 9th Ave)*, in the same block, offers innovative East-West fusion at lower prices (about $15 an entrée) than more highly celebrated fusion restaurants. It's closed Monday. The trendiest restaurant in the area is the cafeteria-style *Pluto's (Map 6; ☎ 415-753-8867, 627 Irving St)*. Hilariously cartoony atomic-age decor doesn't hinder the food, which comes in large portions at unbelievably low prices.

A few blocks closer to Haight St, *Ganges (Map 6; ☎ 415-661-7290, 775 Frederick St)* is a popular but relaxed Indian vegetarian restaurant. It's closed Sunday and Monday.

ENTERTAINMENT

San Francisco's nightlife doesn't hinge on huge, hyperfashionable nightclubs but rather on its eclectic bars, dance clubs and cutting-edge concert spaces. The city also has a number of theater venues, a renowned opera house, a symphony, a ballet company and numerous modern dance companies. Sporting events are also important.

The *San Francisco Chronicle*, especially its Sunday Datebook entertainment supplement, has fairly extensive movie and theater listings. However, the city's most extensive run-down on entertainment possibilities is found in the free weeklies: the *San Francisco Bay Guardian* and the *SF Weekly*.

For tickets to the theater, the big music acts and other shows, call BASS (☎ 510-762-2277) or go to their outlets at Wherehouse or Tower Records stores. TIX Bay Area (☎ 415-433-7827), 251 Stockton St in Union Square, sells half-price tickets to musical performances, opera, dance and theater, on the day of the performance. The TIX booth is open 11 am to 6 pm Tuesday to Thursday (until 7 pm Friday and Saturday). They take cash only and charge a small service fee.

Cafes

San Francisco may not quite rival Seattle – the nation's coffee capital – but caffeine enthusiasts will not be disappointed. Cafes and coffeehouses sometimes straddle several categories: a cafe may be as much a bar and restaurant as it is a cafe. The following listings are essentially cafes where you go to sip coffee and sit around – reading, doodling or simply daydreaming.

Union Square *Café de la Presse (Map 2; ☎ 415-398-2680, 352 Grant Ave)*, across from the Chinatown Gate, is a popular, European-style cafe with an international selection of newspapers and magazines. *Yakety Yak (Map 2; ☎ 415-885-6908, 679 Sutter St)* is a funky coffee shop that also provides Internet access for a small fee.

Civic Center At the funky *Mad Magda's Russian Tea Room & Cafe (☎ 415-864-7654, 579 Hayes St)*, green-haired girls, grungy boys and older Russian women come for

---

Praise the Lord

The Glide Memorial United Methodist Church (☎ 415-771-6300), 330 Ellis St in the Tenderloin, puts on an all-inclusive service each Sunday at 9 am enlivened by a gospel choir, jazz band and psychedelic slide shows. Often 1500 people come for services – not a bad turnout.

The fact that St John Coltrane's African Orthodox Church (☎ 415-621-4054), 351 Divisadero St at Oak St, has a different approach to worship is obvious from the first tentative strains of Coltrane's 'Africa Brass,' which begin each service. Then Bishop Franzo King steps up to the altar blowing a tenor sax, and you know you are in for an amazing experience. Much of the first half of the three-hour service is devoted to an inspired performance of Coltrane's most religious recording, *A Love Supreme* (1964). Services begin every Sunday at 11:45 am.

SAN FRANCISCO

cookies, tarot readings and palmistry ($13 for a sitting).

Momi Toby's Revolution Cafe (☎ 415-626-1508, 528 Laguna St) is a small but airy room with wood-frame windows and a marble-top bar. Coffee, beer, wine, pizzettas and focaccia sandwiches draw you in; the place's vibe makes you want to stay.

Chinatown Birdcages hang above antique tables at the *Imperial Tea Court* (Map 3; ☎ 415-788-6080, 1411 Powell St). Some precious tea varieties are extremely expensive (exceeding $100 per pound), but a pot of refreshing keemun mao feng costs just a few dollars.

North Beach *Caffè Greco* (Map 3; ☎ 415-398-2680, 423 Columbus Ave) prepares a superior espresso, but the place is small and almost too popular. You're more likely to find a table a few doors down at *Caffe Puccini* (Map 3; ☎ 415-989-7033, 411 Columbus Ave). Across the street and down a block, the *Steps of Rome* (Map 3; ☎ 415-397-0435, 348 Columbus Ave) is easily the most Italian of North Beach's cafes, with see-and-be-seen energy rather than old-world charm.

Caffe Trieste (Map 3; ☎ 415-392-6739, 601 Vallejo St) is justifiably one of the most popular cafes in the city. Caffe Trieste harks back to the Beat days; it opened in 1956.

Caffè Malvina (Map 3; ☎ 415-391-1290, 1600 Stockton St) has old-world elegance, and windows along two sides keep it well lit during the day.

The Haight The Upper Haight has only a few noteworthy cafes. The *People's Cafe* (☎ 415-553-8842, 1419 Haight St), near Masonic Ave, serves quality coffee and snacks. *Blue Front Cafe* (☎ 415-252-5917, 1430 Haight St), across the street, serves food and beer as well as coffee, and often has live music.

Lower Haight offers better possibilities for cafes. The sprawling *Horse Shoe* (☎ 415-626-8852, 556 Haight St), between Steiner and Fillmore Sts, attracts the slacker crowd and is open nightly until 1 am. *Cafe International* (☎ 415-552-7390, 508 Haight St) at Fillmore St, draws a quieter clientele and serves salads, sandwiches and light Middle Eastern meals.

The Castro *Cafe Flore* (Map 5; ☎ 415-621-8579, 2298 Market St) is a wood-framed hothouse with a glassed-in patio. The clientele is almost entirely gay, and on warm afternoons it's a lively spot. The *Orbit Room Cafe* (Map 5; ☎ 415-252-9525, 1900 Market St), a postindustrial jazz-age space at the corner of Market and Laguna Sts, attracts a fashionable gay and straight crowd.

The Mission *Cafe Macondo* (Map 5; ☎ 415-863-6517, 3159 16th St) is a model bohemian literary environment, with old couches and leftist Latin-American political posters. *Red Dora's Bearded Lady Cafe and Gallery* (Map 5; ☎ 415-626-2805, 485 14th St), near Guerrero St, is a lesbian coffeehouse that doubles as a gallery and performance space.

Muddy's (Map 5; ☎ 415-647-7994, 1304 Valencia St) is a large, cluttered cafe littered with newspapers and chess and backgammon boards.

Bars & Clubs

The line between bars, clubs and music venues is often fuzzy, with many nightspots playing alternate or dual roles on any given night of the week. South of Market has the biggest concentration of clubs and music venues, while the Mission District and Haight St are lined with bars that are especially popular with the twentysomething crowd.

Union Square The best place to have a drink around Union Square is in the ritzy hotel lounges. Start at the warmly atmospheric *Compass Rose* (Map 2; ☎ 415-774-0167) in the St Francis Hotel, one of the city's most romantic and historic bars. The Clift Hotel's swank, art deco *Redwood Room* (Map 2; ☎ 415-775-4700, 496 Geary St) is open to midnight every night except Friday and Saturday, when there's live jazz until 1 am. The equally swank *Harry Denton's Starlight Room* (Map 2; ☎ 415-395-8595, 450

Powell St), on the 21st floor of the Sir Francis Drake Hotel, has live music during its happy hour (5 to 7 pm).

The *Blue Lamp* (Map 2; ☎ 415-885-1464, 561 Geary St) is a faded but noble old bar that books blues bands most nights. The *Red Room* (Map 2; ☎ 415-346-7666, 827 Sutter St), at the Commodore Hotel, is an extravagant study in reds – red vinyl, red bottles, red bar, red lights. *C Bobby's Owl Tree* (Map 2; ☎ 415-776-9344, 601 Post St), at Taylor St, applies a single-mindedness equal to that of the Red Room, but the focus here is owls.

Biscuits & Blues (Map 2; ☎ 415-292-2583, 401 Mason St), at Geary St, opened only a few years ago but has already become a dependable blues club. Cover charges range from $5 to $10; the Sunday-night gospel dinner is $15, which includes a plate full of Southern cookin'.

Civic Center *Martuni's* (☎ 415-241-0205, 4 Valencia St), at Market St, is a swank and gay-friendly cocktail lounge, often with live piano music.

Despite its questionable Tenderloin address, *Club 181* (Map 2; ☎ 415-673-8181, 181 Eddy St) is a slick supper club with some of the hottest jazz in town. The *Edinburgh Castle* (Map 2; ☎ 415-885-4074, 950 Geary St) has a big selection of British beers on tap and serves excellent fish-and-chips. Trendy *Backflip* (Map 2; ☎ 415-771-3547, 601 Eddy St), in the Phoenix Hotel, is popular with the fashionable crowd. Sunday night DJs pack 'em in.

In Hayes Valley, *Place Pigalle* (☎ 415-552-2671, 520 Hayes St) books jazz bands most nights and charges no cover. The back pool room, where the bands play, is also an art gallery. Devotees of the grape must check out *Hayes & Vine* (Map 2; ☎ 415-626-5301, 377 Hayes St), a sophisticated wine bar.

South of Market The Bay Bridge sails right over the top of the *Gordon Biersch Brewery* (Map 2; ☎ 415-243-8246, 2 Harrison St), an immensely popular after-work gathering place for the suit set. *Kate O'Brien's* (Map 2; ☎ 415-882-7240, 579 Howard St) is a comfortable Irish pub.

A popular spot for sinking a few drinks between clubs is the *20 Tank Brewery* (Map 2; ☎ 415-255-9455, 316 11th St), near Folsom St. You can do the same in hipper *El Bobo* (Map 2; ☎ 415-861-6822, 1539 Folsom St) around the corner.

The *Eagle* (Map 2; ☎ 415-626-0880) at 12th and Harrison Sts, is a quintessential gay leather bar.

Most of SoMa's dance and live-music clubs are scattered along Folsom and 11th Sts. SoMa is also a prime hunting ground for blues and jazz, particularly for 'new jazz.' *Julie's Supper Club* (Map 2; ☎ 415-861-0707, 1123 Folsom St), at 7th St, is a bustling restaurant with live blues and jazz on Friday and Saturday night. *330 Ritch* (Map 2; ☎ 415-541-9574, 330 Ritch St), off Townsend St near 3rd St, also combines jazz and food (tapas). It's closed Sunday.

The two-story *Up & Down Club* (Map 2; ☎ 415-626-2388, 1151 Folsom St), between 7th and 8th Sts, is a hip spot to hear local jazz bands (closed Sunday).

The *Hotel Utah Saloon* (Map 2; ☎ 415-421-8308, 500 4th St), at Bryant St, and the *Covered Wagon Saloon* (Map 2; ☎ 415-974-1585, 917 Folsom St), at 5th St, are bars that host bands several nights a week. You can drink and dance at the fashionable *Cat's Grill & Alley Club* (Map 2; ☎ 415-431-3332, 1190 Folsom St), near 8th St. The decor is surreal, and they serve tapas until late.

Slim's (Map 2; ☎ 415-621-3330, 333 11th St) is an authentic R&B club partly owned by '70s rock star Boz Scaggs; an impressive group of artists pass through.

Right at the corner of 11th and Folsom Sts is the noisy, crowded *Paradise Lounge* (Map 2; ☎ 415-861-6906, 1501 Folsom St). There may be as many as five different shows on three different stages on some nights, ranging from rock to jazz to poetry readings. Earlier in the day, from 3 to 7 pm, there's free pool for all.

Financial District In the opulent Sheraton Palace Hotel (Map 2; ☎ 415-392-8600, 2 New Montgomery St), the *Pied Piper Bar*, with the huge 1909 Maxfield Parrish painting for which it is named, is worth seeing – though

SAN FRANCISCO

the Palace's airy **Garden Court** is an even nicer place for a drink.

The 52nd-floor **Carnelian Room** (Map 2; ☎ 415-433-7500, 555 California St), atop the Bank of America Building, has the best views in the city. Drink prices are as high as the viewpoint. The circular bar at **Equinox** (Map 2; ☎ 415-788-1234, 5 Embarcadero Center), atop the bay-front Hyatt Regency, rotates the full 360°, showing off San Francisco from every conceivable angle.

Nob Hill Topping the list of Nob Hill bars is the **Top of the Mark** (Map 2; ☎ 415-392-3434, 999 California St), the rooftop bar atop the Mark Hopkins Hotel. The Fairmont Hotel (Map 2; ☎ 415-772-5000), at Mason and California Sts, has three cocktail lounges: the **Crown Room**, which resembles the set of any Rock Hudson movie from around 1959; the **Tonga Room**, with hurricanes blowing through the artificial lagoon every half hour; and the elegant **New Orleans Room**, with a piano player or small jazz combo every night.

North Beach The **Vesuvio Cafe** (Map 3; ☎ 415-362-3370, 255 Columbus Ave) looks across Jack Kerouac Alley to City Lights Bookstore. Vesuvio's history as a Beat hangout may make it a tourist attraction, but it continues to be a popular neighborhood bar.

Two other historic bars sit directly across Columbus Ave. **Tosca Cafe** (Map 3; ☎ 415-391-1244, 415-986-9651, 242 Columbus Ave) is as famous for its people-watching opportunities as it is for the arias that emanate from the all-opera jukebox. A trip and stumble away, in tiny William Saroyan Place, **Specs** (Map 3; ☎ 415-421-4112) has a remarkable hodgepodge of memorabilia that appears to have been culled from ports around the globe.

Grant Ave has several good bars, including the tiny **North End Caffe** (Map 3; 1402 Grant Ave) and the equally small **Gathering Caffe** (Map 3; ☎ 415-433-4247, 1326 Grant Ave); the latter often features jazz. The large, very **European Savoy Tivoli** (Map 3; ☎ 415-362-7023, 1434 Grant Ave) has a covered patio looking out onto the street.

At the elegant **Hi-Ball Lounge** (Map 3; ☎ 415-397-9464, 473 Broadway), live and DJ-spun swing music is on the menu most every night. One of the city's swankiest nightclubs, **Bimbo's 365 Club** (Map 4; ☎ 415-474-0365, 1025 Columbus Ave), near Chestnut St, features everything from live swing and rockabilly to alternative rock, country and soul.

Fisherman's Wharf The **Buena Vista Cafe** (Map 4; ☎ 415-474-5044, 2765 Hyde St), near the cable car turnaround, is so popular you may have to wait in line to get in. On Pier 39 the **Eagle Cafe** (Map 4; ☎ 415-433-3689) is a formerly idiosyncratic old bar that, despite an unsympathetic restoration, still stands out amid the hokey Wharf madness.

Lou's Pier 47 (Map 4; ☎ 415-771-0377, 300 Jefferson St) is a restaurant and bar that books live music seven days a week.

The Marina Union St, where many of the watering holes are concentrated, is singles-bar central. **Perry's** (Map 4; ☎ 415-922-9022, 1944 Union St) is a bona-fide cruising spot, as it was when Armistead Maupin wrote it into his Tales of the City novels. The **Pierce Street Annex** (Map 4; ☎ 415-567-1400, 3138 Fillmore St), between Greenwich and Filbert Sts, is another prime pickup spot. The **Union Ale House** (Map 4; ☎ 415-921-0300, 1980 Union St) distinguishes itself with a multitude of beers on tap.

The Haight In the Upper Haight, the **Persian Aub Zam Zam** (☎ 415-861-2545, 1633 Haight St), between Belvedere and Clayton Sts, has achieved cult status largely due to Bruno, the ornery bartender: he only opens when he feels like it, and on some nights he only serves martinis, and then only if you ask nicely. The retro **Club Deluxe** (☎ 415-552-6949), at the famous corner of Haight and Ashbury Sts, is in emphatic denial that the '60s ever happened. Jazz and swing combos are featured Wednesday to Sunday nights (cover $2 to $5). **John Murio's Trophy Room** (☎ 415-752-2971, 1811 Haight St), near Stanyan St, is a rowdy – but fun – neighborhood bar with two dog-eared pool tables. *Club Boomerang* (☎ *415-387-2996, 1840 Haight St*) is a small, crowded venue hosting bands you're never likely to hear from again.

In the Lower Haight, the three blocks of Haight St between Pierce and Webster Sts are home to a jumping enclave of noisy bars where young crowds pass the evening hours. *An Bodhran* (☎ *415-431-4724, 668 Haight St*) is a friendly, low-key Irish bar. The dark *Midtown Bar* (☎*415-558-8019, 582 Haight St*) starts to fill up early in the evening and throbs with action throughout the night. *Noc Noc* (☎ *415-861-5811, 557 Haight St*) has a cavelike interior that often draws comparisons to the Bedrock home of the Flintstones. A few doors down, the *Toronado* (☎ *415-863-2276, 547 Haight St*) has one of the best and broadest tap selections in town. *Mad Dog in the Fog* (☎ *415-626-7279, 530 Haight St*) is a popular British-style pub with dartboards, soccer on TV and tasty pub grub. *Nickie's BBQ* (☎ *415-621-6508, 460 Haight St*) and the *Top* (☎ *415-864-7386, 424 Haight St*) are two noisy joints packed most nights of the week. At the Top, the DJ's music of choice is punk and reggae; at Nickie's, the tunes range from hip-hop and world music to funk and jazz.

The Castro Cruising the Castro is a time-honored activity for the city's large gay community. The *Twin Peaks Tavern* (*Map 5; ☎ 415-864-9470, 401 Castro St*) pioneered large bay windows so the patrons could watch the passing scene.

Detour (*Map 5; ☎ 415-861-6053, 2348 Market St*) has the city's longest happy hour (2 to 8 pm), a superior sound system, chain-link urban playground decor, go-go dancers and a diverse crowd.

The drinkers and people watchers on the balcony opposite Cafe Flore are patrons of the semi-upscale *Metro* (*Map 5; ☎ 415-703-9750, 3600 16th St*). At *Badlands* (*Map 5; ☎ 415-626-9320, 4121 18th St*), the Sunday beer bust (4 to 9 pm) attracted lines that stretched halfway down the block. The diverse gay crowd included leather men, businessmen and punky kids. At this writing, however, it is closed indefinitely for construction. The *Bar on Castro* (*Map 5; ☎ 415-626-7220, 456 Castro St*) draws gays of all stripes.

The Mint (*Map 5; ☎ 415-626-4726*), attached to a hamburger joint at 1942 Market St, draws a diverse karaoke-loving crowd. It's open all day, but things only get interesting after 9 pm, when the karaoke gets started.

The below-the-street-level, '30s-style *Cafe du Nord* (*Map 5; ☎ 415-861-5016, 2170 Market St*), at Sanchez St, is a former speakeasy that features live jazz, rockabilly, West Coast blues and salsa acts.

The Mission The Mission's bars are, like most everything else about the Mission, a funky mix. The *Elbo Room* (*Map 5; ☎ 415-552-7788, 647 Valencia St*) has a swank curved bar that's always packed with scenesters. Upstairs, DJs and live musicians play anything from experimental jazz to hip-hop. The cover charge varies.

At the crowded junction of 16th and Valencia Sts, *Esta Noche* (*Map 5; ☎ 415-861-5757, 3079 16th St*) is a Latino gay bar especially popular with cross-dressers. *Casanova Lounge* (*Map 5; ☎ 415-863-9328, 527 Valencia St*) feels like a Quentin Tarantino set brought to life, and dimly lit *Dalva* (*Map 5; ☎ 415-252-7740, 3121 16th St*) feels like the stage design of a Spanish alley. Up the street, the *Kilowatt* (*Map 5; ☎ 415-861-2595, 3160 16th St*) is in a converted firehouse and draws a hip Mission crowd.

Three blocks north of 16th St, *Zeitgeist* (*Map 5; ☎ 415-255-7505, 199 Valencia St*) is a popular spot for San Francisco's urban biker scene – from bike messengers to motorcyclists. The back patio is a nice place to spend a warm afternoon.

The *Lexington Club* (*Map 5; ☎ 415-863-2052, 3464 19th St*) is the only all-lesbian bar – that's seven days a week – in the city.

The *Lone Palm* (*Map 5; ☎ 415-648-0109, 3394 22nd St*) has a romantic *Casablanca*-like setting that is sometimes enhanced by a pianist and a muted trumpeter.

The *Latin American Club* (*Map 5; ☎ 415-647-2732, 3286 22nd St*), just east of Valencia St, is low-key and popular. The *Make-Out*

Room (Map 5; ☎ 415-647-2888, 3225 22nd St), just down the street, comes furnished with velvet curtains, a concrete floor and a vibrating bed.

There are a few good bars and clubs on Mission St itself. The *Elysium Cafe (Map 5; ☎ 415-282-0337, 2438 Mission St)* is a comfortable, moodily lit bar as well as an excellent restaurant. *Bruno's (Map 5; ☎ 415-550-7455, 2389 Mission St)*, a swank bar-restaurant, books talented jazz groups in two rooms nearly every night (other types of music round out the weekly schedule). There's usually a cover charge of a few dollars. South down Mission St, *El Rio (☎ 415-282-3325, 3158 Mission St)*, at Cesar Chavez St, is a large, upbeat bar and dance club that draws a diverse crowd of gays, lesbians and straights of varying ethnicities.

Dance Clubs
South of Market SoMa nightclubbing requires some local, underground knowledge, as clubs constantly fade in and out. To find out what's going on, check the weekly *San Francisco Bay Guardian* or *SF Weekly* newspapers.

1015 Folsom (Map 2; ☎ 415-431-0700, 1015 Folsom St) is the city's foremost dance club, generally featuring the best in local DJ talent and hosting some of the most popular club nights.

The *Sound Factory (Map 2; ☎ 415-979-8686, 525 Harrison St)* has 15,000 sq feet of dance space in many rooms on many levels. Musical persuasions run the gamut, from house and jungle to Top 40.

The *Endup (Map 2; ☎ 415-543-7700, 995 Harrison St)* is a SoMa institution that attracts a mixed crowd, although Fag Fridays make an obvious pitch for the gay male set. Things run late here, often till after 4 am. The art gallery at *111 Minna St (☎ 415-974-1719, 111 Minna St)* turns into a club at night. It's a cool space that draws a smart SoMa crowd.

Next door to the Paradise Lounge, the *Transmission Theater (Map 2; ☎ 415-861-6909, 314 11th St)* often hosts dance parties, though it isn't strictly a dance club.

Trendy *V/sf (Map 2; ☎ 415-621-1530, 278 11th St)* has become one of the more successful venues in town (some would say too successful). It recently took over the popular, kinky Bondage-a-Go-Go Wednesday night party.

Club Townsend (Map 2; ☎ 415-974-1156, 177 Townsend St) caters primarily to gay men; lesbian parties, such as the monthly Q Club, are also held here. The steady source for lesbian entertainment is the *CoCo Club (Map 2; ☎ 415-626-2337, 139 8th St)*. It isn't strictly a lesbian hangout – all are welcome – and dancing is only one facet of CoCo's constantly evolving scene.

The *Stud (Map 2; ☎ 415-863-6623, 399 9th St)*, at Harrison St, is a sort of elder statesman of SoMa clubs. Though some straights now frequent it, the Stud remains first and foremost a gay establishment.

The *DNA Lounge (Map 2; ☎ 415-626-1409, 375 11th St)* is a big mass-market dance club that had its heyday in the '80s.

North Beach If you're looking for an alternative to the too-cool SoMa dance scene, the place you're looking for just might be *Broadway Studios (Map 3; ☎ 415-291-0333, 435 Broadway)*. This old ballroom (built in 1911) has three bars, a restaurant and a spacious dance floor. Musical persuasions include rock, swing, salsa, funk and tango.

The Castro The population at the *Café (Map 4; ☎ 415-861-3846, 2367 Market St)* is young, ethnically mixed and gets more male as the night goes on. This is one of the only places in the Castro that has a dance floor, and the long deck overlooking Market St is a good place to cool off.

The Mission The club unofficially known as *Liquid (Map 4; ☎ 415-431-8889, 2925 16th St)*, near South Van Ness Ave, hosts a different party every night of the week, and the vibe is consistently good. People still call the place Liquid, even though a lawsuit by a Miami club named Liquid has forced the club to look for a new name. The name may change, but the vibe will remain the same.

Comedy & Cabaret

A number of bars occasionally feature comedy nights, but for the real thing, San Francisco has two immensely popular comedy clubs: the *Punch Line* (☎ 415-397-4337, 444 Battery St), in Maritime Plaza in the Financial District; and *Cobb's Comedy Club* (Map 4; ☎ 415-928-4320, 2801 Leavenworth St), in the Cannery at Fisherman's Wharf. Both clubs usually have two performances nightly, one around 8 pm and one around 11 pm, with a cover charge ranging from $5 to $15 and a two-drink minimum.

Along comedic lines is the everlasting *Beach Blanket Babylon* extravaganza in North Beach (see the Theater section for more information). Also in North Beach is *Finocchio* (Map 3; ☎ 415-982-9388, 506 Broadway), where female impersonators engage in a 'been-there, seen-that' type of comedy routine.

Cinema

Forget those modern multiscreen theaters – San Francisco boasts a bunch of great, old, single-screen dinosaur theaters. Topping the list for cinemas where the building is as interesting as the film is undoubtedly the *Castro Theatre* (Map 5; ☎ 415-621-6120, 429 Castro St), with a magnificent Wurlitzer organ that rises out of the stage.

In business since 1913, the *Clay Theater* (☎ 415-346-1123, 2261 Fillmore St) has been in continuous operation longer than any cinema in the city. It still looks magnificent, if a little worn. The *Lumière* (☎ 415-885-3201, 415-352-0810, 1572 California St), at Polk St, has three screens and shows a mix of art house films and new releases. The art deco *Metro* (Map 4; ☎ 415-931-1685) is in the Marina at Union at Webster Sts. Another art deco gem, the *Balboa* (☎ 415-221-8184, 3630 Balboa St), in the Richmond District, has been operating since 1926 and screens new releases.

The *Casting Couch* (☎ 415-986-7001, 950 Battery St), near Levi's Plaza and the Embarcadero, is a tiny theater that seats just 46 people on luxury loveseat couches. Gourmet snacks are delivered to your seat, and admission is $8.50.

In the Mission, the *Roxie Cinema* (Map 5; ☎ 415-863-1087, 3117 16th St) screens an eclectic selection of films, although the space itself is featureless. At the small *Red Vic Movie House* (☎ 415-668-3994, 1727 Haight St), in the Upper Haight, you can see rare cult films and other interesting oldies and rereleases.

The city hosts the Asian American Film Festival (☎ 415-863-0814) in March at Japantown's *Kabuki 8 Theater* (☎ 415-931-9800, 1881 Post St); the popular San Francisco International Film Festival (☎ 415-931-3456) in April (mainly at the Kabuki and the Castro); the Gay and Lesbian Film Festival in June (mainly at the Castro); and the Jewish Film Festival (☎ 510-548-0556) in July and August (at the Castro).

Performing Arts

Theater San Francisco is not a cutting-edge city for theater, but it has one major company, the *American Conservatory Theater* (ACT; ☎ 415-749-2228), which puts on performances at a number of theaters in the Union Square area, including the *Geary Theater* at 450 Geary St; the *Marines Memorial Theatre* at 609 Sutter St; and the *Stage Door Theatre* at 420 Mason St. The *Magic Theatre* (Map 4; ☎ 415-441-8822), at Building D in Fort Mason Center, is probably the city's most adventurous large theater.

The big spectacular shows – like the Andrew Lloyd-Webber musicals – play at the *Curran Theatre* (☎ 415-474-3800, 445 Geary St), between Mason and Taylor Sts; the *Golden Gate Theatre* (☎ 415-474-3800, 1 Taylor St), at Golden Gate Ave and Market St; and the *Orpheum Theatre* (☎ 415-551-2000) at Market and Hyde Sts.

Many of the jokes will go straight over non-San Franciscans' heads, but *Beach Blanket Babylon* at *Club Fugazi* (Map 3; ☎ 415-421-4222, 678 Green St), in North Beach, is San Francisco's longest-running comedy extravaganza, now into its third decade and still packing them in. There are shows Wednesday to Sunday and cleaned-up matinee performances on weekends (over 21 years of age, except at matinees).

San Francisco also has many small theater spaces – such as the **Marsh** (☎ 415-641-0235, *1062 Valencia St*), **Theater Artaud** (☎ 415-621-7797, *450 Florida St*) and **Theatre Rhinoceros** (☎ 415-861-5079, *2926 16th St*) – that host solo and experimental shows. Check listings in the city's weekly and daily newspapers.

Classical Music The *San Francisco Symphony*, whose musical director is the popular Michael Tilson Thomas, performs September to May in the Davies Symphony Hall (☎ 415-431-5400), Grove St at Van Ness Ave. Tickets are typically $24 to $68, but a limited number of cheap seats go on sale two hours before the performance for $10 to $12, cash only.

The *Herbst Theatre* (☎ 415-392-4400, *401 Van Ness Ave*) in the Veterans Building also has some classical performances. The *San Francisco Conservatory of Music* (☎ 415-759-3475, *1201 Ortega Ave*) puts on a variety of performances at Hellman Hall.

Opera The acclaimed *San Francisco Opera* performs from early September to mid-December at the *War Memorial Opera House* (Map 2; ☎ 415-864-3330, *301 Van Ness Ave*). For only $20, students with a valid ID can sit in the $100 orchestra section; these tickets go on sale two hours before curtain. Standing-room tickets, available for some shows, are $8 and also go on sale two hours before performances.

Dance The *San Francisco Ballet* (☎ 415-703-9400) performs at the opera house and at the *Yerba Buena Center for the Arts* (Map 2; ☎ 415-978-2787, *700 Howard St*) at 3rd St.

San Francisco also has a large and diverse modern dance scene. The *ODC Theater*

Free & Outdoors

Free outdoor entertainment abounds in San Francisco, especially in summer, when many of the city's big performance companies – and some of its smaller ones – sponsor events in the open air.

On summer Sundays the **Stern Grove Festival** (☎ 415-252-6252) presents free performances in the Stern Grove Amphitheater, at Sloat Blvd and 19th Ave in the Sunset. The grove's open-air amphitheater is a beautiful spot to enjoy a picnic while listening to music performed by the San Francisco Symphony or big-name jazz artists.

One of the city's most popular outdoor events is **Shakespeare in the Park** (☎ 415-422-2222). Each year one play is performed in parks throughout the Bay Area, and in September it comes to Golden Gate Park. It's free and starts at 1:30 pm, but the grove, just across Conservatory Drive from the Conservatory of Flowers, fills up much earlier.

The second Sunday in September, also in Golden Gate Park, is **Opera in the Park**, a free, noncostumed concert celebrating the opening of the opera season. It runs from 1:30 to 3:30 pm and draws huge crowds. It's held in Sharon Meadow, at the eastern end of the park near Stanyan St.

The **San Francisco Mime Troupe** (☎ 415-285-1717, 415-285-1720 for schedule information) performs at parks throughout San Francisco and the East Bay all summer. Don't expect any silent, white-faced mimes – this is political musical theater in the commedia dell'arte tradition. It's big, it's fun and it's free.

For a bit of music at lunchtime downtown, the **Noontime Concert Series** (☎ 415-255-9410) puts on a varied repertoire of free classical music performances in Old St Mary's Church, at Grant Ave and California St, every Tuesday at 12:30 pm (donations appreciated). On Fridays during the summer there are **lunchtime jazz concerts** in Justin Herman Plaza and, if you prefer the shade, in Redwood Plaza, next to the Transamerica building.

(Map 5; ☎ 415-863-9834, 3153 17th St) has modern dance nearly every weekend, and the Yerba Buena Center and *Theater Artaud* *(☎ 415-621-7797, 450 Florida St)* also frequently have dance performances. Other than dance at these venues, most modern dance is in small performance spaces scattered throughout the Mission District. Check the weekly newspapers for performances.

SPECTATOR SPORTS

San Francisco's National Football League (NFL) team, the San Francisco 49ers (☎ 415-468-2249), is one of the most successful teams in league history, having brought home no fewer than five Super Bowl championships. The city's National League baseball team, the San Francisco Giants (☎ 415-467-8000), has not been so successful since moving from its original home, the Polo Grounds in Brooklyn, New York. The Giants and 49ers share the cold and windy Candlestick Park (officially 3Com Park), off Hwy 101 in the southern part of the city. By the spring of 2000 the Giants should be playing in their new downtown stadium, Pacific Bell Park (Map 2).

Tickets are available through BASS (☎ 510-762-2277). Ticket brokers, who sometimes charge astronomical prices, include Just Tix (☎ 510-838-0193) and Mr Ticket (☎ 415-292-7328).

SHOPPING

San Francisco's shopping, like its nightlife, is best when the words 'small,' 'odd,' and 'eccentric' come in to play. Sure, there are big department stores and international name-brand boutiques, but the oddities of the Castro, the Haight or the Mission are a lot more fun.

Where to Shop

Union Square San Francisco's downtown shopping concentrates around Union Square and nearby Market St. Macy's (☎ 415-397-3333), Neiman-Marcus (☎ 415-362-3900) and Saks Fifth Avenue (☎ 415-986-4300) make up the square's trio of plush department stores. Nordstrom (☎ 415-243-8500) occupies the top several floors of the stylish

San Francisco Shopping Centre (☎ 415-495-5656), 865 Market St at 5th St, where you'll also find clothing boutiques and a variety of other shops. A huge new Bloomingdale's is scheduled to open next door to the San Francisco Centre in 2001.

Hayes Valley Hayes St between Franklin and Laguna Sts near the Civic Center is a trendy little enclave with a subcultural feel. Most of the shops are up-to-the-minute boutiques featuring local designers, but there are also stores selling tasteful furniture and housewares.

Chinatown Only Fisherman's Wharf rivals Chinatown for sheer quantity of tourist junk, especially along Grant Ave. Instead, explore Chinatown's back streets and alleys for bargain-priced cookware and unusual herbal pharmaceuticals.

Fisherman's Wharf For San Francisco souvenirs, there's no better – or worse – place than Fisherman's Wharf. This garish tourist strip reaches its peak in the claustrophobic assortment of shops, amusement arcades and eateries of Pier 39. The Cannery, Ghirardelli Square and the Anchorage are other, less frenetic, wharf-front shopping centers.

The Marina & Cow Hollow Union St in Cow Hollow is dotted with designer boutiques and gift shops. Only a few blocks north toward the bay is Chestnut St in the Marina, where a host of chain stores like the Gap and Pottery Barn cater to a yuppie crowd.

The Haight Haight St tries hard to sustain its role as a youth-culture mecca; these days it's the place to come for superchunky platform shoes rather than Indian hippie sandals. It's particularly good for vintage clothing and music, especially secondhand CDs and vinyl. The Upper Haight can get very crowded on weekends. There are good shops in both the Upper and Lower Haight.

The Castro & Noe Valley Just south of Market St, Castro St has a bit of everything, including chichi antique shops, men's

SAN FRANCISCO

clothing stores, bookstores and novelty stores, all aimed to one degree or another at an affluent gay crowd. Come as much for the vibe and the people watching as for what's in the stores.

Follow Castro St south, over a high hill, and below lies Noe Valley's 24th St, most easily reached on the Muni J-Church streetcar. This thoroughly San Franciscan street is far from the tourist throng and is packed with a fine selection of clothes, books and food. Along here you'll also find a preponderance of shops filled with maternity wear, recycled kids' clothes and toys.

The Mission Valencia St is a hot spot for recycled clothing and secondhand furniture. Some stores here specialize in overpriced junk, but a few places sell curios of the past at reasonable prices. The interesting shops are spread out along the strip between 16th and 24th Sts and are interspersed with cafes and restaurants.

Cameras

Adolph Gasser (☎ 415-495-3852), in SoMa at 181 2nd St, between Mission and Howard Sts, has a huge range of new and used photographic and video equipment and also processes film. Downtown, Brooks Camera (☎ 415-362-4708), 125 Kearny St between Post and Sutter Sts, sells new cameras and does repairs and rentals.

Fashion

San Francisco is a stylish city, but the great thing is that the style spectrum is far-ranging and diverse – in San Francisco, anything goes, from sharp tailored suits to retro to drag extravagance, and everything in between.

Gap, a San Francisco-based company, has half a dozen city locations, the most prominent being the flagship store in the James Flood Building, at the corner of Market and Powell Sts (☎ 415-788-5909). Banana Republic, owned by Gap, but a bit more upscale than Gap, has stores at 256 Grant Ave (☎ 415-788-3087) and 2 Embarcadero Center (☎ 415-986-5076). The Esprit factory outlet (☎ 415-957-2550), 499 Illinois St at

> ## Adults Only
>
> In the heart of the Mission, there's a tasteful shop providing means for adult entertainment. **Good Vibrations** (☎ 415-974-8980), 1210 Valencia St, specializes in vibrators of all types and sizes, and other paraphernalia, such as sex toys, books and videos. It's open daily 11 am to 7 pm.
>
> Even kinkier is the **Foxy Lady Boutique** (☎ 415-285-4980), 2644 Mission St. It specializes in sex-industry chic, including shiny thigh-high stiletto boots and underwear made of feathers; a grumpy old guy selling lottery tickets staffs the front desk.
>
> If you're into the leather subculture, do your shopping in the Castro or SoMa. **Image Leather** (☎ 415-621-7551), 2199 Market St, is a hard-core leather and fetish gear shop; descend into the 'dungeon' where there's a museum of sorts. **Stormy Leather** (☎ 415-626-1672), 1158 Howard St in SoMa, sells leather and PVC intimate apparel, as well as whips, paddles and collars.

16th St, near Potrero Hill, is a big warehouse with 30% to 50% discounts on apparel by Esprit, another San Francisco start-up.

Designer Clothing If price is no object, head to Wilkes Bashford (☎ 415-986-4380), 375 Sutter St, which carries high-quality men's clothes. MAC, or Modern Appealing Clothing (☎ 415-837-0615), 5 Claude Lane downtown, has a fabulous men's shop filled with designer and retro gear.

There are many great women's clothing stores in San Francisco. Check out the exquisite outfits on offer at the women's MAC (☎ 415-837-1604), 1543 Grant Ave in North Beach. Favorite boutiques in Hayes Valley include Junebug (☎ 415-863-5284), 519 Laguna St, which carries a small but well-chosen assortment of groovy gear (closed Monday); and Asphalt (☎ 415-626-5196), 551 Hayes St, which boasts a large selection by local designers.

Rabat (☎ 415-282-7861), 4001 24th St in Noe Valley, has interesting shoes and drapey, sumptuous clothes. Ambiance (☎ 415-552-5095), 1458 Haight St, has casual and dressy women's clothing plus vintage-style hats and jewelry. Jeremy's (☎ 415-882-4929), 2 South Park in SoMa, has all sorts of big-name designer seconds at bargain prices.

Vintage Clothing Haight St has bumper-to-bumper retro clothing shops, including Martini Mercantile at No 1519 (☎ 415-552-1940) and No 1736 (☎ 415-831-1942), and La Rosa Vintage (☎ 415-668-3744) at No 1171. The emporium-like Wasteland (☎ 415-863-3150), No 1660, is more of a grab bag, with bargain-priced stuff from the '70s, '80s and '90s.

Guys and Dolls (☎ 415-285-7174), 4789 24th St in Noe Valley, is a hidden gem with lots of clothes and accessories from the 1930s and '40s. American Rag (☎ 415-474-5214), 1305 Van Ness Ave, is a huge store with shoes and new and recycled clothes.

If you'd like a change of outfit, trade in the one you're wearing for a new set of duds at Buffalo Exchange, 1555 Haight St (☎ 415-431-7733), and 1800 Polk St (☎ 415-346-5726). Clothes Contact (☎ 415-621-3212), 473 Valencia St, sells clothes by the pound ($8 per lb), with no single item costing more than $8.

Thrift Stores The Mission District has more thrift stores than any other area of town. The biggest are Thrift Town (☎ 415-861-1132), 2101 Mission St; the Salvation Army Thrift Store (☎ 415-643-8040), 1501 Valencia St at 26th St; and the Community Thrift Store (☎ 415-861-4910), 625 Valencia St. Also in the Mission, Goodwill (☎ 415-826-5759), 2279 Mission St, is densely packed with good stuff (plus there's a cafe).

Food & Drink

The Embarcadero farmers' market takes place on Saturday from 8:30 am to 1:30 pm and Sunday 9 am to 1 pm and is well worth a visit. The market is at Green and Front Sts, where they hit the Embarcadero. A less impressive farmers' market is held on United Nations Plaza in the Civic Center on Wednesday and Sunday from 8 am to 5 pm.

If you don't leave San Francisco with an appreciation for **sourdough bread** you haven't tried hard enough. Boudin Bakery (☎ 415-928-1849), 156 Jefferson St in Fisherman's Wharf, is still the best place for classic sourdough. There's another branch in Macy's (☎ 415-296-4740) on Union Square, one in Ghirardelli Square (☎ 415-928-7404), and many others scattered throughout the city.

Ghirardelli is the big name in **chocolate** in this town. You can find Ghirardelli treats all over the city and beyond, but two stores sell it in Ghirardelli Square on the site of the company's old factory: Ghirardelli's Premium Chocolates (☎ 415-474-3938) and Ghirardelli Too (☎ 415-474-1414).

For overseas visitors, taking back a couple bottles of Napa Valley or Sonoma Valley **wine** is a great idea. The Napa Valley Winery Exchange (☎ 415-771-2887), downtown at 415 Taylor St, has small-production and specialist wines. K&L Wines and Spirits (☎ 415-896-1734), 734 Harrison St near the Moscone Center, has a wide range of Californian wines. Also on Harrison St, at No 953, the Wine Club (☎ 415-512-9086) has discounted prices on a huge selection of wines, as well as a help-yourself wine-tasting bar.

Music

The best place for interesting new and used records in all genres is Amoeba Records (☎ 415-831-1200), 1855 Haight St near Stanyan St. This huge emporium, formerly a bowling alley, will keep you occupied for hours. Another place to look for used records, CDs and tapes is Streetlight Records (☎ 415-282-3550), 3979 24th St in Noe Valley.

Of the stores specializing in vinyl, try Flat Plastic Sound (☎ 415-386-5095), 24 Clement St at Arguello Blvd, which stocks classical and rare pop vinyl, and Grooves (☎ 415-436-9933), 1797 Market St, which offers a free search service. The city's longest-running record store, Jack's Record Cellar (☎ 415-431-3047), 254 Scott St at Page St in the Lower Haight, still specializes in 78-rpm discs.

SAN FRANCISCO

For indie music, check out Aquarius Records (☎ 415-647-2272), 1055 Valencia St in the Mission. Discolandia (☎ 415-826-9446), deep in the Mission at 2964 24th St, is the oldest Latin-music store in the Bay Area.

If sheer scale is what you're after, visit the Virgin Megastore (☎ 415-397-4525), 2 Stockton St at Market St, complete with listening stations and a cafe. For a large but bland selection of CDs, go to Tower Records (☎ 415-885-0500) at the corner of Columbus Ave and Bay St close to Fisherman's Wharf. There's another Tower at the corner of Market and Noe Sts in the Castro (☎ 415-621-0588). The Tower Records Outlet (☎ 415-957-9660), 660 3rd St in SoMa, is a good place for a bargain.

Outdoor Gear

Many of these stores sell not only clothing but the necessary equipment for outdoor adventure, including travel guides. They can give good advice, and they have bulletin boards full of information.

The North Face (☎ 415-433-3223), 180 Post St, has high-quality outdoor and adventure gear, though you may get better deals at their factory outlet store in SoMa (☎ 415-626-6444), 1325 Howard St between 9th and 10th Sts. Patagonia (☎ 415-771-2050), 770 North Point St in the Fisherman's Wharf area, is another respected name in outdoor gear. Eddie Bauer (☎ 415-986-7600), 250 Post St, has three floors of outdoor equipment and clothing.

For state-of-the-art snowboards, pay a visit to SFO Snowboarding (☎ 415-386-1666), 618 Shrader St in the Upper Haight. Next door is its sister shop, FTC Skateboarding (☎ 415-386-6693).

Piercings & Tattoos

Numerous body-piercing professionals will pierce parts of your body nowhere near your ears. Nipples and navels are the most popular 'below the neck' piercings, though men can consider half a dozen different ways of putting a pin through their genitals.

Piercing specialists start with the Gauntlet (☎ 415-431-3133), 2377 Market St at Castro St. In the Haight, there's Anubis Warpus

(☎ 415-431-2218), 1525 Haight St, and in the Mission, Body Manipulations (☎ 415-621-0408), 3234 16th St near Guerrero St. Nomad Body Piercing (☎ 415-563-7771), 1808 McAllister St north of the Panhandle, is a friendly place with lush tropical decor.

Tattoos are what you need to go along with your piercings, and Lyle Tuttle Tattooing (☎ 415-775-4991), 841 Columbus Ave in North Beach, will satisfy that need. It also has a small tattoo museum. Some girls might prefer the women-owned and -operated Black & Blue Tattoo (☎ 415-626-0770), 483 14th St in the Mission.

GETTING THERE & AWAY
Air

The Bay Area has three major airports: San Francisco International Airport (SFO), on the west side of the bay; Oakland International Airport, only a few miles across the bay on the east side; and San Jose International Airport, at the southern end of the bay. The majority of international flights use SFO; at Oakland and San Jose 'international' means Mexico and Canada. All three airports are important domestic gateways, but travelers from other US (particularly West Coast) cities may find cheaper flights into Oakland, a hub for discount airlines such as Southwest.

SFO (☎ 650-876-7809) is on the Peninsula, 14 miles south of downtown San Francisco, off Hwy 101. SFO is undergoing massive renovations (scheduled for completion in 2003). In the meantime, the North Terminal is where American, Canadian and United Airlines are based. The South Terminal is home to Air Canada, Alaska Airlines, America West, Continental, Delta, Southwest, TWA and US Airways. And the International Terminal is where you'll find all international airlines (except for the Canadian ones), plus the international services of Alaska Airlines, Delta, Northwest and United.

Information Booths (white courtesy phone ☎ 7-0018) on the lower level of all three terminals operate daily from 8 am to midnight. Travelers' Aid information booths on the upper level operate daily from 9 am to 9 pm. All three terminals have ATMs.

Bus

All bus services (except Green Tortoise) arrive at and depart from the Transbay Terminal (Map 2; ☎ 415-495-1575), 425 Mission St at 1st St, two blocks south of Market St. If you're heading out to neighboring communities you can take AC Transit (☎ 510-839-2882) buses to the East Bay; Golden Gate Transit (☎ 415-932-2000) buses north to Marin and Sonoma counties; SamTrans (☎ 800-660-4287) buses south to Palo Alto and along the coast; and Santa Clara Transportation Agency (☎ 800-894-9908) buses south beyond Palo Alto and to San Jose.

Greyhound Lines (☎ 800-231-2222, www .greyhound.com) has multiple buses daily to Los Angeles ($35/67 one way/roundtrip; eight to 12 hours) and other destinations.

An alternative to Greyhound is the funky Green Tortoise bus service (☎ 415-956-7500, 800-867-8647), with an office at 494 Broadway at Kearny St; all buses leave from the corner of 1st and Natoma Sts in SoMa. The buses have been converted into rolling lounges, and there are stops for cookouts. The north-south trip runs between Seattle and Los Angeles via San Francisco. From San Francisco the fares are: Seattle $59, Portland $49, Eugene $39 and Los Angeles $35. For an extra $10, bicycles are welcome.

Train

CalTrain (☎ 800-660-4287) operates down the Peninsula, linking San Francisco with Palo Alto (Stanford University) and San Jose. The CalTrain terminal is south of Market St at the corner of 4th and Townsend Sts. Muni's N-Judah streetcar line runs to and from the CalTrain station.

The nearest Amtrak (☎ 800-872-7245) terminal is at Jack London Square in Oakland (see the San Francisco Bay Area chapter).

GETTING AROUND
To/From the Airport

SFO operates a ground transportation information hotline (☎ 800-736-2008), weekdays 7:30 am to 5 pm.

SamTrans (☎ 800-660-4287) express bus No 3X ($1) takes 20 minutes to reach the Colma BART station, where you can ride

BART to downtown San Francisco ($2.25). Or take the free CalTrain (☎ 800-660-4287) shuttle on its nine-minute ride to the Millbrae CalTrain station. From there you can ride the CalTrain north to San Francisco ($1.75 between 10 am and 4 pm, $1.25 at other times).

Airport transport buses include the SFO Airporter (☎ 415-495-8404), with three different shuttle services operating every 20 minutes to a list of major hotels. The fare is $10, $18 roundtrip.

Airport shuttle service is provided by Super Shuttle (☎ 415-558-8500) for $13 one way. Lorrie's (☎ 415-334-9000) and Quake City (☎ 415-255-4899) are $10. Others include American Airporter Shuttle (☎ 415-546-6689) and Marin Airporter (☎ 415-461-4222).

Public Transportation

Muni San Francisco's principal public transportation system is the San Francisco Municipal Railway (☎ 415-673-6864), known as Muni, which operates nearly a hundred Muni bus lines (many of them electric trolley buses), Muni Metro streetcars, historic streetcars and the famous cable cars.

The detailed *Street & Transit Map* costs $2 and is available at newspaper stands around Union Square. A free timetable, worth having if you're riding a line with irregular service, is available at Metro stations and on some buses.

Standard Muni fares are $1 for buses or streetcars, $2 for cable cars. Transfer tickets are available at the start of your journey, and you can then use them for two connecting trips within about 90 minutes or so. However, they are *not* transferable to cable cars.

A Muni Pass, available in one-day ($6), three-day ($10) or seven-day ($15) versions, allows unlimited travel on all Muni transportation (including cable cars). They are available from the Visitors Information Center at Hallidie Plaza, the half-price tickets kiosk on Union Square, some hotels and businesses that display the Muni Pass sign in their window. A cheaper Weekly Pass costs $9 and allows free bus and railway travel and discounts on cable car rides.

Negotiating the Neighborhoods

If you're planning on getting around on public transit, you really should pick up a free Muni map at the visitor center. Some of the most important Muni bus routes for visitors include:

No 5 Fulton Along Market, McAllister and Fulton Sts along the north side of Golden Gate Park all the way to the ocean

No 7 Haight From the Ferry Building along Market and Haight Sts, through the Haight, to the southeast corner of Golden Gate Park; daytime only

No 14 Mission Along Mission St through SoMa and the Mission district

No 15 3rd St From 3rd St in SoMa, through the Financial District on Kearny St, through North Beach on Columbus Ave, then along Powell St to the Fisherman's Wharf area

No 18 46th Ave Palace of the Legion of Honor to Sutro Baths along the western edge of Golden Gate Park on the Great Hwy, past San Francisco Zoo and Lake Merced

No 22 Fillmore From Potrero Hill, through the Mission along Fillmore St, past Japantown to Pacific Heights and the Marina

No 24 Divisadero Through Noe Valley, along Castro St then Divisadero St to Pacific Heights

No 26 Valencia Through the historic areas of the Mission, along Valencia St to Market and Polk Sts, and through SoMa along Mission St

No 28 19th Ave From Fort Mason to the Golden Gate Bridge toll plaza and on through the Presidio, Richmond District, Golden Gate Park and south through the Sunset District all the way to Daly City BART

No 30 Stockton From the CalTrain Station in SoMa, along 3rd and Market Sts, then on Stockton St through Chinatown, and Columbus Ave through North Beach to Fisherman's Wharf, Fort Mason and the Palace of Fine Arts

No 32 Embarcadero From the CalTrain Station along the Embarcadero, past the Ferry Building to Fisherman's Wharf

No 33 From Potrero Ave in Potrero Hill, through the Mission on 16th St and then 18th St, through the Castro up to Market St, up Clayton St above the Haight-Ashbury, down Haight St to Stanyan St on the east edge of Golden Gate Park, to Fulton St and then Arguello Blvd in the Richmond District

No 37 Corbett A winding route from the Haight-Ashbury via Buena Vista Park to Twin Peaks

No 38 Geary From the Transbay Terminal along Market St and then Geary Blvd all the way to the Cliff House at the ocean

No 71 Haight-Noriega Along Market and Haight Sts, through the Haight, along the south side of Golden Gate Park on Lincoln Way and then down to Noriega St through the Outer Sunset to the ocean

BART The Bay Area Rapid Transit system (BART; ☎ 650-992-2278) is a subway system linking San Francisco with the East Bay. BART opened in 1972 and is convenient, economical and generally quite safe to use, although caution is required around some BART stations at night and the system shuts down at midnight. Four of the system's five lines pass through the city before terminating at Daly City or Colma.

In the city, the route runs beneath Market St; the Powell St station is the most convenient to Union Square. One-way fares vary from $1.10 to $4.70. From San Francisco

BART stations, a free transfer is available for Muni bus and streetcar services.

Car & Motorcycle

A car is the last thing you want in downtown San Francisco – it's a two-part nightmare of negotiating the hills and parking, not to mention traffic. Remember, on hill streets (with a grade as little as 3%) you must 'curb wheels' so that they ride up against the curb – failing to do so can result in daunting fines.

The AAA (☎ 415-565-2012) has an office at 150 Van Ness Ave. Members can call ☎ 800-222-4357 for emergency road service and towing.

Parking Some of the cheaper downtown parking garages are at 123 O'Farrell St (☎ 415-986-4800; $5 for 6 pm to 6 am) and on Mission St between 4th and 5th Sts (24 hours for $13). The parking garage under Portsmouth Square in Chinatown is very reasonably priced for shorter stops; ditto for the St Mary's Square Garage on California St near Grant Ave, under the square. There are numerous parking restrictions in San Francisco, especially on street-cleaning days and in residential neighborhoods that operate on a permit system. Never doubt the veracity of posted parking signs – 'No Parking 8 am to 10 am' means exactly what it says. Local police are tow and ticket happy. If you suspect your car has been towed, call City Tow (☎ 415-621-8605), 375 7th St between Folsom and Harrison Sts.

Rentals All major car rental operators can be found in San Francisco, particularly at the airports. The downtown offices are: Alamo (☎ 415-882-9440, 800-327-9633) at 687 Folsom St; Avis (☎ 415-885-5011, 800-831-2847) at 675 Post St; Budget (☎ 415-928-7864, 800-527-0700) at 321 Mason St; Dollar (☎ 415-771-5301, 800-800-4000) at 364 O'Farrell St; Hertz (☎ 415-771-2200, 800-654-3131) at 433 Mason St; and Thrifty (☎ 415-788-8111, 800-367-2277) at 520 Mason St.

Want to rent something flashy? Sunbelt Car Rental (☎ 415-772-1919), 150 Powell St, rents convertibles, BMWs, Corvettes, Jaguars, Mustangs and 4WDs. How about a motorcy-

cle? Dubbelju (☎ 415-495-2774), 271 Clara St in SoMa, has BMWs and Harleys.

Taxi

If you need to call a cab, some of the major companies are Luxor Cab (☎ 415-282-4141), De Soto Cab (☎ 415-673-1414) and Yellow Cab (☎ 415-626-2345). Fares start at $1.70 for the first mile and then cost 30¢ per sixth of a mile thereafter.

Bicycle

For most visitors, bicycles will not be an ideal way of getting around the city – there's too much traffic and all those hills are fearsome – but the Bay Area is a great place for recreational bike riding. A bike is the ideal way to explore the Presidio and Golden Gate Park. You can also cycle across the Golden Gate Bridge (it's windy) to Marin County. See the Activities section for more information. Bicycles are allowed on BART, but use is restricted. During morning commute hours (7:05 am to 8:50 am), bikes are allowed in the Embarcadero Station only for trips to the East Bay. During evening commute hours (4:35 pm to 6:45 pm), bicyclists are not allowed on trains to the East Bay; bicyclists traveling from the East Bay into San Francisco must exit at the Embarcadero Station (as indicated by the BART Trip Planner and the All About BART brochure).

Ferry

The opening of the Bay Bridge (in 1936) and the Golden Gate Bridge (in 1937) virtually killed the city's ferries, although in recent years they have enjoyed a modest revival for both commuters and tourists.

The main operator is the **Blue & Gold Fleet**, which runs the Alameda-Oakland Ferry (☎ 510-522-3300) from the Ferry Building at the foot of Market St, and on some runs from Pier 41 at Fisherman's Wharf, to Alameda and Oakland. Transfers are available to and from Muni and AC Transit buses. Blue & Gold's popular ferries to Alcatraz and Angel Island (☎ 415-705-5555, 415-773-1188) leave from Pier 41 at Fisherman's Wharf. To take the ferry to

Sausalito or Tiburon in Marin County, board at Pier 41. (During commute hours, there are a few ferries between Tiburon and the Ferry Building in San Francisco.)

Blue & Gold also operates the Vallejo Ferry (☎ 415-705-5444), which travels to Vallejo from the Ferry Building on weekdays and from Pier 39 at Fisherman's Wharf on weekends and holidays. Finally, Blue & Gold offers a variety of bay cruises and connections to the Six Flags Marine World theme park in Vallejo.

Golden Gate Ferries (☎ 415-923-2000), part of Golden Gate Transit, have regular services from the Ferry Building in San Francisco to Larkspur and Sausalito, in Marin County. Transfers are available to Muni bus services, and bicycles are permitted.

San Francisco Bay Area

To leave San Francisco without exploring the surrounding Bay Area would be an unforgivable oversight. There are day trips to cater to all tastes and budgets, and transportation is generally convenient thanks to the regional bus systems and the BART and CalTrain rail systems.

North of San Francisco, Hwys 1 and 101 provide easy – and often scenic – access to the Bay Area's prime outdoor playgrounds: the Marin Headlands, Angel Island, Mt Tamalpais, Muir Woods and the Point Reyes National Seashore.

The prime attractions in the East Bay, just across the Bay Bridge from San Francisco, are underappreciated Oakland, a culturally and economically diverse community, and off-kilter Berkeley, the birthplace of California cuisine and home to an infamous branch of the University of California. South of San Francisco, via Hwy 101 or I-280, are Palo Alto, home to Stanford University; San Jose, the self-styled 'Capital of Silicon Valley'; and laid-back beach towns such as Half Moon Bay and Santa Cruz.

Marin County

If there's a part of the Bay Area that consciously tries to live up to the California dream, it's Marin County. Just a short drive across the Golden Gate Bridge from San Francisco, Marin is wealthy, laid-back and right in tune with every trend that comes by, from hot tubs to mountain biking to designer pizzas.

Breathtaking views of San Francisco and the bay, an abundance of hiking and biking trails and great climate make Marin County an excellent day trip from the city. Visitors come to Marin for the splendor of Mt Tamalpais (or Mt Tam), Muir Woods, Point Reyes and the wild Pacific coastline, and for the charm of Marin's well-kept artsy communities, such as waterfront Sausalito and woodsy Mill Valley.

Highlights

- Angel Island – walk, bike & camp within sight of San Francisco
- Mt Tamalpais State Park – ride the trails of the mountain bike's birthplace
- Soulful Oakland – get the blues at the 5th Amendment, A&C and Eli's Mile High Club
- Bolinas – a secretive coastal town worth finding
- Berkeley – cappuccino + subversion + soapbox preaching + the Naked Guy
- Santa Cruz – surf dudes, big trees and health spas with a New Age twist

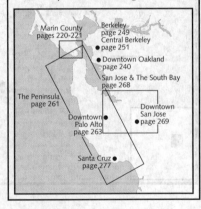

Orientation

Two important routes run through Marin: busy Hwy 101 spears straight through Marin, and quiet Hwy 1 winds its way up the sparsely populated coast (the two highways briefly meet in Mill Valley). Sir Francis Drake Blvd is the thoroughfare that cuts across west Marin from Hwy 101 to the ocean. Tank up before starting out on Hwy 1 – there are no gas stations from Mill Valley all the way north to Bolinas or Point Reyes Station.

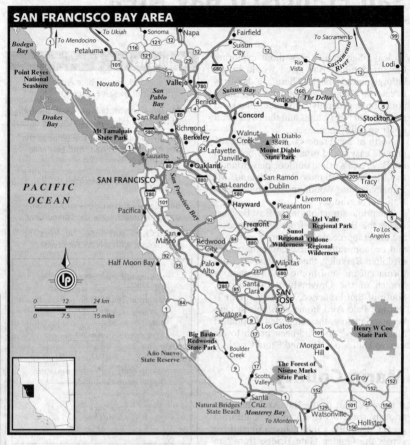

SAN FRANCISCO BAY AREA

From the East Bay, Hwy 580 comes in over the Richmond-San Rafael bridge ($2 toll for westbound traffic) to meet Hwy 101 at Larkspur.

Information
The Marin County Convention & Visitors Bureau (☎ 415-472-7470), in the civic center building in San Rafael, handles tourist information for the entire county. Information is also available from visitor centers in Sausalito and Mill Valley.

Getting There & Away
Even though Marin can be reached by ferry or bus, reliable public transportation between towns – say from Mill Valley to Tiburon – is scarce and getting to some of the coastal towns and parks by bus takes some planning. To thoroughly explore the area, you really need a car.

Bus Golden Gate Transit (☎ 415-923-2000) operates buses from San Francisco to Marin County.

Greyhound (☎ 415-495-1569) runs buses to the San Rafael Transit Center twice a day from San Francisco's Transbay Terminal. The one-way fare is $8/9 on weekdays/weekends.

Gray Line (☎ 415-558-9400) bus tours depart the Transbay Terminal daily at 9, 10 and 11 am and 1:30 pm and make a 3½-hour circuit of Marin ($29), including visits to Sausalito and Muir Woods. Reservations are required.

Ferry Golden Gate Ferries (☎ 415-923-2000) runs from the San Francisco Ferry Building to Sausalito and Larkspur Landing for $4.25 each way. The Blue & Gold Fleet (☎ 415-773-1188) sails from Pier 41 at Fisherman's Wharf in San Francisco to Sausalito and Tiburon. Weekdays, during commute hours, the ferries also operate between the downtown Ferry Building and Tiburon.

MARIN HEADLANDS

The headlands rise majestically out of the water at the north end of the Golden Gate Bridge, their rugged beauty all the more striking given their proximity to the city. A few forts and bunkers are left over from a century of US military occupation, but other than that the area is free of development. Hiking and biking trails, beaches and isolated campgrounds are all nestled within these rolling coastal hills.

Orientation & Information

Heading north across the Golden Gate Bridge, exit at Alexander Ave (the first exit) and dip left under the highway (thus avoiding the busy coach-tour stopping place at Vista Point) and head out west for the expansive views and hiking trailheads. Conzelman Rd snakes up into the hills, where it eventually forks: Conzelman Rd continues west, and McCullough Rd heads inland, joining Bunker Rd toward Rodeo Beach and the Marine Mammal Center.

Information is available from the Golden Gate National Recreation Area (GGNRA; ☎ 415-556-0560) and from the Marin Headlands Visitors Center (☎ 415-331-1540) at Fort Barry on Bunker Rd, near Rodeo Lagoon. The Olmsted & Brothers map *A Rambler's Guide to the Trails of Mt Tamalpais and the Marin Headlands* shows all the trails and elevations.

Things to See

About 2 miles up Conzelman Rd is **Hawk Hill**, where thousands of migrating birds of prey can be seen soaring along the cliffs from late summer to early fall. There are several hiking trails in this area. At the end of Conzelman is the 1877 **Point Bonita Lighthouse**, open 12:30 to 3:30 pm weekends. It's a breathtaking half-mile walk from the parking area. The loop road continues around to **Rodeo Lagoon** and the Marin Headlands Visitors Center on Bunker Rd.

On the hill above the lagoon is the **Marine Mammal Center** (☎ 415-289-7325), which rehabilitates injured, sick and orphaned sea mammals before releasing them to the wild. It's open 10 am to 4 pm daily; free.

The **Headlands Center for the Arts** (☎ 415-331-2787), on the north side of Rodeo Lagoon (take the left-hand Field Rd fork off Bunker Rd and follow the signs), is

> ### An Energetic Marin Roundtrip
>
> Got energy to burn and want a real Bay Area experience? From San Francisco, walk across the Golden Gate Bridge to the Marin Headlands and continue down to Sausalito (about 4 miles, altogether). If it's a summer weekend you may actually overtake cars stuck in traffic jams. Wander the shops and waterfront. Then take Golden Gate Transit bus No 10 to Tiburon ($1.50). You can lunch in either Tiburon or Sausalito. Take the ferry across from Tiburon to Angel Island ($6 roundtrip), rent a bicycle ($10/25 per hour/day) and ride around the island. Then take the Blue & Gold Fleet ferry from Tiburon back to San Francisco ($5.50) and ride the cable car back to downtown ($2). Total cost: $15 in fares plus the cost of bicycle rental.

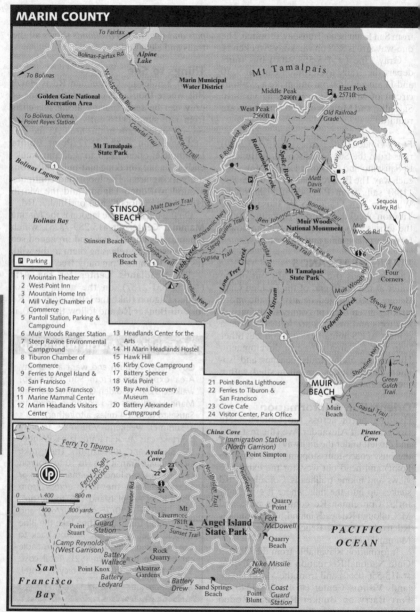

MARIN COUNTY

To Fairfax
Bolinas-Fairfax Rd
Alpine Lake
To Bolinas
W Ridgecrest Blvd
Marin Municipal Water District
Mt Tamalpais
Middle Peak 2490ft ▲
East Peak 2571ft ▲
West Peak 2560ft ▲
P
Old Railroad Grade
Golden Gate National Recreation Area
To Bolinas, Olema, Point Reyes Station
Coastal Trail
E Ridgecrest Blvd
Cataract Trail
Gravity Car Grade
Summit Ave
Mt Tamalpais State Park
Spike Buck Creek
2
Matt Davis Trail
3
P
Panoramic Hwy
Sequoia Valley Rd
Bolinas Lagoon
1
Pantoll Rd
1
P
Rattlesnake Creek
Boojack Trail
STINSON BEACH
Matt Davis Trail
5
Ben Johnson Trail
Muir Woods National Monument
Muir Woods Rd
Bolinas Bay
Panoramic Hwy
Steep Ravine Trail
Deer Park Fire Rd
Dipsea Trail
6
Stinson Beach
Redrock Beach
Webb Creek
Dipsea Trail
Lone Tree Creek
Coastal Trail
Four Corners
Mt Tamalpais State Park
Muir Woods Rd
Miwok Trail
7
Shoreline Hwy
Cold Stream
Redwood Creek
1
Shoreline Hwy
MUIR BEACH
Green Gulch Trail
Muir Beach
Pirates Cove
Coastal Trail

P Parking

1 Mountain Theater
2 West Point Inn
3 Mountain Home Inn
4 Mill Valley Chamber of Commerce
5 Pantoll Station, Parking & Campground
6 Muir Woods Ranger Station
7 Steep Ravine Environmental Campground
8 Tiburon Chamber of Commerce
9 Ferries to Angel Island & San Francisco
10 Ferries to San Francisco
11 Marine Mammal Center
12 Marin Headlands Visitors Center

13 Headlands Center for the Arts
14 HI Marin Headlands Hostel
15 Hawk Hill
16 Kirby Cove Campground
17 Battery Spencer
18 Vista Point
19 Bay Area Discovery Museum
20 Battery Alexander Campground

21 Point Bonita Lighthouse
22 Ferries to Tiburon & San Francisco
23 Cove Cafe
24 Visitor Center, Park Office

Ferry To Tiburon
China Cove
Immigration Station (North Garrison)
Point Simpton
Ayala Cove
23
Ferry to San Francisco
22
24
0   400   800 m
0   400   800 yards
Coast Guard Station
Point Stuart
Camp Reynolds (West Garrison)
Perimeter Rd
No Bridge Trail
Perimeter Rd
Quarry Point
Fort McDowell
Mt Livermore 781ft ▲
Angel Island State Park
Sunset Trail
Quarry Beach
PACIFIC OCEAN
San Francisco Bay
Battery Wallace
Point Knox
Battery Ledyard
Rock Quarry
Alcatraz Gardens
Battery Drew
Sand Springs Beach
Nike Missile Site
Point Blunt
Coast Guard Station

SAN FRANCISCO BAY AREA

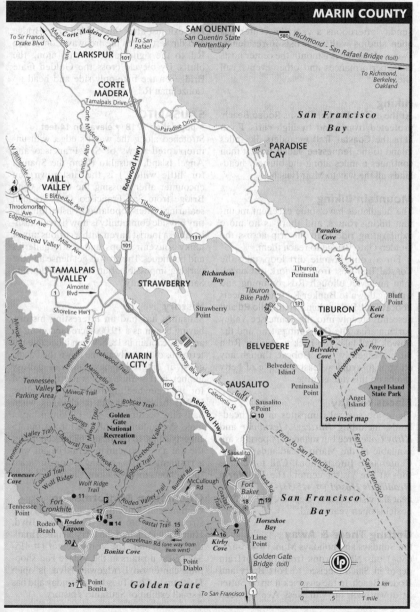

MARIN COUNTY

To Sir Francis
Drake Blvd
LARKSPUR
Corte Madera Creek
To San
Rafael
SAN QUENTIN
San Quentin State
Penitentiary
580 Richmond - San Rafael Bridge (toll)

CORTE
MADERA
Tamalpais Drive

Paradise Drive

PARADISE
CAY

San Francisco
Bay

To Richmond,
Berkeley,
Oakland

W Blithedale Ave
MILL
VALLEY
E Blithedale Ave
Throckmorton
Ave
Edgewood Ave
Homestead Valley
Miller Ave

Camino Alto
Corte Madera Ave
Redwood Hwy
Tiburon Blvd

131

Paradise
Cove

Tiburon
Peninsula
Paradise Drive

TAMALPAIS
VALLEY
Almonte
Blvd
Shoreline Hwy

STRAWBERRY

Richardson
Bay

Strawberry
Point

Tiburon
Bike Path

131

Tiburon
Peninsula

TIBURON

Keil
Cove

Bluff
Point

Miwok Trail
Tennessee Valley Rd
Tennessee Valley Trail
Tennessee
Valley
Parking Area
Miwok Trail
Old
Springs
Chaparral Trail
Wolf Ridge
Wolf Ridge
Trail

Marincello Rd
Oakwood Trail
Bobcat Trail
MARIN
CITY
Golden
Gate
National
Recreation
Area
Miwok Trail
Gerbode Valley
Bobcat Trail
Miwok Trail
Rodeo Valley Trail

Bridgeway Blvd
Caledonia St
SAUSALITO
Sausalito
Point
10
Redwood Hwy

Belvedere
Cove
Belvedere Island
Peninsula
Point

Raccoon Strait
Ferry

Ferry

BELVEDERE

8
9

Angel Island
State Park

see inset map

Angel
Island

SAN FRANCISCO BAY AREA

Tennessee
Cove
Coastal Trail
Tennessee
Point
Fort
Cronkhite
11
Rodeo
Beach
20
Rodeo Lagoon
12
13
14
Conzelman Rd (one way from here west)
Bonita Cove
21
Point
Bonita
Point
Diablo

McCullough
Rd
Bunker Rd
Coastal Trail
15
16
Kirby
Cove
17
Golden Gate
Bridge (toll)

Fort
Baker
18
19
Horseshoe
Bay
Lime
Point

Ferry to San Francisco
Sausalito
Lateral
East Rd
Coastal Trail

San Francisco
Bay

Ferry to San Francisco

Golden Gate
To San Francisco

101
1

0   1   2 km
0   .5   1 mile

LP

a refurbished barrack converted into artists' work spaces and conference facilities. Three Sunday afternoons a year the center has open studios with its artists-in-residence. Two or three times a month the center hosts talks, performances and other events; call ahead.

Hiking

At the end of Bunker Rd sits **Rodeo Beach**, protected from wind by high cliffs. From here the **Coastal Trail** meanders 3½ miles inland to the **Tennessee Valley Trail**. It then continues 6 miles along the blustery headlands, all the way to Muir Beach.

Mountain Biking

The headlands have some excellent mountain biking routes, and there is no more exhilarating ride than the trip across the Golden Gate Bridge to reach them.

For a good 12-mile dirt loop, take the **Coastal Trail** west from the fork of Conzelman and McCullough Rds, bumping and winding down to Bunker Rd where it meets **Bobcat Trail**; Bobcat joins **Marincello Rd** and descends steeply into the Tennessee Valley parking area. The **Old Springs** trail and the **Miwok Trail** take you back to Bunker Rd a bit more gently than Bobcat, though any attempt to avoid at least a couple of hefty climbs on this ride is futile.

Places to Stay

There are several campsites in the headlands, including **Battery Alexander** and **Kirby Cove**. Free but mandatory permits are available at the Marin Headlands Visitors Center (see Information). Call to reserve sites at the visitor center. The HI **Marin Headlands Hostel** (☎ 415-331-2777) is also near the visitor center. Beds are $12, and the hostel is open year round.

Getting There & Away

On Sundays and holidays Muni (☎ 415-673-6864) bus No 76 runs from the CalTrain depot in San Francisco to Fort Barry and Rodeo Beach. In the city, pick it up on Sutter St downtown, on Van Ness Ave between Sutter and Lombard Sts, or on Lombard St in the Marina. By car, take the Alexander Ave exit just after the Golden Gate Bridge and dip left under the freeway. Conzelman Rd, to the right, takes you up along the bluffs. By bicycle cross the Golden Gate Bridge on the bike-only side and head up Conzelman Rd.

SAUSALITO

● **population 7218** ● **elevation 14 feet**

Stretched along the water's edge, with uninterrupted views of San Francisco and Angel Island, Sausalito (from the Spanish for 'little willow') is the first town you encounter after crossing the Golden Gate Bridge from San Francisco. Once a small seafaring center populated by fisherfolk, the tiny bayside community is now fiercely fashionable, a tourist haven with a curious mix of junky souvenir shops and costly galleries and boutiques. The crowds get dense and the parking impossible, but there's no denying Sausalito's beauty.

History

Sausalito has had an interesting history, having begun as a 19,000-acre land grant to an army captain in 1838. When it became the terminus of the railway line down the Pacific coast, it entered a new stage as a busy lumber port with a racy waterfront noted for its freewheeling bars and bordellos. WWII brought dramatic changes when Sausalito became the site of Marinship, a huge shipbuilding yard that turned out 15 Liberty ships, 16 oilers and 62 tankers. After the war a new bohemian period began, with a resident artists' colony living in 'arks' (houseboats moored along the bay).

Orientation & Information

Commercial Sausalito is essentially one street, the waterfront Bridgeway Blvd. Humboldt Park and the ferry terminal mark the town center. The visitor center (☎ 415-332-0505), upstairs in the Village Fair shopping center on Bridgeway Blvd, is open 11:30 am to 4 pm Tuesday to Sunday and has a small exhibit of Sausalito's history.

Things to See & Do

Sausalito's main attraction is its bayside setting, with sailboats silhouetted against the shimmering bay. The town itself also has some sites worth checking out.

The **Plaza de Viña Del Mar Park**, near the ferry terminal, has a fountain flanked by 14-foot-tall elephant statues recycled from the 1915 Panama-Pacific Exposition in Golden Gate Park. Opposite Johnson St, **Ark Row** has a number of so-called arks (houseboats that were once common on the bay).

Housed in one of the old Marinship warehouses on Marinship Way, off Bridgeway Blvd, the Army Corps of Engineers' **Bay Model** Visitor Center (☎ 415-332-3871) houses a model of the San Francisco Bay and the delta, a collection of local art and interesting displays of the history of the Sausalito shipyards. The center is free and open 9 am to 4 pm Tuesday to Saturday.

Moored outside is the *Wapama*, a 1915 wooden steam schooner that looks, for all the world, like Noah's Ark. Free tours are offered on an erratic schedule; call ☎ 415-556-3002 for details.

Just under the north tower of the Golden Gate Bridge, at East Fort Baker, the **Bay Area Discovery Museum** (☎ 415-487-4398) is a hands-on museum specifically designed for children. Permanent exhibits include an underwater sea tunnel, a ceramic studio, a media center and a science lab. The museum has a cafe and a store and is open 10 am to 5 pm Tuesday to Sunday; $7/6 adults/children.

The **Village Fair** (☎ 415-332-1902), 777 Bridgeway Blvd, is a collection of shops and boutiques.

Places to Stay

Accommodation in Sausalito is limited and expensive. The *Alta Mira Hotel* (☎ 415-332-1350, 125 Bulkley Ave), a block back from Bridgeway Blvd, has doubles for $85 (no view) to $135 (bay view and deck). The *Hotel Sausalito* (☎ 415-332-4155, 16 El Portal St), at Bridgeway Blvd, is close to the ferry terminal in the center of Sausalito. Doubles are $125 to $250. The charming, highly romantic *Casa Madrona* (☎ 415-332-0502, 800-288-0502, 801 Bridgeway Blvd) charges $140 to $260.

Places to Eat

Bridgeway Blvd is packed with both moderately priced cafes and expensive restaurants, all catering to tourists. Although the restaurants don't offer the best prices, or in some cases the best food, there's no denying the fabulous views.

Caffè Tutti (☎ 415-332-0211, 12 El Portal Drive), by the Hotel Sausalito, has sandwiches for $6 and pizza and pasta dishes from $7 to $9. The *Waterfront Cafe* (☎ 415-332-5625, 85 Liberty Ship Way), at the marina, is a good place to sit with a coffee and sandwich ($4) and watch the boats.

Caledonia St, a block off Bridgeway Blvd, has a cluster of cheaper places between Johnson and Pine Sts. Try *Cafe Soleil* (☎ 415-331-9355, 37 Caledonia St) for a caffeine hit. *Gatsby's* (☎ 415-332-4500, 39 Caledonia St) serves up deep-dish pizza and is a good place for a beer; it's open for lunch Friday to Sunday, nightly for dinner. For excellent and reasonably priced Thai food (most entrées less than $10), check out *Arawan* (☎ 415-332-0882, 47 Caledonia St). *Sushi Ran* (☎ 415-332-3620, 107 Caledonia St) serves innovative but expensive Japanese cuisine.

Getting There & Away

If you're up for a little adventure, try walking to Sausalito across the Golden Gate Bridge, through Sausalito's luxurious hillside real estate and into downtown. It's also a relatively easy trip by bicycle (downhill going, uphill on the way back).

Bus Golden Gate Transit (☎ 415-923-2000) bus Nos 10 and 50 run daily to Sausalito from San Francisco; catch them at 1st and Mission Sts outside the Transbay Terminal. The one-way fare is $2.20.

Car Driving to Sausalito from San Francisco, take the Alexander Ave exit (the first exit after the Golden Gate Bridge) and follow the signs into Sausalito. There are three municipal parking lots (with meters) north of the town square at Bridgeway Blvd and El Portal Drive.

Ferry The ferry is a fun alternative for getting to Sausalito. Golden Gate Ferries (☎ 415-923-2000) operates to and from the San Francisco Ferry Building for $4.25 one way. The ferries operate up to 10 times daily and the trip takes 30 minutes. The Blue & Gold Fleet (☎ 415-773-1188) sails every hour or so to Sausalito from Pier 41 at Fisherman's Wharf in San Francisco, daily year round. The one-way fare is $5.50, and you can transport bicycles for free.

Getting Around
Sausalito Waterfront Activities & Bike Rental (☎ 415-331-4448), 803 Bridgeway Blvd, rents mountain bikes for $10/35 per hour/day, 10-speed cruisers for $8/29.

TIBURON
• population 8650 • elevation 67 feet
On a peninsula pointing out into the center of the bay, Tiburon – the name comes from the Spanish Punta de Tiburon (Shark Point) – is a bay community that, much like Sausalito, is noted for its gorgeous views. It is connected by ferry with downtown San Francisco and is also the Marin jumping-off point for nearby Angel Island (see the Angel Island entry).

Orientation & Information
The central part of town is comprised of Tiburon Blvd, with Juanita Lane and charming Main St arcing off. Main St, also known as Ark Row, is where the old houseboats have taken root on dry land and metamorphosed into classy shops and boutiques.

Visitor information is available from the Tiburon Peninsula Chamber of Commerce (☎ 415-435-5633), 96B Main St, open 8 am to 4 pm Monday to Thursday, 8 am to 1 pm Friday.

Things to See & Do
Take the ferry from San Francisco, browse as you stroll past the shops on Main St, grab a bite to eat overlooking the bay, and you've seen Tiburon. There are great views over the

town from the hillside **Old St Hilary's Church** (☎ 415-435-1853), 201 Esperanza, a fine 1888 example of carpenter Gothic. It's open 1 to 4 pm Wednesday and Sunday, April to October.

Back toward Hwy 101 the **Richardson Bay Audubon Center** (☎ 415-388-2524), 376 Greenwood Beach Rd, off Hwy 131, is home to a wide variety of waterbirds. The center is open 9 am to 5 pm Wednesday to Sunday; $2 donation. Nature walks take place at 9 am and 1 pm on Sunday.

Windsor Vineyards (☎ 415-435-3113), 72 Main St, is a small winery with free tastings. It's open 10 am to at least 6 pm daily.

Places to Stay
About the only place to sleep is the *Tiburon Lodge* (☎ 415-435-3133, 800-842-8766, 1651 Tiburon Blvd), a modern and classy spot with standard rooms starting at $135 to $175.

Places to Eat
Sam's Anchor Cafe (☎ 415-435-4527, 27 Main St) is a popular local hangout with an unbeatable view. Stop by for lunch (sandwiches $7 to $10) and soak up the sun, or have a daiquiri and lounge on the deck overlooking the bay. Next to Sam's is the *Sweden House Cafe* (☎ 415-435-9767, 37 Main St), offering coffee, a full selection of baked goods, sandwiches ($6 to $8) and salads ($4 to $8). Right on the waterfront, *Guaymas* (☎ 415-435-6300, 5 Main St) is a festive Mexican restaurant. Their specialties include quesadillas stuffed inside fried pastry shells and mesquite-grilled entrées ($10 to $14). The best seats are on the outside patio overlooking the bay.

Getting There & Away
Bus Golden Gate Transit (☎ 415-923-2000) bus No 10 runs from San Francisco ($2.75) and Sausalito ($1.50) via Mill Valley to Tiburon about every half hour on weekdays and hourly on weekends. During the week, commute bus No 8 runs direct between San Francisco and Tiburon.

Car On Hwy 101, look for the offramp for Tiburon Blvd, E Blithedale Ave and

SAN FRANCISCO BAY AREA

Hwy 131; it leads into town and intersects with Juanita Lane and Main St.

Ferry The Blue & Gold Fleet (☎ 415-773-1188) sails daily from Pier 41 at Fisherman's Wharf in San Francisco to Tiburon; ferries dock right in front of the Guaymas restaurant on Main St. The one-way fare is $5.50, and you can transport bicycles for free. Weekdays, during commute hours, the ferries also operate to and from Tiburon and San Francisco's Ferry Building. From Tiburon, ferries also connect regularly to nearby Angel Island.

ANGEL ISLAND
Angel Island State Park (☎ 415-435-1915), which occupies the entire 750-acre Angel Island, is a short ferry ride from either San Francisco or Marin. With a mild Mediterranean climate and fresh ocean breezes, Angel Island is a popular place for walking, biking and even camping.

The island's varied history as a military base, immigration station, WWII Japanese internment camp and US Army missile site has left it with some interesting and thought-provoking old forts and bunkers to poke around in. Most recently it has been the site of a native-plant restoration project.

Things to See & Do
There are 12 miles of roads and trails around the island, including a hike (no bikes) to the summit of **Mt Livermore** (761 feet) and a 5-mile perimeter trail that offers a 360° panorama of the bay. In **Ayala Cove**, the sheltered harbor on the Tiburon side of Angel Island, a small beach backs up to grassy picnic lawns fringed by forest.

The **Immigration Station**, which operated from 1910 to 1940 and was used during WWII to intern Japanese Americans, is open and staffed with docents on weekends and holidays.

Camp Reynolds, on the island's western side, was built as a US Army defense post in 1863 during the Civil War. **Fort McDowell**, on the island's eastern side, was built in 1898 during the Spanish-American War. Both forts offer guided tours. At 1 and 2 pm, a Civil War cannon is fired from the shore near Camp Reynolds.

Places to Stay & Eat
The island has nine *campsites*, costing $10/7 in high/low season. Reserve through Parknet (☎ 800-444-7275).

The *Cove Cafe* (☎ 415-435-0358) at Ayala Cove where the ferry docks, has limited food and ice cream choices. Bring everything you may need – it is an island, after all.

Getting There & Away
From San Francisco, take a Blue & Gold Fleet (☎ 415-773-1188) ferry from Pier 41. From May to November, there are three ferries a day in each direction; at other times there is one ferry a day on weekends and holidays only. Roundtrip tickets are $10.

From Tiburon, take the Angel Island-Tiburon Ferry (☎ 415-435-2131) for $6 roundtrip; add $1 for bicycles. Service is daily in summer, with hourly departures from 10 am to 4 pm. Between September and May, the ferry operates on weekends only.

Getting Around
You can rent bicycles at Ayala Cove for $10/25 per hour/day, and there are tram tours (☎ 415-897-0715) around the island from May to September ($10/7 adults/children).

LARKSPUR & VICINITY
Clustered around Hwy 101 and Sir Francis Drake Blvd are the small inland towns of Larkspur, Corte Madera, Kentfield, Ross, San Anselmo and Fairfax.

In downtown **Larkspur**, charming Magnolia Ave is a fun place for window-shopping, or you can explore the redwoods in nearby Madrone Canyon. On the east side of the freeway, the hulking mass of **San Quentin State Penitentiary**, a maximum security prison, looms above the water.

San Anselmo is noted for its fine selection of antiques shops along San Anselmo Ave. **Fairfax** is another sleepy little town with a relaxed hippie feel to it. Stroll down Broadway Blvd and Bolinas Rd and you'll find an array of cafes and whole-food stores. **Corte Madera** is home to one of the Bay Area's best bookstores, Book Passage (☎ 415-927-0960), 51 Tamal Vista Blvd in the Market Place shopping center. It has an especially good travel section, plus frequent author readings and slide shows in the evenings.

Places to Eat
Housed in an old-style Victorian tucked away in a redwood canyon, the *Lark Creek Inn (☎ 415-924-7766, 234 Magnolia Ave)*, in Larkspur, is one of Marin's best dining experiences. The food is four-star American with a California twist. Entrées are $9 to $18, and reservations are advised.

If you're into microbreweries, *Marin Brewing Company (☎ 415-461-4677, 1809 Larkspur Landing Circle)* is arguably the best in Marin County. The food is pretty good, too. It's something of a pickup scene.

Getting There & Away
Larkspur and the adjoining towns are off Sir Francis Drake Blvd, which you can access from Hwy 101 about 5 miles north of Sausalito.

Golden Gate Ferries (☎ 415-923-2000) offers service from the Ferry Building in San Francisco to Larkspur Landing (not far from the intersection of Hwy 101 and Sir Francis Drake Blvd). The trip takes 30 to 45 minutes and runs weekdays up to 13 times daily ($2.75), weekends up to six times daily ($4.50). You can bring bicycles on the ferry.

SAN RAFAEL
• population 54,000 • elevation 7 feet
San Rafael, the largest town in Marin, is more down to earth and less Marin-like than its neighbors and, consequently, is largely ignored. Just north of San Rafael, Lucas Valley Rd heads off west to Point Reyes Station, passing George Lucas' Skywalker Ranch movie center (oddly enough, Lucas Valley Rd is not named after the creator of *Star Wars*).

Orientation
Fourth St, San Rafael's main drag, is lined with cafes and shops. If you follow it west out of downtown San Rafael, it meets Sir Francis Drake Blvd, which continues west to the coast.

Things to See & Do
The **Mission San Rafael Arcángel** (☎ 415-456-3016), 1104 5th Ave at A St, was founded in 1817, the penultimate Californian mission. In 1833, it was the first to be secularized. The remains of the abandoned mission were torn down in 1870; the present building dates from 1949. The mission's museum is open 11 am to 4 pm Monday to Saturday, from 10 am on Sunday.

The **Marin County Civic Center** (☎ 415-499-7407) complex blends into the hills just east of Hwy 101, 2 miles north of central San Rafael. This is the only government building Frank Lloyd Wright ever built. The lobby has an information kiosk if you want to find out more. The gift shop on the 2nd floor sells a brochure on the building for 25¢. The complex is open 8 am to 6 pm weekdays.

From Hwy 101, take the North San Pedro Rd exit and continue 3 miles east to **China Camp State Park** (☎ 415-456-0766). At the park's entrance, you'll find the abandoned remains of a Chinese fishing village and the small China Camp Museum. Many such small Chinese shrimp-fishing encampments once could be found around San Francisco Bay.

McNear's Beach (☎ 415-499-7816) may not be the most popular beach in Marin, but it has the best weather (it's protected from the dense fog and wind that haunts much of the coast). Follow North San Pedro Rd from Hwy 101 in San Rafael. There's a $2 drive-in fee.

Places to Stay
Walk-in campsites at *China Camp State Park (☎ 415-456-0766)* cost $12 to $16 a night. Reservations are advised on weekends from April to October; for bookings call ParkNet (☎ 800-444-7275).

The simple *San Rafael Inn (☎ 415-454-9470, 865 E Francisco Blvd)* has doubles for $50 to $85. The small *Panama Hotel (☎ 415-457-3993, 4 Bayview St)* has both history and style. Rooms range from $65 (shared bath) to $90 and up (private bath).

SAN FRANCISCO BAY AREA

Places to Eat

San Rafael has a plethora of ethnic possibilities; satisfy your sushi cravings at *Kamikaze* (☎ 415-457-6776, 223 3rd St) in the Montecito shopping center; *My Thai Restaurant* (☎ 415-456-4455, 1230 4th St) has great Thai. For authentic Mexican food, try *Las Camelias* (☎ 415-453-5850, 912 Lincoln Ave).

Getting There & Away

Numerous Golden Gate Transit (☎ 415-923-2000) buses operate between San Francisco and the San Rafael Transit Center at 3rd and Hetherton Sts. Bus No 40 is the only service that takes bicycles across the Golden Gate Bridge.

MILL VALLEY

• population 12,967 • elevation 82 feet

If Sausalito and Tiburon are too touristy for your taste, head inland to Mill Valley, a town in the redwoods that feels like an artist's retreat. Originally a logging town and named after a lumber mill, Mill Valley also served as the starting point for the scenic railway that carried visitors up Mt Tam. The tracks were removed in 1940, and today the Depot Bookstore & Cafe (see Places to Eat) occupies the space of the former station.

Mill Valley visitor information is available from the chamber of commerce (☎ 415-388-9700), 85 Throckmorton Ave.

Things to See

Built around 1835, the saw mill for which the town is named is the oldest standing mill in California. In 1950, it was restored as a state landmark. Between Throckmorton Ave and Old Mill St is Old Mill Park, a wonderful place for a picnic.

Just past the bridge at Old Mill Creek in Old Mill Park, the Dipsea Steps mark the start of the Dipsea Trail. These 676 steps are the challenging beginning to the annual Dipsea Race that runs from Mill Valley to Stinson Beach.

Along East Blithedale and Throckmorton Aves are an array of fine housewares stores and antiques shops, most of them incredibly expensive.

Hiking

The Tennessee Valley Trail, in the Marin Headlands, offers beautiful views of the rugged coastline and is one of the most popular hikes in Marin (the trail can be crowded on weekends). It offers easy, level access to the beach and ocean and is a short 3.8 miles. Go on a clear, calm day, since it can be very windy. From downtown Mill Valley, take Miller Ave to the Shoreline Hwy, as if you were going back to the bridge; turn right onto Tennessee Valley Rd and follow it to the parking lot, where you'll find the trailhead. If you're coming from Hwy 101, take the Mill Valley-Stinson Beach-Hwy 1 exit and turn left onto Tennessee Valley Rd from the Shoreline Hwy.

A more demanding option is the 7-mile Dipsea Trail, which climbs over the coastal range and down to Stinson Beach, cutting through a corner of Muir Woods. The trail starts at Old Mill Park, right in downtown Mill Valley, with a climb up 676 steps in three separate flights. Having surmounted Windy Gap (760 feet), the trail then tumbles down Suicide Hill and clambers right back up Dynamite Hill to reach Lone Tree (1350 feet). From there it's pretty much downhill, apart from short ascents at Insult Hill and Steep Ravine.

Places to Stay

As you travel farther into Marin, you'll find Best Westerns, Travelodges and Holiday Inns clustered close to Hwy 101. The *Holiday Inn Express* (☎ 415-332-5700, 800-258-3894, 160 Shoreline Hwy) is in Mill Valley just 4 miles north of the Golden Gate, off Hwy 101 at the Stinson Beach exit. Doubles are $105 to $130, including a continental breakfast.

The *Mill Valley Inn* (☎ 415-389-6608, 165 Throckmorton Ave) has 16 'casually elegant' rooms and two cottages that run $135 to $165, including breakfast on the sun terrace.

Places to Eat

Mill Valley has plenty of cafes around the center of town, including the *Depot Bookstore & Cafe* (☎ 415-383-2665, 87 Throckmorton Ave), which has been serving

SAN FRANCISCO BAY AREA

extra-strength cappuccinos, sandwiches and light meals (most less than $10) for more than 25 years. *Phyllis' Giant Burgers* (☎415-381-5116, 72 E Blithedale Ave) is the place to go for a one-of-a-kind juicy hamburger ($3 to $5).

Overlooking the Depot, *Piazza D'Angelo* (☎ 415-388-2000, 22 Miller Ave) serves Italian food at reasonable prices – pizzas are $7, pastas $7 to $14, entrées $10 to $17. *Avenue Grill* (☎ 415-388-6003, 44 E Blithedale Ave) is a popular Marin restaurant that specializes in California cuisine (entrées about $15).

Tucked away in a small back courtyard, *El Paseo* (☎ 415-388-0741, 7 El Paseo Ave), between Sunnyside and Throckmorton Aves, is a charming but pricey restaurant specializing in French cuisine. The restaurant is well worth the splurge for a special occasion.

Entertainment
Sweetwater (☎ 415-388-2820, 153 Throckmorton Ave) provides an intimate setting for live music and is a favorite spot for local musicians.

Getting There & Away
From San Francisco or Sausalito, take Hwy 101 north to the Mill Valley-Stinson Beach-Hwy 1 exit. Follow Hwy 1 (here called the Shoreline Hwy) to Almonte Blvd (which becomes Miller Ave), then follow Miller Ave into downtown Mill Valley.

From Tiburon, take Tiburon Blvd west until it becomes East Blithedale Ave and follow it into downtown Mill Valley.

From San Francisco, Golden Gate Transit (☎ 415-923-2000) bus No 10 runs to Mill Valley ($2.25) via Sausalito and continues to Tiburon.

MT TAMALPAIS STATE PARK
Standing guard over Marin County, majestic Mt Tamalpais (Mt Tam) has breathtaking 360° views of ocean, bay and hills rolling into the distance. The rich, natural beauty of 2571-foot Mt Tam and the surrounding area is inspiring – especially considering that it lies within an hour's drive from one of the state's largest metropolitan areas.

Mt Tamalpais State Park was formed in 1928 from land donated by the naturalist William Kent (who also donated the land that became Muir Woods National Monument in 1907). Its 6400 acres of hill and dale are home to deer, fox and bobcat, and over 200 miles of hiking and biking trails crisscross the mountain.

Mt Tam was a sacred place to the coastal Miwok Indians for thousands of years before the arrival of European and American settlers. By the late 19th century, San Franciscans were escaping the bustle of the

SAN FRANCISCO BAY AREA

Lost & Lonely on Mt Tamalpais

With its 6400 sprawling acres of redwood canyons, grasslands and trails, Mt Tam can be daunting to first-time visitors. Yet, there are plenty of guides to help you choose the right trail and find the way home again. Some of the best are the following:

• *Tamalpais Trails* by Barry Spitz; a handy guide with detailed maps and trail descriptions.

• *The Marin Mountain Bike Guide* by Armor Todd; lists trips and trails of some of the best hiking/biking spots in Marin, including Mt Tam.

• *Mt Tam: A Hiking, Running & Nature Guide* and *Hiking Marin: Great Hikes in Marin County* by Don & Kay Martin; with maps, rating charts and detailed descriptions.

• *Rambler's Guide to the Trails of Mt Tamalpais* by Gerald Olmsted; a detailed map with descriptions of the trails.

city with all-day outings on the mountain, and in 1896 the 'world's crookedest railroad' was completed from Mill Valley to the summit. Though the railroad was closed in 1930, Old Railroad Grade is today one of Mt Tam's most popular and scenic hiking and biking paths.

Orientation & Information

Panoramic Hwy climbs from Mill Valley through the park to Stinson Beach. Pantoll Station (☎ 415-388-2070), 801 Panoramic Hwy, is the park headquarters. Detailed park maps are sold here for $1.

Things to See

Driving from Pantoll Station it's 4.2 miles to **East Peak Summit**; take Pantoll Rd and then panoramic Ridgecrest Blvd to the top. Parking is $5 and a 10-minute hike leads to the very top and the best views.

The park's **Mountain Theater** (☎ 415-383-1100) presents plays on six Sundays between mid-May and late June. Ask the rangers at Pantoll Station about the once-a-year astronomy lecture at the theater, under Mt Tam's glorious night sky.

Hiking

The $1 park map is a smart investment, as there are a dozen worthwhile hiking trails in the area.

From Pantoll Station the **Steep Ravine Trail** follows a wooded creek to the coast (about 2.1 miles each way). For a longer hike, veer right (northwest) after 1½ miles onto the Dipsea Trail, which meanders through the trees for 1 mile before ending at Stinson Beach (this is the course of the annual cross-country Dipsea Race, begun in 1904). Grab some lunch, then walk north through town and follow signs for the **Matt Davis Trail**, which leads 2.7 miles back to Pantoll Station, making a good loop. The Matt Davis Trail continues on beyond Pantoll Station, wrapping gently around the mountain with superb views.

Another worthy option is the **Cataract Trail**, which runs along Cataract Creek from the end of Pantoll Rd; it's about 3 miles to Alpine Lake. The last mile is a spectacular rooty staircase as the trail descends alongside Cataract Falls.

Mountain Biking

Bikers must stay on fire roads (and off the single-track trails) and keep speeds under 15 mph (24 kph). The rangers take these rules seriously, even using radar guns on the weekends, and a ticket can result in a $250 fine for the cyclist.

The most popular ride is the **Old Railroad Grade**; for a sweaty, 6-mile, 2280-foot climb, start in Mill Valley at the end of W Blithedale Ave and bike up to East Peak at 2571 feet. It takes about an hour to reach the **West Point Inn** from Mill Valley. For an easier start, begin partway up at the Mountain Home Inn (see Places to Stay) and follow the **Gravity Car Grade** to the Old Railroad Grade and the West Point Inn. From the latter, it's an easy half-hour ride to the summit.

From just west of Pantoll Station, bikers can either take the **Deer Park fire road** through giant redwoods to the main entrance of Muir Woods or the southeast extension of the **Coastal Trail**, which has breathtaking views of the coast before joining Hwy 1 about 2 miles north of Muir Beach. Either option requires a return to Mill Valley via Frank Valley/Muir Woods Rd, which climbs steadily (800 feet) to Panoramic Hwy and then becomes Sequoia Valley Rd as it drops toward Mill Valley. A left turn on Wildomar and two right turns at Mill Creek Park leads to the center of Mill Valley at the Depot Bookstore & Cafe.

Places to Stay

Pantoll Station (☎ 415-388-2070) has 16 first-come, first-served campsites that cost $12 to $16, depending on the season.

Steep Ravine Environmental Campground (☎ 415-456-5218), just off Hwy 1 about 1 mile south of Stinson Beach, has six isolated, beachfront campsites for $10 on weekdays, $11 on weekends. The campground also has rustic five-person cabins overlooking the ocean for $30, but these book out months in advance. Reservations are mandatory and must be made through

The Mountain, the Bike, the Story

On the north side of Mt Tam, just west of Fairfax, Repack Rd begins its treacherous 1.8-mile, 1300-foot descent from the San Geronimo Ridge: a steep downhill through rocky gullies, tight turns, rutted bare rock and stretches of gnarly 20% grade. Early in the 1970s, a band of 15 hard-core downhillers loaded their Schwinn clunkers into pickups and drove up the road as far as they could, pedaling and pushing their bikes the rest of the way to the top. Clad in protective jeans and leather motorcycle boots and gloves, these men – and a few women – were looking for the thrill of speed, and they bombed their one-speed pedal-brake cruisers down to the bottom, leaving clouds of dust behind them.

The Repack Race, as this ride came to be known, was the first mountain-bike race ever held. The first additions to the basic cruiser design were sturdy motorcycle handlebars and brake levers; thumb shifters, to allow riders to shift gears without letting go of their handlebars; drum brakes, which don't require repacking at the bottom of the hill; and the knobbiest tires available.

By the late 1970s, the Repack Race had as many as 50 entrants. A few people already had custom-built prototype mountain bikes, and they were the ones setting Repack records: Joe Breeze created oversized tubing for the frame; Gary Fisher added a 15-speed gear train; Tom Ritchey curved the fork blades for better shock absorption; and Steve Potts, Charlie Cunningham and Mark Slade designed other innovative frames. These folks began selling their hand-built creations, mostly locally, in the latter part of the '70s.

Ritchey MountainBikes, an alliance between Ritchey and Fisher, is one of the better-known frame builders, as is Wilderness Trail Bikes in Mill Valley, which is owned and operated by Potts, Cunningham and Slade. In 1982, Fisher split with Ritchey MountainBikes and switched his production from hand-built frames to mass-produced frames welded in Japan, naming his new company Fisher MountainBikes.

– Beca Lafore

SAN FRANCISCO BAY AREA

Parknet (☎ 800-444-7275). If you'd rather hike to the campground, it's 2.1 miles downhill from Pantoll Station via the Steep Ravine Trail.

The **Mountain Home Inn** (☎ 415-381-9000, *810 Panoramic Hwy*), on the east side of the mountain, has rooms for $130 to $145, including breakfast. With awesome views of the East Bay, the inn is also a great spot for a lunch on the outdoor deck.

Getting There & Away

To reach Mt Tam's Pantoll Station, take Hwy 1 to the Panoramic Hwy and look for the Pantoll signs. On weekends and holidays you can also take Golden Gate Transit (☎ 415-923-2000) bus No 63 from the Golden Gate Bridge toll plaza. It stops at the Mountain Home Inn and Pantoll Station.

MUIR WOODS NATIONAL MONUMENT

The old-growth redwoods at Muir Woods were saved from logging when President Theodore Roosevelt made the site a national monument in 1908. The name honors Sierra Club founder John Muir.

The 550-acre reserve, surrounded on all sides by Mt Tamalpais State Park, is the closest redwood stand to San Francisco, so it can get quite crowded, especially on weekends. Try to come midweek, early in the morning or late in the afternoon, when tour buses are less of a problem. Even at busy times, a short hike will get you out of the densest crowds and onto trails with huge trees and stunning vistas.

Muir Woods National Monument is open 8 am to sunset daily (to 5 pm in winter); $2.

For information contact the Muir Woods ranger station (☎ 415-388-2595).

Hiking

For an easy walk, try the 1-mile **Main Trail Loop**, which leads alongside Redwood Creek to the 1000-year-old trees at Cathedral Grove and returns via **Bohemian Grove**, where the tallest tree in the park stands 254 feet high. The **Dipsea Trail** is a good 2-mile hike up to the top of aptly named Cardiac Hill.

You can also walk down into Muir Woods by following trails from the Panoramic Hwy (such as the Bootjack Trail from the Bootjack picnic area) or from Mt Tamalpais' Pantoll Station campground (via the Ben Johnson Trail).

Getting There & Away

Muir Woods is just 12 miles north of the Golden Gate Bridge. Driving north on Hwy 101, exit at Hwy 1 and continue north along Hwy 1/Shoreline Hwy to the Panoramic Hwy (a right-hand fork). Follow that for about a mile to Four Corners, where you turn left onto Muir Woods Rd (there are plenty of signs). There are no direct buses to Muir Woods.

THE COAST
Muir Beach

The turnoff to Muir Beach from Hwy 1 is marked by the longest row of mailboxes on the North Coast. Muir Beach is a quiet little town with a nice beach, but it has no direct bus service. Just north of Muir Beach there are superb views up and down the coast from the **Muir Beach Overlook**; during WWII, watch was kept from the surrounding concrete lookouts for invading Japanese ships.

The ever-popular and very English-looking *Pelican Inn* (☎ *415-383-6000, 10 Pacific Way*) is the only commercial establishment in Muir Beach. It has a pleasant restaurant and pub-style bar, and rooms for $175. The **Green Gulch Farm & Zen Center** (☎ 415-383-3134), 1601 Shoreline Hwy, is a Buddhist retreat in the hills above Muir Beach. The center's *Lindisfarne Guest House* (☎ *415-383-3134*) has singles/doubles for $70/110 on

weekdays, $85/125 on weekends. Buffet-style vegetarian meals are included.

Stinson Beach

Stinson Beach, 5 miles north of Muir Beach, flanks Hwy 1 for about 3 blocks and is densely packed with galleries and shops, eateries and B&Bs. Stinson's beach is often blanketed with fog; when it's sunny, it's blanketed with surfers, families and gawkers. Nevertheless, it's a nice beach, with views of Point Reyes and San Francisco on clear days, and it's plenty long for a vigorous stroll.

Things to See & Do Three-mile-long **Stinson Beach** is a popular surf spot, but swimming is advised from late May to mid-September only; for updated weather and surf conditions call ☎ 415-868-1922. To reach the beach, take Calle del Arroyo, the only big street heading west out of town; it's about a block to the beach.

About a mile south of Stinson Beach is **Redrock Beach**. It's a popular clothing-optional beach, but it attracts smaller crowds than Stinson Beach, as it requires a steep hike down from Hwy 1.

About 3½ miles north of town, in the hills above the Bolinas Lagoon, the **Audubon Canyon Ranch** (☎ 415-868-9244) is a major nesting ground for great blue herons and great egrets. Visitors can get a bird's-eye view from the trail above the narrow canyon. The ranch is open from 10 am to 4 pm on weekends mid-March to mid-July. A $10 donation is requested. There's a sign for the ranch on the east side of Hwy 1, but keep a sharp lookout for it, because turning around is difficult once you pass it.

Places to Stay There are campsites 1 mile south of Stinson Beach at the *Steep Ravine Environmental Campground*; see the earlier Mt Tamalpais State Park section.

The *Stinson Beach Motel* (☎ *415-868-1712, 3416 Hwy 1*) is a simple, older motel with rooms for $60. Right next door, *Redwoods Haus B&B* (☎ *415-868-1034, 1 Belvedere Ave*) has doubles for $90 to $135, including breakfast and use of the hot tub;

the 'zimmer frei' sign indicates just how many Europeans pass through Stinson Beach. Back from the highway, on Belvedere Ave, is the bigger *Casa del Mar Inn* (☎ 415-868-2124, 37 Belvedere Ave) with rates from $140 to $250.

The *Sandpiper Motel* (☎ 415-868-1632, 1 Marine Way) is closer to the beach and has rooms for $90. It has cottages with kitchens for $115.

Places to Eat The *Sand Dollar Restaurant* (☎ 415-868-0434, 3458 Hwy 1) is a nice local bar (the only one in town that serves hard liquor) and restaurant, with entrées in the $10 to $16 range. Stock up on supplies at *Becker's by the Beach* grocery store, at the intersection of Hwy 1 and Camino del Mar. A block toward the ocean from there is the popular *Parkside Cafe* (☎ 415-868-1272, 43 Arenal Ave). It's famous for its hearty breakfasts ($6 to $9) but also serves Italian-style dinners and good fish. Entrées are $13 to $18.

Getting There & Away From Hwy 101, take the Hwy 1 exit and continue north along Hwy 1/Shoreline Hwy. After about 2 miles, you'll come to a fork (both roads eventually join up in Stinson Beach). The left-hand fork (the continuation of Hwy 1/Shoreline Hwy) goes past Muir Beach and then swings northwest along the coast to Stinson Beach. The right-hand fork (the Panoramic Hwy) winds its way through Mt Tamalpais State Park before dropping down into Stinson Beach. The roads are equally long, equally beautiful and equally curvy. From San Francisco it's a 40- to 50-minute drive on either road, though plan for long traffic delays on weekends.

On weekends, Golden Gate Transit (☎ 415-923-2000) bus No 63 runs to Stinson Beach from the Golden Gate Bridge toll plaza.

Bolinas
• population 1098 • elevation 9 feet

This sleepy beachside community became famous in the 1970s for its disappearing direction signs, removed from Hwy 1 by locals in a successful campaign to save the town from development (and from marauding tourists). The highway department finally tired of replacing the signs and agreed to leave Bolinas to its own devices.

Bolinas has one of the few gas stations along the coast: northbound the next ones are at the Olema Ranch Campground and at Point Reyes Station, southbound you have to go all the way to Mill Valley. The free monthly *Pacific Coastal Post* gives an interesting perspective on the world, as seen from Bolinas.

Things to See & Do For a town so plainly unexcited about tourism, Bolinas offers some fairly tempting attractions. The **Bolinas Museum** (☎ 415-868-0330), 48 Wharf Rd, has exhibits on the art and history of coastal Marin; it's open 1 to 5 pm Friday to Sunday.

There are tide pools at **Duxbury Reef Nature Reserve**, round the end of Duxbury Point. The **Point Reyes Bird Observatory** (☎ 415-868-0655), off Mesa Rd west of downtown, has bird banding and netting demonstrations, a visitor center and a nature trail. The demonstrations are from sunrise to noon daily, and on Wednesdays and weekends from Thanksgiving to May 1.

Beyond the observatory, you can continue to the Palomarin parking lot and access various walking trails; it's only 3 miles past Bass and Pelican lakes to the Alamere Falls at Wildcat Beach.

Places to Stay Although Bolinas residents are famously unenthusiastic about outsiders, the town has a few low-key accommodation possibilities. *Smiley's Schooner Saloon & Hotel* (☎ 415-868-1311, 41 Wharf Rd) is a Bolinas legend – a crusty old bar with a combination salty/Western feel. Rooms are $59. The *Grand Hotel* (☎ 415-868-1757, 15 Brighton Ave), just off Wharf Rd, is very ungrand looking, with two rooms sharing a common bathroom and kitchen for $40 the first night and $30 on subsequent nights.

The *Blue Heron Inn* (☎ 415-868-1102, 11 Wharf Rd) has a few pleasant rooms at $90 to $100, including breakfast across the road at the Shop Cafe. There are several other small B&Bs in town, including the New

SAN FRANCISCO BAY AREA

Agey *Elfriede's Beach Haus* (☎ 415-868-9778, 59 Brighton Ave).

Places to Eat On Wharf Rd, *Smiley's Schooner Saloon & Hotel* is the popular drinking hole in town, and also has food. Down the street, the *Bolinas Bay Bakery and Cafe* has a deli counter, pastries and breads made from organic flour. The $2.50 tamales, made on the premises, are definitely a treat.

Getting There & Away By car, follow Hwy 1 north from Stinson Beach. The turnoff for Bolinas (not signposted) is the first past Audubon Canyon Ranch, on the left. You can also get to Bolinas from Sir Francis Drake Blvd as it winds its way from Fairfax into Lagunitas and Forest Knolls.

There are no buses to Bolinas.

Olema
• population 175 • elevation 60 feet

Though it's basically a one-horse town today, Olema, about 10 miles north of Stinson Beach near the junction of Hwy 1 and Sir Francis Drake Blvd, was the main settlement in West Marin in the 1860s. There was stagecoach service to San Rafael and a weekly steamer to San Francisco, not to mention *six* saloons. In 1875, when the railroad was built through Point Reyes Station instead of Olema, the town's importance began to fade. In 1906, it gained distinction again as the epicenter of the Great Quake, but it has never regained its vital bar scene.

Hiking & Biking About a mile west of Olema, on Sir Francis Drake Blvd, is the trailhead for the **Bolinas Ridge Trail**, a 12-mile series of ups and downs culminating at the Bolinas-Fairfax Rd above the Bolinas Lagoon. Whether you hike it part of the way or take it the full 24 miles roundtrip for a grueling mountain-bike ride, don't miss the spectacular views, especially looking north over Tomales Bay.

Olema's Trail Head Rentals (☎ 415-663-1958), at Hwy 1 and Bear Valley Rd, rents bikes for $7 per hour or $20 per day ($24 on weekends).

Places to Stay Just north of downtown Olema on Hwy 1, the *Olema Ranch Campground* (☎ 415-663-8001) has RV hookups ($25), tent sites ($18) and a laundry – the only one for miles.

Another camping option is the *Samuel P Taylor Park* (☎ 415-488-9897), just 6 miles east of Olema on Sir Francis Drake Blvd. This 2600-acre park has 60 secluded campsites ($12 to $14) in redwood groves, all available on a first-come, first-served basis.

Getting There & Away The drive from San Francisco takes about 1¼ hours via either Hwy 1 or Sir Francis Drake Blvd. On weekends and holidays, take Golden Gate Transit bus No 65 from the San Rafael Transit Center.

Point Reyes Station
• population 675 • elevation 35 feet

With a gas station and an ATM, Point Reyes Station is the hub of West Marin. Essentially a ranch town, Point Reyes was invaded by artists and intellectuals getting 'back to the land' in the '60s. Today it's an interesting blend: art galleries and tourist shops, a saloon that whoops it up on weekends and the occasional smell of cattle on the afternoon breeze.

The weekly paper, the *Point Reyes Light*, has local news and listings of events, restaurants and lodgings, as well as the always-interesting sheriff's calls.

Places to Stay The only cheap choice is the hostel at the nearby Point Reyes National Seashore (see Point Reyes National Seashore section). Otherwise, the *Holly Tree Inn* (☎ 415-663-1554), on Silverhills Rd off Bear Valley Rd, has rooms for $120, and several cottages near Inverness. *Coastal Lodging* (☎ 415-663-1351) has listings for B&Bs and cottages in Point Reyes Station, Inverness and Bolinas.

Places to Eat For delicious fare, including seafood and locally raised beef, try the *Station House Cafe* (☎ 415-663-1515) on Main St. Breakfasts and lunches are $6 to $10, dinner entrées $10 to $15. The *Pine*

Cone Diner (☎ *415-663-1356, 60 4th St*), formerly a truck stop, now has good diner-style food. Across the street, *Tomales Bay Foods and Cowgirl Creamery*, a local market in an old silver barn, has a lunch counter (get your tofu mushroom sandwiches here), cheese, wine and local organic produce. For coffee and pastries, *Bovine Bakery* on Main St is *the* spot.

Entertainment The *Dance Palace* (☎ *415-663-1075, 503 B St*) has weekend events, movies and live music.

Getting There & Away Hwy 1 becomes Main St in town, running right through the center. On weekends and holidays, Golden Gate Transit bus No 65 runs to Point Reyes Station from the San Rafael Transit Center.

Inverness
• population 1422 • elevation 80 feet
The word 'charming' comes to mind when you arrive in this tiny town spread along the west side of Tomales Bay. The downtown has two restaurants and a good grocery store with a deli counter, and several great beaches are just a few miles north.

Blue Waters Kayaking Tours & Rentals (☎ 415-669-2600), 12938 Sir Francis Drake Blvd (at the Golden Hinde Inn), offers **natural history tours** of Tomales Bay, or you can **rent a kayak** and paddle around the bay on your own, exploring secluded beaches and drabbling in rocky crevasses.

Sir Francis Drake Blvd from Hwy 1 leads straight into Inverness. On weekends and holidays, Golden Gate Transit bus No 65 stops here.

Places to Stay & Eat *Manka's Inverness Lodge* (☎ *415-669-1034*), about ¼-mile north of town (follow the signs up Argyle St, off Sir Francis Drake Blvd), was built as a hunting lodge in 1917. Its comfortable, elegant rooms are $95, and the restaurant serves delicious food, including seasonal game.

About a mile past downtown, the *Inverness Valley Inn* (☎ *415-669-7250, 13275 Sir Francis Drake Blvd*) has a hot tub and singles/doubles for $75/85 a night.

Gray Whale Pizza (☎ *415-669-1244*) is the best spot for food downtown, with reasonably priced pizza and snacks.

Point Reyes National Seashore
Point Reyes National Seashore has 110 sq miles of pristine ocean beaches, wind-tousled ridges and diverse wildlife. The enormous peninsula, with its rough-hewn beauty, has excellent hiking and camping opportunities.

Sir Francis Drake

Sir Francis Drake was an extraordinary character: a self-made man, fearless, resourceful, clever, ruthless and very lucky. In 1577, he set off from England in a fleet of five small ships. His mission was exploration and adventure, to be financed by what could best be described as piracy, with the hated Spanish the intended victims.

In 1579, the *Golden Hind* was alone off the California coast. Two of the ships, brought only to carry supplies, had been abandoned. The third ship had sunk with all hands during the rounding of Cape Horn, and the fourth had lost contact and turned back to England. Drake and his crew had found rich pickings at the expense of the Spanish, but the *Golden Hind* was in sorry shape. Somewhere along the Marin County coast, possibly at Drakes Beach near Point Reyes, Drake put in to a sheltered bay and careened his ship (ran it aground at high tide and tipped it on its side to repair the ravaged hull). He stayed there for five weeks, trading with the local Indians and exploring inland, where one of his crew noted that the land was much more welcoming than it appeared from the sea.

Eventually, Drake sailed off on a trip that would carry him right around the world and bring him back to England as a phenomenally wealthy and famous explorer. He cemented his fame by helping defeat the Spanish Armada in 1588.

SAN FRANCISCO BAY AREA

Be sure to bring warm clothing, however, as even the sunniest days can quickly turn cold and foggy.

The Bear Valley Visitor Center (☎ 415-663-1092), on Bear Valley Rd near Olema, is the park headquarters. It has a great deal of information and maps and is open 9 am to 5 pm weekdays, 8 am to 5 pm weekends. There are two additional visitor centers: at Point Reyes Lighthouse (☎ 415-669-1534), open 10 am to 5 pm Thursday to Monday, and the Ken Patrick Center (☎ 415-669-1250) at Drakes Beach, open 9 am to 5 pm weekends and holidays.

Things to See & Do Of all the trails at Point Reyes, one of the most awe-inspiring is the **Earthquake Trail** from the park headquarters at Bear Valley. On the trail you can view a 16-foot gap between the two halves of a once-connected fence line, a lasting testimonial to the power of the 1906 earthquake that was centered in this area. Another trail leads from the visitor center a short way to Kule Loklo, a reproduction of a **Miwok village**.

Limantour Rd, off Bear Valley Rd about 1 mile north of the Bear Valley Visitor Center, leads to the Point Reyes Hostel and to **Limantour Beach**. At the beach there's a trail that runs along Limantour Spit, with Estero de Limantour on one side and Drakes Bay on the other. The **Inverness Ridge Trail** heads from Limantour Rd up to 1282-foot Mt Vision, which has spectacular views of the entire national seashore. You can drive almost to the top of Mt Vision from the other side, so don't be surprised if after hours of hiking you see perfectly refreshed people enjoying the view.

About 2 miles past Inverness, Pierce Point Rd splits off to the right from Sir Francis Drake Blvd. From here you can get to two nice swimming beaches on the bay: Marshall Beach requires a hike from the parking area, while Hearts Desire, in **Tomales Bay State Park**, is directly accessible by car. Pierce Point Rd continues on to the huge windswept sand dunes at **Abbotts Lagoon**, full of peeping killdeer and other shorebirds. At the end of the road is Pierce

Point Ranch, the trailhead for the 3½-mile Tomales Point Trail through the **tule elk reserve**. The tule elk are an amazing sight, standing with their big horns against the backdrop of Tomales Point, with Bodega Bay to the north, Tomales Bay to the east, and the Pacific Ocean to the west.

The **Point Reyes Lighthouse** is at the very end of Sir Francis Drake Blvd. This spot, with its wild terrain and ferocious winds, has the best **whale watching** on the coast. There's also a sea-lion viewing area nearby. The 300-foot lighthouse sits far below the headlands, so its light can shine out below the fog, which often blankets Point Reyes. Lighthouse hours are 10 am to 4:30 pm Thursday to Monday. On weekends there's a shuttle ($2.50) from the Drakes Beach Visitor Center; when it's running the road is closed to private vehicles.

Places to Stay The HI *Point Reyes Hostel* (☎ *415-663-8811*) is just off Limantour Rd. Nightly costs are $12 to $14 per person, including use of a family room and kitchen facilities.

The Point Reyes reserve doesn't have any drive-in campsites (the nearest are in Olema – see the previous section). Instead it has four hike-in campgrounds with pit toilets and tables (no wood fires). Sites cost $10; call ☎ 415-663-1092 for information, ☎ 415-663-8054 for reservations. The *Coast* campground is 1.8 miles from the visitor center, and *Wildcat* is 6.3 miles; both are beautiful sites near the beach. The other two campgrounds, *Sky* (1.7 miles) and *Glen* (4.5 miles), are farther inland.

If you're looking for a hotel or B&B, see the previous sections on Inverness and Point Reyes Station.

Places to Eat Halfway from Inverness to the Point Reyes Lighthouse, look for the sign to the *Johnson's Drakes Bay Oysters* (☎ *415-669-1149*) for delicious, fresh cheap oysters. It's open 8 am to 4 pm daily, except Monday.

Getting There & Away By car you can get to Point Reyes a few different ways. The

Gray Whales

Gray whales may be seen at various points along the California coast, and the Point Reyes Lighthouse is a superb viewpoint for observing these huge creatures on their annual 6000-mile migration. During the summer, the whales feed in the Arctic waters between Alaska and Russian Siberia. Around October, they start to move south down the Pacific coast of Canada and the US to sheltered lagoons in the Gulf of California, by the Mexican state of Baja California.

The whales, led by the pregnant cows, pass Point Reyes in December and January. They're followed by pods of females and courting males, usually in groups of three to five, and then by the younger whales. The whales usually spend about two months around Baja California, during which time the pregnant whales give birth to calves 15 or 16 feet long and weighing 2000 to 2500 pounds. The newborn whales put on 200 pounds a day, and in February the reverse trip begins.

Gray whales live up to 50 years, grow to 50 feet in length and weigh up to 45 tons. Spotting whales is a simple combination of patience and timing. Spouting, the exhalation of moist, warm air, is usually the first sign that a whale is about. A series of spouts, about 15 seconds apart, may be followed by a sight of the creature's tail as the whale dives. If you're lucky, you may see whales spy hopping (sticking their heads out of the water to look around) or even breaching (leaping clear out of the water). Bring binoculars; whales are typically a quarter to a half mile out to sea, though they're closer to shore on the southbound leg of the journey.

Bay & Delta Charters (☎ 415-332-6811) runs all-day, naturalist-led whale-watching expeditions ($59 per person) on weekends during both migration seasons. They depart from Sausalito for the Farallon Islands, 28 miles outside the Golden Gate. Reservations are required.

curviest is along Hwy 1, through Stinson Beach and up to Olema. The less-winding way is to take Hwy 101 to San Rafael, then follow Sir Francis Drake Blvd all the way to the tip of Point Reyes. For the latter route, take the Central San Rafael exit and head west on 4th St, which turns into Sir Francis Drake Blvd. By either route, it's about 1½ hours to Olema from San Francisco.

Just north of Olema, where Hwy 1 and Sir Francis Drake Blvd come together, turn left onto Bear Valley Rd. Less than a mile farther, on the left, is the Bear Valley Visitor Center, with access to trails leading all over the southern portion of the national seashore. To reach the actual point of Point Reyes, go past the visitor center back to Sir Francis Drake Blvd and bear left; follow this road to the point, about an hour's drive.

On weekends and holidays, Golden Gate Transit (☎ 415-923-2000) bus No 65 stops at the Bear Valley Visitor Center, but that's as close to the national seashore as you can get on the bus.

East Bay

Linked to San Francisco by the Bay Bridge, the East Bay mostly consists of dense suburbs that range from poor neighborhoods on the bayside flats to exclusive enclaves high in the hills. Gritty Oakland and opinionated Berkeley, each with a distinct personality, dominate the East Bay, which was originally known as Contra Costa (Spanish for 'opposite coast'), a name that still applies to one of the East Bay's counties.

Somewhat surprisingly, miles of woodsy parkland cover the ridgeline above Berkeley and Oakland, and Mt Diablo towers in the background.

OAKLAND
• **population 396,300** • **elevation 42 feet**

To Oakland's critics, it will always be associated with street crime, run-down buildings and desolate docks. Never mind that

Oakland's climate is generally warmer and less foggy than San Francisco's. Never mind that Oakland is a city of remarkable racial and economic diversity, with an enduring jazz and blues scene, attractive parks, a bustling Chinatown, a top-rate museum, several thriving neighborhoods and plenty of good restaurants.

Despite what you may have heard, under-appreciated Oakland is a low-key and very livable city. Though it has always languished in San Francisco's more glamorous shadow, Oakland has enough attractions to justify a foray across the bay.

History

The Oakland area's earliest inhabitants were Ohlone Indians. In 1820, the land was included in the enormous *rancho* granted to Mexican soldier Luis Maria Peralta, but, in 1850, three US citizens 'leased' what is now downtown Oakland and Jack London Square from the Peralta family. In short order they sold the land off in lots, and Oakland was born.

The city took off in 1869, with the completion of the first transcontinental railway. As the railroad's West Coast terminus, Oakland grew rapidly into a business and industrial center and a busy port. Things remained that way through the 1920s, until the Great Depression, which hit Oakland hard. Gertrude Stein, who had lived in Oakland during her school years, returned to her old neighborhood in 1934 and was distraught over its dissolution. Her words of despair at the loss of her old home –'There is no *there* there' – have become the most misquoted phrase ever attached to the city of Oakland.

The completion of the Bay Bridge in 1936 provided a needed boost, as did WWII-era industries such as shipbuilding. The 1940s saw a lively blues scene take shape in Oakland, vestiges of which are still hanging on. In the 1960s, the city was the scene of some violently repressed draft riots, as well as the founding of the Black Panther Party for Self-Defense. In more recent years, as San Francisco's shipping traffic has declined, Oakland's has strengthened. Today, Oakland

is the fourth-largest container port in the country. The huge container cranes hovering threateningly above the Oakland docks are said to have inspired the Imperial Walkers that George Lucas dreamed up for *The Empire Strikes Back*.

Revitalization efforts have spruced up some of downtown Oakland, but much of that area is still somewhat forlorn, and in the evenings the whole area empties out. Parts of the city remain in the grip of urban decay, plagued by drug trafficking, gangs and economic depression, but others are ripe for discovery. There are indications that the city may soon be on the upswing, especially if you believe the promises of Oakland's new mayor, Jerry Brown, a former governor of California.

Orientation

Oakland is a long, slender city. I-880 traces the bay at the city's western edge, and I-580 parallels I-880 about 1½ miles inland.

West Oakland is heavily industrial, with residential pockets and housing projects. Just east are the downtown and Lake Merritt areas. North Oakland encompasses upscale Piedmont and Rockridge. East Oakland is best avoided, unless you're headed to the Oakland Coliseum or the Western Aerospace Museum. The city's major parks run along the hills that form its eastern border.

Broadway is the backbone of downtown Oakland, running from Jack London Square at the waterfront all the way north to Piedmont and Rockridge. Telegraph Ave branches off Broadway at 15th St and heads straight to Berkeley; east from Broadway, Grand Ave runs to Lake Merritt.

Downtown BART stations are on Broadway at both 12th St and 19th St; other stations are near Lake Merritt and in Rockridge.

Information

The Oakland Convention & Visitors Authority (☎ 510-839-9000, 800-262-5526), 550 10th St, is in the convention center. Some information is available from the booth by the Jack London Square parking lot.

SAN FRANCISCO BAY AREA

The Black Panthers

In October 1966, against a backdrop of enduring racism and an insurgent civil rights movement, two Oakland college students founded the Black Panther Party for Self-Defense. Steeped in left-wing revolutionary philosophy, the party called for full employment, adequate housing and universal health care for African Americans and all other minorities. It also made some more disputatious demands, such as the immediate release of all black people from prison and the payment of reparations to compensate for slavery.

Black Panther minister of defense Huey Newton and chairman Bobby Seale attracted scores of young black recruits in Oakland and across the nation, and the party made a point of reaching out to groups in other ethnic communities who shared their left-wing principles. Their growing numbers, their politics and their revolutionary elements – the guns, the militaristic garb, the strongly worded rhetoric – unnerved white America and brought some criticism from blacks as well.

Events such as the infamous march of armed Panthers into the California legislature – a protest against a bill that would strip them of their right to carry guns – are well remembered. Less so are the party's community programs, which enjoyed much success. Their daily free breakfasts for poor black kids, begun in 1969, subsequently inspired similar government programs; they distributed groceries to families in need; and they were directly responsible for the installation of a traffic light at a busy Oakland intersection where schoolchildren had been killed trying to cross.

Gun battles between Panthers and police shook West Oakland and other US cities, and to this day neither side agrees who started the battles or why. The FBI, meanwhile, engaged in a systematic and ultimately successful program to infiltrate and destroy the party. But that was not all that brought the Panthers down – intense disputes between party leaders also weakened the party, and by the end of the 1970s it was pretty much defunct.

In 1996, the Dr Huey P Newton Foundation (☎ 510-986-0660) instituted the **Black Panther Legacy Tour**. Led by former chief of staff David Hilliard, the 2½-hour bus tour takes visitors to sites such as the corner where the traffic light was installed, the first free-breakfast site, and the spot where Newton was killed by a drug dealer in 1989. Followed by a question and answer session, the tour is both sobering and hopeful, weaving in aspects of Oakland and US history and leaving participants with much food for thought. It runs once a week and costs $22.50 for adults, $18.50 for students.

Oakland's many fine new and used bookstores include Walden Pond (☎ 510-832-4438), 3316 Grand Ave; Diesel (☎ 510-653-9965), 5433 College Ave; and Pendragon (510-652-6259), 5560 College Ave. If you're interested in African-American literature or history, check out Marcus Bookstore (☎ 510-652-2344), 3900 Martin Luther King Jr Way.

The *Oakland Tribune* is Oakland's daily newspaper. The free *East Bay Express* is an alternative weekly newspaper with good coverage of Oakland and Berkeley. There are Wells Fargo ATMs at City Center and near the 19th St BART station. Post offices are at the corner of 15th and Franklin Sts and in the Federal Building at Clay and 14th Sts.

Downtown

The pedestrianized **City Center**, off Broadway between 12th and 14th Sts, forms the heart of downtown Oakland. The twin towers of the Federal Building are on Clay St, just behind it. At 13th and Franklin Sts, the 1923 **Tribune Tower** is an Oakland icon that has been closed since the '89 quake. The tower's former occupant, the *Oakland Tribune* newspaper, is scheduled to reoccupy the building in 2000. The beautiful 1914 beaux arts **City Hall**, on 14th St between Broadway and Clay St, is worth a close look.

The buildings along 9th St off Broadway constitute Old Oakland's **Victorian Row**. They date from the 1860s to the 1880s and are the backdrop for a Friday **farmers' market**; though the buildings are quite attractive, many of them stand without tenants.

For another taste of old Oakland, walk over to tranquil **Preservation Park** (☎ 510-874-7580), at 13th St and Martin Luther King Jr Way, where 16 restored Victorian houses, dating from 1870 to 1911, have been collected from all over the city and arranged to approximate a late-19th-century Oakland neighborhood.

East of Broadway, **Chinatown** centers around Franklin and Webster Sts, as it has since the 1870s. Much smaller than San Francisco's Chinatown, it nevertheless bustles with commerce and has many good restaurants.

North of the center, where Telegraph Ave angles off Broadway, stands the 1913 flatiron **Cathedral Building**. At Broadway, between 20th and 21st Sts, is the **Paramount Theatre**, a restored 1931 art deco masterpiece. Tours ($1) of the theater are usually offered at 10 am on the first and third Saturdays of the month. (For information on shows at the theater, see Entertainment.)

Downtown Oakland has plenty of other buildings adorned with art nouveau or art deco details; unfortunately, many stand empty and are in need of care. The abandoned 1928 **Fox Oakland Theatre**, at Telegraph Ave and 19th St, was once the largest cinema west of Chicago. The sign outside, with its rust and chipping paint, is the image of faded splendor. Other notable buildings are the 1916 **OTIG Co** building, at 15th and Franklin Sts, and the **Financial Center Building**, 405 14th St. Wander the streets off Broadway and you'll come across others.

From May through October, the City of Oakland runs free 90-minute **walking tours** of historic downtown streets, City Hall and Preservation Park. Reservations are recommended; call ☎ 510-238-3234.

Jack London Square

The waterfront where writer and adventurer Jack London once raised hell now bears his name. It has been difficult converting a decaying industrial area into a tourist zone, but Oakland has certainly been trying, with some success. A new Amtrak station opened at the east end of the square in 1995. Also in the mid-1990s, the city and the Port of Oakland poured $4 million into the renovation of the space where swanky jazz club Yoshi's now resides, hoping the venue would lure attention to the square. Several chain restaurants dot the area, and there's a **farmers' market** every Sunday.

It is said that London was a regular patron of the 1880 **Heinhold's First & Last Chance Saloon**, maintained in all its period glory and still open for business. Across from the saloon is a replica of Jack London's **Yukon cabin**, and if ever a building looked out of place, it's this one.

In the lagoon at **Jack London Village**, a waterfront shopping center at the square, is a sorry replica of London's boat, the *Razzle Dazzle*, from which he used to poach oysters in San Francisco Bay. Also in the Village is the small **Jack London Museum** (☎ 510-451-8218), with a variety of exhibits about the author; it's open 10:30 am to 6 pm Wednesday to Saturday, 11:45 am to 6 pm Sunday; $1. The **Ebony Museum** (☎ 510-763-0745) is there as well, displaying African and African-American art. It's open 11 am to 6 pm Tuesday to Saturday, noon to 5 pm Sunday; free.

The USS *Potomac* (☎ 510-839-7533), Franklin D Roosevelt's 'floating White

SAN FRANCISCO BAY AREA

DOWNTOWN OAKLAND

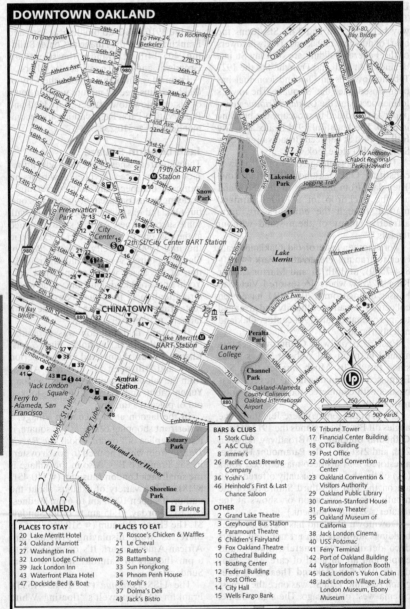

BARS & CLUBS
1 Stork Club
4 A&C Club
8 Jimmie's
26 Pacific Coast Brewing
    Company
36 Yoshi's
46 Heinhold's First & Last
    Chance Saloon

OTHER
2 Grand Lake Theatre
3 Greyhound Bus Station
5 Paramount Theatre
6 Children's Fairyland
9 Fox Oakland Theatre
10 Cathedral Building
11 Boating Center
12 Federal Building
13 Post Office
14 City Hall
15 Wells Fargo Bank

16 Tribune Tower
17 Financial Center Building
18 OTIG Building
19 Post Office
22 Oakland Convention
    Center
23 Oakland Convention &
    Visitors Authority
29 Oakland Public Library
30 Camron-Stanford House
31 Parkway Theater
35 Oakland Museum of
    California
38 Jack London Cinema
40 USS Potomac
41 Ferry Terminal
42 Port of Oakland Building
44 Visitor Information Booth
45 Jack London's Yukon Cabin
48 Jack London Village, Jack
    London Museum, Ebony
    Museum

PLACES TO STAY
20 Lake Merritt Hotel
24 Oakland Marriott
27 Washington Inn
32 London Lodge Chinatown
39 Jack London Inn
43 Waterfront Plaza Hotel
47 Dockside Bed & Boat

PLACES TO EAT
7 Roscoe's Chicken & Waffles
21 Le Cheval
25 Ratto's
28 Battambang
33 Sun Hongkong
34 Phnom Penh House
36 Yoshi's
37 Dolma's Deli
43 Jack's Bistro

P Parking

SAN FRANCISCO BAY AREA

House,' is moored at Clay and Water Sts by the ferry dock. It's open 10 am to 2 pm Wednesday and Friday, 11 am to 3 pm Sunday; $3. In the spring and summer, free boat tours of the **Port of Oakland** (☎ 510-272-1200), also at Clay and Water Sts, operate 10 am to 2 pm Wednesday to Friday, 11 am to 3 pm Sunday.

Lake Merritt

Lake Merritt, Oakland's visual centerpiece, is an urban jewel and a popular place to stroll or go running (a 3½-mile track circles the lake). Lake Merritt was once a tidal marsh teeming with waterfowl. It became a lake in 1869 with the damming of an arm of the Oakland Estuary, and the following year the state legislature designated Lake Merritt a wildlife refuge, the first in the US. The lake still supports some migratory waterfowl, and it's still connected to the estuary, so its 155 acres are saltwater. Like other Bay Area parks, Lake Merritt is fine during the day, but be careful there at night.

Lakeside Park, at the northern end of the lake, includes **Children's Fairyland** (☎ 510-452-2259), which has enticing fairy-tale-themed rides and displays. It's open 10 am to 4 pm daily in summer, Wednesday to Sunday in spring and fall, Friday to Sunday in winter; $5 for unlimited rides. For a jaunt on the lake, rent a vessel at the park's **boating center**. Hourly charges are $6 for canoes or rowboats, $8 for kayaks, $12 for pedal boats. From June through September, boats are available 9 am to 6 pm weekdays, 9 am to 7 pm weekends; October to May you can rent 10:30 am to 5 pm daily, except Monday.

In the late 19th century, Lake Merritt was lined with fine homes, but only one remains: the 1876 **Camron-Stanford House** (☎ 510-836-1976), 1418 Lakeside Drive, taken over by the city in 1907. You can go on a tour, but the best aspect of the house is really its wonderful lakeside setting and the hint it gives of how Oakland looked in its Victorian heyday. Tours take place on 11 am to 4 pm Wednesday, 1 to 5 pm Sunday; $4.

The two main commercial streets skirting Lake Merritt are **Lakeshore Ave** on the eastern edge of the lake and **Grand Ave**, running along the north shore. Their stores offer more to neighborhood residents than to visitors, but both have some nice spots for eating or drinking – see Places to Eat and Entertainment for suggestions.

Oakland Museum of California

The Oakland Museum (☎ 510-238-3401), 1000 Oak St at 10th St, is really three museums: one for ecology, one for history and one for art. The 10th St entrance leads to the 1st-floor **Hall of California Ecology**, which presents well-designed, engaging dioramas of California ecosystems – tidal, coastal redwood, desert, high Sierra and so on.

On the 2nd floor is the **Hall of California History**. The crowded displays follow a time line from before the Spanish arrival up through the present, touching on the tragic, the opulent, the ingenious and the kitschy. Check out the shiny steam fire pump from 1898 and the series of displays glimpsing elements of the California dream: the beach culture, the car culture, the suburban culture, the flower-power culture.

The 3rd floor houses the surprisingly good **Gallery of California Art**, which has a fair number of landscape paintings and a lively collection of contemporary art.

The museum has a cafe, store and multi-level rooftop garden. It's open 10 am to 5 pm Tuesday to Sunday (10 am to 9 pm Friday); $5/3 adults/children. The Lake Merritt BART station is a block away, and there's a moderately priced parking lot beneath the museum.

North Oakland

North of downtown Oakland, Broadway becomes a strip of car dealerships so lengthy the city gave it a name: Broadway Auto Row. Just past that is tony **Piedmont**, whose commercial center is Piedmont Ave, which branches off Broadway and is wall-to-wall antique stores, coffeehouses and fine restaurants.

The main drag in **Rockridge** is College Ave, which leads off Broadway farther north and bustles with contented people and well-behaved dogs. College Ave runs into

Stein & London

Neither of Oakland's famous writers was actually born in Oakland. Gertrude Stein, the daughter of a wealthy stockbroker, was born in 1874 in Pennsylvania, then lived in Vienna and Paris before coming to Oakland for her school years. After college she moved to Paris, where she lived until her death just after the end of WWII. Stein was famous mainly for being famous, and she courted and encouraged many of the seminal artists and writers of her era, most notably Picasso and Hemingway. Her attempts to emulate cubist art in her writing ensured she would be an unread writer, and her best-known book is probably *The Autobiography of Alice B Toklas*, which is actually her own autobiography, not that of her long-term partner Alice B Toklas.

Born in San Francisco in 1876, Jack London was the son of a spiritualist (mom) and an Irish astrologer (dad, who soon deserted the family). London began to turn his life into an adventure story while still a teenager, poaching oysters in the San Francisco Bay with his own boat, the *Razzle Dazzle*, working on a ship to Japan, riding freight trains around the USA as a hobo and enthusiastically embracing socialism. Self-educated, he entered the University of California, Berkeley, but soon quit to join the 1897 Klondike gold rush.

Back from Alaska, and still broke, he threw himself into writing with spectacular energy, turning out everything from songs to horror stories. His first book, *The Son of the Wolf*, was published in 1900, and for the next 16 years he averaged three books a year. London soon became the highest-paid writer in the USA, but he burned through the cash even faster. In 1910, he turned to farming in the Sonoma Valley (see the Wine Country chapter) and, in 1916, died in somewhat mysterious circumstances, officially from kidney disease but quite possibly a drug-overdose suicide.

Berkeley, and the whole length of the avenue is lined with boutiques, bookstores, pubs, cafes and – a recent addition – upscale restaurants. Exiting BART at the Rockridge station puts you in the thick of things.

The Oakland Hills

East from downtown the streets become convoluted, winding through exclusive communities such as Montclair before reaching the ridgeline, where a series of parks edges the hills. The area around the junctions of Hwys 13 and 24 was the site of the disastrous October 1991 fire that killed 26 people and destroyed more than 3000 houses. The houses have been rebuilt, but the vegetation is kept sparse to avoid a repeat of the blaze.

For a nice day hike without traveling far, the large East Bay parks are ideal. Information, including the excellent *Regional Parks* booklet, is available from the East Bay

Regional Parks District (☎ 510-562-7275), 2950 Peralta Oaks Court. Off Hwy 24, the **Robert Sibley Volcanic Regional Preserve** is the northernmost of the Oakland Hills parks. It has great views of the Bay Area from its Round Top Peak (1761 feet), an old volcano cone.

From Sibley, Skyline Blvd runs south past **Redwood Regional Park** and the adjacent **Joaquin Miller Park** to **Anthony Chabot Regional Park**. A hike or mountain-bike ride through the groves and along the hilltops of any of these sizable parks will make you forget you're in an urban area. At the southern end of Chabot Park is the enormous Lake Chabot, with an easy trail along its shore and paddleboats for rent.

AC Transit bus No 64 will put you in the vicinity of Joaquin Miller Park, but not on the weekend; the No 46 runs along Skyline Blvd during commute hours.

East Oakland

East Oakland, beginning south of downtown Oakland, goes on and on, one numbered block after another, before finally blending into San Leandro. Most visitors simply pass through East Oakland on the way to or from the airport or Coliseum, which is probably a good idea.

The **Oakland-Alameda County Coliseum** (☎ 510-569-2121) beside I-880 is home to the Oakland A's baseball team, the Golden State Warriors basketball team and the Oakland Raiders football team (see Spectator Sports below).

If you're traveling to or from Oakland International Airport, consider a brief stop at the **Western Aerospace Museum** (☎ 510-638-7100), at Hangar 6 opposite North Field; turn off the airport entrance road northbound onto Doolittle Drive and watch for the aircraft. The museum's collection includes a Lockheed Electra (like the one Amelia Earhart disappeared in back in 1937) and a Harrier jump jet. The museum's pride and joy is the huge four-engined British Short Solent flying boat. The museum is open 10 am to 4 pm Wednesday to Sunday; $4. An internal inspection of the Solent costs an extra $2.

Places to Stay

When it comes to accommodations, Oakland is no competition for San Francisco. San Francisco has many more economical hotels, and BART service makes a visit from San Francisco an easy alternative to staying in the East Bay. Still, some campsites are available, and if you want to experience East Bay luxury, Oakland offers several options.

Camping There are 75 tent sites ($15) and RV spaces ($20) at *Anthony Chabot Regional Park* (☎ 510-639-4751), all available first-come, first-served. It's a good spot if you're car camping and want to spend a few nights in the Bay Area (as San Francisco offers no tent camping at all). The park is a few miles south of Oakland off I-580.

Downtown At the stately 1927 *Lake Merritt Hotel* (☎ 510-832-2300, 800-933-4683, 1800 Madison St) breakfast is included and can be enjoyed in the glassed-in dining room overlooking the lake. Rates range from $109 for a standard room to $179 for a deluxe suite.

The *Oakland Marriott* (☎ 510-451-4000, 800-228-9200, 1001 Broadway) is a modern deluxe hotel across from the Oakland Convention Center. There are nearly 500 rooms with nightly costs ranging from $139 to $175. The nearby, smaller *Washington Inn* (☎ 510-452-1776, 495 10th St) has rooms starting at $99, including continental breakfast.

Jack London Square The *London Lodge Chinatown* (☎ 510-451-6316), 423 7th St at Broadway, is conveniently central, only six blocks from the 12th St BART station and a stone's throw from Chinatown and Jack London Square. Featureless but large rooms are $45/55.

The *Jack London Inn* (☎ 510-444-2032, 444 Embarcadero West) is clean and relatively cheap with rooms for $75 to $90 a night. Right on the waterfront at the end of Broadway, the *Waterfront Plaza Hotel* (☎ 510-836-3800, 10 Washington St) is more expensive, at $170 (no view) to $190 (harbor view).

Dockside Bed & Boat (☎ 510-444-5858, 800-436-2574, 77 Jack London Square) has a number of boats moored in the square's marina; you can spend the night on one of them for $95 to $195 weekdays, $115 to $275 weekends.

Oakland Hills To experience the indulgence of a spa without traveling to Calistoga, head to the *Claremont Resort and Spa* (☎ 510-843-7924, 800-551-7266) at Ashby and Domingo Aves, near Rockridge on the Berkeley border. It offers various weekend deals, from the Escape Package ($179), which includes use of the fitness center and swimming pools, to the Spa Sampler ($355), which gives you the same, plus a 50-minute massage and breakfast.

Oakland Airport There are a cluster of hotels in South Oakland, beside the I-880 freeway or on the short Hegenberger Rd axis between the Oakland-Alameda Coliseum and the airport. These include, from cheapest to most expensive, a *Motel 6* (☎ *510-638-1180, 8480 Edes Ave*), with double rooms for $55 to $70; the *Holiday Inn Oakland Airport* (☎ *510-562-5311, 500 Hegenberger Rd*), with doubles for $85 to $110; and the *Hilton Oakland Airport* (☎ *510-635-5000, 800-445-8667, 1 Hegenberger Rd*), with rooms starting at $120.

Places to Eat

Downtown The glossy City Center development has a collection of popular, budget-priced lunch spots, which are particularly good when the sun is shining and you can eat outside. *Ratto's* (☎ *510-832-6503, 821 Washington St*) is an Oakland institution (since 1897), serving generous salads and sandwiches. It has a full deli selling olives, cheese and international delicacies. Also popular at lunchtime, *Le Cheval* (☎ *510-763-8495, 1007 Clay St*), between 10th and 11th Sts, serves delicious Vietnamese food in spacious environs. The lemongrass tofu and baked clay pot dishes won't let you down; dishes range from $5 to $9.

Oakland's Chinatown may be less picturesque than San Francisco's, but it's just as busy and provides equally tasty and economical dining opportunities. *Phnom Penh House* (☎ *510-893-3825, 251 8th St*) and *Battambang* (☎ *510-839-8815, 850 Broadway*) are excellent, affordable Cambodian restaurants with main dishes for less than $9. Battambang's eggplant in lime sauce is a tasty treat. *Sun Hongkong* (☎ *510-465-1940, 389 8th St*) has fresh seafood for $5 to $7 a plate.

Jack London Square Good inexpensive food is plentiful at Jack London Square. *Dolma's Deli* (☎ *510-839-1951, 201 Broadway*) does great falafel sandwiches. The *Happy Belly Deli & Cafe* (☎ *510-835-0446*), in Jack London Village, serves tasty sandwiches and salads ($6 to $8) on an outdoor deck.

For a bit more money, you can feast on sushi at *Yoshi's* (☎ *510-238-9200, 510 Embarcadero West*). Take off your shoes, relax at the sunken tables and enjoy *unagi* (barbecued eel) and spicy tuna rolls ($4 to $4.50). Entrées such as *chirashi* (raw fish over a bowl of rice) are also good, costing around $11. If you're feeling flush, try *Jack's Bistro* (☎ *510-444-7171*) in the Waterfront Plaza Hotel. The Mediterranean seafood and poultry entrées range from $14 to $19.

Lake Merritt The incomparable *Roscoe's Chicken & Waffles* (☎ *510-444-5705, 336 Grand Ave*) serves exactly that, plus soul food staples; main dishes are $5 to $9, sides $1.50 to $3. The waffles are stellar.

Arizmendi (☎ *510-268-8849, 3265 Lakeshore Ave*), past the freeway overpass, is a bakery co-op that sells scrumptious gourmet pizza by the slice from 11:30 am to 2 pm and 4:30 pm to 7 pm. If you miss the pizza, try the equally good focaccia or any of the hearty pastries or breads. Popular, homey *Spettro* (☎ *510-465-8320, 3355 Lakeshore Ave*) is open for dinner 5 pm to 10 pm daily and for lunch 11:30 am to 2 pm Tuesday to Friday. Its creative menu includes the savory butternut squash cannelloni (entrées $12 to $15).

In an old house northeast of the Grand Lake Theatre, the *Autumn Moon Cafe* (☎ *510-595-3200, 3909 Grand Ave*) serves creative breakfast and lunch dishes ($6 to $10) and hearty dinners ($10 to $16). The chocolate bread pudding is to die for.

North Oakland In Piedmont, *Tropix Backyard Cafe* (☎ *510-653-2444, 3814 Piedmont Ave*) serves good Creole and Jamaican food ($6 to $11, about $5 for tapas) on its colorful back patio. *Bay Wolf* (☎ *510-655-6004, 3853 Piedmont Ave*) is one of the East Bay's best-known restaurants. Emphasizing Mediterranean cuisine, it serves excellent appetizers (around $8) and main courses ($14 to $18) such as halibut served on a pillow of white bean puree. The restaurant has a heated front porch hidden from the street, so you can dine outside even on chilly evenings.

If you're searching for something simpler, *Barney's Gourmet Hamburgers* (☎ *510-655-7180, 4162 Piedmont Ave*) serves the best burgers you'll find anywhere – and that goes for the veggie burgers, too. There's another Barney's in Rockridge at 5819 College Ave.

Also in Rockridge is ever-popular **Zachary's Pizza** (☎ 510-655-6385, *5801 College Ave*), serving Chicago-style pizza stuffed with an array of fresh ingredients; prices range from $11 to $23. The cheery, aromatic **Red Tractor Cafe** (☎ 510-595-3500, *5634 College Ave*) serves peerless, affordable comfort food such as sweet potato pudding ($1.50) and chicken pot pie ($6.25); the breakfasts are good, too.

The atmosphere at **Mama's Royal Cafe** (☎ 510-547-7600, *4012 Broadway*), near 40th St, is rather tumbledown, but that keeps the prices reasonable ($5 to $9). With hefty breakfasts and strong coffee, it attracts lots of students from the nearby art school. Get there early or be prepared to wait.

Entertainment

Bars & Clubs If you're downtown and thirsting for a brew, the **Pacific Coast Brewing Company** (☎ 510-836-2739, *906 Washington St*) makes its own. Sing-along enthusiasts should head for the **Alley** (☎ 510-444-8505, *3325 Grand Ave*), where Rod Dibble has been tickling the ivories from 9 pm to closing Tuesday to Saturday since 1960. **Ben & Nick's** (☎ 510-923-0327, *562 College Ave*) in Rockridge, serves a score of microbrews in an easygoing atmosphere, and there's good pub food as well. Also on College Ave is the **Hut** (☎ 510-653-2565, *5515 College Ave*), with good deals on pitchers of beer from 5 to 9 pm weekdays.

For live music, Oakland's most famous venue is **Yoshi's** (☎ 510-238-9200, *510 Embarcadero West*) at Jack London Square. It bills itself as a world-class jazz club, and that's no lie. **Kimball's East** (☎ 510-658-2555, *5800 Shellmound*) in Emeryville, northwest of Oakland, is another club for big-name jazz.

If you're looking for the blues, **Eli's Mile High Club** (☎ 510-655-6661, *3629 Martin Luther King Jr Way*), near 37th St, presents blues bands, mostly local, six nights a week. It's not in the best neighborhood, so if you go, take a cab. In downtown Oakland, the **A&C**

Club (☎ 510-893-4100, *1950 San Pablo Ave*) has two blues shows on Sunday, one of them a jam, and hosts an all-day blues fest every second Saturday. **Jimmie's** (☎ 510-268-8445, *1731 San Pablo Ave*) calls itself 'a grown folks' club.' They've got jazz on Sunday and blues and R&B a few nights a week.

The narrow, lively **5th Amendment** (☎ 510-832-3242, *3255 Lakeshore Ave*) books jazz and blues bands and has a friendly, flirty atmosphere.

Blue Oakland

When thousands of blacks moved to the Bay Area in the 1940s to work in the ship-yards and other wartime industries, they brought the blues with them. From the mid-1940s through the '50s, Oakland – specifically West Oakland – was home to a thriving blues scene. Clubs peppered 7th St, Union St and Grove St (now Martin Luther King Jr Way), and most of the era's blues musicians spent time in the clubs' smoky environs. Lowell Fulsom and Jimmy McCracklin are two bluemen whose enduring music is closely associated with Oakland blues. Ivory Joe Hunter got his start in Oakland.

Unlike Chicago blues, which included the harmonica and could trace its roots to Mississippi, Oakland blues originated in Texas and Louisiana, resulting in 'a slow, draggier beat and a kinda mournful sound,' in the words of Bob Geddins, the man credited with defining and nurturing the style.

In the 1960s, the blues faded from favor. When the popularity of rock threw the spotlight back on the genre, it was the Chicago style, not the Oakland style, that enjoyed a renaissance. West Oakland's underground blues clubs hung on, but in the 1970s the sound began to evolve, incorporating the harmonica and other elements. You can still find blues clubs in Oakland, but no longer are they dominated by the historic Oakland blues sound.

What remains of Oakland's early-1990s underground rock scene can be found at the **Stork Club** (☎ 510-444-6174, 2330 Telegraph Ave) downtown, which books an eclectic lineup of indie folk singers and local progressive bands.

Theaters & Cinemas They don't show movies often at the **Paramount Theatre** (☎ 510-465-6400), at Broadway and 21st St, but when they do it's an experience. The theater is home to the Oakland East Bay Symphony (☎ 510-446-1992) and the Oakland Ballet (☎ 510-465-6400) and periodically books big-name bands and musicians for concerts.

The grand old **Grand Lake Theatre** (☎ 510-452-3556, 3200 Grand Ave) has been carved up into a multiplex and shows first-run Hollywood releases. So does the multiplex **Jack London Cinema** (☎ 510-433-1320), on Washington St at Jack London Square. At the **Parkway Theater** (☎ 510-814-2400, 1834 Park Blvd) second-run films are $3, and you can watch them from comfy couches with a beer, slice of pizza or sandwich in your hand.

Spectator Sports

The **Golden State Warriors** (☎ 888-479-4667) are the Bay Area's only NBA basketball team. They play at the New Arena at the Oakland-Alameda County Coliseum. The **Oakland A's** (☎ 510-638-0500), the Bay Area's American League baseball team, play at the Oakland Coliseum's outdoor stadium. And for better or worse, Oakland's prodigal NFL team, the **Raiders** (☎ 800-949-2626), are once again playing at the Coliseum after a few years' sojourn in Los Angeles (still a touchy subject for Bay Area sports fans).

You can book tickets for football, baseball or basketball games through BASS (☎ 510-762-2277). Bleacher seats for A's games are $5 to $8 and have a good view. More expensive seats range from $11 to $20. For most baseball games, it's no problem to just turn up and save the BASS booking fee. Tickets to see the Warriors and Raiders play are another story – book as far ahead as possible.

Getting There & Away

You can arrive in Oakland by air, bus, Amtrak train, BART or even ferry. From San Francisco by car, you cross the Bay Bridge and then enter Oakland by I-580 or I-980.

Air Oakland International Airport (☎ 510-577-4000) is almost directly across the Bay from San Francisco International Airport. If you're traveling within the US (the only international departures from Oakland are to Canada and Mexico), arriving or departing the Bay Area through this less-crowded alternative can make good sense, especially since discount carriers such as Southwest Airlines (☎ 800-435-9792) use Oakland Airport, not San Francisco.

Bus AC Transit (☎ 510-839-2882) runs a number of convenient buses from San Francisco's Transbay Terminal, at Mission and 1st Sts, to downtown Oakland and Berkeley and between the two East Bay cities. A score of buses goes to Oakland from San Francisco during commute hours, but only the O runs both ways all day and on weekends; you can catch it at the corner of 6th and Washington Sts in San Francisco. The fare to and from Oakland is $2.20.

Between Berkeley and downtown Oakland ($1.25) take the No 15 Bus, which runs from BART's 12th St station in downtown Oakland into Berkeley via Martin Luther King Jr Blvd; or the No 40, which runs up and down Telegraph Ave between the two city centers. The No 51, which runs along Broadway in Oakland and then along College Ave in Berkeley, is less direct but has some handy stops, including the UC Berkeley campus and the Berkeley Marina.

Greyhound (☎ 800-231-2222) buses operate direct from Oakland to Vallejo, San Francisco, San Jose, Santa Rosa and Sacramento (the San Francisco terminal has many more direct-service options). Oakland's seedy Greyhound station (☎ 510-834-3213) is at 2103 San Pablo Ave.

Train Amtrak (☎ 800-872-7245) trains operating up and down the coast run through

Oakland (San Francisco does not have an Amtrak station).

Oakland's Amtrak station (☎ 510-238-4306) is at Jack London Square. From here you can catch AC Transit bus Nos 58, 72 or 73 to downtown Oakland, or take a ferry across the bay to San Francisco. If you're keen on taking a bus directly to San Francisco, you should disembark at the Emeryville Amtrak station (see the following Berkeley section) – a bus there meets all incoming Amtrak trains and then leaves for San Francisco's Transbay Terminal.

BART Within the Bay Area, the most convenient way to get to Oakland and back is by BART (Bay Area Rapid Transit; ☎ 415-992-2278, 510-465-2278). Trains run like clockwork every several minutes from 4 am to midnight on weekdays, every 10 to 15 minutes 6 am to midnight on Saturday, from 8 am to midnight Sunday.

To downtown Oakland, catch a Richmond- or Pittsburg/Bay Point-bound train. Fares to the 12th or 19th St stations from downtown San Francisco are $2.20; to Rockridge, $2.50. For Lake Merritt ($2.20) or the Oakland Coliseum/Airport station ($2.75), take a Fremont- or Dublin/Pleasanton-bound BART train. The Rockridge stop is on the Pittsburg/Bay Point line.

A BART-to-Bus transfer ticket, available from white AC Transit machines near BART station exits, costs 60¢.

Ferry Ferries are the slowest and most expensive, but undoubtedly the most enjoyable, way of traveling between San Francisco and Oakland. From San Francisco's Ferry Building, the Alameda/Oakland ferry (☎ 510-522-3300) sails to Jack London Square (up to 12 trips a day on weekdays, six to eight on weekends), where it docks at Clay and Water Sts. The ride takes about 20 minutes. The one-way fare is $4.50; buy tickets on board. You can get a free transfer between the ferry and AC Transit or MUNI buses.

Getting Around
To/From the Airport A taxi from the Oakland airport to downtown Oakland

costs about $18, to San Francisco about $50. Shuttles to the Coliseum BART Station run every 10 minutes for $2, 6 am to midnight Monday to Saturday, 9 am to midnight Sunday. AC Transit Bus No 58 operates between Oakland Airport and Jack London Square (via the Coliseum BART Station); local fare is $1.10.

SuperShuttle (☎ 510-268-8700) operates door-to-door shuttles to Oakland and San Francisco destinations for $12 to $21. To destinations farther afield, down the peninsula or South Bay, fares go up to $45.

Bus AC Transit (☎ 510-839-2882) has a comprehensive bus network within Oakland. Bus No 13 will take you from 14th St downtown to Lake Merritt and Lakeshore Ave. From Broadway downtown, the No 58 goes to Grand Ave, the No 59 to Piedmont Ave, and the No 51 to College Ave. One-way bus fares are $1.25.

BERKELEY
• population 107,800 • elevation 183 feet
Berkeley, long renowned for its mixture of bizarre street life and activist politics, is dominated by the huge campus of the University of California, Berkeley (UCB). Though Berkeley has mellowed since its '60s heyday, it remains a mecca of liberalism and student politics. The student sector isn't all there is to Berkeley. As the birthplace of both the Free Speech Movement and the California culinary revolution, Berkeley is anything but one-dimensional.

Telegraph Ave is Berkeley's most interesting thoroughfare, where you'll find pierced urban urchins begging money 'for beer or dog food,' street vendors, buttoned-down professors, pot-legalization activists, the down-and-out homeless and a cast of street personalities like the Hate Man and the Bubble Lady.

Orientation
Berkeley is bordered by the bay to the west, the hills to the east and Oakland to the south. I-80 runs along the town's western edge, next to the marina; from here University Ave heads east to the campus.

SAN FRANCISCO BAY AREA

Subverting the Dominant Paradigm

Berkeley students have always been passionate about their beliefs. As far back as the 1930s, student activists were rallying against social injustice and human rights violations, but it wasn't until the '60s that the city became famous – or, to many, infamous – as the nation's premier domestic battleground.

By 1964, students had already vocalized their opposition to President Kennedy's Bay of Pigs invasion, Senator Joseph McCarthy and the House Un-American Activities Committee hearings. But when a peaceful sit-in at Sproul Hall on the campus was disrupted by police on September 30, the revolution began to gain momentum. Freedom of speech and anti-Vietnam War sentiment were the primary issues, and over the next five years UC Regents (the administration) and then-governor Ronald Reagan led a harsh campaign of violent antiprotest reprisal that included arrests in the thousands, veritable armies of riot police, multiple tear-gas assaults, even a 17-day-long occupation by the National Guard.

The spring of 1969 was the height of the turmoil, and an unlikely symbol emerged at its heart: People's Park. In April, a derelict plot of land owned by the university was dubbed 'Power to the People Park.' Hundreds of hippies came armed with trees and flowers to create a center for their counterculture. In May, shortly after the land was consecrated by the Berkeley Free Church, the university seized the land, erecting fences overnight. Riots resulted in which hundreds were injured and one man was killed by stray gunfire.

Shattuck Ave crosses University Ave one block west of campus, forming the main crossroads of the downtown area. To the north is the Northside, including the 'Gourmet Ghetto'; to the south is the downtown Berkeley BART station.

The only navigational difficulties are the one-way streets near the campus' south side and the barriers set up to prevent traffic through many residential areas, making crossing these areas in a straight line nearly impossible. There's a pay-parking structure on Durant near Telegraph.

Information

The helpful Berkeley Convention & Visitors Bureau (☎ 510-549-7040, 800-847-4823), 2015 Center St near the downtown BART station, is open 9 am to 5 pm weekdays. There's also a 24-hour recorded information line (☎ 510-549-8710).

Campus maps and information are available from the university's visitor services center (☎ 510-642-5215), 101 University Hall, 2200 University Ave at Oxford St. It also offers free campus tours, departing at 10 am Monday to Saturday.

The Berkeley Historical Society (☎ 510-848-0181), 1931 Center St, offers occasional but excellent Sunday walking tours ($7).

University of California, Berkeley

The Berkeley campus of the University of California is the oldest and second-largest university in the state. The decision to found the college was made in 1866, when the campus area was ranchland. The first students arrived in 1873; today UCB has almost 30,000 students, more than a thousand professors, and more Nobel laureates than you could point a particle accelerator at.

From Telegraph Ave, enter the campus via Sproul Plaza and Sather Gate, a center for people watching, soapbox oration and pseudotribal drumming. Alternatively, enter from Center and Oxford Sts, near the downtown BART station.

Interesting campus sights include the **Museum of Paleontology** (☎ 510-642-1821) in the ornate Valley Life Sciences Building. This research museum is mostly closed to the public, but you can peek at exhibits in the atrium, including a Tyrannosaurus rex skeleton and the bones of local dinos. The atrium

BERKELEY

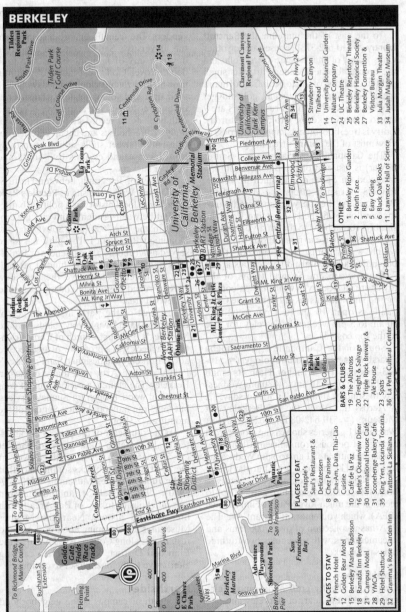

Tilden Regional Park

Claremont Canyon Regional Preserve

University of California, Clark Kerr Campus

University of California, Berkeley

Elmwood District

North Berkeley BART Station

Berkeley BART Station

see Central Berkeley map

San Francisco Bay

Golden Gate Fields (Race Track)

ALBANY

Solano Ave Shopping District

Fourth Street Shopping District

Berkeley Marina

Cesar E Chavez Park

Shorebird Park

Adventure Playground

Aquatic Park

San Pablo Park

ML King Jr Civic Center Park & Plaza

Gourmet Ghetto

Indian Rock Park

Live Oak Park

Codornices Park

La Loma Park

Strawberry Canyon Trailhead
13 Strawberry Canyon Trailhead
14 University Botanical Garden
17 Nature Company
24 UC Theatre
25 Berkeley Repertory Theatre
26 Berkeley Historical Society
27 Berkeley Convention & Visitors Bureau
33 Julia Morgan Theater
34 Judah Magnes Museum

OTHER
1 Berkeley Rose Garden
2 North Face
3 REI
5 Easy Going
6 Black Oak Books
11 Lawrence Hall of Science

BARS & CLUBS
19 The Albatross
20 Freight & Salvage
22 Triple Rock Brewery & Ale House
23 Spats
36 La Peña Cultural Center

PLACES TO EAT
4 Fatapple's
4 Saul's Restaurant & Delicatessen
6 Chez Panisse
8 Cha-Am, Dara Thai-Lao Cuisine
10 Café de la Paz
16 Bette's Oceanview Diner
30 International House Café
31 Sconehenge Bakery Café
35 King Yen, Locanda Toscana, Trattoria La Siciliana

PLACES TO STAY
7 French Hotel
12 Golden Bear Motel
15 Berkeley Marina Radisson
18 Ramada Inn Berkeley
21 Campus Motel
28 YMCA
29 Hotel Shattuck
32 Gramma's Rose Garden Inn

SAN FRANCISCO BAY AREA

is open during university terms, 8 am to 9 pm weekdays and 1 to 5 pm weekends; free.

To the east of the museum, the **Bancroft Library** (☎ 510-642-3781) houses, among other gems, a copy of Shakespeare's First Folio and the records of the Donner Party. Its small public exhibits of historical Californiana include the surprisingly small gold nugget that sparked the 1849 gold rush. Hours are 9 am to 5 pm weekdays, 1 to 5 pm Saturday. Entry is free, but you must apply for a pass to view most of the library's treasures.

The **Campanile** (officially named Sather Tower) is just east of the Bancroft Library. Modeled on St Mark's Basilica in Venice, the 328-foot spire offers fine views of the Bay Area. At the top, you can stare up into the carillon of 61 bells – ranging from the size of a cereal bowl to that of a Volkswagen – and, if you arrive at noon during the week, watch a carillonist play one of three booming daily recitals; other recitals are at 7:50 am and 6 pm. Several floors of the tower are an ossuary in which the paleontology department stashes old bones. The Campanile is open 10 am to 4 pm weekdays, 10 am to 5 pm weekends. The elevator ride to the top costs $1.

South of the Campanile is the **Phoebe Hearst Museum of Anthropology** (☎ 510-643-7648) at 103 Kroeber Hall. Its small exhibits are open 10 am to 4:30 pm Wednesday to Sunday, 10 am to 9 pm Thursday; $2.

Across the street, the **UC Berkeley Art Museum** (☎ 510-642-0808), 2626 Bancroft Way, has 11 galleries showcasing works from a range of periods, from ancient Chinese to modern. Hours are 11 am to 5 pm Wednesday to Sunday (11 am to 9 pm Thursday); $6/4 adults/children. The complex also houses a bookstore, cafe and sculpture garden, not to mention the much-loved **Pacific Film Archive** (PFA), which you enter off Durant Ave. The PFA has a collection of over 7000 films and documentaries, with screenings two to three times per week.

Southside

Despite its slightly gruff appearance, **Telegraph Ave** is the heart of Berkeley and one of the most colorful streets in the entire Bay Area, pumping out a steady sidewalk flow of students and shoppers, vagrants and vendors. The frenetic energy buzzing from the university's Sather Gate on any given day is a mix of honking horns and loud debates over God's real name, of youthful post-hippies reminiscing about days before their time and young hipsters who sneer at tie-dyed nostalgia. Telegraph Ave is packed with bookstores, record shops, clothing boutiques, coffeehouses and cheap eateries, not to mention street stalls selling everything from incense and crystals to T-shirts and bumper stickers.

Just east of Telegraph, between Haste St and Dwight Way, is the site of **People's Park**, a marker in local history as a political battleground between residents and city government in the late '60s (see 'Subverting the Dominant Paradigm'). The park has since served as a (unofficial) residence for Berkeley's homeless. A publicly funded restoration in the early '90s gave the park new grass, a relaid basketball court and a sand volleyball area.

Just east of the park, at the corner of Bowditch St and Dwight Way, stands Bernard Maybeck's 1910 **First Church of Christ Scientist**. Maybeck was a professor of architecture at UC Berkeley and designed San Francisco's Palace of Fine Arts, plus many homes in Berkeley. The church, a curious mix of concrete and wood, is open for Sunday services, but tours run only on the first Sunday of the month, at 12:15 pm.

To the southeast of the park is the architecturally notable **Julia Morgan Theater** (☎ 510-845-8542), 2642 College Ave at Derby St, and three blocks southeast of that is the **Judah Magnes Museum** (☎ 510-549-6950), 2911 Russell St, an old mansion museum housing tokens of Bay Area Jewish life, art and history. Near the Magnes Museum is the charming nook of shops and restaurants along College Ave known as the Elmwood District, which offers a calming alternative to the buzz closer to campus.

Northside

Just north of campus is the neighborhood known as Northside, filled with lovely

CENTRAL BERKELEY

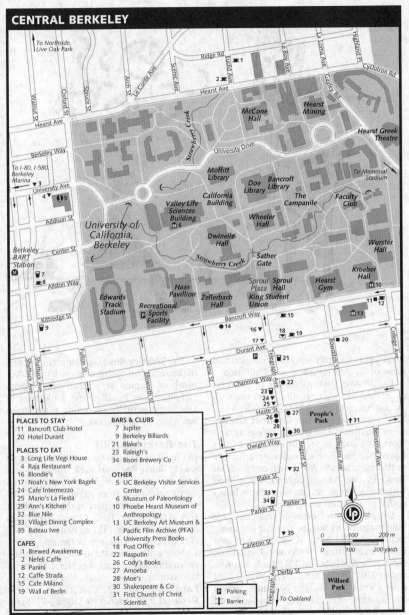

To Northside, Live Oak Park

Ridge Rd

Euclid Ave

La Loma Ave

Le Roy Ave

Highland Pl

Cyclotron Rd

Hearst Ave

Walnut St

Oxford St

Spruce St

Arch St

Le Conte Ave

Scenic Ave

Gayley Rd

Hearst Mining

McCone Hall

Hearst Greek Theatre

Strawberry Creek

University Drive

Berkeley Way

To I-80, I-580, Berkeley Marina

University Ave

Addison St

Moffitt Library

Doe Library

Bancroft Library

The Campanile

Faculty Club

To Memorial Stadium

California Building

Valley Life Sciences Building

University of California, Berkeley

Wheeler Hall

Center St

Dwinelle Hall

Wurster Hall

Berkeley BART Station

Allston Way

Strawberry Creek

Sather Gate

Kroeber Hall

Edwards Track Stadium

Recreational Sports Facility

Haas Pavillion

Zellerbach Hall

Sproul Plaza

Sproul Hall

King Student Union

Hearst Gym

Kittredge St

Shattuck Ave

Fulton St

Ellsworth St

Dana St

Telegraph Ave

Bancroft Way

Durant Ave

Channing Way

Haste St

People's Park

Dwight Way

Bowditch St

College Ave

Regent St

Hillegass Ave

Benvenue Ave

Blake St

Parker St

Carleton St

Derby St

Willard Park

To Oakland

PLACES TO STAY
11 Bancroft Club Hotel
20 Hotel Durant

PLACES TO EAT
3 Long Life Vegi House
4 Raja Restaurant
16 Blondie's
17 Noah's New York Bagels
24 Cafe Intermezzo
25 Mario's La Fiesta
29 Ann's Kitchen
32 Blue Nile
33 Village Dining Complex
35 Bateau Ivre

CAFES
1 Brewed Awakening
2 Nefeli Caffe
8 Panini
12 Caffe Strada
15 Cafe Milano
19 Wall of Berlin

BARS & CLUBS
7 Jupiter
9 Berkeley Billiards
21 Blake's
23 Raleigh's
34 Bison Brewery Co

OTHER
5 UC Berkeley Visitor Services Center
6 Museum of Paleontology
10 Phoebe Hearst Museum of Anthropology
13 UC Berkeley Art Museum & Pacific Film Archive (PFA)
14 University Press Books
18 Post Office
22 Rasputin
26 Cody's Books
27 Amoeba
28 Moe's
30 Shakespeare & Co
31 First Church of Christ Scientist

P Parking
Barrier

0   100   200 m
0   100   200 yards

SAN FRANCISCO BAY AREA

homes, parks, stately schools of religion and some of the best restaurants in California.

Euclid Ave, with its cluster of peaceful cafes and stores near the junction with Hearst Ave, is the center of Northside. A few blocks northwest is the **Gourmet Ghetto**, along Shattuck Ave between Virginia and Rose Sts. Food – especially the deified Chez Panisse – is the main attraction here. Farther northwest is **Solano Ave**, which crosses from Berkeley into Albany. Solano Ave is lined with funky shops, restaurants, places to sip coffee or wine and movie theaters.

Over the years, Northside residents have built magnificent homes. You can see many examples of Bernard Maybeck's Arts and Crafts architecture – with carved wood and handcrafted details – at 1515 La Loma Ave and at 2704, 2711, 2733, 2751, 2754 and 2780 Buena Vista Way. Wander Northside streets to examine the elaborate gardens and Asian-influenced front gates of local homes.

The **Berkeley Rose Garden**, eight terraces of Technicolor blooms, is on Euclid Ave south of Eunice St, several blocks from campus. Quiet benches and a plethora of almost perpetually blooming roses make this a worthy destination.

The Berkeley Hills

In the hills east of town is Berkeley's crown jewel, **Tilden Regional Park**. The 2079-acre park has more than 30 miles of trails of varying difficulty, from paved paths to hilly scrambles, including part of the magnificent Bay Area Ridge Trail. Other attractions include a carousel ($1), miniature railroad ($1.50), children's farm, botanical garden, 18-hole golf course (☎ 510-848-7373) and an environmental education center. Lake Anza is a favorite area for picnics. You can swim in Lake Anza for $2. Call the East Bay Regional Park District (☎ 510-562-7275) for information and brochures with maps. AC

SAN FRANCISCO BAY AREA

Transit bus No 67 runs to the park from the downtown BART station.

The **Lawrence Hall of Science** (☎ 510-642-5132), on Centennial Drive near Grizzly Peak Blvd, is named after Ernest Lawrence, who won the Nobel Prize (the first one for UC Berkeley) for his invention of the cyclotron particle accelerator and was a key member of the WWII Manhattan Project, which developed the first atomic bomb. He also invented and patented the color-TV picture tube. The Hall of Science itself has a huge collection of exhibits on subjects ranging from lasers to earthquakes. Outdoor exhibits, including a 60-foot model of a DNA molecule, compete with the breathtaking bay view for your attention. Hours are 10 am to 5 pm daily; $6/4. AC Transit buses No 8 and No 65 run to the hall from the downtown BART station, as does the university's Hill Service Shuttle from the Hearst Mining Circle.

Another great find in the hills is the **University Botanical Garden** (☎ 510-642-3343), 200 Centennial Drive in Strawberry Canyon, below the Hall of Science. With over 13,000 species of plants, the garden is one of the most varied collections in the US. It too can be reached by the Hill Service Shuttle. It's open 9 am to 4:45 pm daily; free.

The nearby **fire trail** is a woodsy walking loop around Strawberry Canyon that gives great views of town and of the off-limits Lawrence Berkeley National Laboratory. Enter at the trailhead at the parking lot on Centennial Drive just southwest of the Botanical Garden; you'll emerge near the Lawrence Hall of Science.

West Berkeley

Hidden within a highway-side industrial area in West Berkeley lies the glitz and glam of the three-block street mall known as the **4th St Shopping District**. This small area offers the finest in upscale shopping; if you don't want to shop, take a stroll along the **Berkeley Marina**, where seagulls defend their airspace from an almost daily blitz of colorful kites. Construction of the marina began in 1936 and continued through the 1940s and '50s. The pier jutting out from the

marina has much older origins; it was originally built in the 1870s and was replaced by a 3-mile-long ferry pier in 1920. Part of the original pier has been rebuilt.

Places to Stay

If you decide to sleep in Berkeley, there are hotels and motels all along University Ave from I-80 to the UC Berkeley campus, but the quality is not always good.

The Berkeley Convention & Visitors Bureau (see Information) can recommend local hotels. The Berkeley and Oakland Bed & Breakfast Network (☎ 510-547-6380) can recommend (more expensive) private homes that offer lodging, from private suites to garden cottages. If you're looking to splurge, head to the Claremont Resort and Spa on the Berkeley-Oakland border (see Places to Stay in the Oakland section).

Hostels Berkeley doesn't have an official hostel, but it does have a *YMCA* (☎ 510-848-6800, 2001 Allston Way) in the heart of downtown Berkeley. Small – sometimes *very* small – singles/doubles/triples with shared bath are $33/40/50, including use of the sauna and swimming pools. Advance bookings are recommended.

Southside Directly across the road from the UC Berkeley campus, the *Bancroft Club Hotel* (☎ 510-549-1000, 2680 Bancroft Way) has 22 comfortable rooms, all nonsmoking, at $80 to $100.

Only a block back from the campus, the *Hotel Durant* (☎ 510-845-8981, 800-238-7268, 2600 Durant Ave) is a larger 140-room hotel with a popular bar. Nightly costs are from $79 to $105.

The *Hotel Shattuck* (☎ 510-845-7300, 2086 Allston Way), in the center of downtown Berkeley, is a large, older hotel with 175 rooms starting at $100, including continental breakfast. It's just off Shattuck Ave, close to BART.

The campus area has several B&Bs. *Gramma's Rose Garden Inn* (☎ 510-549-2145, 2740 Telegraph Ave) at Stuart St, has 40 rooms, all with attached bath, in two older and three newer buildings. If you can put up with the cloying name, nightly costs are $99 in the main house, $110 to $165 in the other buildings. That includes breakfast, wine in the evenings, and coffee or tea at any time. The smaller *Elmwood House* (☎ 510-540-5123, 800-540-3050), in a well-kept Victorian home on College Ave in the Elmwood District, has two rooms with shared bath ($69 to $80) and two with private bath ($75 to $100). Due to the inn's small size, we've been asked not to list their address – call for reservations and directions.

Elsewhere in Berkeley University Ave, which runs from I-80 straight to the UC Berkeley campus, is dotted with motels with prices from dirt cheap to medium range. One of the more respectable options is the 117-room *Ramada Inn Berkeley* (☎ 510-849-1121, 920 University Ave), near 7th St. Comfortable doubles start at $79.

Typical of cheaper University Ave motels is the simple but well kept, 23-room *Campus Motel* (☎ 510-841-3844, 1619 University Ave), near California St. Singles/doubles start at $45/60. The *Golden Bear Motel* (☎ 510-525-6770, 1620 San Pablo Ave) near Cedar St, is a slightly better class of motel, though not in a great area. Doubles are $54 to $60.

Right in the Gourmet Ghetto, the 18-room *French Hotel* (☎ 510-548-9930, 1538 Shattuck Ave) is a modern building with very straightforward rooms at $95 single or double. It has a popular cafe downstairs.

The *Berkeley Marina Radisson* (☎ 510-548-7920, 200 Marina Blvd) is Berkeley's biggest and glossiest hotel. It's on the waterfront with great views across the bay. Although it's far from almost everything else in Berkeley, it has a free shuttle to BART. Doubles cost $99 (weekends) to $149 (weekdays).

Places to Eat
Telegraph Ave, on the Southside near the UC Berkeley campus, is packed with cafes, cheap food stands and restaurants that cater to all budgets. Along University Ave in downtown Berkeley, you'll find more of the same. The Northside – or the Gourmet

Ghetto, as it's known by Bay Area gourmands – is the district that helped give birth to California cuisine, and not surprisingly it's home to some top-flight restaurants.

Southside Fast-moving lines and a hefty slice for $2 to $3 make *Blondie's* (☎ 510-548-1129, 2340 Telegraph Ave) Berkeley's best stop for a slice of pizza. Though the chain is now corporate-owned, *Noah's New York Bagels* (☎ 510-849-9951, 2344 Telegraph) still has the best bagels ($1 and up).

Cafe Intermezzo (☎ 510-849-4592, 2442 Telegraph Ave) holds the title for the biggest and best sandwiches and salads, both for around $5. *Mario's La Fiesta* (☎ 510-848-2588, 2444 Telegraph Ave) is the place for large servings of Mexican food. *Ann's Kitchen* (☎ 510-548-8885, 2498 Telegraph Ave) serves up diner-food options and is a busy breakfast joint.

Better sit-down meals are down Telegraph Ave past Dwight Way. *Blue Nile* (☎ 510-540-6777, 2525 Telegraph) serves up truly finger-licking-good Ethiopian food and tasty honey wine in a most peaceful setting. Across at No 2556 is the Village, a low-key wooden complex that offers Indian food at both *New Delhi Junction* (☎ 510-486-0477) and *Annapurna* (☎ 510-845-9100), Korean barbecue at *Koryo* (☎ 510-548-2525), Japanese dishes at *Norikonoko* (☎ 510-548-1274) and Swiss fondue at *Fondue Fred* (☎ 510-549-0850). Entrées at each cost $8 to $12. *Bateau Ivre* (☎ 510-849-1100, 2629 Telegraph Ave), a bit farther down the street, is a classy French restaurant (entrées $8 to $17) that's also good for beer, wine, coffee or snacks. On sunny days, you can dine on the outdoor patio. It's closed on Monday.

There's a handful of good restaurants near the Berkeley BART station. For tasty sushi head to *Tokyo's Bliss* (☎ 510-644-1570, 2134 Oxford St), where a generous combination goes for $15. *Long Life Vegi House* (☎ 510-845-6072, 2129 University Ave) dishes up cheap and plentiful Chinese vegetarian and seafood specialties. Across the street at *Raja Restaurant* (☎ 510-848-7252, 2160 University Ave), try a vegetarian thali ($8.95) or tandoori prawns ($14.75).

SAN FRANCISCO BAY AREA

Near the Ashby BART station, the **Sconehenge Bakery Cafe** (☎ 510-845-5168, *2787 Shattuck Ave*) serves excellent breakfasts and lunches for $4.50 to $5.95. The bakery offers things like sweet-potato bear claws. It's closed Sunday.

In the Elmwood District, College Ave is lined with restaurants. For years **King Yen** (☎ 510-845-1286, *2995 College Ave*) has served what is arguably some of Berkeley's best Chinese food (entrées $6 to $10). A pang for Italian could lead you to one of two Elmwood restaurants: Tuscan-oriented **Locanda Toscana** (☎ 510-848-5544, *2985 College Ave*) and **Trattoria La Siciliana** (☎ 510-704-1474, *2993 College Ave*), a few doors down. Both are medium-priced ($15 to $25 for a meal) and have remarkably similar pseudo-Italian charm.

Northside Carnivores weary of veggie-happy Berkeley head to **Fatapple's** (☎ 510-526-2260, *1346 Martin Luther King Jr Way*), beloved for its delicious hamburgers ($5 to $7) and pies ($3 a slice).

Two superb Thai restaurants sit at the corner of Shattuck Ave and Cedar St. **Cha-Am** (☎ 510-848-9664, *1543 Shattuck Ave*) has succulent curries ($6.95) and veggie offerings. Its neighbor, **Dara Thai-Lao Cuisine** (☎ 510-841-2002, *1549 Shattuck Ave*), serves food from Thailand and Laos.

The mood is Spanish at nearby **Cafe de la Paz** (☎ 510-843-0662, *1600 Shattuck Ave*), which serves tapas and other Spanish and Latin-American dishes.

The deli part of **Saul's Restaurant & Delicatessen** (☎ 510-848-3354, *1475 Shattuck Ave*) offers take-out sandwiches and bakery items. The restaurant serves excellent Jewish and Eastern European food (matzo brei, latkes, spaetzel, etc). It's difficult to spend more than $10 on a dish here; special dinners are offered on Jewish holidays.

Got lots of cash? Worship at Alice Waters' feet at **Chez Panisse** (☎ 510-548-5525 *for dinner reservations, 1517 Shattuck Ave*). Menus change nightly. Downstairs they serve phenomenal prix fixe meals – pasta in shellfish broth, beef tenderloin with black truffles – for $38 to $68 per person (the price of a

Alice Waters

meal rises as the week progresses), plus a 15% service charge (this is the tip). The upstairs cafe offers a la carte fare such as oven-baked calamari or grilled swordfish ($10 to $19). For a world-famous temple of gastronomy, the place has retained a welcoming atmosphere. Book your reservations several weeks in advance.

West Berkeley The 4th St Shopping District has a small collection of restaurants. Among the notables is **Bette's Oceanview Diner** (☎ 510-644-3230, *1807 4th St*) The diner-style food is good, but long waits for tables can be very frustrating.

Entertainment

Cafes A mainstay for Berkeley students and locals alike, coffeehouses dot the town, and the smell of fresh grounds wafts from the early morning till late in the evening. The most popular Southside places are **Caffe Strada** (☎ 510-843-5282, *2300 College Ave*), with a tree-shaded patio; **Cafe Milano**

SAN FRANCISCO BAY AREA

(☎ 510-644-3100, 2522 Bancroft Way), with a skylit loft; **Wall of Berlin** (☎ 510-540-8449, 2517 Durant Ave), offering strong java and sidewalk seats; and the cafe at the **International House** (or 'I-House'; ☎ 510-642-9932), at the top of Bancroft Way at Piedmont Ave, where you can hang out with the university's foreign students.

On the Northside, **Brewed Awakening** (☎ 510-540-8865, 1807 Euclid Ave) offers a quiet place to read and people watch. Across the street is wee **Nefeli Caffe** (☎ 510-841-6374, 1854 Euclid Ave). **Panini** (☎ 510-849-0405), off Shattuck near the Berkeley BART station, is a sunny oasis in which to sip joe or nibble a snack.

Bars & Clubs **Blake's** (☎ 510-848-0886, 2367 Telegraph Ave) is a popular spot for live music, notably local blues and rock bands (downstairs with a cover), with bars on three floors, a menu of tolerable eats and two pool tables. **Raleigh's** (☎ 510-848-8652, 2438 Telegraph Ave), a nightly frat-boy haven, has a shuffleboard and two pool tables crammed in the back and a nice outdoor patio. **Bison Brewery Co** (☎ 510-841-7734, 2598 Telegraph Ave) serves its own brews and has a pool table and small balcony upstairs and live music on weekends.

Downtown, **Jupiter** (☎ 510-843-8277, 2180 Shattuck Ave) is considered by many to be the best place for beer, with a long list of microbrews on tap, a beer garden in back, good pizza and live bands in better weather. **Berkeley Billiards** (☎ 510-848-1766, 2367 Shattuck Ave) has 20 full-size tables, plenty of straight cues, and beer and wine at the bar.

Farther north, near the Gourmet Ghetto, saloonlike **Spats** (☎ 510-841-7225, 1974 Shattuck Ave) is Berkeley's best place for a mixed drink. It's filled with antique and cushy furniture and offers a long menu of exotic alcoholic beverages. Nearby, **Triple Rock Brewery & Ale House** (☎ 510-843-2739, 1920 Shattuck Ave) offers a good range of its own brews, some hearty eats and a small outdoor patio on the roof.

In West Berkeley, the **Albatross** (☎ 510-843-2473, 1822 San Pablo Ave), nicknamed

'the Bird' by locals, is a long-standing dive bar known for its strong drinks.

Berkeley's major live music venues include **Freight & Salvage** (☎ 510-548-1761, 1111 Addison St), near San Pablo Ave, for folk music and **La Peña Cultural Center** (☎ 510-849-2568, 3105 Shattuck Ave), near the Ashby BART station, with live music, comedy, theater and poetry with a Latin American flavor. Both venues charge covers ($3 to $15).

Cinemas Berkeley's excellent art cinemas include the **Pacific Film Archive** (☎ 510-642-1124), in the Berkeley Art Museum, with nightly international and classic films, and the **UC Theatre** (☎ 510-843-3456, 2036 University Ave) downtown, with an eclectic menu of new, classic and camp films that changes nightly.

Theater & Dance The respected **Berkeley Repertory Theatre** (☎ 510-845-4700, 2025 Addison St), in downtown Berkeley, hosts classical and modern theater. Dance and music of all types and styles, performed by national and international groups, are featured at **Zellerbach Hall** (☎ 510-642-9988) on the south side of the UC Berkeley campus; tickets for campus events can be bought at the adjoining Cal Performances Ticket Office (☎ 510-642-9988).

Spectator Sports

Sporting venues in Berkeley include the university's 76,000-seat **Memorial Stadium**, which dates from 1923. This is the site (in alternating years) of the November Big Game, a famous football clash between UC Berkeley and Stanford University. Call ☎ 800-462-3277 for ticket information on all UC Berkeley teams. Football tickets are easier to get than basketball tickets, which are often sold out weeks in advance.

Shopping

Telegraph Ave offers everything from handmade sidewalk-vendor jewelry to head-shop paraphernalia, but its most appealing shops are irrefutably its terrific book and music stores.

Books Cody's Books (☎ 510-845-7852), 2454 Telegraph Ave, has one of the widest selections of new books in the world and regular author appearances. Moe's (☎ 510-849-2087), at No 2476, offers four floors of new and used book browsing, and Shakespeare & Co (☎ 510-841-8916), at No 2499, is literally stacked to the ceiling with new and used books. University Press Books (☎ 510-548-0585), 2430 Bancroft Way, stocks works by UC Berkeley professors and has other brainy academic titles.

Northside bibliophiles love Black Oak Books (☎ 510-486-0698), 1491 Shattuck Ave, with new and used books and a full calendar of author appearances. Easy Going (☎ 510-843-3533), 1385 Shattuck Ave near Rose St, is a long-standing and excellent travel bookstore.

Music For music, mass quantities of new and used CDs, tapes and records (yes, lots of vinyl) can be found at both Rasputin (☎ 510-848-9004), 2401 Telegraph Ave, now in its third and largest location, and Amoeba (☎ 510-549-1125), at No 2455, where the extent of its inventory and selection hits you immediately upon entering.

Outdoor Gear In West Berkeley, north of the 4th St Shopping District, check out the Nature Company's original store (☎ 510-649-5448), 740 Hearst St at 4th St, as well as the huge REI store (☎ 510-527-4140), 1338 San Pablo Ave near Gilman St, for outdoor gear. Near REI is the Wilderness Exchange (☎ 510-525-1255), 1407 San Pablo Ave, the Berkeley outdoorperson's favorite little shop for new and used gear. North Face (☎ 510-526-3530), a well-respected brand of outdoor gear, is based in Berkeley at 5th and Gilman Sts.

Getting There & Away

Bus AC Transit (☎ 510-817-1717) runs a number of buses from San Francisco's Transbay Terminal, at Mission and 1st Sts, to Berkeley. The most convenient bus is the F line, which runs from the Transbay Terminal to downtown Berkeley (the stop is near the Berkeley BART station) every 15 to 20 minutes on weekdays only ($2.75). The trip takes 30 minutes.

Between Berkeley and downtown Oakland, take AC Transit bus No 15 ($1.25), which runs to and from Berkeley and Oakland's 12th St BART station via Martin Luther King Jr Way, or bus No 40, which runs up and down Telegraph Ave between the two centers. The No 51 runs along Broadway in Oakland and then along College Ave in Berkeley, past the UC campus and down to the Berkeley Marina (near campus, catch the No 51 on Bancroft Way; in downtown Berkeley, catch it on Shattuck Ave near the BART station).

BART The easiest way to travel between San Francisco, Oakland and Berkeley is on BART (☎ 510-465-2278), with trains running every 10 minutes or so from 4 am to midnight on weekdays, with more limited service from 6 am on Saturday and from 8 am on Sunday.

To Berkeley, catch a Richmond-bound train to one of three BART stations: Ashby, Berkeley (the main station is at Shattuck Ave and Center St) or North Berkeley. The fare is $2.50 to $2.70 from downtown San Francisco, $1.10 from downtown Oakland. After 8 pm on weekdays, 7 pm on Saturday and all day Sunday, there is no direct service from San Francisco to Berkeley; you need to catch a Pittsburg/Bay Point train and transfer at 12th St station in Oakland.

A BART-to-Bus transfer ticket, available from white AC Transit machines near station exits, costs 60¢.

Car & Motorcycle With your own motorized wheels you can approach Berkeley from San Francisco by taking the Bay Bridge and then following either I-80 (for University Ave, downtown Berkeley and the UC campus) or Hwy 24 (for College Ave and the Berkeley Hills).

Parking near campus is tough. Two university-run parking areas – one on College Ave between Durant Ave and Channing Way, the other on Bancroft Way between Telegraph Ave and Dana St – charge 75¢ per half hour. The situation improves in the evenings and on weekends, when the other university lots open to the public for a flat $3 fee.

Getting Around

Public transit and your feet are the best options for getting around crowded central Berkeley. Berkeley TRiP (Transit, Ride Sharing & Parking; ☎ 510-644-7665) has all sorts of public and alternative transport information. Its Commute Store is at 2033 Center St, near the downtown Berkeley BART station.

AC Transit operates public buses in and around Berkeley; see Getting There & Away. The university's Campus Transit (☎ 510-642-5149) offers bus service from the downtown BART station to campus; the one-way fare is 25¢. From its stop at the Hearst Mining Circle, you can connect with the Hill Service Shuttle, which runs along Centennial Drive to the higher parts of the campus; the fare is 50¢.

Missing Link (☎ 510-843-4763), 1961 Shattuck Ave, rents mountain bikes for about $35 per day. They also sell new bikes at the main store across the street.

BEYOND THE HILLS

Head east from San Francisco on I-80, across the Bay Bridge, past Oakland and Berkeley on Hwy 24, and into the Caldecott Tunnel, and you will emerge on the other side of the Berkeley Hills in suburbia. The tunnel doesn't just bring an attitude adjustment; it also heralds a climatic change. The east side of the range is fog free, hotter in summer and colder in winter. BART runs through the hills to Walnut Creek, Pleasant Hill, Concord and Pittsburg/Bay Point.

County Connection buses (☎ 925-676-7500) serve Walnut Creek, Concord and beyond; fares are only 50¢ with BART-to-Bus transfer tickets, which are issued free at BART stations.

Briones Regional Park

Briones (☎ 925-370-3020) is a 3500-acre park situated smack in the middle of suburbia, next to the affluent village of Lafayette. Briones is geared toward hikers, with over 20 miles of well-maintained, uncrowded trails (some of which wind through a working cattle ranch) with spectacular views of the Diablo Valley. Briones' claim to fame is the massive concentration of newts (a bit like salamanders) that populate it during the cool, wet fall months, when rain-fed freshwater ponds appear almost as if by magic.

From Oakland, take Hwy 24 east through the Caldecott Tunnel to the Orinda exit. Turn left onto Camino Pablo (which becomes San Pablo Dam Rd) and follow it to Bear Creek Rd. Then turn right. You will see the sign for Briones on the right.

Danville

• population 39,150 • elevation 368 feet

The city of Danville, set in the shadow of Mt Diablo, looks like the archetype of the perfect upper-middle-class Californian suburb – with 2.3 shiny new cars in each driveway and 2.3 smiling kids in-line skating past the neatly trimmed lawns of each home. The only reason to stop in Danville is to see the surprisingly good auto museum. The home of playwright Eugene O'Neill is interesting, but you can't simply drop by – advance reservations are required.

Blackhawk Museums Blackhawk Plaza is a somewhat bizarre shopping center with upscale pretensions, situated at the corner of Crow Canyon Rd and Camino Tassajara, 5 miles from the Sycamore Valley Rd exit on I-680. Kenneth Behring, a car dealer turned real estate magnate, developed Blackhawk and built two museums here for the University of California. The **Blackhawk Auto Museum** (☎ 925-736-2280) must be one of the world's most luxurious car museums. Nothing here is mundane: the Ferraris are rare ones; the Bugatti collection is amazing; and the museum has plenty of double-barreled names: Rolls-Royce, Talbot-Lago, Hispano-Suiza, Isotta Fraschini, Pierce-Arrow. When you've visited the museum, don't miss the car showroom in the adjacent shopping plaza, just in case you'd like to take one home.

SAN FRANCISCO BAY AREA

The adjoining **UC Berkeley Museum** is less thrilling – it has paleontology displays from the university's collection, including a mastodon skeleton unearthed nearby.

The museums are open 10 am to 5 pm Wednesday to Sunday; $8/5 adults/children for entry to both museums.

Tao House Eugene O'Neill built Tao House with his 1936 Nobel Prize money and wrote *The Iceman Cometh, Long Day's Journey into Night* and some of his other late works here. Free tours (☎ 925-838-0249) operate at 10 am and 12:30 pm Wednesday to Sunday, but the tours must be booked in advance, because you have to be picked up by a bus from downtown Danville; the neighbors don't want tourists parking in their neighborhood.

Getting There & Away From San Francisco, I-80 takes you across the Bay Bridge and Hwy 24 goes through the Caldecott Tunnel out to Walnut Creek, where you merge with I-680 to Danville.

Mt Diablo State Park
Mt Diablo (3849 feet) is over 1000 feet higher than Mt Tamalpais in Marin County. On a clear day (early on a winter morning for the clearest weather) the views from Mt Diablo can be amazing: west over the bay and out to the Farallon Islands, east over the Central Valley to the Sierra.

Mt Diablo State Park (☎ 925-837-2525) has 50 miles of hiking trails (and thickets of poison oak off the trails), which can be approached from Walnut Creek or Danville. The park office is at the junction of the two entry roads, from where a steep road climbs up to near the summit of Mt Diablo. The park charges a $5 day-use fee. Simple campsites cost $12 per night (reservations are not required). Park wildlife includes deer, foxes, coyotes, bobcats and even mountain lions.

Dublin, Livermore & Altamont
South of Danville, I-680 and I-580 cross at Dublin. I-580 runs east from Dublin toward I-5, passing through the bland suburb of Liv-

ermore, which is home to the University of California's **Lawrence Livermore National Laboratory**. The vast majority of the USA's nuclear weapons are designed at this high-security R&D center. This was also the primary development center for President Reagan's unsuccessful Star Wars missile-defense program. You can learn more about the laboratory and its role in weapons development at the visitor center (☎ 925-423-3272) on Greenville Rd, 2 miles south of I-580. It's free and open 1:30 to 4:30 pm weekdays.

The Bay Area bids farewell to departing visitors with a final high-tech sight. The consistently windy **Altamont Pass** is dotted with an eerie collection of wind generators; this wind farm is a pioneering site for the turning of a stiff breeze into kilowatts. The remains of the old **Altamont Speedway** stands at the junction where I-580 bends south and I-205 continues east. The film *Gimme Shelter* tells the story of the disastrous 1969 Rolling Stones concert at the speedway, when Hell's Angels hired by the Stones for security beat a concertgoer to death with pool cues, right in front of the stage, an event which brought flower power and the Woodstock era to a crashing end.

SAN PABLO & SUISUN BAYS
It's easy to forget that there are more bays to the north of the San Francisco Bay. The Richmond-San Rafael Bridge, linking Contra Costa County with Marin, is the dividing line between San Francisco Bay and San Pablo Bay. In turn, the narrow Carquinez Straits leads to Suisun Bay and then the Sacramento River. Richmond, north of Berkeley is home to the gargantuan WWII Kaiser Shipyards and an equally enormous oil refinery. The Richmond BART station is adjacent to the Amtrak station, if you're taking a train north or east.

The towns along the Carquinez Straits had a brief boom in the gold rush era, and the gradual outward crawl of Bay Area suburbs is threatening to wake them from their long ghost town slumbers. Port Costa was once the southern terminus for huge railway ferries that shuttled across from Benicia on the northern side of the strait.

Vallejo
• **population 111,400** • **elevation 60 feet**
For one week in 1852 Vallejo was considered as a possible site for the California state capital; then the legislature changed its mind. In 1854, Vallejo did become the site of the first US naval station on the West Coast. The **Vallejo Naval & Historical Museum** (☎ 707-643-0077), 734 Marin St, tells the story. It's open 10 am to 4:30 pm Tuesday to Saturday; $2.

One of the Bay Area's big tourist attractions, **Six Flags Marine World** (☎ 707-643-6722) offers traditional theme-park rides along with animal shows featuring sharks, killer whales, dolphins, seals and sea lions. The park is on Marine World Parkway, 5 miles north of Vallejo. It's open weekdays 10 am to 10 pm, weekends 10 am to 11 pm; $32/22 (children under 48 inches cost $16).

Monday to Saturday visitors can take the BART (☎ 415-992-2278, 510-465-2278) to Richmond; free shuttle buses run to the park. The Blue & Gold Fleet (☎ 415-773-1188 or 707-643-3779 for information, 415-705-5555 for tickets) runs ferries from San Francisco's Pier 41 at Fisherman's Wharf to Vallejo for $7.50 each way. Ferries run daily mid-April to late October, weekends only the rest of the year. Amtrak (☎ 800-872-7245) and Gray Lines (☎ 415-558-9400) also stop near the park.

Benicia
• **population 27,850** • **elevation 33 feet**
For a short time after the 1849 gold rush, Benicia was a port to rival San Francisco. For one year, from February 1853 to February 1854, Benicia was also the state capital. Only some fine old buildings hint at that lost glory. The town was founded in 1847 by Robert Semple, leader of the 'Bear Flag Revolt' (see Sonoma in the Wine Country chapter), on land deeded to him by Mariano Guadalupe Vallejo, the Mexican leader whom he had overthrown in the revolt just one year earlier. The town was named for Vallejo's wife, Francisca Benicia. The visitor

center (☎ 707-745-2120), 601 1st St, has a walking-tour leaflet. Today, Benicia is having a modest revival as a relaxed arts and crafts center.

The 1852 **Old State Capitol** (☎ 707-745-3385), at 1st and W G Sts, is now a museum, open 10 am to 5 pm daily; $2. The only other building open to the public, the adjacent 1840s **Fischer-Hanlon House** at 117 W G St, keeps erratic hours. There are, however, many interesting old houses around town, including a number that were built on the East Coast and shipped around the Cape Horn. The rectory of St Paul's Episcopal Church, 122 E J St, started life in Connecticut in 1790 and was dismantled and shipped to Benicia in 1868.

Benicia Transit (☎ 707-745-0815) operates buses from the Pleasant Hill BART station to Benicia ($1.50).

Martinez
• **population 36,100** • **elevation 23 feet**
Less than 15 miles north of Walnut Creek, sleepy Martinez was the birthplace of baseball slugger 'joltin' Joe DiMaggio. It also has the **John Muir National Historic Site** (☎ 925-228-8860), the house where the pioneering conservationist and Sierra Club founder lived from 1890 until his death in 1914. The house was built by his father-in-law in 1882. For visitors expecting something in tune with Muir's hearty outdoors image, the house can be a disappointment, since it reflects his in-laws' tastes and lifestyle more than his own. The grounds include the 1844 Martinez Adobe, part of the ranch on which the house was built. The house is 2 miles south of Martinez, at 4202 Alhambra Ave, and is open 10 am to 4:30 pm Wednesday to Sunday; $2.

The Peninsula

San Francisco is the tip of a 30-mile peninsula, sandwiched between the Pacific Ocean to the west and the San Francisco Bay to the east. San Francisco, with all its style, attitude and edge, disappears almost as soon as you start driving south on Hwy 101: city gives way to suburbia that continues to San Jose and beyond. Down Hwy 101, Palo Alto and Stanford University are the first real reasons to stop after leaving San Francisco. The alternative north-south route, scenic I-280, has a few places of interest en route to Palo Alto.

Hwy 1 runs down the Pacific coast via Half Moon Bay and a string of interesting beaches to Santa Cruz. Highway 101 runs down the other side of the San Francisco Peninsula to Santa Clara, where Hwy 17 makes its way across to Santa Cruz. These two routes can be combined into an interesting loop or extended to the Monterey Peninsula.

SAN FRANCISCO TO PALO ALTO

South of the San Francisco peninsula, I-280 is the dividing line between the densely populated South Bay area and the rugged and lightly populated Pacific coast. With its sweeping bends, I-280 is a more scenic choice than gritty, crowded Hwy 101. Unfortunately, these parallel north-south arteries are both clogged with traffic during the weekday commute.

Colma

• **population 1280** • **elevation 100 feet**

Off I-280 just beyond Daly City is Colma, the graveyard for San Francisco ever since cemeteries were banned within the city limits. Notables buried here include sculptor Beniamino Bufano, gunslinger Wyatt Earp and jeans inventor Levi Strauss. There's also a bizarre pet cemetery filled with all manner of small oddly shaped graves.

Get a cemetery tour leaflet from the Colma Town Hall (☎ 650-997-8300), 1198 El Camino Real at Serramonte Blvd (there's an exit off I-280 for Serramonte Blvd).

Filoli

Filoli (☎ 650-364-2880) is a superb country estate, 10 miles northwest of Palo Alto and a few miles north of the small town of Woodside. The house was built between 1915 and 1917 by wealthy gold-mine owners Mr and Mrs William Bowers Bourn II. It combines English country house style with uniquely

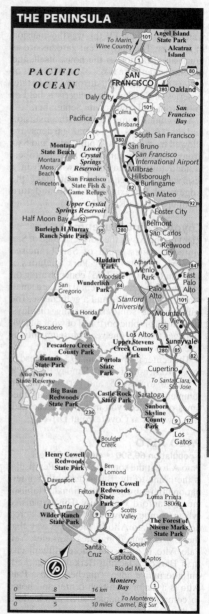

THE PENINSULA

To Marin, Wine Country

PACIFIC OCEAN

Angel Island State Park
Alcatraz Island

SAN FRANCISCO
Oakland
Daly City
Colma
Brisbane
Pacifica
San Francisco Bay
South San Francisco
San Bruno
San Francisco International Airport
Montara State Beach
Lower Crystal Springs Reservoir
Montara
Moss Beach
Millbrae
Hillsborough
Burlingame
Princeton
San Francisco State Fish & Game Refuge
San Mateo
Upper Crystal Springs Reservoir
Foster City
Half Moon Bay
Belmont
Burleigh H Murray Ranch State Park
San Carlos
Redwood City
Huddart Park
Atherton
Menlo Park
East Palo Alto
Woodside
San Gregorio
Wunderlich Park
Palo Alto
Stanford University
La Honda
Mountain View
Pescadero
Los Altos
Upper Stevens Creek County Park
Sunnyvale
Pescadero Creek County Park
Butano State Park
Portola State Park
Cupertino
Año Nuevo State Reserve
To Santa Clara, San Jose
Big Basin Redwoods State Park
Castle Rock State Park
Saratoga
Sanborn Skyline County Park
Los Gatos
Boulder Creek
Henry Cowell Redwoods State Park
Ben Lomond
Henry Cowell Redwoods State Park
Loma Prieta 3806ft ▲
Davenport
Felton
UC Santa Cruz Wilder Ranch State Park
Scotts Valley
The Forest of Nisene Marks State Park
Santa Cruz
Soquel
Capitola
Aptos
Rio del Mar
Monterey Bay
To Monterey, Carmel, Big Sur

0   8   16 km
0   5   10 miles

SAN FRANCISCO BAY AREA

Californian design elements. If it looks strangely familiar, you may have been watching too much TV; this was the mansion in *Dynasty*. The magnificent gardens are as much an attraction as the house itself, and docents lead nature hikes of the 620 acres of undeveloped land that surround the estate. A series of Sunday jazz concerts is held at Filoli from mid-May to late September.

Self-guided tours ($10) of the mansion and its 16 acres of formal gardens are allowed from 10 am to 2 pm Friday and Saturday, mid-February to late October. Guided tours are available with advance reservations. To reach the estate, take the Edgewood Rd exit from I-280 and turn north up Cañada Rd.

Coyote Point Museum

Right on the bay at the northern edge of San Mateo, 4 miles south of San Francisco Airport, Coyote Point Park includes a museum (☎ 650-342-7755) concentrating on ecological and environmental issues, a small zoo of 'local' wildlife and a golf course. The museum has some fascinating displays, including a graphic portrayal of what a hawk manages to eat in one year. Museum entry is $3/2.

The center is open 10 am to 5 pm Tuesday to Saturday, noon to 5 pm Sunday. Parking is supposed to cost $5, and certainly will in summer and on weekends, though at other times of the year you may not be charged. Exit Hwy 101 at Coyote Point Drive.

PALO ALTO
• population 60,500 • elevation 23 feet

Palo Alto, at the south end of the Peninsula, is the home to the Bay Area's other internationally renowned educational establishment, Stanford University. This expansive sylvan campus, covering 8200 leafy acres, dominates Palo Alto in the same way that the UC campus dominates Berkeley. Yet, Palo Alto is a glossier, more affluent city than Berkeley, lacking Berkeley's wacked-out alternative edge – maybe because Palo Alto is a major high-tech center and home to computer companies such as Hewlett-Packard.

Orientation

Palo Alto and adjacent Menlo Park are bordered by Hwy 101 to the north and I-280 to the south. In between it's bisected by El Camino Real, which also divides the town from the campus. University Ave is Palo Alto's main street and continues, with a name change to Palm Drive, straight into the heart of the Stanford campus. The extensive Stanford Shopping Center is on El Camino Real just north of campus. Approach East Palo Alto, on the east side of Hwy 101, with caution; it's a world away from affluent Palo Alto.

Palo Alto means 'tall tree' in Spanish, and the town's namesake timber is beside the San Francisquito Creek, where the railway line crosses it, just north of the city center.

Information

The chamber of commerce (☎ 650-324-3121), 325 Forest Ave, is open 9 am to 5 pm weekdays. For entertainment listings get a copy of the free *Palo Alto Weekly* newspaper. *The Art of Palo Alto Site Map*, available at the chamber of commerce, covers Palo Alto's large selection of public art – murals and sculptures.

Bookstores Like any good university town, Stanford has plenty of bookstores. Stacey's (☎ 650-326-0681) is a good general bookshop downtown at 219 University Ave. Away from downtown, Kepler's Bookshop (☎ 650-324-4321), 1010 El Camino Real in Menlo Park, is a bright, modern store with a popular adjacent cafe. The area's premier travel bookshop is Phileas Fogg (☎ 650-327-1754) in the Stanford Shopping Center.

Stanford University

Leland Stanford was one of San Francisco's robber barons and a former governor of California. When the Stanfords' only child died of typhoid during a European tour in 1884, the Stanfords decided to build a university in his memory. Stanford University opened in 1891, just two years before Leland Stanford's death, but the university grew to become a prestigious and wealthy institution. The campus was built on the site of the

Stanfords' horse-breeding farm, and as a result, Stanford is still known as 'The Farm.'

The Stanford University Information Booth (☎ 650-723-2560) is in the Memorial Auditorium in front of Hoover Tower, just east of the Main Quad. It's open 8 am to 5 pm weekdays, from 9 am weekends. Free one-hour walking tours of the campus depart from the Information Booth daily at 11 am and 3:15 pm. Despite the campus' size, parking can be a real pain. If the scarce parking-meter spots are occupied, buy an all-day parking permit ($6) at the information booth.

Auguste Rodin's *Burghers of Calais* bronze sculpture marks the entrance to the **Main Quad**, an open plaza where the original 12 campus buildings, in a mix of Romanesque and mission revival styles, were joined by the **Memorial Church** in 1903. The church is noted for its beautiful mosaic-tiled frontage, stained-glass windows and organ with 7777 pipes.

East of the Main Quad, the 285-foot-high **Hoover Tower** offers superb views of the campus. The tower houses the university library and offices and part of the right-wing Hoover Institution on War, Revolution & Peace. At the entrance level there are exhibits concerning President Herbert Hoover, who was a student at Stanford. The ride to the top costs $2. The tower is open 10 am to 4:30 pm daily, except during final exams, breaks between sessions and some holidays.

The **Cantor Center for Visual Arts** (☎ 650-723-4177), formerly the Stanford Museum of Art, was reopened in January 1999, following nearly 10 years of renovations to repair damage from the 1989 earthquake. Admission to the collection, spanning Greek and Roman artifacts to modern works, is free. Open 11 am to 5 pm Wednesday to Sunday (to 8 pm Thursday).

Immediately south is the stunning open-air **Rodin Sculpture Garden**, with a large collection of sculpture by Auguste Rodin, including reproductions of his towering *Gates of Hell*. There's plenty more sculpture dotted around the campus, all detailed in the free *Guide to Outdoor Sculpture* leaflet,

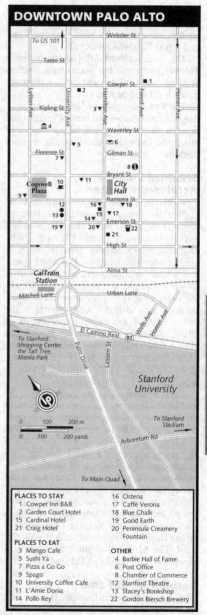

DOWNTOWN PALO ALTO

PLACES TO STAY
1 Cowper Inn B&B
2 Garden Court Hotel
15 Cardinal Hotel
21 Craig Hotel

PLACES TO EAT
3 Mango Cafe
5 Sushi Ya
7 Pizza a Go Go
9 Spago
10 University Coffee Cafe
11 L'Amie Donia
14 Pollo Rey
16 Osteria
17 Caffè Verona
18 Blue Chalk
19 Good Earth
20 Peninsula Creamery Fountain

OTHER
4 Barbie Hall of Fame
6 Post Office
8 Chamber of Commerce
12 Stanford Theatre
13 Stacey's Bookshop
22 Gordon Biersch Brewery

available at the museum. Tours of the outdoor sculpture, on the first Sunday of the month, leave from the Main Quad at 2 pm; call ☎ 650-723-3469 for details.

The free **Stanford Art Gallery**, between Hoover Tower and the Main Quad, displays student-produced art and hosts temporary exhibits (closed Monday).

The **Red Barn**, part of Leland Stanford's original farm, stands just west of campus and is open daily. Hiking and biking trails lead from the barn into the foothills west of campus.

Stanford Linear Accelerator Center

Few drivers speeding by Stanford on I-280 realize that things are speeding by beneath them at far higher velocities. The Stanford Linear Accelerator Center (SLAC), run by the university's physics department, goes right under the freeway. Positrons (positively charged subatomic particles) hurtle down a straight 2-mile path in a 4-inch-diameter linac (an accelerator beam tube), on their way to high-speed impacts at the other end of the tube. Experiments at SLAC, which opened in 1961, proved that the protons and neutrons that make up the atomic nucleus are made of even more fundamental particles called 'quarks.' Chalk up a Nobel Prize for that discovery.

Later a storage ring was tagged on to the end of the linac, so positrons and electrons could be streamed in, traveling in opposite directions at close to the speed of light. The resulting collisions revealed the existence of the psi (comprising a quark and an anti-quark) and of a new type of quark, charmingly named a 'charm.' That was good enough for another Nobel Prize.

Visitors are welcome to have a peek during free tours that operate several times each week, usually at 10 am or 1 pm. Advance reservations are required; call ☎ 650-926-2204. The SLAC is about 2 miles west of campus at 2575 Sand Hill Rd, east of I-280.

Barbie Hall of Fame

This quirky museum features Barbie, Ken and their doll friends in more than 20,000 incarnations, from Barbie as a nun to Ken (totally killing his wimpy image) in his Desert Storm camouflage fatigues. The museum also has a varied assortment of Barbie equipment – her stretch limousine, windsurfer, catamaran, motorcycle, horse, etc – and Barbie's myriad outfits over the years. The rather risqué lingerie are presumably all presents from Ken. The museum (☎ 650-326-5841) is at 433 Waverly St near University Ave. It's open 1:30 to 4 pm Tuesday and Thursday, 1:30 to 4:30 pm Wednesday and Friday, 10 am to noon and 1:30 to 4:30 pm Saturday; $6.

Places to Stay

Hostels HI's *Hidden Villa* hostel (☎ 650-949-8648, 26870 Moody Rd) is in the Los Altos Hills, 2 miles west of I-280. Beds are $12. The hostel is closed June to August, and reception is closed 9:30 am to 4:30 pm daily. The hostel is in a great location, close to many hiking trails, but don't plan to get there by public transport.

Downtown Palo Alto The cheapest hotel in downtown Palo Alto is the *Craig Hotel* (☎ 650-853-1133, 164 Hamilton Ave). This no-frills residential hotel rents most rooms by the week and month, though a few doubles are usually available without/with bath for $39/56. The hotel's clean and safe, but it's certainly nothing to get excited about.

The resolutely old-fashioned *Cardinal Hotel* (☎ 650-323-5101, 235 Hamilton Ave) has a terrific central location. Comfortable rooms with shared bath cost $70 to $80, with private bath $90 to $120.

The 14-room *Cowper Inn B&B* (☎ 650-327-4475, 705 Cowper St), close to downtown, has two rooms without bath for $65 and $85, the rest with bath starting at $130. Prices include breakfast.

A good splurge is the elegant *Garden Court Hotel* (☎ 650-322-9000, 520 Cowper St). Rooms come with VCRs, T-1 Internet hookups, fax machines and more. Doubles are $180 to $320.

Elsewhere For cheap accommodation try the motels along El Camino Real. Just north

SAN FRANCISCO BAY AREA

of the Stanford campus in Menlo Park, you'll find the dull but thoroughly respectable **Best Western Riviera** (☎ *650-321-8772, 15 El Camino Real*), with rooms for $99/139 on weekends/weekdays. Continue a block farther to the cheaper **Stanford Arms** (☎ *650-325-1428, 115 El Camino Real*), priced from $55 to $65. Palo Alto's **Coronet Motel** (☎ *650-326-1081, 2455 El Camino Real*), just north of Page Mill Rd, is fairly close to the campus' south side. It can be a bit noisy, but at $60 to $65 it's good value.

There's a collection of simple motels with rooms from $55 to $75 a bit farther out, including the **Townhouse Inn** (☎ *650-493-4492, 4164 El Camino Real*) and the **Country Inn** (☎ *650-948-9154, 4345 El Camino Real*). The **Super 8 Palo Alto** (☎ *650-493-9085, 3200 El Camino Real*), 2 miles south of campus, has a pool and rooms from $65 to $75.

Places to Eat

There are dozens of good restaurants, from cheap eats to elegant bistros, in the compact blocks of downtown Palo Alto – mainly on University Ave between Cowper and Emerson Sts.

Budget Founded in 1923, but looking as if yesterday was the opening day, the wonderfully authentic **Peninsula Creamery Fountain** (☎ *650-323-3131, 566 Emerson St*), at Hamilton Ave, is famous for its frothy milkshakes. It's open for breakfast, lunch and dinner, until at least 10 pm nightly. The **University Coffee Cafe** (☎ *650-322-5301, 271 University Ave*) serves coffee, microbrewery beer, wine and some great sandwiches. **Caffè Verona** (☎ *650-326-9942, 236 Hamilton Ave*) serves light meals and is popular for a quick, reasonably priced lunch.

Pollo Rey (☎ *650-473-0212, 543 Emerson St*) offers cheap, cheerful and filling Tex-Mex food; you can eat well for less than $6. **Pizza a Go Go** (☎ *650-322-8100, 335 University Ave*), a popular pizzeria, is open late most nights.

Mid-Range The **Mango Cafe** (☎ *650-325-3229, 435 Hamilton Ave*) brings the flavors of Jamaica and Trinidad & Tobago to suburban Palo Alto (quite a feat). Entrées are a bargain at $6 to $10. The cafe is open for lunch on Friday, for dinner Monday to Saturday.

Popular **Blue Chalk** (☎ *650-326-1020, 630 Ramona St*) is a multilevel Cajun restaurant, bar and pool hall. Lunch entrées are $5 to $9, dinner entrées $7 to $12. You'll pay about the same for a full meal at **Sushi Ya** (☎ *650-322-0330, 380 University Ave*), a tiny sushi bar (closed Sunday).

At the **Good Earth** (☎ *650-321-9449, 185 University Ave*), the menu is an amazingly international creation, stretching from burgers to Mexican to Cajun to Malaysian. Entrées are $7 to $10.

Top End **Osteria** (☎ *650-328-5700, 247 Hamilton Ave*), at Ramona St, cooks up hearty Italian food from Tuscany. This stylish and popular restaurant has pasta dishes starting at $9, entrées at $13. Lunch is served weekdays, dinner Monday to Saturday.

L'Amie Donia (☎ *650-323-7614, 530 Bryant St*) is one of Palo Alto's most pleasant French restaurants, with a casual elegance that blends smoothly with its French country cuisine. Entrées are $12 to $17. It's open Tuesday to Saturday for dinner only.

For a real splurge try Wolfgang Puck's **Spago** (☎ *650-833-1000, 265 Lytton Ave*). The inventive California cuisine is delicious but pricey – entrées are $15 to $25. Reservations are a must. The kitchen is open on weekdays for lunch and dinner, on weekends for dinner only.

Entertainment

You can have a drink or play pool at **Blue Chalk** (☎ *650-326-1020, 630 Ramona St*). Microbrewed beer is the drink of choice at the trendy **Gordon Biersch Brewery** (☎ *650-323-7723, 640 Emerson St*). **The Edge** (☎ *650-324-3343, 260 California Ave*), southeast of campus, is a bar and dance club with a youngish (sometimes *very* young) crowd. The cover charge is $2 to $7.

The **Stanford Theatre** (☎ *650-324-3700, 221 University Ave*) screens Hollywood classics accompanied by a 'mighty' Wurlitzer organ.

Getting There & Away

Palo Alto is about 30 miles south of San Francisco and 15 miles north of San Jose. CalTrain's (☎ 800-660-4287) San Francisco-San Jose-Gilroy service runs via Menlo Park, Palo Alto and Stanford. There are hourly departures on weekdays, every two hours or so on Saturday. San Francisco to Palo Alto takes about an hour and costs $4. Palo Alto to San Jose takes half an hour for $2.75. Palo Alto's CalTrain Station is beside Alma St, just north of University Ave.

Buses arrive and depart Palo Alto at the Transit Center, adjacent to the CalTrain station. SamTrans' (☎ 800-660-4287) bus No 7F operates between San Francisco and Palo Alto up to 40 times daily on weekdays. The fare for the 90-minute trip is $3. The Santa Clara Transportation Agency (☎ 800-894-9908) serves Palo Alto and the Santa Clara Valley. Bus No 300 (weekdays only) runs between Stanford University, Palo Alto and San Jose, while the No 22 (daily) runs from Palo Alto to San Jose. The fare for either is $1.10 each way.

Getting Around

The free SLAC Line shuttle runs from Stanford University (in front of Hoover Tower) to the SLAC from 7 am to 5:30 pm, and with the CalTrain station during commute hours. There's free two-hour car parking all over town, or you can park all day for $1 at the CalTrain station. See the Stanford University entry above for parking on campus.

The Bike Connection (☎ 650-424-8034), 2086 El Camino Real, southeast of campus, rents bikes for $20 to $25 per day. There's a network of bicycle routes around town.

AROUND PALO ALTO
NASA-Ames Research Center & Moffett Field

Moffett Field is right beside Hwy 101, a few miles south of Palo Alto. The NASA-Ames Research Center (☎ 650-604-6497), at the north side of the field, conducted specialized research into hyper-velocity flight, and its gigantic wind tunnel is still used for advanced aerospace research. Turn off Hwy 101 at the Moffett Field exit and turn left immediately in front of the main gate to reach the visitor center. A one-third scale model of a space shuttle fronts the center, along with a U2 spy plane and other aerospace hardware. Inside are various exhibits about NASA. The center is open 8 am to 4:30 pm weekdays; free.

Much more interesting than a visit to the center is a tour of the actual research facilities. These are also free but must be booked four to six weeks in advance by calling ☎ 650-604-6274. The two-hour tour involves a 2-mile walk and may include visits to the wind tunnel, flight simulation facilities or the centrifuge.

Until recently, most of Moffett Field was used by the US Navy, but from Hwy 101 the hangar on the field looks as if it was designed for a zeppelin, which is pretty close to the truth. In the 1930s, the US Navy had two 785-foot-long dirigibles, the USS *Akron* and the USS *Macon*. Filled with helium (an inert gas, unlike the explosive hydrogen that brought down the *Hindenburg*), these craft were like flying aircraft carriers, each carrying five fighter planes that could be launched and retrieved while in flight. In 1933, just eight days before the 1100-foot-long hangar was to be dedicated, the *Akron* crashed in a storm off New Jersey, killing 73 crew members, including Rear Admiral Moffett, the Navy's visionary of lighter-than-air crafts. In 1935, in a near identical disaster, the *Macon* crashed into the sea off Big Sur. There's a model of the *Macon*, without a single word of explanation, in the NASA-Ames displays, though you must go to the Maritime Museum in Monterey (see Central Coast chapter) for information about the crash and the recent discovery of the wreckage.

Silicon Valley

Don't look for Silicon Valley on the map – it doesn't exist. Silicon is the basic element used to make the silicon chips that form the basis of modern microcomputers. Since the Santa Clara Valley – stretching from Palo Alto down through Mountain View, Sunnyvale, Cupertino and Santa Clara to San Jose – is thought of as the birthplace of the microcomputer, it's been dubbed 'Silicon

Valley.' Not only does the valley not exist on the map, it's pretty hard to define even at ground level. The Santa Clara Valley is wide and flat, and its towns are essentially a string of shopping centers and industrial parks linked by a maze of freeways. It's hard to imagine that even after WWII this was still a wide expanse of orchards and farms.

There's very little to see in Silicon Valley; the cutting-edge computer companies are secretive and not keen on factory tours. Their anonymous-looking buildings – expanses of black glass are an architectural favorite – hint at their attitude. The Tech Museum in San Jose gives some of the valley's technological flavor. You can also check out the **Intel Museum** (☎ 408-765-0503), 2200 Mission College Blvd in Santa Clara, which has displays on the birth and growth of the computer industry with special emphasis, not surprisingly, on Intel's pivotal role. The museum is open 8 am to 5 pm weekdays; free.

Since the computer business is famed for its garage start-ups, enthusiasts may want to drive by 367 Addison Ave, just five blocks south of University Ave in downtown Palo Alto, to see the garage where William Hewlett and David Packard started computer giant Hewlett-Packard.

SAN JOSE
- population 894,000 • elevation 87 feet

San Jose, California's oldest Spanish civilian settlement, was founded in 1777 as El Pueblo de San José de Guadalupe. The city had a brief period as the state capital from 1849 until 1851, when the capital shifted to Sacramento.

Now a flat, sprawling city with more than a hint of Los Angeles in its makeup, San Jose is the capital of Silicon Valley and the third-largest city in California (after Los Angeles and San Diego). San Jose is no competition for San Francisco when it comes to attracting visitors, but when it comes to money and growth San Jose is the Bay Area king. Over the past 30 years, industrial parks and high-tech computer firms, along with look-alike housing suburbs that stretch for miles, have taken over the city's former orange groves and farmland.

Orientation
Downtown San Jose is at the junction of Hwy 87 and I-280. Highway 101 and I-880 complete the box. San Jose State University is just east of downtown. Santa Clara University is 8 miles northwest and close to San Jose International Airport.

Information
The helpful Convention & Visitors Bureau (☎ 408-977-0900) has two offices, the most convenient at 150 W San Carlos St inside the San Jose Convention Center. It's open 8 am to 5:30 pm weekdays. The San Jose events hotline (☎ 408-295-2265) will tell you what's happening and where, or you can pick up a free copy of the weekly *Metro* newspaper.

The visitor bureau's *Historical Walking Tour* leaflet outlines an interesting and easy-to-follow downtown tour.

Plaza Park
This leafy square in the center of downtown San Jose is a part of the city's original Spanish plaza. The **Cathedral Basilica of St Joseph** at San Fernando and Market Sts was the pueblo's first church; originally built in adobe in 1803, it was replaced by a second adobe church in 1845, replaced again by a wooden church in 1869, which burned down and was replaced yet again in 1877, by the present building.

Tech Museum of Innovation
This excellent technology museum has exhibits on everything from high-tech bicycles to the production of silicon chips. There are also numerous interactive displays, including a host of robotic exhibits. The museum (☎ 408-795-6100), 201 S Market St at Park Ave, opposite Plaza Park, moved in 1998 to increase its exhibit space and make room for a towering 300-seat IMAX theater. Entry is $8 for the museum or IMAX theater, $13.50 for joint entry. The hours are 10 am to 5 pm Tuesday to Sunday.

San Jose Museum of Art
The city's excellent art gallery (☎ 408-294-2787), 110 S Market St at San Fernando St, has a strong permanent exhibit of 20th

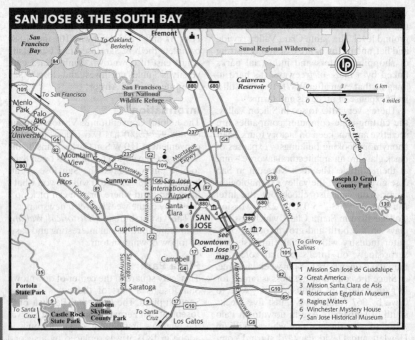

SAN JOSE & THE SOUTH BAY

1 Mission San José de Guadalupe
2 Great America
3 Mission Santa Clara de Asís
4 Rosicrucian Egyptian Museum
5 Raging Waters
6 Winchester Mystery House
7 San Jose Historical Museum

SAN FRANCISCO BAY AREA

century art and a variety of imaginative changing exhibits. The modern wing was added in 1991 to a building that started life as the post office in 1892, was damaged by the 1906 earthquake and became an art gallery in 1933. The gallery is open 10 am to 5 pm Tuesday to Sunday (10 am to 8 pm Thursday); $7/4.

Peralta Adobe & Fallon House

These very different houses (☎ 408-993-8182) are across the road from each other and have a visitor center at 175 W St John St at San Pedro St. The Peralta Adobe dates from 1797 and is the last survivor from the original Spanish pueblo, which at that time would have stretched from the Peralta Adobe to around the Fairmont Hotel by Plaza Park. The building is an example of a Californian adobe structure at its most basic, and the two rooms have been furnished as they might have been during their occupa-

tion by the Gonzales and Peralta families. Luis Maria Peralta came to the Bay Area at age 16 and died an American citizen and a millionaire, the owner of a large chunk of the East Bay.

Thomas Fallon married the daughter of an important Mexican landowner, built this fine Victorian house in 1854-55 and went on to become mayor of San Jose.

Joint house tours take place at 12:15, 2 and 3 pm Tuesday to Sunday; $6. Or pay $10 for a joint ticket that includes admission to the San Jose Historical Museum.

Children's Discovery Museum

This downtown tech museum for kids has hands-on science and space displays, plenty of nifty toys to play with and an adjacent playground with oversized animal sculptures. Whoopee! The museum (☎ 408-298-5437) is at 180 Woz Way (which is named after Steve Wozniak, the co-founder of

Apple, now a fifth-grade teacher) and is open 10 am to 5 pm Tuesday to Saturday, from noon Sunday; $6/4 adults/children.

Rosicrucian Egyptian Museum

The Rosicrucian Order has a large center at the corner of Naglee and Park Aves, about 4 miles west of downtown San Jose. The order is devoted to the study of mysticism and metaphysics, and the whole center has an Egypt-meets-San Jose look. The centerpiece is the extensive Egyptian Museum (☎ 408-947-3636), with a collection of pharaonic artifacts, including statues, jewelry, household items and mummies. Tours depart regularly at a complete reproduction of a Egyptian nobleman's subterranean tomb. The museum is open 9:30 am to 5 pm daily; $7/5.

The complex also has one of the oldest **planetariums** in the US. It's being renovated and is closed until further notice. Call ☎ 408-947-3635 before visiting.

San Jose Historical Museum

An interesting collection of historic buildings brought from all over San Jose are on display at this open-air museum (☎ 408-287-2290), 3 miles southeast of the city center, at 1600 Senter Rd in Kelley Park. The centerpiece is a half-scale replica of the 237-foot-high 1881 Electric Light Tower. The original tower was a pioneering attempt at street lighting, intended to illuminate the entire town center. It was a complete failure but, lights or not, was left standing as a central landmark until it toppled over in 1915. Other buildings include a hotel, an 1888 Chinese temple and a post office. The Trolley Restoration Barn restores historic trolley cars to operate on San Jose's light-rail line. The trolleys are also run on the park's own short line.

The museum is open noon to 5 pm Tuesday to Sunday; $6, or $10 for a combined ticket with the Peralta Adobe and Fallon House.

Winchester Mystery House

The real mystery here is how anybody managed to build such a ridiculous house, which is little more than a hodgepodge of

DOWNTOWN SAN JOSE

Ⓜ Light Rail Stop

PLACES TO STAY
6 Hotel De Anza
13 Fairmont Hotel
18 Crown Plaza San Jose
19 San Jose Hilton & Towers
21 Hyatt Sainte Claire
30 San Jose Convention Inn

PLACES TO EAT
4 Tied House
5 White Lotus
7 Blake's Steakhouse
8 Don Pedro's
9 Bella Mia
16 Casa Castillo
22 Original Joe's
25 Cafe Matisse
6 Eulipia
31 Emile's

BARS & CLUBS
27 The Agenda
28 The Usual
29 Cactus Club

OTHER
1 Fallon House
2 Post Office
3 Peralta Adobe
10 Greyhound Station
11 Cathedral Basilica of St Joseph
12 San Jose Museum of Art
14 Pavilion Shopping Center
15 Tech Museum of Innovation
17 Center for the Performing Arts
20 San Jose Public Library
23 Children's Discovery Museum
24 Convention & Visitors Bureau

silly rooms all jammed together like a child's build-a-house game. Sarah Winchester inherited the Winchester rifle fortune and, so it is surmised, spent the rest of her life building this sprawling mansion because the spirits of those killed by her husband's guns told her to do so.

The house (☎ 408-247-2101) is 10 miles west of central San Jose, at 525 S Winchester Blvd, just north of I-280. Most people shell out $13.95 for the 65-minute guided introductory tour, which includes a self-guided romp through the gardens and entry to a guns and rifles exhibit. The 50-minute Behind the Scenes tour is for diehards willing to pay $10.95 to see the house's basement, plumbing facilities and other underwhelming features. A combined tour is $21.95. All tours are offered, every 30 minutes or so, from 9:30 am to 4 pm daily.

Places to Stay

San Jose's lodging scene is grim. The only cheap options are the HI hostel (difficult to reach without a car) and the string of motels along The Alameda, many of which are overpriced considering what you get. Hotels downtown are busy year round, thanks to San Jose's copious conventions and trade shows.

Hostels HI's *Sanborn Park Hostel* (☎ 408-741-0166, 15808 Sanborn Rd) is off Hwy 9 in Sanborn County Park, 12 miles west of San Jose. There are dorm beds and some private rooms, all priced at $8.50 for HI members, $11.50 for nonmembers (50% reduction for those under age 18). The hostel has an 11 pm curfew, and reception is closed until 5 pm. Bring food; the nearest shops and restaurants are 4 miles away in Saratoga. Getting to the hostel by public transport is nearly impossible, as it involves four changes of bus.

Hotels & Motels Dozens of motels line The Alameda as it heads west from downtown out to Santa Clara University (take Santa Clara St west; it becomes The Alameda). One of the nicer choices along this stretch is the *Arena Hotel* (☎ 408-294-6500, 817 The Alameda), with rooms from $85 to $129.

The motel-style *San Jose Convention Inn* (☎ 408-298-3500, 455 S 2nd St), near the convention center, is the only budget option in downtown San Jose. Rooms are $70 and there's a pool. The rates may rise in 1999 when it becomes part of the Ramada hotel chain.

The central *Crown Plaza San Jose* (☎ 408-998-0400, 282 Almaden Blvd), across from the convention center, has spiffy rooms starting at $109 on weekends, $189 on weekdays. The art deco *Hotel De Anza* (☎ 408-286-1000, 233 W Santa Clara St) has prices to match its plush comforts. This is Silicon Valley, so every room has three phones, dedicated data lines and fax ports. Rooms are $150 on weekends, $220 and up on weekdays.

Other possibilities include the *Hyatt Sainte Claire* (☎ 408-295-2000, 800-824-6835, 302 S Market St), across from the convention center. Rooms are $150 to $270. The luxurious *Fairmont Hotel* (☎ 408-998-1900, 170 S Market St), right on Plaza Park, has rooms for $160 to $250 during the week, with prices dropping to $140 on weekends. The vast *San Jose Hilton & Towers* (☎ 408-287-2100, 300 Almaden Blvd) is a deluxe high-rise attached to the convention center. It's geared towards business travelers and is priced accordingly ($175 to $350).

Places to Eat

There are plenty of places to choose from along S 1st St and on San Pedro St by San Pedro Square. Mexican restaurants cluster along S 1st St and along E Santa Clara St, Vietnamese restaurants along E Santa Clara St from 4th to 12th Sts. San Jose's small Japantown, around Jackson St and its intersections with 4th, 5th and 6th Sts, has some good mid-range Japanese restaurants.

Many San Jose restaurants close around 9:30 or 10 pm.

Budget & Mid-Range *Original Joe's* (☎ 408-292-7030, 301 S 1st St), a San Jose landmark, serves standard Italian dishes ($6 to $10) for an appreciative audience. The chrome-and-glass dining room is loaded with 1950s charm.

SAN FRANCISCO BAY AREA

Cafe Matisse (☎ *408-298-7788, 415 S 1st St*) is one of the city's best spots for coffee, vegan goodies and lounging on big fluffy couches.

Casa Castillo (☎ *408-971-8132, 200 S 1st St*) turns out honest Mexican food in a pleasant, low-key setting. The same goes for *Don Pedro's* (☎ *408-977-0303, 43 Post St*), which has economical lunch specials for $5.50.

White Lotus (☎ *408-977-0540, 80 Market St*) is an unpretentious vegetarian restaurant that makes Asian stir-frys and noodle dishes.

San Pedro Square is chockablock with restaurants, bars and cafes. *Tied House* (☎ *408-295-2739, 65 N San Pedro St*) is a microbrewery with cheap beer and a standard burgers-and-the-like menu. *Blake's Steakhouse* (☎ *408-298-9221, 17 N San Pedro Sq*) serves thick cuts of prime beef and is probably San Jose's most popular steakhouse (entrées $7 to $15). The menu also has chicken, seafood and some vegetarian items. The kitchen is open 11:30 am to 10 pm weekdays, 5 to 10 pm weekends.

Top End *Eulipia* (☎ *408-280-6161, 374 S 1st St*), at San Carlos St, was a San Jose pioneer of California cuisine and does a popular prix fixe menu at $27. The restaurant is open Tuesday to Friday for lunch, daily except Sunday for dinner. *Bella Mia* (☎ *408-280-1993, 58 S 1st St*), farther up the street, is a popular Italian restaurant that's surprisingly reasonable; you can eat quite well for less than $20.

San Jose's best-known splurge is *Emile's* (☎ *408-289-1960, 545 S 2nd St*). The setting is romantic, the Californian-European cuisine is delicious, and the prices are sky high (entrées $15 to $30). It's open nightly for dinner, on Friday only for lunch.

Entertainment
Head to S 1st St for the best selection of bars. The *Agenda* (☎ *408-287-4087, 17 San Salvador St*), a few doors down the street, is a bar and restaurant that hosts live jazz and swing. The *Usual* (☎ *408-535-0330, 400 S 1st St*) has live rock shows and regular DJ dance nights. *Cactus Club* (☎ *408-491-9300, 417 S 1st St*) has a similar format.

The *Center for the Performing Arts* (☎ *408-288-2828, 255 Almaden Blvd*) is home to San Jose's symphony and ballet company.

Spectator Sports
The beleaguered San Jose Sharks, the city's NHL hockey team, play their home games at the *San Jose Arena* (☎ *408-287-9200*), a massive glass-and-metal stadium at the corner of Santa Clara and Autumn Sts. Tickets are $16 to $80; you can also buy your tickets, for a surcharge, through Ticketmaster (☎ 408-998-8497). The NHL season runs September to April.

Somewhat against the odds, Major League Soccer (MLS), the USA's professional soccer league, is doing quite well. The San Jose Clash play their home MLS games at *Spartan Stadium* (☎ *408-985-4625*), on 7th St near Alma Ave. The MLS season is from late March to mid-October, and Clash tickets cost $13 to $20.

Getting There & Away
The quickest and most convenient connection between San Jose and San Francisco is with CalTrain, a commuter rail service that operates daily up and down the Peninsula.

Air San Jose International Airport (☎ 408-277-4759), at the junction of Hwy 101 and I-880, is 'international' only insofar as it offers flights to Canada and Mexico. The airport has two terminals, with American, Reno Air and Southwest using Terminal A; Alaska, Delta, Mexicana, Northwest, TWA, United, US Airways and others using Terminal C.

Bus & BART Greyhound (☎ 408-295-4151), 70 Almaden Ave, operates buses to San Francisco ($7) and Los Angeles ($27 to $33). Apart from Greyhound there are no direct San Jose-San Francisco buses. If you don't mind changing buses, the least inconvenient option is SamTrans' (☎ 800-660-4287) bus No 22 from San Jose to Stanford University, then bus No 7F from Stanford to San Francisco. The full fare is $4.50.

From San Jose by bus and BART, take express bus No 180 to the Fremont BART station ($2) and catch a BART train to Oakland, Berkeley or across to San Francisco (about $2.50).

Train CalTrain (☎ 800-660-4287) makes more than 40 trips a day between San Jose and San Francisco; the 90-minute trip costs $5.25 each way. Trains leave every 15 minutes during rush hour, hourly at other times. San Jose's CalTrain station is at 65 Cahill St, just south of The Alameda. You can reach the station from central San Jose on bus No 64 ($1.10). For the same fare the Light Rail (see Getting Around) will take you to CalTrain's Tamien station, south of downtown San Jose.

The Cahill St CalTrain station is also the Amtrak station, and San Jose is on the Oakland-Los Angeles route.

Car & Motorcycle 'Do you know the way to San Jose,' Dionne Warwick warbled sweetly in the Burt Bacharach hit. Well, San Jose is right at the bottom end of the San Francisco Bay, about 40 miles from Oakland (via I-880) or San Francisco (via Hwy 101 or I-280). Although I-280 is slightly longer, it's usually quicker than heavily congested Hwy 101, which typically takes about 1½ hours. On the East Bay side, I-880 runs between Oakland and San Jose, and I-680 comes in from Dublin.

Getting Around

To/From the Airport Every 10 minutes, the free Light Rail shuttle runs from both terminals to the Metro Airport Light Rail station, where you can catch the San Jose Light Rail to downtown San Jose for just $1.10. Super Shuttle (☎ 408-225-4444) offers door-to-door bus service to most Silicon Valley destinations for $12 to $16. A taxi between the airport and downtown costs about $15.

Public Transport San Jose Light Rail (☎ 408-321-2300) runs 20 miles north-south from the city center, as far as Almaden and Santa Teresa in the south and, via the Civic Center, the airport and Great America in the north (see Around Jose). Fares are $1.10 for a two-hour pass, $2.50 for a day pass.

San Jose's historic trolley cars, dating from 1903 to 1928, operate along the central five-block 'transit mall' and north as far as the Civic Center. These vintage vehicles run, weather permitting, every 20 minutes from 10:30 am to 5:30 pm. Fares are the same as for the Light Rail.

Santa Clara County Transportation Agency buses (☎ 800-894-9908) run all over Silicon Valley. Regular bus fares are the same as for the Light Rail, though express buses cost more at $1.75.

AROUND SAN JOSE
Mission San José de Guadalupe

Founded in 1797, the Mission San José de Guadalupe was the 14th mission in the chain of missions in California. Its large Indian population and fertile agricultural lands made it one of the most successful, until a major earthquake struck in 1868, virtually leveling the mission's original 1809 church, which was replaced by a wooden one. In 1979, the wooden church was sold and moved to San Mateo; the adobe church seen today is a reasonably faithful reconstruction of the 1809 structure. A statue of St Bonaventure, in a side altar, dates from around 1808 and survived the 1868 earthquake. The adjacent living quarters, now housing a small mission museum, are original.

The mission (☎ 510-657-1797) is at 43300 Mission Blvd in Fremont, at the foot of Mission Peak Regional Preserve. From I-880 or I-680, take the Mission Blvd exit to Washington Blvd. The museum and mission are open 10 am to 5 pm daily; $2.

Mission Santa Clara de Asís

The eighth mission in California is 8 miles from downtown San Jose on the Santa Clara University campus in Santa Clara. The mission started life in 1777, on the Guadalupe River. Floods forced the first move; the second site was only temporary; the third church burned; the fourth church, a substantial adobe construction, was finished in 1784, but an earthquake in 1818 forced the move to the present site. That church, the fifth, was completed in 1822, but in 1926 it burned down, so the present church, an enlarged version of the 1822 church, completed in 1928, is the sixth church on the fifth site.

Many of the roof tiles came from the earlier buildings, and the church is fronted by a wooden cross from the original mission of 1777. The only remains from the 1822 mission are a nearby adobe wall and an adobe building. The first college in California was opened at the mission in 1851. The college grew to become Santa Clara University, and the mission church is now the college chapel.

Across the old mission plaza, the free **De Saisset Museum** (☎ 408-554-4528) houses art and history collections and is open 11 am to 4 pm Tuesday to Sunday. Santa Clara University is within walking distance of the Santa Clara CalTrain station.

Raging Waters
This water theme park (☎ 408-270-8000) at Tully and White Rds, 13 miles east of the center at Lake Cunningham Regional Park, features slides, pools and high-speed, high-adrenaline water rides. It's open May to September; $21.99.

Great America
Paramount's Great America (☎ 408-988-1776), off Hwy 101 at Great America Parkway in Santa Clara, is an amusement park that throws you into rides re-creating various Paramount movies including *Top Gun*, *Days of Thunder* and *Star Trek*. June through August the park is open daily; in spring and fall it opens weekends and holidays. Park entry is $31.99.

SAN FRANCISCO TO HALF MOON BAY
One of the real surprises of the Bay Area is how fast the urban landscape disappears along the rugged and largely undeveloped coast. In the 70 miles from San Francisco to Santa Cruz, the coast road, winding Hwy 1, passes beach after beach, many of them hidden from the highway. Most beaches along Hwy 1 are buffeted by wild and unpredictable surf, making them more suitable for sunbathing than swimming. The state beaches along the coast don't charge an access fee, but parking usually costs $5.

A cluster of isolated and supremely scenic HI hostels, at Point Montara (22 miles south of San Francisco) and Pigeon Point (36 miles), makes this an interesting route for cyclists, though narrow Hwy 1 itself can be a stressful, if not downright dangerous, road for inexperienced cyclists.

Pacifica & Devil's Slide
Pacifica and Point San Pedro, 15 miles from downtown San Francisco, signal the end of the urban sprawl. This area also marks the end of Hwy 1 whenever the Devil's Slide, an unstable cliff area just a mile to the south of Pacifica, assaults the highway with mud and boulders following heavy winter storms. Rebuilding and repairs always seem to be delayed by arguments between developers and conservationists about just what should be done about this problem stretch of road. A circuitous bypass is usually cobbled together.

Collecting a suntan or catching a wave are the attractions at **Rockaway Beach** in Pacifica and the more popular **Pacifica State Beach**.

Gray Whale Cove to Miramar Beach
Just south of Point San Pedro is **Gray Whale Cove State Beach**, one of the coast's popular 'clothing optional' beaches. There's a bus stop with steps down to the beach and a parking lot ($5 parking fee). **Montara State Beach** is just a half-mile south.

From the town of **Montara**, 22 miles from San Francisco, trails climb up from the Martini Creek parking lot into **McNee Ranch State Park**, which has hiking trails aplenty.

Point Montara Lighthouse HI Hostel (☎ 650-728-7177), Hwy 1 at 16th St, started life as a fog station in 1875, after two steamers wrecked on the shallow ledge offshore. The hostel is adjacent to the current lighthouse, which dates from 1928. This very popular hostel has a living room, kitchen facilities, an outdoor hot tub and an international clientele. Reception is open 7 to 9:30 am and 5 to 9:30 pm. Dorm beds are $12 for HI members, $15 for others; a few private rooms go for the normal per person rate plus a $10 room charge. In summer reservations are usually essential, especially on weekends. SamTrans buses will let you off close to the hostel if you ask nicely.

Montara has a number of B&Bs at lower price levels than Half Moon Bay ($100 to $115 per night as opposed to $120 to $135). These include *Goose & Turrets* (☎ 650-728-5451, 835 George St) and the *Farallone Inn* (☎ 650-728-8200, 1410 Main St).

South of the lighthouse, the **Fitzgerald Marine Reserve** at Moss Beach is an extensive area of natural tidal pools. A good place to eat in Moss Beach is the *Moss Beach Distillery* (☎ 650-728-5595) at Beach Way and Ocean Blvd. The restaurant sits on a cliff and is claimed to be haunted by the 'Blue Lady,' who wanders the cliffs awaiting the return of her piano-playing lover.

South of here is a stretch of coast called Pillar Point. Fishing boats bring in their catch at the Pillar Point Harbor, some of which gets cooked up in seafront restaurants at Princeton; the *Shorebird Wharf Cafe* (☎ 650-728-5541, 390 Capistrano Rd) is popular, though it was temporarily closed for renovation at the time of writing.

To the south, just 2 miles north of Half Moon Bay on Hwy 1, quiet **Miramar** is one of the most popular surfing breaks along the coast. The *Harbor View Inn* (☎ 650-726-2329, 51 Alhambra Ave), right near Pillar Point Harbor, has ocean-view rooms from $75 to $85.

HALF MOON BAY
• population 11,100 • elevation 69 feet

Half Moon Bay is the main town between San Francisco (28 miles north) and Santa Cruz (40 miles south), and it's just across the Santa Cruz Mountains from San Jose (43 miles east). Half Moon Bay developed as a beach resort back in the Victorian era. The long stretches of beach still attract weekenders and a few hearty surfers.

Half Moon Bay spreads out along Hwy 1 (called Cabrillo Hwy in town) but is small enough to merit the epithet 'sleepy.' The main drag, if you can call it that, is a five-block stretch of Main St that's lined with shops, cafes, restaurants and a few upscale

B&Bs. Visitor information is available 10 am to 4 pm weekdays at the Half Moon Bay Coastside Chamber of Commerce (☎ 650-726-8380), 520 Kelly Ave.

Things to See & Do
Pumpkins are a major crop around Half Moon Bay, and the pre-Halloween harvest is celebrated in an annual Pumpkin Festival. Brew-Ha-Ha is a June beer festival; the Bluegrass Festival brings music in September; and there are a host of other festivals and celebrations through the year; contact the chamber of commerce for details.

Inland **Purissima Creek Redwoods** has trails for cyclists and walkers. Seahorse (☎ 650-726-2362), on Hwy 1 about 1 mile north of the Hwy 92 junction, organizes guided horse rides along coastal and beach trails. A 90-minute ride is $35; the Early Bird special, a two-hour ride from 8 am to 10 am, is just $25.

Places to Stay & Eat
Overnighting at Half Moon Bay can be very cheap or rather expensive. The cheap options are the spartan campsites at *Half Moon Bay State Beach* (☎ 650-726-8820), just west of town ($5 day-use fee). Its 56 sites are first-come, first-served and cost $16 per night. The showers are c-c-cold.

The *Ramada Limited* (☎ 650-726-9700, 3020 N Cabrillo Hwy) has rooms for $60 to $85 on weekdays, $80 to $95 on weekends, which is about as low as prices go in Half Moon Bay.

San Benito House (☎ 650-726-3425, 356 Main St) is one of the more moderately priced Half Moon Bay B&Bs, at $77/95 for doubles with shared/private bath. The *Old Thyme Inn* (☎ 650-726-1616, 779 Main St) is a Queen Anne Victorian circa 1899; very 'cute' and therefore more expensive.

Cameron's Restaurant & Inn (☎ 650-726-5705, 1410 S Cabrillo Hwy), 1 mile south of the Hwy 92 junction, is a popular English-style pub in a century-old building, with a large selection of beers and a range of food. The three upstairs rooms ($69 to $99) are large and quite comfortable if you don't mind some barroom noise.

Getting There & Away SamTrans (☎ 800-660-4287) bus No 1L operates from the Daly City BART Station down the coast to Half Moon Bay ($1.10). Buses 1L and 96C (limited service) go from Montara down the coast to Half Moon Bay; some 96C services continue down the coast to San Gregorio, Pescadero, Año Nuevo and Waddell Creek.

HALF MOON BAY TO SANTA CRUZ

More beaches lie south of Half Moon Bay, starting with **San Gregorio State Beach**, 10 miles to the south. It has a clothing-optional stretch to the north, but the beach can get so chilly that only polar bears would find the idea appealing.

Pomponio and Pescadero state beaches are farther down the coast, on the way to the pleasant little town of **Pescadero**. Bird watchers enjoy the **Pescadero Marsh Reserve**, where guided walks take place on weekends year round. In mid-August, Pescadero hosts the annual Pescadero Arts & Fun Fest, with live music, arts & crafts and food.

The HI *Pigeon Point Lighthouse Hostel* (☎ 650-879-0633) on Hwy 1 at Pigeon Point, 5 miles south of Pescadero, uses the old lighthouse keeper's quarters and features an outdoor hot tub. The 110-foot lighthouse, one of the tallest in America, was built in 1872. The hostel is such a pleasant place that, especially on weekends and throughout the summer, advance reservations are essential. Dorm beds are $12 for HI members, $15 for others. Some private rooms are available for an additional $10. Reception is open 7:30 to 9:30 am and 4:30 to 9:30 pm.

Inland, large stretches of the hills are protected in a patchwork of parks that, just like the coast, remain remarkably untouched despite the huge urban populations only a few miles to the north and east. The drive east on Hwy 84 through La Honda to Palo Alto winds through impressive stands of trees. The tiny township of **La Honda**, 9 miles east of San Gregorio State Beach, is surrounded by four parks offering campsites and lots of opportunities for hiking or mountain biking. La Honda's *Applejacks Inn* (☎ 650-747-0331) offers backyard bar-becue, Harleys and a whole lot of local color. If you've come looking for the grizzly side of Americana, look no farther. There's live music on Saturday nights.

Big Basin Redwoods State Park (☎ 831-338-8860), off Hwy 236 about 9 miles northwest of Boulder Creek, encompasses 25 sq miles of the largest redwoods in the Southern Coastal Mountain Range, as well as rivers and streams, wildlife and many miles of hiking trails. The old-growth forests contain stands of fir, cedar, bay, madrone and oak. Big Basin was California's first state park, signed into law in 1902 after a heated battle between local conservationists and logging interests. Many of the redwoods here are over 1500 years old. The park has 115 tent/RV sites ($14 to $16), 32 walk-in sites (secluded in a thick redwood grove at Wastahi Campground) and 36 tent cabins with wood-burning stoves ($40 to $50). Reserve through Parknet (☎ 800-444-7275).

Año Nuevo State Reserve

A visit to the elephant seal colony on Año Nuevo Beach is a wonderful experience, but at the mid-winter peak season, you must plan well ahead. The beach is 5 miles south of Pigeon Point, 27 miles north of Santa Cruz.

Elephant seals were just as fearless two centuries ago as they are today, but unfortunately, club-toting seal trappers were not in the same seal-friendly category as camera-toting tourists. Between 1800 and 1850, the elephant seal was driven to the edge of extinction. Only a handful survived around the Guadalupe Islands off the Mexican state of Baja California. With substitutes for seal oil and more recent conservationist attitudes, the elephant seal made a comeback, reappearing on the Southern California coast from around 1920. In 1955, they returned to Año Nuevo beach and today the reserve is home to 3000 or more in the peak season.

The peak season is during the mating and birthing time, December 15 to the end of March, when visitors are only allowed on heavily booked guided tours. For the peak of the peak season, mid-January to mid-February, it's recommended you book eight weeks ahead. Although the park office

Elephant Seals

Elephant seals follow a precise calendar: between September and November young seals and the yearlings, who left the beach earlier in the year, return and take up residence. In November and December, the adult males return and start the ritual struggles to assert superiority; only the largest, strongest and most aggressive 'alpha' males gather a harem. From December through February, the adult females arrive, pregnant from last year's beach activities, give birth to their pups and, about a month later, mate with the dominant males.

At birth an elephant seal pup weighs about 80 pounds and, while being fed by its mother, puts on about 7 pounds a day. A month's solid feeding will bring the pup's weight up to about 300 pounds, but around March, the females depart, abandoning their offspring on the beach. For the next two to three months the young seals, now known as 'weaners,' lounge around in groups known as 'pods,' gradually learning to swim, first in the rivers and tidal pools, then in the sea. In April, the young seals depart, having lost 20% to 30% of their weight during this prolonged fast.

(☎ 650-879-0227) can advise on your chances of getting a place, bookings can only be made through Parknet (☎ 800-444-7275). Tours cost $4, plus $4 for parking. From the ranger station it's a 3-mile roundtrip walk to the beach and the visit takes 2½ hours. If you haven't booked, bad weather can sometimes lead to last-minute cancellations. The rest of the year, from April 1 to December 15, advance reservations are not required.

SANTA CRUZ
• population 54,600 • elevation 20 feet

Santa Cruz, a popular weekend escape from San Francisco (70 miles north), is just as beautiful as Monterey (40 miles south), but with a far more authentic 'beach town' vibe. Santa Cruz caters to health-conscious hippies instead of wealthy yuppies – this is, after all, where Ken Kesey launched his notorious LSD odysseys in the 1960s and where songwriter Neil Young still lives. It's also home to the University of California, Santa Cruz (UCSC) and the university's 10,000 left-of-center students.

Santa Cruz grabbed national headlines after the 1989 Loma Prieta earthquake, when the Pacific Garden Mall was decimated and a number of people were killed by collapsing buildings. Things are mostly back to normal, but 'normal' in an offbeat Santa Cruz way. The city is serene and quiet most of the year except on summer weekends, when crowds swarm the beaches and the Santa Cruz Beach Boardwalk.

Orientation
Santa Cruz stretches for a long way along the coast, blending into Capitola, a slightly lower-key beach resort. Santa Cruz itself can be a little confusing, with roads winding up and downhill and disappearing then reappearing as they cross the San Lorenzo River. Pacific Ave is the main street of downtown Santa Cruz, with Front St one block east.

The University of California campus is about 2½ miles northwest of the center.

Information
The Visitor Information Center (☎ 831-425-1234), 701 Front St, can help find accommodations. It's open 9 am to 5 pm Monday to Saturday, 10 am to 4 pm Sunday.

Metro Santa Cruz, the town's free weekly newspaper, has event, film and restaurant listings. Bookshops include the big Bookshop Santa Cruz (☎ 831-423-0900) at 1520 Pacific Ave and the equally mammoth Gateways Books (☎ 831-429-9600) at 1018 Pacific Ave (enter on Cathcart St).

Santa Cruz Beach Boardwalk
The 1906 boardwalk (☎ 831-423-5590) is the oldest beachfront amusement park on the West Coast. Its most famous rides include the half-mile-long Giant Dipper, a wooden roller coaster built in 1924, and the 1911 Looff carousel – both National Historic Landmarks.

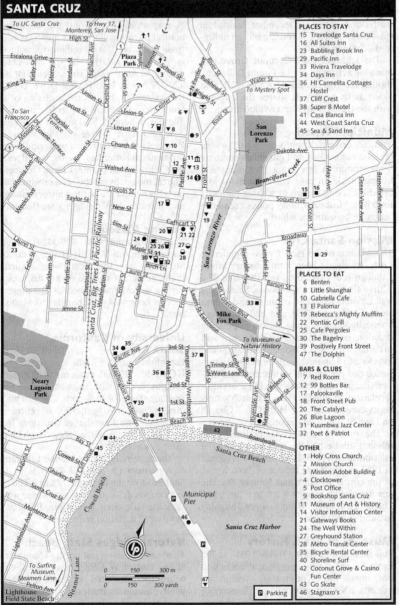

SANTA CRUZ

PLACES TO STAY
15 Travelodge Santa Cruz
16 All Suites Inn
23 Babbling Brook Inn
29 Pacific Inn
33 Riviera Travelodge
34 Days Inn
36 HI Carmelita Cottages
   Hostel
37 Cliff Crest
38 Super 8 Motel
41 Casa Blanca Inn
44 West Coast Santa Cruz
45 Sea & Sand Inn

PLACES TO EAT
6 Benten
8 Little Shanghai
10 Gabriella Cafe
13 El Palomar
19 Rebecca's Mighty Muffins
22 Pontiac Grill
25 Cafe Pergolesi
30 The Bagelry
39 Positively Front Street
47 The Dolphin

BARS & CLUBS
7 Red Room
9 99 Bottles Bar
17 Palookaville
20 Front Street Pub
26 The Catalyst
28 Blue Lagoon
31 Kuumbwa Jazz Center
32 Poet & Patriot

OTHER
1 Holy Cross Church
2 Mission Church
3 Mission Adobe Building
4 Clocktower
5 Post Office
9 Bookshop Santa Cruz
11 Museum of Art & History
14 Visitor Information Center
21 Gateways Books
24 The Well Within
27 Greyhound Station
35 Bicycle Rental Center
40 Shoreline Surf
42 Coconut Grove & Casino
   Fun Center
43 Go Skate
46 Stagnaro's

SAN FRANCISCO BAY AREA

The boardwalk is open daily June to August, on weekends and some holidays in winter and closed in December. Individual rides cost about $3, or you can buy an unlimited ticket for $19.95.

The adjacent 1907 **Coconut Grove** still hosts big acts in its ornate Grand Ballroom, though the Big Band era of the 1930s and '40s was its heyday. It shares the building with the Casino Fun Center video arcade.

Municipal Wharf

You can drive right onto the wharf, where seafood restaurants and gift shops compete for attention. A few shops rent poles and fishing tackle, in case you're keen to join fisherfolk along the wharf waiting patiently for a bite. Most days, noisy pods of sea lions sunbathe beneath the wharf.

Mission Santa Cruz

The 'Mission of the Holy Cross,' founded in 1791, has always been a rather sorry affair, although it did give the town its name. The 12th of the Californian missions, Santa Cruz was isolated from the comings and goings along El Camino Real and had an uneconomically small Ohlone Indian population (missions needed Indians to Christianize and to do the hard work). Worse, the mission was too close to a Spanish settlement – sad experience had proven that settlements and missions did not mix. The mission fell apart after secularization, and the mission church simply disappeared. Today the Holy Cross Church on High St stands on the original site.

The only original construction is the **mission adobe** building on School St. The **mission church** (☎ 831-426-5686) was rebuilt in 1932, as a half-size replica of the original, at the corner of High and Emmet Sts. The mission church is open 9 am to 5 pm daily. The adobe is open 10 am to 4 pm Thursday to Sunday, in summer.

Museum of Art & History

This small museum (☎ 831-429-1964), at 705 Front St, has a so-so permanent collection but hosts more interesting temporary exhibits. It's open noon to 5 pm Tuesday to Sunday (to 7 pm Friday); $3, free for students.

Santa Cruz City Museum of Natural History

A gray whale figure fronts this worthwhile natural history collection; a highlight is the fossil skeleton of a 12-million-year-old sea cow, a local relative of the still-extant dugong of Australasia. The museum (☎ 831-429-3773) is at 1303 E Cliff Drive, close to the waterfront, but on the east side of the San Lorenzo River. It's open 10 am to 5 pm Tuesday to Sunday; $2 donation requested.

Like Pacific Grove on the Monterey Peninsula, Santa Cruz is a wintering retreat for monarch butterflies (see the boxed text in the Central Coast chapter). From October to March, monarchs can be seen in Santa Cruz on trees behind the natural history museum and also at Natural Bridges State Beach.

Surfing Museum

The tiny museum (☎ 831-429-3429) at Lighthouse Point, on W Cliff Drive, overlooks Steamer Lane, the most popular surfing break in Santa Cruz. Inside are displays on surfing, surfers and surfboards. The museum is open noon to 4 pm Thursday to Monday; free.

University of California, Santa Cruz

Established in 1965 in the hills above town, UCSC has 10,000 students and a rural campus dotted with interesting buildings and fine stands of redwoods. Campus buildings include two galleries, a renowned arboretum and a number of structures from the Cowell Ranch of the 1860s, on which the campus was built.

The university's **Long Marine Laboratory & Aquarium** (☎ 831-459-4308) is at 100 Shaffer St, on the west side of town. The collection includes aquariums and a blue whale skeleton. It's open 1 to 4 pm Tuesday to Sunday; $2 donation requested.

Natural Bridges State Beach

This scenic beach is just north of Santa Cruz at the end of W Cliff Drive. Besides the beach, there are tidal pools and leafy trees where monarch butterflies hibernate in great big bunches from November to March.

Unfortunately, the eponymous natural bridge washed away a few years ago.

Spas

Santa Cruz's New Agey spas are ideal places to unwind. Hourly rates for communal hot tubs are $7 to $12, a bit more for private facilities. Spas are generally 'clothing optional,' but don't get the wrong idea. Contact The Well Within (☎ 831-458-9355), 417 Cedar St at Elm St, or Kiva House (☎ 831-429-1142), 702 Water St. Both also provide massage therapy in a strictly non-sexual atmosphere, with rates beginning at $35 for half-hour sessions.

Swimming & Surfing

The north side of Monterey Bay is warmer than the south, which is cooled in summer by the upwelling waters from the Monterey Canyon. As a result, beach activities are much more feasible in Santa Cruz than at Monterey.

Surfing is popular in Santa Cruz, especially at Steamer Lane (called 'Steamers' locally). Other favorite surf spots are Pleasure Point Beach, on E Cliff Drive toward Capitola, and Manresa State Beach, beyond Capitola. You can rent surfboards (around $20 per day) and surfing gear at Go Skate (☎ 831-425-8578), 601 Beach St, or Shoreline Surf (☎ 831-458-1380), 125 Beach St.

Want to learn to surf? Richard Schmidt (☎ 831-423-0928) or Club Ed (☎ 831-459-9283) will have you standing and surfing the first day out. Both charge $70 for two-hour group lessons, all equipment included. Private lessons are $50 to $70 per hour.

Whale Watching & Harbor Cruises

Whale-watching trips depart from the municipal wharf, last three hours and cost $17 to $20. The main season runs November to April, with the greatest concentration of sightings occurring from mid-December to

---

Riding the Big Tree

The arrival of the Southern Pacific Railway put Victorian-era Santa Cruz on the tourist map. The first railroad line was built in 1875 and carried freight from the Santa Cruz wharf 7 miles up the San Lorenzo River Canyon to Felton. The spectacular route, and the Big Trees redwood grove near Felton, soon attracted tourists as well as freight.

In 1880, a narrow gauge line across the Santa Cruz Mountains linked San Francisco, Oakland and San Jose, to bring visitors to Felton and then down to the beach. In 1940, a severe storm washed out the line from the Bay Area to Felton, and the line was never repaired. Afterwards the short Santa Cruz-Felton line reverted to freight use. A plan to build a second rail line to San Francisco, known as the Ocean Shore Railroad, was plagued by the difficult and unstable terrain (just as Hwy 1 is today), and it never consisted of more than random stretches connected by ferry services. The 1906 earthquake finished the line off.

In 1985, passenger services restarted as the **Santa Cruz, Big Trees & Pacific Railway** (☎ 831-335-4400). The short, slow, hugely scenic trip between Santa Cruz's boardwalk and Roaring Camp, a recreated 1880s logging town outside Felton, takes two hours. From mid-June to early September trains operate twice daily; the rest of the year they run on weekends and holidays. The roundtrip cost is $15.

From Roaring Camp, you can take the second railway trip on the narrow-gauge steam locomotives of the **Roaring Camp & Big Trees Railroad**. The 75-minute roundtrip to the Big Trees redwood stand costs $13.50. This route operates daily in summer, on weekends and holidays year round. It's possible to drive to the Roaring Camp depot and catch a train from there; take Hwy 17 to Scotts Valley, exit at Mt Herman Rd and follow that west for 3½ miles, turn left on Graham Hill Rd and continue for ½ mile.

early February. Harbor cruises run year round and cost $6 to $10. For current boat timetables, call Stagnaro's (☎ 813-427-2334), which has a kiosk on the municipal wharf.

Diving

Ocean Odyssey (☎ 831-475-3483), 2345 S Rodeo Gulch Rd, offers two-dive orientation trips (usually beach dives near Monterey) for $80, or $130 if you need full equipment.

Bicycling

The hills behind Santa Cruz offer many interesting rides up. Henry Cowell Redwoods State Park is a particularly popular getaway, or try the W Cliff Drive coast ride from the municipal wharf to Natural Bridges State Beach. The Bicycle Rental Center (☎ 831-426-8687), 131 Center St, rents bikes at $7/25 per hour/day. Numerous shops along Beach St also rent bikes.

Places to Stay

If economy is important, Santa Cruz is a much better deal than nearby Monterey. There are campsites in the vicinity, an HI hostel and a vast range of reasonable motels, as well as pricier B&Bs and a few upper-end hotels. Remarkably there are few of the hi-rise hotels you might expect in such a popular beach town, and surprisingly little beachfront construction.

Camping There are many available *campsites* in the mountains and on the beach. Call Parknet (☎ 800-444-7275) for reservations at Big Basin Redwood State Park at Boulder Creek (see the previous Half Moon Bay to Santa Cruz section); at Henry Cowell Redwood State Park near Felton; at New Brighton State Beach in Capitola; at Seacliff State Beach in Aptos; or at Sunset State Beach in Watsonville.

The *Santa Cruz KOA Kampground* (☎ 813-722-0551) is in Watsonville near the beach, 15 miles south of downtown, but tent sites are expensive at $32.

Hostels HI's *Carmelita Cottages Hostel* (☎ 831-423-8304, 321 Main St) is one of the finest in Northern California, just two blocks from the beach and five blocks from downtown. Beds are $13 to $15 and check-in is from 5 to 10 pm. Advance reservations are advised.

Hotels Recommending motels and hotels in Santa Cruz is a fairly hopeless task – there are many, and many are unmemorable. Prices vary considerably depending on proximity to the beach, whether it's a weekday (cheaper) or weekend (pricier), and whether it's winter (cheaper) or summer (far more expensive). On a midweek day in winter, motels offer rooms for as little as $35. On a summer weekend, the same room may fetch upwards of $110.

Hwy 1, or Mission Rd (as it's known within the town limits) has many motels. As you travel farther from the beach, you get more room for less money. Other good hunting grounds are on the streets running back from Beach St and the boardwalk, home to some real dives (rooms by the hour); along Riverside Ave near the boardwalk; and along Ocean St on the other side of the San Lorenzo River.

Days Inn (☎ 831-423-8564, 325 Pacific Ave) is a standard motel in the no-man's land between downtown Santa Cruz and the waterfront. Rooms drop as low as $55 in the off-season and climb to $90 to $130 in peak season. Other standard motels close to the beach include the *Super 8 Motel* (☎ 831-426-3707, 338 Riverside Ave), with rooms from $60 to $135 (slightly cheaper in winter).

At Best Western's comfortable *All Suites Inn* (☎ 831-458-9898, 500 Ocean St), at Soquel Drive, all rooms are suites and cost $85 to $160 off-season, $95 to $185 in season.

The *Pacific Inn* (☎ 831-425-3722, 330 Ocean St) occupies a former apartment building, and all the rooms are spacious. The swimming pool and hot tub are added bonuses. Rooms range from $38 (low season) to $105 (high season).

At the *Travelodge Santa Cruz* (☎ 831-426-2300, 525 Ocean St), prices can drop to $70 or so off-season and climb to $135 in season. The swimming pool is handy on hot summer days. The *Riviera Travelodge*

(☎ 831-423-9515, 619 Riverside Ave) has similar rates and facilities.

The **Casa Blanca Inn** (☎ 831-423-1570, 800-644-1570, 101 Main St), at Beach St, is one of the nicer beachside motels. Most of its 40 rooms have unobstructed ocean views, though rooms overlooking Beach St can be noisy. Rooms are priced from $78 to $195.

If 'location, location, location' are your three key requirements, then the **Sea & Sand Inn** (☎ 831-427-3400, 201 W Cliff Drive) deserves its higher prices. The neat and tidy motel is right on the cliff edge and every room looks across the bay. Rates are $90 to $190, depending on the season.

The only 'big' hotel is **West Coast Santa Cruz** (☎ 831-426-4330, 800-662-3838, 175 W Cliff Drive). There are 172 rooms, most with ocean views, plus a pool, sauna, restaurant and bar. Rooms start at $109 on weekdays, $129 on weekends.

B&Bs The five-room **Cliff Crest** (☎ 831-427-2609, 407 Cliff St) is close to the beach and boardwalk. Rooms in this attractive Victorian mansion range from $105 to $155. Or try the 12-room **Babbling Brook Inn** (☎ 831-427-2437, 1025 Laurel St). It's not so conveniently located, but with attractive rooms and a garden complete with a stream and waterfall. Rooms range from $145 to $195.

Places to Eat

For organic fruits and vegetables you'd be hard pressed to find better shopping than at the **farmers' market**, held from 2:30 to 6:30 pm every Wednesday on Cedar St between Walnut and Lincoln Sts.

Budget Start the day at **Rebecca's Mighty Muffins** (☎ 831-429-1940, 514A Front St), which sells more than 30 varieties of delectable muffins. The **Bagelry** (☎ 831-429-8049, 320A Cedar St), near the corner of Maple St, is another popular breakfast spot.

Cafe Pergolesi (☎ 831-426-1775, 418 Cedar St), a student coffeehouse, is a Santa Cruz landmark, with a balcony overlooking the street and great cakes and pies.

For cheap eats, pizzerias and Mexican restaurants are scattered all over Santa Cruz. Or there are burger-and-fries alternatives such as **Positively Front Street** (☎ 831-426-1944, 44 Front St), a lively bar and restaurant. Pasta and pizza also feature on its menu. **Pontiac Grill** (☎ 831-427-2290, 429 Front St) is an authentic interpretation of a '50s diner, with burgers for $4.50 to $7. It's open daily to at least 11 pm.

Little Shanghai (☎ 831-458-2460, 1010 Cedar St) is a cheap, simple and popular Chinese restaurant.

Mid-Range Winner of many 'Best Mexican Restaurant' awards, **El Palomar** (☎ 831-425-7575, 1336 Pacific Ave) serves safe Mexican staples that are nonetheless quite good. The bar is a trendy pickup scene. The **Gabriella Cafe** (☎ 831-457-1677, 910 Cedar St) is a tranquil candlelit restaurant with a menu featuring pasta, seafood and numerous local wines (entrées $7 to $15). **Benten** (☎ 831-425-7079, 1541 Pacific Ave), a popular sushi bar, has reasonable prices, considering what you get (closed Tuesday).

The municipal wharf is loaded with seafood restaurants, most of which have great views and inflated prices. An exception is **The Dolphin** (☎ 831-426-5830), a straightforward diner-style restaurant with fresh-off-the-boat seafood entrées at $8 to $12.

Entertainment

The **Poet & Patriot** (☎ 831-426-8620, 112 2nd St), on Cedar Sq (enter off Cedar St), aims for the English pub style. Or there's the **99 Bottles Bar** (☎ 831-459-9999, 110 Walnut Ave), a nice place for a beer. The subdued **Red Room** (☎ 831-426-2994, 1003 Cedar St) serves cocktails to Santa Cruz's hipster crowd. The **Front Street Pub** (☎ 831-429-8838, 516 Front St) is a popular microbrewery that also serves good pub grub.

The **Kuumbwa Jazz Center** (☎ 831-427-2227, 320 Cedar St) is a pleasant bar, occasional dance spot and frequent live music venue. There's a cluster of nightspots along Pacific Ave. **Palookaville** (☎ 831-454-0600, 1133 Pacific Ave) is a well-known bar-dance venue. There's live music most nights at the **Catalyst** (☎ 831-423-1336, 1011 Pacific Ave). **Blue Lagoon** (☎ 831-423-7117, 923 Pacific

SAN FRANCISCO BAY AREA

Ave) is popular with the local gay crowd, as well as with students and those seeking loud techno and retro tunes on weekend nights.

Getting There & Away

Without your own wheels, the easiest way to reach Santa Cruz is on a Greyhound bus. There are no commuter train services to or from Santa Cruz.

Bus Greyhound (☎ 831-423-1800), next to the Metro Center at 425 Front St, operates a San Francisco-Santa Cruz-Monterey-Santa Barbara-Los Angeles route twice a day in each direction. Fares are $13 to San Francisco, $10 to Monterey, $37 to Los Angeles.

Connections to Santa Cruz from the Cal-Train/Amtrak station in San Jose take 45 minutes and cost $7. Monterey-Salinas Transit bus No 28 connects to Salinas via Castroville, No 29 via Prunedale. On weekdays, Hwy 17 Express Bus Services take just over an hour to San Jose. Inquire at the Metro Center (see Getting Around) about where to pick it up.

The Santa Cruz Airporter (☎ 831-423-1214) runs shuttle buses to the airports at San Jose ($30) and San Francisco ($35).

Car & Motorcycle Santa Cruz is 40 miles north of Monterey via Hwy 1 and 35 miles west of San Jose via winding Hwy 17. From San Francisco, 70 miles north, the most scenic but slowest route is Hwy 1 down the coast; it's faster to take I-280 and then cross over the mountains via Hwy 17. Another option, much longer but worth it for the mountain scenery, is I-280 to Hwy 85 to Hwy 9.

Getting Around

Santa Cruz Metropolitan Transit (☎ 831-425-8600) operates from the Metro Center at 920 Pacific Ave. Useful services include bus No 3B to Natural Bridges State Beach, No 35 to Felton and on up to Ben Lomond and Boulder Creek, No 40 (limited service) to Davenport and the north coast beaches and the No 69 to the Capitola Transit Center. One-way trips are $1; a day pass costs $3.

AROUND SANTA CRUZ

The **Mystery Spot** (☎ 831-423-8897) is a fine old-fashioned tourist trap that has scarcely changed from the day it opened in the 1940s. On this steeply sloping hillside compasses point crazily, mysterious forces push you around, balls roll uphill and buildings lean at silly angles. It's open 9 am to 5 pm daily, and this good, clean, harmless fun costs $4. The Mystery Spot is 3 miles north of town on Branciforte Drive; take Water St to Market St, turn left and continue up into the hills.

SAN JUAN BAUTISTA

• population 1650 • elevation 220 feet

In this pleasantly sleepy semi-ghost town, California's 15th mission, fronted by the only original Spanish plaza in the state, is precariously perched right on the edge of the San Andreas Fault. The critical scenes in Hitchcock's *Vertigo* take place at the mission.

San Juan Bautista is on Hwy 156 about 2 miles east of Hwy 101, between San Jose and Salinas on the way to Monterey. San Juan Bautista has many attractive old buildings, a few motels and a string of restaurants and cafes along 3rd St. Away from the plaza, San Juan Bautista looks almost frozen in time.

Mission San Juan Bautista

The mission (☎ 831-623-4528) was founded in 1797, and construction of its **church** started fitfully in 1803. The interior, completed in 1816, was painted by an American sailor who jumped ship in Monterey and may well have been the first US resident of California. The church was built with three aisles, but at some point the outer aisles were walled off. They were destroyed in the 1906 earthquake and were not repaired until the 1970s, when the inner archways were opened up to make this the largest of California's mission churches. The bell tower was also added at that time. Note the footprints of bears and coyotes on the red-tiled floor – the animals probably walked across the tiles as they were hardening, a reminder of what a rugged place California was two centuries ago. The mission church is open 9:30 am to 4:45 pm daily; $2 donation requested.

In the Spanish era, the area had a large Indian population and over 4000 of them are buried in the old **cemetery** beside the mission's northeastern wall. The ridge along the north side of the church is the actual line of the San Andreas Fault.

North of the cemetery, a section of the old El Camino Real, the 'King's Highway,' can be seen. This Spanish road, built to link the missions, was the first road in the state. In many places Hwy 101 still follows the original route.

The Plaza & Town

The buildings around the expansive old Spanish plaza are part of the state historic park, open 10 am to 4:30 pm daily; $2. The **Plaza Hotel** started life as a single-story adobe in 1814 and was enlarged and converted into a hotel in 1858; in its time it was a very popular overnight stagecoach halt.

The adjacent **Castro House** was built for José Maria Castro, who led a successful 1836 revolt against the unpopular Governor Juan Gutiérrez, then repeated the performance in 1843, when he helped usurp and deport Governor Micheltorena. In 1848, the house was bought by the Breen family, survivors of the Donner Party, which was stranded for

111 days in the Sierra Nevadas during the extraordinarily severe winter of 1846 (see 'The Donner Party' in the Sierra Nevada chapter). The Breens made a quick gold rush fortune in 1848, and the house remained with the family until 1933.

The large blacksmith shop and the **Plaza Stable** of about 1861 hint at San Juan Bautista in its heyday, when as many as 11 stagecoaches a day passed through, many on the busy San Francisco-Los Angeles route. The completion of the railway in 1876 bypassed San Juan Bautista, and the town became a sleepy backwater.

AROUND SAN JUAN BAUTISTA

Gilroy, 14 miles north of San Juan Bautista via Hwy 101, claims to be the garlic capital of the world, and celebrates this achievement with an annual Garlic Festival (☎ 408-842-1625) held on the last full weekend in July.

Castroville, 15 miles southwest at the junction of Hwy 156 and Hwy 1, is also a world capital, but this time it's for artichokes. In fact, nine out of 10 US artichokes come from Castroville, and yes, there's an annual Artichoke Festival in September (☎ 408-633-3402).

Wine Country

Only about 7% of California wine comes from the Wine Country, the parallel Napa and Sonoma valleys. Most California wine comes from the heavily agricultural Central Valley, but that's the bulk stuff, California plonk. The Wine Country is where, back in the 1970s, the state's independent wineries began producing award-winning vintages that quickly garnered worldwide acclaim. Many of California's high-quality wines are still produced in the Napa and Sonoma valleys, though in recent years there's been an explosion of topflight wineries throughout the state.

The two valleys, Napa and Sonoma, lie about 1½ hours' drive north of San Francisco. Napa Valley, the farther inland of the two, has more than 230 wineries. Sonoma Valley is low-key and far less commercial than Napa, with only about 50 wineries. If you have time to visit only one of them, make it Sonoma. That said, both offer the same rustic beauty of vineyards, wildflowers and green and golden hills. The valleys can be covered on a hectic day trip from San Francisco, but to do them each justice, allow two full days for exploring and wine tasting.

Spring and fall are the best times to visit. Summers tend to be hot and dusty, as well as decidedly crowded. Fall combines fine weather with the grape harvest and the 'crush,' when the wine-making season gets under way with the pressing of the grapes. However, wine isn't all these valleys have to offer; there's Spanish and Mexican history in Sonoma, lots of outdoor activities, mud baths and spas at Calistoga, literary connections with two important writers and cartoon connections with two popular cartoonists in Santa Rosa.

History

Early Spanish and Mexican settlers produced some wine in the Napa and Sonoma valleys, but Hungarian count Ágoston Haraszthy started the modern wine business in 1857 when he bought land in Sonoma

Highlights

- Sunrise, champagne and hot air – the valleys look great from a balloon
- Harbin Hot Springs – ready for a naked massage?
- Valley of the Moon – a Sonoma winery noted for its exquisite ports
- Clos Pegase – one of Napa's best wineries
- Oakville Grocery & Cafe – gourmet sandwiches worth the drive

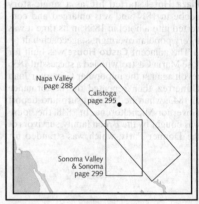

Napa Valley
page 288

Calistoga
page 295

Sonoma Valley & Sonoma
page 299

Valley and began cultivating grapes for wine production. By the late 1860s there were already 50 vintners in Napa Valley.

Later in the century things started to go bad, a double assault from cheap imports and the arrival of the deadly root louse phylloxera, fresh from devastating the vineyards of Europe. The wine business was still stumbling from these attacks when Prohibition delivered the knockout in 1919. Remarkably, a handful of wineries continued in business, producing sacramental wine.

Prohibition ended in 1933, but it was not until the 1960s that wine production really got back into high gear. In 1976, at a blind

WINE COUNTRY

wine-tasting competition in France, Chateau Montelena's 1973 Chardonnay and a '73 Cabernet Sauvignon from Stag's Leap outscored French Bordeaux wines, putting Napa Valley on the international wine map.

Wine Tasting

These days few Napa Valley wineries offer free tastings. If you want to sample the wines you'll have to pay, usually $3 to $10 for two to three varieties; sometimes a complimentary wine glass is included. In Sonoma Valley, on the other hand, free tastings are still the rule rather than the exception. In any case, you don't want to do too much tasting – visiting five or six wineries in a day is usually quite enough. Most wineries are open all day every day for tastings, but call ahead if you absolutely, positively don't want to miss a tasting or tour.

Wineries will generally have their wines on sale, but don't come to the wineries looking for bargains. The wines are usually on sale at full retail price and can often be found cheaper at liquor stores and supermarkets. Of course, wines from some of the

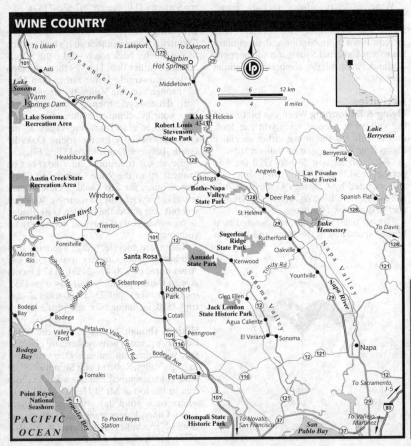

WINE COUNTRY

smaller boutique wineries, as well as special vintages or reserves, will be available only from the wineries themselves or from a very restricted list of outlets.

There are hundreds of wineries in the valleys, so those mentioned in this chapter are just a sampling of both the better-known larger places and the quirkier and more interesting smaller places. At some wineries, facilities for visitors consist of little more than a tasting room. Others may have displays, museums, art galleries and guided or do-it-yourself tours of the wine-making process.

Wine Country whites include Fumé Blanc, Riesling, Gewürztraminer, Chenin Blanc and California Chardonnay. Reds include Pinot Noir, Merlot and Beaujolais; the robust Cabernet Sauvignon and peppery Zinfandel are probably the premier California reds.

Activities

Flying & Ballooning When you get tired of the valleys at ground level you can look down on them from above, either on glider flights from Calistoga or on balloon trips.

Glider flights cost $80 to $120 for one person, or $125 to $180 for two people, and are operated by Calistoga Gliders (☎ 707-942-5000), 1546 Lincoln Ave, at the Gliderport in downtown Calistoga.

Hot-air balloon flights are operated by a host of specialists in the Napa and Sonoma valleys, many of them in Yountville. Balloon flights are usually early in the morning (around 7 am), when the air is coolest; sometimes they include a champagne breakfast after you land. The cost is $175 to $185 per person, and advance reservations are recommended. Some operators make two flights, so you have an opportunity to ride on one flight and follow in the pursuit vehicle on the other.

In Yountville, call Balloons Above the Valley (☎ 707-253-2222) or Napa Valley Balloons (☎ 707-944-0228); in Napa, try Adventures Aloft (☎ 707-944-4408); in Santa Rosa, try Sonoma Thunder (☎ 707-538-7359).

Bicycling Bicycling around the Wine Country is popular, although it's best to stick to the quieter back roads – take the Silverado Trail rather than Hwy 29 through Napa Valley and Arnold Drive rather than Hwy 12 through Sonoma Valley. Both valleys are fairly flat and cycle-friendly, but you'd better have your hill-climbing abilities tuned up if you want to ride from one valley to the other, particularly by the trying Oakville Grade, between Oakville and Glen Ellen.

Bicycles, if transported in a box, can be brought up to the Wine Country on Greyhound buses for $10. Golden Gate Transit will take bicycles only on route No 40, which will bus you across the Golden Gate Bridge as far as San Rafael (beyond that you're on your own).

There are bicycle rental agencies in a number of Wine Country towns. Getaway Adventures (☎ 800-499-2453), 1117 Lincoln Ave in Calistoga, offers half-day trips ($55, including bike) and 25- to 30-mile all-day trips ($90, including bike and picnic lunch).

Hiking Though hiking is not the Wine Country's primary activity, there are places to take some time out and enjoy the landscape. In Napa Valley, Robert Louis Stevenson State Park is undeveloped and has a 5-mile dusty trail to the top of Mt St Helena (4343 feet), where on a good day you'll get excellent views. Other, longer trails are in developed Bothe-Napa Valley State Park (☎ 707-942-4575), which charges a $5 day-use fee.

In Sonoma Valley, check out the trails at some of the wineries.

Getting There & Away

From San Francisco, public transportation can get you to the valleys, but it's not the ideal way of working your way among the wineries. Amtrak goes to Martinez (south of Vallejo), and from there you can catch a connecting bus to the main Napa Valley centers.

Tours from San Francisco are operated by Gray Lines (☎ 415-558-9400), which has a daily 9 am departure from the Transbay Terminal, at 1st and Mission Sts. This nine-hour, $43 tour covers both Napa and Sonoma valleys and includes visits to two or three wineries and a stop to shop and lunch on your own.

Bus Greyhound (☎ 800-231-2222) runs twice daily from San Francisco's Transbay Terminal up through Napa Valley to Calistoga ($14 one way, three hours) via Oakland, Vallejo, Oakville and St Helena. Call for services north past Calistoga and to Sonoma.

Napa Valley Transit (☎ 800-696-6443) operates buses from the Vallejo Ferry Terminal through Napa Valley to Calistoga; the buses are labeled Route 10, and the fare to Calistoga is $2.10.

Golden Gate Transit (☎ 707-541-2000, 415-923-2000) bus No 90 runs from San Francisco to Sonoma; catch it at 1st and Mission Sts, across from the Transbay Terminal. The fare is $2.

Once you're there, Sonoma County Transit (☎ 707-576-7433, 800-345-7433) has buses around the Sonoma Valley.

Car & Motorcycle By car or motorcycle from San Francisco, take Hwy 101 north to the Hwy 37 exit at Novato. Follow Hwy 37 northeast for a few miles to Hwy 121 and continue north to the junction of Hwys 12 and 121. For Sonoma Valley, take Hwy 12 north; for Napa Valley, take Hwy 12/121 east. Just before the town of Napa Hwy 12/121 splits: Hwy 121 turns left (north) and joins up with Hwy 29 (also known as the St Helena Hwy); Hwy 12 merges with the southbound extension of Hwy 29. From the East Bay, you can reach Hwy 29 directly from Hwy 80 via Vallejo. Don't worry if this sounds confusing; the signs to Napa and Sonoma are well marked.

If you drive from San Francisco, keep in mind that Hwy 29 backs up on weekend evenings between 4 and 7 pm, which will slow your return.

Napa Valley

Napa Valley is the longer of the two valleys (around 30 miles long), lies farther inland and has more wineries. The city of Napa, at the valley's southern end, is the region's main hub but is of minimal interest. Better places for a pause are St Helena and, at the northern end of the valley, Calistoga – a name famous for mineral water rather than wine.

Two roads run north-south along the valley: Hwy 29 (the St Helena Hwy) and the more scenic Silverado Trail, just a mile or two east. If you're driving, it's worth the effort to get away from these main roads. The Oakville Grade and rural Trinity Rd (which leads southwest to Hwy 12 in Sonoma Valley) are curvaceous and beautiful; Mt Veeder Rd leads through some pristine mountain scenery. Yountville Cross and Yountmill Rds provide an equally bucolic link between the Silverado Trail and Hwy 29.

A popular way to explore the valley is on the **Napa Valley Wine Train** (☎ 707-253-2111, 800-427-4124), 1275 McKinstry St, Napa, which serves a daily lunch ($63) and dinner ($70) in a 1915 vintage Pullman dining car that travels from Napa to St Helena and back. Champagne brunch ($57) is served Saturday, Sunday and holidays. A daily deli car (lunch only) is more affordable ($25). The 36-mile roundtrip takes three hours, and it's a beautiful ride. The train leaves from McKinstry St near 1st St.

NAPA VALLEY WINERIES

Many of the more than 230 wineries in Napa Valley are small operations without the facilities or desire to welcome visitors. Wineries that do offer tastings and tours are

WINE COUNTRY

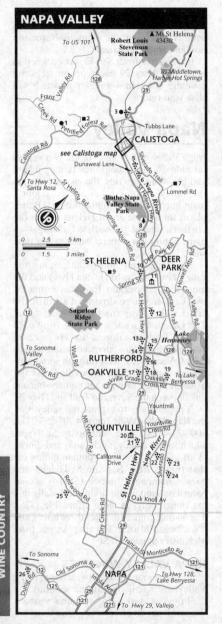

NAPA VALLEY

PLACES TO STAY
2 Triple-S-Ranch
7 Calistoga Ranch Club
9 White Sulphur Springs Resort

WINERIES
4 Château Montelena
5 Clos Pegase
6 Sterling Vineyards
10 Beringer
12 V Sattui
13 Niebaum-Coppola Estate
14 Grgich Hills Cellar
15 Beaulieu
16 Cakebread Cellars & St Supéry

17 Robert Mondavi
18 Opus One
19 Villa Mt Eden
21 Domaine Chandon
22 Pine Ridge
23 Stag's Leap
24 Clos du Val
25 Hess Collection & Winery
26 Domaine Carneros

OTHER
1 Petrified Forest
3 Old Faithful Geyser
8 Bale Grist Mill State Historic Park
11 Silverado Museum
20 Napa Valley Museum

usually open from 10 or 11 am to 4 or 5 pm daily. Call ahead if you'd like a tour, because they usually depart at set hours and sometimes require reservations.

The following wineries are listed in south-north order.

Domaine Carneros This 137-acre estate (☎ 707-257-0101), 1240 Duhig Rd at Hwy 12/121, Napa, is partly owned by French champagne maker Taittinger and is housed in an exotic-looking château. The winery itself is in the Carneros region, southwest of Napa and halfway to Sonoma Valley. There's a tasting room and a visitor center (open 10:30 am to 6 pm daily). Tours are offered at 11 am and 1 and 3 pm Monday to Thursday, every hour from 11 am to 4 pm Friday to Sunday. Reservations are not required.

Hess Collection & Winery Wine and art merge in this decidedly top-end winery (☎ 707-255-1144), 4411 Redwood Rd, Napa, with a wonderful but expensive art gallery spread over three floors. The winery is open 10 am to 4 pm daily. Tastings are $3 (don't miss the Cabernet Sauvignon), and self-guided estate tours are free. The winery is equidistant between the Napa and Sonoma valleys.

Clos du Val This winery (☎ 707-259-2200), 5330 Silverado Trail, Yountville, is not much to look at, but a visit to Clos du Val is worthwhile if you enjoy high-quality Zinfandels and Cabernet Sauvignons. Tastings are offered 10 am to 5 pm daily; the $5 fee can be applied to the purchase of a bottle.

Stag's Leap It was a Stag's Leap Cabernet Sauvignon that bested the French back in 1976, and they continue to produce exceptional wines. Stag's Leap (☎ 707-944-2020), 5766 Silverado Trail, Yountville, also makes an internationally acclaimed Chardonnay. Tastings ($5) are offered 10 am to 4:30 pm daily.

Pine Ridge This is a small, low-key winery (☎ 707-253-7500), 5901 Silverado Trail, Yountville, known for its red wines – the Merlot is especially good. Tastings are offered 11 am to 5 pm daily. It's $5 to sample the current releases, $7 for limited releases and $10 for the reserve vintages. Winery tours are offered at 10:15 am and 1 and 3 pm daily.

Domaine Chandon French champagne maker Moët-Hennesey has several 'new world' wineries where they make 'sparkling wine' (rather than champagne, since the French insist that champagne is only champagne when it comes from the Champagne region of France). The winery (☎ 707-944-2280), 1 California Drive, west of St Helena Hwy, Yountville, is open 10 am to 6 pm daily and has interesting displays, an informative tour, tastings ($8) and an exquisite restaurant (see Yountville Places to Eat).

Robert Mondavi This is a big commercial winery (☎ 707-226-1395), 7801 St Helena Hwy, Oakville, with a mission-looking design fronted by a Beniamino Bufano statue. Despite its size and the sometimes oppressive crowds, it puts on an informative tour on the wine-making process. Tastings cost $2 to $5 per glass, although if you take the free hour-long tour, offered hourly 10 am to 4 pm, you're rewarded with a free tasting. Reservations are required for the three- to four-hour 'In-Depth Tours.'

Opus One From the St Helena Hwy, the winery building is quite a sight, looking like a cross between an art deco ocean liner and an Aztec pyramid. Unfortunately, Opus One (☎ 707-963-1979), 7900 St Helena Hwy, Oakville, is a high-end winery that charges a staggering $25 to sample its award-winning reds and whites. Tastings are offered 10:30 am to 3:30 pm daily.

Villa Mt Eden This winery (☎ 707-944-2414), 8711 Silverado Trail, Oakville, is small, which means that it's less crowded and a bit more down-to-earth than most others. Free tastings are offered 10 am to 4 pm daily. The winery itself is in a fine old building.

Cakebread Cellars This lesser-known winery (☎ 707-963-5221), 8300 St Helena Hwy, Rutherford, produces some of the valley's finest whites, including its signature Chardonnay and Sauvignon Blanc. There are no tours. Tastings ($5, $10 for reserve wines) are offered 10 am to 4:30 pm daily.

St Supéry The historic 1882 Atkinson House fronts this modern winery (☎ 707-963-4507), 8440 St Helena Hwy, Rutherford, which has some of the most innovative displays in the valley, including interesting explanations of wine colors and aromas. Tastings are $3, and there's a free self-guided tour. The winery is open 9:30 am to 5 pm daily.

Grgich Hills Cellar This winery (pronounced GIRR-gich) has an unpretentious tasting room (free on weekdays, $3 on weekends); it may be small, but these may be the wines with which you compare all the rest. The cellar (☎ 707-963-2784), 1829 St Helena Hwy, Rutherford, is open 9:30 am to 4:30 pm daily. Tours are by appointment.

Beaulieu Beaulieu, French for 'beautiful place' and named after an area in France, was founded in 1900 by a French immigrant and is now one of the largest Napa wineries (☎ 707-963-2411), 1960 St Helena Hwy, Rutherford. Tastings are free at the visitor

WINE COUNTRY

center (open 10 am to 5 pm daily), but cost $18 for five glasses at the reserve cellar (open 10:30 am to 4:30 pm daily).

Niebaum-Coppola Estate The former Inglenook estate (☎ 707-963-9099), 1991 St Helena Hwy, Rutherford, was purchased by filmmaker Francis Ford Coppola in the mid-1980s, and since then it has consistently produced some of the valley's finest reds. An added bonus is the movie memorabilia from Coppola's films *The Godfather* and *Dracula*. Tastings ($7.50) are offered 10 am to 5 pm daily.

V Sattui This large winery in an old stone building (☎ 707-963-7774), 1111 White Lane, St Helena, loudly encourages picnicking; its deli sells great breads, cheeses and of course, wine. Table-wine tastings are free, and it's open 9 am to 5 pm daily.

Beringer Beringer (☎ 707-963-4812), 2000 Main St, St Helena, is fronted by the regal 1883 Rhine House and is the oldest continuously operating winery in Napa. It was founded by German brothers Jacob and Frederick Beringer in 1876 and survived Prohibition by manufacturing sacramental and medicinal wines. The free tour includes a visit to the extensive tunnels that burrow into the hill behind the winery. Free tastings are offered 9:30 am to 4:30 pm daily.

Sterling Vineyards The gimmick at Sterling Vineyards (☎ 707-942-3344), 1111 Dunaweal Lane, Calistoga, is a gondola ride that carries you to the hilltop, which has superb views across the valley. Wines here are known for their quality; the winery itself is architecturally interesting. A $6 ticket includes a tour and tasting. The winery is open 10:30 am to 4:30 pm daily.

Clos Pegase This well-respected winery (☎ 707-942-4981), 1060 Dunaweal Lane, Calistoga, combines architecture, art and wine and is one of Napa Valley's highlights. Interesting sculptures dot the grounds of the 1987 Michael Graves-designed buildings, and modern art graces the visitor center. There

are free tours at 11 am and 2 pm. Tastings, offered 10:30 am to 5 pm daily, are $2.50 at the visitor center or $2 per glass at the reserve cellar.

Chateau Montelena At the north end of the valley, Chateau Montelena (☎ 707-942-5105), 1429 Tubbs Lane, Calistoga, has a beautiful lake with Chinese-style bridges and pavilions, a fine stone château and picnic grounds for winery customers. There's a $5 tasting fee. It's open 10 am to 4 pm daily.

NAPA
• population 69,300 • elevation 17 feet
Napa may be the main town in the valley, but there's little reason to pause in this workaday center. Napa had a brief history as a river port before railways enticed the traffic away. There are a few interesting old buildings around town; stop by the visitors bureau for a walking-tour leaflet. The tiny Napa County Historical Society Museum (☎ 707-224-1739), 1219 1st St, has simple displays on wine making and local history; it's worth a quick peek.

Orientation & Information
Napa is sandwiched between the Silverado Trail and the St Helena Hwy. Coming from San Francisco on Hwy 12/121, turn left (north) onto the St Helena Hwy (confusingly labeled Hwy 121/29 within the town limits). To reach the downtown area, exit Hwy 121/29 at 1st St and follow it east. Napa's main drag, 1st St, is lined with shops and restaurants.

The Napa Valley Visitors Bureau (☎ 707-226-7459), at 1310 Napa Town Center, right off 1st St, is the biggest and most active information center in the valley. It's open 9 am to 5 pm daily, and the staff will make room reservations for you.

Activities
Napa Valley Bike Tours (☎ 707-255-3377), 4080 Byway East just off the St Helena Hwy, rents bicycles for $7/22 per hour/day. When business isn't too busy they also offer one-way rentals: for an extra $25 you can ride to

WINE COUNTRY

Calistoga, for example, and they will pick you up and return you and the bike to Napa.

For information on hot-air ballooning, see the Activities section at the beginning of this chapter.

Places to Stay

The plain *Discovery Inn* (☎ 707-253-0892, *500 Silverado Trail*) is southeast of the town center on Hwy 121. Basic doubles are $40 to $50.

The *Travelodge* (☎ 707-226-1871) is centrally located at the corner of 2nd and Coombs Sts. Once renovations are finished it should be a good value, at $79/89 weekdays/weekends.

The *Napa Valley Budget Inn* (☎ 707-257-6111, *3380 Solano Ave*) is just west of the St Helena Hwy off Redwood Rd. The simple but clean motel has a pool and rooms starting at $56/65 weekdays/weekends. One of the nicer motel options is the *John Muir Inn* (☎ 707-257-7220, 800-522-8999, *1998 Trower Ave*), at the corner of Trower Ave and the St Helena Hwy. Rooms are $80 to $85 on weekdays, $90 to $95 on weekends.

If money is no object, the *Silverado Country Club* (☎ 707-257-0200, *1600 Atlas Peak Rd*) is a swank resort in the hills 3½ miles east of Napa. One-bedroom condominiums cost $169/199 weekdays/weekends, two-bedroom condos $209/239. The resort has two golf courses, tennis courts and myriad swimming pools. From the St Helena Hwy, turn right (east) on Trancas St (which becomes Monticello Rd) and go left at Atlas Peak Rd.

Places to Eat

Downtown Joes (*902 Main St*), on the riverbank at the end of 2nd St, incorporates a microbrewery and restaurant and operates from breakfast to dinner. Right across the junction is *PJ's Cafe* (☎ 707-224-0607, *1001 2nd St*), a standard diner offering straightforward burgers, sandwiches, pastas and pizzas.

The *Napa Valley Coffee Roasting Co* (☎ 707-224-2233, *948 Main St*) at the corner of 1st and Main Sts, is a good breakfast spot in a historic building. In the shopping center

by Napa's clock tower are two popular Mexican places: *Taquería Tres Hermanos* (☎ 707-224-6062, *1122 1st St*) and *Don Perico Restaurant* (☎ 707-252-4707, *1025 1st St*).

The *Foothill Cafe* (☎ 707-252-6178, *2766 Old Sonoma Rd*), in the J&P Shopping Center, is a casual respite from the glamour of other Napa attractions and offers reasonably priced sandwiches and light entrées ($8 to $12) 4:30 to 9:30 pm Wednesday to Sunday.

Bistro Don Giovanni (☎ 707-224-3300, *4110 St Helena Hwy*) is a stylish Italian spot with a good wine list and delicious wood-oven-cooked pizzas. Entrées are $13 to $17, and reservations are required most evenings.

If romance is called for and you're feeling flush, make advance dinner reservations at the *Vintner's Court* (☎ 707-257-0200, *16 Atlas Peak Rd*), at the Silverado Country Club. The setting and service are impeccable, and the kitchen excels at creative California cuisine.

YOUNTVILLE

• **population 3630**   • **elevation 100 feet**

Yountville (pronounced YAWNT-vill), one of the larger towns in the valley, is 9 miles north of Napa and 21 miles south of Calistoga. Yountville straddles the St Helena Hwy, though most of its restaurants and shops are on Washington St, which runs parallel to and just east of the highway. Yountville has a handful of places to stay and plenty of famous high-end restaurants, but otherwise St Helena and Calistoga, farther north, make better bases.

Yountville's modernist 40,000-sq-foot **Napa Valley Museum** (☎ 707-944-0500), 55 Presidents Circle, off California Drive, chronicles Napa's cultural history and showcases local paintings. It's open 10 am to 5 pm Wednesday to Monday; $4.50.

Squashed between Washington St and the St Helena Hwy is Vintage 1870, Yountville's rather twee shopping center. More useful is the chamber of commerce (☎ 707-944-0904), across the street at 6515 Yount St. You can also try the Napa Valley Tourist Office (☎ 707-944-1558), 6488 Washington St.

Places to Stay

Yountville is a pricey place to stay. *Petit Logis* (☎ 707-944-2332, 6527 Yount St) is an upscale motel-cum-inn with rooms for $125/150 weekdays/weekends (including full breakfast). Nicer and even more expensive is the *Napa Valley Lodge* (☎ 707-944-2468, 2230 Madison St), at the corner of Madison and Washington Sts, with 55 rooms priced from $135 to $225.

Places to Eat

Since all of the places mentioned here are favorites, dinner reservations are strongly recommended. *The Diner* (☎ 707-944-2626, 6476 Washington St), a popular spot, proclaims that it has 'legendary food.' In fact, it's merely above-average diner food at above-average diner prices. The Diner is perhaps best for breakfast. Next door is a branch of the popular California chain *Ristorante Piatti* (☎ 707-944-2070). The food is high-quality Italian, with pastas and pizzas from $9 to $15.

Domaine Chandon (☎ 707-944-2892, 1 California Drive), just off the St Helena Hwy, is a recommended splurge, with delicious California cuisine served on a leafy patio. Jackets are required at dinner, but most agree that the effort is well worth the price (entrées are $12 to $25). It's closed in January.

It's nearly impossible to get reservations at Yountville's elegant *French Laundry* (☎ 707-944-2380, 6640 Washington St). If you succeed, prepare yourself for a superb prix-fixe lunch ($29 or $38) or dinner ($58 or $72). The menu features traditional French dishes with a distinct California twist.

Between Yountville and Oakville is *Mustards Grill* (☎ 707-944-2424, 7399 St Helena Hwy), which consistently gets rave reviews for service and food (steaks, seafood and pastas). Entrées are $8 to $15.

OAKVILLE

• **population 250** • **elevation 150 feet**

The tiny settlement of Oakville is just a few miles north of Yountville. Though it has no sights to speak of, Oakville is well endowed with wineries (10 and counting). It also has the *Oakville Grocery & Cafe* (☎ 707-944-

8802, 7856 St Helena Hwy), just north of Oakville Cross Rd; it's one of the best gourmet delis in the Napa and Sonoma valleys, with delicious sandwiches ($5 to $7.50) and a large selection of salads, breads and cheeses.

RUTHERFORD

• **population 210** • **elevation 170 feet**

Like Oakville, Rutherford is neither a town nor a village but rather a loose-knit collection of wineries, private homes and roadside antiques and gift shops. It also has one of the valley's most popular restaurants, *Auberge de Soleil* (☎ 707-963-1211, 180 Rutherford Hill Rd), off the Silverado Trail. This is a quintessential Wine Country dining experience – French with a California twist – and is priced accordingly ($30 to $40 a meal, or more).

There is camping near Rutherford on the shores of Lake Berryessa, at the privately owned *Lake Berryessa Marina Resort* (☎ 707-966-2161, 5800 Knoxville Rd). Seventy sites for tents ($15) and about 50 with hookups for RVs ($21) are complemented by a full-service marina. The RV sites and marina are open year round, but tent sites are available only from March to late October. Reservations are recommended in summer. To get there from Rutherford, take Hwy 128 (Sage Canyon Rd) about 11 miles east and go left (north) on Berryessa Knoxville Rd for 9 miles.

ST HELENA

• **population 5925** • **elevation 255 feet**

The St Helena Hwy runs right through the small town of St Helena (pronounced ha-LEE-na) and is called Main St in town. St Helena has many interesting old buildings to walk around and plenty of restaurants, but it can get uncomfortably busy on summer weekends.

The chamber of commerce (☎ 707-963-4456), 1010 Main St, Suite A, is open 10 am to 5 pm weekdays, until 3 pm Saturday. St Helena Cyclery (☎ 707-963-7736), 1156 Main St, rents bicycles for $7/25 per hour/day.

The free **Silverado Museum** (☎ 707-963-3757), 1490 Library Lane, has a fascinating collection of Robert Louis Stevenson memorabilia. In 1880, the famous author – at that time sick, penniless and unknown – stayed in an abandoned bunkhouse at the old Silverado Mine with his new wife, Fanny Osbourne. His novel *The Silverado Squatters* is based on his time there. The museum is open noon to 4 pm Tuesday to Sunday. To reach Library Lane, turn east off the St Helena Hwy at the Adams St traffic lights and cross the railway tracks.

Places to Stay

See the following Calistoga section for information on camping at Bothe-Napa Valley State Park, midway between St Helena and Calistoga.

Pleasant *El Bonita Motel* (☎ 707-963-3216, 195 Main St) has rooms for $95 to $150 in high season (summer, holidays and weekends), $79 to $109 in low season. Right in the center of town, the *Hotel St Helena* (☎ 707-963-4388, 1309 Main St) dates from 1881 and has 18 rooms (some with private bathroom) for $165 to $195 in high season, $112 to $165 in low season. The *Harvest Inn* (☎ 707-963-9463, 800-950-8466, 1 Main St) offers 54 rooms in a Tudor-style building. It has two pools, lots of luxuries and prices from $120 to over $300.

California's oldest resort, *White Sulphur Springs Resort* (☎ 707-963-8588, 3100 White Sulphur Springs Rd) is a peaceful place, with hot springs, a swimming pool and a redwood grove. Private cottages are $135/155 weekdays/weekends, rooms at the inn are $105/115, and smaller rooms with shared bathroom in the Carriage House are $85/95. Driving north on the St Helena Hwy, go *past* the Sulphur Springs St exit and continue into St Helena; after the first traffic light turn left (west) onto Spring St (which becomes White Sulphur Springs Rd) and continue straight for 3 miles.

Places to Eat

The *Model Bakery* (1357 Main St) serves great scones, muffins and coffee (closed Monday). *Gillwoods Cafe* (☎ 707-963-1788, 1313 Main St) is a straightforward diner. *Armadillo's* (1304 Main St) is a bright Mexican restaurant with reasonable prices.

St Helena has some interesting places for a classy meal, but remember to make reservations. *Pairs Parkside Cafe* (☎ 707-963-7566, 1420 Main St) is simple, reasonably priced ($7 to $12 a meal), romantic and memorable – a real find. The menu covers everything from homemade soups to decadent pasta and meat dishes.

On the southern edge of town, just off Main St, *Tra Vigne* (☎ 707-963-4444, 1050 Charter Oak Ave) is a stylish Italian restaurant with a reputation for some of the best food in the valley (entrées $18 to $25). The *Cantinetta*, in Tra Vigne's walled garden patio, is a deli and wine shop that serves quicker, less-expensive meals than the main restaurant.

The *Wine Spectator Greystone Restaurant* (☎ 707-967-1010, 2555 Main St) is run by the renowned Culinary Institute of America.

CALISTOGA

• population 4900 • elevation 365 feet

Calistoga is probably the most attractive town in Napa Valley, with numerous places to stay and eat. 'Calistoga' is synonymous with the bottled water that brandishes its name (Guiseppe Musante began bottling Calistoga mineral water here in 1924), yet more than pure mineral water bubbles up from below. Calistoga's natural hot springs have spawned a collection of spas where you can indulge in the local specialty, a hot mud bath.

It's said the town's curious name came from tongue-tied Sam Brannan, who founded the town in 1859 with the heartfelt belief that it would emulate the New York spa town of Saratoga, perhaps as the 'Calistoga' of 'Sara-fornia.'

Orientation & Information

Calistoga's shops and restaurants are strung along Lincoln Ave, stretching from the St Helena Hwy across to the Silverado Trail. City Hall, on Washington St, was built in 1902 as the Bedlam Opera House. The 1868 Old Railroad Depot on Lincoln Ave closed down in 1929 and now houses shops and restaurants.

The Chamber of Commerce & Visitors Center (☎ 707-942-6333), 1458 Lincoln Ave behind the Old Railroad Depot, is open to

Sam Brannan

Born in Maine in 1819, Sam Brannan was a larger-than-life character who roamed the US working in printing and newspapers. In 1845, he headed to California to found a Mormon colony. His passion for religious pioneering quickly faded, however, and in 1847 he founded San Francisco's first newspaper. It was Sam Brannan who, in 1848, announced to the world that gold had been discovered in the Sierra foothills, sparking the gold rush. The healthy properties of Calistoga's spas and springs were his next discovery. His luck ran out toward the end of his colorful life, and he died penniless in 1888.

at least 4 pm daily. The Calistoga Bookstore (☎ 707-942-4123), 1343 Lincoln Ave, has a wide variety of books.

Things to See
Created by an ex-Disney animator, the **Sharpsteen Museum** (☎ 707-942-5911), 1311 Washington St, has a collection of dioramas showing scenes from the town's colorful history, and a restored cottage from Brannan's original Calistoga resort. (The only Brannan cottage still at its original site is at 106 Wapoo Ave, near the Brannan Cottage Inn.) The museum is free and open noon to 4 pm daily.

Activities
For information on glider flights and hot-air balloon rides, see the Activities section at the beginning of this chapter.

Spas & Mud Baths Basking up to your neck in a tub full of mud is all the rage in Calistoga. The town has a collection of hot-spring spas and mud-bath emporiums where you can be buried in hot mud and emerge much better for the experience. Mud-bath packages take 60 to 90 minutes and cost from around $45. You start semi-submerged in hot mud, then take a shower, then soak in hot mineral water. An optional steam bath

and a cooling towel-wrap follow. The treatment can be extended to include a massage, pushing the cost up to $90 or more.

Baths can be taken solo or, in some establishments, as couples. Variations can include thin mud baths (called *fango* baths), herbal wraps, seaweed baths and all sorts of exotic massages. Discount coupons are sometimes available from the visitor center. It's wise to book ahead, especially on summer weekends.

Besides Harbin Hot Springs (see 'A Harbin Memoir' boxed text) and the White Sulphur Springs Resort (see St Helena Places to Stay), you can try the following spa centers in downtown Calistoga:

Dr Wilkinson's Hot Springs
  (☎ 707-942-4102) 1507 Lincoln Ave
Golden Haven Hot Springs
  (☎ 707-942-6793) 1713 Lake St
Lincoln Avenue Spa
  (☎ 707-942-5296) 1339 Lincoln Ave
Nance's Hot Springs
  (☎ 707-942-6211) 1614 Lincoln Ave

Bicycling Getaway Adventures (☎ 707-942-0332), 1117 Lincoln Ave, rents bicycles for $25 per day. Bikes can also be rented at similar rates from Palisades Mountain Sports (☎ 707-942-9687), 1330B Gerrard St, behind the post office on Washington St.

Places to Stay
Camping & Cabins There are tent ($10) and RV ($18) sites a few blocks north of the town center at the *Napa County Fairgrounds* (☎ 707-942-5111, 1435 Oak St). The scenery is a bit better at the *Bothe-Napa Valley State Park* (☎ 707-942-4575), 3 miles south of Calistoga on the St Helena Hwy. Tent sites ($15) can be reserved by calling ParkNet (☎ 800-444-7275).

Economizers can head south on the Silverado Trail to the *Calistoga Ranch Club* (☎ 707-942-6565, 580 Lommel Rd). The 167-acre grounds have tent sites ($19), four-person cabins ($50 and up) and a swimming pool. (See the Napa Valley map.)

Two and a half miles northwest of town is the *Triple-S-Ranch* (☎ 707-942-6730, 4600

Mt Home Ranch Rd), where cabins start at $65. There's a swimming pool. The ranch is closed from January to the end of March. (See the Napa Valley map.)

Hotels Right in the center of town, the *Calistoga Inn & Brewery* (☎ 707-942-4101, *1250 Lincoln Ave*) is a historic hotel with 18 simple rooms with shared bathroom, priced at $49 on weekdays, $65 on weekends.

Just north of the town center, the *Comfort Inn* (☎ 707-942-9400, *1865 Lincoln Ave*) is a large motel with rooms as low as $65 on a winter weekday, and up to $105 on a summer weekend.

B&Bs Close to the center of town, *The Elms B&B* (☎ 707-942-9476, *1300 Cedar St*) has seven comfortable and well-equipped rooms priced from $115 to $155 on weekdays, $125 to $180 on weekends. The *Brannan Cottage Inn* (☎ 707-942-4200, *109 Wapoo Ave*) is on the National Register of Historic Places and charges $115 to $155.

Spa Hotels Several hotels double as spas, and vice versa. Besides Harbin Hot Springs (see 'A Harbin Memoir' boxed text), try the *Roman Spa Motel* (☎ 707-942-4441, *1300 Washington St*), which includes free use of its three mineral pools (mud baths and massage packages are extra). Standard rooms are $77/106 weekdays/weekends, and rooms with kitchens are $90/122.

Rooms at *Nance's Hot Springs* (☎ 707-942-6211, *1614 Lincoln Ave*) have kitchenettes and cost $70 midwinter, $95 and up in summer. Spa treatments are extra.

Though it may seem expensive, the *Euro Spa & Inn* (☎ 707-942-6829, *1202 Pine St*), a few blocks back from Lincoln Ave, is not a bad deal. Two 90-minute spa packages (mud bath, sauna and more) are included in the room rates, which are $189/279 weekdays/weekends.

The popular *Mount View Hotel* (☎ 707-942-6877, *1457 Lincoln Ave*) combines historic style with modern facilities (mud baths and swimming pool). Rooms are $120 on weekdays, $150 and up on weekends. This is a great place to splurge.

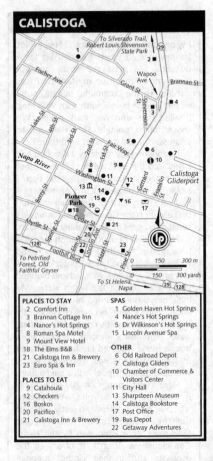

CALISTOGA

PLACES TO STAY	SPAS
2 Comfort Inn	1 Golden Haven Hot Springs
3 Brannan Cottage Inn	4 Nance's Hot Springs
4 Nance's Hot Springs	5 Dr Wilkinson's Hot Springs
8 Roman Spa Motel	15 Lincoln Avenue Spa
9 Mount View Hotel	
18 The Elms B&B	**OTHER**
21 Calistoga Inn & Brewery	6 Old Railroad Depot
23 Euro Spa & Inn	7 Calistoga Gliders
	10 Chamber of Commerce &
PLACES TO EAT	Visitors Center
9 Catahoula	11 City Hall
12 Checkers	13 Sharpsteen Museum
16 Boskos	14 Calistoga Bookstore
20 Pacifico	17 Post Office
21 Calistoga Inn & Brewery	19 Bus Depot
	22 Getaway Adventures

Places to Eat

Lincoln Ave has plenty of dining possibilities. Starting at the Foothill Blvd end there's *Pacifico* (☎ 707-942-4400, *1237 Lincoln Ave*), with excellent and reasonably priced Mexican food; the *Calistoga Inn & Brewery* (☎ 707-942-4101, *1250 Lincoln Ave*), with tasty microbrews and moderately priced California cuisine; and *Boskos* (☎ 707-942-9088, *1364 Lincoln Ave*), a popular pizzeria and pasta specialist. *Checkers* (☎ 707-942-9300, *1414 Lincoln Ave*) is part of a small gourmet-pizza chain.

A Harbin Memoir

My one and only experience at Harbin Hot Springs started when I signed up for a *wassertanzen* massage, mostly because the name sounded so mysterious. I was directed to the communal mineral pool, where I met a tall Swedish man with long flowing hair who was stark naked. We shook hands politely. He asked me to undress. Um, did he mean right there?

Conquering my modesty, I disrobed and eased into the pool, where a dozen other naked people paid me little attention. I began wondering what sort of massage I had gotten myself into. Then I remembered that *wasser* is the German word for water. I could only guess at the meaning of *tanzen*.

For the next hour, the Swedish man and I engaged in something not unlike a naked water ballet. My body was contorted, and I was grabbed, pulled, whisked and plunged under and through the warm water. My initial nervousness turned into stoic acceptance, which in turn became relaxation. By the end I was honestly enjoying this underwater pummeling, despite the odd looks from a friend who had finished her shiatsu massage early and was wondering why I was dancing in the pool with a naked man.

Harbin Hot Springs (☎ 707-987-2477) is about 4 miles beyond Middletown, which in turn is 12 miles directly north of Calistoga, beyond the Robert Louis Stevenson State Park. Run by the Heart Consciousness Church, it offers all the usual spa stuff in their 'clothes optional' pools; for massage appointments, call ☎ 707-987-3801. There's also a simple vegetarian restaurant (for spa guests only).

Dorm accommodations cost $30 to $45, and you must bring your own linen. Camping facilities are also available, as are rooms with shared bathroom ($75/105 weekdays/weekends), rooms with private bathroom ($100/150) and fully equipped cabins ($185 and up).

– Scott McNeely

The food at upscale *Catahoula* (☎ 707-942-2275, 1457 Lincoln Ave), in the Mount View Hotel, is hearty Cajun fare (entrées $12 to $20). The best seats are those at the bar (which has a separate, less-expensive dinner menu), where you can watch owner-chef Jan Birnbaum at work. Catahoula is closed Tuesday.

AROUND CALISTOGA
Bale Grist Mill State Historic Park

There are good picnicking opportunities at this small state park (☎ 707-963-2236), and a mile-long hiking trail that leads to the adjacent Bothe-Napa Valley State Park. Also here is a 36-foot wheel, dating from 1846, that once ground the local farmers' grain to flour.

The mill and park are visible from the St Helena Hwy, midway between St Helena and Calistoga, and are open 10 am to 5 pm daily; admission is $2. In early October, the living history festival, Old Mill Days, is celebrated here.

Old Faithful Geyser

Featured in *National Geographic* in 1948, Calistoga's slightly smaller version of Yellowstone's Old Faithful spouts off on a fairly regular 50-minute cycle, shooting boiling water 60 feet into the air. The geyser (☎ 707-942-6463) is about 2 miles north of town at 1299 Tubbs Lane, off the Silverado Trail. The site is open 9 am to 6 pm daily (to 5 pm in winter). Entry is $6, and local newspapers often have discount coupons.

Petrified Forest

Three million years ago, a volcanic eruption at Mt St Helena blew down a stand of redwood trees between Calistoga and Santa Rosa. The trees all fell in the same direction, pointing away from the center of the blast and were covered in ash and mud. Over the millennia the trunks of these mighty trees were petrified or turned into stone and gradually the overlay eroded away to expose the trunks. The first stumps were discovered in 1870, and a monument marks the visit to the petrified forest by Robert Louis Stevenson in 1880. He described his visit in *The Silverado Squatters.*

The forest (☎ 707-942-6667) is at 4100 Petrified Forest Rd, 1½ miles north of town off Hwy 128 (see the Napa Valley map). It's open 10 am to at least 4:30 pm daily; $4.

Robert Louis Stevenson State Park

The long-extinct volcano cone of Mt St Helena closes off the end of the valley, 8 miles north of Calistoga, in this undeveloped state park (☎ 707-942-4575), at the end of Hwy 29 (see the Napa Valley map). It's a tiring 5-mile climb to the peak's 4343-foot summit, but clear weather will reward walkers with superb views. The park includes the site of the old Silverado Mine where Stevenson and his wife, Fanny, honeymooned in 1880. Entry is free.

Sonoma Valley

'Slonoma,' the locals' term for their relaxing, livable wine town, hints at the low-key charms of the 17-mile-long Sonoma Valley. With its family-owned wineries and quiet rural back roads, the 'Valley of the Moon' (Jack London's literary name for the region) is a much more enjoyable place to wander around than the somewhat sterile Napa Valley.

The town of Sonoma, at the southern end of the valley, is surrounded by wineries and has a fascinating history. Santa Rosa, at the northern end, is the valley's 'metropolis.' The main road through the valley is the Sonoma Hwy (Hwy 12), but make an effort to explore some of the quiet lanes and roads just off the highway.

If you have excess energy after visiting the Sonoma Valley wineries, you can drive northwest to the small, high-quality wineries around Healdsburg or along the Russian River near Guerneville (see the North Coast chapter).

SONOMA VALLEY WINERIES

The wine is just as good as Napa Valley's, but the wineries in Sonoma Valley are less crowded, and free tastings are still the norm. In contrast to the 230-plus Napa wineries, there are only 50 or so here. If you don't have a car, the town of Sonoma makes a good base, as there are several wineries within easy bicycling distance of the town center.

The following wineries are listed in south-north order, beginning a few miles south of the town of Sonoma. You can purchase winery maps and load up on discount coupons at the southern branch of the Sonoma Valley Visitors Bureau (☎ 707-935-4747), on the grounds of the Viansa winery. It's open 9 am to 5 pm daily.

Viansa The views are idyllic from this small hilltop winery (☎ 707-935-4700), 25200 Arnold Drive, off Hwy 121, a few miles southeast of Sonoma in what's actually known as the Carneros region. Free tastings are offered 10 am to 5 pm daily, and there are free self-guided tours of the grounds.

Gundlach-Bundschu One of Sonoma Valley's oldest wineries, Gundlach-Bundschu (☎ 707-938-5277), 2000 Denmark St, Sonoma, was founded by a Bavarian immigrant in 1858. Although grapes continued to be grown on the property right through Prohibition, wine production did not recommence until 1973. The winery is reached by a winding road and has a peaceful lake and

sedate hiking trails. Free tastings are offered 11 am to 4:30 pm daily.

Buena Vista This historic winery (☎ 707-938-1266), 18000 Old Winery Rd, Sonoma, dates back to 1857, when it was purchased by the pioneering Hungarian vintner Count Ágoston Haraszthy. It has a fine old building with art displays. Free tastings, offered 10:30 am to 5 pm daily, are held in the Press House. Guided tours are offered at 11 am and 2 pm on most days (reservations are recommended).

Sebastiani There are regular guided tours of this venerable old winery in the heart of the town of Sonoma (☎ 707-938-5532), 389 4th St E. It was founded by monks in 1825 and purchased in 1904 by Samuele Sebastiani. Free tastings are offered 10 am to 5 pm daily, and the last tour is at 4 pm.

Ravenswood This low-key winery in the hills behind Sebastiani (☎ 707-938-1960), 18701 Gehricke Rd off Lovall Valley Rd, Sonoma, is famous for its award-winning Zinfandel. There's a daily winery tour at 10:30 am (reservations required), and free tastings 10 am to 4:30 pm daily.

Valley of the Moon This small, relaxed winery (☎ 707-996-6941), 777 Madrone Rd, Glen Ellen, is just far enough off busy Hwy 12 to escape heavy traffic. The modern winery is not much to look at, but the Merlot, Zinfandel and vintage port are superb. Free tastings are offered 10 am to 4:30 pm daily.

Benziger On the road up to Jack London State Historic Park, this interesting and educational winery (☎ 707-935-3000), 1883 London Ranch Rd, Glen Ellen, includes a do-it-yourself walk through the grapevines and tractor-trailer tours of the whole winery, which is open daily 10 am to 5 pm. Interesting art exhibits include a display of wine label artwork. There's also a picnic area. Unfortunately, not all the free tasting wines are up to snuff – the whites are especially mediocre. It's worth paying $5 to sample the reserve wines.

Chateau St Jean There's a short self-guided tour of this beautiful, sprawling winery (☎ 707-833-4134), 8555 Sonoma Hwy (Hwy 12), Kenwood, which is noted for its whites (the Gewürztraminer is especially good) and for its pleasant picnic area. Free tastings are offered 10 am to 4:30 pm daily.

SONOMA
• **population 9200** • **elevation 81 feet**
The small town of Sonoma makes an excellent base for exploring the surrounding vineyards. The town can be oppressively crowded on summer weekends, when traffic clogs the otherwise peaceful streets that border green and leafy Sonoma Plaza. This plaza – plus the adjacent Sonoma Mission and 19th-century barracks – loudly proclaims the town's Mexican heritage.

Sonoma has celebrations, cook-offs, concerts and wine auctions that take place throughout the year. Check with the visitors bureau for details.

History
Believe it or not, Sonoma was the site of a second American revolution, this time against Mexico. In 1846, California was an uneasy place. Mexico had neither the resources nor the energy to effectively manage far-flung centers like Sonoma, and the growing number of American settlers was leading to increased tension.

General Mariano Guadalupe Vallejo, the last Mexican governor of California, suggested that an American takeover was in the best interests of the region. Sensing an opening, American frontiersmen occupied the lightly guarded Sonoma presidio and declared independence. They dubbed California the Bear Flag Republic, after the battle flag they had fashioned. The unfortunate Vallejo was thereafter bundled off to imprisonment in Sacramento.

Despite its early success, the republic was short-lived. Only a month later the Mexican-American War broke out and California was taken over by the US government. The abortive revolt did, however, give California its state flag, which still proclaims 'California Republic.'

WINE COUNTRY

SONOMA VALLEY & SONOMA

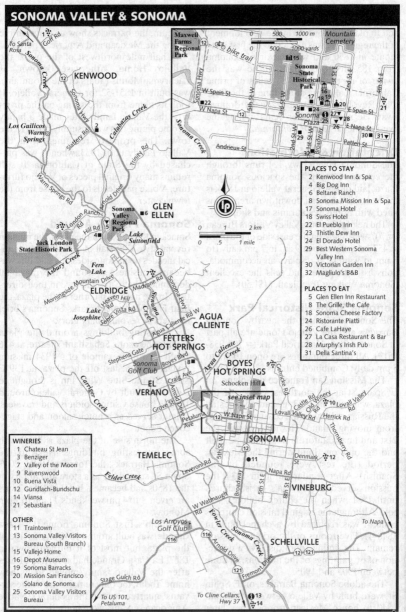

To Santa Rosa

Golf Rd

Sonoma Creek

KENWOOD

Los Guilicos Warm Springs

Calabazas Creek

Slattery Rd

Trinity Rd

Warm Springs Rd

Arnold Drive

London Ranch Rd

Hill Rd

Sonoma Valley Regional Park

GLEN ELLEN

Jack London State Historic Park

Asbury Creek

Fern Lake

Lake Suttonfield

Morningside Mountain Drive

Heaven Hill Rd

Sobre Vista Rd

Lake Josephine

ELDRIDGE

Madrone Rd

Sonoma Creek

Sonoma Hwy

AGUA CALIENTE

Agua Caliente Rd W

FETTERS HOT SPRINGS

Stephens Gate

Boyes Blvd

Agua Caliente Creek

BOYES HOT SPRINGS

Sonoma Golf Club

Schocken Hill

Craig Ave

EL VERANO

Carriger Creek

Grove St

Arnold Drive

Castle Rd

Old Winery Rd

Lovall Valley

Lovall Valley Rd

Herrick Rd

Thornsberry Rd

Petaluma Ave

W Napa St

SONOMA

see inset map

Denmark St

Napa Rd

TEMELEC

Felder Creek

Leveroni Rd

5th St W

Broadway

5th St E

8th St E

VINEBURG

To Napa

W Watmaugh Rd

Los Arroyos Golf Club

Fowler Creek

Sonoma Creek

SCHELLVILLE

Stage Gulch Rd

To US 101, Petaluma

To Cline Cellars, Hwy 37

Arnold Drive

Fremont Drive

Inset map (Sonoma)

Maxwell Farms Regional Park

bike trail

0   500   1000 m
0   500   1000 yards

Mountain Cemetery

Sonoma State Historical Park

5th St W

W Spain St

W Napa St

2nd St W

Andrieux St

Sonoma Plaza

Broadway

E Spain St

E Napa St

Patten St

1st St E

PLACES TO STAY

2 Kenwood Inn & Spa
4 Big Dog Inn
6 Beltane Ranch
8 Sonoma Mission Inn & Spa
17 Sonoma Hotel
18 Swiss Hotel
22 El Pueblo Inn
23 Thistle Dew Inn
24 El Dorado Hotel
29 Best Western Sonoma Valley Inn
32 Victorian Garden Inn
32 Magliulo's B&B

PLACES TO EAT

5 Glen Ellen Inn Restaurant
8 The Grille, the Cafe
18 Sonoma Cheese Factory
24 Ristorante Piatti
26 Cafe LaHaye
27 La Casa Restaurant & Bar
28 Murphy's Irish Pub
31 Della Santina's

WINERIES

1 Chateau St Jean
3 Benziger
7 Valley of the Moon
9 Ravenswood
10 Buena Vista
12 Gundlach-Bundschu
14 Viansa
21 Sebastiani

OTHER

11 Traintown
13 Sonoma Valley Visitors Bureau (South Branch)
15 Vallejo Home
16 Depot Museum
19 Sonoma Barracks
20 Mission San Francisco Solano de Sonoma
25 Sonoma Valley Visitors Bureau

WINE COUNTRY

Vallejo, whose name pops up all over the town, was soon back in Sonoma and continued to play a major role in the development of the region. He was elected to the first state senate in 1850 and was mayor of Sonoma from 1852 to 1860. Although he was the owner of more than 273 sq miles of prime California real estate at the time of the Bear Flag Revolt, his fortune gradually drained away. He spent his later years writing the five-volume *History of California*.

Orientation & Information

The Sonoma Hwy (Hwy 12) runs through the center of town. The spacious Sonoma Plaza, laid out by General Vallejo in 1834, is the heart of the small downtown area and is lined with hotels, restaurants and shops.

The helpful Sonoma Valley Visitors Bureau (☎ 707-996-1090), on the east side of the plaza at 453 1st St E, is open 9 am to 7 pm daily (to 5 pm in winter). It displays an accommodations list with prices and sells the excellent 'Sonoma Walking Tour' leaflet ($1.50).

Sonoma State Historical Park

The Sonoma Mission, the nearby Sonoma Barracks and the Vallejo Home are all part of Sonoma State Historical Park (☎ 707-938-1519). All three buildings are open 10 am to 5 pm daily. Combined entry is $2.

The **Mission San Francisco de Solano**, on E Spain St at the northeast corner of the plaza, was built in 1823, in part to forestall the Russian colony on the coast at Fort Ross from moving inland. The mission was the 21st and final California mission to be built and the only one built during the Mexican period (the rest were founded by the Spanish). After secularization in 1834, the mission served as Sonoma's parish church until 1881, when the church building was sold. Although the original mission church is gone, it was replaced by a chapel built in 1840-41. Five rooms of the original mission remain. The dining room displays a collection of 61 paintings of the missions, all done between 1903 and 1905.

The adobe **Sonoma Barracks**, on E Spain St, were built by Vallejo between 1836 and 1840 to house Mexican troops. They later became American military quarters before starting a long and varied civilian life. Now a museum, the barracks show displays on life during the Mexican and American periods.

A half mile northwest of the plaza, the **Vallejo Home**, otherwise known as Lachryma Montis (Tears of the Mountain), was built in 1851-52 for General Vallejo. It took its name from the spring on the property; the Vallejo family later made a handy income piping this water supply down to the town. The property remained with the Vallejo family until 1933, when it was purchased by the State of California. It still retains many original pieces of Vallejo furniture. A bike path leads to the house from the town center.

Sonoma Plaza & Around

Smack in the middle of the plaza, the mission revival-style **City Hall** of 1906-08 has identical facades on all four sides. It's said this was because businesses around the plaza all demanded that City Hall face in their direction. In the northeast corner of the plaza, the **Bear Flag Monument** marks Sonoma's brief moment of revolutionary glory.

Interesting buildings around the plaza include the exotic **Sebastiani Theatre**, at 476 1st St E, a fine example of a 1934 mission revival cinema. Just off the plaza, at 139 E Spain St, the **Blue Wing Inn** is thought to have been built by General Vallejo around 1840 to house visiting soldiers and travelers. It later served as a hotel, saloon and stagecoach depot.

The north side of the plaza is lined with some interesting buildings. Next to the Sonoma Barracks, the **Toscano Hotel,** 20 E Spain St, started life as a store and library in the 1850s and became a hotel in 1886. Tours are given 1 to 4 pm weekends, 11 am to 1 pm Monday.

Vallejo's first Sonoma home, **La Casa Grande**, was built around 1835 on this side of the plaza, but most of it burned down in 1867. La Casa Grande had a variety of uses after the Vallejo family moved to its new home. Today, the only remains are of the servants' quarters, where the general's Native American servants were housed.

WINE COUNTRY

Depot Museum

North of the plaza in Depot Park, the Depot Museum (☎ 707-938-1762) has art and historical exhibits. The museum building has had a checkered history. In the 1880s, a railway line ran along Spain St to the plaza; the depot building was built on the north side, and the railway company gradually took over most of the plaza, until public protests against the railway's encroachment on public land forced its move to Depot Park.

The railway closed down in 1917, but when the old building was being converted into a museum it burned down. The current building is a 1978 replica of the original. A bicycle trail now follows the route the train once took through town. The museum is open 1 to 4 pm Wednesday to Sunday; admission is free.

Traintown

At Traintown (☎ 707-938-3912), 1 mile south of the plaza on Broadway, a miniature steam engine makes 20-minute trips for $3.75. There's also a Ferris wheel ($1.50), merry-go-round ($1) and petting zoo. From October to May, the train operates every 20 minutes from 10 am to 5 pm Friday to Sunday. June to September it runs daily.

Bicycling

Sonoma Valley Cyclery (☎ 707-935-3377), 20093 Broadway, rents bicycles for $20 to $25 per day. Bikes are $5/25 per hour/day at Good Time Bicycles (☎ 707-938-0453), 18503 Sonoma Hwy (Hwy 12), north of the center toward Santa Rosa.

Places to Stay

Camping The nearest campground is in *Sugarloaf Ridge State Park* (☎ 707-833-5712, 2605 Adobe Canyon Rd), just north of Kenwood. You can reserve sites ($15) by calling ParkNet (☎ 800-444-7275).

If you're in a pinch, there are also sites for tents ($29) and RVs ($35) at the *Petaluma KOA* (☎ 707-763-1492, 20 Rainsville Rd), off Hwy 101, in the city of Petaluma. You'll get more peace and quiet at *Spring Lake Regional Park* in Santa Rosa (see Santa Rosa Places to Stay).

Hotels & Motels The cheapest option is *El Pueblo Inn* (☎ 707-996-3651, 806 W Napa St), with standard motel rooms starting at $75 on weekdays, $90 on weekends. The *Best Western Sonoma Valley Inn* (☎ 707-938-9200, 550 2nd St W), a block west of the plaza, is an OK deal during the week ($80 to $115) but a bit expensive on weekends, when there's a two-night minimum stay ($160 to $195 per night).

There are a number of stylish older hotels right on the plaza. The fine old *Swiss Hotel* (☎ 707-938-2884, 18 W Spain St) has just five elegant rooms, all different and all with wavy floors and walls to show just what a historic place it is. Rates are $100 to $120 weekdays, $110 to $130 weekends. The *Sonoma Hotel* (☎ 707-996-2996, 110 W Spain St) has renovated rooms for $155 to $220. At *El Dorado Hotel* (☎ 707-996-3030, 405 1st St W), rooms have balconies, there's a pool and breakfast is included in the price ($120/150 weekdays/weekends).

Outside of town, in Glen Ellen, are the plantation-style *Beltane Ranch* (☎ 707-996-6501, 11775 Sonoma Hwy), where rooms range in price from $130 to $180, and the homey and similarly priced *Big Dog Inn* (☎ 707-996-4319, 15244 Arnold Drive), where the owners breed St Bernards.

B&Bs The four-room *Magliulo's B&B* (☎ 707-996-1031, 681 Broadway) is a short distance south of Sonoma Plaza and has rooms for $85 (shared bathroom) to $110 (private bathroom). The *Victorian Garden Inn* (☎ 707-996-5339, 316 E Napa St) charges from $95 to $175 a night. The old house dates from 1870 and has a swimming pool. The *Thistle Dew Inn* (☎ 707-938-2909, 171 W Spain St) has six rooms ranging in price from $120 to $185.

Spa Hotels The ultimate splurge is the peacefully pink *Sonoma Mission Inn & Spa* (☎ 707-938-9000, 800-862-4945, 18140 Sonoma Hwy), at Boyes Hot Springs. It's the perfect spot for an indulgent weekend getaway – especially if you sign up for one of the $750-a-night rooms. Other rooms spiral gradually down in price to $175 a night.

WINE COUNTRY

Nonguests can use the spa facilities on weekdays and Sunday afternoon.

The incomparable **Kenwood Inn & Spa** (☎ 707-833-1293, 10400 Sonoma Hwy), north of Glen Ellen, is a luxurious 12-room getaway charging $250 to $375 a night.

Places to Eat

If you're stocking up for a picnic, **Sonoma Cheese Factory** (☎ 800-535-2855), right on Sonoma Plaza, is the 'Home of Sonoma Jack' and has everything you'll need, including free cheese tastings. A **farmers' market** takes place every Friday morning on the plaza.

Cafe LaHaye (☎ 707-935-5994, 140 E Napa St) is great for breakfast ($5 to $10). The Mexican roots of the region shine at **La Casa Restaurant & Bar** (☎ 707-996-3406, 121 E Spain St), an inexpensive favorite near the mission.

Della Santina's (☎ 707-935-0576, 133 E Napa St) is a small trattoria that cooks up yummy Tuscan food ($7 to $20) for eat-in or take-out. If you're craving wood-oven-cooked pizzas, head to the moderately priced **Ristorante Piatti** (☎ 707-996-2351, 405 1st St W), in El Dorado Hotel.

Murphy's Irish Pub (☎ 707-935-0660, 464 1st St E), in an alley off the plaza, has good pub grub, beer and live music.

The Grille (☎ 707-938-9000, 18140 Sonoma Hwy), at the Sonoma Mission Inn & Spa, is one of Sonoma Valley's 'in' places, and advance reservations are a must. The food is classic California cuisine, with entrées from $15 to $25. It's easier to get a table at **The Café**, the spa's less-expensive bistro.

An excellent place for California cuisine in Glen Ellen is the **Glen Ellen Inn Restaurant** (☎ 707-996-6409, 13670 Arnold Drive). Entrées are $15 to $30.

JACK LONDON STATE HISTORIC PARK

Napa Valley has Robert Louis Stevenson, Sonoma has Jack London, and this park (☎ 707-938-5216), off Hwy 12, past the small settlement of Glen Ellen, traces the last years of London's short life. Shuffling occupations from Oakland fisherman to Alaska gold prospector to Pacific yachtsman – and of course, novelist on the side – London finished by taking up farming. He bought Beauty Ranch in 1905 and moved there permanently in 1910; today, he would have been called an organic farmer. With his wife, Charmian, he lived and wrote in a small cottage while his huge mansion, Wolf House, was being built. On the eve of its completion in 1913 it burned down. The cause was never determined but it was probably arson; the staunchly socialist London certainly had enemies. The disaster was a devastating blow, and although he toyed with the idea of rebuilding, he died (in 1916) before construction got under way.

After his death, Charmian built the House of Happy Walls, which is now preserved as a Jack London **museum**. It's a half-mile walk from there to the remains of Wolf House, passing London's **grave** along the way. Other walking paths wind around the farm to the cottage where he lived and worked. Trails, some of them open to mountain bikes, lead farther into the park. Be warned that thickets of poison oak await those who wander off the trails.

The park and its attractions are open 10 am to 5 pm daily. Entry is free, if you don't count the $6 parking fee.

SANTA ROSA

• population 136,100 • elevation 164 feet

Two cartoonists and a horticulturist are Santa Rosa's claims to fame. This sprawling city is the Wine Country's major population center and offers reasonably priced accommodations, but there's not a lot of reason to hang around. The Sonoma County Harvest Fair (☎ 707-545-4200) runs from late July to early August, a busy but excellent time to stop by.

Orientation & Information

The Santa Rosa Visitors Bureau (☎ 707-577-8674) is in the railroad depot at 9 4th St (take the downtown Santa Rosa exit off Hwy 12 or Hwy 101). It's open 8:30 am to 5 pm weekdays, 10 am to 3 pm weekends.

The main shopping stretch is along 4th St, which abruptly ends at Hwy 101 but reemerges on the other side in the historic Railway Square area. There are a number of downtown parking lots with free parking for the first 1½ hours.

Luther Burbank Home & Gardens

Luther Burbank (1849-1926), a pioneering horticulturist, developed many of his hybrid plant and tree species at his 19th-century Greek Revival home, at the corner of Santa Rosa and Sonoma Aves. The extensive gardens (☎ 707-524-5445) are free and open 8 am to 5 pm daily. The house and adjacent Carriage Museum, each with displays on Burbank's life and work, are open 10 am to 4 pm Tuesday to Sunday from April through October; admission is $3.

Church of One Tree

Robert Ripley was a Santa Rosa cartoonist who spent his life tracking down oddities to publish in his syndicated 'Believe It or Not!' column, which first appeared in 1918. A museum dedicated to Ripley was once housed in the Church of One Tree, a church built entirely from a single redwood tree. The museum is permanently closed, but there are plans to keep the church within Julliard Park, across Santa Rosa Ave from the Luther Burbank Home & Gardens.

Snoopy's Gallery

Cartoonist Charles Schulz is a long-term Santa Rosa resident, and his Peanuts cartoon strip can claim to have added 'security blanket' to the dictionary. The gallery has an awesome collection of Peanuts paraphernalia, while the mezzanine level recounts the story of the cartoon's worldwide success.

Snoopy's Gallery (☎ 707-546-3385) is at 1667 W Steele Lane beside the Redwood Empire Ice Arena, 2½ miles north of downtown off Hwy 101. It's open 10 am to 6 pm daily; admission is free.

Places to Stay

Camping Tent sites are $15 at *Spring Lake Regional Park* (☎ 707-539-8092), which is on Summerfield Drive adjacent to Annadel State Park. From downtown Santa Rosa, go east on 4th St, turn right on Farmer's Lane, go *past* the first Hoen St and turn left on the *second* Hoen St, go straight for a bit and then turn left on New Anga St, which leads to the park entrance. In total, it's a 4-mile drive.

Hotels & Motels The *Astro Motel* (☎ 707-545-8555, 323 Santa Rosa Ave) is beside Julliard Park and very close to downtown. This plain and simple motel has some of the lowest prices in town (doubles $38 to $50). The large *Days Inn* (☎ 707-573-9000, 175 Railroad St) is just off 3rd St west of Hwy 101, on the edge of Railroad Square. Rooms start at $89.

Historic *Hotel La Rose* (☎ 707-579-3200), in the Railroad Square area at 308 Wilson St, has comfortable rooms from $105 to $175.

Places to Eat

Almost any appetite can be satisfied downtown along 4th St, where there are also a number of bookstores, some with their own coffee bars. *Checkers* (☎ 707-578-4000, 523 4th St) is a sister restaurant to the popular Calistoga pizza and pasta specialist. *Caffe Portofino* (☎ 707-523-1171, 535 4th St) is a bustling and entertaining dinner stop, with pasta and meat entrées for around $10. Across the road, the *Santa Rosa Cantina* (☎ 707-523-3663, 500 4th St) is a big and bright Mexican eatery with reasonable prices. For Mediterranean cuisine with a vegetarian tilt, try *Fourth St Bistro* (☎ 707-526-2225, 645 4th St), where entrées cost $6 to $10.

The much pricier *Mixx* (☎ 707-573-1344, 135 4th St), at Davis St, has an eclectic menu and stays open reasonably late (closed Sunday).

Getting There & Away

Golden Gate Transit (☎ 707-541-2000, 415-923-2000) has daily buses from San Francisco's Transbay Terminal to Santa Rosa ($5.30) via Petaluma (Nos 72, 74 and 80). Sonoma County Transit (☎ 707-576-7433, 800-345-7433) has local bus routes up the Sonoma Valley. Greyhound has services from San Francisco to Santa Rosa and farther north along Hwy 101.

WINE COUNTRY

Sacramento Valley

As you head north from Sacramento, the northern reaches of the Central Valley are like the rest of the valley – flat, agricultural, very hot in summer, often shrouded in low-lying tule fog in winter. This chapter follows Hwys 70 and 99 through the valley. Along the route you'll find some delightful places to visit, from sleepy mining towns to vibrant, youthful university towns.

SACRAMENTO
- **population 396,500** - **elevation 25 feet**

On weekdays, Sacramento, California's capital, is a lively, get-things-done city filled with politicians, political aides and conventioneers. On weekends, the downtown empties out after sunset and feels like a ghost town. This is when tourists and residents of the Sacramento and San Joaquin valleys show up and populate Old Sacramento, Sutter's Fort and the very big, and very popular, Arden Fair Mall and Downtown Plaza shopping malls. Its skyline, impressive from afar, sprang up in the 1980s at the expense of street-level businesses.

The city's social climate depends partially on who is in office and what convention is in town. As the state capital, Sacramento has a stable economy, aided by the Port of Sacramento (the second-largest export harbor in the US), California State University Sacramento (known for its business school) and the satellite medical facilities of the University of California at Davis. All said, Sacramento isn't a boring place to visit, though California does have more appealing cities.

History
In 1839, Swiss immigrant John Sutter arrived in California and proposed to build an outpost north of San Francisco for the Mexican government. The government gave Sutter 76 sq miles of land around the confluence of the American and Sacramento rivers where, with the aid of local Miwok tribes, Sutter built an adobe fort, planted crops and

Highlights

- California State Railroad Museum – worth a trip to Sacramento for its interactive displays and classic locomotives
- California State Capitol – see where the decisions get made
- Marysville's Chinatown – a harbor of Buddhist traditions
- Chico – a vibrant yet laid-back university town

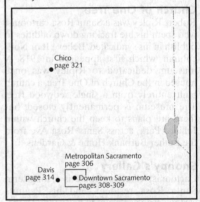

Chico
page 321

Metropolitan Sacramento
page 306

Davis
page 314

Downtown Sacramento
pages 308-309

ran cattle. As the only outpost between San Francisco and Vancouver, British Columbia, Sutter's Fort became a bastion of security and general rendezvous.

When James Marshall discovered gold in the tailrace of Sutter's lumber mill near Coloma in 1848, hundreds of thousands of people flocked to California, most of whom traveled through Sutter's Fort. Sam Brannan built several structures west of the fort, along the Sacramento River, to benefit from the new influx of miners. (See the boxed text 'Sam Brannan' in the Wine Country chapter.) Sutter gave his fort to his son, who christened the newly sprung town 'Sacramento.'

Though plagued by fires and flood, the riverfront settlement prospered and became the state capital in 1850.

Orientation

Sacramento sits at the confluence of the Sacramento and American rivers, roughly halfway between San Francisco and Lake Tahoe.

I-5 runs along the western edge of downtown between the city and the Sacramento River and becomes Hwy 99 when it leaves town to the north. I-80 goes west to San Francisco and northeast to Reno by way of Donner Pass and north Lake Tahoe. The I-80 Business route (Bus 80) cuts through downtown. Hwy 50 branches off Bus 80 toward Placerville and South Lake Tahoe.

Downtown, numbered streets run north-south, with 3rd St as the main thoroughfare going south (one way), and 5th St as the main thoroughfare going north (one way); lettered streets run east-west, with Capitol Ave (also called Capitol Mall) replacing M St.

Information

Sacramento's main Visitor Information Center (☎ 916-442-7644) is in Old Sacramento at 1101 2nd St and is open 9 am to 5 pm daily. The Convention and Visitor's Bureau (☎ 916-264-7777), 1421 K St, has bus schedules and information on current events. It is open 8 am to 5 pm weekdays.

The *Sacramento Bee*, the local daily newspaper, maintains an automated local information line (☎ 916-552-5252) covering weather, events and museum hours.

Money There's a concentration of banks downtown on J St, near the Downtown Plaza Mall. Regular banking hours are 9 am to 6 pm weekdays. The American Express office (☎ 916-441-1780), 515 L St, is open 9:30 am to 5:30 pm weekdays.

Post & Communications The main post office (☎ 916-263-7181) is at 2000 Royal Oaks Drive, and there's a small branch in the visitor center in Old Sacramento open 9 am to 5 pm daily.

Bookstores The best selection of Sacramento and California history books is in the gift shop of the capitol, open 9 am to 6 pm daily.

The Avid Reader (☎ 916-443-7323), across from the capitol at the corner of 10th and L Sts, has a good selection of maps, travel guides and photo books.

Laundry City Suds (☎ 916-443-1914), at the corner of 19th and L Sts, is open 7 am to 11 pm daily.

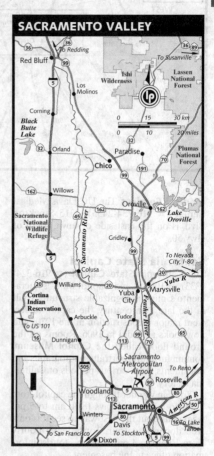

SACRAMENTO VALLEY

METROPOLITAN SACRAMENTO

1 Virgin Sturgeon
2 Canterbury Inn
3 Beverly Garland Hotel
4 Post Office
5 Red Lion Sacramento Inn
6 Granada Inn
7 UC Davis Medical Center

Medical Services The UC Davis Medical Center (☎ 916-734-2455), 2315 Stockton Blvd, is on the east side of town, south of Hwy 50.

California State Capitol

The **California State Capitol** (☎ 916-324-0333), at 10th St and Capitol Mall, is Sacramento's most recognizable structure. Built in the late 19th century, the capitol underwent major reconstruction in the 1970s and now looks as it did in 1906. Rooms on the ground floor, called the **Capitol Museum**, contain furniture, portraits, photographs and documents from various periods of California history.

You can wander through the capitol from 7 am to 6 pm weekdays (8:30 am to 5 pm weekends), but the best way to see it is on a free docent-led tour. Tours leave hourly from 10 am to 4 pm from the tourist information office in the basement.

The **Assembly** and **Senate rooms**, decorated in green and red respectively, are open to the public whenever each legislative body is in session. Sessions are held most Thursdays, beginning at 9:30 am, and can last from

20 minutes to 18 hours. For information, go to the Bills Office, in the basement next to the gift shop.

The 40 acres surrounding the capitol make up the **Capitol Park**, with trees from all over the world – a nice place to picnic or escape summer's heat. In the east end is a powerful and somewhat graphic Vietnam War memorial.

On 11th St, one block north of the capitol, are a smattering of graceful buildings. Look for the ornately embellished **Elks Lodge No 6**, built in the 1930s, and, at the corner of K and 11th Sts, the **Cathedral of the Blessed Sacrament**, built in the 1890s in the style of a 19th-century French cathedral.

Old Sacramento

Once a bustling river port filled with hopeful gold seekers, Old Sacramento (Old Sac) boasts California's largest concentration of buildings on the National Register of Historic Places, though they now contain candy stores, T-shirt shops and restaurants.

Besides the California State Railroad Museum, Old Sac's best feature is its riverfront setting. The **Spirit of Sacramento** (☎ 916-552-2933, 800-433-0263), an 1842 paddle wheeler, makes one-hour narrated tours of the Sacramento River worth the $10 ticket. The boat leaves hourly in summer from the L St dock across from the visitor center.

At Old Sac's north end, near where the notorious 'Big Four' – Leland Stanford, Mark Hopkins, Collis P Huntington and Charles Crocker – masterminded fundraising campaigns and track-laying strategies for the first transcontinental railroad, is the excellent **California State Railroad Museum** (☎ 916-445-6645, 916-445-7387), 125 I St, at 2nd St. Its well-displayed collection of locomotives, freight and passenger cars, toy models and memorabilia took 14 years to acquire. Tickets costs $6, and include entrance to the restored **Central Pacific Passenger Depot**, across the plaza from the museum entrance. Both are open 10 am to 5 pm daily. From here, on weekends from April to September, you can board a steam-powered passenger train ($5) for a short jaunt along the riverfront.

Next door to the railroad museum, the **Discovery Museum** (☎ 916-264-7057), 101 I St, has hands-on exhibits and a good display of gold rush-era artifacts. The museum is open from 10 am to 5 pm May to September, noon to 5 pm October to April (closed Monday); $4.

The decor in **Fat City** (☎ 916-446-6768), 1001 Front St, one of the city's best-known restaurants, is worth a look; the bar came from Leadville, Colorado, in 1876, and the stained glass 'Lady Wearing Purple' won first prize at the 1893 Chicago World's Fair.

Sutter's Fort State Historic Park

Now hemmed in by office buildings and medical centers, Sutter's Fort State Historic Park (☎ 916-455-4422), at the corner of 27th and L Sts, was once the only trace of civilization for hundreds of miles. Built by John Sutter, the fort welcomed European immigrants who, like Sutter, were eager to escape the rigidity of Europe and start anew in America.

The fort is restored to its 1850s appearance, complete with original furniture and equipment. Upon entering, you're given a handheld radio, which narrates a self-guided tour. The fort is open 10 am to 5 pm daily; $3. During Living History Days, usually held the first weekend of each month, docents dress in period costume and carry on with life as it would have been in the 1850s; admission then goes up to $5.

California State Indian Museum

On the north side of Sutter's Fort, the California State Indian Museum (☎ 916-324-0971), 2631 K St, has a thorough display of Native American costumes, handicrafts, tools and basketry. It is open 10 am to 5 pm daily; $3.

Crocker Art Museum

Housed in the Victorian-style home of Margaret and Judge Edwin B Crocker (tycoon Charles Crocker's brother) – which is a piece of art in itself – this museum (☎ 916-264-5423), at the corner of 3rd and O Sts, holds the first publicly displayed art collection in the western US. It also houses a good

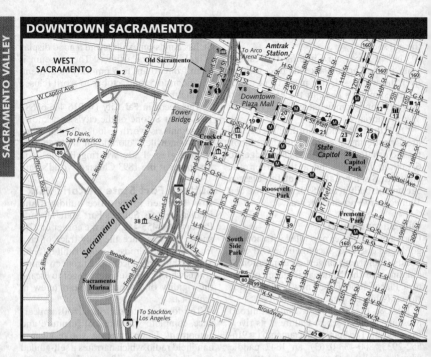

DOWNTOWN SACRAMENTO

show of California art after 1945 and hosts traveling exhibits. Museum hours are 10 am to 5 pm Tuesday to Sunday (to 9 pm Thursday); $4.50.

Leland Stanford Mansion

This mansion (☎ 916-324-0575), at the corner of 8th and N Sts, was built in 1859 by Leland Stanford. Under constant restoration, the mansion can be visited on a limited basis for free. The tour offered is unique in that it reveals flood-damaged floors and ceilings, as well as odd things found in the walls during restoration. Call for tour times.

Wells Fargo History Museum

Located in the Wells Fargo Center, at 400 Capitol Mall, this museum (☎ 916-440-4161) has a collection of original documents, photographs and lithographs from Sacramento's early days. Naturally, the museum's theme is Wells Fargo's 'instrumental role in settling

the West' – a reference to the first messenger's trip across the Sierra in 1852. The museum is open 10 am to 5 pm weekdays; free.

Governor's Mansion State Historic Park

Built in 1877 and acquired by the state in 1906, Sacramento's original governor's mansion (☎ 916-324-7405), 1526 H St, has housed 13 governors and their families. The mansion's furniture and architecture is as eclectic as the folks who've lived there, which makes the guided tours of the mansion (hourly from 10 am to 5 pm daily) worth the $3 cost of admission.

Towe Ford Museum

The 157 beautifully restored Ford cars and trucks housed in the Towe Ford Museum (☎ 916-442-6802), 2200 Front St, just west of I-5/Hwy 99 on the Sacramento River, are

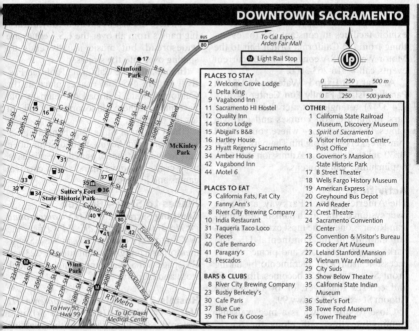

DOWNTOWN SACRAMENTO

To Cal Expo,
Arden Fair Mall

Ⓜ Light Rail Stop

PLACES TO STAY
2 Welcome Grove Lodge
4 Delta King
9 Vagabond Inn
11 Sacramento HI Hostel
12 Quality Inn
14 Econo Lodge
15 Abigail's B&B
16 Hartley House
23 Hyatt Regency Sacramento
34 Amber House
42 Vagabond Inn
44 Motel 6

PLACES TO EAT
5 California Fats, Fat City
7 Fanny Ann's
8 River City Brewing Company
10 India Restaurant
31 Taqueria Taco Loco
32 Pieces
40 Cafe Bernardo
41 Paragary's
43 Pescados

BARS & CLUBS
8 River City Brewing Company
23 Busby Berkeley's
30 Cafe Paris
37 Blue Cue
39 The Fox & Goose

OTHER
1 California State Railroad
   Museum, Discovery Museum
3 Spirit of Sacramento
6 Visitor Information Center,
   Post Office
13 Governor's Mansion
   State Historic Park
17 B Street Theater
18 Wells Fargo History Museum
19 American Express
20 Greyhound Bus Depot
21 Avid Reader
22 Crest Theatre
24 Sacramento Convention
   Center
25 Convention & Visitor's Bureau
26 Crocker Art Museum
27 Leland Stanford Mansion
28 Vietnam War Memorial
29 City Suds
33 Show Below Theater
35 California State Indian
   Museum
36 Sutter's Fort
38 Towe Ford Museum
45 Tower Theatre

SACRAMENTO VALLEY

enough to make any car enthusiast drool. Next door, the gift shop has a large collection of automobile memorabilia and picture books. Both are open 9 am to 6 pm daily; $5.

Tower Enclave

Around the landmark Tower Theatre (☎ 916-443-1982), an art-film house at 16th St and Broadway, are the flagships for the nationwide Tower chain of stores (☎ 800-275-8693), including Tower Records, Tower Books and Tower Video. You might find the stores ugly and cramped, but you'll understand their popularity when you see endless selections of CDs, books and videos. There's even a Tower Cafe (☎ 916-441-0222), reflecting the popular coffee culture in Sacramento and other California cities.

Cal Expo

Site of the California State Fair, which is held every summer, Cal Expo, east of I-80

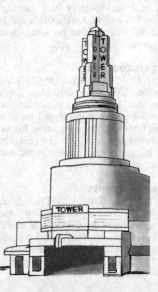

from the Cal Expo exit (see the Metropolitan Sacramento map), has 700 acres of exhibit facilities in constant use for everything from the California Bridal Fair to the Motor World USA convention. For current events, call ☎ 916-263-3000.

Also at Cal Expo is **Waterworld USA & Paradise Island Family Fun Center** (☎ 916-924-3747), a tangle of water slides, bumper cars, miniature golf courses and carnival games. The wave pool – where you can surf mini breakers – is a big hit. The park is open 10:30 am to 6 pm daily. Admission is $16.99, not including game tokens.

Activities

The American River Parkway, a 23-mile river system on the north bank of the American River is one of the most extensive riparian habitats in the continental US. The park's network of trails and picnic areas is accessible from Old Sacramento by taking Front St north until it becomes Jiboom St and crosses the river, or by taking the Jiboom St exit off I-5/Hwy 99.

Close to downtown is a nice walking/running/bicycling path along the Sacramento River levee, accessible from the west end of J St. McKinley Park, bordered by Alhambra and McKinley Blvds and H and 33rd Sts, has a public pool, tennis courts, playground and picnic areas.

Organized Tours

Sacramento Gray Line (☎ 916-927-2877, 800-356-9838), 2600 North Ave, has a city tour that runs four buses continuously, allowing you to hop off and on at major attractions and shopping areas. Prices vary according to season, but are generally $28 per person (a bit cheaper in the winter). Reservations are necessary.

Special Events

During Gold Discovery Days, held the weekend closest to January 28th – the day James Marshall discovered gold at Sutter's Mill – people dress in period costumes at Sutter's Fort State Historic Park and can be found making barrels, pounding iron and baking bread.

The Sacramento Jazz Jubilee (☎ 916-372-5277), held the last weekend in May, attracts big names from all over the US. Venues are widespread, but music usually ends up spilling over into the streets.

In mid-June, the California Railroad Festival (☎ 916-445-7387) takes place at the California State Railroad Museum in Old Sacramento, where old locomotives roll out for the occasion.

The California State Fair is held at Cal Expo from mid-August to mid-September, and includes a rodeo, agriculture displays, arts, crafts, food vendors, rides, carnival games and live music.

Places to Stay – Budget

Camping Sacramento's *KOA Campground* (☎ 916-371-6771, 3951 Lake Rd W), near the W Capitol Ave exit off I-80, in West Sacramento, has a few grassy tent sites for $23 and RV spaces for $29. Amenities include a pool, store and laundry.

Hostels The brand-new *Sacramento HI Hostel* (☎ 916-443-1691, 900 H St), in a restored 1885 Victorian, is within walking distance of the capitol, Old Sac and the train station. There are eight dorm rooms and two private rooms with a total of 70 beds, a nice common area, kitchen facilities and laundry room. Beds are $13, $16 for non-HI-AYH members. The hostel attracts an international crowd and is a good place to find rides to San Francisco and Lake Tahoe. Office hours are daily 7:30 to 9:30 am and 5 to 10 pm.

Motels Prices at most Sacramento motels are lower on weekends, unless there's a convention in town. On slow weekends, top-end places often cut their prices in half. Most chain motels are north of downtown off the I-80 Cal Expo exit. Closer to downtown, off the J St exit, are *Motel 6* (☎ 916-457-0777, 1415 30th St) and *Vagabond Inn* (☎ 916-454-4400, 1319 30th St); both charge around $45/50 single/double.

The *Quality Inn* (☎ 916-444-3980, 818 15th St) is centrally located, has clean, fresh rooms for $54/67 and a small pool. Nearby, the *Econo Lodge* (☎ *916-443-6631, 711 16th St*) has comparable rooms and rates.

Sacramento's concentration of cheap, independent motels is in West Sacramento along W Capitol Ave – a depressing strip, best avoided by solo travelers after dark. Rooms cost $25 to $35 and are generally clean, but the carpet, beds and plumbing may be older than you. The nicest place is the *Welcome Grove Lodge* (☎ *916-371-8526, 600 W Capitol Ave*), with quiet rooms for $32/43.

At the far west end, the *Granada Inn* (☎ *916-372-2780, 4751 W Capitol Ave*) is part of a small chain of truckers' motels. It has newly decorated but noisy rooms for $36/43 and a 24-hour coffee shop next door.

Places to Stay – Mid-Range

Sacramento's mid-level accommodations cater to business people. Weekend rates are usually $20 to $30 cheaper than those listed here. Most accommodations offer free airport shuttle service and are near places to eat.

Another *Vagabond Inn* (☎ *916-446-1481, 909 3rd St*) is within walking distance to most attractions but is practically beneath the freeway overpass. It has a heated pool and rooms for $75/85.

Near Cal Expo and the Arden Fair shopping mall, the *Beverly Garland Hotel* (☎ *916-929-7900, 1780 Tribute Rd*) has a restaurant, spa and pool, and rooms for $89. In the same area, the *Canterbury Inn* (☎ *916-927-0927, 1900 Canterbury Rd*) is a good value with rooms for $74, and an outdoor pool and spa.

Places to Stay – Top End

Hotels Besides being a novelty, the *Delta King* (☎ *916-444-5464, 800-825-5464*), housed on a paddle wheeler similar to the *Spirit of Sacramento*, is docked at the L St landing in Old Sac – an unbeatable location. State rooms, which are small compared to similarly priced hotel rooms, cost $109 to $140.

Across from the capitol and convention center, the *Hyatt Regency Sacramento* (☎ *916-443-1234, 1209 L St*) caters to guests who wear suits (very *nice* suits). Rooms start at $190, and amenities include a pool, spa, fitness center and two restaurants.

Near Cal Expo, the *Red Lion Sacramento Inn* (☎ *916-922-8041, 1401 Arden Way*) has Sacramento's most deluxe accommodations, with a resortlike layout, including indoor and outdoor pools, a spa, fitness center, several restaurants and a nightclub with live music and dancing. Rooms start at $138 but can be as little as $74 on weekends.

B&Bs Sacramento's B&Bs are in a residential neighborhood north of the capitol, within walking distance of downtown. Prices include a full breakfast. *Abigail's B&B* (☎ *916-441-5007, 2120 G St*) has five rooms, each with a private bathroom, patio and hot tub for $95 to $165.

Nearby, the Arts and Crafts-style *Hartley House* (☎ *916-447-7829*), at the corner of 22nd and G Sts, has rooms with large windows, private bath, TV and telephone for $110 to $165.

Sacramento's best-known B&B, the *Amber House* (☎ *916-444-8085, 1315 22nd St*) has a nice porch swing, rooms with private bath (some even have in-room Jacuzzis), TV, VCR and telephone for $130 to $200.

Places to Eat

Sacramento's eating scene is increasingly diverse. It has several terrific restaurants where you can have first-rate food and atmosphere for around $10. Otherwise you've got overpriced cafes open weekdays for lunch only, and nice restaurants where dinner costs around $20 per person.

The best bet for everything from coffee and pastries to pasta and wine is *Cafe Bernardo* (☎ *916-443-1180, 2726 Capitol Ave*), which has outdoor seating and an adjacent martini bar (very popular around happy hour).

Pieces (☎ *916-441-1949, 1309 21st St*) sells enormous slices of pizza ($1.50) and is open late. Also under $5, *Taquería Taco Loco* (☎ *916-447-0711, 2326 J St*), has excellent fish tacos, burritos and 'Beach Blanket Bingo' decor – bright colors, surfboards and beach-scene murals. Main courses at *India Restaurant* (☎ *916-448-9046, 729 J St*) are $8 to $12 for dinner, around $4 for lunch.

Fanny Ann's (☎ 916-441-0505, 1023 2nd St), in Old Sac, is more of a bar than a restaurant and its walls are cluttered with enough stuff to make you claustrophobic, but they make the best burger in town ($5, with fries). Much more upscale is the *River City Brewing Company (☎ 916-447-2739)*, in the Downtown Plaza Mall, near the K St entrance. Beer ($3.50 a pint) is the focus, but plenty of good food – burgers are $8, appetizers $4 to $10, pastas and pizzas around $12 – is consumed.

West of I-5, in an old barge on the north bank of the American River, the *Virgin Sturgeon (☎ 916-921-2694, 1577 Garden Hwy)* is the locals' favorite spot for seafood ($8 to $14), barbecued ribs ($7) and Cuban black beans and rice ($5). The outside patio gets crowded with boaters drinking Bloody Marys on summer weekends.

For a splurge, try one of the restaurants owned by the Fat or Paragary families – both synonymous with good food in Sacramento. *California Fats (☎ 916-441-7966, 1015 Front St)*, in Old Sac, has an Asian twist. Next door, *Fat City (☎ 916-446-6768, 1001 Front St)*, has Old Sacramento ambience and a straight-forward selection for $8 to $16. *Paragary's (☎ 916-456-5121, 2726 N St)*, at the corner of 28th St, is the epitome of good taste – white tablecloths, wood paneling, large pieces of colorful art, a great wine list and quality pasta, meat and fish for $8 to $15.

Entertainment
Pick up a copy of the *Sacramento News & Review*, available at cafes, restaurants and music stores, for a list of current happenings around town. It's published on Thursday. Preferred Seating Ticket Service (☎ 916-498-1400) has fair prices and information on all the shows and sporting events in town.

Cinema The *Tower Theater (☎ 916-443-1982)*, at 16th St and Broadway, shows classic, foreign and alternative films in its old theater, and new releases in its recently renovated auditorium.

Bars & Clubs The *River City Brewing Company (☎ 916-447-2739)*, in the Down-town Plaza Mall near the K St entrance, has an upscale, chic-industrial setting and good microbrews. On the top floor of the Hyatt Regency, *Busby Berkeley's (☎ 916-443-1234, 1209 L St)* has a great view and an over-40 crowd. Tucked away in a residential neighborhood, *The Fox & Goose (☎ 916-443-8825, 1001 R St)* has live music (usually blues or reggae) after 9 pm Wednesday to Sunday nights.

Cafe Paris (☎ 916-442-2001), on K St, between 23rd and 24th Sts, is a popular dance club with a $3 to $8 cover. The *Blue Cue (☎ 916-442-7208)*, above a festive, sophisticated Mexican restaurant at the corner of J and 28th Sts, is a good spot for pool and beer, with a well-dressed crowd. The *Crest Theater (☎ 916-442-7378, 1013 K St)* hosts a variety of live music.

Performing Arts The *Community Center Theater (☎ 916-264-5181, 1301 L St)* is in the Sacramento Convention Center. It's home to Sacramento's opera, ballet and symphony, and most big-name entertainers who come to town play here. For schedules and ticket information, call the box office. The intimate *B Street Theater (☎ 916-443-5300, 2711 B St)* hosts off-Broadway plays of contemporary playwrights.

Spectator Sports
The Kings, Sacramento's professional basketball team, play home games at the *Arco Arena (☎ 916-928-6900)* from November to May. Every game in the Kings' history has been sold out, but tickets are often available at the arena box office right before game time. Tickets cost $15 to $65. Call for schedule information.

Shopping
Shopping is a major activity in Sacramento, with most of it done in the Arden Fair Mall, north of downtown off Bus 80 near Cal Expo, and at the Downtown Plaza Mall, which takes up the blocks of downtown between 3rd, 7th, J and L Sts. Both have stores, restaurants, movie theaters and ATMs. The Downtown Plaza has a good brewery (see Places to Eat).

Getting There & Away

Air The small but busy Sacramento International Airport (☎ 916-929-5411), 15 miles north of downtown off I-5, is serviced by Alaska, America West, American, Delta, Horizon Air, Northwest, Southwest, United and TWA.

Bus Greyhound (☎ 916-482-4993, 916-444-7270), near the capitol at the corner of 7th and L Sts, goes to San Francisco ($13, three hours) every hour on the half-hour from 6:30 am to 7:30 pm; later buses leave less frequently. Seven buses daily leave for Los Angeles ($37, 10 hours), nine go to Reno ($23, three hours) and three go to Seattle ($56, 26 hours).

Train Sacramento's Amtrak depot is between downtown and Old Sac at 4th and I Sts. Trains leave daily for Seattle ($150, 20 hours), Los Angeles ($54, 14½ hours) and San Diego ($55 to $69, 14 hours); ticket prices depend on availability. Trains to San Francisco ($14 to $18, four hours) leave three times daily.

Getting Around

To/From the Airport Numerous shuttle services connect Sacramento's airport to downtown ($11), West Sacramento ($20) and Davis ($16, 20 minutes). There are complimentary phones in the airport terminals and an information booth in front of Terminal 6. Shuttles pick up from the median curb in front of the restaurant building.

Taxi service to downtown is about $24 for one to four people. Top-end hotels provide free shuttle service to/from the airport, the Convention Center and various points downtown, though on weekdays only.

Bus The Downtown Area Shuttle (DASH; ☎ 916-321-2877) has weekday service along J and L Sts and goes to most tourist sights. Sacramento Regional Transit buses run from 5 am to 12 midnight daily and cost $1.25 for a one-hour ride, including one transfer. Sacramento's light-rail system (also run by Regional Transit) stops along K St but is mostly used for the commute to outlying communities.

Car Most car rental agencies have booths at the airport in the car rental terminal (serviced by a free shuttle from the main airport terminals). These include Alamo (☎ 916-646-6020), Avis (☎ 916-922-5601), Budget (☎ 916-922-7317), Hertz (☎ 916-927-3882) and National (☎ 916-568-2415).

Companies not at the airport tend to be a bit cheaper. These include Enterprise (☎ 916-446-6444), Senator Ford (☎ 916-392-4225) and Thrifty (☎ 916-922-8387), each of which will arrange a pick-up or drop-off at the airport, bus or train station.

Taxi Service is regulated and costs $2.80 for the first mile and $2.20 for each additional mile. Sacramento Independent Taxi (☎ 916-457-4862) and Yellow Cab (☎ 916-444-2222) are Sacramento's two main companies. The Hyatt Regency on L St always has a surplus of cabs.

DAVIS

• **population 28,400** • **elevation 45 feet**

Davis is an attractive college town centering around the University of California at Davis (UCD), one of the top schools in the US for veterinary medicine, agriculture and wine making. Besides having more bikes per capita than any other town in the US, Davis has the highest level of education per capita in the US and stands as a progressive outpost amid the conservative agricultural towns of the Sacramento Valley. The student population and year-round community have a mutual respect for each other and together support a vibrant cafe, pub and performing arts scene. Naturally, Davis is much more fun to visit from September to May when classes are in session.

Orientation

I-80 skirts the south edge of town, with the Davis/Olive St exit giving the easiest access to downtown, via Richards Blvd and 1st St. Lettered streets run north-south, and numbered streets run east-west.

UCD lies southwest of downtown, bordered by A St, 1st St and Russell Blvd. The campus' main entrances are from I-80 via Old Davis Rd or from downtown via 3rd St.

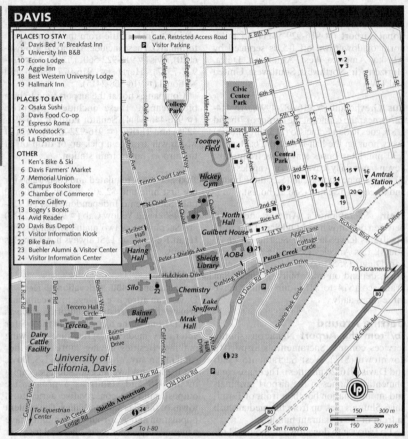

DAVIS

PLACES TO STAY
- 4 Davis Bed 'n' Breakfast Inn
- 5 University Inn B&B
- 10 Econo Lodge
- 17 Aggie Inn
- 18 Best Western University Lodge
- 19 Hallmark Inn

PLACES TO EAT
- 2 Osaka Sushi
- 3 Davis Food Co-op
- 12 Espresso Roma
- 15 Woodstock's
- 16 La Esperanza

OTHER
- 1 Ken's Bike & Ski
- 6 Davis Farmers' Market
- 7 Memorial Union
- 8 Campus Bookstore
- 9 Chamber of Commerce
- 11 Pence Gallery
- 13 Bogey's Books
- 14 Avid Reader
- 20 Davis Bus Depot
- 21 Visitor Information Kiosk
- 22 Bike Barn
- 23 Buehler Alumni & Visitor Center
- 24 Visitor Information Center

Gate, Restricted Access Road
Visitor Parking

Information

Davis' small chamber of commerce and visitor center (☎ 530-756-5160), 228 B St, has a good city map for $2.50, a dining and lodging guide and schedules for regional transportation (including Amtrak). For information about current events around town, you can check the bulletin boards in cafes, bookstores and campus buildings. UCD's campus information line (☎ 530-752-2222) can connect you to any department or building on campus.

For books, the Avid Reader (☎ 530-758-4040), 617 2nd St, has a good selection and is open until 11 pm. Bogey's Books (☎ 530-757-6127), 733 E St, deals in used and out-of-print books. The campus bookstore (☎ 530-752-6846), in the student union, has a large book selection, plus UCD souvenirs.

Things to See & Do

The Davis Art Association publishes a small brochure (available at the chamber of commerce) with information about art in public spaces. The one-room, nonprofit **Pence Gallery** (☎ 530-758-3370), 212 D St, has exhibits of contemporary California art and frequently hosts lectures. It is open noon to 4 pm Tuesday to Saturday; free.

Free **UCD campus tours** are offered at 11:30 am and 1:30 pm on weekends, and on weekdays by appointment. For information, call ☎ 530-752-8111, or stop by the Buehler Alumni & Visitors Center on Old Davis Rd. Campus maps are available at the visitor center and at all campus entrances. A scenic, paved 3-mile trail runs through the **Shields Arboretum**. The **Equestrian Center** (☎ 530-752-2372) offers hour-long trail rides for $21.

The **Davis Farmers' Market**, held in the park at 4th and C Sts, features food vendors, street performers and live bands from 8 am to noon on Saturdays, and from 5:30 to 8:30 pm (2 to 6 pm October to April) on Wednesdays.

Cycling is popular here, probably because the only hill around is the bridge that crosses over the freeway. A favorite destination is to Lake Berryessa, around 30 miles west. For bike rental information, see the Getting Around section.

Places to Stay

Reservations are imperative in May and September.

Motels The **University Park Inn** (☎ 530-756-0910, 1111 Richards Blvd), on the south side of I-80, is the only motel in Davis that is not downtown. There's a pool, and rooms with microwaves and refrigerators go for $70/105 single/double.

Rooms at the **Econo Lodge** (☎ 530-756-1040, 800-424-4777, 221 D St) are a little worn but include a refrigerator, small microwave and coffeemaker for $54/60.

Directly across from UCD's east entrance, the **Aggie Inn** (☎ 530-756-0352, 245 1st St) has homey rooms for $76/85, free coffee and pastries, and an outdoor spa. Also near the campus, at the corner of 2nd St, the **Best Western University Lodge** (☎ 530-756-7890, 800-528-1234, 123 B St) has nice rooms for $66/72.

The **Hallmark Inn** (☎ 530-753-3600, 800-753-0035, 110 F St) has a small pool and rooms for $79.

B&Bs The **Davis Bed 'n' Breakfast Inn** (☎ 530-753-9611, 422 A St) features an old-fashioned living room and cozy rooms with private baths for $50/55.

A block away, the **University Inn Bed and Breakfast** (☎ 530-756-8648, 304 A St) has complimentary fruit, chocolates and coffee, and rooms with private baths for $50 to $65.

Places to Eat

Davis' student population demands cheap, convenient food and coffee by the gallons. **Espresso Roma**, on E St, between 3rd and 2nd Sts, is a good spot to get caffeinated and it's open late. The **Davis Food Co-op** (☎ 530-758-2667), at the corner of 6th and G Sts, has bulk items and a good deli.

Woodstocks (☎ 530-757-2525, 219 G St) has Davis' best (or, at least, most popular) pizza; it's sold by the slice ($1.25) for lunch, by the pie ($15 for a large) for dinner. **Osaka Sushi** (☎ 530-758-2288, 630 G St) has sushi to rival San Francisco's best, plus excellent sashimi, tempura and teriyaki dinners for $8 to $14. They also have a floating sushi bar, where you serve yourself from colored plates (each color represents a price, from $1.50 to $3.75) going around on boats and pay according to the number of plates stacked up when you're through.

For Mexican, **La Esperanza** (☎ 530-753-4449), at the corner of 2nd and G Sts, is highly recommended. Lunches cost $5 to $7, complete dinners $7 to $12. South of the freeway, **Sudwerk** (☎ 530-758-8700, 2001 2nd St) serves home-brewed beer, bratwurst and sauerkraut, burgers and large salads; complete meals cost around $10.

Getting There & Away

Across from the student store in UCD's Memorial Union (called 'mu') is a ride board where students who need or are willing to give rides (usually to the Bay Area) post notices.

Bus Yolobus (☎ 530-666-2877) makes a continuous loop between Davis and the Sacramento airport from 5 am to 11 pm daily and costs $1 one-way. The trip from Davis to Sacramento takes 25 minutes. Buses stop at various points on the UCD campus, and along 5th St, F St and Russell Blvd.

Unitrans (☎ 530-752-2877) has red buses (some double-decker) that shuttle people around town and the UCD campus for 50¢. Buses stop at blue and white ASUCD signs, and run from 7:30 am to 11:30 pm Monday to Saturday.

Greyhound has daily service to San Francisco ($13) from the Davis Bus Depot.

Train Davis' Amtrak station (☎ 530-758-4220) is at the corner of 2nd and H Sts, on the southern edge of downtown. Seven eastbound trains go to Sacramento ($4.50) and Reno ($11), and seven westbound trains go to San Francisco ($12) daily. The Seattle–Los Angeles train stops early in the morning heading north, late at night going south.

Getting Around

Nearly every street has a bike lane with its own stoplight. When driving around, and especially when pulling out from a parking space, be aware of bike traffic – it's the primary mode of transportation here. Ken's Bike & Ski (☎ 530-758-3223), 650 G St, rents bikes for $10 per day; the Bike Barn (☎ 530-752-2575), on the UCD campus, has similar rates.

YUBA CITY & MARYSVILLE

These two county seats (of Sutter and Yuba counties) are joined by two bridges spanning the Feather River and basically function as one: Yuba City (population 33,900) provides shopping malls, automotive stores and a newly revitalized Main St, while Marysville (population 12,550) entertains tourists with its historic downtown. Water issues are of utmost importance to both towns, since they sit in the middle of a flood plain and depend, almost exclusively, on rice production for economic livelihood. Because of floods caused by early mining practices, Marysville is entirely surrounded

by levees whose construction is a much debated mystery; no one has record of what's under the grass that covers them, although the theory is dirt that may have been dredged from the river, or gravel. Yuba City's Sikh population, one of the largest in California, is a major part of the cultural climate and should be thanked for the excellent Indian restaurants around town.

History

As the head of the Feather River, Marysville boomed during the gold rush when nearly all people and supplies destined for the northern mines passed through its gates. A large Chinese population settled here to work in the mines and remained in Marysville to work on the railroad when it pushed through in the early 1900s.

In 1841, John Sutter established Hock Farm, the first large-scale agricultural project in Northern California, just south of present-day Yuba City. Its proximity to Marysville's port made it an agricultural trade center. The rich and elite built their houses in Yuba City (along 2nd St), giving the town great political sway, and in 1899 Yuba City became the seat of Sutter County.

Orientation & Information

Hwy 99 runs north-south along Yuba City's western edge and is connected to the twin cities by Hwy 20 (called Colusa Ave in Yuba City and 10th St in Marysville). Bridges span the Feather River at 10th and 5th Sts.

Yuba City's historic district lies south of Hwy 20 along Plumas Ave and 2nd St. The heart of Marysville's central business and historic district is between 1st and 5th Sts, and B and E Sts.

The best place to pick up brochures and walking-tour maps is at the Mary Aaron Museum (see the next section). Marysville's main post office is at the corner of 4th and C Sts, right across from Wells Fargo Bank.

Things to See

Yuba City's **Community Memorial Museum of Sutter County** (☎ 530-741-7141), 1333 Butte House Rd, chronicles Sutter County history from the Maidu Indians to present-day farmers and has some amusing 1850s photographs. It's open 9 am to 5 pm Tuesday to Friday, noon to 4 pm weekends; free.

South of central Yuba City on 2nd St are the 1899 **Sutter County Courthouse**, **Hall of Records** and graceful houses that reflect Victorian, Italianate and Classical architecture. Julia Morgan (of Hearst Castle fame) designed the **Kline-Smith House** at 364 2nd St.

In Marysville, the **Mary Aaron Museum** (☎ 530-743-1004), housed in an 1855 Gothic Revival brick structure at 704 D St, has changing art and history exhibits; it's open 1 to 4 pm Tuesday to Saturday. One block east is St Joseph's Cathedral, built in 1855.

At the southern end of B, C and D Sts, is Marysville's **Chinatown**, where the Suey Sing Chamber of Labor & Commerce, 305 1st St,

is still the community's hub, and the Buddhist Church, 110 B St, is its central place of worship. The **Bok Kai Temple**, at the southern end of D St behind the Silver Dollar Saloon, is the only temple in California dedicated to Bok Kai (the water god; the museum spells it 'Bok Eye'). The temple is open only on Bomb Day (the first Sunday in March), at the end of the two-day Bok Kai Festival. Its exterior ornamentation can be seen from the top of the levy, directly behind the temple.

Places to Stay

Accommodations are concentrated along Hwys 99 and 20 in Yuba City. *Motel Orleans* (☎ *530-674-1592, 730 N Palora Ave*), at the junction of Hwys 99 and 20, has an outdoor pool and modern rooms for $42/46. Across

---

Joss Houses

'Joss,' which in pidgin English means 'deity,' is a corruption of the Portuguese word *deus* (god) – a term used by early navigators to describe idols they found in the East Indies. Joss houses were the principal places of worship for Chinese miners and often the only public symbol of Chinese culture in mining towns.

The exterior of a joss house was usually very simple, while the interior was decorated with rich and symbolic ornamentation. The main images represented were the 'God of Sombre Heavens,' 'God of War,' 'God of Medicine' and 'God of Wealth,' combining characteristics of Buddhism, Taoism and Confucianism. Men came to the joss house to ask special favors of a god, or to offer prayers and supplication.

The rituals required in order to 'talk' with a god were very formal. A man entered the joss house, bowed with clasped hands, lit the appropriate candles and incense, knelt on a mat and called the god by name three times. He then took two semi-oval blocks of wood called 'Yum Yeung Puey' and tossed them into the air. If both blocks landed in the same position it was an unfavorable omen. If one block faced up and the other faced down, it meant that the god had to be persuaded.

The worshipper then knocked his head on the ground three times, offered his petition and then shook a cylindrical pot of numbered bamboo slips until one of the slips fell out. The priest or joss-house keeper checked the number before looking up the omen in an ancient text. The priest then beat drums and rang the joss-house bells while the worshipper burned paper money as final payment. At last, the fortune was told.

A few joss houses still survive in California. The Chinese Temple in Oroville is open for tours daily. The Bok Kai Temple in Marysville is open only once a year, during the Bok Kai Festival. Nevada City's Firehouse Museum No 1 (see the Gold Country chapter) has a reconstructed altar from an 1860s joss house and a good collection of related Chinese relics. In Chico, the Chico Museum holds an impressive re-creation of an old Taoist temple altar. In Weaverville, the Joss House State Historic Park holds an ornate altar, sent from China, that's more than 3000 years old (see the Northern Mountains chapter).

Hwy 99, the **Days Inn** (☎ *530-674-1711, 700 N Palora Ave)*, has a spa, pool, nice lobby and rooms for around $75. **Vada's Motel** (☎ *530-671-1151, 545 Colusa Ave)* has budget rooms for $33/42.

In Marysville, the **Vagabond Inn** (☎ *530-742-8586)*, at the corner of 10th and H Sts, is a good choice, with a small pool and $40/50 rooms.

Places to Eat

For good coffee, sandwiches and salads, try the arty **Java Retreat** (☎ *530-671-5282, 728 Plumas St)*, in Yuba City, or **Mahler Coffee & Tea Co** (☎ *530-741-3211, 316 D St)*, in Marysville. Both are inexpensive and open from around 6 am until late.

The **Szechwan Restaurant** (☎ *530-743-0660, 223 1st St)* has a reputation for serving the most authentic Chinese food in Marysville ($6 to $9), and the **Silver Dollar Saloon** (☎ *530-642-9020)*, at the corner of D and 1st Sts, serves Marysville's best burgers, barbecued chicken and ribs (not a place recommended for vegetarians!) for $6 to $14. The bar came around Cape Horn in the 1850s and is laden with silver dollars. Live country bands stir up a crowd on Friday and Saturday nights.

For excellent Indian food, try **Taste of India** (☎ *530-751-5156, 1456 Bridge St)*, across from Raley's supermarket, one block west of Hwy 99. The lunch buffet ($6; not served Sunday) has a vast number of choices. Full dinners are around $9.

Getting There & Away

Greyhound buses leave from Marysville's Union Bus Station (☎ 530-742-7121) at 905 5th St and go to Sacramento four times daily ($12, one hour) and once daily to San Francisco ($12, three hours) and Los Angeles ($35, 14 hours).

OROVILLE

• **population 12,300** • **elevation 170 feet**

Oroville's biggest claim to fame is the Oroville Dam, 9 miles northeast of town; its construction in the 1960s created Lake Oroville. The dam and the recreational opportunities afforded by the Lake Oroville

State Recreation Area are the prime attractions for visitors.

The Oroville Area Chamber of Commerce (☎ 530-538-2542, 800-655-4653), 1789 Montgomery St, has information on the entire area. It's open 9 am to 4:30 pm weekdays. The Feather River Ranger Station, La Porte Ranger District (☎ 530-534-6500), 875 Mitchell Ave, has maps and information about the Plumas National Forest. For current road conditions, especially if you'll be heading up into the mountains in winter, phone ☎ 800-427-7623.

Things to See & Do

The **Chinese Temple** (☎ 530-538-2496), 1500 Broderick St, was built in 1863 to serve Oroville's Chinese community, which was the second largest in California after San Francisco's. Tours of the temple and grounds are given from 11 am to 4:30 pm Thursday to Monday, 1 to 4 pm Tuesday and Wednesday (closed December 15 to January 31).

You can see chinook salmon jumping the fish ladder during their annual migration from September to November at the **Feather River Fish Hatchery** (☎ 530-538-2222), 5 Table Mountain Blvd, off Hwy 70 on the north bank of the Feather River. The hatchery is open 7:30 am to sunset daily; the office is open 8 am to 4 pm Monday to Friday.

Nine miles northeast of Oroville, Oroville Dam and Lake Oroville are part of the **Lake Oroville State Recreation Area**. At 770 feet, this dam across the Feather River is the tallest in the US and the largest earthen dam ever built. It's a popular place for recreation. The Lake Oroville State Recreation Area Visitor Center (☎ 530-538-2219), 917 Kelly Ridge Rd, has free pamphlets detailing self-guided driving, bicycling and hiking tours in the area. It's open 9 am to 5 pm daily.

Hiking trails include the **Feather Falls Trail** to the 640-foot Feather Falls, a good all-day hike, and the ¼-mile **Bald Rock Trail** to a giant outcropping with huge, unusually shaped rocks.

Hwy 70 heads northeast from Oroville into the mountains, snaking up through the magnificent **Feather River Canyon**. When the

Ishi

In the early morning of August 29, 1911, a frantic barking of dogs woke the butchers sleeping inside a slaughterhouse outside Oroville. When they came out, they found their dogs holding a man at bay – a Native American clad only in a loincloth, who was starving, exhausted, afraid and spoke no English.

They called the sheriff, who took the man to the jail until something could be decided. Newspapers declared a 'wild man' had been discovered, and people thronged in, hoping to see him. Local Indians came and tried to communicate with him in Maidu and Wintu, but to no avail; his language was different from those of the surrounding tribes.

Anthropologists from the University of California, Berkeley, Professors Alfred L Kroeber and Thomas Talbot Waterman, read the accounts in the news. Waterman took the train to Oroville and, using lists of vocabulary words of the Yana Indians who once lived in this region, discovered that the man belonged to the Yahi, the southernmost tribe of the Yana, which was believed to be extinct.

Waterman took 'Ishi,' meaning 'man' in the Yahi language, to the museum at the university, where he was cared for and brought back to health. Ishi spent his remaining years there, telling the anthropologists his life story and teaching them his tribal language, lore and ways.

Ishi's tribe had been virtually exterminated by settlers before Ishi was born. In 1870, when he was a child, there were only about 12 or 15 Yahi left, hiding in remote areas in the foothills east of Red Bluff. Ishi, his mother, sister and an old man were all that were left of the Yahi by 1908. In that year, the others died and Ishi was left alone. On March 25, 1916, Ishi died of tuberculosis at the university hospital, and the Yahi disappeared forever.

The book *Ishi in Two Worlds: A Biography of the Last Wild Indian in North America*, by Theodora Kroeber, Professor Kroeber's wife, tells Ishi's story. In Oroville, you can drive to the site of the slaughterhouse where he was found, but all that remains is a monument by the side of the road. Part of the Lassen National Forest in the foothills east of Red Bluff, including Deer Creek and other areas where Ishi and the Yahi lived, is now called the Ishi Wilderness. If you go to Berkeley, you can also see the exhibit on Ishi at the university museum.

leaves change color in fall, this is a beautifully scenic drive.

Special Events

Held for one week in May, Feather Fiesta Days celebrates the discovery of gold at Bidwell Bar on the Feather River in 1848. Bidwell Bar is now submerged by the lake, but townsfolk gather on the shore in period costume to celebrate their history.

Places to Stay & Eat

The Lake Oroville State Recreation Area Visitor Center has maps and details of US Forest Service (USFS) campgrounds; make reservations through Parknet (☎ 800-444-7275).

Houseboats can be rented at **Bidwell Canyon Marina** (☎ 530-589-3165, 800-637-1767), on the south end of the lake, or at the **Lime Saddle Marina** (☎ 530-877-2414, 800-834-7517), on the west branch of the Feather River. Both places also rent boats for getting to those boat-in campgrounds.

Running along the east side of Hwy 70, Feather River Blvd is 'motel row,' with chain motels in the $35 to $50 range.

Jean's Riverside B&B (☎ 530-533-1413, jeansbandb@yahoo.com, 1142 Middlehoff Lane) is in a secluded spot on the west bank of the Feather River, just off Oro Dam Blvd. Rooms and suites, most with river views, private Jacuzzis and Franklin woodstoves, are $65 to $125. Overlooking the lake, the

SACRAMENTO VALLEY

Lake Oroville B&B (☎ *530-589-0700, 240 Sunday Drive*), in Berry Creek, has six rooms from $75 to $135.

The *Cornucopia Restaurant & Pie Shop* (☎ *530-534-9025, 515 Montgomery St*), on the east side of Hwy 70, is open 24 hours, serving sandwiches, burgers, fries, steaks, fish and more for around $5 to $6 at lunch, $6 to $10 at dinner. *Cassidy's* (☎ *530-533-7565, 491 Oro Dam Blvd*) is open 24 hours on Friday and Saturday, 5 am to 10 pm the rest of the week.

Getting There & Away
Greyhound buses heading north and south stop at the 1st Stop, 2401 5th Ave, a couple of blocks east of Hwy 70.

CHICO
• population 49,000 • elevation 200 feet
Chico is a university town, with a vibrant youthful feel and more going on than you'd expect from a city its size.

Chico was founded in 1860 by John Bidwell, who came to California in 1841 and proceeded to make himself one of its most illustrious early pioneers. In the late 1840s, he purchased 40 sq miles here, called the Rancho del Arroyo Chico. In 1868, after a term as a California congressman in Washington, DC, he married Annie Ellicott Kennedy, daughter of a prominent Washington official. They moved to the new mansion he had built, now the Bidwell Mansion State Historic Park. After John died in 1900, Annie continued as a philanthropist there until her death in 1918.

Downtown Chico is flat, relatively compact and easy to get around – just look for the compass directions on the streets to figure out if you are heading east or west. The Esplanade and Main St divide east and west addresses.

Orientation & Information
The Chico Chamber of Commerce & Visitor Center (☎ 530-891-5559, 800-852-8570), 300 Salem St, at the corner of 3rd St, offers free maps, plenty of information on things to do, and a monthly calendar of events. It's open 9 am to 5 pm weekdays, 10 am to 3 pm on summer Saturdays.

The AAA (☎ 530-891-8601) is at 2221 Forest Ave, near Hwy 99.

From mid-May to late September, the weather is very hot, with 90° to 105°F (32° to 40°C) days cooling off to the 70s at night.

There's a post office at the corner of 5th and Broadway Sts, opposite the City Plaza.

The Bookstore, 118 Main St, has tons of quality used books. Tower Books & Records, 211 Main St, is open 9 am to midnight daily, making browsing a popular nighttime activity in Chico.

Pick up a copy of the excellent free weekly *Chico News & Review* to find out what's happening around town; it comes out every Thursday. Alternative newspapers include the *Chico Alternative* and the *Weekly Synthesis*.

Things to See
Chico's most prominent landmark is **Bidwell Mansion State Historic Park** (☎ 530-895-6144), 525 The Esplanade, built from 1865 to 1868 as the opulent home of Chico's founders John and Annie Bidwell. Tours are given hourly from noon to 4 pm weekdays, 10 am to 4 pm weekends. A stately Victorian home, the **Stansbury Home** (☎ 530-895-3848), at the corner of Salem and W 5th Sts, offers tours from 1 to 4 pm on most weekends.

Chico Museum (☎ 530-891-4336), in the former 1904 Carnegie Library, at the corner of Salem and W 2nd Sts, contains a historical museum, a re-creation of an old Taoist temple altar and rotating exhibits. It's open noon to 4 pm Wednesday to Sunday.

Ask for a free map of the **Chico State University (CSU)** campus to guide yourself around, or inquire about guided tours at the University Admissions office (☎ 530-898-4428, 800-542-4426), at the corner of Hazel and W 2nd Sts. Information on campus events is available at the CSU Information Center (☎ 530-898-4636), in the Bell Memorial Union, at the corner of Chestnut and W 2nd Sts.

Internationally renowned glass art is made at **Orient & Flume Art Glass** (☎ 530-893-0373), 2161 Park Ave, a couple of miles south of downtown. You can see the glass being blown from 7 am until around 10 am or noon on weekdays.

The **Satava Art Glass Studio** (☎ 530-345-7985), 819 Wall St, is smaller but is another option to see glassblowing and glass art. The gallery is open 10 am to 5:30 pm Wednesday to Friday, 9 am to 4 pm Saturday. Glassblowers at work can be seen 9 am to 2 pm weekdays.

The **Sierra Nevada Brewery** (☎ 530-893-3520), 1075 E 20th St, where award-winning ales and lagers are made, offers free half-hour brewery tours at 2:30 pm Tuesday to Friday, continuously from noon to 3 pm Saturday, and at 2:30 pm Sundays.

The historic 1894 **Honey Run Covered Bridge** is the only covered bridge in California whose roof consists of three separate sections, each one at a different height. Take the Skyway exit off Hwy 99 on the southern outskirts of Chico, head east about a mile, turn left onto Honey Run-Humbug Rd; the bridge is 5 miles along, in a small park.

Activities

The extensive Bidwell Park stretches 10 miles northwest along Chico Creek, starting from downtown. In 1937, *The Adventures of*

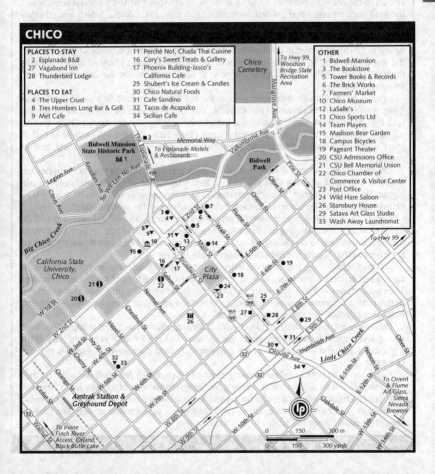

CHICO

PLACES TO STAY
2 Esplanade B&B
27 Vagabond Inn
28 Thunderbird Lodge

PLACES TO EAT
4 The Upper Crust
8 Tres Hombres Long Bar & Grill
9 Met Cafe
11 Perchè No!, Chada Thai Cuisine
16 Cory's Sweet Treats & Gallery
17 Phoenix Building-Jasco's California Cafe
25 Shubert's Ice Cream & Candies
30 Chico Natural Foods
31 Cafe Sandino
32 Tacos de Acapulco
34 Sicilian Cafe

OTHER
1 Bidwell Mansion
3 The Bookstore
5 Tower Books & Records
6 The Brick Works
7 Farmers' Market
10 Chico Museum
12 LaSalle's
13 Chico Sports Ltd
14 Team Players
15 Madison Bear Garden
18 Campus Bicycles
19 Pageant Theater
20 CSU Admissions Office
21 CSU Bell Memorial Union
22 Chico Chamber of Commerce & Visitor Center
23 Post Office
24 Wild Hare Saloon
26 Stansbury House
29 Satava Art Glass Studio
33 Wash Away Laundromat

Robin Hood was filmed here; parts of *Gone with the Wind* were filmed here in 1938, and, in 1950, *The Red Badge of Courage* was shot here. In the park, the Chico Creek Nature Center (☎ 530-891-4671), about 2 miles east of downtown, offers **nature exhibits**, events and park maps. For **swimming**, there's a pool at the Five Mile Recreation Area, about 5 miles northeast of downtown in the park. More remote natural swimming holes are in upper Bidwell Park: Bear Hole is 2.5 miles upstream from where the paved road ends; farther upstream, Salmon Hole and Brown Hole are popular for skinny-

John & Annie Bidwell

John Bidwell, founder of Chico, was one of California's most prominent pioneers. Born in New York in 1819, he left home to attend school in Ohio, then continued west to Missouri and on to the Mexican province of Alta California. In the spring of 1841, several years before the gold rush, he organized the first overland wagon train to California, which arrived safely in November 1841.

Soon after arriving, Bidwell began working for John Sutter. He supported the Bear Flag Revolt in 1846 and served in the Mexican-American War, attaining the rank of general. After the war he returned to Sutter's Fort and was present when James Marshall discovered gold there in January 1848. Bidwell carried the news to San Francisco, and the California gold rush followed soon after.

Later in 1848, Bidwell discovered gold at Bidwell Bar on the middle fork of the Feather River, now submerged beneath Lake Oroville. The following year he began purchasing the land that he loved the most in California: the 26,000-acre Rancho del Arroyo Chico. California agriculture was still in an experimental stage at the time, and Bidwell became one of its most ardent enthusiasts, importing and experimenting with a great variety of plants, animals and farming techniques.

Entering politics, he was elected first to the state assembly, then to the state senate, and finally, in 1865, the year the Civil War ended, to the US House of Representatives in Washington, DC. In Washington, he came into contact with the Kennedy family, most notably their eldest daughter, Annie, whom he came to love 'more than all the world beside.'

Annie, 20 years his junior, refused his proposal of marriage, and Bidwell returned to California in March 1867. Hoping to attract Annie to come to California and become his wife, he turned his attention to organizing his ranch, planting crops and trees, and renewing work on the mansion that is now the Bidwell Mansion State Historic Park.

The two wrote long, impassioned letters to one another for many months, wherein he agreed not to pester her about love or marriage in exchange for her continued friendship. Then on October 7, 1867, she wrote to him a historic letter. It began, 'Perhaps the contents of this note will surprise you, perhaps not,' and in it she agreed to marry him, leave her home in Washington and live on his ranch in Chico.

They were married in Washington in April 1868 and returned to Chico in May. They lived a long and happy life here. They never had children, but the Bidwells kept very busy in the highest political and social circles of the growing state, and they were benefactors to many charitable causes.

Annie and John both loved the growing town of Chico, which John had laid out near their mansion. After John died in 1900, Annie gave their favorite part of all their lands, the land near upper Chico Creek, to the city for a park; this is Bidwell Park today. Annie remained at the mansion in Chico until her death in 1918, continuing in the public service. The Bidwells are still beloved figures in Chico.

dipping. Park maps, showing trails and swimming holes, are available at the chamber of commerce and are published in the *Chico News & Review*.

In summer, **tubing** on the Sacramento River is popular; inner tubes can be rented at places along Nord Ave. Tubers enter the river at the Irvine Finch Launch Ramp, on Hwy 32, a few miles west of Chico, and come out at the Washout off River Rd.

CSU Adventure Outings (☎ 530-898-4011), on the ground floor of the Bell Memorial Union, organizes a wide variety of fun adventure outings, open to students and nonstudents alike.

Special Events
Several annual summerlong outdoor events are popular family attractions. Free concerts are given in the City Plaza on Friday evenings from mid-May to late September; a similar free series featuring alternative rock bands is held in the plaza on Wednesday evenings from late May to late October. Shakespeare in the Park (☎ 530-891-1382), at Cedar Grove in lower Bidwell Park, runs from mid-July to the end of August.

Places to Stay
Camping The *Woodson Bridge State Recreation Area* (☎ 530-839-2112, 800-444-7275), about 25 miles north on Hwy 99, then west toward Corning, has a pleasant campground with tent and RV sites on the riverbank for $12. *Black Butte Lake* (☎ 530-865-4781), about a 35-minute drive west from Chico past Orland, is another option. Neither site has hookups.

Motels & Hotels Good-value motels are found in three convenient areas in Chico: downtown, on The Esplanade and beside Hwy 99 at the Cohasset Rd exit. Since this is a campus town, graduation and homecoming ceremonies (in May and October respectively) can fill up hotels and raise the price. Downtown motels include the *Thunderbird Lodge* (☎ 530-343-7911, 715 Main St), with rooms for $38 on weekdays, $44 on weekends, and the similarly priced *Vagabond Inn* (☎ 530-895-1323, 630 Main St). The *Rio Lindo Motel* (☎ 530-342-7555, 2324 The Esplanade) is a good deal at $34/38. The quiet and secure *Safari Motel* (☎ 530-343-3201, 2352 The Esplanade) charges $51/55.

The *Holiday Inn* (☎ 530-345-2491, 800-310-2491, 685 Manzanita Court), north of town just off Hwy 99 (take Mangrove Ave north from downtown), is the largest and fanciest hotel in Chico, with a restaurant, bar, dancing on weekends and rooms for $62 to $85. There are cheap chain hotels along this strip as well.

B&Bs The *Esplanade B&B* (☎ 530-345-8084, 620 The Esplanade), opposite the Bidwell Mansion, has five rooms from $65 to $85. In an attractive almond orchard, *Johnson's Country Inn* (☎ 530-345-7829, 3935 Morehead Ave), just over a mile from downtown (take W 5th St southwest), has four rooms from $80 to $125 (10% cheaper on weekdays). *Music Express Inn* (☎ 530-345-8376, icobeen@aol.com, 1091 El Monte Ave), just over 2 miles from downtown (take Hwy 32 east), has 12 rooms for $58/85 on weekdays, $75 or $85 on weekends. *L'Abri B&B* (☎ 530-893-0824, 800-489-3319, 14350 Hwy 99), about seven minutes north of downtown, has three rooms, each with private entrance, for $65 and $75 weekdays, or $80 and $90 weekends.

Places to Eat
Natural food supermarkets include *Chico Natural Foods* (☎ 530-891-1713, 818 Main St). An outdoor *farmers' market* (☎ 530-893-3276) is held in the city parking lot at the corner of Wall and E 2nd Sts from 7:30 am to 1 pm year round on Saturdays; from June to December it's also held from 5:30 to 8:30 pm on Wednesdays in the Chico Mall parking lot near Gottschalks.

For a down-home breakfast, *Kalico Kitchen* (☎ 530-343-3968, 2396 The Esplanade) serves ample portions of good inexpensive food with fast, friendly service and air-conditioning. Inexpensive Mexican fare can be found at *Tacos de Acapulco* (☎ 530-892-8176, 429 Ivy St), at the corner of W 5th St. Boasting 'the biggest burrito in Chico,' it's open 8 am to 3 am daily and is popular with students. *Tres Hombres Long Bar & Grill* (☎ 530-342-0425, 100 Broadway) is good fun for drinking and people-watching.

For a good moderately priced meal, try any of the following. *Cory's Sweet Treats & Gallery* (☎ 530-345-2955, 230 W 3rd St) is a popular breakfast and Sunday brunch spot. The *Upper Crust* (☎ 530-895-3866, 130 Main St) has fine baked goods and light meals. *Perchè No!* (☎ 530-893-4210, 119 W 2nd St) has Belgian waffles, Italian gelato and espresso. *Met Cafe* (☎ 530-345-0601, 128 Broadway) is a popular coffeehouse with European flair and live music on weekend evenings.

A Chico favorite, *Jasco's California Cafe* (☎ 530-899-8075), upstairs in the Phoenix Building, at the corner of Broadway and W 3rd St, serves excellent California-style food, gourmet pizza and good lunch specials. *Cafe Sandino* (☎ 530-894-6515, 817 Main St) has a relaxed atmosphere and features vegetarian food from around the world, with daily lunch and dinner specials. *Chada Thai Cuisine* (☎ 530-342-7121, 117-B W 2nd St) serves authentic vegetarian Thai food for lunch and dinner daily except Sunday.

Gashouse Pizza (☎ 530-345-3621, 2359 The Esplanade) earned the title 'living legend' when it was voted 'best pizza in Chico' in the *Chico News & Review* readers' poll for five years running.

The expensive *Sicilian Cafe* (☎ 530-345-2233, 1020 Main St) is famous for its superb family-style Italian dinners.

For dessert, try *Shubert's Ice Cream & Candy* (☎ 530-342-7163, 178 E 7th St), a beloved Chico landmark. They've made delicious homemade ice cream and confections for more than 60 years.

Entertainment

The *Madison Bear Garden* (☎ 530-891-1639, 316 W 2nd St), at the corner of Salem St, is a fun restaurant/saloon popular with college students, with dancing and nightly drink specials. The *Wild Hare Saloon* (☎ 530-342-5202, 116 W 5th St) has live music and dancing nightly. *LaSalle's* (☎ 530-893-1891, 229 Broadway), the *Brick Works*

(☎ 530-898-9898), at the corner of Wall and E 2nd Sts, and *Team Players* (☎ 530-896-1868, 319 Main St) are weekend dance spots popular with young people.

The *Sierra Nevada Taproom & Restaurant* (☎ 530-345-2739, 1075 E 20th St), at the Sierra Nevada Brewery, is a popular bar and restaurant featuring ales and lagers. The *Chico Brewhouse* (☎ 530-894-2149, 250 Cohasset Rd) is an elegant pub, restaurant and sports bar with live music. For live music in a coffeehouse atmosphere, check out *Met Cafe* (☎ 530-345-0601, 128 Broadway) and *Perchè No!* (☎ 530-893-4210, 119 W 2nd St).

For theater, concerts, art exhibits and other cultural events at the CSU campus, contact the CSU Box Office (☎ 530-898-5791) or the CSU Information Center (☎ 530-898-4636) in the Bell Memorial Union.

The *Pageant Theatre* (☎ 530-343-0663, 351 E 6th St) screens international and alternative films; Monday is bargain night.

Getting There & Around

The Chico airport is small and flights are expensive; if you must fly, head to Sacramento instead.

Butte County Transit (☎ 530-534-9999) has buses to Paradise, Oroville and Gridley every day except Sunday. The Greyhound depot (☎ 530-343-8266) is at the Amtrak station, at the corner of W 5th and Orange Sts. Four buses heading north and south depart daily. The train station is unattended, but the schedule for train and Amtrak Thruway bus connections is posted on the wall. Tickets can be purchased at travel agencies.

Notices from people offering or seeking shared rides are posted on the ride board in the Bell Memorial Union on the CSU campus.

Rental car companies in town include Enterprise (☎ 530-899-1188), 2267 The Esplanade. There are more companies at the airport.

Bicycles can be rented from Campus Bicycles (☎ 530-345-2081), 330 Main St and Chico Sports Ltd (☎ 530-894-1110), 240 Main St.

RED BLUFF

• **population 13,000** • **elevation 304 feet**

Red Bluff is a small, relaxing town where Victorian homes border quiet, shady, tree-lined streets, and ice-cream socials and rodeos bring the community together. Because it's at the junction of I-5 and Hwy 99, many people pass through, and it's a convenient base for visits to Lassen Volcanic National Park (see the Northern Mountains chapter).

Orientation & Information

Most of Red Bluff is on the west bank of the Sacramento River, on the west side of I-5. The town's main intersection is the corner of Antelope Blvd and Main St. The historic Victorian neighborhood is in the blocks west of Main St. Many motels, fast-food places and 24-hour gas stations and restaurants serving drive-through travelers are on Antelope Blvd near the junction of I-5.

Main St offers many services, including the Red Bluff-Tehama County Chamber of Commerce (☎ 530-527-6220, 800-655-6225) at 100 Main St. It's open 8:30 am to 4 pm Monday, until 5 pm Tuesday to Thursday, until 4:30 pm Friday.

Things to See & Do

The chamber of commerce offers free maps and a brochure for a self-guided tour of the Victorian homes. **The Kelly-Griggs House Museum** (☎ 530-527-1129), 311 Washington St, a classical Victorian home with period furnishings and exhibits, is open for tours from 1 to 4 pm Thursday to Sunday. There are many antique stores both on and off Main St.

On a beautiful bluff overlooking the Sacramento River, the **William B Ide Adobe State Historic Park** (☎ 530-529-8599), 21659 Adobe Rd, preserves the original adobe home and grounds of pioneer William B Ide. Ide came to California with his wife and children in 1845, 'fought' in the 1846 Bear Flag Revolt at Sonoma to win California's independence from Mexico, and was named president of the short-lived California Republic. To get to the park, turn east from Main St onto Adobe Rd about a mile north of downtown and go about another mile, following the signs.

The **Red Bluff Lake Recreation Area** is on the east bank of the Sacramento River, on the southeast side of town. It has interpretive hiking trails through various habitats, bicycle paths, boat ramps, a wildlife viewing area with excellent birding, and a 2-acre native and drought-tolerant plant garden. The visitor center, called the **Sacramento River Discovery Center** (☎ 530-527-1196), on Sale Lane, at the Diversion Dam, has interactive hands-on displays about the river; it's open 11 am to 4 pm daily, except Monday.

Opposite the discovery center, the **US Fish & Wildlife Interpretive Display & Fish Ladders** has year-round educational displays on chinook salmon and steelhead trout; both migrate up the Sacramento River to spawn. The fish ladders are active from May 15 to September 15, when the dam is in place and impedes fish passage in the main part of the Sacramento River. The fish are most abundant from September to December.

Rafting and **inner tubing** on the Sacramento River are popular in summer, but you'll have to bring your own gear. Chico and Redding are the nearest places for rentals.

Places to Stay

The *Sycamore Grove Camping Area* (☎ 530-824-5196), beside the river in the Red Bluff Lake Recreation Area, is a quiet, attractive USFS campground. Campsites are $10, first-come, first-served. They also have a large group campground, Camp Discovery, where cabins are available and reservations are required. The *Bend RV Park* (☎ 530-527-6289) is on the Sacramento River about 4 miles north of Red Bluff. Tent sites are $14, RV sites with full hookups $18; discounted weekly and monthly rates are offered. Take the Jellys Ferry Rd exit from I-5, 4 miles north of Red Bluff and head east for 2½ miles, following the signs.

Most motels are along Antelope Blvd and Main St. The newly renovated *Travel Lodge* (☎ 530-527-6020, 800-587-7878, 38 Antelope Blvd) is an attractive motel with singles/doubles for $39/48. The *Sky Terrace Motel*

(☎ 530-527-4145, 99 Main St) has rooms for $27/32, with cheaper weekly rates. The **Lamplighter Lodge** (☎ 530-527-1150, 210 S Main St) has rooms for $38/42.

A few Victorian homes have been turned into B&Bs. The **Jeter Victorian Inn B&B** (☎ 530-527-7574, 1107 Jefferson St) offers five rooms from $65 to $140 and a separate cottage for $95. The **Jarvis Mansion B&B** (☎ 530-527-6901, 1313 Jackson St) has four rooms from $65 to $90, each with private bath.

Places to Eat

The following restaurants are moderately priced. **The Feedbag** (☎ 530-527-3777, 200 S Main St) is popular with locals and is famous for its giant flapjacks at breakfast. **Collectibles & Delectables** (☎ 530-529-4624, 521 Walnut St), three blocks west of Main St, features great coffee and interesting baked goods. The **Green Barn** (☎ 530-527-3161), on the corner of Antelope Blvd and Chestnut Ave, is a long-established family restaurant serving pancakes, burgers, sandwiches, and other American fare. It's popular with both locals and travelers. For Mexican food, try **Francisco's Mexican Restaurant** (☎ 530-527-5311, 480 Antelope Blvd), in the Holiday Market shopping center, or **La Comida** (☎ 530-527-5424, 360 S Main St).

A bit more upscale, **Wild Bill's Rib-Steakhouse & Saloon** (☎ 530-529-9453, 500 Riverside Way), just off Antelope Blvd and one block east of Main St, has a beautiful dining room and deck overlooking the river. There are plenty of other selections aside from ribs and steaks, and they have 'ribs to go' from 4 to 10 pm.

Getting There & Away

Greyhound buses head north and south on I-5. The Greyhound station (☎ 530-527-0434) is at 22825 Antelope Blvd, at the corner of Hwy 36 E, beside the Salt Creek Deli.

Mt Lassen Motor Transit (☎ 530-529-2722) operates a mail and passenger bus from Red Bluff to Susanville and back every day except Sunday. It departs from the Greyhound station at 8 am, arriving in Susanville at 1 pm, with stops along the way at Mineral (for Lassen Volcanic National Park), Chester (for Lake Almanor) and Westwood. The bus departs Susanville at 1:30 pm for the return trip.

Gold Country

California's 'Gold Country,' also known as the 'Mother Lode,' extends 300 miles along Hwy 49 (named in reference to the year the big rush to this area occurred) through the western Sierra Nevada foothills. Besides beautiful scenery and an abundance of opportunities for outdoor recreation, the area has a wealth of restored mining towns and an up-and-coming wine industry that people liken to the Napa Valley of 30 years ago.

Most places to stay and eat – especially in well-preserved towns such as Nevada City and Sutter Creek – are on the expensive side since they cater to (or are owned by) escapees from the San Francisco or Sacramento area who are used to more than preground coffee and doughnuts. Cheaper motel accommodations are found in service towns such as Auburn, Jackson and Grass Valley, which are less than attractive in themselves but generally not far from historic sites. Unfortunately, it's virtually impossible to travel the region without a car; San Francisco, Sacramento and Reno are the cheapest places to rent one.

History

California's gold rush started when James Marshall was inspecting the lumber mill he was building for John Sutter near present-day Coloma. He saw a fleck of gold in the mill's tailrace water and pulled out a gold nugget 'roughly half the size of a pea.' Marshall consulted Sutter, who tested the gold by methods described in an encyclopedia, and the two men found the piece to be of high quality. Sutter, however, wanted to finish his mill and thus made an agreement with his laborers that they could keep all the gold they found in their spare time if they kept working. Before long, word of the find leaked out.

Sam Brannan, for example, went to investigate the rumors just a few months after Marshall found his nugget. He went to Coloma (the little town by Sutter's Mill – see later in this chapter) to investigate. After finding 6oz of gold in one afternoon, he

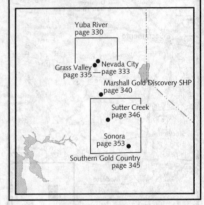

Highlights

- Amador County vineyards – Napa Valley wishes it looked so good
- Calaveras Big Trees State Park – the trees are big, the crowds are not
- Downtown Murphys – the definition of charming
- Empire Mine State Historic Park – equipment, buildings and a mine owner's home

Yuba River
page 330

Grass Valley
page 335

Nevada City
page 333

Marshall Gold Discovery SHP
page 340

Sutter Creek
page 346

Sonora
page 353

Southern Gold Country
page 345

returned to San Francisco and paraded through the streets, gold dust in hand, proclaiming, 'There's gold in the Sierra foothills!' Convinced that there was money to be made, he bought every piece of mining equipment in the area – from handkerchiefs to shovels. When gold seekers needed equipment for their adventure, Brannan sold them goods at a 100% markup and was a rich man by the time the first folks hit the foothills. (See the boxed text 'Sam Brannan' in the Wine Country chapter for what happened after that.)

By the time construction of the mill was finished, in the spring of 1848, gold seekers had begun to arrive. The first wave came from San Francisco. The new miners found

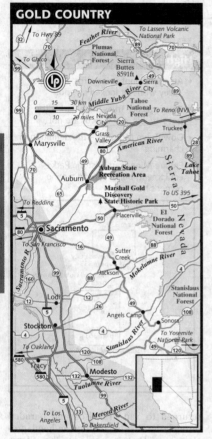

GOLD COUNTRY

To Hwy 89 · To Lassen Volcanic National Park
Feather River · Plumas National Forest · Sierra Buttes 8591ft
Downieville · Sierra City
Middle Yuba River
0   15   30 km
0   10   20 miles
Nevada City · Tahoe National Forest · To Reno (NV)
Grass Valley · Truckee
Marysville
American River
Auburn State Recreation Area · Lake Tahoe
Auburn
Marshall Gold Discovery State Historic Park · To US 395
To Redding
Placerville · El Dorado National Forest
Sacramento
To San Francisco
Sutter Creek
Mokelumne River
Jackson
Stanislaus National Forest
Lodi
Angels Camp · Sonora
Stockton · To Yosemite National Park
To Oakland
Tracy · Stanislaus River
Modesto
Tuolumne River
To Los Angeles · Merced River
To Bakersfield

miners believed was the source of all the gold found in the streams and riverbeds. (Since then, geologists have discovered that the kind of mother lode that miners dreamed of does not and cannot exist.)

Most prospectors didn't stick around after the initial diggings petered out. In 1859, when the Comstock Lode was found on the eastern side of the Sierra in Virginia City, Nevada (see coverage of the Comstock Lode in the Facts about Nevada section), many left. Those who did stay signed on with large operations, such as the Empire Mine in Grass Valley, which were financed by businesses or private fortunes. Gold-extraction processes became increasingly complex and invasive, culminating in the practice of hydraulic mining, by which miners drained lakes and rivers to power their water cannons and blast away entire hillsides (see the boxed text 'Getting the Gold'). After various environmental and agricultural battles ensued at Malakoff Diggins (see Malakoff Diggins State Historic Park later in this chapter), operators found the price of extraction too great to justify staying in business.

Currently, specimen gold – gold that is still attached to a piece of quartz, making it ideal for museum display – fetches higher prices than gold ore. The largest piece ever found is owned by Kautz Ironstone Vineyards in Murphys (see Things to See & Do in the Murphys section). Several large-scale, open-pit mines, primarily owned by out-of-state corporations, still exist. Locals will tell you (though guardedly) that there's still plenty of gold in the hills – most easily found in rivers and streams after a heavy rain.

Northern Gold Country

In response to James Marshall's find, most people headed straight for the area around Coloma, eventually called the Northern Mines (or Northern Diggins). Sacramento was the jumping-off point, where people abandoned river travel and bought the supplies needed to head into the hills. Valleys

gold so easily that they thought nothing of spending (or gambling away) all they had in one night, knowing that they could find just as much again the next day. They spread the word boastfully, thinking there was plenty of gold for all. By the end of 1848, San Francisco was nearly depleted of able-bodied men, while towns near the 'diggins' – as the mines were called – swelled with thousands of people. News spread to Oregon, the East Coast and South America, and by 1849, more than 60,000 people migrated to California to find the mother lode – the big deposit that

and tributaries of the Yuba, Feather, Bear and American rivers held the first sizable settlements, with Grass Valley and Nevada City as the hubs.

The towns in the Northern Mines area (from Nevada City to Placerville) are some of the most picturesque in the Gold Country – perched on mountainsides, entrenched in canyons and bordered by Tahoe National Forest. I-80, which connects Sacramento, Lake Tahoe and Reno, Nevada, offers easy access to most of them, though Hwy 49 is more scenic.

YUBA RIVER

The northernmost segment of Hwy 49 follows the North Yuba River through some remote, stunning parts of the Sierra Nevada. There are many trails (including part of the Pacific Crest Trail) for hikers, mountain bikers and skiers. The best source of trail and camping information is the Downieville Ranger Station (☎ 530-288-3231), open in the summer, or the North Yuba Ranger Station (☎ 530-288-3231) on Hwy 49 where it crosses the North Fork of the Yuba River.

The California State Park System owns 2000 acres of land along the South Yuba River and leases another 5000 acres from the Bureau of Land Management. Through the South Yuba River Project, the system hopes to acquire even more river access and connect Malakoff Diggins and South Yuba River state parks with hiking trails. Some of these trails are already in place, including the Independence Trail, which starts from the south side of the South Yuba River bridge on Hwy 49 and goes for about a mile. Get maps from the Forest Service Headquarters in Nevada City (see the Nevada City section), from the North Yuba Ranger Station or from either of the parks.

GOLD COUNTRY

Getting the Gold

California gold exists in two kinds of deposits: lode, in which gold quartz is buried deep in the ground, and placer, which originated in lodes but has been moved to the earth's surface, sometimes at the bottom of a creek, over the centuries by erosion and weathering. Mining techniques rely on the fact that gold is heavier than the gravel, dirt and sand surrounding it and will settle to the bottom of a receptacle while other debris is washed away.

Already separated from its earthen bed, and usually washed to stream and river bottoms, placer gold is the easiest to get. Miners plunge a pan into a streambed, swirl gravel and sand around and let the gold settle to the bottom while the other stuff splashes over the sides. This 'panning' was the most popular technique in early California mining.

To process larger amounts of gravel, miners used sluice boxes – long rectangular boxes outfitted with tin riffles (series of ridges) and sieves. Dirt was shoveled into the box and the stream passed over it, washing dirt away and catching gold dust in the riffles. Sometimes gas-powered dredges vacuumed the bottom of a river or stream, depositing the debris into large sluice boxes. Dredges are still used in mining and are visible in remote areas along riverbanks.

To get to lode deposits, miners go far into the earth, into the hard rock surrounding gold quartz. The labor and equipment required for hard-rock mining are so great that most hard-rock mines can be owned only by large companies such as the Anaconda Company, which mined Montana, Nevada and California, or wealthy families such as the Bournes, who operated Grass Valley's Empire Mine. Hard-rock mining blasts a vertical or inclined tunnel into the earth, in which miners descend via elevators or railroad cars, which also bring the ore to the surface. The ore is then put through a stamp mill, which crushes the ore fine enough to be sluiced.

Until it was banned in 1884 (see the section on Malakoff Diggins State Historic Park later in this chapter), hydraulic mining was also used to mine lodes. In that process, water cannons blasted entire hillsides away and miners sluiced the debris that came washing down.

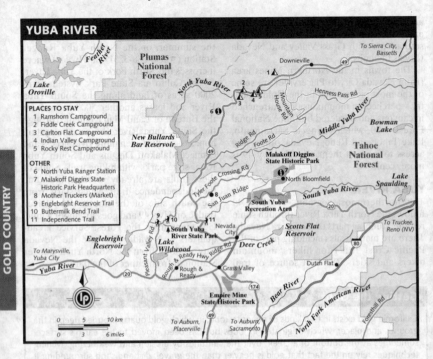

YUBA RIVER

PLACES TO STAY
1 Ramshorn Campground
2 Fiddle Creek Campground
3 Carlton Flat Campground
4 Indian Valley Campground
5 Rocky Rest Campground

OTHER
6 North Yuba Ranger Station
7 Malakoff Diggins State
  Historic Park Headquarters
8 Mother Truckers (Market)
9 Englebright Reservoir Trail
10 Buttermilk Bend Trail
11 Independence Trail

Between the Middle and South Forks of the Yuba lies San Juan Ridge – home to alternative and spiritual communities, hippies and (so some say) marijuana crops. **Mother Truckers** is where folks on the ridge buy organic groceries and catch up on local news. The store is 3 miles east of Hwy 49 on Tyler Foote Crossing Rd, which leads to Malakoff Diggins State Historic Park.

Sierra City
• **population 250** • **elevation 4187 feet**
At Sierra City, Butcher Ranch Rd turns north from Hwy 49 toward the **Sierra Buttes**, probably the closest thing to the Alps you'll find in California without hoisting a backpack. The scale here is much smaller, but the tight cluster of jagged peaks has the same awe-inspiring effect.

At Bassetts, 9 miles north of Sierra City, the Pacific Crest Trail crosses Hwy 49 and Gold Lake Rd and heads north through the Gold Lakes region. There's a vast network of trails here, good for backpacking as well as casual hikes. Get the *Lakes Basin, Downieville – Sierra City* map ($1.50) from the Sierra Country Store (☎ 530-862-1181) on Hwy 49.

Downieville
• **population 350** • **elevation 2899 feet**
This charming little gold rush town once had a population of 5000 and was known for being rough – its first justice of the peace was also the local saloon keeper, and the first woman to hang in the Mother Lode did so from Downieville's gallows. Nowadays the town is known for the **Downieville Downhill**, a mountain bike course that descends 5000 vertical feet in 12.4 miles and is rated the best downhill route in the USA by a popular bicycle magazine. Downieville Outfitters (☎ 530-289-0155), in the heart of Downieville, spends all summer shuttling people to

the top of the course ($10) and fixing their bikes at the bottom. Bike rental ranges from $25 for a basic mountain bike to $45 for one with shock absorbers that will make the trip more comfortable. West of Downieville, Hwy 49 passes numerous campgrounds and trailheads in the Tahoe National Forest. *Carlton Flat*, *Fiddle Creek*, *Indian Valley*, *Rocky Rest* and *Ramshorn* campgrounds all have first-come, first-served sites ($7) along the Yuba River: information is available at the Downieville Ranger Station or at the Downieville Grocery (☎ 530-289-3596).

Malakoff Diggins State Historic Park

Malakoff Diggins, with its restored town site, good museum, red stratified cliffs and gigantic mounds of tailings left behind by years of hydraulic mining, is worth a full day's exploration.

The world's first water cannons – designed specifically for hydraulic mining – cut a 200-foot canyon through ancient bedrock during the 1850s to unearth rich veins of gold. Rubble washed down from the hillsides, and the tailings dropped back into the South and Middle Forks of the Yuba River. This eventually created a problem when the waste reached the flat Sacramento Valley floor: by the 1860s, 20-foot mud glaciers blocked the rivers and caused severe flooding each spring during the Sierra snowmelt. After a year of heated courtroom (and barroom) debate between farmers and miners, most hydraulic mining practices were prohibited. North Bloomfield, the small mining community at the center of Malakoff's operation, went bankrupt and fell dormant.

The Malakoff Diggins State Historic Park Headquarters and Museum (☎ 530-265-2740) shows an interesting movie and sells literature and maps. Most of North Bloomfield's structures have been restored to their original condition and now house a few

Mining Glossary

arastra – a round, shallow pool with a turnstile in the middle to which several boulders and a mule's harness were attached; gold-bearing rocks were placed in the pool with a small amount of water, and as the mule walked, the boulders crushed the rocks to fine gravel, which was then panned or sluiced

dredge – a gas-powered pump used for vacuuming the sand and gravel at the bottom of a stream or river; it usually had a spout to deposit the debris into a sluice box

head frame – a big, wooden trestle-like structure that supports ropes and cables; used for lowering people and things into the mines

ore – pieces of rock, usually about the size of a grapefruit, containing gold

Pelton waterwheel – a waterwheel that had, instead of the usual single large bucket at every rung, a split bucket that redirected water into the bucket behind it so that no water was wasted and more force per turn was gained

stamp mill – a large metal or wooden frame from which hung several 'stamps,' long metal rods with solid cylinders at the end; cranks operated by water or horse power brought the stamps to the top of the frame, usually at various intervals, then let them fall with full weight to the surface below, where ore was placed

tailings – the leftover debris from a miner's sluice box

GOLD COUNTRY

operating stores. Admission to the park, including the museum, costs $5 per vehicle.

The park has primitive campsites, three developed campgrounds with $14 sites (reservable at ☎ 800-444-7275) and four rental cabins (converted old miners' cabins), plus many picnic areas and a network of hiking trails. There are no RV hookups.

The turn-off for the park, Tyler Foote Crossing Rd, is 11 miles north of Nevada City on Hwy 49 and goes northeast for 17 miles to the park entrance. The road crosses a 5000-foot pass and hits washboard gravel just before the park entrance; a 4WD vehicle is often necessary during the winter. Call the park headquarters for road information.

South Yuba River State Park

The longest single-span wood-truss covered bridge in the US, all 251 feet of it, crosses the South Yuba River here at Bridgeport (not to be confused with a California town in the eastern Sierra with the same name – see the Eastern Sierra section). Maps and information are available from the state park headquarters (☎ 530-432-2546) next to the bridge. The bridge – built for private commercial use in 1862 – is indeed interesting, but probably not worth the curvy, 7-mile drive (westward off of Hwy 49 on Pleasant Valley Rd). The park does offer gold panning in the summer and fall, as well as year-round bird walks on the last Sunday of each month. The hiking and swimming are definitely well worth the trip and can be enjoyed for at least half a day. The Buttermilk Bend trail skirts the South Yuba for 1.4 miles, offering river access and wonderful wildflower viewing around April. There's also a 1-mile trail to Englebright Reservoir, which has placid waters and several undeveloped campsites.

NEVADA CITY & GRASS VALLEY
- populations 2820 & 8291
- elevations 2525 & 2420 feet

Nevada City can probably trace its liberal roots to Aaron Sargent, a transplanted New England journalist who helped organize the Republican Party in California and later served in Congress and the Senate. Local

history has it that he authored the 19th Amendment (with input from his friend Susan B Anthony). He introduced a railroad bill in Congress that was signed into law by Abraham Lincoln and led to the construction of the transcontinental railroad. Thanks to the hippies (who arrived in the 1970s) and folks from Los Angeles and the Bay Area (who are still arriving), the town still seems progressive. The arts are a big part of life here – there are three theater companies, two alternative film houses and live music performances almost every night. The downtown is well preserved and has a quaint feel that makes it one of the best places in the Gold Country to spend a few days.

The flip side is found in Grass Valley, where area residents buy groceries, service their cars and get their pets groomed. Its historic business district, while still intact, is dwarfed by a sprawl of strip malls, gas stations and fast food restaurants, which sprang up when building codes were tossed aside in the name of progress during the mid- to late 1980s. The two towns are so intertwined that they share a newspaper – the *Union* - in which 'NC' denotes Nevada City and 'GV,' Grass Valley.

History

In 1851 George Knight followed a wayward cow to the slope of Gold Hill and stubbed his toe on a piece of gold-filled quartz. Rumor of the find spread quickly, and within three years Grass Valley had a population of 3000. Nevada City became – and remains – the area's cultural hub and the county seat for Grass Valley's thriving industry.

Grass Valley's mines – notably George Bourne's Empire Mine – were among the first shaft mines in California. They showed mine owners and investors that, with promotion of a company's stock and the use of large-scale operations, there were big bucks to be made in lode mining. The Empire Mine was the first mining company to sell stock. Because of the labor needed in the Empire Mine, Grass Valley was bigger than Los Angeles and San Diego in the 1860s and became the largest and longest-lived mining town in California.

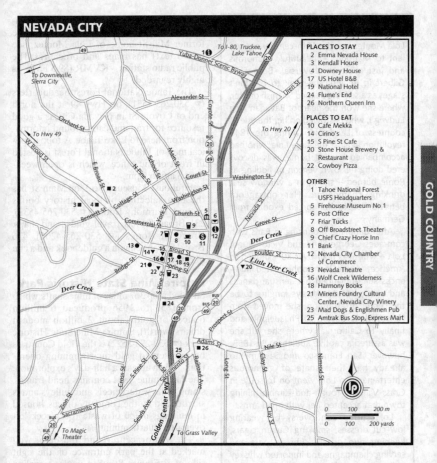

NEVADA CITY

PLACES TO STAY
2 Emma Nevada House
3 Kendall House
4 Downey House
17 US Hotel B&B
19 National Hotel
24 Flume's End
26 Northern Queen Inn

PLACES TO EAT
10 Cafe Mekka
14 Cirino's
15 S Pine St Cafe
20 Stone House Brewery & Restaurant
22 Cowboy Pizza

OTHER
1 Tahoe National Forest USFS Headquarters
5 Firehouse Museum No 1
6 Post Office
7 Friar Tucks
8 Off Broadstreet Theater
9 Chief Crazy Horse Inn
11 Bank
12 Nevada City Chamber of Commerce
13 Nevada Theatre
16 Wolf Creek Wilderness
18 Harmony Books
21 Miners Foundry Cultural Center, Nevada City Winery
23 Mad Dogs & Englishmen Pub
25 Amtrak Bus Stop, Express Mart

GOLD COUNTRY

Orientation

Hwy 49/20 spans the 5 miles separating the two towns; Hwy 49 turns northwest at Nevada City toward the Yuba River. Nevada City's streets, often crammed with pedestrians and horse-drawn carriages, are best navigated on foot. Broad St is the main thoroughfare, reached by the Broad St exit off Hwy 49/20.

Grass Valley's main thoroughfares are Mill St and W Main St (the heart of the historic business district) and E Main St, which goes north to the shopping centers and mini-malls,

continues north as the Nevada City Hwy and heads on into Nevada City as Sacramento St. S Auburn St divides E and W Main St.

Information

Nevada City's Chamber of Commerce and Downtown Association (☎ 530-265-2692, 800-655-6569), 132 Main St at the east end of Commercial St, has an immaculate public toilet and many brochures on recreation, lodging, restaurants and entertainment. It's in Ott's Assay Office, where James J Ott assayed the first ore samples from Nevada's

Grass Valley's Lola Montez

Lola Montez was the 19th-century equivalent to Madonna – beautiful, glamorous and just a bit controversial. Born Eliza Gilbert in Ireland, she took to London's stages as a self-proclaimed Spanish dancer, where she won the heart of Bavarian king Ludwig I, who bestowed on her the title of countess of Landsfeld. During the 1848 revolution against the king, Lola, who had accompanied Ludwig home, was discovered doing her own version of fiddling as Rome burned – sitting in a window seat drinking champagne. Her outrageous behavior led to her forced exodus from Germany.

After dabbling in dancing in Paris with comrades George Sand and Victor Hugo, Lola – who was now over 30 – moved to America, where less sophisticated audiences still applauded her sensual dances and exotic beauty. Always longing to be the center of attention, she moved from New York to Boston to Philadelphia and finally to California, where she felt she was assured a captive audience. By 1853, however, San Francisco and Sacramento already had their share of glamorous entertainers, so Lola went on to settle in Grass Valley, a rough-and-tumble mining town that accepted her with open arms.

Lola stirred controversy by wearing low-cut dresses, smoking Cuban cigars, keeping two grizzly cubs as pets and serving champagne and imported whiskey at her European-style 'salons,' at a time when women were expected to bake bread, keep clothes clean and not have their own wealth. Considered heavenly by the miners and hellish by miners' wives, Lola was Grass Valley's most famous citizen until the Australian gold rush drew her south to fresh audiences that had not had a chance to tire of her shows. Her former home, now the chamber of commerce, is still a Grass Valley landmark.

Comstock Lode. In Grass Valley, the Downtown Association (☎ 530-272-8315), in the former Mill St home of Lola Montez (see boxed text) has maps and brochures. The public radio station – KVMR (89.5 FM) – is highly regarded.

The Tahoe National Forest headquarters (☎ 530-265-4531), on Hwy 49 at the north end of Coyote St in Nevada City, is a good resource for trail and campground information from here to Lake Tahoe. A topographical map of Tahoe National Forest is posted in front of the office, which is open weekdays 8 am to 5 pm.

Firehouse Museum No 1, on Main St, has the best selection of local history books around. Harmony Books (☎ 530-265-4531), 231 Broad St, has travel guides and maps. Broad St Books (☎ 530-265-4204), 426 Broad St, can sell you a guidebook and a cup of espresso.

Empire Mine State Historic Park

Situated atop 367 miles of mine shafts, which from 1850 to 1956 produced 6 million ounces of gold (about 2 billion modern dollars' worth), Empire Mine State Historic Park (☎ 530-273-8522) is the Gold Country's best-preserved gold quartz mining operation – worth at least a half-day's exploration. The large mine yard contains head frames, stamp mills, waterwheels and pulleys and is surrounded by the company offices, housed in buildings made of waste rock (rock left over after quartz mining).

The visitor center and museum, well marked at the park entrance on the right side of E Empire St when you're traveling east, shows a worthwhile movie and offers free ranger-led tours every hour. If you miss the tour, be sure to see the color-coded mine system model in the room adjacent to the visitor center. Next to the largest head frame in the mine yard is a stairway that leads 40 feet down into the main mine shaft.

On the other side of the visitor center you'll find stately buildings that belonged to the Bourne family, under whose ownership the Empire Mine prospered. You can visit the elegant country club, English manor home, gardener's house and rose garden on

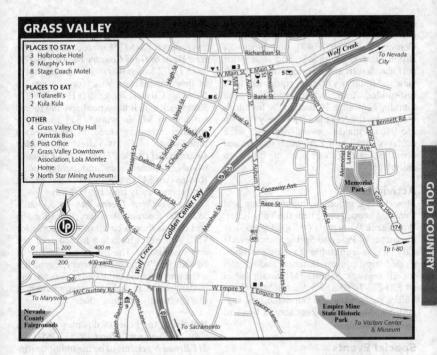

GRASS VALLEY

PLACES TO STAY
3 Holbrooke Hotel
6 Murphy's Inn
8 Stage Coach Motel

PLACES TO EAT
1 Tofanelli's
2 Kula Kula

OTHER
4 Grass Valley City Hall
  (Amtrak Bus)
5 Post Office
7 Grass Valley Downtown
  Association, Lola Montez
  Home
9 North Star Mining Museum

GOLD COUNTRY

a docent-led tour; check the visitor center for the day's schedule.

Hiking trails begin near the old stamp mill in the mine yard and pass abandoned mines and equipment. A trail map is available at the visitor center. The park is 2 miles east of Grass Valley via the Empire St exit off Hwy 49. The park and visitor center (see the Grass Valley map) are open 9 am to 6 pm daily (10 am to 5 pm in winter); $3.

North Star Mining Museum

Grass Valley's North Star Mine used the largest Pelton waterwheel ever made (see mining glossary in boxed text). The mine's old stone powerhouse on the west bank of Wolf Creek, at Mill St's south end, is now a museum (☎ 530-273-4255) with a small collection of Pelton waterwheels (and their prototypes), mining equipment and artifacts. A few shady, creek-side tables behind the museum make nice picnic spots. The museum is open 10 am to 5 pm daily May to October; a donation is requested.

Firehouse Museum No 1

Housed in Nevada City's original firehouse, this museum (☎ 530-265-5468), 214 Main St, has an extensive Chinese collection – including the entire altar of an 1862 Joss House (see the boxed text 'Joss Houses' in the Sacramento Valley chapter). It also has and a haunted photograph that supposedly houses a living spirit, and attracts parapsychologists by the busload. The museum, which is across the street from the post office, is open 11 am to 4 pm daily April to October; free.

Miners Foundry Cultural Center

Built in 1856, Nevada City's foundry produced the first Pelton waterwheel, which revolutionized hydraulic mining. After WWII, the foundry made Health Master juicers, which became popular with health gurus. Now it's the Miners Foundry Cultural Center (☎ 530-265-5040), one block off Broad St at 325 Spring St, and is used for performance art and private parties. You can view the foundry's original equipment on a self-guided tour, which starts at the foundry's entrance. Housed in the foundry's old garage, the **Nevada City Winery** (☎ 530-265-9463) makes award-winning wine (notably Syrah and Zinfandel) on site and operates a tasting room, open noon to 5 pm daily; free.

Activities
Most hiking, mountain biking, skiing and kayaking happen on or near the Yuba River. Wolf Creek Wilderness (☎ 530-265-9653), at the corner of Pine and Spring Sts in Nevada City, has a reputable kayaking school, guided trips, equipment rental and apparel for all seasons. Samurai Mountain Bikes (☎ 530-272-7790), 153 S Auburn St in Grass Valley, rents bikes and can make trail suggestions. Mountain bikers should head to Downieville.

Special Events
As home to the Nevada County Fairgrounds, Grass Valley hosts most of the area's large events, including the Sierra Festival of the Arts in late May, the annual Father's Day Weekend Bluegrass Festival in June (the Tour of Nevada City Bicycle Classic is on the same weekend) and the weeklong Nevada County Fair in mid-August. There is the popular Jazz Jubilee, which is held at Nevada City's Miners Foundry Cultural Center on the third weekend in May, and many Christmas-themed events in December.

Places to Stay
It's worth paying a little extra to stay in Nevada City, especially if you're going for the quaint B&B experience. Otherwise, there are a few cheap independent inns and plenty of chain motels near the Golden Center Freeway (Hwy 49) in Grass Valley. Weekend prices are around $10 higher than weekday prices, which are the ones listed here.

Motels The **Stage Coach Motel** (☎ 530-272-3701, 405 S Auburn St), in Grass Valley, has rooms for $45 ($65 for four people). The **Best Western Gold Country Inn** (☎ 530-273-1393, 11972 Sutton Way), about 2 miles north of downtown Grass Valley on the way to Nevada City, is east off Hwy 49/20's Brunswick exit. It has a pool, spa and rooms for $60 to $75 in winter, $75 to $89 in summer. Standing alone on Hwy 49 two miles south of Grass Valley, the **Golden Chain Motel** (☎ 530-273-7279) has 4 acres of woods, a picnic area and heated pool. Rooms cost $48 to $78 and are noisy except for the ones away from the highway.

The **Northern Queen Inn** (☎ 530-265-5824, 400 Railroad Ave) has rooms for $66 and chalets that sleep up to five people for $110. Amenities include a heated pool, spa and restaurant. The inn is on the site of Nevada City's Chinese cemetery; legend has it the graves of the cremated bodies are still in the ground, though the grave markers, if there were any, are long gone.

Hotels In the heart of downtown Nevada City, the **National Hotel** (☎ 530-265-4551, 211 Broad St) claims to be the oldest continuously operating hotel west of the Rocky Mountains. The building was constructed in the 1850s; the furnishings (1960s vintage) have seen better days. Rooms are $68 any day of the week. A few doors up Broad St, the **US Hotel B&B** (☎ 530-265-7999) has elegantly restored rooms starting at $95, including breakfast and complimentary wine in the evening.

In Grass Valley, the **Holbrooke Hotel** (☎ 530-273-1353, 212 W Main St) is a good choice. It has Mark Twain's signature in the hotel register and very nice rooms for $75 to $155, including breakfast.

B&Bs Two blocks from downtown Nevada City, the **Kendall House** (☎ 530-265-0405, 534 Spring St) has wonderful owners (who are friendly, well informed and good cooks to boot) and a heated pool; rooms are $105 to $160. In town, the **Emma Nevada House** (☎ 530-265-4415, 800-916-3662, 528 E Broad St) is in the childhood home of 1890s opera

JOHN ELK III

Lobby in the Paramount Theatre, Oakland

JOHN ELK III

Claremont Resort and Spa, in the Oakland Hills

JOHN ELK III

Sproul Plaza and the Campanile, UC Berkeley

NANCY KELLER

Chinese Temple, Oroville

JOHN ELK III

Capitol dome, Sacramento

JOHN ELK III

Beringer winery, Napa Valley

South Yuba River State Park

Mt Shasta

Lava tube, Lava Beds National Monument

JOHN ELK III

NANCY KELLER

JOHN ELK III

Mt Lassen reflected in Manzanita Lake, Lassen National Park

Rafting on the Trinity River

Castle Crags State Park

star Emma Nevada. It has a hot tub and six rooms for $100 to $155. A few doors down, the *Downey House* (☎ 530-265-2815, 800-258-2815, 517 W Broad St) has southwest decor, nice gardens and rooms for $90 to $120 midweek, and $95 to $120 on weekends, with a discount for staying two nights or more. The *Flume's End* (☎ 530-265-9665, 317 S Pine St), in Nevada City, is beside Deer Creek on 3 acres, but only a few blocks from town. Rooms are $85 to $140.

Near Grass Valley's historic center, *Murphy's Inn* (☎ 530-273-6873, 318 Neal St) has eight Victorian-style rooms, which cost $105 to $155.

Places to Eat
Open until midnight, Nevada City's *Cafe Mekka* (☎ 530-478-1517, 237 Commercial St), whose overstuffed couches, brocade-and-gauze drapes and heavy wooden screen attract an eclectic young crowd, has food for around $7, eye-popping desserts and live acoustic music on weekends. Also in Nevada City, the *S Pine St Cafe* (☎ 530-265-0260, 110 S Pine St) between Broad and Spring Sts, is a good choice for breakfast.

Cowboy Pizza (☎ 530-265-2334, 315 Spring St) has excellent pizzas (with many veggie options) for around $16 for a large; it

is open Wednesday through Sunday. For a hearty Italian meal among locals, try *Cirino's* (☎ 530-265-2246, 309 Broad St), where reservations are recommended (especially on Wednesday, when they make pizza) even though the atmosphere is totally casual. Dinners are $6 to $11. In the town's original brewery building, the *Stone House Brewery & Restaurant* (☎ 530-265-3960, 107 Sacramento St) produces top-notch ales, lagers and porters. The affordable bar menu, served in the lively brewpub, has food for $5 to $8 and is as good as the restaurant menu ($7 to $15) served upstairs.

In Grass Valley, *Tofanelli's* (☎ 530-272-1468, 302 W Main St) is well known for its friendly service and good food (especially breakfast). Most items are under $10. *Kula Kula* (☎ 530-274-2229, 207 W Main St) serves outstanding Japanese food for $6 to $11 (around $5 for lunch) and has live piano music on Saturday night.

Entertainment
The Prospector section of the *Union* comes out Thursdays, with a listing of what's going on around the area; it's widely available. Harmony Books on Broad St in Nevada City is a good spot to find out about music and theater events.

The Cornish Pastie

Though the mines are long closed, Grass Valley folks still love their Cornish pasties (pronounced PAST-eez), pastry pockets stuffed with meat and potatoes and resembling turnovers or calzones. Introduced by tin miners from Cornwall, England, pasties were inexpensive, easy to make and traveled well in a miner's lunch pail. In fact, a three-level lunch pail was invented around the pastie: the bottom level held hot tea, which kept the pasties on the second level warm; sweets and tobacco took up the third level.

Although Grass Valley's pastie shops advertise 'original ingredients' and '100-year-old recipes,' you probably wouldn't want to eat a true 1850s pastie, made with bacon grease, salted beef and months-old potatoes. Today's versions are usually made with vegetable shortening and filled with everything from apples to broccoli and turkey.

Ask any older woman in the area where you can get the best pastie around, and she'll inevitably answer 'in my kitchen.' Should you *not* get invited, a reliable place to sample a pastie is *Marshall's Pasties* (☎ 530-272-2844, 203 Mill St). It has a cramped counter downstairs and a few well-worn tables upstairs. Thanks to modern technology, Marshall's now uses a microwave to warm up the product of their 100-year-old recipe.

Bars For drinking and darts in Nevada City, try *Mad Dogs & Englishmen Pub* (☎ 530-265-8173, 211 Spring St), which has live entertainment on weekends. The *Chief Crazy Horse Inn* (☎ 530-265-9933, 203 Commercial St) has a mixed crowd (hard-core 6am-2am whiskey drinkers along with just-got-off-the-trail outdoorsy types), DJ music and pool tables. One block away but worlds apart, *Friar Tucks* (☎ 530-265-9320, 111 Pine St) is a cozy wine bar with a slightly older crowd and live music nightly.

Cinemas Probably the smallest, friendliest and most environmentally conscientious movie house in California (management serves popcorn in real bowls, coffee in real mugs and bakes fresh brownies for intermission; they don't rely on paper and plastic products), the *Magic Theater* (☎ 530-265-8262, 107 Argall Way), south of downtown Nevada City, shows nightly films for $3 (Monday to Thursday) or $4 (Friday to Sunday). The 1865 brick *Nevada Theater* (☎ 530-265-6161, 4401 Broad St) is California's first theater building. It's used for live theater and screens current films Friday to Sunday night.

Theater The area's biggest productions are by the professional *Foothill Theatre Company* (☎ 530-265-8587), which uses the Miners Foundry Cultural Center and Nevada Theater as venues. *Apollo Theater Company* (☎ 530-692-8620) produces several operas each year, most often staged at St Joseph's Cultural Center in Grass Valley. For offbeat entertainment in an intimate setting, check out what's on at the *Off Broadstreet Theater* (☎ 530-265-8686, 305 Commercial St), a dessert theater that presents mostly adult comedies.

Getting There & Away
Amtrak runs two buses daily (both in the morning) between the Nevada City-Grass Valley and Sacramento ($20). In Nevada City, buses stop at the Express Mart store, 301 Sacramento St at Hwy 49. In Grass Valley, they stop in front of City Hall, 125 E Main St.

Getting Around
The Gold Country Stage (☎ 530-477-0103) travels between the towns of Grass Valley and Nevada City ($1 per ride, $2 for an all-day pass) Monday to Friday from 7:30 am to 6 pm, with night runs from 5:30 to 9:45 pm. In Nevada City the bus stops at the corner of Broad and Coyote Sts; in Grass Valley it stops in front of the post office on E Main St. The Main St Trolley makes the same trip for the same reasonable rates; it leaves from the National Hotel on Broad St in Nevada City. Call for a current schedule (☎ 530-265-4551).

AUBURN
• population 12,500 • elevation 1255 feet

In 1856 Auburn started its own minor railroad to compete with trains running from Sacramento to Folsom by bringing people farther north and east, closer to the mines. The Sacramento-Folsom line eventually shut down, while Auburn's railroad became part of Central Pacific's transcontinental route. Interstate 80 follows this route between the Bay Area and Lake Tahoe and is a commuter passage for people who live in Auburn and work in Sacramento. Auburn's proximity to I-80 makes it one of the most visited towns in the Gold Country, though it's mostly a service center town with strip malls, automotive stores and fast food restaurants. The historic part of town (called Old Town) is nice and can be explored in an hour or so without venturing far from the interstate, but folks traveling Hwy 49 to more picturesque Gold Country towns needn't bother stopping here.

Orientation & Information
Auburn lies east of I-80, with the Old Town south of the noticeable Placer County Courthouse (a large yellow building, very visible from the freeway) and the new part of town spreading north and east; Lincoln Way and High St form an 'X' (the town's main intersection and junction of the old and new sections) about a block east of the courthouse. There are supermarkets, gas stations and chain motels on Hwy 49, and several banks near the 'X.' Old Town contains Auburn's

not-too-glitzy antiques stores, neon-signed bars and good restaurants.

Housed in the old Auburn railroad depot at the north end of Lincoln Way, the Auburn Area Chamber of Commerce (☎ 530-885-5616) has museum, lodging and dining guides. It's open 9 am to 5 pm weekdays.

Things to See & Do
Auburn's best history displays are at the **Placer County Museum**, on the 1st floor of the stately Placer County Courthouse. The museum is open 10 am to 4 pm Tuesday to Sunday and is free. The courthouse is open 8 am to 5 pm daily.

More educational and less polished is the **Gold Country Museum**, toward the back of the fairgrounds on High St, open 10 am to 3:30 pm Tuesday to Friday, 11 am to 4 pm weekends. The $1 admission is also good for the **Bernhard Museum Complex**, 291 Auburn-Folsom Rd (at the south end of High St), built in 1851 as the Traveler's Rest Hotel. The museum has displays depicting the typical life of a 19th-century farm family, including the requisite winery and carriage house. It's open 10 am to 3:30 pm Tuesday to Friday, noon to 4 pm weekends. Information about these three museums, and all other Placer County museums, is available by calling ☎ 530-889-6500.

Places to Stay & Eat
The only motel in downtown Auburn is the slightly shabby **Elmwood Motel** (☎ 530-885-5186, 588 High St), with an outdoor pool and rooms for $40/45 single/double.

At the north end of Lincoln Way, 3 miles north of downtown, the **Best Western Golden Key** (☎ 530-885-8611) has a heated pool and rooms for around $70. Alongside I-80 on Auburn Ravine Rd are a few motels, including the **Auburn Inn** (☎ 530-885-1800, 800-272-1444, 800-626-1900), which has a spa, pool and rooms for $60/65, and the small **Foothills Motel** (☎ 530-885-8444) with a pool, hot tub, friendly owners and rooms for $50/65.

Old Town has good restaurants, while downtown has coffee shops where you can dine on grilled-cheese sandwiches and coleslaw with the over-60 crowd.

Awful Annies (☎ 530-888-9857, 160 Sacramento St), a local favorite in Old Town, serves breakfast and lunch indoors or outdoors on a deck for $4 to $8. **Cafe Delicias** (☎ 530-888-2050, 1591 Lincoln Way) in Old Town is the best place for Mexican food (around $6); walk around back to see their tortillas being made by hand.

Try **Bootleggers** (☎ 530-889-2229, 210 Washington St) for a splurge. It's housed in Auburn's original city hall. Prices are $8 to $18 for lunch and dinner.

Getting There & Away
Amtrak has one train and two buses per day to Sacramento ($7.50, 1¼ hours). All leave from the train platform and bus shelter at 277 Nevada St at the corner of Fulweiler (about 2 miles north of the historic part of Old Town). Tickets are sold on board.

AUBURN STATE RECREATION AREA
About 4 miles south of Auburn, the North and Middle Forks of the American River converge below a bridge on Hwy 49. In summer this is a popular spot for sunning and swimming, though signs clearly warn that the current is strong and dangerous. Numerous trails in the area are shared by hikers, mountain bikers and horses. Boaters have an entire campground and boating trail exclusively for them.

The best place to get maps and information is the Auburn State Recreation Area California Department of Parks and Recreation office (☎ 530-885-5648), on Hwy 49 halfway between the bridge and Auburn. Hours are 8 am to 4:30 pm weekdays; trail and campground information is available from a box outside. For mountain bike rentals try Bike & Hike (☎ 530-885-3861) in Auburn at 227 Palm Ave.

One of the most popular trails is the **Western States Trail**, which connects Auburn State Recreation Area to Folsom Lake State Recreation Area and Folsom Lake. It is the site of an annual '100 Miles in One Day' horseback ride, which starts in Soda Springs (near Truckee – see the Lake Tahoe section in the Sierra Nevada chapter) and ends in

Auburn. The trail is also the route for the annual Western States 100-mile endurance run, held each year in June.

COLOMA
• **population 1100** • **elevation 750 feet**

Originally known for its proximity to Sutter's Mill (site of California's first gold discovery), Coloma is now famous for its white-water rafting. Situated on the South Fork of the American River, about 11 miles north of Placerville, all that makes up the 'town' is Marshall Gold Discovery State Historic Park and a few choice campgrounds and businesses along Hwy 49. Jungle Java (☎ 530-642-1996), at 7291 Hwy 49, acts as Coloma's tourist information center and general year-round rendezvous.

Marshall Gold Discovery State Historic Park

The South Fork of the American River and Hwy 49 run right through Marshall Gold Discovery State Historic Park. Though you can see most of the park by just driving through, its hiking trails, restored buildings and replica of Sutter's Mill warrant a few hours out of the car. The State Park Visitors Information Center & Museum (☎ 530-622-3470), on Bridge St just off Hwy 49, shows a worthwhile movie and has a good mining exhibit.

You can make a loop tour by car up to the James Marshall Monument, marked by a statue at the miner's grave site, or hike up the Monument Trail, which passes old mining equipment and a nice designated picnic area (as well as scenic clearings and rock outcroppings that are also fine for picnicking). The visitor center sells a good interpretive trail map for $1.50.

Panning for gold is a popular recreational pastime here – you can pay $3 to pan at a private operation (on Hwy 49 across from the visitor center), where you're assured to find some 'color,' as the old-time miners used to call the gold as it appeared in their pans. Or take a chance and try the river's east bank, just across the bridge from the mill replica. Pans are available from the visitor center, and demonstrations are given most

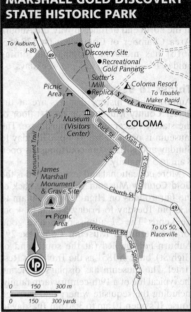

MARSHALL GOLD DISCOVERY STATE HISTORIC PARK

weekends from May to September. At the end of September, the World Gold Panning Championships attract a large crowd.

The park is open 8 am to sunset daily (the visitor center closes at 6 pm from May to September, at 5 pm the rest of the year). Admission is $5 per car, collected at the museum.

White-Water Rafting

The American River offers some of California's most accessible white-water rafting. Accessibility means crowds on most weekends, but it also means a wide choice of trips and outfitters. The season is usually from May to mid-October. Jungle Java, on Hwy 49 in Coloma, is a good place to find out about river conditions and trip availability.

Half-day trips usually start upstream at Chile Bar sand bar and end near Marshall Gold Discovery State Historic Park. Full-day trips put in at the Coloma Bridge and

GOLD COUNTRY

take out at Salmon Falls, near Folsom Lake. The half-day options start in Class III water and are action-packed to the end (full-day trips start out slowly, then build up to Class III as a climax). The full-day trips include lunch, which is often a gourmet affair. Recommended for their meticulous equipment, knowledgeable guides and tasty food, Whitewater Connection (☎ 800-336-7238) has half-day trips for $69 weekdays ($89/84 Saturday/Sunday), full-day trips for $89 weekdays ($109/$99 Saturday/Sunday) and two-day trips starting at $195.

Another good bet, for the same reasons, is Whitewater Voyages (☎ 800-488-7238, www .whitewatervoyages.com), whose friendly guides will make you feel at home on the river for half-day trips (weekends only, $68), full-day trips ($99 weekdays, $112/106 Saturday/Sunday) or two-day trips ($199 Monday to Thursday, $225 Friday and Sunday, $238 Saturday). Mariah Wilderness Expeditions (☎ 510-233-2303, 800-462-7424) is also recommended and has similar prices. Cheaper operators offer no-frills service.

A free and fun pastime is watching people navigate the Trouble Maker Rapid, upstream from the bridge next to Sutter's Mill in the state park. The Coloma Club (☎ 530-626-6390), 7171 Hwy 49, is a bar, restaurant and hangout that comes alive with guides and river rats when the water is high.

Places to Stay & Eat
Most rafting companies own private campgrounds for their guests who do overnight trips. If the campgrounds are not full, however, they often let those who do day trips stay for around $12.

The *American River Resort* (☎ 530-622-6700), just south of the state park, has a restaurant and bar, a playground, a pond and farm animals. Reservations are necessary only in summer. Tent and RV sites cost $28, and cabins rent for $115 to $130. Across the river, the *Coloma Resort* (☎ 530-621-2267) gets just as crowded but has more space at each campsite (fewer trees, though). Tent and RV sites cost $28 ($30 on weekends) Tent cabins are $40 and units with a kitchen and bath go for $75.

Camp Lotus (☎ 530-622-8672), 1 mile west of Coloma (take the Lotus Rd turnoff from Hwy 49), has 10 RV spaces but is primarily for tenters. Showers here are hot, the toilets flush and sites cost $15 on weekdays, $21 on weekends. No dogs are allowed. They close from November to April.

The *Golden Lotus B&B* (☎ 530-621-4562, 1006 Lotus Rd) is highly recommended by locals; rooms cost $89 to $128.

PLACERVILLE
• population 8800 • elevation 1866 feet

'Old Hangtown,' as Placerville is fondly known, has always relied on travelers passing through for its livelihood. Originally it was a destination for gold seekers who reached California by following the South Fork of the American River. In 1857 the first stagecoach to cross the Sierra Nevada linked Placerville to Nevada's Carson Valley – a route that eventually became part of the nation's first transcontinental stage route. Today, Placerville is a gas and food stop for people traveling between Sacramento and South Lake Tahoe on Hwy 50. An hour's stop reveals a bustling and well-preserved downtown and some great antiques shops.

History
Jared Sheldon and William Daylor, who planted the first wheat in the Sacramento Valley, came east during the summer of 1848 to sell some cattle to the miners at Coloma and decided to poke around a previously unmined area about 12 miles southeast of modern-day Placerville. They found about $17,000 worth of gold in one week, but they were so dedicated to their farm that they returned to it and hired some Miwok Indians (for 50¢ per day) to do the digging for them. Other miners came to settle here, calling the place 'Dry Diggins,' since the most gold was discovered near the surface of dry streambeds, where it could be extracted with knives, spoons and pointed sticks.

At the peak of the gold rush, gold was found regularly enough to obviate crime, and what crime did occur was dealt with by 'miners' law,' such as tying a criminal to a tree stark naked in the middle of mosquito season. As more people arrived and the gold became harder to find, crime ran rampant and makeshift miners' courts became common. The courts' sentences increased in severity until, in 1849, five men charged with robbery and attempted murder were met with a unanimous 'Hang them!' In short order, the men were taken to a tree on Main St and strung up. After that event, Dry Diggins was given the name Hangtown. By 1854, when the growing community boasted a church, a temperance union, a theater and several restaurants, and placer mining was supporting an increasing number of miners and their families, the name of the town was changed to Placerville.

Orientation & Information

Main St, the heart of downtown Placerville, runs parallel to Hwy 50 between Canal St and Cedar Ravine Rd. Hwy 49 meets Main St at the west edge of downtown. Mini-malls and fast food restaurants lie at both ends of Main St but are concentrated toward the east end of town.

The El Dorado County Chamber of Commerce (☎ 530-621-5885, 800-457-6279), 542 Main St, has information on Gold Country and the Lake Tahoe area and is open 9 am to 5 pm weekdays. On weekends and holidays they have a staffed information booth in an old caboose at the junction of Main St and Hwy 49. The Wine Smith (☎ 530-622-0516), 346 Main St, is open Tuesday to Sunday and sells a good recreation guide to El Dorado County for $1. Banks and several good bookstores are on Main St; the post office is one block south on Sacramento St.

Things to See & Do

Most buildings along Main St date back to the 1850s, including the El Dorado County Courthouse, 543 Main St, and Placerville Hardware, 441 Main St, the oldest continuously operating hardware store west of the Mississippi River. An old photograph in front of the store shows early Placerville and the hangman's tree.

The Placerville Historical Museum (☎ 530-626-0773), housed in the Fountain &

Tallman Soda Works Building at 524 Main St, has a small collection of soda factory relics and Placerville photographs. It's free; hours are noon to 4 pm Friday to Sunday.

One mile north of town on Bedford Ave, Gold Bug Park (☎ 530-642-5238) is on the site of four mining claims that yielded gold from 1849 to '88. You can visit the Gold Bug Mine for $3 (including hard hat) and explore the museum, stamp mill and picnic grounds free. It's open 10 am to 4 pm daily May through October, and weekends only in March, April and November (closed December to February).

The El Dorado County Historical Museum (☎ 530-621-5865), on the El Dorado County Fairgrounds west of downtown Placerville (exit north on Placerville Drive from Hwy 50), is an extensive complex of restored buildings, mining equipment and re-created businesses. It's open 10 am to 4 pm Wednesday to Saturday, noon to 4 pm Sunday. Admission is free.

In early October, the Dixieland Jazz Jubilee attracts big-name musicians from all over the country. Call ☎ 530-621-5885 for information.

Places to Stay

The *Placerville KOA* (☎ 530-676-2267), 6 miles west of Placerville on Hwy 50 (exit north on Shingle Springs Drive), sits on 18 acres of land and has a store, laundry and pool. Tent sites are well shaded, though not grassy, and cost $20 during the winter and $22 in the summer. Hookups cost $22 to $29, and cabins are available in the $39 to $44 range.

In downtown Placerville, the *Cary House Hotel* (☎ 530-622-4271, 300 Main St) is completely nonsmoking. It has newly restored rooms that reflect their bordello history, starting at $75 (including breakfast). Ask for a room in the back to avoid street noise.

The large pink *Combellack-Blair House B&B* (☎ 530-622-3764, 3059 Cedar Ravine Rd), two blocks south of Main St, has three Victorian-style rooms for $110. The *Chichester-McKee House B&B* (☎ 530-626-1882, 800-831-4008, 800 Spring St), north of Hwy 50 at Hwy 49, charges from $80 to $110,

Places to Eat

Fast food restaurants – well marked and highly visible from Hwy 50 – abound in Placerville, but 'real' food is found downtown. *Gelato D'Oro Cafe* (☎ 530-626-8097, *311 Main St*) is a good place for coffee and pastries, light meals and live music. A newspaper clipping on display attests to the fact that Frank Sinatra once ate at *Lil' Mama D Carlo's* (☎ 530-626-1612, *482 Main St*), which is a favorite stop for performers en route to South Lake Tahoe. It's a small, casual place with homemade pasta for under $10 (closed Monday). For Mexican food, *La Casa Grande* (☎ 530-626-5454, *251 Main St*) is popular with the locals for sit-down meals (around $7), while *Creekside Cantina* (☎ 530-626-7966, *451 Main St*) makes good burritos for less than $5 (closed Sunday).

Entertainment

Placerville's bars are akin to the neighborhood watering holes in the Midwest: they open at 6 am, get a yearly cleaning on Christmas and are great for people who want to soak up local color. Marked by vintage signs, the *Hangman Tree* (☎ 530-622-3878, *305 Main St*) and *Liars' Bench* (☎ 530-622-0494, *255 Main St*) are good for catching the ol' Hangtown scene, as is *Gil's* (☎ 530-621-1402, *372 Main St*).

Getting There & Away

Amtrak has three buses daily to Sacramento ($8, one hour). The bus stop is in front of the Buttercup Pantry Restaurant, just south of Hwy 50 at the corner of Pacific and Main Sts.

Tickets to Sacramento on Greyhound, which also has three buses daily, cost $11. Greyhound also runs three buses to Stateline (see South Lake Tahoe in the Sierra Nevada chapter) for $19. The Greyhound stop is at 1750 Broadway. It's closed Saturday afternoon and Sunday.

AROUND PLACERVILLE
Apple Hill

In 1860, a miner planted a Rhode Island greening apple tree on what is now the property of the Larsens, and thus began what is now the prolific Apple Hill, a 20-sq-mile area east of Placerville and north of Hwy 50 where there are now more than 60 growers. The miner's Rhode Island greening still stands (a major gimmick for the Larsens, who operate a museum) and is flanked by Granny Smiths, pippins, red and yellow delicious, Fujis from Japan and braeburns from New Zealand. Apple growers sell directly to the public, usually from September to around December.

A decent map of Apple Hill is available at the Apple Hill Visitors Center in the Camino Hotel, near the Camino exit off Hwy 50 (☎ 530-644-7692). For a condensed Apple Hill tour, take the Camino exit north onto Barkley Rd until it becomes Larsen Drive. Follow Larsen Drive (which will become Cable and then Mace Rd) until it meets Pony Express Trail back beside Hwy 50. White signs emblazoned with bright red apples mark connecting side roads and byways.

Favorite stops to buy apples, cider, pies and handicrafts are Larsen's Apple Barn, 2461 Larsen Drive; Boa Vista Orchards, 2952 Carson Rd; High Hill Ranch, just off Carson Rd at 2901 High Hill Rd; Bolsters Hilltop Ranch, 2000 Larsen Drive; and Argyres Orchard, 4220 N Canyon Rd.

El Dorado County Farm Trails

The El Dorado County Farm Trails Association (☎ 530-621-2363) tries to 'keep small farming alive in a rural lifestyle that stands at the doorstep of urban development,' a promotional flyer says. They have marked a 100-mile route with blue, red and yellow El Dorado County Farm Trails signs indicating that the adjacent farm sells directly to the public and welcomes visitors. Maps and information are available at the El Dorado County Chamber of Commerce in Placerville or by calling the association.

Wineries

El Dorado County wines are becoming popular and frequently show up on Bay Area menus. To compete with the Napa and Sonoma markets, area wineries have invested a good deal in their properties, and most offer free tastings on weekends. You can pick up a map at the chamber of commerce or at Wine Smith in Placerville, or from the El Dorado Winery Association (☎ 916-967-1299, 800-306-3956, www .eldoradowines.org), PO Box 1614, Placerville, CA 95667.

Some noteworthy wineries, all north of Hwy 50, are Lava Cap Winery (☎ 530-621-0175), 2221 Fruitridge Rd; Madrona Vineyards (☎ 530-644-5948), just north of Carson Rd on High Hill Rd; and Boeger Winery (☎ 530-622-8094) at 1709 Carson Rd. During Passport Weekends, held in March and April, one 'passport' gets you into seven wineries that offer special tastings and tours.

Southern Gold Country

As people realized that the topography and geology of the Cosumnes, Calaveras, Stanislaus and Tuolumne rivers were similar to the environs of gold-bearing rivers up north, they started exploring the southern foothills and found equally rich deposits. Miners from Mexico, who came north over the Gila Trail (a trade and travel route between Silver City, New Mexico, and the Gold Country that was established after the Mexican-American War), were some of the earliest and most productive prospectors on the scene. When the Argonauts (as young Americans searching for gold were called) arrived in mid-1849, they thought it was unfair for 'foreigners' to make such an easy living off American land and so imposed a $20 per person foreign miners tax, which sent many people back over the border.

These Southern Mines, which extend from Placerville south to Mariposa, were originally reached via Stockton. Some good skiing lies east of the southern Gold Country, notably along Hwy 4 (out of Murphys) and Hwy 108 (out of Sonora). The wine industry in Amador County is booming, thanks to some excellent Zinfandels produced in 1995 and 1996 and to the friendliness of small-winery owners.

PLYMOUTH
• population 814 • elevation 1086 feet

This little town, on Hwy 49 about 3 miles north of the Hwy 16 intersection, is growing quickly as the surrounding vineyards welcome more tourists each year. The town is mostly a service center, with a grocery store and gas station, but the large *Far Horizons 49er Village RV Park and Campground* (☎ 209-245-6981) on Hwy 49 isn't a bad place to spend the night. Amador County wineries are concentrated east of Plymouth on Steiner and Shenandoah Rds.

Wineries
The Swiss-born Uhlingers began the wine industry here when they planted vines in 1856. The region wasn't really developed until the 1960s, however, when grapes that were traditionally sold to large wine makers for blending started yielding juice and skin of high enough quality to be made into wine on their own. Amador County is best known for its Zinfandel, a peppery wine with hints of berries and black currants. Tasting at the small, family-run wineries is very laid back and almost always free. Maps are available at motels and chambers of commerce, and from the Amador Vintners Association (☎ 209-245-4309), PO Box 667, Plymouth, CA 95669.

Head east from Plymouth on Shenandoah Rd, which eventually becomes Steiner Rd. Signs indicate where the wineries are and which ones are open (some are closed weekdays). Highly recommended are Story Winery and Karly, both off Shenandoah Rd on Bell Rd; Young's Vineyard; Vino Noceto (for their Sangiovese wine); and Sobon Estate (☎ 209-245-6554), which has a wonderful wine museum (open 10 am to 5 pm daily) with 12,000-gallon redwood barrels and memorabilia from around the area.

AMADOR CITY
• population 210 • elevation 620 feet

Literally a bend in the road (Hwy 49, some 30 miles south of Placerville), Amador City is among the smallest incorporated townships in California. Once home to the Keystone Mine – one of the most prolific gold produc-

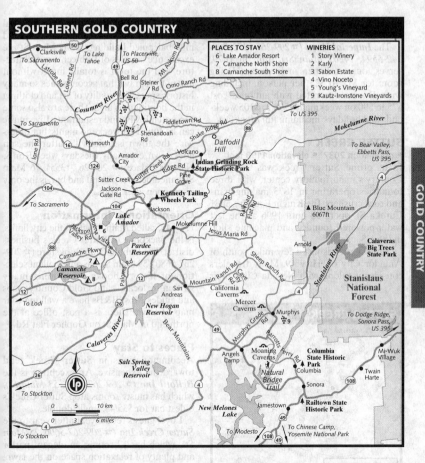

SOUTHERN GOLD COUNTRY

PLACES TO STAY
6 Lake Amador Resort
7 Camanche North Shore
8 Camanche South Shore

WINERIES
1 Story Winery
2 Karly
3 Sabon Estate
4 Vino Noceto
5 Young's Vineyard
9 Kautz-Ironstone Vineyards

GOLD COUNTRY

ers in California – the town lay deserted from 1942 (when the mine closed) until the 1950s, when a family from Sacramento bought the dilapidated buildings and converted them into antiques shops. Now the town has half a dozen shops and an excellent specialty store for birders. The **Amador Whitney Museum** (☎ 209-267-0928), on Main St, has biannual exhibits about the women of the Gold Country. It's open noon to 4 pm weekends; free.

Stop by the Imperial Hotel to pick up a walking-tour map. Behind Amador City's old firehouse (the building with a bright red garage door and bell tower in front) is a stone arastra once used to grind gold-laced quartz (see the boxed text on 'Mining Glossary'). The arastra still works and is put to use during the Jose Amador Fiesta in late April, held in honor of Jose Maria Amador, a miner and rancher whose name is now a creek, a town and a county. With Spanish dancing and music, demonstrations of gold mining techniques and arts and crafts booths, the festival makes an entertaining half-day. Call the Imperial Hotel of the

Amador County Chamber of Commerce (☎ 209-223-0350) for information.

The *Imperial Hotel* (☎ *209-267-9172, 800-242-5594, 14202 Main St)*, built in 1879, serves gourmet dinners in an elegant dining room for $12 to $25 per person, including wine. Rooms, decorated with antiques, cost $75 to $90 on weeknights, $90 to $105 weekends and holidays, including full breakfast.

SUTTER CREEK
• population 2037 • elevation 1198 feet

In its prime, Sutter Creek was the Gold Country's main foundry center, with three foundries operating in 1873 making pans and rock crushers. The Knight Foundry, at 81 Eureka St, operated until 1996 as the last water-powered foundry and machine shop in the US.

Sutter Creek is just a few miles south of Amador City on Hwy 49. Many travelers consider it (along with Nevada City) their

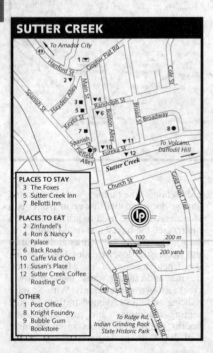

SUTTER CREEK

To Amador City
Hanford St
Gopher Flat Rd
Spanish St
Main St
Hayden Alley
Randolph St
Keyes St
Boston Alley
Cole St
Broad St
Broadway
Spanish St
Eureka St
Fenleaf Alley
Sutter Creek
To Volcano,
Daffodil Hill
Church St
Gold Dust Trail
Denny Axle
Lenby Axle
To Ridge Rd,
Indian Grinding Rock
State Historic Park
Sutter Hill Rd

PLACES TO STAY
3 The Foxes
5 Sutter Creek Inn
7 Bellotti Inn

PLACES TO EAT
2 Zinfandel's
4 Ron & Nancy's Palace
6 Back Roads
10 Caffe Via d'Oro
11 Susan's Place
12 Sutter Creek Coffee Roasting Co

OTHER
1 Post Office
8 Knight Foundry
9 Bubble Gum Bookstore

0   100   200 m
0   100   200 yards

favorite Gold Country town. Its residential areas and the raised, arcaded sidewalks and high-balconied buildings along Main St are excellent examples of 19th-century architecture, and the town is totally intact without any of the sprawl that accompanies so many historic spots. The quality of art and clothing in the boutiques is high. There are also some top-notch B&Bs and restaurants. Live music can be found on weekend nights, but otherwise the town is quietsville after the sun goes down, especially Tuesdays when Ron & Nancy's Palace (☎ 209-267-1355), 76 Main St, a mediocre restaurant and bar, is the only place open after 5 pm.

Orientation & Information
Hwy 49, called Main St within the city limits, is the backbone of Sutter Creek's business district. The Bubble Gum Bookstore (☎ 209-267-5680), 59 Main St, has an excellent selection of history books – including many written by locals – and Gold Country maps and guides. Most B&Bs have a walking-tour map of town. There is a post office at the north end of Main St on Gopher Flat Rd.

Places to Stay
Accommodations in Sutter Creek tend toward the expensive. An exception is the *Bellotti Inn* (☎ *209-267-5211, 53 Main St)*, which has musty rooms atop Sutter Creek's oldest bar for $35/45, single/double.

Loyal guests return year after year to the *Sutter Creek Inn* (☎ *209-267-5606, 75 Main St)*, which has 17 rooms, an elegant parlor and plenty of relaxation space on the lawn. Rooms are decorated with antiques, fireplaces and gently swinging beds, which are suspended from the ceiling by cables. The cost is $65 to $115 during the week and $95 to $175 on weekends. Reservations are advised. Next door, *The Foxes* (☎ *209-267-5882, 77 Main St)*, has seven plush rooms with televisions, designer furniture and bathrobes. Prices are $135 to $210.

Places to Eat
Sutter Creek's coffeehouses serve hearty sandwiches and baked goods. The local favorite is *Back Roads* (☎ *209-267-0440,*

GOLD COUNTRY

74-A Main St), just off Main St, which has a lively atmosphere and serves big sandwiches and hot lunch specials for around $6. **Sutter Creek Coffee Roasting Co** (☎ 209-267-5550, 20 Eureka St) has great coffee and pastries.

You can taste most of the local wines at **Susan's Place** (☎ 209-267-0945, 15 Eureka St), then order a glass of your favorite and have a salad or cheese board (around $9) to go with it – so very chic. Susan also makes picnics to go, with prices depending upon what is ordered. **Zinfandel's** (☎ 209-267-5008), at the corner of Main and Hanford Sts and open Thursday through Sunday, is said to be the finest restaurant in the area, famous for its eclectic California menu. Entrées are $12 to $25. **Caffe Via d'Oro** (☎ 209-267-0535, 36 Main St) is a bit more casual. They have pastas and pizzas for around $12, interesting salads and a good local wine list. All three of these places are closed Tuesday.

AROUND SUTTER CREEK

You can see most of these sights in one day, though each is worthy of at least a few hours (more if you want to hike around the state park) and can be reached from Jackson just as easily as from Sutter Creek.

Indian Grinding Rock State Historic Park

This park (☎ 209-296-7488), on the Pine Grove-Volcano Rd off Hwy 88 (2 miles southwest of Volcano, 1 mile from Pine Grove), is sacred ground for the local Miwok Indians. In it you can see a limestone outcropping covered with petroglyphs – 363 originals and a few modern additions – and mortar holes called *chaw'ses* used for grinding acorns into meal. The 1185 holes are thought to be the most on any one rock in California.

Adjacent to the rock are replica Miwok structures and the **Regional Indian Museum**, which has good displays about northern Miwok culture and gives free tours of the park on weekends. Big Time Days, a traditional Miwok festival held the fourth weekend in September, is worth visiting. On weekends and in summer you pay the $5 day-use fee at the entrance gate; otherwise use a self-registration envelope.

There are a few nice hiking trails through the park and a spacious **campground** with rest rooms (no showers) and 21 first-come, first-served sites that cost $6.

Volcano
• elevation 2053 feet

Volcano feels more like an outpost than a town. It was a Unionist enclave during the Civil War, and these days it is far less developed than other Gold Country towns. Hand-painted signs in front of buildings give amusing insights into Volcano's colorful past. The town lays claim to the first astronomical observation site, the first private law school and the first library in California. Large granitic sandstone rocks line Sutter Creek, which runs through the center of town. The rocks, now flanked by picnic tables, were blasted from surrounding hills by hydraulic processes, then scraped clean of gold-bearing dirt.

Volcano's two year-round businesses (others close from November to April) are the Country Store on Main St, which claims continuous operation since 1852, and the bar of the **St George Hotel** (☎ 209-296-4458), whose eclectic collection of historical and contemporary 'stuff' is mesmerizing. The St George has been refurbished by a young couple from the Bay Area who charge $65 to $80 for a room and a healthy breakfast; the restaurant is a popular weekend destination, with brunch for around $8. Volcano does see a fair bit of a tourism when Daffodil Hill is in bloom, and on weekends from April to November when the **Volcano Theater Company** (☎ 209-223-4663) produces live dramas in the restored Cobblestone Theater (tickets are $12).

Reach Volcano by going northeast from Jackson on Hwy 88 and turning north at Pine Grove, or by the scenic, winding Sutter Creek Rd, which enters the town of Sutter Creek (see above) as Church St, near the east end of Main St.

Daffodil Hill

Between mid-March and mid-April, Daffodil Hill, 2 miles northeast of Volcano, is blanketed with more than 300,000 daffodils.

The McLaughlin and Ryan families have operated the hilltop farm since 1887 and keep hyacinths, tulips, violets, lilacs and the occasional peacock among the daffodils. The hill is open daily when the flowers are in bloom. There's no fee, but donations toward next year's planting are appreciated.

JACKSON
• **population 3809** • **elevation 1200 feet**
From 1860 to 1920, when the Kennedy and Eureka mines were in full swing, Jackson was the area's primary entertainment center, known for its saloons, gambling halls and bordellos. Businesses geared toward tourism now occupy these historic structures (most of them well preserved), though Jackson is more of a 'take care of business' town than a charming historic village. It's the Amador County seat and supports a large service industry, mostly spread along the fringes of town.

It's also where Hwy 88 turns east from Hwy 49 and heads over the Sierra near Kirkwood ski resort (see South Lake Tahoe in the Sierra Nevada chapter). At the junction there's a 24-hour Safeway supermarket and the Amador County Chamber of Commerce (☎ 209-223-0350), which has loads of brochures and the free *Amador County: A County for All Seasons* guide, which has walking tours of most towns in the area. There's a laundry west of the junction on the north side of Hwy 49.

Amador County Museum
Perched on a hill overlooking downtown, this museum (☎ 209-223-6386, 225 Church St), two blocks north of Main St, contains general Gold Country history displays, a 1908 baseball uniform and a .32-caliber stealth cane that belonged to the judge who owned the house in which the museum is situated. There are some impressive pieces of mining equipment in the surrounding gardens, plus an old locomotive and several carriages. Hours are 10 am to 4 pm Wednesday to Sunday; donation requested. Across Church St, a plaque in front of the elementary school marks the site of the first synagogue in the Mother Lode.

Kennedy Tailing Wheels Park
A mile from downtown Jackson via North Main St, this park doesn't look like much at first glance, but it is a unique sight in the Gold Country. It contains four iron and wood wheels, 58 feet diameter (they look like fallen carnival rides), that transported tailings from the Eureka Mine over two low hills into an impounding dam by way of gravity flumes. The wheels aren't terribly old – they were built in 1914 after the state legislature forbade mining operations to dump toxic tailings into rivers – but they are marvelous examples of engineering and craftsmanship. Be sure to climb to the top of the hill behind the wheels to see the impounding dam.

On weekends you can tour the old Eureka Mine, visible from Hwy 49. Call ☎ 209-223-9542 for information.

Mokelumne Hill
• **elevation 1474 feet**
Mokelumne Hill is 8 miles south of Jackson on Hwy 49. Known locally as 'Moke Hill,' it was first settled by French trappers in the early 1840s. When gold was discovered in 1848, Moke Hill became the principal mining town of Calaveras County and the county seat from 1853 to '56. Now Moke Hill is a good place to see historic buildings without the common glut of antiques stores and gift shops.

Not pronounced in French fashion, *Hotel Leger* (☎ 209-286-1401, 8304 Main St) has a classic bar (established in 1851) with a potbelly stove, ceiling fans and marble tables. Its Thursday night calamari dinners and Saturday afternoon live bands attract large crowds. Rooms cost about $70.

Places to Stay & Eat
Jackson's small, inexpensive motels are on the outskirts of town near Hwys 49 and 88. The *Country Squire Motel* (☎ 209-223-1657, 1105 N Main St) is between downtown and Kennedy Tailing Wheels State Park. It has a nice lawn, free breakfast and rooms for $45 to $60. The *Amador Motel* (☎ 209-223-0970, 12408 Kennedy Flat Rd) has a small garden, outdoor pool and 10 rooms for $45 during the week and $55 on weekends. The *Jackson*

Gold Lodge (☎ 209-223-0486), a half-mile west of downtown on Hwy 49/88, has an outdoor pool and spacious rooms and cottages for $50 to $80.

Mel's and Faye's Diner Drive-In (☎ 209-223-0853), where Main St meets Hwy 49, is a local institution and favorite stop for travelers. Breakfast begins at 5 am, though Mel's is best known for $5 burgers – served in paper-lined baskets with mounds of french fries – and coffee milkshakes. *Teresa's Restaurant* (☎ 209-223-1786, 1229 Jackson Gate Rd), a mile out of town, has been dishing up four-course Italian dinners for three generations. Meals cost around $11 per person; closed Wednesday and Thursday.

LAKE AMADOR & THE PARDEE & CAMANCHE RESERVOIRS

Southwest of Sutter Creek and Jackson, the Mokelumne River feeds Lake Amador and the Pardee and Camanche reservoirs. Pardee Reservoir, open February to November, is exclusively a fishing lake; the other two – especially Camanche – are popular for waterskiing and windsurfing. Bass and sunfish are the most common fish, though Camanche also has trout and kokanee salmon. The major access route is Buena Vista Rd, between Hwy 88 and Hwy 12. The lakes are about two hours from the Bay Area, but most traffic is from Sacramento and local areas. You can get the obligatory fishing license and tackle, rent boats and launch boats at any of the resorts listed here.

The Camanche Recreation Company operates resorts on both sides of the reservoir. *Camanche South Shore* (☎ 209-763-5178), on Camanche Parkway just north of Hwy 12, has shady tent sites for $15, RV hookups for $20 and cottages for $75 ($95 April to September). On the other side of the reservoir, *Camanche North Shore* (☎ 209-763-5121), on Liberty Rd (North Camanche Parkway), has identical prices but a younger crowd and less shade. It also has motel rooms for $35 ($49 April to September). *Lake Amador Resort* (☎ 209-274-4739), 3 miles south of Hwy 88 on Jackson Valley Rd, has tent sites for $18.

SAN ANDREAS
• population 2200 • elevation 1008 feet

San Andreas is about 15 miles south of Jackson on Hwy 49. As the seat of Calaveras County, it has utilitarian businesses concentrated along the highway. The old town, north of Hwy 49 along N Main St, is noteworthy for its county courthouse which houses an art gallery, restored jail and jail-yard where notorious stagecoach robber Black Bart awaited trial. Also here is the **Calaveras County Museum** (☎ 209-754-3910), which has one of the area's best history displays. The courthouse is open 10 am to 4 pm daily; $1.

In Cave City, 9 miles east of San Andreas (take Mountain Ranch Rd to Cave City Rd), are the spectacular **California Caverns** (☎ 209-736-2708), which John Muir described as 'graceful flowing folds deeply placketed like stiff silken drapery.' Regular tours take 60 to 90 minutes and cost $4. For $75 you can take a Wild Cave Expedition tour, which lasts four hours and includes some serious spelunking. The caverns are open daily mid-May to mid-October.

Homey rooms at *Bonnie's Inn* (☎ 209-754-3212), on Hwy 49 toward the west end of town, start at $60. Across Hwy 49, *The Robin's Nest* (☎ 209-754-1076) has rooms for $65 to $115, including a five-course breakfast.

ANGELS CAMP
• population 2582 • elevation 1379

Angels Camp, about 12 miles south of San Andreas on Hwy 49, is one of the less prosperous towns in the region, though it's famous as the place where Mark Twain gathered notes for his short story 'The Celebrated Jumping Frog of Calaveras County.' The town makes the most of this historic tie – there are smiling frogs painted on the sidewalk along Main St, the International Frog Jump Competition is held the third weekend in May and Mark Twain Days are celebrated on Fourth of July weekend. While nearby Murphys has new businesses sprouting up at a fast pace, in Angels Camp 'For Sale' signs hang on many buildings along Main St.

The town was founded by George Angel in 1849 as a service center for surrounding gravel and quartz mines. Hard-rock mining peaked in the 1890s, when 200 stamp mills ran around the clock. Remains of the last mine are visible in Utica Park at the west end of Main St.

The **Angels Camp Museum** (☎ 209-736-2963), 753 S Main St, documents the area's mining heyday with photographs, relics and 3 acres of old equipment. It's open 10 am to 3 pm March to November.

Places to Stay & Eat

The *Jumping Frog Motel* (☎ *209-736-2191, 330 Murphy Grade*) at the corner of Main and Church Sts, has friendly owners and simple rooms around a courtyard for $38 to $53. Farther east on Main St, the new *Angels Inn Motel* (☎ *209-736-4242*) has a pool and rooms for $69 to $79.

La Hacienda Restaurant (☎ *209-736-6711, 15 S Main St*) is a favorite for chiles rellenos, enchiladas and tostadas. Dinners are around $8, lunches around $6.

MURPHYS

• **population 3229** • **elevation 2171 feet**
Murphys, 7 miles east of Hwy 49 on Murphys Grade Rd, is named for Daniel and John Murphy, who in the early 1840s set up a trading post and mining operation on Murphy Creek in conjunction with the local Maidu Indians. The town's Main St, which looks like a cross between a Norman Rockwell painting and the set of a John Wayne western, is among the liveliest in the Gold Country and has some of the best restaurants, galleries and wineries around.

Things to See & Do

On Main St you'll find three wine-tasting rooms, Black Sheep Vintners, Milliaire Winery and Stevenot Winery (all free and open daily). Also you'll find **Murphy's Old Timers Museum** (☎ 209-728-1160), free with a suggested $1 donation and open 11 am to 4 pm weekends. It has a good photo collection and Maidu basket exhibit, and the 'Wall of Relative Ovation,' dedicated by the mostly silly gold rush-era organization called E Clampus Vitus, a men's social organization that still exists today.

Two miles south of town via Six Mile Rd (next to the Murphys Historic Hotel) **Kautz-Ironstone Vineyards** (☎ 209-728-1251) is a large winery with beautiful grounds, a small deli and a jewelry shop where the largest piece of specimen gold ever found – 44lbs! – is on display. Crowds are common here, but the wine-tasting room is spacious. Be sure to taste their 'Symphony' wine, made from a grape hybrid created by students from UC Davis (see the Davis section in the Sacramento Valley chapter).

In the opposite direction, 1 mile from downtown on Sheep Ranch Rd, **Mercer Caverns** (☎ 209-728-2101) were discovered in 1885 by Walter Mercer, who, after a long day of gold prospecting, tried to find some water to quench his thirst but found a cool stream of air coming out of the ground instead. A 45-minute guided tour takes you past enormous stalactites, stalagmites and vaulted chambers with names such as 'Chinese Meat Market' and 'Organ Loft.' They're open 10 am to 4:30 pm daily (until 6 pm Friday and Saturday) October to May. June to August they're open 9 am to 6 pm Sunday through Thursday (until 8 pm Friday and Saturday). September hours are 10 am to 6 pm daily; $7.

Places to Stay & Eat

Most accommodations in Murphys are expensive B&Bs. Check nearby Angels Camp or Arnold for cheaper alternatives.

Known as the Murphys Hotel, the *Murphys Historic Hotel & Lodge* (☎ *209-728-3444, 800-532-7684, fax 209-728-1590, 457 Main St*) is touted as the best place to stay and eat locally. It definitely has old-time Murphys flavor. Rooms are $70 weekdays, $80 weekends. Lunch costs $6 to $10, and dinner specialties such as prime rib and fresh salmon are $9 to $18. Reservations are a good idea for dinner.

The *Redbud Inn* (☎ *209-728-8533, 800-827-8533*), directly across Main St from the Murphys Hotel, has 13 rooms (most have a fireplace, balcony and hot tub) for $95 to $245. The *Dunbar House 1880 Bed &*

Breakfast (☎ *209-728-2897, 800-692-6006*), on the east end of Main St, has a beautiful garden and four antique-laden rooms for $135 to $190 a night.

The best place for sophisticated breakfast and lunch ($4 to $8) is *Grounds* (☎ *209-728-8663, 402 Main St*). *Sun China* (☎ *209-728-1294, 386 Main St*) serves decent Chinese food for around $8 (closed Mondays). *Murphys Bagel Barn* (☎ *209-728-1511, 140 Main St*) and the *Coffee Roasting Co*, next to each other on the east end of Main St, are good at what they do and have a faithful local clientele.

EBBETTS PASS
• elevation 8730 feet

Hwy 4 heads northeast from Murphys, passes through Calaveras Big Trees State Park, crosses Ebbetts Pass and descends to meet Hwy 89, and eventually Hwy 395, on the eastern side of the Sierra. The pass is closed most of the winter, but the road is usually plowed up to **Bear Valley Ski Area** (☎ 209-753-2301), a popular resort with 2000 feet of vertical rise, 11 lifts, $35 tickets and a cross-country ski center (☎ 209-753-2834).

Arnold, 18 miles east of Murphys and 2 miles from the state park, is the biggest community along Hwy 4 and has some affordable accommodations. The *Arnold Timberline Lodge* (☎ *209-795-1053*), the only place that gets cable TV, has old but clean rooms with fireplaces for $49 to $145. *Ebbetts Pass Lodge Motel* (☎ *209-795-1563*) has raggedy rooms facing the highway, with kitchenettes and new bathrooms, starting at $59. The *Tamarack Pines Inn B&B* (☎ *209-753-2080*) has the newest facilities in the area and cross-country ski trails from their backyard; double rooms are $90 in the summer and $45 during the low season. Rooms with kitchenettes sleep four and are around $90 during the low season and $20 to $30 more in the summer. *Mr B's Diner* (☎ *209-795-0601*) has good, solid, economical all-American food ($3 to $8) and a friendly atmosphere.

Calaveras Big Trees State Park
This park, at about 5000 feet, is a great place to hike and camp among giant sequoia trees.

Though small and undeveloped, it is easily accessible (4 miles northeast of Arnold on Hwy 4) and not too crowded.

It has two giant sequoia groves, 6000 acres of pine forest and the Stanislaus River and Beaver Creek, which offer good trout fishing and great swimming. During the winter, the North Grove stays open for snow camping and cross-country skiing. The entrance fee is $5 per car year round.

The North Grove Campground is at the park entrance, where the visitor center, ranger station (☎ 209-795-2334) and main parking lots are. Less crowded is the Oak Hollow Campground, 9 miles farther on the park's main road.

The **North Grove Big Trees Trail**, a 1-mile self-guided loop, begins next to the visitor center and winds along the forest floor past the 'Big Stump' and a tree named Mother of the Forest. A 4-mile trail that branches off from the self-guided loop climbs out of the North Grove, crosses a ridge and descends 1500 feet to the Stanislaus River.

Not accessible by car, and devoid of any picnic areas or campgrounds, the **South Grove** is a designated nature preserve in the

Giant sequoias (right) are stockier than their cousins, the coastal redwoods (left).

GOLD COUNTRY

park's most remote reaches. From the Beaver Creek picnic area (half a mile from the visitor center), follow the 9-mile **South Grove Trail**. You don't have to hike the whole thing to have a memorable experience.

MURPHYS TO SONORA

There are two routes between Murphys and Sonora: Hwy 49, which heads southwest and passes through Angels Camp, and Parrot's Ferry Rd (county road E18), which crosses a picturesque bridge over the Stanislaus River.

North of the bridge is **Moaning Caverns** (☎ 209-736-2708), least impressive of the underground chambers in the area but worth the $7.95 entrance fee if you don't plan on visiting any others. The big attraction here is a 100-foot spiral staircase that takes you into the cave, and the chance to rappel 180 feet on a three-hour, $75 Adventure Tour.

Between the caverns and the bridge, the **Natural Bridge Trail** leads down to the Stanislaus River, where the water has carved an immense passage through the hills. The river actually seems to flow from an immense grotto, a sight well worth the half-mile hike. The trailhead is on a dead-end road (across from an outhouse), well marked from Parrots Ferry Rd; park anywhere along the dead-end road.

Columbia State Historic Park
• elevation 2143 feet

Columbia is on Parrots Ferry Rd, which runs north off of Hwy 49 about 2½ miles north of Sonora. It is known as the 'Gem of the Southern Mines' and considered one of the best-preserved gold rush towns. Columbia has four central blocks that are now a State Historic Park. The houses on the fringe of these blocks blend in so well that it's hard to tell what's park and what's not. Within the park, preserved 1850s buildings house historical displays, and concessionaires wear period costumes and sell old-fashioned products. The blacksmith and shoemaker use traditional methods, and a horse-drawn carriage is the only vehicle allowed on the streets.

Limestone and granite boulders (they look like whale vertebrae or dinosaur bones) are noticeable around town. These were washed out of the surrounding hills by hydraulic mining and scraped clean by prospectors. There's a good explanation of this kind of mining at the Columbia Museum (☎ 209-532-4301) at the corner of Main and State Sts. The free museum, open 10 am to 4:30 pm daily, also has some interesting ore specimens and a slide show about Columbia's history.

The restaurant at the *City Hotel* (☎ 209-532-1479) is run by students of Columbia College's Culinary Arts Program and serves some of the fanciest food in the Gold Country; dinner costs around $40 per person, wine included. The *Fallon Hotel* (☎ 209-532-1470) is home to the Sierra Repertory Theater, whose musical productions draw crowds from near and far. Shows run year round Wednesday to Sunday, and tickets cost $12 to $17. Both hotels were established in 1857 and have restored rooms for $60 to $115, including a continental breakfast. Be warned: the streets are usually empty after 6 pm.

SONORA
• population 4386 • elevation 1796 feet

Settled in 1848 by miners from Sonora, Mexico, who arrived via the Gila Trail, this town was, in its heyday, a cosmopolitan center. It had Spanish plazas, elaborate saloons and the Southern Mines' largest concentration of gamblers, drunkards and gold. The Big Bonanza Mine, at the north end of Washington St where Sonora High School now stands, yielded 12 tons of gold in two years (including a 28lb nugget). Still bustling as the Tuolumne County seat and a thoroughfare for Sierra Nevada travelers, Sonora is a good spot from which to explore the surroundings. Its downtown is well preserved, has quality shopping and is lively even after the sun goes down.

Orientation & Information

Sonora Pass (Hwy 108 en route to US 395) and Tioga Pass (Hwy 120 on the eastern edge of Yosemite National Park) cross the Sierra Nevada east of Sonora (see the Sierra Nevada chapter).

The center of downtown Sonora is the T-shaped intersection of Washington and Stockton Sts, with Washington being the main thoroughfare. Businesses on Washington St include banks, bookstores and restaurants. The Tuolumne County Visitors Bureau (☎ 209-533-4420, 800-446-1333), 55 W Stockton St, is helpful with information on recreation, road conditions and lodging. They also have Yosemite National Park information, including maps, current road and weather conditions, and a free phone line to lodgings near the park. The bureau is open 9 am to 7 pm Monday to Thursday, 9 am to 8 pm Friday, 10 am to 6 pm Saturday and 10 am to 5 pm Sunday in summer. During the winter the hours are 10 am to 6 pm Monday through Saturday.

Stop by the Sierra Nevada Adventure Company (☎ 209-532-5621), 173 S Washington St, for maps, equipment and friendly advice on where to climb, hike and fish.

Things to See

Housed in the former Tuolumne County Jail, the **Tuolumne County Museum** (☎ 209-532-1317), 158 W Bradford St, two blocks west of Washington St, is a good museum with $100,000 worth of gold on display. It's free and open daily.

Residential neighborhoods, off the north end of Washington St, are lined with restored Victorian houses, and the spooky old **cemetery** at the west end of Jackson St has many graves from that same era. **St James Episcopal Church**, a local landmark on N Washington St north of Elkin St, built in 1860, has been in continuous use since then and is now simply called the 'Red Church.' The Tuolumne County Historical Society publishes a walking tour map called *Sonora: A Guide to Yesterday*, available at the museum and at the visitor bureau.

In late September, the Tuolumne County Wild West Film Festival, at the Mother Lode

GOLD COUNTRY

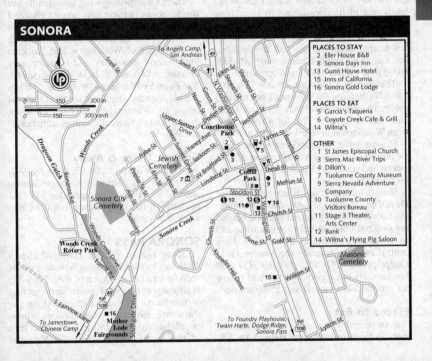

SONORA

PLACES TO STAY
2   Eller House B&B
8   Sonora Days Inn
13 Gunn House Hotel
15 Inns of California
16 Sonora Gold Lodge

PLACES TO EAT
5   Garcia's Taqueria
6   Coyote Creek Cafe & Grill
14 Wilma's

OTHER
1   St James Episcopal Church
3   Sierra Mac River Trips
4   Dillon's
7   Tuolumne County Museum
9   Sierra Nevada Adventure Company
10 Tuolumne County Visitors Bureau
11 Stage 3 Theater, Arts Center
12 Bank
14 Wilma's Flying Pig Saloon

To Angels Camp, San Andreas

To Jamestown, Chinese Camp

To Foundry Playhouse, Twain Harte, Dodge Ridge, Sonora Pass

Fairgrounds east of Stockton St on South-gate Drive, features a rodeo, street fair and outdoor screenings of classic westerns. For information, call the visitor center.

White-Water Rafting

The Tuolumne River is known for its Class IV rapids and its population of golden eagles and red-tailed hawks. The Stanislaus River is more accessible and more heavily traveled. Sierra Mac River Trips (☎ 209-532-1327, 800-457-2580), PO Box 366, Sonora, CA 95370, has a good reputation and offers a wide variety of trip lengths and destinations. Day trips cost $180, two-day trips are $375. The trips leave from Groveland (a 45-minute drive toward Yosemite), but with enough advance notice the guides can usually arrange transportation from Sonora.

Places to Stay

Columbia College, 6 miles north of Sonora on the way to Columbia State Park, often lends one of its dormitories to Hostelling International ($12 per person). The location is remote and woodsy – highly scenic but not convenient to *anything* – and the facilities are nice. Call student housing (☎ 209-533-3039) to see if the hostel is in operation.

The **Inns of California** (☎ 209-532-3633, 350 S Washington St) has a pool, hot tub and modern rooms for $60/155, $75/155 on weekends and in summer. Ask for a room away from Washington St to avoid traffic noise.

Rooms in the historic **Gunn House Hotel** (☎ 209-532-3421, 286 S Washington St) are quaint and cost $45/75, including a continental breakfast.

Sonora's historic inn is now the **Sonora Days Inn** (☎ 209-532-2400, 160 S Washington St) with a modern motel addition behind the original hotel; motel rooms start at $49 to $69, hotel rooms at $59 to $79. Less central but very friendly, the **Sonora Gold Lodge** (☎ 209-532-3952, 800-363-2154, 480 Stockton St) has a pool, hot tub and rooms for around $44 (winter) and $59 (summer).

Places to Eat

Sonora probably has twice as many restaurants as most towns its size. **Wilma's** (☎ 209-

532-9957) on S Washington St is good for local color and for what they call 'just plain good ol' food' from 6 am to 9 pm; the pies ($3 a slice) and huge barbecue dinners ($7 to $11) are famous. **Garcia's Taqueria** (☎ 209-588-1915, 145 S Washington St), upstairs, makes fat burritos for under $5 and has a good beer selection. The **Coyote Creek Cafe & Grill** (☎ 209-532-9115, 177 S Washington St) is a bit expensive but locals swear by it. Prices run $6 to $11 for pasta, salads and daily specials.

Entertainment

The free and widely available weekend supplement of the **Union Democrat** comes out on Fridays and lists movies, music, performance art and events for all of Tuolumne County. Many bars and cafes have live music on weekend nights with no cover – **Wilma's Flying Pig Saloon** (☎ 209-532-9957) and **Dillon's** (☎ 209-533-1700), both on Washington St, are reliable.

There's a surprisingly big, high-quality live theater scene in these hills. Sonora's **Stage 3 Theater** (☎ 209-536-1778, 208 S Green St), in the Arts Center behind the Bank of America at the corner of Washington and Stockton Sts, does off-Broadway and contemporary dramas; tickets are $12 ($8 on Thursdays). The **Foundry Playhouse** (☎ 209-532-0345), in the old foundry one block south of the post office on Washington St, does musicals, dramas and some locally written stuff; tickets are $8 to $16.

Getting There & Away

Wy's Guides Tours (☎ 209-536-9004, 888-997-1849) runs daily shuttles between Sonora and the San Francisco airport for $45 ($81 roundtrip); reservations are required one week in advance.

SONORA PASS

Heading east of Sonora, Hwy 108 climbs 4000 feet before it crosses Sonora Pass at 9628 feet and drops down to meet Hwy 395 at Bridgeport (see the Eastern Sierra section of the Sierra Nevada chapter). Along the route are mountain communities whose populations average 150 and roads that lead to the surrounding Stanislaus National

Forest. It's most economical to buy gas and provisions in Sonora, but there are plenty of markets, gas stations and motels at these higher elevations – many of which offer a good dose of local flavor.

Ranger stations at Mi-Wuk Village and the turnoff for Pinecrest-Dodge Ridge have information on trails and campgrounds. Eleven miles east of Sonora, **Twain Harte** is a woodsy town established in 1924 as an overnight stop between Lake Tahoe and Yosemite Valley, and named after authors Mark Twain and Bret Harte, who lived here briefly. The *Wildwood Inn* (☎ *209-586-2900, 888-400-2620*) isn't a bad place to spend a few days, and *The Rock* (☎ *209-586-2080*) has good food and live music.

In winter, Hwy 108 is usually closed at the turnoff to **Dodge Ridge** (☎ 209-965-4444), 32 miles from Sonora, which offers a good number of downhill trails and is popular with snowboarders. Lift tickets are $39 ($25 weekdays); ungroomed cross-country trails are free.

JAMESTOWN
• **population 1900** • **elevation 1405 feet**
Three miles south of Sonora, just south of the Hwy 49/108 junction, Jamestown (affectionately called 'Jimtown' by area residents) was the site of three major booms. The first came with Tuolumne County's first gold strike in 1848; the second arrived when the railroad did in 1897; the third occurred in the 1920s when Jamestown became construction headquarters for dams on the Stanislaus and Tuolumne Rivers. Besides a wealth of antiques shops, three terrific old hotels and a very slick Harley-Davidson store, Jamestown has the best gold panning in the Southern Mines area. There are two 'pay $3 get a little gold dust' operations on Main St, which can be fun. Gold Prospecting Expeditions (☎ 209-984-4653, 800-596-0009), 18170 Main St, runs trips that last from a half-hour ($10) to two days ($135) and even offers a three-day college-accredited gold-prospecting course ($595). One of the more popular tours includes a 5-mile float down the Stanislaus River ($79 adults, $49 if under 18) with lunch.

Railtown 1897 State Historic Park
This area (☎ 209-984-3953), south of Main St on 5th Ave, has a 26-acre collection of trains and railroad equipment and was the backdrop for the film *High Noon*. The $6 admission includes a ride on the *Mother Lode Cannon Ball*, a narrow-gauge railroad once used to transport ore, lumber and miners to and from the mines. The train makes a one-hour loop past old mines and equipment. It usually runs Saturdays and Sundays from April to October, and Saturdays only during the winter. The park is open year round.

Places to Stay & Eat
If you want to stay in one of Jamestown's historic beauties, make reservations in advance and plan on spending $70 to $135; breakfast is usually included. Good choices are the *Royal Hotel* (☎ *209-984-5271*) and the *Jamestown Hotel* (☎ *209-984-3902*), both on Main St.

In general, you get more for your money by staying in Sonora and eating in Jamestown, provided you're hungry for Chinese or Mexican food. *Kamm's Chinese Restaurant* (☎ *209-984-3105, 18208 Main St*) serves top-notch food, as does *Morelia Mexican Restaurant* (☎ *209-984-1432, 18148 Main St*). Both are casual, under $10 and often crowded.

CHINESE CAMP
• **elevation 1260 feet**
Chinese Camp, 10 miles south of Sonora on Hwy 49, was founded in 1849 by Chinese miners. During the 1850s, the town had an all-Chinese population of about 5000, most of whom worked in the mines and on railroad building crews. The 'Trees of Heaven,' pines planted for railroad ties but never used, hide many of the old structures. The trees and the dilapidated buildings are about the only visible remains of this time. There is a small branch of the Tuolumne County Visitors Bureau (☎ 209-984-4636) in the old general store at the corner of Hwy 49 and Main St, open daily in the summer.

Northern Mountains

Natural beauty is definitely the attraction here. This chapter covers some of California's grandest features, including majestic Mt Shasta, Lassen Volcanic National Park and Lava Beds National Monument, not to mention Shasta Lake and many other sparkling mountain lakes surrounded by lush forests. There are plenty of places mentioned in this chapter that many native Californians will never see, thinking them too remote. The relaxed, uncrowded nature of tourism up here makes it especially enjoyable – you can find all the services you need without competing with thousands of other visitors.

Mt Shasta Area

You'll probably never forget your first glimpse of Mt Shasta. Naturalist and Sierra Club founder John Muir wrote: 'When I first caught sight of it I was 50 miles away and afoot, alone and weary. Yet all my blood turned to wine, and I have not been weary since.'

Many people are attracted to the mountain for its reputed spiritual qualities; others are attracted by its beauty and its recreational possibilities. Camping, hiking, skiing, soaking in hot springs, mountain biking and scenic driving are all popular activities here.

The **Shasta-Trinity National Forest** extends in patches for 2.1 million acres, from Six Rivers National Forest in the west all the way to Modoc National Forest in the east. Within the forest are some of northern California's prime recreational attractions, including Trinity-Clair Engle Lake, Whiskeytown Lake, Lewiston Lake, Shasta Lake and Mt Shasta. It also includes Trinity Alps Wilderness, Mt Shasta Wilderness, Castle Crags Wilderness, Chanchelulla Wilderness and part of Yolla Bolly-Middle Eel Wilderness. A 154-mile section of the Pacific Crest Trail passes through the forest, as do the 9-mile Sisson-

Highlights

- Mt Shasta – 'Lonely as God, white as a winter moon'
- Lassen Volcanic National Park – a living lesson in volcanic landscapes
- Lava Beds National Monument – lava tube caves, ancient petroglyphs and the eerie labyrinth of Captain Jack's Stronghold
- Mountain lakes – clear, clean, sparkling blue, surrounded by mountains and emerald-green forests
- Spring and fall migrations – birds filling the air at the Klamath Basin National Wildlife Refuges

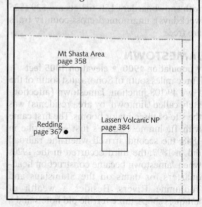

Mt Shasta Area page 358

Redding page 367

Lassen Volcanic NP page 384

Callahan National Recreation Trail and the 8-mile South Fork National Recreation Trail.

The Shasta-Trinity National Forest Headquarters (☎ 530-244-2978, www.r5.fs.fed.us/shastatrinity), 2400 Washington Ave in Redding, is a good resource for information about all types of activities. The Mt Shasta Visitors Bureau puts out a free pamphlet, *Things to See & Do*, which is also a fine place to look for recreation suggestions.

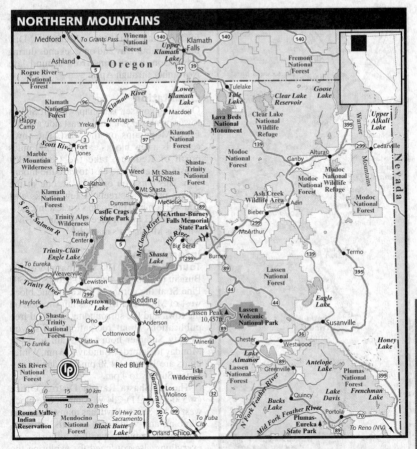

NORTHERN MOUNTAINS

MT SHASTA – THE TOWN

- **population 3500** - **elevation 3561 feet**

The town of Mt Shasta is dwarfed by its namesake mountain, which rises 10,600 feet above it. When European fur trappers arrived in the area in the 1820s they found several small Indian tribes including the Shasta, Karuk, Klamath, Modoc, Wintu and Pit. By 1851, hordes of gold rush miners had arrived, disrupting the Indians' traditional livelihood. The railroad transported logs and workers for a new and booming lumber

industry and, since the town was surrounded by many 'dry' towns, Mt Shasta became a bawdy, good-time place for lumberjacks.

Originally called Strawberry Valley for the abundant wild strawberries that grew here, the town was renamed Sisson, after its principal landowner, postmaster and innkeeper. It was given the name Mt Shasta in the 1920s. Today, New Age residents have replaced the lumberjacks.

With a number of good places to stay and eat, and a quiet, friendly atmosphere, the

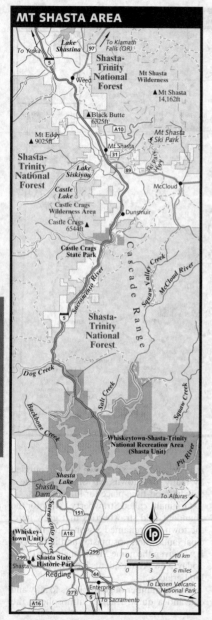

MT SHASTA AREA

NORTHERN MOUNTAINS

town makes an excellent base for exploring the area's natural wonders. The busiest times in Mt Shasta are from Memorial Day through Labor Day and on weekends during ski season, which runs from around late November through April.

Orientation

Orienting yourself is a snap, with Mt Shasta towering above you on the east side and the Eddy Mountains on the west. The town center is a few blocks east of I-5, 60 miles north of Redding; take the Central Mt Shasta exit and head east toward the mountain. This puts you on Lake St, one of the town's principal streets. A few blocks east you will come to the town's busiest intersection, where Lake St meets Mt Shasta Blvd, which is Mt Shasta's main drag.

Information

Tourist Offices The Mt Shasta Visitors Bureau (☎ 530-926-4865, 800-926-4865), 300 Pine St at the corner of Lake St, one block west of Mt Shasta Blvd, has information on the town and the surrounding area and free publications about recreation in Siskiyou County. Summer hours are 9 am to 5 pm Monday to Saturday, Sunday to 3 pm. Winter hours are 10 am to 4:30 pm Monday to Saturday, Sunday to 4 pm.

The Mt Shasta Ranger District Office (☎ 530-926-4511), 204 W Alma St one block west of Mt Shasta Blvd, has maps, mountain climbing and wilderness permits, information, good advice, weather reports and everything else you need for exploring the mountain and the Shasta-Trinity area. It's open 8 am to 4:30 pm weekdays year round; from May to October it's also open Saturday (same hours) and Sunday to noon.

The AAA office (☎ 530-926-5221), 111-B W Lake St, is beside the gas station on the southwest corner of Mt Shasta Blvd and Lake St.

Bookstores Several shops carry interesting books about Mt Shasta, covering topics from geology to folklore. Check out the Golden Bough Bookstore (☎ 530-926-3228), 219 N Mt Shasta Blvd; Crystal Wings Bookstore

(☎ 530-926-3041), 226 N Mt Shasta Blvd; and Village Books (☎ 530-926-1678), 320 N Mt Shasta Blvd. The Sisson Museum also has a good selection of books.

Things to See & Do

Most of Mt Shasta's attractions are in the surrounding area, but the town also has a few places worth visiting. In the 26-acre **Mt Shasta City Park**, on Nixon Rd about a mile north of the town center, the headwaters of the **Sacramento River** gurgle up from the ground in a large, cool spring. The park also contains hiking trails, picnic spots and sports areas, a gazebo and children's playground.

The **Sisson Museum** (☎ 530-926-5508) and the **Mt Shasta Fish Hatchery** (☎ 530-926-2215) are side by side at 1 Old Stage Rd, ½ mile west of I-5. The museum features exhibits on the geology and history of the town and the mountain. The hatchery has large ponds where you can see and feed several types of trout.

Fifth Season Sports (☎ 530-926-3606), 300 N Mt Shasta Blvd at Lake St, rents mountain climbing, camping and backpacking gear, mountain bikes, skis, snowshoes and snowboards. The House of Ski & Board (☎ 530-926-2359), 316 Chestnut St, rents hiking, skiing and snowboarding gear. Sportsmen's Den (☎ 530-926-2295), 402 N Mt Shasta Blvd, also rents sporting, skiing and snowboarding gear.

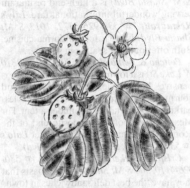

Wild strawberries

Places to Stay

Camping *Lake Siskiyou Camp-Resort* (☎ 530-926-2618), on the lakeside at Lake Siskiyou, is a great camping destination, with a swimming beach as well as canoe, fishing boat and paddle boat rentals. Rates run from $10.50 for a dry tent site to $22.50 for an RV site with cable TV hookup. Self-contained RV lodging units are available for $50 to $85.

A few blocks north of the center of town, *Mt Shasta KOA* (☎ 530-926-4029, 800-562-3617, 900 N Mt Shasta Blvd), off E Hinckley St, charges $15 to $21 for tents, $20 to $25 for RVs, and $31 to $39 for cabins, with off-season discounts.

Check with ranger stations in Mt Shasta and in McCloud (see the McCloud section, later in this chapter) for USFS campgrounds. The rangers at Mt Shasta recommend the following: *McBride Springs*, on Mt Shasta, with running water, no showers and pit toilets ($10 per site); *Panther Meadows*, also on Mt Shasta, with a Wintu Indian sacred spring above it; *Castle Lake* (☎ 530-542-3333), about 13 miles southwest of Mt Shasta, with free camping for tents only (six campsites) but no drinking water; *Gumboot Lake*, 15 miles southwest of Mt Shasta, with free camping for tents only (purify your own drinking water); *Toad Lake*, 15 miles from Mt Shasta town (not a designated campground but lovely; you go down a gravel road and walk in the last half-mile); and *Sims Flat*, 20 miles south of Mt Shasta just off I-5, beside the Sacramento River ($12 per site). The road to Toad Lake is a great 4WD experience. High-clearance standard-drive vehicles can also make the trip.

Hostels *Alpenrose Cottage Hostel* (☎ 530-926-6724, 204 E Hinckley St), a few blocks north of the center of town, attracts visitors from around the world. It's clean, open all day and costs $15 ($90 per week; children half-price), including sheets and towels. Proprietor Betty Brown is a fountain of information. Reservations are recommended.

Motels *Finlandia* (☎ 530-926-5596, 1612 S Mt Shasta Blvd) is a good budget bet. Recently refurbished rooms, some with a view of the mountain, are $34 to $75; guests can enjoy an outdoor hot tub and an authentic Finnish sauna.

Several other decent motels are spread out along S Mt Shasta Blvd. Most have pools and hot tubs and charge from $40 to $50 in summer. Try the *Travel Inn* (☎ 530-926-4617), *Econo Lodge Motel* (☎ 530-926-3145, 800-500-3145), or the *Mountain Air Lodge & Ski House* (☎ 530-926-3411).

Rooms at the *Evergreen Lodge* (☎ 530-926-2143) and *Pine Needles Motel* (☎ 530-926-4811) are newly renovated and reasonably priced ($45 to $60).

A fancier motel, the *Strawberry Valley Inn* (☎ 530-926-2052, 1142 S Mt Shasta Blvd), has rooms for $50/55 (single/double), including a breakfast buffet, wine in the evening, a garden and a terrace with a view of the mountain. Its sister motel, the *Strawberry Valley Court* (☎ 530-926-2052, 305 Old McCloud Rd), has several brick cabins with private garages for $50/56.

The more expensive *Best Western Tree House Motor Inn* (☎ 530-926-3101), I-5 and Lake St, has rooms starting at $73.

B&Bs & Resorts The *Mt Shasta Ranch B&B* (☎ 530-926-3870, 1008 WA Barr Rd), a mile or two west of town, has a main house with four bedrooms with private baths for $95 each; in the rear is a carriage house with five bedrooms sharing two bathrooms, and a kitchen for guests' use, for $40 to $70 single, or $50 to $70 double. They have billiards, Ping-Pong and a Jacuzzi.

The Wagon Creek Inn (☎ 530-926-0838, 1239 Woodland Park Drive), at Old Stage Rd, is a log-cabin lodge with rooms for $75 to $95. *Ward's Big Foot Ranch* (☎ 530-926-5170, 1530 Hill Rd) is a delightful B&B on a farm with spacious grounds and one guest room with private bath and a view of Mt Shasta for $65/70.

Mt Shasta Resort (☎ 530-926-3030, 800-958-3363, 1000 Siskiyou Lake Blvd) is Mt Shasta's poshest place to stay, with a golf course, a fine restaurant-lounge and all the amenities. Lodge rooms are $89, one-bedroom chalets are $108 to $132 and two-bedroom chalets are $158 to $172.

Places to Eat

The Bagel Cafe & Bakery (☎ 530-926-1414, 315 N Mt Shasta Blvd) has plenty of healthy selections and is a relaxed place to hang out. Hours are 6 am to 5 pm Monday to Friday, 7 am to 4 pm Saturday, and 8 am to 4 pm Sunday. *Has Beans Coffeehouse* (☎ 530-926-3602, 1011 S Mt Shasta Blvd) has superb locally roasted coffee and live entertainment on weekends. Both are moderately priced.

Wendie's Italian Restaurant (☎ 530-926-4047, 610 S Mt Shasta Blvd) is great for a home-style breakfast, lunch or dinner. Other good Italian dinner houses include *Mike & Tony's* (☎ 530-926-4792, 501 S Mt Shasta Blvd), open for dinner only; *Michael's Restaurant* (☎ 530-926-5288, 313 N Mt Shasta Blvd), open for lunch and dinner Tuesday to Friday; and the *Piedmont Restaurant* (☎ 530-926-2402, 1200 S Mt Shasta Blvd), open for dinner Tuesday to Saturday and from 1 to 9:30 pm Sunday. Of the four, only Michael's might be considered a bit pricey.

A popular hangout, *Willy's Bavarian Kitchen* (☎ 530-926-3636, 107 Chestnut St) at Mt Shasta Blvd, serves German food with vegetarian options and has a small beer garden with a view of the mountain. *Serge's* (☎ 530-926-1276, 531 Chestnut St), one block east of Mt Shasta Blvd, serves French cuisine with creative variations (worth prices that are slightly on the high side); there's seating indoors or on the mountain-view terrace.

The *Trinity Cafe* (☎ 530-926-6200, 622 N Mt Shasta Blvd) is a high-end restaurant serving wonderful international fare. *Lily's Restaurant* (☎ 530-926-3372, 1013 S Mt Shasta Blvd) is great for California cuisine. Both offer outdoor seating in summer.

Poncho & Lefkowitz (☎ 530-926-1006, 310 W Lake St) is a town favorite, serving up inexpensive home-style Mexican food and gourmet hot dogs from a trailer in the Payless parking lot, with tables out under a tent. For Mexican meals on the opposite end of the economic spectrum, try the upmarket *Lalo's* (☎ 530-926-5123, 520 N Mt Shasta Blvd).

Crispi's Market & Delicatessen (☎ 530-926-4110, 900 S Mt Shasta Blvd) boasts that they have 'the best deli sandwiches in town.' Natural foods markets include *Berryvale*

Natural Foods Grocery (☎ *530-926-1576, 305 S Mt Shasta Blvd)* next to the post office, and the *Mountain Song Natural Foods Market* (☎ *530-926-3391)* in the Mt Shasta Shopping Center off W Lake St.

Entertainment
The *Vet's Club Bar* (☎ *530-926-3565, 406 N Mt Shasta Blvd)* has live music (mostly rock & roll) and dancing on Thursday, Friday and Saturday nights. *Has Beans Coffeehouse* (see Places to Eat) has live entertainment on weekends.

Getting There & Away
Greyhound buses heading north and south on I-5 stop opposite the Vet's Club, 406 N Mt Shasta Blvd.

The STAGE bus (☎ 530-842-8295) includes the town of Mt Shasta in its local route, which also serves McCloud, Dunsmuir, Weed, Yreka and Montague; other buses connect at Yreka for Fort Jones, Greenview, Etna, Klamath River and out to Happy Camp.

In winter, the California Highway Patrol (CHP) has a recorded report (☎ 530-842-4438) that gives weather and road conditions for all Siskiyou County roads.

MT SHASTA – THE MOUNTAIN
• elevation 14,162 feet

'Lonely as God, white as a winter moon,' wrote Joaquin Miller of Mt Shasta in *Life Among the Modocs*. Dominating the landscape for 50 miles around and visible for more than 100 miles from many parts of northern California and southern Oregon, Mt Shasta is a notable landmark. Though not California's highest peak – it ranks sixth – it is especially magnificent because it rises alone on the landscape, unrivaled by other mountains.

Mt Shasta is part of the vast Cascade volcanic chain that to the south includes Lassen Peak and to the north, Mt St Helens and Mt Rainier. The presence of thermal hot springs indicates that Mt Shasta is dormant, but not extinct; smoke was seen puffing out of the crater on the summit in the 1850s, though the last eruption was probably a few hundred years ago. The mountain has two cones: the main cone has a crater about 200 yards across, and the younger, shorter cone on the western flank, called Shastina, has a crater about half a mile wide.

Hiking, climbing, mountain biking, skiing and snowshoeing, as well as plain old

NORTHERN MOUNTAINS

The Strange Legends of Mt Shasta

Mt Shasta has been inspiring legends since long before Europeans arrived on the scene. Indigenous people had their own legends about the mountain, some remarkably similar to more modern stories. Several of these modern legends are – to say the least – a bit unusual, but there are those who believe them. One story has it that a race of Lemurians – refugees from the lost continent of Lemuria, now thought to be submerged beneath the Pacific Ocean – live inside the mountain. Variations on the theme say that a race of little people, invisible people or a mystic brotherhood live inside the mountain. GW Ballard, founder of Mt Shasta's St Germain Foundation (also known as 'I AM'), claims to have had a mystical meeting with the group's namesake on the mountain in the summer of 1930. The foundation now distributes 'Golden Cities' maps with details on how to locate vortexes and be party to updated prophecies.

Many believe Mt Shasta is a center or magnet for spiritual energy, or that a vortex of spiritual energy is formed by the triangle of Mt Shasta, Mt Eddy and Castle Crags. There are spirit-conscious people who live or visit here because they believe their own spiritual powers increase when they are near Mt Shasta. Still others say that your characteristics – whatever they may be – will be intensified by the mountain's energy for good or for ill. Of course, there are plenty of people who think that all this spiritual stuff is a bunch of nonsense!

sightseeing, are all popular activities on the mountain. The ranger station sells topographical maps, and staffers there can advise you on current conditions.

Information

The best place for information of all kinds is the Mt Shasta Ranger District Office (☎ 530-926-4511); see the Information section for Mt Shasta – The Town.

Hiking

A treeless, black volcanic cone on the north side of the town of Mt Shasta, **Black Butte** rises almost 3000 feet. A 2½-mile trail to the top is steep and rocky in many places, and, as there is neither shade nor water, heat can be a problem in summer. Allow two to five hours or more for a round-trip; wear good hiking shoes and bring plenty of water. The ranger station has a pamphlet about the climb.

Rangers can also direct you to any of the many access points along the **Pacific Crest Trail**, including those at Gumboot Lake, Deadfall Lake, Toad Lake and Castle Crags State Park. Two easy sections the rangers recommend are the relatively flat, 4-mile trail to **Deadfall Lake** and the 2-mile section from Gumboot Lake to **Seven Lakes Basin**.

Or try the 9-mile **Sisson-Callahan National Recreation Trail**, a historic route established in the mid-1800s by prospectors, trappers and cattle ranchers to connect the mining town of Callahan with the town of Sisson, now called Mt Shasta.

Climbing

Climbing to the summit is best done in summer from around May to August. How long it takes to climb up and back depends on the route selected, the physical condition of the climbers and weather conditions. Though the round-trip could conceivably be done in one day with 12 or more hours of solid hiking, it's best to allow at least two days and spend a night on the mountain. Though the hike to the summit is only about 6 miles, it is a vertical climb of more than 7000 feet, so acclimatizing to the elevation is important. Also, you'll need crampons, an ice ax and a helmet, all of which can be rented locally. Rock slides and unpredictable weather can be hazardous, so novices should contact the ranger station for a list of available guides.

There's a fee to climb the mountain; a three-day pass costs $15; an annual pass is $25. Contact the Mt Shasta Ranger District Office for details. You must have a free wilderness visitor's pass any time you go into the wilderness, whether on the mountain or in the surrounding area.

Driving

You can drive up the mountain for a fine view at any time of year. The Everitt Memorial Hwy (Hwy A10) goes up to 7900 feet; to get on it, simply head east on Lake St from downtown Mt Shasta and keep going. Everitt Vista Point is a highlight – the short interpretive walk from the parking lot leads to a stone-walled outcropping affording exceptional views of Mt Lassen to the south, the Eddys and Marble Mountains to the west and the whole Strawberry Valley below.

The Mt Shasta ranger station offers a free map for a round-the-mountain drive, starting at Mt Shasta and finishing at Weed. This may be possible only in late summer, depending on how much winter snowfall is still around.

Mt Shasta Ski Park

On the south slope of Mt Shasta, off Hwy 89 heading toward McCloud, the Mt Shasta Ski Park (☎ 530-926-8610, snow reports 530-926-8686) is open in winter for skiing and snowboarding, usually from late November to April, depending on snowfall. The park has a 1390-foot vertical drop and 27 alpine runs; rentals, instruction and weekly specials are available. This is also northern California's largest night-skiing operation (14 trails, two lifts, 1100-foot vertical drop).

The ski park is open in summer, from around late June to early September, for scenic chairlift rides and admission to an educational exhibit on volcanoes. Mountain bikers can take the chairlift up and come whooshing back down. There's also a 24-foot-high climbing tower. Special events are often scheduled, including outdoor concerts. Summer hours are 10 am to 5 pm daily.

Lakes near Mt Shasta

There are a number of stunning mountain lakes near Mt Shasta, including **Lake Siskiyou** (the largest), 2½ miles southwest of the town of Mt Shasta on Hwy 26. Stop at **Box Canyon Dam** to see a picturesque 200-foot-deep canyon. Another 10 miles up in the mountains, southwest of Lake Siskiyou on Castle Lake Rd, is Castle Lake, an unspoiled site surrounded by granite formations and pine forest. Swimming, fishing, picnicking and free camping are popular here in summer; in winter, people ice-skate on the lake. **Lake Shastina**, about 15 miles northwest of Mt Shasta off of Hwy 97 on Big Springs Rd, is another nearby beauty.

The Mt Shasta ranger station distributes a pamphlet, *Alpine Lakes of the Mt Shasta Ranger District*, with details on 50 nearby lakes. Some of them are accessible only by dirt roads or hiking trails and are great for getting away from it all. You can camp beside any of the lakes, as long as you get a free campfire permit from the ranger station and set up your camp at least 200 feet from the water.

DUNSMUIR

• **population 2170** • **elevation 2300 feet**

Eight miles south of Mt Shasta on I-5, 6 miles north of Castle Crags State Park, and nestled into the forested Sacramento River Canyon, the picturesque town of Dunsmuir is known for its pristine landscapes and good fishing.

The Dunsmuir Chamber of Commerce (☎ 530-235-2177, 800-386-7684), 4118 Pine St, has free maps, walking guide pamphlets and information about the town. It's open 10 am to 4 pm daily (11 am to 3 pm in winter).

Things to See & Do

The peaceful Dunsmuir City Park beside the Sacramento River is worth visiting; go around behind the steam engine near the north side of the chamber of commerce and follow the winding road until you reach the park. On the way is the Alexander Dunsmuir Fountain, which coal baron Dunsmuir

gave to the town after its founders named their city after him.

The town was built by the Southern Pacific Railroad, and it was originally called Pusher for the auxiliary 'pusher' engines that muscled heavy steam engines up a steep grade nearby. Originally, it was just a railroad camp. Around 1886 or '87 it was moved a mile down the road and renamed Dunsmuir.

Dunsmuir has two waterfalls worth visiting. **Hedge Creek Falls** is a five-minute walk from a lovely little botanical garden on Dunsmuir Ave. In the garden, look for the viewpoint overlooking the river. A short walk upstream on a forest trail brings you to the falls.

Mossbrae Falls is the larger and more spectacular of the two. Turn west from Dunsmuir Ave onto Scarlett Way, passing under an archway marked 'Shasta Retreat.' Park by the railroad tracks and walk upstream for about half an hour until you reach a railroad bridge built in 1901. Backtracking slightly from the bridge, you will find a little path going down through the trees to the river and the falls.

Note: Be *extremely careful* of trains as you walk by the tracks – the river's sound can make it impossible to hear them coming.

Places to Stay

Certainly the most unusual place to stay in Dunsmuir is a vintage railroad caboose at the ***Railroad Park Resort*** *(☎ 530-235-4440, 800-974-7245, 100 Railroad Park Rd)*, 1 mile south of town (take the Railroad Park exit off I-5). A caboose or a cabin costs $65/70 ($10 cheaper in winter). There's also a campground with tent/RV sites for $16/22. ***Cave Springs Resort*** *(☎ 530-235-2721, 888-235-2721, 4727 Dunsmuir Ave)*, overlooking the Sacramento River, has motel rooms from $39 to $53, cabins with kitchens from $32 to $46, mobile homes from $49 to $69, RV spaces for $14 (no tents) and vacation homes from $85 to $150. Weekly rates are lower. ***The Oak Tree Inn*** *(☎ 530-235-2884, 6604 Dunsmuir Ave)*, at the south end of town, is another comfortable, relaxed lodging in an attractive setting; regular rooms are $45, with larger suites available. Several other motels along Dunsmuir Ave are in the $40 to $50 range. *The Cedar Lodge* (☎ 530-235-4331, 4201 Dunsmuir Ave) is notable for its aviary of exotic birds.

The Dunsmuir Inn B&B (☎ 530-235-4543, 888-386-7684, 5423 Dunsmuir Ave) comes highly recommended by travelers. You can cook in the kitchen or barbecue in the yard. The five guest rooms, all with private baths, are $60 to $70.

Places to Eat
Shelby's (☎ 530-235-0654, 4917 Dunsmuir Ave) is Dunsmuir's most popular eatery, with a friendly, small-town atmosphere, moderate prices, delicious food and unusual selections with generous portions for all meals. *Cafe Maddalena* (☎ 530-235-2725, 5801 Sacramento Ave), also with mid-range prices, is downhill from Main St. It specializes in magnificent country-style Italian food. The restaurant closes for about four months every winter, when Maddie goes back to visit her home in Italy. Dinners are served Thursday through Sunday. *The Railroad Park Resort* (see Places to Stay) offers dining in vintage railroad cars – a little on the expensive side, but definitely something different.

Getting There & Away
The Greyhound bus stops in front of the Cecchetini Bookshop (☎ 530-235-4047), 5814 Dunsmuir Ave. The STAGE bus serves Dunsmuir, Mt Shasta and other local destinations (see Mt Shasta – The Town).

The Amtrak station at 5750 Sacramento Ave, one block east of Dunsmuir Ave, where you can catch the north-south *Coast Starlight* train, is the only train stop in Siskiyou County. Buy tickets at local travel agencies or from the conductor aboard the train, but call Amtrak to make a reservation.

CASTLE CRAGS STATE PARK
Castle Crags State Park is adjacent to and within a portion of the Castle Crags Wilderness Area. It features soaring spires of ancient granite with elevations ranging from 2000 feet along the Sacramento River to more than 6000 feet at the top of the Crags.

Castle Crags Peak tops out at 6544 feet. The park is just off I-5, 6 miles south of Dunsmuir. The crags are similar to the granite formations of Yosemite National Park and the eastern Sierra, and Castle Dome here resembles Yosemite's famous Half Dome.

There are 28 miles of hiking trails. They include the gentle, 1-mile Indian Creek Nature Trail; the moderately strenuous, 1-mile Root Creek Trail; the strenuous, 2.7-mile Crags Trail-Indian Springs Trail; and 7 miles of the Pacific Crest Trail, which passes through the park at the base of the crags. There's fishing in the Sacramento River at the picnic and camping area on the opposite side of I-5.

The office at the park entrance (☎ 530-235-2684) is open daily and has all the information you could want. Day use is $5 per vehicle.

Camping
Camping is allowed only at designated camping sites within the park. These are open all year, even in winter when there is snow. *Parknet* (☎ 800-444-7275) takes reservations from mid-May to mid-September, when campsites cost $16; the rest of the year it's first-come, first-served (sites cost $12). There is running water and hot showers, but no hookups. Or you can camp free in the Shasta-Trinity National Forest surrounding the park; you must have a free campfire permit, issued at park offices.

Across I-5 in Castella, the small, quiet *Cragview Valley Park* (☎ 530-235-0081) has tent sites for $10 and RV sites with/without hookups for $15/12. Also across the highway, the state park's riverside picnic area has camping for $16.

THE LAKES
Shasta Lake
About 15 minutes north of Redding on I-5 is Shasta Lake, the largest reservoir in California. It is a popular place, surrounded by hiking trails and campgrounds, and teeming with just about anything that will float.

The Shasta Lake Ranger District Office of the Shasta-Trinity National Forest (☎ 530-275-1589) offers free pamphlets with maps and information about fishing, boating and hiking trails around the lake. From I-5, take the Mountaingate Wonderland Blvd exit, 10 miles north of Redding, and turn right on Holiday Rd. The office is open 8 am to 4:30 pm daily in summer, and the same hours, weekdays only, the rest of the year.

At the south end of Shasta Lake on Shasta Dam Blvd (Hwy 151) is **Shasta Dam**, the second most massive dam in the US. Its 487-foot spillway is the largest artificial waterfall in the world – as high as a 60-story building, and three times higher than Niagara Falls. The dam was built from 1938 to 1945; Woody Guthrie wrote 'This Land Is Your Land' while he was here working on the dam. Free tours are given every day, departing from the Shasta Dam Visitors Center (☎ 530-275-1554).

Lake Shasta Caverns (☎ 530-238-2341, 800-795-2283) is a network of limestone and marble caves. Tours operate daily and include a boat ride across Lake Shasta to get to the caves ($15, $7 for children ages four through 12, free for ages three and under). The tour lasts around two hours, with one hour inside the caves. Bring a sweater, as the temperature inside is 58°F (14°C) year round. Take the Shasta Caverns Rd exit from I-5, about 20 minutes north of Redding, and follow the signs.

Places to Stay The USFS operates many campgrounds around the lake, some accessible by road, others only by boat, for $10 to $15 per site.

There are plenty of commercial campgrounds around the lake, including the *Antlers RV Park & Campground* (☎ 530-238-2322, 800-642-6849), which is at the end of Antlers Rd in Lakehead and has tent and RV sites from $17.50 to $26.50. It's a family-oriented campground, with a marina and a snack bar with outdoor tables. *Holiday Harbor Resort* (☎ 530-238-2383, 800-776-2628) has tent and RV camping (mostly RV) for $23. It's on Holiday Harbor Rd off Shasta Caverns Rd right next to the lake. You'll find it has a big marina and a restaurant that serves breakfast and lunch. The *Lakeshore Inn* (☎ 530-238-2003, 20483 Lakeshore Dr)

has tent and RV sites ($18 to $20), as well as a restaurant, bar and a swimming pool. The *Shasta Lake RV Resort* (☎ 238-2370, 800-374-2782, 20433 Lakeshore Dr) has both tent and RV sites for $14.50 to $21.50.

Camping outside organized campgrounds requires a campfire permit, available free from any National Forest Service office.

Houseboats and other boats can be rented from a number of marinas, including *Antlers Resort & Marina* (☎ 530-238-2553, 800-238-3924, 20679 Antlers Rd), *Jones Valley Resort* (☎ 530-275-7950, 800-223-7950, 22300 Jones Valley Marina Dr), *Shasta Marina* (☎ 530-238-2284, 800-959-3359, 18390 O'Brien Inlet Rd), and the *Silverthorn Resort Marina* (☎ 530-275-1571, 800-332-3044, 16250 Silverthorn Rd). If you want to rent a houseboat, reserve one as far in advance as possible – many are booked a full year ahead, especially for the summer months.

There are several places to eat around Shasta Lake, including restaurants and snack bars at the resorts and marinas. The *Tail of the Whale* (☎ 530-275-3021, 10300 Bridge Bay Rd) at the Bridge Bay Resort is one of the lake's often recommended restaurants – you can sit out on a deck right over the lake, with a beautiful view. It's medium priced. The bar here, The Pelican, is also popular. The restaurant at the lakeside *Holiday Harbor Resort*, on Holiday Harbor Rd just off Shasta Caverns Rd, is good for breakfast and lunch.

Whiskeytown Lake

Whiskeytown Lake, which takes its name from an old mining town, is 8 miles west of Redding on Hwy 299. When the lake was created in 1965 by the construction of a 282-foot dam for power generation and Central Valley irrigation, the few remaining buildings of old Whiskeytown were moved and the site was submerged.

Today, people come to the lake for activities ranging from gold panning to waterskiing. Boats can be rented at Oak Bottom Marina, just off Hwy 299.

The Whiskeytown Visitors Center (☎ 530-246-1225), on the northeast point of the lake just off Hwy 299, offers free maps as well as information about Whiskeytown Unit, which is one of the three units comprising the Whiskeytown-Shasta-Trinity National Recreation Area. The center is open 9 am to 5 pm daily in summer and 10 am to 4 pm in winter. There's a day-use fee of $5 per vehicle (or $30 for an annual pass) to visit the lake.

Places to Stay *Brandy Creek Campground*, in a grove of trees beside the lake, offers RV camping for $14 in summer, $7 the rest of the year, on a first-come, first-served basis for self-contained RVs only (no tents). Information is available at the Whiskeytown Visitors Center. The *Oak Bottom Campground*, larger than Brandy Creek and in a more open setting, allows both tent and RV camping and it accepts reservations through Parknet. Various primitive campsites are also available around the lake.

Lewiston Lake

Twenty-six miles west of Redding, off of Hwy 299 on Trinity Dam Blvd, Lewiston (population 1500) makes a pleasant rest stop. It's right beside the Trinity River, where there's a campground and good fishing below the bridge. About 1½ miles north, tiny Lewiston Lake is a peaceful alternative to the other lakes in the area, because of its 10mph boat speed limit. The water is kept at a constant level, providing a nurturing habitat for fish (especially rainbow, brook and brown trout) and waterfowl. It is a stopover for a number of migrating bird species – early in the evening you may see ospreys and bald eagles diving for fish.

Places to Stay & Eat Several USFS and commercial campgrounds are spaced around the lake. The lovely *Lakeview Terrace Resort* (☎ 530-778-3803, 800-291-0308, 89 Lakeview Terrace Dr) offers cabins, camping and boat rentals. The Pine Cove Marina (☎ 530-778-3770, 888-876-8804), the only marina on the lake, offers free information about the lake and its wildlife, plus boat and canoe rentals and guided wildlife tours on the lake.

The *Lewiston Hotel* (☎ 530-778-3823), on Deadwood Rd in the center of town, was built in 1899 and is no longer a functioning hotel. It is, however, a hangout with a lot of character, serving excellent drinks and dinners. The bar opens at 3 pm and the restaurant at 6 pm Thursday to Sunday. *Mama's Restaurant* (☎ 530-778-3177), on Trinity Dam Blvd in Lewiston, serves excellent lunches.

Also in town, on Rush Creek Rd at Turnpike Rd, the *Old Lewiston Bridge RV Resort* (☎ 530-778-3894, 800-922-1924) offers tent and RV camping beside the river bridge and has trailers for rent. The riverside *Old Lewiston Inn B&B* (☎ 530-778-3385, 800-286-4441), on Deadwood Rd in the center of town, has seven rooms and a hot tub; basic B&B in rooms with private bath is $75/85. The inn also offers all-inclusive fly-fishing packages and two-night romantic getaways. The *Lewiston Valley Motel* (☎ 530-778-3942, 4789 Trinity Dam Blvd) is a basic, clean motel with rooms for $40.

Trinity-Clair Engle Lake

Just north of Lewiston Lake, Trinity Lake (sometimes called Clair Engle Lake) is California's third-largest artificial lake. It attracts multitudes, who come for the swimming, fishing and other water sports. The west side of the lake, accessible off of Hwy 299 via Hwy 3, has most of the campgrounds, RV parks, motels, boat rentals and restaurants. The east side is quieter, with more secluded campgrounds, some accessible only by boat. The ranger station in Weaverville (☎ 530-623-2121) has information on USFS campgrounds.

REDDING

• population 80,000 • elevation 560 feet

At the north end of the Sacramento Valley, shadowed by mountain ranges on three sides, Redding is a rather quiet town. The area was called Poverty Flat by miners, because there wasn't much there. When the railroad came north, Poverty Flat was chosen as the site for the railroad terminus, and a town was laid out there around 1872. The new city was named after Benjamin B Redding, who was a land agent for the railroad. For about 10 years Redding was the railroad terminus, while railroad track construction pushed northward into the Sacramento Canyon, where construction was much more difficult.

Many travelers spend a few days here, as it makes a convenient base for day trips to Lassen Volcanic National Park, Shasta Lake, the Lake Shasta Caverns, Whiskeytown Lake, Shasta State Historic Park, Lewiston, Weaverville and other northern mountain destinations.

The big Turtle Bay Museums project (see Things to See and Do), scheduled for completion by summer 2001, may make a visit to Redding attractive in itself. Straddling the Sacramento River, the project includes a spectacular footbridge designed by internationally known engineering architect Santiago Calatrava of Spain.

Orientation & Information

Downtown Redding is bordered by the Sacramento River on the north and east; its major thoroughfares are Pine and Market Sts. Standard hotels and chain restaurants can be found south of downtown, at the Cypress St exit off of I-5 and Hilltop Drive east of I-5.

The Redding Convention and Visitors Bureau (☎ 530-225-4100, 800-874-7562), 777 Auditorium Drive, is open 8 am to 5 pm weekdays, 9 am to 5 pm weekends.

Shasta-Trinity National Forest Headquarters (☎ 530-244-2978, camping reservations ☎ 800-280-2267), 2400 Washington St off Park Marina Drive, has maps and free camping permits for all seven national forests in northern California. It's open most of the year 7:30 am to 4:30 pm weekdays (until 5 pm in summer).

The Shasta Cascade Wonderland Association (☎ 530-365-7500, 800-474-2782), at the south end of the Shasta Factory Outlets Mall in Anderson, about 10 miles south of Redding on Hwy 273, it offers interesting

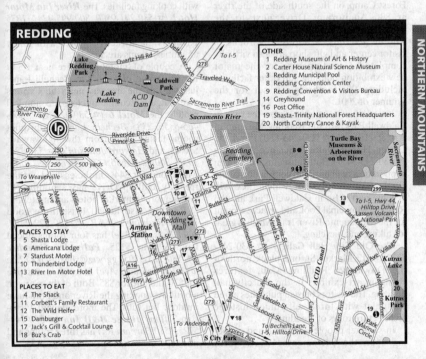

REDDING

OTHER
1 Redding Museum of Art & History
2 Carter House Natural Science Museum
3 Redding Municipal Pool
8 Redding Convention Center
9 Redding Convention & Visitors Bureau
14 Greyhound
16 Post Office
19 Shasta-Trinity National Forest Headquarters
20 North Country Canoe & Kayak

PLACES TO STAY
5 Shasta Lodge
6 Americana Lodge
7 Stardust Motel
10 Thunderbird Lodge
13 River Inn Motor Hotel

PLACES TO EAT
4 The Shack
11 Corbett's Family Restaurant
12 The Wild Heifer
15 Damburger
17 Jack's Grill & Cocktail Lounge
18 Buz's Crab

NORTHERN MOUNTAINS

displays and a wealth of tourist information. It's open 9 am to 6 pm Monday to Saturday, 10 am to 6 pm Sunday.

Things to See & Do

On the north side of Redding, on both sides of the Sacramento River, sits the **Turtle Bay Museums and Arboretum on the River** complex (☎ 530-243-8850, www.turtlebay .org). The ambitious 300-acre project should be completed by summer 2001.

It is expected to be a major cultural and scientific center for visitors of all ages, with an emphasis on the Sacramento River watershed. It will feature natural and re-created wildlife exhibits such as otter and salmon ponds, an aviary and an arboretum. There will also be interactive exhibits on art, history, the forest and the natural sciences, as well as extensive gardens.

Phase I of the expansion was finished in 1997, with the opening of Paul Bunyan's Forest Camp, on the south side of the river at 836 Auditorium Drive next to the Redding Convention Center. The first wildlife exhibits, arboretum gardens, a visitor center and gift shop are also virtually completed. Grand opening for the major new exhibition building and other facilities, including the footbridge, is set for the summer of 2001.

Just north of downtown, across the river in Caldwell Park, are the Redding Museum of Art & History (☎ 530-243-8801) and the Carter House Natural Science Museum (☎ 530-243-5457). Both museums will remain in operation here until full completion of the Turtle Bay complex, of which they will become part. Also in Caldwell Park are the Redding Municipal Pool, and an access point for the Sacramento River Trail, which is great for hiking and bicycling.

The **Old City Hall Gallery** (☎ 530-241-7320), 1313 Market St, one block north of the Downtown Redding Mall, features changing art exhibits in the old city hall building. The visitors bureau publishes a free pamphlet with three self-guided historic architecture tours of Redding.

In summer people go rafting and canoe-ing upon the Sacramento River. North

Country Canoe & Kayak (☎ 530-244-1940), 2525 Park Marina Drive, offers sales and rentals of a wide variety of canoes, kayaks and rafts. Rentals cost $30 for canoes, $25 to $29 for kayaks and $49 to $69 for rafts, for a 12.6-mile trip down the river, which includes a shuttle service to bring you back again when you've finished. Redding Sports Ltd (☎ 530-221-7333), 950 Hilltop Drive, rents recreational equipment for every season. Call ☎ 530-221-7334 for their 24-hour snow report.

Places to Stay

Downtown, the *Thunderbird Lodge (☎ 530-243-5422, 1350 Pine St)* is a homey motel charging $30/32. Nearby are the *Stardust Motel (☎ 530-241-6121, 1200 Pine St)* with rooms for $29/34, and the *Shasta Lodge (☎ 530-243-6133, 1245 Pine St)* with rooms for $35. The *Americana Lodge (☎ 530-241-7020, 1250 Pine St)* has rooms for $28, some with cooking facilities. The *River Inn Motor Hotel (☎ 530-241-9500, 800-995-4341, 1835 Park Marina Drive)*, near the Sacramento River, is an attractive motel with many amenities; rooms are $55.

A couple of 'motel rows' are near I-5 at the south end of town. On Bechelli Lane, just west of the freeway near the Cypress Ave exit, are a couple of clean, economical motels: the *Motel 6 (☎ 530-221-0562, 800-466-8356, 2385 Bechelli Lane)*, with quiet rooms facing away from the highway for $36/42, and *Howard Johnson's (☎ 530-223-1935, 800-446-4656, 2731 Bechelli Lane)*, with rooms for $44. On the east side of the freeway, Hilltop Drive has a number of larger, more upmarket hotels and motels.

Redding also has at least three good B&Bs. *Redding's B&B (☎ 530-222-2494, 1094 Palisades Ave)* has four rooms priced from $75 to $125. *Palisades Paradise (☎ 530-223-5305, ggoetz@shasta-co.k12.ca .us, 1200 Palisades Ave)* has two rooms, one for $70 and one for $85. Both of these are on a bluff overlooking the River and both have outdoor hot tubs. The more elegant Victorian *Tiffany House B&B Inn (☎ 530-244-3225, 1510 Barbara Rd)* has three rooms and one separate cottage priced $85 to $135.

NORTHERN MOUNTAINS

Places to Eat

Inexpensive eateries downtown include *The Shack* (☎ 530-241-5126, 1325 Eureka Way), *Corbett's Family Restaurant* (☎ 530-241-2303, 1455 Pine St) and *Wild Heifer* (☎ 530-241-2575, 1177 Shasta St) at East St. *Damburg* (☎ 530-241-0136, 1320 Placer St) is a charming, old-fashioned burger joint and soda fountain with a 1930s atmosphere. *Buz's Crab* (☎ 530-243-2120, 2159 East St) serves inexpensive seafood dishes, fresh daily.

Moving upmarket, *Jack's Grill & Cocktail Lounge* (☎ 530-241-9705, 1743 California St) has a reputation for choice steaks. They don't take reservations and you may have a long wait for a table, but it's worth it. *Nello's Place* (☎ 530-223-1636, 3055 Bechelli Lane) at Hartnell Ave, a Redding landmark, is an Italian dinner house with music and dancing. There's an 'early bird' discount if you arrive before 6:30 pm (7 pm in summer).

Fast-food restaurants can be found on Cypress Ave, just east of I-5.

Getting There & Around

The Greyhound bus station (☎ 530-241-2531), 1321 Butte St at Pine St, is open 24 hours daily.

The Amtrak train station is at 1620 Yuba St, one block west of the Downtown Redding Mall. Buy tickets on the train or at a travel agency; the station is not staffed.

The Redding Area Bus Authority or RABA (☎ 530-241-2877) has 11 city routes, plus express routes to Burney, which is about 30 miles northeast of Redding on Hwy 299. Buses operate 6:30 am to 6:30 pm weekdays, 9:30 am to 6:30 pm Saturday, with no service on Sunday.

SHASTA STATE HISTORIC PARK

Six miles west of downtown Redding on Hwy 299, Shasta State Historic Park preserves the ruins of the gold rush mining town of Shasta (not to be confused with the town of Mt Shasta covered earlier in this chapter), including an old courthouse that is now a museum (☎ 530-243-8194), open 10 am to 5 pm Wednesday to Sunday. When the gold rush was at its height, everything and everyone had to pass through Shasta.

But when the railroad bypassed it to set up in Poverty Flat, poor Shasta lost its reason for being. Fortunately, the entire town has been preserved as a state historic park. The Courthouse Museum, Masonic lodge, two stores and a bakery are still functioning buildings, and there are several private homes that are still lived in. You can also see one long row of brick buildings, which are now in ruins.

WEAVERVILLE
● **population 3500** ● **elevation 2045 feet**

Weaverville, a small gem of a town at the foot of the spectacular Trinity Alps, is on the National Register of Historic Places. Situated on Hwy 299, 42 miles west of Redding and 100 miles east of Eureka, it is the seat of Trinity County, a mountain and forest area that's 75% federally owned. With its 3223 sq miles, Trinity County is the size of Delaware and Rhode Island together, yet has a total population of only 15,000, not one traffic light or parking meter and no incorporated towns. Its only government is five elected county supervisors.

The Weaverville Ranger District office (☎ 530-623-2121), 210 N Main St, has maps, information and permits for all the lakes, national forests and wilderness areas in and near Trinity County, with specifics on hiking trails, camping areas and recreation sites. It's open 8 am to 4:30 pm weekdays, and on major summer holiday weekends. The Trinity County Chamber of Commerce (☎ 530-623-6101, 800-421-7259), 211 Trinity Lakes Blvd (Hwy 3), has summer hours 9 am to 5 pm weekdays, and some weekends; winter hours are 9 am to 4 pm weekdays.

Things to See & Do

You can spend some very pleasant hours just strolling around town, visiting art galleries, crafts shops, museums and historic places. Plaques on the outsides of the buildings tell when they were built and what they were. **Weaverville Joss House State Historic Park** (☎ 530-623-5284), in the center of town, is the oldest continuously used Chinese temple in California; its ornate altar, sent from China, is more than 3000 years old. It's open from 10 am to 4 pm – seven days a week in summer, Saturdays only in winter, and Wednesday to Sunday in springtime and autumn. The **Weaverville Drug Store** at 219 Main St, proclaims itself 'California's Oldest Living Pharmacy.' It was established in 1853 and is a living museum as well as a functioning business.

A farmers' market is held from 5 to 7 pm on Wednesdays June to October in the parking lot of the Weaverville Community Service District building, 716 Main St.

In the fall, the vibrant colors of changing leaves attract people to the Trinity Scenic Byway and to the Trinity Heritage National Scenic Byway (see sections on both routes in this chapter). Self-guided tour information is available at the Trinity County Chamber of Commerce and at the ranger district office.

Places to Stay
The ranger station has information on many USFS campgrounds in the area, especially around Trinity-Clair Engle Lake.

The *Weaverville Hotel* (☎ 530-623-3121, 203 Main St) in the center of town, is a charming 1861 hotel that's old-fashioned, comfortable and well cared for. The seven rooms, each with private bath or shower, are $39.50, including free tea or coffee in the morning. The reception desk is below the hotel, at Brady's Sport Shop. At the west end of town, the *Red Hill Motel* (☎ 530-623-4331) is a quiet place with six free-standing cabins, two duplexes, and four motel units. Prices are $30/35, higher for accommodations with kitchens or for family units. It's on Red Hill Rd just off Main St, a block west of the center of town and behind the county library, which is opposite the ranger station. Several other motels are on Hwy 299, on the east side of town.

Places to Eat
Along Main St, try the *Pacific Brewery Restaurant & Bar* (☎ 530-623-3000, 401 Main St) for American-style food, or *Noell's Garden Cafe* (☎ 530-623-3121, 252 Main St) for healthful continental cuisine. *La Casita* (☎ 530-623-5797, 252 Main St), downstairs, serves Mexican food. *Trinideli* (☎ 530-623-

5856), at the corner of Trinity Lakes Blvd (Hwy 3) and Center St, is a good deli serving gourmet sandwiches. *La Grange Cafe* (☎ 530-623-5325, 315 N Main St) has award-winning continental food and a friendly atmosphere – if the weather is nice, sit out on the patio. You can find places that stay open later along Nugget Lane, at the east end of town, including *Marino's* (☎ 530-623-6466), with Nino Marino on one side (Italian) and Marino's on the other side (a steakhouse), and the *Sawmill Saloon* (☎ 530-623-4436), a bar with pool tables that serves lunch and dinner.

Mountain Marketplace (☎ 530-623-2656, 222 S Main St), in the center of town, is a natural foods grocery store with a juice bar and vegetarian deli.

Getting There & Away
A local bus makes a weekday Weaverville-Lewiston loop via Hwy 299 and Hwy 3. Another local bus runs between Weaverville and Hayfork, a small town about 30 miles to the southeast on Hwy 3. Trinity Transit (☎ 530-623-5438) can provide details.

TRINITY SCENIC BYWAY
Starting in Redding and heading west, Hwy 299, known as the Trinity Scenic Byway, winds through scenic, rugged mountains for 150 miles to Arcata, on the coast not far from Eureka. The highway runs along the meandering Trinity River and through the Shasta-Trinity and Six Rivers national forests, past Whiskeytown Lake and historic towns, including Shasta and Weaverville. In autumn the changing color of the leaves is a special treat.

TRINITY HERITAGE NATIONAL SCENIC BYWAY
This 111-mile scenic drive heads north from Weaverville on Hwy 3, goes over 9025-foot Mt Eddy and finally meets I-5 just north of Weed. You can do all or only part of the tour; it takes all day to do the whole thing. The section north of Coffee Creek is made impassable by snow in winter. There are good places to stop for a picnic or hike – the route intersects with various hiking trails, including

NORTHERN MOUNTAINS

the historic Sisson-Callahan National Recreation Trail and the Pacific Crest Trail, which you can take south from the road for 3 miles of easy grade for a pleasant day hike to the Deadfall Lakes Basin.

McCLOUD
• population 1600 • elevation 3238 feet
McCloud, a tiny, historic mill town at the foot of the south slope of Mt Shasta, is on the north side of Hwy 89, some 9 miles east of I-5. As the closest settlement to the Mt Shasta Ski Park, McCloud is worth a visit both for itself and for recreation in the surrounding area.

Information
The McCloud Chamber of Commerce (☎ 530-964-3113, 877-964-3113, o-mcloud@inreach.com, www.mccloudca.com), at 205 Quincy Ave, is open 10 am to 4 pm weekdays. The Ranger District office (☎ 530-964-2184), two blocks east of town, has information on camping and recreation in the area. It's open 8 am to 4:30 pm weekdays.

Things to See & Do
McCloud Lake is 9 miles south of town on Squaw Valley Rd; it is small, peaceful and good for swimming and picnicking.

The **McCloud River Loop**, a 6-mile dirt road along the Upper McCloud River, begins at Fowlers Camp, 5½ miles east of McCloud, and emerges onto Hwy 89 about 11 miles east of town. You'll pass three waterfalls (the Lower, Middle and Upper McCloud River Falls), a riparian habitat for bird-watching in Bigelow Meadow, and a hiking trail. The drive can easily be done by car or bicycle.

There are several good area hiking trails, including the **Squaw Valley Creek Trail** (not to be confused with the ski area near Lake Tahoe), an easy 5-mile loop south of town, with swimming, fishing, and picnicking along the way.

Other hiking trails include the short **Ah-Di-Na Nature Trail** and a portion of the Pacific Crest Trail, both accessible from the Ah-Di-Na campground, which is on Squaw Valley Rd south of the town of McCloud.

Ask at the ranger office for a free pamphlet outlining these routes and directions to the trailheads.

Saunter down to see some square dancing at McCloud Dance Country (☎ 530-964-2252), a 1906 dance hall at the corner of Broadway and Pine Sts. Open dances are held every Friday and Saturday evening in summer, with rounds at 7:30 pm and squares starting at 8 pm.

Fishing is popular on Lake McCloud, the Upper McCloud River (stocked with trout) and at Squaw Valley Creek. Ah-Di-Na is popular for fly-fishing.

Places to Stay
Camping There are seven or eight USFS campgrounds nearby, including *Fowler's Camp*. The ranger station can give you details. The campgrounds have a range of facilities and prices. Three charge fees ranging from $8 to $12; the others are free but more primitive (no running water). Six miles south of town on the road to Lake McCloud, *Friday's Retreat* (☎ 530-964-2878, 530-529-0698) in Squaw Valley near Squaw Valley Creek has tent/RV sites for $12/16.50. They offer weekly and

monthly discounts, a fly-fishing pond and a fly-fishing school. The **McCloud Dance Country RV Park** (☎ *530-964-2252*), at the corner of Squaw Valley Rd and Hwy 89, is big, popular and open April through October. Tent sites are $14, water-and-electric sites $17 and full hookup sites $21.

B&Bs McCloud is a small town, but it has a number of fine B&Bs. Perhaps the most notable is the **McCloud B&B Hotel** (☎ *530-964-2822, 800-964-2823, 408 Main St)*, in the town center. A registered historic landmark, this grand hotel from 1916 has been lovingly restored to a luxurious standard; it opened with great hoopla in May 1995. Seventeen spacious rooms, each with private bath, are $74 to $114; suites with private Jacuzzi run $124 to $163.

The **Stoney Brook Inn** (☎ *530-964-2300, 800-369-6118, 309 W Colombero)* has a retreat-like atmosphere. It features a hot tub and sauna, Native American sweat lodge, therapeutic massage by appointment and a variety of rooms with rates from $36 to $85 (for double occupancy), some with fully equipped kitchen. Weekly rates are available off-season.

McCloud River Inn (☎ *530-964-2730, 800-261-7831, 325 Lawndale Court)* is a Victorian-style building listed on the National Register of Historic Places. Five guest rooms, each with private bath, are $70 to $150, including gourmet breakfast. **Hogan House B&B** (☎ *530-964-2882; rtoreson@ snowcrest.net, 424 Lawndale Court)*, in one of McCloud's original old homes, has four rooms for $65 apiece.

Places to Eat
Try the simple little **McCloud Soda Shoppe & Cafe** (☎ *530-964-2747, 245 Main St)* in the Old Mercantile Building, an old-fashioned, all-American cafe and soda fountain. Also in the center of town are **Raymond's Ristorante** (☎ *530-964-2099, 424 Main St)* for Italian, the **Briar Patch** (☎ *530-887-1239, 140 S Squaw Valley Rd)* for Mexican and American, the **Cozy Corner** (☎ *530-964-2683)* for breakfast and lunch, **Jilly's Summit Club**

(☎ *530-964-2227, 127 W Colombero Ave)* for pizza, pasta and sandwiches, and **Mac's Frosty** (☎ *530-964-3139, 125 Broadway Ave)*. The **McCloud River Inn** (☎ *530-964-2130, 325 Lawndale Court)* has an espresso shop, which serves light lunches.

McCloud's most unusual dining experience is the **Shasta Sunset Dinner Train** (☎ *530-964-2142, 800-733-2141)*, on Main St in the center of town. This is a three-hour train ride with a four-course gourmet dinner served in 1915-vintage restored dining cars. In summer, the train leaves at 6 pm Wednesday to Saturday, with several routes going west and east from McCloud; cost is $70 per person, plus tax and tip. Also in summer, one-hour afternoon open-air train rides are offered. Trips are scaled back in autumn; call for details.

McARTHUR-BURNEY FALLS MEMORIAL STATE PARK
This state park (☎ *530-335-2777)*, about 40 miles east of McCloud on Hwy 89 (6 miles north of Hwy 299), is the home of McArthur-Burney Falls, Lake Britton and a number of hiking trails, picnic and camping areas. Fed by a spring, the falls run with the same amount of water and at the same temperature, 48°F (9°C), year round. Clear, lava-filtered water comes surging not only over the top, but also from springs in the rocks right across the waterfall's face, adding up to some 100 million gallons flowing over the falls each day.

There's a lookout point beside the parking lot, with trails going up and down the creek from the falls. A nature trail heading downstream brings you to Lake Britton. Other trails include a section of the Pacific Crest Trail, a trail to Lake Britton Dam (1½ miles, pretty flat) and Rock Creek (a bit more strenuous), and one to Baum Lake and the Crystal Lake Hatchery (pretty flat).

About 10 miles northeast of McArthur-Burney Falls is the 6000-acre **Ahjumawi Lava Springs State Park**, known for its abundant springs and its rivers and lava flows. It can only be reached by boats that are launched at Rat Farm, 3 miles north of the town of McArthur. There is camping in Ahjumawi at nine primitive campsites (three separate campgrounds with three sites each). The fee is $7 per site. Arrangements can be made by calling McArthur-Burney park.

Regular campsites in McArthur-Burney park are $16/14 in summer/winter, with hot showers; day use is $5 per vehicle. The park is open all year, with camping even when there's snow on the ground.

ASH CREEK WILDLIFE AREA
Ash Creek Wildlife Area, one of the most remote in California, lies east of McArthur, along Hwy 299 near the junction of Hwy 139. The area's **Big Swamp**, about 3000 acres of natural wetlands, provides a protected habitat for dozens of bird species as well as for antelope and deer. Maps and information are available at the Department of Fish & Game office in Bieber (☎ 530-294-5824), just southwest of the wildlife area on Hwy 299.

STEWART MINERAL SPRINGS
To get to Stewart Mineral Springs, go 10 miles north of the town Mt Shasta on I-5, passing Weed; take the Edgewood and Gazelle exit, turn west and follow the signs for 4 miles to 4617 Stewart Springs Rd (☎ 530-938-2222).

Stewart Springs was founded in 1875 by one Henry Stewart, after Indians brought him here to heal when he was near death. He attributed his recovery to the healthful properties of the mineral waters, said to draw toxins out of the body. Today, you can soak in mineral water in small individual rooms with claw-foot tubs, emerging periodically to run to the sauna down the hall; the cost is $15 per day, or $12 if you're spending the night.

Other available amenities are massage, body wrap, Native American sweat lodge purification, a meditation room and a sunbathing deck. Lodging options include camping ($10), teepees ($15), dorms ($25), apartments ($30 to $65) and cabins with kitchens ($45).

YREKA
• **population 7200** • **elevation 2625 feet**
About 40 miles north of Mt Shasta on I-5, Yreka is inland California's northernmost city. A modern town with its roots in the gold rush, Yreka is a good stopping place to eat or to stay.

Most places of interest are along Main and Miner Sts, including the Yreka Chamber of Commerce (☎ 530-842-1649, 800-669-7352, www.yrekachamber.com), 117 W Miner St, open 9 am to 5 pm daily in summer, weekdays only in winter. The Klamath National Forest Headquarters (☎ 530-842-6131), 1312 Fairlane Rd, is open 8 am to 4:30 pm weekdays. The AAA office (☎ 530-842-4416) is at 500 N Main St.

Things to See & Do
Yreka is proud of its **Yreka Western Railroad**, fondly known as the Blue Goose. The 1915 Baldwin steam engine, pulling both covered and open-air cars, chugs at 10 mph through the Shasta Valley to the tiny town of **Montague**, 7½ miles away, with Mt Shasta looming in the distance. The train depot is just east of I-5, at the Central Yreka off-ramp. The depot opens an hour before the train leaves. In it are a 1000-foot working model railroad, historic railroad memorabilia and a gift shop. Call for departure times and reservations; tickets are $9, $4.50 for children three to 12 (☎ 530-842-4146, 800-973-5277).

The **Siskiyou County Museum** (☎ 530-842-3836), 910 S Main St, has an outdoor section with several historic buildings brought from around the county. Behind the museum is the Yreka Creek Greenway. Pathways wind through the trees, and there are informative plaques along the creek, as well as several good picnic areas. The **Siskiyou County Courthouse**, 311 4th St, was built in 1857 and has a collection of gold nuggets in the foyer.

Places to Stay
Klamath National Forest operates several campgrounds in the area; the forest headquarters has information. *Waiiaka Trailer Haven* (☎ 530-842-4500, 240 Sharps Rd) has

NORTHERN MOUNTAINS

What's in a Name?

You may ask yourself, 'Why Yreka?' When, in 1851, Abraham Thompson discovered gold in nearby Black Gulch, there was no town to name. Only six weeks later, more than 2000 prospectors were on hand, raising a tent city with a few rough shanties and cabins thrown in. Originally known as Thompson's Dry Diggings, the settlement expanded to its present site, beside what is now Yreka Creek, and was renamed Shasta Butte City. In 1852, when Siskiyou County was formed, the town won the title of county seat by only one vote over Deadwood, in Scott Valley. Its name was then changed again, to Wyreka, later Yreka, the Shasta Indian name for Mt Shasta.

tent/RV sites at $10/22; it's not the most attractive place, but it is in town.

Several comfortable motels are found up and down Main St, including the *Ben Ber Motel* (☎ 530-842-2791, 1210 S Main St) and the *Klamath Motor Lodge* (☎ 530-842-2751, 1111 S Main St), which has a swimming pool and a shady lawn. The *Heritage Inn* (☎ 530-842-6835, 306 N Main St) has rooms set back from the street. All of these charge around $30/40, single/double, in summer, with winter discounts. There are more motels at the south end of town, just off I-5 at the Fort Jones exit. For a bit more luxury, the *Best Western Miner's Inn* (☎ 530-842-4355, 122 E Miner St) at the Central Yreka exit, has two heated swimming pools and charges $49/54.

Places to Eat

There are a number of moderately priced eateries in Yreka. *The Peasantry Restaurant* (☎ 530-842-5418, 322 W Miner St) is locally famous for its omelets and sourdough pancakes at breakfast, and avocado sandwiches at lunch. *Poor George's* (☎ 530-842-4664, 108 Oberlin Rd), at the south end of town a couple of doors west of Main St, is another

place locals rave about, with large portions, good prices and a friendly hometown atmosphere. Don't be discouraged by the outside appearance, it's nice inside. *Grandma's House* (☎ 530-842-5300, 123 E Center St), between Main St and I-5, is popular for its home-style cooking and salad bar. *Nature's Kitchen* (☎ 530-842-1136, 412 S Main St) serves healthy vegetarian dishes and espresso drinks.

For Chinese food at good prices try *Ming's* (☎ 530-842-3888, 210 W Miner St) or the *China Dragon* (☎ 530-842-3444, 520 S Main St). *Lalo's* (☎ 530-842-2695, 219 W Miner St) serves good Mexican food. *Nancy's Old-Fashioned Soda Fountain* (☎ 530-842-0808, 117 W Miner St), which shares space with the chamber of commerce, is a small-town soda fountain with sundaes, hot dogs and thick malts.

Getting There & Away

Bus Buses running along I-5 stop at the Greyhound depot (☎ 530-842-3145), 825 N Main St.

STAGE bus line has daily buses running throughout the region. The weekday Scott Valley route connects Montague, Yreka, Fort Jones, Greenview and Etna. Twice a week buses go from Yreka down the Klamath River to Happy Camp and back. The STAGE office (☎ 530-842-8295) is at 411 4th St.

Car About 25 miles north of Yreka on I-5, Siskiyou Summit (elev 4310 feet) catches many storms in winter and closes often – even when the weather is just fine on either side. Check the CHP's recorded information line (☎ 530-842-4438) for road conditions before you travel. The same number provides information on winter road conditions for all of Siskiyou County.

The fastest and easiest route between Yreka and the coast is the freeway. You take I-5 north through Ashland, Medford and Grant's Pass, Oregon, then head south on Hwy 199 to Crescent City. The trip takes about 3½ hours. Highways 96, 3 and 299 will also get you to the coast; they are quite scenic but are also slow and winding.

SCOTT VALLEY

Southwest of Yreka, Hwy 3 passes through Scott Valley, a pristine agricultural area nestled between towering mountains. This is where the Scott Bar Mine operated for 110 years. At the north end of the valley, 18 miles from Yreka, is **Fort Jones**, with its small museum of Native American artifacts. Another 12 miles brings you to **Etna**, known for its tiny Etna Brewing Company & Pub (☎ 530-467-5277) at 131 Callahan St. Free tours of the brewery are available by arrangement, and food is served in the pub. The *Sengthong Thai (☎ 530-467-5668, 434 Main St)* is a popular restaurant for dinner; people come all the way from Mt Shasta and Weaverville to dine here. The atmosphere is informal and the prices very reasonable. Continuing south, Hwy 3 passes over Scott Mountain Summit (5401 feet) and joins the Trinity Heritage National Scenic Byway, passing Trinity Lake and finally arriving at Weaverville.

KLAMATH NATIONAL FOREST

With 1.7 million acres, Klamath National Forest covers a large portion of California's extreme north. It's bordered on the west by Six Rivers National Forest, by Trinity Alps Wilderness on the south and by the Oregon border on the north. It extends in a patchwork pattern east to Yreka, with one far-flung district extending north beyond that, all the way to Lava Beds National Monument (see the Northeastern California section). The Klamath National Forest Supervisor's Office (☎ 530-842-6131) is at 1312 Fairlane Rd, Yreka.

The forest includes three major rivers – the Klamath, Salmon and Scott – providing opportunities for everything from slow, lazy canoeing and inner-tubing to challenging Class V white-water rafting and kayaking. Rafts, canoes and kayaks can be rented, and a number of tour companies offer organized river trips; the ranger stations can provide details.

The forest also incorporates parts of five wilderness areas. The 223,500-acre **Marble Mountain Wilderness**, just west of Scott Valley, has close to 100 lakes, part of the Pacific Crest Trail and is relatively easy to get to. The 500,000-acre **Trinity Alps Wilderness,** north of Weaverville, features Alpine terrain, lakes, streams and a 400-mile system of trails. The 12,000-acre **Russian Wilderness**, which is about 6 miles west of the tiny town of Callahan, includes high, craggy granite formations and more than 20 lakes. The 153,000-acre **Siskiyou Wilderness**, on the west side of the forest, is rugged and seldom visited. A small portion of the **Red Buttes Wilderness** is also within the forest, though most of it is in the Rogue River National Forest across the Oregon border. Topographic maps and advice on current conditions for all of these wilderness areas are available at the ranger stations; specific phone numbers are available through the Klamath National Forest Supervisor's Office.

Northeastern California

Where the high desert plateaus of Modoc and Lassen counties give way to the mountains of the northern Sierras, life seems to proceed at a slower pace. People appear genuinely happy to greet a visitor. So far removed is this corner of the state from big-city living that many native Californians never see it. It's worth taking the time to visit and experience these spectacular but little-known areas. Heavy winter snows may be a deterrent if you don't like cold-weather sports, but the rest of the year it's quite easy to travel here – traffic congestion and smog are definitely not problems.

KLAMATH BASIN NATIONAL WILDLIFE REFUGES

Six national wildlife refuges form the Klamath Basin National Wildlife Refuges. The Tule Lake and Clear Lake refuges are wholly within California, Lower Klamath refuge straddles the California-Oregon border, and the Upper Klamath, Klamath Marsh and Bear Valley refuges are across the border in Oregon. Bear Valley and Clear Lake (not to be confused with the Clear

NORTHERN MOUNTAINS

Lake just east of Ukiah) are closed to the public to protect their delicate habitats, but the rest are open during daylight hours daily. There is a small admission fee, which is used for enhancement of the refuges.

These refuges provide habitats for birds migrating along the Pacific Flyway; 75 to 80% of all the birds on the flyway stop, some only temporarily, some to mate, make nests and raise their young. There are always birds here, and during the spring and fall migrations, there can be hundreds of thousands of waterfowl.

The spring migration peaks in March (the first northbound birds begin to arrive in February), and some years more that a million birds fill the skies. In April and May, songbirds, waterfowl and shorebirds arrive, some to stay and nest, others to rest and build up their energy before they continue north. In summer around 45,000 ducks, 2600 Canada geese and many other water birds are raised here. The fall migration begins in early September, and within two months peak numbers of more than a million birds are present.

In cold weather, the area hosts the largest wintering concentration of bald eagles in the lower 48 states, with 500 to more than 1000 in residence from December to late February. The Tule Lake and Lower Klamath refuges are the easiest places to see these eagles, as well as other raptors (including hawks and golden eagles).

The Tule Lake and Lower Klamath refuges attract the largest numbers of birds, and auto trails have been set up; a free pamphlet from the visitor center shows the routes, and there's a $3-per-vehicle fee.

Self-guided canoe trails have been established in three of the refuges. Canoe trails in the Tule Lake and Klamath Marsh refuges are open July 1 to September 30, but no canoe rentals are available. Canoe trails in

Wildlife Refuge Tour

California is on the Pacific Flyway, a migratory route for hundreds of species of birds heading south in the winter and north in the summer. Flyway regulars include everything from tiny hummingbirds, finches, swallows and woodpeckers to eagles, swans, geese, ducks, cranes and herons.

Wildlife refuges are established to protect habitats for many kinds of wildlife; in northern California they mostly safeguard wetlands used by migrating waterfowl. There are birds to see year round, but the most spectacular views are to be had during the spring and fall migrations.

The Klamath Basin National Wildlife Refuges are all within about an hour's drive of one another. About a 1½-hour drive east of the Tule Lake Wildlife Refuge is the Modoc National Wildlife Refuge at Alturas. Another detour brings you to the Ash Creek Wildlife Area near the junction of Hwys 299 and 139, about an hour southwest of Alturas. Others are just over the border in Nevada and Oregon.

A ranger-suggested route for touring the refuges begins at the Ash Creek Wildlife Area southwest of Alturas on Hwy 299. After visiting the nearby Modoc National Wildlife Refuge, try the large Sheldon National Wildlife Refuge across the border in Nevada, about a 1½-hour drive from Alturas; and the Hart Mountain National Antelope Refuge in Oregon, about two hours from Alturas or Sheldon. From Hart Mountain it's about a 90-minute drive north to the Malheur National Wildlife Refuge in southeastern Oregon. Then, heading southwest again, visit the Klamath Basin National Wildlife Refuges in southern Oregon and northern California.

There are few hiking trails in the refuges, as management prefers people to be as unobtrusive as possible by staying on defined driving routes or in canoes.

Rangers can supply information about wildlife in their own and in nearby refuges. A free pamphlet called National Wildlife Refuges shows all the refuges in the US.

the Upper Klamath refuge are open year round; canoes can be rented at Rocky Point, on the west side of Upper Klamath Lake.

Information

The Klamath Basin National Wildlife Refuges Visitor Center (☎ 530-667-2231, www.klamathnwr.org) is on Hill Rd, 5 miles west of Hwy 139 near the town of Tulelake, on the west side of the Tule Lake refuge. Follow the signs from Hwy 139 or from Lava Beds National Monument (see the Lava Beds National Monument section). This information center services all six refuges. It has an interesting six-minute slide program about the birds and the refuges, as well as information on these and other wildlife refuges. It's open weekdays 8 am to 4:30 pm, weekends and holidays until 4 pm.

Places to Stay

There's camping nearby at Lava Beds National Monument. A couple of motels are on Hwy 139 near the tiny town of Tulelake: *Park Motel* (☎ 530-667-2913), half a mile south of town, and *Ellis Motel* (☎ 530-667-5242), half a mile north of town. Both charge around $39 for regular rooms; the Ellis also has kitchenette units for $5 more.

LAVA BEDS NATIONAL MONUMENT

Lava Beds National Monument, off Hwy 139 immediately south of Tule Lake National Wildlife Refuge, is a remarkable 9-by-8-mile landscape of volcanic features that include lava flows, craters, cinder cones, spatter cones, shield volcanoes and remarkable lava tubes.

Lava tubes are formed when hot, spreading lava cools and hardens on the surface and sides, where it's exposed to cold air. The inside lava is thus insulated, keeping it hot and flowing, which leaves an empty tube as the process continues. Nearly 400 such tubular caves have been found in the monument, and many more are likely to be discovered as the monument continues to be explored and more caves are found.

From near the visitor center on the south side of the park, a short loop drive provides access to many lava tube caves with names like Mushpot, Hercules Leg and Blue Grotto. The visitor center provides free flashlights for cave explorations; you can buy a special caver's 'bump hat' for a nominal price. It's essential you use a high-powered flashlight, wear good shoes (lava is sharp) and not go exploring alone. In Mushpot, the cave nearest the visitor center, lighting and informative signs have been installed.

Other notable features of the region include the tall black cone of **Schonchin Butte**, where there's a magnificent outlook; **Mammoth Crater**, the source of most of the area's lava flows; and ancient **petroglyphs** at the base of a high cliff at the north end of the monument. A leaflet explaining the origin of the petroglyphs and their probable meaning is available in the visitor center. Look for the hundreds of birds' nests in holes high up in the cliff face.

Also worth seeing is the intriguing **Captain Jack's Stronghold** at the north end of the monument. A brochure will guide you through the Stronghold trail; allow plenty of time to be halted in your tracks, meditating on the history and the labyrinthine landscape. The brochure and other books about the Modoc War (see the boxed text) are available at the visitor center.

Just opposite Captain Jack's Stronghold and the petroglyphs is the Tule Lake Wildlife Refuge, open during daylight hours. The visitor center (☎ 530-667-2282, www .nps.gov/labe), at the south end of the monument, has free maps and information about the monument and its volcanic features and history. From Memorial Day through Labor Day it's open 8 am to 6 pm daily; the rest of the year it closes at 5 pm.

Places to Stay

A tree-shaded, 42-site campground is beside the visitor center. Camping costs $10 a night in summer, $6 in winter when there's no running water, though there's always water available at the visitor center. A couple of motels are on Hwy 139 in nearby Tulelake (see the Klamath Basin National Wildlife Refuges section).

Captain Jack's Stronghold

The eerie labyrinth of lava formations known as Captain Jack's Stronghold, at the north end of Lava Beds National Monument, is the site of an important episode in American history, the Modoc War. Here Modoc subchief Kientpoos, known as Captain Jack, led a band of about 150 Modoc men, women and children in fighting off a six-month-long siege by a US Army force that eventually numbered over 600. As the Modoc War dragged on it became a great shame to the US Army – a sort of Vietnam War for its era.

Prior to the siege, conflicts between the Modocs and early white settlers had led to efforts to confine the tribe on a reservation near Upper Klamath Lake, 70 miles north of the lava beds. After experiencing hardships and harassment on the reservation, Captain Jack had led his followers back home to the Lava Beds area.

Fighting erupted when soldiers sent from Fort Klamath came to arrest Captain Jack and return his people to the reservation. Using the natural cover of the stronghold, the Modocs were able to fight the army to a standstill throughout the rough winter of 1872-73. In the end, the Modocs were defeated and Captain Jack and five of his followers were hanged at Fort Klamath – a tragic end to a tragic conflict.

MODOC NATIONAL FOREST

Modoc National Forest covers almost 2 million acres of California's northeast corner. At Medicine Lake Highlands, 14 miles south of Lava Beds National Monument on Lava Beds Medicine Lake Rd on the western edge of the forest, Medicine Lake is a stunning crater lake surrounded by pine forest and volcanic formations. Several flows of obsidian (shiny, black volcanic glass) came out of the volcano that formed Medicine Lake, which is in a caldera, or collapsed volcano. Pumice eruptions were followed by flows of obsidian.

Four campgrounds are spaced around the lake, a great place for camping and swimming. Notable geologic features of the area include the 570-acre **Medicine Lake Glass Flow**, the 8760-acre **Burnt Lava Flow** and the 4210-acre **Glass Mountain Glass Flow**. Roads are closed by snow from around mid-November to mid-June, but the area is still popular for winter sports, and accessible by cross-country skiing and snowshoeing.

Devil's Garden, north of Alturas in the central part of the forest, is an open plateau full of western juniper and other greenery.

The Warner Mountains, on the east side of the forest, are a spur of the Cascade Range. About 80 miles from north to south and 10 miles from east to west, the Warners are divided at Cedar Pass (elev 6305 feet), east of Alturas, into the North Warners and South Warners. At the pass, Cedar Pass Ski Hill (☎ 530-233-3323, 530-233-3152) offers downhill and cross-country skiing. Close by are the *Cedar Pass* and *Stough Reservoir* USFS campgrounds.

The **South Warner Wilderness Area** contains 77 miles of hiking and riding trails; the best time to use them is from July to mid-October. Weather on the Warners is extremely changeable, and snowstorms have occurred there at all times of year, so always be prepared.

In the South Warners, 160-acre Blue Lake offers camping and fishing, with a campground open from Memorial Day to mid-October. The 1½-mile Blue Lake Trail, beginning at the campground, and the 5½-mile High Grade Trail in the North Warners are two of the forest's most popular trails.

Maps and information about the forest is available at the Modoc National Forest Supervisor's Headquarters in Alturas (see the section on Alturas Orientation and Information).

ALTURAS
• **population 3000** • **elevation 4372 feet**
Small and friendly, Alturas is the seat of Modoc County and the principal service town for the state's northwestern cattle and alfalfa ranchers. 'Where the West Still Lives' – the Modoc County slogan – is fitting;

major annual events include spring and fall cattle drives, the rodeo and the county fair.

On the high, flat desert of the Modoc Plateau, with the Warner Mountains towering in the east and beyond them, Surprise Valley, the town is removed from the rest of California not only by attitude but by geography. But considering that Alturas is only a three-hour drive from Redding, Reno or Mt Shasta, and 1½ hours from Susanville or Klamath Falls, it isn't that hard to get to. If you do go to Alturas, you'll find friendly people, good places to stay and eat and plenty to see and do, including a wildlife refuge just 3 miles away.

Orientation & Information

Alturas is at the junction of Hwy 299 and US 395. Most businesses are along Main St in the 1-mile section south of its T-junction with 12th St (Hwy 299) at the north end of town. County Rd 56, which crosses Main St at the south end of town, between the museum and the chamber of commerce, heads east to the wildlife refuge and Dorris Reservoir.

The Alturas Chamber of Commerce (☎ 530-233-4434), 522 S Main St, is open 9 am to 4:30 pm weekdays. The Modoc National Forest Supervisor's Headquarters (☎ 530-233-5811), on 12th St (Hwy 299) a few blocks west of town, has information and permits for all types of recreation in the area. It's open 8 am to 5 pm weekdays.

Things to See & Do

The **Modoc County Museum** (☎ 530-233-6328), 600 S Main St, boasts hundreds of interesting historical items and a remarkable collection of books with stories about the Wild West history of Modoc County. It's open from 10 am to 4 pm, Tuesday to Saturday, May to October. The 1914 beaux arts **Modoc County Courthouse**, at the corner of Modoc and Court Sts, has a lovely stained-glass window and historical displays in the rotunda.

Murals around town portray Modoc County life with scenes such as the spring and fall cattle drives, the rodeo and the wildlife refuge.

The **Modoc National Wildlife Refuge**, 3 miles southeast of Alturas, is worth a visit. A signboard provides a map and suggests an auto tour. The sign has tips for bird-watchers, and information on the Pacific Flyway and the 232 species of birds found here. For pamphlets and more information about the birds, check with the rangers at refuge headquarters (☎ 530-233-3572), open 8 am to 4:30 pm weekdays. You'll see the most birds if you come in early morning; bring binoculars.

Birds are present throughout the year, but peak numbers can be seen during the spring and fall migrations (mid-March to late May, September to October). From mid-December to mid-February fewer birds visit the frozen wetlands, though bald eagles can still be seen. The refuge is open every day, sunrise to sunset; free.

A bit east of the refuge, on County Rd 56, Dorris Reservoir allows swimming, boating and waterskiing from June to October. From mid-October to January there's no public access at all, as the reservoir becomes a wildlife refuge.

Places to Stay

Sully's Trailer Lodge (☎ 530-233-2253) is right in town, one block east of the museum on County Rd 197 at the corner of County Rd 56; it's a quiet park with tent/trailer spaces for $11/15. A USFS campground, *Cedar Pass*, is on Hwy 299, about a 15-minute drive east of Alturas. It is situated by a stream and under large trees and is free, as is the *Stough Reservoir* campground a few miles farther east on Hwy 299. Information is available at forest headquarters.

The *Niles Hotel* (☎ 530-233-3261, 304 S Main St) is a beautifully restored historic landmark with comfortable rooms done in vintage decor for $25 to $115.

On Hwy 299, about a mile east of Main St, the *Rim Rock Motel* (☎ 530-233-5455) has a view of the Warner Mountains, as does the nearby *Drifters Inn Motel* (☎ 530-233-2428). Both have rooms for around $30/35. There are more motels on N Main St, also in the $30-to-$40 range.

Dorris House (☎ 530-233-3786), a B&B on the shore of Dorris Reservoir, has four rooms in a two-story 1912 ranch house for $40/45 single/double.

Places to Eat

The *Beacon Coffee Shop Restaurant* (☎ 530-233-2623, 206 N Main St), at the corner of 2nd St, is a home-style restaurant good for all meals, open 6 am to 10 pm daily. Its specialties are roasted chicken and barbecued ribs, to eat in or take out. Other family restaurants are the *Wagon Wheel* (☎ 530-233-5166, 308 W 12 St), closed Monday, and *Jerry's Restaurant* (☎ 530-233-3332, 449 N Main St), open 24 hours.

The *Act One Espresso Bar & Bakery* (128 N Main St) is a restaurant, coffeehouse and bakery with organic and vegetarian food, and a variety of baked goods; closed Sunday.

Nipa's (☎ 530-233-2520, 1001 N Main St) serves an imaginative selection of tasty Thai, French and California cuisine, 11 am to 9 pm daily. *King Wah* (☎ 530-233-4657, 404 W 12th St) serves Chinese food. For additional international fare, the *Brass Rail Restaurant* (☎ 530-233-2906), half a mile east of town on Hwy 299, serves up family-style Basque dinners. A landmark, it's open for lunch from noon to 2 pm, dinner from 5:30 to 10 pm; closed Monday.

For fine dining, the restaurant at the *Niles Hotel* (see Places to Stay) serves lunch and dinner and specializes in prime rib.

SURPRISE VALLEY & CEDARVILLE

• **population 1500** • **elevation 4460 feet**

Long and narrow, Surprise Valley is bordered on the west by the Warner Mountains and on the east by the high, flat, dry peaks of Nevada's Hays Canyon Range. The biggest surprise is the valley's alkaline lakes – eerie and white with nothing living in them, and often dry.

Surprise Valley's 'big town' is tiny Cedarville (population 800), 24 miles east of Alturas, which feels like an old Wild West town. The Warner Mountain Ranger District Office (☎ 530-279-6116), 385 Wallace St, one block off Main St, has information on the mountains and other local natural wonders.

Cedarville offers several places to stay and to eat. From May to October there's camping at the *Modoc County Fairgrounds* (☎ 530-279-2315). Tent sites are $7; RV or trailer sites are $10, with electrical hookups and access to water (bring your own hose). The *Drew Hotel* (☎ 530-279-2423) with rooms for $31/41, and the *JK Metzker House* (☎ 530-279-2650), with rooms for $70 including breakfast, are historic places on Main St in the center of town. The *Sunrise Motel* (☎ 530-279-2161), Hwy 299 on the west side of town, has rooms for $36/47.

For food, try the *Country Hearth Restaurant & Bakery* (☎ 530-279-2280) or the *Tumbleweed Cafe* (☎ 530-279-6363), both on Main St.

Twenty-six miles north of Cedarville are Fort Bidwell – originally a fort but now a small town – and the Fort Bidwell Indian Reservation.

SUSANVILLE

• **population 16,000** • **elevation 4255 feet**

On a high desert plateau, Susanville feels remote from the rest of the world, though it doesn't really take that long to get to other places. At the junction of Hwy 36 and Hwy 139 (4 miles off US 395), the town is 38 miles east of Chester and Lake Almanor, 85 miles northwest of Reno and 96 miles south of Alturas. Primarily a center for the surrounding cattle and timber district, Susanville experienced a jump in economic activity and population in 1992, when construction began on an expansion of the state prison at the west end of town.

Susanville is not a tourist destination, but if you happen to be traveling through this part of California, it offers basic services. The Susanville Railroad Depot (☎ 530-257-3252), 601 Richmond Rd, operates as a visitor center from May to October; it's open 9 am to 5 pm Friday to Monday. The Lassen County Chamber of Commerce (☎ 530-257-4323), 84 N Lassen St, is open 9 am to noon and 1 to 5 pm weekdays. The Lassen National Forest Supervisor's Office (☎ 530-257-2151), 55 S Sacramento St at Main St, has maps and information about the forest and is open 8 am to 4:30 pm weekdays.

The town's oldest building is named after Susanville's founder, Isaac Roop. **Roop's Fort** was a trading post on the Nobles Trail, a California immigrant route, in 1853. The town was incorporated in 1900. Roop's Fort, at 75 N Weatherlow St, now houses the Lassen Historical Museum (☎ 530-257-3292), open weekdays in summer.

Places to Stay & Eat

Sixteen miles northwest of Susanville, the large *Eagle Lake* attracts visitors from late spring until fall for swimming, fishing, boating, water-skiing and camping. Five campgrounds, administered through Lassen National Forest, are on the south shore of the lake. A bit more peaceful with boat ramps but no real marina, *Antelope Lake* is about 15 miles south of town and has three campgrounds administered by the Plumas National Forest.

Motels along Main St, none of them exceptional, range from $30/35 to $46/50. They include the *River Inn Motel* (☎ 530-257-6051), *Susanville Inn* (☎ 530-257-4522) and the *Super 8 Motel* (☎ 530-257-2782, 2975 Johnstonville Rd) at Main St. The *Roseberry House B&B* (☎ 530-257-5675, 609 N St), two blocks north of Main St, has four rooms from $60 to $85.

Main St has plenty of fast-food restaurants and several historic cafes. A plaque outside the *Pioneer Cafe* (☎ 530-257-2311, 724 Main St) – a combination bar, billiards room and cafe – declares that a saloon has been on this site since 1862, and that this is the oldest established business in northeastern California. Other historic cafes on Main St include the *Grand Cafe* (☎ 530-257-4713, 730 Main St), established in 1909, and the *St Francis Cafe* (☎ 530-257-4820), at the Old St Francis Hotel at the corner of Main and South Union Sts. These three eateries are inexpensively to moderately priced.

Getting There & Away

A bus, operated by Mt Lassen Motor Transit (☎ 916-529-2722) between Red Bluff and Susanville, stops on the way at Mineral (for Lassen Volcanic National Park), Chester (for Lake Almanor) and Westwood. It operates every day except Sunday (see Red Bluff in the Sacramento Valley chapter for details).

LAKE ALMANOR, CHESTER & WESTWOOD

Lake Almanor, about 30 miles west of Susanville on Hwy 36, is in an area perfect for relaxing and enjoying nature year round. It takes about an hour to drive around the lake's 52-mile shoreline.

Chester (population 2250), rather charming and small, is the main town near the lake. Its chamber of commerce and ranger station have information about every type of lodging and recreation in, on and around the lake, in the surrounding Lassen National Forest and in nearby Lassen Volcanic National Park. The Chester-Lake Almanor Chamber of Commerce (☎ 530-258-2426, 800-350-4838), 529 Main St (Hwy 36), is open 9 am to 4 pm weekdays. The Almanor Ranger Station of the Lassen National Forest (☎ 530-258-2141), on Main St (Hwy 36) about a mile west of town, is open 8 am to 4:30 pm weekdays.

In Westwood, a tiny town a few miles east of Chester on Hwy 36, is a historical museum that features the story of Paul Bunyan and Babe the blue ox, as well as other local legends; phone for hours (☎ 530-256-2352).

Also in Westwood is the start of the historical **Bizz Johnson Trail**, which runs for 25 miles between Westwood and Susanville. Harold 'Bizz' Johnson was a congressman who worked on acquiring the land and establishing this trail. It was once part of the old Southern Pacific right-of-way, and in the 1980s Johnson was instrumental in turning it from rail to trail. It can now be traveled by foot, mountain bike, horseback or cross-country skis (no motorized vehicles). It's easiest to do the trail in the Westwood-to-Susanville direction, as it's mostly downhill that way; pamphlets are available in Chester and Susanville at their chambers of commerce, and at the Susanville Railroad Depot, which is also the trail terminus (see section on Susanville).

Bodfish Bicycles & Quiet Mountain Sports (☎ 530-258-2338), at 152 Main St,

Chester, rents bicycles, cross-country skis and snowshoes and sells canoes and kayaks. Boats and other water sports equipment can be rented at many places around the lake.

Places to Stay

Camping There's plenty of camping around the lake and in the surrounding Lassen and Plumas national forests, both of which have sites on the lake's south shore. Nearest to Chester, the *North Shore Campground* (☎ 530-258-3376), 2 miles east of town on Hwy 36, has tent/RV sites ($15/18) right by the water.

Motels The *Seneca Motel* (☎ 530-258-2815, 545 Cedar St) at Martin Way, is quieter than places right on the highway. It's pleasant and old-fashioned, with a picnic and barbecue area and free kitchen use; rooms are $31/37, higher for family units. The *Antlers Motel* (☎ 530-258-2722, 268 Main St) has rooms for $35/40, plus larger family units and weekly rates. The *Timber House Lodge* (☎ 530-258-2729) and the *Black Forest Lodge* (☎ 530-258-2941) also have motel rooms (see Places to Eat).

B&Bs The *Bidwell House* (☎ 530-258-3338, 1 Main St) is the relocated summer home built by John and Annie Bidwell (see the boxed text on John and Annie Bidwell in the Sacramento Valley chapter). Rooms are $75 to $150, with a separate cottage for $150. The *Cinnamon Teal B&B* (☎ 530-258-3993, 227 Feather River Drive) has three rooms from $65 to $85 and a suite for $95.

Places to Eat

Chester is your best bet for getting something to eat around the lake. The *Kopper Kettle Cafe* (☎ 530-258-2698, 243 Main St) is great for breakfast and lunch, with home-style food and giant portions; half-orders are available. It has great hospitality and small-town atmosphere – lots of locals eat here. On weekends it's open 24 hours; weekdays it closes at 3 pm. The *Knotbumper Restaurant* (☎ 530-258-2301, 274 Main St), with an expanded deli menu and medium prices, is a cozy place for lunch or dinner.

The *Timber House Restaurant* (☎ 530-258-2989), at the corner of Main and First Sts, is a restaurant and bar known for steak, prime rib and seafood. The 'early-supper specials' from 4:30 to 6:30 pm are about half price. *Creekside Grill* (☎ 530-258-1966, 278 Main St) offers eclectic California cuisine. *Benassi's Restaurant* (☎ 530-258-2600, 118 Watson Rd) at Main St, serves northern Italian cuisine. About 10 miles west of Chester on Hwy 36, the *Black Forest Lodge* (☎ 530-258-2941) is recommended for its German and American cuisine and for trout fresh from the restaurant's own ponds. You can sit on the terrace, which overlooks the ponds, and order rainbow trout for breakfast, lunch or dinner. Hours are seasonal; call for times.

Getting There & Away

The Mt Lassen Motor Transit bus between Red Bluff and Susanville stops at Chester, Mineral and Westwood every day except Sunday (☎ 916-529-2722).

LASSEN NATIONAL FOREST

Lassen National Forest covers 1.2 million acres in an area called the 'crossroads,' where the granite Sierras, the volcanic Cascades, the Modoc Plateau and the Central Valley meet. The forest surrounds Lassen Volcanic National Park and contains three recreation areas – Eagle Lake, Lake Almanor and Hat Creek – all with campgrounds.

Special points of interest include a ⅓-mile walk through the **Subway Cave** lava tube; the 1½-mile volcanic **Spatter Cone Trail**; 7700-foot **Antelope Peak**; the 900-foot-high, 14-mile-long **Hat Creek Rim** escarpment; and **Willow** and **Crater Lakes**. If you're feeling ambitious, you can do a 170-mile loop drive, the **Scenic Byway**, passing many points of interest. It takes about five hours to do the whole thing, or you can do only part of it. From Red Bluff, pick up the trail at the junction of Hwy 36 and Hwy 89. From Chico, pick it up when you hit Hwy 36, from Hwy 32. If you're coming from Oroville on Hwy 70, take Hwy 89 toward Chester, and as soon as you hit Lake Almanor you're on it (there's one loop that goes around Lake

Almanor). When coming from Susanville, take either Hwy 36 toward Chester, or Hwy 44 west. From Redding, pick it up at the junction of Hwy 44 and Hwy 89; from that point, either take Hwy 89 south through Lassen Park or continue east toward Susanville on Hwy 44. The best place to get information about the Scenic Byway is from the Almanor Ranger District Office (☎ 530-258-2141), 900 E Hwy 36, Chester, about a mile west of Chester.

The forest contains 460 miles of hiking trails, including 120 miles of the Pacific Crest Trail. Other major trails include the Bizz Johnson Trail, the 18-mile Hole-in-the-Ground to Black Rock Trail, the 6-mile Spencer Meadows National Recreation Trail, and the 3⅓-mile Heart Lake National Recreation Trail.

The forest also contains three wilderness areas. The **Caribou Wilderness** and **Thousand Lakes Wilderness** are best visited from mid-June to mid-October; the **Ishi Wilderness**, at a much lower elevation in the Central Valley foothills east of Red Bluff, is more comfortable to visit in the spring and fall, as summer temperatures often climb to over 100°F (37°C).

The Lassen National Forest Supervisor's Office (☎ 530-257-2151) is at 55 S Sacramento St in Susanville (see the Susanville section earlier in this chapter). District ranger offices include Almanor Ranger District (☎ 530-258-2141), Eagle Lake Ranger District (☎ 530-257-4188) and Hat Creek Ranger District (☎ 530-336-5521).

LASSEN VOLCANIC NATIONAL PARK

Lassen Volcanic National Park is a living lesson in volcanic landscapes. Lassen Peak, the world's largest plug-dome volcano, rises 2000 feet over the surrounding landscape to 10,457 feet above sea level. The park also contains boiling hot springs and mud pots, steaming sulfur vents, fumaroles, lava flows, tube caves, cinder cones, craters and crater lakes. The road through the park wraps around Lassen Peak on three sides and provides access to the geothermal areas, lakes and hiking trails. The park contains 150 miles of hiking trails, including a 17-mile section of the Pacific Crest Trail, and seven campgrounds.

Lassen Peak is classified as an active volcano. The most recent eruption took place in 1915, when it blew a giant cloud of smoke, steam and ash 7 miles into the atmosphere. The national park was created the following year to protect the volcanic landscape. Some areas destroyed by the blast, such as the appropriately named Devastated Area, are slowly recovering.

It's only possible to drive through the park in the summer, usually from around June to October. There have even been times that the road has been closed by snow, as much as 40 feet of it, well into July. A day-use pass, valid for seven days, is $10 per vehicle.

Information

When you enter the park you'll be given a free pamphlet with a map and general information. Topographic maps and more specialized publications about the park's history and natural features are also available at the park entrances or at the park headquarters.

Park headquarters (☎ 530-595-4444) are on Hwy 36 about a mile west of the tiny town of Mineral, open 8 am to 4:30 pm weekdays most of the year, daily in summer. The Southwest Information Station is at the park's southern entrance; at the northern gate is an entrance station, quite near the Manzanita Lake Visitor Center and Loomis Museum (☎ 530-595-4444, ext 5180), which is open 9 am to 5 pm daily in summer.

Places to Stay

Seven campgrounds are within the park, with many more in the surrounding Lassen National Forest. *Manzanita Lake Campground* is the only one with RV hookups and showers; all the others do have bathrooms. Campgrounds in the park are usually open from around late May to late October, depending on snow conditions; campsites are $8 to $14, first-come, first-served. Various lodges, cabins and small resorts are nearby outside the park; a list is published in the park newspaper. Chester, Red Bluff and

NORTHERN MOUNTAINS

LASSEN VOLCANIC NATIONAL PARK

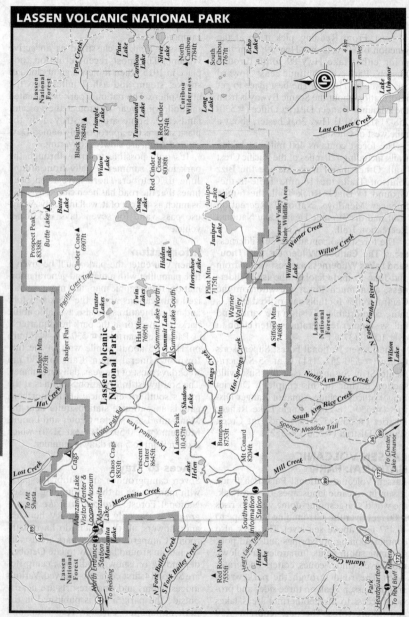

Redding all make convenient bases for visits to the park.

Getting There & Away

The park has two entrances. The north entrance, at Manzanita Lake, is 47 miles east of Redding via Hwy 44. The south entrance is reached up a 5-mile road taking off from Hwy 89, at a turnoff 5 miles east of Mineral, where the park headquarters is found. From this turn-off on Hwy 89, it is 48 miles west to Red Bluff, 25 miles east to Chester, 60 miles east to Susanville and 65 miles southeast to Quincy.

A bus between Red Bluff and Susanville, stopping on the way at Mineral, Chester and Westwood, operates daily except Sunday (see Red Bluff in the Sacramento Valley chapter). Mineral is the stop closest to the park. There's no public transport within the park, though, or on the 5 miles between Hwy 36 and the park entrance.

QUINCY
• population 5000 • elevation 3432 feet

Quincy is nestled in a valley in the northern High Sierra, southeast from both Lassen Volcanic National Park and Lake Almanor via Hwy 89. With its relatively dense population, tiny Quincy is the county seat and the 'big city' of Plumas County. It makes a pleasant stop if you're driving through the Sierra on Hwy 70, which joins with Hwy 89 as it passes through the town, or if you're traveling from the Central Valley to the mountains on Hwy 70, through the magnificent Feather River Canyon.

The **Feather River** is the county's namesake (*plumas* is Spanish for 'feathers'). Its icy waters are popular for swimming and fishing in summer. **Bucks Lake**, a 20-minute drive from Quincy west on Bucks Lake Rd, is another summer hangout; in winter, snow renders the road to the lake impassable to cars. Plumas National Forest is handy to Quincy and is great for camping, hiking and fishing.

Orientation

Hwys 70 and 89 make up Quincy's main artery. Passing through town, it splits into two one-way streets, with traffic on Main St heading east, and traffic on Lawrence St heading west. Most everything you need is on, near, or between these two streets, which form the center of Quincy's low-key commercial district. Jackson St, running parallel to (and one block back from) Main St, is another important thoroughfare.

Information

The Plumas County Visitors Bureau (☎ 530-283-6345, 800-326-2247) on Hwy 70, half a mile west of town, has a helpful staff. It's open 8 am to 5 pm weekdays, with Saturday hours (also 8 am to 5 pm) in summer.

The Plumas National Forest Supervisor's Office (☎ 530-283-2050), 159 Lawrence St, has maps and information, which it will send you free if you phone. The office is open 8 am to 4:30 pm weekdays.

The Mt Hough Ranger District Office (☎ 530-283-0555), 39696 Hwy 70, 4 miles west of Quincy, also has information and is open the same hours.

The AAA office (☎ 530-283-1014), 20 Crescent St, is at the west end of town where Hwy 70 becomes Main St.

Things to See

The large 1921 **Plumas County Courthouse** at the west end of Main St is the area's most impressive structure, with huge interior marble posts and staircases and a 2000lb bronze-and-plate-glass chandelier in the lobby.

In the block behind the courthouse, the Plumas County Museum (☎ 530-283-6320), 500 Jackson St at the corner of Coburn St, is worth a stop. Exhibits with hundreds of historical photos and relics cover the county's pioneer days, its early mining and timber industries, construction of the Western Pacific Railroad and the Maidu Indians. It's open 8 am to 5 pm weekdays, plus 10 am to 4 pm on weekends and holidays from May to September; $1.

The visitor bureau offers a free pamphlet outlining a 30-minute **Heritage Walk**, and another for an 8-mile historic driving tour of the area surrounding Quincy, the American Valley.

Activities

There are a lot of winter activities in the area, especially at Bucks Lake. Cross-country ski gear and snowshoes can be rented at Sierra Mountain Sports (☎ 530-283-2323), 501 W Main St. Ask the visitor bureau for their Winter Recreation pamphlet.

Places to Stay

If you plan to stay in or around Quincy in summer, it's a good idea to make reservations, as it's a small town in a tourist-heavy area.

There's plenty of camping near Quincy in the Plumas National Forest and at Bucks Lake (see those sections later in this chapter).

There are a number of adequate motels on Hwy 70, which is called Crescent St at the west end of town. At the east end of town, the *Ranchito* (☎ 530-283-2265, 2020 E Main St) consists of several buildings on woodsy 3-acre grounds bisected by a brook. Rooms are $44/51, higher for kitchen units. Also on the east end, *Lariat Lodge* (☎ 530-283-1000, 800-999-7199, 2370 E Main St) has rooms for $41/47.

The *Gold Pan Motel* (☎ 530-283-3686, 800-804-6541, 200 Crescent St) has rooms for $39/42. The *Spanish Creek Motel* (☎ 530-283-1200, 233 Crescent St) has a spa, barbecue and picnic area; rooms are $42/48 in summer, $38/42 in winter. The *Pine Hill Motel* (☎ 530-283-1670), on Hwy 70 a mile west of Quincy, is a rustic place with rooms and cabins for $50/55 with kitchen, $45/50 for efficiency units, $40/45 without kitchen.

The *Feather Bed B&B* (☎ 530-283-0102, 800-696-8624, 542 Jackson St) at Court St, just behind the courthouse, has seven rooms for $80 to $130.

Places to Eat

The *Morning Thunder Cafe* (☎ 530-283-1310, 557 Lawrence St) is good for breakfast and lunch. *Ragged Jack Cafe & Bakery* (☎ 530-283-1974, 189 W Main St) serves breakfast and lunch and has an extensive selection of healthful ethnic and vegetarian foods. *Moon's* (☎ 530-283-0765, 497 Lawrence St) is good for dinner and has Italian food and steaks, homemade dishes, great aromas and ambience; it's open from 5 pm onward daily except Monday. The *Quincy Natural Foods* market (☎ 530-283-3528, 30 Harbison St) is just off Main St, near The Loft.

The small, cozy *Ten-Two Dinner House* (☎ 530-283-1366, 8270 Bucks Lake Rd) in Meadow Valley on the road to Bucks Lake, about a 15-minute drive from Quincy, is among the best restaurants in the area. In summer you can sit outside by the creek. It's a bit pricey but serves superb food with all-natural ingredients and has a changing menu with great specials. It's open daily year round; reservations recommended.

BUCKS LAKE

About 17 miles southwest of Quincy on Bucks Lake Rd (Hwy 119) and 32 miles northeast of Oroville, Bucks Lake is a clear mountain lake surrounded by pine forest. It's popular in summer for camping, hiking, fishing, boating and waterskiing. Boats are for rent at Bucks Lake Marina and Bucks Lakeshore Resort (see Places to Stay). Bucks Lake Stables (☎ 530-283-2532) offers trail rides and pack trips. The Pacific Crest Trail passes through the Bucks Lake Wilderness, and there are other good hiking trails, too.

In winter, the road to the lake is closed by snow, but it's still popular for cross-country skiing. Winter sports gear can be rented in Quincy.

The lake adjoins the 21,000-acre Bucks Lake Wilderness, a section of the Plumas National Forest. Any of the forest ranger stations have information about hiking, fishing and camping on the lake and in the wilderness area.

Places to Stay & Eat

Several USFS campgrounds offer basic facilities for $3 to $12. Any Plumas National Forest Ranger station will have details; make reservations through Parknet (☎ 800-444-7275). *Bucks Lake Marina* (☎ 530-283-4243) offers camping, housekeeping cabins, and boat and kayak rentals. There's also the *Haskins Valley Pacific Gas & Electric (PG&E) Campsite* (☎ 916-386-5164). Most campgrounds and services are open from around June to October.

Bucks Lake Lodge (☎ 530-283-2262, 16525 Bucks Lake Rd) has a campground and various sizes of housekeeping cabins, for two to 10 people, for $54 to $95; it's open all year, with boat rentals and fishing tackle in summer and cross-country skiing in winter. The restaurant at the lodge is known for good food; locals often drive out from Quincy for dinner. Bucks Lake Lodge, the **Timberline Inn** (with rooms for $75 to $95) and the elegant new **Haskins Valley Inn B&B** (with rooms for $125) are operated by the same family and are together on Bucks Lake Rd; they can all be reached at the one telephone number.

Bucks Lakeshore Resort (☎ 530-283-6900) is a full-service lakeshore lodge with a restaurant, bar and country store, open year round. In summer it operates a campground, cabins and boating marina; in winter, it's a cross-country skiing resort.

PLUMAS-EUREKA STATE PARK

Within Plumas-Eureka State Park, some 30 miles southeast of Quincy, is **Johnsville**, an Old West mining town still inhabited today. You can also see the mining camp where more than $8 million worth of gold was processed. Gold was discovered here in March 1851, and mining continued until WWII. Eureka Peak (elevation 7450 feet), originally named Gold Mountain, is still the site of an estimated 67 miles of mining shafts and air vents. An old stamp mill and other historical features are preserved, and the park visitor center (☎ 530-836-2380) doubles as a mining history museum.

Summer activities include hiking, with three main trails ranging from easy to strenuous; fishing at Jamison Creek, Eureka Lake and Madora Lake; and activities and interpretive programs put on by the park visitor center. Nearby Graeagle Stable (☎ 530-836-0430) offers trail rides, riding lessons and a children's summer camp.

In winter, there's cross-country and downhill skiing in the park at the **Plumas-Eureka Ski Bowl** (☎ 530-836-2317, 530-836-2380), with two poma lifts (a spring-loaded, rope-towed pole with a small disk on the bottom; you ride by placing the disk between your legs and letting the pole drag you up the mountain), a rope tow and a 650-foot vertical drop. The bowl has a relaxing atmosphere, good for beginning and intermediate skiers; it's open weekends and holidays, usually from late December to mid-March, depending on snow conditions.

Outside the ski bowl, there are other cross-country ski areas in the park, as well as other trails nearby in the Lakes Basin Recreation Area (see the Lakes Basin Recreation Area section later in this chapter). Cross-country skiers also start off from Gold Lake Rd, which runs between Graeagle on Hwy 89 and Bassetts on Hwy 49. Cross-country skis can be rented at Blairsden Mercantile (☎ 530-836-2589) in nearby Blairsden.

Places to Stay & Eat

There's family camping in the park on a first-come, first-served basis from May to mid-October (dates depend on snow conditions each year); campsites are $16 in summer, $12 in spring or fall. Other camping is nearby in Plumas National Forest; contact the Mohawk Ranger Station (☎ 530-836-2575) in Blairsden for details.

Layman Resort (☎ 530-836-2356), on Layman Rd just off Hwy 70, 4½ miles west of the small town of Graeagle (follow the sign at the turnoff), is a fun place, right on the Middle Fork of the Feather River. Originally built in late '20s and early '30s, it has 13 rustic housekeeping cabins, and a great swimming hole (Dad's Hole) and swimming beach right on the river. Its small, quaint and charming, with log cabins, a community lodge building, shuffleboard and campfires. Cabins are $50 to $95 a night. Closes in winter.

River Pines Resort (☎ 530-836-2552, 800-696-2551, 8296 Hwy 89), a quarter-mile north of the village of Graeagle (between Graeagle and Blairsden), is one of the nicer lodgings in the area. It has a swimming pool and a popular restaurant, and is within walking distance of the Middle Fork of the Feather River. Its 45 units include motel units and suites ($65 to $225) as well as self-contained cabins ($80 to $105), with weekly rates available.

NORTHERN MOUNTAINS

The **White Sulphur Springs B&B** (☎ 530-836-2387, 800-854-1797) on Hwy 89, three miles south of the village of Graeagle, is just north of the Whitehawk Ranch golf course and residential community. It occupies an 1852 hotel that was a stagecoach stop, and still has many of the original antique furnishings. Its spacious grounds feature warm mineral springs, an Olympic-size swimming pool and a sweeping view of the Mohawk Valley. Ample country breakfasts are served. It has six units, most with private bath – four in the main house, plus two separate cottages. Prices are $85 to $140 per night.

There are many options for vacation home rentals in and around Graeagle. Graeagle has six golf courses, including three championship golf courses, two nine-hole golf courses and a huge new championship golf course scheduled to open in 2000. All the golf courses also offer lodging. Information is available at the Plumas County Visitors Bureau in Quincy and the Eastern Plumas County Chamber of Commerce in Portola.

Cheaper accommodations are found in Portola, about 10 miles east on Hwy 70 (see Portola section later in this chapter).

Getting There & Away

The park is near the intersection of Hwys 70 and 89; turnoffs are marked on both highways. The park is 5 miles west of Hwy 89, on County Road A-14.

LAKES BASIN RECREATION AREA

The Lakes Basin Recreation Area contains dozens of pristine lakes, many accessible only by hiking and horse trails. It lies south of Graeagle, off Hwy 89. It is accessible by Gold Lake Rd (Hwy 24), which runs north-south from Hwy 89, south of Graeagle, to Hwy 49, north of Sierra City. Gold Lake Rd is not snowplowed in winter, making it popular for cross-country skiing.

Gold Lake, the largest lake, has a boat landing and is the home of the Gold Lake Stables (☎ 530-836-0940) for trail rides and pack trips. The Pacific Crest Trail and many other trails traverse the area; the Round-Lake Loop trail, a 3.7-mile (three-hour)

loop trail passing nine mountain lakes, is great for hiking and horseback riding. The trailhead is at the parking lot of Gold Lake Lodge, just north of Gold Lake, off Gold Lake Rd.

Both Tahoe and Plumas national forests have organized campgrounds that are in the area (Tahoe, ☎ 530-288-3231; Plumas, ☎ 530-836-2575), or you can backpack and camp freely anywhere in the area. Rustic accommodations and dining are available at several old-fashioned lakeside lodges; the Plumas County Visitors Bureau in Quincy has details. Some of the lodges are booked up a year in advance, so you must reserve early; several are also open for casual dining.

Free maps and information about the area are available from the Plumas County Visitors Bureau in Quincy (☎ 530-283-6345, 800-326-2247).

PORTOLA
• population 2200 • elevation 4850 feet
A small mountain town straddling the Middle Fork of the Feather River, Portola's pride and joy is its Portola Railroad Museum (☎ 530-832-4131), with 36 locomotives and more than 80 freight and passenger cars and cabooses. The museum is open from mid-March to mid-December daily 10 am to 5 pm; $2. Train rides are given from 11 am to 4 pm on summer weekends, or you can arrange to run a locomotive yourself, with an instructor, for $95 to $125; call ☎ 530-832-4532 for details.

Seven miles north of Portola, in the Plumas National Forest, **Lake Davis** is good for trout and bass fishing year round. **Frenchman Lake** is also popular, but it's farther away. Go southeast toward Reno for 20 miles to the turnoff at Chilcoot, then 12 miles north to the lake.

The Eastern Plumas County Chamber of Commerce (☎ 530-832-5444, 800-995-6057) is on Hwy 70, a short distance from town. It's open 10 am to 2 pm weekdays, until 4 pm in summer.

Places to Stay & Eat

There's camping at Lake Davis in summer, or a bit further afield, at Plumas-Eureka

State Park, about 15 miles west of Portola, and at Frenchman Lake. Otherwise, there are several trailer camps along Hwy 70, west of Portola.

The *Sierra Motel* (☎ 530-832-4223, 380 E Sierra Ave [Hwy 70]), has rooms for $38/44. The *Sleepy Pines Motel* (☎ 530-832-4291, 74631 Hwy 70), just west of town, has rooms starting at $44. *Pullman House B&B* (☎ 530-832-0107, 256 Commercial St), with six rooms from $60 to $85, is conveniently situated in town, opposite the Good & Plenty Cafe. The *Silver Lady B&B* (☎ 530-832-1641, 100 Escondido Way), with three rooms from $45 to $55, is in the Delleker district, about a mile west of town. The friendly little *Good & Plenty Cafe* (☎ 530-832-5795, 239 Commercial St) is open 6 am to 2 pm daily, serving ample portions of good food. *Canyon Cafe* (☎ 530-832-9947, 448 W Sierra Ave [Hwy 70]) is open 24 hours. Both are quite reasonably priced. For dinner, try the *Log Cabin* (☎ 530-832-5243, 64 E Sierra Ave [Hwy 70]), a local landmark specializing in German food, sometimes with live music. *Alpine Moon* (☎ 530-832-5360, 165 E Sierra Ave) serves lunch on weekdays and dinners nightly except Monday. Prices at these two are in the medium range.

PLUMAS NATIONAL FOREST

Covering 1.2 million acres (1825 sq miles) in the northern Sierra Nevada, the Plumas National Forest extends roughly from Lake Oroville in the southwest, to Lake Almanor in the northwest, to Honey Lake in the northeast, and to Frenchman and Davis lakes in the southeast. The mountains are covered with evergreen forest, mostly ponderosa and sugar pine, and Douglas, red and white fir. The forest contains more than 100 lakes and some 1000 miles of rivers and streams, including the Feather River Canyon, through which you can travel for miles on Hwy 70.

The forest has more than 50 campgrounds and dozens of hiking trails. Maps and information are available from the Plumas National Forest Supervisor's Office (☎ 530-283-2050), 159 Lawrence St, Quincy; the Mt Hough Ranger District Office (☎ 530-283-

0555), 39696 Hwy 70, Quincy; the Beckworth Ranger District Office (☎ 530-836-2575) off Hwy 70, west of Blairsden; or from the La Porte Ranger District Office (☎ 530-534-6500), 875 Mitchell Ave, Oroville.

Western Mountains

Between the Central Valley and the coast, the Coastal Mountain Range is national forest land all the way from the Oregon border south to just above Clear Lake, at the north end of the Wine Country. North of the Central Valley, the Coastal Range fans out into other mountain ranges: the Cascades, the Siskiyou Mountains, the Trinity Alps, the Salmon Mountains, the Marble Mountains and the Scott Bar Mountains. At higher elevations are evergreens, including ponderosa pine, sugar pine, incense cedar, and red, white and Douglas fir; at lower elevations are hardwoods, including oak, cottonwood, dogwood and beech.

SIX RIVERS NATIONAL FOREST

Hugging the west side of the Klamath and Trinity national forests and the Siskiyou and Trinity Alps wilderness areas, Six Rivers National Forest is a long, narrow green swath. It extends more than 100 miles from north to south but only about five to 10 miles from east to west, starting at the Oregon border and going south all the way to the Yolla Bolly-Middle Eel Wilderness on the north end of Mendocino National Forest.

The six rivers for which the forest is named are the Eel, Klamath, Mad, Smith, Trinity and Van Duzen. The forest has 15 campgrounds, but you can camp anywhere in the forest with a free campfire permit.

There are four separate ranger districts:

Lower Trinity Ranger District (☎ 530-629-2118), 580 Hwy 96, Willow Creek

Mad River Ranger District (☎ 707-574-6233), Hwy 36, Mad River

Orleans Ranger District (☎ 530-627-3291), Hwy 96 at Ishi Pishi Rd, Orleans

Smith River NRA, also known as Gasquet Ranger District (☎ 707-457-3131), Hwy 199, Gasquet

The Six Rivers National Forest Supervisor's Office (☎ 707-442-1721) is at 1330 Bayshore Way, Eureka.

MENDOCINO NATIONAL FOREST

Sixty-five miles long from north to south and 35 miles wide, the Mendocino National Forest includes more than 1 million acres of forested mountains and canyons. Elevations range from 750 feet at Grindstone Creek Canyon in the Sacramento Valley foothills on the east side of the forest up to 8092-foot South Yolla Bolly Mountain in the north.

Several recreation areas – Lake Pillsbury, Middle Creek-Elk Mountain, Letts Lake, Fouts, Eel River and Plaskett Lake – have campgrounds. There are 42 campgrounds within the forest, but you can camp anywhere for free with a free campfire permit.

The forest has three national recreation trails: the Ides Cove Loop Trail in the Yolla Bolly Wilderness, the Travelers Home Trail at the Middle Fork of the Eel River and the Sled Ridge Trail beginning at Middle Creek Campground. What it does *not* have is a single paved road, although almost all of the roads have been graded and are now accessible to two-wheel-drive vehicles.

Lake Pillsbury, probably the forest's most visited spot, attracts hikers, campers, boaters and anglers, but being rather remote – 11 miles up a gravel road – it's still uncrowded. The *Lake Pillsbury Resort* (☎ 707-743-1581) has camping, cabins, fishing boat rentals and a grocery store. There's also camping at four USFS campgrounds, all operated by PG&E (☎ 916-386-5164). Two wilderness areas are within the forest: the 37,000-acre Snow Mountain Wilderness, with its 52 miles of hiking trails, and part of the Yolla Bolly-Middle Eel Wilderness, with its 40 miles of hiking trails.

Information

The forest is divided into separate ranger districts. The Mendocino National Forest Supervisor's Office (☎ 530-934-3316) is at 825 N Humboldt Ave, Willows. Its recorded information line (☎ 530-934-2350) operates 24 hours.

YOLLA BOLLY-MIDDLE EEL WILDERNESS

The 147,000-acre Yolla Bolly-Middle Eel Wilderness, between the North and South Yolla Bolly Mountains at the headwaters of the middle fork of the Eel River, includes territory from the Mendocino, Shasta-Trinity and Six Rivers national forests. The name Yolla Bolly comes from the Wintu Indian language: *yo-la* meaning 'snow-covered' and *bo-li* meaning 'high peak.'

The best time to visit is in June or July, though it's possible to visit some areas from early May to mid-October. Precautions must be taken for erratic weather conditions at all times of year. Information on current weather conditions is available from the Yolla Bolla Ranger District Office (☎ 530-352-4211) on Hwy 36 West, five miles west of Platina. Part of the Shasta-Trinity National Forest, this ranger district manages the northern part of the Yolla Bolly-Middle Eel Wilderness. It keeps up with current weather information, and also sends out information packets about the Yolla Bolly-Middle Eel Wilderness.

CLEAR LAKE
- elevation 1340 feet

Just south of Mendocino National Forest, bordered by Hwy 20 on the northeast, Hwy 29 on the west and south and Hwy 53 on the southeast, Clear Lake is a popular recreational lake with a shoreline more than 100 miles long. Mt Konocti, towering over the water at 4200 feet, is classified as an active volcano, and the lake itself is of volcanic origin. In late summer, thriving algae sometimes gives the lake a murky green appearance; at other times of year it's clear. The algae makes the lake a great habitat for fish, especially bass, and it's also home to a variety of birds. You'll often hear the terms 'upper lake' (the northwest portion) and 'lower lake' (the southeast portion), as the lake narrows in the middle to form two sections.

Clearlake (population 11,900), on the southeastern shore on Hwy 53, covers the largest area and is home to more people than any other town on the lake. Lakeport (population 4540), on the northwest shore, is the Lake County seat. Other communities around the lake include Kelseyville, Clearlake Oaks, Glenhaven, Lucerne and Nice. Middletown, another sizable Lake County town, is about 20 miles south of Clearlake at the junction of Hwy 29 and Hwy 175.

Information

The Lake County Visitor Information Center (☎ 707-263-9544, 800-525-3743), 875 Lakeport Blvd, has information on everything around the lake and the county. Summer hours are 8:30 am to 5:30 pm weekdays, 10 am to 4 pm Saturday; winter hours are 8:30 am to 5 pm Tuesday to Friday, 10 am to 2 pm Saturday.

Also helpful are the Greater Lakeport Chamber of Commerce (☎ 707-263-5092, www.lakeportchamber.com), 290 South Main St, Lakeport, and the Clearlake Chamber of Commerce (☎ 707-994-3600, www.clearlake .ca.us) 4700 Golf Ave, Clearlake. They are both open 9 am to 5 pm weekdays.

Things to See & Do

In Lakeport, the 1871 **Old County Courthouse**, 255 N Main St, is a state historic landmark. Inside, the small but interesting **Lake County Museum** (☎ 707-263-4555) has Pomo Indian artifacts and other historical exhibits; it's open 11 am to 4 pm Wednesday to Saturday, plus Sundays in summer. In Lower Lake, the **Lower Lake Historical Schoolhouse Museum** (☎ 707-995-3565), 16435 Morgan Valley Rd, a reconstructed classroom with historical displays, is open the same hours.

Library Park on the lakeshore in Lakeport has picnic areas, a children's playground and a gazebo where concerts are held.

Clear Lake State Park (☎ 707-279-4293, 707-279-2267), 5300 Soda Bay Rd, Kelseyville, on the lake's southwest shore, has hiking trails, fishing, boating and camping. There's also a visitor center with interpretive exhibits on the area's geology, natural history and Native American culture, with slide shows and films. Campsites in four campgrounds are $15 to $20 from April through September, when reservations are

available through Parknet (☎ 800-444-7275); the rest of the year they are $12 and are first-come, first-served.

Anderson Marsh State Historic Park (☎ 707-994-0688) in Lower Lake has a large marshy area, a 35-acre Pomo Indian archaeological site, a model Pomo Indian village, the restored historic John Still Anderson Ranch House, hiking trails and bird watching. Free two- to three-hour nature and bird-watching walks, sponsored by the Redbud Audubon Society (☎ 707-994-1545), are held at 9 am the first Saturday of each month.

The *Clear Lake Queen* (☎ 707-994-5432), based at the Ferndale Resort, 6190 Soda Bay Rd, Kelseyville, is an elegant three-story paddle wheel steamboat offering sightseeing cruises on the lake, with dining, a bar and live music; reservations required.

Boats can be rented from a number of places including On the Waterfront (☎ 707-263-6789), 60 3rd St, and Disney's Water Sports (☎ 707-263-0969), 401 S Main St, both in Lakeport. Boats can also be rented from Blue Fish Cove (☎ 707-998-1769), 10573 E Hwy 20, Clearlake Oaks, and from the marina at the Konocti Harbor Resort (see Places to Stay).

Outrageous Waters Water Park & Fun Center (☎ 707-995-1402), Hwy 53 at Dam Rd, Clearlake, has water slides and a children's pool and is open daily from Memorial Day through Labor Day. They also have a Grand Prix racetrack (with motorized go-carts for children or adults) and an arcade that are both open daily year round.

Wineries

Four wineries around the lake have tasting rooms:

Guenoc & Langtry Estate Vineyards & Winery (☎ 707-987-2385), 21000 Butts Canyon Rd, Middletown; self-guided tours.

Ployez Winery (☎ 707-994-2106), 1171 S Hwy 29, Lower Lake; tours by appointment.

Steele Wines (☎ 707-279-9475), off Hwy 29, between Kelseyville and Lakeport; tours by appointment.

Wildhurst Vineyards (☎ 707-279-4302), 3855 Main St, Kelseyville.

Places to Stay

Places to stay and eat can be found all around the lake, with everything from campgrounds to lavish resorts and B&Bs and from snack shacks to fine dinner houses. The Lake County Visitor Information Center and the chambers of commerce in Lakeport and Clearlake have information.

Konocti Harbor Resort & Spa (☎ 707-279-4281, 800-660-5253) on Konocti Bay, off Soda Bay Rd on the lakeshore about 4 miles from Kelseyville, is the most comprehensive resort on the lake. It has 250 rooms, a marina, sauna, spa, fitness center, tennis, miniature golf and restaurant. Boats and fishing gear can be rented at the marina. The resort also has entertainment venues, including a 5000-seat outdoor amphitheater and 1000-seat indoor space. Rooms are $49 to $229.

Lakeport has many motels and restaurants. Lakeshore motels include the *Anchorage Inn* (☎ 707-263-5417, 950 N Main St), with rooms for $52 to $135 in summer, $40 to $89 in winter; the *Clear Lake Inn* (☎ 707-263-3551, 1010 N Main St), with rooms for $69/79 in summer, $38/45 in winter; and the *Skylark Shores Motel Resort* (☎ 707-263-6151, 1120 N Main St), with rooms from $66 to $116 in summer, $45 to $80 in winter.

In Clearlake, the big, 68-room *Best Western El Grande Inn* (☎ 707-994-2000, 800-528-1234, 15135 Lakeshore Drive) has many amenities and is one block from the lake; rooms and suites are $67 to $89. On the lakeshore, *Days Inn* (☎ 707-994-8982, 800-300-8982, 13865 Lakeshore Drive) has it own pier and 20 rooms for $55/45 in summer/winter. Also on the lakeshore in Clearlake, *Tamarack Lodge* (☎ 707-995-2424, 13825 Lakeshore Drive) has 10 cottages with kitchenettes, plus boat rentals and moorings. *Garner's Resort* (☎ 707-994-6267, 6235 Old Hwy 53) is a campground with 45 tent and RV sites for $15/16, plus boat rentals and moorings and a swimming pool.

In Clearlake Oaks, the *Lake Marina Resort Motel* (☎ 707-998-3787, 800-498-3787, 10215 E Hwy 20), on the lakeshore, has boat rentals, launching and moorings, and 12 rooms with kitchenettes for $40 to $50.

In Glenhaven, the *Lake Place Resort* (☎ 707-998-3331, 9515 Harbor Drive), on the lakeshore, has nine waterfront cottages with kitchens for $75/85 on weekdays/weekends in summer, $55/60 in winter, plus RV sites for $20/15 in summer/winter. They have a hot tub, free kayaks and boat launching and mooring.

In Nice, the *Featherbed Railroad Co* (☎ 707-274-8378, 800-966-6322, 2870 Lakeshore Blvd) is a unique B&B – all of its nine rooms are converted railroad cabooses, most with Jacuzzis inside! Rates are $86 to $146.

Places to Eat

Lakeport has several good places to eat. *Park Place* (☎ 707-263-0444, 50 3rd St) is one of the town's most popular restaurants, specializing in pasta dishes and salads, all moderately priced. It's open 11 am to 9 pm daily and has a deck overlooking the lake; reservations suggested.

The more expensive *Anthony's* (☎ 707-263-4905, 2509 Lakeshore Blvd) is a popular Italian dinner house; reservations suggested. The *Dutch Treat* (☎ 707-262-0631, 150 N Main St) is a European-style coffeehouse with coffee and pastries in the morning, lunch daily and Sunday champagne brunch. You can buy your goodies there and take them over to Library Park, a great picnic spot.

In Clearlake, *Kathie's Inn* (☎ 707-994-9933, 14677 Lakeshore Drive) is a casual steak and seafood restaurant good for lunch and dinner, with ample portions and moderate prices. In Lower Lake, *Robert's* (☎ 707-995-3569, 16170 Main St) is a moderately priced restaurant serving French country cuisine. In Kelseyville, the *Sicilian Country Steakhouse* (☎ 707-279-0704, 5685 Main St) is popular for its authentic Sicilian and Italian cuisine.

Entertainment

Headline entertainment is presented regularly at the 5000-seat outdoor amphitheater and the 1000-seat indoor concert hall at the *Konocti Harbor Resort & Spa* (see Places to Stay).

Getting There & Away

Greyhound has a daily San Francisco-Lakeport bus that makes 15 stops along the way and takes five hours. The bus leaves Lakeport in the morning and returns from San Francisco in the afternoon. There is no depot in Lakeport, but the bus will make a flag stop anywhere on Main St. Driving time between San Francisco and Clear Lake is about 2½ to three hours.

NORTHERN MOUNTAINS

North Coast

From Bodega Bay and the beautiful Russian River resort area up to the Oregon border, California's rugged North Coast holds some of the state's finest attractions, including forests of old-growth coast redwoods and a rocky, brooding coastline still being carved by crashing waves.

North of the Golden Gate Bridge, the Pacific Coast Hwy (Hwy 1) and the Redwood Hwy (Hwy 101) fork. Heading north, Hwy 1 snakes along the coast past tiny coastal towns and magnificent scenery – rocky, windswept beaches; craggy cliffs punctuated by coves, bays, rivers and quiet estuaries; grasslands that are green in winter, golden in summer and full of wildflowers in spring; and ancient forests of redwood trees. Hwy 101 heads north through a series of fertile inland valleys before entering the great redwood forests.

The North Coast also has many other highlights, including lakes, rivers, bays and coastal lagoons; charming towns; a historic railroad (the 'Skunk Train'); and an individualistic culture very different from what you find in the big cities.

Summers on the North Coast tend to be pleasantly cool and fresh but also often foggy. Winters are usually cold and rainy. Spring can be windy. Many people's favorite time of year to visit is in autumn, when the sky is clear and the weather balmy.

Russian River

A 1½- to two-hour drive north of San Francisco, the lower Russian River is a beautiful area of magnificent scenery, with the river coursing through a hilly landscape of coastal redwood forest, vineyards and a few tiny towns. A popular resort area offering endless activities and a laid-back attitude and pace of life, it attracts lots of visitors in summer; the rest of the year it's a lot quieter.

The Russian River begins in the mountains north of Ukiah and flows south, touch-

Highlights

- Redwood National Park – awe-inspiring ancient forests of the tallest trees on Earth
- Mendocino – an artsy coastal town tenaciously hugging a windswept bluff
- Skunk Train – a historic steam train winding over redwood-forested mountains
- Kinetic Sculpture Race – an amphibious race featuring the quirkiest vehicles you'll ever see

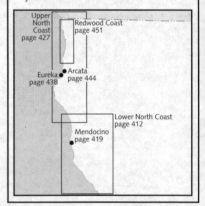

ing Ukiah, Hopland, Cloverdale and Healdsburg along the way, then makes a sharp turn west towards the ocean just south of Healdsburg. This area of the lower river, after it has made the turn, is known as the Russian River resort area, or simply the Russian River, named for the early-19th-century sea otter pelt hunters who came from Russia and settled the area. Little towns near the river include Forestville, Rio Nido, Guerneville, Monte Rio and Duncans Mills. Small towns away from the river include Cazadero and Occidental.

Guerneville (population 7000), the river's biggest town, has resorts, restaurants and many other services, and the liveliest ambience of any of the river towns. Four miles downriver, past the Northwood golf course, Monte Rio has a river beach, a bridge, a couple of places to stay and eat, and the turnoff to Occidental. The Bohemian Grove, where bigwigs of politics and industry congregate for a camp-out each summer, is in the hills outside town. Farther downriver, Duncans Mills, with a population of only 26 souls, is a tiny restored historic town. Occidental, a few miles south of Monte Rio via the Bohemian Hwy, is an idyllic little historic town in the redwoods and a good destination for a scenic redwoods drive; Cazadero, in the mountains a few miles north of the river, has a remote, away-from-it-all feel.

Orientation & Information

River Rd, connecting Hwy 101 just north of Santa Rosa with Hwy 1 on the coast at Jenner, is the main artery of the lower Russian River region, hugging the river all the way from Forestville to the coast. Hwy 116, coming northwest from Cotati through Sebastopol and on to Guerneville, is another important route.

The Russian River Chamber of Commerce (☎ 707-869-9000), 16209 1st St, Guerneville, is open 10 am to 5 pm weekdays, 11 am to 4 pm Saturday. The Russian River Region Visitors Bureau (☎ 707-869-9212, 800-253-8800), 14034 Armstrong Woods Rd, Guerneville, is open 9:30 am to 5 pm weekdays, with additional summer hours 10 am to 5 pm Saturday and 10 am to 3 pm Sunday. It also operates the Russian River Region Visitor Information Center at the Korbel Champagne Cellars (☎ 707-869-2772), 13250 River Rd, Guerneville, open 10 am to 3:45 pm daily.

Activities

Many sandy beaches and swimming holes along the river make pleasant spots for picnics, swimming and relaxing. Canoes, paddleboats, inner tubes and other craft are available in summer at Johnson's Beach (☎ 707-869-2022), at the river end of Church St in downtown Guerneville. Rentals are

reasonable: canoes $15 per day; kayaks $15 per day ($5 per hour on weekends); paddleboats $5 per hour; rowboats $15 per day or $5 per hour; and inner tubes $3 per day.

Burke's Canoe Trips on the Russian River (☎ 707-887-1222), 8600 River Rd, Forestville, rents canoes for a variety of trips on the river from around May to October. Their basic full-day canoe trip costs $35, including a shuttle to bring you back to the starting point. Prices vary for other trips. Overnight camping is available at their campground in a redwood grove beside the river. Russian

River canoe trips are also available from April to October from WC 'Bob' Trowbridge Canoe Trips (see the Healdsburg Canoeing & Kayaking section).

There's year-round fishing in the Russian River, with king and silver salmon from late August to November, steelhead from November to April, shad in late May and June and bass and catfish in summer. King's Sport & Tackle (☎ 707-869-2156), 16258 Main St, Guerneville, is the local center for fishing gear and information.

Salmon

From late summer through autumn, the rivers of Northern California host thousands of salmon swimming upriver from the ocean to spawn. Of the six Pacific species of salmon, two are predominant in Northern California: chinook (also called 'king' or 'spring' salmon) and coho (also called 'silver' salmon). Chinook are the world's largest species of salmon; most chinook are around 3 feet long and weigh about 23lb, though they have been known to reach 80lb or even 100lb. Coho salmon are smaller, around 2 feet long and weigh in around 10lb.

The salmon swim upriver in autumn, returning to spawn in the same river where they were hatched. After spawning, when a female may lay anywhere from 2000 to 17,000 eggs, the adult salmon die. The eggs, which were buried in gravel, hatch after two to four months. The baby salmon remain hidden in the gravel for several more months, receiving nourishment from a yolk sac. Some species head seaward as soon as they emerge from the gravel; others may spend up to three years in freshwater before making the trip out to sea.

Upon reaching the ocean, the salmon range far and wide, some migrating thousands of miles. They live in the ocean for anywhere from six months to seven years. When their time comes to spawn, they return to the river where they were hatched, swim upstream to spawn and the cycle begins anew.

Most young salmonids migrating downstream never reach the ocean. Hazards they encounter along the way include water pollution, dams and reservoirs, rivers affected by loss of natural habitat in their watersheds and being eaten by animals or birds. At sea, they risk being preyed upon by other fish and commercial fisherfolk.

When they return to their home rivers to spawn, they face threats from commercial and noncommercial fishing, dams, pollution and loss of habitat.

Salmon numbers have declined drastically in recent years in most of Northern California's rivers, due to a combination of adverse factors. In the Mattole River watershed, for example, it's estimated that historically anywhere from 4000 to 10,000 adult salmon once returned to the river to spawn each year. After a post-WWII logging boom, salmon numbers began to decline until, in 1990, only around 100 fish were counted. Thanks to volunteer habitat restoration and restocking efforts, by 1996 it was estimated that around 1000 adults returned to spawn.

Salmon restoration efforts are an important issue in Northern California. Hatcheries play an important role, releasing thousands of young salmon into rivers and streams each year. Fish ladders are constructed beside many dams to allow the fish to swim upstream to spawn.

Another very important aspect of salmon restoration is to protect the rivers from pollution and to protect the natural habitats on a watershed-by-watershed basis. Coho salmon, for example, which are listed as a threatened species in California, need cool, shaded, clear streams for spawning. Redwood forests provide the ideal habitat; haphazard logging threatens the salmon's ability to persist, both by cutting down on shade and by causing streams to become full of sediment.

Armstrong Redwoods State Reserve

The Armstrong Redwoods State Reserve (☎ 707-869-2015), 17000 Armstrong Woods Rd, about 2 miles north of Guerneville, is an 805-acre park preserving a magnificent stand of old-growth redwood forest set aside by Colonel Armstrong, an early lumberman here. This is the only remaining public grove of virgin redwoods in this area. There's a $5 day-use fee to drive into the park, but you can park at the entrance and walk or bicycle in for free – the amazing grove of giant trees is right near the entrance.

The park has hiking and equestrian trails, interpretive nature trails, an outdoor amphitheater and camping at Bullfrog Pond (see Camping under Places to Stay). The Armstrong Woods Pack Station (☎ 707-887-2939) operates year-round trail rides, with everything from 1½ hour horseback rides to full-day lunch rides and three-day pack trips.

Wineries

The Korbel Champagne Cellars (☎ 707-887-2294), 13250 River Rd, Guerneville, is a picturesque 1886 winery producing premium, award-winning sparkling wine. Free tours and tastings are offered daily year round; there's also the Russian River Brewing Company, a wine shop and a gourmet deli with outdoor patio seating.

Other wineries in the area include the Mark West Estate Winery (☎ 707-544-4813), 7010 Trenton-Healdsburg Rd, in Forestville. The winery has a picnic area and offers tasting, and tours by appointment.

Topolos at Russian River Vineyards (☎ 707-887-1575, 888-867-6567), 5700 Gravenstein Hwy N (Hwy 116) in Forestville, offers wine tasting, dining and winery tours by appointment.

Special Events

Big events in Guerneville include the Stumptown Days Parade, Rodeo & BBQ the third weekend in June (Father's Day weekend); the Russian River Blues Festival at Johnson's Beach in June; the Russian River Jazz Festival in September; and the Russian Heritage Christmas in December.

Places to Stay

For a complete listing of the accommodations available in every category, contact the chamber of commerce or one of the visitor centers..

Camping Within Armstrong Redwoods State Reserve, the Austin Creek State Recreation Area has drive-in campsites at *Bullfrog Pond* for $12; it has cold water but no showers. Primitive hike-in and equestrian backcountry trail campsites are $10. All camping is first-come, first-served year round.

Many commercial campgrounds are in Guerneville and along the river. *Johnson's Beach Campground & Cabins* (☎ 707-869-2022, 16241 1st St), on the river in downtown Guerneville, has tent sites for $8 for the first person, $2 for each additional person. RV sites cost $15 and up, with full hookups.

Schoolhouse Canyon Campground (☎ 707-869-2311, 12600 River Rd), near the river, has a private river beach. Tent and RV sites are $20 for the first two people on weekdays, $25 for one to three people on weekends ($5 for each additional person any time). For RV sites, add $2 to these prices for electric and water (no full hookups available).

The *Casini Ranch Family Campground* (☎ 707-865-2255, 800-451-8400, 22855 Moscow Rd) is in Duncans Mills, on the river. Tent sites cost $19 for two people. RV sites with water, electricity and cable are $22 per night; $25 per night with full hookups (including sewer hookups).

Hotels, Resorts & Cottages The area has everything from simple family-style resorts with old wooden cabins to lively (or, in some cases, quieter) gay resorts.

Cazanoma Lodge (☎ 707-632-5255, 1000 Kidd Creek Rd), in Cazadero on a large acreage with a waterfall and a fine restaurant, has three suites, one sleeping room and two cabins, with prices from $70 to $140. *Fife's* (☎ 707-869-0656, 16467 River Rd), an attractive, mostly gay resort right on the river, in Guerneville, has one-room cabins with private bath for $55 to $85 on weeknights, $85 to $105 on weekends.

NORTH COAST

Johnson's Beach Resort (☎ 707-869-2022, 16241 1st St), right on the beach in downtown Guerneville, has cabins for $150 to $175 per week.

At *Riverlane Resort* (☎ 707-869-2323, 800-201-2324, 16320 1st St), on the river in downtown Guerneville, two-room cabins for four people cost $70 midweek, $90 on weekends and holidays. Studio cabins for two people are $50 midweek, $60 on weekends and holidays. A studio cabin with fireplace is $55 midweek, $70 on weekends and holidays. The *Creekside Inn & Resort* (☎ 707-869-3623, 800-776-6586, www.creeksideinn .com, 16180 Neeley Rd), in Guerneville, has rooms and cottages. Cottages cost $75 to $200 per night. The Creekside's two suites each cost $149, and rooms with shared bath are $60 to $80.

Rio Villa Beach Resort (☎ 707-865-1143, www.riovilla.com, 20292 Hwy 116), on the river in Monte Rio, has 19 rooms, including duplex cottages, rooms with kitchenettes and private balconies, two deluxe studios and two freestanding cabins with fireplaces, all with private bath. Prices are $69 to $139 Sunday to Thursday; $84 to $179 Friday and Saturday.

B&Bs In Monte Rio, look for the *Huckleberry Springs Country Inn & Spa* (☎ 707-865-2683, 800-822-2683, 8105 Beedle Rd), a 60-acre mountaintop retreat with sweeping views from the deck, pool or spa. The four cottages go for $125 single, $145 to $165 double. The *Raford House* (☎ 707-887-9573, 800-887-9503, 10630 Wohler Rd), in Healdsburg, is a restored 1880 Victorian summerhouse on a knoll overlooking a lovely vineyard, with seven rooms for $110 to $175. *Rio Inn* (☎ 707-869-4444, 800-344-7018), just off River Rd in Rio Nido, has 10 rooms for $99 to $149. The *Ridenhour Ranch House Inn* (☎ 707-887-1033, 888-877-4466, 12850 River Rd), in Guerneville, beside the Korbel Champagne Cellars, has eight rooms with private bath for $95 to $145. The luxurious *Applewood Inn* (☎ 707-869-9093, 13555 Hwy 116), in Guerneville, has 16 rooms for $135 to $275 and an elegant restaurant (see Places to Eat).

Places to Eat

Guerneville The *Hub Cap Cafe & Deli* (☎ 707-869-2393, 16337 Main St), in the center of town, is open from very early till very late daily, with great home cooking for low prices; interesting daily dinner specials cost $6. There are both inside and sidewalk tables.

The *taco truck* parked in the Safeway parking lot on Main St is popular for its delicious, inexpensive Mexican food. *Mi Casita* (☎ 707-869-9626, 16380 Mill St) is a good little Mexican restaurant with burritos for around $5, meals for $7.

Andorno's Pizza Cafe (☎ 707-869-0651, 16205 1st St) serves pizza, pasta, burgers and sandwiches inside or on the outdoor deck in the rear. A large pepperoni pizza is $13.

The *Coffee Bazaar* (☎ 707-869-9706, 14045 Armstrong Woods Rd), in the Cinnabar building, is a local hangout, popular for its for coffee, baked goods and ice cream. *Brew Moon* (☎ 707-869-0201, 16248 Main St) is a tiny coffeehouse.

For fine dining, the *Applewood Restaurant* (☎ 707-869-9093, 13555 Hwy 116), across the Guerneville Bridge at the beautiful Applewood Inn, is an elegant restaurant winning rave reviews; it's open for dinner Tuesday to Saturday. Entrées are $12 to $23, and reservations are essential. *Fife's* (☎ 707-869-0656, 16467 River Rd), at the resort of the same name, offers attractive gourmet dining both indoors and outside, with breakfast and brunch served on the deck overlooking the pool. Dinner entrées are $13 to $19.

Around the River Every little town along the river has places to eat. In Forestville, the *Forestville Inn Mexican Restaurant* (☎ 707-887-1242, 6625 Front St), right in the town center, serves Mexican food inside or outside in a lovely Spanish-style courtyard, especially pleasant in summer. Nearby, *Chez Marie* (☎ 707-887-7503, 6675 Front St) is a pleasant little dinner house serving a country French menu Friday to Sunday, Cajun-Creole on Wednesday and Thursday. *Journey's End* (☎ 707-887-9647, 6544 Front St) is a pleasant coffeehouse serving food, baked goods and great coffee. *Spancky's* pizzeria and the

Tahoe Chinese Restaurant are up the hill in the little shopping center.

Duncans Mills has the excellent little *Cape Fear Cafe* (☎ 707-865-9246, 25191 Hwy 116), with a varied menu of interesting foods; it's open 9 am to 3 pm daily for breakfast, lunch and brunch, dinner Thursday to Sunday, with seating indoors and out on the patio. Lunches are around $6 to $7; dinners $11 to $17. *Wine & Cheese Tasting of Sonoma County* (☎ 707-865-0565, 25179 Hwy 116) offers tastes of Sonoma County's finest wines, cheeses, breads and desserts, with casual seating both indoors (with a cozy fireplace in winter) and al fresco. Cost is $6 for three wine tastings and $6 for three cheeses; for $13 you get a little spread of three wines, three cheeses, bread and crackers. The *Blue Heron Restaurant* (☎ 707-865-9135, 25300 Steelhead Blvd) is an old favorite for dinner, though it's a bit expensive for what you get, by river standards.

North of the river, Cazadero also has good eateries, especially the *Cazanoma Lodge* (☎ 707-632-5255, 1000 Kidd Creek Rd), with its fine German and American dinners (for around $14) and Sunday brunch. A trout farm provides fresh fish. It's open March to December.

Entertainment

Most of the area's nightlife happens in Guerneville. *Main Street Station* (☎ 707-869-0501, 16280 Main St) has live jazz several nights weekly, and serves pizza, sandwiches and salads. The *Rainbow Cattle Company* (☎ 707-869-0206, 16220 Main St) is a popular gay bar. The *Bullpen* (☎ 707-869-3377, 16246 1st St) is a bar in the center of town with a mixed gay and straight crowd. The bar at *Fife's* resort (see Places to Stay) is another attractive and popular gay bar. Just west of Guerneville, the *Northwood Roadhouse* (☎ 707-865-2454, 19400 Hwy 116), in Monte Rio, has live dance music on Saturday nights in summer.

Getting There & Away

Sonoma County Transit (☎ 707-576-7433, 800-345-7433) has a daily bus route (No 20) connecting Santa Rosa and the Russian River area, plus a weekday route (No 28) serving Guerneville, Monte Rio, Duncans Mills and Rio Nido.

OCCIDENTAL
• population 500   • elevation 558 feet

This lovely little town is nestled in the redwood-covered hills a few miles south of the Russian River and west of Sebastopol (see the Lower North Coast map). Founded as a logging town in the 19th century, Occidental attracts visitors for its charming ambience, interesting little shops and fine places to eat. The two Italian family-style restaurants are the town's most prominent features. The scenic drive to Occidental, whichever way you come, is one of the highlights of western Sonoma County.

Places to Stay

The historic 1879 *Union Hotel* (☎ 707-874-3635, 707-874-3555, 3703 Main St) offers lodging in 11 motel rooms behind the old hotel, which is now a restaurant and saloon; rooms are $60 weekends, $44 weekdays. Across the street, *Negri's Occidental Hotel Lodge* (☎ 707-874-3623, 3610 Bohemian Hwy) has a swimming pool and 24 rooms for $70 on weekends, $45/55 single/double the rest of the week. *The Inn at Occidental* (☎ 707-874-1047, 800-522-6324, 3657 Church St) is a Victorian B&B with eight rooms for $190 to $270, $180 to $255 midweek.

Places to Eat

The *Union Hotel* (☎ 707-874-3555) dining room and *Negri's Italian Dinners* (☎ 707-823-5301), opposite one another on Main St right in the center of town, have been attracting visitors to Occidental for ample family-style Italian meals since the 1930s. Dinners at both restaurants cost $10 to $15.

The Union Hotel also has the *Union Cafe* for coffee and baked goods, open from 6 am daily. *Howard's Station Cafe* (☎ 707-874-2838, 75 Main St), in the center of town, is great for breakfast and lunch.

Entertainment

At the Union Hotel, the *Union Hotel Saloon* (☎ 707-874-3555), a popular gathering spot and watering hole for friendly locals, looks like it hasn't changed a thing since it was built in 1879; live music is occasionally presented on weekends.

SEBASTOPOL
• population 7750 • elevation 97 feet
An attractive little town in a countryside of rolling hills and apple orchards 50 miles north of San Francisco and 12 miles west of Santa Rosa (see the Lower North Coast map), Sebastopol is famous for Gravenstein apples, the area's major crop; also making inroads are vineyards and wineries. Sebastopol is also getting a reputation among antique buffs for its many shops. Historic Main St was spruced up several years ago and now sports many interesting little boutiques. The big weekend flea market is another attraction.

Orientation & Information
The crossroads of Hwys 116 and 12 is Sebastopol's major intersection. Hwy 116, called Main St in the center of town, is the main commercial street; in the heart of town, southbound highway traffic uses Main St, and northbound traffic uses Petaluma Ave, one block to the east. At the north end of Main St, the road makes a 90° turn at the Safeway store, after which the street becomes Healdsburg Ave; continuing north out of town towards Forestville and the Russian River, about 8 miles away, it's called Gravenstein Hwy N. South of town, heading towards Cotati, Hwy 116 is called Gravenstein Hwy S; this is where you'll find most of the antique shops and the flea market.

The Sebastopol Area Chamber of Commerce & Visitor Center (☎ 707-823-3032, 877-828-4748), 265 S Main St, is open 9 am to 5 pm weekdays, 11 am to 2 pm Saturday.

Wineries
Local vineyards include the Taft Street Winery (☎ 707-823-2049), 2030 Barlow Lane, and Sebastopol Vineyards (☎ 707-829-9463), 8757 Green Valley Rd; both offer tasting. The Sebastopol Fine Wine Co (☎ 707-829-9378), 6932 Sebastopol Ave, Suite A, is a wine shop and tasting room right in town.

Special Events
Annual events in Sebastopol include the Apple Blossom Parade & Festival in April; the Kate Wolf Memorial Music Festival in June; the Gravenstein Apple Fair in August; the Sebastopol Celtic Festival in September; and the Russian River Valley Holidays Showcase in November.

Places to Stay
There are three B&Bs in the countryside surrounding Sebastopol. The *Gravenstein Inn* (☎ 707-829-0493, 3160 Hicks Rd) is a national historic landmark; built in 1872, it was one of the first big farmhouses in the area. The inn has a 6-acre apple orchard, a wisteria arbor, extensive gardens and a heated swimming pool; its four rooms are $100 to $135. *Raccoon Cottage* (☎ 707-545-5466) is a private country cottage amid oaks, fruit trees and English gardens, renting for around $70 to $95 a night, depending on the length of stay. The new *Vine Hill Inn* (☎ 707-823-8832, 3949 Vine Hill Rd), beside a vineyard, has a swimming pool, private decks and four rooms with private bath for $125 and $150.

New in 1998, the large *Holiday Inn Express Hotel & Suites* (☎ 707-829-6677, 1101 Gravenstein Hwy S) is a luxurious hotel with 82 rooms for $79 to $179.

Places to Eat
The *East West Cafe & Bakery* (☎ 707-829-2822, 128 N Main St) is a great place to eat, hang out and enjoy the coffee, healthy food and comfortable atmosphere. *Lucy's Cafe* (☎ 707-829-9713, 110 N Main St) serves organic foods and has won great reviews.

Coffee Catz (☎ 707-829-6600, 6761 Sebastopol Ave), a 'roastery and coffee club' is in the Gravenstein Station. It has historic railway cars on display and is popular for coffee, cafe fare and live music most nights. *Powerhouse Brewing Company* (☎ 707-829-9171, 268 Petaluma Ave), is a microbrewery serving good food, with occasional live music. *101 Main St Bistro & Wine Bar* (☎ 707-829-3212, 101 S Main St) serves innovative foods and a large selection of wines by the glass.

Viva Mexico (☎ 707-823-5555, 841 Gravenstein Hwy S), a simple little take-out restaurant with tables under an awning in the front,
serves tasty Mexican food. They also have a
larger, indoor branch, *Viva Mexico Tropi-cal*
(☎ 707-824-8482, 7235 Healdsburg Ave). The
Thai Pot (☎ 707-823-1324, 6961 Sebastopol
Ave) offers Thai food to eat there or to go.
Mary's Pizza Shack (☎ 707-829-5800, 790
Gravenstein Hwy N) serves up famous pizza
in a family-style pizza parlor. *Pasta Bella*
(☎ 707-824-8191, 796 Gravenstein Hwy S)
serves Italian food at affordable prices.

Sebastopol's favorite fancy restaurant,
Chez Peyo (☎ 707-823-1262, 2295 Gravenstein Hwy S), 2 miles south of town, is
popular for its French country cuisine.
Dishes range from around $10 to $20.

Entertainment

Jasper O'Farrell's (☎ 707-823-1389, 6957
Sebastopol Ave) is a traditional Irish-style
pub with decent pub food and live music or
other entertainment every night. The *Main
Street Theatre* (☎ 707-823-0177, 104 N Main
St) presents theater performances. *Sebasto-
pol Cinemas* (☎ 707-829-3456, 6868 McKinley
St) has five screens.

Shopping

Ordinary browsers and antique buffs alike
will enjoy the many antique shops and col-
lectibles on the south end of town and along
Gravenstein Hwy S. The Sebastopol Antique
Mall (☎ 707-823-1936), 755 Petaluma Ave,
houses many varied shops. Sebastopol
Center for the Arts (☎ 707-829-4797), 6821
Laguna Park Way, hosts exhibits of local and
nationally known artists, with a strolling Art
Walk the first Thursday of each month.

Midgley's Country Flea Market (☎ 707-
823-7874), 2200 Gravenstein Hwy S, is the
region's largest flea market, held on Saturday and Sunday.

The Sebastopol Certified Farmers'
Market, held 10 am to 1 pm Sunday May to
October, is a popular farmers' market held
at the downtown plaza, at the corner of
Petaluma and McKinley Aves. The free
Sonoma County Farm Trails pamphlet pro-
vides a map and information on dozens of

nearby farms where you can buy everything
from apples to wreaths, with a chart showing
when each is harvested.

Getting There & Away

Sonoma County Transit (☎ 707-576-7433,
800-345-7433) operates several daily bus
routes connecting Sebastopol with Santa
Rosa, Cotati/Rohnert Park, Occidental and
the Russian River area.

The Mendocino Transit Authority (MTA;
☎ 707-884-3723, 800-696-4682) has a daily
Coast Bus that comes down the coast from
Point Arena, turning inland south of Bodega
Bay, stopping at Bodega and Sebastopol en
route to Santa Rosa. It goes south every
morning and returns every afternoon.

Along Hwy 101

North of Santa Rosa, Hwy 101 heads north
through a series of fertile valleys, joining the
Pacific Coast Hwy (Hwy 1) at Leggett.

Some highlights of this area include the
Sonoma and Mendocino County wine
country regions, Lakes Sonoma and Mendocino, the picturesque Anderson Valley and
the two hot springs near Ukiah. The highway
passes along the upper Russian River from
Healdsburg north to Calpella, north of
Ukiah.

HEALDSBURG
• **population 9750** • **elevation 103 feet**
Healdsburg (see the Lower North Coast
map) is a small, pleasant town centered
around a shady Spanish-style plaza. The
Russian River, Lake Sonoma and over 60
wineries all within a half-hour drive attract
more than a million visitors to Healdsburg
each year – a figure that seems hard to
believe when you stroll around the unpre-
suming little plaza.

Orientation & Information
The heart of town is the appealing Healdsburg Plaza, bordered by Healdsburg Ave
and Center, Matheson and Plaza Sts. The
Healdsburg Chamber of Commerce & Visitors Bureau (☎ 707-433-6935, 800-648-9922

NORTH COAST

within California), 217 Healdsburg Ave a block south of the plaza, is open 9 am to 5 pm weekdays, 10 am to 2 pm weekends. The chamber of commerce has information on many activities, including hot-air ballooning, train rides, golf, tennis, art galleries, spas, tours, antique shops, farm trails and more.

Things to See & Do

The shady, green Healdsburg Plaza is surrounded by shops and cafes; free concerts are held here on summer Sunday afternoons. The **Healdsburg Museum** (☎ 707-431-3325), 221 Matheson St, has exhibits on northern Sonoma County history, and a nice collection of Pomo and Wappo baskets, plus changing exhibits. It's open 11 am to 4 pm Tuesday to Sunday; free.

You can obtain a **walking tour** guidebook to Healdsburg's historic homes from the Healdsburg Museum, City Hall at 401 Grove St or Toyon Books (☎ 707-433-9270), 104 Matheson St.

Healdsburg Veterans Memorial Beach, on the river about a mile south of the plaza, is popular for swimming, fishing, canoeing and picnics in summertime.

Canoeing & Kayaking

WC 'Bob' Trowbridge Canoe Trips (☎ 707-433-7247, 800-640-1386), 13840 Old Redwood Hwy, rents canoes and kayaks ($30/40 half day/full day) from April to October for a variety of trips on the Russian River. They operate the Alexander Valley Campground (see Camping under Places to Stay).

Getaway Adventures (☎ 707-763-3040, 800-499-2453) offers canoeing and kayaking trips on the river and coast.

Special Events

Major annual events include the Russian River Wine Road Barrel Tasting in March, the Healdsburg Harvest Century Bicycle Tour in mid-July, and Harvest Time in the Alexander Valley in October, plus myriad holiday events throughout the year.

Places to Stay

Camping *Alexander Valley Campground* (☎ 707-433-7247, 800-640-1386, 2411 Alexan-

der Valley Rd), operated by WC 'Bob' Trowbridge Canoe Trips, has 75 campsites on the bank of the Russian River; $8 per person.

There's also camping at Lake Sonoma (see the Around Healdsburg section) and at the *Cloverdale Wine Country KOA Camping Resort* (☎ 707-894-3337, 800-368-4558, 26460 River Rd), in Cloverdale, about 15 miles north of Healdsburg, with tent/RV sites for $25/28, cabins $42.

Motels On the north edge of town at the Dry Creek Rd exit from Hwy 101, the *Healdsburg Travelodge* (☎ 707-433-0101, 800-499-0103, 178 Dry Creek Rd) has 25 rooms for around $109/89 on weekends/weekdays in summer (they're cheaper in winter). The *Best Western Dry Creek Inn* (☎/ 707-433-0300, 800-222-5784, 198 Dry Creek Rd) has 104 rooms for around $99 to $149 in summer, $94 in winter.

Older motels on Healdsburg Ave, a few blocks south of the plaza, include the *Fairview Motel* (☎ 707-433-5548, 74 Healdsburg Ave), with rooms for $46 to $80, and the *L&M Motel* (☎ 707-433-6528, 70 Healdsburg Ave), with rooms starting at $60/50 in summer/winter, slightly higher for rooms with kitchenette.

B&Bs In town, the *Healdsburg Inn on the Plaza* (☎ 707-433-6991, 800-431-8663, 110 Matheson St) has a solarium and 11 rooms on an upper floor for $145 to $245. The *George Alexander House* (☎ 707-433-1358, 800-310-1358, 423 Matheson St), in a 1905 Queen Anne Victorian three blocks east of the plaza, has four rooms for $145 to $235. The *Camellia Inn* (☎ 707-433-8182, 800-727-8182, 211 North St) has nine bedrooms in an elegant 1869 Italianate Victorian town house for $80 to $165. The *Haydon Street Inn* (☎ 707-433-5228, 800-528-3703, 321 Haydon St), also in a Queen Anne Victorian, has eight rooms, including two in a separate cottage, for $95 to $165.

In the countryside north of town, the *Belle de Jour Inn* (☎ 707-431-9777, 16276 Healdsburg Ave) has a room in the carriage house and five cottages for $165 and $275. Half a mile west of town, the *Madrona Manor*

(☎ 707-433-4231, 800-258-4003, 1001 Westside Rd) has 20 rooms in a luxurious country mansion with a swimming pool, carriage house and garden suite for $155 to $255.

Places to Eat

On Healdsburg Ave south of the plaza, the *Singletree Inn* (☎ 707-433-8263, 165 Healdsburg Ave) is a pleasant, old-fashioned place for breakfast and lunch.

Bistro Ralph (☎ 707-433-1380, 109 Plaza St) is a casual but elegant little restaurant with good food, serving lunch on weekdays and dinner nightly.

A block north, *Ravenous* (☎ 707-431-1770, 117 North St), beside the Raven Theatre, is very popular for its interesting food and enjoyable ambience. *CK House* (☎ 707-433-4122, 336 Healdsburg Ave) is an attractive Chinese restaurant.

About five minutes' drive north of town, *Cafe at the Winery* (☎ 707-433-3141, 400 Souverain Rd), at the Chateau Souverain winery in Geyserville, is a favorite for its French country cuisine and its attractive ambience, with a view overlooking the rolling vineyards. It's open for lunch daily, and for dinner Friday to Sunday. Dinners cost about $30 per person, and reservations are recommended.

Entertainment

Tamale Malone's Cantina (☎ 707-431-1856, 245 Healdsburg Ave) serves Mexican food and offers nightly entertainment, with live dance music on weekends. The *Bear Republic Brewing Company* (☎ 707-433-2337, 345 Healdsburg Ave) features handcrafted award-winning ales, live music on Friday and Saturday nights and gives brewery tours by appointment.

Getting There & Around

Bus Greyhound (☎ 800-231-2222) serves Healdsburg with two northbound and two southbound buses daily, departing from a flag stop at the bench in front of the Exxon station on Dry Creek Rd. Sonoma County Transit (☎ 707-576-7433, 800-345-7433) has a daily local bus route (No 60) to and from Santa Rosa and north to Cloverdale.

Bicycle If you'd like to tool around by bike, Healdsburg Spoke Folk Cyclery (☎ 707-433-7171), 249 Center St, rents bicycles. Maps are available at the chamber of commerce. Or call Getaway Adventures (☎ 707-763-3040, 800-499-2453). Getaway Adventures offers guided one- to six-day bicycle trips around the wine country.

AROUND HEALDSBURG
Wineries

Smack in the middle of the northern Sonoma County wine country, Healdsburg is surrounded by more than 60 wineries and vineyards. Those mentioned here are the more famous, but there are plenty of others, including tiny family wineries that can be the most charming of all. The chamber of commerce has a complete listing.

Chateau Souverain (☎ 707-433-8281), 400 Souverain Rd, Geyserville; tasting, cafe

Clos du Bois (☎ 707-857-3100, 800-222-3189), 19410 Geyserville Ave, Geyserville; tasting

Dry Creek Vineyard (☎ 707-433-1000, 800-864-9463), 3770 Lambert Bridge Rd, Healdsburg; tasting, picnic area

Ferrari-Carano Vineyards & Winery (☎ 707-433-6700), 8761 Dry Creek Rd, Healdsburg; tasting, tours by appointment

Hop Kiln Winery (☎ 707-433-6491), 6050 Westside Rd, Healdsburg; historic tasting room, picturesque picnic area and pond

Simi Winery (☎ 707-433-6981), 16275 Healdsburg Ave, Healdsburg; tasting, picnic area and a 'dynamic tour program recognized as one of the wine industry's best'

Lake Sonoma

Eleven miles northwest of Healdsburg, 2700-acre Lake Sonoma is popular for camping and water recreation. Formed by Warm Springs Dam in 1983, the lake has two major arms and many smaller coves.

The dam, 319 feet high and 3000 feet long, is on the south end of the lake. Nearby, the visitor center (☎ 707-433-9483) has historical exhibits, maps for the 40 miles of hiking trails and other information. An aquarium and a salmon and steelhead hatchery are behind the visitor center.

NORTH COAST

About a half mile west of the dam, the Lake Sonoma Marina (☎ 707-433-2200) rents every type of water recreation you can think of, from canoes to houseboats. To get the lake from Hwy 101, take the Dry Creek Rd exit on the north end of Healdsburg and head northwest for 11 miles, through beautiful Dry Creek Valley's vineyards, a very scenic drive.

Camping around the lake includes 100 sites at Liberty Glen Campground, a developed drive-in campground with hot showers. It's on a ridge overlooking the south arm of the lake; sites are $16 year round and rarely crowded. Fifteen primitive boat-in or hike-in campgrounds ($10 per site) are dotted around the lake. To make reservations, contact the National Recreation Reservation Service (☎ 877-444-6777); campsite reservations are accepted year round.

HOPLAND

• **population 80** • **elevation 486 feet**

This little three-block town on Hwy 101 (see Lower North Coast map) is known as the gateway to the Mendocino County wine country. The town was named for its most prominent crop: hops. Hops were grown here starting in 1866, but Prohibition brought the industry to a halt. The town languished until 1977, when Fetzer Vineyards renovated the old high school and opened it as a wine-tasting room. The event that put Hopland back on the map was the opening of the Mendocino Brewing Company in 1983, the first brewpub to open in California since Prohibition and the second in the nation. Now one of Northern California's best known brewpubs, the Mendocino Brewing Company attracts visitors from near and far, as do the Fetzer and Milone wineries, and the Jepson Vineyards north of town.

Another interesting attraction is the **Real Goods Solar Living Center** (☎ 707-744-2100, www.realgoods.com), 13771 S Hwy 101. They offer free tours of their 12-acre site at 11 am and 3 pm Friday to Sunday. Tours include solar and wind power generators, three ponds, water fountains, a large building constructed of straw bales, sustainable

gardens and more. They also have a summer internship program. Real Goods is open 10 am to 7 pm Monday to Saturday, 10 am to 6 pm Sunday (hours may be shorter in winter).

The Sol Fest Summer Solstice Celebration, organized by the Institute for Solar Living, is held at the Real Goods Solar Living Center site each year on the closest weekend to summer solstice. The celebration includes well-known speakers and music groups; booths with vendors; workshops on sustainable living, including hay bale construction, solar and wind power, sustainable gardening and many other topics; and tours of the 12-acre site.

The Hopland Chamber of Commerce (☎ 707-744-1379) or the chamber of commerce in Ukiah (see Ukiah Orientation & Information) can provide information about Hopland.

Wineries

Many of the area's wineries have tasting rooms. These include:

Brutocao Cellars (☎ 707-744-1664, 800-433-3689), 13500 S Hwy 101; developing Schoolhouse Plaza, with a tasting room (open 10 am to 5 pm Monday to Thursday, 10 am to 6 pm Friday to Sunday), restaurant, bar, deli, bakery, wine shop, outdoor concert area and six Olympic-size boccie courts

Fetzer Vineyards Tasting Room & Visitor Center (☎ 707-744-1250), 13601 Eastside Rd; tasting room, deli, gift shop, gardens and picnic areas; open 9 am to 5 pm daily

Jepson Vineyards Winery Distillery (☎ 707-468-8936), 10400 S Hwy 101; tasting 10 am to 5 pm daily, picnic grounds, tours by appointment

Milone Family Winery (☎ 707-744-1396, 800-564-2582), 14594 S Hwy 101; tasting room; open daily 10 am to 5 pm

Places to Stay & Eat

The *Thatcher Inn & Restaurant* (☎ 707-744-1890, 800-266-1891, 13401 S Hwy 101) is a charming, beautifully restored 1890 Victorian hotel with 20 double rooms from $130 to $180 in summer, $95 to $135 in winter; breakfast included. Dinner is served in the dining room and on the garden patio daily in summer, weekends in winter. *Fetzer Vineyards* (☎ 707-744-1250, *13601 Eastside Rd*) also operates a B&B.

The *Mendocino Brewing Company* (☎ 707-744-1361, 707-744-1015, *13351 S Hwy 101*) is famous for its award-winning Red Tail Ale and other brews. The tavern hosts occasional live music; the brewery also has a pleasant outdoor beer garden and the *Hopland Brewery Tavern Restaurant*.

Next door, *The Cheesecake Lady* (☎ 707-744-1469, *13325 S Hwy 101*) is a pleasant cafe famous for a wide variety of award-winning cheesecakes and other goodies. Across the street, the *Bluebird Cafe* (☎ 707-744-1633, *13340 S Hwy 101*) is a pleasant cafe.

ANDERSON VALLEY

A beautiful agricultural valley with vineyards, apple orchards, sheep pastures, oak trees and redwood groves, Anderson Valley is northwest of Hopland and southwest of Ukiah (see Lower North Coast map). Visitors primarily come here to visit the wineries and to make the 25-mile scenic drive along Hwy 128 from Yorkville to Navarro. Tiny **Boonville** and **Philo** are the valley's principal towns.

Boonville is linguistically famous for its unique language, 'Boontling,' developed here around the turn of the century, when Boonville was a pretty remote place; the language was developed so that the locals could communicate privately around outsiders, as well as for their own amusement. Try asking for a 'horn of zeese' (a cup of coffee) or some 'bahl gorms' (good food) while you're there.

Orientation & Information

Highway 128 travels 57 twisty miles between Hwy 101 at Cloverdale and Hwy 1 on the coast at Albion. Hwy 253, heading west 19 miles from Hwy 101 just south of Ukiah to Boonville, is an alternate route and the easiest way to get here from Ukiah.

Information about Anderson Valley is available from the chamber of commerce in Ukiah (see Orientation & Information in the Ukiah section).

Things to See & Do

The valley has over a dozen wineries (see the Around Ukiah section), most offering wine tasting, some offer tours as well. Hiking, bicycling, fishing, canoeing and kayaking are other popular activities. The **Anderson Valley Historical Society Museum**, housed in a historic little red schoolhouse on Hwy 128 just west of Boonville, has exhibits of photos and artifacts from the valley's history.

Places to Stay & Eat

The *Shenoa Retreat Center* (☎ 707-895-3156, *18520 Van Zandt Rd*), in Philo, open May through October, offers camping, cabins and luxurious cottages for individuals and groups, with delicious vegetarian meals available. The *Wellspring Renewal Center* (☎ 707-895-3893, *8550 Ray's Rd*), an interfaith retreat center in Philo, offers camping and cabins for individuals and groups. Camping costs $9 per night per adult, $4 per child. Cabins without plumbing are $22 per adult and $9 per child, or $24 for a single person. Cabins with plumbing are $32 per adult and $11 per child, or $36 for a single person.

Other Philo lodgings include the *Anderson Valley Inn* (☎ 707-895-3325, *8480 Hwy 128*), with four rooms for $35/45 single/double; the *Philo Pottery Inn* (☎ 707-895-3069, *8550 Hwy 128*), with five rooms from $95 to $115; and the *Pinoli Ranch Country Inn* (☎ 707-895-2550, *3280 Clark Rd*), with three rooms from $90 to $105.

In Boonville, there's the *Boonville Hotel* (☎ 707-895-2210, *14050 Hwy 128*), with 10 rooms at prices ranging from $74 to $200; the *Anderson Creek Inn* (☎ 707-895-3091, *12050 Anderson Valley Way*), with five rooms for $110 to $170; and the *Toll House Inn* (☎ 707-895-3630, *15301 Hwy 253*), with three rooms for $125 and $145.

Several places to eat are dotted around the valley but probably the best known is the *Buckhorn Saloon* (☎ 707-895-3369, *14081 Hwy 128*), in Boonville, a microbrewery and pub serving homemade beers and pub food. The *Boont Berry Farm* (☎ 707-895-3576, *13981 Hwy 128*) is another favorite. The *Boonville Hotel* (☎ 707-895-2210, *14050*

Hwy 128) serves lunch and dinner; reservations recommended for dinner.

UKIAH

• **population 15,000** • **elevation 635 feet**

Ukiah is the Mendocino County seat and the largest town in the area. In the fertile Yokayo Valley, Ukiah is surrounded by vineyards, wineries and pear orchards. Ukiah doesn't have many tourist attractions right in town, but it has plenty of places to stay, eat, shop, etc, and many places to visit nearby, including several wineries, two fine hot springs and Lake Mendocino.

Orientation & Information

State St, running north-south a few blocks west of Hwy 101, is Ukiah's 'main drag,' with most of the town's businesses, motels and restaurants.

The Greater Ukiah Chamber of Commerce (☎ 707-462-4705), 200 S School St, one block west of State St, has information on Ukiah and all of Mendocino County. It's open 9 am to 5 pm weekdays.

The Bureau of Land Management office (BLM; ☎ 707-468-4000), 2550 N State St, has maps and information for the surrounding wilderness areas, including camping. The AAA office (☎ 707-462-3861) is at 601 Kings Court.

Things to See & Do

The **Sun House-Grace Hudson Museum** (☎ 707-467-2836), 431 S Main St, a block east of State St, is an art, history and anthropology museum focusing on the paintings of Grace Hudson (1865-1937), famous in her day for her sensitive depictions of Pomo Indian subjects, and the Pomo basket collection and ethnological work of her husband John Hudson (1857-1936). Guided tours are given of their home, the Sun House, built in 1911; the museum is in the rear. It's open 10 am to 4:30 pm Wednesday to Saturday, noon to 4:30 pm Sunday; donation requested.

The **Ukiah Flea Market** (☎ 707-468-4626), voted 'one of the best flea markets in Northern California,' is held every Saturday and Sunday at the Ukiah Fairgrounds, 1055 N State St, beginning at 7 am.

A **farmers' market** is held Tuesday and Saturday May through October, with fresh local produce, entertainment and local talent. On Tuesday, the market is held from 3 to 6 pm on the corner of Clara and School Sts. On Saturday, it's held 8:30 am to noon at Orchard Plaza, on Orchard Ave at the corner of Perkins St.

Special Events

The chamber of commerce has information on these and other annual events: Cinco de Mayo in May; 4th of July Concert & Fireworks; the Redwood Empire 12th District Fair in August; the Fabulous Flashback Car Show in September; the Ukiah Country PumpkinFest, an arts and crafts fair, children's carnival and fiddle contest, with continuous live music, in October; and Small Town Christmas in December, with a musical program, tree lighting and truckers' light parade.

Places to Stay

South State St has many motels to choose from. *Motel 6* (☎ 707-468-5404, 800-466-8356, 1208 S State St) has rooms for $36/42 single/double in summer, $36/42 in winter. *Holiday Lodge* (☎ 707-462-2906, 1050 S State St) has a swimming pool, picnic and barbecue area, free continental breakfast and rooms for $48/53 in summer, $39/45 in winter. The *Economy Inn* (☎ 707-462-8611, 406 S State St) has rooms for $58/48 in summer/winter. *Days Inn* (☎ 707-462-7584, 800-329-7466, 950 N State St) has single/double rooms for $51/58 in summer, $47/53 in winter.

The *Sanford House B&B Inn* (☎ 707-462-1653, 306 S Pine St) offers five rooms in a 1904 Queen Anne Victorian in a quiet neighborhood close to downtown; rooms are $75/100, all with private bath.

Places to Eat

The *Maple Restaurant* (☎ 707-462-5221, 295 S State St) is a long-time old-fashioned family coffee shop popular with locals for its inexpensive breakfast and lunch. *Schat's Courthouse Bakery & Cafe* (☎ 707-462-1670, 113 W Perkins St) is a cheerful, old-fashioned bakery and cafe with checkered tablecloths, tasty baked goods, lunches and coffee. A sandwich costs about $4.50; open 6 am to 6 pm weekdays, 8 am to 4:30 pm Saturday. *Ellie's Mutt Hut & Vegetarian Cafe* (☎ 707-468-5376, 732 S State St) serves a varied menu of tasty vegetarian and meat dishes for around $6.50.

The Coffee Critic (☎ 707-462-6333, 476 N State St) is a pleasant coffeehouse serving specialty coffees and teas from around the world. They sometimes host live music on weekends.

Angelo's Italian Restaurant (☎ 707-462-0448, 920 N State St) is a family restaurant serving authentic Italian food for very reasonable prices, with plenty of vegetarian dishes on the menu. *El Azteca Mexican Restaurant* (☎ 707-463-1330, 1631 S State St) is a similarly authentic Mexican family restaurant serving tasty, inexpensive Mexican food. The *North State Cafe* (☎ 707-462-3726, 263 N State St) offers 'a casual experience in fine dining,' with a quality menu of steak, seafood, pasta and vegetarian selections.

Entertainment

For people interested in it, cultural entertainment in Ukiah is presented by the Mendocino Ballet (☎ 707-463-2290), Ukiah Symphony Orchestra (☎ 707-485-9155), Ukiah Civic Light Opera (☎ 707-462-9155), Ukiah Players Theatre (☎ 707-462-9226, 707-462-1210), Near & Arnold's School of Performing Arts & Cultural Education – SPACE (☎ 707-462-9370) and the Ukiah Community Concert Association (☎ 707-463-2738). Mendocino College (☎ 707-468-3000) presents performances, including theater, dance and music. The chamber of commerce has dates and details for all of these events.

In summer, *Sunday Concerts in the Park* presents concerts outdoors at Todd Grove Park.

Other entertainment includes live music and country & western dancing at the *Silver Tip Saloon* (☎ 707-462-9227, 720-A N State St); dancing on weekends at the *Perkins St Grill & Lounge* (☎ 707-463-0740, 228 E Perkins St); square dancing

(visitors welcome) every Thursday night and a couples' dance every Friday night at the *Frank Zeek Elementary School* (☎ 707-463-5245, 1060 N Bush St); and billiards and darts competitions at *Rack 'Em Up Quality Billiards & Darts* (☎ 707-468-1421, 401 S State St).

Five miles north of Ukiah, the *Shodakai Coyote Valley Casino* (☎ 707-485-0700, 7751 N State St) has 24-hour gambling and occasional live music. The *Sho Ka Wah Casino* (☎ 707-744-1395, 13101 Nokomis Rd), off Hwy 175 14 miles south of Ukiah, has a bingo parlor, 24-hour gambling and occasional entertainment.

Getting There & Away

MTA (☎ 707-462-1422, 800-696-4682), 241 Plant Rd, operates a weekday bus starting in Gualala, heading north to the Navarro River junction. There it turns inland on Hwy 128, goes through the Anderson Valley to Ukiah and returns. At Navarro, this bus connects with Mendocino Stage buses going to Mendocino and Fort Bragg.

A daily MTA bus travels the Mendocino-Fort Bragg-Willits-Ukiah-Santa Rosa route in the morning, returning in the afternoon. A Monday-to-Saturday bus travels the Ukiah-Potter Valley-Willits-Redwood Valley and return route. Another weekday route operates between Willits and Laytonville.

The Mendocino Stage (☎ 707-964-0167) operates daily buses on the Fort Bragg-Willits-Ukiah-Santa Rosa and return route.

Greyhound (☎ 800-231-2222) operates two northbound and two southbound buses daily on Hwy 101. They stop at the MTA bus stop, 241 Plant Rd, just outside the airport gate.

AROUND UKIAH
Wineries

Ukiah sits in the heart of the Mendocino County wine country. The Ukiah Chamber of Commerce has a free color pamphlet with a map and information on 35 local wineries and vineyards. Almost all offer tasting, most during scheduled hours, some by appointment only; a few offer tours as well. Some of the area's better-known wineries include:

Dunnewood Vineyards (☎ 707-462-2987), 2399 N State St, Ukiah; tasting, picnic grounds, gift shop, tours by appointment

Hidden Cellars (☎ 707-462-0301), 13265 S Hwy 101, Hopland; tasting

Husch Vineyards (☎ 707-895-3216), 4400 Hwy 128, Philo; tasting

Parducci Wine Cellars (☎ 707-462-9463), 501 Parducci Rd, Ukiah; tasting, tours, gifts

Redwood Valley Cellars (☎ 707-485-0322), 7051 N State St, Redwood Valley; tasting, picnic areas

Scharffenberger Cellars (☎ 707-895-2065), 8501 Hwy 128, Philo; tasting daily, tours available by appointment

Vichy Springs

Just a five-minute drive east of Ukiah, the Vichy Springs Resort (☎ 707-462-9515), 2605 Vichy Springs Rd, is a famous old hot springs with the distinction of being the only warm and naturally carbonated ('champagne') mineral baths in North America. Opened in 1854 and named after the world-famous Vichy Springs in France, this spring is the oldest continuously operating mineral springs spa in California; the two cottages here, built in 1854, are the two oldest structures standing in Mendocino County.

Around the turn of the century, Vichy Springs was a bustling place, popular for day trips from San Francisco; literary luminaries, including Mark Twain, Jack London and Robert Louis Stevenson, all came here for the restorative properties of the waters, which can be drunk as well as bathed in.

Facilities include a heated outdoor mineral hot tub, 10 indoor and outdoor tubs with natural 90°F (32°C) waters, a grotto with a ladle for sipping the effervescent waters, and a massage room. The 700-acre grounds feature hiking trails to the old Cinnabar mine shaft, up Grizzly Creek, and to a 40-foot waterfall, with 20 more miles of trails nearby.

Overnight accommodations include 12 rooms, built of redwood in the 1860s, for $99/135 single/double; five creekside rooms for $130/155; and three one- and two-bedroom cottages with kitchen for $160/195. All prices include a fine buffet breakfast and use of the grounds. RV parking costs $15, plus the all-day use fee.

All-day use of the springs costs $30, or $18 for two hours or less. Swimsuits are required. Swedish massage and herbal facials are available.

To get to Vichy Springs from Hwy 101, take the Vichy Springs Rd exit and follow the signs; the resort is 3 miles east.

Orr Hot Springs

The Orr Hot Springs Resort (☎ 707-462-6277), 13201 Orr Springs Rd, about 13 miles northwest of Ukiah, is a famous old hot springs where clothing is optional. Facilities include a communal redwood hot tub, an outdoor tile-and-rock heated pool, four individual porcelain tubs, a cold swimming pool, sauna, steam room, massage room, gardens, camping areas, lodging, a library, lounge and a communal kitchen (bring your own food). Day-use of the springs, 10 am to 10 pm daily, costs $19 ($10 on Monday).

Overnight lodging rates include full use of all facilities. Options include camping, with walk-in tent sites and a vehicle camping area, for $36 per person Thursday to Sunday, $34 Monday to Wednesday; a dorm room holding up to 12 people on futons for the same prices as camping; private rooms for $115 Thursday to Sunday, $95 Monday to Wednesday, some with private bath; and private cottages with kitchen for $150 Thursday to Sunday, $130 Monday through Wednesday.

To get there from Hwy 101, take the N State St exit, go north a quarter mile to Orr Springs Rd, turn west and keep going for 13 miles. Orr Springs Rd is a winding mountain road, and it takes at least 30 to 45 minutes to drive those 13 miles.

Lake Mendocino

This is a 1822-acre lake formed in 1958 by the completion of Coyote Dam on the East Fork of the Russian River and set in rolling hills just 5 miles northeast of Ukiah. It's a popular spot for camping and water recreation. In summer, boats are available to rent; the marina (☎ 707-485-8644) is on the north end of the lake. Coyote Dam, 3500 feet long and 160 feet high, is on the lake's southwest corner; the east part of the lake is a 689-acre protected wildlife habitat. A hiking trail circles most of the lake.

This valley is the ancestral home of the Pomo Indians. The Pomo Visitor Center (☎ 707-485-8285), on Marina Drive, on the north side of the lake, is modeled after a Pomo roundhouse and has interesting exhibits on the Pomo, the valley and the US Army Corps of Engineers, who built the dam and manages the lake. The visitor center is open seasonally, usually from around April to October.

The US Army Corps of Engineers office (☎ 707-462-7581), 1160 Lake Mendocino Drive, near the lake, has information on camping and other recreational activities. It's open 7:45 am to 4:30 pm weekdays.

The lake has nearly 300 varied campsites ($8 to $16 in summer, $14 in winter) in four campgrounds, most with hot showers. Reservations are possible for some, others are first-come, first-served. Call the National Recreation Reservation Service (☎ 877-444-6677).

For the most convenient access to Lake Mendocino, turn east from Hwy 101 onto Hwy 20, a few miles north of Ukiah; before long you'll see the lake on your right. Turn right from Hwy 20 onto Marina Drive and follow the signs to the marina, visitor center and campgrounds.

WILLITS
• population 5400 • elevation 1377 feet
Willits is a small, nondescript, but friendly, little town on Hwy 101, 22 miles north of Ukiah. Ranching, the timber industry and industrial manufacturing are the mainstays of its economy; for visitors, Willits' greatest claim to fame is that it's the eastern terminus of the Skunk Train.

The Willits Arch, which originally towered over Virginia St in Reno, Nevada, was given to Willits in 1990; after extensive redesign, the arch was erected in Willits in 1995. It now stands proudly over Hwy 101, just south of the Hwy 20 west intersection.

Orientation & Information
Hwy 101 (Main St) winds its way through the center of town. On the south end of town is the intersection of Hwy 101 and Hwy 20, which heads 34 miles west to the Mendocino coast. The Willits Chamber of Commerce (☎ 707-459-7910, www.willits.org), 239 S Main St, is open 10 am to 4 pm weekdays.

Things to See & Do
The **Skunk Train**, operating the 34 miles between Willits and Fort Bragg, is Willits' primary tourist attraction (see Fort Bragg later this chapter). The Skunk Train depot is at 299 E Commercial St, three short blocks east of Hwy 101.

Two blocks farther east, the **Mendocino County Museum** (☎ 707-459-2736), 400 E Commercial St, offers exhibits on Mendocino County history and culture, collections of Yuki and Pomo Indian basketry and local artifacts. Outside the museum, the Roots of Motive Power exhibit has occasional demonstrations of steam logging and other historic machinery, and the Redwood Empire Railroad History Project offers occasional demonstrations of a steam locomotive. The museum is open 10 am to 4:30 pm Wednesday to Sunday; free.

Golf in the Redwoods (☎ 707-459-6761) is said to be one of the most picturesque nine-hole golf courses in Northern California.

Special Events
The Celtic Renaissance Faire (☎ 707-459-3263), held in May, features traditional Highland Scottish games, music, dance, jugglers, food, arts and crafts. Also in May, pre-1970 automobiles gather on display at the Community Festival & Bob Hanson Memorial Car Show (☎ 707-459-7910). Willits Frontier Days & Rodeo (☎ 707-459-6330), with rodeos, Western dance, a parade, BBQ, pancake breakfast, junior rodeo, talent show and entertainment, is held the week of the 4th of July. Held since 1926, it's billed as 'the oldest continuous rodeo in California' and attracts many visitors. In September, the Roots of Motive Power Festival & Lumberjack Handcar Races (☎ 707-459-2736) sports

a working display of antique steam logging equipment and fun handcar races.

Places to Stay

Camping The *Willits/Ukiah KOA Resort* (☎ 707-459-6179, 800-562-8542), on Hwy 20, about 1½ miles west of Hwy 101, has a Skunk Train depot, hiking trails, a swimming pool, a children's playground and plenty of family activities and amenities. Tent/RV sites are $24/28, one-room 'kamping kabins' are $40.

Hidden Valley Campground (☎ 707-459-2521, 29801 N Hwy 101), 6½ miles north of town, has tent/RV sites for $15/17. Camp 20 of the *Jackson Demonstration State Forest* (☎ 707-964-5674), 15 miles west of Willits on Hwy 20, offers primitive camping and day-use with recreational activities. The campsites are free, but require a camping permit from the on-site camp host. Campsites have barbecue pits, picnic tables and pit toilets, but no running water.

Motels Several motels are found along Hwy 101, some offering Skunk Train packages. The *Skunk Train Motel* (☎ 707-459-2302, 500 S Main St) has regular rooms for $32, rooms with kitchen for $40 to $50. Next door, the *Pepperwood Motel* (☎ 707-459-2231, 452 S Main St) has regular rooms for $50 to $55 in summer, $35 to $40 in winter, $10 more with kitchen.

The *Old West Inn* (☎ 707-459-4201, 1221 S Main St) is a Western theme motel with rooms for $45 to $69 in summer, $45 to $55 in winter. The *Pine Cone Motel* (☎ 707-459-5044, 1350 S Main St) has rooms for $48 and up in summer, $38 to $42 off-season, more for a two-bedroom unit with kitchen. The *Lark Motel* (☎ 707-459-2421, 1411 S Main St), with free Skunk Train pickup and delivery, has rooms for $40/30 in summer/winter. The *Holiday Lodge Motel* (☎ 707-459-5361, 800-835-3972, 1540 S Main St) has a swimming pool, free Skunk Train pick-up and delivery, and rooms for $45/50 single/double in summer, $40/45 off-season, including continental breakfast.

The *Baechtel Creek Inn* (☎ 707-459-9063, 800-459-9911, 101 Gregory Lane) is a more upscale motel with a swimming pool and spa, and rooms for about $100 in summer, $69/79 single/double off-season, but cheaper with a Skunk Train package, available only in summer.

Places to Eat

Ardella's Kitchen (☎ 707-459-6577, 35 E Commercial St), a block east of Hwy 101, is the locals' favorite for breakfast, with good food and plenty of conversation; open 6 am to noon Tuesday to Saturday. Popular lunch spots include the *Loose Caboose Cafe* (☎ 707-459-1434, 10 Wood St), just off Main St, a cheerful little restaurant with train decor, and *Juliana's Cafe* (☎ 707-459-2910, 235 S Main St).

The *Tsunami Restaurant* (☎ 707-459-4750, 50 S Main St) serves nontraditional Japanese and 'Mendonesian' cuisine, primarily organic, plus chicken and fish. *Gribaldo's Cafe* (☎ 707-459-2256, 1551 S Main St), popular with local old-timers, serves breakfast, lunch and dinner; specialties include beef ribs and ostrich meat. *El Mexicano* (☎ 707-459-5702, 166 S Main St), operated by a friendly Mexican family and popular with locals, serves delicious, inexpensive Mexican food. *Perko's Restaurant* (☎ 707-459-3850, 1740 S Main St) is a dependable chain restaurant open 6 am to 10 pm daily.

The *Rib Rack* (☎ 707-459-8688, 889 S Main St), in the Safeway shopping center beside the arch, is a fun place with sawdust on the floor, cow and cowboy murals on the walls, and seating inside and out. BBQ ribs and other meats are the specialty, but they serve lots of other dishes, including daily seafood specials, vegetarian selections, homemade desserts and local microbrews.

Fresh produce from local farmers is available at the *Willits Farmers' Market*, held 3 to 6 pm Thursday May to October, in the Willits City Park on State St, one block east of Hwy 101.

Entertainment

The cozy *Willits Community Theatre* (☎ 707-459-2281) hosts award-winning productions year round.

NORTH COAST

Getting There & Away

Greyhound buses (☎ 707-459-2210, 800-231-2222) plying Hwy 101 stop at a flag stop in front of McDonald's, 1488 S Main St, with two northbound and two southbound buses daily.

MTA (☎ 800-696-4682) operates a bus on the Mendocino-Fort Bragg-Willits-Ukiah-Santa Rosa route in the morning, returning in the afternoon daily. Monday to Saturday a bus travels the Ukiah-Potter Valley-Willits-Redwood Valley and return route. Another weekday route operates between Willits and Laytonville.

The Mendocino Stage (☎ 707-964-0167) operates daily buses on the Fort Bragg-Willits-Ukiah-Santa Rosa route and return route.

Lower North Coast

Appropriately known as the Pacific Coast Hwy, Hwy 1 twists and snakes along the rugged coastline from Bodega Bay until it turns inland to meet the Redwood Hwy (Hwy 101) at Leggett, about 160 miles north of Bodega Bay.

The coast is usually cool and foggy in summer, cold and rainy in winter. The best times of year to visit are spring and autumn, especially around September and October when the fog lifts, the ocean sparkles blue and the summer tourists have mostly gone home. In summer and on autumn weekends, the many fine campgrounds along the coast tend to fill up, so reserving in advance is practically a necessity.

Highlights of this part of the north coast include the picturesque town of Mendocino and its environs, the popular Skunk Train between Fort Bragg and Willits, the many fine state parks, historic Fort Ross built by the Russians and of course the rugged beauty of the coastline itself.

Beaches range from wide swaths of windswept dunes to secluded rocky coves. Tidepools are a special treat at low tide, when you can see starfish, mussels, sea urchins, anemones, hermit crabs and other marine creatures go about their business.

Unlike the coasts of Southern California, here you're more likely to need a warm jacket or windbreaker than a bikini and suntan oil. Rather than sunbathing and swimming, walking on the sand, exploring tidepools, searching for unusual shells and driftwood, gazing at the horizon and watching the sunset are the main attractions. Other activities include surfing, surf fishing, deep-sea fishing, crabbing, river fishing for salmon (in season on the Russian River the end of May to mid-September) and steelhead trout (in season around December to April), and abalone diving (in season April, May, June, August, September, October and November).

Whale watching is a popular attraction from December to April, when the gray whales migrate along the Pacific coast. You can spot the whales from almost any point or headland jutting into the sea, or on whale-watching boat trips from Bodega Bay and Fort Bragg. Harbor seal colonies can be seen at Jenner, by the mouth of the Russian River, and at MacKerricher State Park north of Fort Bragg.

Getting There & Away

MTA (☎ 800-696-4682) and the Mendocino Stage operate several coastal bus routes, and connect the coast with inland points along Hwy 101 including Willits, Ukiah and Santa Rosa. See the Mendocino Getting There & Away section for details on these routes.

In Santa Rosa, Golden Gate Transit buses (☎ 707-541-2000) operate to and from San Francisco and the Bay Area; Sonoma County Transit buses (☎ 707-576-7433, 800-345-7433) connect with other points in Sonoma County, including the Russian River and Sonoma; and Greyhound (☎ 707-545-6495, 800-231-2222) connects with points farther afield.

BODEGA BAY

• population 950 • elevation 45 feet

Bodega Bay is a small fishing town on an attractive bay. Visitors come here to hike or for whale watching at Bodega Head, to enjoy the beaches and tidepools, to fish, surf and enjoy the fresh seafood for which the

LOWER NORTH COAST

Sinkyone Wilderness State Park

Leggett

Standish-Hickey State Recreation Area

Round Valley Indian Reservation

Mendocino National Forest

To Eureka

Covelo

South Fork Eel River

Eel River

Rockport

Westport-Union Landing State Beach

Laytonville

Middle Fork Eel River

Black Butte ▲ 7448ft

Branscomb Rd

Branscomb

Westport

Longvale

Eel River

Lake Pillsbury

MacKerricher State Park

Skunk Train

Noyo River

Willits

Fort Bragg

Jackson State Forest

Jug Handle State Reserve

Caspar

Russian Gulch State Park

Mendocino

Van Damme State Park

Comptche – Ukiah Rd

Comptche

Coast Range

Montgomery Woods State Reserve

E Side Potter Valley Rd

Mendocino National Forest

Little River

Flynn Creek Rd

Albion

Navarro River Redwoods State Park

Off Springs Rd

Low Gap Rd

Lake Mendocino

Greenwood State Beach

Elk

Navarro River

Philo

Ukiah

Upper Lake

Nice

Indian Valley Management Area

Hendy Woods State Park

Boonville

Cow Mountain Recreation Area

Clear Lake

Lakeport

Manchester State Park

Point Arena Lighthouse

Manchester

Mountain View Rd

Hopland

Anderson Valley

Kelseyville

Clearlake

Point Arena

Fish Rock Rd

Mailliard Redwoods State Reserve

Schooner Gulch State Beach

Anchor Bay

Gualala

Lake Sonoma Recreation Area

Cloverdale

Alexander Valley

Russian River

Middletown

PACIFIC OCEAN

Annapolis

Lake Sonoma

Annapolis Rd

Sea Ranch

Dry Creek Rd

Healdsburg

Calistoga

Stewarts Point

Stewarts Point – Skaggs Springs Rd

Westside Rd

Windsor

To Napa Valley

Kruse Rhododendron State Reserve

Seaview Rd

Salt Point State Park

Ft Ross Rd

Cazadero

Fort Ross State Historic Park

Guerneville

River Rd

Forestville

Santa Rosa

To Sonoma

Jenner

Monte Rio

Occidental

Graton Rd

Sebastopol

Rohnert Park

Sonoma Coast State Beaches

Bodega

Bodega Hwy

Cotati

Bodega Bay

Valley Ford

To Olema, Pt Reyes, Muir Beach

Tomales

Dillon Beach

Petaluma

To San Francisco

0   10   20 km
0   5   10 miles

town is known. In summer, even when it's hot inland, Bodega Bay is almost always breezy and fresh.

Long inhabited by Pomo Indians, the bay takes its name from Juan Francisco de la Bodega y Quadra, captain of the Spanish ship *Sonora,* which entered the bay on October 3, 1775. The area was settled by Russians in the early 19th century, and farms were established to grow wheat and other items for the Russian fur-trapping empire that stretched from Alaska all the way down the coast to Fort Ross. The Russians pulled out of the area in 1842, abandoning the fort and their farms; American settlers moved in. In more recent history, the tiny town of Bodega, about 2 miles south of Bodega Bay and then 2 miles inland on the Bodega Hwy, was the setting for Alfred Hitchcock's film *The Birds.*

Orientation & Information

Hwy 1 runs along the east side of Bodega Bay. You can get to the Bodega Head peninsula by turning seaward from Hwy 1 onto E Shore Rd, then turning right at the stop sign onto Bay Flat Rd; going straight at this stop sign brings you to the marina and the Sandpiper Cafe.

The Sonoma Coast Visitor Information Center (☎ 707-875-9435), 850 Hwy 1 opposite the Tides Wharf, is open 9 am to 7 pm or 8 pm daily, depending on the season. The Bodega Bay Area Chamber of Commerce (☎/fax 707-875-3422) provides information for the Bodega Bay area, from Valley Ford north to Fort Ross.

Bodega Bay also has several art galleries; you can obtain information from the chamber of commerce or the visitor center.

Activities

Doran Regional Park (see Camping under Places to Stay) has fine beaches and picnic areas, but there's a $3 day-use fee to go there; see Sonoma Coast State Beaches later in this chapter for information on free beaches.

Year-round **sportfishing** and **whale-watching** trips (December to April), are offered by the New Sea Angler and Jaws,

reached through the Bodega Bay Sport Fishing Center (☎ 707-875-3344), 1500 Bay Flat Rd, beside the Sandpiper Cafe. The Predator (☎ 707-875-3495) and the Dandy (☎ 707-875-2787) are also available for charter. Reserve in advance, as they are quite popular. Wil's Fishing Adventures (☎ 707-875-2323), 1580 Eastshore Rd, offers harbor cruises as well as fishing and whale watching. Bait, tackle and fishing licenses are available at the Boat House (☎ 707-875-3495), 1445 Hwy 1, and the Bodega Bay Sport Fishing Center.

Bodega Bay Pro Dive (☎ 707-875-3054), 1275 Hwy 1, offers **diving** instruction, gear rentals and dive trips. Bodega Bay Surf Shack (☎ 707-875-3944), 1400 Hwy 1, Suite E, rents surfboards, boogie boards, sea kayaks, bicycles and wet suits, and it also offers **surfing** instruction.

Activities on land include **hiking** at Bodega Head, where there are several good trails including a 3½ mile trail to the Bodega Dunes Campground. Candy & Kites (☎ 707-875-3777), 1415 Hwy 1, sells a wide variety of single-line and dual-control sport kites; Bodega Head is usually windy. Chanslor Stables (☎ 707-875-3333), 2660 Hwy 1, about a mile north of Bodega Bay, offers **horseback riding** on the beach, along Salmon Creek and at other scenic spots in the area. The Bodega Harbour Golf Course (☎ 707-875-3538) is an 18-hole Scottish-style **golf** course.

Special Events

The Bodega Bay Fishermen's Festival held in April is the big event of the year, attracting thousands of visitors; activities include the blessing of the fishing fleet, a flamboyant parade of decorated boats and vessels of all kinds, an arts and crafts fair, outdoor food stalls, dances, races, a kite-flying contest and more.

Places to Stay

Camping Campgrounds here are popular and often full in summer and on balmy autumn weekends. *Sonoma County Regional Park* (☎ 707-527-2041) operates *Doran Park* (☎ 707-875-3540) and *Westside Campground*

(☎ 707-875-2640), both right beside the bay, with beaches, hot showers, fishing and boat ramps. Doran Park has four exposed and rather windswept camping areas on the narrow spit of land between the bay and the ocean; to get there, turn seaward from Hwy 1 onto Doran Beach Rd. Westside Campground, on the bay side of Bodega Head, is also quite open and exposed. Campsites are $15 at both places; day-use is $3.

Hotels, Motels & B&Bs The *Bodega Harbor Inn* (☎ 707-875-3594, *1345 Bodega Ave*), half a block from Hwy 1, is the most economical lodging in town, with cottage-style rooms from $53 to $75. The *Bodega Coast Inn* (☎ 707-875-2217, *800-346-6999 within California, 521 Hwy 1*), with a fine view of the bay, has rooms from $109 to $239 (winter $99 to $219). The *Inn at the Tides* (☎ 707-875-2751, *800-541-7788, 800 Hwy 1*) has rooms starting at $132/154 on weekdays/weekends in summer, $149/179 in winter. The attractive 83-room *Bodega Bay Lodge* (☎ 707-875-3525, *800-368-2468, 103 Hwy 1*) has rooms starting at $150.

The *Chanslor Guest Ranch & Horse Stables* (☎ 707-875-2721, *2660 Hwy 1*), about a mile north of Bodega Bay, has horse riding and a variety of B&B rooms starting at $70. *Bay Hill Mansion B&B* (☎ 707-875-3577, *800-526-5927, 3919 Bay Hill Rd*), on the north end of town, is a beautiful Queen Anne Victorian with five rooms ($130 to $225) and a panoramic view overlooking the bay and ocean.

Vacation Rentals Vacation home rentals are an option, but they tend to be expensive, upwards of $100 a night. Try *Vacation Rentals International* (☎ 707-875-4000, *800-548-7631*), *Bodega Bay & Beyond* (☎ 707-875-3942, *800-888-3565*), *Coastal Vistas* (☎ 707-875-3000, *800-788-4782*) or the *Bodega Harbor Inn* (☎ 707-875-3594).

Places to Eat
The *Tides Wharf Restaurant* (☎ 707-875-3652, *835 Hwy 1*) and the nearby *Lucas Wharf Restaurant & Bar* (☎ 707-875-3522, *595 Hwy 1*) are the two largest and best-known restaurants. Specializing in seafood, they sit right on the waterfront, with big picture windows affording a view of the fisherfolk unloading their catch from the docks. At Tides Wharf, lunches are $11 to $16; dinners $13 to $22. At Lucas Wharf, they serve the same menu for lunch and dinner, with prices ranging from $10 to $40 for the lobster.

Smaller, cheaper and more popular with locals, the *Sandpiper Dockside Cafe & Restaurant* (☎ 707-875-2278, *1410 Bay Flat Rd*) is a casual, cheerful place offering fresh seafood and other fare and a fine view of the pier, the marina and the bay. To get there, turn seaward from Hwy 1 onto E Shore Rd and go straight at the stop sign to the marina.

Getting There & Away
MTA (☎ 707-884-3723, *800-696-4682*) operates a bus daily from Point Arena to Santa Rosa and back, via Bodega Bay.

SONOMA COAST STATE BEACHES
The 12-mile stretch of rocky coast heading from Bodega Bay to Jenner contains 14 state beaches, collectively known as the Sonoma Coast State Beaches (☎ 707-875-3483). South to north they are the Bodega Dunes, Salmon Creek, Miwok, Coleman, Arched Rock, Marshall Gulch, Carmet, Schoolhouse, Portuguese, Gleasons, Rock Point, Duncan's Landing, Wright's and Goat Rock state beaches.

Some of these are tiny beaches tucked away in little coves; others are wide expanses of tawny sand. Goat Rock State Beach is at the mouth of the Russian River, across the river from the townof Jenner; north of Jenner are Russian Gulch and Vista Point.

Camping is available at two of the beaches and at two inland sites. One mile north of Bodega Bay, *Bodega Dunes Campground* has campsites among high sand dunes; sites are $16 (hike/bike sites $3 per person), with hot showers available. Six miles north of Bodega Bay, *Wright's Beach* has beachside sites without much privacy. They have bathrooms, but no showers; sites are $20. Reservations are made through Parknet (☎ 800-444-7275) year round.

On Willow Creek Rd, inland from Hwy 1 just south of the Russian River Bridge, the **Willow Creek** and **Pomo Canyon** walk-in environmental campgrounds are first-come, first-served; sites are $10, with parking nearby. Willow Creek has no water; Pomo Canyon has cold water faucets. Both are open April through November, depending on weather.

JENNER
• population 160 • elevation 12 feet

The tiny, picturesque town of Jenner is perched on the hills at the mouth of the Russian River. Stop at the Hwy 1 turnouts just north of the town for a view of the harbor seal colony at the river mouth; pups are born March through August.

The Jenner Visitor Center (☎ 707-865-9433), opposite the gas station, has displays on the Russian River estuary, and the seabirds and marine mammals that frequent it.

Bridgehaven (☎ 707-865-2473) at the south end of the Russian River Bridge has tent/RV sites for $20 ($15 in winter). **River's End** (☎ 707-865-2484, 707-869-3252, 11048 Hwy 1) has a restaurant, hotel rooms and cabins for $125, and campsites without facilities for $10, all with a splendid river view.

Jenner Inn & Cottages (☎ 707-865-2377, 800-732-2377), Hwy 1 in the center of town, is Jenner's most prominent building and landmark, with rooms for $75 to $215 (breakfast included); more expensive vacation rental homes, many on the waterfront; and a restaurant for guests.

Seagull Gifts & Deli (☎ 707-865-2594), Hwy 1, opposite the gas station, offers deli fare, espresso and outdoor tables.

FORT ROSS STATE HISTORIC PARK
Eleven miles north of Jenner on Hwy 1, Fort Ross was the southernmost American outpost of the 19th-century Russian fur trade. In March 1812, a group of 25 Russians and 80 Native Alaskans from the Kodiak, Kenai and Aleutian tribes arrived and began to build the wooden fort at Fort Ross, near the site of Meteni, a Kashaya Pomo Indian village. The fort was established as a base for sea otter hunting operations, for growing wheat and other crops to supply Russian settlements in Alaska and as a base for trade with Spanish Alta California. The Russians dedicated the fort on August 13, 1812, and occupied it until 1842, abandoning it because the sea otter population was decimated and the agricultural production was never as great as hoped.

Fort Ross today is an accurate historical reconstruction of the Russian fort; only one building is original. Most of the original construction was sold, dismantled and carried away to Sutter's Fort in California's Central Valley during the gold rush.

The fort is open 10 am to 4:30 pm daily; $6 per vehicle. The visitor center (☎ 707-847-3286) has good displays on the history of the fort and an excellent library on California history, nature and other topics. On Living History Day, held the last Saturday in July, costumed volunteers bring the fort's history back to life.

Places to Stay
Within the park, about ¾ mile south of the fort, the **Reef Campground** has 21 campsites (cold running water, no showers) nestled into a sheltered seaside gully. The campground is open April to November; sites are $12 and are first-come, first-served.

At Timber Cove, about 2½ miles north of Fort Ross on Hwy 1, there's camping at **Sea Coast Hideaways** (☎ 707-847-3278), on a bluff overlooking the sea and a private, secluded beach in a little cove. Sites are $21/19 with/without hookups; amenities include hot showers, an outdoor hot tub, boat rentals, scuba gear rentals, fishing bait and tackle, and more. They also rent private homes and cabins in the area, starting at $195 for two nights. Also on Hwy 1 at Timber Cove, the luxurious **Timber Cove Inn** (☎ 707-847-3231) has rooms starting at $78 on weekdays, $110 on weekends. The lodge has a restaurant serving all meals.

Two miles north of Timber Cove on Hwy 1, **Stillwater Cove Regional Park**

NORTH COAST

(☎ 707-847-3245) has 22 campsites under Monterey pines; hot showers are available and the sites, all first-come, first-served, are $15 (hike/bike sites $3 per person). About a half mile north, the **Stillwater Cove Ranch** (☎ 707-847-3227, 22555 Hwy 1) has six guest rooms for $40 to $70 on weekdays, $10 more on weekends. A mile farther north, the **Salt Point Lodge** (☎ 707-847-3234, 23255 Hwy 1) has 16 rooms, some with an ocean view and all with accessible hot tub, for $50 to $137.

SALT POINT STATE PARK

Salt Point State Park (☎ 707-847-3221, 707-865-2391) is a 6000-acre coastal park with hiking trails, picnic areas, tidepools, a pygmy forest, the 317-acre Kruse Rhododendron State Reserve, two campgrounds, and an underwater reserve at Gerstle Cove that is one of California's first underwater parks, good for snorkeling and diving. Day-use is $5 per vehicle.

The **Kruse Rhododendron State Reserve** is a short distance inland; to get there, turn east from Hwy 1 onto Kruse Ranch Rd and follow the signs. Growing abundantly in the filtered light of the redwood forest, the rhododendrons reach heights of 30 feet or more, with a magnificent display of pink blossoms in springtime, usually around mid-April to late May.

The two campgrounds, **Woodside** and **Gerstle Cove**, both signposted from Hwy 1, offer campsites under Monterey pines; they have cold running water but no showers. Campsites are $16 (hike/bike sites $3 per person), or $14 for walk-in environmental campsites on the east side of Woodside campground, about half mile from the parking area. The campgrounds are open year round; make reservations through Parknet (☎ 800-444-7275) from March through November.

GUALALA
• population 585 • elevation 60 feet
This tiny coastal town was founded in 1858 as a lumber mill town. The **Gualala Point Regional Park** (☎ 707-785-2377), 1 mile south of town, has an attractive campground with hot showers in a redwood grove beside

the Gualala River, on the east side of Hwy 1; sites are $15 per vehicle (hike/bike sites $3 per person) and are first-come, first-served year round. Hiking trails lead along the river, to the beach and coastal bluffs, and to Whale Watch Point. The **Gualala River Park** (☎ 707-884-3533), another campground in a redwood grove beside the Gualala River, is open in summer; to get there, turn east from Hwy 1 onto Old State Rd on the south end of town and follow the signs. Tent/RV sites cost $22/25.

The historic 1903 **Gualala Hotel** (☎ 707-884-3441), on Hwy 1 at the center of town, has a saloon, a restaurant and 19 comfortable rooms for $48 with shared bath, $60 to $71 with private bath. The **Gualala Country Inn** (☎ 707-884-4343) and the **Surf Motel** (☎ 707-884-3571), both on Hwy 1 in town, have rooms for $79 to $149. The **Whale Watch Inn B&B** (☎ 707-884-3667), overlooking the sea 5 miles north of town, is more expensive, with rooms for $170 to $270.

POINT ARENA
• population 440 • elevation 220 feet
Point Arena is a small fishing town on a windswept point where a lighthouse has stood for over a century. The **Point Arena Lighthouse & Museum** (☎ 707-882-2777) is open 11 am to 2:30 pm daily, with guided tours; $3. The present lighthouse, 115 feet high, is the second to stand on this spot; the original, built in 1870, was toppled by the 1906 earthquake.

At the lighthouse, several former US Coast Guard homes are available as vacation rentals, should you wish to settle in for a week or so. Phone the **Point Arena Lighthouse Keepers** (☎ 707-882-2777) for details. On Hwy 1 in town, the **Sea Shell Inn** (☎ 707-882-2000, 135 Main St) has rooms starting at $50, and the **Point Arena B&B** (☎ 707-882-3455, 300 Main St) has three rooms for $55. A mile west of town at Arena Cove, overlooking Point Arena's small cove and pier, the **Coast Guard House Inn** (☎ 707-882-2442) has six rooms from $115 to $175. The more expensive historic **Wharfmaster's Inn** (☎ 707-882-3171), a restored 1862 Victorian that was originally the wharfmaster's home, has 22 rooms in four buildings starting at $110 on weekdays, $135 on weekends.

Good places to eat on Main St include the popular *Point Arena Cafe* (☎ 707-882-2110) for breakfast and lunch, and *Pangaea* (☎ 707-882-3001) for dinner, with world-class, eclectic California cuisine. At Arena Cove, the *Galley Restaurant & Bar* (☎ 707-882-2189) has a fine view over the cove and pier; *Cosmic Pizza* (☎ 707-882-1900) is downstairs.

MANCHESTER STATE BEACH

Seven miles north of Point Arena, a half mile north of the tiny town of Manchester, a turnoff from Hwy 1 leads to Manchester Beach, a long, wide beach with two camp-grounds. The *Mendocino Coast-Manchester Beach KOA* (☎ 707-882-2375, 800-562-4188), the fancier of the two campgrounds, has attractively landscaped grounds with camp-sites spread among Monterey pines, a heated swimming pool, hot tub spa, cooking pavilion, hot showers, laundry, children's playgrounds, hiking trails and more. The cost is $28 for tents, $32 to $35 for RVs, $41/49 for one-/two-room cabins.

Farther along on the same road, *Manchester State Park* (☎ 707-937-5804) has a campground in the coastal scrub near the beach with cold running water (no showers), plus 10 walk-in environmental campsites hidden in the dunes, a 1.1-mile walk from the parking area; these have creek water, but no treated water. Campsites are $12 year round (hike/bike sites $3 per person), first-come, first-served.

ELK

• population 250 • elevation 140 feet

Elk is a very tiny coastal town; its most notable feature is the **Greenwood State Beach**, with picnic areas but no camping. The state beach has a visitor center (☎ 707-877-3458), usually open on weekends; exhibits use historic photographs and artifacts to tell the area's history.

Several B&Bs take advantage of the quiet beauty of the coast. They include the *Griffin House at Greenwood Cove* (☎ 707-877-3422, 5910 S Hwy 1), with garden/ocean-front cottages starting at $95/165; the *Elk Cove Inn* (☎ 707-877-3321, 6300 S Hwy 1), with rooms and cottages starting around $100; the *Sandpiper House* (☎ 707-877-3587, 800-894-9016, 5520 S Hwy 1), with lodgings starting at $130; and the *Harbor House* (☎ 707-877-3203, 800-720-7474, 5600 S Hwy 1), with rooms starting at $195, breakfast and dinner included.

Elk has several good restaurants: the *Greenwood Pier Cafe* (☎ 707-877-9997), the *Roadhouse* (☎ 707-877-3285) and *Bridget Dolan's Irish Pub & Dinner House* (☎ 707-877-1820). The *Harbor House* (☎ 707-877-3203) and the *Elk Cove Inn* (☎ 707-877-3321) serve meals for guests and nonguests in dining rooms overlooking the ocean.

NAVARRO RIVER REDWOODS STATE PARK

The Navarro River, with Hwy 128 snaking along beside it, meets the sea about 5 miles north of Elk and 10 miles south of Mendocino. The Navarro River Redwoods State Park (☎ 707-937-5804), beginning at the river mouth and extending upriver along Hwy 128 for 12½ miles, has two camp-grounds. The *Navarro Beach Campground*, at the intersection of Hwys 1 and 128, has pit toilets but no water; campsites $5. The *Paul M Dimmick Campground*, off Hwy 128 about 8 miles east of Hwy 1, has flush toilets and water in summer; campsites here are $12. Both campgrounds are open year round, and are first-come, first-served.

HENDY WOODS STATE PARK

Inland about 20 miles along Hwy 128, Hendy Woods State Park (☎ 707-937-5804) offers picnic areas, hiking trails and a *camp-ground* with hot showers. Campsites cost $16; reservations are available through Parknet (☎ 800-444-7275) from mid-May through September. The rest of the year they're first-come, first-served. Day-use of the park is $5 per vehicle.

ALBION

• Population 350 • Elevation 178 feet

The tiny town of Albion, hugging the north side of the Albion River mouth, 5 miles south of Mendocino, was originally a logging village and is now mostly a fishing and tourist town. It has two commercial docks, two campgrounds – *Schooner's Landing Campground* (☎ 707-937-5707) and the *Albion River Campground & Fishing Village* (☎ 707-937-0606) – and several B&Bs. Based at Schooner's Landing Campground, Dive Crazy Adventures (☎ 707-937-3079), offers kayak rentals and tours, fishing and diving charters and whale watching. The Albion River provides 4½ miles of navigable river for kayaking, or you can kayak out into the bay.

The pricey *Albion River Inn* (☎ 707-937-1919, 3790 N Hwy 1), with a beautiful view overlooking Albion Bay, has an excellent seafood restaurant serving dinner every night, and 20 guest rooms for $170 to $260.

VAN DAMME STATE PARK

Three miles south of Mendocino, Van Damme State Park is best known for its unusual **pygmy forest**. A combination of acidic soil and an impenetrable layer of hardpan just below the surface created a natural bonsai forest with decades-old trees growing only a few feet high. A raised wheelchair-accessible boardwalk provides easy access to the pygmy forest. To get there, turn east from Hwy 1 onto Little River Airport Rd, a half mile south of the Van Damme State Park entrance, and go 3½ miles. Or you can hike up from the camping area on the 3½-mile Fern Canyon Scenic Trail, which crosses back and forth over Little River.

Other features of the park include a visitor center (☎ 707-937-4016), with a museum, videos and summer programs. A 30-minute marsh loop trail departs from near the visitor center. Lost Coast Kayaking (☎ 707-937-2434), based in Fort Bragg, offers two-hour sea cave kayak tours.

The park has 74 campsites with hot showers in two areas, one just off Hwy 1 and one in a highland meadow. Campsites ($16) are open year round, with reservations possible through Parknet (☎ 800-444-7275) April to October. There are also 10 walk-in environmental sites ($12), a 1¾-mile hike up Fern Canyon from the parking lot inside the park.

A $5 day-use fee per vehicle is charged to drive into the park, but you can walk in for free if you park in the parking lot on the beach side.

Maps and information are available at the park's entrance kiosk (☎ 707-937-0851), at the visitor center (☎ 707-937-4016) or at the Mendocino State Parks Headquarters (see Information under Mendocino later in this chapter).

MONTGOMERY WOODS STATE RESERVE

This new reserve (☎ 707-937-5804) contains 1300 acres of old-growth redwoods in five groves. A 2-mile loop trail traverses all five groves, going up one side of Montgomery Creek and back down the other. Picnic tables and pit toilets are at the beginning of the trail, near the parking area. This is a day-use park; no camping. The park is about 5 miles east of Comptche on the Comptche-Ukiah Rd, which intersects Hwy 1 about a quarter mile south of Mendocino.

MENDOCINO

• population 1100 • elevation 90 feet

The picturesque little town of Mendocino, perched on a bluff overlooking the Pacific Coast, is noted for its Cape Cod architecture and its active artistic community. Built as a lumber mill town in the 1850s by transplanted New Englanders, Mendocino thrived in the late 19th century, with ships transporting the redwood timber from Mendocino Bay to San Francisco. Activity declined after the mills shut down in the 1930s, until the town was rediscovered by artists in the 1950s and became a bohemian haven. Tourists have been following the artists to Mendocino ever since. The entire town, with its historic buildings lovingly restored, is on the National Register of Historic Places.

Attractions for visitors include art galleries and shops, charming Victorian B&Bs and other quality places to stay and eat, a couple historic house museums and the natural beauty of the coast. Mendocino is a very popular tourist destination in summer, when it gets overrun; the rest of the year the ambience is more relaxed.

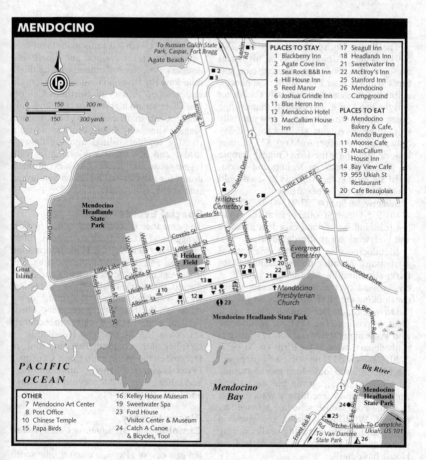

MENDOCINO

PLACES TO STAY
1 Blackberry Inn
2 Agate Cove Inn
3 Sea Rock B&B Inn
4 Hill House Inn
5 Reed Manor
6 Joshua Grindle Inn
11 Blue Heron Inn
12 Mendocino Hotel
13 MacCallum House Inn
17 Seagull Inn
18 Headlands Inn
21 Sweetwater Inn
22 McElroy's Inn
25 Stanford Inn
26 Mendocino Campground

PLACES TO EAT
9 Mendocino Bakery & Cafe, Mendo Burgers
11 Moosse Cafe
13 MacCallum House Inn
14 Bay View Cafe
19 955 Ukiah St Restaurant
20 Cafe Beaujolais

OTHER
7 Mendocino Art Center
8 Post Office
10 Chinese Temple
15 Papa Birds
16 Kelley House Museum
19 Sweetwater Spa
23 Ford House Visitor Center & Museum
24 Catch A Canoe & Bicycles, Too!

Information

The Ford House Visitor Center & Museum (☎ 707-937-5397), 735 Main St, has maps, books and information about the town and the nearby state parks, plus exhibits on natural and cultural history. Hot cider and interesting videos are always available – it's a good place to relax and unwind. It's open 11 am to 4 pm daily. A $1 donation is requested to tour the museum.

The Mendocino State Parks Headquarters (☎ 707-937-5804), on the east side of Hwy 1, at Russian Gulch State Park, 2 miles north of Mendocino, has information on all the state parks in the area. It's open 8 am to 4:30 pm weekdays.

Things to See & Do

The **Mendocino Art Center** (☎ 707-937-5818, 800-653-3328), 45200 Little Lake St, is the artistic heart of Mendocino, with two art galleries, live theater productions, arts and crafts fairs and a nationally recognized program of over 200 art classes; write or phone to request a schedule of classes (PO Box 765, Mendocino, CA 95460). Mendocino also has many other art galleries; the visitor center has a complete list.

The **Kelley House Museum** (☎ 707-937-5791), 45007 Albion St, is a historical museum in an 1861 home. The museum features artifacts, over 15,000 historical photos, a library for research about early California and the local area, and exhibits that change every two months. It's open 1 to 4 pm daily from June to August (Friday to Monday only from September to May); $2. Another historic building is the 1852 **Chinese Temple** on Albion St between Kasten and Woodward Sts; look in the windows to see the old Chinese altar and other artifacts.

Sweetwater Spa (☎ 707-937-4140, 800-300-4140), 955 Ukiah St, offers private or group hot tubs and saunas and excellent massage and bodywork, all at affordable prices.

Mendocino also has some fine natural attractions. **Mendocino Headlands State Park**, surrounding Mendocino village, is crisscrossed by trails, with pleasant walks overlooking the bluffs and rocky coves.

On weekends, free guided walks are a pleasant pastime. The 1½ hour **Mendocino Bird Walk** along the Mendocino Headlands trails departs from Papa Birds (☎ 707-937-2730, 800-845-0522) on Albion St (opposite the MacCallum House Inn) most Saturday mornings at 10 am; bring binoculars and warm clothing. A free **history walk** departs from the Ford House; schedule arranged by request. **Wildflower walks** are given in spring and **whale-watching walks** during whale season, December to March; the Ford House has details.

At **Big River**, a quarter mile south of Mendocino on Hwy 1, Catch A Canoe & Bicycles, Too! (☎ 707-937-0273, 800-320-2453), just inland from Hwy 1 on the Comptche-Ukiah Rd, rents mountain bikes, canoes, outrigger canoes, and single and double kayaks for self-guided trips up the 8-mile-long Big River tidal estuary, the longest undeveloped estuary in Northern California. There are no highways or buildings, only beaches, salt marshes, stream beds, historic logging sites – including century-old train trestles, wooden pilings and log dams – forest and abundant wildlife. A private logging road up the river provides unofficial access for bicycles and hikers on Sundays in summer, daily in winter.

Special Events
The chamber of commerce office in Fort Bragg (see Fort Bragg Orientation & Information later in this chapter) has information on these and other events in the area. The first weekend in March there's the Mendocino Whale Festival, with wine tasting, whale-watching walks and strolling musicians; in July, there's the Mendocino Music Festival, a one- to two-week summer concert series on the Mendocino Headlands; in October, an Abalone Festival; and in December, the Mendocino Coast Christmas Festival, with tree lighting, music, inn tours and other events in Mendocino, Fort Bragg and Little River.

Places to Stay
Camping The *Mendocino Campground* (☎ 707-937-3130), on the Comptche-Ukiah Rd just east of Hwy 1, a quarter mile south of Mendocino, is an attractive campground with hot showers, plenty of trees, a nature

---

Mendocino, Star of the Silver Screen

Though Mendocino is only a tiny town, over 50 films for TV and the silver screen have been shot here, starting with *The Promise*, a 1916 silent film. Some of the better-known motion pictures filmed here include *East of Eden* (1954), starring James Dean; *The Island of the Blue Dolphins* (1964), filmed on the south Mendocino coast; *The Summer of '42* (1970); *Same Time, Next Year* (1978); and the well-known *Murder, She Wrote* TV series (1984-88), starring Angela Lansbury.

trail and campsites for $17/19 on weekdays/ weekends. About 5 miles north of Mendocino, the **Caspar Beach Campground** (☎ 707-964-3306, *14441 Cabrillo Drive*), in a sheltered gully beside Caspar Beach, has tent/RV sites for $18/25. There's plenty more camping in nearby state parks; see their separate sections.

Hotels & B&Bs Accommodations in Mendocino, most in restored Victorian homes, all have charm, character, comfort, high style and high price tags. If you want something cheaper, try the less expensive motels in Fort Bragg, 10 miles to the north.

Mendocino Coast Reservations (☎ 707-937-5033, 800-262-7801, *1000 Main St*) makes reservations and provides information for over 70 vacation homes and 30 B&Bs in the area.

The 1878 *Mendocino Hotel* (☎ 707-937-0511, 800-548-0513, *45080 Main St*), overlooking the sea, has an elegant Victorian dining room, a more casual garden bar and cafe and rooms from $85 to $275. The 1882 *MacCallum House Inn* (☎ 707-937-0289, 800-609-0492, *45020 Albion St*) also has a fine restaurant, and rooms from $100 to $190.

Other places right in town include the *Seagull Inn* (☎ 707-937-5204, 888-937-5204, *44594 Albion St*), with rooms from $45 to $145; the *Headlands Inn* (☎ 707-937-4431), at the corner of Albion and Howard Sts, with rooms from $100 to $195; and the *Blue Heron Inn* (☎ 707-937-4323, *390 Kasten St*), at the corner of Albion St, with a good restaurant and three rooms from $80 to $95. *McElroy's Inn* (☎ 707-937-1734, *998 Main St*) has four rooms from $80 to $110.

Sweetwater Inn & Spa (☎ 707-937-4076, 800-300-4140, *44840 Main St*) offers a variety of accommodations in Mendocino and Little River – cottages with private hot tubs and ocean views, fanciful water-tower units, pet units and more. Prices ($55 to $225) include free use of the spa (see Things to See & Do).

On Little Lake Rd, you'll find the *Joshua Grindle Inn* (☎ 707-937-4143, *44800 Little Lake Rd*), with rooms for $100 to $175, and the most expensive place in town, *Reed Manor* (☎ 707-937-5446), which faces Little Lake Rd but has its entrance through the block on Palette Drive, with rooms starting at $175. Nearby, at the corner of Lansing St, the *Hill House Inn* (☎ 707-937-0554, *10701 Palette Drive*) has rooms from $130 to $225.

Farther out on Lansing St, overlooking the ocean, are the *Agate Cove Inn* (☎ 707-937-0551, 800-527-3111, *11201 Lansing St*), with ocean-view cottages from $109 to $250, and the *Sea Rock B&B Inn* (☎ 707-937-5517, *11101 Lansing St*), with ocean-view cottages and deluxe units for $85 to $250. The *Blackberry Inn* (☎ 707-937-5281, 800-950-7806, *44951 Larkin Rd*), north of town, has various accommodations running from $95 to $145.

Three miles south of Mendocino, **Little River** also has places to stay and eat, including the *Inn at Schoolhouse Creek* (☎ 707-937-5525, 800-731-5525, *7051 N Hwy 1*), with 13 cottages, and the 24-unit *SS Seafoam Lodge* (☎ 707-937-1827, 800-606-1827, *6751 N Hwy 1*); both have hot tubs.

Places to Eat

For a fine view of the bay, you can't beat the aptly named *Bay View Cafe* (☎ 707-937-4197, *45040 Main St*) opposite the Ford House, with an upstairs dining room and outdoor deck. Breakfast, lunch and dinner are served; it's especially known for its good breakfasts.

The *Mendocino Bakery & Cafe* (☎ 707-937-0836, *10483 Lansing St*) is great for casual, inexpensive dining and just hanging out. In addition to their baked goods, they have a variety of soups, salads, hot meals, pizzas, plus a pleasant outdoor patio alongside the indoor cafe. In the rear, *Mendo Burgers* (☎ 707-937-1111) serves up popular beef, turkey and veggie burgers.

Moving up the economic spectrum, *Cafe Beaujolais* (☎ 707-937-5614, *961 Ukiah St*), open for dinner nightly, is probably Mendocino's most famous restaurant; reservations are definitely a good idea. Next door is the *955 Ukiah St Restaurant* (☎ 707-937-1955).

You can dine on European cuisine in Victorian elegance at the fancy dining room of the *Mendocino Hotel* (☎ 707-937-0511,

45080 Main St); breakfast and lunch are served daily in the hotel's *Garden Bar & Cafe*. Another fine old Victorian inn, the *MacCallum House Inn* (☎ 707-937-5763, *45020 Albion St*) also has an elegant restaurant, open for dinner nightly (closed January to mid-February). Or there's the smaller *Moosse Cafe* (☎ 707-937-4323), at the Blue Heron Inn at the corner of Kasten and Albion Sts, open for lunch, dinner and Sunday brunch.

Entertainment

The Mendocino Art Center and the many galleries around town always have something going on. *Mendocino Theatre Company* (☎ 707-937-4477) performances are presented at the Mendocino Art Center's *Helen Schoeni Theatre*.

Getting There & Away

The Mendocino Stage (☎ 707-964-0167) operates several bus routes. One route runs buses every day from Fort Bragg to Willits, Ukiah, Santa Rosa and back. Weekday buses include the Fort Bragg-Mendocino-Navarro and return route, and another route connecting Fort Bragg and Mendocino.

MTA (☎ 800-696-4682) operates eight bus routes. One bus travels the Mendocino-Fort Bragg-Willits-Ukiah-Santa Rosa route every morning and returns in the afternoon. Another route goes daily from Point Arena to Santa Rosa and back, via Jenner, the Russian River and Sebastopol. In Santa Rosa, you can connect with Golden Gate Transit (☎ 707-541-2000), Sonoma County Transit (☎ 707-576-7433, 800-345-7433) and Greyhound (☎ 707-545-6495, 800-231-2222). Another weekday route starts in Gualala, heads north, turns inland on Hwy 128 at Navarro, goes through the Anderson Valley to Ukiah, and returns in the afternoon; in Navarro, it connects with Mendocino Stage's Fort Bragg-Mendocino-Navarro bus.

OLD MILL FARM

The Old Mill Farm School of Country Living (☎ 707-937-0244), on a rolling ridgetop adjacent to Big River, 7 miles inland from Mendocino, is a living early-20th-century self-sustaining organic farm with rustic cabins. The site allows visitors to experience the work and the wonders of small farm life. The land has hiking trails, a swimming hole, forests and other natural beauties, plus organic gardens, a goat dairy, barns, etc. Accommodations include a hiker's hut ($50 to $60 for two nights, $160 per week), a family cabin ($90 for two nights, $270 per week), a group camp ($50 to $75 per night) and sweat lodge with tent camping and group events available; they also will barter for arts and crafts or for work exchange.

JUG HANDLE CREEK FARM

Five miles north of Mendocino, the Jug Handle Creek Farm (☎ 707-964-4630, jughandl@mcn.org) offers accommodations in a 120-year-old farmhouse up on a hill on the east side of Hwy 1. The farmhouse has a nature center and library, a fully equipped kitchen where you can cook and seven bedrooms for $18 per person from April to September, $15 the rest of the year, $20 on holidays. There are also three cabins at $25 per person, with use of the house facilities. Guests are expected to do one hour of chores per day. Bring your own sleeping bag or bedding; towels are provided. This is a popular place, especially with university students (who get a discounted rate of $12/10 per person in summer/winter), so it's a good idea to reserve in advance, especially for weekends.

RUSSIAN GULCH STATE PARK

Two miles north of Mendocino on Hwy 1, Russian Gulch State Park has scenic trails, a small waterfall, rocky headlands, a small sandy beach, many trees and rhododendrons, picnic areas and attractive campsites with hot showers and plenty of vegetation. Camping is available only from April through October, with reservations through Parknet (☎ 800-444-7275); the 30 campsites are $16 (hike/bike sites $3 per person). Day-use parking is $5.

The Mendocino State Parks Headquarters (☎ 707-937-5804) is on the east side of Hwy 1, opposite the campground entrance.

JUG HANDLE STATE RESERVE

Midway between Mendocino and Fort Bragg, the Jug Handle State Reserve has an 'ecological staircase' – five wave-cut terraces ascending in steps from the seashore, each about 100 feet and 100,000 years removed from the one before it. Each terrace has its own distinct geology and vegetation; on one level is a pygmy forest similar to the better-known one at Van Damme State Park. A pamphlet for a 5-mile self-guided **ecological staircase nature trail** is available at the parking area just off Hwy 1, or from the Mendocino State Parks Headquarters at Russian Gulch State Park. Other features of the reserve include a half-mile Headlands loop trail and a sandy beach in a lovely little cove just north of the parking lot.

JACKSON DEMONSTRATION STATE FOREST

Heading east over the mountains for 34 miles from Fort Bragg to Willits, Hwy 20 passes through the 816-sq-mile Jackson Demonstration State Forest. Demonstration trails, with signs to explain the ecology, history and management of the redwood forest, include the Forest History Trail, the Tree ID Trail and the Chamberlain Creek Demonstration Trail.

The forest contains two main camping areas, *Camp One* and *Camp 20*, each with a number of separate campgrounds, some open seasonally, some year round. The campgrounds are primitive – bring your own water. Camping is free, but you need a free campfire permit, available from the resident camp hosts, or at the Department of Forestry office (☎ 707-964-5674), 802 N Main St, Fort Bragg. This office also has maps, permits and information about the forest. It's open 8 am to noon and 1 to 5 pm weekdays.

FORT BRAGG

● **population 6100** ● **elevation 80 feet**

Fort Bragg is about 10 miles north of Mendocino on Hwy 1. Less conspicuously touristy than Mendocino, Fort Bragg has less-expensive food and lodging, making it a good alternative base for visiting the area.

The town takes its name from the fort established here in 1857, named for Colonel Braxton Bragg, a veteran of the Mexican War. The fort was abandoned in 1867; in 1885, a lumber company was established on the old fort site, and in the same year, the California Western Railroad, later nicknamed the Skunk Train, was established to get the big redwood trees out of the forest and down to the coast. Today, the Skunk Train is a popular tourist attraction.

Orientation

Fort Bragg is basically a 'Main Street' town, Main St being Hwy 1. Most everything you need is on or just off the main drag. Several antique stores, boutiques, a movie theater, the post office and a few restaurants are on Franklin St, which runs parallel to Main St, one block to the east. Fort Bragg's commercial district, with its boat docks and several good restaurants, lies in the 2 miles between Pudding Creek on the north end of town and the Noyo River and Noyo Harbor at the south end.

Information

The Fort Bragg-Mendocino Coast Chamber of Commerce (☎ 707-961-6300, 800-726-2780, chamber@mcn.org; www.mendocinocoast .com), 332 N Main St, has abundant information about Fort Bragg, Mendocino and the surrounding area. It's open 9 am to 5 pm weekdays, 9 am to 3 pm Saturday.

Things to See & Do

Fort Bragg's pride and joy is the **Skunk Train** (☎ 707-964-6371, 800-777-5865), with a variety of historic engines and cars making daily runs between Fort Bragg and Willits, about 40 miles over beautiful redwood-forested mountains. The train got its nickname in 1925 when passenger service was established using stinky gas-powered steam engines. Today, the historic steam and diesel locomotives have no odor, and the ride is a delightful trip through the mountains, the redwood forest and along Pudding Creek and the Noyo River, crossing 30 bridges and passing through two deep mountain tunnels.

NORTH COAST

The Skunk Train operates daily except Thanksgiving, Christmas and New Year's Day. Departures are from both ends of the line; you can take the train one way or roundtrip in either direction or go just to Northspur, the halfway point. Phone to check the schedule. Tickets cost $35 for a full-day roundtrip, $25 for half-day round-trips to Northspur, or one-way trips between Fort Bragg and Willits (children half price). The depot in Fort Bragg is at the foot of Laurel St, one block west of Main St, in the center of town. In Willits, the depot is on E Commercial St, three blocks east of Hwy 101.

The **Guest House Museum** (☎ 707-961-2823), 343 N Main St, built in 1892, holds historical photos and relics of Fort Bragg's logging history. It's open 10:30 am to 2:30 pm Tuesday to Sunday (Friday to Sunday in winter); $2.

The **Mendocino Coast Botanical Gardens** (☎ 707-964-4352), 18220 N Hwy 1, 2 miles south of town, cover 47 acres from the highway out to the coastal bluffs; the admission price of $6 includes a trail map. The gardens are open 9 am to 5 pm daily March to October, 9 am to 4 pm November to February.

On the north end of town, **Glass Beach** is named for the sea-polished glass found there; it's reached by a short trail leading towards the sea from Elm St, off Main St. Other coastal trails lead around both sides of **Noyo Harbor** at the south end of town.

Activities

A number of small boats at Noyo Harbor offer deep-sea fishing, coastal cruises and whale-watching cruises December through April (they say you see the most whales from late January to March). Signs for many of the boats are posted around Noyo Harbor and at the chamber of commerce; they include Anchor Charters (☎ 707-964-4550), the *Misty II* (☎ 707-964-7161), the *Noyo Belle* (☎ 707-964-3104), the *Patty C* (☎ 707-964-0669), the *Tally Ho II* (☎ 707-964-2079) and the *Telstar* (☎ 707-964-8770).

Sub-Surface Progression (☎ 707-964-3793), 18600 N Hwy 1, a mile south of town, offers

snorkeling and scuba diving tours, guided kayak trips, abalone diving tours, deep-sea fishing and whale watching, and all necessary gear. Abalone season is from April 1 to June 30 and from August 1 to November 30.

Ricochet Ridge Ranch (☎ 707-964-7669), 24201 N Hwy 1, opposite MacKerricher State Park just north of town, offers horse rides on the beach and into the redwoods.

Special Events

The chamber of commerce has information on events in Fort Bragg, Mendocino and the surrounding region. Events include the Fort Bragg Whale Festival on the third weekend in March, featuring microbrewed beer tasting, a crafts fair, a 10K Whale Run and whale-watching trips; the Rhododendron Show the last weekend in April; the World's Largest Salmon BBQ at Noyo Harbor on the Saturday closest to the 4th of July; Paul Bunyan Days on Labor Day weekend, celebrating California's logging history with a fiddlers' contest, parade and children's games; and various Christmas celebrations including a Lighted Truck Parade, tree lighting, music and more.

Places to Stay

Camping *Woodside RV Park & Campgrounds* (☎ 707-964-3684, 800-207-8772, 17900 N Hwy 1), about a mile south of town, has plenty of trees; tent/RV sites are $16/21. Across the road, the *Pomo RV Park & Campground* (☎ 707-964-3373, 17999 Tregoning Lane) has tent/RV sites for $18/24.

Motels Starting from the south end of town, the *Coast Motel* (☎ 707-964-2852, 18661 Hwy 1), about a quarter mile south of Hwy 20, has 28 rooms, some with kitchen, starting at $36. *Surf Motel* (☎ 707-964-5361, 1220 S Main St) has 54 rooms starting at $62/45 in summer/winter. The *Tradewinds Lodge* (☎ 707-964-4761, 800-524-2244, 400 S Main St) is one of the largest motels in town, with 92 rooms starting at $65/45 in summer/winter. The *Ebb Tide Lodge* (☎ 707-964-5321, 800-974-6730, 250 S Main St) is an attractive motel with 31 rooms starting at $49/40 in summer/winter. The *Fort Bragg*

Motel (☎ 707-964-4787, 800-253-9972, 763 N Main St) has a variety of rooms for $40 and up.

Colombi Motel (☎ 707-964-5773, 647 Oak St), is said to be the 'cheapest and cleanest motel in town.' Operated by a friendly family, it's five blocks east of Hwy 1, in a quiet residential area. Rooms are $40 (weekends $45), with family rooms and kitchenettes available. A laundry facility is next door; check in at the grocery store across the street.

The *Beach House Inn* (☎ 707-961-1700, 100 Pudding Creek Rd) is on the north bank of Pudding Creek, opposite the beach, on the north end of town. New in 1998, it's a lovely motel with 30 large, well-appointed rooms, some with fireplace, hot tub, private ocean-view balcony and other amenities, for $59 to $150.

B&Bs Fort Bragg has several good B&Bs. As in Mendocino, most are in large, beautifully restored historic homes. The *Rendezvous Inn* (☎ 707-964-8142, 800-491-8142, 647 N Main St) has rooms for $75 to $110 (less in winter) and a fine restaurant. The *Country Inn B&B* (☎ 707-964-3737, 632 N Main St) has rooms for $89 to $139. The *Grey Whale Inn* (☎ 707-964-0640, 800-382-7244, 615 N Main St) has rooms for $88 to $165.

The superb *Weller House Inn* (☎ 707-964-4415, 877-893-5537, 524 Stewart St) has rooms for $100 to $175 on weekends, $20 less on weekdays, third day free. It is Fort Bragg's most luxurious B&B. Their water tower, the highest vantage point in Fort Bragg, has a hot tub at the top.

On a bluff overlooking the Noyo River at the south end of town, the *Lodge at Noyo River* (☎ 707-964-8045, 800-628-1126, 500 Casa del Noyo Rd) has rooms with rates running from $105 to $149.

Places to Eat

For breakfast you can't beat *Eggheads* (☎ 707-964-5005, 326 N Main St) a popular little restaurant serving over 50 kinds of omelets and other breakfast specialties, ½lb burgers and other treats at lunch. A few doors up, the *Fort Bragg Grille* (☎ 707-964-

3663, 356 N Main St) is also popular for breakfast and lunch. For hearty food, there's the *Home Style Cafe* (☎ 707-964-6106, 790 S Main St).

For fine dining, try the *Rendezvous Inn* (☎ 707-964-8142, 800-491-8142, 647 N Main St), serving dinner Wednesday to Sunday; reservations recommended. The *North Coast Brewing Company Taproom & Grill* (☎ 707-964-2739, 455 N Main St) is a popular restaurant and pub.

Don't miss the *Headlands Coffeehouse* (☎ 707-964-1987, 120 E Laurel St). A half block east of Main St, it's a great place to enjoy many varieties of coffee, light meals and baked goods. Next door, *Cafe Prima* (☎ 707-962-0753, 124 E Laurel St) has an African chef and serves delicious ethnic-inspired dishes; Swahili cuisine is their specialty. *Viraporn's Thai Cafe* (☎ 707-964-7931), on Chestnut St half a block east of Main St, is a casual, inexpensive little Thai restaurant open for lunch weekdays, dinner nightly. Nearby, *D'Aurelio & Sons* (☎ 707-964-4227, 438 S Franklin St) is popular for pizza and pasta, with an inexpensive menu and casual family atmosphere; it's open evenings only.

Noyo Harbor has several good seafood restaurants. Probably the most attractive is the *Wharf Restaurant & Lounge* (☎ 707-964-4283) with a beautiful view of the harbor. Nearby, *Cap'n Flint's* (☎ 707-964-9447) is a more casual restaurant with that same great harbor view. Also at the harbor, *El Mexicano* (☎ 707-964-7164) is an inexpensive family restaurant serving home-style Mexican food.

Entertainment

Live acoustic music or poetry readings take place every evening at the *Headlands Coffeehouse* (☎ 707-964-1987, 120 E Laurel St). The *North Coast Brewing Company* (☎ 707-964-2739, 455 N Main St) has a lively pub scene.

The *Fort Bragg Footlighters Little Theater* (☎ 707-964-3806), at the corner of Laurel and McPherson Sts, features 1890s-style musicals, comedy and melodrama at 8 pm on Wednesday and Saturday in summer. The Gloriana Opera Company performs operettas and musicals year round at the *Gloriana Theatre* (☎ 707-964-7469, 721 N Franklin St). Concerts, dance and other performing arts are also shown here. *Opera Fresca* (☎ 707-937-0420), a local opera company, performs at various venues. In Caspar, about 5 miles south of Fort Bragg, the *Caspar Inn* (☎ 707-964-5565) features rock, R&B, world beat and other music Thursday, Friday and Saturday nights; Wednesday is open-mike night.

Getting There & Around
See the Mendocino section for bus information. The Tradewinds Lodge (☎ 707-964-4761, 800-524-2244), 400 S Main St, rents bicycles by the hour, day or week.

MacKERRICHER STATE PARK
On the coast about 3 miles north of Fort Bragg, MacKerricher State Park (☎ 707-937-5804) covers 8 miles of rugged coastline from Pudding Creek in the south to Ten Mile River in the north, with beaches, sand dunes, coastal bluffs, tidepools and an 8-mile coastal hiking trail. Other attractions include Lake Cleone, a freshwater lake good for fishing, nonmotorized boating and hiking, and Laguna Point, a good spot for watching harbor seals year round and whales in season. Horseback rides on the beach and into the redwoods are offered by the Ricochet Ridge Ranch (☎ 707-964-7669), on Hwy 1, opposite the park.

The park's attractive campgrounds offer hot showers and 142 drive-in sites nestled in the trees, plus 10 more attractive and secluded walk-in sites just 50 yards from the parking area. The walk-in sites are first-come, first-served year round; other sites can be reserved through Parknet (☎ 800-444-7275) from April through mid-October. It's wise to reserve in advance, as this is a very popular park. Campsites are $16 year round (hike/bike sites $3 per person). There's no day-use fee to visit the park.

WESTPORT
• population 100 • elevation 120 feet
Clinging to a coastal bluff 14 miles north of Fort Bragg on Hwy 1, Westport is only a tiny village today. In the late 1800s and early 1900s it was a much more important place – a shipping port with a population of 3000 and the longest logging chute in California.

There's camping a couple of miles north of town at the *Westport-Union Landing State Beach* (☎ 707-937-5804), with primitive sites on a treeless coastal bluff for $12 (hike/bike sites $3 per person). Half a mile north of town, the *Wages Creek Beach Camp* (☎ 707-964-2964, 37700 N Hwy 1) has hot showers and campsites near the beach for $17.

Other accommodations in Westport include the *Pelican Lodge & Inn* (☎ 707-964-5588) with a restaurant, the *Westport Inn* (☎ 707-964-5135), the *Seagate Guest House* (☎ 707-964-5595), the *De Haven Valley Farm* (☎ 707-961-1660) and the *Howard Creek Ranch* (☎ 707-964-6725).

Upper North Coast

Hwy 1 (the Pacific Coast Hwy) and Hwy 101 (the Redwood Hwy) join at Leggett, a small settlement 45 miles north of Fort Bragg. From Leggett, Hwy 101 heads north by an inland route for about 80 miles until it meets the sea at Eureka on Humboldt Bay, California's largest bay north of San Francisco. Along the way it passes through some awe-inspiring groves of ancient redwoods in several state parks, notably the Humboldt Redwoods State Park, with its famous Avenue of the Giants. Even if you're only driving north or south on Hwy 101 on your way to somewhere else, it's definitely worth getting off the highway and driving on the beautiful Avenue of the Giants instead.

Eureka, a fishing and former lumbering town on Humboldt Bay, is the largest town on California's far north coast; it's known for its many fine old Victorian buildings and its delicious fresh seafood. A little farther north, Arcata is a pleasant university town with a youthful ambience reminiscent of the 1960s. The Humboldt and Arcata bays are good for bird watching, with several wildlife refuges.

North of Arcata, the highway hugs the coast most of the way to the Oregon border, about another 100 miles, passing magnificent scenery for its entire distance; the spectacular virgin groves of giant redwood trees in the Redwood National & State Parks are unforgettable.

Highways crossing the Coast Range, connecting the coast with the interior, are slow, winding and scenic, mostly snaking through the mountains in river canyons.

Hwy 36, between Fortuna and Red Bluff, is extremely winding and a particular ordeal to traverse. Hwy 299 between Arcata and Redding, dubbed the Trinity Scenic Byway, is also a long haul, with about 3½ hours of mountainous curves, but it's a beautiful drive and the primary connection between the coast and the interior. From Hwy 299, scenic Hwy 96 branches northwards and goes up the Trinity and Klamath river valleys, through Happy Camp, to join I-5 just north of Yreka, just south of the Oregon border.

Heading northwards from Crescent City into Oregon, you can keep on hugging the coast on Hwy 101, which continues as the coast highway in Oregon, or you can head inland on Hwy 199, called the Smith River National Scenic Byway, through the Smith River National Recreation Area.

LEGGETT
• population 200 • elevation 952 feet
If you're traveling north, Leggett is where you'll catch your first glimpse of the ancient redwood forests. Beside the South Fork of the Eel River, Leggett is a very small settlement; you can easily drive right through it and never know you've been there. But it does have some fine places to stay and to linger, if you're so inclined.

The **Chandelier Drive-Thru Tree Park** (☎ 707-925-6363), on Drive-Thru Tree Rd (Hwy 271), has 200 acres of virgin redwood forest with picnic areas, nature walks and the Chandelier Tree, which has a square hole allowing cars to drive through. The park is open 8 am to dusk daily; $3 per vehicle.

The 1012-acre **Standish-Hickey State Recreation Area** (☎ 707-925-6482), on Hwy 101, has virgin and second-growth redwoods, swimming holes and fishing in the

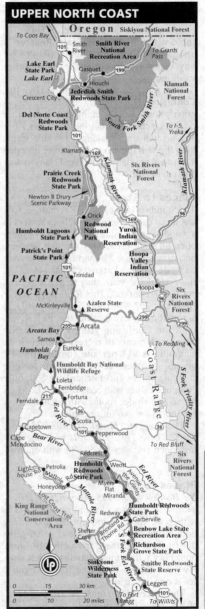

UPPER NORTH COAST

NORTH COAST

Eel River, picnic areas, camping and hiking trails ranging from easy to strenuous. A couple of miles farther north on Hwy 101, the **Smithe Redwoods State Reserve** is another redwood grove, but it doesn't have any camping, developed trails or other facilities.

Nine miles north of Leggett on Hwy 101, **Confusion Hill** (☎ 707-925-6456) has a gravity house, water running uphill and other oddities, a children's petting zoo, a snack bar and a small train making a 1¼ mile scenic loop through the forest. In summer it's open 9 am to 7 pm daily, in winter 11 am to 4 or 5 pm daily; $3.

Places to Stay

The Standish-Hickey State Recreation Area has three *campgrounds* with hot showers in a wooded area beside the river, two of them open all year. From May through September, campsites are $16 and reservations can be made through Parknet (☎ 800-444-7275); the rest of the year, they're $12 and first-come, first-served. The *Redwoods River Resort* (☎ 707-925-6249, 75000 Hwy 101), in a redwood grove beside the Eel River, opposite Confusion Hill, is a fun family place, with plenty of recreational activities. Camping is $17 per site (more with RV hookups); other accommodations include camping cabins (no kitchen) for $30, fully equipped cabins with beds, linen and kitchen for $60, and lodge rooms with kitchen access for $60/76 for two/four people.

The *Leggett Motel* (☎ 707-925-6266, 67672 Drive-Thru Tree Rd) has nine old-fashioned cottages for $35/40 with one/two beds.

Places to Eat

Ne-Bob's (☎ 707-925-1066, 62674 Drive-Thru Tree Rd), is a pleasant restaurant-cafe with good food at good prices and tables both inside and on the lattice-covered patio out front. To get there from Hwy 101, turn onto Hwy 1, then immediately turn left onto Hwy 271 (Drive-Thru Tree Rd), and you'll see it on your right.

The *Price's Peg House* (☎ 707-925-6444, 69501 Hwy 101), opposite the Standish-

Hickey State Recreation Area, is a deli and country store with tables inside and outside.

Getting There & Away

Greyhound buses going north and south on Hwy 101 stop at the Price's Peg House. Buses also stop at the Bell Glen Resort by request.

RICHARDSON GROVE STATE PARK

Richardson Grove State Park (☎ 707-247-3318) is a popular 1500-acre park in a lovely virgin redwood grove where many of the trees are more than 1000 years old and more than 300 feet tall. The South Fork of the Eel River runs through the park, and there are ranger-led campfire programs and interpretive nature walks in summer.

The park has three campgrounds, one open year round, with hot showers. Camping reservations can be made through Parknet (☎ 800-444-7275) from May through September when campsites are $16; the rest of the year, sites are $12 and first-come, first-served. Also in the park, the Richardson Grove Lodge (☎ 707-247-3415) operates a gift shop, grocery store and three rustic one-bedroom cabins for $60, each with kitchenette, private bath, barbecue, picnic tables and propane heating; cabins are available April through November.

BENBOW LAKE

The 1200-acre **Benbow Lake State Recreation Area** (☎ 707-247-3318) is on the banks of the South Fork of the Eel River, where a summer dam forms the 26-acre Benbow Lake every year from mid-June to Labor Day in early September. The lake is right on Hwy 101, 2 miles south of Garberville; take the Benbow exit.

Various special events are held at Benow Lake throughout the year, especially at Thanksgiving and all through December until New Year's Day. Summer events on Benbow Lake include Jazz on the Lake, the Summer Arts Fair and Shakespeare on the Lake.

The *campsites* at Benbow Lake State Recreation Area are open year round and have hot showers. The sites, in a grove of oak trees, tend to be loud because they're near the highway. It's $16 per site from May through September, when reservations can be made through Parknet (☎ 800-444-7275); the rest of the year they're $12 and first-come, first-served. Two full-hookup sites are $21/17 in high/low season.

Beside the lake, the elegant ***Benbow Inn*** *(☎ 707-923-2124, 800-355-3301, 445 Lake Benbow Drive)*, is a large Tudor-style country inn opened in 1926 and now a national historic landmark. Rooms are $110 to $295, with off-season discounts. The restaurant here is world class (reservations recommended).

GARBERVILLE
• **population 1800** • **elevation 479 feet**
Garberville, and its tiny sister town of Redway 2 miles away, became famous on the underground grapevine in the 1970s for the *sinsemilla* (highly potent, seedless marijuana) grown in the surrounding hills; you still see many lefties and back-to-the-landers around, though the '70s salad days are long gone. Today, Garberville and Redway are quiet little towns with a few good places to eat and basic services; though it's tiny, this is 'town' for the surrounding rural areas.

Information
In the Jacob Garber Square, the Garberville-Redway Area Chamber of Commerce (☎ 707-923-2613, 800-923-2613), Suite E, 773 Redwood Drive, at the corner of Church St, has plenty of brochures and information on the region. It's open 10 am to 5 pm weekdays and sometimes on Saturdays in summer. For local news, unusual music and other interesting broadcasting, check out KMUD radio (91.1 FM).

Special Events
Reggae on the River is the major event of the year, drawing around 10,000 fans for 'the best reggae fest in the US,' a three-day event held the first weekend in August at French's Camp, beside the Eel River, 8 miles south of Garberville. Tickets, sold for both days only (no one-day tickets available), go on sale March 1 and sell out quickly; the Reggae on

the River Hotline (☎ 707-923-4583) has information and ticket details.

Other events include the Avenue of the Giants Marathon in May; the Redwood Run, a Harley-Davidson run through the redwoods, usually the first weekend in June; the Garberville Rodeo, the second weekend in June; the Hemp Festival in November; the Harvest Ball, also in November; and the Winter Arts Fair in mid-December, with magnificent arts and crafts.

Places to Stay
The closest camping to town is in the Benbow Lake State Recreation Area (see Benbow Lake).

Several motels are on Redwood Drive. The ***Lone Pine Motel*** *(☎ 707-923-3520, 912 Redwood Drive)*, has a swimming pool, hot tub and other amenities; rooms are $42 to $63 from May to October, $38 to $48 from November to April. The ***Humboldt Redwoods Inn*** *(☎ 707-923-2451, 987 Redwood Drive)* is another fine motel, with rooms for $50 to $72 in summer, $45 to $54 in winter. Fancier motels include ***Motel Garberville*** *(☎ 707-923-2422, 948 Redwood Drive)*, with single/double rooms for $52/58 in summer, $42/48 in winter, and the ***Best Western Humboldt House Inn*** *(☎ 707-923-2771, 800-528-1234, 701 Redwood Drive)*, with rooms for $83/69 in summer/winter.

Places to Eat
One of Garberville's best-loved restaurants, the small ***Woodrose Cafe*** *(☎ 707-923-3191, 911 Redwood Drive)*, has been serving delicious organic food since 1977, with both meat and vegetarian selections. The ***Eel River Cafe*** *(☎ 707-923-3783, 801 Redwood Drive)* is a local favorite for breakfast and lunch, as is the small ***Cafe Garberville*** *(☎ 707-923-3551, 770 Redwood Drive)*. The ***Waterwheel Restaurant*** *(☎ 707-923-2031, 924 Redwood Drive)* is a basic family restaurant with reasonable prices. At dinner there's a choice of Italian food or steaks and seafood.

Calico's Deli & Pasta *(☎ 707-923-2253, 808 Redwood Drive)* is a deli with salads, soups and a full Italian menu. ***Sicilito's*** *(☎ 707-923-2814, 445 Conger St)*, one block east of Redwood Drive, is a fun restaurant with American, Mexican and Italian food, pizza, steak, seafood and hamburgers. A big-screen TV provides entertainment, as does the decor with hundreds of historic items. *Cadillac Wok* (☎ 707-923-2343, 373 Sprowel Creek Rd), just west of Redwood Drive, is good for Chinese food.

The *Mateel Cafe* (☎ 707-923-2030, 3342 and 3344 Redwood Drive), in Redway, is one of the area's most famous restaurants. French chef Pierre Gaudé offers a deliciously unique culinary experience in a casual setting, with excellent prices; open 11:30 am to 9 pm Monday to Saturday. The *Brass Rail Inn* (☎ 707-923-3188, 3188 Redwood Drive), Redway, an attractive old roadhouse, is good for steak and seafood dinners.

Getting There & Away
Greyhound operates two northbound and two southbound buses daily on Hwy 101. They stop at the Singing Salmon (☎ 707-923-3388), 432 Church St, half a block east of Redwood Drive.

HUMBOLDT REDWOODS STATE PARK
The 80-sq-mile Humboldt Redwoods State Park holds some of the world's most magnificent old-growth redwood forest. Some of the most famous features of the park include the awe-inspiring Founders Grove, Rockefeller Forest and the Avenue of the Giants. The Park Visitor Center (☎ 707-946-2263), on the Avenue of the Giants just south of Weott, has information about the park, the redwoods, history and natural history, with useful books and maps. In summer it's open 9 am to 7 or 8 pm daily, 10 am to 4 pm in winter.

The Avenue of the Giants is a 32-mile stretch of scenic highway winding through numerous groves of old-growth redwoods, running parallel to Hwy 101 and the Eel River. A free Avenue of the Giants Auto Tour map and brochure is available at either end of the avenue and at the park visitor center. The southern entrance to the avenue is 6 miles north of Garberville, the northern entrance is a few miles south of Fortuna, and there are several other access points.

A number of the park's spectacular trees have been given names, including the Giant Tree – the world-champion coast redwood – in the Rockefeller Forest. That honor was held by the Dyerville Giant, in Founders Grove, until it fell in March 1991, when hit by another falling tree; a walk along the length of the 362-foot Dyerville Giant, with the width of its trunk towering high overhead, helps you appreciate how huge these ancient trees are. The Founders Tree, in Founders Grove, is another spectacular tree, as are the Tall Tree (also called the Rockefeller Tree) and the huge Flatiron Tree in the Rockefeller Forest. The Flatiron Tree fell in January 1995.

The park has more than 100 miles of trails for hiking, biking and horseback riding, ranging in difficulty from easy to strenuous. Easy hiking trails through Founders Grove, the Rockefeller Forest, the Drury-Chaney Loop Trail and the High Rock Trail are all popular, and there are plenty of others; a booklet with maps and directions for 22 spectacular walks is available at the visitor center.

Happy Horse Hill (☎ 707-943-3008), 1989 Elk Creek Rd, Myers Flat, offers one-hour horseback rides through the forest for $20 per person; children welcome, reservations appreciated.

Places to Stay
Camping The park has three developed and two environmental campgrounds, five trail camps, a hike-bike camp, two group camps and an equestrian camp. The developed campgrounds, all with hot showers, include *Burlington*, beside the park visitor center and open year round, *Hidden Springs* and *Albee Creek*, open from late May to mid-October. Reservations for these are available through Parknet (☎ 800-444-7275) from May through September when campsites are $16; the rest of the year, campsites are $12 and first-come, first-served.

Motels Several of the tiny towns along the Avenue of the Giants have attractive motels. Starting from south to north, the *Madrona*

Motel & Resort (☎ 707-943-1708, 2907 Avenue of the Giants), in Phillipsville (population 250), is simple, quaint and old-fashioned, with single/double rooms for $38/45.

The *Miranda Gardens Resort* (☎ 707-943-3011, 6766 Avenue of the Giants), in Miranda, right beside the Eel River, is a lovely place, with a heated swimming pool and children's playground. Rooms start at $65/55 in summer/winter; deluxe cottages, some with kitchen, whirlpool and fireplace, are $110 to $175.

In Myers Flat (population 200), the *Log Chapel Inn* (☎ 707-943-3315, 12840 Avenue of the Giants) is a simple place with single/double rooms for $35/40. Across the road, the *Historic Myers Inn* (☎ 707-943-3259, 800-500-6464, 12913 Avenue of the Giants) is a B&B in a newly refurbished historic stagecoach stop, with 10 rooms with private bath for $125.

Farther north in Redcrest (population 350), the *Redcrest Resort* (☎ 707-722-4208, 26459 Avenue of the Giants) has cabins starting at $45 ($5 more with kitchen), tepees for $20, campsites at $14/20 for tents/RVs.

SCOTIA
• **population 1000** • **elevation 164 feet**

Scotia is a rarity in the modern world: it's one of the last 'company towns' left in California, entirely owned and operated by the Pacific Lumber Company (PALCO), which runs the largest redwood lumber mill in the world. PALCO built the town beside the giant lumber mill in 1887 for its employees and their families. Today, Scotia is a manicured, organized, wholesome little town providing housing and services for some 270 families.

The three interesting things to do in Scotia – besides just strolling around and seeing what it feels like to be in a company town – are to take a tour of the giant lumber mill, visit the fisheries exhibit and stop by the museum. The **Scotia Museum & Visitors Center** (☎ 707-764-2222 ext 247), on Main St, at the corner of Bridge St, is open 8 am to 4 pm weekdays in summer.

Free self-guided tours of the lumber mill are offered from 7:30 to 10:30 am and

11:30 am to 2 pm weekdays. In summer, when the museum is open, you must stop by there to pick up your free permit for the tour; the rest of the year, permits are available at the guard shack at the mill entrance. The mill tour takes about 1 to 1½ hours and allows you to see everything from the debarking of the giant trees to their conversion to board lumber.

A new educational fisheries display is in the visitor parking lot near the mill entrance. The exhibit, open year round, has salmon and steelhead fish ponds and provides information about the lumber company's various fishery and in-stream enhancement projects.

Another nearby attraction is PALCO's demonstration forest, about 4½ miles south of Scotia, with a picnic area and nature hike. In summer, it's open 8 am to 4 pm daily.

Places to Stay & Eat
The *Scotia Inn* (☎ 707-764-5683, 888-764-2248), on Main St, is an attractive historic inn with rooms from $65 to $195. The dining room is open for dinner 5 to 9 pm Wednesday to Sunday year round; in summer, they also serve weekday lunches and a Sunday brunch. The inn also has a steak-and-potato pub, open from 5 to 9 pm nightly year round, for more casual dining.

Groceries, sandwiches, salads, coffee and the like are available at *Hoby's Market* (☎ 707-764-3623), opposite the inn. Otherwise there are several motels and little restaurants in Rio Dell, across the river from Scotia.

Getting There & Away
Redwood Transit System operates a bus route serving Scotia (see Eureka later in this chapter).

GRIZZLY CREEK REDWOODS STATE PARK
This park (☎ 707-777-3683), on the banks of the Van Duzen River, 18 miles east of Hwy 101 on Hwy 36, has redwood groves, campgrounds, activities and a museum inside a restored stagecoach stop. Campgrounds with hot showers are open year round; campsites are $16/12 in summer/winter.

Headwaters Forest

No place on Earth could feel more profoundly peaceful than Northern California's ancient redwood forests, with their quiet dignity and their thick carpet of rich, fragrant duff and loam. But some of these forests are at the center of a raging conflict between the lumber industry on the one hand and conservationists on the other, both of which are powerful groups in Northern California.

One grove in particular, a grove of old-growth redwood trees known as the Headwaters Forest, has been at the center of the conflict for a number of years. Southeast of Eureka, north of Hwy 36 near the tiny town of Stafford, this 3500-acre grove is California's largest remaining tract of unprotected ancient redwoods. The forest is owned by the Pacific Lumber Company (PALCO), which was, until 1986, a family-owned operation that practiced selective logging. Then Charles Hurwitz, CEO of Houston-based Maxxam Corporation, leveraged $750 million in junk bonds to buy out PALCO and take over its board of directors. To pay off the junk bond debt, Maxxam transformed PALCO's selective logging policy into one of clear-cutting the last of the ancient redwoods, doubling and even tripling the former rate of cut (a redwood tree 300 feet tall and 18 feet in diameter can fetch $200,000).

For several years, PALCO's harvesting of timber in Headwaters Forest has met vigorous objection from several groups of concerned environmentalists, who argue that this beautiful grove of trees (many over 1000 year old) must not be destroyed, but rather respected and preserved. 'Once it's gone, it's gone forever,' could be said to be their motto.

From the point of view of PALCO and the timber industry, environmentalists and demonstrators have no right to interfere with the harvesting of timber. The forest is the timber company's private property, and to them, lumber is a perfectly legitimate industry. From the point of view of the demonstrators, destruction of the ancient redwood forests is an unforgivable crime, a mistake that can never be remedied, and they feel compelled to do whatever is necessary to protect it, even throwing their own bodies in the way of harm to the ancient trees.

FERNDALE
• population 1240 • elevation 30 feet

Ferndale is an idyllic little dairy farming community founded in 1852 that feels as if time has somehow passed it by. About 20 miles south of Eureka, the town has many century-old buildings and homes still in use; they are well preserved and lovingly tended by their inhabitants. The town has two museums, various places to stay, and pleasant restaurants and art and antique shops along Main St, but Ferndale is not just a tourist trap – it's an authentic, charming 19th-century farming village in an otherwise busy world. So it should come as no surprise that the entire town is a state historic landmark, listed on the National Register of Historic Places.

Orientation & Information

'Downtown' Ferndale is a five-block section of Main St lined with Victorian-era buildings and shops. The *Victorian Village of Ferndale* map, with a visitors' guide and walking tour, is available free from a rack at the Kinetic Sculpture Museum, where you'll also find many other brochures from a number of Main St merchants.

The Ferndale Chamber of Commerce (☎ 707-786-4477) has a telephone recording with information about current events, and they will send out information upon request.

Things to See & Do

The first thing you should do in Ferndale is to take a historic walk around town, seeing the fine old Victorians and the interesting

Headwaters Forest

Demonstrators have gone into the Headwaters Forest to try to forcibly prevent logging there. In September 1998, 24-year-old David 'Gypsy' Chain of Austin, Texas, was accidentally killed by a falling tree while protesting logging near the Grizzly Creek redwood grove. In the same month, controversy raged about methods used by police in dealing with pro-forest demonstrators, including police swabbing demonstrators' eyes with concentrated pepper spray to break up a demonstration. Julia Butterfly, meanwhile, had been up in her tree for almost a year (see the boxed text 'Julia Butterfly & Luna, the Tree She Loves'), on a campaign to raise public awareness about the importance of protecting the old-growth redwood forests from destruction.

In September 1998, after years of conflict and demonstrations held to protect Headwaters Forest, an agreement was reached for public purchase of the forest. The federal government put up $250 million, and the state $245 million, for joint purchase of 7500 acres of PALCO's old-growth redwood groves, including the Headwaters Forest, a couple of other nearby old-growth groves and some already-logged land connecting them. The purchase is being made with the stipulation that the land and the old redwoods be set aside for public use. Eventually the Headwaters Forest will probably become a park, to be preserved for future generations.

Environmentalists are not completely happy with the arrangement – they had hoped for a larger purchase of 60,000 acres, which would have spared six groves of ancient redwoods and the partly logged land between them, which could be rehabilitated to provide habitat for a number of endangered species, including the northern spotted owl, marbled murrelet and coho salmon. They claim that the buffer area around the forest is insufficient to serve as adequate habitat protection.

At this writing, money had yet to change hands, and it's possible that further adjustments to the agreement could yet be made. But at a minimum, it looks as if the dedication of demonstrators in the long fight to preserve the Headwaters Forest has finally triumphed, and that this grove will be saved. For information and updates, see www.wildcalifornia.org.

shops on Main St. As the original settlers began to grow wealthy from the successful dairy farms they operated, some built large, ornate Victorian mansions known as 'butterfat palaces.' The **Gingerbread Mansion**, at 400 Berding St, now a B&B (see Places to Stay), is the most famous, but there are plenty of other interesting old homes and buildings in town.

The **Ferndale Museum** (☎ 707-786-4466), one block west of Main St at the corner of Shaw and 3rd Sts, has hundreds of artifacts and exhibits on the area's history. It's open 11 am to 4 pm Wednesday to Saturday, 1 to 4 pm Sunday.

Kinetic sculptures that have run in the annual Arcata-to-Ferndale Kinetic Sculpture Race (see the 'Kinetic Sculpture Race' boxed text) are on display at the **Kinetic Sculpture Museum**, 580 Main St, open 10 am to 5 pm daily; donations are appreciated. For information on the museum and the Kinetic Sculpture Race, call the Hobart Gallery (☎ 707-786-9259).

Special Events

The chamber of commerce has information on many events held in Ferndale throughout the year, including the Tour of the Unknown Coast bicycle race, on Mother's Day weekend in May; the Kinetic Sculpture Race, on Memorial Day weekend; the Scandinavian Festival and Parade, in June; the Humboldt County Fair & Horse Races (☎ 707-786-9511), which takes place over 10 days in mid-August; Oktoberfest, a full

NORTH COAST

Julia Butterfly & Luna, the Tree She Loves

At this writing, Julia 'Butterfly' Hill, 25, a preacher's daughter from Jonesboro, Arkansas, had been living on an 8-foot platform in a 200-foot-tall, 1000-year-old redwood named Luna for 18 months, near the tiny town of Stafford.

She ascended the tree on December 10, 1997, resolving to stay in it to prevent the Pacific Lumber Company from cutting the tree. This particular tree was chosen because it was the largest old-growth redwood tree in a grove of ancient redwoods slated for cutting. Her efforts did save this tree – but Pacific Lumber went ahead and cut all the other trees on the hillside, leaving Luna standing alone.

Butterfly has remained in the tree through storms, taunts, threats, nearby helicopter salvage logging and attempts by the lumber company to forcibly remove her, and has vowed that her feet will not touch earth again until she has done everything she can to make a difference in saving the ancient redwood forests. Earth First! activists provide her with food and contact with the outside world. Communicating by cellular telephone and walkie-talkie, she has given many interviews with national media, with the object of drawing attention to the plight of the old-growth redwood forests and the need to preserve them. For information and updates, see www.lunatree.org.

weekend of ethnic foods, music and dancing held each October; and the Christmas Celebrations, including a Lighted Tractor Parade, tree-lighting ceremony, arts and crafts sales, horse-and-carriage rides, concerts and theater productions.

Places to Stay

Camping The *Humboldt County Fairgrounds* (☎ 707-786-9511), at the corner of Van Ness and 5th Sts, offers camping on the lawn in front of the fairgrounds, with tent/RV sites for $5/15. To get there from Main St, turn west onto Van Ness St, on the north side of town, and go a few blocks down.

Hotels & Motels The *Francis Creek Inn* (☎ 707-786-9611, 577 Main St) has four comfortable, homey rooms for $55, with Danish pastries and coffee in the morning. The *Ferndale Laundromat & Motel* (☎ 707-786-9471, 632 Main St) has two units at $45, each with two bedrooms, kitchen and private bath. The *Fern Motel* (☎ 707-786-5000, 332 Ocean Ave) has rooms and suites for $65 to $125.

Hotel Ivanhoe (☎ 707-786-9000, 315 Main St), at the corner of Main St and Ocean Ave, is a grand historic hotel that was the town's original stagecoach stop. At this writing, the hotel was being restored; eventually there will be 10 rooms, each with private bath, for around $70 to $100. The hotel's northern Italian restaurant is a local favorite (see Places to Eat).

B&Bs Ferndale's elegant Victorians are naturals for B&Bs, and there are several excellent ones from which to choose. The *Gingerbread Mansion Inn* (☎ 707-786-4000, 800-952-4136, 400 Berding St), at the corner of Berding and Brown Sts and one block east of Main St, is a fancy 1899 Queen Anne-Eastlake Victorian mansion, the most photographed home in Ferndale. Now converted to a four-star B&B, it offers the utmost in service and elegance, with 11 large rooms from $140 to $350.

The *Shaw House* (☎ 707-786-9958, 703 Main St) was the first permanent structure to be built in Ferndale; the town's founder,

Seth Shaw, started building the gabled Carpenter Gothic Victorian home in 1854, though it was not completed until after his death in 1872. The house, called 'Fern Dale' for the six-foot-tall ferns that grew here, housed the new settlement's first post office, of which Shaw was the postmaster – and that's how the town of Ferndale got its name. Today, the Shaw House is a B&B with seven rooms from $85 to $145.

The *Creekside Inn* (☎ 707-786-9610, 1099 Van Ness Ave), in a pleasant 1895 Victorian beside the creek, offers 'bed no breakfast,' but you do get tea, coffee and cookies in the morning; two bedrooms sharing one bath are $50 each. *Grandmother's House* (☎ 707-786-9704, 861 Howard St) is a Queen Anne Victorian with three guest rooms for $65/75. They are happy to accept children and families.

Bartlett House (☎ 707-786-4010, 483 Shaw Ave), just off Main St, has two rooms for $85 and $95, each with private bath; it's open only on weekends, reservations essential. The *Queen of Harts B&B* (☎ 707-786-9716, 831 Main St) is a new B&B in an original Victorian home. Currently it has two rooms and will be expanding to five, each with private

bath, for $95 to $120, including full breakfast and afternoon tea.

Places to Eat
There are plenty of good eateries along the few blocks of Main St, including a bakery and coffeehouse, several lunch places, a candy-making shop and more.

For dinner, the northern Italian restaurant at the *Hotel Ivanhoe* (☎ 707-786-9000, 315 Main St), at the corner of Main St and Ocean Ave, is popular with locals and visitors alike (main courses are $8 to $16). Their chicken cacciatore special on Thursday nights is a popular weekly draw.

Curley's Grill (☎ 707-786-9696, 460 Main St) is another local favorite, with California casual dining, lots of grilled food, generous portions, moderate prices and friendly service. Tables are indoors and on the shady back patio. It's open 11:30 am to 9 pm daily, and for breakfast on weekends.

Entertainment
The *Ferndale Repertory Theatre* (☎ 707-786-5483, 447 Main St), a top-quality theater company, has productions year round. If one is on while you're in the area, don't miss it – this is Ferndale's pride and joy.

LOST COAST
California's 'Lost Coast,' with its southern border where Hwy 1 turns inland north of Rockport, and its northern border around Ferndale, became 'lost' when the state's highway system was put in place earlier this century. The steep, rugged King Range, which rises just above 4000 feet less than 3 miles inland, with near-vertical cliffs plunging into the sea, and the high rainfall (averaging 100 inches annually) exacerbating the unstable soil and rock conditions, all conspired to make it next to impossible to build a highway here. So the Pacific Coast Hwy was routed inland and, in time, legislation was passed to protect the region from development. Today, the Lost Coast is one of California's most pristine coastal areas.

The south part of the Lost Coast is composed of the King Range National Conservation Area and the Sinkyone Wilderness

---

Kinetic Sculpture Race

The Kinetic Sculpture Race was born in 1969 when Ferndale artist Hobart Brown decided to spruce up his son's tricycle to make it more interesting, creating a wobbly, five-wheeled red 'pentacycle.' Initially, five odd contraptions raced down Main St on Mother's Day, at the end of the Ferndale Arts Festival. The race was expanded in the early '70s to two days coming from Fields Landing, on Humboldt Bay south of Eureka; by now it has grown to a three-day, 38-mile amphibious event, coming all the way from Arcata and attracting thousands of spectators and usually around 40 to 60 entrants (but one year there were 99). The race is held every year on Memorial Day weekend.

NORTH COAST

State Park. The area north of the King Range is more accessible, but the scenery is not as dramatic. Shelter Cove, the only sizable community on the Lost Coast, is an isolated settlement on a remote cove 25 miles west of Garberville.

The best time to visit the Lost Coast is probably in spring and autumn, when there's a good chance of clear weather. If you'll be doing any hiking along the coast, late spring (around late April and early May) is an especially good time as not only might the weather cooperate, but you can view the migrating California gray whales.

North of the King Range

The northern section of the Lost Coast is accessible year round via Mattole Rd, which is paved. It takes about three hours to drive the 68 miles from Ferndale in the north, out to the coast at Cape Mendocino and then cut inland again to reach Humboldt Redwoods State Park and Hwy 101. Don't expect wild redwood forests like those found on Hwy 101 – the vegetation here is mostly grassland and pasture with scattered cattle ranches. You'll pass through three tiny towns: **Capetown**, **Petrolia** and **Honeydew**. The only gas station is at the Honeydew post office/market/hangout, but it's open sporadically and can't be counted on; be sure to fill your gas tank before you start the drive. Allow plenty of time, as the road is slow going. Though the drive is pleasant enough, the wild, spectacular scenery of the Lost Coast is not here, but farther south in the less accessible regions.

There's camping ($12 per vehicle) at the *AW Way County Park* (☎ 707-445-7651), on Mattole Rd, 6 miles southeast of Petrolia, between Petrolia and Honeydew.

King Range National Conservation Area

The 94-sq-mile King Range National Conservation Area, operated by the BLM, covers 35 miles of virgin wilderness coastline, with ridge after ridge of steep mountains plunging almost vertically into the surf, and the rugged King Range, with King's Peak the highest point at 4087 feet. The

BLM office in Arcata administers the conservation area, so it's the best place to obtain current information. Maps are available from the BLM offices in Arcata and Ukiah. For camping outside developed campgrounds, you'll need a free campfire permit, available from the California Department of Forestry (CDF) or the BLM offices in Arcata and Ukiah.

Hiking One of the area's most attractive and alluring features is the **Lost Coast Trail**, following 24 miles of coast from the Mattole Rivermouth Campground on the north end to Black Sands Beach at Shelter Cove on the south end. The prevailing northerly winds make it best to hike the trail from north to south. Highlights include an abandoned lighthouse at Punta Gorda, remnants of old shipwrecks, tidepools and a great abundance of marine and coastal wildlife including sea lions, seals and more than 300 species of birds. The trail is mostly level, passing along beaches and over rocky outcrops; consult tide tables, as some rocky outcroppings are passable only at low tide. The hike takes three to four days from end to end.

A good shorter day hike along part of the Lost Coast Trail, with beautiful tidepools along the way, can be made by starting at the Mattole Campground trailhead and hiking 3 miles south along the coast to the abandoned lighthouse at Punta Gorda, and back again,. The Mattole Campground is easy to reach; it's at the ocean end of Lighthouse Rd, a 4-mile road which intersects with Mattole Rd just southeast of Petrolia.

Other notable trails in the King Range are the **King Crest Trail** and the **Chemise Mountain Trail**, both designated as national recreation trails. The 16-mile King Crest Trail is a fairly easy trek along the main coastal ridge north of Shelter Cove. From the end of the Lost Coast Trail at Black Sands Beach at Shelter Cove, you can hike up the hill through the Shelter Cove community (about 5 miles on a paved road) to the Wailaki and Nadelos recreation sites, which are trailheads for the Chemise Mountain Trail, a ridge trail which connects with the Lost Coast Trail in the Sinkyone Wilderness State Park.

Shelter Cove

A seaside resort and retirement community with beautiful homes on a windswept cove just above Point Delgada, Shelter Cove is surrounded by the King Range National Conservation Area. It's a remote place, with just one access road – a 23-mile paved road winding west over the mountains from Garberville and Redway, which takes a good hour to drive.

Places to Stay & Eat The *Shelter Cove Campground & Deli* (☎ 707-986-7474, 492 Machi Rd), right in town, has hot showers and 100 campsites at $15/25 for tents/RVs. The deli has tables both inside and out on an ocean-view deck; fish and chips is their specialty. There's free camping in undeveloped campsites at Black Sands Beach or the nearby Wailaki and Nadelos recreation sites.

Other places to stay at Shelter Cove include the *Shelter Cove Beachcomber Inn* (☎ 707-986-7733, 7272 Shelter Cove Rd); the *Shelter Cove Motor Inn* (☎ 707-986-7521, 205 Wave Drive); and the *Marina Motel* (☎ 707-986-7595, 533 Machi Rd). The *Cove Restaurant* (☎ 707-986-1197, 210 Wave Drive), features fresh local seafood, California cuisine and has live music on weekend nights.

Sinkyone Wilderness State Park

The 7367-acre Sinkyone Wilderness State Park, named for the Sinkyone Indians who once lived here, is another pristine stretch of coastline. The Lost Coast Trail continues here for another 22 miles, from Whale Gulch on the north end to the Usal Beach Campground at the south end, 6 miles north of Hwy 1, and takes at least three days to hike.

Near the north end of the park, the Needle Rock Ranch House (☎ 707-986-7711) serves as a visitor center where you can check in, register for a campsite and get maps and trail guides. Upstairs in the ranch house are two unfurnished bedrooms available for 'indoor camping'; reservations can be made up to nine weeks in advance.

To get to the Needle Rock Ranch House, drive west from Garberville and Redway on Briceland Rd for 21 miles through White-

thorn to Four Corners, where you turn left (south) and continue about another 4 miles down a very rugged road to the ranch house; it takes about 1½ hours. There's also road access to the Usal Beach Campground at the south end of the park; from Hwy 1, about 3 miles north of Rockport, the unpaved County Rd 431 takes off from the highway at milepost 90.88 and goes 6 miles up the coast to the campground. These roads are not maintained during rainy months and quickly become impassable.

EUREKA

• population 27,800 • elevation 44 feet

The largest town on California's far north coast, Eureka hugs the shore of Humboldt Bay, a long, narrow bay that is the state's largest bay and seaport north of San Francisco, with a significant fishing fleet. At first glance, when you drive into town on Hwy 101, which goes right through the town, Eureka doesn't look too impressive – the highway is a thunder of traffic, motels, fastfood joints, gas stations and so on, giving a bad impression. Getting away from the highway, however, especially if you go into Old Town just a couple of blocks away, you find beautiful historic Victorian homes, an attractively refurbished commercial district, many good restaurants and other attractions.

Information

The Eureka-Humboldt County Convention and Visitors Bureau (☎ 707-443-5097, 800-346-3482), 1034 2nd St, at the corner of L St, has maps and information about Eureka, Arcata and all of Humboldt County. It's open 9 am to noon and 1 to 5 pm weekdays. The Eureka Chamber of Commerce (☎ 707-442-3738, 800-356-6381), 2112 Broadway, also has visitor information; it's open 9 am to 5 pm Monday to Wednesday, 9 am to 7 pm Thursday and Friday, 10 am to 4 pm weekends.

The Six Rivers National Forest Headquarters (☎ 707-442-1721), 1330 Bayshore Way, off Broadway on the south end of town near Henderson St, has maps and information about the forest. It's open 8 am to 4:30 pm weekdays.

NORTH COAST

EUREKA

PLACES TO STAY
18 Carter House B&B, Bell Cottage,
   Carter Cottage
19 Hotel Carter
29 Eureka Inn Annex Downtowner
   Motel
30 Eureka Inn
33 Cornelius Daly Inn
34 Weaver's Inn
35 Abigail's Elegant Victorian Mansion

PLACES TO EAT
1 Cafe Marina & Woodley's Bar
8 Los Bagels Bakery & Cafe
9 Cafe Waterfront Oyster Bar & Grill,
   Eureka Baking Company
12 Tomaso's
14 The Sea Grill
16 Lost Coast Brewery & Cafe
19 Hotel Carter Restaurant
23 Casa Blanca
26 Eureka's Seafood Grotto
30 Rib Room, Bristol Coast Cafe

OTHER
2 Blue Ox Millworks Historical Park
3 MV Madaket Dock
4 Hum-Boats
5 Adorni Recreation Center
6 Adorni Amphitheater
7 Romano Gabriel Wooden
   Sculpture Garden
10 Old Town Gazebo
11 Going Places
13 Clarke Memorial Museum
15 Ritz Club
17 Eureka-Humboldt County
   Convention & Visitors Bureau
20 Carson Mansion
21 Library
22 Humboldt Bay Maritime Museum
24 Greyhound Bus Station
25 Northern Mountain Supply
27 Post Office, Courthouse
28 Pro Sport Center
31 AAA
32 Post Office

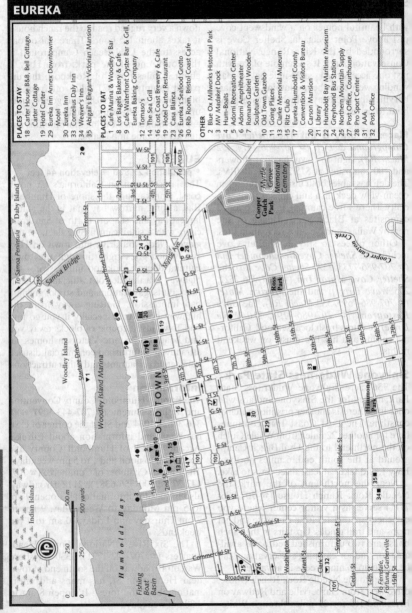

For a good selection of travel guidebooks and maps, visit Going Places (☎ 707-443-4145), 328 2nd St. The AAA office (☎ 707-443-5087) is at 707 L St.

Things to See & Do

Old Town, along 2nd and 3rd Sts from C St to M St, is a pleasant place to stroll. Formerly Eureka's down-and-out area, Old Town has been refurbished into a district of trendy boutiques, shops, art galleries, cafes and restaurants.

Eureka has many fine old Victorian homes. The free *Eureka Visitors Map,* available at the tourist offices, shows routes for scenic and architectural drives and walks. The most famous Victorian of all is the ornate **Carson Mansion** at the east end of 2nd St at M St. Home of lumber baron William Carson in the 1880s, it's said that it took 100 men a full year (1884-85) to build the mansion. Today, it's occupied by a private club, Ingomar, and is not open to the public. The pink house at 202 M St, opposite Carson Mansion, is an 1884 Queen Anne Victorian designed by the same architects and built as a wedding gift for Carson's eldest son.

The **Clarke Memorial Museum** (☎ 707-443-1947), 240 E St, at the corner of 3rd St, in the former Bank of Eureka building, has an especially impressive American Indian collection and thousands of other items pertaining to early Humboldt County history. The museum's largest historical artifact is the structure itself. Built 1911-12, the building was the leading bank in Eureka until the 1950s, and today it is on the National Register of Historic Places. The museum is open noon to 4 pm Tuesday to Saturday; free, but donation requested. Another museum, the small **Humboldt Bay Maritime Museum** (☎ 707-444-9440), 1410 2nd St, a block east of Carson Mansion, is open 11 am to 4 pm daily; free.

A relic of Eureka's more recent past is the **Romano Gabriel Wooden Sculpture Garden**, displayed in a large glass case in a little triangular plaza just off the sidewalk on 2nd St, between D and E Sts. For 30 years Gabriel's sculptures delighted locals. After he passed away in 1977, the city moved the collection from his front yard to preserve it.

The **Blue Ox Millworks Historical Park** (☎ 707-444-3437, 800-248-4259), at the bay end of X St, is another interesting historical place, where antique tools and mills are used in the production of gingerbread trim and other decoration for old Victorian buildings. A real working museum owned and operated by Eric and Viviana Hollenbeck, this is one of few places in the world where you can see this being done; a one-hour tour takes you through the entire mill and other historical buildings. The $5 admission is well worth it (discounts for seniors, children and groups). It's open 9 am to 5 pm Monday to Saturday, with possible Sunday hours in summer.

Yet another historic site in Eureka is the **Fort Humboldt State Historic Park** (☎ 707-445-6567), just off Broadway St on the south end of town; turn inland onto Highland Ave and you'll see the entrance gate. Ulysses S Grant was stationed at Fort Humboldt in 1853. He went on to become a general, led the Union Army to victory in the Civil War in 1865, and became president of the US in 1869. The fort was established in 1853 on a high bluff affording a view of Humboldt Bay and its entrance. It has indoor and outdoor exhibits about logging, two museums, and one original and one reconstructed fort building. Steam engine rides are given the third Saturday of each month in summer. Open 9 am to 5 pm daily (museums till 4 pm); free.

Sequoia Park & Zoo (☎ 707-442-6552), 3414 W St, is a beautiful redwood grove with bicycle and hiking trails, picnic areas, a children's playground, duck pond and tiny zoo. The park is always open. The zoo is open 10 am to 7 pm Tuesday to Sunday from May to September, closing at 5 pm the rest of the year; free, but donation suggested.

Activities

One of Eureka's most delightful activities is the Humboldt Bay Harbor Cruise on the MV *Madaket* (☎ 707-445-1910). The oldest passenger vessel in continuous use in the US, the *Madaket* was built here and launched

NORTH COAST

Eureka's History

Humboldt Bay is said to have been formed some 10,000 years ago, at the end of the last ice age, when the sea rose and flooded an inland valley. About 14 miles long, the bay was home to the Wiyot Indians before Europeans arrived. Although various early European explorers had plied the coast of California, the bay's narrow entrance kept it from being discovered until 1806, when Captain Jonathan Winship of the US vessel *O'Cain*, which was chartered to the Russian-American Fur Company sailed into the bay, searching for sea otters.

The bay was not settled at that time, however, and it seems to have been forgotten. Legend or history – it's hard to tell which, as accounts differ – relate that the bay was rediscovered, and the town of Eureka founded, when whaler James T Ryan sailed into the bay in spring of 1850, shouting, 'Eureka!' (Greek for 'I've found it!'). That was a popular expression at the time, and this was not the only place to be named Eureka. Nevertheless, the name stuck here, the town was founded, and later on, when the first state congress met, 'Eureka' was adopted as the California motto and put on the new state seal. The bay was named after German explorer and naturalist Baron Alexander von Humboldt.

During the 1840s and '50s, when miners were active on the Trinity and Klamath rivers farther inland, Eureka and Arcata were important supply bases and trading posts for the mining camps. It wasn't long before lumbering became as important as mining, and then surpassed it. By 1854, there were seven lumber mills in Eureka, and more in Arcata, with schooners taking the lumber to San Francisco and other burgeoning coastal settlements. At one point, over 75 lumber mills were in operation around Humboldt Bay. Railroad systems were laid down to get the big trees from the forests to the mills; the trains required a strong engine and many flatbed cars to do the job. The first overland connection between Humboldt Bay and the outside world came in 1914 with the establishment of the Northern Pacific Railroad coming north from San Francisco.

Today, most of the lumber mills have closed, with only one, the Louisiana Pacific pulp mill on the Samoa Peninsula opposite Eureka, left in operation.

June 6, 1910. The vessel has served in Humboldt Bay since then, ferrying passengers and workers to the lumber mills and other places around the bay for many years before the Samoa Bridge was built in 1972. The cruise passes many places of interest around the bay, while a host tells stories about history and natural features, giving you an experience you could never get from land. The 1¼ hour cruises depart several times daily from May to October, from the dock at the foot of C St; phone for reservations and the current schedule.

Hum-Boats (☎ 707-443-5157), at the bay end of F St, offers kayak and sailboat rentals, instruction and tours, ecotours, a water taxi, sailboat charters, sunset sails and full-moon kayak rides. Northern Mountain

Supply (☎ 707-445-1711), 125 W 5th St, at the corner of Commercial St, rents canoes, hard-shell and inflatable kayaks and camping and backpacking gear. The Pro Sport Center (☎ 707-443-6328), 508 Myrtle St, at the corner of 5th St, rents scuba and abalone diving gear, inflatable boats, skiing, snowboarding, camping gear and bicycles.

Special Events

Many enjoyable events are held every year in Eureka, including the Redwood Coast Dixieland Jazz Festival in March; the Rhododendron Festival in April; the Tour of the Unknown Coast bicycle race in May; a series of summer concerts in Sequoia Park from June to August; the Humboldt Arts Festival in July and August, featuring concerts, plays and art exhibits; Blues on the Bay the last weekend in August; and the December Christmas Celebrations, including a Truckers' Christmas Convoy Parade and the Eureka Inn Christmas Celebration.

Places to Stay

Camping The *Eureka KOA* (☎ 800-562-3136), KOA Drive, on the east side of Hwy 101 about 4 miles north of Eureka, has tent/RV sites ($20/23), cabins ($35) and cottages ($110), with discounts in winter. The *Fortuna KOA* (☎ 707-725-3359, 800-562-0532), Hwy 101, at the Kenmar Rd exit, 18 miles south of Eureka, has tent/RV sites for $21/27 and one- and two-room cabins for $36/40, with winter discounts. There's also camping on the Samoa Peninsula, across the bay from Eureka.

Motels Dozens of motels line Hwy 101 where it goes through town, but they are exposed to the roar of highway traffic; you'll get a more peaceful sleep away from the highway noise.

The *Bayview Motel* (☎ 707-442-1673, 2844 Fairfield St), just off Henderson St near the corner of Broadway, is close to the highway but it's quiet, perched on a high bluff overlooking the bay, and is reasonably priced.

Also away from the highway, the *Eureka Inn Annex Downtowner Motel* (☎ 707-443-5061, 424 8th St), at the corner of E St, has an outdoor heated swimming pool, indoor sauna and hot tub, and 72 spacious rooms that are clean, quiet and comfortable. Rooms are $54, including continental breakfast.

Hotels Eureka has two elegant, classic hotels. The luxurious Tudor-style *Eureka Inn* (☎ 707-442-6441, 518 7th St), between F and G Sts, is on the National Register of Historic Places. It has every amenity, including a heated swimming pool, sauna and hot tub, fine restaurants, a pub and 100 rooms starting at $110.

Another elegant place, the *Hotel Carter* (☎ 707-444-8062, 707-445-1390, 800-404-1390, 301 L St), at 3rd St, has earned numerous awards for best inn, best restaurant, best

breakfast, etc. Its room rates of $125 to $295 include a fabulous breakfast, plus wine and hors d'oeuvres each evening, with dinner available in the hotel restaurant (see Places to Eat). The same hospitable owners/hosts, Mark and Christi Carter, also operate the Carter House B&B, Bell Cottage and Carter Cottage on the opposite corner (see B&Bs).

B&Bs Eureka's elegantly restored Victorians are a natural for B&Bs. The Eureka B&B Reservation Service (☎ 707-441-1215) books several B&Bs around town. Summer prices are listed here; all offer discounts in winter.

Abigail's Elegant Victorian Mansion (☎ 707-444-3144, 1406 C St), at 14th St, is a national historic landmark that's like an interactive living-history museum, justly famous for the friendly hospitality of its hosts; its four guest rooms are $85 to $185, including a horseless carriage ride around Eureka in your choice of a 1929 Model A Ford coupe with a rumble seat, a 1925 Chevrolet touring car or a 1928 Ford touring car. The *Cornelius Daly Inn* (☎ 707-445-3638, 800-321-9656, 1125 H St), at 12th St, is a 1905 Colonial Revival mansion with generous grounds, a garden patio and rooms from $85 to $150. *Weaver's Inn* (☎ 707-443-8119, 800-992-8119, 1440 B St), in an 1883 Queen Anne Victorian with extensive gardens, has four guest rooms for $75 to $125 (singles $10 less).

The *Carter House B&B* (☎ 707-444-8062, 1033 3rd St), with rooms for $125 to $285; *Bell Cottage* (☎ 707-444-8062, 1023 3rd St), with the same prices; and *Carter Cottage* (☎ 707-444-8062, 1027 3rd St), a luxurious 1000-sq-foot private house for $495, are all in a row and are operated by the elegant Hotel Carter on the opposite corner, where guests enjoy the hotel restaurant's sumptuous breakfasts and evening wine and hors d'oeuvres.

In rural Loleta, about 10 miles south of Eureka, between Eureka and Ferndale, *Southport Landing* (☎ 707-733-5915, 444 Phelan Rd), an 1890 Early Colonial Revival mansion at the end of a country lane on the shore of Humboldt Bay, overlooking the

Humboldt Bay National Wildlife Refuge, has four guest rooms from $85 to $115.

Places to Eat

An outdoor *farmers' market* is held at the Old Town Gazebo at the corner of 2nd and F Sts 10 am to 1 pm Tuesday from July to October.

Eureka's best-known eatery, the *Samoa Cookhouse* (☎ 707-442-1659) is the 'last surviving cookhouse in the West.' An old lumber camp cookhouse, with a museum in one part of the building, the whole place is like a slice out of Eureka's lumbering past. Diners are seated all together at long tables covered with checkered cloths, then served all-you-can-eat of course after course of hearty dishes. Dinner includes soup, salad, two types of meat, potatoes, vegetables, apple pie and coffee, tea or iced tea for $12; breakfast and lunch are similarly hearty meals for $7 and $8 respectively. It's on the Samoa Peninsula, a few minutes northwest of Eureka, over the Samoa Bridge; follow the signs. It's open 6 am to 3:30 pm and 5 to 9 pm Monday to Saturday, from 6 am to 9 pm Sunday. Seating is first-come, first-served.

There are many other good places to eat right in town, mostly in Old Town. The gourmet restaurant at the *Hotel Carter* (☎ 707-444-8062, 707-445-1390, 800-404-1390, 301 L St), at 3rd St, has won many national and international awards for excellence; it's famous both for its breakfasts, which consists of a four-course meal and lavish buffet served every morning from 7:30 to 10 am, and its gourmet dinners served from 6 to 9 pm nightly. Dinners feature a five-course vegetarian and five-course meat-and-fish meal, in addition to the a la carte menu. There's a 50-page wine list. Reservations are recommended for both breakfast and dinner.

Eureka's other fine hotel, the *Eureka Inn* (☎ 707-442-6441, 518 7th St), between F and G Sts, offers elegant dining in its Rib Room, which specializes in prime rib; breakfast and lunch are served in the Bristol Rose Cafe.

For simpler fare, *Los Bagels Bakery & Cafe* (☎ 707-442-8525, 403 2nd St), at the corner of E St, is a branch of the popular Arcata cafe-bakery-hangout; it's open 7 am to 5 pm, closing earlier on Sunday and altogether on Tuesday. Around the corner, the *Eureka Baking Company* (☎ 707-445-0520, 108 F St) has a wide variety of baked goods, sandwiches, soups, great coffee and a few tables.

Eureka has many fine seafood restaurants. The *Cafe Waterfront Oyster Bar & Grill* (☎ 707-443-9190, 102 F St), at the corner of 1st St, with a view of Humboldt Bay, is a fun, pleasant place that's popular for seafood and not too expensive, with dinners for $10 to $16. *The Sea Grill* (☎ 707-443-7187, 316 E St) is also known for good seafood, for $13 to $19.

Eureka's Seafood Grotto (☎ 707-443-2075), a casual restaurant at the corner of 6th St and Broadway, is a bustling family-style eatery with large portions and reasonable prices: $7 for the fish and chips, $10 for snapper, $15 for the seafood platter and $29 for the lobster. *Cafe Marina & Woodley's Bar* (☎ 707-443-2233), on Woodley Island, with decks and a view overlooking the marina, is another pleasant place for seafood. Dinners range from $10 to $16.

For excellent Italian food, visit *Tomaso's* (☎ 707-445-0100, 216 E St). You'll know you're nearby when you smell the enticing aromas wafting onto the sidewalk. Famous dishes here include the spinach pies, tomato pies, chicken cannelloni and seafood Provençale.

Casa Blanca (☎ 707-443-6190, 1436 2nd St), at the corner of P St, beside the Maritime Museum, is a favorite for Mexican food, with indoor and outdoor dining and live music on Friday nights.

The *Lost Coast Brewery & Cafe* (☎ 707-445-4480, 617 4th St), is a fun, popular microbrewery, pub and cafe serving a variety of brews and pub food.

Entertainment

The *Eureka Inn* (☎ 707-442-6441, 518 7th St), has live music upstairs in the Palm Lounge Thursday to Sunday nights; downstairs Mirrors is a quieter bar. The *Ritz Club* (☎ 707-445-8577), at the corner of 3rd and F Sts, has DJ dance music Thursday to Saturday nights and other entertainment. The **Lost Coast Brewery & Cafe** (☎ *707-445-4480, 617 4th St*) is a popular pub. A pitcher of their beer costs $7.75.

Getting There & Around

The Arcata-Eureka Airport, on Hwy 101 about 20 miles north of Eureka, is served by two airlines: Horizon Air (☎ 800-547-9308) and United Express (☎ 800-241-6522).

Greyhound (☎ 707-442-0370, 800-231-2222), 1603 4th St, at Q St, operates two northbound and two southbound buses daily.

The Redwood Transit System (☎ 707-443-0826), 133 V St, operates buses weekdays between Scotia in the south and Trinidad in the north, with stops at all the little towns along the way, including Fortuna and Arcata; these buses make a number of stops along 4th and 5th Sts as they pass through Eureka. Local city buses are operated by Eureka Transit Service (☎ 707-443-0826), with service Monday to Saturday.

Car rental companies in and near Eureka include Avis (☎ 707-839-1576, 800-831-2847), Budget (☎ 707-839-4374, 800-527-0700), Enterprise (☎ 707-443-3366, 800-325-8007) and Hertz (☎ 707-839-2172, 800-654-3131).

The Pro Sport Center (☎ 707-443-6328), 508 Myrtle St at the corner of 5th St, rents bicycles by the full or half day.

AROUND EUREKA
Samoa Peninsula

The 7-mile-long, half-mile-wide Samoa Peninsula is the north spit of Humboldt Bay; it's said the place got its name from its resemblance to Pago Pago Harbor. The peninsula's most famous attraction is the **Samoa Cookhouse** (see Eureka Places to Eat), but it has other attractions too.

You can go to the beach anywhere along the peninsula, walking west through the dunes. At the south end of the peninsula, the **Samoa Dunes Recreation Area** offers picnic areas and access to the bay and the ocean, and it provides opportunities for fishing; it's operated by the Bureau of Land Management (☎ 707-825-2300). The recreation area is open from sunrise to sunset; free.

There's camping at the Samoa Boat Ramp County Park (☎ 707-445-7651), on the bay side of the peninsula, about 4 miles south of the Samoa Bridge, for $10 a night. There's not much to it – basically it's just some picnic tables and a toilet block beside a parking lot.

Humboldt Bay National Wildlife Refuge

On the south end of Humboldt Bay, this refuge (☎ 707-733-5406) is an important one for more than 200 species of birds migrating on the Pacific Flyway each year. Peak season for most species of waterbirds and raptors is from September through March, and peak season for black brant geese and migratory shorebirds is from mid-March to late April, but many birds can be seen year round, including shorebirds, gulls, terns, cormorants, pelicans, egrets and herons. The refuge also harbors seals. It has two interpretive trails; a free map is available at the refuge entrance and from tourist offices. To reach the refuge, turn seaward from Hwy 101 at the Hookton Rd exit, 11 miles south of Eureka, and follow the signs. It's open sunrise to sunset daily.

ARCATA
• **population 16,450** • **elevation 33 feet**

Five miles north of Eureka, Arcata is a pleasant university town overlooking Arcata and Humboldt bays with a youthful, laid-back ambience reminiscent of the 1960s. Humboldt State University (HSU), the northernmost campus in the state university system, is strong on environmental studies – and forestry. A recent referendum to change the school's mascot from a lumberjack to the endangered marbled murrelet lost by a narrow margin.

When it was founded by the Union Timber Company in 1850, Arcata was called Union Town; in 1860, the name was changed to Arcata. Originally a depot and base for the Trinity gold fields in the mountains to the east and for nearby lumber camps, Arcata grew and became a lumber town with a number of mills. In the late 1850s, author Bret Harte worked in Arcata as a journalist; the town became the setting for some of his stories.

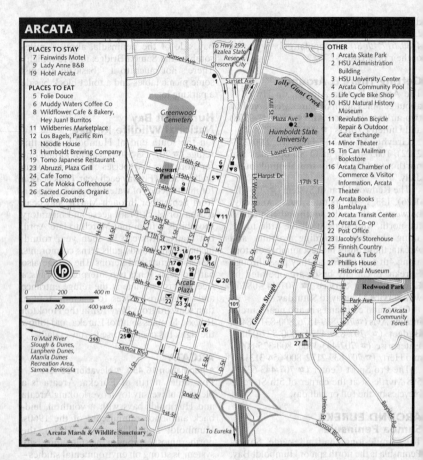

ARCATA

PLACES TO STAY
7 Fairwinds Motel
1 Lady Anne B&B
19 Hotel Arcata

PLACES TO EAT
5 Folie Douce
6 Muddy Waters Coffee Co
8 Wildflower Cafe & Bakery,
   Hey Juan! Burritos
11 Wildberries Marketplace
12 Los Bagels, Pacific Rim
   Noodle House
13 Humboldt Brewing Company
19 Tomo Japanese Restaurant
23 Abruzzi, Plaza Grill
24 Cafe Tomo
25 Cafe Mokka Coffeehouse
26 Sacred Grounds Organic
   Coffee Roasters

OTHER
1 Arcata Skate Park
2 HSU Administration
   Building
3 HSU University Center
4 Arcata Community Pool
5 Life Cycle Bike Shop
10 HSU Natural History
   Museum
11 Revolution Bicycle
   Repair & Outdoor
   Gear Exchange
14 Minor Theater
15 Tin Can Mailman
   Bookstore
16 Arcata Chamber of
   Commerce & Visitor
   Information, Arcata
   Theater
17 Arcata Books
19 Jambalaya
20 Arcata Transit Center
21 Arcata Co-op
22 Post Office
23 Jacoby's Storehouse
25 Finnish Country
   Sauna & Tubs
27 Phillips House
   Historical Museum

Orientation

Arcata is an attractive town sloping down a hill toward Humboldt Bay. At the top of the hill are HSU and Hwy 101. G and H Sts, connecting with Hwy 101 at the north end of town, are the main streets going from the freeway into town, with G St going one-way up the hill and H St going one-way downhill. The heart of the town is Arcata Plaza, between G and H Sts and 8th and 9th Sts. Finding addresses is a snap in downtown; the streets are all laid out on a grid, with numbered streets crossing lettered streets.

The Giuntoli Lane exit off Hwy 101, where several budget hotels are found, is a couple of miles north of town. Hwy 299, the Trinity Scenic Byway going east to Weaverville and Redding, intersects Hwy 101 about a mile north of town.

Information

The Arcata Chamber of Commerce & Visitor Information Center (☎ 707-822-3619, 800-908-9464), 1062 G St beside the Arcata Theater, is open 10 am to 4 pm Monday to Thursday, 10 am to 5 pm Friday, 9 am to 5 pm

NORTH COAST

Saturday. The free *Map Guide to Arcata* has plenty of useful information about the town and the region.

In fall 1999, their office is scheduled to move to large new quarters at 1635 Heindon Rd, a couple of miles north of town (take the Giuntoli Lane exit from Hwy 101), where it will operate a California Welcome Center serving all Humboldt County, Del Norte County and the state; hours will be 9 am to 5 pm daily.

The BLM office (☎ 707-825-2300), 1695 Heindon Rd, a couple of miles north of town, has information on the Lost Coast and the King Range National Conservation Area. In October 1999, this office will move into the new California Welcome Center.

Arcata has a couple of excellent bookstores, with books you don't usually find elsewhere. The Tin Can Mailman (☎ 707-822-1307), 1000 H St, at the corner of 10th St, is a magnificent store with more than 125,000 used books of all kinds on two floors. Arcata Books (☎ 707-822-1024), 959 H St, is fascinating, with over 200,000 used, new, rare and antiquarian books.

Things to See & Do

Around **Arcata Plaza** are many restaurants, shops and historic buildings. The chamber of commerce's free town map offers historical descriptions and a route for a self-guided walking tour of historic homes and their architectural styles. The large 1857 **Jacoby's Storehouse** building, at the corner of H and 8th Sts, at the southwest corner of the plaza is a registered national historic landmark, as is the 1915 **Hotel Arcata**, at the corner of G and 9th Sts at the northeast corner of the plaza. The 1914 **Minor Theater**, 1013 10th St, is another historic building, though its not registered.

Taking up most of the northeast side of town, **Humboldt State University** (HSU; ☎ 707-826-3011) has a large, attractive campus with an art gallery, cultural and sporting events and more (see Entertainment). **HSU Center Activities** (☎ 707-826-3357), on the 2nd floor of the University Center, beside the clock tower on campus, offers myriad activities, outings, trips, classes,

workshops and sporting-gear rentals at affordable prices; nonstudents are welcome.

On the east end of 11th and 14th Sts, **Redwood Park** is lovely, with redwood trees and picnic areas. Adjoining the park is the extensive **Arcata Community Forest**, a beautiful 600-acre redwood forest crisscrossed by 18 trails, with dirt roads and paved roads good for hikers and mountain bikers. A free Community Forest map is available from the chamber of commerce.

The **HSU Natural History Museum** (☎ 707-826-4479), 1315 G St, is a small museum with exhibits including fossils, live animals of the north coast, a tidepool tank, an observation beehive, tsunami and seismic exhibits and more. It's open 10 am to 4 pm Tuesday to Saturday; free, but donations appreciated.

The **Phillips House Historical Museum** (☎ 707-822-4722), at the corner of 7th and Union Sts, is a historic 1854 home museum open for guided tours 1 to 4 pm Sunday, or by appointment; admission by donation.

The **Finnish Country Sauna & Tubs** (☎ 707-822-2228), at the corner of 5th and J Sts, is blissful, with an assortment of private saunas and hot tubs in a lovely garden out behind the Cafe Mokka. The hot tubs and saunas are popular, especially on weekends; phone ahead for a reservation. It's open noon to 11 pm daily (until 1 am Friday and Saturday). The **Arcata Community Pool** (☎ 707-822-6801), 1150 16th St, offers swimming, hot tub, exercise room and more.

The popular new **Arcata Skate Park**, Sunset Ave near Jay St, offers challenges for beginning to advanced skaters. It has three bowls with rails, a 4-foot-tall fun box and a snake run with lots of vertical edges. Safety gear is required. Open daily during daylight hours; free.

The **Arcata Marsh & Wildlife Sanctuary** (☎ 707-826-2359), on the shores of Humboldt Bay at the foot of I St, is great for birding. The Audubon Society offers guided walks every Saturday at 8:30 am, departing from the parking lot at the bay end of the road. Friends of Arcata Marsh give guided tours every Saturday at 2 pm, departing from the Marsh Interpretive Center, 600

South G St. The sanctuary has walking trails and many points of interest; pick up a free map from the chamber of commerce.

Special Events

Arcata's most famous annual event is the three-day Kinetic Sculpture Race on Memorial Day weekend, the last weekend in May (see Ferndale Special Events). Other events include the Arcata Bay Oyster Festival, the second Saturday in June; the July 4th Jubilee; the September North Country Fair; and Pastels on the Plaza, the first Saturday in October.

Places to Stay

Camping There's good camping at *Patrick's Point State Park* (☎ 707-677-3570, 4150 Patrick's Point Drive), 16 miles north of Arcata, and farther north at *Humboldt Lagoons State Park* (☎ 707-488-2041, 15336 Hwy 101). Closer in, the **Clam Beach County Park** (☎ 707-445-7491), on Hwy 101, about 8 miles north of town, offers primitive camping in the dunes; facilities include pit toilets, a few cold water faucets, picnic tables and fire rings. Campsites are $8 per vehicle.

Hotels & Motels *Hotel Arcata* (☎ 707-826-0217, 800-344-1221, 708 9th St), at the corner of G St on the north side of the plaza, is a beautifully restored 1915 hotel with charming, comfortable rooms for $66, all with private bath and claw-foot tubs.

The *Fairwinds Motel* (☎ 707-822-4824, 1674 G St), at 17th St, has OK rooms, but the noise from Hwy 101 just a few feet behind the motel is loud; singles/doubles are $40/45.

Other motels are 2 miles north of town at Hwy 101's Giuntoli Lane exit. They include *Motel 6* (☎ 707-822-7061, 800-466-8356), with rooms for $38/44; *Comfort Inn* (☎ 707-826-2827, 800-221-2222), with rooms starting at $49/59; *North Coast Inn* (☎ 707-822-4861), with rooms starting at $65; and *Best Western Arcata Inn* (☎ 707-826-0313, 800-528-1234), with rooms starting at $52/56, higher with Jacuzzi.

B&Bs The *Lady Anne B&B* (☎ 707-822-2797, 902 14th St), at I St, has five rooms with private bath in a fancy Queen Anne Victorian mansion for $80 to $105. *Cats' Cradle B&B* (☎ 707-822-2287, 815 Park Place), overlooking town and within walking distance to Redwood Park, has three rooms and one suite for $65 to $120.

Places to Eat

The *Arcata Co-Op* (☎ 707-822-5947), at the corner of 8th and I Sts, is a large natural-foods supermarket open 7 am to 9 pm daily. *Wildberries Marketplace* (☎ 707-822-0095), 13th and G Sts, at the top of the hill, is an attractive marketplace with an award-winning deli, bakery, natural juice bar and outdoor deck. From May to November, a *farmers' market* meets 9 am to 1 pm Saturday on the Arcata Plaza.

Los Bagels (☎ 707-822-3150, 1061 I St) is great for coffee, bagels and other baked goods and general hanging out. The *Cafe Mokka Coffeehouse* (☎ 707-822-2228), at the corner of 5th and J Sts, has a Bohemian atmosphere and international newspapers. It's open noon to 11 pm daily (till 1 am Friday and Saturday).

Pacific Rim Noodle House (☎ 707-826-7604, 1021 I St) is popular for its inexpensive, eclectic mix of Pacific Rim foods (Thai, Korean and more), with outside tables and take-out food. Up the hill, the *Wildflower Cafe & Bakery* (☎ 707-822-0360, 1604 G St), at 16th St, offers baked goods and tasty, wholesome, inexpensive organic vegetarian meals. *Hey Juan! Burritos* (☎ 707-822-8433, 1642½ G St) is a hip, cheap little Mexican cafe and with just five tables; a basic but good, filling meal is around $4.

The *Humboldt Brewing Company* (☎ 707-826-2739, 856 10th St), at the corner of I St, serves lunch, dinner and pub food (including delicious buffalo wings) in addition to its good homemade brews.

Arcata also has several more substantial restaurants, where reservations are a good idea. *Abruzzi* (☎ 707-826-2345) is a good Italian dinner house on the downstairs level of the historic Jacoby's Storehouse building, at the corner of 8th and H Sts; the entrance is easiest to find if you walk around the corner onto H St, to the rear of the building.

NORTH COAST

Upstairs, the *Plaza Grill* (☎ 707-826-0860) has a fun, lively atmosphere; it's open for dinner from 5 pm until late in the evening nightly.

Popular, quality gourmet restaurants with an international flair include *Folie Douce* (☎ 707-822-1042, 1551 G St), a tiny restaurant with gourmet pizza as well as more exotic fare and a 270-item wine list; it's open for dinner only, closed Sunday and Monday. *Tomo Japanese Restaurant* (☎ 707-822-1414), in the Hotel Arcata at the corner of 9th and G Sts, on the north side of the plaza, is a popular sushi bar and restaurant.

Entertainment

Jambalaya (☎ 707-822-4766, 915 H St), near the plaza, offers live jazz, blues and other music, plus weekly jam nights, poetry nights and more; the schedule is posted at the door. On the south side of the plaza, *Cafe Tomo* (☎ 822-4100, 773 8th St) is a restaurant, bar and dance hall with varied music every night. The *Humboldt Brewing Company* (☎ 707-826-2739, 856 10th St) features live music Thursday to Saturday nights.

For mellower sounds, check out the *Cafe Mokka Coffeehouse* (☎ 707-822-2228), at the corner of 5th and J Sts, with live acoustic music (usually European folk) on weekend evenings. *Sacred Grounds Organic Coffee Roasters* (☎ 707-822-0690, 686 F St), at the corner of 7th St, has live music on weekends. *Muddy Waters Coffee Co* (☎ 707-825-6833, 1603 G St) has a fireplace, cozy ambience and live music on weekends. It's open 6 am to midnight daily.

The *Arcata Theater* (☎ 707-822-5171, 1036 G St) and the *Minor Theater* (☎ 707-822-5171, 1013 H St) have frequently changing movies and bargain matinees.

HSU's *Center Arts* (☎ 707-826-4411, 707-826-3928) sponsors performances, concerts, international music and cultural events.

Getting There & Around

The Arcata Transit Center (☎ 707-822-3775) is off F St at 10th St. Greyhound buses traveling on Hwy 101 stop here, with two northbound and two southbound buses daily. Redwood Transit System's weekday Trinidad-Scotia buses (see Eureka Getting There & Around), and Arcata city buses, also stop here. Daily Amtrak Thruway buses connect with Amtrak trains at Martinez; buy tickets at travel agencies.

Revolution Bicycle Repair & Outdoor Gear Exchange (☎ 707-822-2562), 1360 G St, rents mountain bikes, cruisers, bike racks and other gear. Life Cycle Bike Shop (☎ 707-822-7755), 1593 G St, rents bicycles, helmets and car racks. Both are full-service bicycle shops.

AROUND ARCATA

For good wildlife viewing, head to **Mad River Slough & Dunes**. A trail passes mudflats, salt marsh and tidal channels. Over 200 species of birds can be seen here around the year, with migrating waterfowl in spring and autumn, songbirds in spring and summer, shorebirds in autumn and winter, and abundant wading birds year round. To get there from Arcata, go west on Samoa Blvd for about 3 miles, then turn right at the Manila turnoff (Young St).

The 475-acre **Lanphere Dunes Unit** of the Humboldt Bay National Wildlife Refuge (☎ 707-822-6378), formerly known as the **Lanphere-Christensen Dunes**, is one of the finest examples of dune succession on the entire Pacific coast. West of Arcata, the undisturbed sand dunes can reach heights of over 80 feet. Because the environment is fragile, access is by tour only. Friends of the Dunes (☎ 707-444-1397) lead tours the first and third Saturday of each month, 10 am to noon, rain or shine, departing from the Pacific Union School parking lot at 3001 Janes Rd in Arcata. Bring a jacket and soft-soled shoes.

A couple of miles south of Lanphere-Christensen Dunes, the 100-acre **Manila Dunes Recreation Area** (☎ 707-445-3309) is open to the public, with access from Peninsula Drive. Friends of the Dunes offer guided walks the second and fourth Saturday of each month, 10 am to noon, rain or shine, and restoration workdays on the third Saturday. Friends of the Dunes also offers special seasonal walks; call for recorded information.

NORTH COAST

Azalea State Reserve (☎ 707-445-6547) is on Hwy 200, 1 mile east of Hwy 101, about 3 miles north of Arcata. It's lovely when the azaleas bloom, usually from around late April to late May, but not so dramatic at other times.

TRINIDAD
• **population 360** • **elevation 175 feet**

About 12 miles north of Arcata, this attractive, affluent little historic town on Trinidad Bay looks freshly painted and well cared for. Attractions here include hiking on Trinidad Head and the beautiful Trinidad State Beach, surfing on Luffenholtz Beach, visiting the museum and old lighthouse and just strolling around.

The town and bay have a long history. Originally settled by Tsurai Indians, Trinidad Bay was discovered by European explorers several times, beginning in 1595. The Spanish sea captains Hezeta and Bodega anchored here on June 9, 1775, and named the bay 'La Santisima Trinidad' (the Holy Trinity), placing a monument to the Spanish king on Trinidad Head where the white granite cross is today. But it wasn't until the 1850s that Trinidad became the site of a booming settlement, after Josiah Gregg and seven companions tramped over the mountains from the Klamath and Trinity gold fields in 1849. Searching for a convenient sea transport link to the mining regions, they rediscovered the bay and went on to rediscover Humboldt Bay as well.

Like Eureka and Arcata, Trinidad became an important base and supply port for the inland gold fields, with schooners bringing supplies up from San Francisco and returning with redwood lumber from the north coast forests.

Orientation & Information

The town is small and it's easy to get your bearings. Taking the Trinidad exit from Hwy 101 brings you to the town's major intersection, the corner of Main St, Patrick's Point Drive and Scenic Drive, where an information kiosk is stocked with free town maps and tourist brochures. The *Discover Trinidad* brochure has a good town map showing hiking trails on Trinidad Head and Trinidad State Beach.

From this corner, Patrick's Point Drive heads north along coastal bluffs past motels, campgrounds and B&Bs to Patrick's Point State Park. Scenic Drive heads south to Luffenholtz Beach. Or, if you go about three blocks straight ahead on Main St, you come to the entrance to Trinidad State Park.

The Trinidad Chamber of Commerce (☎ 707-441-9827) does not have a staffed office, but you can phone for information about the town.

Things to See & Do

Several attractive hiking trails are at **Trinidad State Beach** and **Trinidad Head**; the free town map from the information kiosk shows where they are. The state beach, on an exceptionally beautiful cove, has picnic areas and is for day-use only. The Trinidad Head Trail, with a fine view of the coastline and excellent whale watching in season, starts from the parking lot at the base of the head.

The **Trinidad Memorial Lighthouse** is at the corner of Trinity and Edwards Sts, on a bluff overlooking Trinidad Bay.

Half a block inland from the lighthouse, the **Trinidad Museum** (☎ 707-677-3883), 529-B Trinity St, has exhibits on the area's natural and human history. It's open May to September on Friday, Saturday and Sunday noon to 3 pm. The **Humboldt State University Marine Laboratory** (☎ 707-826-3671), two blocks farther down Edwards St toward Trinidad Head, has a touch tank, several aquariums, a giant whale jaw, a three-dimensional map of the ocean floor off the coast, and other displays. It's open 9 am to 5 pm weekdays year round, plus 10 am to 5 pm weekends when school is in session.

Scenic Drive, which indeed provides a very scenic drive along the coastal bluffs, passes several tiny coves with a view back toward Trinidad Bay for 2 miles before opening onto the long, broad expanse of **Luffenholtz Beach**, which farther south is called Little River State Beach and then Clam Beach County Park. The long, regular waves at Luffenholtz Beach make it a popular surfing beach; there's also surfing at

Trinidad State Beach. North of town, along Patrick's Point Drive, you can see and hear California sea lions barking on the rocks just offshore.

Trinidad is famous for its good fishing, both from the shore and by boat. Sportfishing trips can be arranged through Bob's Boat Basin & Gift Shop (☎ 707-677-3625), Salty's Sporting Goods (☎ 707-677-3874), Shenandoah Charters (☎ 707-677-3344) and Trinidad Bay Charters (☎ 707-839-4743, 800-839-4744). The harbor is at the bottom of Edwards St, at the foot of Trinidad Head.

Places to Stay
Camping & Cottages Five miles north of town, Patrick's Point State Park is excellent for camping (see the Patrick's Point State Park section). On Patrick's Point Drive, heading north from town along the coast, are several campgrounds and lodgings. The **Emerald Forest** (☎ 707-677-3554, 753 Patrick's Point Drive) has tent/RV sites for $18/23 and rustic cabins for $59 to $150, cheaper in winter. **Viewcrest Lodge** (☎ 707-677-3393, 3415 Patrick's Point Drive) has tent/RV sites for $14/20, and nine cottages for $65 to $120. Closer in, the **Hidden Creek RV Park** (☎ 707-677-3775, 199 N Westhaven Drive), just east of Hwy 101 at the Trinidad exit, has tent/RV sites for $12/19.

The **Bishop Pine Lodge** (☎ 707-677-3314, 1481 Patrick's Point Drive) is a peaceful, old-fashioned place with 13 cottages starting at $60/50 in summer/winter, $8 more with kitchen; medium-size cottages with two queen-size beds start at $70/60; rooms in a duplex building with shared outdoor Jacuzzi are $80 year round; and two two-bedroom cottages are $86 and $95 ($10 less off-season).

Motels The **Trinidad Inn** (☎ 707-677-3349, 1170 Patrick's Point Drive) has rooms for $60 to $110 (winter $45 to $95), with kitchens available on request. The **Sea Cliffe Motel** (☎ 707-677-3485, 1895 Patrick's Point Drive) has three rooms, two with kitchen, for $44/46. **Patrick's Point Inn** (☎ 707-677-3483, 3602 Patrick's Point Drive), has 10 rooms for $50 to $80 in summer, $40 to $60 in winter.

B&Bs Trinidad has three excellent B&Bs. Right in town, overlooking the harbor and Trinidad Head, the **Trinidad Bay B&B** (☎ 707-677-0840, 560 Edwards St) has four rooms in an attractive Cape Cod-style home for $125 to $155. The **Lost Whale Inn** (☎ 707-677-3425, 800-677-7859, 3452 Patrick's Point Drive) has eight rooms, five with ocean view, for $140 to $170 in summer (winter $30 less). Trinidad's newest B&B, the **Turtle Rocks Oceanfront Inn** (☎ 707-677-3707, 3392 Patrick's Point Drive) has three ocean-front acres, with a sea lion colony on the Turtle Rocks just offshore; spacious rooms with glass-paneled decks and spectacular ocean views are $90 up to $180 for a two-room suite.

Places to Eat
At the harbor, the **Seascape Restaurant** (☎ 707-677-3762), specializing in seafood, is open 7 am to 8:30 pm daily. In town, the **Trinidad Bay Eatery & Gallery** (☎ 707-677-3777), at the corner of Trinity and Parker Sts, is pleasant for breakfast and lunch.

The **Larrupin' Cafe** (☎ 707-677-0230, 1658 Patrick's Point Drive), north of town, is Trinidad's most famous restaurant; people drive from miles around to dine here. The ambience is comfortable and the varied international menu features many savory mesquite-grilled specialties. Dinners cost $17 to $22. The cafe is open for dinner 5 to 9 pm Thursday to Monday, and reservations are recommended.

On Luffenholtz Beach, about 2 miles south of town, **Merryman's** (☎ 707-677-3111, 100 Moonstone Beach Rd), is a popular, upscale restaurant right on the beach, with great sunset views. Dinners cost $17 to $25.

Getting There & Away
Trinidad is served by Redwood Transit System buses; see the Eureka Getting There & Around section for information.

PATRICK'S POINT STATE PARK
Patrick's Point State Park (☎ 707-677-3570), 4150 Patrick's Point Drive, is a beautiful 640-acre park on a coastal bluff jutting out into the Pacific.

NORTH COAST

The park's many features include the long, broad Agate Beach, where people collect sea-polished agates on the sand; the Rim Trail, a 2-mile walk along the bluffs all around the edge of the point, with access to several rocky outcrops excellent for whale watching in season; a nature trail and several other hiking trails, some on and around unusual rock formations, including Ceremonial Rock and Lookout Rock; extensive tidepools at Palmer's Point, Abalone Point and Agate Beach; a native plant garden; and colonies of seals and sea lions. Also very interesting is Sumeg, a replica of a traditional Yurok Indian village, with traditional-style Yurok buildings of hand-hewn redwood, where Native Americans gather to hold traditional ceremonies; you are welcome to walk around the village and to enter the buildings.

The park has three campgrounds, all with hot showers and attractive, secluded sites. The *Abalone Campground* and the *Penn Creek Campground* are sheltered under trees, while the *Agate Campground*, overlooking Agate Beach, has sites open to the sun. Parknet (☎ 800-444-7275) offers reservations May through September, when sites are $16; the rest of the year sites are $12, first-come, first-served. Day-use is $5.

HUMBOLDT LAGOONS STATE PARK

Humboldt Lagoons State Park (☎ 707-488-2041) stretches for miles along the coast, with long sandy beaches and two large coastal lagoons – Big Lagoon and Stone Lagoon – both excellent for bird watching. Outside the park on the north end, about a mile north of the Stone Lagoon Visitor Center, Freshwater Lagoon is also good for birding. The Stone Lagoon Visitor Center on Hwy 101 opens seasonally, usually May to September, when there are volunteers.

The park operates two environmental campgrounds: *Stone Lagoon*, with six boat-in environmental campsites, and *Dry Lagoon*, with six environmental campsites, all $7 per site, first-come, first-served. *Humboldt County Parks* (☎ 707-445-7651) operates a drive-in campground in a cypress grove beside Big Lagoon; campsites with flush toilets and cold water, but no showers, are $11 and first-come, first-served.

ORICK
• population 340 • elevation 34 feet

This tiny town is unremarkable in itself, but the Redwood National & State Parks Information Center here is a highly recommended stop if you're heading north. Some of the parks' most attractive features, including Lady Bird Johnson Grove, Tall Trees Grove and Fern Canyon, are near Orick.

The Redwood National & State Parks Information Center (☎ 707-822-7611 ext 5265) beside the beach on Hwy 101 a mile south of town, is the best source of maps and information about the parks; pick up your free permit here to visit Tall Trees Grove in Redwood National Park. It's open 9 am to 5 pm daily.

Two miles north of town, *Rolf's Park Cafe* (☎ *707-488-3841*), Hwy 101 at the corner of Davison Rd, the turnoff for Fern Canyon, is operated by a German chef, Rolf Rheinschmidt, and his sons Stefan and Gerry. People travel far out of their way to come and eat here; the food is magnificent, with a menu encompassing many unusual ingredients, including elk, buffalo and wild boar, plus a wide variety of German and seafood dishes, with generous portions and interesting selections for all meals. Breakfasts are around $6 to $8; lunches are $7 to $9; dinners are around $14 to $16. Their specialty meats are available at all meals and cost a bit more. Their winter break is from December 1 to March 15. *Rolf's* also operates eight motel rooms, with singles/doubles for $33/43; contact Rolf's Park Cafe for information.

REDWOOD NATIONAL PARK
Special attractions of this 177-sq-mile park include the Lady Bird Johnson Grove and Tall Trees Grove.

The **Lady Bird Johnson Grove**, where this national park was dedicated, features an easy 1-mile loop trail. To get to the grove, turn east off Hwy 101 onto Bald Hills Rd and go 2½ miles.

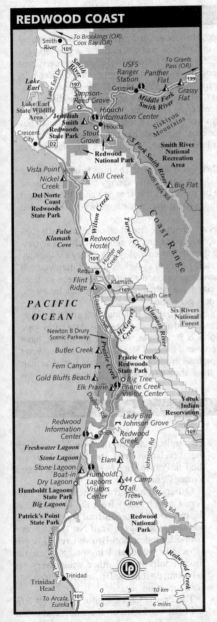

REDWOOD COAST

To Brookings (OR),
Coos Bay (OR)

Smith
River

101

Lake
Earl Dr

Smith River

USFS
Ranger
Station

Panther
Flat

To Grants
Pass (OR)

199

Lake
Earl

197

Simpson-
Reed Grove

Gasquet

Middle Fork
Smith River

Grassy
Flat

Lake Earl
State Wildlife
Area

Jedediah
Smith
Redwoods
State Park

Hiouchi
Information Center

Hiouchi

Stout
Grove

Siskiyou
Mountains

Crescent
City

D2

Redwood
National Park

S Fork Smith River

Smith River
National
Recreation
Area

Vista Point

Nickel
Creek

Mill Creek

Del Norte
Coast
Redwoods
State Park

South Fork Rd

Big Flat

Wilson Creek

False
Klamath
Cove

Redwood
Hostel

Turwar Creek

Coast Range

Requa

101

Flint
Ridge

Hunter Creek Rd

Klamath

169

Klamath Glen

PACIFIC
OCEAN

Coastal Drive

McGarvey Creek

Klamath River

Six Rivers
National
Forest

Newton B Drury
Scenic Parkway

Butler Creek

Fern Canyon

Gold Bluffs Beach

Elk Prairie

Prairie Creek

Davison Rd

Prairie Creek
Redwoods
State Park

Big Tree

Prairie Creek
Visitor Center

Yurok
Indian
Reservation

Redwood
Information
Center

Orick

Lady Bird
Johnson Grove

Redwood
Creek

169

Johnson Rd

Freshwater Lagoon

Stone Lagoon

Elam

Stone Lagoon
Boat-in

Dry Lagoon

Humboldt
Lagoons
State Park

Big Lagoon

Patrick's Point
State Park

Humboldt
Lagoons
Visitors
Center

44 Camp

Tall
Trees
Grove

Bald Hills Rd

Redwood
National
Park

Patrick's Point Dr

Redwood Creek

Trinidad
Head

Trinidad

101

To Arcata,
Eureka

0   5   10 km

0   3   6 miles

Farther along on Bald Hills Rd, **Tall Trees Grove** is a remarkable redwood grove, home to several of the world's tallest trees. Only 50 vehicles are allowed to visit the grove each day; pick up a free permit from the park information center in Orick.

Several long hiking trails, including the beautiful 8.2-mile **Redwood Creek Trail**, also allow access to Tall Trees Grove. A free backcountry permit, available at the park visitor center, is required to hike this trail, and it can only be done from Memorial Day to Labor Day, when summer footbridges are in place; outside this season, the bridges are down and water levels fluctuate. You can also come on horseback; ask at the visitor center for information. The center also has details on many other good trails in the park.

Primitive camping is allowed all along Redwood Creek, from 1 mile up the trail all the way to the park boundary; camping is in the creekbed, on the gravel. Limited primitive camping is also available elsewhere in the park; check with rangers for details. Camping along Redwood Creek requires a free backcountry permit, available from the park information center in Orick.

PRAIRIE CREEK REDWOODS STATE PARK

This 23-sq-mile park features the beautiful Fern Canyon, many miles of wild and untouched coastline and beaches, prairies with herds of large Roosevelt elk, over 70 miles of trails and some spectacular scenic drives. Day-use of the park is $5, but no fee is charged to drive through on the famous Newton B Drury Scenic Parkway.

The 8-mile **Newton B Drury Scenic Parkway**, passing through amazingly beautiful virgin redwood forests, runs parallel to Hwy 101 and is well worth taking. Along the way are many turnouts, with hiking trails branching off for endless explorations through the forest. **Big Tree**, near the south end of the parkway, is just 100 yards down a paved path from the parking area beside the road. **Cal Barrel Rd** is a popular scenic drive, intersecting the Newton B Drury Scenic Parkway about a quarter mile south of Big Tree; it's 3 miles to the end of the road. Other

The Tallest Trees on Earth

Though they once covered much of the Northern Hemisphere, today redwood trees grow only in three small areas of the world, two of them in California and one in China, with a separate and unique species growing in each of these places. Coast redwoods (Sequoia sempervirens) are found in a narrow 450-mile-long strip along the Pacific coast from central California to southern Oregon. They can live up to 2200 years, grow to 367.8 feet tall (the tallest tree ever recorded) and achieve a diameter of 22 feet at the base, with bark up to 12 inches thick.

Unlike most trees, which have a deep taproot, coast redwoods have no taproot and their root system is shallow in relation to their height – only 10 to 13 feet deep and spreading out 60 to 80 feet around the tree. The structure of coast redwoods has been compared to a nail standing on its head. The trees sometimes fall due to wind, but they are very flexible and sway in the wind as if they're dancing.

Redwood trees are named for the color of their wood and bark. The high tannin content of their wood makes it resistant to insects and disease; the thick, spongy bark is even more resistant and has a high moisture content. The bark insulates the trees and gives them a great resistance not only to insects and disease but also to fire; ancient redwoods have lived through many naturally occurring forest fires.

Cones growing on the ends of the branches are about the size of an olive, and each contains up to 50 or 60 seeds. Coast redwoods reproduce not only by seed, but also by sprouting from their parents' roots and stumps, using the established root systems; they are the only coniferous trees in the world that can reproduce by sprouts as well as seeds. Often you will see a circle of redwoods standing in a forest, sometimes around a wide crater; these are trees that sprouted from one parent tree, which may have deteriorated into humus long ago, leaving the ring of trees standing to form the next generation.

Four parks, all with spectacular redwood forests – Redwood National Park and the Prairie Creek Redwoods, Del Norte Coast Redwoods and Jedediah Smith Redwoods state parks – are managed cooperatively as the Redwood National & State Parks. Together these parks have been declared an International Biosphere Reserve and a World Heritage Site. The Redwood National Park Trail Guide pamphlet shows hiking trails in all four parks and has a general map and information about each trail. Each of the three state parks also has its own information center with more detailed maps.

scenic drives in the park include the **Coastal Drive** heading past **Gold Bluffs Beach** to **Fern Canyon**, an enchanting canyon with sheer 60-foot-high walls covered with several species of ferns. An easy half-mile loop trail takes you through the canyon and up into the redwoods. Fern Canyon is right beside the beach, about 1½ miles north of the Gold Bluffs Beach Campground. To reach Fern Canyon, turn west from Hwy 101 onto Davison Rd, follow a gravel road for 4 miles until you reach the beach, then go another 4 miles north along the beach road.

This park has 28 hiking trails, ranging from very easy to strenuous. Several short,

easy trails, including the Five-Minute Trail, the Revelation Trail, the Nature Trail and the Elk Prairie Trail, begin at the Elk Prairie Visitor Center.

Other notable trails include the easy Fern Canyon Loop Trail, the Coastal Trail, the moderate Ossagon Trail and the strenuous half-mile Zigzag Trail No 1. The South Fork-Rhododendron-Brown Creek Loop is especially wonderful in spring when the rhododendrons and other wildflowers are in bloom; do it in the Brown Creek to South Fork direction.

The Prairie Creek Visitor Center (☎ 707-464-6101 ext 5300), on the south end of the

Newton B Drury Scenic Parkway, 6 miles north of Orick, is usually open 9 am to 5 pm daily.

The park has two developed campgrounds, two backcountry campsites ($3 per person) and one environmental campsite ($7 per site). *Elk Prairie*, an attractive developed campground with hot showers, is in the redwoods beside Elk Prairie, where herds of Roosevelt elk are often seen, just off the south end of the Newton B Drury Scenic Parkway. From May through September, campsites are $16 and reservations are possible through Parknet (☎ 800-444-7275); the rest of the year, the campsites are $12, first-come, first-served.

Gold Bluffs Beach, the other developed campground with hot showers, is on the beach about 1½ miles south of Fern Canyon. The campsites are open and exposed, but windbreaks have been erected around many of the sites. Prices are the same as at Elk Prairie; campsites are first-come, first-served year round.

KLAMATH
• **population 1420** • **elevation 28 feet**

Besides the Klamath River, the town of Klamath's most noticeable landmark is the giant statue of Paul Bunyan and Babe the Blue Ox towering over the parking area at the entrance to the **Trees of Mystery** (☎ 707-482-2251, 800-638-3389), on Hwy 101, 5 miles north of the Klamath River Bridge. The featured attraction is a 30- to 45-minute walk along a trail passing a number of unusual trees, redwood carvings and other oddities; $6.50/4 adults/children.

The **End of the Trail Museum**, in a separate section of the Trees of Mystery complex, is an outstanding museum of Native American arts, crafts and other artifacts, definitely worth a stop; free.

Klamath River Jet Boat Tours (☎ 707-482-7775, 800-887-5387) offers jet boat tours of the Klamath River May through October, with morning, afternoon, lunch and dinner trips. The trip is fully narrated, with plenty of stops for photos of the remarkable views and the abundant wildlife, including bears, elk, deer, otters, mink, eagles, osprey and

hawks, and seals and sea lions at the river mouth.

Klamath has a drive-through tree, called the **Tour-Thru Tree**, 400 yards off the highway. Access to the tree is during daylight hours and it costs $2 to drive through. This is one of several such trees along Hwy 101.

Various hiking trails and scenic drives in the Klamath area wind through Redwood National & State Parks; the park map shows where they are.

Fishing is good in the Klamath River. The Salmon Festival in August, with a salmon barbecue and traditional Yurok arts, crafts and dances, is hosted by the Yurok Indians and is Klamath's major event of the year. The Klamath River Jet Boat Marathon is held in June. The Klamath Chamber of Commerce (☎ 800-200-2335) has information on attractions and events in Klamath.

Places to Stay
Camping & Cabins Klamath has about 16 private campgrounds and RV parks, some with cabins. The *Mystic Forest RV Park* (☎ 707-482-4901, 15875 Hwy 101), about ¾ mile south of the Trees of Mystery, has hot showers, spa, swimming pool, recreation room and tent/RV spaces for $14/16. The *Chinook RV Resort* (☎ 707-482-3511, 17465 Hwy 101), 1½ miles north of the Klamath River Bridge, has tent/RV spaces for $17.

Camp Marigold (☎ 707-482-3585, 800-621-8513, 16101 Hwy 101), 4 miles north of the Klamath Bridge, is a charming, relaxed, old-fashioned little resort with camping, cabins with kitchens and a six-bedroom lodge. Tent/RV spaces are $10/15, with hot showers and full hookups available. Cabins are $42 to $72, cheaper off-season or weekly; lodge rooms $165.

Riverwoods Campground (☎ 707-482-5591, 1661 W Klamath Beach Rd), on the south bank of the Klamath River, 2 miles west of Hwy 101, is bordered by Redwood National Park on three sides and by the Klamath River on the fourth side; tent/RV sites are $12/16.

Hostels The HI *Redwood Hostel* (☎ 707-482-8265, 14480 Hwy 101), about 7 miles

Humanity vs the Redwood

In the past 150 years, what nature hadn't already done to reduce the range of the coast redwood, humans have done. California's gold rush of the 1850s is well known; less well known is the similar 'timber rush' that was going on at the same time on the North Coast. The ancient redwood forests were decimated for lumber to build California's new settlements, including San Francisco.

Timber continues to be the primary industry on the North Coast, though it's been drastically reduced in recent times. Most of the ancient forests are gone now; those that remain are largely found in state and national parks; only about 6000 acres of unprotected old-growth redwood forest remains. Conflict between environmentalists and loggers continues to rage on the North Coast. In 1918, the Save-the-Redwoods League began working to preserve the last remnants of the old-growth redwood forests for future generations, buying old-growth groves from the lumber companies and dedicating them as state and national parks and reserves. Today, the league (☎ 415-362-2352, www.savetheredwoods.org), 114 Sansome St, Room 605, San Francisco, CA 94104, is still working to protect the last remaining virgin redwood forests. Other groups also work to protect the great trees; the Save-the-Redwoods League has information about such groups.

north of Klamath, is in the large, historic DeMartin House on the coast overlooking the beautiful False Klamath Cove. It adjoins a couple of fine hiking trails, including the Coast Trail and the Redwood Hostel Trail. Bunks in separate-sex dorm rooms are $12 to $14 a night; reservations are advised, as it's very popular. Check-in is 7:30 to 9:30 am and 4:30 to 9:30 pm. The hostel is closed from 9:30 am to 4:30 pm; there's an 11 pm curfew.

Motels On Hwy 101, opposite the Trees of Mystery, *Motel Trees* (☎ 707-482-3152) has a tennis court, restaurant and 23 rooms for $44/48 single/double (winter $35).

The *Klamath Inn* (☎ 707-482-1425, 451 Requa Rd), west of Hwy 101 on the north bank of the Klamath River, is a renowned country inn with an eventful history. Built in 1885 as a town hotel, the Klamath Inn, and the majority of the town, burned down in 1913; most of the town, including the inn, was rebuilt in 1914.

Originally there were other buildings around it, but over the years, something or other happened to all the other buildings – fires, floods, etc. But this one building has survived; it's still there on the bank of the Klamath River, about a mile in from the ocean and has a beautiful view of the river. Its 10 rooms are $59 to $95, including breakfast.

Places to Eat

The restaurant at the *Klamath Inn* (☎ 707-482-1425, 451 Requa Rd) is a local favorite. It's open for dinner nightly (in winter, dinner and lodging by reservation); reservations recommended.

The *Forest Cafe* (☎ 707-482-5585, 15499 Hwy 101 S), beside Motel Trees, is open every day and is moderately priced: breakfast and lunch are around $5 to $10, dinner around $7 to $17.

DEL NORTE COAST REDWOODS STATE PARK

This 7000-acre park contains beautiful redwood groves and 8 miles of unspoiled coastline. Over 30 miles of hiking trails range from a half mile to 20 miles in length, and in difficulty from easy to strenuous. **Enderts Beach** on the north end of the park, accessible from Enderts Beach Rd or the Last Chance/Coastal Trail, has magnificent tidepools at low tide, as does **Hidden Beach**, about 2 miles south of False Klamath Cove, accessible by the Coastal Trail or the Hidden Beach Trail.

Maps and information about the park are available at the Redwood National & State Parks Headquarters in Crescent City and at the Redwood National & State Parks Information Center in Orick.

Mill Creek Campground (☎ 707-464-6101 ext 5112), a developed campground with hot showers and 145 campsites, is in a redwood grove 2-1/2 miles east of Hwy 101; the turnoff is about 7 miles south of Crescent City. The campground is normally open from May through September; campsites are $16 from Memorial Day to Labor Day, when reservations are accepted through Parknet (☎ 800-444-7275), and $12 on a first-come, first-served basis the rest of the year. The park also has a couple of hike/bike campgrounds ($3 per person). Day-use fee is $5.

CRESCENT CITY
• population 8800 • elevation 44 feet

On a crescent-shaped bay, Crescent City is the only sizable coastal town north of Arcata. Although Crescent City has been here since 1853, when it was founded as a port and supply center for inland gold mines, it has very few old buildings, as over half the town was destroyed by a tsunami (tidal wave) in 1964. The town has been rebuilt, and it's a pleasant enough place when the sun is shining. Like the rest of the North Coast, however, Crescent City is often socked in by fog in the summer and is cold and wet in winter, with about 100 inches of

Crescent City's Great Tsunami

On March 28, 1964, most of downtown Crescent City was destroyed by a great tidal wave or, more accurately, a tsunami. Here's how it happened.

At 3:36 am a giant earthquake – at 8.5 on the Richter scale, the most severe earthquake ever recorded in North America – occurred in Alaska on the north shore of Prince William Sound. The first of the giant ocean swells created by the earthquake reached Crescent City a few hours later. Altogether there were four waves, each higher than the last. The swells were so huge that they did not crest and break like ordinary waves on the shore; when each wave came, it simply seemed as if the level of the entire ocean were rising.

The third wave came almost up into the town. By this time, residents were awake, had heard about the Alaska earthquake and were fearful of what might happen. When the third wave receded, some residents rejoiced, thinking the danger was over. Then a very eerie thing happened: the water in the bay receded until the entire bay was empty of water, leaving boats that had been anchored offshore sitting in the mud.

When the fourth wave surged in, the frigid water rose all the way up to 5th St, knocking buildings off their foundations, carrying away cars, trucks and anything that wasn't bolted down, and even a lot of things that were. Many residents stayed in their houses as they floated off their foundations, adrift.

By the time the fourth wave receded, it had destroyed 29 blocks of the town, damaging or displacing more than 300 buildings. Five bulk gasoline storage tanks exploded; 11 people were killed and three were never found.

In the wake of the tsunami, the townspeople came together to help one another, and aid poured in. Many old-timers are still remembered for their heroic acts during and after the wave, helping to save their neighbors and to rebuild the town.

Today, you can still see the effects of the tsunami that changed the town forever. In odd places, you may come upon a giant piling weighing several tons, which had washed up onto land and was never removed.

This is why, although Crescent City is a historic town, there are virtually no historic buildings to be seen here. The waterfront is now a broad, grassy expanse of park. And the modern little downtown shopping center, built to replace some of the town's old businesses, has an unusual but very appropriate name – Tsunami Landing.

rain falling annually. Fishing, including shrimp and crab, and the Pelican Bay maximum security prison just outside town are the town's main economic bases.

Orientation & Information

It's virtually impossible to get lost in Crescent City's small 'downtown' area. Hwy 101 passes along the east side of town, with southbound traffic on L St and northbound traffic on M St. The tiny commercial area is centered along 3rd St.

The Crescent City-Del Norte County Chamber of Commerce (☎ 707-464-3174, 800-343-8300), 1001 Front St, has free town maps and plenty of information on the surrounding areas. In summer it's open 9 am to 7 pm weekdays, 9 am to 5 pm weekends; it's open 9 am to 6 pm weekdays only the rest of the year.

The Redwood National & State Parks Headquarters (☎ 707-464-6101), 1111 2nd St, at the corner of K St, has free maps and information about all four parks under its jurisdiction. It's open 9 am to 5 pm daily.

Things to See & Do

The 1856 **Battery Point Lighthouse** (☎ 707-464-3089), at the south end of A St, is still in operation on a tiny, picturesque little offshore island, which you can easily walk to at low tide. From April through September, the lighthouse is open as a museum, with tours for $2; hours vary, depending on tides, so phone for schedule.

The **Del Norte Historical Society Museum** (☎ 707-464-3922), 577 H St at 6th St, has historical exhibits that include a fine collection of local Tolowa and Yurok Indian artifacts, exhibits on Del Norte County's pioneer past, the '64 tsunami and a giant lens from St George Reef lighthouse. It's open 10 am to 4 pm Monday to Saturday May through September; $2.

Ocean World (☎ 707-464-3522), 304 Hwy 101 S, on the south side of town, is a small aquarium, and not nearly as impressive as some of California's huge coastal aquariums. But if you're not jaded by visits to more lavish aquariums, a stop here is very enjoyable. The friendly staff takes you on an informative 45-minute guided tour, explaining all about the local marine life. The tour is followed by a sea lion show. There's also a great gift shop. In summer, the aquarium is open 8 am to 8 pm daily; it's open 9 am to 5 pm daily in winter; $6.

You can see cheese being made at the **Rumiano Cheese Company** (☎ 707-465-1535), at the corner of 9th and E Sts. There's a cheese-tasting room, too. In summer, it's open 8:30 am to 4 pm weekdays, 8:30 am to noon Saturday. Winter hours are 8:30 am to 3:30 pm weekdays.

Special Events

Special events in and near Crescent City include the World Championship Crab Races the third weekend in February; the Easter Seals Charity Ball in March; the State of Jefferson Championships in April; the Coastal Aires Cabaret in May; the Crescent City Bay Blues Festival in early June; the Gasquet Raft Races in July; the Del Norte County Fair in August; and Drums on the Beach in September. The Sea Cruise Classic Car Show features over 50 classes of car-show competition, plus music, dance, food and brews, the first weekend in October. The Christmas Light Parade and Tree Lighting takes place in late November.

Places to Stay

Camping State parks near Crescent City have plenty of good camping; see their separate sections.

Del Norte County (☎ 707-464-7230) operates three campgrounds, all with running water and flush toilets, but no showers; reservations are accepted. The nearest to Crescent City, *Florence Keller Park*, has camping and picnic areas in a beautiful redwood grove, with campsites for $10. To get there, take Hwy 101 north from town for 3 miles; take the Elk Valley crossroad, turn left (west) and follow the signs. *Ruby VanDeventer* campground, in a redwood grove on the Smith River, is on Hwy 197, 5 miles east of Hwy 101, about 12 miles northeast of Crescent City and 5 miles west of Jedediah Smith State Park; campsites $10. *Clifford Kamph Memorial Park*, a small campground for tents only, is on the beach, 2 miles south of the Oregon border; campsites are $5.

Five miles north of town, the **Crescent City Redwoods KOA** (☎ 707-464-5744, 800-562-5754, 4241 Hwy 101 N) is a 21-acre campground with 10 acres of redwoods and many amenities, including hot showers, laundry, recreation areas, nature trails and more. Summer/winter rates are $20/17 for tents, $25/22 for RVs, $37/32 for one-room 'kamping kabins' and $44/39 for two-room 'kamping kabins.' It's often closed in January and February.

Motels A great many motels line Hwy 101, often with lots of highway noise.

Half a mile south of town, the **Curly Redwood Lodge** (☎ 707-464-2137, 701 Hwy 101 S) is a pleasant, comfortable older motel opposite the harbor, with covered parking and large, attractive rooms for $60/37 in summer/winter. The entire motel was built from the lumber of just one curly redwood tree; a brochure at the desk tells the story. Next door, the **Super 8 Motel** (☎ 707-464-4111, 685 Hwy 101 S) has rooms for $69/44 in summer/winter. It's not as attractive as the Curly Redwood Lodge, but some of the rooms face away from the highway.

The **Crescent Beach Motel** (☎ 707-464-5436, 1455 Hwy 101 S), 2 miles south of town on a pleasant stretch of beach, has 27 rooms, most with ocean views and patios, for $69/47 in summer/winter. Also south of town, the **Bay View Inn** (☎ 707-465-2050, 800-446-0583, 310 Hwy 101 S) has pleasant rooms for $59/45.

B&Bs The **Lighthouse Cove B&B** (☎ 707-465-6565, 215 S A St) near the Battery Point Lighthouse, has a suite for $120 (continental breakfast) or $135 (full breakfast), with a glassed-in oceanfront sitting room and spacious outdoor deck overlooking the sea.

Places to Eat

Glen's Restaurant & Bakery (☎ 707-464-2914, 722 3rd St) is a bright and cheerful place for an inexpensive breakfast, lunch or early dinner. Old-fashioned and friendly, this is one of the town's longtime favorites. From

October 1947, it was situated at 1238 2nd St until 1964. when the '64 tidal wave moved it to its present location. It's open 5 am to 6:30 pm Tuesday to Saturday.

On the north side of town, at the corner of Hwy 101 and Northcrest Drive, the **Good Harvest Espresso Bar & Cafe** (☎ 707-465-6028, 700 Northcrest Drive, No A) has slightly higher prices. It is known for its good, healthy food; open for breakfast and lunch.

The **Jefferson State Brewery** (☎ 707-464-1139, 400 Front St) has a pleasant medium-priced restaurant serving delicious foods, including vegetarian pannini sandwiches, penne al pesto pasta, fresh salmon, fish-and-chips and traditional French onion soup. They brew six styles of beer, plus homemade nonalcoholic ginger beer and root beer, and serve the best wine-by-the-glass of any restaurant in town. It's open 11 am to 11 pm daily; free brewery tours are offered each Saturday at 6 pm.

The **Da Lucciana Ristorante Italiano** (☎ 707-465-6566, 575 Hwy 101 S) is a favorite with locals for seafood, steaks and Italian food. Dinner entrées are around $15. Half a mile south of town and one block west of Hwy 101, the **Harbor View Grotto** (☎ 707-464-3815), at the corner of Citizens Dock Rd and Starfish Way (follow the signs from Hwy 101), with a harbor and beach view, is popular for seafood, steak, prime rib and simpler fare.

Thai food aficionados rave about the **Sea West Thai Restaurant** (☎ 707-487-1573, 6655 Lake Earl Drive), in Fort Dick, a small town about 11 miles north of Crescent City. From the outside, the Sea West looks like just an average restaurant, but the food is superb. Most dishes are around $6 to $7. It's open for dinner only. Thai food is served Tuesday to Saturday nights, Monday night it's American food; closed Sunday.

Getting There & Away

North of town, the small Crescent City airport is served by United Express (☎ 800-241-6522).

The Greyhound bus station (☎ 707-464-2807), 500 E Harding Ave, just east of Northcrest Drive about a mile north of the downtown area, has two northbound and two southbound buses daily. Locally, Redwood Coast Transit (☎ 707-464-9314, 707-464-4314) operates a bus route between Crescent City, Klamath and Redwood National Park, with many stops along the way. The bus makes two runs a day, Monday to Saturday.

Car rental companies in Crescent City include U-Save Auto Rental (☎ 707-464-7813) and Coast Auto Center (☎ 707-464-8344).

JEDEDIAH SMITH REDWOODS STATE PARK

On Hwy 199, about 10 miles northeast of Crescent City, Jedediah Smith Redwoods is the northernmost of California's redwood state parks. A few miles inland, at the confluence of the Smith River and Mill Creek, the park is often sunny in summer, when Crescent City is foggy.

There's a lovely picnic area on the bank of the Smith River, near the campground (see Places to Stay in this section) and a fine swimming hole; the easy ½ mile **Stout Grove Trail**, departing from the other side of the campground and crossing the river over a summer footbridge, takes you to **Stout Grove**, the park's most famous redwood grove. Several other trails can also be started near the campground and picnic area. Altogether the park has 19 hiking trails, ranging in length from a half mile to 8 miles, and in difficulty from easy to strenuous.

Hiouchi, on Hwy 199 about a mile east of the park, is a useful stop for campers. Lunker Fish Trips (☎ 707-458-4704, 800-248-4704), 2095 Hwy 199 in Hiouchi, rents inner tubes, rafts and inflatable kayaks and mountain bikes in summer. In fall, winter and spring they offer guided wilderness and fishing trips for salmon, steelhead and cutthroat trout on the Smith, Eel, Klamath and Mattole rivers (all 'big fish' rivers).

Maps and information about the park are available at the Hiouchi Information Center (☎ 707-464-6101 ext 5112) in Hiouchi, about 5 miles east of Hwy 101; it's open 9 am to 5 pm daily May through October. The center has historic photos and a Tolowa Indian

canoe. Jedediah Smith State Park Visitor Center (☎ 707-464-6101 ext 5112), at the campground, is open 9 am to 5 pm daily in summer; the rest of the year it's open by request. Information and maps are also available at the Redwood National & State Parks Headquarters (☎ 707-464-6101), 1111 2nd St, in Crescent City. Day-use is $5 per vehicle.

Places to Stay

Within the park, the *Jedediah Smith Campground*, in a beautiful redwood grove beside the Smith River on Hwy 199, about 5 miles east of Hwy 101, is a developed campground with hot showers and 107 campsites. Campsites are $16 May through September, when reservations are made through Parknet (☎ 800-444-7275); the rest of the year, sites are $12 and first-come, first-served.

A couple of other accommodations are available in Hiouchi. The *Hiouchi Hamlet RV Resort* (☎ 707-458-3321), opposite the Hiouchi Motel, has tent sites for $15, RV sites for $20 with full hookups. The *Hiouchi Motel* (☎ 707-458-3041, 2097 Hwy 199) has 17 rooms for $27 single, $50 and $55 double.

LAKE EARL STATE PARK

Half a mile north of Crescent City, Lake Earl State Park includes 5000 acres of wildlife habitat in a varied terrain with beaches, sand dunes, marshes and other wetlands, meadows, wooded hillsides and two lakes – Lake Earl and the smaller Lake Talawa, connected to Lake Earl by a narrow waterway.

Over 250 bird species can be seen in the wildlife area, with resident as well as migrating birds; deer, coyote, raccoons, sea lions, seals and migrating gray whales are also spotted. Cutthroat trout can be caught in the lakes. Wildflowers are a special attraction in spring and early summer. The park has about 20 miles of hiking and horseback trails, most of them level and sandy.

The Lake Earl State Park Headquarters (☎ 707-464-6101), 1375 Elk Valley Rd, has maps and information about the park, as does the Lake Earl Wildlife Area Headquarters (☎ 707-464-6101), 2591 Old Mill Rd. Free information and park maps are also available

NORTH COAST

in Crescent City at the Redwood National & State Parks Headquarters and the chamber of commerce office.

The park has two primitive **campgrounds**: a walk-in environmental campground where you must provide your own water, and a walk-in and equestrian site with non-potable water. Both are quiet and private; cost is $7 for the environmental site, $4 per horse-and-rider in the equestrian site, both first-come, first-served. To register for camping in summer, you must go to Jedediah Smith Redwoods State Park, or Del Norte Coast Redwoods State Park's Mill Creek Campground. Campfire wood is provided in summer. No day-use fee is charged for use of the park.

NORTH TO OREGON

From Crescent City, two routes go north into Oregon. Hwy 101, the Coast Highway, crosses into Oregon about 20 miles north of Crescent City and continues up the coast towards Brookings and Coos Bay.

Three miles north of Crescent City, Hwy 199 branches off from Hwy 101 and heads northeast into Oregon by an inland route towards Cave Junction and Grants Pass, where it meets I-5. On the way, Hwy 199 follows the middle fork of the Smith River, passing first through Jedediah Smith Redwoods State Park and then continuing on through the Smith River National Recreation Area. This route has been dubbed the Smith River National Scenic Byway; free brochures about the route and about the national recreation area are available from the park office on Hwy 199 at Gasquet, a few miles beyond Hiouchi.

Consult Lonely Planet's *Pacific Northwest* travel guide if you're heading up into Oregon.

NORTH COAST

Central Coast

California's Central Coast stretches from Monterey Bay to Ventura Harbor, 273 miles of unadulterated beauty clinging to the edge of the continent.

Monterey Peninsula

Spectacular coastal scenery, a colorful history as the old Spanish and Mexican capital of California, a superb aquarium and lots of money all come together on the Monterey Peninsula, which juts into the Pacific just over 100 miles south of San Francisco. Historic Monterey and easygoing Pacific Grove, on the northern tip of the peninsula, are linked by the scenic 17-Mile Drive to the wealthy little enclave of Carmel to the south. Beyond Carmel, the wild scenery of Point Lobos makes a fine introduction to the awesome Big Sur coastline.

Getting Around

Monterey-Salinas Transit (MST; ☎ 831-899-2555) operates buses around the peninsula, inland to Salinas and south to Big Sur. The whole peninsula (which includes Monterey, Pacific Grove, Pebble Beach and Carmel) counts as one zone, and a single journey costs $1.50, or $3 for a day pass. The fare from the peninsula south to Big Sur or inland to Salinas is $3. An all-zones day pass is $6.

MONTEREY BAY

Monterey Bay is one of the world's richest and most varied marine environments. It boasts a majestic coastline, famous kelp forests and a diverse range of marine life, including mammals such as sea otters, seals and sea lions, elephant seals, dolphins and whales. The protected waters of the Monterey Bay National Marine Sanctuary extend approximately 50 miles out to sea from San Simeon in the south to San Francisco in the north, where they merge into the Gulf of the Farallones National Marine Sanctuary.

Highlights

- Monterey – adobe buildings, Cannery Row, and the stunning Monterey Bay Aquarium, for close encounters of the fishy kind

- Big Sur – a coastal ribbon of velvety hillsides, rugged cliffs and vistas that touch the soul

- Hearst Castle – kitsch or cult?

- San Luis Obispo – a down-to-earth college town with a rare community spirit

- Santa Barbara – a quintessential California coastal town, relaxed, friendly and handsome, with lots of nature and history for good measure

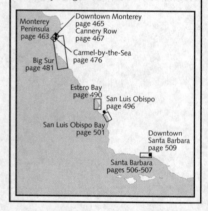

Monterey Peninsula page 463
Downtown Monterey page 465
Cannery Row page 467
Carmel-by-the-Sea page 476
Big Sur page 481
Estero Bay page 490
San Luis Obispo page 496
San Luis Obispo Bay page 501
Downtown Santa Barbara page 509
Santa Barbara pages 506-507

Starting only a few hundred yards offshore from Moss Landing, the Monterey Canyon plummets to a depth of over 10,000 feet. In summer, the upwelling currents carry cold water from this deep submarine canyon, sending a rich supply of nutrients up toward the surface level to feed the bay's diverse marine life. These frigid currents also account for the bay's generally low water temperatures and the fog that often blankets the peninsula in summer.

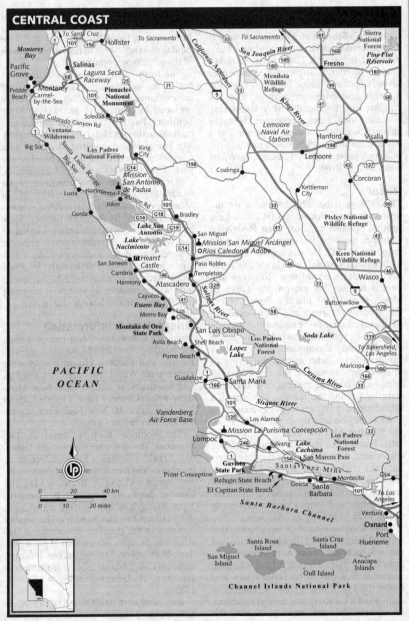

CENTRAL COAST

To Santa Cruz
Hollister
To Sacramento
To Sacramento
Sierra National Forest
Pine Flat Reservoir

Monterey Bay
Pacific Grove
Salinas
Laguna Seca Raceway
Fresno

Pebble Beach
Monterey
Carmel-by-the-Sea
Pinnacles National Monument
Mendota Wildlife Refuge

Palo Colorado Canyon Rd
Soledad
Lemoore Naval Air Station
Hanford
Visalia

Ventana Wilderness
King City
Lemoore

Big Sur
Los Padres National Forest
Corcoran

Lucia
Mission San Antonio de Padua
Coalinga
Pixley National Wildlife Refuge

Gorda
Bradley
Kettleman City
Kern National Wildlife Refuge
Wasco

Lake San Antonio
Lake Nacimiento
San Miguel
Mission San Miguel Arcángel
Rios Caledonia Adobe

San Simeon
Hearst Castle
Paso Robles
Templeton

Cambria
Harmony
Atascadero
Buttonwillow

Cayucos
Estero Bay
Morro Bay
Los Osos
Salinas River
Soda Lake
To Bakersfield, Los Angeles

Montaña de Oro State Park
San Luis Obispo
Los Padres National Forest

Avila Beach
Shell Beach
Lopez Lake
Maricopa

PACIFIC OCEAN
Pismo Beach
Guadalupe
Santa Maria
Cuyama River

Vandenberg Air Force Base
Los Alamos
Sisquoc River

Lompoc
Mission La Purísima Concepción
Solvang
Lake Cachuma
San Marcos Pass
Los Padres National Forest

Gaviota State Park
Point Conception
Santa Ynez Mtns
Ojai

Refugio State Beach
El Capitan State Beach
Goleta
Montecito
Santa Barbara
To Los Angeles

0   20   40 km
0   10   20 miles
Santa Barbara Channel
Ventura
Oxnard
Port Hueneme

Santa Rosa Island
Santa Cruz Island
Anacapa Islands

San Miguel Island
Gull Island
Channel Islands National Park

MONTEREY

- **population 30,000** • **elevation 25 feet**

California's Spanish and Mexican history is encountered elsewhere, but nowhere is evidence of the state's Latin heritage richer than in Monterey. The city has numerous lovingly restored adobe buildings from the Spanish and Mexican periods, and it's enlightening to spend a day wandering about the town's historic quarter. Monterey also offers a fine maritime museum and a world-famous aquarium, not to mention the relative tourist traps of Fisherman's Wharf and Cannery Row.

History

The Ohlone tribe, who had been on the peninsula since around 500 BC, may have spotted Spanish explorer Juan Rodríguez Cabrillo, the first European visitor, who sailed by in 1542. He was followed in 1602 by Sebastián Vizcaíno, who landed near the site of today's downtown Monterey and named it after his patron, the Duke of Monte Rey. A long hiatus followed before the Spanish returned in 1770 to establish Monterey as their first presidio in Alta California. The expedition was led by Gaspar de Portolá and accompanied by Father Junípero Serra, who started the string of Spanish missions along the coast. A year later, Serra decided to separate church and state by shifting the mission to Carmel, a safe distance from the military presence.

Monterey became the capital of Alta California after Mexico broke from Spain in 1821. Freed from the tight Spanish trading constraints, it also became a bustling international trading port where East Coast Yankees mixed with Russian fur traders and seafarers carrying exotic goods from China.

The stars and stripes were temporarily raised over Monterey in 1842 when Commodore Thomas Jones, hearing a rumor that war had been declared between Mexico and the US, took the town. A red-faced withdrawal took place a few days later when the rumor turned out to be false. When war really did break out in 1846, Commodore John Sloat's takeover was almost reluctant; he clearly did not want to repeat the mistake. The American takeover signaled an abrupt change in the town's fortunes, for San Jose soon replaced Monterey as the state capital, and the 1849 gold rush drained much of the remaining population.

The town spent 30 years as a forgotten backwater, its remaining residents eking out an existence from whaling, an industry replaced by tourism in the 1880s. After Southern Pacific Railroad entrepreneurs built the luxurious Hotel del Monte, wealthy San Franciscans discovered Monterey as a convenient getaway. The former hotel is now part of the US Navy's postgraduate school.

Around the same time, fishermen began to capitalize on the teeming marine life in Monterey Bay, and the first sardine canneries soon opened. By the 1930s, Cannery Row had made the port the 'Sardine Capital of the World,' but overfishing and climatic changes caused the industry's sudden collapse in the 1950s. Fortunately, in more recent decades, tourism came to the rescue once again; modern Monterey is an enormously popular and heavily visited city.

Orientation & Information

Monterey's downtown is a compact area surrounding Alvarado St, which ends with Portola and Custom House plazas, near Fisherman's Wharf. This area is known as Old Monterey, as distinct from New Monterey where Cannery Row is located, about a mile northwest. New Monterey segues straight into Pacific Grove.

The Monterey Visitors Center has two branches. The office at Camino El Estero and Franklin St has a huge collection of brochures and free direct-call phones to 40-plus hotels and motels. Between May and October, hours are 9 am to 6 pm daily (to 5 pm Sunday); otherwise it's 9 am to 5 pm daily (10 am to 4 pm Sunday). The smaller center is at the chamber of commerce, 380 Alvarado St, open 8:30 am to 5 pm weekdays. Both offices are for walk-in information only. A 24-hour phone information service is available by calling ☎ 831-649-1770.

Bay Books (☎ 831-375-1855), 316 Alvarado St, has a superb range of books and a

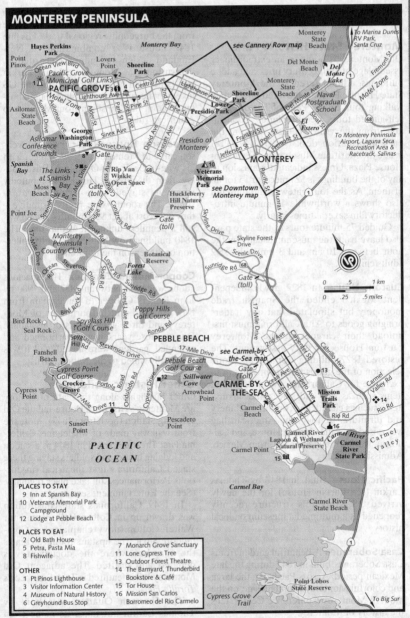

MONTEREY PENINSULA

PLACES TO STAY
9 Inn at Spanish Bay
10 Veterans Memorial Park Campground
12 Lodge at Pebble Beach

PLACES TO EAT
2 Old Bath House
5 Petra, Pasta Mia
8 Fishwife

OTHER
1 Pt Pinos Lighthouse
3 Visitor Information Center
4 Museum of Natural History
6 Greyhound Bus Stop
7 Monarch Grove Sanctuary
11 Lone Cypress Tree
13 Outdoor Forest Theatre
14 The Barnyard, Thunderbird Bookstore & Café
15 Tor House
16 Mission San Carlos Borromeo del Rio Carmelo

coffee bar. Kinko's Copies (☎ 831-373-2298) has a branch at 799 Lighthouse Ave.

Monterey State Historic Park

Old Monterey is home to an extraordinary assemblage of 19th-century brick and adobe buildings, administered as the Monterey State Historic Park and covered on a 2-mile walking tour called 'Path of History.' For self-guided tours, free brochures are available from the visitor centers or from the park information desk (☎ 831-649-7118) inside the Maritime Museum on the Custom House Plaza. Unless indicated, admission to any of the buildings is $2 apiece, or $5 for all of them. As the tour gateway, the museum also shows a worthwhile 14-minute introductory film several times hourly.

Guided 75-minute tours of the state park also leave from the museum, usually on the hour between 10 am and 3 pm daily; $5/2 adults/children.

Custom House In 1822, newly independent Mexico ended the Spanish trade monopoly but stipulated that any traders bringing goods to Alta California must first unload their cargoes at the Monterey Custom House for duty assessment. The restored 1827 building displays an exotic selection of the goods traders brought in to exchange for Californian cow hides – food items such as rice and spices and 'luxury' items such as chandeliers, liquor, machinery and furniture. In 1846, the American flag was raised over the Custom House, and California was formally annexed from Mexico. Admission is free.

Pacific House Built in 1847 by Thomas Larkin (see Larkin House) for the newly arrived US Army, this structure recently reopened as a multimedia museum on local history.

Casa Soberanes A beautiful garden fronts Casa Soberanes, built in 1842 during the late Mexican period. Across Pacific St, the large and colorful **Monterey Mural** mosaic, on the modern Monterey Conference Center, tells the history of Monterey.

Larkin House Thomas Larkin arrived from New England in 1832 and made a fortune from the burgeoning regional trade. His fine 1842 house is a combination of New England design and adobe construction, known today as Monterey colonial. Larkin was US consul in Monterey during the US takeover; he subsequently played an important role in the transition from Mexican to American rule.

Stevenson House Robert Louis Stevenson came to Monterey in 1879 to meet with his wife-to-be, Fanny Osbourne. This building, then the French Hotel, was reputedly where he stayed while writing *Treasure Island*. The rooms were pretty primitive – they only cost about $2 a month – but he was still a penniless unknown at that time. The 1840 building now houses a superb collection of Stevenson memorabilia.

Cooper-Molera Complex This spacious adobe was built between 1827 and 1900 by John Rogers Cooper (a sea captain from New England and harbormaster of Monterey) and three generations of his family. During those years, it was partitioned and extended, gardens were added, and it was eventually willed to the National Trust.

Other Historic Buildings

Other highlights along the Path of History are Monterey's **First Brick House** and the **Old Whaling Station** (both from 1847) – note the front walkway made of whalebone. **California First Theatre** opened in 1844 as a saloon and lodging house, and soldiers staying there staged California's first theatrical productions. Performances still take place regularly. (See the Entertainment section.)

In 1849, California's state constitution was drawn up in **Colton Hall**, named for Walter Colton, navy chaplain for Commodore Sloat. The upstairs room re-creates the chamber where the document was debated and drafted. The adjacent **Old Monterey Jail** is featured in John Steinbeck's *Tortilla Flat*.

The **Sherman Quarters** was built by Thomas Larkin but takes its name from

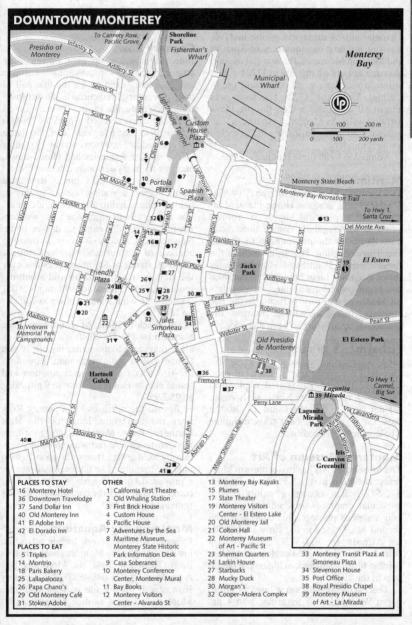

DOWNTOWN MONTEREY

PLACES TO STAY
16 Monterey Hotel
36 Downtown Travelodge
37 Sand Dollar Inn
40 Old Monterey Inn
41 El Adobe Inn
42 El Dorado Inn

PLACES TO EAT
5 Triples
14 Montrio
25 Paris Bakery
25 Lallapalooza
26 Papa Chano's
29 Old Monterey Café
31 Stokes Adobe

OTHER
1 California First Theatre
2 Old Whaling Station
3 First Brick House
4 Custom House
6 Pacific House
7 Adventures by the Sea
8 Maritime Museum,
   Monterey State Historic
   Park Information Desk
9 Casa Soberanes
10 Monterey Conference
   Center, Monterey Mural
11 Bay Books
12 Monterey Visitors
   Center - Alvarado St

13 Monterey Bay Kayaks
15 Plumes
17 State Theater
19 Monterey Visitors
   Center - El Estero Lake
20 Old Monterey Jail
21 Colton Hall
22 Monterey Museum
   of Art - Pacific St
23 Sherman Quarters
24 Larkin House
25 Starbucks
28 Mucky Duck
30 Morgan's
32 Cooper-Molera Complex

33 Monterey Transit Plaza at
   Simoneau Plaza
34 Stevenson House
35 Post Office
38 Royal Presidio Chapel
39 Monterey Museum
   of Art - La Mirada

famed General Sherman of the Civil War, who lived there in 1847. The **Royal Presidio Chapel**, built of stone and adobe in 1795, was the military headquarters of Spanish and Mexican Monterey. The original mission church was built on this site in 1770 but was moved a year later to its permanent site in Carmel. Until the 1820s, the town was almost all contained within the presidio's fortified walls. As Monterey expanded, it all gradually disappeared, leaving the chapel as a sole reminder.

Admission to all these buildings is free.

Maritime Museum

The Maritime Museum of Monterey (☎ 831-373-2469) is in Customs House Plaza. Monterey has a plentiful supply of retired admirals who regularly donate their naval miscellanies to the museum, so there's an excellent collection. Highlights include the Fresnel lens of Point Sur Lighthouse (later called Point Sur Light Station), a great ship-in-a-bottle collection and interesting displays on Monterey's history, particularly the rise and rapid fall of the sardine business. The museum is open 10 am to 5 pm daily; $5/2.

Fisherman's Wharf

Like its larger namesake in San Francisco, the wharf is a tourist trap at heart, but good fun nevertheless. You'll find a plentiful supply of restaurants. Noisy seals make regular visits to the wharf, and it's also the base for a variety of boat trips, including whale-watching expeditions.

Monterey Museum of Art

The Museum of Art has two centers in Monterey. The branch at 559 Pacific St (☎ 831-372-5477) has changing exhibits with particular emphasis on Californian artists, and a superb photographic collection. The second site, housed in the early adobe villa La Mirada (☎ 831-372-3689), 720 Via Mirada, has exhibits that explore early Californian history and look at life on the peninsula in the 1920s.

The Pacific St museum is open 11 am to 5 pm Wednesday to Saturday, 1 to 4 pm

Sunday. La Mirada has the same hours but is closed Wednesday as well; $3.

Cannery Row

John Steinbeck's novel *Cannery Row* immortalized the sardine-canning business that Monterey lived on for the first half of the 20th century. Predictions that overfishing could decimate the business were ignored when the catch reached a peak of 250,000 tons in 1945. Just five years later, the figure had crashed to 33,000 tons, and by 1951 most of the sardine canneries had closed down, many of them mysteriously catching fire.

Steinbeck described Cannery Row as 'a poem, a stink, a grating noise, a quality of light, a tone, a habit, a nostalgia, a dream.' The cannery bells summoned the workers whenever the ships came in, day or night. Nowadays, Cannery Row is a bustling enclave of restaurants, bars and tourist shops. A statue of Steinbeck presides over the new incarnation of his old stomping ground, La Ida Cafe, which still stands at 851 Cannery Row but is now known as Kalisa's La Ida Cafe.

Steinbeck's Spirit of Monterey Wax Museum (☎ 831-375-1010) is a fairly hokey affair that seeks to dramatize historic life on Cannery Row with more than a hundred life-size wax figures, plus animation and sound effects. Hours are 9 am to 9 pm daily; $6.95/2.95.

Toward the north end of Cannery Row, near the aquarium, look for the **New Cannery Row Mural**, a 400-foot-long wooden fence covered with colorful paintings by local artists. It was put up in 1989 to hide the eyesore of an undeveloped site for a proposed hotel. Originally scheduled for completion in 1993, the construction site has remained untouched.

Monterey Bay Aquarium

Cannery Row's one worthwhile attraction justifies a trip to the Monterey area all on its own. Opened in 1984, the Monterey Bay Aquarium (☎ 831-648-4888), 886 Cannery Row, stands on the site of what was once Monterey's largest sardine cannery. Apart

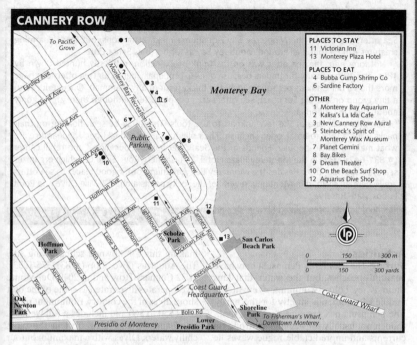

CANNERY ROW

To Pacific Grove

Eardley Ave
David Ave
Irving Ave
Prescott Ave
Hoffman Ave
McClellan Ave
Laine St
Beldon St
Archer St
Spencer St
Pine St

Monterey Bay Recreation Trail

Public Parking

Foam St
Wave St
Cannery Row
Lighthouse Ave
Hawthorne St
Drake Ave
Dickman Ave
Reeside Ave

Monterey Bay

Hoffman Park

Oak Newton Park

Scholze Park

San Carlos Beach Park

Coast Guard Headquarters

Bolio Rd

Presidio of Monterey

Lower Presidio Park

Shoreline Park

Coast Guard Wharf

To Fisherman's Wharf, Downtown Monterey

PLACES TO STAY
11 Victorian Inn
13 Monterey Plaza Hotel

PLACES TO EAT
4 Bubba Gump Shrimp Co
6 Sardine Factory

OTHER
1 Monterey Bay Aquarium
2 Kalisa's La Ida Cafe
3 New Cannery Row Mural
5 Steinbeck's Spirit of
  Monterey Wax Museum
7 Planet Gemini
8 Bay Bikes
9 Dream Theater
10 On the Beach Surf Shop
12 Aquarius Dive Shop

0   150   300 m
0   150   300 yards

---

from temporary displays, its state-of-the-art exhibits are devoted to the rich marine life of the Monterey Bay.

Life-size models of whales and other marine mammals hang from the beamed ceiling. Star exhibits include the gigantic **kelp forest**, where 7-inch-thick acrylic panels separate visitors from more than 300,000 gallons of water, and marine creatures swim between the towering fronds of kelp; feeding takes place twice a day.

Children love the **touch tanks**, where they can pick up sea stars and other shallow-water creatures, and the pool where bat rays can be gently stroked.

Sea otter feeding is a prime attraction for adults and children alike and usually takes place at 10:30 am, and 1:30 and 3:30 pm daily. At most other times, these charming creatures can be seen basking in the **tide pool** outside the aquarium, where they are

quite free to roam around as they please. Harbor seals also drop in here.

A spectacular $55 million aquarium extension that re-creates the open ocean – dubbed the Outer Bay Wing – opened in March 1996. The highlight here is the other-worldly **jellyfish exhibit**, which displays dozens of varieties of these ethereal organisms in darkened galleries. Jellies pulse and glide as meditative music fills the rooms. Also mind-boggling is the million-gallon tank teeming with ocean sunfish, sharks, tuna and a green sea turtle.

The aquarium is open 10 am to 6 pm daily (from 9:30 am in summer and during holidays); $16/13/7 adults/seniors/children. To avoid long lines in summer and on week-ends and holidays, get your tickets in advance from your hotel or by calling ☎ 800-756-3737. There's an excellent shop and a restaurant on the premises.

Some Critters You 'Otter' Not Miss

Sea otters are one of the Monterey Bay Aquarium's major attractions, but these charming creatures can be found all around Monterey Bay as far north as Santa Cruz.

Not long ago, the sea otter was on the brink of extinction, ruthlessly hunted down by 18th- and 19th-century fur traders because of its exceptionally dense fur (sea otters can have more than a million hairs per square inch, the thickest fur of any mammal). Once reduced to a tiny group on the Big Sur coast, sea otters are now protected, although there are still only about 2500 in California.

Sea otters are one of the few animals to use tools. They may be seen floating on their backs using a rock to break open shellfish. Their playful nature and laid-back appearance are what make them so popular. Friends of the Sea Otter has an educational and retail center (☎ 831-642-9037) in the Monterey Plaza Hotel, 381 Cannery Row, Suite Q, which organizes sea otter spotting trips. Besides the Monterey Bay Aquarium, other good places to see otters are Fisherman's Wharf in Monterey, several of the rocky points along 17-Mile Drive and Point Lobos State Reserve.

Activities

Surfing The Monterey Peninsula may have beautiful beaches, but the water that laps them is icy cold; swimming, even in the middle of summer, is strictly for the hardy. The peninsula has some great surfing spots, though not usually for beginners. Strong rip currents and unpredictable rogue waves lie in wait for the unwary, not to mention the presence of those famous sharks. Local surfers vote Asilomar State Beach (in Pacific Grove) and Moss Landing (north of Monterey and Marina) as having the best and most consistent breaks. For surf gear and rentals, head to On the Beach (☎ 831-646-9283) at 693 Lighthouse Ave.

Diving The Monterey Bay's famous kelp forests teem with diverse marine life,

making this a renowned scuba diving site. The Aquarius Dive Shop (☎ 831-375-1933), at 32 Cannery Row and at 2040 Del Monte Ave, operates dives rated as some of the best shore dives in the country. Equipment rental costs $50 to $60 and includes a full wet suit, hood and gloves for comfort in the bay's chilly waters. Dives, with a maximum of four people per guide, cost $50 for a single tank dive, $80 for a two-tank dive.

Kayaking Monterey Bay Kayaks (☎ 831-373-5357), 693 Del Monte Ave, rents open and closed kayaks for $25 per day, offers instruction courses every weekend and operates a range of natural history tours. Their 3½-hour kayaking tour costs $45.

Whale Watching The season is from December to March. Whale-watching boats leave from Fisherman's Wharf, with two-hour trips costing $15 on average.

Bicycling Thanks to stunning scenery and paved bike paths, cycling is a very popular peninsula activity. Try the Monterey Peninsula Recreational Trail, which travels for 18 car-free miles along the waterfront from Asilomar State Beach in Pacific Grove to Castroville, passing by Fisherman's Wharf and Cannery Row in Monterey.

For bike rentals, try Adventures by the Sea (☎ 831-372-1807), with outlets at 201 Alvarado St (the waterfront end), 299 Cannery Row and at Lovers Point. Rental rates are $6 per hour, $18 per half day or $24 per day, and they also rent in-line skates and kayaks. Bay Bikes (☎ 831-646-9090), 640 Wave St, is another respected rental outfit.

Special Events
The Monterey Peninsula stages numerous events throughout the year, including the popular Monterey Wine Festival (☎ 831-656-9463) in late March/early April and the internationally famed Monterey Jazz Festival (☎ 831-373-3366) in September; reserve tickets well in advance for either. Two Pebble Beach events also fill the area to capacity: the AT&T Pebble Beach National Pro-Am golf tournament in late January and the Concours d'Élégance classic car exhibit in August.

Places to Stay
Monterey is not noted for bargain accommodations. If you're economizing, consider staying in Santa Cruz, only 40 miles north, instead; the nearest youth hostel is there as well. Prices in Monterey are seasonal and skyrocket in summer and on weekends year round. Central reservation agencies include Monterey Peninsula Reservations at ☎ 888-655-3424 and Roomfinder Service at ☎ 831-624-1711 or ☎ 800-847-8066.

Camping The *Veterans Memorial Park* (☎ 831-646-3865) has 40 primitive campsites without electricity and enforces a three-day maximum stay. Sites are first-come, first-served and cost $15 for vehicles or $3 for walk-ins. Take Hwy 68 to Skyline Forest Drive, head east to Skyline Drive, where you turn north (left); from here it's about a mile to the park.

For more creature comforts, the *Laguna Seca Recreation Area* (☎ 831-758-3604, 888-588-2267 for reservations) has 185 spaces, showers, hookups and other facilities for RVs ($22) and tent campers ($18). It's 9 miles east on Hwy 68 toward Salinas. A third option, also with a full range of amenities, is

the private *Marina Dunes RV Park* (☎ 831-384-6914, 3330 Dunes Drive), in the town of Marina, some 9 miles north of Monterey along Hwy 1. RV and tent sites range from $20 to $33.

Motels, Hotels & B&Bs A group of economical motels can be found about 2½ miles east of Old Monterey on N Fremont St around the junction of Casa Verde, just south of Hwy 1 and just east of Hwy 68. Off-season prices can dip as low as $35 here, although you're looking at $60 to $80 in the Best Westerns and Travelodge category. This group includes the *Vagabond Motel* (☎ 831-372-6066, 2120 N Fremont St), *Super 8 Motel* (☎ 831-373-3081, 2050 N Fremont St), *Travelodge* (☎ 831-373-3381, 2030 N Fremont St), and two Best Westerns – the *Ramona Inn* (☎ 831-373-2445, 2332 N Fremont St) and the *De Anza Inn* (☎ 831-646-8300, 2141 N Fremont St).

Closer to downtown Monterey, *El Dorado Inn* (☎ 831-373-2921, 800-722-1836, 900 Munras Ave) has fairly basic rooms with an old-fashioned feel (some with fireplace), that range from $39 to $145, including a small in-room breakfast.

For more charm, try *El Adobe Inn* (☎ 831-372-5409, 800-433-4732, fax 831-624-2967, 936 Munras Ave), a neat and well-kept property a short stroll south of downtown. Rooms are $69 to $129, including continental breakfast and use of a hot tub. Equally convenient is the *Sand Dollar Inn* (☎ 831-372-7551, 800-982-1986, fax 831-372-0916, 755 Abrego St); its 34 rooms range from just $29 to $110, again with breakfast.

The historic *Monterey Hotel* (☎ 831-375-3184, 800-727-0960, fax 831-373-2899, 406 Alvarado St) is in a beautiful building right in the heart of Old Monterey. Rooms are furnished old-world style and range from $109 to $279, including a satisfying continental breakfast. Moving right up the price scale, the 285-room *Monterey Plaza Hotel* (☎ 831-646-1700, 800-334-3999, fax 831-646-5937, 400 Cannery Row) commands an impressive location: its rooms don't just overlook the bay – they're built right out over it! Rates start at $195, topping out at $295.

Monterey has plenty of upscale B&Bs, like the large and luxurious *Victorian Inn* (☎ 831-373-8000, 800-232-4141, fax 831-373-4815, 487 Foam St), near Cannery Row. Rates vacillate between $159 and an astronomical $339, though discounts may be available on slow days. In the same vein, the *Old Monterey Inn* (☎ 831-375-8284, 800-350-2344, fax 831-375-6730, 500 Martin St) oozes charm by the gallon but the price of admission is stiff: $200 to $350.

Places to Eat

The *Old Monterey Café* (☎ 831-646-1021, 489 Alvarado St) is resolutely old-fashioned, with plate-warping breakfasts served till closing, plus soups, sandwiches and salads. It's a good choice for the budget-conscious, with most menu items under $10; open 7 am to 2:30 pm daily. Across the street, *Papa Chano's* (☎ 831-646-9587, 462 Alvarado St) is a simple Mexican eatery with fresh tacos and big burritos under $5. Practically next door is the hip *Lallapalooza* (☎ 831-645-9036, 474 Alvarado St), which has a dozen martinis and updated versions of mid-priced American classics served in a stylish setting. For a quick bite, the *Paris Bakery* (☎ 831-646-1620, 271 Bonifacio Place), at Washington St, does great sandwiches and aromatic coffee.

The historic *Stokes Adobe* building now houses a highly regarded restaurant of the same name (☎ 831-373-1110, 500 Hartnell St). The varied menu focuses on the rich, rustic flavors of Mediterranean country cooking, featuring steak, duck breast, pork chop and chicken dishes. 'Small plates' cost $3 to $8; 'large plates' start at $12.

Seafood restaurants abound along the wharf. Touristy but fun, *Bubba Gump Shrimp Co* (☎ 831-373-1884, 720 Cannery Row) is a rollicking theme restaurant based on the movie *Forrest Gump*; clam chowder goes for $3.25, and shrimp dishes start at $11.50. Movie stills decorate the lobby, and you may even run into 'Forrest' himself (the restaurant is not above hiring a Tom Hanks look-alike to greet the customers). Nearby, the *Sardine Factory* (☎ 831-373-3775, 701 Wave St) has over-the-top decor and expensive, though delicious, seafood. Jackets are required at this dinner-only restaurant.

In downtown Monterey, *Montrio* (☎ 831-648-8880, 414 Calle Principal) has classy decor with Mexican touches, friendly service and an inspired menu of California eclectic cuisine. Lunches average $10; dinner entrées range from $11 to $22. The desserts are killer. Try the chocolate brioche bread pudding with espresso crème anglaise and white chocolate sorbet or the caramelized quince mascarpone napoleon with ginger ice cream and caramel sauce.

Dinner on the flower-framed patio of *Triples* (☎ 831-372-4744, 220 Oliver St), tucked into a car-free avenue behind the Doubletree Hotel, is a romantic and memorable experience. Medium-deep pockets, though, are required for Italian main courses ranging from $16 to $26.

A bit outside of town, in a rustic 1917 homestead and recommended by locals, is *Tarpy's Roadhouse* (☎ 831-647-1444, 2999 Monterey/Salinas Hwy 1), at Hwy 68 and Canyon Del Rey. It garners accolades for its comfort and its updated versions of classic American dishes. Main courses range from $10 to $24; yummy sandwiches and salads can be had for less than $10.

Entertainment

For comprehensive 'what's on' listings, restaurant reviews and other information, pick up a free copy of the *Coast Weekly* and *Go!* available in bookstores, restaurants and at the visitor centers.

Coffeehouses *Morgan's* (☎ 831-373-5601, 498 Washington St) makes some of the best coffee in town. It's a nice relaxed place with live music. *Starbucks* (☎ 831-373-5282, 461 Alvarado St) and *Plumes* (☎ 831-373-5282), at Alvarado and Franklin Sts, are other popular coffee shops.

Bars & Clubs The *Mucky Duck* (☎ 831-655-3031, 479 Alvarado St) is an English-style pub in Old Monterey. Most of the activity at night, however, is around Cannery Row. Upstairs on the 3rd floor, *Planet Gemini* (☎ 831-373-1449, 625 Cannery Row) has live music or comedy on Thursday to Saturday nights with a cover charge of around $6 (entrance off Hoffman Ave).

Theater & Cinema The *California First Theatre* (☎ 831-375-4916), at Pacific and Scott Sts, puts on Victorian melodramas and musical revues in a venue that's stood the test of time, and was indeed California's first theater.

Local cinemas include the multiscreen *Galaxy 6* (☎ 831-655-4619, 280 Del Monte Center); *Lighthouse Cinemas* (☎ 831-372-7336, 525 Lighthouse Ave), in Pacific Grove; the fine old *State Theater* (☎ 831-372-4555, 417 Alvarado St); and the *Dream Theater* (☎ 831-372-1494, 301 Prescott Ave).

Getting There & Away

Air Seven airlines, including American and United, operate flights out of Monterey Peninsula Airport (☎ 831-648-7000) on Olmsted Rd, about 4 miles southeast of the town center. Service includes direct connections to Los Angeles and San Francisco. Other reasonably close airports are those in San Francisco and San Jose (see those sections). Monterey-Salinas Airbus (☎ 800-291-2877) provides shuttle service ($30 or $55 roundtrip) 10 times daily.

Bus Greyhound buses (☎ 831-373-4735) operate twice a day between Los Angeles and San Francisco via Monterey. They stop at the Exxon gas station at 1042 Del Monte Ave, just east of El Estero Lake. Fares to San Francisco are $18 ($35 roundtrip), to Los Angeles $37 ($73 roundtrip), and to Santa Cruz $10.

Train The nearest Amtrak station is in Salinas, a stop for the *Coast Starlight* on its route from Seattle to Los Angeles. A free shuttle bus connects the Amtrak station in Salinas with downtown Monterey. Call ☎ 800-872-7245 for information.

Car & Motorcycle Monterey is 120 miles south of San Francisco (scenic and slow by Hwy 1, quicker via Hwys 101 and 156). If you're heading down the Big Sur coast and you don't already have your own wheels, it's worth considering renting some. The coast doesn't lend itself to public transportation; stopping and starting is what it's all about.

Getting Around

The Monterey Transit Plaza at Simoneau Plaza at the south end of Alvarado St is the terminal for Monterey services. Useful routes include Nos 1 and 14 to downtown Pacific Grove (No 1 goes via Cannery Row); Nos 4, 5, 22 and 24 to Carmel (No 22 continues south to Point Lobos and Big Sur); and Nos 20 and 21 to Salinas, including the Amtrak station.

MST's the WAVE (Waterfront Area Visitors Express; ☎ 831-899-2555), with four routes connecting downtown Monterey with Cannery Row, Fisherman's Wharf and Pacific Grove, runs 9 am to 6:30 pm daily between Memorial Day and Labor Day; all-day passes are $2/1.

Monterey traffic can be horrendous on summer weekends, and parking can be a serious problem, especially around Cannery Row. The public garage at Foam St and Hoffman Ave is convenient and charges $1 per hour, a relative bargain. All major national companies – Budget, Hertz, National, etc – have offices in Monterey; Rent-a-Wreck (☎ 831-373-3356) is at 95 Central Ave in Pacific Grove.

AROUND MONTEREY
Laguna Seca Raceway

Just off Hwy 68, about midway between Salinas and Monterey, the Laguna Seca Raceway (☎ 831-648-5100, 800-327-7322) attracts auto racing fans for an annual round of the Indy Car World Series, and motorcycle enthusiasts for a round of the World Superbike Championship. Back in the early '50s, races used to take place on a road circuit in the Del Monte Forest at Pebble Beach, but the track was very unsafe and the Laguna Seca track replaced it in 1956.

Salinas

• **population 120,000** • **elevation 55 feet**

Just 17 miles east of Monterey, Salinas is the birthplace of John Steinbeck and a major agricultural center that's been nicknamed California's 'salad bowl.' Easily reached by public transportation or via Hwy 68, this working farming town makes a strong contrast with the conspicuous affluence of other peninsula cities. Its historic center stretches out along Main St, with the chamber of commerce (☎ 831-424-7611) at 119 E Alisal St, three blocks east of Main St. Seasonal highlights include the Steinbeck Festival (☎ 831-753-6411) in August, the California Rodeo (☎ 800-771-8807) in July and the California International Airshow (☎ 831-758-1983) in September or October.

National Steinbeck Center With the opening of the state-of-the-art 37,000-sq-foot National Steinbeck Center (☎ 831-796-3833, www.steinbeck.org), 1 Main St, in summer 1998, Salinas is paying fitting homage to its Nobel Prize-winning native son. John Steinbeck was born in Salinas in 1902. His literary explorations were influenced and inspired by the people and daily life of the area; his observations on Cannery Row in Monterey, for example, resulted in the eponymous 1945 book.

The heart of the center is an interactive exhibit that chronicles the writer's life and works in a creative and engaging fashion. Each of seven themed galleries stages scenes from famous books like *The Grapes of Wrath*, *East of Eden* and *Of Mice and Men*, incorporates quotes and artifacts like letters and books and features a small theater showing film clips. Prized exhibits include Rocinante, the customized camper in which Steinbeck traveled around America while researching *Travels with Charley*. Not to be missed is the short biographical film, which provides a thorough introduction to the man and his volatile career.

The center is open 10 am to 5 pm daily; $7 adults, $6 seniors and students, $4 for ages 11 to 17.

Two blocks west, at 132 Central Ave and Stone, stands the **Victorian house** that was Steinbeck's birthplace and boyhood home. It's now a fancy restaurant (☎ 831-424-2735), open for lunch daily except Sunday.

John Steinbeck (1902-68)

Traipse through the word houses built by many West Coast writers, and you'll encounter the large footprints of John Steinbeck, just leaving the room. Steinbeck is as thoroughly an American writer as Mark Twain. And, arguably, no writer has ever been more defined by the land in which he lived and by the people he lived among.

A roughneck, Stanford dropout, social critic, humorist, screenwriter and war correspondent, Steinbeck grew up and worked with the desperate people who toiled, often on the edge of starvation, in the fields of his native Salinas. His knowledge of the human condition was largely shaped by his observations of the eternal struggle to hold on to some shred of human dignity in the face of utmost poverty. The honesty of his feelings about life's inequities is nowhere more powerful than in his greatest novel, *The Grapes of Wrath*, which garnered him a Pulitzer Prize. It's the wrenching story of a family of 1930s dust bowl farmers who reach the end of their road in the farm fields of California and whose trials, humiliation and ultimate defeat are met with stoicism and nobility. This theme – of redemption in the face of disaster – is one that echoes through much of Steinbeck's work.

When awarded the Nobel Prize for Literature in 1962, Steinbeck said in his acceptance speech: 'Literature...grew out of the human need for it, and it has not changed much except to become more needed. The writer is delegated to declare and to celebrate man's proven capacity for greatness of heart and spirit – for gallantry in defeat, for courage, compassion and love.' Reading Steinbeck is still to be put in touch with something profoundly American.

– David Peevers

Steinbeck is buried in the **Garden of Memories Cemetery** family plot, also in Salinas.

Places to Stay Thanks to its proximity to Monterey and its relative abundance of inexpensive motels, Salinas makes for a good alternative base for exploring the peninsula. *Econo Lodge* (☎ 831-422-5111, 180 Sanborn Rd), *Days Inn* (☎ 831-759-9900, 1226 De La Torre St), *Comfort Inn* (☎ 831-758-8850, 144 Kern St), *Holiday Inn Express* (☎ 831-757-1020, 131 John St), *Super 8 Motel* (☎ 831-422-6486, 1030 Fairview Ave) and *Vagabond Inn* (☎ 831-758-4693, 131 Kern St) are among the chain properties represented here, with year-round rates starting at $50 or $60.

Getting There & Away MST buses (☎ 831-424-7695) for the Monterey Peninsula (No 20 via Marina or No 21 via Hwy 68; $3) stop at the Transit Center at 110 Salinas St and also at the Amtrak station.

PACIFIC GROVE
• population 16,000 • elevation 55 feet

Founded as a Methodist summer retreat in 1875, Pacific Grove's Victorian origins are still reflected in its architecture and overall small-town feel, albeit a decidedly upscale one. Until about a decade ago, Pacific Grove, between the Cannery Row and 17-Mile Drive, used to be little more than a quiet, laid-back bedroom community. The opening of the Monterey Bay Aquarium in 1984 not only revitalized Cannery Row, but also brought more tourists to Pacific Grove, spurring the creation of a slew of sophisticated B&Bs and restaurants to accommodate them. No longer a more economical base for peninsula explorations, the town has blossomed into a pleasant community and destination of its own.

Orientation & Information
Lighthouse Ave is the main shopping street of Pacific Grove and continues southeast to Monterey. The Visitor Information Center (☎ 831-373-3304, 800-656-6650, fax 831-373-3317), at the chamber of commerce, is a block north at the corner of Central and

Forest Aves. Hours are 9:30 am to 5 pm weekdays, 10 am to 4 pm Saturday.

Museum of Natural History
Fronted by a model of a gray whale, this museum (☎ 831-648-3116), 165 Forest Ave, has some of that old-fashioned 'dead zoo' flavor that used to be typical of natural history museums. But there are also interesting exhibits about Big Sur, sea otters and the monarch butterflies for which Pacific Grove is famous. If you're in town during butterfly season (roughly October to March), you can see them cluster by the millions either at the **Monarch Grove Sanctuary** or at **George Washington Park**, both within a short driving distance. The Butterfly Parade, marking the return of the monarchs to Pacific Grove, is in October. The museum itself is open 10 am to 5 pm, closed Monday; free.

Point Pinos Lighthouse
Continue through Pacific Grove, along Ocean View Blvd, right to the northern tip of the Monterey Peninsula to find the oldest continuously operating lighthouse on the West Coast. It's been warning ships of this hazardous point with the same lenses and prisms and in the same building since 1855. There are exhibits on its history and on local shipwrecks. The lighthouse (☎ 831-648-3116) is open 1 to 4 pm weekends; free.

Places to Stay
Pacific Grove used to be a cheaper alternative to Monterey and Carmel, but as the town has gone more upscale, it's become harder to find affordable accommodations. Less-expensive lodgings are on 'motel row' on the northern end of Lighthouse Ave. Here, *Pacific Grove Motel* (☎ 831-372-3218, 800-858-8997, fax 831-372-8842), at Lighthouse and Grove Acres Aves, has a pool and spa, a pleasantly quiet setting and rooms ranging from $39 to $121. *Wilkie's Inn* (☎ 831-372-5960, 800-253-5707, fax 831-655-1681, 1038 Lighthouse Ave) offers continental breakfast with its $55 to $115 rates.

Closer to downtown is the *Larchwood Inn* (☎ 831-373-1114, 800-525-3373, fax 831-665-5048), which has 48 rooms, most of them

Monarch Butterflies

Butterflies are frail, no? Well, nobody told that to the monarch butterflies that spend their whole winter in Pacific Grove and other choice Central Coast communities.

Monarchs follow a remarkable migration pattern, starting in the spring along the central California coast and heading north and east. These migrating monarchs live for about four weeks, during which time they fly north, mate, lay their eggs on milkweed leaves and die. In three to six days the eggs hatch, and the larva or caterpillars start out on a 15- to 20-day milkweed eating binge, which increases their weight by a factor of over 2500. The caterpillar then suspends itself from a stem or leaf and enters the chrysalis, or pupa, stage, from which a butterfly emerges about 10 days later. Once its wings have dried and hardened, the new monarch starts off on another four-week journey to the north.

Over the spring and summer four or five successive generations of monarchs travel farther and farther north, crossing the border into Canada and traveling as far as milkweed, their food source, extends. Finally, as the nights lengthen and temperatures drop, the northward migration ends in early October, and the final generation turns south to fly 2000 miles back to their wintering grounds. Covering as much as 100 miles a day and flying as high as 10,000 feet, the monarchs start turning up back in California in October.

The wintering generation of monarchs lives for six to nine months, clustering on trees at a number of favorite sites along the central California coast. In late winter, rising temperatures and longer hours of daylight trigger their dormant sex drive; mating takes place, and by March the monarchs are again heading north.

California monarchs have developed a 'homing' fondness for imported Australian eucalyptus trees. In Pacific Grove, monarchs cluster by the thousands in trees found in George Washington Park and in the Monarch Grove Sanctuary on Grove Acre Ave. Natural Bridges State Park in Santa Cruz, Pismo Beach and the San Simeon Natural Preserve near Hearst Castle are other favorite monarch sites.

---

with gas fireplace; there's also a guest laundry and fee-based sauna and spa. Rates are $59 to $110.

Pacific Grove boasts plenty of B&Bs, but for a special treat the charm and comfort of the *Martine Inn* (☎ 831-373-3388, 800-852-5588, fax 831-373-3896, 255 Ocean View Blvd) are hard to beat. Staying here means savoring the ambience of your room (some with fireplace) furnished with stylish American antiques, enjoying wine and appetizers at cocktail hour, retiring to the sound of waves crashing against the rocky shoreline and waking up to a hearty breakfast. The owner is an antique car aficionado; ask to see the classic MG roadsters in his garage. Rates are fairly reasonable starting at $135 and cresting at $245.

In nearby Pebble Beach, on 17-Mile Drive (see the next section), are two swank hotels for the fat-wallet crowd. Near the northern entrance of the drive, the *Inn at Spanish Bay* (☎ 831-647-7500, 800-654-9300, fax 831-644-7955) has rooms starting at $305. On the opposite end, not far from the southern entrance, is the *Lodge at Pebble Beach* (☎ 831-624-3811, 800-654-9300, fax 831-644-7960), which asks $350 and up.

Places to Eat
Peppers Mexicali Café (☎ 831-373-6892, 170 Forest Ave) blends Mexican and Latin American flavors with some distinctly Californian ingredients to produce well-priced dishes like salmon tacos and swordfish fajitas. It's closed Tuesdays.

On Lighthouse Ave, you'll find several no-nonsense diners, as well as *Bookworks* (☎ 831-372-2242, 667 Lighthouse Ave), which combines a bookstore with a popular cafe.

Lighthouse Ave also has an international bunch of eateries like **Pasta Mia** (☎ 831-375-7709, 481 Lighthouse Ave), one of the best Italian restaurants on the peninsula, and the stylish **Petra** (☎ 831-649-2530, 477 Lighthouse Ave), with excellent Middle Eastern fare.

Pasta from $7 and seafood for $9 to $13 are the order of the day at the popular and much recommended **Fishwife** (☎ 831-375-7107, 1996½ Sunset Drive), close to the intersection with 17-Mile Drive at Asilomar. A good spot for romantic dinners is the **Old Bath House** (☎ 831-375-5195, 620 Ocean View Blvd); the menu here is heavy on fish and fowl, including Muscovy duck, priced at $20 and up.

17-MILE DRIVE

Monterey, Pacific Grove and Carmel are linked by the spectacularly scenic 17-Mile Drive, which winds through Pebble Beach, a resort and residential area that most potently symbolizes the peninsula's affluence. Open sunrise to sunset, entry is via five gates and costs $7.25 per car, including a guide map. Bicycles enter free, but on weekends and holidays bicyclists can use only the Pacific Grove gate. Use caution when biking, as drivers tend to be *very* distracted by the sights.

Pebble Beach has fancy hotels (the Lodge at Pebble Beach and the Inn at Spanish Bay – see Places to Stay in the preceding section), golf courses (seven of them, including the famous Pebble Beach Golf Course) and the 5000-acre Del Monte Forest. 17-Mile Drive winds around the rugged coastline and up into the forest, but it's the coastal stretch that's the most interesting and makes a fine, if somewhat circuitous, method of getting from Pacific Grove to Carmel.

From the Pacific Grove gate, the drive winds by **Spanish Bay**, where Gaspar de Portolá dropped anchor in 1769. Rocky **Point Joe** has been the site of several shipwrecks, when mistaken for the entrance to Monterey Bay. Sea lions, harbor seals and many birds can be seen around **Bird Rock**, where there is a 1-mile nature walk. A little farther, **Seal Rock** and then **Fanshell Beach** also attract seals and other bay life.

Cypress Point Lookout offers one of the finest views along the whole drive, though somewhat spoiled by an ugly wire fence. The road continues through **Crocker Grove**, with its Monterey cypress and finally reaches the **Lone Cypress**, inspiration for far too many local artists and photographers and also the (copyrighted!) symbol of the Pebble Beach Company, which is now trying to claim copyright to all uses of the image, even in paintings.

CARMEL-BY-THE-SEA
• **population 4500** • **elevation 20 feet**
Carmel began as a planned seaside resort in the 1880s and by the early 1900s had already established a reputation as a slightly bohemian retreat. The artistic flavor survives, but these days 'wealthy' and 'homogenous' are just as descriptive; Carmel positively glows with self-satisfaction. It's easy to see why this perfect vision of a Californian seaside village exerts such an attraction; woodsy Carmel has a neat grid of picturesque homes, an impressive coastal frontage, upscale shopping streets and a beautiful Spanish mission.

Orientation & Information

Visitor information is available from the Carmel Business Association (☎ 831-624-2522), on San Carlos St, between 5th and 6th Aves. It's open 9 am to 5 pm weekdays, 11 am to 3 pm Saturday and on Sunday in the summer.

The town's charming appearance is ensured by local bylaws, which forbid streetlights, mailboxes in the central area and even high heels! Residents have to pick up their mail from the post office. There are also no street numbers, so addresses always specify the block and side of street. Even public phones, garbage cans and newspaper vending boxes are picturesquely rehoused with shingles.

The town's artistic temperament may still be strong, but affluence has brought a distinctly right wing brand of bohemianism. In *Freedom of Speech*, a local free paper, a page

CENTRAL COAST

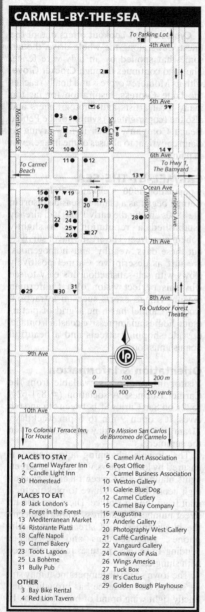

CARMEL-BY-THE-SEA

To Parking Lot
4th Ave
5th Ave
6th Ave
To Carmel Beach
To Hwy 1, The Barnyard
Ocean Ave
7th Ave
8th Ave
To Outdoor Forest Theater
9th Ave
10th Ave
Monte Verde St
Lincoln St
Dolores St
San Carlos St
Mission St
Junipero Ave

To Colonial Terrace Inn, Tor House
To Mission San Carlos de Borromeo de Carmelo

PLACES TO STAY
1 Carmel Wayfarer Inn
2 Candle Light Inn
30 Homestead

PLACES TO EAT
8 Jack London's
9 Forge in the Forest
13 Mediterranean Market
14 Ristorante Piatti
18 Caffè Napoli
19 Carmel Bakery
23 Toots Lagoon
25 La Bohème
31 Bully Pub

OTHER
3 Bay Bike Rental
4 Red Lion Tavern

5 Carmel Art Association
6 Post Office
7 Carmel Business Association
10 Weston Gallery
11 Galerie Blue Dog
12 Carmel Cutlery
15 Carmel Bay Company
16 Augustina
17 Anderle Gallery
20 Photography West Gallery
21 Caffè Cardinale
22 Vangaurd Gallery
24 Conway of Asia
26 Wings America
27 Tuck Box
28 It's Cactus
29 Golden Bough Playhouse

devoted to 'what a good thing a gun can be' probably says it all.

There's a Books Inc (☎ 831-625-0440) on Ocean Ave, between Mission and San Carlos. Try Travels at the corner of Ocean Ave and Dolores St for travel books. Carmel's best-known and largest book outlet is the Thunderbird Bookshop & Café (☎ 831-624-1803) in the Barnyard shopping center, just outside of town.

Mission San Carlos de Borromeo de Carmelo

The original Monterey mission was founded by Padre Junípero Serra in 1769, but poor soil and, probably more importantly, the military presence of the presidio forced the move to the riverside site in Carmel in 1771. Although Serra founded 20 other missions in California, this one, his second, remained his base. He died here in 1784 and was buried in the mission church beside his compatriot Padre Juan Crespi.

The mission church was originally built of wood, then replaced by an adobe structure and, in 1793, by the present stone church. In the 19th century, the mission went into decline; it was secularized in 1834 and virtually abandoned in 1836 when the padre moved to Monterey. The ruin was roofed over in 1884, which at least slowed the decay, but restoration didn't really commence until 1931. Today it is one of the most attractive and complete of the California missions, with a superb museum relating the story of Serra and the missions.

The mission (☎ 831-624-1271) is at 3080 Rio Rd, off Hwy 1 on the south side of Carmel. It's open 9:30 am to 4:30 pm (from 10:30 am Sunday). In summer, it stays open until 7:30 pm. A $2/1 donation is suggested for entry to the museum and church.

Tor House

Poet Robinson Jeffers was one of the creators of the Carmel ethos, and his strikingly rugged home, Tor House (☎ 831-624-1813 Monday to Thursday, 831-624-1840 Friday and Saturday), 26304 Ocean View Ave, off Scenic Rd, has become a pilgrimage point. Tours operate hourly from 10 am to 4 pm

Friday and Saturday, and the cost is $5/1.50. Numbers are limited to six per tour, so it's wise to book by phoning ahead.

Places to Stay

The whole Monterey Peninsula has a reputation as an expensive place to stay, and prices reach their apogee in Carmel's selection of sleek small hotels and cozy B&Bs. Many places impose a two-night minimum stay on weekends and rooms can be hard to find, particularly on summer weekends. A free room finder service is offered at ☎ 800-847-8066.

People with RVs can go 4 miles up Carmel Valley Rd and turn right on Schulte Rd to *Carmel-by-the-River* (☎ 831-624-9329). This place takes RVs only and charges around $40.

There's nothing cheap in Carmel – Motel 6s are definitely not welcome. Right in the center, at Lincoln St and 8th Ave, the *Homestead* (☎ 831-624-4119, fax 831-624-7688) has comfy rooms and cottages, all with attached bathroom, from $60 to $100. The *Carmel Wayfarer Inn* (☎ 831-624-2711, 800-624-2711, fax 831-625-1210), at Mission St and 4th Ave, is a charming country inn dating back to 1919, with rooms costing $80 to $110, including homemade breakfast.

An excellent bet is the equally central and friendly *Candle Light Inn* (☎ 831-624-6451, 800-433-4732, fax 831-624-6732), on San Carlos St, between 4th and 5th Aves, which has snug and comfortable rooms with coffeemakers. It's run by a friendly French woman who's a treasure trove of information about great restaurants. As a special touch, continental breakfast is left outside your room in a basket. Rates are $119 to $209. Less central, but near the beach, is the *Colonial Terrace Inn* (☎ 831-624-2741, fax 831-626-2715), at San Antonio and 13th Aves. The well-equipped rooms start at $86, though deluxe digs are as much as $236. Both premises are part of the Inns by the Sea group, which can be booked through ☎ 800-433-4732.

Places to Eat

Carmel restaurants can be surprisingly down-to-earth and the prices are not always as outlandish as you might expect. The *Carmel Bakery* (☎ 831-626-8885), on Ocean Ave between Dolores and Lincoln Sts, has been *the* place for baked goods since 1935. Head to the *Mediterranean Market* (☎ 831-624-2022), at Ocean Ave and Mission St, for gourmet picnic goodies to take to the beach or to Point Lobos State Reserve (see the Around Carmel section).

Another good place is the *Thunderbird Bookshop & Café* (☎ 831-624-9414), at the Barnyard shopping center, which serves inexpensive soups, salads and sandwiches in a setting that includes a fireplace and a patio overlooking a lovely garden.

The Fabulous Toots Lagoon (☎ 831-625-1915), on Dolores St, between Ocean and 7th Aves, has been turning out straightforward food of the steak-and-ribs, pizza-and-pasta variety for a couple of decades. Prices are very reasonable for Carmel with main courses starting at $10; the bar is a popular gathering spot for locals. *La Bohème* (☎ 831-624-7500), on Dolores St near 7th Ave, lays on the European romantic look with a shovel, but the three-course French meal, which changes daily and costs about around $25, is a good value.

Jack London's (☎ 831-626-2336), tucked into an alley off San Carlos St between 5th and 6th Aves, has been a Carmel mainstay since 1973 and serves inexpensive, no-nonsense fare (burgers are around $7) and a selection of local microbrews.

Even more atmosphere reigns at the *Bully III* (☎ 831-625-1750), at Dolores St and 8th Ave, which has upscale pub grub at sensible prices (entrées cost less than $10); prime rib is a specialty.

One of the best and most fun places in town is the *Forge in the Forest* (☎ 831-624-2233), at the corner of 5th and Junípero Aves. You can dine on the flowery patio or in the rustic interior, where there's an authentic blacksmith's forge. The food is American/Californian and mid-priced, and there's a daily happy hour with free appetizers. *Ristorante Piatti* (☎ 831-625-1766), at the corner of 6th and Junípero Aves, is a stylish Italian spot with sunny decor and main courses costing $10 to $16.

CENTRAL COAST

Caffé Napoli (☎ 831-625-4033), on Ocean Ave near Lincoln St, is a hugely popular small, southern-Italian restaurant with pizzas and pastas priced around $9, plus other dishes.

Entertainment

For great coffee, locals swear by *Caffé Cardinale (☎ 831-626-2095)*, in an alley off Ocean Ave between San Carlos and Dolores Sts, which roasts its beans on the premises but closes at 6 pm. Lots of places have popular bars but the *Red Lion Tavern (☎ 831-625-6765)*, in a lane off Dolores St, between 5th and 6th Aves, has that unique British pub flair. The *Tuck Box (☎ 831-624-6365)*, on Dolores St near 7th Ave, is equally British, but here it's tea and scones rather than beer (closed Monday and Tuesday).

On summer weekends, outdoor performances take place at the *Outdoor Forest Theatre (☎ 831-626-1681)*, on Mountain View between Forest and Guadalupe Sts. The *Carmel Bach Festival (☎ 831-624-1521, 831-624-2046 for tickets)* is held from mid-July to early August. The *Golden Bough Playhouse (☎ 831-622-0100)*, on Monte Verde St, at 8th Ave, is the home of the Pacific Repertory Theatre.

Shopping

Shopping is a favorite pastime for locals and visitors alike, and Carmel has plenty of outlets to satisfy the urge. Not chain shops, mind you; they're banned in central Carmel, although the definition of 'chain' must be different when applied to Italian and English stores, because you will find places such as Benetton and Crabtree & Evelyn.

Unique shops are here en masse, with a particular abundance of art and craft galleries and shops selling all those things you don't need but are nice to have anyway. Carmel galleries are laden with happy dolphin sculptures, oil paintings of local scenery (would you believe paintings of golf courses?) and pictures by artists who discovered impressionism a century too late. What follows is a list of places that provides a flavor for the types of boutiques you'll find.

Anderle Gallery (☎ 831-624-4199), Lincoln St between Ocean and 7th Aves – tribal arts, crafts from Southeast Asia, particularly Indonesia, Korean antiques

Augustina (☎ 831-624-2403), Lincoln St between Ocean and 7th Aves – rhinestone cowboy gear, fringed leather jackets, appliquéd boots and the like

Carmel Art Association (☎ 831-624-6176), Dolores St between 5th and 6th Aves – founded in 1927, presents works by local artists

Carmel Bay Company (☎ 831-624-3868), Ocean Ave at Lincoln St – filled with books, accessories and gewgaws for house and garden

Carmel Cutlery (☎ 831-624-6699), Dolores St at 6th Ave – 'collectible knives' is the subtitle: knives (lots of them), scissors, swords and the odd battle-ax

Conway of Asia (☎ 831-624-3643), Dolores St at 7th Ave – oriental rugs and interesting artifacts from Tibet, the subcontinent and northern Southeast Asia

Galerie Blue Dog (☎ 831-626-4444), 6th Ave between Lincoln and Dolores Sts – George Rodriguez has decided when you do something good, you might as well stick to it; here find his surreal paintings of his dog Tiffany, who died in 1980

It's Cactus (☎ 831-626-4213), Mission St between Ocean and 7th Aves – colorful Mexican, African and Central and South American crafts, an interesting and fun shop, with a friendly owner

Photography West Gallery (☎ 831-625-1587), Dolores St between Ocean and 7th Aves – interesting photography by a variety of established and up-and-coming photographers

Vanguard Gallery (☎ 831-622-9034), Lincoln St between Ocean and 7th Aves – Vargas nudes, those cheesecake pinups of the '50s that have assumed the position of high art

Weston Gallery (☎ 831-624-4453), 6th Ave between Dolores and Lincoln Sts – any commentary on Carmel galleries has to mention this one; yes, Edward Weston was a Carmel native, Ansel Adams helped create a Carmel school of photography, and some of the work displayed here is terrific

Wings America (☎ 831-626-9464), northwest corner of Dolores St and 7th Ave – a big boy's toy shop full of aviation memorabilia and superb (and commensurately expensive) wooden models of aircraft

Getting There & Around

Carmel is only 5 miles south of Monterey by Hwy 1. See the Monterey Getting Around section for bus information.

Free unlimited car parking can be found at Vista Lobos Park at 3rd Ave and Torres St. Bay Bike Rentals (☎ 831-625-2453) is on Lincoln St between 5th and 6th Aves.

AROUND CARMEL
Point Lobos State Reserve

Point Lobos (☎ 831-624-4909) makes a wonderful finale to the peninsula and a fitting introduction to the spectacular scenery of Big Sur. The reserve, with its dramatically rocky and convoluted coastline, takes its name from the *Punta de los Lobos Marinos*, or the 'point of the sea wolves,' named by the Spanish for the howls of the resident sea lions. Point Lobos encompasses 554 land acres as well as 750 submerged acres, which are good for scuba diving, though permits are required (call ☎ 831-624-8413 for details). There's a terrific selection of short walks, most of them less than a mile in length, which take in the wild and inspiring scenery. Favorite destinations include **Sea Lion Point** and **Devil's Cauldron**, the latter a blowhole and whirlpool that gets splashy at high tide. At the end of the main road, **Bird Island** is good for bird watching and for starting out on long hikes.

The reserve entrance is on the west side of Hwy 1, about 4 miles south of Carmel. It's open 9 am to 7 pm daily (to 5 pm in winter); $7 per vehicle, free for walk-ins.

Carmel Highlands

The 12-mile stretch between Carmel and Big Sur is popular for scuba diving and bird watching. Cypress and redwood trees are plentiful, and sea lions like to hang out on the offshore rocks. South of Point Lobos is Carmel Highlands, where million-dollar homes cling to cliffs above the Pacific. En route you pass **Garrapata State Park**, an off-the-beaten-track state park with rest rooms, picnic tables and barbecues. The trail leading down to the beach is one of the few shore access points between Carmel and Big Sur. The $7 day-use fee is avoided by parking on Hwy 1.

Upper Central Coast

The austere Santa Lucia Range runs from Point Sur to Morro Bay, separating the Pacific Ocean from the San Joaquin Valley. The range's western edge plunges directly into the sea while the east side's rolling foothills support ranches and vineyards. Travel here is either along Hwy 1 (along the coast) or Hwy 101 (on the east side of the mountains). The two highways converge in San Luis Obispo and north of Salinas. Once you get on Hwy 1 between those two cities you're pretty much committed, so be sure you have the time for this slower, scenic route. The narrow, slow and winding Nacimiento-Fergusson Rd (G18), which cuts across the Santa Lucia mountains, is the only road connecting the highways between San Simeon and Carmel. The road passes nearby the remote Mission San Antonio de Padua (see Along Hwy 101 later in this chapter).

Scenic Hwy 1 offers one of the most dramatically beautiful drives in the world. It journeys along some of California's most spectacular coastline, where wind and water are continually shaping the Santa Lucia Range into cliffs and rocky promontories. Coastal redwoods grow along the Big and Little Sur rivers, and the Ventana Wilderness supports the Santa Lucia fir which is endemic to the area. Tourist 'sights' consist of coves, campgrounds and state parks until you reach Hearst Castle in San Simeon.

Hwy 101 is more interesting than I-5, which runs through the desert farther inland, but not nearly as scenic as Hwy 1. Hwy 101 follows the route of the old El Camino Real, built to connect California's missions. The scenery is mostly rolling fields and pastures, but the highway does provide access to several historical sites and Pinnacles National Monument.

BIG SUR
• population 1100 • elevation 155 feet

Big Sur is an experience rather than one tangible place. Its raw beauty is awe inspiring, its folksy residents endearing. There are no traffic lights, banks or shopping centers, and when the sun goes down, the moon and stars are the only streetlights.

Big Sur must be explored by car, since you'll want to make frequent stops to take in the rugged beauty and stunning vistas that reveal themselves after every hairpin turn.

Driving Hwy 1

Completed in 1937, after 18 years of construction (mostly with convict labor), Hwy 1 is California's first Scenic Highway, and it certainly deserves the title. The curvy two-lane road isn't meant for quick travel; driving straight from Carmel to San Luis Obispo takes about five hours. Taking in the brilliant coastal scenery here is mandatory; towering, golden cliffs plummet down to the rock-strewn sea, which can change from peacock blue to the deep purple of a marlin's back in a heartbeat. Photographers are advised to load up on film and to plan on spending all the daylight hours making the trip. You will, quite literally, find yourself pulling off the road every hundred yards or so for that perfect shot. From December to March, whales migrating north from Baja make a fantastic roadside attraction.

If you enjoy driving, you will *love* the banks and swerves of this road. But your patience can be tested: summer brings fog and heavy traffic, and the highway is often closed during winter storms. Just relax and let the road reveal one incredibly beautiful vista after another. Buy gas in Carmel or San Luis Obispo to avoid exorbitant gas prices (sometimes more than double the regular price), and bring your own food for picnicking. Beach access is limited since much of the land along Hwy 1 is private (trespassing laws are strictly enforced), and swimming is discouraged because of undertows and rip currents. Trails that do lead to the beach require tennis shoes or sturdy sandals.

Although it's only 90 miles from Carmel to San Simeon, driving along this narrow two-lane highway is slow going, especially in summer when traffic is dense and it may be difficult and dangerous to pass slower vehicles. Be on the lookout for bicyclists as well; Hwy 1 is a popular route. Allow at least four hours to cover the distance. Traveling after dark is perilous and futile, since you won't be able to see any of the countryside. Keep this in mind, especially if you're in the area during short winter days.

History

The Esselen tribe, known to date back at least 3000 years in the area, occupied settlements along the coast, surviving primarily on acorns, rabbit, deer, bear and sea mammals. They were wiped out by diseases brought by the Spanish before the first US settlers arrived.

Big Sur was named by Spanish settlers living in Carmel's mission who referred to the unexplored wilderness as *el pais grande del sur* (the big country to the south). They named the two coastal rivers *el rio grande del sur* (the big river to the south) and *el rio chiquito del sur* (the little river to the south). The names were made official by the arrival of Big Sur's post office in the 1900s.

In 1852, John Rogers Cooper (also known as Juan Bautista Rogerio Cooper) filed claim to Rancho El Sur, stretching from Cooper Point to the mouth of the Little Sur River. Cooper Point and the headquarters for the ranch are now part of Andrew Molera State Park.

Homesteaders arrived in the early 1900s and supported the canning and lumbering industries. At the turn of the century, Big Sur supported a larger population than it does today. Electricity arrived in the 1950s and TV reception in the 1980s.

In the 1950s and '60s, Big Sur became a favorite retreat for writers and artists, including Henry Miller, who lived here from 1947 to 1964, and Beat Generation members Lawrence Ferlinghetti and Jack Kerouac. Today, Big Sur still attracts its share of New Age mystics and 'artistic' and eccentric types.

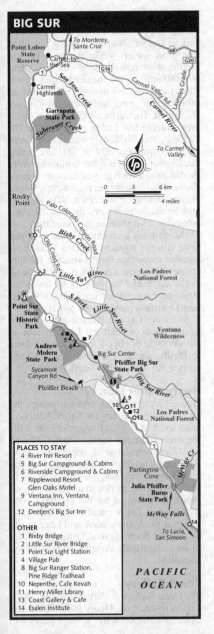

BIG SUR

PLACES TO STAY
4 River Inn Resort
5 Big Sur Campground & Cabins
6 Riverside Campground & Cabins
7 Ripplewood Resort,
   Glen Oaks Motel
9 Ventana Inn, Ventana
   Campground
12 Deetjen's Big Sur Inn

OTHER
1 Bixby Bridge
2 Little Sur River Bridge
3 Point Sur Light Station
4 Village Pub
8 Big Sur Ranger Station,
   Pine Ridge Trailhead
10 Nepenthe, Cafe Kevah
11 Henry Miller Library
13 Coast Gallery & Cafe
14 Esalen Institute

Orientation & Information

Rocky Point marks Big Sur's northern end, and the Esalen Institute defines the southern end. Tourists often wander into businesses along Hwy 1 and ask, 'How much farther to Big Sur?' In fact, there is no town of Big Sur, though you may see the name on many maps.

If Big Sur has a hub, it is Big Sur Center (called the Village), which is really just a cluster of shops 15 miles south of Rocky Point. Here lie the post office and the Big Sur Bazaar (☎ 831-667-2197), a combination market, deli and all-purpose shop, which stocks camping supplies, film, maps and regional natural history books. This is the most affordable place to get food if you're on a budget, and they stock a variety of picnic supplies. It's open until 8 pm daily, until 6:30 pm off-season.

El Sur Grande, a free newspaper published once a year, lists all of Big Sur's campgrounds, parks and businesses. It is available at nearly every stop along Hwy 1 or by contacting *El Sur Grande* (☎ 831-667-2100), PO Box 87, Big Sur, CA 93920.

For information about Los Padres National Forest, the Ventana Wilderness or the state parks, stop by the Big Sur Ranger Station (☎ 831-667-2315, 831-667-2423), about 3 miles south of the Village shops. The office is open 8 am to 4:30 pm daily and has maps posted. For road information, call ☎ 831-757-2006. The nearest medical services are at Community Hospital of the Monterey Peninsula (☎ 831-624-5311), reached by taking the westbound Hwy 68 exit off Hwy 1.

Bixby Bridge

Bixby Bridge spans Bixby Creek in a graceful 320-foot arch, 2 miles south of Rocky Point. Completed in 1932 and originally called the 'Rainbow Bridge,' it is composed of 600,000 pounds of steel reinforcement and 825 truckloads worth of concrete.

Before the bridge was built, travelers had to trek 14 miles inland on what's called the **Old Coast Rd**, which heads east from Bixby Bridge's north side and reconnects with Hwy 1 across from Andrew Molera State

Park. Brave travelers can still make the adventure with a sturdy car.

Little Sur River Bridge

South of Bixby Bridge, Hwy 1 rises to the lofty Hurricane Point headlands, then drops to the low-lying **Little Sur River Bridge**. Here the Little Sur River makes a gentle sweep – a favorite subject for local artists – before it meets the sea, turning the water bright blue with its heavy limestone deposits. During the dry season the river forms a lagoon behind a sandbar. **Pico Blanco**, the white-and-green-striped mountain to the east, stands 3709 feet tall and was revered by the Esselen Indians as the sacred birthplace of man and beast.

Point Sur State Historic Park

About 19 miles south of Carmel is **Point Sur**, that imposing volcanic rock that looks like an island but is actually connected to land by a sand bar. Atop the rock, 361 feet above the surf, is the 1899 **Point Sur Light Station**, which was in operation until 1972. Lighthouse enthusiasts can take a three-hour tour on weekends (plus on Wednesday in summer); $5 adults, $3 teens and $2 ages five to 12. Call ☎ 831-625-4419 for the current schedule.

Andrew Molera State Park

Once part of Juan Bautista Cooper's 9000-acre Rancho El Sur, Andrew Molera State Park (☎ 831-667-2315) has $3 walk-in campsites equipped with fire pits, vault toilets and drinking water. Among eucalyptus trees, just north of the meadow, is the **Cooper Cabin**, the oldest structure in Big Sur. A gentle ½-mile trail leads past the campground and sycamore trees to a beautiful beach where the Big Sur River runs into the ocean. From here, several trails head south along the bluffs above the beach.

Molera Horseback Tours (☎ 831-625-5486, 800-942-5486), in a barn near the entrance to Andrew Molera State Park, offers two-hour guided trail rides for around $40 between April and January. Beyond their barn is the **Molera Educational Sanctuary & Ornithology Center**, open 9 am to 4 pm weekdays.

Pfeiffer Big Sur State Park

Pfeiffer Big Sur State Park is the largest state park in Big Sur. Named after Big Sur's first European settlers – Michael and Barbara Pfeiffer, who arrived in 1869 – the park occupies 680 acres of the former Pfeiffer Ranch Resort and contains the original homestead cabin and the graveyard where the Pfeiffers are buried. The rustic administration buildings and **Big Sur Lodge** were built in the 1930s by the Civilian Conservation Corps (CCC). Campsites ($14 to $24) are beside the Big Sur River in a flat-bottomed valley shaded by redwood groves; facilities include showers and laundry but no hookups. Reservations through Parknet (☎ 800-444-7275) may be made from April through October; otherwise, it's first-come, first-served.

Hiking trails loop through the park and head into the adjacent Ventana Wilderness. Summer crowds are the drawback to this otherwise idyllic scene. The Pine Ridge Trailhead, in the south end of the parking lot, is the major access point for the Ventana Wilderness. Overnight parking costs $6 per car.

Sycamore Canyon Rd, the second major turnoff south of Point Sur Light Station on the west side of Hwy 1, winds 2 miles down to **Pfeiffer Beach**. The road is rugged and narrow but the beach is worth the trip.

Henry Miller Library

Housed amid gardens and sculptures, the Henry Miller Library (☎ 831-667-2574), 3 miles south of Big Sur Ranger Station, is Big Sur's most cultured venue. It was the home of Miller's great friend, the painter Emil White, until his death in 1989 and is now run by a nonprofit agency. The library has all of Miller's written works, many of his paintings, translations of his books and a great collection of Big Sur and Beat Generation material. Grabbing a book and hanging out on the deck is encouraged. Official hours are 11 am to 5 pm daily, except Monday (but call ahead); $1.

Coast Gallery

The Coast Gallery & Cafe (☎ 831-667-2301), 2 miles south of the Henry Miller Library, is made of redwood water storage tanks that originally served the Oakland Naval Facility. The gallery was a showplace for bohemian artists' work in the 1950s, but now has a haphazard collection of works by local artists and craftspeople and is largely geared toward tourists. Open 9 am to 5 pm daily.

Partington Cove

From the west side of Hwy 1, a well-marked fire road descends ½ mile along Partington Creek to Partington Cove, named for John Partington, who built the original dock there in the 1880s. Originally, the cove was used for loading tanbark, a cross between an oak and a chestnut whose bark was used in tanning leather; during Prohibition it was an alleged landing for bootleggers. You can still see a wooden footbridge and tunnel (built in the 1870s), as well as the old dock's fittings, which were revived during the construction of Hwy 1 in the 1920s.

Julia Pfeiffer Burns State Park

Julia Pfeiffer Burns State Park (☎ 831-667-2315) extends 2 miles south from Partington Cove along both sides of Hwy 1 and features redwood, tan oak, madrone and chaparral. At the park entrance (on the east side of Hwy 1) are forested picnic grounds along McWay Creek and an old cabin (on the creek's north side, just past the picnic area) that housed the Waters, the first homesteaders on the land now occupied by the state park. The Waters built Saddle Rock Ranch here in the 1900s. The Ewoldsen Trail offers good views of the ocean and the Santa Lucia mountains.

The park's highlight is California's only coastal waterfall, 80-foot **McWay Falls**, which drops straight into the sea (onto the sand at low tide). To reach the waterfall viewpoint, take the trail heading west from the park entrance and cross beneath Hwy 1. Nearby, two walk-in campsites sit on a semi-protected bluff. Rates are $14 to $16; for reservations, call Parknet at ☎ 800-444-7275. Camper registration is at Pfeiffer Big Sur campground, about 12 miles north.

Esalen Institute

Marked only by a lighted sign reading 'Esalen Institute, By Reservation Only,' Esalen is world renowned for its seminars and natural hot springs. Workshops deal with anything that 'promotes human values and potentials,' from African dance to yoga to exploring the inner game of golf. In business for decades, it's sort of the 'old timer' of the New Age.

The Esalen baths are fed by a natural hot spring and sit on a ledge above the ocean, below the center's main building. Tubs formerly available to the public for late-night soaking were destroyed by the fury unleashed by El Niño in 1998, but they may be replaced by the time you read this; call first.

When space is available, you can stay at Esalen and use their new baths without participating in a seminar. Accommodations are in standard rooms and cost $125 per room (one or two people) from October through March and $150 per person in peak season. Dorms, sleeping four to six people, are $85 per person ($95 in peak season). Rates include three meals. For room reservations or to book a seminar, call ☎ 831-667-3005. For a free catalog with seminar dates and details, call ☎ 831-667-3000.

Ventana Wilderness

The 167,000-acre Ventana Wilderness is the backcountry of the Big Sur coast. It lies within the northern part of Los Padres National Forest, which straddles the Santa Lucia Range and runs parallel to the Big Sur coast for its entire length. Most of the wilderness is covered with oak and chaparral, though canyons cut by the Big Sur and Little Sur rivers support virgin stands of coastal redwoods. Scattered pockets of the endemic Santa Lucia fir grow in rocky outcroppings at elevations above 5000 feet.

The Ventana is especially popular with backpackers (day hikers usually stick to coastal trails). One favorite destination is **Sykes Hot Springs**, natural hot mineral pools (ranging from 98° to 110°F) framed by redwoods, about 11 miles from the wilderness boundary via the **Pine Ridge Trail** – the gateway into the wilderness.

The trailhead is at the Big Sur Ranger Station and has parking, fresh water and rest rooms. The Pacific Valley Ranger Station

(☎ 831-927-4211), south of Big Sur, gives access to the southern half of the wilderness. A good access point in this area is from the Kirk Creek Campground (see Southern Big Sur).

Backcountry and fire permits are available from both ranger stations. Note that the Ventana has the country's largest concentration of mountain lions (one cat per 10 square miles). See Dangers & Annoyances in the Facts for the Visitor chapter.

Places to Stay

Aside from camping, it's impossible to find cheap accommodations in Big Sur. Rooms at the relatively small number of cabins, inns and motels are pricey and often booked up weeks, if not months, in advance, especially in summer and on weekends year round. Make reservations early or count on staying outside Big Sur limits.

Camping All three state parks in Big Sur offer camping (see listings with each park description, mentioned earlier, for details).

Private campgrounds include *Big Sur Campground & Cabins* (☎ 831-667-2322), which has tent sites and trailer sites with hookups on the Big Sur River for $26 and summer tent cabins for $45. Cabins with bathrooms and kitchens are $80 to $130. The camp store stocks the basics, and there are laundry facilities, hot showers, volleyball and basketball courts and a playground. A half mile to the south, *Riverside Campground & Cabins* (☎ 831-667-2414) has similar prices and facilities. Another option is the *Ventana Campground* (☎ 831-667-2688) set in a 40-acre redwood grove, where secluded campsites for two cost $25; they attract a relatively subdued crowd.

Inns & Resorts Cabins at the *Ripplewood Resort* (☎ 831-667-2242) cost $60 to $99, tax inclusive, and have kitchens and private bathrooms. The cabins along the river are peaceful and surrounded by redwoods, but those on Hwy 1 can be quite noisy. Their coffee shop is good for breakfast and lunch, with $4 omelets and superb burgers for $5. The adjacent market stocks fresh produce

and picnic supplies. Next door, the *Glen Oaks Motel* (☎ 831-667-2105) has clean and simple rooms with phones for $45/55.

Deetjen's Big Sur Inn (☎ 831-667-2377) is a rustic conglomeration of rooms, redwoods and wisteria along Castro Creek. Rooms cost $75 to $180 and get booked far in advance, though you benefit from a last-minute cancellation. Exactly why this place is so popular is a mystery, since the staff can be quite unwelcoming.

The *Ventana Inn* (☎ 831-667-2331, 800-628-6500, fax 831-667-2419), a stylish yet low-key country inn, regularly garners accolades from travel experts and has served as the Big Sur hideaway of a huge stable of Hollywood A-list members, including Robert Redford, Tom Cruise and Mel Gibson. An aura of serenity and romance pervades the complex, which integrates a Japanese bathhouse, sauna and sun deck, plus two pools. Rooms are equipped with a spa, fireplace and robes. Such luxury has its price: $260 to $725 per night. Below the ritzy resort is the Ventana Campground.

Places to Eat

The *Village Pub* (☎ 831-667-2355), next to the River Inn Resort, is a good place for a beer and a game of darts, and it's where locals congregate to watch major televised events (few people in Big Sur have their own TV). The cook makes wonderful soups, fish-and-chips and veggie burgers for mostly under $5.

Known for its elaborate gardens, cliffside location and eccentric owners who have lived in Big Sur since 1949, *Nepenthe* (☎ 831-667-2345) is a scenic place for a drink at sunset. The bar and dining room have redwood beams and panoramic glass windows facing the sea and they open onto a patio that sprawls atop the cliffs. The menu incorporates local produce, fresh herbs, game and seafood. More affordable and just below the main restaurant, *Cafe Kevah* has salads, soups and sandwiches for under $10; it's open daily from 9 am to 4 pm.

Even if you can't afford to stay at the *Ventana Inn*, you can still sample its unique ambience over dinner in the romantically rustic restaurant (☎ 831-667-2331) – which is not to say that eating here is cheap. But you definitely get your money's worth, with impeccable service and dishes that are both artistic and tasty and complemented by a stunning wine list. If you're confused, ask your server for a recommendation.

SOUTHERN BIG SUR

South of the Esalen Institute, Hwy 1 straightens out considerably and there is a wider sweep of lowlands between mountain and sea. The landscape is barren and wild compared to Big Sur's river-fed valley, and services are few and far between.

Lopez Point, a prominent south-facing promontory, defines the northern end of Lucia Bay. The *Lucia Lodge* (☎ *831-667-2391*) sits 500 feet above the bay with cabins for $75 to $150, and has a restaurant with a fabulous southwest view and overpriced lunch and dinner.

A half mile south of the lodge, a large white cross on the highway marks the entrance to the **New Camaldolese Hermitage**. The monks in this self-sufficient community devote their lives to prayer and meditation. Silent and nondirected retreats are open to men and women. For information, call ☎ 831-667-2456.

About 4 miles south of Lucia, *Kirk Creek Campground* (☎ *831-385-5434*) has 33 tent and trailer sites (no hookups) on a first-come, first-served basis. Though rather unprotected, it offers easy access to a sandy beach and has flush toilets. Rates are $10 in winter and $15 in summer.

On the Nacimiento-Fergusson Rd, which cuts over to Hwy 101, are the *Nacimiento Campground* and *Ponderosa Campground*. Both have tent sites with vault toilets for $6, but other than that they are pretty primitive. Nearby, the Nacimiento Ridge gives views of the ocean and eastern foothills of the Santa Lucia Range. About 4 miles south of the turnoff is the aforementioned Pacific Valley Ranger Station.

One of the nicest spots between Big Sur and San Simeon, *Plaskett Creek Campground* (☎ *831-385-5434 for information*), south of Pacific Valley on the east side of Hwy 1, has 43 large, grassy sites shaded by

Monterey cypress (first-come, first-served) for $10/15 winter/summer. Trails to the beach leave from the west side of the highway, directly across from the campground, and about ½ mile to the north is a turnout for the **Sand Dollar Beach** picnic area, which has trails to the longest sandy beach in the area.

About 2 miles south of Sand Dollar Beach is a series of coves known for their jade deposits. In 1971, three divers recovered a 9000-pound jade boulder that measured eight feet long and brought in $180,000. The best time to find jade, which is black or blue-green and looks dull until you dip it in water, is during low tide or after a big storm.

Named for an offshore outcropping that looks like a fat lady, **Gorda** (Spanish for 'fat') is best known for its annual Jade Festival, held the first weekend in October. The Gorda General Store & Deli (☎ 805-927-3918) has camping supplies, and the adjacent *Whale Watchers Cafe* serves food from 8:30 am to 8 pm. Gas prices are steep, but the station has clean rest rooms and public showers. Six cabins from $125 to $175 and four newer rooms with full amenities, such as whirlpool and hot tubs, go for $150. Rates are negotiable depending on the season, and they arrange whale-watching tours and visits to local seal colonies. Contact the General Store & Deli.

HEARST CASTLE

Imagine driving up the winding road to the imposing castle looming above and arriving there for dinner at the 50-foot dining table. Charlie Chaplin is to your right, a reigning queen is on your left and the newest screen heartthrob is batting eyes at you over the roast pheasant. All of this takes place under the intense scrutiny of newspaper magnate William Randolph Hearst – one of the most powerful men in the world – who literally launched the Spanish-American War to sell his newspapers. Well, you never made the list of the world's most desirable dinner guests, but you can still relive the moment at Hearst Castle.

Perched high on a hill dubbed 'The Enchanted Hill' by Hearst, and overlooking vast pastureland and the Pacific Ocean, the castle is a monument to wealth and ambition. It sprawls out over 127 acres of lushly landscaped gardens, accentuated by shimmering pools and fountains and statues from ancient Greece and Moorish Spain.

The compound has a total of 165 rooms in four houses, all of them furnished with Italian and Spanish antiques and enhanced by any of 41 fireplaces and 61 bathrooms.

There's a lavish private chapel and numerous entertainment rooms.

Hearst's art collection was so vast that an accurate calculation of its size or value was never possible. Spanish cathedral ceilings covered with flags from the Palio in Siena, Italy, hover above a French refectory table. The display of wealth borders on grotesque, and the amalgam of styles and periods is enough to make any architect or historian

The Man & His Castle: William Randolph Hearst (1863-1951)

According to the Orson Welles film *Citizen Kane*, William Randolph Hearst died an unhappy and tormented man, an interpretation that must be considered as Hollywood taking major license with reality. Born into great wealth in San Francisco in 1863, Hearst was the only son of George and Phoebe Apperson Hearst, who had come west from Missouri. His father was a self-made man who owed his considerable wealth to interests in gold and silver mining ventures, including the Comstock Lode in Nevada. When he was 10 years old, his mother took little William on a grand tour of Europe, where he developed his lifelong penchant for art and culture.

Hearst went on to Harvard, where he had his first brush with journalism, but he didn't grasp the true object of his desire – his father's *Examiner* newspaper – until 1887. With a $20 million fortune behind him, Hearst could afford to make enemies where other papers could not, namely in the arenas of business and politics. His papers covered stories that others wouldn't touch and became the voice and champion of working class laborers and, though not openly, democratic ethics.

Over time, Hearst acquired and built a tremendous publishing empire, encompassing more than 50 newspapers across the US. Outselling his competition became Hearst's obsession. He invented news if there wasn't any; the Spanish-American War is often directly attributed to reports in the Hearst papers of the crimes committed by the Spanish in Cuba, which never happened. Hearst created the 'banner headline' and used it as a bludgeon to become the king of yellow journalism and muckraking. The *San Francisco Examiner* and *Good Housekeeping* and *Cosmopolitan* magazines are still run by the Hearst Corporation, though at press time, the *Examiner* was in danger of folding.

After inheriting the family fortune upon his mother's death in 1919 (George died in 1891), Hearst picked San Simeon, where he had spent many summers as a boy, as the site of his new private home, *La Cuesta Encantada*, the Enchanted Hill, now known as Hearst Castle. He hired renowned architect Julia Morgan to turn his vision into a reality. Though originally a reasonably sized project, the house grew to accommodate Hearst's expansive interest in art and in Hollywood actress Marion Davies. As Hearst purchased cathedral ceilings, refectory tables, Grecian urns and Roman columns, Davies invited Hollywood's elite to spend weekends at 'the ranch,' playing tennis, swimming, watching movies in a full-scale theater and driving through the zoo and gardens stocked with exotic animals and plants.

When Hearst died in 1951, the enormous project was still unfinished. But photos and reports from his last years reveal a man – surrounded by his wealth and the accolades of Hollywood's beautiful and talented – who seemed, in spite of his bizarre excesses, oddly contented with what he had done.

grimace. But to visit the castle is to 'ooh' and 'aah' at Hearst's casual, if clumsy, attempt at becoming royal. And the subterranean pool, where Errol Flynn and his ilk dallied, is worth the price of admission all by itself.

Information

Hearst Castle, a state historical monument, is open for tours daily except on Thanksgiving, Christmas and New Year's Day. The first tour starts at 8:20 am; the last leaves at 3:20 pm (there may be a 4:20 pm tour in summer). Tours last 1¾ hours (including 30 minutes on the bus between the Visitor Center and the castle) and cost $14 for adults, $8 for kids six to 12, free for kids under six. Tour frequency ranges from one per hour in winter to up to six per hour at peak times. The castle gets really busy between May and September and on holiday weekends, and tours often sell out in advance, so be sure to make reservations via Parknet (☎ 800-444-4445).

All tours start at the Visitor Center at the bottom of the hill. Besides the ticket office, the center also offers food service, two gift shops and a free exhibit on Hearst and his castle. Also at the Visitor Center is the **National Geographic Theater** (☎ 805-927-6811), with its five-story large-screen theater, which regularly shows an entertaining and educational 40-minute film on Hearst's life and the construction and life at the castle. A second feature (*The Mysteries of Egypt* at the time of research) screens several times daily. Admission is $7 for adults, $5 for children; double features are $12/8.

Organized Tours

There are four tours of the estate; all include visits to the estate's stunning Greco-Roman outdoor **Neptune Pool** and the indoor **Roman Pool**, lined with gold and Venetian glass.

Tour 1 This is the best tour for first-timers. In Casa Grande, the main house, you'll visit the huge Assembly sitting room, the refectory (dining room), the billiards room and the theater where old home movies of celebrities frolicking at the castle are shown. You'll also see the esplanade, gardens and the Casa del Sol guest cottage.

Tour 2 This tour shows off the upper floors of Casa Grande, including Hearst's Gothic-style private suite and study, the library with 5000 books and ancient Greek vases, the well-equipped and surprisingly modern pantry and kitchen, and the beautiful Doge Suite, modeled after the Doge's Palace in Venice.

Tour 3 Good for those interested in architecture, this tour takes you to the north wing of Casa Grande, which is the least altered part of the entire estate and was built in Hearst's final years (totally different from anything else). You'll also see a video about Hearst Castle's construction and all rooms of Casa del Monte, a 10-room guest cottage.

Tour 4 This tour, available April to October, shows a 'hidden terrace and gardens,' once part of the original plans but covered up in later construction and rediscovered during more recent restoration. The tour also covers the esplanade, a guest cottage, the pool dressing rooms and the wine cellar of Casa Grande.

Evening Tour Offered on selected Fridays and Saturdays in spring and fall only, the hugely popular evening tours feature docents in period dress 'acting' as Hearst's guests and staff. Besides touring the most extraordinary rooms of Casa Grande, you'll also see the guest cottage Casa del Mar and the pools and gardens illuminated by hundreds of lights. These tours last 2¼ hours and cost $25/13.

SAN SIMEON
• population 460 • elevation 20 feet

San Simeon began life in the 1850s as a whaling station. In 1865, George Hearst bought 45,000 acres of land and established a beachside settlement on the west side of Hwy 1, across from today's entrance to Hearst Castle. The Hearst Corporation still owns most of the land here, and the Julia Morgan houses formerly inhabited by Hearst Castle staff are now home to the cowboys who run the corporation's 80,000-acre cattle ranch. **Sebastian's Store**, a California historical landmark built in 1852, is still going strong. It has a good inventory of food, plus Hearst souvenirs, a nice cafe and post office. Adjacent to the buildings, William Randolph Hearst State Beach has a pleasant sandy stretch with intermittent rock outcroppings and a rickety wooden pier ($5 day-use fee).

Three miles south of the original San Simeon (just off the Hearst Corporation's property), modern San Simeon is a mile-long strip of unexciting motels and restaurants. The San Simeon Chamber of Commerce (☎ 805-927-3500, 800-342-5613, fax 805-927-6453) is at 9255 Hearst Drive and open 9 am to 5 pm, closed Sunday.

Along Hearst and Castillo Drives, which run parallel to Hwy 1, the *San Simeon Lodge* (☎ 805-927-4601, 9520 Castillo Drive) is a no-frills place with rooms costing $35 to $70. The *Silver Surf Motel* (☎ 805-927-4661, 800-621-3999, fax 805-927-3225, 9390 Castillo Drive) has a small indoor pool and spa, and rooms for as low as $29, though you're more likely to shell out $45 to $65.

San Simeon State Park

Six miles south of the original San Simeon, San Simeon State Park includes a long sandy beach and, on the east side of Hwy 1, the 134-site *San Simeon Creek Campground* and the *Washburn Campground* with 60 sites. Sites at San Simeon Creek, which has hot showers and flush toilets, cost $14 to $18; sites at Washburn are primitive and cost $7. For reservations call Parknet at ☎ 800-444-7275.

Within the state park are the **Santa Rosa Creek Natural Preserve**, which provides habitat for the endangered tidewater goby (a fish); the **San Simeon Natural Preserve**, which is a popular wintering spot for monarch butterflies; and the **Pânu Cultural Preserve**, the site of archeological finds dating back 6000 years. A 3.3-mile trail leads through the park.

CAMBRIA
• population 5400 • elevation 65 feet

About ½ mile inland, Cambria is a self-proclaimed artists' village surrounded by hills, and an excellent base for visits to Hearst Castle. The town's considerable charm almost completely disappears under the feet of summer tourists, but from late October to late May it's a good place to spend the afternoon amidst shops and art galleries. Most commercial activity is centered on Main St.

Moonstone Beach (Cambria's coastal half), named for the opalescent stones once abundant here, has low bluffs and an accessible white sand beach across from a strip of mid- and high-priced motels. At the beach's northern end, **Leffingwell Landing** offers dramatic views and a picnic area shaded by Monterey cypress.

South of Cambria, off Hwy 1, minuscule **Harmony** (population 18) is a quirky slice of Americana. It consists of an old creamery that houses artists' workshops, and it deserves a quick browse.

Places to Stay

Cambria's lodgings are concentrated along Moonstone Beach Drive, though the most affordable places are in the Village. Prices fluctuate with the seasons and can be as much as double the base rate on weekends and from May to September.

The **Blue Bird Motel** (☎ 805-927-4634, 1880 Main St) is one of the most affordable options, with rooms starting at $42 and cresting at $78; some have a refrigerator and fireplace. The **Creekside Inn** (☎ 805-927-4021, 800-269-5212, 2618 Main St) charges $35 to $70 and has 21 rooms, including some with a balcony facing a creek.

For beachside accommodations, try the **Cambria Shores Inn** (☎ 805-927-8644, 800-433-9179, 6276 Moonstone Beach Drive); rooms cost $45 to $95.

Places to Eat

Soto's Market (☎ 805-927-4411, 2244 Main St) has heaping sandwiches for around $3. **Linn's** (☎ 805-927-0371, 2277 Main St) has a huge menu and is famous for its chicken pot pie ($6) and desserts. Locals also recommend the **Sow's Ear Cafe** (☎ 805-927-4865, 2248 Main St) and the **Brambles Dinner House** (☎ 805-927-4716, 4005 Burton Drive), the latter housed in a cute English-style cottage. Both are casual places with a continental menu heavy on seafood, ribs and chicken, with main courses ranging from $10 to $22.

ESTERO BAY

Estero Bay is a long, shallow, west-facing bay with Cayucos at its north end and Montaña de Oro State Park at its south end. Morro Bay, a deep inlet guarded by Morro Rock and separated from the ocean by a 12-mile long sand spit, sits about halfway between the two and has most of Estero Bay's services and tourist activity. Morro Rock is the bay's unmistakable landmark, used as a navigation marker since the Portolá expedition in 1769.

Cayucos

• population 3000 • elevation 60 feet

At the bay's north end, small and slow-paced Cayucos (ki-YOU-kiss) offers a glimpse of local beach life without hordes of tourists. The town developed around the mouth of Cayucos Creek and a wharf and warehouse built by Captain James Cass in 1867. Ocean Ave, which parallels Hwy 1, is the main thor-

oughfare and lined with early-20th-century buildings, shops and restaurants.

Cayucos' gentle waves are good for beginning surfers. Fishing off the pier is allowed even without a license and the shoreline is easily explored by kayak. Good Clean Fun (☎ 805-995-1993), south of the pier at 136 Ocean Front St, rents kayaks for $35 per day and surfboards for $5 per hour.

Morro Bay

• population 9700 • elevation 100 feet

Apart from its commercially developed Embarcadero with its tourist-geared shops and restaurants, Morro Bay is still an honest-to-goodness fishing town. The bay itself is a giant estuary which harbors two dozen threatened and endangered species, including the brown pelican, sea otter and steelhead trout. In winter, about 120 migratory bird species make the bay their home.

Morro Bay's landmark is **Morro Rock**, one in a chain of nine volcanic peaks between Morro Bay and San Luis Obispo that is about 23 million years old. It got its name in 1542 from Juan Rodríguez Cabrillo who thought it resembled a Moorish turban. A pair of peregrine falcons nest among its high crevices. An aesthetic eyesore, but apparently not a deterrent to birds or tourists, is the trio of cigarette-shaped smokestacks of the coal power plant on the northern edge of the town. The plant borders **Morro Strand State Beach**, with its lovely wide sandy beach. Also here is a campground (see Places to Stay).

Morro Bay's **Chamber of Commerce** (☎ 805-772-4467, 800-231-0592, fax 805-772-6038, www.morrobay.com), 880 Main St, is open 8 am to 5 pm weekdays and 10 am to 3 pm Saturday.

Starting just south of Morro Rock, the Embarcadero is good for people-watching and is also the main stage of the popular Morro Bay Harbor Festival in October, and the launching area for boat tours.

The *Tiger's Folly II* paddle wheeler makes $6 harbor tours and features Dixieland jazz; for information, inquire at the Harbor Hut Restaurant (☎ 805-772-2257, 1205 Embarcadero). For views of kelp forests and

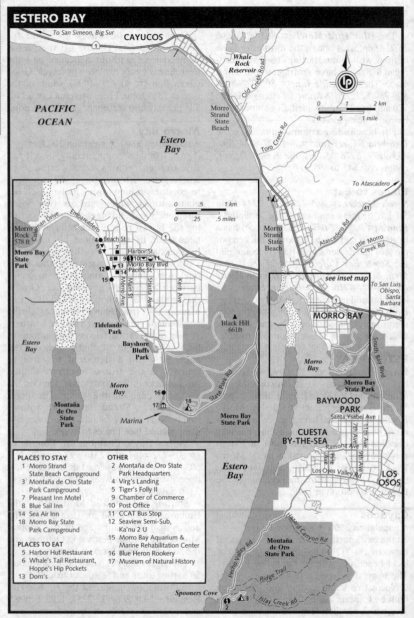

ESTERO BAY

PLACES TO STAY
1 Morro Strand
   State Beach Campground
3 Montaña de Oro State
   Park Campground
7 Pleasant Inn Motel
8 Blue Sail Inn
14 Sea Air Inn
18 Morro Bay State
   Park Campground

PLACES TO EAT
5 Harbor Hut Restaurant
6 Whale's Tail Restaurant,
   Hoppe's Hip Pockets
13 Dorn's

OTHER
2 Montaña de Oro State
   Park Headquarters
4 Virg's Landing
5 Tiger's Folly II
9 Chamber of Commerce
10 Post Office
11 CCAT Bus Stop
12 Seaview Semi-Sub,
   Ka'nu 2 U
15 Morro Bay Aquarium &
   Marine Rehabilitation Center
16 Blue Heron Rookery
17 Museum of Natural History

schools of fish, take a spin on the *Seaview* (☎ 805-772-9463), a semi-sub which plies the waters daily from Marina Square at 699 Embarcadero; $12.50/5.50 adults/children. If you'd rather do your own exploring, rent a canoe or kayak from Ka'nu 2 U (☎ 805-772-3349) next door. Rentals are $10 and $8 per hour, respectively, though rates drop for half-day and full-day rentals. Introductory three-hour tours are $32.50 and $39.50.

If you want to try your hand at **fishing**, Virg's Landing (☎ 805-772-1222, 800-762-5263), at 1215 Embarcadero (on the north end), is as good a place as any on the Central Coast. Daily trips are $36 per day ($25 half-day); poles rent for $7. An open ocean license is required and can be purchased at Virg's.

About midway along the Embarcadero and entered through a gift shop, the **Morro Bay Aquarium & Marine Rehabilitation Center** (☎ 805-772-7647) helps nurse sick seals, sea lions and otters back to health. The $2 admission includes a bag of smelt to feed to the resident animals, which greedily perform hilarious tricks. The aquarium itself is old-fashioned and low-key and showcases local denizens of the sea. It's usually open 9:30 am to 5:30 pm daily, with extended summer hours.

The Embarcadero ends at **Tidelands Park**, which has a grassy picnic area and playground. If you head up the stairs from the park and go right on Main St, you can take a scenic walk (about 2 miles) through Bayside Bluffs Park to Morro Bay State Park.

Places to Stay   At Morro Strand State Beach there's a 104-site *campground* (☎ 805-772-8812) in a parking lot setting with flush toilets and cold showers. Sites are $14 to $18, and it's open on a first-come, first-served basis year round.

Motels cluster around Main and Harbor Sts. In the off-season, room prices are often negotiable when you show up in person, but during the summer and the Harbor Festival reservations are imperative. Chain motels downtown include the *Econo Lodge* (☎ 805-772-5609, 1100 Main St), *Travelodge* (☎ 805-772-1259, 1080 Market Ave), at Beach St, and *Best Western El Rancho* (☎ 805-772-

2212, 2460 Main St), which all charge from around $55 in winter and $90 in summer.

Among the cheapest options is the 25-room *Sea Air Inn* (☎ 805-772-4437, 845 Morro Ave), at Morro Bay Blvd, which has spiffy digs for $35 to $55 in winter, $40 to $70 in summer, including continental breakfast. Their most expensive rooms have in-room hot tubs and ocean views.

Doing justice to its name is the flower-festooned *Pleasant Inn Motel* (☎ 805-772-8521, 888-772-8521, fax 805-772-1550, 235 Harbor St), which has a B&B-type flair and 10 prettily appointed rooms costing $39 to $58. Nearby is the rambling *Blue Sail Inn* (☎ 805-772-7132, 800-336-0707, 851 Market Ave); the rooms have balconies and ocean views but no air-conditioning and cost $65 to $95 year round.

Places to Eat   Locals recommend the *Whale's Tail Restaurant* (☎ 805-772-7555, 945 Embarcadero) for its tasty fish and pasta for around $10. Slightly cheaper bistro-style fare is on the menu at *Hoppe's Hip Pockets* (☎ 805-772-5371, 901 Embarcadero), which also has picture-perfect views of Morro Rock.

In business since 1942, *Dorn's* (☎ 805-772-2269, 801 Market St), above the Embarcadero, is a Morro Bay institution known for its clam chowder, fresh fish and extensive wine list. The decor is elegant, but anything goes for attire. Full dinners cost around $18, though you can make a meal of appetizers, chowder and bread for under $12.

Getting There & Away   Bus service between Morro Bay, San Luis Obispo and San Simeon is provided by Central Coast Area Transit (☎ 805-541-2228). Fares depend on distance traveled; unlimited day passes are $3. The main stop is at Morro Bay State Park between Harbor St and Piney Way.

Morro Bay State Park

This state park is quite developed and incorporates an 18-hole golf course, a marina with kayak rentals and a campground within its 1965 acres. The **Morro Bay Museum of Natural History** (☎ 831-772-2694) has a good

Chumash exhibit and a Discovery Center. Hours are 10 am to 5 pm daily; $3/1. Just north of the museum is a eucalyptus grove that harbors a large great blue heron rookery; from late February to May, you can spot them feeding their young.

The ***Morro Bay State Park Campground*** (☎ 805-772-7434), in the park's southern end about 2 miles from downtown, has beautiful sites fringed by eucalyptus and cypress trees; $14 for tents, up to $24 for RVs. There is hot water and trails lead to the beach. For reservations, call Parknet at ☎ 800-444-7275.

Montaña de Oro State Park

About 6 miles southwest of Morro Bay, Montaña de Oro State Park covers 8000 acres of undeveloped mountain and seaside terrain. Its coastal bluffs are a favorite spot for hiking, biking and horseback riding. The northern half of the park includes a row of sand dunes (some 85 feet high) and the 12-mile-long sand spit that separates Morro Bay from the Pacific. The park's southern section consists of fingerlike bluffs and an ancient marine terrace, which after seismic uplifting is now a series of 1000-foot peaks. In the spring, the mountains are blanketed by bright wildflowers that give the park its name, which means 'mountain of gold' in Spanish.

South of the park entrance, **Spooner Cove** is a popular beach and picnic area. Nearby is the park headquarters (☎ 805-528-0513), which doubles as a natural history museum and is open 11 am to 3 pm October to March, noon to 4 pm March to September. The adjacent day-use facilities cost $5. You can park at any of the trailheads or turnouts along Pecho Valley Rd for free.

Several hiking trails, including the **Bluff Trail**, which skirts the cliffs and has beach access points, and the **Alan Peak Trail**, which climbs to the park's highest point (1649 feet), start from the parking lot next to the headquarters. The best access to the sand dunes is along the **Hazard Canyon Reef Trail**, on Pecho Valley Rd, about halfway between the park entrance and headquarters. With a 4WD, you can reach the sand spit via Sand Spit Rd (also called 'Army' and 'Dune Buggy Rd'), which intersects Pecho Valley Rd ½ mile north of the park entrance.

Montaña de Oro State Park Campground (☎ 805-528-0513) is Estero Bay's nicest campground. It winds along a narrow canyon, near hiking trails and beaches, with each site near the creek or against the hillside. A 12-mile, 20-minute drive along a windy road is required to reach the campground, so it's not a quick place to crash. Sites cost $10 to $11, including use of picnic tables, fire pits and pit toilets and drinking water, but no showers. For reservations (mandatory from April to September), call Parknet at ☎ 800-444-7275.

To reach the park from Hwy 1, exit at South Bay Blvd, which heads south through the community of Baywood Park and dead-ends at Los Osos Valley Rd. Turn west and follow the road until it becomes Pecho Valley Rd, which leads straight into the park.

ALONG HWY 101

Small agricultural towns along the inland route, Hwy 101, offer little in the way of accommodations, but good Mexican restaurants abound. The stretch between Carmel and San Luis Obispo (about 100 miles) is easily traveled in one day. If you want to stay overnight, there is camping at Pinnacles National Monument and plenty of motels in Paso Robles.

Pinnacles National Monument

Pinnacles National Monument (☎ 831-389-4485, www.nps.gov/pinn), 12 miles northeast of Hwy 101, gets its name from the spires and crags which rise abruptly up to 1200 feet out of the oak- and chaparral-covered hills of the Salinas Valley. The rocks are remains of an ancient volcano that formed along the San Andreas Rift Zone about 23 million years ago. Their arches, spires, crags and lumps are the result of millions of years of erosion.

Orientation & Information The rock formations divide the park into East Pinnacles and West Pinnacles. East Pinnacles is reached via Hwy 146, which cuts west off Hwy 25 about 30 miles south of Hollister. For West Pinnacles, catch Hwy 146 going east off Hwy 101 at Soledad. While there is no road connecting the two sides, you can hike from one to the other in about an hour. Information, maps, books and bottled water are available from the Bear Gulch Visitor Center (east district) and the Chaparral Ranger Station (west district). The monument is open for day-use only (no overnight camping) and there's a $5 fee per vehicle, valid for seven consecutive days. The park is busiest in March, April and May and may fill to capacity by noon on some weekends.

Activities The devastation wrought by El Niño-induced floods in 1998 temporarily closed the park; some hiking trails were still off-limits at the time of writing, while others were in rather bad shape. Check with the visitor center or the ranger station about their current status. Although the Pinnacles' volcanic tufa is a bit crumbly, rock climbing is popular here. Climbing access signs direct people to the best spots, most of which are on the east side. Other activities include birding and wildflower walks in spring.

Places to Stay The privately owned *Pinnacles Campground* (☎ 831-389-4462), outside the East Pinnacles entrance off Hwy 146, has 78 tent sites and 36 RV hookups. Rates are $7 per person and include hot showers. There's also a swimming pool and convenience store. Off Hwy 101, Soledad has a bank, gas station, market, a few Mexican restaurants and some budget motels.

Mission San Antonio de Padua

This mission's remote location makes it a pain to reach, but it's well worth the trip. The lack of surrounding development is thanks to the US military, which owns the land, now Fort Hunter Ligget, an active army base. The mission was founded in 1771 by Father Junípero Serra and built with Indian labor from Salinas. The interior is quite elaborate, but the highlight is the mission grounds where you can see the remains of a grist mill, rip saw, corral, reservoir and irrigation system. Plan on spending two hours at the mission and another hour driving to and from. For information, call ☎ 831-385-4478.

The mission is open 8 am to 4 pm (from 11:30 am Sunday); free. Museum hours are the same; donation requested.

A quarter mile before the mission's entrance, on a small hill, is the Spanish-style Hacienda Inn – originally called the **Milpitas Ranch House** – designed by Julia Morgan for William Randolph Hearst. The inn is now owned by the military, but has a dining room and bar which are open to the public. Lunch and dinner are served weekdays, and the bar is open nightly. The food is neither gourmet nor military grub, but you can get a big steak and all the trimmings for around $10.

Getting There & Away From the north, take the Jolon exit (just before King City) and follow Jolon Rd (G14) 20 miles south to Mission Rd. From the south, take the Hwy 101 exit marked San Antonio Mission/Lake San Antonio Recreation Area (north of Bradley) and head 22 miles northwest on G18. You'll pass a few markets and gas stations on the north shore of Lake San Antonio (good for swimming) and pass through a military checkpoint. From here, Mission Rd goes another 5 miles to the mission.

You can also reach the mission from Hwy 1, via the Nacimiento-Fergusson Rd.

Paso Robles
• population 15,500 • elevation 721 feet

Traditionally the hub of surrounding ranches, Paso Robles is a lively town with a decidedly western feel. Recently, ranchers have found wine grapes more lucrative than beef, so vineyards are replacing cattle and Paso Robles is becoming increasingly chic. The city council recently restored the old town square into a lovely park. The chamber of commerce and visitor center (☎ 805-238-0506, 800-406-4040, fax 805-238-0527), 1225 Park St, has maps and information and is open 8:30 am to 5 pm weekdays, 10 am to 4 pm Saturday.

A surprising highlight is the **Helen Moe Antique Doll Museum** (☎ 805-238-2740), on Hwy 101 at Wellsona Rd, which has a stunning collection of about 1000 dolls displayed in period rooms. The most prized possession is a 16th-century doll that once belonged to

King Edward VI of England. Hours are 10 am to 5 pm Monday to Saturday; $3/1.

About 25 miles east off Hwy 101, on Route 46, a monument marks the spot where James Dean died in a car crash on September 30, 1955, at the age of 24.

Places to Stay & Eat Paso Robles' accommodations are concentrated along Spring St, the town's main thoroughfare. The *Melody Ranch Motel (☎ 805-238-3911, 800-909-3911 in California only, 939 Spring St)* has basic rooms costing $36 to $48 and a small pool. Quite a bit nicer, the *Adelaide Inn (☎ 805-238-2770, 800-549-7276 in California only, 1215 Ysabel Ave)* has 67 rooms for $38 to $52, nice landscaping and a heated pool.

Across from the town square, the historic *Paso Robles Inn (☎ 805-238-2660, 1103 Spring St)* served as a stage stop in the early 1900s, and has been functioning as a hotel and restaurant ever since. Rooms are priced at $69 and the restaurant is good and has a folksy atmosphere. The *Black Oak Restaurant (☎ 805-238-6330, 1535 24th St)*, an upscale coffee shop popular with locals, serves meaty main courses from $12 to $22. *Lolo's Mexican (☎ 805-239-5777, 305 Spring St)* is an inexpensive Mexican eatery.

Mission San Miguel Arcángel

North of Paso Robles off Hwy 101, Mission San Miguel Arcángel (☎ 805-467-3256), 775 Mission St, is the most accessible and one of the most authentic of the California missions. Established in 1797 as a stopover between Mission San Antonio de Padua and Mission San Luis Obispo de Tolosa, Mission San Miguel was number 16 in the chain of 21 missions. The current structure dates back to 1818 and has not been significantly altered since, as is evident from its rough and water-stained appearance. Murals painted by Chumash Indians, using pigment from local rock, are visible in the main church. It's still run by Franciscan fathers.

A self-guided walking tour begins in the gift shop and goes through the mission's interior rooms and garden; allow half an hour. Check out the enormous cactus in front of the mission. It was planted about the

same time the mission was built. Hours are 9:30 am to 4:30 pm daily; donations are appreciated. Mass is held on Sundays and church holidays.

Rios Caledonia Adobe

A quarter mile south of the mission is the Rios Caledonia Adobe (☎ 805-467-3357), which stands on mission property that Governor Pio Pico illegally sold to Petronillo Rios in 1846. Using Chumash labor, Rios built the two-story adobe as a ranch headquarters and hacienda for his family, later turning it into an inn and stage stop on the route between Los Angeles and San Francisco. Original adobe bricks are visible where the whitewash has peeled off. The adobe is open 10 am to 4 pm daily; free.

Lake Nacimiento

About 17 miles northwest of Paso Robles (reached via Lake Nacimiento Rd, clearly marked from Hwy 101), Lake Nacimiento is best visited on the way to or from Mission San Antonio de Padua, unless you are a water-skier, in which case it deserves priority status. With its sprawling inlets, the pine- and oak-fringed reservoir is considered one of the best waterskiing spots in the US. The lake is crowded with boats from April to October (especially on weekends and holidays) and has a real party atmosphere.

Most lakeshore property is privately owned. *Lake Nacimiento Resort (☎ 805-238-3256, 800-323-3839)*, the only public access, charges a $10 day-use fee per vehicle ($7 in winter), which includes use of a swimming pool, hot tub and other facilities. The restaurant serves good breakfast and lunch and marginal dinners during summer. Campsites cost $22 (there are hookups for RVs), trailers start at $95 and lodge accommodations start at $150 and rise steeply to $355; reservations are advised. Power boat rentals cost $55 to $150 per hour or up to $275 per day, and canoes, kayaks and pedal boats rent for $5 to $10 per hour.

Paso Robles Wine Country

The wine country surrounding Paso Robles is worth a day's exploration, as it has not yet attained the notoriety, throngs of people or price level of Napa or Sonoma. Most wineries are concentrated along Hwy 46 and west of Hwy 101 just north of Templeton. There are also several along Vineyard Drive, which intersects with Hwy 101 south of Templeton.

Most vineyards have tasting rooms and offer free tours. Try **Meridian Vineyards** (☎ 805-237-6000), on Hwy 46, some 7 miles east of Hwy 101, open daily except Tuesday, and **Jan Kris Vineyard** (☎ 805-434-0319), on Bethel Rd, between Vineyard Drive and Hwy 46 west, open daily. **Bonny Doon** (☎ 805-239-5614), 3 miles west of Hwy 101 on Hwy 46 west, is known for dessert wines. They're open for tasting from 11 am to 5:30 pm daily.

Lower Central Coast

The lower Central Coast is dominated by San Luis Obispo and Santa Barbara, both lively college towns with plenty of places to stay and eat and lots to see and do. South of San Luis Obispo, Southern California development begins in earnest and the highways become less interesting, used more as travel corridors than exploration routes. Hwy 101 is the primary north-south thoroughfare, though Hwy 1 offers a glimpse of small towns populated by farmworkers and surrounded by sugar beet and lettuce fields.

SAN LUIS OBISPO
- **population 40,308** • **elevation 234 feet**

San Luis Obispo (SLO; pronounced Sun loo-ISS Obispo) is a lively yet low-key town with a high quality of life and vibrant community spirit. It's centered physically around Mission San Luis Obispo de Tolosa and culturally around California Polytechnic State University (Cal Poly). From September to May, music flows from pubs and cafes on Higuera St (the main drag) where you can hear everything from New Age electric grunge to Dixieland in one block. When school is not in session, the town is quieter and the year-round population of ranchers and oil refinery employees is more visible.

The best day to visit is Thursday, when the famous San Luis Obispo Farmers' Market takes over Higuera St (between Osos and Broad Sts) from 6 to 9 pm, turning the downtown into a giant street party. Truly excellent barbecues belching smoke, strolling families and fantastic music make this one of the liveliest evenings you'll have anywhere in California. Interestingly, other cities have studied this phenomenon, tried to launch their own version of it, and failed. There's just something about SLO.

SLO's reasonably priced accommodations and proximity to beaches, state parks and Hearst Castle (45 miles north), make it a good Central Coast hub.

History
Legend has it that Father Junípero Serra rang a bell on the bank of San Luis Creek to attract local Chumash Indians of the Tixlini community. When they came to find what the jingle was all about, Father Serra read from the Bible and said mass. Together, Father Serra and the Chumash built Mission San Luis Obispo de Tolosa, which became the center of community life.

Orientation
SLO's downtown is wonderfully walkable. Its main arteries are Higuera (pronounced HI-gera) St, which travels one way going southwest and Marsh St, parallel to Higuera St, running one way northeast. Most shops, restaurants and bars are located along here. One block north of Higuera St is Monterey St, which heads east from Mission Plaza and has most of the hotels and motels. San Luis Creek, once used to irrigate mission orchards, flows through downtown parallel to Higuera St.

The best exits from Hwy 101 are Marsh St (south) and Monterey St (north). Parking is free for the first 90 minutes in several downtown parking garages.

Information
The SLO Chamber of Commerce (☎ 805-781-2777, www.sanluisobispocounty.com), 1031 Chorro St, provides a free phone line to local hotels and motels, plenty of free

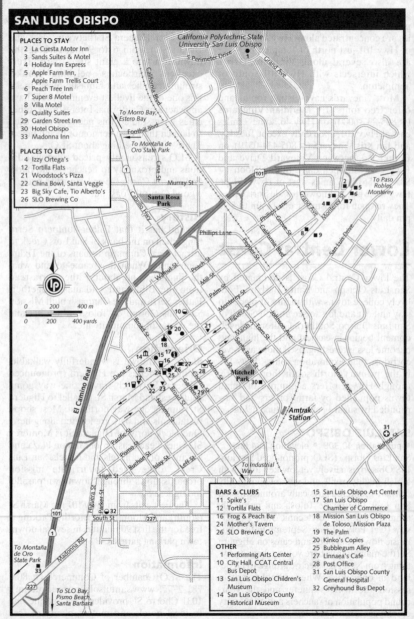

SAN LUIS OBISPO

PLACES TO STAY
2 La Cuesta Motor Inn
3 Sands Suites & Motel
4 Holiday Inn Express
5 Apple Farm Inn,
   Apple Farm Trellis Court
6 Peach Tree Inn
7 Super 8 Motel
8 Villa Motel
9 Quality Suites
29 Garden Street Inn
30 Hotel Obispo
33 Madonna Inn

PLACES TO EAT
4 Izzy Ortega's
12 Tortilla Flats
21 Woodstock's Pizza
22 China Bowl, Santa Veggie
23 Big Sky Cafe, Tio Alberto's
26 SLO Brewing Co

California Polytechnic State
University San Luis Obispo
S Perimeter Drive
Grand Ave

To Morro Bay,
Estero Bay

Foothill Blvd

To Montaña de
Oro State Park

California Blvd

Murray St

Santa Rosa
Park

Phillips Lane

Phillips Lane

To Paso
Robles,
Monterey

To Montaña
de Oro
State Park

To SLO Bay,
Pismo Beach,
Santa Barbara

To Industrial
Wtiy

Amtrak
Station

Mitchell
Park

Bishop St

BARS & CLUBS
11 Spike's
12 Tortilla Flats
16 Frog & Peach Bar
24 Mother's Tavern
26 SLO Brewing Co

OTHER
1 Performing Arts Center
10 City Hall, CCAT Central
   Bus Depot
13 San Luis Obispo Children's
   Museum
14 San Luis Obispo County
   Historical Museum

15 San Luis Obispo Art Center
17 San Luis Obispo
   Chamber of Commerce
18 Mission San Luis Obispo
   de Toloso, Mission Plaza
19 The Palm
20 Kinko's Copies
25 Bubblegum Alley
27 Linnaea's Cafe
28 Post Office
31 San Luis Obispo County
   General Hospital
32 Greyhound Bus Depot

printed matter and a useful $2 city map. Hours are 10 am to 5 pm Sunday and Monday, 8 am to 5 pm Tuesday and Wednesday, 8 am to 8 pm Thursday and Friday and 10 am to 8 pm Saturday.

Banks are along Higuera and Marsh Sts, and the post office (☎ 805-541-3062) is at the corner of Marsh and Morro Sts. Kinko's Copies (☎ 805-543-3363), at Monterey and Morro Sts, is open 24 hours.

SLO County General Hospital (☎ 805-781-4800) is ½ mile southeast of Monterey St at 2180 Johnson Ave.

Mission San Luis Obispo de Tolosa

The mission (☎ 805-543-6850) occupies a solid block of Monterey St, between Chorro and Broad Sts, and contains an excellent **museum** with extensive Chumash and mission period exhibits. Established in 1772 by Fathers Junípero Serra and José Cavaller as the fifth of the California missions, it is often called 'Prince of the Missions.'

Its **church** is decorated with colorful woodwork and has high open-beam ceilings made from logs carried 40 miles from the Santa Lucia mountains by the Chumash. The mission is open 9 am to 5 pm daily; free, though a $2 donation is suggested upon entering the museum. The church is still active and celebrates mass on weekends and religious holidays.

In front of the mission, **Mission Plaza** is a shady space with several restored adobes and an amphitheater overlooking San Luis Creek. On the plaza's south end is the **San Luis Obispo Art Center** (☎ 805-543-8562), which shows local artists' paintings, sculpture and photography and hosts visiting exhibits – usually from San Francisco. Hours are noon to 5 pm Tuesday to Sunday; free.

San Luis Obispo County Historical Museum

This museum (☎ 805-543-0638), at 696 Monterey St, across the street from the mission, is housed in SLO's 1904 Carnegie Library Building. Better than the average county museum, it has historical samplings from Chumash, nautical and Victorian worlds. It is

open 10 am to 4 pm Wednesday to Sunday and is free.

San Luis Obispo Children's Museum

Entertaining for kids of all ages, the Children's Museum (☎ 805-544-5437), 1010 Nipomo St, has hands-on activities and interactive displays that teeter between being educational and fun. Hours are 10 am to 5 pm Thursday to Tuesday (less in the off-season); $4 (free if under two).

California Polytechnic State University

The Cal Poly campus is home to 17,000 students and has a nice hilly setting north of downtown. Free daily student-run **campus tours** (☎ 805-756-2792) lead past the campus' 1960s buildings to the fields where agriculture projects are in process. The school is renowned for its 'learn by doing' approach and also famous for its engineering and architecture programs. Also on campus is the new **SLO Performing Arts Center** (see the Entertainment section).

Another unlikely highlight is the **Shakespeare Press Museum** (☎ 805-756-1108), which contains a gold rush-era collection of printing presses and type sets. The collection belonged to Charles Palmer, an antiques collector and poet who earned the nickname 'little Shakespeare' in California's gold fields. It's open by appointment only, but they'll do what they can to show you around, even at short notice; free.

Bubblegum Alley

One of the most bizarre sights in this pretty town is the narrow alley where the walls are blanketed with thousands of wads of discarded chewing gum. How this local fetish ever began, no one knows. But the result resembles modern art (Jackson Pollock comes to mind) and is both impressive and repulsive. Look for the entrance to Bubblegum Alley between 733 and 737 Higuera St.

Activities

Hiking There are plenty of good hikes around SLO, many of which start from Poly

Canyon Rd on the Cal Poly campus. Hiking maps and parking information are available at the booth on the right as you enter the campus. Parking in designated lots costs around $2.50 per day.

Popular day hikes lead to Bishop Peak and Cerro San Luis Obispo, which offer panoramic views of San Luis Obispo Bay and surrounding ranch land. A hiking map and description sheet is available from the chamber of commerce.

Bicycling   Bike shops and the chamber of commerce sell the excellent *San Luis Obispo County Bike Map* ($1). The SLO Bikeway runs for 20 miles via Cal Poly, downtown and Laguna Lake. Rentals are available from Alamo Bicycle Touring Company (☎ 805-781-3830) for $25 per day ($15 for three hours), which offers delivery and pick-up services since they don't have a shop.

Special Events

In April, SLO's streets are adorned during the Italian Street Painting Festival. The Mozart Festival in July and August features Mozart's works performed by musicians from all over the world. For more information, contact the chamber of commerce.

Places to Stay

Camping   Campgrounds in the SLO vicinity include those in Montaña de Oro State Park (see Estero Bay earlier in this chapter) and in Pismo Beach (see the Pismo Beach section later in this chapter).

Hostels   The 20-bed *Hostel Obispo* (☎ 805-544-4678, fax 805-544-3142, 1617 Santa Rosa St) is a well-kept Hostelling International facility in a converted Victorian, which gives it a bit of a B&B feel. It's on a lovely tree-lined street just one minute from the Amtrak station and a 10-minute walk from downtown. Single-sex dorm accommodations, with four or five beds per room, cost $16 to $18; the two private rooms are $37 and $40. Prices include an all-you-can-eat pancake breakfast, and common areas include a well-equipped kitchen and a lounge area with fireplace. Check-in is from

5 to 10 pm, and the hostel is closed from 9:30 am to 5 pm. Free on-site parking.

Motels, Hotels & B&Bs   SLO's motels are concentrated on the north end of Monterey St. *La Cuesta Motor Inn* (☎ 805-543-2777, 800-543-2777, fax 805-544-0696, 2074 Monterey St) has a pool and Jacuzzi, free continental breakfast and afternoon tea, free local calls and 72 rooms from $87 to $110. The *Peach Tree Inn* (☎ 805-543-3170, 800-227-6396, fax 805-543-7673, 2001 Monterey St) is friendly and folksy with a flowery lobby. Room rates are $49 to $69 and include a hearty breakfast; children under 16 stay free.

The *Sands Suites & Motel* (☎ 805-544-0500, 800-441-4657, fax 805-544-3529, 1930 Monterey St) has rooms away from the street and a comfortable lobby. Their $59 to $99 rates are a good value, though they leap to $79 to $129 in summer. Owned by a friendly family, the *Villa Motel* (☎ 805-543-8071, 1670 Monterey St) has newly renovated units for $33 to $49, climbing as high as $79 in summer.

Chain hotels represented in SLO include the *Best Western Royal Oak Motor Hotel* (☎ 805-544-4410, 214 Madonna Rd), *Best Western Somerset Manor* (☎ 805-544-0973, 1895 Monterey St), *Holiday Inn Express* (☎ 805-544-8600, 1800 Monterey St), *Days Inn* (☎ 805-549-9911, 2050 Garfield St), *Howard Johnson Express* (☎ 805-544-5300, 1585 Calle Joaquin), *Super 8 Motel* (☎ 805-544-7895, 1951 Monterey St) and the *Vagabond Inn* (☎ 805-544-4712, 210 Madonna Rd).

An excellent bet is the hacienda-style *Quality Suites* (☎ 805-541-5001, 800-228-5151, fax 805-546-9575, 1631 Monterey St), with its flower-intense courtyard area, pool and spa. Suites sport refrigerator, microwave, VCR, stereo system and TV. A full cooked-to-order American breakfast and a happy hour with free drinks and snacks are included in the rates of $110 to $130, which occasionally dip below $100.

Another good choice is the *Apple Farm Inn* (☎ 805-544-2040, 800-255-2040, fax 805-541-5497, 2015 Monterey St), a frilly Victorian country inn with an antique mill house and a popular restaurant. Rooms cost $119 to $239 and include welcome baskets and afternoon guest reception. Rates at the adjacent *Apple Farm Trellis Court* (same phone numbers) are $99 to $129, with family suites cresting at $149.

The most atmospheric stay is at the historic *Garden Street Inn* (☎ 805-545-9802, 1212 Garden St), a lovely B&B with 13 themed rooms and suites costing $90 to $160; rates include a big breakfast and wine and cheese reception.

Over the top, eccentric, tacky, outlandish, amazing, 'only in America' – these are just a few ways to describe the *Madonna Inn* (☎ 805-543-3000, 800-543-9666, fax 805-543-1800), a landmark on Madonna Rd just west of Hwy 1/101. This is the upper stratosphere of bad taste, the breeding ground of kitsch. Get an eyeful of the gingerbread exterior before plunging into a fantasyland filled with scarlet plastic booths, synthetic flower arrangements, undulating chandeliers and heart-shaped chairs. Don't miss the waterfall urinal in the men's rest room that's activated when you...activate it. Staying at the inn means taking your pick from 109 themed rooms, including the Caveman Room, carved from solid rock, or the Austrian Room, with crystal chandeliers and white baroque furniture. Prices range from $90 to $200. The Madonna Inn is worth seeing even if you don't stay here, and fortunately strolling is not discouraged by management.

Places to Eat

SLO has a good variety of ethnic food, and most restaurants have a vegetarian selection. *Woodstock's Pizza* (☎ 805-541-4420, 1000 Higuera St) is SLO's landmark pizza joint – fast, greasy and always crowded. Pizzas come on white or whole wheat crust and cost around $16 for a large, $2.50 per slice. From 11 am to 3 pm on weekdays, $4 will get you all the pizza you can eat and all the soda you can drink.

The *SLO Brewing Co* (☎ 805-543-1843, 1119 Garden St), between Higuera and Marsh Sts, has good burgers, veggie burgers, grilled meats and fish, and large salads, all for under $10. The atmosphere is loud and the homemade brews are worth sampling.

Another winner with young people is *Big Sky Cafe* (☎ 805-545-5401, 1121 Broad St), a tall-ceilinged dining room that serves light and creative world cuisine at student prices (mostly under $10). The Big Sky noodle bowl, blackened chicken salad, and Japanese eggplant sandwich are outstanding favorites.

For good, healthy Mexican food, line up with the locals at the no-nonsense *Tío Alberto's* (☎ 805-546-9646, 1131 Broad St), where you can seriously fill up on burritos, tacos and tamales for under $5. South of the border fare is also on the menu at *Tortilla Flats* (☎ 805-544-7575, 1051 Nipomo St), though it's more famous for its 50 varieties of tequila (see Entertainment). Another lively Mexican place with everything under $10 is *Izzy Ortega's* (☎ 805-543-3333, 1850 Monterey St) inside the Holiday Inn Express.

China Bowl and *Santa Veggie* are all-you-can-eat Chinese restaurants in the 600 block of Higuera St that serve Americanized fare for the budget-minded, with buffets costing less than $10.

Entertainment

Coffeehouses *Linnaea's Cafe* (☎ 805-541-5888, 1110 Garden St), just across from the Brewing Co, is artistic and tiny and hosts folk and acoustic guitarists. The back patio is atmospheric, with a fountain and plenty of plants.

Bars *Mother's Tavern* (☎ 805-541-3853, 729 Higuera St) is the college crowd's favorite for boozing and carousing. Across the street, the *Frog & Peach Bar* (☎ 805-595-3764) has a wide beer selection, subdued British atmosphere and live jazz on Friday and Saturday nights.

Spike's (☎ 805-544-7157, 570 Higuera St) is a beer-lover's dream with around 70 different beers available (45 on tap). If somehow you manage to guzzle one of everything, you get a T-shirt to commemorate what's left of your liver. The *SLO Brewing Co* (☎ 805-543-1843, 1119 Garden St) is popular for billiards and beer and has live bands, usually Thursday to Saturday nights. The college crowd also flocks to *The Graduate* (☎ 805-541-0969, 990 Industrial

Way), which is also a dance club with live music nightly except Monday.

Tortilla Flats (☎ 805-544-7575, *1051 Nipomo St*) serves 50 varieties of tequila (a sampler of four is $20) and frequently offers happy-hour specials.

Cinema *The Palm* (☎ 805-541-5161, *817 Palm St*) is an old-style movie house that shows foreign and classic films nightly. Tickets are $6 ($3 on Monday).

Performing Arts Pride of the town is the new $30 million *Performing Arts Center*, in a daring building by Albert Bertoli on Grand Ave on the Cal Poly campus. The 1350-seat auditorium is styled after a European opera house and offers fine acoustics. For tickets or information, call ☎ 805-756-2787, 888-237-8787 in California.

Getting There & Away

Air The small SLO County Airport (☎ 805-541-1038), south of downtown between Hwy 1/101 and Broad St, offers some 40 flights daily, including service to Los Angeles and San Francisco by American Eagle (☎ 800-433-7300).

Bus Greyhound runs six daily buses to Los Angeles ($29) and to Santa Barbara ($19), and five to San Francisco for $38 (fares are one-way). The Greyhound station (☎ 805-543-2121) is south of downtown, one block east of Higuera St, at 150 South St.

Buses of the Central Coast Area Transit (CCAT; ☎ 805-541-2228) travel north to Morro Bay, where you can catch a bus to Cayucos, Cambria and San Simeon. Another line goes out to the SLO Bay communities. The central bus station is on Osos St opposite the SLO City Hall. Fares depend on distance; unlimited day passes are $3. Schedules are available at the chamber of commerce.

Train SLO is the northern terminus of Amtrak's *San Diegan* route, with daily service to destinations like Santa Barbara, Los Angeles and San Diego. The *Coast Starlight* between Seattle and Los Angeles (via Sacramento) also stops at SLO daily. The Amtrak station is at the southern end of Santa Rosa St.

Getting Around

SLO's downtown is best explored on foot, though the weary can hop on the free SLO Trolley, which makes a continuous loop along Marsh, Higuera, Nipomo, Monterey and Palm Sts, from noon to 5 pm daily (until 9 pm Thursday to coincide with the farmers' market). The SLO city bus system (☎ 805-541-2877) operates several routes covering all corners of the city, including regular trips to Cal Poly. Fares are 75¢. An excellent service is provided by the nonprofit Ride-On organization, which offers rides within SLO County for just $4 between 9 pm and 3 am on Thursday, Friday and Saturday nights.

SAN LUIS OBISPO BAY

About 8 miles southwest of San Luis Obispo, the small communities of Avila Beach, Shell Beach, Pismo Beach, Grover Beach and Oceano border San Luis Obispo Bay, the bay Cabrillo called *Todos Santos* (all saints) because of its beauty. When Mission San Luis Obispo de Tolosa was built in 1772, the bay was its main port, connected to San Luis Obispo by narrow-gauge railroad.

Today, the bay is bordered by oil refineries and beach towns that survive on tourism. If you hear a steady siren for three to five minutes, tune your radio to 920 AM, 1400 AM or 98.1 FM; Diablo Nuclear Power Plant, just east of the bay, might be doing something weird.

Getting Around The beach communities are linked by the Coastal Cruiser Trolley (☎ 805-541-2277), which operates between 10 am and 6 pm daily from mid-June to early September, with weekend service to 5 pm the rest of the year. The fare is just 25¢.

Avila Beach
• **population 400** • **elevation 20 feet**
Farthest north on San Luis Obispo Bay, Avila Beach is reached via a lovely sycamore- and maple-lined glen that follows San Luis Creek to the sea. Avila's main drag

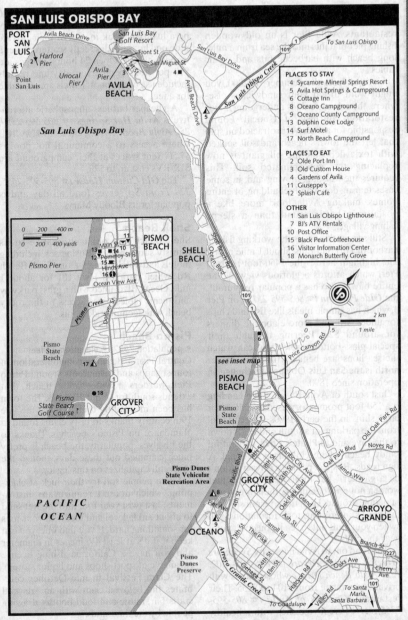

SAN LUIS OBISPO BAY

PLACES TO STAY
4 Sycamore Mineral Springs Resort
5 Avila Hot Springs & Campground
6 Cottage Inn
8 Oceano Campground
9 Oceano County Campground
13 Dolphin Cove Lodge
14 Surf Motel
17 North Beach Campground

PLACES TO EAT
2 Olde Port Inn
3 Old Custom House
4 Gardens of Avila
11 Giuseppe's
12 Splash Cafe

OTHER
1 San Luis Obispo Lighthouse
7 BJ's ATV Rentals
10 Post Office
15 Black Pearl Coffeehouse
16 Visitor Information Center
18 Monarch Butterfly Grove

is beachside Front St, referred to as 'the boardwalk,' which has a few shops and restaurants. Avila Pier is an old wooden fishing pier that juts into the sea from a mile-long beach with barbecue pits and picnic tables.

Until at least the summer of 2000, you might want to eat your sandwiches elsewhere, though, as Avila is undergoing major restoration courtesy of Unocal. Found responsible for a massive, protracted oil spill that left the town's beach and soil soaked with toxic deposits, the oil giant is now replacing the contaminated soil. This requires the hoisting, moving and, in some cases, tearing down and rebuilding, of entire homes, making Avila look more like a postatomic battleground than a sleepy fishing village.

Still scenic, though, is the working fishing harbor of Port San Luis, about 1 mile north. The highlight here is the 1460-foot **Harford Pier**, which affords a glorious view of the entire bay. It also has a popular restaurant, the *Olde Port Inn* (☎ *805-595-2515*), on Pier 3, which has simple meals like fish and chips for under $10, and more elaborate dinners for around $20. Peering through their special glass-bottom tables, you can watch the sea lions laze beneath the pier. Farther north is the **San Luis Obispo Lighthouse**, in operation since 1890.

Just south of Avila Beach, **Cave Landing** is a 150-foot promontory used as a dock for large ships in the early 1900s. A rocky trail from the parking lot's south end leads down to the cave and to **Pirate's Cove**, a beautiful sandy beach where clothing is optional. A sign reads, 'Respect people's privacy – don't be a gawker!' but locals recommend that women not go alone unless there are plenty of people around. High tides, responsible for the cove's interesting rock formations, will sweep your stuff out to sea if you don't put it near the cliffs.

The road out to Avila passes by *Sycamore Mineral Springs Resort* (☎ *805-595-7302, 1215 Avila Beach Drive*), whose rooms with private spas range from $104 to $135. Their restaurant, *Gardens of Avila* (☎ *805-595-7365*) serves creative dishes with a healthy accent for under $10 at lunch and under $20 for dinner. The best deal here, though, may be a luxuriant soak in one of their private redwood hot tubs, discreetly scattered over a woodsy hillside. Open 24 hours, charges are $10 per hour per person; daytime rentals include use of the pool. Towels are available for a fee.

A cheaper but less atmospheric alternative is *Avila Hot Springs* (☎ *805-595-2359, 250 Avila Beach Drive*), closer to Hwy 101, where access to a communal hot pool is $7.50. Tent spaces at their campground are $18, RVs cost up to $28.

The *Old Custom House* (☎ *805-595-7555, 324 Front St*) serves food all day and is popular for its Bloody Marys.

Shell Beach

Shell Beach is a quiet alternative to its touristy surroundings. Businesses, including motels and hotels, stretch along Shell Beach Rd, which parallels Hwy 101 for about 1 mile. Ocean Blvd, lined with a grass parkway and picnic tables, gives access to the rocky beach with teeming tide pools.

Pismo Beach
• **population 7937** • **elevation 33 feet**
Central Pismo Beach, a conglomeration of tourist shops and restaurants around Pismo Pier, borders a wide sandy beach that extends south for about 10 miles. The town has been invaded by tourists since the late 19th century thanks to tasty clams found in abundance on Pismo's beaches. Thanks to the bivalves' popularity, the beach is pretty much clammed out these days, though the town still capitalizes on this legacy.

Some people still try their luck at clamming, which doesn't require any instruments: Just twist your foot into the wet sand to about ankle level and feel with your toes for something hard. If you find one, you can keep it if it's at least 4½ inches in diameter and you have a California fishing license (available at sport shops and liquor stores). The **Clam Festival** in mid-October celebrates the beloved clam with an arts and crafts fair, music and food booths, drawing people by the thousands.

For visitor information, call ☎ 800-443-7778, log onto www.pismobeach.org, or visit the office at 581 Dolliver St, which is usually open 9 am to 5 pm (10 am to 4 pm Sunday).

Monarch Butterfly Grove If you're in Pismo between late November and March, be sure to visit this secluded spot, the winter home for millions of these beautiful migrating critters (see 'Monarch Butterflies' boxed text) Forming dense clusters in the tops of eucalyptus and pine trees, they perfectly blend into the environment and are easily mistaken for leaves. Access to the grove is via the North Beach Campground, south of town off Hwy 1. Docent-led walks are offered regularly.

Pismo Dunes Preserve This extensive network of coastal dunes south of the Pismo proper is often used as a movie set (*The Sheik* with Rudolph Valentino was one of the earliest films shot here). Access is via Oso Flaco Lake Rd. Part of the dunes is set aside as the **Pismo Dunes State Vehicular Recreation Area**, where all-terrain vehicle fans can have a field day. BJ's ATV Rentals (☎ 805-481-5411), 197 Grand Ave, in Grover Beach, offers rentals by the hour ($32 to $52, depending on the size of the bike). There's also a primitive **campground** (☎ 805-473-7220) where sites cost $6; reserve through Parknet at ☎ 800-444-7275.

Places to Stay – Camping There are plenty of campgrounds in the Pismo area, including **North Beach Campground** (☎ 805-489-2684), about 1 mile south of the Pismo Pier off Hwy 1. It has 103 grassy sites in the dunes, shaded by eucalyptus trees; there's easy beach access trails and flush toilets, but there are no hookups. **Oceano Campground** (☎ 805-489-2684) is near the entrance to Pismo Dunes in the small community of Oceano and popular with dune warriors. Sites cost $14 to $24 at both places and, in summer, can be reserved through Parknet at ☎ 800-444-7275. Only a few of the sites have hookups. A quieter option is nearby **Oceano Memorial Campground** (☎ 805-781-5200), opposite the Memorial

County Park. There are flush toilets and fire pits and 22 spaces ($18 to $21, all with hookups) available on a first-come, first-served basis.

Places to Stay – Motels & Inns Pismo Beach has dozens of motels, but rooms fill up quickly and prices skyrocket between May and September and during the Clam Festival. Midweek rates are usually lower. Close to the beach, the **Surf Motel** (☎ 805-773-2070, 250 Main St) has singles for $40 to $65 and doubles from $45 to $75. Rates include coffee and donuts in the mornings and use of the heated pool. The shoreside **Dolphin Cove Lodge** (☎ 805-773-4706, fax 805-773-4214, 170 Main St) is a friendly, non-smoking property where ocean-view rooms are $60 to $90 year round, including small continental breakfast. A bit of gossip: James Dean enjoyed trysting here with Pier Angeli.

Just north of town is the brand-new, English country-style **Cottage Inn** (☎ 805-773-4617, fax 805-773-8336, 888-440-8400, 2351 Price St), with a spectacular bluff-top setting and charming rooms ranging from $79 to $199, including breakfast.

Places to Eat There are several good chowder houses directly up from the pier on Pomeroy St, including **Splash Cafe** (☎ 805-773-4653, 197 Pomeroy St), where you can get rich and chunky clam chowder in a sourdough bread bowl or a grilled ahi tuna sandwich for under $5. Across the street, the **Black Pearl Coffeehouse** (☎ 805-773-6631) has java, baked goods and a young local scene. Ironically, the best place in town has nothing to do with fish: **Giuseppe's** (☎ 805-773-2870, 891 Price St) specializes in reasonably priced pizzas and Southern Italian food and is a winner with visitors and locals alike.

SANTA YNEZ VALLEY

The Santa Ynez Valley, dotted with vineyards and ranches, is set between the Santa Ynez and San Rafael mountains, a lovely coastal region known for its warm climate and rolling hills.

CENTRAL COAST

Lompoc

• population 41,516 • elevation 104 feet

Lompoc (pronounced lom-poke) is the largest town along Hwy 1 as it winds between Pismo Beach and Santa Barbara, forced inland by **Vandenberg Air Force Base** and its Missile Test Center which occupies the coast. A free 2½-hour tour of the base departs at 10 am on Wednesdays (no children under 10). You'll need to make reservations at least one week ahead; call ☎ 805-734-8282 ext 63595. Non-US citizens need to bring a passport.

Lompoc itself is a quiet military town with wide shady streets. It is surrounded by hills turned into a brilliant mosaic of wildflowers in the spring. The **Lompoc Museum** (☎ 805-736-3888), in a lovely neoclassical-style villa at 200 S H St, has a collection focused on Chumash and regional artifacts. Hours are 1 to 5 pm Tuesday to Friday, to 4 pm weekends; free.

For visitor information, visit the Lompoc Chamber of Commerce (☎ 805-736-4567), 111 S I St.

Mission La Purísima Concepción Just

east of Hwy 1, on Hwy 246 about 3 miles northeast of the town center, this beautiful mission (☎ 805-733-3713) is one of two run by the State Park Service. Totally restored in the 1930s by the CCC, its buildings are fully intact and decorated as they were during the mission period – right down to blankets on the cots and grinding stones in the courtyard. The mission fields still support livestock, and the gardens are planted with medicinal plants and trees once used by the Chumash. Also here are fountains and ground-level troughs where women did the wash – one for the Indians and one for the mission women. The original mission was actually 3 miles south but was rebuilt here, by Chumash Indians, after a major earthquake in 1812.

Surrounding the mission are 15 miles of hiking and horse trails. At the park entrance is a museum and bookstore with a good selection of local history books and a free trail map. Park hours are 9 am to 5 pm daily; mission buildings close at 4 pm. Admission is $5 per car.

Solvang

• population 5,149 • elevation 496 feet

In 1911, three Danish farmers established the Atterdag College folk school in the Santa Ynez Valley to pass on their Danish traditions to future generations. The small farming community of Solvang, whose name means 'sunny field,' grew up around the school. Today, the quasi-Danish town is a cutesy conglomeration of bakeries, gift shops and galleries.

The one redeeming piece of culture is the **Elverhøj Museum** (☎ 805-686-1211), housed in a replica 18th-century Jutland farmhouse, two blocks south of the main shopping district, at the corner of 2nd St and Elverhoy Way. Essentially a local history museum, its collection of *papierklip* (paper cut-out) art, period clothes and furniture, farm tools and old photographs is worth a look. Hours are 1 to 4 pm Wednesday to Sunday; free.

Amid the faux-front stores and European flags downtown is the **Hans Christian Andersen Museum** (☎ 805-688-2052), in the Book Loft building at 1680 Mission Drive. It has a decent-size collection of old books, manuscripts, letters and photographs, plus paper cut-outs inspired by Andersen's sleepy-time favorites. Open 10 am to 5 pm daily.

Solvang's cultural loner is the **Old Mission Santa Inés** (☎ 805-688-4815), 1760 Mission Drive, hemmed in by civilization and a parking lot, which was once a vegetable garden. Founded at the height of missionary prosperity in 1804, the mission is an active parish and school. If you are planning to visit other missions, don't bother with this one. Hours are 9 am to 5:30 pm daily (to 7 pm May to September); $3, free if under 16.

Places to Eat Among the many Danish bakeries, locals recommend *Birkholms* (☎ 805-688-3872, 1555 Mission Drive) for shortbread cookies and pastries. They have indoor and outdoor tables where you can have a coffee with your sweets.

The *Solvang Restaurant* (☎ 805-688-4645, 1672 Copenhagen Drive) serves *aebleskivers* (ball-like pancakes dusted with powdered sugar) as well as 'normal' American breakfasts and lunches for under $8. The heavily advertised split pea soup of **Pea Soup Andersen's** (☎ 805-688-5581), 3 miles west of Solvang, in Buellton at the Hwy 246/101 junction, is actually quite good.

SANTA BARBARA
• **population 90,000** • **elevation 50 feet**
Sandwiched between the Pacific Ocean and Santa Ynez Mountains, this affluent and pretty city charms with its red tile roofs, white stucco walls and seaside lassitude reminiscent of small Mediterranean villages. It is one of the Central Coast highlights and a popular getaway for those needing peaceful sanctuary.

Five colleges in the area, including the University of California at Santa Barbara (UCSB), give the town a youthful vivacity and balance Santa Barbara's yachting and retirement communities. Downtown Santa Barbara has outstanding architectural integrity, a masterpiece of a courthouse and noteworthy art and natural history museums. Rising abruptly and majestically to the north, the Santa Ynez foothills offer great hiking and camping opportunities.

History
Until about 200 years ago, Chumash Indians thrived in the Santa Barbara area, living in villages along the coast and in the Santa Ynez Mountains. In 1542, Juan Rodríguez Cabrillo entered the channel, put up a Spanish flag and went on his way. Sebastián Vizcaíno, a cartographer for the Duke of Monte Rey, landed in the harbor on December 4, 1602 (the feast day of St Barbara), and literally put Santa Barbara on the map. But being claimed and named by Spain didn't affect Santa Barbara's Chumash until the arrival of missionaries in the mid-1700s.

The padres converted the Chumash against their will, made them construct the mission and presidio and taught them to wear clothes and to change their traditional diet of acorn mush, roots and fish to meat. The Indians contracted European diseases and were decimated, though today the tribe is again very much alive and well.

Easterners started arriving in force with the 1849 gold rush, and by the late 1890s Santa Barbara was an established vacation spot for the rich and famous. The American Film Company, founded at the corner of Mission and State Sts in 1910, was the largest in the world for about three of its 10 years in existence. Thanks to the local film commission, the movie and TV business continues to thrive in the city. Each March, independent US and international films are shown at the Santa Barbara International Film Festival.

Orientation
Downtown Santa Barbara is laid out in a square grid whose main artery is State St, which runs north-south. Lower State St (south of Ortega St) has a large concentration of bars and shady characters, while upper State St (north of Ortega St) is where the nice shops and museums are. Cabrillo Blvd hugs the coastline and turns into Coast Village Rd as it enters the eastern suburb of Montecito.

Santa Barbara is surrounded by small affluent communities: Hope Ranch to the west, Montecito and Summerland to the east. UCSB is just west of Hope Ranch in Isla Vista, and most of Santa Barbara's college crowd lives around the campus or in neighboring Goleta.

Information
The Tourist Information Center (☎ 805-965-3021), at the corner of Garden St and Cabrillo Blvd, has maps, brochures and a busy but helpful staff. Summer hours are 9 am to 5 pm daily (from 10 am Sunday), fewer hours in winter. The privately operated Hot Spots Visitors Center (☎ 805-564-1637, 800-793-7666), inside a 24-hour cafe at 36 State St, is staffed from 9 am to 9 pm (to 4 pm Sunday). Both maintain a touch-screen computer for information and free hotel reservations.

For a free destination guide, leave your name and address at ☎ 800-676-1266, or check out www.santabarbara.ca.com, which has the same information.

Numerous banks and ATMs are on State St. Paul Brombal's Exchange Services (☎ 805-687-3641), 4 miles north of downtown at 3601 State St, exchanges 40 foreign

SANTA BARBARA

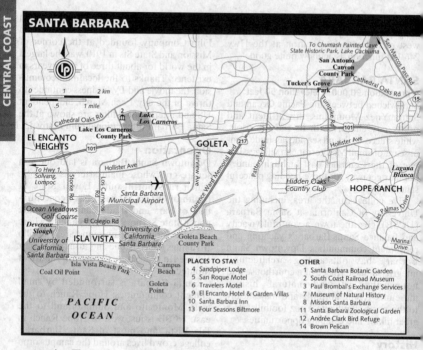

PLACES TO STAY
4 Sandpiper Lodge
5 San Roque Motel
6 Travelers Motel
9 El Encanto Hotel & Garden Villas
10 Santa Barbara Inn
13 Four Seasons Biltmore

OTHER
1 Santa Barbara Botanic Garden
2 South Coast Railroad Museum
3 Paul Brombal's Exchange Services
7 Museum of Natural History
8 Mission Santa Barbara
11 Santa Barbara Zoological Garden
12 Andrée Clark Bird Refuge
14 Brown Pelican

currencies. The main post office is at 836 Anacapa St. For fax and computer services try Kinko's (☎ 805-966-1114), 1030 State St.

The Red Tile Tour

This self-guided 12-block walking tour is an excellent way to take in all major downtown sights and historic landmarks, including the Santa Barbara County Courthouse, Museum of Art, Historical Museum and El Presidio (all described here). Pick up a free map from the Tourist Information Center or Hot Spots.

Santa Barbara County Courthouse

The 1929 courthouse (☎ 805-962-6464), 1100 Anacapa St, is one sight not to be missed. Built in Spanish-Moorish Revival style, it features hand-painted ceilings, wrought-iron chandeliers and tiles from Tunisia and Spain. You're free to explore on your own between 8:30 am and 5 pm (from 10 am on week-

ends), but the best way to see it is on a free docent-led tour offered at 2 pm Monday to Saturday and also at 10:30 am Monday, Tuesday and Friday. If you miss it, be sure to see the mural room and go up the 80-foot clock tower for your panoramic shots of the city.

Santa Barbara Museum of Art

This well-regarded regional museum (☎ 805-963-4364), 1130 State St, has a varied permanent collection with works by Monet, Matisse and Chagall, Hopper and O'Keeffe, as well as Asian art and classical sculpture. A new wing built in early 1998 added exhibit space, a cafe and a children's gallery. Hours are 11 am to 5 pm Tuesday through Saturday (to 9 pm Friday) and noon to 5 pm Sunday; $5 adults, $3 seniors, $1.50 students. Admission is free for children under six and for everyone on Thursday and the first Sunday of the month.

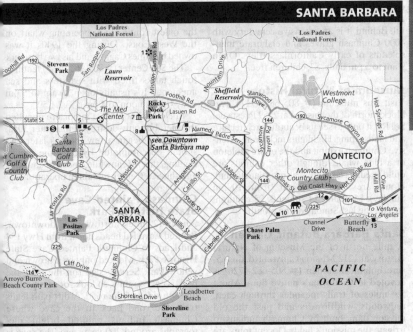

Santa Barbara Historical Museum

Located in an adobe complex at 136 E De La Guerra St, this educational museum (☎ 805-966-1601) has an exhaustive collection of Santa Barbara memorabilia, including antique furniture, an intricately carved coffer that belonged to Padre Junípero Serra and exhibits on Santa Barbara's involvement in toppling the last Chinese monarchy. Guided tours are given at 1:30 pm Wednesday and weekends. Hours are 10 am to 5 pm Tuesday through Saturday (from noon Sunday); free.

El Presidio de Santa Barbara State Historic Park

One of four in California, this 18th-century former Spanish fort (☎ 805-966-9719), in the 100 block of E Cañon Perdido St, harbors some of the city's oldest structures and is undergoing constant restoration and recon-

struction. Founded in 1782 to protect the missions between Monterey and San Diego, the presidio also acted as a social and political hub, and as a stopping point for Spanish military traveling along the coast. Be sure to visit the chapel, whose interior explodes in kaleidoscopic color and features some interesting trompe l'oeil effects. Hours are 10:30 am to 4:30 pm daily; free but donation requested.

Mission Santa Barbara

Called the 'Queen of the Missions,' Mission Santa Barbara (☎ 805-682-4713), 2201 Laguna St, sits on a majestic perch a half mile north of downtown. It was established on December 4, 1786 (the feast day of St Barbara), as the 10th California mission. Three adobe structures preceded the current stone one, from 1820; its main facade integrates neoclassical-style columns. Today, the mission still functions as a Franciscan friary as well as a parish church and museum. The church features Chumash wall decorations, and the gardens in the courtyard are peaceful. Behind it is an extensive cemetery with 4000 Chumash graves and elaborate mausoleums of early California settlers. Open 9 am to 5 pm daily; $3, children free.

Museum of Natural History

Visit this museum (☎ 805-682-4711), two blocks north of the mission at 2559 Puesta del Sol Rd, if only to see its beautiful architecture and landscaping. Highlights include an extensive Chumash exhibit and the entire skeleton of a blue whale, though other exhibits are quite mediocre. There's also a planetarium. Hours are 9 am to 5 pm (from 10 am Sunday); $5 adults, $4 students, $3 children, free on the last Sunday of the month.

Santa Barbara Botanic Garden

A mile north of the Museum of Natural History, at 1212 Mission Canyon Rd, this 65-acre botanical garden (☎ 805-682-4726) is devoted to California's native flora. About 5½ miles of trails meander through cacti, redwoods, wildflowers and past the old mission dam, built by Chumash Indians to irrigate the mission's fields. Docent tours are offered daily (except Wednesday) at 2 pm and also at 10:30 am on Thursday and Sunday. Garden hours vary by season but are roughly 9 am to sunset; $5 for adults, $3 for teens and seniors, $1 for kids ages five to 12, free for kids under five.

Santa Barbara Zoological Garden

The zoo (☎ 805-962-5339), 500 Niños Drive, has gorgeous gardens as well as 700 animals from around the world, including big cats, monkeys, elephants and giraffes. The 100-year-old vegetation was once part of a palatial estate. Hours are 10 am to 5 pm daily; $7/5/5 adults/seniors/children.

Just west of the zoo at 1400 E Cabrillo Blvd, the **Andrée Clark Bird Refuge** consists of a lagoon, gardens and a path from which to observe nesting freshwater birds; free.

Stearns Wharf

This rough wooden pier extending into the harbor from the south end of State St is a favorite place to eat seafood and watch sea lions. Built in 1872 by John Peck Stearn, it is the oldest continuously operating wharf on the West Coast. During the 1940s it was owned by James Cagney and his two brothers.

The **Sea Center** (☎ 805-962-0885) features touch tanks filled with sea stars and sea anemones. It's usually open 10 am to 5 pm daily (tanks noon to 4 pm); $3/2/1.50.

In November 1998, a major fire engulfed the pier, but only destroyed the outer 20%. Rebuilding began a few months later and should be completed by the time you're reading this. Meanwhile, most restaurants and the Sea Center remain in operation.

Chumash Painted Cave State Historic Park

About 12 miles northwest of downtown, Painted Cave Rd heads north from Hwy 154 and leads to Chumash Painted Cave State Historic Park. Marked only by a brown and yellow Park Service sign (on the left), the park is easy to miss, so look for cars parked on both sides of the road. A dirt path leads from the road back to the cave where Chumash Indians painted bright pictographs around 200 years ago. The cave is protected by a metal screen, so a flashlight is helpful for getting a good view.

South Coast Railroad Museum

This museum (☎ 805-964-3540), 300 N Los Carneros Rd, ¼ mile from the Los Carneros exit off Hwy 101, occupies a 1901 Southern Pacific Railroad depot in Goleta, 8 miles northwest of downtown Santa Barbara. It holds a sizable collection of railroad artifacts, old photographs and a 300-sq-foot model railroad. Hours are 1 to 4 pm Wednesday to Sunday. The best time to visit is 2 to 3:30 pm Wednesday and Friday or 1:15 to 3:45 pm weekends, when you can ride the miniature train. Admission (and the train ride) is free.

Beaches

East Beach is the long sandy stretch between Stearns Wharf and Montecito; it's Santa Barbara's largest and most popular beach. At its east end, across from the Biltmore

DOWNTOWN SANTA BARBARA

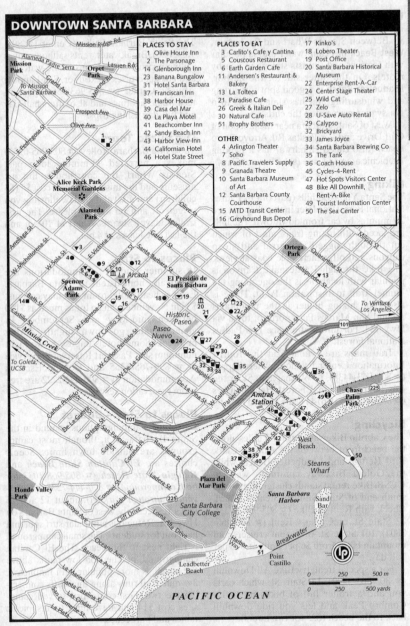

PLACES TO STAY
1 Olive House Inn
2 The Parsonage
14 Glenborough Inn
23 Banana Bungalow
31 Hotel Santa Barbara
37 Franciscan Inn
38 Harbor House
39 Casa del Mar
40 La Playa Motel
41 Beachcomber Inn
42 Sandy Beach Inn
43 Harbor View Inn
44 Californian Hotel
46 Hotel State Street

PLACES TO EAT
3 Carlito's Cafe y Cantina
5 Couscous Restaurant
6 Earth Garden Cafe
11 Andersen's Restaurant & Bakery
13 La Tolteca
21 Paradise Cafe
26 Greek & Italian Deli
30 Natural Cafe
51 Brophy Brothers

OTHER
4 Arlington Theater
7 Soho
8 Pacific Travelers Supply
9 Granada Theatre
10 Santa Barbara Museum of Art
12 Santa Barbara County Courthouse
15 MTD Transit Center
16 Greyhound Bus Depot

17 Kinko's
18 Lobero Theater
19 Post Office
20 Santa Barbara Historical Museum
22 Enterprise Rent-A-Car
24 Center Stage Theater
25 Wild Cat
27 Zelo
28 U-Save Auto Rental
32 Calypso
32 Brickyard
33 James Joyce
34 Santa Barbara Brewing Co
35 The Tank
36 Coach House
45 Cycles-4-Rent
47 Hot Spots Visitors Center
48 Bike All Downhill, Rent-A-Bike
49 Tourist Information Center
50 The Sea Center

Hotel, Armani swimsuits and Gucci sunglasses abound at **Butterfly Beach**.

Between Stearns Wharf and the harbor, **West Beach** has calm water and is popular with families and tourists staying in nearby motels. On the other side of the harbor, **Leadbetter Beach** is a good spot for surfing and windsurfing and has stair access to a grassy picnic area atop the cliffs.

West of Santa Barbara near the junction of Cliff Drive and Las Positas Rd, **Arroyo Burro Beach** (also called Hendry's) has a parking lot, picnic area and cafe (see Places to Eat).

Hiking

The Santa Ynez foothills (part of Los Padres National Forest, see later in this chapter) are 20 minutes by car from downtown. The hills are laced with hiking trails, most of which cut through rugged chaparral and steep canyons and offer incredible coastal views. The hike through Rattlesnake Canyon is popular with locals, as is the one along the Tunnel Trail to Inspiration Point. There is also good hiking higher in the mountains around San Marcos Pass, north of town via Hwy 154. For information, see Los Padres National Forest.

Trail maps are available at the Tourist Information Center, Pacific Travelers Supply (☎ 805-963-4438), 12 W Anapamu St, or the Los Padres National Forest Headquarters (☎ 805-683-6711), 6144 Calle Real in Goleta.

Bicycling

The Cabrillo Bikeway runs for 3 miles along the beachfront between the Andrée Clark Bird Refuge and Leadbetter Beach, while the Goleta Bikeway continues west to UCSB. Bike rental stands cluster around the south end of State St, near Stearns Wharf. Check with Rent-A-Bike (☎ 805-966-6733), 22 State St, or Cycles-4-Rent (☎ 805-966-3804), 101 State St. Both rent cruisers and mountain bikes from $6 per hour or $15 per half day.

For a special treat, try Bike All Downhill (☎ 805-963-3700), 14 State St, which carts you and a trailer full of bikes up to La Cumbre Peak and lets you ride downhill back to the beach ($25 for two hours).

Sailing, Fishing & Whale Watching

The Santa Barbara Sailing Center (☎ 805-962-2826), Breakwater, rents sailboats, gives sailing instruction and runs whale-watching and coastal cruises. Next door, Sea Landing Aquatic Center (☎ 805-963-3564) guarantees whale sightings and also offers half-day and full-day fishing trips.

Organized Tours

The Santa Barbara Trolley (☎ 805-965-0353) makes a narrated 90-minute loop past Stearns Wharf, the courthouse, the art museum and the mission. Tickets cost $5 ($3 children) and are valid all day, allowing you to get off and on as you please. The first trolley leaves Stearns Wharf at 10 am and the last one leaves at 4 pm.

Places to Stay

In summer, budget accommodations are practically nonexistent in Santa Barbara. Even a cheap motel room that may cost just $35 in November can go for as much as $150 between mid-May and September. In general, rates go down slightly during midweek. Some hotels impose a two-night minimum stay. Passport Reservation Service at ☎ 800-765-6255 and Coastal Escapes Accommodation at ☎ 800-292-2222 are free room reservation services.

Places to Stay – Budget

Camping Camping options abound in the Santa Barbara area, though most campgrounds are outside town limits. Scenic choices are *El Capitan State Beach* and *Refugio State Beach* (☎ *805-968-1033 for both campgrounds,* ☎ *800-444-7275 for reservations through Parknet)*, about 12 and 15 miles, respectively, west of Santa Barbara on Hwy 101. Refugio is a popular surf spot and hangout for students. The small campground is right next to the beach. The El Capitan campground, perched on low bluffs above the beach, is more popular with families. A 2½-mile trail runs along the bluffs connecting the two. First-come, first-served campsites cost $14 and have flush toilets, picnic tables and barbecues.

Private campgrounds closer to town are *El Capitan Canyon* (☎ 805-968-2214, 805-685-3887 for reservations, 11560 Calle Real) and *Rancho Oso Campground* (☎ 805-683-5686) on Paradise Rd.

Hostels Santa Barbara's only hostel is the 56-bed *Banana Bungalow* (☎ 805-963-0154, 800-346-7835, fax 805-963-0184, 210 E Ortega St), a fairly run-down affair in a barrel-like corrugated tin structure. There's no curfew, no lock-out, and no real chance of getting a good night's sleep when the place is full. Beds in 'semiprivate' dorms sleeping eight cost $18; bunks in a large communal room are $15. In summer, there's a busy activity schedule with barbecues, hiking trips, volleyball competitions and the like. US travelers are OK for stays of up to three days.

Hotels & Motels An excellent bet is the friendly 54-room *Hotel State Street* (☎ 805-966-6586, fax 805-962-8459, 121 State St), near the beach. Clean and newly renovated, it attracts Europeans and sophisticated budget travelers. Each room has a sink and towel, but bathrooms are shared. Midweek rates start at $35, but usually are more in the $55 to $75 range, but at least they hold pretty much steady year round.

One block closer to the beach, the *Californian Hotel* (☎ 805-966-7153, fax 962-9781, 35 State St) was in the process of renovation at the time of writing. Rates were $100/110 but are bound to be higher after summer 1999.

On upper State St is a cluster of motels that are fairly affordable in the off-season, though rates shoot up in summer; you might do better at one of the properties listed in the mid-range section. The small *Travelers Motel* (☎ 805-687-6009, fax 805-687-0419, 3222 State St) has simple rooms from $35 to $45, with prime season rates of $65 to 150. The *San Roque Motel* (☎ 805-687-6611, 800-587-5667, fax 805-687-7116, 3344 State St) charges from $42/48 single/double (though up to $150/160 in peak season). Rates at the *Sandpiper Lodge* (☎ 805-687-5326, 800-405-6343, fax 805-687-2271, 3525 State St) hold fairly steady year round at $80.

Places to Stay – Mid-Range

Most of Santa Barbara's mid-priced motels are along Cabrillo Blvd, west of State St. The *Sandy Beach Inn* (☎ 805-963-0405, 122 W Cabrillo Blvd) has a flowery lobby, wine and cheese in the afternoon and rooms for $95 to $165 in winter and $145 to $265 in summer. One block west is the pleasant *Beachcomber Inn* (☎ 805-965-4577, 805-965-9937, 202 W Cabrillo Blvd), which offers a small pool, sun deck and 32 rooms, some with kitchens, starting at $80 but topping out at $255. *La Playa Motel* (☎ 805-962-6436, 212 W Cabrillo Blvd) has similar facilities, a snug, frilly lobby and charges $65 off-season, $95 to $195 the rest of the year.

Another cluster of hotels is on Bath St just off Cabrillo Blvd. Easily the best deal in this area is the delightful *Franciscan Inn* (☎ 805-963-8845, fax 805-564-3295, 109 Bath St), which has a nice pool, spa and guest laundry and is run with efficiency and charm. A generous breakfast is served in the morning. The very reasonable rates start at $69 in winter, with kitchen suites costing $99; in summer, rates leap to $89/119 – still an excellent price.

Small and simple, the *Harbor House* (☎ 805-962-9745, fax 888-474-6789, 104 Bath St) has individually decorated rooms for $78 to $88 in winter, $140 in summer. Another good option is *Hotel Santa Barbara* (☎ 805-957-9300, 888-259-7700, 533 State St), which offers European spirit, a central location and pleasantly decorated rooms costing from $89 during off-season to $209 for a mini-suite when things warm up. *Casa del Mar* (☎ 805-963-4418, 800-433-3097, fax 805-966-4240, 18 Bath St) has 20 rooms with kitchens and fireplaces for around $100 to $160 in winter, $124 to $209 in summer.

Places to Stay – Top End

Hotels Most high-end accommodations are north of downtown in the hills and east in Montecito, though an excellent choice near the beach is the *Harbor View Inn* (☎ 805-963-0780, 800-755-0222, fax 805-963-7967, 36 W Cabrillo Blvd), whose large pool and spa are integrated into a nicely landscaped garden. Year-round rates start at $130 and crest at $330.

Long considered *the* hotel in Santa Barbara, *El Encanto Hotel & Garden Villas* (☎ 805-687-5000, 800-346-7039, fax 805-687-3903, 1900 Lasuen Rd) sits on a hill above the mission with a great view of downtown and the ocean. Nestled among 10 acres of lush gardens, its secluded cottages with private patios start at $229 and zoom to $1450.

The *Santa Barbara Inn* (☎ 805-966-2285, 800-231-0431, fax 805-966-6584, 901 E Cabrillo Blvd) is a full-service convention facility right across from the beach. Winter rates are reasonable at $109 to $169, but summer prices start at $150. Also popular among the well-heeled is the *Four Seasons Biltmore* (☎ 805-969-2261, 800-332-3442, fax 805-565-8323, 1260 Channel Drive), in Montecito. Situated on 20 acres, this place caters to the golf and tennis crowd. Rooms here start at $250.

B&Bs The six-room *Olive House Inn* (☎ 805-962-4902, 800-786-6422, fax 805-899-2754, 1604 Olive St), near the mission, is housed in a 1904 Craftsman-style villa. It has a terraced garden, large sun deck and rooms costing $110 to $180. Next door, *The Parsonage* (☎ 805-962-9336, fax 805-962-2285, 1600 Olive St) is in a 1892 Victorian, which isn't nearly as neat but charges from $155 to around $300.

Also in a residential neighborhood three blocks west of State St, the no-smoking *Glenborough Inn* (☎ 805-966-0589, 800-962-0589, fax 805-564-8610, 1327 Bath St), between Victoria and Sola Sts, has 11 rooms that cost $100 to $250 year round.

Places to Eat

Santa Barbara's 'restaurant row' is in the 500 and 600 blocks of State St. A local institution, the *Greek & Italian Deli*, at the corner of State and Ortega Sts, has great sandwiches, gyros, Greek salad and hot lunch specials for around $5. Three blocks south, the *Natural Cafe* (☎ 805-962-9494, 508 State St) serves Zen burgers, Buddha burritos and Yogananda lasagna for under $7. The *Earth Garden Cafe* (☎ 805-899-2778, 1225½ State

St) is similar with a 98% organic menu, including many choices fit for vegans.

The *Paradise Cafe* (☎ 805-962-4416, 702 Anacapa St) is a nice and peaceful spot with a romantic outdoor patio. Their menu features no-nonsense salads and burgers for under $10 and more substantial oak grilled meats and seafood for around $20. Lunch is slightly cheaper. Also in downtown is the *Couscous Restaurant* (☎ 805-899-4780, 1231 State St), perfect for those who like culinary adventures. Their seven-course ceremonial Moroccan feasts are served on low circular brass tables and often accompanied by belly dancing. Prices range from $17.50 to $25.

Beachside dining options include the reliably excellent *Brophy Brothers* (☎ 805-966-4418) in the Santa Barbara Yacht Harbor. A lively restaurant and oyster bar where locals go for superb seafood, its top choices include clam chowder and *cioppino* (seafood stew), all served with chewy sourdough bread. Entire meals can be had for around $10.

On Arroyo Burro Beach, west of town, is the *Brown Pelican* (☎ 805-687-4550), an informal cafe with view of the waves, whose fare includes mouthwatering salads, sandwiches and seafood (the clam chowder is terrific). It's also a nice place for breakfast.

La Tolteca (☎ 805-963-0847, 616 E Haley St), in an industrial part of town, is a 'mexicatessen' with famously authentic enchiladas and tamales to eat there or to take out. Prices are $1.70 to $6. More expensive, but also more central, is the colorful *Carlito's Cafe y Cantina* (☎ 805-962-7117, 1324 State St).

To stock up on fresh produce, visit the *farmers' market*, held Tuesday late afternoons on the 500 block of State St and Saturday mornings at the corner of Santa Barbara and Cota Sts.

Entertainment

The free *Independent* is published on Thursday and has thorough events listings and reviews. Also good is the *Santa Barbara News-Press* which has a daily events calendar and special Friday issue called 'Scene' that details the week's happening.

JOHN ELK III

Hwy 1 along the Central Coast

Jellyfish at the Monterey Bay Aquarium

JOHN ELK III

California sea otter

LEE FOSTER

JOHN ELK III

DAVID PEEVERS

Public art in San Luis Obispo: Street Painting Festival and Bubblegum Alley

JOHN ELK III

Pinnacles National Monument

JOHN ELK III

Children's rodeo, Salinas

RICK GERHARTER

Forestiere Underground Gardens, Fresno

Lupine, Tuolumne Meadows

Yosemite Valley

DL Bliss State Park, Lake Tahoe

Bodie State Historic Park

Marmot

Devils Postpile National Monument

Sequoia National Park

Hot Creek Geological Site, Owens Valley

Mono Lake

Coffeehouses New coffeehouses and cafes spring up in Santa Barbara almost weekly, so your best bet is to cruise State St (between Cota and Anapamu Sts) for an appealing scene. *Andersen's Restaurant & Bakery* (☎ 805-962-5085, 1106 State St), an old-fashioned European-style coffeehouse, is a local favorite. Another good choice is the 24-hour *Hot Spots* (☎ 805-564-1637, 36 State St).

Bars & Clubs Santa Barbara's raging afterdark scene revolves around lower State St and Ortega St. Most places have happy hour and college nights, when the booze is cheap and the atmosphere rowdy. Such places include *Calypso* (☎ 805-966-1388, 514 State St) and *Zelo* (☎ 805-966-5792, 630 State St). *The Tank* (☎ 805-963-9680, 416 State St) has aquariums for decor and dancing on weekends. Looking like a cross between a warehouse and a love den, the *Wild Cat* (☎ 805-962-7970, 15 W Ortega St) is the ultimate '70s revival lounge with a diverse crowd and good mix of music. *Soho* (☎ 805-962-7776, 1221 State St), above McDonald's, has live jazz nightly and only charges admission for weekend and big-name shows. Regional touring acts appear at the *Coach House* (☎ 805-962-8877, 110 Santa Barbara St).

Good pubs include the literary *James Joyce* (☎ 805-962-2688, 513 State St), with its wooden ceiling, crackling fireplace and friendly crowd; the *Brickyard* (☎ 805-899-2820, 525 State St), which has 85 beers on tap and caters to an edgier rock 'n' roll scene; and the *Santa Barbara Brewing Co* (☎ 805-730-1040, 501 State St), whose more sedate decor draws in a slightly more mature drinking crowd.

Theater To find out current theater happenings, call the *Santa Barbara Performing Arts League* (☎ 805-892-2250 ext 5545) 24-hour hotline.

The *Lobero Theater* (☎ 805-963-0761, 33 E Cañon Perdido St), California's oldest continuously operating theater, is home to the Lobero Theater Foundation and Santa Barbara Chamber Orchestra, and presents musicals, comedies, children's theater and films.

Built in 1930, the *Granada Theatre* (☎ 805-966-2324, 1216 State St) hosts – among others – the Santa Barbara Civic Light Opera, which performs an annual series of musicals and operettas. The *Arlington Theater* (☎ 805-963-4408, 1317 State St) is home to the Santa Barbara Symphony and also contains a movie theater.

The *Center Stage Theater* (☎ 805-963-0408), on the upper level of the Paseo Nuevo Center, hosts small productions and the Great Globe Shakespeare Company.

UCSB stages occasional events in *Campbell Hall*, a large performing arts center, and in the *Halten Theater*, both on campus. For information call ☎ 805-893-3535.

Shopping

Shops along State St feature clothing, knickknacks, antiques and books. Paseo Nuevo, between Cañon Perdido and Ortega Sts, is a charming outdoor mall anchored by Nordstrom and Robinsons-May department stores, plus various retail chains like the Gap and Victoria's Secret. La Arcada, 1114 State St, at Figueroa St, is a historical red-tile passageway designed by Myron Hunt (builder of the Rose Bowl in Los Angeles) and filled with boutiques, restaurants and whimsical public art. Another lovely, flower-festooned courtyard is the Historic Paseo, opposite Paseo Nuevo.

Getting There & Away

Air The small Santa Barbara Airport (☎ 805-683-4011), 8 miles west of downtown off Hwy 101 at 500 Fowler Rd, has commercial service to Los Angeles and San Francisco on commuter planes. Major airline carriers include American Eagle, Skywest Delta Connections and United Express.

For shuttle service to/from Los Angeles International Airport (LAX), there's the Santa Barbara Airbus (☎ 805-964-7759) with several departures daily costing $35, $65 roundtrip.

Bus Greyhound has nine daily buses to Los Angeles for $12, and six to San Francisco for $35; roundtrip fares save a few dollars each way. The Greyhound bus station, a magnet for transient types, is downtown at 33 W Carrillo St.

Train Three southbound Amtrak trains and one northbound train leave daily from Santa Barbara's train depot (☎ 805-963-1015), 209 State St. The general fare to Los Angeles is $20 and to San Francisco (via Oakland) is $67.

Car & Motorcycle Santa Barbara is bisected by Hwy 101. For downtown, take the Garden St or Cabrillo Blvd exits. Parking on the street and in any of the 10 municipal lots is free for the first 90 minutes (all day Sunday). There's no charge for beach parking on weekdays between Labor Day and Memorial Day.

Getting Around

Bus The Downtown-Waterfront Shuttle bus runs every 10 to 15 minutes from 10:15 am to 6 pm between downtown and Stearns Wharf. A second route travels from the zoo to the yacht harbor at 30-minute intervals. The fare is 25¢ per ride; transfers between routes are free.

Santa Barbara Metropolitan Transit District (MTD) buses cost $1 per ride and operate daily (less on weekends) throughout downtown and also west to Goleta and east to Carpenteria (via Montecito and Summerland). The MTD Transit Center (☎ 805-683-3702), downtown at 1020 Chapala St, has details on routes and schedules.

Car Avis, Budget and Hertz have kiosks in the main airport terminal, as well as downtown. The most affordable rent-a-car service is U-Save Auto Rental (☎ 805-963-3499), 510 Anacapa St. Enterprise Rent-A-Car (☎ 805-966-3097) has a branch at 624 Santa Barbara St.

LOS PADRES NATIONAL FOREST

Los Padres National Forest starts in the Santa Ynez foothills just east of Santa Barbara and extends north and west over one million acres. (This is the southern part of the forest, the northern port is at Big Sur.) Forest headquarters (☎ 805-683-6711) are at 6144 Calle Real in Goleta and are a great

source for maps and information on hiking, mountain biking, camping and other outdoor activities. If you are traveling by car, you must have the National Forest Adventure Pass in order to make use of the facilities, including hiking trails, in the forest (see boxed text in the Outdoor Activities chapter).

The best access to the forest from Santa Barbara is via Hwy 154 northwest. Paradise Rd, which crosses Hwy 154 north of San Marco Pass, offers the best access to developed facilities. At the Paradise Rd/Hwy 154 junction, the **Cold Springs Tavern** (☎ 805-967-0066) is *the* gathering point for hikers and campers – a fun place to have a beer. They also serve good burgers and fries for under $10.

About 5 miles up the road is a USFS ranger station, open 8 am to 5 pm Monday to Saturday, with posted maps and information. There are three **campgrounds** before the ranger station and one just past it, all of which are near the Santa Ynez River and cost $8.

At **Red Rocks** (clearly marked from the ranger station), the Santa Ynez River pools among rocks and waterfalls, making a great swimming and sunning spot. Many hiking trails radiate out from here.

At the bottom of San Marcos Pass, surrounded by oaks, **Lake Cachuma County Park** is a haven for anglers and boaters and also has a large **campground** (☎ 805-688-4658) with $13 tent spaces, picnic tables, barbecues, flush toilets and 100 RV hookups. Sites are first-come, first-served and fill quickly on weekends. Check with forest headquarters for details about the several dozen, mostly primitive, campgrounds within the forest.

WINE COUNTRY

Fog and ocean breezes flowing into the valleys carved into the coastal mountains around Santa Barbara create microclimates well suited for growing grapes. About three dozen wineries, mostly family-run, are scattered throughout the county, producing Chardonnays as well as Pinot Noir, Merlot, Cabernet Sauvignon and other varietals. Many vineyards are open for touring and operate tasting rooms. Those worth a visit include Gainey (☎ 805-688-0558), 3950 E Hwy 246, in Santa Ynez; Zaca Mesa (☎ 805-688-9339), 6905 Foxen Canyon Rd, in Los Olivos; and Firestone (☎ 805-688-3940), 5017 Zaca Station Rd, in Los Olivos. For in-depth touring, pick up a free winery map at the Tourist Information Center in Santa Barbara.

OJAI & AROUND

About 35 miles southeast of Santa Barbara and 14 miles inland from Ventura off Hwy 33, Ojai (pronounced oh-hi, and meaning 'nest' to the Chumash) is a town that has long drawn artists and the spiritually inclined. Several religious institutes, includ-ing the Krishnamurti Foundation and the Krotona Institute of Theosophy, have set up residence here. Ojai is famous for the rosy glow which emanates both from its mountains at sunset – the so-called Pink Moment – and from the faces emerging from spa treatments. In fact, the scenery here is so stunning that Frank Capra felt the Ojai Valley worthy of representing a mythical Shangri-La in his 1937 movie *Lost Horizon*.

As a resort, Ojai flourished about 20 years ago but now looks a tad aged. The exception is the *Ojai Valley Inn (☎ 805-646-5511, 800-422-6524)*, on the west end of town, and well signed from the highway. The Inn has a putting green, croquet court and restaurants. The Arcade Plaza, a maze of mission revival-style buildings on Ojai Ave (the main thor-oughfare), contains cutesy shops and art galleries. Bart's Books (☎ 805-646-3755), two blocks north of Ojai Ave at 302 W Mar-tilija St, is worth at least a half-hour browse.

The *Farm Hostel (☎ 805-646-0311)*, on Hwy 33, about 10 minutes from downtown Ojai, is indeed a working family farm with 250 organic fruit trees. Beds in this non-smoking, vegetarian facility are just $12; an international passport is required.

About 10 miles outside of town, **Lake Casitas** has lovely coves and inlets and was the site of the 1984 Olympic canoeing and rowing events. This being a reservoir, swim-ming is not permitted. The 9 miles of the Ojai Valley Trail are a haven for outdoor recre-ationists, including joggers and bicyclists.

VENTURA
• population 103,000 • elevation 100 feet
Ventura's historic downtown is centered on Main St, north of Hwy 101 via Seaward Ave. The Visitors Center (☎ 805-648-2075), at 89C South California St, is open daily. Main Street has a world-class assortment of antique and thrift shops that could easily entertain bargain hunters for an entire day. Of cultural interest is the cluster of museums centered around the 1809 **Mission San Buenaventura** (☎ 805-643-4318), 211 E Main St. A fraction of its former self but still beautifully decorated, the church is the only one in California that has not missed a Sunday service in more than 100 years. Hours are 10 am to 5 pm daily.

The mission's original foundations and related artifacts are among items on display in the adjacent **Albinger Archaeological Museum** (☎ 805-648-5823), open 10 am to 4 pm Wednesday to Sunday. Across the street at 100 E Main St, the **Ventura County Museum of History & Art** (☎ 805-653-0323) has two rooms dedicated to Chumash history as well as some 300 miniature histor-ical figures created by George Stuart. Hours are 10 am to 5 pm, closed Monday; $4/1.

Ventura Harbor, southwest of Hwy 101 via Harbor Blvd, is where boats depart for the Channel Islands. Even if you don't embark on an island adventure, **Channel Islands National Park Headquarters** (☎ 805-658-5730), 1901 Spinnaker Drive, has an interesting natural history display and a three-story lookout from where you can see the islands on a clear day. Next door is Island Packers, the main outfitter for island excursions (see the next section).

CHANNEL ISLANDS NATIONAL PARK
The Channel Islands are an eight-island chain lying off the coast from Newport Beach to Santa Barbara. The five northern islands – San Miguel, Santa Rosa, Santa Cruz, Anacapa and Santa Barbara – and their surrounding ocean comprise the

Channel Islands National Park. Isolated from the mainland and located in a transition zone between warm water from the tropics and cold water from Arctic seas, the islands have unique flora and fauna and extensive tide pools and kelp forests.

Originally inhabited by the Chumash and Gabrielino Indians (who were taken to the mainland missions in the early 1800s), the islands were owned by sheep ranchers and the US Navy until the mid-1970s, when conservation efforts began. San Miguel, Santa Rosa, Anacapa and Santa Barbara islands are now owned by the National Park Service, which also owns 20% of Santa Cruz (the other 80% belongs to the Nature Conservancy).

Anacapa, which is actually three separate islets, is the closest to the mainland and thus gets the most visitors. A visitor center and picnic area sits atop the island's narrow plateau (reached by 153 steps); snorkeling and swimming are possible in Frenchy's Cove. **Santa Cruz**, the largest islet, is laced by hiking trails and is probably the best island for exploring on your own. Popular activities include swimming, snorkeling, scuba diving and kayaking. **Santa Barbara** is home to the humongous northern elephant seal and is a remote playground for birds and marine wildlife. Beautiful sandy beaches, nearly 200 bird species and the Painted Cave are highlights on **Santa Rosa**. Rangers tell us that **San Miguel** – the most remote island – is the most exciting for its unusual natural formations (Caliche Forest, made of calcium-carbonate castings of trees) and for the six species of seals and sea lions cohabiting on Point Bennett beaches.

Beautiful any time of year, the islands receive most visitors between May and September; the nicest times to visit, though, are during spring wildflower season (in April and May) and in September and October, when the weather conditions are calmest.

Places to Stay

Camping is free and permitted year round on Anacapa and San Miguel; from April to November on Santa Rosa and Santa Barbara; and from May to November on San Miguel. All campgrounds are primitive, and you must pack everything in (and out, including trash), including water.

The campground on Santa Barbara is large, grassy and surrounded by hiking trails, while the one on Anacapa is high, rocky and isolated. Camping on San Miguel, with its unceasing wind, fog and volatile weather, is only for the hardy. Santa Rosa's campground is sheltered by a canyon with wonderful views of Santa Cruz, whose own site is located within a eucalyptus grove. Free camping permits are required and issued by the park headquarters. For camping reservations ($2.50 per site), call ☎ 800-365-2267.

Getting There & Away

Two boat and one air concessionaire offer campers transportation to/from the islands as well as half-day and one-day excursions. Island Packers (☎ 805-642-1393, 805-642-7688 for recorded information), 1867 Spinnaker Drive, adjacent to the park headquarters, offers packages to all islands with a focus on Anacapa. Rates are $37/20 adults/children for the eight-hour East Anacapa trip and $32/20 for the six-hour East Anacapa trip. Overnight campers pay $48/30; for an extra $6, you can bring along a kayak (for rent from several outfitters in the area; check the phone book or ask for a list at the park headquarters). Their whale-watching tours cost $57/52 for a full day or $22/15 for a half day.

Truth Aquatics (☎ 805-962-1127) operates out of offices at 301 W Cabrillo Blvd in Santa Barbara and specializes in the other islands, especially Santa Cruz, with day trips costing $60/45. Tours offered by either operator include an optional ranger-led nature walk and, where available, time for swimming and snorkeling.

Most trips require a minimum number of participants and may be canceled any time because of surf and weather conditions. In any case, landing is never guaranteed, again because of changeable weather and surf conditions. Channel crossings take from one to five hours. Reservations are suggested for weekend, holiday and summer trips and require a credit card or advance payment.

Those prone to seasickness might want to consider taking a trip with Channel Islands Aviation (☎ 805-987-1301) instead. The company operates one-day trips to Santa

Rosa for $85/65 adults/children; camper transportation is $150. Planes leave year round from airports at Camarillo and Santa Barbara.

San Joaquin Valley

The San Joaquin Valley extends roughly 300 miles from Stockton to Bakersfield, between the Sierra Nevada and the Coast Range. The San Joaquin River's major tributaries – the Kings, San Joaquin, Merced, Tuolumne, Stanislaus and Calaveras rivers – flow west from their headwaters in the Sierra Nevada. They then join the San Joaquin proper, which flows north to the delta, where it meets the Sacramento River and flows to the Pacific. Together the Sacramento and San Joaquin valleys constitute the Central Valley or Great Valley (or Great Central Valley).

The San Joaquin Valley is very important to California's economy. Often called the most productive valley in the world, the San Joaquin Valley produces much of the United States' walnuts, almonds, grapes, peaches, apricots, plums, oranges, olives, tomatoes and cotton, and holds five of the country's top 10 agricultural counties. Crops are cultivated on an enormous scale, with most land in the hands of big corporations that own at least 5000 acres each and use pesticides, massive irrigation systems and Mexican laborers. Human and environmental rights activists point angry fingers at these farming practices for overtaxing the land and exploiting workers. Faced with such issues, many small-time farmers can't compete with corporate farms and are increasingly enticed by a 'sure thing': an average of 15,000 acres of farmland goes to commercial and real estate development each year (in 1997 this reduced a $13 billion crop to $11 billion). John Steinbeck painted a classic literary portrait of farming life during the depression in the Great Valley in *The Grapes of Wrath*.

For travelers, the San Joaquin Valley is a corridor to be passed through quickly – especially from June to September, when temperatures often reach 100°F (37°C) by 11 am. I-5 offers a streamlined route (popular with truckers) between San Francisco and Los Angeles, which takes about six hours to drive; the only roadside attractions are gas stations and fast-food stops. Hwy 99 follows

Highlights

- Kern River – raft through rapids in a thrilling white-water ride
- Blossom Trail – a florid drive through Central Valley fruit orchards
- Forestiere Underground Gardens – 70 subterranean acres of fruits and flowers

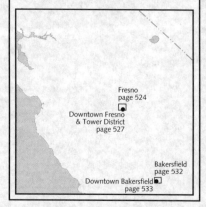

Fresno
page 524

Downtown Fresno
& Tower District
page 527

Bakersfield
page 532

Downtown Bakersfield
page 533

an old wagon route, parallel to the railroad, between Bakersfield and Sacramento, connecting the valley's important towns. Listening to the radio reveals true valley culture: a mix of Christian rock, country and western and Mexican folk.

THE SACRAMENTO DELTA

The Sacramento Delta, where the Sacramento and San Joaquin rivers meet and flow toward the Carquinez Strait, contains 1000 miles of waterways. In the 1930s the Bureau of Reclamation issued an aggressive water redirection program, the Central Valley and California State Water Projects, that dammed California's major rivers and directed 75% of their supply through the Central Valley for agricultural use and use in Southern California. The siphoning has affected the Sacramento Delta, its wetlands

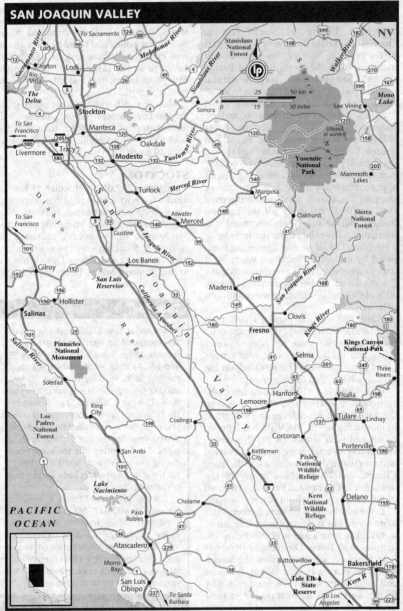

SAN JOAQUIN VALLEY

To Sacramento

Locke

Sacramento River

Mokelumne River

Stanislaus National Forest

NV

124
88
99
12
Isleton
Lodi
88
26
12
Rio Vista
The Delta
Stockton
49
4
Stanislaus River
Sonora
108
395
182
270
167
Sierra

0   25   50 km
15   30 miles

Lee Vining
Mono Lake

To San Francisco
5
Manteca
120
108
Oakdale
Tuolumne River
49
120
120 (closed in winter)
158
203

To San Francisco
580
Tracy
205
580
Livermore
132
Modesto
132
Nevada
Yosemite National Park
Mammoth Lakes

Diablo
San
Turlock
Merced River
Mariposa
140
49
Oakhurst
Sierra National Forest

To San Francisco
5
33
Atwater
Merced
140
140
99
41

Gustine
San Joaquin River
152
145
San Joaquin River
168

101
Gilroy
152
152
Los Banos
Joaquin
33
Madera
145
Kings River

156
Hollister
156
California Aqueduct
145
Clovis
180

Salinas
101
Fresno
Kings Canyon National Park

Salinas River
San Luis Reservoir
180
Selma
245
Three Rivers

25
Range
41
201
63
198

Pinnacles National Monument
Soledad
Valley
Lemoore
Hanford
Visalia
198

Los Padres National Forest
King City
198
Coalinga
Tulare
Lindsay
65
137

101
San Ardo
33
Corcoran
Porterville
190

Lake Nacimiento
Kettleman City
5
Pixley National Wildlife Refuge
43

PACIFIC OCEAN
Cholame
46
41
Kern National Wildlife Refuge
43
Delano
155

Paso Robles
41

46
Atascadero
229
33

Morro Bay
1
Buttonwillow
58
Bakersfield
178
58

San Luis Obispo
227
To Santa Barbara
Tule Elk State Reserve
To Los Angeles
99
223
Kern R

and estuaries, and has been a source of environmental, ecological and political debate ever since. Before the Shasta, Folsom, Oroville and Friant dams were built, as part of the projects, most of this water flowed naturally from the rivers into the Pacific through San Francisco Bay. A natural annual flood cycle purged the delta of impurities that settled and saltwater that encroached during the dry season, and the waterways stayed pretty healthy. After WWII, agricultural production in the San Joaquin Valley grew enormously, and the use of chemical pesticides and fertilizers became commonplace. Simultaneously, dams appeared on many of the delta's tributaries, stopping the annual floods and redirecting the flow that once took all the harmful buildup out to sea. Soon afterward, the Sacramento River had to be redirected into a peripheral canal to avoid being contaminated by the delta's backflow. Water is let back into the delta from control points along the canal and further redirected to supply 40% of California's drinking water and 45% of its irrigation.

While still a major part of California's political and environmental arena, the delta is also a favorite place for boating, water skiing and duck hunting (the river's woes aren't apparent when you're sitting on the deck of a houseboat drinking margaritas).

Hwy 4 and Hwy 12 head east from I-80 and connect to Hwy 160, which runs atop the Sacramento River levee and is Main St in most delta towns. **Rio Vista** has a public beach and boat launch facility. Northeast, **Isleton** has an interesting main street lined with corrugated tin buildings with faded Chinese characters above many of the doors. Isleton's Crawdad Festival, at the end of June, draws people from all over the state.

Locke was built by Chinese farmers after a fire wiped out Walnut Grove's Chinatown in 1912. The town's one street sits below the highway and levee. Dilapidated buildings lean toward each other over the street, giving the place a broken feeling. Its shops and galleries are worn by age and proximity to the water, but so picturesque in their decrepitude that one could imagine that

they have been touched up to gain the effect. Locke's unlikely centerpiece is *Al the Wop's*, a grungy bar with crumpled dollar bills on the ceiling and faded pictures on the wall. People come here to drink heavily and eat huge steaks ($15) served family-style with pasta, bread, fries and salad on checkered tablecloths.

More in touch with the town's heritage is the **Dai Loy Museum**, an old gambling hall filled with photos and relics from some of Locke's original families. The museum is open 10 am to 5 pm weekends; $1.

STOCKTON
• **population 239,000** • **elevation 15 feet**
Stockton's port connects to San Francisco via a deep-water channel, making it an important loading and unloading point for San Joaquin Valley agriculture. During the gold rush, Stockton was the main disembarkation point for men and goods headed to the Southern Mines. Today, many neigh-

---

Tule Fog

Radiation or tule (TOO-lee) fog causes an average of 24 deaths per year on San Joaquin Valley roads, including Hwy 99 and I-5. As thick as proverbial pea soup, the fog limits visibility to about 10 feet, making driving conditions almost impossible. The fog is thickest from November to February, when cold mountain air settles on the warm valley floor and condenses into fog as the ground cools at night. The fog often lifts for a few hours during the afternoon, just long enough for the ground to warm back up and thus perpetuate the cycle.

Call the California Highway Information Network (☎ 800-427-7623) to check road conditions before traveling through the valley. If you end up on a fog-covered road, drive with your low beams on, keep a good distance from the car in front of you, stay at a constant speed, avoid sudden stops and never try to pass other cars.

borhoods in Stockton are potentially dangerous conglomerations of boarded-up buildings and dilapidated houses, with the area around University of the Pacific (UOP) as the main exception. The excellent Haggin Museum, however, is worth a visit, and the historic Magnolia District is of interest to architecture buffs.

Things to See & Do

Stockton's main thoroughfares are Pacific Ave (which becomes Center St south of Harding Way) and El Dorado St going north-south, and Park St, Weber St and Harding Way going east-west. Maps and information are available at the Stockton-San Joaquin Convention & Visitors Bureau (☎ 209-943-1987, 800-350-1987), downtown off Center St at 46 W Fremont St.

Most visitors exit I-5 at Pershing Ave and head two blocks north to the **Haggin Museum** (☎ 209-462-4116), 1201 N Pershing Ave. It has an excellent collection of American landscape paintings, including works by Albert Bierstadt, famous for his portraits of Yosemite Valley, some colorful horse-drawn fire engines and Native American (mostly Yokut and Pomo) trading and ceremonial baskets. Hours are 1:30 to 5 pm Tuesday to Sunday; $2 donation requested.

Victory Park, surrounding the museum, is a shady picnic or barbecue spot with large trees and a duck pond. In the evening people run laps around the park (clockwise, always clockwise).

About 1 mile east of the Haggin Museum via Acacia St (on Victory Park's south side), the **Magnolia District** stands as testimony to Stockton's more prosperous days. Eden Park, on Acacia between El Dorado and Hunter Sts, is a good place to park your car. From here, walk one block north on Hunter to Magnolia St, where most of the beautiful homes – Queen Anne, Arts and Crafts and California Bungalow styles – are located. The visitor bureau has a detailed pamphlet on the history and architecture.

The garish **Hotel Stockton**, downtown at the corner of Weber and El Dorado Sts, is in a sad state of disrepair. Looking like a California mission in drag, the hotel was built in 1910 for $500,000 and hosted Stockton's most important guests during its heyday.

Places to Stay

There is a well-located **Days Inn** (☎ 209-948-6151) at the corner of Weber and Center Sts, near I-5 downtown. Rooms cost $66 and various discounts are available. In a more suburban location, north of downtown, the **Acorn Inn** (☎ 209-478-2944, 4540 N El Dorado St) has a pool and rooms for around $40 per night (cheaper by the week).

Places to Eat

A well-established and equally worn standby, **Ye Olde Hoosier Inn** (☎ 209-463-0271, 1537 N Wilson Way), is open 6:30 am to 2:30 pm Monday to Thursday (until 8pm Friday and Saturday, until 7pm Sunday) for big breakfasts ($3 to $6), excellent burgers (from $6) and a variety of steaks ($11 to $16). Folksy antiques hang about the walls, among them a lantern that supposedly belonged to Mark Twain. The **Valley Brewing Co** (☎ 209-464-2739, 157 W Adams St) opens daily from 11:30 am to around 11 pm for handcrafted beers, pizzas, large salads, pastas and hot sandwiches; a beer and a bite costs around $10. For authentic Mexican food, Miguel's (☎ 209-951-1931, 7555 Pacific Ave) will do the trick – in a no-frills atmosphere – for under $7.

MODESTO

• population 181,463 • elevation 87 feet

Despite Modesto's agricultural roots, its most famous product is George Lucas, who immortalized Modesto in his movie *American Graffiti* and gave it the reputation as 'cruising capital of the world.' The cruising tradition ended in 1992, when things got a bit out of control and gang-related incidents increasingly threatened general safety. Now weekend cruising is prohibited, though people still rev their engines mighty loud and seem to take great care of their cars.

A massive revitalization project, centered around the intersections of 10th and J Sts, will replace two blocks of historic (but very run-down) structures with an open pedestrian plaza and is due to be finished around

2004. This seems to be pumping the town with optimism: J St is already welcoming new businesses, sophisticated cafes and an art scene driven by the newly renovated State Theater, 1307 J St, which has films or live music nightly.

The area's biggest employers – the Ernest & Julio Gallo wineries and the Tri-Valley Growers' cannery (the largest fruit cannery in the world) – will likely remain the same. The Modesto Arch, at the corner of 9th and I Sts, delineates the good and bad parts of town – avoid the area west of 9th St after dark.

Things to See & Do

Housed in the 1912 city library, the **McHenry Museum** (☎ 209-577-5366), at the corner of 14th and I Sts, has a mishmash of medical, dental, mining and farm equipment. The museum is open noon to 4 pm Tuesday to Sunday. In the museum basement, the **Central California Art League Gallery** (☎ 209-529-3369) has regional arts and crafts displays.

One block away, at I and 15th Sts, the **McHenry Mansion** (☎ 209-577-5344), built in 1889, showcases replica rugs and wallpapers and original Victorian furniture. One-hour tours are given 1 to 4 pm Sunday to Thursday, and noon to 3 pm Friday. In the blocks east of the museum and mansion, especially along 14th St and Sycamore Ave, are numerous homes built in the early 20th century. The chamber of commerce (☎ 209-577-5757) has a free detailed walking-tour map.

Places to Stay

McHenry Ave, which runs north from Needham St downtown to become Hwy 108, is the lifeline of modern Modesto and has ample chain motels and restaurants. A good choice close to downtown is the *Chalet Motel* (☎ 209-529-4370, 115 Downey St), which has a pool and $38/42 single/double rooms. Next to the McHenry Mansion is the *Best Western Town House Lodge* (☎ 209-524-7261, 909 16th St), with $54/58 rooms, free breakfast and a pool. The *Doubletree Hotel* (☎ 209-526-6000, 1150 9th St) is Modesto's convention center and nicest accommodation, with a restaurant,

spa and rooms starting at $104; special rates are available midweek and for various club members.

Places to Eat

DeVa (☎ 209-572-3382), at the corner of 12th and J Sts, is a coffeehouse and bistro that serves breakfast until 11 am, huge salads, interesting sandwiches and hot items like crab cakes and pasta for around $7.

Maker of some really fine beers, *St Stan's Brewery* (☎ 209-524-4782, 821 L St) is a brewery, pub and restaurant. Tours are given on Saturdays at 2 pm (reservations are required). The pub lets you sample different brews ($3), and the restaurant serves mediocre salads, pasta, burgers and chicken for $6 to $11; appetizers are a better value.

India Oven (☎ 209-572-1805, 1022 11th St) serves good Indian food and has an all-you-can-eat lunch buffet for $6. *Tresetti's World Caffe* (☎ 209-572-2990, 927 11th St) is a good lunch spot (dinners are $20 and up) and has an outstanding regional wine list. It also has a bar and holds free wine tastings every Tuesday.

OAKDALE

• **population 14,400** • **elevation 155 feet**

On the way to Yosemite, 13 miles east of Modesto on Hwy 108, Oakdale is home to the western division of **Hershey Chocolate USA** (☎ 209-848-8126), just off the highway at 120 S Sierra Ave. A mosaic of sweets, the visitor center sells every Hershey product available. Free factory tours leave the visitor center every half-hour from 8:30 am to 3 pm weekdays.

MERCED

• **population 61,862** • **elevation 171 feet**

What Merced has going for it is a friendly hostel and handy public transportation to and from Yosemite National Park. Hwy 140, which meets Hwy 99 in Merced, is a scenic route into the park and one of the few that is open year round. Merced will also be home to the University of California's newest campus, which should be complete by 2002. As for downtown, it might rejuvenate after the university is built, but until then should be avoided after dark.

Orientation & Information

Downtown Merced is east of Hwy 99 along Main St, between J and R Sts. Numbered streets run parallel to Hwy 99, with 16th St as the main drag. The newer part of town – mostly fast-food restaurants, gas stations and the Merced Mall – is east of downtown along Olive St. The Merced Chamber of Commerce/Convention & Visitor's Bureau (☎ 209-384-7092), 690 W 16th St at the west end of N St (adjacent to the bus depot), has information about Merced and Yosemite and is open 8:30 am to 5 pm weekdays.

Things to See & Do

The stately **Merced County Courthouse**, built in 1874, houses a local history museum (☎ 209-723-2401) open 1 to 4 pm Wednesday to Sunday. About 6 miles north of Merced, off the Atwater exit from Hwy 99, the **Castle Air Museum** (☎ 209-723-2178) has a worthwhile display of restored military aircraft, uniforms and WWII propaganda. Hours are 10 am to 4 pm daily; $5.

The Merced Farmers' Market is held Saturday morning at the corner of 19th and N Sts, and there's a street fair from 6 to 9 pm Thursdays at the same place. If you stay long enough to explore, there is a nice path along both sides of Bear Creek and a beautiful city park on the north side of the creek between M and R Sts.

Places to Stay

Hostels The *Merced Home Hostel* (☎ 209-725-0407) is a family-style hostel in the home of longtime Merced residents who know tons about Yosemite. There are two rooms (each with two beds) and kitchen facilities, though the family likes everyone to eat meals together and often prepares dinner for all who are staying there. The hostel gets full quickly on weekends from May to September. The hostel will pick up or drop off people traveling from bus and train stations. It closes during the day and has an 11 pm curfew. Call between 5:30 and 10 pm for information, reservations and directions. For HI-AYH members, a bed is $12; nonmembers pay $15.

Motels If hosteling isn't your thing, try the *Happy Inn* (☎ 209-722-6291), east of Hwy 99 on Motel Drive, next to Carrows Restaurant, which has clean rooms for around $30. There are other chain motels along Motel Drive, all with rooms for $50 to $60.

Places to Eat

The *Taquería Azteca* (☎ 209-722-8223), across from the bus station, has decent Mexican takeout for under $5. *Maria's* (☎ 209-722-3360, 259 W Main St), at the corner of Main St and Martin Luther King Jr Blvd, is in a funky log cabin building and has been a favorite for over 30 years; meals are $4 to $7. Also good is *Victoria's* (☎ 209-388-0160, 950 Motel Drive), which makes its own tortillas and has an all-you-can-eat lunch buffet for $5.

Getting There & Away

Bus VIA buses (☎ 209-384-1315) depart for Yosemite several times daily (check with VIA for a current schedule) from Merced's bus station at 690 W 16th St (at the west end of N St). The buses meet north- and southbound Amtrak trains and stop at motels, the KOA and Yosemite Bug hostel (both in Midpines; see the Yosemite chapter) on Hwy 140 just outside the park entrance; it's a 2½-hour trip. A roundtrip ticket costs $38 ($20 one-way) and includes park entrance fee. If you're planning on staying at the hostel and visiting the park several times, buy a roundtrip ticket to Midpines and then get individual bus tickets, which are a few bucks cheaper, from the hostel. The VIA drivers are helpful if you have questions.

Greyhound buses operate from the same station and go to Los Angeles ($28, 6¼ hours) 11 times daily and San Francisco ($26, six hours) five times daily.

Train The Amtrak station (☎ 209-722-6862, 800-872-7245) is at the corner of 24th and K Sts, near the Merced County Courthouse and is open 7:15 am to 8:45 pm daily, although it closes at mealtimes. There are four northbound trains per day connecting Merced to Oakland ($26, 2½ hours), and four southbound trains that go to Los Angeles ($38) via a bus connection in Bakersfield (three hours to Bakersfield, then 2½ hours to Los Angeles). Buses to Yosemite meet the early train from San Francisco and the afternoon train from Los Angeles.

Car & Motorcycle Enterprise Rent-a-Car (☎ 209-722-1600), 1334 Main St, charges $90 for a three-day weekend rental with unlimited miles. If you call ahead, an agent will meet you at the train or bus station.

FRESNO
• **population 411,600** • **elevation 296 feet**
Wine maker Francis Eisen started the raisin business in Fresno in 1862, when he accidentally let his grapes dry on the vine. Irrigation from the Friant-Kern Canal then turned this desert into farmland, and Fresno became home to millionaires who made fortunes on citrus and raisin crops. Fresno County is still one of the United States' most productive counties, leading the country in grape, plum, cotton and nectarine yields. California State University, Fresno (student population 19,000) is considered one of the best agricultural schools in the US.

Demographically, Fresno is a prime example of 'leapfrog' development: a developer buys cheap land a mile or two from town, builds a shopping center and waits for another developer to build tract homes to fill the space between town and the new development. This has happened over and over again, making the city an urban sprawl of old and new shopping centers, old and new neighborhoods and enough traffic lights to frustrate even people from Los Angeles. The Mexican, Armenian, Chinese and (more

FRESNO

PLACES TO STAY	OTHER
1 Red Roof Inn	3 Forestiere Underground Gardens
2 Howard Johnson Express Inn & Suites	6 Fresno Art Museum, Radio Park
4 Picadilly Inn	7 Chaffee Zoological Gardens, Playland, Storyland
PLACES TO EAT	8 Kearney Mansion
5 Kim's Restaurant	

recently) Hmong populations so vital to Fresno's large-scale agricultural output generally occupy the 'old' pieces of this patchwork. Not surprisingly, Fresno is also the country's largest test ground for fast-food chains.

Orientation & Information

Fresno is large and sprawling, with little of interest between distinct sights. Getting around on foot is unenjoyable, if not impossible. The historic, mostly decrepit, downtown lies between Divisadero St, Hwy 41 and Hwy 99. Extending north and east of downtown, Fresno's newer developments are connected by the thoroughfares of Shaw, Shields and Olive Aves (going east-west) and Palm and Blackstone Aves (going north-south). Hwy 41 is handy for going north-south, as it has exits at most major boulevards.

The Fresno City & County Convention & Visitor's Bureau (☎ 559-233-0836, 800-788-0836), open 8 am to 5 pm weekdays, is downtown at 808 M St but will be moved to the historic water tower at the corner of Fresno and O Sts. The Radisson Hotel and Conference Center (☎ 559-268-1000) has maps and brochures in its lobby, which is open 24 hours. Services, including banks and pharmacies, are on most major thoroughfares north of downtown.

Forestiere Underground Gardens

If you see only one thing in Fresno, make it the underground gardens of Baldasare Forestiere (☎ 559-271-0734), marked by a large yellow sign on Shaw Ave, one block east of Hwy 99. After migrating from Sicily in the 1890s, Forestiere bought 70 acres of land, with hopes of planting citrus groves. He found, however, that the soil beneath his land was solid hardpan, making it impossible for him to plant anything. To escape the intense summer heat, he dug a basement out of the hardpan beneath his house and found that, with proper illumination from skylights, he could grow trees in pots beneath the ground. Eventually Forestiere cleared out some 70 subterranean acres for crops and his own living quarters. By altering the skylights, he engineered a year-round

SAN JOAQUIN VALLEY

growing season and was able to sustain himself and sell his produce – over 20 different crops – at local markets. He even had a pond stocked with trout and cod.

After Forestiere died in 1946, his family preserved the gardens and registered them as a historic landmark. Weekend tours leave hourly from noon to 2 pm; $6. In summer, tours are also offered Wednesday to Friday.

Museums

The **Fresno Art Museum** (☎ 559-441-4221), 2233 N 1st St in Radio Park, is Fresno's pride and joy. One of its more interesting twists is an exhibition of art related to social change featuring about 30 artists per year. The permanent collection has bits and pieces from France and South America, including some post-impressionist graphics. Hours are 10 am to 5 pm Tuesday to Friday and noon to 5 pm on weekends; $2 (free on Tuesdays).

A favorite with children, the **Fresno Metropolitan Museum** (☎ 559-441-1444), downtown at 1555 Van Ness Ave, has three floors of hands-on science exhibits and a small laser show. The museum also has Fresno's best exhibit on William Saroyan – the author and playwright who commuted between Paris and his native Fresno. Hours are 11 am to 5 pm daily; $5.

Historic Homes

Built in 1888 by Dr TR Meux, who had been a surgeon for the Confederate army during the Civil War, the **Meux Home** (☎ 559-233-8007), at the corner of Tulare and R Sts, is a good example of Victorian architecture. The well-trained docents give an educational spiel on the Victorian era, a time 'when people loved to think about death and pretend sex didn't exist.' Though the only original parts of the house are its windows, light fixtures and hardware, period furniture and clothing is displayed throughout. The house is open Friday to Sunday from noon to 3:30 pm (closed in January), and tours are given on request; $4.

More interesting but less central, the **Kearney Mansion** (☎ 559-441-0862), 7 miles west of downtown on Kearney Blvd, belonged to M Theo Kearney, one of Fresno's first raisin barons. The house was built in 1903 and is beautifully restored with about half of its original furnishings and exquisite art nouveau wallpapers. Tours are given hourly from 1 to 3 pm Friday to Sunday for $3.

Tower District

Fresno's Tower District, at the east end of Olive Ave, around Wishon, Fern and Fulton Sts, was revived when the 1939 **Tower Theater** (☎ 559-485-9050) was renovated and turned into a center for the performing arts. Surrounding the theater are used-clothing stores, record shops, bookstores and cafes that cater to Fresno's gay community and thirty-something crowd. This is Fresno's best neighborhood for browsing and people watching, but remember this *is* Fresno (not San Francisco). Weekend nights are especially lively, when restaurants fill up around 9 pm and people hang out to see and be seen. Pick up a copy of *Talk of the Tower*, available at most stores and cafes, which lists the current events and exhibits around the neighborhood.

Roeding Park

On Olive Ave just west of Hwy 99, Roeding Park is a shady spot to picnic and escape the summer heat. There is a $1 per vehicle entrance fee. The park is also home to the **Chaffee Zoological Gardens** (☎ 559-498-2671), or simply 'the zoo.' The small but well-tended zoo has a good collection of average zoo animals – monkeys, lions, tigers, elephants – plus a great tropical rain forest arboretum. The zoo is open 9 am to 5 pm daily March to October, 10 am to 4 pm November to February; $4.95. For an extra $2, you can purchase a plastic key at the gift shop, which activates recorded information at exhibits throughout the zoo – fun for people under 10.

Adjacent to the zoo are **Playland** and **Storyland,** which can keep children entertained for at least half a day. There is no admission fee to enter Playland, but its mini roller coasters, rides and games cost 50¢ a pop. Storyland has oversize fairy-tale figures, castles and cottages that 'come to life' when you insert a magic key sold at the entrance for $2. Performances of children's stories like 'Hansel and Gretel,' 'Sleeping Beauty' and 'Jack and the Beanstalk' take place on weekends.

Playland is open year round. Storyland is open 10 am to 4 pm weekdays May to September, 10 am to 5 pm weekends (October to April, weekends only). Admission is $3/2. For information call ☎ 559-264-2235.

Special Events

During the third weekend in April, nearby Clovis hosts the biggest two-day rodeo in California, complete with rodeo events, a carnival and a street dance on Saturday night. A completely different crowd attends the Tower District's music, dance and arts festival (☎ 559-237-9734) at the end of May. On August 14, the eve of the Feast of the Immaculate Conception, is the Blessing of the Grapes, an Armenian tradition celebrating the first fruit of the season. The Fresno Fair, the largest in California, takes place the first two weeks in October and ends with a huge Ragtime Festival where costumed people play music and dance in the streets.

Places to Stay

If you're looking for a quick, highway-side rest stop, continue north or south, since

SAN JOAQUIN VALLEY

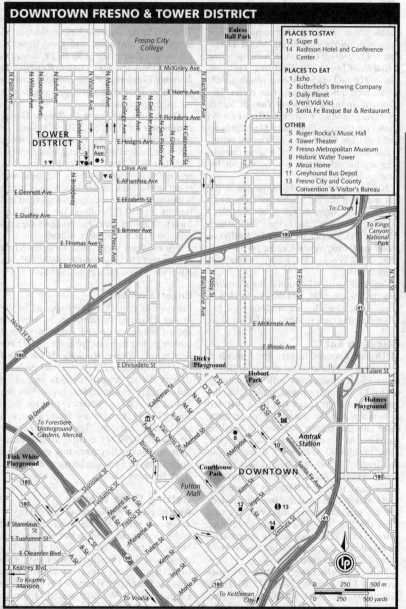

DOWNTOWN FRESNO & TOWER DISTRICT

PLACES TO STAY
12 Super 8
14 Radisson Hotel and Conference
      Center

PLACES TO EAT
1   Echo
2   Butterfield's Brewing Company
3   Daily Planet
4   Veni Vidi Vici
10 Santa Fe Basque Bar & Restaurant

OTHER
5   Roger Rocka's Music Hall
4   Tower Theater
7   Fresno Metropolitan Museum
8   Historic Water Tower
9   Meux Home
11 Greyhound Bus Depot
13 Fresno City and County
      Convention & Visitor's Bureau

SAN JOAQUIN VALLEY

Fresno's accommodations are the valley's most expensive. There are several cheap hotels, which are not all that comfortable or even necessarily safe, along Motel Drive, east of Hwy 99 off Olive Ave. A better value is *Red Roof Inn* (☎ 559-276-1910), one block east of Hwy 99 via Shaw Ave, where $36/39 buys a nice, quiet room and free coffee. The *Howard Johnson Express Inn & Suites* (☎ 559-277-3888), a block farther east on Shaw Ave (next to Forestiere Underground Gardens), has $79 rooms (each with a refrigerator and microwave) and a large complimentary breakfast; this is a good spot for families and groups.

If you need to stay downtown near the bus and train station, you've got a choice of the very basic *Super 8* (☎ 559-268-0621, 2127 Inyo St) between L and Van Ness, which charges $45/55, or the upscale *Radisson Hotel and Conference Center* (☎ 559-268-1000, 2233 Ventura St), where rooms cost around $107.

Another high-end option is the *Picadilly Inn* (☎ 559-226-3850, 800-468-3586, 2305 W Shaw Ave), which has an outdoor pool, hot tub and restaurant. Rooms cost $94 to $130.

Places to Eat

McDonald's opened its very first franchised restaurant in Fresno at the corner of Blackstone and Simpson Aves, with 10 hamburgers for $1. The menu is now modern, but the restaurant's architecture has been restored to how it was in the '50s, with glass on three sides and the golden arches built into the structure. At the other end of the spectrum, *Echo* (☎ 559-442-3246, 609 E Olive Ave), in the Tower District, has been rated by the *San Francisco Chronicle* as one of Northern California's top five restaurants. The restaurant raises its own meat and organic produce and has original Frank Lloyd Wright chairs from the late '40s. The nightly fixed-price menu ($15 to $25, depending on the night) is an excellent value; dinner a la carte will cost at least $25 per person.

Other upscale Tower District favorites are *Veni Vidi Vici* (☎ 559-266-5510, 1116 N Fulton St), one block south of Olive Ave, which has an outdoor patio with live music

on weekends, and the *Daily Planet* (☎ 559-266-4259, 1211 N Wishon Ave), next to the Tower Theater, which has sophisticated supper club ambience and great desserts. Lunch at either place is $6 to $9, dinner is $11 to $15. A few doors down, *Butterfield's Brewing Company* (☎ 559-264-5521) makes good beer and has decent appetizers, though meals are overpriced.

Downtown, the *Santa Fe Basque Bar & Restaurant* (☎ 559-266-2170, 935 Santa Fe Ave), across from the train station, looks more like a seedy bar than a place to eat. The bar is a hangout for Fresno's few remaining Basque old-timers, but the dining room in the back serves family-style meals with soup, salad, meat, vegetables, bread and dessert for $10 ($7 without the meat). The food isn't always great, but portions are generous and the atmosphere is lively.

For excellent Vietnamese food, try *Kim's Restaurant* (☎ 559-225-0406, 5048 N Maroa Ave), where you can eat well for $10.

Entertainment

Fresno's after-dark scene happens in the Tower District. In summer, movies are shown outdoors on the sides of several buildings, and many of the restaurants have live music. *Roger Rocka's Music Hall* (☎ 559-266-9493, 1226 N Wishon) presents decent Broadway productions and often sells out. The entertainment is good for the $18-to-$22 price range; dinner plus the show costs $32, but the money is better spent at a bona fide restaurant. The *Tower Theater* (☎ 559-485-9050, 815 E Olive St) gets headliners and many Bay Area folk groups. It is open 10 am to 5 pm weekdays and 10 am to 2 pm Saturday.

Getting There & Away

Air The Fresno Air Terminal, east of Hwy 41 at the east end of Shields Ave, is antiquated and expensive to fly in or out of. Your best bet is to take a bus or train from Los Angeles or San Francisco, since most flights to and from Fresno stop at one of these hubs anyway. The airport is serviced by American Eagle, Delta, Westair/United Express, Skywest and US Airways. Bus No 26 runs from the airport's main entrance to downtown (near the courthouse at Van Ness and Tulare Sts) from 6:40 am to 6:30 pm daily and costs 75¢. For information call Fresno Transit (☎ 559-488-1122).

Bus Greyhound connects Fresno to Los Angeles 16 times daily ($21, five hours), San Francisco eight times daily ($22, 4¾ hours) and Las Vegas twice a day ($48, nine hours). The bus depot (☎ 559-268-1829) is in a sketchy part of downtown at 1033 Broadway St.

Hwy 41 goes north to Yosemite, and Hwy 180 (Kings Canyon Rd) goes east to Kings Canyon and Sequoia national parks. The regular VIA/Gray Line bus tour from Merced to Yosemite will pick you up in Fresno if you call in advance. You can take a one-day tour (lunch is included) or get dropped off in the park, provided you have lodging or campground reservations (or a backcountry permit). The fare is $60 roundtrip.

Train Fresno is on the main Amtrak route between Oakland ($27, 4½ hours) and Bakersfield ($18, two hours) with a connection to Los Angeles for another $7 (3¾ hours). The train station (☎ 559-486-7651, 800-872-7245) is downtown at the corner of Tulare and Q Sts and gets four northbound and four southbound trains daily.

Getting Around

Inspired by conventioneers who want to eat in the Tower District but stay downtown, Golden Eagle Trolleys operate from 4 pm to midnight Wednesday to Saturday and make a tour of downtown and the Tower District every 20 minutes. The $2 ticket (available from the driver) is good for the night, so you can get on and off the trolley as many times as you'd like.

BLOSSOM TRAIL

To make an attraction of the profuse blossoms on the fruit orchards each spring, the Fresno City & County Convention & Visitor's Bureau has mapped out a 67-mile route, designated the 'Blossom Trail,'

through peach, plum, nectarine, almond and citrus groves, whose flowers usually blossom from late February to late March. You certainly don't need to do the *whole* trail to enjoy the flowers – just getting off Hwy 99 and into the fields for a few miles is enough for most people. If you're driving to or from Yosemite or Kings Canyon and Sequoia national parks, you don't need to make a special effort to see the flowers, as you'll be heading right through the orchards anyway.

If you want to go for the whole Blossom Trail, pick up a map at Fresno's convention and visitor's bureau (see Orientation & Information in the Fresno section) or at **Simonian Farms** (☎ 559-237-2294), 2629 Cloves Ave at Jensen St, east of Hwy 99, where you can buy dried fruit and nuts. The average driving time for the trail is 2½ hours, and crop identification signs line the route.

A better option for people driving through on Hwy 99 is to take the Reedly exit (13 miles south of Fresno) and head east for about 5 miles to the **Circle K Ranch**. The stretch between the ranch and Hwy 99 is flanked by fruit trees, and the ranch has a terrific shop with plenty of free samples (open 9 am to 6 pm daily). About 10 miles farther east, **Reedly** has one of the best-preserved Main Streets in the valley, with most buildings dating from around 1890. The Mennonites were instrumental in settling the town and still are a big part of the population. The Mennonites are a Protestant Christian sect, founded in the 16th century, who oppose military service and acceptance of public office, and favor simple living; they make their own clothes and grow much of their own food. They run the **World Craft Center** (☎ 559-638-3560), 1012 G St between 10th and 11th Sts, open 9:30 am to 4 pm weekdays and 10 am to 2 pm Saturday. You can see weavers at the loom and, on Monday mornings, the Mennonite Women's Quilting Guild stitching away.

Nearly enveloped by Fresno's suburbs, **Clovis** also has a restored downtown, which has become increasingly popular with antiques hounds. Clovis is east of Fresno via Ashlan Ave.

HANFORD

• population 44,890 • elevation 247 feet

Hanford has a compact, restored downtown that centers around the 1896 **Kings County Courthouse**. Most of Hanford's brick buildings along Court and 7th Sts were built by railroad agencies in the early 1900s and are on the National Register of Historic Places. Learn more about them at the **Hanford Carnegie Museum** (☎ 559-584-1367), 109 E 8th St, where tours starting at noon are available by appointment Tuesday to Saturday. Predating these is Hanford's **Taoist Temple**, built in 1893 in 'China Alley,' heart of a once-bustling Chinatown. To reach China Alley from downtown, take 7th St (away from the railroad tracks) to Green St and turn left; China Alley is clearly visible on the right.

Places to Stay & Eat

Downtown Motel (☎ *559-582-9036, 101 N Redington St)*, between 6th and 7th Sts, is the area's most affordable place to stay. Rooms cost $38/41 singles/doubles.

The one lasting business in China Alley is the landmark *Imperial Dynasty Restaurant (☎ 559-582-0196, 406 China Alley)*, owned by the same family since 1894. Oddly enough, the restaurant serves pricey continental cuisine ($8 to $15) and is known for its cordon bleu and escargots.

Housed in the old jail on the courthouse's ground floor, the *Bastille (☎ 559-582-9741, 113 Court St)* serves good margaritas and tap beer and has live music starting at 8 pm Monday to Saturday. Recently they've hosted big-name contemporary jazz shows like Spyro Gyra and Hiroshima. Across the street, the 1924 art deco Fox Theater (☎ 559-584-7423) gets a fair share of important country & western singers including Merle Haggard and George Jones.

Getting There & Away

Amtrak trains connect Hanford to Oakland ($40, five hours) and Bakersfield ($22, 1 hour 35 minutes) with a connection to Los Angeles ($6, 3 hours 20 minutes) four times daily. The train station *(☎ 559-582-5236)* is off 7th St at 200 Santa Fe Ave.

VISALIA

• population 93,290 • elevation 331 feet

Visalia is probably the nicest town between Stockton and Los Angeles, and a good place to stay en route to Sequoia and Kings Canyon national parks. Its downtown – centered on the intersection of Court and Main Sts, three blocks north of Hwy 198 – has undergone more thorough revitalization than other valley towns and is pleasant for strolling. It also has several good coffeehouses, restaurants and sport shops. As the Tulare County seat, Visalia remains prosperous even when crop prices drop.

Things to See & Do

The original Victorian and Craftsman-style homes in Visalia are real architectural gems and, though interspersed with not-so-nice homes and run-down apartment buildings, are worth viewing on foot. Get information on the self-guided **Heritage Tour** from the visitor center (☎ 559-738-3435, 800-524-0303) next to the convention center at 301 E Acequia St, open 9 am to 5 pm weekdays. If you want a quick look at some homes, head north from Main St on N Willis St to Race Ave, turn right (east) and go two blocks to Encina St; the 700-block of N Willis is lined with Craftsman bungalows, and the 500 and 600 blocks of Encina have many beautifully restored homes from the late 19th century.

South of downtown on Hwy 63 (Mooney Blvd), **Mooney Grove Park** is a vast sprawl of shaded grass where people picnic, run and fly kites. Within the park is the **Tulare County Museum** (☎ 559-733-6616), open 10 am to 4 pm Thursday to Monday; $2 donation requested. The museum has a typical collection of photographs, clothing and farm equipment from the 19th and early 20th centuries. Visalia's **Chinese Cultural Center** (☎ 559-625-4545), between Hwy 99 and downtown, one block south of Hwy 198 on Akers Rd, is built in the traditional Chinese style – without nails. The building is primarily used for private parties, though anyone can go in and have a look at the collection of Chinese games, vases, serving vessels and books. It's open 11 am to 6 pm Wednesday to Sunday.

Between Visalia and Bakersfield, downtown **Tulare** (west of Hwy 99) has several buildings from its heyday as a railroad hub. The most notable, at 160 South K St, now houses the Crafter's Outlet Mall, which has 150 vendors of crafty, antiquey, lacy things. Tulare's other outlet mall – very visible and heavily advertised on Hwy 99 – is the Horizon Outlet Mall, where name-brand items by Ralph Lauren, Reebok and Bass are marked up by 200% so they can then be 'discounted' by 50%. The bargains are few and hard to find.

Places to Stay & Eat

Helpful staff at the visitor information center will book accommodations at no charge. Downtown, the ***Best Western Visalia Inn Motel*** (☎ 559-732-4561, 623 W Main St) has quiet rooms for around $65. The ***Lamplighter Inn*** (☎ 559-732-4511, 3300 W Mineral King Ave), 2 miles west of downtown, has similar prices and a pool.

Visalia has some great restaurants that attract people from all over the valley. Locals like ***Colima*** (☎ 559-733-7078, 111 E Main) for Mexican food at under $10. For a splurge, try the ***Vintage Press*** (☎ 559-733-3033, 216 N Willis). The French bistro decor is authentic and the menu is 'ooh-la-la,' with prices starting at $9 and going up to $22. For a healthy meal under $7, head to ***Watson's Veggie Garden*** (☎ 559-635-7355, 615 W Main St), open 10 am to 4 pm weekdays.

Getting There & Away

Visalia is serviced by Greyhound, which has seven daily buses to Los Angeles ($14, 3¾ hours) and five daily to San Francisco ($31, six hours). Visalia's bus station (☎ 559-734-3507), 1927 E Mineral King Ave, is 1 mile east of downtown. Amtrak shuttle buses stop here to make the train connection in Hanford; for information call Amtrak (☎ 559-582-5236).

BAKERSFIELD

• population 245,570 • elevation 408 feet

At the northern foot of the Tehachapi Mountains, Bakersfield is a rich town, thanks to oil (the Kern River oil field was discovered here in 1899 and is still California's richest), country music (it's the birthplace of Buck Owens) and race cars – in that order. Though Bakersfield resembles the rest of the San Joaquin Valley, with its conservative, agriculture-based political and social views, it is gaining a liberal contingent as folks from Los Angeles settle in its suburbs (a four-bedroom house costs around $150,000 here – about a quarter of what it would cost in Los Angeles) and do business over the Internet. Bakersfield's large Latino population is gaining affluence faster than in other parts of California, buying small farms and businesses.

If you don't visit in midsummer, when temperatures rarely drop below 100°F (37°C), Bakersfield is not that bad of a place, though it is hardly one of California's top destinations. The downtown is a pleasant mix of restored buildings and new county offices; several cafes and clubs host live music and performance art. Buck Owens' multimillion-dollar country & western bar attracts people from all over the valley. California State University, Bakersfield (known for its petroleum engineering department), boasts a student population of 6000 (though it doesn't do much for the social scene, since most students commute home to valley towns on weekends). Bakersfield also has some of the best Basque restaurants in California, run by families whose not-so-distant ancestors tended sheep on Colonel Thomas Baker's 136-sq-mile field, from which the town got its name.

History

The Yowlumne branch of the Yokuts lived in a village near what is now 16th and F Sts downtown. In 1776 Friar Francisco Garces came, trying to find a route between Sonora, Mexico, and Monterey, and declared what is now the Bakersfield area part of New Spain. Not much was done about it after he left to continue his journey to Monterey, and not many outsiders came to the area until Colonel Thomas Baker came from Iowa in 1852, built a dam across the Kern River to control flooding and turned what was called 'Kern Island' into an enormous field where he planted cotton and raised sheep. Basques

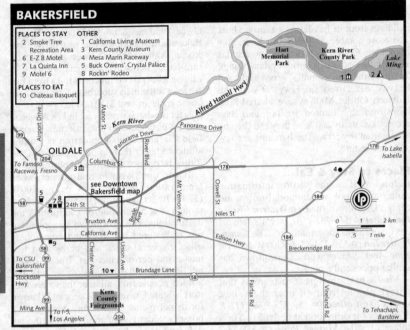

BAKERSFIELD

PLACES TO STAY	OTHER
2 Smoke Tree Recreation Area	1 California Living Museum
6 E-Z 8 Motel	3 Kern County Museum
7 La Quinta Inn	4 Mesa Marin Raceway
9 Motel 6	5 Buck Owens' Crystal Palace
	8 Rockin' Rodeo

PLACES TO EAT
10 Chateau Basquet

came in the 1890s to tend sheep on 'Baker's field' (at the time, the only fenced-in land between Los Angeles and Sacramento), and by the time farmers from Arkansas and Oklahoma took refuge here during the Dust Bowl years of the '30s, Bakersfield was an incorporated town.

Orientation

The Kern River flows north of downtown, separating the business district from unsightly oil fields. Truxton and Chester Aves are the main downtown thoroughfares; numbered streets run parallel to Truxton, lettered streets run parallel to Chester Ave. Many businesses are in the malls along Stockdale Hwy and Ming Ave, south of downtown off Hwy 99.

Information

The Greater Bakersfield Chamber of Commerce (☎ 661-327-4421), 1725 Eye St, has a

Recreation Profile that is helpful, but only limited information on lodging. The main post office (☎ 800-275-8777) is downtown at 1730 18th St. There's a Bank of America with ATM at the corner of Chester and Truxton Aves.

Museums

The pioneer village at the **Kern County Museum** (☎ 661-861-2132), north of downtown at 3801 Chester Ave, is definitely worth visiting if you're traveling with kids. The village is composed of old houses, offices and cabins brought from their original locations, restored and furnished as they were in their original state. You can enter quite a few of them, including an old oil warehouse with an exhibit on the history of oil. The main museum has a mediocre local history collection with a Bakersfield twist – Merle Haggard's cowboy boots. The museum is open 9 am to 5 pm weekdays, 10 am to 5 pm

Saturday and noon to 5 pm Sunday; $5 (ticket sales stop at 3:30 pm, and the pioneer village starts to shut down around 4 pm).

Surrounded by a small park and lovely sculpture garden, the **Bakersfield Museum of Art** (☎ 661-323-7219), 1930 R St, has changing exhibits of regional and California art that are generally of good quality. Hours are Tuesday to Saturday 10 am to 4 pm; $3.

Northwest of Bakersfield on Alfred Harrel Hwy, the **California Living Museum** (☎ 661-872-2256) is a zoological and botanical garden whose unspectacular displays concentrate on California animal and plant life. It's not really worth a trip in itself, but it is a nice stop on the way to or from Lake Isabella. Hours are 9 am to 5 pm Tuesday to Sunday; $3.

Raceways

Bakersfield's raceways, in full swing from March to October, are probably its biggest tourist draw. A night at these races gives you a chance to drink Budweiser, chew tobacco and curse loudly as souped-up cars scream by. Weekend events, some with high-profile sponsors and large cash prizes, draw people from all over the state. Smaller races get a local crowd. Ticket prices vary from $7 to $18. Except for really big events, tickets are available at the gate only.

The **Famoso Raceway** (☎ 661-399-2210) is a quarter-mile drag strip famous for its Budweiser-sponsored race in January. At the Friday night Test-N-Tune 'grudge races,' you can drive up in any kind of vehicle (provided you have a valid driver's license and the car has seat belts) and speed around the track, competing against other drivers who have paid for the privilege. It costs $10 to run your car and $5 to watch. To reach the raceway, take the Hwy 46 exit off Hwy 99, turn right onto Famoso Rd and go east 4 miles; from downtown, take Hwy 65 north and go west on Famoso Rd.

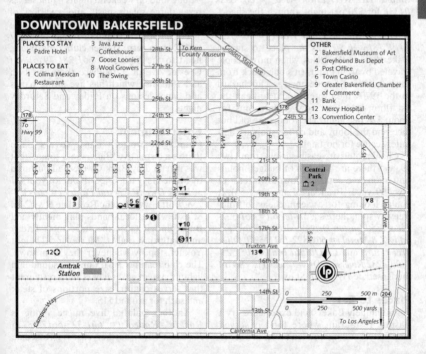

DOWNTOWN BAKERSFIELD

PLACES TO STAY
6 Padre Hotel

PLACES TO EAT
1 Colima Mexican Restaurant

3 Java Jazz Coffeehouse
7 Goose Loonies
8 Wool Growers
10 The Swing

OTHER
2 Bakersfield Museum of Art
4 Greyhound Bus Depot
5 Post Office
6 Town Casino
9 Greater Bakersfield Chamber of Commerce
11 Bank
12 Mercy Hospital
13 Convention Center

Home to NASCAR events, the **Mesa Marin Raceway** (☎ 661-366-5711) is a half-mile oval where cars do 25 to 100 laps at speeds way over 100 miles an hour. Races are held Thursday, Friday and Saturday nights, usually around 7:30 pm.

Special Events
California State University, Bakersfield, hosts an annual jazz festival, held downtown in mid-May, which is gaining more popularity each year for big-name artists like BB King, Dianne Schurr and Natalie Cole.

Arts and crafts, antiques, livestock, carnival rides and rodeo events come together at the Kern County Fair, held in September at the Kern County Fairgrounds, near downtown at 1142 South P St.

Places to Stay
Camping is available at Lake Ming, 10 miles east of downtown off Alfred Harrel Hwy, at **Smoke Tree Recreation Area** (☎ 661-832-0433), for $20 per night, though the shadeless sites are hardly worth it.

Downtown, the **Padre Hotel** (☎ 661-322-1419, 1813 H St) was *the* place to stay in Bakersfield in the 1940s, when most people traveled by train or bus (it's one block from the bus station). Condemned as a fire hazard in the 1970s, the owner fought to keep the 1st floor open and now rents rooms for about $28 per night. The rooms are old but nice, and the lobby and coffee shop are definitely cause for nostalgia.

Chain motels are easily visible from Hwy 99, and there are a bunch of budget motels on Union Ave, south of downtown (east of Hwy 99 via E Brundage Lane/Hwy 58). If you're looking for a clean, cheap, off-the-freeway spot, there's a **Motel 6** (☎ 661-327-1686, 1350 Easton Drive). Also available are an **E-Z 8 Motel** (☎ 661-392-1511, 5200 Olive Tree Court) and **La Quinta Inn** (☎ 805-525-7400, 3232 Riverside Drive), near Hwy 99 off the Rosedale Hwy/24th St exit.

Places to Eat
For a uniquely Bakersfield experience, try a Basque restaurant where food is served family-style at long wooden tables in a series of courses: first soup, then salad, then the entrée (usually lamb chops, or pork or beef stew) accompanied by rice or noodles, vegetables and bread, followed by dessert. A full meal costs around $15, but most places have a light meal (everything but the meat) for under $10. **Wool Growers** (☎ 661-327-9584, 620 E 19th St) is Bakersfield's oldest Basque restaurant, where other restaurant owners washed their first dishes. One of the least expensive Basque restaurants is **Chateau Basque** 661-325-1316, 101 Union Ave), where pickled tongue is one of the usual courses.

If Basque isn't sounding good, the **Colima Mexican Restaurant** (☎661-631-1188), at the corner of 19th St and Chester Ave, is highly recommended. Large burritos cost $5; traditional seafood dishes served with homemade tortillas cost around $10 and breakfast costs under $5. **Goose Loonies** (☎ 661-631-1242, 1623 19th St) is a sports bar – quite loud on weekend nights – that serves pizza, large salads, pasta and a variety of Greek dishes for around $10.

For an upscale Cajun or Italian meal ($7 to $12) in a retro supper club atmosphere, head to the **Swing** (☎ 661-281-7946), off Chester Ave on 17th Place (between 17th and 18th Sts), which has live swing bands and dance lessons on Friday and Saturday nights.

Entertainment
Country & western music lovers claim there's a distinctive 'Bakersfield sound' that was invented by Buck Owens and nurtured by Merle Haggard. Check it out for yourself at **Buck Owens' Crystal Palace** (☎ 661-328-7560), off Hwy 99 at the Rosedale Hwy/24th St exit, where local bands play nightly and Buck himself takes the stage most Friday and Saturday nights. Merle and Dwight Yokum stop by whenever they're in town. The club features a $1.5 million sound and lighting system, several bars and a restaurant that serves country-size portions of steak and such for around $15.

Another palatial live music venue is **Rockin' Rodeo** (☎ 661-323-6617, 3745 Rosedale Hwy), farther east on Rosedale

Buck Owens

buses meet southbound trains and continue over the Grapevine, on I-5, to Los Angeles (2½ hours). Tickets from Bakersfield to Los Angeles cost $14.50; if you're buying a ticket from a point farther north (Modesto, Fresno, Hanford), the Bakersfield-Los Angeles leg costs around $7 and is incorporated into the price of the ticket.

Greyhound connects Bakersfield to Los Angeles and San Francisco several times a day. Schedules and fares change often, so it is a good idea to check with the bus company as you make your plans. The Greyhound depot (☎ 661-327-5617), downtown at 1820 18th St, is a lively place with a 24-hour cafeteria, lockers and numerous taxis outside.

KERN RIVER

Designated a Wild and Scenic River, the Kern starts near Mt Whitney and journeys 170 miles to its final destination in the valley. It is dammed in two places to create **Lake Isabella**, which supplies irrigation water to the southern San Joaquin Valley. About 70 miles east of Bakersfield, Lake Isabella is California's largest freshwater lake; it's a fingery body of water with coves and rock promontories, surrounded by chaparral-covered mountains.

The lake actually lies in the southern Sierra, but most people access it through Bakersfield. Hwy 178 follows the Kern River's edge between Bakersfield and Lake Isabella, through Sequoia National Forest and past USFS campgrounds and picnic areas. Summer temperatures in this area hover around 105°F (40°C), and there is little protection from the sun. People naturally spend most of their time on or in the water.

The town of Lake Isabella (pop 10,000) is a strip of markets, banks, gas stations and restaurants on the south end of the lake. Here, Hwy 155 heads north, around the west side of lake, to **Kernville** (pop 4800), a cute little town that straddles the Kern River about 2 miles from the lake's shore and is the hub for rafting on the Kern. The town swarms with visitors on summer weekends, but otherwise is very serene.

Hwy, where performances range from rock to country to rap. Five bars take care of the crowds, who work themselves into a thirst on several dance floors. There's a $4 cover charge most weeknights; prices go up substantially on weekends.

Less expensive and considerably less involved are the jazz, folk and blues shows on Thursday to Saturday nights at *Java Jazz Coffeehouse* (☎ 661-324-5717), a whimsically restored Victorian at the corner of 19th and D Sts. Downtown is great for bar hopping on Friday and Saturday nights: just follow the flow of people. The *Swing* (see Places to Eat) is good for dancing; the *Town Casino* (in the Padre Hotel) has a local clientele; and *Goose Loonies* (see Places to Eat) is the place to drink beer and watch sports.

Getting There & Away

There are four Amtrak trains per day between Bakersfield and Oakland ($42 to $55; 6½ hours) from the train station (☎ 661-395-3175) at the corner of 16th and F Sts; these trains stop in Hanford, Fresno, Merced, Modesto and Stockton. Amtrak

River Running

The Upper Kern and Forks of the Kern (both sections of river north of Kernville) are known for their white water and are popular with adventurous rafters and kayakers; the Lower Kern (south of Lake Isabella) is a good family river. In both cases, the Kern is known as the 'working man's river,' because you often have to paddle – continuously – for control and navigation. It's not a good river for a leisurely float.

About six rafting companies operate out of Kernville; all offer competitive prices and run trips from May to August, depending on the river conditions. Sierra South (☎ 760-376-3745) runs 12 'Lickety Split' trips ($19; one hour) per day. They also have half- and full-day trips ($73/$130) with Class III and IV rapids. Mountain & River Adventures (☎ 760-376-6553) runs all their trips on Class I, II and III water – a good choice for families and those who might be frightened. One-hour and three-hour trips cost $18 and

A River *Roars* Through It: The 'Killer Kern'

When the runoff from winter snows begins in spring, parts of the Kern become a surging monster of a river – charging through steep gorges in the Sequoia National Forest – with some of the fastest and fiercest rapids anywhere. At other times of the year, and on other sections, the passage is considerably more tame and can be enjoyed by nearly everyone.

Having guided the rivers of the Northwest myself in what seems like an earlier incarnation, I was ready to hit the water again on a tour of the Lower Kern with Whitewater Voyages (☎ 800-488-7238, fax 510-758-7238, www.whitewatervoyages.com), a Kern outfitter with a permanent base on the river. Between April and September, this company runs one- to three-day trips on various stretches of the Kern – mild to menacing – and acquits itself professionally and with aplomb.

'Wet and wild' was definitely the norm on the Lower Kern two-day run I had picked (Class III and IV). It all began rather placidly on day one with a lovely float through beautiful forests and past bizarrely carved granite boulders that – when the water's high – throw up enormous waves and treacherous hydraulic holes. We camped on a sublime bend in the river where – after a gourmet dinner of steak, chicken, salads and Dutch oven brownies – we slept like babes while the Kern murmured sweetly to us.

The following day, our group of four was joined by 23 other adventurers, and our armada of rafts headed into the Class III and IV sections downriver. This was wild. I got to relive my former river-rat life by pulling three 'swimmers' – launched from other rafts while bumping through various cataracts – to welcome and sputtering safety. One of our boats wrapped around a boulder for about a half-hour and another raft popped – gimping home after a hasty patch job. There were bruises, cuts and abrasions to be sure, but the river had done its work. The macho were meek, the reclusive were raucous and the timid were tigers. That's what a great river can do to you.

Like other companies operating on the Kern, Whitewater Voyages also does half-day and one-day trips on the Upper Kern (Class III to IV) and the distinctly Class V Thunder Run. Those who hunger for the extreme should worship at the forks of the Kern run, where the river drops 60 feet per mile through solid granite walls in a seemingly unending series of furious Class IV and Class V rapids that will all but erase your id, ego and taints of civilization. But be warned: you have to be tough, experienced and comfortable with running on the edge to go here. This is liquid madness and rolling thunder, and people *do* die – many of them unprepared or drunken yahoos.

– David Peevers

$34, respectively. They also rent mountain bikes for $20/30, half-day/full day.

Hiking

North of Kernville, Hwy 122/Mtn 99 enters dense pine forests interspersed with grassy meadows where there are a few opportunities to hike around. One of the nicest hikes is the **River Trail,** which starts on the east side of Hwy 122/Mtn 99 at the Johnsondale Bridge, 19 miles north of Kernville. Information is available from the Cannell Meadow Ranger Station (☎ 760-376-3781), downtown Kernville at 105 Whitney Rd. It's open 8 am to 5 pm daily in the summer and 8:30 am to 4:30 pm weekdays during the winter.

Places to Stay

There are five USFS campgrounds along the 10-mile stretch between Lake Isabella and Kernville, and another five north of Kernville on Hwy 122/Mtn 99. Most campgrounds between the two towns are right on the lake and are used by water-skiers and people with boats, while those north of Kernville are a bit less crowded and are surrounded by trees. Sites have concrete platforms (which RV owners love), nonflush toilets and a price tag of $12; campsites are first-come, first-served but should be reserved (which costs an extra $9) at least a week in advance for weekends and holidays through National Forest Recreation Reservations (☎ 800-280-2267).

Kernville's motels are woodsy and have quite reasonable rates. On the hill just above the town square, the *Kern Lodge Motel* (☎ *760-376-2224*) has newly remodeled rooms for $60 to $100. One block north, the *McCambridge Lodge* (☎ *760-376-2288*) has older facilities with rooms for $47 to $70 and a two-night minimum on weekends. Right next to the town square and the river, the *River View Lodge* (☎ *760-376-6019*) has rooms for $50 to $90.

Sierra Nevada

Over 400 miles long and 60 to 80 miles wide, the Sierra Nevada creates a massive barrier along most of eastern California, separating the Central and Owens valleys. This impressive range (the longest in the continental US) is one big block of granite, tilted westward along a series of faults, with a steep eastern side and gently rolling western foothills. The highest peaks, including Mt Whitney, are in the southeastern part of the range along the Sierra Nevada crest. Yosemite, Kings Canyon and Sequoia national parks sit high in the west, with the Gold Country at their feet. Between the crest and foothills lies a granite world woven with canyons, rivers, lake basins and meadows – some of California's most majestic and pristine scenery. You'll need backpacking equipment and good hiking boots (or skis) to visit much of the Sierra. If you're looking for a beer and a bed after a day on the trail, Lake Tahoe, Yosemite and Mammoth Lakes are good destinations.

Geology

About 140 million years ago, the Pacific Plate dove beneath the westward moving North American Plate, its surface melting into magma with the intense heat and friction. While some of the magma rose to the surface through volcanoes (like those around Mammoth Lakes), most cooled to form the granite block that would become the Sierra Nevada. Over the next 50 to 80 million years, this granite block uplifted along faults on its eastern side, tilting west to form an asymmetrical range. As the mountains rose, the streams draining them became fast-flowing rivers and started carving V-shaped valleys (trending east-northwest) into the western slope. Glaciers, which covered the higher parts of the range about 3 million years ago, scraped the V-shaped valleys into U-shaped valleys and left behind the Sierra's most remarkable topography – erratic boulders, scoured peaks and valleys such as Yosemite and Kings Canyon.

Highlights

- Lake Tahoe – gambling, hiking, skiing and 300 days of sunshine
- Mono Lake – funky volcanic formations in view of the Eastern Sierra
- Yosemite – why John Muir fell in love with the Sierra
- Kings Canyon & Sequoia – backpackers' paradise and the earth's largest living things

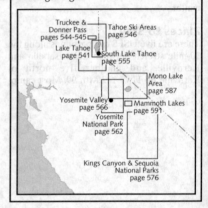

The Sierra's lower western slope, around 2000 feet, is covered with California black oak, chaparral, manzanita and high grasses characteristic of its mild climate. Above 2000 feet, this foliage gives way to dense conifer forests of pine and fir, meadows and large rock outcroppings. In what is called the High Sierra, above 9000 feet, soil was carried away by glacial activity, leaving a polished granite landscape of peaks, basins and ridges where foxtail and white-bark pines, lichen and heather are about all that grow. The Sierra tops out on its eastern side along the Sierra crest, where peaks rise to about 9000 feet near Lake Tahoe and get gradually higher in the south, where they reach above 14,000 feet.

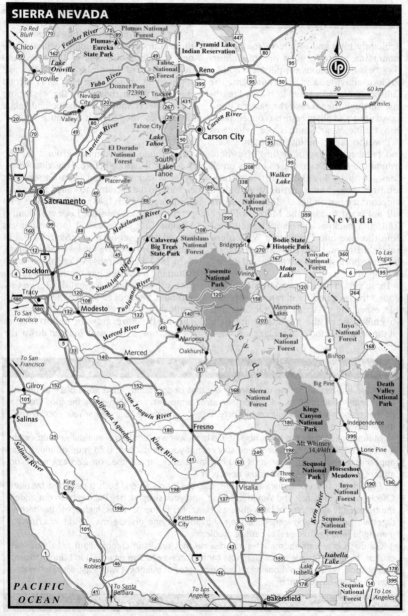

SIERRA NEVADA

Lake Tahoe

Brilliantly blue and totally surrounded by mountains, Lake Tahoe is one of California's best destinations for people who like outdoor activities and entertainment. The California-Nevada state line cuts lengthwise through the lake, so the eastern shore has casinos and glitzy resorts (concentrated in Stateline, near South Lake Tahoe) as well as the skiing, hiking, mountain biking and lake activities you'll find elsewhere around the lake. Skiers have choices on all sides – with 14 downhill resorts, six cross-country areas and seemingly unlimited backcountry possibilities. Mountain bikers will not want to miss the Marlette Flume Trail, and backpackers should head west from the lake into Desolation Wilderness. Emerald Bay and DL Bliss State Park, on the west shore, should not be missed if Hwy 89 is open.

There's good public transportation to and around the lake, and room rates are reasonable, especially in April, May, October and November, when the mountains are bare but the weather is too cold for lake activities.

A desire to drive around the lake is instinctual, but not necessarily the best way to see it. First of all, it's a long drive – about three hours without stopping – with the lake only visible about 70% of the time. And during much of the winter a round-the-lake trip isn't an option, since Hwy 89 (Emerald Bay Rd), which runs along the west shore and connects South Lake Tahoe and Tahoe City, closes when there is too much snow.

History

Lake Tahoe was summer ground for the Washo Indians long before it was 'discovered' by gold seekers headed from Carson City, Nevada, to the Sacramento Valley during California's gold rush (1848). As California's gold petered out, the Comstock Lode was found in Virginia City, Nevada, and fortune hunters crossed back over the mighty Sierra by way of Squaw Valley or along the lake's south shore.

In 1862, Fish Ferguson Coggins & Smith Company harvested hay on the flatlands of the north shore, near present-day Tahoe City and built a schooner to take the hay to the south shore, where it fetched $250 per ton. The north shore grew in importance as logging operations sent lumber down the

SIERRA NEVADA

Outdoor Dangers & Annoyances

Bears are hooked on people food and know that campgrounds are a good place to find it. Never leave food unattended in picnic areas or campsites, and always use the food storage containers provided. For more on the increasing 'bear problem,' see 'Bears, Your Food & You' in the Activities chapter.

Mountain lion sightings have increased in the lower western Sierra, especially in areas with lots of deer. Rangers recommend you stay calm if you meet a lion; hold your ground, try to appear large by raising your arms or grabbing a stick, and if the lion gets aggressive or attacks, fight back, shout and throw objects at it.

Ticks may carry Lyme disease or borelliosis (relapsing fever), both transmitted by bite. Check your clothes, hair and skin after hiking, and your sleeping bag if it has been out under the trees. Early symptoms of both diseases are similar to the flu: chills, high fever, headache, digestive problems and general aching. Advanced Lyme disease may result in arthritis, meningitis, and neurological or cardiac problems.

Giardiasis is a water-borne intestinal disease that results in chronic diarrhea, abdominal cramps, bloating, fatigue and weight loss (not a fun way to slim down). Don't drink stream, lake or snow water without boiling it for five minutes or treating it with a giardia-rated water filter or iodine-based purifier.

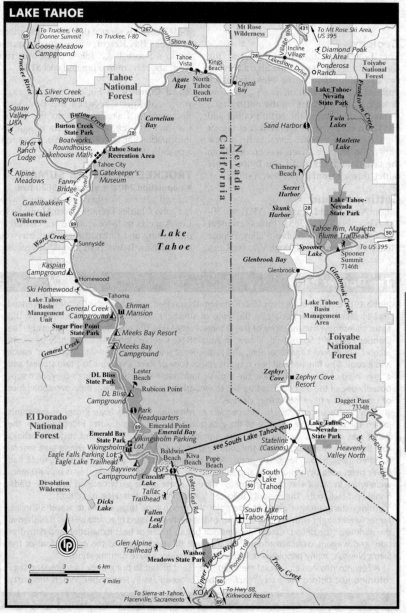

SIERRA NEVADA

Truckee River to help build the transcontinental railroad.

Geology

The Tahoe Basin formed between the Carson Range (east) and the Sierra Nevada (west) when the Sierra Nevada block uplifted 50 to 80 million years ago. Lava flowing from Mt Pluto, on the north shore, formed a dam across the basin's outlet and created a lake several hundred feet higher than the present one. Eventually a new outlet, the Truckee River, was eroded from the lava dam; it remains Lake Tahoe's only outlet, flowing from its northwest shore.

Getting Around

Tahoe Area Rapid Transit (TART; ☎ 530-581-6365, 800-736-6365) buses connect Tahoe City, Truckee, Squaw Valley, Alpine Meadows, Tahoe Vista, Incline Village, Kings Beach, Homewood and Tahoma, and include a shuttle to Truckee. In summer, TART extends service down the west shore to Meeks Bay Resort, where you can transfer to a South Lake Tahoe bus. Buses run from about 6 am to 6 pm and cost $1.25.

Road Conditions For current updates on route conditions between the Bay Area, Sacramento, Lake Tahoe and the Reno/Carson City area, call the Caltrans highway information line (☎ 800-427-7623). It requires a push-button telephone.

TRUCKEE & DONNER SUMMIT
• population 2400 • elevation 5820 feet

Named after a Northern Paiute chief who led John Charles Frémont from Montana to Los Angeles in 1846, Truckee is a charming old mining and railroad town that survives on tourism. It has restaurants, interesting

---

The Donner Party

In the 19th century, more than 40,000 emigrants traveled west along the California Overland Trail in search of a better life in the 'land of sunshine.' High drama was common on this arduous journey, but the story of the Donner Party takes the prize for morbid intensity. The Donner Party left Springfield, Illinois, in April 1846. George Donner had a family of seven; Jacob Donner had a family of five; and James Reed had a family of seven, two hired hands and a cook. The families had two wagons apiece (one of Reed's wagons had two stories) and a large herd of livestock, to make the trip as comfortable as possible. Though they were supposedly one of the best outfitted parties to embark on the journey west, their overabundance of supplies may have led to their demise.

They had a smooth trip to Independence, Missouri, where a large group of emigrants joined them, increasing the size of the group to about 87 people. After Independence, the going was slow, and by July, they were running behind schedule. When Lansford Hastings told them of a 'shortcut' around the south end of the Great Salt Lake that would save several hundred miles, it sounded pretty good. What Hastings didn't mention was that this route had never been used by wagons (he also said that the Great Salt Lake Desert was only 40 miles wide when in fact it was more than 80). Though some in the party decided to go the traditional Fort Hall route, the majority followed the Donners via this 'Hastings cutoff.'

Things started to get grim. At one point the group took three weeks to travel 36 miles. James Reed fought with another member of the party and killed him, and he was banished in the middle of the desert. Oxen and livestock began to die of heat exhaustion and dehydration, and wagons were abandoned. By the time the party reached the eastern foot of the Sierra Nevada, many people were walking and provisions were running short.

A few months earlier, several men had been sent ahead to bring back supplies, and they returned just before the party reached the Truckee Pass in November. When the party

shops and some nightlife. In winter, ski shuttles connect Truckee to most major resorts on the Lake Tahoe north shore and at Donner Summit.

West of Truckee, via I-80, Donner Lake is surrounded by small, woodsy resorts and private cabins and is a low-key alternative to Tahoe action. The Donner Party lodged near the lake during their fateful winter. Donner Summit, east of the lake, is the name given to the area around 7239-foot Donner Pass (on I-80), which includes five ski resorts (four downhill and one cross-country). If you plan on staying at one of the bunkhouses (see Places to Stay) in Donner Summit, you'll need your own transportation to get to Truckee and Lake Tahoe.

History
Built in 1863 as Coburn's Station, Truckee was a rendezvous for miners and lumber-jacks, with its fair share of saloons, gambling halls and bordellos. In 1868, during the race to finish the first transcontinental railroad, workers built east and west from Truckee, making it a railroad center. A few years later it was the site of the West's first big train robbery – the Verdi Robbery – when seven bandits made off with $41,000 in gold.

Orientation
Historic downtown Truckee is along Commercial Row, which becomes Donner Pass Rd (to Donner Lake and the state park) at the west end of town. West River St runs along the Truckee River, parallel to Commercial Row. Bridge St constitutes the town's east border, connecting I-80 and Hwy 267, which goes southeast to Lake Tahoe's north shore. Most services, gas stations and markets are west of downtown at the junction of Donner Pass Rd and Hwy 89.

The Donner Party

encountered a fierce snowstorm that made the mountains impassable, they were not too concerned: they had food to last a month and certainly the weather would clear by then. But the snow fell for weeks on end, until it reached a depth of over 20 feet – the most snow recorded in a hundred years.

By winter, the party was split in three: about half were camped at Truckee (now Donner) Lake; most of the others (including George Donner, who had slashed his hand trying to carve a new wagon axle) were at Alder Creek, about 6 miles from the lake; the Breen family, a family of 10, was in a cabin built two years before by another emigrant party.

James Reed, the fellow banished in the desert, made it to Sutter's Fort, California, by mid-October. Fearing that his family was trapped by winter storms, he put together the first rescue party, which arrived at the camps in mid-February. With most livestock and oxen buried in snow, people were surviving on boiled ox hides. Since many were too weak to travel, the rescue party could evacuate only six people.

By the time the second rescue party came in March, people had resorted to cannibalism. Journals and reports tell of 'half-crazed people living in absolute filth, with naked, half-eaten bodies strewn about the cabins.' Again, only a few of the strongest survivors could be rescued. By mid-April, when a final rescue party arrived, the only person remaining at the lake camp was Lewis Keseberg. At the Alder Creek Camp, the rescuers found George Donner's body cleansed and wrapped in a sheet, but no sign of Tasmen Donner, George's wife, who had refused to leave her husband even though she was strong enough to go with earlier rescue parties. Keseberg admitted to surviving on the flesh of those who had died, but denied the accusations that he had killed Tasmen Donner for fresh meat. He spent the rest of his life trying to clear his name.

Altogether, 40 people survived, 47 people perished.

Information

The Truckee Donner Visitor Center (☎ 530-587-0476), housed in the train depot at the west end of Commercial Row, has maps, brochures, local bus schedules and a public rest room.

The Sierra Mountaineer (☎ 530-587-2025), at the corner of Bridge and Jiboom Sts, in Truckee's first structure, has a good selection of maps, guides and camping/climbing equipment; their staff is helpful and can make trail recommendations. Truckee Books (☎ 530-582-8302), at Bridge and W River Sts, has a good local and natural history selection and is open 9:30 am to 6 pm daily. The USFS Truckee Ranger Station (☎ 530-587-3558) is 1 mile northeast of town on Hwy 89.

Museums

The free **Old Truckee Jail Museum** (☎ 530-582-0893), at the corner of Jiboom and Spring Sts, has some interesting relics from the Old West days. It's open 11 am to 4 pm weekends. The **Western Ski Sport Museum** (☎ 530-426-3313) at Boreal (take the Boreal/Castle Peak exit off I-80) is worth a look. It's open 11 am to 5 pm Wednesday to Sunday; $2 donation requested.

Donner Memorial State Park

On the east end of Donner Lake, this park is on one of three sites where the Donner Party spent the winter of 1846 waiting to continue over Donner Pass to Sutter's Fort. A memorial on the south side of I-80 shows how high the snow got that year.

The Emigrant Trail Museum (☎ 530-582-7894) does a great job chronicling the Donner Party's journey and has a worthwhile film; open 9 am to 4 pm daily. Admission is $2 and can be used toward the park's $5 day-use fee. From the museum, the Emigrant Trail winds through the forest past

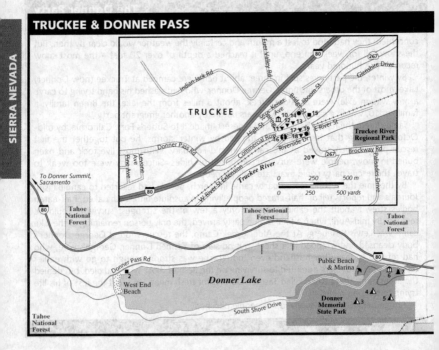

TRUCKEE & DONNER PASS

SIERRA NEVADA

TRUCKEE

Truckee River Regional Park

To Donner Summit, Sacramento

Tahoe National Forest

Tahoe National Forest

Tahoe National Forest

Public Beach & Marina

Donner Lake

Donner Memorial State Park

West End Beach

Tahoe National Forest

other cabin sites and a memorial erected in 1918. Though its history is gruesome, the park is lovely and has a nice campground (see Places to Stay), sandy beach and cross-country ski trails.

Donner Lake

Because of its small size, Donner Lake is much warmer than Lake Tahoe, making swimming quite comfortable. The wind comes up in the afternoon, so waterskiing isn't as popular as windsurfing here. Most campers and boaters go to the beach and marina on the east end of the lake at the state park, which is nice but small. Families favor West End Beach ($4), at the west end of Donner Pass Rd, for its volleyball, basketball, snack stand and roped-off swimming area. Docks along the lake's north shore (visible from Donner Pass Rd) are public and free (unless fenced off) and quieter than the beaches.

Activities

Several equipment rental shops cater to activities in all seasons. Besides the Sierra Mountaineer (see Information), Porter's Ski & Sport (☎ 530-587-1500), in the Lucky/Longs Center at the I-80/Hwy 89 junction, has just about everything for the outdoors: skis, tents, backpacks, fishing gear, bikes and all the clothes and accessories. For guided backcountry tours and skills seminars, Alpine Skills International (☎ 530-426-9108) is highly respected. Their base camp is at Donner Pass, where they offer a 'bunk & breakfast' (see Places to Stay), but you must register in advance for their courses. Call for a catalog, or write to PO Box 8, Norden, CA 95724.

Ski areas around Donner Lake are smaller and less flashy than Squaw Valley and Alpine (see later this chapter), but they are still good. Most are west of town, off I-80 or Donner Pass Rd, and all have full-service

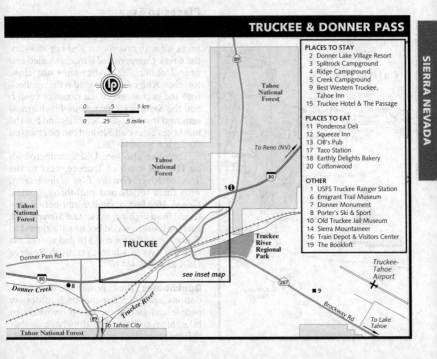

TRUCKEE & DONNER PASS

SIERRA NEVADA

0   .5   1 km
0 .25 .5 miles

Tahoe National Forest

Tahoe National Forest

Tahoe National Forest

To Reno (NV)

TRUCKEE

see inset map

Donner Pass Rd

Donner Creek ● 8

Truckee River

To Tahoe City

Tahoe National Forest

Truckee River Regional Park

Brockway Rd

Truckee-Tahoe Airport

To Lake Tahoe

PLACES TO STAY
2 Donner Lake Village Resort
3 Splitrock Campground
4 Ridge Campground
5 Creek Campground
9 Best Western Truckee, Tahoe Inn
15 Truckee Hotel & The Passage

PLACES TO EAT
11 Ponderosa Deli
12 Squeeze Inn
13 OB's Pub
17 Taco Station
18 Earthly Delights Bakery
20 Cottonwood

OTHER
1 USFS Truckee Ranger Station
6 Emigrant Trail Museum
7 Donner Monument
8 Porter's Ski & Sport
10 Old Truckee Jail Museum
14 Sierra Mountaineer
16 Train Depot & Visitors Center
19 The Bookloft

lodges with rentals, ski schools, equipment shops and a restaurant or cafeteria. In Truckee, **Tahoe Donner** (☎ 530-587-9444) has 600 vertical feet, and a $40 beginner's special, including ticket, rentals and lessons (lift tickets are $26). Locals recommend **Sugar Bowl** (☎ 530-426-3651), south of Donner Pass Rd, for steep terrain and good atmosphere. The lodge area resembles a Tyrolean village, not too surprising since the place was founded by Walt Disney. The ski area has eight lifts, 1500 vertical feet and a $42 lift tickets.

Though small, **Boreal** (☎ 530-426-3666) – with its 10 lifts, 600 vertical feet and $28 tickets – has some fun terrain and three 'parks' for kids, snowboarders, etc; night skiing (until 9 pm) is included in the ticket price. **Donner Ski Ranch** (☎ 530-426-3635), off Donner Pass Rd, with six lifts and 750 vertical feet, has Lake Tahoe's cheapest tickets – $23 ($10 midweek). For not-too-committed skiers,

Soda Springs (☎ 530-426-3666) has a great snow-tubing area as well as two lifts; $15 lets you ski and tube, and includes tube rental.

For cross-country skiers, Donner Memorial State Park has marked, ungroomed trails for a $5 day-use fee. South of I-80 off Soda Springs Rd, the **Royal Gorge Cross Country Ski Resort** (☎ 530-426-3871) is the largest cross-country ski resort in the US, with almost 200 miles of trails and four surface lifts. Hard-core skiers consider this *the* spot, but it's expensive ($20 on weekends, $17 midweek) and not really worth it unless you've skied all the other terrain around here.

With 43 miles of groomed trails, **Tahoe Donner** (☎ 530-587-9484) has $15 passes and night skiing from 5 to 8 pm Wednesday to Saturday. In addition, **Northstar-at-Tahoe** (☎ 530-562-1010) has 40 miles of trails for $15 (see Skiing under Tahoe City later this chapter).

Places to Stay

Camping The Donner Memorial State Park campground is divided into three areas, all with rest rooms and hot showers: the *Creek Campground* is nicely shaded and near Donner Creek, but sites are close together; *Ridge Campground* is the smallest, with the best access to the campfire center; and the *Splitrock Campground* is the most removed from day-use activities and has the most sites. Sites cost $16 and can be reserved through ☎ 800-444-7275.

There are also nice USFS campgrounds on Hwy 89 south of Truckee, next to the Truckee River: *Granite Flat* is the largest, with flush toilets and pull-through sites; *Goose Meadow* is smaller and better protected from highway noise; and *Silver Creek* gets the most crowded because it's closest to Tahoe City. All sites cost $16 and are reservable (10 days in advance) through Reserve USA at ☎ 877-444-6777.

Bunkhouses These hostel-like accommodations are great for meeting outdoorsy people and getting the scoop on where to bike, hike and ski. The drawback is that they're around 20 miles from Lake Tahoe

TAHOE SKI AREAS

and can't be reached by public transportation. Most have dorm accommodations (bring a sleeping bag, pillow and towel), a community lodge and free breakfast. *Alpine Skills International* (☎ 530-426-9108) offers a 'bunk & breakfast' for $27.50. The Sierra Club's *Clair Tapaan Lodge* (☎ 530-426-3632) charges $43 per person ($39 for Sierra Club members) and has a few private rooms. Run by the Associated Students of the University of California at Berkeley, *Cal Lodge* (☎ 530-426-3392) charges $28 ($33 Friday and Saturday) for bed, breakfast and dinner.

Hotels & Lodges A stage stop in the 1860s, home to railroad laborers in the 1870s, then a lumbermen's boarding house for many years, the *Truckee Hotel* (☎ 530-587-4444, 800-659-6921, 10007 Bridge St), just off Commercial Row, is the most historic lodging option. Its recent restoration, homey atmosphere and nice decor also make it no most pleasant. Rooms with a sink but no private bathroom cost $85 to $125, standard rooms are $115 to $125, including breakfast.

Southeast of town, toward Tahoe City on Hwy 267, the *Best Western Truckee Tahoe Inn* (☎ 530-587-4525) has lovely views and is on the Truckee Trolley route; rooms are $84 to $105.

Donner Lake Village Resort (☎ 530-587-6081, 800-621-6664, 15695 Donner Lake Rd) has decent condos and suites for $70 to $125 ($10 more with a view), a private beach, marina and pool; snowshoeing and snowmobiling are available in winter.

Built in the 1920s, the *Rainbow Lodge* (☎ 800-500-3871), off I-80 at Royal Gorge Cross Country Ski Resort, has classic mountain lodge charm, with a huge fireplace and cozy rooms for $108 ($75 without private bath). Ski trails are right out the door.

Places to Eat
Earthly Delights Bakery (☎ 530-587-7793), on W River St, is a good spot for coffee, pastries and bread. Among the restaurants on Commercial Row, *Squeeze Inn* (☎ 530-587-9814) serves excellent breakfast and lunch ($5 to $8), and the *Ponderosa Deli* (☎ 530-

587-3555) has sandwiches on homemade bread for under $5. *Taco Station*, in an old rail car on W River St, has cheap but decent Mexican food.

The Passage (☎ 530-587-7619), in the Truckee Hotel, and *Cottonwood* (☎ 530-587-5711), off Hwy 267 on a hill southeast of town, are local hangouts with live music most weekends. Both have excellent food for $11 to $25 and a good bar scene with affordable appetizers.

Getting There & Around
Amtrak (trains and motorcoaches) and Greyhound buses both stop at the Truckee train depot, in the same building as the visitor center at the west end of Commercial Row. There are five Greyhound and Amtrak buses to Reno/Tahoe International Airport ($8) and five to Sacramento/San Francisco ($18/32) daily. There's one eastbound train to Reno ($12) and a westbound train to Emeryville/San Francisco ($49) daily. Tickets are sold at the ticket counter one hour before departure in summer, on board in winter.

The Truckee Trolley (☎ 530-546-1222) leaves from the train depot at the west end of Commercial Row hourly from 7:30 am to 6:30 pm, with one route to Donner Memorial State Park and West End Beach, and another to the Northstar resort on Hwy 267. One-way fare is $1; an all-day pass is $2.

SQUAW VALLEY USA
This mountain valley near the headwaters of the Truckee River was explored in the 1880s by miners looking for a short route over the Sierra to the silver mines in Nevada. In 1955, Alexander Cushing developed Squaw Valley USA (☎ 530-583-6955) into a resort equipped to host the 1960 Olympic winter games. In 1997, the mountainside facilities were overhauled and updated, and a deluxe golf course and conference center – the Resort at Squaw Creek – were added. Now 'Squaw' is a year-round village with restaurants, plenty of lodging (see Places to Stay in Tahoe City) and enough activities to make the lazy person wince.

Summer and winter activities are based from the main lodge at the bottom of the

SIERRA NEVADA

gondola, which also has equipment rental shops, restaurants, visitor information and lift-ticket sales. Squaw has 40 chairlifts, 2830 vertical feet and some of the best skiing in California; lift tickets are $48 ($31 half day).

In summer, High Camp, at the top of the gondola (8200 feet), serves as a scenic spot for bungee jumping, ice skating and outdoor swimming. A roundtrip ride on the gondola is $14 ($5 after 5 pm and for kids). With either ice skating or swimming the tickets costs $19/10 adults/children, for both it costs $21/12. Hours are 9:30 am to 3:30 pm daily in May, June and October, 9 am to 9 pm from July to September. You can take a mountain bike on the gondola (free) and ride down, or take a two-hour ($35) or half-day ($55) clinic at Dirt Camp (☎ 800-771-3478) at the bottom of the mountain.

Other activities include horseback riding at Squaw Valley Stables (☎ 530-583-7433) for $17 an hour and golf at the Resort at Squaw Creek (☎ 800-327-3353).

TAHOE CITY

- population 3092 • elevation 6240 feet

The largest town on Lake Tahoe's northern shore, Tahoe City has been the lake's primary boating community since Italian and Portuguese fishermen settled here in the 1860s. Its location – at the Hwy 89/28 junction – makes it a much visited place, though it lacks a real downtown since most businesses are in small shopping centers strung along the lakeshore. This is, however, the place where people congregate after a day on the lake or in the mountains. There are

several marinas and a nice beach central to town activity (near the popular Boatworks Mall). On Hwy 89, just south of the Hwy 28 junction, the Truckee River flows through floodgates and passes beneath **Fanny Bridge**, named for the most prominent feature when people lean over the railings to look at fish.

Orientation & Information

Tahoe City's businesses start south of Fanny Bridge, just north of the Granlibakken Conference Center Resort, on Hwy 89. Hwy 28 heads northeast from Hwy 89 as N Lake Blvd, Tahoe City's main drag. From this junction, Hwy 89 goes north (as River Rd) to Squaw Valley and Truckee, and south, along the lake's west side, to South Lake Tahoe. Hwy 28 continues around the lake's north and east shore.

East of the junction, next to the Bank of America, the North Lake Tahoe Resort Association and Visitor Information Center (☎ 530-583-3494, 800-824-6348) has lodging, dining, shopping and activities information 9 m to 5 pm weekdays. The Book Shelf (☎ 530-581-1900), in the Boatworks Mall, has good maps, Lake Tahoe books and guides and is open 10 am to 9 pm daily (10 am to 8 pm Sunday).

Gatekeeper's Museum

Near the south end of Fanny Bridge on Hwy 89, this museum (☎ 530-583-1762) has a large Native American basket collection and old Tahoe memorabilia including ski equipment and photos. The surrounding park is nice for picnicking. The free museum is open 11 am to 5 pm Wednesday to Sunday. In summer, the 1908 Watson Log Cabin (on N Lake Tahoe Blvd near the public beach) is open 1 to 5 pm daily.

Activities

Porter's Ski & Sport (☎ 530-583-2314), 501 N Lake Blvd, is a good source for trail maps and equipment. They rent mountain bikes and in-line skates ($6 per hour, $20 per day), water skis ($15 per day) and alpine/cross-country skis for $16/8 per day; ski rentals cost $3 less on weekdays. Dave's Ski Shop (☎ 530-583-6415), on N Lake Tahoe Blvd next to Safeway, is good for snowboard rentals, and the Back Country (☎ 530-581-5861) has telemark equipment and snowshoes for rent.

A nice paved path along the Truckee River, north of town, is popular for running, walking, skating and biking.

Hiking & Bicycling There are some great day hikes in the Granite Chief Wilderness, east of Tahoe City. The Five Lakes and Whiskey Creek trails, from the Alpine Meadows parking lot, give steep but immediate access to beautiful alpine lakes and the Pacific Crest Trail; from here you can access backcountry trails, good for overnight trips – no wilderness permits required.

A trailhead for the Tahoe Rim Trail is just off Hwy 89 (north of Fanny Bridge) on Fairway Drive, across from the Fairway Community Center. No bikes are allowed for the first 8 miles of this stretch, but you can access the bikeable part via dirt roads in Burton Creek State Park, 1½ miles northeast of town off Hwy 28 (see Lake Tahoe map); maps are available at Porter's. Watson Lake, 12 miles from the trailhead, is a good overnight destination for hikers.

Skiing Between Tahoe City and the turnoff for Squaw Valley USA is the road to **Alpine Meadows** (☎ 530-583-4232, 800-441-4423), a top-notch resort with a nice lodge and some great off-the-beaten-path terrain. Locals like Alpine for its friendly atmosphere and steep backside bowls. It has 12 lifts, 1800 vertical feet and $47/35 full-day/half-day lift tickets.

Northstar-at-Tahoe (☎ 530-562-1010), off Hwy 267 (toward Truckee), is a year-round resort whose runs are popular with families and intermediate skiers. Northstar has 11 lifts, a gondola, 2200 vertical feet, cross-country and snowshoe terrain and loads of other activities; lift tickets are $45. Good discounts are available if you stay at the resort; call central reservations (☎ 800-466-6784) for prices.

Northeast of town off Hwy 28, via Fabian and Village Rds, **Lakeview Cross-Country Ski Center** (☎ 530-583-9353) has 40 miles of groomed trails that wander through Burton

Creek State Park. It has a well-respected ski school ($38 per lesson, including rentals and a ski pass; $15 rentals only) and a nice lodge. Passes are $15.

River Running The Truckee River is gentle and wide as it flows northwest from the lake – perfect for novice rafters who like to drag a six-pack behind the boat. Raft companies set up along Hwy 89 in town and charge $25 to $60 per boat. They provide transportation back from the River Ranch Lodge (☎ 530-583-4264) at the end of the run. The lodge is famous for its strawberry margaritas and big patio overlooking the roughest part of the ride.

Places to Stay

Accommodations get booked far in advance for 4th of July and Labor Day weekends, December 26 to January 1, and the weeks before and after Easter Sunday (depending on snowfall). Squaw Valley Central Reservations (☎ 800-545-4350) books motel rooms, condos and houses in the Squaw Valley area, though sometimes they have places available at other locations on the north shore and in Reno, Nevada. North Tahoe Lodging (☎ 800-824-6348) is a similar operation with slightly better prices. This is an affordable way to go for long stays and larger groups. Tahoe Vista and Kings Beach (see later this chapter) have a bunch of affordable motels and cabins and are serviced by bus year round.

Camping Just outside of town on Hwy 28, the *Tahoe State Recreation Area* (☎ 530-583-3974) has flush toilets, showers and 31 sites close to the lake for $16 (for reservations, call Parknet at ☎ 800-444-7275). There are three USFS campgrounds north of town on Hwy 89, listed under Truckee (see earlier this chapter).

Motels Downtown, the *Tahoe City Inn* (☎ 800-800-8246, 790 N Lake Blvd) is the most affordable in town with $55 rooms ($70 to $95 on summer weekends). The *Pepper Tree Inn* (☎ 530-583-3711, 800-624-8590, 645 N Lake Blvd) is a good value with basic rooms for $66 to $76. For a splurge, the **Tahoe Marina Lodge** (☎ *530-583-2365, 800-748-5650*) is a good choice. They have lakeside rooms for $92, condos starting at $120 and a private beach.

Places to Eat
Look for the free *North Lake Tahoe/Truckee Dining Guide* newspaper, published monthly, which has sample menus and coupons. The **Bridgetender** (☎ *530-583-3342*), on the south end of Fanny Bridge, has a wood stove, pool table, daily beer specials and great burgers for around $5. The view at **Lakehouse Pizza** (☎ *530-583-2222*), in Lakehouse Mall on N Lake Tahoe Blvd, is terrific and they make good pizzas ($16 for a large), hot sandwiches ($6) and salads ($4) for a local crowd. **Rosie's Cafe** (☎ *530-583-8504, 640 N Lake Blvd*) and **Jakes** (☎ *530-583-0188*), in the Boatworks Mall, are both recommended for nice meals (main courses start around $12) and happy hour appetizer specials.

For a deluxe dinner that might break the bank (prices start at $22), everyone and their mother recommends **Wolfdale's Cuisine Unique** (☎ *530-583-5700, 790 N Lake Blvd*), which serves gourmet food from a small, seasonal menu and has an extensive wine list.

Entertainment
Both the *North Tahoe Truckee Week* and the Action section of the *Tahoe World* paper come out Thursday and list current happenings in and around Tahoe City. They are available free at most area markets, motels and restaurants.

Favorite bars include **Pierce St Annex** (☎ *530-583-5800*), behind Safeway on N Lake Tahoe Blvd, which has music and dancing nightly; the **Nawty Dawg**, next to Bank of America on N Lake Tahoe Blvd, which draws a young, local crowd; and the **Bridgetender** (☎ *530-583-3342*). **Elevation** (☎ *530-583-4867*), across from Safeway on N Lake Tahoe Blvd, gets funk, reggae and swing bands from around California and has DJed music several nights per week. (For jazz, check out **Cottonwood** and **The Passage** in Truckee.)

Lake Tahoe Stats
Lake Tahoe is the third-deepest lake in North America, with its greatest depth measured at 1645 feet and its average depth 1000 feet. The bottom of the lake, about 4500 feet in elevation, is lower than the Carson Valley floor, at the bottom of the Carson Range in Nevada. The lake is 22 miles long, 12 miles wide and has about 72 miles of shoreline.

Getting Around
In summer, the Tahoe City Trolley zips people around town for free, stopping at the malls, Gatekeeper's Museum and requested destinations. TART (see the introduction to this section) buses connect to places east and south.

NORTH & EAST SHORES
Between Tahoe City and Glenbrook, Nevada, are a handful of lakeside communities that buzz with tourist activity from June to September and, not as loudly, from December to whenever the snow melts. While the towns are not very exciting – usually just motels and shopping centers strung along Hwy 28 – they have good Lake Tahoe beach access and affordable accommodations. Since these motels depend on tourism, room rates are always negotiable. The lake's northern California-Nevada state line crosses Hwy 28 at Crystal Bay (where a sad conglomeration of casinos tries to look like South Lake Tahoe), placing the entire east shore in Nevada. Park trails on this side of the lake are outstanding in summer, and the biking and hiking on Lake Tahoe Nevada State Park's Marlette Flume Trail is legendary.

Tahoe Vista
• **population 1144** • **elevation 6232 feet**
This strip of motels along Hwy 28 (N Lake Blvd) is quite woodsy and more serene than Kings Beach, its larger neighbor immediately east. North Tahoe Regional Park is

north of the highway, at the end of National St, with hiking, biking, cross-country ski trails and nice picnic facilities.

Places to Stay *Beesley's Cottages* (☎ 530-546-2448, 6674 N Lake Blvd) are cute and whimsical and surrounded by a grassy lawn that slopes down to the lake. Rooms in the small, basic motel are $74; one-bedroom cottages start at $100. Across the road, the *Cedar Glen Lodge* (☎ 530-546-4281, 800-341-8000) has friendly owners and new rooms for $55 to $105. Straddling the highway, the *Vista Shores Resort* (☎ 800-535-9671, 6731 N Lake Blvd) has mountain-side rooms for $55 to $85 and lakeside cottages starting at $110, plus a private beach and swimming pool.

Kings Beach
• **population 2796** • **elevation 6254 feet**
Kings Beach is home to many of the Latino folks who work in Lake Tahoe's casinos. Off the highway, the difference in standard of living between those who work in the casinos and those who play in them (and live on the lake's west shore or in Incline Village) is clear. On the highway are a good bunch of affordable motels, a few popular restaurants and (on the lake side) the North Tahoe Beach Center (☎ 530-546-2566), which has health-spa facilities ($7 per day), a sandy beach and canoe and kayak rentals.

Places to Stay & Eat The *Sun & Sand Lodge* (☎ 530-546-2515, 800-547-2515, 8308 N Lake Blvd) has a beach, discounted lift tickets, free breakfast and rooms for $50 to $85. The *Falcon Lodge & Suites* (☎ 530-546-2583, 800-682-4631, 8258 N Lake Blvd) has similar facilities and $40 rooms in fall and spring. The *Big 7 Motel* (☎ 530-546-2541, 800-354-8940, 8141 N Lake Blvd) charges $35 to $60 year round because they are across the highway from the lake.

The lakeside bar at *Steamers* (☎ 530-546-2218, 8290 N Lake Blvd) is popular in summer, and their food – pizzas, sandwiches and salads – is very good for under $8. *Gar-Woods Grille* (☎ 530-546-3366, 5000 N Lake

Blvd) is popular for steak, seafood ($7 to $14) and live music.

Incline Village, Nevada
• **population 4329** • **elevation 6269 feet**
Incline's Lakeshore Drive, which skirts the lake while Hwy 28 (Tahoe Blvd) swings northeast, is lined with million-dollar homes and private beach clubs – the lake's most prominent displays of wealth. A paved bike path along Lakeshore Drive has good views of the water. Businesses in Incline Village are along Village Blvd, between Hwy 28 and Lakeshore Drive, and at the Village Blvd/Hwy 28 junction. The Village Ski Loft and Boutique (☎ 775-831-3537) is a good place for bike and ski rentals, and the Incline Village Chamber of Commerce and Visitors Bureau (☎ 775-832-1606), on Hwy 28 at the east end of town, has local maps and lodging information.

Golfers should check out **Incline Championship Golf Course** (☎ 775-832-1144), north of Hwy 28 via Country Club and Fairway Drives, one of the lake's most popular public courses. Northeast of town, off Hwy 28 and Country Club Drive, **Diamond Peak Ski Resort** (☎ 775-831-3249) has downhill skiing with seven chairlifts and mostly intermediate runs; lift tickets are $38 ($19 on Wednesday). The adjacent **Diamond Peak Cross Country and Snowshoe Center** (☎ 775-832-1177) has 25 miles of groomed cross-country trails, a snow play park and some fun 'adventure' snowshoe trails where you navigate through woodsy obstacle courses; day passes are $15.

Mt Rose, Nevada
• **elevation 8900 feet**
Mt Rose, north of Incline Village off Hwy 431 (Mt Rose Hwy, which connects with US 395 to Reno), has the profile of a woman lying on her back with clasped hands resting on her stomach. An early miner, looking at her from Reno, named the mountain Rose, after his sweetie.

The Mt Rose Wilderness lies northwest of the highway, with good access from the Mt Rose Summit and Tahoe Meadows Trailhead, a half mile west of the summit. Self-register wilderness permits are at the trailheads, where there are posted maps, rest rooms and free parking. The wilderness is interspersed with private land, so get a good map before doing any overnight trips (day hikes are generally OK).

On the other side of the highway, **Mt Rose Ski Area** (☎ 775-849-0704) is low-key, uncrowded and popular with locals. It has five lifts, 1440 vertical feet of ski terrain and interesting views of both wilderness and Reno. Lift tickets are $38 ($15 for women on Thursday).

Ponderosa Ranch, Nevada
For a worn-out piece of Western Americana, visit the Ponderosa Ranch (☎ 775-831-0691), off Hwy 28 just south of Incline Village, where the Western TV classic *Bonanza* was filmed. Tours of the Cartwright Ranch include old film clips, a barn full of props and antiques used on the set and a staged gunfight on 'Main Street.' The ranch also has a petting zoo, shooting gallery and old buildings which function as stores and restaurants. The ranch is open April to October 9:30 am to 5 pm daily (weather permitting); $12.

Sand Harbor, Nevada
If it weren't for the swarms of summer tourists, Sand Harbor would be ideal. It sits on the northeast shore of Lake Tahoe, where two sand spits have formed a beautiful shallow bay with brilliant turquoise water and white sand beaches. **Diver's Cove**, a popular scuba spot, is at the north end of the harbor, where the lake bottom drops off and underwater rock formations attract fish.

The area is managed by the Nevada State Park Service, which charges $5 per vehicle and maintains a small visitor center (☎ 775-831-0494) with good maps and hiking information. The beach has lifeguards, rest rooms, a snack stand and boat rentals. In July and August, the harbor hosts a reputable **Shakespeare Festival** (☎ 800-486-2463) with outdoor performances beside the lake. Tickets are $11 to $16 and sell out quickly.

Lake Tahoe Nevada State Park
This excellent state park spans most of the ridge along the lake's east shore, encompassing beaches, lakes and miles of trails. There are beach access points all along Hwy 28 – mostly undeveloped, word-of-mouth spots where you'll see cars parked along the highway but no parking lot or trailhead. There are two official parking lots (across from each other on the highway) for Chimney Beach, often full by 10 am.

At the park's south end, at the Hwy 50/Hwy 28 junction, **Spooner Lake** has the most facilities and the best park information. The lake is stocked with trout and has rest rooms, nice picnic facilities ($4 per vehicle) and a cross-country ski area (☎ 775-749-5349) with 56 miles of groomed trails ($12 trail pass) and a rental facility.

The **Marlette Flume Trail** (the flume) follows the path of an old flume that carried logs by water to lumber mills and mines at Virginia City. The trail heads north from Spooner Lake with the Tahoe Rim Trail, then goes around the west side of Marlette Lake (the Rim Trail goes around the east side). The trail's west side drops straight down to the lake, making it quite treacherous for all but very experienced mountain bikers. It's also great for hiking and cross-country skiing. There is a scenic primitive campsite on the east side of Marlette Lake and at Twin Lakes, about 2 miles north. The sites are first-come, first-served and cost $7.

WEST SHORE
The west shore of Lake Tahoe, between Emerald Bay and Tahoe City, has some of the lake's nicest state parks and swimming beaches. The 'towns' along Hwy 89 – Meeks Bay, Tahoma, Homewood and Sunnyside – are little more than gatherings of cabins and resorts inhabited by Bay Area families who have had cabins here since the 1920s. TART buses connect these communities to Tahoe City and (in summer) South Lake Tahoe. Ski Homewood (☎ 530-525-2992) is the area's only ski hill, a small, friendly affair with nine lifts, $35 lift tickets and a separate hill (formerly Tahoe Ski Bowl) entirely for beginners.

Sunnyside
The deck of *Sunnyside Lodge* (☎ 530-583-7200, 1850 W Lake Blvd) is *the* place to be in

the summer. They serve lunch, dinner and loads of cocktails around sunset, when people are just coming off the trails. They also have pricey lakeside accommodations ($160 to $210) and a full-service marina with boat rentals and a water-ski school ($89 per hour for three people).

Just north, across the highway, Cyclepaths (☎ 530-581-1171) rents bikes ($10 per hour) and in-line skates ($7 per hour) and is a good source of hiking, biking and skiing information.

Homewood

This place revolves around its ski hill in winter and also has good backcountry ski access to Desolation Wilderness via Black Canyon (clearly marked from Hwy 89). West Side Sports (☎ 530-525-0310) is a good place for trail information and equipment rentals. *Kaspian*, a mile north of Homewood on the west side of Hwy 89, is the lake's only bicycle campground, with $5 first-come, first-served sites. At the base of Ski Homewood, the *Homeside Motel* (☎ 530-525-9990) is one of the best little spots on the lake. The owner bakes each morning for the guests and keeps the rooms in great shape. It's $65 for a double, $85 for a room with a kitchenette for four people.

Tahoma

Tahoma has the west side's concentration of places to stay and eat, as well as a post office and the area's general rendezvous, the *PDQ Tahoma Market* (☎ 530-525-7411), a well-stocked deli and market open until 9 pm daily. Just north of the market, the *Tahoma Meadows B&B* (☎ 530-525-1553, 800-355-1596) has a beautiful garden and darling cabins for $85. Next door, the microscopic *Stony Ridge Cafe* (☎ 530-525-0905) serves excellent breakfasts and lunch ($4 to $8) until 3 pm.

The *Norfolk Woods Inn* (☎ 530-525-5000, 6941 W Lake Blvd) has a variety of plush rooms and rustic cabins for $90 to $125, including breakfast. Across the highway, *Tahoe Cedars Lodge* (☎ 530-525-7515) has small cabins for $55, and its own beach.

Sugar Pine Point State Park

Between Meeks Bay and Tahoma, Sugar Pine Point is a well-run park with a swimming pier, tennis courts and a nature center; there's a $5 day-use fee. The **Ehrman Mansion** (☎ 530-525-7982), a beautiful 1920s estate, is the park's major attraction. It is open 10 am to 5 pm daily; free.

On the west side of Hwy 89 is the park's densely forested *General Creek Campground* with 175 year-round sites and hiking and cross-country ski trails. Sites ($16) are reservable through ☎ 800-444-7275 in summer. In winter they cost $12 and are first-come, first-served.

Meeks Bay

This long, shallow bay with a wide sweep of shoreline stays light longer than other spots along the lake, because it has a meadow on its west side that lets in the afternoon sun. It also has warm water by Tahoe standards.

Meeks Bay Resort (☎ 530-525-6946) was recently purchased by the Washo Indian tribe, who spruced up the cabins and gave the place a face-lift. Cabins rent for around $85 for two people, $325 for eight people per week, and tent sites are $15. Adjacent is the lovely USFS *Meeks Bay Campground*, with $16 sites (reserve at ☎ 800-280-2267) but no hot water.

DL Bliss State Park

If you only have one day on the lake, this park is a good place to spend it. Some of the prettiest sections of the lake, Rubicon Point and Lester Beach (called 'DL Bliss Beach') harbor boast clear turquoise water, white sand and big boulders which people jump off into the lake – beware of low water and protruding rocks should you decide to take the plunge. From the beach's south end you can connect with the Rubicon Trail (the official trailhead is just past the park entrance), a 4-mile hiking trail which skirts the water's edge, south to Emerald Point. Beach and trailhead parking costs $5 and is extremely limited – the lots usually fill up by 10 am, in which case you must walk the steep 1½ miles from the park entrance to the beach.

SIERRA NEVADA

The large **DL Bliss Campground** (☎ 530-525-7277) has flush toilets, potable water, tables and fire pits. Sites ($19) are reservable through ☎ 800-444-7275.

EMERALD BAY

This long, narrow bay off the southwest corner of the lake is one of Lake Tahoe's major attractions (according to Eastman-Kodak it's the most photographed thing in the US). It contains the lake's only island and has waters that truly justify its name. Hwy 89 wraps around the bay's southern rim, affording great views from pull-outs and designated scenic points. The Eagle Falls parking lot, on Hwy 89 just as it turns north, has rest rooms and a short trail to Eagle Falls; trails from the west side of Hwy 89 lead to Desolation Wilderness. There's a $3 parking fee. For campground information, see Places to Stay under South Lake Tahoe.

Below Hwy 89 at the lake's edge, **Vikingsholm** (☎ 530-525-7277) is reached by boat or a steep 1-mile descent from the Vikingsholm parking lot (just past the Eagle Falls lot) on Hwy 89. This storybook mansion, built by Laura Knight in 1928, incorporates preindustrial craftsmanship and Scandinavian design with carved wooden ceilings and furniture in Viking motif. The $3 tour, given from 10 am to 4 pm daily June to September (weekends only the rest of the year) is worthwhile. The stone ruins atop Fannette Island were once Laura Knight's teahouse.

One of the most enjoyable ways to see the bay is by boat. The *Tahoe Queen* (☎ 530-541-3364) and MS *Dixie II* (☎ 775-588-3508), both out of South Lake Tahoe, make daily excursions year round. For details, see Lake Tours later this section.

SOUTH LAKE TAHOE

• **population 22,400** • **elevation 6260 feet**

Here at the southeastern extent of the lake, the state line cuts through the trees dividing Stateline (Nevada) and South Lake Tahoe (California). The subcommunities here (Al Tahoe, Meyers, Marla Bay) started as food and lodging stops for people traversing the Sierra, but now merge as a monotonous string of commercial development.

Boxy casinos loom above the lake and swaths of ski runs loom above the casinos, while Hwy 50 (Lake Tahoe Blvd) lines the lake with mini-malls, motels and, on the Nevada side, 'chapels' where you can get hitched in 15 minutes for $45 – rings and flowers included.

There is only a small gap in the development where the lake is visible from Hwy 50; the best views are from the Heavenly Valley ski area and the top floors of casinos, and the best beach access is west of town off Hwy 89. The south shore's concentration of million-dollar homes and boats is in the Tahoe Keys, a network of docks and waterways northwest of Hwy 50 via Tahoe Keys Blvd. The best part about South Lake Tahoe is its affordable food and lodging and its ceaseless entertainment.

Orientation

Hwy 50 (Lake Tahoe Blvd) wraps around the south shore of the lake between Spooner Summit and the Y where it joins Hwy 89 (Emerald Bay Rd). Hwy 89 is often closed west of the Tallac Historic Site when there is heavy snow.

Traffic along Hwy 50 is a real problem: it gets totally jammed around noon and 5 pm and on weekends, while in winter Sunday evenings (when skiers head back down the mountain) are the worst. A good alternate route is Pioneer Trail, which branches east off Hwy 89/Hwy 50 (south of the Y and reconnects with Hwy 50 at Stateline. The speed limit is strictly enforced along Pioneer Trail.

Information

The South Lake Tahoe Chamber of Commerce (☎ 530-541-5255), 3066 Lake Tahoe Blvd, has brochures, maps and a friendly staff. A smaller branch at the junction of Hwys 89 and 50 is primarily a bathroom stop and orientation point for people coming down the hill.

For topographical maps, head to the USFS station (☎ 530-573-2600), just past where Emerald Bay Rd forks, or the Lake Tahoe Visitor Center at the Tallac Historic Site (see that section). The Sierra Bookshop

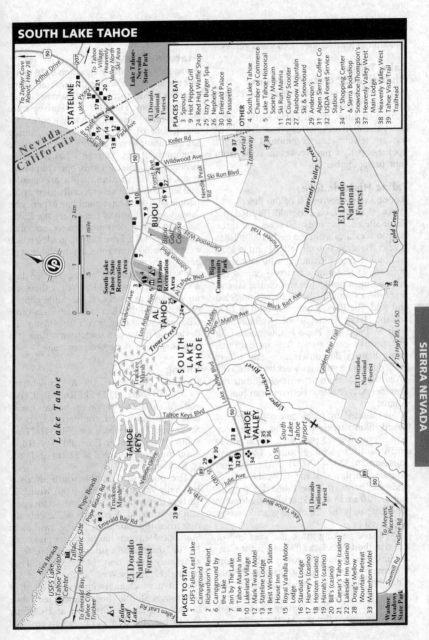

SOUTH LAKE TAHOE

PLACES TO EAT
3 Sprouts
9 Hot Pepper Grill
24 Red Hut Waffle Shop
25 Izzy's Burger Spa
26 Nephele's
30 Emerald Palace
36 Passaretti's

OTHER
4 South Lake Tahoe
   Chamber of Commerce
5 Lake Tahoe Historical
   Society Museum
11 Ski Run Marina
23 Country Scooter
27 Rainbow Mountain
29 Anderson's
31 Alpen Sierra Coffee Co
32 USDA Forest Service
   Station
34 'Y' Shopping Center
   & Sierra Bookshop
35 Snowshoe Thompson's
37 Heavenly Valley West
   Main Lodge
38 Heavenly Valley West
39 Tahoe Vista Trail
   Trailhead

PLACES TO STAY
1 USFS Fallen Leaf Lake
   Campground
2 Richardson's Resort
6 Campground by
   the Lake
7 Inn by The Lake
8 Tahoe Marina Inn
10 Lakeland Village
12 Mark Twain Motel
13 Stateline Lodge
14 Best Western Station
   House Inn
15 Royal Valhalla Motor
   Lodge
16 Stardust Lodge
17 Harvey's (casino)
18 Horizon (casino)
19 Harrah's (casino)
20 Bill's (casino)
21 Caesar's Tahoe (casino)
22 Lakeside Inn (casino)
28 Doug's Mellow
   Mountain Retreat
33 Matterhorn Motel

SIERRA NEVADA

(☎ 530-541-6464), in the shopping center at the fork in Emerald Bay Rd, has a great selection of local history books and guides.

Lake Tahoe Historical Society Museum

Next door to the chamber of commerce, this museum (☎ 530-541-5458) has a rustic collection of 'stuff' from early settlers, and some nice Native American (mostly Washo) baskets, jewelry and ceremonial garb. It's open noon to 4 pm weekends, daily from June to September; $1.

Tallac Historic Site

About 3 miles northwest of the junction of Hwys 50 and 89, on Emerald Bay Rd, the Tallac site encompasses 150 acres and three luxurious estates from the early 1900s. Elias 'Lucky' Baldwin bought Tallac Point in 1880 and built a resort including a hotel, casino, promenade and tennis courts – one of the few and most opulent places on the lake at that time. Eventually the estate was parceled and sold. The Pope Estate was built in 1894 and the Heller Estate, dubbed Valhalla, was built in 1924. The Pope Estate acts as an interpretive center and has art exhibits, living history demonstrations and offers guided tours on summer weekends. Valhalla is the site of various activities, including the Summer Arts & Music Festival from June to August.

Surrounded by pines and connected by paved hiking/biking paths, the entire area now serves as a big park with beach access and beautiful picnic grounds. The **Tallac Museum** (☎ 530-541-5227) in the Baldwin house is worth a visit for its Washo exhibit and old photos of Lake Tahoe. It opens in summer 10 am to 4 pm Thursday to Monday, weekends only the rest of the year; donation requested.

Near the parking lot at the west end of the site, the USFS Lake Tahoe Visitor Center has good natural history exhibits, short interpretive trails and a Stream Profile Chamber where you can watch trout and salmon through an underwater window. It's open daily in summer. During the October and November salmon run, the forest service puts on an annual Kokanee Salmon Festival here.

Stateline, Nevada
• population 28,000 • elevation 6329 feet
For about a half mile, Hwy 50 resembles the Las Vegas Strip on a much smaller scale. Caesars Tahoe, Harrah's and Harvey's are the 'big three' **casinos**, with lavish entertainment, tons of slot machines and gaming tables, multiple restaurants and resortlike accommodations. Harrah's has a terrific Family Fun Center for kids, open until midnight. The Horizon and Bill's are smaller and less flashy; Bill's is especially friendly for people who don't have gambling experience. About a mile north of the others, the Lakeside Inn has a local atmosphere and nice view of the lake. Free gaming guides, which explain casino game rules, are available at all casinos.

Casinos are open 24 hours a day, 365 days a year. As in Reno and Las Vegas, there are no windows or clocks on the walls, climate control is in full effect and waitresses bring free cocktails as long as you are playing – all devices to make you forget what time it is and how much money you are losing.

Skiing

Rainbow Mountain Ski & Snowboard (☎ 530-541-7482), 1133 Ski Run Blvd, convenient to Heavenly Valley, has an excellent reputation and competitive prices. Snowshoe Thompson's (☎ 530-541-1776), south of the fork in Emerald Bay Rd, is good for people headed to Sierra-at-Tahoe or Kirkwood .

The big resort on the south shore is **Heavenly Valley** (☎ 775-586-7000), with 3500 vertical feet (wow!), 23 lifts and a tram operating year round. A gondola will eventually run from the mountain to the casinos at Stateline. Heavenly has two parts: Heavenly North (the Nevada side), accessible from Kingsbury Grade, north of Stateline off Hwy 50; and Heavenly West, at the end of Ski Run Blvd, which intersects Hwy 50 south of the casinos. Shuttles from South Lake Tahoe motels and casinos drop off at Heavenly West where the tram is. Lift tickets cost $49

($33 half day); discount tickets are available at most Safeway stores. The tram ride offers one of the most spectacular lake views anywhere, especially for those who might not get into the mountains under their own steam. There are beginner ski runs at the top, a level hiking trail (open in summer) and a lodge and restaurant. Summer tram hours are 10 am to 6 pm daily and extended when the restaurant is serving dinner; tickets are $15 ($10 after 6 pm).

West of where Hwy 50 crosses Echo Summit and descends to the lake, **Sierra-at-Tahoe** (☎ 530-659-7453) gets less crowded than Heavenly and is a good choice for day-trippers from the Bay Area (though you won't get to see the lake). It has 10 lifts, 2212 vertical feet and some really fun terrain. Lift tickets are $46. They run a shuttle to motels and casinos every half-hour.

About 40 miles southwest on Hwy 88 (via Hwy 89), **Kirkwood Resort** (☎ 559-258-6000, 800-967-7500) is set in a high-elevation valley that gets better snow and holds it longer than almost anywhere else. The drive through Hope Valley to get there is beautiful and, especially for advanced and extreme skiers, the skiing and snowboarding is worth the drive. It has 11 lifts, 2000 vertical feet, cliffs, cornices and epic open bowls. Lift tickets cost $43 ($32 half day). Kirkwood also has a full cross-country trail system with 80km of groomed track. The cross-country lodge is on Hwy 88 just before the main Kirkwood entrance. Trail passes are $12.

Hiking

The chamber of commerce and the USFS visitor center at Tallac have free hiking information and a good recreation map of Lake Tahoe for $7. A favorite hike is up Mt Tallac (5 miles), the glacier-gouged peak above the lake's southwest corner. The Tallac Trailhead, south of Hwy 89 via a rough road, just past the Tallac Historic Site (across from Baldwin Beach), also gives access to Desolation Wilderness (see Desolation Wilderness section).

There is also good hiking from the Glen Alpine Trailhead at Fallen Leaf Lake, south of Hwy 89 via Fallen Leaf Lake Rd, and from the Eagle Lake Trailhead, found on Hwy 89 at Emerald Bay.

A scenic but expensive hike is along the Tahoe Vista Trail from the top of the Heavenly Valley tram (see the Skiing section). Spooner Summit is a good place to start day hikes.

Bicycling

The USFS visitor center at Tallac sells good mountain biking maps ($2.50). There is a paved bike path from Lakeview Rd (at the stoplight at Rufus Allen and Lake Tahoe Blvds, just past the chamber of commerce) to the Baldwin Beach turnoff on Emerald Bay Rd. The path skirts the lake at times, goes through the Tahoe Keys and passes the Tallac Historic Site. Country Scooter (☎ 530-544-9814), near the path at 800 Emerald Bay Rd, rents bikes, skates and scooters. Andersen's (☎ 530-541-0500), at 645 Emerald Bay Rd, is also good, as are the numerous well-marked rental shops along Lake Tahoe Blvd.

Boating & Swimming

There is a free public beach and picnic area across from the chamber of commerce at the small South Lake Tahoe State Recreation Area. On Emerald Bay Rd, there are some nice beaches – Pope, Kiva and Baldwin – with good swimming and picnic tables and barbecues (day-use fee of $5 per car).

Ski Run Marina (☎ 530-544-0200), on the lake at the foot of Ski Run Blvd, has the best boat rental rates: $80 per hour for a jet ski, $90 per hour for a power boat.

Reminiscent of summer camp, Richardson's Resort (☎ 800-544-1801) is on Emerald Bay Rd, with a nice beach, kayak and canoe rentals ($12 per hour) and a general store. On the other side of Stateline, 4 miles north of the casinos, Zephyr Cove Resort (☎ 775-588-3508) is a woodsy resort with a swimming area, boat rentals, volleyball courts and an outdoor bar and restaurant. Both swarm with kids in summer and charge a day-use fee (around $3).

Lake Tours

Touring the lake by boat is worthwhile. The *Tahoe Queen* (☎ 530-541-3364) leaves from

SIERRA NEVADA

the Ski Run Marina, on the lake at the foot of Ski Run Blvd, for two-hour cruises to Emerald Bay ($17) and back. They also have sunset dinner cruises with live music ($22) and, in winter, a fun ski package ($78) that includes a boat trip to the north shore, bus ride, lift ticket to Squaw Valley and boat trip home with cocktails and live music.

The MS *Dixie II* (☎ 775-588-3508) leaves from Zephyr Cove Resort, 4 miles north of Stateline on Hwy 50. Their prices and itinerary are identical to the *Tahoe Queen*; they also have a champagne brunch cruise ($22), which skirts the lake's east shore.

Places to Stay

The South Lake Tahoe Visitor's Authority (☎ 800-698-2463) makes free room reservations which often include meals, casino shows and lift tickets. Most casino hotels offer good deals from September to mid-November and March to May. Harrah's and Caesars offer packages including a double room, breakfast, lift tickets, transportation to/from the lifts (usually Heavenly Valley) and a few gaming tokens for about $100 per person, per night (two-night minimum).

Camping Camping in South Lake Tahoe ain't cheap, and it's only possible when the snow melts. Information is available at the USFS visitor center on Emerald Bay Rd.

On the west side of Emerald Bay, the *Bayview Campground* is right off Hwy 89 and the *Eagle Point Campground* is on the tip of picturesque Eagle Point, overlooking the lake. Both have $14 sites, reservable through ☎ 800-444-7275. The USFS *Fallen Leaf Lake Campground*, south of Emerald Bay Rd on Fallen Leaf Lake (take Fallen Leaf Lake Rd), has very scenic $14 sites that fill up quickly on weekends; reserve one (at least ten days in advance) through Reserve USA (☎ 877-444-6777).

Right in the thick of things, the *Campground by the Lake*, behind the chamber of commerce on Lake Tahoe Blvd, has hot showers, flush toilets and $20 sites. There is good beach access, but lots of noise from the highway. The *South Lake Tahoe KOA* (☎ 530-577-3693) is south of town at the

Hwy 50/Hwy 89 junction, with $23 tent sites, $29 for water and electric hookup.

Hostels *Doug's Mellow Mountain Retreat* (☎ 530-544-8065, 3787 Forest Ave), south of Lake Tahoe Blvd, between Ski Run Blvd and Wildwood Ave, is an independent hostel run by a hard-core ski bum. Doug's beds cost $15 and carry no curfew.

Motels & Hotels There are hundreds of small motels in the area, mostly near Stateline along Lake Tahoe Blvd and on the small streets off Ski Run Blvd. Rooms go for $50 to $65 at the low-end places (down to $25 in April, May, October and November), $80 to $130 at the high-end places, with lower rates on weekdays. The *Matterhorn Motel* (☎ 530-541-0367, 2187 Lake Tahoe Blvd) is well run and good for people with their own transportation. Rooms are $49/$59.

Behind the Liquor Barn on Lake Tahoe Blvd, the *Tahoe Marina Inn* (☎ 530-541-2180) has nice rooms for $70 to $90, with lake views, an outdoor pool and a quiet sandy beach. On the other side of the road, the *Inn by the Lake* (☎ 530-542-0330, 800-877-1466, 3300 Lake Tahoe Blvd) is an upscale convention motel with elegant rooms (some with lake views) starting at $98. There are restaurants, boat rentals, and a shuttle stop for Heavenly Valley and casino buses within walking distance of these places.

At Stateline, there is an especially good concentration of motels on the lake side of Hwy 50, across from the casinos, between Stateline Blvd and Park Ave. The *Mark Twain Motel* (☎ 530-544-5733, 800-232-6363, 947 Park Ave) has friendly owners and clean rooms for $30 on weekdays, $65 on weekends. Also on Park Ave, *Stateline Lodge* (☎ 530-544-3340, 800-826-8885) is old-fashioned through and through – from the sign to the owners. Rooms are $45 midweek, $75 on weekends. The nicest place in this pocket is the *Best Western Station House Inn* (☎ 530-542-1101, 800-822-5888, 901 Park Ave). Rooms cost $98 midweek, $108 on weekends, with a full breakfast. Across from the lake, the *Royal Valhalla Motor Lodge* (☎ 530-544-

2233, 800-999-4101, 4104 Lakeshore Blvd) has a nice pool, private beach and rooms for $59 to $79 midweek and $84 to $104 weekends.

On Lake Tahoe Blvd between Ski Run Blvd and Stateline, you'll find a *Motel 6*, *Super 8*, *Rodeway Inn*, *Quality Inn* and *Holiday Inn Express*. The *Stardust Lodge* (☎ *530-544-5211, 4061 Lake Tahoe Blvd)* has studios for $60 to $95 and one-bedroom units with kitchenettes that sleep two to six people ($125 to $150).

Casinos These multilevel coin boxes in Stateline tend to be overpriced, but offer all kinds of amenities, including health spas, 24-hour room service and shuttles to and from ski areas. Rooms ($85 to $130) are typically clean and boring unless you get a suite, which might have a lake view or in-room Jacuzzi, and cost an extra $100. *Harrah's* (☎ *775-588-6611, 800-427-7247, fax 775-586-6607)* and *Harvey's* (☎ *775-588-2411, 800-427-8397, fax 775-588-4732)* have the nicest decor, with Harvey's having a new gym and spa. Rooms at *Caesars Tahoe* (☎ *775-530-3515, 800-367-4554, fax 775-586-2102)* are a bit worn, but guests have free access to the indoor pool surrounded by plants and waterfalls. The *Horizon* (☎ *775-588-6211, 800-322-7723, fax 775-588-4732)* has the most basic rooms for $10 to $20 less than its neighbors.

Resorts In South Lake Tahoe, next door to the Tahoe Marina Inn, *Lakeland Village* (☎ *530-544-1685, 800-822-5969, 3535 Lake Tahoe Blvd)* is a good spot for families. They have a private beach with an outdoor grill, a lakeside clubhouse and cabins for up to 10 people with kitchens, lofts and fireplaces; prices start at $100. On Emerald Bay Rd, the very busy *Richardson's Resort* (☎ *530-541-1801)* has a campground, cabins that sleep two to eight people ($85 in winter, $540 per week in summer), a historic hotel ($59 in winter, $80 in summer) and a modern lakeside inn ($70 in winter, $80 in summer). There's also a beach, marina, riding stables, cross-country ski trails and restaurant.

In Hope Valley, southeast of Lake Tahoe on Hwy 88, *Sorensen's* (☎ *530-694-2203, 800-423-9949)* is a magical year-round resort with woodsy cabins, a cozy dining room and access to cross-country ski and hiking trails and good fishing. B&B rooms cost $70 to $110 ($10 more in winter), and cabins cost $90 to $115 for two to four people, $400 for six.

Places to Eat
The daily *Tahoe Tribune*, available widely, is loaded with two-for-one dining coupons. The *Alpen Sierra Coffee Co* (☎ *530-541-7449, 822 Emerald Bay Rd)* is the local hangout for coffee, pastries and gossip. The *Red Hut Waffle Shop* (☎ *530-541-9024, 2723 Lake Tahoe Blvd)* often has a long line for breakfast ($5 to $7). *Meyer's Downtown Cafe* (☎ *530-573-0228)*, on Hwy 50, in Meyers, is very good and a favorite with locals headed to Kirkwood or Sierra-at-Tahoe; prices are $4 to $6. North of Stateline, the *Zephyr Cove Lodge* (☎ *775-588-6644)*, 4 miles north of the casinos on Hwy 50, is truly rustic and makes a fun breakfast or lunch destination (dinners are a bit overpriced). Their pancakes ($4) and mushroom sour cream burger ($6.50) are famous.

Bright lights and loud clinking aside, casinos offer the best values in town. *Harrah's*, *Harvey's* and the *Horizon* offer all-you-can-eat buffets for around $10 (locals recommend the Horizon), and every casino has a 24-hour coffee shop. *Llewellyns*, on the top floor of Harvey's, is one of the south shore's most elegant restaurants and has an unbeatable view. Main courses start at $18.

For good burgers ($4 to $6), try *Izzy's Burger Spa* (☎ *530-544-5030, 2591 Lake Tahoe Blvd)*. *Sprouts* (☎ *530-541-6969)*, across from the chamber of commerce on Lake Tahoe Blvd, is a natural-foods cafe with big sandwiches, black bean burritos and fresh smoothies for around $6.

Hot Pepper Grill (☎ *530-542-1015, 3490 Lake Tahoe Blvd)* has healthy Mexican takeout for around $5, and *Emerald Palace* (☎ *530-544-7165)*, on Emerald Bay Rd, has an all-you-can-eat buffet for $7. *Nephele's* (☎ *530-544-8130)*, on Ski Run Blvd, and *Passaretti's* (☎ *530-541-3433)*, south of the fork in Emerald Bay Rd, are cozy and recommended for nice-but-not-too-expensive dinners; main courses are $7 to $12.

SIERRA NEVADA

Getting There & Away

Greyhound and Amtrak buses leave from Harrah's (at the back of the casino) five times daily to Sacramento ($18, two hours) and San Francisco ($12, seven hours). The 'Gambler's Special,' which includes $10 in gaming tokens and costs $24 roundtrip to San Francisco, is available from Greyhound at limited times. Tickets can be bought at the desk inside the casino.

The *Tahoe Casino Express* (☎ 775-785-2424, 800-446-6128) connects South Lake Tahoe and Stateline to the Reno/Tahoe International Airport with 14 shuttles daily ($17, one hour) that stop at Harrah's, Harvey's, Horizon and Caesars.

Getting Around

The South Lake Tahoe Stage (☎ 530-542-6877) buses run 24 hours a day and make frequent stops along Lake Tahoe Blvd between the Lakeside Inn (north of Stateline) and the Hwy 50/Hwy 89 junction. The fare is $1.50.

Most casinos have free shuttles that run until 2 am and will stop at any motel. In winter, the Heavenly Valley shuttle ($2) runs from the Main Lodge at Heavenly West to all the casinos, the intersection of Hwy 50 and Ski Run Blvd, and several motel areas.

DESOLATION WILDERNESS

This wilderness area, the most heavily used per acre in the US, spreads south and west from Lake Tahoe, encompassing 100 sq miles of forests, lakes and peaks. Contrary to what its name suggests, the wilderness is vibrantly beautiful and alive with trees, birds, fox, deer, bears and marmots. Retreating glaciers formed Desolation Valley, sweeping away its soil and leaving huge, polished rock faces in its upper elevations. Trees don't grow in this area, but coniferlike shrubs grow as big as trees, and wildflowers sprout between the rocks. Camping on these smooth, flat granite surfaces is great, and hiking and climbing is fast and easy.

A wilderness permit quota system limits overnight camping from June 15 to the first weekend in September. Permits cost $5 per person, per night for the first two nights and are free after that. There are an equal number of first-come, first-served permits (given on the day of departure) and reservable permits; reservations are made by calling USFS (☎ 530-573-2674) and cost a flat rate of $5. All permits must be obtained in person at the USDA Forest Service station, the USFS South Lake Tahoe Visitor Center in South Lake Tahoe or the Camino Ranger Station on Hwy 50; maps and information are available at all three. Day hikers can self-register at the trailheads.

From Hwy 50, the best access is from Wrights Lake, at the north end of Wrights Lake Rd, where there is plenty of parking, posted maps and a nice *campground* with $16 sites (reservable through ☎ 800-444-7275). There's also access from Echo Lake, though you have to hike for about 2 miles past private homes and cabins before reaching the wilderness. Trailheads from South Lake Tahoe are south of Hwy 89 (Emerald Bay Rd), across from the Tallac Historic Site, and at Emerald Bay.

Yosemite National Park

With over 3 million visitors per year, Yosemite is one of the most visited places in the US – and for good reason. Seeing photographs of the valley's glacier-swept profile, with Half Dome on one side and El Capitan on the other, is no substitute for experiencing it in person. Waterfalls thunder from granite walls that stretch 3000 feet above the valley floor, which is covered with meadows and groves and swept by the Merced River. East of the valley, lone 13,000-foot granite peaks rise above flowery meadows and gemlike lakes. Even with the crowds, traffic and congestion, Yosemite is awesome and stunning. And with tourist activity concentrated in 6% of the park (mostly in Yosemite Valley), outdoors enthusiasts need only hit the trails to find solitude and wilderness.

The western part of the park is densely forested with a mild climate, resembling the foothills to the west, while the east side along the Sierra Nevada crest is a sub-alpine environment. Yosemite Valley, on the southwest side of the park, is the park's top destination, home to most visitor facilities and campgrounds. Tuolumne Meadows, off the Tioga Rd (closed in winter), is the high-country hub.

History

The Ahwahneechee, a group of Central Valley Miwok and Eastern Sierra Paiute, lived in the Yosemite area for 4000 years before whites set foot in Yosemite Valley. Their main staples were black oak acorns and fish from the Merced River, though occasionally they trapped deer and rabbits. During the fall and winter they lived in the valley, then in spring headed to the eastern high country where they traded with Paiute from the Mono Lake area.

In 1833, a group of explorers looking for a trans-Sierra route saw Yosemite Valley from its eastern rim but did not descend its steep walls.

In the 1850s, as miners settled the Sierra's western foothills, the Mariposa Battalion was formed to find 'threatening' Native Americans living in the mountains. On one of these missions, the battalion followed a group of Ahwahneechee into the valley – they were the first non-Native Americans to enter Yosemite Valley. Four years later, James Mason Hutchings, a San Francisco newspaperman, organized the first tourist party to the valley, which included artist Thomas Ayers. Ayers' sketches of the trip were the first printed publicity advertising Yosemite's scenic wonders.

As visitors increased, conservationists such as Hutchings and Frederick Law Olmsted recognized the importance of protecting the valley and the grove of giant sequoia trees south of the valley. In 1864, Abraham Lincoln signed a bill preserving and protecting these two areas under the Yosemite Grant to California. This was the first state park in the world, and the foundation of what is now the national park system. With major campaigning led by John Muir, the area around the valley and grove were established as Yosemite National Park in 1890, and in 1906 the valley and grove themselves were ceded by the state of California to be included in the national park.

From 1890 to 1914, the US Army managed and administered the park. During the Spanish-American War, the first civilian rangers were employed, and in 1914 the first 'park rangers' were authorized by the Department of the Interior. By the mid-1970s, traffic and congestion were bad enough to cast a smoggy haze over the valley floor. To alleviate this problem, the General Management Plan (GMP) – a 'blueprint for improving and preserving the park for the next century' – was developed in 1980.

On public review since then, the GMP has been amended several times – most recently by the 1996 Draft Yosemite Valley Implementation Plan/Supplemental Environmental Impact Statement, which presents four alternatives that deal with changes in the Valley's 'developed areas, natural resource management, cultural resource management, interpretation and visitor services and park operations.'

The least involved alternative calls for no action in addition to the GMP, while the most aggressive alternative (and the one most likely to pass) calls for 147 acres to be restored to natural conditions, 82 acres to be redesigned and 38 acres to be developed to accommodate relocated facilities and functions. Regardless of which alternative is voted in, it looks like there will be an orientation and transfer facility at the west end of the valley (either at Taft Toe or Pohono Quarry), where people will leave their cars and use a shuttle bus system to enter the valley. Changes to campgrounds and circulation within the valley are also proposed, but haven't been developed in detail.

> In the face of Yosemite scenery cautious remonstrance is vain; under its spell one's body seems to go where it likes with a will over which we seem to have scarce any control.
>
> – John Muir, *The Yosemite*, 1911

SIERRA NEVADA

YOSEMITE NATIONAL PARK

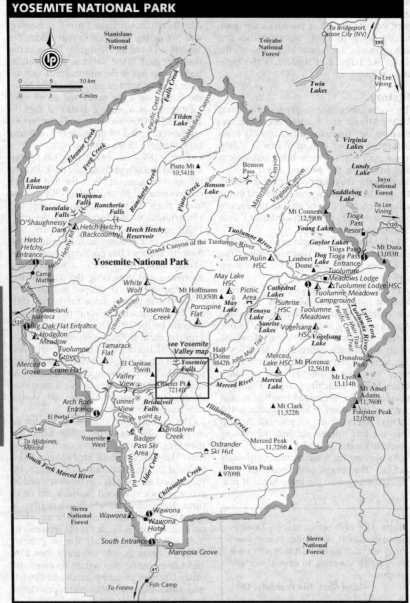

SIERRA NEVADA

Geology

As the Sierra block uplifted and tilted west, the slow-moving Merced River increased in flow and cut a 3000-foot canyon into the rock – the V-shaped Yosemite Valley.

An ice age covered the valley with glaciers for about 2½ million years. As the glaciers retreated (about 14,000 years ago), they scoured Yosemite's V into a U, breaking off enormous granite slabs along vertical 'joints' formed by stress and strain when the granite was forming beneath the earth's surface. Yosemite has six types of granite – a high concentration for such a small area – and each has its own rate of erosion. So while some walls withstood the glacial action, others crumbled, giving Yosemite Valley its unique profile. El Capitan, a 3593-foot granite monolith, is flanked by rock slides (mostly covered with trees) of weaker granite.

Over the past 6000 years about 10,000 feet of sediment has collected on the bottom of Yosemite's U, creating a flat valley floor. Tenaya Canyon, in the valley's northeast corner, is a good example of a U-shaped valley that hasn't been filled in. Several retreating glaciers, remnants of a mini-ice age about 600 years ago, persist at high elevations around Tuolumne Meadows.

Flora & Fauna

Yosemite's wide range of elevations nurture diverse species of trees, plants, birds and other animals. At lower elevations, the most common native trees are small leaf maple, black oak, ponderosa pine, dogwood (which bloom with big white flowers in spring) and incense cedar (the cedar's shaggy red bark makes it look like a giant sequoia or redwood, but its wood is much harder and its needles are flat). Higher elevations harbor ponderosa and Jeffrey pines and Douglas fir trees – all of them shorter than low-elevation trees because of the harsher climate.

Giant sequoias grow in three isolated groves in the park: the Mariposa Grove, off Hwy 41; the Tuolumne Grove, off the Tioga Rd; and the Merced Grove, which is off Big Oak Flat Rd near the Big Oak Flat Entrance.

Wildflowers bloom in April and May in the valley, late May and June at higher elevations. The best place to see wildflowers – lupine, iris, shooting star, Indian paintbrush, monkey flower, mule ear, Mariposa lily – is around Tuolumne Meadows.

Wildlife, except Western gray squirrels and mule deer, is most abundant outside Yosemite Valley. In 1986, California bighorn sheep, native to the area, were reintroduced after being wiped out by hunting and disease. The herd lives in the high country on the park's eastern edge, sometimes seen from Hwy 120. American black bears, which can be golden to dark brown to black, roam all parts of the park.

Steller's jays are numerous in the valley and are known for swiping food off campground tables. More rare and interesting are peregrine falcons, which raise their young on rock ledges above the valley floor.

There are numerous endangered, threatened and sensitive species in the park, including the golden eagle, Yosemite toad, Sierra Nevada red fox and California wolverine. The Yosemite Wilderness Center, in Yosemite Village, is a good place to get information.

When to Go

It's quite simple: In summer, the entire park is accessible, all visitor facilities are open and everything from backcountry campgrounds to ice cream stands are at maximum capacity. In winter, there are fewer people, trails are often inaccessible due to snow (but you can downhill and cross-country ski) and visitor facilities are scaled down to a bare minimum. Spring and fall generally offer the calm of winter with the weather (especially mid-September to mid-October) of summer.

Orientation

There are three primary approaches to Yosemite: Hwy 41 from Fresno, which enters at South Entrance and goes on to pass Wawona and Glacier Point Rd; Hwy 140 from Merced, which passes El Portal and enters at Arch Rock Entrance; and Hwy 120 from the San Francisco Bay Area and Manteca, which enters at Big Oak Flat

Entrance, traverses the park as the Tioga Rd (closed in winter) and heads east to Lee Vining and Mono Lake (in the Eastern Sierra) via Tioga Pass. Directions are well signed, and all roads access Yosemite Valley.

Information

For recorded park information, campground availability and road and weather conditions, call ☎ 559-372-0200. For lodging information and reservations, call ☎ 559-252-4848; for any other type of reservation (horseback riding, sightseeing tours, etc) call ☎ 559-252-4848. The NPS also maintains a thorough website (www.nps.gov/yose).

Yosemite's entrance fee is $20 per vehicle, $10 for people on foot, bicycle or horseback. It is valid for seven continuous days; a one-year pass to Yosemite is $40. Upon entering the park, you'll receive an NPS map and the *Yosemite Guide*, a quarterly newspaper with current ranger programs, park activities and a shuttle bus map and schedule.

Gas prices are about 30% higher in the park, and gas stations often close after dark.

Impassable Tioga Pass

Hwy 120, the main route into Yosemite National Park from the Eastern Sierra, climbs through Tioga Pass, the highest pass in the Sierra, at 9945 feet. On most maps of California, you'll find a parenthetical remark – 'closed in winter' – printed on the map near the pass. While true, this statement is also misleading. The Tioga Rd is usually closed from the first heavy snowfall in October to May or June. If you are planning a trip through Tioga Pass in the spring, you're likely to be out of luck. According to the park's official policy, the earliest date that the road through the pass will be plowed is April 15, yet the pass has only been open in April once since 1980. So call ahead (☎ 559-372-0200) for road and weather conditions before heading for Tioga Pass.

There are gas stations at Wawona, El Portal, the Tioga Rd-Big Oak Flat Rd junction (closed in winter; see 'Impassable Tioga Pass' boxed text), Tuolumne Meadows and in the valley near Yosemite Lodge.

Visitor Centers   There are ranger stations with maps, information and posted campground availability at all park entrances, but the Valley Visitor Center (☎ 559-372-0299) in Yosemite Village is definitely information central for the entire park. Here, you'll find a kiosk out front for simple questions and lodging information, a park concessions courtesy phone, a message board and museum-quality exhibits about the park. The bookstore (open 9 am to 6 pm daily) has a good selection of maps and guides. The Yosemite Wilderness Center, near the visitor center, issues wilderness permits and has topographical maps and trip planning guides.

In the high country, the Tuolumne Meadows Visitor Center (☎ 559-372-0263) has hiking maps of the area and general guidebooks. A half mile east, the Tuolumne Meadows Store (☎ 559-372-1328) is well stocked with topo maps and camping supplies. A ranger kiosk, just off the road near Tuolumne Meadows Lodge, issues wilderness permits. There are smaller centers at Big Oak Flat and Wawona, each with a market.

There are campfire programs and ranger-led walks at Crane Flat/Big Oak Flat, Wawona, Tuolumne Meadows and at Valley Visitor Center, Curry Village and Yosemite Lodge in Yosemite Valley. Look in the *Yosemite Guide* for a current schedule.

Money   There is a Bank of America (open 8 am to 4 pm daily) and a 24-hour ATM in Yosemite Valley (next to the Village Store). The bank cashes personal checks with a driver's license, state ID or passport. The Village Store (open until 10 pm), Tuolumne Meadows Store, Curry Village Store and Wawona Grocery Store will cash a check for $20 over your purchase. Shops and restaurants accept traveler's checks in US dollars only; American Express cards are not accepted anywhere in the park.

Post & Communications The post office in Yosemite Village accepts general delivery mail and has a fax machine; the zip code is 95389.

Books A really good general guidebook is *The Complete Guidebook to Yosemite* by Steven P Medley, available for $12 at the valley and Tuolumne Meadows visitor centers and most gift shops. Jeffrey P Schafer's *Yosemite National Park: A Natural History Guide to Yosemite and Its Trails* is a great hiking companion and includes a detailed map of the park. Sierra Club Books recently reprinted John Muir's *The Yosemite* and added photographs by Galen Rowell, a well-respected nature photographer; it sells for around $20. Other books such as *My First Summer in the Sierra* and *The Mountains of California* present Muir at his eloquent, tree-loving best; they can be found in used bookstores and at gift shops for $5 to $10.

Photography Any aspiring Ansel Adams should check out sunrise at Mirror Lake or Yosemite Falls, and sunset from Valley View, Tunnel View or Glacier Point. Sentinel Bridge, near Housekeeping Camp (in Yosemite Valley), offers an epic shot of Half Dome. Slide and print film is widely available and reasonably priced.

Free camera walks led by professional photographers leave the Ahwahnee Hotel or Valley Visitor Center daily at 8:30 am; check the *Yosemite Guide* for information on walks during your visit.

Laundry & Showers In the valley, there is a coin-op laundry at Housekeeping Camp, open in summer 8 am to 11 pm daily, and another at Curry Village, open 8 am to 6 pm daily year round. Showers are available at Housekeeping Camp and Curry Village for $2 (free for camp guests). Those at Curry Village are much nicer, but closed from noon to 4 pm and 10 pm to midnight. You can also get a shower for $2 at the Tuolumne Meadows Lodge.

Useful Organizations The Yosemite Institute (☎ 559-372-9300), PO Box 487, Yosemite National Park, CA 95389, is a well-respected nonprofit group that offers hands-on environmental education programs in the park. Many of their courses are for Elderhostel and school groups, but they have weekend programs for individuals year round. The Yosemite Fund (☎ 800-469-7275) raises money for preserving and restoring the park, in cooperation with the National Park Service. Its most interesting scheme is their four-color, $50 Yosemite California license plates.

Dangers & Annoyances Black bears, which can be golden to dark brown to black, are not generally aggressive but may attack when startled, and mother bears may charge to protect their cubs. They also have a keen interest in things they associate with food (especially processed food) and caution must be used when camping in Yosemite. For details, be sure to read the boxed text 'Bears, Your Food & You' in the Activities chapter.

Emergency For emergencies, call ☎ 911. A medical clinic (☎ 559-372-4637) and dental clinic (☎ 559-372-4200) are in Yosemite Valley, on the Ahwahnee Hotel road near Yosemite Village. Hours vary, but doctors can be reached by phone 24 hours a day.

Yosemite Valley

Its 3000-foot, sheer granite walls towering above lush meadows and forest really let you *know* you're in Yosemite. Yosemite Village is a good starting point from which to see the valley's star attractions. To avoid traffic and angst, get around by free shuttle bus, bicycle (available for rent in Yosemite Village and Camp Curry; $18 per day), or on foot. Most sights are within a mile of each other.

Next to the Valley Visitor Center, a free museum complex houses the **Yosemite Museum Gallery**, which has changing exhibits, and the **Indian Cultural Exhibit**, with a large Miwok and Paiute basket collection and nice gift shop. Hours are 9 am to 4:45 pm daily (closed noon to 1 pm). Behind the museum, a self-guiding interpretive trail winds through the **Indian Village of the Ahwahnee**, a reconstructed Miwok-Paiute village still used for religious ceremonies; it's open dawn to dusk and admission is free. These sights are OK if you're keenly interested in the subject matter, otherwise it's better to spend your time out-of-doors.

About a quarter mile east of the village, the **Ahwahnee Hotel** is a picture of elegance and rustic grace. Built in 1927 for $1.25 million, the Ahwahnee was the park's first resort, a popular destination for adventurous well-to-do tourists. The structure is of local granite, pine and cedar, decorated with leaded glass, sculpted tile and, inside, Native American rugs and Turkish kilims. Wander through even if you aren't staying there.

West of the village, near Yosemite Lodge, is an easy path to the base of **Yosemite Falls**, whose double-tiered stream is visible from all over the valley. Together, the upper and lower falls cascade 2425 feet – the tallest waterfall in North America. The viewing point at the base only shows the lower falls,

but the path leading to it gives a good view of both. Across the valley, a short jaunt from the Bridalveil Fall parking lot leads to the base of 620-foot **Bridalveil Fall**. The Ahwahneechee call the fall *Pohono* (Spirit of the Puffing Wind), as gusts often blow the falls from side to side. This fall is especially nice around sunset.

At the valley's southeast end, where the Merced River courses around two small islands, **Happy Isles** is the starting point for several popular hikes and home to the Happy Isles Nature Center (open May to October; free). The center has hands-on nature exhibits and free 'Explorer Packs' full of games, books and educational toys for kids.

One of the best views in the park is from **Glacier Point**, 3214 feet above the valley floor on the south rim. You can reach the point via Glacier Point Rd (off Hwy 41) by car, tour bus (from the valley; $10 each way),

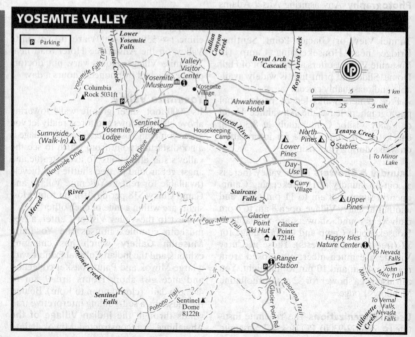

YOSEMITE VALLEY

cross-country skis or on foot via the Panorama Trail or Four Mile Trail. Take the bus one way and hike up or down. On the valley's south side, at the east end of the Wawona Tunnel, **Tunnel View** gives the classic Yosemite Valley view. On the other side of the valley, just west of El Capitan Meadow, **Valley View Turnout** is a good place to ogle **El Capitan** – at 3593 feet from base to summit, it is the world's largest granite monolith. Look closely and you'll probably see ropes, haul bags and climbers reckoning with its sheer face.

Tuolumne Meadows & Tioga Rd

At 8500 feet, Tuolumne Meadows is the largest sub-alpine meadow in the Sierra. Its wide open fields and clear blue lakes are a dazzling contrast to Yosemite's densely forested valley. The surrounding granite peaks – part of the Sierra Nevada crest – appear small and close, though most are between 10,000 and 13,000 feet. This area is more typically 'High Sierra' than it is 'Yosemite': in summer, it blooms with wildflowers and services hikers on the John Muir Trail, and in winter it sits under a blanket of snow, crisscrossed by backcountry skiers and snowshoers.

The Tioga Rd (Hwy 120), originally built as a mining road in 1882, is the only road to traverse the park from east to west. Tioga Pass at its east end (outside park boundaries) is the highest pass in the Sierra, at 9945 feet (closed in winter; see the 'Impassable Tioga Pass' boxed text). Besides great scenery, the road offers relatively uncrowded campgrounds, excellent day hikes and the chance to see climbers at close range. At the road's west end, just after its junction with Big Oak Flat Rd, are two giant sequoia groves: the Merced Grove, the most serene in the park, since it requires a 2-mile hike to reach (the trailhead is on the south side of the road, near a post marked B-10), and the Tuolumne Grove, the park's smallest, cut through by a 6-mile loop road.

It is 46 miles from the Tioga Pass Entrance to the Big Oak Flat Entrance, about a two-hour drive. Tuolumne Meadows, which stretches for about 2 miles, about 16 miles west of the Tioga Pass entrance, is the only place with services along the way.

Wawona

• population 313 • elevation 4012 feet

Sixteen miles south of the valley, Wawona is Yosemite's historical center, home to the park's first headquarters and site of its first tourist facilities. The Wawona Grocery Store (☎ 559-375-6574) acts as 'downtown' Wawona, with a post office, deli and bus stop. The **Pioneer History Center** has an outdoor collection of stage coaches and some of the first buildings in the park (relocated from various points), including remnants of Clark's Station, built by the park's first guardian in 1857. Nearby, the **Wawona Hotel**, built in 1875, is a picture of vintage elegance, with manicured grounds, a covered porch and wooden deck chairs for anyone to use.

A free bus (or your car) takes you 6 miles from Wawona (2 miles from the park's South Entrance) to the **Mariposa Grove** of giant sequoia trees – once John Muir's favorite grove. Probably much to his dismay, a trip to the grove these days is about as unnatural as a nature experience gets: a diesel powered open-air tram ($8) makes the 2-mile drive through the trees to the Mariposa Grove Museum. Walking along the trail is somewhat better but still crowded and exposed to tram noise; the longer outer loop trail gets relatively little traffic. There's a good interpretive map (50¢) at the trailhead on the east end of the parking lot.

Despite the tourist racket, the trees themselves are impressive – several are over 3000 years old and 300 feet high. The Wawona Tunnel Tree, which toppled over in 1969, was the famous drive-through tree that first gave the grove its notoriety.

Hetch Hetchy

After an environmental debate that knocked the wind out of John Muir, the 1913 Raker Bill allowed the City of San Francisco to construct O'Shaughnessey Dam in the Hetch Hetchy Valley, blocking the Tuolumne River to create Hetch Hetchy Reservoir. The 8-mile-long reservoir now submerges an area said to be as beautiful as Yosemite Valley,

SIERRA NEVADA

while it supplies the majority of San Francisco's water and hydroelectric power.

The area around Hetch Hetchy gets the park's least amount of traffic. Its low elevation and arid landscape make it less scenic than other parts of Yosemite, but it is a good place to start long trips into the park's quiet northern reaches. There is a nice backpackers' camp at the reservoir's west end (near the dam), popular with people who know the park well. A gentle 6-mile hiking trail crosses the dam, goes through a tunnel and heads along the north shore past Tueeulala, Wapama and Rancheria Falls. This is a good afternoon trip in spring or fall, but should be completed before 3 pm in summer when temperatures soar. At Rancheria Falls, the trail splits to go northeast through the Tiltill Valley and east (and eventually north) through Pleasant Valley to the Sierra's high country.

Hiking

Yosemite has more than 800 miles of trails that go far beyond the beaten tourist path. The best way to enjoy the park's natural splendor is to take to the backcountry, even if it is only 2 miles in and only for half a day. Besides the two most popular areas mentioned below, there's good hiking in Hetch Hetchy (see Hetch Hetchy section). Distance mongers should consider hiking between Tuolumne Meadows and the valley floor.

Yosemite Valley There are several classic hikes from the valley that are breathtakingly beautiful and totally crowded. Most popular is the paved Mist Trail from Happy Isles Nature Center to Vernal Falls. It's ½ mile to the bottom and another steep 1½ miles to the top. While not extraordinary considering the crowds, the hike offers essential Yosemite scenery. Strong hikers should continue up the switchbacks 1½ miles (3½ miles via the more gentle horse trail) to Nevada Falls, where crowds are dispersed and views are even better.

Good for viewing waterfalls, Half Dome and the valley, the Panorama Trail goes from Happy Isles Nature Center to Glacier Point. It's a tough 8½ miles going up, but coming down is a cinch. For $10 you can ride the bus one way to/from Glacier Point; check bus schedules in the *Yosemite Guide* or at Yosemite Village, Curry Village, Yosemite Lodge or the Ahwahnee Hotel.

At the valley's east end, a paved trail goes to **Mirror Lake**. Ansel Adams took many a photo here, as early morning and evening light catches the reflection of Half Dome in the lake. From here, a 3-mile trail makes a loop along Tenaya Creek, with nice views of its U-shaped canyon.

Arduous, but worthwhile for waterfall enthusiasts, the hike to the top of **Yosemite Falls** gains 2700 feet of elevation in 3½ miles. Now that's steep. The trail leaves from behind Sunnyside walk-in campground, passes Columbia Point, the top of Lower Yosemite Falls (a good turn-around point for some) and continues to the top of the upper falls. Once at the top, it's worth going just a little farther (about a mile) to Yosemite Point for a stunning view of Half Dome.

Tuolumne Meadows There are loads of small glacial lakes in this area, making for good day-hike destinations. Just west of the Tioga Pass Entrance, the trail to Gaylor Lakes advances immediately to a high-altitude environment: it's 1 mile to Middle Gaylor Lake, another two to the upper lakes. The altitude and steep terrain make this one quite difficult.

The John Muir Trail parallels the Lyell Fork of the Tuolumne River at Tuolumne Meadows, connecting the visitor center, campground and lodge. This is an easy 2-mile section with nice swimming holes, meadows and dome views.

A steep 1½-mile trail from the Dog Lake parking lot (near Tuolumne Meadows Lodge) heads around the east side of Lembert Dome to Dog Lake, whose grassy shore is good for picnicking and swimming. From here you can continue 5 miles to Young Lakes or go back around the west side of the dome to end up at the Tuolumne Meadows stables.

West along the Tioga Rd, trailheads are well marked for the Cathedral Lakes, Sunrise Lakes and May Lake trails, all highly recommended. From May Lake you can climb 2 steep miles (unmarked) to the top of Mt Hoffmann, the geographical center of the park, for a panoramic view.

Backpacking

Wilderness permits (free) are required year round for all overnight trips. A quota system limits the number of people leaving from each trailhead each day: half of the quota is available first-come, first-served no earlier than 24 hours before you want to begin; the other half may be reserved (☎ 559-372-0740) from 24 weeks to two days before your trip for a $3 fee.

Before you get your permit, know how many people are in your party, your entry and exit dates, your starting and ending trailheads and your principle destination. Permits can be obtained from the Yosemite Valley Wilderness Center, Wawona Ranger Station, Tuolumne Valley Permit Kiosk (off the Tioga Rd near Tuolumne Meadows Lodge), Big Oak Flat Information Station and Hetch Hetchy Entrance Station. The best place for camping and backpacking supplies is at the Curry Village Mountain Sport Shop (☎ 559-372-8396) in Yosemite Valley. The Tuolumne Meadows Store (☎ 559-372-1328; open May to October) has sleeping bags and pads, stoves, foul weather gear and a good selection of freeze-dried faux-food.

Legendary Half Dome

NANCY KELLER

According to Native American legend, one of Yosemite Valley's early inhabitants went down from the mountains to Mono Lake, where he wed a Paiute named Tesaiyac. The journey back to the valley was difficult, and by the time they reached what was to become Mirror Lake, Tesaiyac had decided that she wanted to go back down to live with her people at Mono Lake. Her husband refused to live on such barren, arid land with no oak trees from which to get acorns. With a heart full of despair, Tesaiyac began to run toward Mono Lake, and her husband followed her. When the powerful spirits heard quarreling in Yosemite, they became angry and turned the two into stone: he became North Dome and she became Half Dome. The tears she cried made marks as they ran down her face, thus forming Mirror Lake.

True or not, Half Dome is Yosemite's most distinctive monument. It is 87 million years old and has a 93% vertical grade – the sheerest cliff in North America. Climbers come from around the world to grapple with its legendary 'north face,' but good hikers can reach its summit via an 8½-mile trail from Yosemite Valley. The trail gains 4900 feet in elevation and has cable handrails for the last 200 yards. The hike *can* be done in one day, but is more enjoyable if you break it up by camping (Little Yosemite Valley is the most popular spot) one night along the way.

SIERRA NEVADA

The Yosemite Mountaineering School (☎ 559-372-8344 from September to May, 559-372-8435 from June to August) has three and four-day guided backpacking trips for $100 to $225 per person, per day depending on how many people are in your party. The school also rents backpacks ($8 per day), sleeping bags ($10), pads ($2) and bear canisters ($3) – necessary for storing food. Be aware of Yosemite's altitude range, especially in the valley where steep trails gain altitude quickly, and in the Tuolumne Meadows area where trails start at around 9000 feet. Take it slow and allow your body to acclimatize.

Rock Climbing

With 3000-foot granite monoliths and a mild climate, Yosemite is a climber's mecca. When you see a person hanging from the mass of Half Dome or a single light shining from El Capitan in the middle of the night, the meaning of 'Go Climb A Rock' (a well-known Yosemite slogan) becomes clear. Most climbers stay at Sunnyside walk-in campground in the valley. People looking for climbing partners or equipment post notices on the bulletin board here, and resident climbers are helpful in suggesting routes. The best place to go for equipment and printed information is the Curry Village Mountain Sport Shop (☎ 559-372-8396) in Yosemite Valley. They have climbing books to loan, maps and a knowledgeable staff. Climbers recommend the *Climber's Guide to the High Sierra* by Steve Roper.

The Yosemite Mountaineering School (see the Backpacking section) has beginner and intermediate rock-climbing classes ($80) daily, private guided climbs for one to three people ($220 for one person, $310 for two people and $405 for three) and a highly recommended Alpencraft Seminar every Monday to Friday ($375) and Monday to Wednesday ($210). Equipment is provided, and climbing shoes are for rent ($6); rentals are only available with a lesson.

The meadow across from El Capitan, and the northeast end of Tenaya Lake (off the Tioga Rd), are good for watching climbers dangle from granite (binoculars – for rent for around $3 – are needed for a really good view). Look for the haul bags first – they're bigger, more colorful and move around more than the climbers, thus they are easier to spot.

Horseback Riding

Stables, all of which are managed by Yosemite Concession Services (YES), are located at Tuolumne Meadows (☎ 559-372-8427), Wawona and in Yosemite Valley. The season usually runs from early April to mid-October at Wawona and in the valley, and from May to September at Tuolumne. Rates are $35 for two hours, $46 for four hours and $68 all day (about nine hours). No experience is needed, but reservations are advised, especially at the valley stables.

River Running

Floating the Merced River, from Curry Village to Sentinel Bridge, is a leisurely way to soak up Yosemite Valley views. Raft rentals are available at Curry Village for $15, including equipment and shuttle service back to the village (two person minimum). Paddles, life jackets and the shuttle ride cost $2 each with your own raft or inner tube. Rafting above Yosemite Stables or below Cathedral Beach Picnic Area is forbidden.

Winter Activities

According to locals, Yosemite is at its best when the snow falls. Accommodations are cheaper, the park is less crowded and the weather in the valley stays mild. Roads in the valley are plowed, and Hwys 41, 120 and 140 are usually kept open, conditions permitting (Hwy 140 is almost always open). The Tioga Rd, though, closes with the first snow fall (see 'Impassable Tioga Pass' boxed text). Be sure to bring snow chains with you as prices double once you hit the foothills.

There is a big ice-skating rink at Curry Village, a snow play area at Crane Flat Campground and a free shuttle from the valley to **Badger Pass Ski Area** (☎ 559-372-1244), California's oldest ski area. It is primarily a beginner and intermediate hill, with 10 chairlifts, 900 vertical feet, $35 lift tickets, a good ski school and full-service lodge.

Anyone staying at a YES accommodation (basically any lodge/motel in the valley) gets one free Badger Pass lift ticket per night (except Friday and Saturday).

For cross-country skiing, there are 28 miles of groomed trails (free) from Badger Pass (including a scenic 10-mile trail to Glacier Point) and marked backcountry trails to the valley's south rim. The **Yosemite Cross Country Ski School** (☎ 559-372-8444) offers learn-to-ski packages ($46), guided tours ($37) and equipment rentals ($16). There are marked, ungroomed trails from the Crane Flat Campground on the park's north side (no facilities).

Two backcountry ski huts with beds, cooking facilities, bathrooms, wood stoves and water are available for overnight stays: the Yosemite Association (☎ 559-372-0740) operates the Ostrander Ski Hut, in a gorgeous spot on the bank of Ostrander Lake; the Cross Country Ski School (☎ 559-372-8444) operates the Glacier Point Hut. Reservations are required for both.

Organized Tours

While tours are good for covering a lot of ground with someone else in the driver's seat, four of the five tours offered – all from Yosemite Valley – are in big tour buses and make few stops. Your best bet is the two-hour Valley Floor Tour ($17) in an open-air tram, which stops at major points of interest, including Yosemite Falls, Bridalveil Falls and El Capitan; the moonlight version of this is spectacular (summer only). Other tours are listed in detail in *Yosemite Magazine* and at departure points: Yosemite Lodge, Curry

John Muir

Born in Scotland in 1838, John Muir came to America with his father in 1849 and settled near the Fox River in Wisconsin. After studying botany and geology at the University of Wisconsin, he set out on what would be a never ending journey through the wilds. He accompanied research expeditions to the Arctic and the Yukon and discovered Glacier Bay in Alaska. But more than anywhere else, Muir is synonymous with the Sierra Nevada. He spent most of his life studying the range's geology and plant life and scouting the area between Yosemite Valley and Mt Whitney, where the 200-mile John Muir Trail now pays him tribute.

Though he discovered 75 glaciers and mapped much of the Sierra for the first time, Muir is best known for his eloquent writings. His love for the outdoors was so passionate that he spent most of his time in solitude, among trees, cliffs, rocks and waterfalls, using his pen to commune with the environment.

Yosemite was his special love. In *My First Summer in the Sierra* (1911), he wrote about his first view of Yosemite Valley:

Never before had I seen so glorious a landscape, so boundless an affluence of sublime mountain beauty. The most extravagant description I might give of this view to any one who has not seen similar landscapes with his own eyes would not so much hint at its grandeur and the spiritual glow that covered it.

Muir's articles and lobbying efforts were the foundation of the campaign that established Yosemite as a national park in 1890. He died in 1914, one year after losing the battle against the creation of the Hetch Hetchy Reservoir to the city of San Francisco.

SIERRA NEVADA

Village (summer only), the Ahwahnee Hotel and Village Store (mid-May to mid-October) in Yosemite Village.

Places to Stay

Camping All campsites in the park are $12 to $18 and include a picnic table, fire pit and bear box (for storing food). In Yosemite Valley (where camping can be like sleeping in a motel with very thin walls), *Upper Pines Campground* is open year round, *Lower Pines Campground* is open March to October and *North Pines Campground* is open April to October. Reservations (see Campground Reservations) are required at all of these. Upper Pines has the most trees and nicest sites but is farthest from Yosemite Village, while North Pines, across the river, is near the stables and has nice group and backpacker sites. *Sunnyside Walk-in Campground*, the cheapest and most popular with climbers, is open year round and sites are first-come, first-served.

Outside the valley, *Wawona* and *Hodgon Meadow* campgrounds are open year round. Reservations are required from May to September; sites are first-come, first-served the rest of the year. *Tuolumne Meadows Campground* is open July to September; half the sites are by reservation only, half are first-come, first-served. *Crane Flat Campground*, where reservations are required, is open June to September. *Bridalveil Creek*, *Tamarack Flat*, *White Wolf*, *Porcupine Flat* and *Yosemite Creek* campgrounds are open May to September on a first-come, first-served basis – these are the most likely to have a spot when the rest of the park is full. Of these, Porcupine Flat is really woodsy, Tamarack Flat is set back from the road with sites along Tamarack Creek, and White Wolf is near the busy White Wolf Lodge, where you can get a meal for around $12. At *Hetch Hetchy Campground*, at the end of Hetch Hetchy Rd, you need a wilderness permit to camp.

You can make reservations up to five months in advance, beginning the 15th of each month. Do this by phone (☎ 800-436-7275) with a Visa, MasterCard or Discover, or by sending a check or money order to NPRS, PO Box 1600, Cumberland, MD 21502. The advantage of using the phone is that if your first (or second, or third) choice is unavailable, you can stay on the line until you find something. Try to call early on the 15th, as campgrounds fill up fast. You may also make reservations via the Internet at http://reservations.nps.gov.

Don't fret if reservations are full. Except during Labor Day, 4th of July and Veterans Day weekends, there are usually spots at first-come, first-served campgrounds if you arrive by check-out time (10 am in the valley, noon everywhere else).

High Sierra Camps The six High Sierra Camps (HSC) are set about 9 miles apart in the park's high country near Tuolumne Meadows. Each has canvas tents for four to six people, a communal dining room, and bathroom with running water and hot showers. Beds have sheets and down comforters, and meals (breakfast and dinner) are very hearty. This is a great way to experience the backcountry without having to carry much food or equipment. The cost is $45 per person, per night including two meals. If there happens to be a cancellation (which is rare), hikers not staying at the camp can get a meal for around $10.

The camps are (clockwise) at Tuolumne Lodge, Vogelsang, Merced Lake, Sunrise Lake, May Lake and Glen Aulin. Tuolumne Lodge, just off the Tioga Rd, gets nonhikers and is a popular start/end point for the loop. May Lake is 1 mile off the road, thus popular for one-night trips. A short season (late June to September) and high demand requires a lottery for reservations. Applications are accepted from October 15 to November 30, and the lottery is in December. For an application, call ☎ 559-252-4848.

Cabins & Lodges Yosemite Concession Services manages all noncamp accommodations in the park, including cabins and tent cabins. Their 'Plan Your Visit to Yosemite Map, Activity and Rate Guide,' with seasonal rates and a send-in reservation form, is available at visitor centers or from Yosemite Reservations (☎ 559-252-4848), 5410 E

Home Ave, Fresno, CA 93727. Places get booked well in advance for summer months.

In Yosemite Valley, **Curry Village** has tent cabins – basically a wooden platform with a double bed, mirror, plastic sides and a roof – for $42; these are very close together. Wooden cabins without bath ($60) are a bit nicer but still crowded together, while those with bath ($76) are spacious and cozy. There are also modern rooms here, right in the thick of Curry Village activity, for $92.

Yosemite Lodge gets large tour groups and has the park's most popular restaurant and bar. Standard rooms cost $97, and modern 'lodge' rooms with TV and phone cost $107. There are also cabins for $85. The park's deluxe accommodations are at the elegant **Ahwahnee Hotel**, where rooms and cottages start at $230 and are usually booked a year in advance.

In Tuolumne Meadows, the **Tuolumne Meadows Lodge** has canvas tent cabins with four beds, a wood stove and candles (no electricity) for $44. This is a fun place to stay if you want to feel like you're roughing it in style. A mile north of the Tioga Rd, **White Wolf Lodge** is in a charming world of its own. The lodge has a great porch and rustic dining room, tent cabins ($44), wood cabins with bath ($68) and a lovely campground.

Built in 1879, the graceful **Wawona Hotel** has rooms for $103 ($74 without bath) and a terrific porch.

Outside the Park The best deal around is the **Yosemite Bug Hostel** (☎ 559-966-6666), on Hwy 140, in Midpines (near Mariposa). Beds are $15 (plus a 10% resort tax) and there's a kitchen and a good, cheap restaurant on the premises. Usually you can find a ride to the park with a fellow hosteler; otherwise the hostel sells roundtrip tickets to/from the park on the VIA bus, which runs between Yosemite and Merced (see Getting There & Away). The last VIA bus to the hostel leaves Merced at 3:15 pm. If you take this bus, buy a ticket from Merced to the hostel only. You can then buy tickets to the park from the hostel at half price. If you take an early bus from Merced, buy a ticket to the park so you can spend the day in the

park (the hostel closes daily 10 am to 5 pm) before going back on a Merced-bound bus in the afternoon. The hostel is often booked in summer, so call for a reservation or show up early in the morning. The VIA bus also stops at the KOA in Midpines.

Other non-YES accommodations include **Yosemite West Cottages** (☎ 559-372-4567), which has studio apartments and houses with stocked kitchens and maid service starting at $95 for two people and reaching $325 for 12 people. The cottages are in a private development within the park, halfway between Wawona and Yosemite Valley on Hwy 41. Farther from park activities, the **Redwoods Guest Cottages** (☎ 559-375-6666), 1 mile east of Wawona on Chilnualna Falls Rd, has one- to five-bedroom units with kitchen and fireplace starting at $105; there's a three-night minimum. Accommodations near the park, in the small towns along major access routes, tend to be overpriced, especially in summer.

At Tioga Pass, 2 miles east of park boundaries, are four nice USFS campgrounds with flush toilets, picnic tables and fire grates. The rustic **Tioga Pass Resort** (☎ 559-372-4471) has housekeeping cabins and motel rooms for around $450 a week, including breakfast.

Places to Eat

Bringing your own food saves money, but can be a hassle because you must remove it all from your car (or backpack or bicycle) and store it in a locker or bear box. The best spots for self-catering are the **Village Store** in Yosemite Village and the **Curry Village Store** – both open until 10 pm daily. The **Wawona Store** is also good.

Prices at restaurants are reasonable and most menus have vegetarian items. Popular with climbers, the **Terrace Lounge** at Curry Village has good pizza ($15 large), pitchers of beer and a nice deck. Next to it, the **Dining Pavilion** is a self-service cafeteria with mediocre breakfast, lunch and dinner for around $5. In Yosemite Village, the **Pasta Place** serves (what else?) large portions of noodles with a choice of sauce and Caesar salad for $7.

Locals like the **Mountain Broiler Room** at Yosemite Lodge for its patio and casual

SIERRA NEVADA

atmosphere, but the food is overpriced, with OK prime rib, steak and seafood dinners starting at $16. A worthwhile dining splurge is the **Ahwahnee Hotel Dining Room** (☎ 559-372-1489), where the room itself is a feast for the eyes and the food is truly gourmet. Go for a scone and coffee ($5) just for the experience. Breakfast and lunch are under $15, dinner is around $25 per person. Reservations and coat and tie (for men) are required at dinner.

On the park's east edge, the **Tioga Pass Resort** is small and rustic and serves excellent pancakes. The **Tuolumne Meadows Store** has good picnic items, and the grill next door has food for under $5.

Entertainment
There are often evening programs at the **Ahwahnee Hotel** (a great setting) that aren't publicized but are open to anyone; check the marquee in the lobby for the night's offerings.

The park's most noteworthy entertainer is actor Lee Stetson, who does a one-man show about the life of John Muir. One of three different performances ('The Spirit of John Muir' is recommended) is given nightly (except Sunday) in the **Valley Visitor Center** auditorium, behind the center's main building. Tickets are $7, children $3.

Getting There & Away
Yosemite is one of the easiest national parks to reach by public transportation. VIA buses (☎ 559-384-1315) meet Amtrak trains and Greyhound buses in Merced (see the San Joaquin Valley chapter) and depart for Yosemite daily at 7 and 10:40 am, and 3:15 pm; it's a three-hour ride. The bus stops at motels, the KOA and Yosemite Bug Hostel (both in Midpines) on Hwy 140, then travels to Yosemite Village and Curry Village, both in Yosemite Valley.

A roundtrip ticket costs $38 ($20 one way), including park entrance fee. If you're planning on staying at the hostel and visiting the park several times, buy a roundtrip ticket to Midpines and then get individual bus tickets from the hostel for half price. The VIA drivers are helpful if you have questions.

Greyhound buses and Amtrak trains connect Merced with Los Angeles, San Francisco and Bakersfield.

Getting Around
In Yosemite Valley, a free shuttle bus runs from 7 am to 10 pm September to October, 9 am to 10 pm October to mid-November. The shuttles operate at 20-minute intervals; stops include all day-use parking lots and campgrounds, Yosemite Village, Curry Village, Yosemite Lodge, the Ahwahnee Hotel and popular trailheads. From mid-May to September the shuttle also goes to Tuolumne Meadows (2½ hours one way).

Bike rentals are available at Yosemite Lodge and Curry Village for $5.50 per hour, $20 per day. A two-way bike path (clearly marked on the NPS map) makes a 6-mile loop around the valley, passing all campgrounds, picnic areas and visitor facilities; spur trails go to the Happy Isles Nature Center and toward Mirror Lake.

YOSEMITE GATEWAYS
The small towns on Yosemite's western fringe are mostly old mining towns that now thrive on the park's overflow. These are good places to stay if you arrive without a tent or room reservation. From the east, the nearest town is Lee Vining, 9 miles east of Tioga Pass (closed in winter; see 'Impassable Tioga Pass' boxed text). The Mariposa County Visitor Center (☎ 559-966-2456, 800-208-2434) publishes a hefty, detailed brochure with lodging and activities information for Mariposa, El Portal, Midpines, Buck Meadows and Fish Camp, available by mail (PO Box 425, Mariposa, CA 95338); or visit visitor@yosemite.net.

Oakhurst & Around
Situated at the junction of Hwys 41 and 49, Oakhurst is the last place with normal gas prices, supermarkets, banks and auto parts stores before entering the park from the south. While most traffic is Yosemite bound, a fair amount of people pass through Oakhurst en route to Bass Lake, a popular fishing and boating spot. The City Park and Fresno Flats Historical Park, both southeast

of Hwy 41 near the historic town center, offer shady spots to stretch your legs.

Chain motels are your best bet here, though they're relatively expensive. The *Shilo Inn* (☎ 559-683-3555), *Best Western Yosemite Gateway* (☎ 559-683-2378) and *Holiday Inn Express* (☎ 559-642-2525) are all on Hwy 41. Each has a pool and rooms for around $80 ($95 from June to September).

Fifteen miles north, **Fish Camp** is smaller and less commercial. Its *Marriott Tenaya Lodge* (☎ 559-683-6555) is a luxurious place to stay, with two pools, a fitness center, woodsy grounds and cozy log rooms starting at $160.

Mariposa & Around

About halfway between Merced and Yosemite Valley at the Hwy 140/49 junction, Mariposa (population 7269) is the largest and most interesting town near the park. Born as a mining and railroad town during the gold rush, it has a stately courthouse built in 1854 (the oldest in continuous use west of the Mississippi), and a History Center (☎ 559-966-2924; open 10 am to 4 pm daily), at the east end of town across from Happy Burger, with mediocre mining and railroad exhibits. The **California State Mining & Mineral Museum** (☎ 559-742-7625), a mile south of town off Hwy 49 at the fairgrounds, is worth a stop ($2; closed Monday and Tuesday).

The *Mother Lode Lodge* (☎ 559-966-2521) and *Mariposa Lodge* (☎ 559-966-3607), both on Hwy 140, are good places to stay with singles/doubles costing around $65/75.

El Portal Just west of the park's Arch Rock entrance, El Portal sprawls for about 7 miles along Hwy 140. *Savage's Trading Post*, at its west end where the South and Main Forks of the Merced River meet, is the town's well-known tourist trap – a gift shop and restaurant erected on the site of a trading post used by miners and Miwok in the 1850s. The adjacent *Red Bug Lodge* (☎ 559-379-2301) has decent rooms for $80. Farther east, the *Cedar Lodge Resort* (☎ 559-379-2612) and *Yosemite View Lodge* (☎ 559-379-2681) each have a pool, restaurant and $85 rooms.

Hwy 120 West

From the Big Oak Flat Entrance, it's 22 miles to **Groveland**, an adorable highwayside town with restored gold rush-era buildings. The *Hotel Charlotte* (☎ 559-962-6455), in the middle of town on Hwy 120, has vintage rooms for $67 ($58 with shared bath), including breakfast. Four miles east of Groveland on Hwy 120, *Sugar Pine Ranch* (☎ 559-962-7823, 888-800-7823) is an excellent destination for people with a car. Rooms on the 60-acre ranch are $100 to $150 and include a beautiful breakfast. Farther east at Buck Meadows, the *IMA Yosemite West Gate* (☎ 559-962-5281) has standard rooms from $99, and the *Buck Meadows Lodge* has a market and coffee shop open until 9 pm most of the year. Visitor facilities are sparse along this route, but there are two good spots to swim – Don Pedro Reservoir, 11 miles west of Groveland, and Rainbow Bridge on the Tuolumne River, 3 miles east of Buck Meadows.

Kings Canyon & Sequoia National Parks

South of Yosemite, on the Sierra's western slope, the adjacent Kings Canyon and Sequoia national parks encompass some of the world's most incredible pieces of nature. Giant sequoias stand as the most massive living trees on earth, and the awesome canyon of the South Fork of the Kings River rivals any in the Sierra. Despite this superlative world, crowds are sparse thanks to relative inaccessibility. There's none of that usual amusement park atmosphere. Popular as hiking and backpacking parks, there are few drive-by sites but loads of trails for all ability levels. Each park has its own history and defining characteristics, but they are administered as one unit.

History

The Potwisha Indians, subtribes of Central Valley Yokuts, lived as hunter-gatherers in

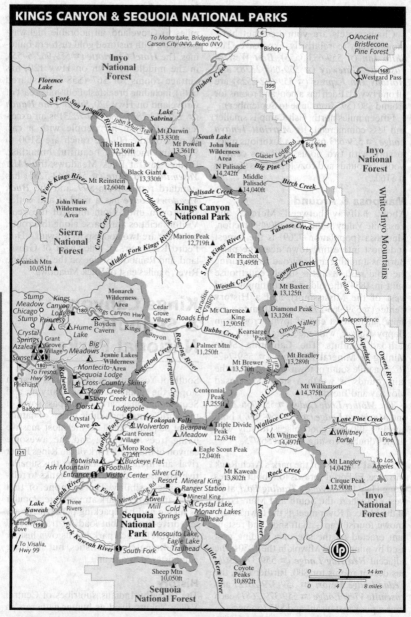

KINGS CANYON & SEQUOIA NATIONAL PARKS

To Mono Lake, Bridgeport,
Carson City (NV), Reno (NV)

Bishop

Inyo
National
Forest

Ancient
Bristlecone
Pine Forest

Westgard Pass

Florence
Lake

S Fork San Joaquin River

Bishop Creek

Lake
Sabrina

John Muir Trail

Mt Darwin
13,830ft

South
Lake

John Muir
Wilderness
Area

Glacier Lodge Rd

Big Pine

The Hermit ▲
12,360ft

Mt Powell
13,361ft

Big Pine Creek

Inyo
National
Forest

N Kings River

Mt Reinstein
12,604ft

Black Giant ▲
13,330ft

Goddard Creek

N Palisade
14,242ft

Middle
Palisade
14,040ft

Birch Creek

Palisade Creek

White-Inyo Mountains

John Muir
Wilderness
Area

Sierra
National
Forest

Crown Creek

Middle Fork Kings River

Kings Canyon
National Park

Marion Peak
12,719ft

S Fork Kings River

Mt Pinchot
13,495ft

Taboose Creek

Sawmill Creek

Owens Valley

Spanish Mtn
10,051ft ▲

Paradise Valley

Woods Creek

Mt Clarence
King
12,905ft

Mt Baxter
13,125ft

Diamond Peak
13,126ft

Independence

Owens River

Monarch
Wilderness
Area

Cedar
Grove
Village

Roads End

Bubbs Creek

Kearsarge
Pass

Onion Valley

LA Aqueduct

395

Stump
Meadow
Chicago
Stump

Kings
Canyon
Lodge

180

Hume
Lake

Boyden
Cavern

Kings
Canyon

Roaring River

Palmer Mtn
11,250ft

Mt Bradley
13,289ft

Crystal
Springs

Grant
Grove
Village

Big
Meadows

Kings Canyon Hwy

Azalea
Sunset

180

To Fresno,
Hwy 99

Pinehurst

Jennie Lakes
Wilderness
Area
Montecito
Sequoia Lodge
Cross-Country Skiing
Stony Creek
Stony Creek Lodge

Sugarloaf Creek

Ferguson Creek

Mt Brewer
13,570ft

Mt Williamson
14,375ft

Redwood Cr

Centennial
Peak
13,255ft

John Muir Trail

Tyndall Creek

Wallace Creek

Lone Pine Creek

Badger

Dorst

Lodgepole

Tokopah Falls

Wolverton

Bearpaw
Meadow

Triple Divide
Peak
12,634ft

Mt Whitney
14,497ft

Whitney
Portal

Lone
Pine

Crystal
Cave

Marble Fork

Giant Forest
Village

Moro Rock
6725ft

Buckeye Flat

Eagle Scout Peak
12,040ft

Mt Kaweah
13,802ft

Kern River

Rock Creek

Mt Langley
14,042ft

To Los
Angeles

Ash Mountain
Entrance

Potwisha

Foothills
Visitor Center

E Fork

Silver City
Resort

Mineral King Rd

Mineral King
Ranger Station

Cirque Peak
12,900ft

Inyo
National
Forest

Kaweah River

Lake
Kaweah

Three
Rivers

198

S Fork Kaweah River

Atwell
Mill

Cold
Springs

Mineral King

Crystal Lake,
Monarch Lakes
Trailhead

Lemon
Cove

To Visalia,
Hwy 99

J21

Sequoia
National
Park

Mosquito Lake,
Eagle Lake
Trailhead

Little Kern River

South Fork

Sheep Mtn
10,050ft

Coyote
Peaks
10,892ft

Sequoia
National Forest

SIERRA NEVADA

0   7   14 km
0   4   8 miles

the western foothills along the Marble Fork of the Kaweah River. In 1858, they led Hale Tharp, a cattleman from Three Rivers, into the Giant Forest along the west side of Moro Rock. Tharp spent summers here for the next 30 years and entertained John Muir, who wrote of the area in magazines and periodicals.

The gold rush brought logging and grazing to the Grant Grove area and mining to Mineral King, causing alarm among early conservationists. Visalia journalist George Stewart, called the 'Father of Sequoia National Park,' started a stir in the San Joaquin Valley with newspaper articles about the effects of logging the big trees. Valley farmers sent their message to Washington, DC, via representatives and, in 1890, Sequoia became the second national park in the US, with the 4 sq miles around Grant Grove becoming Grant Grove National Park a few months later. Kings Canyon was designated a national park in 1940, encompassing Grant Grove and nearby Redwood Mountain.

Flora & Fauna

The parks' low foothills (to 5000 feet) are covered with manzanita, California blue oak and the tall yucca, whose fragrant flowers bloom in early spring. The foothills are usually the only area in which you have to watch for rattlesnakes while hiking, though occasionally rattlers do appear at higher elevations.

From 5000 to 9000 feet, forests include sugar, ponderosa, Jeffrey and lodgepole pine; fir; and incense cedar. A 200-mile stretch north of the Kings River encompasses eight giant sequoia groves, while the remaining 67 are concentrated along a 60-mile belt south of the river. Deer and Douglas squirrels are predominant, though coyotes and bobcats also roam these elevations.

In the high country, above 9000 feet, forests give way to stark granite landscapes dotted with lakes and foxtail and white-bark pine.

Black bears are common and can be destructive in seeking out human food. Proper food storage is required. Check bulletin boards at visitor centers and most parking lots for current instructions (see

'Bears, Your Food & You' boxed text in the Activities chapter).

Orientation & Information

For 24-hour recorded information, call ☎ 559-565-3341. Thorough website information about all aspects of the parks is at www.nps.gov/seki. The entrance fee to both parks is $10 per car, $5 for people on foot or bike. Upon entering the parks, you'll receive a good NPS map and quarterly newspaper with phone numbers, hours and descriptions for all visitor facilities, including those in the nearby national forests.

Near the Hwy 180/Generals Hwy/Kings Canyon Hwy junction, Grant Grove Village is a focal point of the parks. There's a market,

Giant Sequoias

In the same family as the California coast redwood and Dawn sequoia (recently discovered in China), the giant sequoia (*Sequoiadendron giganteum*) grows only on the Sierra's western slope, between 5000 and 7000 feet. Giant sequoias are the largest living things on earth in terms of volume. They can grow to 300 feet tall, 40 feet in diameter and live up to 3000 years – the eldest is estimated to be 3500 years old. The main cause of death for the trees is their own size – they topple under their own weight, not supported by their fragile roots.

Sequoia groves might be more abundant if the trees weren't so finicky. They require plenty of groundwater for their wide, shallow root system, a heavy snowpack to trim limbs and dead branches so they won't blow over in a storm, and frequent fires (their thick, soft bark is full of air – very fire resistant) to pop open their tight cones and free the seeds inside. Aside from Yosemite, look for sequoia groves around Kings Canyon and Sequoia national parks and the similarly gigantic California coast redwood tree along the Pacific coast.

SIERRA NEVADA

showers ($3), post office and laundry open year round. The Grant Grove Visitor Center (☎ 559-335-2856) has a good history exhibit and the true-to-scale 'Sequoia Room.' Cedar Grove Village, at the bottom of Kings Canyon (31 miles northeast of Grant Grove Village), has a visitor center (☎ 559-565-3793), market and deli, lodge, showers ($3) and laundry. Services are open from 8 am to 7 pm daily from late May to mid-October, though the visitor center closes in early September.

Smaller information stations are at Lodgepole (closed from mid-October to late May) and the Foothills Visitor Center, 1 mile north of the Ash Mountain Entrance at the south end of Sequoia National Park (open in summer 8 am to 5 pm daily, 9 am to 4:30 pm October to May). All visitor centers have day-hike and topo maps, books and information for both parks. Books and maps are also available from the Sequoia Natural History Association (☎ 559-565-3759).

There's an ATM at Grant Grove Village, but otherwise there are no banks or check cashing facilities in the parks (most places will accept personal and traveler's checks). Camping supplies are limited and of marginal quality. Gas is not available in the parks. The nearest banks and sporting goods stores are in Reedley, 45 miles west off Hwy 180, and Three Rivers, 8 miles southwest on Hwy 198.

In Mineral King (see Mineral King section later this chapter) there's a ranger station (☎ 559-565-3768) with maps and a small mining exhibit, open 7 am to 3:30 pm daily from May to September. Three miles west of the ranger station, the Silver City Resort has showers, a small market and, usually, gas. It is open until mid-September. Mineral King Rd closes for the winter, from November to the end of May.

KINGS CANYON HWY

About 4 miles north of Grant Grove, the Kings Canyon Hwy enters Sequoia National Forest for its 2000-foot descent to Cedar Grove Village along the South Fork of the Kings River. Views from the road – massive granite ridges, peaks and domes in the distance, with logging roads and clear-cut as foreground – show a major difference

between national park and national forest land-use policies. They also give a glimpse of the stunning backcountry that makes the canyon a favorite place among serious hikers and climbers.

The canyon itself is the deepest in the lower 48 states at 8200 feet. At its west end is a world of rust, chartreuse and golden rock sloping down to the river in big chunks and bladelike ridges. Toward its east end, near Cedar Grove Village, walls are sheer and farther apart, and the valley gains a floor to become U-shaped. Six miles past Cedar Grove Village, Roads End is just that, with trailheads, overnight parking and a ranger kiosk (called the Backpackers Information Station; see Mineral King Hiking & Backpacking) that issues wilderness permits. The road into the valley, and trails leading from it, are the main attractions.

Hume Lake

Created in 1900 as a dam for logging operations, Hume Lake is now surrounded by a thick forest of second-growth pine, incense cedar and fir. The 3-mile road from Kings Canyon Hwy (about 7½ miles south of Grant Grove) to the lake is well marked and maintained but rarely used outside of hunting season (mid-September to November). A primitive USFS *campground* on the lake's south end has sites ($7) near the water.

Converse Basin

About 3½ miles north of Grant Grove, two marked forest service roads (about a mile apart) head west from the highway through what John Muir in *The Mountains of California* (1894) called 'the northernmost assemblage of Big Trees that may fairly be called a forest.' About five years after Muir's visit, lumbermen turned the forest into a sequoia cemetery. The first road goes to Converse Basin Grove, where the Chicago Stump stands. This is the remains of a tree that was supposedly bigger than the General Sherman tree (see Giant Forest & Lodgepole later this chapter) – until it was cut down and sent to Chicago for the 1892 Colombian Exposition, where disbelieving Easterners called it a 'California hoax.' The second road goes 2 miles north to Stump Meadow, where a concentration of stumps and fallen logs make good picnic platforms and photo subjects (especially with black and white film). A half mile past the meadow, a marked trail from the road goes to the Boole Tree, third-largest of the big trees and the only old one surviving in the area.

Boyden Cavern

This limestone cave has whimsically shaped formations – stalagmites, stalactites, domes – near its entrance. While interesting to visit, it can be skipped if you're planning to see Crystal Cave (see that section under Generals Hwy), which is larger and more impressive but requires more walking to see. The entrance/ticket booth (☎ 559-736-2708), 11 miles west of Cedar Grove on the highway, sells $6 tickets for the 45-minute tour from 10 am to 5 pm daily, as long as the road is open. Half a mile past the cave on the left (north), a road cut reveals an incredible black and white marble vein, a glimpse of what lies within most of the canyon walls.

GENERALS HWY

Built between 1921 and 1934, this road connects Grant Grove (in Kings Canyon National Park) to Giant Forest and the rest of Sequoia, giving access to the main visitor facilities, campgrounds and, most importantly, the trees everyone comes to see. Along its 48 miles between Grant Grove (in the north) and the Ash Mountain Entrance Station, the highway winds from about 6500 feet, where the big trees are, to chaparral-covered foothills at around 2000 feet. You can drive the full distance in about two hours and totally defeat the purpose of being here. You should allow for time out of the car – the only way to experience the trees. You could easily spend a day at each site along the way.

Grant Grove

When the bill to create Sequoia National Park was before Congress in 1890, DK Zumwalt, a resident of Visalia, persuaded the bill's sponsor to establish General Grant National Park around the small sequoia grove standing among clear-cut forests. The thumblike 4 sq miles, surrounded by Sequoia National Forest, stood as one of the smallest national parks for 50 years until being absorbed into Kings Canyon National Park in 1940.

From behind the excellent Grant Grove Visitor Center (see Orientation & Information under Kings Canyon & Sequoia National Parks) a road goes northeast 2 miles to **Panoramic Point**, a good spot to view Kings Canyon and start scenic hikes. A mile northwest from the village, the **General Grant Grove** encompasses the General Grant Tree, estimated to be over 2000 years old, and the Fallen Monarch, a massive tree which housed early pioneers, sheepherders and US Cavalry horses.

Redwood Mountain Grove

About 6 miles south of Grant Grove, this is the most extensive concentration of sequoias and one of the most pristine since it is not accessible by car. A 7-mile trail loops through the grove along Redwood Creek (flanked by azalea blossoms in May and June). The trees here are dense though not as huge as in Giant Forest. The trail is on the south side of the highway across from the Quail Flat turnoff, about ½ mile east of the Redwood Mountain Overlook (no facilities).

Giant Forest & Lodgepole

The Giant Forest area is Sequoia's core and a good destination for first-time visitors to the park. 'Discovered' in 1858 by Hale Tharp and named by John Muir in 1875, these three sq miles contain the parks' most massive trees, including General Sherman – the largest living tree on earth. At the north edge of the forest, **Lodgepole** has an excellent visitor center (☎ 559-565-3782) with natural history exhibits and a slide show. Five miles south, Sequoia's first guest facilities were recently removed from **Giant Forest Village** to protect the trees' fragile root system. A museum of the sequoias is scheduled to open here before 2000.

The centerpiece of Giant Forest, halfway between Lodgepole and Giant Forest Village, is the **General Sherman Tree** and

Congress Trail. A parking lot gives access to the short trail around the big tree. The 2-mile, paved Congress Trail passes impressive tree groupings such as the 'House' and 'Senate.' To get away from the crowds, continue to the 5-mile Trail of the Sequoias, which puts you in the heart of the forest.

There are also nice meadows in Giant Forest where you can see the trees in their entirety – top to bottom. At the south edge of Giant Forest Village, **Crescent Meadow Rd** leads to a lovely area (good for picnics) surrounded by meadows and several easy hikes, including one to Tharp's Log where Hale Tharp spent summers in a fallen tree. Before reaching Crescent Meadow, the road passes **Moro Rock**, a solid granite monolith often compared to Yosemite's Half Dome. The best part about this rock is the ¼-mile carved granite staircase that leads to its very top, where the view is unbeatable.

Crystal Cave

Discovered in 1918 by two fishermen, this cave extends around 3 miles into the earth and has formations estimated to be 10,000 years old. It was formed by an underground river that cut soft marble into large chambers and passageways which filled as the water table rose. Cascade Creek eventually eroded a mouth to the cave, draining the water and exposing the rock to air. Secondary formations – stalagmites and stalactites – grew on floors and ceilings in the form of curtains, domes, columns, 'cave bacon' and 'cave popcorn,' all of milky-white marble. The 50-minute cave tour covers a half mile of chambers and includes detailed interpretation. Tickets ($5) are available at the Lodgepole and Foothills visitor centers (not at the cave) and can sell out in summer; tours are every half hour from 11 am to 4 pm daily May to mid-September. The cave itself is northwest of Generals Hwy, up a steep and narrow road, about a 90 minutes' drive from both visitor centers; the ½-mile trail from the parking lot to the cave is mostly stairs.

Foothills

At about 2000 feet, the foothills surrounding the south end of Generals Hwy have a hot, dry environment compared to the rest of the park. Potwisha Indians lived here until the early 1900s, relying primarily on acorn meal as a staple. A vivid pictograph can be seen at Hospital Rock picnic area, once a Potwisha village site, below the sheer face of the rock that dominates the valley. Swimming holes abound along the Marble Fork of the Kaweah River, especially near Potwisha Campground (see Places to Stay); be careful of the powerful current.

MINERAL KING

The Mineral King Rd heads southeast from Hwy 198, between Three Rivers and the Ash Mountain Entrance at the south end of Sequoia National Park. This curvy, steep and narrow 25-mile road manages to weed out all but those with a mission. This is the park's backpacking mecca and a good place to find solitude year round. The valley sits at 7500 feet, surrounded by serrated peaks, lake basins and mountain passes that reach upwards of 11,000 feet. The metamorphic rock here is softer than the granite found in other parts of the Sierra, so the valley's walls are sloped instead of sheer and rusty red and purple in color. These odd characteristics led early explorers to think the area was loaded with precious metals. From the 1860s to 1890s, the valley (called Beulah) witnessed heavy silver mining and lumber activity. There are still remnants of old shafts and stamp mills around, though it takes some exploring to find them. In 1965, the Walt Disney Corporation proposed the development of a massive ski area in the valley, but the debate ended when Congress affixed the area to the national park.

Hiking & Backpacking

With trail mileage 10 times greater than road mileage, these parks are a backpacker's dream. Kings Canyon and Mineral King offer the best backcountry access, while the USFS Jenny Lakes Wilderness Area (accessible from Big Meadows Trailhead near Big Meadows Campground in neighboring Sequoia National Forest) has pristine meadows and lakes at lower elevations. Trails are usually open by mid-May.

SIERRA NEVADA

Wilderness permits, required for all overnight trips, are available at the ranger station nearest your trailhead. Free first-come, first-served permits are available the morning of departure or after 1 pm the afternoon before. To ensure you get to go where you want, when you want (especially in July and August), make a reservation ($10) at least three weeks in advance through Wilderness Permit Reservations (☎ 559-565-3708).

Topo maps and hiking guides are available at ranger stations and visitor centers. For trail conditions and backcountry information, call ☎ 559-565-3708. The Bearpaw Meadow Camp (see Places to Stay) offers an overnight destination for those without proper camping gear.

Kings Canyon You needn't bring a tent to enjoy the canyon's trails. There are numerous gentle paths along the valley floor which offer views of the enticing peaks on all sides. The Cedar Grove day-hike map ($2), available at the visitor center and market, is useful for these hikes. The Zumwalt Meadow Loop is really nice but often crowded, while the 1-mile connecting trail from Roads End to the meadow is less traveled: together they make a good trip. From Roads End, the Bubbs Creek trail offers a good view but climbs a set of nasty switchbacks before putting you next to the creek, while the Paradise Valley Trail follows the river the entire way. (Mist Falls, 4 miles from the trailhead, makes a good destination on this trail.) Both connect with the John Muir/Pacific Crest Trail to form the 43-mile Rae Lakes Loop – a very popular trip. The Copper Creek Trail heads north through somewhat lower terrain.

The Backpackers Information Station at Roads End has a posted map that shows mileage and the location of bear-proof food storage boxes (which may determine where you camp), and a very up-to-date information and message board. During peak season, wilderness permits for popular areas (such as Paradise Valley and the Rae Lakes Loop) are limited: rangers issue permits at the station from 7:15 am to 2:45 pm daily,

with permits for the following day not issued until 1 pm. The rest of the year permits are self-register.

Generals Hwy The day-hike map for Giant Forest, available at visitor centers ($2), is useful for making sense of the 40 miles of trails concentrated in its 3 sq miles. Trails here are quite gentle, with most of them along meadows and the forest floor. The 5-mile Trail of the Sequoias passes the most 'famous' named trees along the Congress Trail, then makes its way past Jeffrey pines, rock outcroppings and fern grottoes. With Moro Rock accessible by car, the Moro Rock Trail from Giant Forest Village stays uncrowded and offers views of the San Joaquin Valley. The High Sierra Trail, from the Crescent Meadow parking lot, is good for views east.

The Lodgepole area offers glacial scenery and some long hikes into high lake basins; trailheads are behind the visitor center at the back of the campground. The short and easy Tokopah Falls Trail skirts the Marble Fork of the Kaweah River and ends at a multilevel cascade. The Twin Lakes Trail climbs hard for the first mile, mellows out at Cahoon Meadow, then climbs along Clover Creek to the lakes at the foot of Siliman Crest – a good day's adventure.

Mineral King When the ranger station is closed, get topo maps at the Foothills Visitor Center (☎ 559-565-3341), 1 mile east of the Ash Mountain Entrance. Be aware of the high elevation, even on short hikes. Nice day hikes go to Crystal, Monarch, Mosquito and Eagle lakes. For long trips, locals recommend the Little Five Lakes Basin and, farther along the High Sierra Trail, Kaweah Gap, surrounded by the sawtooth Black Kaweah, Mt Stewart and Eagle Scout Peak – all above 12,000 feet.

Winter Activities

Grant Grove and Giant Forest offer great snowshoeing and cross-country skiing on marked trails. Since the Generals Hwy is not always open between the two, you're best to choose one or the other as a destination.

SIERRA NEVADA

Trails from Grant Grove connect with those in the Sequoia National Forest and some that are maintained by Montecito Sequoia Lodge (☎ 559-565-3388), a private resort on the Generals Hwy. Grant Grove Village (including the market and restaurant) is in full swing, with ski and snowshoe rentals, nightly programs at the visitor center, cabin and campground accommodations and naturalist-guided snowshoe walks on weekends only. At Wolverton, 2½ miles south of Lodgepole, you'll find a cafeteria, small market and snow play area. Ski activity here is at the Sequoia Ski Touring Center (☎ 559-565-3435), an excellent day-use facility with rentals, lessons and a retail shop.

Places to Stay

Accommodations in Kings Canyon National Park are managed by Kings Canyon Park Service (☎ 559-335-5500), a private concessionaire that handles all reservations. Starting in 1999, Sequoia's accommodations will be handled by Delaware North Parks Service (DNPS; ☎ 888-252-5757). Grant Grove is the only lodge open year round (others close from early October to May).

Camping

Campgrounds are first-come, first-served, with $10 sites, flush toilets, bear boxes, tables and fire pits. Exceptions are **Lodgepole** and **Dorst** where sites must be reserved through ☎ 800-365-2267. DNPS also operates the **Bearpaw Meadow Camp**, 11½ miles from Giant Forest on the High Sierra Trail, where hikers can stay for about $50 per night including showers, two meals, bedding and towels. The necessary reservations are made through the DNPS Reservations Department.

Kings Canyon In the national forest along Kings Canyon Hwy (before the road descends), the **Princess Campground** has $14 sites (reservable through Reserve USA ☎ 877-444-6777) next to a huge meadow. Down in the canyon at Cedar Grove are four NPS campgrounds, all near the village. **Sentinel** and **Sheep Creek** have riverside sites (arrive by noon on weekends to snag one) and thick incense cedar and pine groves nearby, while **Moraine** and **Canyon View** (tenters only) are above the river on a steep embankment with sparse ground cover.

Generals Hwy The biggest concentration of NPS campgrounds is in the Grant Grove area. Across from the visitor center, **Sunset** has hillside sites, some of which overlook the western foothills and San Joaquin Valley, while sites at **Azalea** are well dispersed with some bordering a meadow. **Crystal Springs** is the least attractive, with neither ground cover nor privacy. Campgrounds are first-come, first-served, with $12 sites.

South of Grant Grove on Sierra National Forest land, **Big Meadow Campground**, 6 miles northeast of the highway on a well-marked road, has two units with pit toilets and $10 sites. Just off the highway, **Stony Creek Campground** (☎ 800-280-2267) is one of the nicest around, with $11 creekside sites that get the afternoon sun, and flush toilets. Half of the 49 sites are reservable. A bit farther south, the NPS **Dorst Campground** is near the small Muir Grove of Sequoias and is quite secluded. **Lodgepole**, an enormous but very nice campground behind the Lodgepole Visitor Center and market, has sites along the Marble Fork of the Kaweah River, close to good fishing and hiking.

In the foothills, **Buckeye Flat** and **Potwisha** both have riverside sites near swimming holes. These are good in spring and fall, when the higher elevations get cold; they're hot and buggy in summer.

Mineral King There are two campgrounds on Mineral King Rd: **Atwell Mill**, about 5 miles west of the ranger station, and **Cold Springs**, across from the ranger station, which has two loops along the river and some secluded spots off the road; both have pit toilets and $7 sites.

Motels & Lodges

Kings Canyon Motel rooms at the **Cedar Grove Lodge** (☎ 559-335-5500) have a private bath and two big beds but hardly justify the $76 price. Though a bit isolated, the **Kings Canyon Lodge** (☎ 559-335-2405), on Kings Canyon Hwy, halfway between Cedar Grove Village and Grant Grove Village, is a better value. Rooms with private bath cost $69, cabins are $70 to $150 and sleep up to six people.

Generals Hwy **Grant Grove Lodge** (☎ 559-335-5500) has rustic cabins for around $40, housekeeping cabins with private bath for around $75 and a new motel with rooms starting at $85. Privately owned **Montecito Sequoia Lodge** (☎ 559-565-3388), 9 miles south of Grant Grove, is open to nightly guests from September to May, but often booked with camp groups in summer (if there's an extra bed, they'll gladly put you in it). It maintains its own cross-country ski trails and has a pool and hot tub. Spring and fall rates are around $85 per person, including breakfast and dinner; winter rates are $20 more, including lunch and a trail pass.

About halfway between Grant Grove and Giant Forest, **Stony Creek Lodge** (☎ 559-335-5500) has a big river-rock fireplace in its main room and old but nice motel rooms with private bath for $78 (closed September to May).

Mineral King **Silver City Resort** (☎ 559-561-3223), 3 miles west of the ranger station, has rustic cabins for around $75 and a charming little cafe with excellent pie – good thing, since that's all that they serve on Tuesday and Thursday. It's open from late May to early September.

Places to Eat
The **Lodgepole Market** is the largest in the parks, though the **Grant Grove Market** (open year round) is your best bet after September.

The **Grant Grove Restaurant**, open from 7 am to 8 pm year round, has a comfortably average coffee shop atmosphere, with food to match (under $10). From May to October, the **Lodgepole Deli** serves fresh salads, sandwiches and pizza until 8 pm ($5 to $12), and has a nice patio.

Kings Canyon Lodge (☎ 559-335-2405), on Kings Canyon Hwy, halfway between Cedar Grove Village and Grant Grove Village, has a charming cafe with breakfast and lunch ($4 to $7) daily, dinner (around $8) on weekends and a full bar. The only real choice in Kings Canyon is the **Cedar Grove Snack Bar**, which serves fast food for under $5.

Getting There & Away
The parks spread from the western Sierra Nevada foothills east to the Sierra Nevada crest, though roads only penetrate the very western portion. Hwy 180 makes a gentle climb from Fresno to the Big Stump Entrance Station, 4 miles west of Grant Grove; from here you can go north into Kings Canyon or south along Generals Hwy. In the south, Hwy 198 runs from Visalia through Three Rivers past Mineral King Rd to the Ash Mountain Entrance Station, at the south end of the Generals Hwy. In winter, Generals Hwy is often closed between Grant Grove and Giant Forest, making Route 245 (west of the park) the best connection between the two.

THREE RIVERS
• **population 3100** • **elevation 6000 feet**
Eight miles southwest of the Ash Mountain Entrance Station, this little river town is an access hub for the parks and weekend getaway for San Joaquin Valley residents. Sierra Drive, the main drag, is lined with woodsy motels, stores and artists' studios and galleries. Midway through town, Three Rivers Village has a post office, good pizza parlor and the best market (open 8 am to 6 pm daily, until 5 pm Sunday) for buying supplies en route to the parks.

The Naturedome (☎ 559-561-6560), 42249 Sierra Drive, is a geodesic dome (built in harmonious convergence with nature spirits) with a large deck overlooking the Kaweah River. It features local artists' work, live music and workshops on everything from meditation to finger painting. The River Envy Iris Farm (☎ 559-561-3630), 43429 Sierra Drive, produces a variety of irises, including some genetically engineered to smell like grape juice and orange popsicles! The farm is open to the public from April 1 to June 4 (prime blooming season), during which the display grounds bloom with a rainbow of colors, and staff is on hand to answer questions. During the Three Rivers Redbud Festival, held the first weekend in May, artisans set up booths along Sierra Drive, and hundreds of people converge for general merrymaking.

Eastern Sierra

The Sierra Nevada's eastern slope rises abruptly from the Owens Valley Floor to jagged 14,000-foot peaks marking the Sierra Nevada crest. Many consider this the best side of the Sierra because it offers direct access to alpine scenery, high mountain lakes and lush meadows. Creeks and rivers that tumble from the mountains into the Owens River carve canyons which serve as infiltration points to the otherwise daunting barrier. Most of these drainages are designated national recreation areas, with developed campgrounds, small resorts and well-marked trailheads. Roads are usually paved, and some are plowed in winter, giving access to backcountry ski trails. Most trails cross the Sierra Nevada crest, accessing wilderness areas and national parks in the west.

The arid Owens Valley lies at the base of the mountains, with the ancient White Mountains, nearly as high but much older than the Sierra, to the east. Once as prosperous as the Central Valley in agriculture, Owens Valley is now a desertlike wasteland, drained by the California Aqueduct to provide water to Los Angeles.

For those who don't enjoy the outdoors, the Eastern Sierra holds little in the way of diversions, and US 395 – the main route running along the eastern flanks of the mountains – is a long haul that is often brutally hot in summer.

Orientation

The Eastern Sierra extends from Bridgeport in the north to Hwy 178 in the south. The mountains are lowest and easiest to access north of Bishop, where Mammoth Lakes provides a good destination for hikers, bikers and skiers; Bridgeport is popular with anglers. From Bishop south, where the peaks are highest and the Owens Valley slopes gently downwards, getting into the mountains often requires a long drive up curvy, narrow roads. The easiest access to high, dramatic scenery is from Bishop Creek (near Bishop) and Whitney Portal (near Lone Pine). South of Lone Pine, the Owens Valley tilts south while the Sierra Nevada tops out along peaks over 14,000 feet, including 14,497 foot Mt Whitney – the highest in the contiguous US.

Two-lane US 395 runs the length of the range. Well-marked roads head west into the mountains. Little towns along the highway offer accommodations, food, camping, gasoline and supplies. In winter, the road is nearly deserted (unless the ski resorts at Mammoth and June Lake have received fresh snow) and many facilities in the smaller towns are closed.

Pack Trips

Trails to the Eastern Sierra's high country are short, steep and often rocky – better navigated by horse or mule than by hiking with a heavy pack. Several outfitters offer 'spot trips' and full-service trips, including Agnes Meadows Pack Train (☎ 760-934-2345, 800-292-7758) in Mammoth Lakes; Bishop Pack Outfitters (☎ 760-873-4785) in Bishop; and Rock Creek Pack Station (☎ 760-935-4493 in summer, 760-872-8331 in winter), also in Bishop. Also see the relevant entry in the Activities chapter.

Wilderness Permits

If you're planning an overnight trip to the John Muir, Ansel Adams, Golden Trout and Hoover wilderness areas, you will need to pick up a wilderness permit. These are not needed for the Inyo Mountains or South Sierra wilderness, unless you're headed for a place that does require permits. Trail quotas are in effect for 37 trails in the Inyo National Forest from late June to mid-September. Permits may be picked up at the ranger stations or reserved at ☎ 888-374-3773 daily 8 am to 4:30 pm. For details about trails in the Mt Whitney Zone, see the boxed text later this chapter.

Getting Around

Greyhound buses travel US 395 between Los Angeles and Carson City (Nevada), stopping in Lone Pine, Independence, Big Pine, Bishop, Mammoth Lakes, Lee Vining and Bridgeport.

Each summer several hiker/backpacker shuttles are operated by sporting goods stores and/or climbing schools. Your best bet is to ask at a store in Bridgeport, Mammoth Lakes, Bishop or Lone Pine. Backpacker Shuttle Service (☎ 760-872-2721), in Bishop, has a good reputation. Occasionally, resorts and lodges also provide rides to/from their location to the nearest town for a negotiable fee.

BRIDGEPORT

• population 500 • elevation 6500 feet

Bridgeport is the first town of any importance between Carson City and Mammoth Lakes. Its main street is as American as apple pie, with classic old storefronts and an impressive 1880 courthouse trimmed in red and surrounded by a gracious lawn. A few blocks away in the old Bridgeport schoolhouse, the Mono County Museum (☎ 760-932-5281) has one of the better historical collections in the Eastern Sierra. It's open 10 am to 5 pm daily May to October; free.

Bridgeport is famous among fisherfolk who flock to Virginia Lakes, the Bridgeport Reservoir, the East Walker River and Twin Lakes Bridgeport for record catches of brown and rainbow trout, carp and perch. The other main attractions here are hot springs – for those who aren't afraid of nudity or washboard roads – and Bodie State Historic Park, one of California's best-preserved ghost towns.

Orientation & Information

Hwy 395 jogs east through Bridgeport as Main St, with the turnoff to Twin Lakes at the west end of town and the turnoff to Bridgeport Lake at the east end. Hwy 270 to Bodie heads east from US 395 south of the city limits. The Bridgeport Ranger Station (☎ 760-932-7070), just south of town on the highway, has posted maps and issues permits (required from July 1 to August 15) for the Hoover Wilderness, accessible by trail from Twin Lakes. The best place for fishing information is Ken's Sporting Goods (☎ 760-932-7707), 258 Main St, which has lots of maps, plus fishing, hunting and camping gear.

Places to Stay & Eat

All businesses are on Main St. Built as a stage stop on the road to Bodie, the *Bridgeport Inn* (☎ 760-932-7380) has been in operation since 1877. Nostalgic 'spirits' allegedly cruise the halls, though the rooms are purportedly 'ghost free.' Rates are $49 to $65, and there's a charming bar and restaurant.

The *Silver Maple Inn* (☎ 760-932-7383) has friendly owners, well-kept grounds and nice rooms for $60 to $80. From late October to May, the *Walker River Lodge* (☎ 760-932-7021) is one of only two places open. They have a heated pool, hot tub and rooms for $80 to $120 in summer, from $70 in winter. Also open year round is the *Best Western Ruby Inn* (☎ 760-932-7241), across from the courthouse, which charges $75 to $135 in summer, $65 to $95 the rest of the year.

About 8 miles south of town, off the road to Twin Lakes on Robinson Creek, *Doc and Al's Robinson Creek Resort* (☎ 760-932-7051) has new cabins that sleep 4 to 10 people ($65 to $96), with showers and kitchens, and rustic cabins with a communal shower and toilet ($40). Rental trailers go for $47 to $60. Campsites cost $13 ($17 with a full hookup) with use of all facilities.

Locals drink, play pool and eat pizza at *Rhino's Bar & Grille* (☎ 760-932-7345) but recommend the *Virginia Creek Settlement* (☎ 760-932-7780), 14 miles south on US 395, for good steaks and Italian food for around $12.

TWIN LAKES

With most places open for fishing season from June to November, this is primarily a summer destination. It's revered for its trout, Kamloop and Kokanee salmon, as well as its trails to the Hoover Wilderness and the eastern, lake-riddled reaches of Yosemite National Park.

SIERRA NEVADA

The road to Twin Lakes intersects US 395 at Bridgeport and heads 12 miles through pastures and foothills, past several nice campgrounds on Robinson Creek, before reaching the lower lake. Here, a dirt road goes south to *Lower Twin Lakes* and *Sawmill*, both USFS campgrounds with pit toilets, water and $10 sites on the lake's quiet east shore. At the west end of the upper lake, the road ends at *Mono Village* (☎ 760-932-7071), a huge affair that offers cheap but fairly crowded accommodations, boat rental and launch facilities and a greasy spoon restaurant. They're open from April to October and have a huge campground with $11 tent sites and $17 hookups. Motel rooms range from $50 to $60 and cabins, all with private bath, are $55 to $115. Trailheads begin behind Mono Village and at the terminus of the Lower Twin Lake/Sawmill Campground Rd, which has a day-use parking lot.

BUCKEYE HOT SPRINGS

These are the area's best hot springs and some the hardest to find. The springs surface atop a steep embankment above Eagle Creek and trickle down into pools outlined with rocks. The largest pool, right next to the creek, is cold when the creek is high. A smaller one, next to a solo tree at the top of the embankment, commands a great view of the surrounding forest. Buckeye Hot Springs Rd runs between US 395 (north of Bridgeport) and Twin Lakes Rd, which originates in Bridgeport and goes west; the springs are about 11 miles from both, at a turnout on the south side of the road. West of the springs, at a bridge spanning Eagle Creek, a road goes 2 miles to the USFS *Buckeye Campground* with tables, fire grates, potable water, pit toilets and $7 sites. You can camp for free in undeveloped spots along Eagle Creek on both sides of the bridge.

BODIE STATE HISTORIC PARK

The combination of its remote location and unrestored buildings makes Bodie one of California's most authentic and best preserved ghost towns. Gold was discovered along Bodie Creek in 1859, and within 20 years the place grew from a rough mining camp to an even rougher mining town, with a population of 10,000 and a reputation for lawlessness with gambling halls, brothels and no fewer than 65 saloons. More than $100 million worth of ore came from the surrounding hills, but when the gold supply petered out, people moved on (mostly to the Comstock Lode in Nevada) and left Bodie's buildings to the elements. Five percent of them still remain, maintained by the State Park Service, but untainted by restoration.

An excellent museum and visitor center (☎ 760-647-6445), open 10 am to 6 pm daily from May to September, has historical maps, exhibits and free daily guided tours. The park is open 8 am to 7 pm late May to September, otherwise to 4 pm. Entry is $5 per vehicle. Hwy 270, which connects Bodie and US 395 (13 miles), is unpaved for the last 3 miles and often closed in winter after heavy snowfall. There are no developed campgrounds, but dispersed camping in the surrounding area is allowed with a campfire permit, available from the Bridgeport Ranger Station (☎ 760-932-7070).

VIRGINIA LAKES & LUNDY LAKE

South of Bridgeport, US 395 parallels Virginia Creek until it reaches Conway Summit (8138 feet) and drops down into the Mono Basin. The view south from the summit shows the area's topography, with Mono Lake, backed by the Mono Craters, backed by June and Mammoth mountains – all products of volcanic activity.

Just north of Conway Summit, the Virginia Lakes Rd heads west along Virginia Creek to a cluster of lakes flanked by Dunberg Peak and Black Mountain. A trailhead at the end of the road gives access to the Hoover Wilderness and the Pacific Crest Trail which continues down Cold Canyon to Yosemite National Park. There is a cluster of lakes at around 9000 feet elevation 2½ to 5 miles from the trailhead) said to have some of the Eastern Sierra's best fishing. In high snow seasons, the small cascades that fall from lake to lake turn into crashing waterfalls. *Virginia Lakes Resort* (☎ 760-647-

6484), at the road's end, has snug cabins, a cafe and a general store that sells fishing tackle and licenses.

Between Conway Summit and Mono Lake, Hwy 167 heads east to Hawthorne, Nevada; Lundy Lake Rd goes about 5 miles west to Lundy Lake. This is a gorgeous spot, often overlooked and thus uncrowded. The lake is long and narrow, with steep canyons – great for hiking – feeding its west end. A mining town sat above the lake's northwest end from 1879 to 1884, evident from the old mining equipment and tailings scattered about. The *Lundy Lake Resort* has cabins costing $45 to $65, tent ($7.50) and RV spaces ($10), showers, laundry, boat rentals and a store. A few miles past the resort, on a good dirt road, is trailhead parking for the Hoover Wilderness with self-register wilderness permits. From here you can head over Lundy Pass to Saddlebag Lake, 2 miles north of Tioga Pass and just outside Yosemite National Park.

MONO LAKE

This glistening expanse of alkaline water that spreads lazily across the white-hot desert landscape is North America's second-oldest lake. Though the basin and lake are ice age remnants, formed more than 700,000 years ago, the area's most interesting features come from volcanic-related activity. Appearing like dripped sand castles on and near the lake shore, Mono's tufa (pronounced TOO-fah) towers form when calcium-bearing freshwater springs bubble up through alkaline water.

The Mono Basin Scenic Area Visitor's Center & Ranger Staten (☎ 760-647-3044), just north of Lee Vining off US 395, has a beautiful view of the lake, good interpretive displays and information. It's closed Tuesday and Wednesday. Also a worthwhile stop, the Mono Lake Committee Visitor Center (☎ 760-647-6595, www.monolake.org) in Lee Vining on the west side of US 395, has maps, a great selection of books and a free 15-minute slide show about the lake's natural and political history. You'll find environmental activists here who are passionate about what Mono Lake means. They also offer interpretive talks and hikes, photo excursions and canoe tours. Hours are 9 am to 5 pm daily in winter, to 10 pm in summer.

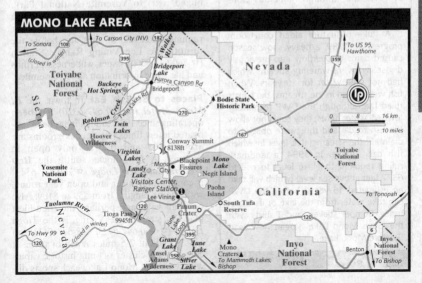

MONO LAKE AREA

SIERRA NEVADA

There are examples of tufa towers all around the lake, but the best concentration is at the **South Tufa Reserve** ($2 fee, Golden Passports honored) on the lake's southern rim. Here a mile-long interpretive trail explains the towers' formation. The best place for swimming is at Navy Beach, just east of here, though there are no showers

Mono Lake

In 1941, the City of Los Angeles Department of Water and Power (DWP) bought most of the Mono Basin and diverted four of the five streams feeding Mono Lake to the California Aqueduct to provide water to Los Angeles. Over time, the lake level dropped 40 feet and doubled in salinity. In 1976, David Gaines began to study the environmental concerns surrounding the lake's depletion and found that it would totally dry up within about 20 years. As the major breeding ground for California gulls and habitat of eared grebes and red-necked phalaropes, this was a major threat to California's bird population. Gaines formed the Mono Lake Committee in 1979 and, through numerous campaigns and court battles, managed to win water from the City of LA.

A fluke of nature aided courtroom progress. In 1989, a heavy snow season caused dams to overflow into previously dry spillways, re-watering streams which had not seen water for 10 years. When fish were found in the streams, the courts ruled that although the DWP technically 'owned' water rights, they could not allow the fish to die and thus were obliged to maintain the streams at a level in which fish can survive. In 1994, a landmark ruling required the lake level to rise to 6377 feet above sea level (which will take an estimated 15 years) before the DWP can take water from the lake or its tributaries. Bumper stickers and T-shirts with the 'Save Mono Lake' slogan now read 'Restore Mono Lake.'

and the salt deposits forming on your skin can be quite irritating.

Away from the lakeshore, between the South Tufa Reserve and Hwy 120, is **Panum Crater**, the youngest (about 640 years old) and smallest of the Mono Craters which string south to Mammoth Mountain. There is a nice trail around the crater rim (about 30 to 45 minutes), and a short but steep 'plug trail' that puts you at the crater's center among rock formations in shiny black obsidian and pumice stone.

On the north shore are the **Black Point Fissures**, narrow crags that opened when Black Point's lava mass cooled and contracted about 13,000 years ago. Reaching the fissures requires a substantial – but worthwhile – hike (east of the County Park off US 395 or south of Hwy 167), that is usually hot and very dry. Check in at one of the visitor centers before heading out.

Lee Vining
• population 315 • elevation 6780 feet

This is Mono Lake's utilitarian addition, where you can eat, sleep and gas up. It is also where Hwy 120 heads west over Tioga Pass (closed in winter; see 'Impassable Tioga Pass' boxed text) to Yosemite National Park. There are six creekside campgrounds just west of town, off Hwy 120, with pit toilets, running water and $7 sites. Just before the turnoff, the Lee Vining Ranger Station (☎ 760-647-3000) issues wilderness permits and has some information about Yosemite.

Places to Stay & Eat In town, the *El Mono Motel* (☎ 760-647-6310) has been operating since 1927, though it has been renovated a few times (no phones); rooms are around $65 and they're only open in summer. A few blocks south, the *Best Western Lakeview Lodge* (☎ 760-647-6543) is considerably nicer and open year round, with rooms ranging from $59 to $109. Also open all year, and perhaps the friendliest place to stay in Lee Vining, is the *Tioga Lodge* (☎ 760-647-6423, 888-647-6423), on US 395, about 2½ miles north of town. It consists of a cluster of snug historic cabins with a view of Mono Lake; each sports different decor, from rustic to frilly. There's a restaurant, though it was closed when we visited in winter. Rates are a reasonable $55 in winter, going up to $70 to $95 in season.

Bodie Mike's Pizza (☎ 760-647-6432) is a good night spot for pizza, salad and beer (under $10); open summer only. For big breakfasts, sumptuous sandwiches (around $7) and plenty of local color, go to *Nicely's Restaurant* (☎ 760-647-6477). *Walking Taco* (☎ 760-647-6477) is a casual Mexican eatery with cheap burritos and fresh tacos.

JUNE LAKE LOOP
Between Mono Lake and Mammoth Lakes, Hwy 158 makes a 16-mile loop west of US 395. This scenic route passes Grant, Silver, Gull and June lakes, flanked by massive Carson Peak to the west and Reversed Peak to the east. The area could detain outdoorsy types for a good week, though it's just as easily a nice half-hour detour off US 395. All of the lakes are good for trout fishing, and Grant and Silver lakes both have free public boat launches. June Lake Village, a cute gathering of small businesses, is at the south end of the route. The mountains immediately west are part of the Ansel Adams Wilderness, which runs into Yosemite National Park, easily reached by trail. There's an unstaffed information kiosk at the loop's southern end entrance.

June Mountain Ski Area
On the south end of the loop near June Lake, this resort (☎ 760-648-7733) is friendly and less crowded than Mammoth. Rising some 10,135 feet above sea level, June Mountain offers 500 acres of skiing with eight lifts, including two high-speed quads and 2600 vertical feet. Lift tickets are $40, $30 for teens and $20 for children.

Activities
At Silver Lake, the Frontier Pack Station (☎ 760-648-7701 in summer, 760-873-7971 in winter) has one-hour rides for $20 and weeklong trips to Yosemite for about $500. Silver Lake Resort (☎ 760-648-7525) rents boats and fishing tackle for $8/hour and also sells fishing licenses. Between the resort and

pack station, the Rush Creek Trailhead is a departure point for wilderness trips with a day-use parking lot, posted maps and self-registration permits. From June to October a wilderness permit quota is in effect. People embarking on multiday hikes should reserve a permit through the wilderness permit hotline at ☎ 888-374-3773. However, if the day's quota (currently 34) hasn't been filled with advance reservations, people without permits may pick one up on a first-come, first-served basis from the kiosk at the trailhead from 8 am to 4 pm daily. Gem and Agnew Lakes make spectacular day hikes, while Thousand Island and Emerald Lake (both on the Pacific Crest/John Muir Trail) are good overnight destinations.

Places to Stay & Eat
The *Silver Lake Campground* has grassy sites ($7) next to Rush Creek and is near the Silver Lake Resort. There are two campgrounds on June Lake, each with running water and $14 sites: the *June Lake Campground* is small and shady but crowded; the *Oh Ridge Campground*, on an arid ridge above the lake's south end, has nice views and beach access but not much shade. Reservations may be made through Parknet at ☎ 800-444-7275. Across from Oh Ridge is a private campground with a store, hot showers ($3) and $12 sites.

The *Silver Lake Resort* (☎ 760-648-7525) is a locus of activity, with a store and woodsy cabins for between $60 to $185. Their cafe serves breakfast and lunch only. Between Silver and Gull lakes, the *Fern Creek Lodge* (☎ 760-648-7722, 800-621-9146) isn't lakeside, but has nice cabins with kitchen and fireplace for around $48 (up to $200 for up to eight people). They have a well-stocked store and a restaurant and a laundry are across the street.

In June Lake Village, the *Heidelberg Inn* (☎ 760-648-7718) has an old Bavarian exterior with modern American rooms for around $80 a night during off-season, and a couple of large suites. Summer and winter rates are from $99 to $119. *Boulder Lodge* (☎ 760-648-7533) has a pool, tennis courts and worn-in rooms and cabins starting at

$49. The **Tiger Bar** (☎ 760-648-7551) is *the* place to be in the evening (especially during ski season) for burgers, fish and beer – though they also do good breakfasts and lunch.

MAMMOTH LAKES

Mammoth Lakes is mostly just called 'Mammoth,' an indication of how much attention the lakes themselves get. While the pocket of alpine lakes west of town are as beautiful as any in the Sierra, Mammoth Mountain, with its world-class skiing and summertime mountain bike park, attracts more visitors. The town is basically a conglomeration of shopping centers and condominiums, with no particular center, spread over a few sq miles. Its lack of charm is made up for by its friendly, laid-back atmosphere, good restaurants, not-*too*-pricey accommodations and the stellar surroundings.

But something's afoot in Mammoth and, if planners have their way (and it looks like they will), Mammoth will soon become one of North America's premier ski resorts, offering up serious competition to Whistler, Keystone, Aspen and Vail (see boxed text).

Orientation & Information

At the Mammoth Lakes turnoff from US 395, Rte 203 heads west for 3 miles to central Mammoth. At the first major intersection, Rte 203 becomes Main St, and Old Mammoth Rd heads south (left) to Old Mammoth, the original town site. Main St spills into Lake Mary Rd, which leads to Mammoth Basin and several lakes. Heading north (right) from the intersection, Minaret Rd leads to the Mammoth Mountain Ski Area and to Devils Postpile beyond. Most businesses are on Main St between the intersections and south on Old Mammoth Rd where it crosses Meridian Blvd.

The Mammoth Lakes Ranger Station (☎ 760-924-5500) and Mammoth Lakes Visitors Bureau (☎ 760-934-2712, 800-367-6572, 888-466-2666, fax 760-934-7066, www.visit mammoth.com) share a building on the north side of Hwy 203, just before Old Mammoth Rd. This one-stop information center issues wilderness permits and has accommodations and campground listings, road and trail condition updates and information on local attractions. A smaller visitors bureau is inside the Minaret Village Mall at the Old Mammoth Rd/Meridian Blvd junction. Both are open 8 am to 5 pm daily. Also at the shopping center are a bank, supermarket, movie theater and bookstore. A good source for up-to-date information about Mammoth is the free weekly *Mammoth Times* (www.mammothtimes.com) distributed around town.

Mammoth Hospital (☎ 760-934-3311), 185 Sierra Park Rd, has a 24-hour emergency room.

Historic Mammoth

Believe it or not, Mammoth did not spring to life with the invention of the chairlift. It was originally a mining and lumber town with stamp mills, sawmills, flumes, waterwheels and a rough-and-tumble main street of tent cabins and saloons. Most of the town, on the west end of Old Mammoth Rd, was burned to cinders, but a 14-foot flywheel and some other old structures remain. The free **Mammoth Museum** (☎ 760-934-6918), just east of where Old Mammoth Rd turns abruptly west, has photographs of the original settlement and gives out tour maps for the old town. It's open 9:30 am to 4:30 pm daily June through October.

Mammoth's origin as a ski resort had humble beginnings in the 1930s when just a few adventurous souls made use of simple rope tows installed around the mountain. One of these pioneers was Dave McCoy, who fell in love with area and eventually built up the destination ski resort that Mammoth Mountain has become today. The first chairlift went up in 1955. In 1986, McCoy also bought adjacent June Mountain (see earlier this chapter). Ultimately, he hopes to connect both ski areas.

Mammoth Mountain Ski Area

This is a true recreationist's resort, where playing hard and having fun are more important than whose name is on your ski parka. For a 24-hour snow report, call ☎ 888-766-9778. The mountain (☎ 760-934-0745,

MAMMOTH LAKES

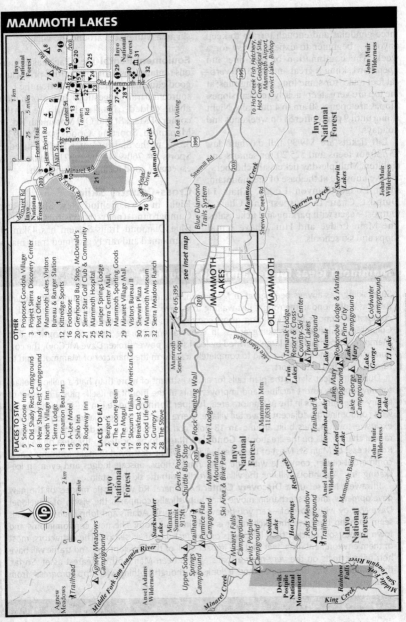

PLACES TO STAY
5 Snow Goose Inn
7 Old Shady Rest Campground
8 New Shady Rest Campground
10 North Village Inn
11 Sierra Lodge
13 Cinnamon Bear Inn
15 A-Lee Motel
19 Shilo Inn
23 Rodeway Inn

PLACES TO EAT
2 Berger's
6 The Looney Bean
14 The Mogul
17 Slocum's Italian & American Grill
18 Breakfast Club
22 Good Life Cafe
24 Grumpy's
28 The Stove

OTHER
1 Proposed Gondola Village
3 Project Sierra Discovery Center
4 Post Office
9 Mammoth Lakes Visitors Bureau & Ranger Station
12 Kittredge Sports
16 Footloose
20 Greyhound Bus Stop, McDonald's
21 Sierra Star Golf Club & Community
25 Mammoth Hospital
26 Juniper Springs Lodge
27 Sierra Center Mall,
   Mammoth Sporting Goods
29 Minaret Village Mall,
   Visitors Bureau II
30 Sherwin Plaza
31 Mammoth Museum
32 Sierra Meadows Ranch

SIERRA NEVADA

888-462-6668, www.mammoth-mtn.com), an inactive volcanic peak, has 27 chairlifts, three gondolas and enough terrain to keep anyone – beginner to expert – busy for a week. The combination of tree-line and open bowl skiing is great and the 3100 vertical feet make for some long cruising runs; at the top are very steep, nearly vertical, slopes. Slopes are open 8:30 am to 4 pm daily. Night skiing until 9 pm is offered on weekends and holidays.

Lift tickets are $49/39 full day/half day, $37/30 for teens and $25/20 for seniors and children. Multiple-day tickets are cheaper.

Five hubs are at the base of the mountain: Main Lodge, Canyon Lodge, Chair 14 Outpost, Chair 15 Outpost and Chair 2 Outpost – each with parking and ticket sales. The Main Lodge and Hut 2 have rental shops and ski schools.

Since parking lots fill quickly, it's best to use the free shuttle buses that connect the ski area with places around the village.

Equipment Rental The village has numerous rental shops with competitive prices and good equipment; their staff is often the best source for trail suggestions and information about guided trips. Try Footloose, at the corner of Main St and Old Mammoth Rd, or Mammoth Sporting Goods (☎ 760-934-3239), in the Sierra Center Mall. Kittredge Sports (☎ 760-934-7566), 3218 Main St, is especially good for backpacking gear.

Cross-Country Skiing

Right in town, behind New Shady Rest Campground (near the visitors bureau), Blue Diamond Trails System has 43km of ungroomed and rarely groomed trails main-

Mammoth Ideas for a Mammoth Mountain

Sure, skiing has always been great in Mammoth, but many have long regarded the quaint town as a diamond in the rough, just waiting to receive its final polish. In comes Intrawest, a corporation famous for revitalizing resort communities and operator of Whistler (in British Columbia) and five other skiing areas. In cooperation with the town of Mammoth and Mammoth Mountain (still largely owned by local skiing power broker Dave McCoy), the corporation has come up with a plan to completely transform the character of Mammoth and to turn it into a first-rate resort.

Dubbed Project Sierra, the plan calls for an investment of more than half a million dollars for new upscale resort facilities and improvements at the mountain itself, plus a number of luxury developments in the Mammoth area. **Juniper Springs Lodge** is a ski-in/ski-out lodge with condominiums adjacent to a retail village. **Sierra Star** is a master-planned community of exclusive town homes built around an 18-hole golf course and a Nordic center. The most radical change will be the creation of **Gondola Village**, to be located in the area on Minaret Rd just east of Main St. Most of the older buildings will be destroyed to make room for a new commercial center, complete with fine restaurants, shops, upscale lodges and even an ice-skating rink. A gondola will link the village directly with the ski mountain.

Intrawest has set up a **Discovery Center** on Minaret Rd with scale models of the new developments and a saccharine movie that hubristically compares the vision of developer Dave McCoy with those of – can you believe this? – Ansel Adams and John Muir! Few locals seem to mind this, and the excitement is high in Mammoth. The new condominiums and town homes sold quicker than lift tickets on the first day of ski season. The detractors, most of them environmentalists, fear that the impact of all of this development and traffic will have horrifying effects on the very nature that's always been Mammoth's greatest asset. So far, their influence has been minor, and it looks as though nothing will stop 'progress' from steamrolling Mammoth.

tained by the USFS. South of town on Old Mammoth Rd (where it veers west), Sierra Meadows Ranch (☎ 760-934-6161) has 25km of groomed track in a wide open meadow (good for beginners) with views of Mammoth Mountain and Mammoth Rock. The Tamarack Cross Country Ski Center (☎ 760-934-2442), 2½ miles outside of town on Lake Mary Rd, has 30km of groomed track and skating lanes, marked backcountry trails and a rustic lodge (see Places to Stay) with rentals and lessons; day passes and rentals are $15 each.

Hiking

There are three main trailheads, all with parking lots and access to good day hikes and longer trails over the Sierra crest. Horseshoe Lake, in Mammoth Basin, is at a high elevation so you needn't hike far to reach alpine scenery; it has a good trail down into Reds Meadow. Also in Mammoth Basin, Lake Mary gives easy access to small alpine lakes backed by the impressive Mammoth Crest. Trails from Agnew Meadows (toward Devils Postpile, accessible by shuttle bus) go north along the Pacific Crest/John Muir Trail into the Minaret Wilderness, surrounded by some of the Sierra's most stunning sawtooth peaks and cirque lakes. In winter, many of these trails (especially to Reds Meadow) are popular with backcountry skiers.

Other Activities

In summer, the Main Lodge at Mammoth Mountain has a **rock-climbing wall**, orienteering courses and outdoor concerts, while the ski runs are used as a **Mountain Bike Park** ($20 lift ticket, $35 bike rentals). This is the site of the NORBA Championship Series Mountain Bike Races in mid-July, the fastest mountain bike race on the circuit. **Fishing** is a popular activity, though you will need a license, available at sports shops.

Places to Stay

Mammoth has lots of lodging options, but prices fluctuate wildly. In general, summer rates are about 25% lower than those listed below, and midweek stays any time of year are cheaper than weekend stays. Rates sky-

rocket during holiday periods. Many motels and lodges also offer packages that include lift tickets and are often a good deal. The visitors bureau does not make reservations but operates a lodging referral at ☎ 888-466-2666.

Camping The USFS 'Campground Schedule,' available at the ranger station, lists campground fees, capacities and elevations. The nicest campgrounds are on the shores of *Twin Lakes*, *Lake Mary* and *Lake George*. They're first-come, first-served, with flush toilets and $13 sites. There are seven USFS campgrounds off Minaret Rd, out toward Devils Postpile, on the Middle Fork of the San Joaquin River. All of these offer great fishing and hiking and cost $12. They're first-come, first-served and fill up quickly. The 21-site campground at *Devils Postpile* itself is $8. Less picturesque but closer to town are *New Shady Rest* and *Old Shady Rest* campgrounds behind the visitors bureau on Rte 203. These have $12 first-come, first-served sites, flush toilets, ranger programs and lots of kids. All campgrounds, except New Shady Rest, are open from late June through October only.

Condominiums Mammoth abounds with holiday condominiums, rustic to luxurious, often owned by wealthy Southern Californians as an investment and occasional getaway. Condo stays are an excellent and affordable option, especially for groups of four or more. For availability, contact Mammoth Reservations Bureau (☎ 800-462-5571) or Central Reservation of Mammoth (☎ 800-321-3261).

Motels , Inns & Lodges The *North Village Inn* (☎ 760-934-2525, 800-257-3781), at the corner of Lake Mary and Minaret Rds, is a rambling lodge with snug cabins starting at $39. The *A-Lee Motel* (☎ 760-934-6709, 1548 Tavern Rd) is another inexpensive lodging option, with no-frills rooms costing $54 to $77. A bit nicer, the *Rodeway Inn* (☎ 760-934-2515, fax 760-934-7319, 164 Old Mammoth Rd) has 156 rooms, a cozy lobby, pool, hot tub and sauna, and rooms and suites that go for $49 to $159 in winter, and start at $64 in summer. The **Sierra Lodge** (☎ 760-934-8881, 800-356-5711 in Southern California), on Main St, halfway between Old Mammoth and Minaret Rds, is a good choice, with new rooms costing $85 to $130.

Hard to beat for comfort and amenities is the **Shilo Inn** (☎ 760-934-4500, 800-222-2244, 2963 Main St), near the town entrance. The spacious lobby has a crackling fireplace, the spacious mini-suites have microwaves and refrigerators, and they provide a free, filling continental breakfast. The best part, though, is the large fitness area, complete with workout room, a large indoor pool, hot tub, steam room and sauna. Rates are reasonable, ranging from $105 to $135 in winter and $85 to $119 in summer.

On the shore of Lower Twin Lake, **Tamarack Lodge Resort** (☎ 760-934-2442, 800-237-6879) is charming, rustic and run by friendly people. The cozy lodge has a fireplace, bar and reading area and excellent restaurant. Accommodations are in the lodge or in cabins scattered about the resort area. It's a popular cross-country ski spot. Winter rates are $55 to $145, cabins start at $90.

B&Bs **Snow Goose Inn** (☎ 760-934-2660, 800-874-7368, fax 760-934-5655, 57 Forest Trail) pampers guests with lavish breakfasts and evening appetizers and also has an outdoor hot tub. Rates are $78 to $98. The **Cinnamon Bear Inn** (☎/fax 760-934-2873, 800-845-2873, 133 Center St) has colonial decor, a nice woodside location and the same amenities. Rooms here cost $69 to $129.

Places to Eat

Mammoth has plenty of places to get that morning coffee jolt and fuel up on carbos for a day on the slopes, including the **Breakfast Club** (☎ 760-934-6944, 2987 Old Mammoth Rd); **The Stove** (☎ 760-934-2821, 644 Old Mammoth Rd); and **The Looney Bean** (☎ 760-934-1345, 3280 Main St). Vegetarians, vegans or the simply health-conscious flock to the **Good Life Cafe** (☎ 760-934-1734), behind the Chart House on Old Mammoth Rd, which has delicious salads and wraps. Some of the best burgers ($4.25)

in town are at **Berger's** (☎ 760-934-6622), on Minaret Rd north of the Main St intersection, though they also do steak and ribs. Another steak joint is the reliably good **The Mogul** (☎ 760-934-3039, 1528 Tavern Rd), where your waiter doubles as your chef.

Grumpy's (☎ 760-934-8587), on Old Mammoth Rd near Meridian Blvd, is a popular hangout and smokefree sports bar that is busy year round; the straightforward menu features chili, burgers, Mexican fare and sandwiches.

A lively atmosphere reigns at **Slocum's Italian & American Grill** (☎ 760-934-7647), on Main St east of Old Mammoth Rd, which serves creative pasta, grilled meat and fish for $15 to $20. A nice place for a special dinner is the **Restaurant at Convict Lake** (see Convict Lake section later this chapter).

Getting There & Away

Mammoth Airport, southeast of town off US 395, is mostly for private planes, though TW Express (☎ 800-221-2000) has one daily flight to San Francisco and two to Los Angeles.

Greyhound buses stop at the McDonald's parking lot, across from the visitors bureau on Rte 203. The southbound bus comes through at 12:30 pm, the northbound at 1:30 am; buy tickets onboard.

AROUND MAMMOTH LAKES
Devils Postpile
National Monument

This monument's 60-foot, multisided columns of blue-gray basalt are the most conspicuous and interesting product of the area's volcanic activity. The columns formed when lava, which flowed through Mammoth Pass, cooled and fractured vertically. A glacier came through later to give them their cracked, shiny surface. Surrounding the monument, **Reds Meadow** has terrific camping and fishing, and a well-worn 1½-mile trail through fire-ravaged forest to Rainbow Falls, a 101-foot sheet cascade. Reds Meadow Pack Station (☎ 760-934-2345) has a reputable horseback-riding school and pack trips into the Minarets Wilderness. There's no access to the monument in winter.

The area is only open from around June to October and must be visited by shuttle, since Minaret Rd (the only access) is closed to cars 7:30 am to 5:30 pm, unless you have 11 or more people or a permit to camp at one of the area's campgrounds. Shuttles leave about every 15 to 30 minutes from the Mammoth Mountain Inn, across from the ski area's Main Lodge ($9 roundtrip). They stop at campgrounds, viewpoints, the Devils Postpile Visitor Center (where the ½-mile trail to the columns begins) and Reds Meadow Pack Station; you can get on and off as much as you like. The entire one-way trip takes about 45 minutes.

Convict Lake

Five miles south of Mammoth and 2 miles west of US 395, this is one of the prettiest lakes in the area, with pellucid emerald water and embraced by two massive peaks – Mt Morrison and Laurel Mountain. The lake is named for a group of convicts who only made it this far after a jail break. A gentle trail skirts the lake, through aspen and cottonwood trees, and a trailhead on the southeast shore goes to Genevieve, Edith, Dorothy and Mildred lakes in the John Muir Wilderness.

Below the lake on an arid ridge, the USFS *Convict Lake Campground* has terraced sites ($10) and flush toilets. Nearby, the *Restaurant at Convict Lake* (☎ 760-943-3803) is popular with Mammoth locals. It has a nice bar and upscale dining with pasta, leg of lamb, grilled venison and the like for dinner (around $20).

Hot Creek Geological Site

Heading south of Mammoth on US 395, turn east at the sign for Hot Creek Fish Hatchery (☎ 760-934-2664). At the hatchery itself, you can see the trout tumbling in outdoor ponds. Continue for about 2 miles until reaching the steaming hot springs and pools at the bottom of a volcanic basin. Water from the mountains filters through cracks in the earth's crust and gets heated up by magma. The steam vents, creating springs of boiling water in what becomes a natural cauldron. It's possible to soak in the pools,

though this is potentially dangerous since sections can be scaldingly hot. Pay attention to posted signs and take care when bathing.

BISHOP
• population 3700 • elevation 4150

The largest town south of Mammoth Lakes, Bishop is a major pit stop for Southern Californians on a weekend recreation mission. The old part of town has classic Western Americana character, with covered sidewalks, classic 1950s neon signs and hunting and fishing stores aplenty. If you like country music, chewing tobacco and mounted antlers, this is a good place to imbibe (any bar will do). The new parts of town, along the highway north and south, are just utilitarian sprawl with fast-food restaurants, chain motels and gas stations. During 'Mule Days,' held annually on Memorial Day weekend, Bishop hosts mule auctions, mule races, mule parades, mule rodeo, etc – and everyone becomes a cowhand or, at least, a mulehand. More than 40,000 people descend on the town for the event.

Orientation & Information

Bishop has US 395's sharpest curve, where it meets Hwy 6 (to Benton, Nevada) at a right angle. The town extends south of this junction for about 3 miles along Main St. The White Mountain Ranger Station (☎ 760-873-2500), 798 N Main St, issues wilderness permits and has trail and campground information for the White Mountains, Big Pine, and Rock and Bishop Creek recreation areas. A few doors south at No 690 is the visitor center (☎ 760-873-8405, www.bishop visitor.com), open 9 am to 4:30 pm weekdays and 10 am to 4 pm weekends.

Laws Railroad Museum

On Hwy 6, 4 miles northeast of Bishop, this extensive collection (☎ 760-873-5950) of historic buildings is worth a stop. The central exhibit is the 1883 Laws railroad depot, a train and passenger depot that serviced the narrow-gauge line used to transport people and agricultural products from near Carson City to just south of Lone Pine through the then-fertile Owens Valley. Other historic buildings,

SIERRA NEVADA

including Bishop's first church, have been moved here and hold antiques and exhibits of all kinds. It's open 10 am to 4 pm daily; $2.

Paiute Shoshone Indian Cultural Center

Just west of central Bishop, the land is part of the Bishop Indian Reservation, the northernmost of four in the Owens Valley. The center (☎ 760-873-4478), 2300 W Line St, acts as administrative headquarters and a gathering place for tribal members. There's also a gift shop and museum showcasing the basketry, tools, clothing and dwellings of the Paiute and Shoshone tribes, including a sweat house and a cooking shelter. Hours are 9 am to 5 pm weekdays, 10 am to 4 pm weekends; in winter 10 am to 3 pm daily; $2/1.

Activities

The Owens River Gorge, 9 miles north of town on the east side of US 395, has excellent **rock climbing**, as do the Buttermilk Hills, west of town on both sides of Hwy 168; the latter are also good for bouldering. Most of the staff at Wilson's Eastside Sports (☎ 760-873-7520), 224 N Main St, are experienced climbers with good route suggestions; the shop rents equipment and sells maps and guidebooks.

Nine miles west of town, Hwy 168 heads into the Sierra along both forks of Bishop Creek. The south fork ends at South Lake, surrounded by jagged peaks, and the north fork ends at Sabrina Basin, with Lake Sabrina and North Lake as its dual centerpiece. **Fishing** is good in all of the lakes (North Lake is least crowded), and **hiking** trails lead through the John Muir Wilderness to Sequoia National Park. Rainbow Pack Station (☎ 760-873-8877, 800-443-2848), within Parcher's Resort near South Lake, has one-hour **horseback rides** for $20. At North Lake, Bishop Pack Outfitters (☎ 760-873-4785, 800-316-4252) is recommended for long pack trips.

Places to Stay

Camping On the south edge of town, family-style **Brown's Campground** (☎ 760-

873-8522, 760-872-6911 in winter) has grassy sites for $10 ($13 with hookups), showers, laundry and other amenities.

Eleven USFS campgrounds along Bishop Creek, 9 miles west of town via Hwy 168, are surrounded by trees and are close to fishing and hiking. A ranger kiosk on the highway (just before the road splits) has maps and information. **Willow Campground** on the south fork, and **Sabrina Campground** on the north, are recommended.

Motels Most places in Bishop are along US 395, with unexciting rooms for $40 to $60. Rooms at the **Village Motel** (☎ 760-872-8155, 286 Elm St), one block east of US 395 at the north end of town, are old but clean. The **Outdoorsman Motor Lodge** (☎ 760-873-6381, 651 N Main St) has a nice guest lobby, plus free coffee and donuts. A bit newer, the **Comfort Inn** (☎ 760-873-4284, 805 Main St) has a pool, spa and rooms for $70 to $90. Bishop's deluxe accommodations are the **Creekside Inn** (☎ 760-872-3044, 800-273-3550, 725 N Main St), with two pools and hot tub, continental breakfast and rates ranging from $79 to $129.

Places to Eat

A much hyped spot, **Erick Schat's Bakkery** (☎ 760-873-7156, 763 N Main St) has been making shepherd bread and other baked goodies since 1938. They also have a snack bar and espresso drinks. **Amigos Mexican Restaurant** (☎ 760-872-2189, 285 N Main St) serves Mexican food, including good fish tacos and ceviche. Popular with locals is **Bar-B-Q Bills** (☎ 760-872-5535, 187 S Main St), an old-fashioned self-service eatery with delicious sandwiches. The **Pizza Factory** (☎ 760-872-8888, 912 N Main St) tosses the best pies in towns starting at $3.60. **Whiskey Creek** (☎ 760-873-7174, 524 N Main St) has a nice bar and patio, good food and the town's best atmosphere.

Getting There & Away

The Greyhound bus station (☎ 760-872-2721) is at 201 S Warren St, one block west of Main St.

BISHOP TO LONE PINE
Big Pine & Big Pine Creek

While the town of Big Pine is nothing too exciting in itself, it offers a place to stay while exploring the Ancient Bristlecone Pine Forest. The visitor center (☎ 760-938-2114, 888-374-3773) is at 126 S Main St and is open 8 am to 4:30 pm daily.

The **Bristlecone Motel** (☎ 760-938-2067, 800-263-3927, 101 N Main St) has large, faded rooms with phone and TV ($35). They also have showers ($3) for nonguests. The **Big Pine Motel** (☎ 760-938-2282, 370 S Main St) and the **Starlite Motel** (☎ 760-938-2011, 511 S Main St) are the other two options and have similar rooms and rates.

West of Big Pine via Glacier Lodge Rd (the only stoplight in town), **Big Pine Creek Canyon** has good camping, fishing and hiking. Campsites ($9) have pit toilets; an information kiosk at the canyon entrance has information and issues wilderness permits. The scenery here is not spectacular compared to canyons farther north, but trails lead to the Palisade Glacier – the southernmost in the US and largest in the Sierra. Glacial runoff turns the lakes below a milky turquoise color that looks great on film. It's a 3-mile hike to the first waterfalls, another 1½ miles before you reach a lake, then another two to see the glacier; experienced mountaineers climb its icy face with crampons and ice picks – fun to watch.

Ancient Bristlecone Pine Forest

The Great Basin bristlecone pines found here are the oldest living things on earth; some of them are over 4000 years old. The oldest trees are squatty and gnarled, with exposed roots and wide-reaching limbs. Soil depletion takes place at a rate of 6 inches per 1000 years here, revealing the age of those trees whose roots are a few feet above ground. Visiting the forest is an all-day affair but worth the time and effort, if only for the astonishing view of the Sierra Nevada and Owens Valley from atop the White Mountains. Dry and stark, this range was once higher than the Sierra but is much older and thus heavily eroded.

To reach the forest, head northeast from US 395 on Hwy 168 (just north of Big Pine) to White Mountain Rd, turn left and follow the curvy road for 10 miles to the Schulman Grove Visitor Center (☎ 760-873-2500 for recorded information) and parking lot. The trip should take about one hour. Admission to the forest is $2 per person or $5 per car; Golden Passports are valid.

From here self-guided trails ($1 brochures at the trailhead) lead through different groves. The longest one, 4½ miles, offers views of the Sierra and Deep Springs Valley (east) and passes the Methuselah 'Forest of the Ancients,' home of our planet's oldest living things. A dirt road (popular with mountain bikers) continues on past the Patriarch Grove Picnic Area, a little-used facility around a stand of bristlecone pines, to the Mt Bancroft High Altitude Research Station, run by the University of California, Berkeley.

The only place to stay up here – from May through October – is at **Grandview Campground** before the visitor center, which has an awesome view and $7 sites; bring your own water.

Independence

• **population 1000** • **elevation 3925 feet**

This sleepy highway town, named for a Civil War fort founded here on Independence Day 1862, has a few unlikely attractions. One block west of US 395, on Market St, is Mary Austin's (author of *Land of Little Rain*) childhood home with a nostalgia-ridden plaque on the gate. Farther west on Market St, the **Eastern California Museum** (☎ 760-878-0258) has an excellent Paiute basket collection and exhibit about Manzanar (see Manzanar National Historic Site). It promises to be even more interesting after completion of a thorough renovation still underway at the time of this writing. It's open 10 am to 4 pm, except Tuesday.

West of town via Onion Valley Rd (Market St in town), Onion Valley has two nice **campgrounds** (open from June to mid-September; $11) and a trailhead for the Kearsarge Pass Trail, an old Paiute trade route that's good for day hiking. This also offers the shortest backside access to Kings Canyon National Park. Golden Trout Lakes, northwest from the trailhead, is a strenuous and poorly marked trail. A herd of California bighorn sheep live south of Onion Valley around Shepherd Pass.

Places to Stay Independence has a small but excellent *HI hostel* (☎ 760-878-2040, fax 760-878-2833, 211 N Edwards St), at the historic 1927 Winnedumah Hotel, once the home away from home for the Hollywood elite filming in the nearby Alabama Hills (see Alabama Hills under Lone Pine later this chapter). There's a kitchen, patio, garden and fireplace, TV room, library and rental bicycles. Rates are $18 per bunk, including breakfast and linens.

Manzanar National Historic Site

Two months after the Japanese bombed Pearl Harbor, President Roosevelt signed an executive order requiring all West Coast Japanese – most of them American citizens – to be placed in internment camps. Manzanar was the first of 10 such camps, built in 1942 among pear and apple orchards, 5 miles south of Independence (off US 395). At full operation, Manzanar held 10,000 people in its 6000 acres, bordered by barbed wire and guarded by sentry posts.

Little remains of the camp – which only became a historic site in 1973 – except for the pagoda-like police post and sentry house by the entrance, and a few concrete foundations. Roads through the camp are very sandy, so your best bet is to park at the entrance and explore on foot. The best educational material and artifacts regarding the site are in the Eastern California Museum in Independence. As of now, there are no facilities and only a few interpretive displays at the site.

LONE PINE
- **population 2800** - **elevation 8371 feet**

Lone Pine is famous for three things: the Alabama Hills, Mt Whitney and the turnoff for Death Valley. Founded in the 1800s as a supply post for Owens Valley ranchers and

farmers, Lone Pine experienced one boom during the 1850s mining activity, and another a century later when movie stars such as Cary Grant, Gary Cooper and Hopalong Cassidy made movies in the Alabama Hills, just west of town. Nowadays, recreationists are more numerous than movie stars and Lone Pine has turned into somewhat of a tourist crossroads, 90 miles from Death Valley and 14 miles from Whitney Portal, the departure point for ambitious hikers.

South of Lone Pine, US 395 passes what *was* Owens Lake and continues through the desertlike southern part of the Owens Valley. From here you can see where the Sierra Nevada tapers to an unexciting end, arid and stark compared to its northern reaches.

Orientation & Information

Hwy 395 runs through Lone Pine as Main St, lined with motels, gas stations, restaurants and a bank. Whitney Portal Rd heads west from US 395 at the town's one stoplight, and Hwy 136 to Death Valley heads southeast from US 395 about 2 miles south of town.

The Interagency Visitor Center (☎ 760-876-6222), 2 miles south of town at the US 395/136 junction, has exhibits, books, maps, and trail and campground information for Death Valley and all of the Sierra Nevada, plus clean rest rooms and potable water; it's open 8 am to 5 pm daily year round. The Mt Whitney Ranger Station (☎ 760-876-6200), on Main St, in Lone Pine, issues wilderness permits and has local trail and road conditions posted. It's open 7 am to 4:30 pm in summer, otherwise 8 am to 5 pm.

Alabama Hills

These hills consist of big red boulders and outcroppings surrounded by sage and scrub. If the scene looks familiar, it's because numerous old Westerns, including *How the West Was Won* and *Gunga Din*, were made here. Movie Rd, west of town via Whitney Portal Rd, makes a loop around the hills and passes near most of the film locations (the Interagency Visitor Center has a history sheet and map for locating the exact spots). The films take center stage at the Lone Pine

Film Festival, held the first weekend in October. When Hollywood's elite were in town, they stayed at the Dow Hotel (still in operation) and carved their names (still visible) in the walls at the trading post on Main St. There are no developed trails among the hills, but the sparse brush makes for easy wandering – just keep an eye out for rattlesnakes.

Places to Stay & Eat

The one star attraction among Lone Pine's typical highway motels is the historic **Dow Hotel** (☎ 760-876-5521, 800-824-9317, 310 S Main St), which lodged movie stars like John Wayne when they came to make movies in the Alabama Hills. Built in 1922, the place has been updated but still retains much charm. There is a comfortable lobby, TV room and library and an outdoor pool. Rooms in the hotel ($23 to $40) share a bath, while those in the modern motel section ($56 to $62) each have their own. Other good lodging options include the **Mt Whitney Motel** (☎ 760-876-4207, 800-845-2362, fax 760-876-8818, 305 N Main St), with a pool and quiet, modern rooms for $36 to $55; and the **Best Western Frontier** (☎ 760-876-5571, 1008 S Main St), south of town, with standard rooms for $50 and deluxe rooms for up to four for $79, including a light breakfast.

Locals recommend 24-hour **PJ's Cafe** (446 S Main St) and **Caffeine Hannah's** (☎ 760-876-0016, 150 S Main St), a coffeehouse and hangout for locals and hikers; they make great smoothies. For healthy Mexican fare, head to **Nacho Grill** next to **Bonanza** (☎ 760-876-4768, 104 N Main St), a family restaurant.

Twenty miles south of Lone Pine in Olancha, the **Ranch House** (☎ 760-764-2363) has down-home American food served in a rustic space with tall ceilings, big wooden booths and red-checkered tablecloths. A short drive further south is the surprising **Still Life Cafe** (☎ 760-764-2044), run by a French couple who serve gourmet food at reasonable prices ($10 to $15); the menu changes daily and is posted on a blackboard.

AROUND LONE PINE
Whitney Portal

You needn't be a mountain climber to enjoy this pine oasis, tucked away below the Sierra's highest peaks, 13 miles west of Lone Pine via Whitney Portal Rd (closed in winter). Though most traffic is headed to the highest point of the lower 48 states – 14,497-foot Mt Whitney – there are trails, campgrounds and waterfalls right at the portal. **Whitney Portal** campground has lovely terraced sites next to a creek ($12) with pit toilets and potable water. The drawback is availability: most sites are reservable (☎ 800-280-2267) and the others fill up quickly. There's a better chance at the nearby first-come, first-served **Whitney Trailhead** campground with the same facilities and $6 sites. The tiny Whitney Portal Store sells maps, outdoor gear and a few groceries, and the small restaurant makes good burgers and 12-inch pancakes that cost 'a buck' each – eat three and they're free! This is also the place to get trail information from people coming off the mountain.

The Whitney Trail is nice for hiking even if you don't hit the top. Before Whitney Portal Rd was paved, climbers started the Whitney ascent in Lone Pine. Four miles of this early trail were recently restored to create the Whitney Portal National Recreation Trail, a scenic low-elevation hike between the Portal and **Lone Pine Campground**, well signed on Whitney Portal Rd. The campground itself is hot and dry but a good alternative if the Portal campground is full; sites are $10 with running water and composting toilets.

Hiking anywhere in the Mt Whitney Zone requires a wilderness permit for both day hikers and backpackers. For most other sections of the Inyo National Forest, only those embarking on overnight trips need permits (see 'Climbing Mt Whitney' boxed text on how to obtain permits).

Horseshoe Meadows

Six miles from Lone Pine off Whitney Portal Rd, Horseshoe Meadows Rd heads south and climbs a series of steep switchbacks to reach Horseshoe Meadows Recreation Area at

Climbing Mt Whitney

At 14,497 feet, Mt Whitney is the highest point in the contiguous United States, climbed by over 2000 people a year. Though the trail to the summit is well marked and maintained, it challenges the average body with its elevation gain: about 6000 feet over 11 miles (an unmarked 'Mountaineers Route' makes the same climb in 4 miles). Most people in good physical condition can make the climb, especially if they take a few days to do it. Altitude sickness is a common problem, and rangers recommend spending a day or two at the first base camp to adjust. A second camp is halfway up the mountain. If you go for it, be sure to get detailed information from the ranger station in Lone Pine before heading out. A recommended guide is *Climbing Mt Whitney*, by Walt Wheelock and Wyrme Burti, sold at the ranger station for $6.95.

Often the biggest problem is getting a wilderness permit for the Mt Whitney Zone, required for all overnight trips as well as for day hikes on the Mt Whitney Trail past Lone Pine Lake. A quota system, in effect from May 22 to October 15, limits numbers to 50 overnight and 150 day hikers. Reservations are accepted six months to two days prior to trail entry. Getting permits for midweek trips or for late summer treks is easier. Contact the Inyo National Forest Wilderness Reservation Service (☎ 888-374-3773, www.sierrawilderness.com), 126 S Main St, PO Box 430, Big Pine, CA 93513 for reservations. The office is open 8 am to 4:30 pm weekdays. Fees range from $2 to $4.

10,000 feet. The elevation makes for a desolate landscape with squat trees scattered sparsely over a sand and rock ground cover. Most people come here to fish and hike the trails which head into the Golden Trout Wilderness. Cottonwood Lakes, home to the native golden trout, is a popular day-hike destination with good fishing. Longer hikes, over

the Sierra crest, lead to Sequoia National Park in the west. The trailheads are well marked from a day-use parking lot at the end of the approach road, where there is also a picnic area and *campground* with large, open sites ($6) and flush toilets. The Cottonwood Pack Station (☎ 760-878-2015), the only business up here, does trips into High Sierra Camps.

Los Angeles

LA is a survivor. It seems to always be at the mercy of nature's whims (from devastating earthquakes and drought to mud slides and brush fires) and society's vagaries (from race riots to sordid crimes of passion). Yet it continues to flourish, attracting a United Nations of immigrants. LA is a place that no traveler should omit from a must-see list.

The big houses, fast cars, fancy clothes, elegant restaurants and designer drugs – of which LA has more than its share – are not only the aggrandizement of the 'American dream' but also statements of LA mentality: what you see may be gone tomorrow, so live life to the fullest today.

In Southern California, where cinema is the ultimate art form, and 'The Industry' willingly shields its public from the 'real world,' it's sometimes hard to separate fact from fiction. You can't avoid The Industry if you try: round one corner, police have cordoned off a major building while filming takes place inside; and every other person you speak to is really a budding actor/writer/producer, who just happens to be serving cocktails or parking cars to get by.

The city of Los Angeles is relatively small compared to the metropolis with which its name is synonymous. Hollywood, for instance, is a part of LA, but West Hollywood and Beverly Hills are independent cities. A network of freeways both makes sense and nonsense of this urban sprawl. Consequently, Angelenos have an almost total dependence on the automobile.

HISTORY

The earliest residents of the LA area were the Gabrielino and Chumash Indians, who arrived between 5000 and 6000 BC. The Gabrielinos were hunter-gatherers who lived inland (their staple food was the acorn, finely ground and made into bread or porridge), while the Chumash lived on the coast as sea trawlers.

The first European known to have laid eyes upon the Los Angeles Basin was Juan

---

> ### Highlights
>
> - Downtown LA – around the globe in a day
> - Getty Center – good art, better views, best architecture
> - Venice Beach – freaks, dudes and babes on the beach
> - Catalina Island – 26 miles and a world away from the big city

---

Rodríguez Cabrillo, who sailed the coast in 1542. From Santa Monica Bay, he observed a brown haze over the landscape – from campfires at the Gabrielino village of Yangna – and called the bay *Bahia de los Fumos*, or 'Bay of Smokes.' LA's fabled smog has apparently been around longer than most folks imagine.

The Mission Era

Greater LA has two missions: Mission San Gabriel Arcángel (1771) and Mission San Fernando Rey de España (1797), both of which have been carefully restored, and both of which can still be visited. The Gabrielinos who built their communities around these missions had no previous concept of heaven or hell but were forced to trade hard labor for salvation, exposing themselves to a variety of diseases, from measles to syphilis, that almost wiped out their people.

In 1781, the missions embarked on a plan to create separate agricultural communities to produce food and support the missions' expansion. Forty-four *pobladores* (settlers) were assigned from San Gabriel to establish a new town near the village of Yangna, on the banks of a cottonwood-lined stream about 9 miles southwest of the mission. The town they established, El Pueblo de Nuestro Señora la Reina de los Angeles del Río Porciúncula (The Town of Our Lady the Queen of the Angels of the Porciuncula River), was named for a saint whose feast day had just been celebrated.

Los Angeles, as the pueblo became known, grew into a thriving farming community. Taking full advantage of long sunny days, the settlers developed orange and olive groves, vineyards and wheat fields and sustained cattle, sheep and horses.

Ranchos

Upon Mexican independence in 1821, many of that new nation's citizens looked to California to satisfy their thirst for private land. By the mid-1830s, the missions had been secularized, with a series of governors doling out hundreds of free land grants and giving birth to the rancho system. The *rancheros*, as the new landowners were called, prospered and quickly became the social, cultural and political fulcrums of California.

Joseph Chapman, a blond Boston millwright-cum-pirate, became the first Yankee Angeleno in 1818; he was known as *El Inglés*, 'the Englishman.' Others followed slowly; by the mid-1830s, only 29 US citizens resided in Los Angeles. But these few bought entire shiploads of imported goods from seafarers in exchange for full cargoes of hides. In setting up a system of credit for rancheros, these men established California's first banking system.

Jedediah Smith, who established the first overland route to the western states, arrived at Mission San Gabriel Arcángel in 1826. Kit Carson, John Charles Frémont's scout and a legend of the American West, helped pave the Santa Fe Trail to Los Angeles in 1832. But most Easterners didn't know much about Los Angeles until 1840, when Richard Henry Dana's *Two Years Before the Mast* gave an account of his mid-1830s experience in the coastal hide-and-tallow trade. 'In the hands of an enterprising people, what a country this might be,' Dana wrote of Los Angeles, then with a population of just over 1200.

From Small Town to Big City

With California statehood, LA was incorporated on April 4, 1850. It was an unruly city of dirt streets and adobe homes, of saloons, brothels and gambling houses that thrived on the fast buck. But by 1854, Northern California's gold rush had peaked, and the state was thrust into a depression. As unemployed miners swarmed to LA and other cities, banks and businesses that had harnessed their futures to miners' fortunes closed their doors.

But a bit of wheeling and dealing brought a railroad spur line to LA in 1876, via the San Joaquin Valley. In 1885, the Atchison, Topeka & Santa Fe Railroad directly linked LA across the Arizona desert to the East Coast.

Coincidental with the arrival of the railroad was the establishment of the citrus industry in Southern California. As California oranges found their way onto New York grocery shelves, coupled with a hard-sell advertising campaign, Easterners heeded the advice of crusading editor Horace Greeley to 'Go West, young man.' LA's population jumped from 2300 in 1860 to 11,000 in 1880 and more than 50,000 in 1890. It reached 100,000 in 1900. Never mind that LA didn't have a natural harbor or a supply of fresh water adequate to support even a small town.

The first of these needs was addressed by the construction of a harbor at San Pedro, 23 miles south of City Hall. Work began in 1899; the first wharf opened in 1914, coinciding with the completion of the Panama Canal. Suddenly 8000 miles closer to the Atlantic seaboard, San Pedro became the busiest harbor on the West Coast.

Bringing drinking water to the blossoming city would require a much more complex solution, as the sporadic flow of the Los Angeles River (as the Río Porciúncula became known) and water from a few artesian wells were clearly insufficient.

In 1904, city water bureau superintendent William Mulholland visited the Owens Valley, on the southeastern slopes of the Sierra, and returned with a startling plan. Voters gave him the $24.5 million he needed to build an aqueduct to carry melted snow from the mountains to the city, and by November 1913, Owens River water was spilling into the San Fernando Valley. The system remains controversial, especially to Owens Valley ranchers and to environmentalists, but it supplies more than 75% of the city's water to this day. Most of the rest, as well as Southern California's electricity, comes from dams on the Colorado River, 300 miles east.

Quenching LA's Thirst

The growth of semi-arid Los Angeles into a megalopolis is inextricably linked to water. Burgeoning population levels after the turn of the 20th century made it clear that groundwater levels would be insufficient to support the city and certainly wouldn't sustain further growth. Water had to be imported, and Fred Eaton, a former LA mayor, and William Mulholland, city water bureau superintendent, knew just how and where to get it: by aqueduct from the Owens Valley, at the foot of the Eastern Sierra, some 250 miles to the northeast.

Work on Mulholland's aqueduct began in 1908. An amazing feat of engineering – crossing barren desert floor as well as rugged mountain terrain – the aqueduct opened to great fanfare on November 5, 1913. An extension to the Mono Basin in 1940 lengthened it by 105 miles. The Owens Valley, though, would never be the same.

With most of Owens Lake drained, the once fertile valley became barren, causing farms to close and businesses to go bust. A bitter feud between valley residents and the city ensued; some foes even used dynamite to sabotage the aqueduct.

To this day, LA's Department of Water and Power owns 307,000 acres in Inyo and Mono counties, and the controversy and resentment toward the thirsty giant to the south persists.

🚲 🚲 🚲 🚲 🚲 🚲

To the Present

LA's population soared to 1 million by 1920 and 2 million by 1930, largely because of the discovery of oil, in 1892, by Edward Doheny near Downtown LA. Exporting the oil also caused a boom in shipping and related harbor industries.

During WWI, the Lockheed brothers and Donald Douglas established aircraft manufacturing plants in the area. Two decades later, with another world war brewing, the aviation industry employed enough people to help lift LA out of the depression. By the end of WWII, billions of federal dollars had poured into Southern Californian military contracts and thousands of families had moved to the region to work at the plants.

The influx of aviation employees caused a new real estate boom, creating whole new suburbs south of LA. Lakewood, just north of Long Beach, for instance, was developed almost overnight by McDonnell Douglas to house the aviation company's employees.

At the same time, thousands of African-American workers came to LA from Texas and Louisiana, causing a vibrant community to develop in South Central LA. What had been just a small colony before the war had grown into one of the nation's great black cultural centers by the '50s.

More than 14 million people now live within a 60-mile radius of Downtown LA. The city of LA proper boasts 3.5 million. In LA County, whites represent about 35%, Latinos 42%, blacks 10%, Asians and Pacific Islanders 12% and Native Americans less than 1%. Today, if LA County were a nation of its own, its gross national product would rank 21st, ahead of Sweden and Austria.

'The Industry'

Nothing symbolizes 20th-century LA more than the film industry. Independent producers were attracted to the area as early as 1908, because LA's sunny climate allowed indoor scenes to be shot outdoors – essential with the unsophisticated photo technology of the day. The diversity of the landscape around LA was a further attraction: any location, from ocean to desert to alpine forest, could be depicted nearby.

Studios were constructed in Culver City and Universal City, but the capital of filmdom was the LA suburb of Hollywood. Soon moviegoers were succumbing to the romance of Southern California as portrayed in silent films. Organ music accompanied one-reel comedies and Westerns that made stars of Charlie Chaplin and Tom Mix. Directors like DW Griffith and Cecil B DeMille became luminaries in their own right. 'Talkies' soon eclipsed the silent films, and color cinematography later made the movies seem more real than ever. Fads followed popular movies, shaping styles around the world.

Movies are still one of the city's major moneymakers. Between 1990 and 1996, employment in the film industry skyrocketed from 143,300 to 224,300, generating more than $26 billion in revenue. And the future continues to be bright for 'The Industry,' with demand for films expected to grow a further 7% by 2001.

GEOGRAPHY & GEOLOGY

LA County encompasses geographical extremes, from subtropical desert and 74 miles of seacoast to a pair of offshore islands and at least one peak above 10,000 feet. The area straddles one of the world's major earthquake fault zones, dominated by the great San Andreas Fault. Quakes rated above 6.0 on the Richter scale have wreaked death and destruction in LA five times this century – with epicenters near Long Beach in 1933, in the San Fernando Valley in 1971 (Sylmar) and 1994 (Northridge), and two in 1992 in the Big Bear region. Angelenos live in fearful knowledge that the 'Big One' may strike any moment.

CLIMATE

LA has a pleasant and temperate Mediterranean climate, protected from extremes of temperature and humidity by the mountain ranges to its north and east. The average Los Angeles temperature is around 70°F (21°C), with summer highs usually in the mid-80s to low 90s and winter lows typically in the mid-50s to low 60s. Offshore breezes keep beach communities 10° to 15°F cooler than areas inland or in the San Fernando Valley. Morning coastal fog also contributes to the cooling effect. Evenings tend to be cool, even at the peak of summer. Rain falls almost exclusively between November and April, with extended storms raging in January and February.

ORIENTATION

Covering 464 sq miles, the city of Los Angeles is vast indeed. Yet its meandering boundaries comprise only a fraction of 4083-sq-mile LA County. There are 88 incorporated cities within the county, many of them independent (like Santa Monica, Beverly Hills, West Hollywood and Culver City), but surrounded by the city of LA.

LA County occupies a broad coastal plain, framed on its west and south by the Pacific Ocean, on its north by the San Gabriel Mountains, and on its east by smaller ranges that run to the Mojave Desert. The Santa Monica Mountains separate Hollywood and Beverly Hills from the San Fernando Valley to the north; Orange County, home of Disneyland and Laguna Beach, extends along the coast to the south.

Getting around in LA need not be hard if you have a car and a basic understanding of its freeway network – eight freeways tangle like knotty vines near the Downtown core. (See 'Major Freeways' under Getting Around for a list of LA's freeways.) Some communities, though, like Beverly Hills and West Hollywood, aren't served by freeways at all.

Maps

For navigating within particular neighborhoods, you should find the maps in this book comprehensive enough. To get around the city, though, you ought to obtain more detailed street maps. These are available at gas stations, bookstores or the Automobile Association of Southern California (see the phone book for the branch nearest you).

INFORMATION
Tourist Offices

Maps, brochures, lodging information and tickets to theme parks and other attractions are available at the Los Angeles Convention and Visitors Bureau's (LACVB) information centers. The Downtown office (Map 2; ☎ 213-689-8822, fax 213-624-1992), 685 S Figueroa St, Los Angeles, CA 90017, is open 8 am to 5 pm weekdays, 8:30 am to 5 pm Saturday. The Hollywood branch (Map 3; ☎ 323-689-8822), 6541 Hollywood Blvd, is open from 9 am to 5 pm daily except Sunday. The LACVB also maintains a 24-hour multilingual events hotline you can call at ☎ 213-689-8822.

Money

Many banks exchange major currencies and traveler's checks and usually have the best rates. Los Angeles International Airport (LAX) has currency exchange offices in all terminals. Overall, exchange rates are not great and you might do better changing your money into dollars or traveler's checks in your home country.

Los Angeles has hundreds of banks, the most prevalent being Bank of America, First Federal and Union Bank. Thomas Cook (☎ 800-287-7362 for all branches) has branches in Beverly Hills at 452 N Bedford St and 9461 Wilshire Blvd, and in West Hollywood at 8901 Santa Monica Blvd. American Express is at 8493 W 3rd St (Map 6; ☎ 310-659-1682), near the Beverly Center mall; in Downtown at 901 W 7th St (Map 2; ☎ 213-627-4800); and in Santa Monica at 1250 4th St (Map 7; ☎ 310-395-9588).

Taxes In Los Angeles, the state sales tax of 7.25% is supplemented by an additional 1% county tax. At hotels, motels and hostels in LA County, a 'transient occupancy tax' is tacked onto room rates. The tax ranges from 11.85% in Pasadena to 14% in Los Angeles.

Post & Communications

The main post office (Map 2; ☎ 213-617-4543) is the Terminal Annex, 900 N Alameda St in Downtown. Handier post offices are: 325 N Maple Drive in Beverly Hills (Map 6; ☎ 310-247-3400); 1248 5th St in Santa Monica (☎ 310-576-2626); and 967 E Colorado Blvd in Pasadena (☎ 626-405-0879). If none of these are close by, check the phone book or call ☎ 800-275-8777.

Thanks to a growing population and cellular phones and other new technology, there is now a confusing patchwork of area codes within the LA area. Current codes are:

213	Downtown Los Angeles
310	Beverly Hills, Westside, Santa Monica, Hermosa Beach, Redondo Beach, Manhattan Beach, Venice, San Pedro
323	Hollywood, Silver Lake, Mid-City, East LA, South Central
562	Long Beach
626	Pasadena, San Marino
818	San Fernando Valley, Burbank, Glendale, North Hollywood

Internet Resources

Web resources abound in Los Angeles.

@LA
www.at-la.com
well organized and comprehensive, links to more than 26,000 sites sorted in 24 categories and countless subcategories; searchable

City of Los Angeles
www.ci.la.ca.us
official City of LA site, with city news to city-sponsored events, links to libraries, museums, events

Yahoo! Los Angeles
www.yahoo.com/Regional/U_S_States/California/Metropolitan_Areas/Los_Angeles_Metro/
lots of links to sites in such categories as education, health, travel and transportation, events, entertainment as well as the Yellow Pages

LA Times
www.latimes.com
online version of the daily *LA Times*, with international and local news. Also try the *Times'* www.latimes.com/home/destla, with information on nightlife, shopping, beaches, hiking and sights; www.calendarlive.com has up-to-date events news and links to hotels, museums, books, activities, etc; searchable

LA Weekly
www.laweekly.com
online version of LA's main entertainment weekly, with access to a back-issue archive

Travel Agencies

Council Travel (Map 6; ☎ 310-208-3551) is at 10904 Lindbrook Drive in Westwood, with STA's (Map 6; ☎ 310-824-1574) branch close by at 920 Westwood Blvd. Another STA (Map 7; ☎ 310-824-1574) office is at 120 Broadway, Suite 108, in Santa Monica.

Bookstores

Excellent travel bookstores include Traveler's Bookcase (Map 4; ☎ 323-655-0575), 8375 W 3rd St near the Beverly Center; California Map & Travel Center (Map 7; ☎ 310-396-6277), 3312 Pico Blvd in Santa Monica; and Distant Lands (Map 8; ☎ 626-449-3220), 56 Raymond Ave in Pasadena. All stock a wide range of Lonely Planet books. Another

Email & Internet Access

Reaching out and touching someone via cyberspace is not a problem in LA, where cybercafes are prevalent. Santa Monica has the World Cafe (☎ 310-392-1661), 2820 Main St, and the Interactive Cafe (☎ 310-395-5009), 215 Broadway, near Third Street Promenade. Cyber Java (☎ 310-581-1300), 1029 Abbot Kinney Blvd in Venice, is one of LA's oldest cybercafes. A cross between a cafe and a computer lab, it has a helpful and knowledgeable staff and enough gadgets to give you an office away from the office. There's a second, 24-hour branch (☎ 323-466-5600), 7080 Hollywood Blvd at La Brea Blvd in Hollywood. In Long Beach, you'll find Megabyte Coffeehouse, 4135 E Anaheim St, open to at least midnight daily.

great place to stock up on maps, guides and travel gear is Nations (☎ 310-318-9915), 502 Pier Ave, Hermosa Beach.

For general interest, head to Book Soup (Map 4; ☎ 310-659-3110), 8818 Sunset Blvd, West Hollywood, which also has a global range of newspapers and magazines. Dutton's Brentwood (Map 7; ☎ 310-476-6263) at 11975 San Vicente Blvd caters to a literary, educated clientele. Vroman's (Map 8; ☎ 626-449-5320), 695 E Colorado Blvd in Pasadena, is Southern California's oldest (since 1894) bookstore. The Midnight Special Bookstore (Map 7; ☎ 310-393-2923), 1318 Third Street Promenade in Santa Monica, has lots of books by minority writers, feminists and radical authors.

For movie memorabilia, old magazines, posters, scripts and stills, try Movie World (☎ 818-845-1563) at 212 N San Fernando Blvd in Burbank. In Hollywood, try Larry Edmunds Bookshop (Map 3; ☎ 323-463-3273), 6644 Hollywood Blvd, and the Collectors Book Store (Map 3; ☎ 323-467-3296), 6225 Hollywood Blvd. The Collectors Book Store is closed on Sunday and Monday.

Libraries

The Downtown Central Library (Map 2; ☎ 213-228-7000), 630 W 5th St, is the repository of 2.1 million books and 2.5 million historical photographs. Hours are 10 am to 5:30 pm Monday and Thursday to Saturday, noon to 8 pm Tuesday and Wednesday and 1 to 5 pm Sunday. Other excellent public libraries are the Beverly Hills Library (Map 6; ☎ 310-288-2220), 444 N Rexford Drive; Santa Monica Library (Map 7; ☎ 310-458-8600), 1343 6th St, and the Glendale Central Library (☎ 818-548-2020), 222 E Harvard St. All universities and colleges also have libraries.

Laundry

Most hostel-style accommodations and many mid-priced motels offer coin-operated laundry facilities. More upscale hotels, however, often charge exorbitant prices for one-day service. If you don't want to do your own wash, ask at your hotel for the nearest Laundromat.

Medical Services

Hospitals with international reputations include Hollywood Presbyterian Medical Center (Map 3; ☎ 323-660-5350), 1300 N Vermont Ave; Cedars-Sinai Medical Center (Map 4; ☎ 310-855-5000), 8700 Beverly Blvd, on the border of Beverly Hills and West Hollywood; UCLA Medical Center (Map 6; ☎ 310-825-9111), 10833 LeConte Ave, in Westwood. Have your insurance card ready.

For nonemergency and outpatient treatment, check the Yellow Pages for a doctor near you. State-subsidized clinics where fees are generally assessed according to your ability to pay include the Venice Family Clinic (Map 7; ☎ 310-392-8630), 604 Rose Ave in Venice, and the Los Angeles Free Clinic, which has branches at 6043 Hollywood Blvd in Hollywood (Map 3; ☎ 323-462-4158) and at 8405 Beverly Blvd near the Beverly Center mall (Map 4; ☎ 323-653-1990).

Emergency

In case of emergency, phone ☎ 911 for assistance from police, fire department, ambulance or paramedics. Other organizations you might need to contact in case of emergency include:

AIDS Hot Line
  ☎ 800-342-2437

Alcohol & Drug Referral Hotline
  ☎ 800-252-6465

Crisis Response Unit
  ☎ 800-833-3376

Poison Information Center
  ☎ 800-777-6476

Rape & Battering Hotline
  ☎ 310-392-8381

Suicide Prevention Hotline
  ☎ 800-333-4444

Dangers & Annoyances

Much has been written about crime in Los Angeles through the years, though overall

---

What's Free in LA

Museums (always free)

Wells Fargo History Museum (Downtown)
California Science Center (Exposition Park)
California African American Museum (Exposition Park)
USC Fisher Gallery (Downtown)
Hollywood Exhibit at Hollywood Roosevelt Hotel (Hollywood)
Frederick's of Hollywood Lingerie Museum (Hollywood)
Getty Center (Westside)
Malibu Lagoon Museum (Malibu)
Travel Town Museum (Griffith Park)
Museum in Black (Leimert Park)
Museum of African American Art (Leimert Park)
Civil Rights Museum at the Center (Watts)
Watts Towers (Watts)
Cabrillo Marine Aquarium (San Pedro)

Museums (sometimes free)

Japanese American National Museum (Downtown) – 3rd Friday of the month
Museum of Contemporary Art (Downtown) – Thursdays 5 to 8 pm
Geffen Contemporary (Downtown) – Thursdays 5 to 8 pm
Heritage Square Museum (Mt Washington/Highland Park) – Fridays 10 am to 3 pm
Huntington Library, Art Collection & Botanical Gardens (San Marino/Pasadena) – 1st Thursday of the month
Page Museum of La Brea Discoveries (Mid-City) – 1st Tuesday of the month

Tours

Los Angeles Times (Downtown)
Music Center of Los Angeles County (Downtown)
Olvera St Walking Tour (Downtown)
Pacific Design Center (West Hollywood)
Campus Tour USC (Downtown)
Campus Tour UCLA (Westside)
Campus Tour Art Center College of Design (Pasadena)
Campus Tour Caltech (Pasadena)

Historic Sights

Avila Adobe – Olvera St (Downtown)
Mann's Chinese Theater Forecourt (Hollywood)
Greystone Park (Beverly Hills)
Griffith Park Observatory (Griffith Park)
Cemeteries: Forest Lawn Memorial Park (Hollywood Hills) and Forest Lawn Cemetery (Glendale), Hollywood Memorial Park Cemetery, Westwood Memorial Park Cemetery
Brand Library and Art Galleries (Glendale)
Wrigley Mansion (Pasadena)

Entertainment & Activities

Wine Tastings at San Antonio Winery (Downtown)
Sierra Club guided hikes
Monday nights at Coronet Theater
Swing dancing lessons at the Derby (see Entertainment)
Coffeehouse poetry readings, concerts (see Entertainment)

---

figures have gone down in recent years. If you take ordinary precautions, chances are you won't be victimized.

Though crime may occur even in 'good' neighborhoods (as the string of murders, including that of a German tourist, in Santa Monica in 1998 showed), it's worth knowing about – and avoiding – 'bad' neighborhoods, especially after dark. These neighborhoods include sections of Hollywood (around Hollywood Blvd), Venice Beach, South Central LA and East LA; in all these areas drug dealing and gang activity are rampant.

Thefts are rare in major hotels with good security, but they are not uncommon in cheap motels. Keep your room locked and use safes, where available. Street people and panhandlers – usually harmless – abound in certain areas such as Downtown and Santa Monica.

DOWNTOWN (MAP 2)

Perennial doubters and incorrigible cynics will never believe it, but LA *does* have a center. Few areas of LA have as much to offer per sqare mile as Downtown. It is rich in history (this is, after all, the birthplace of the city), architecture, restaurants and cultural institutions. In fact, it's possible to 'travel around the world' in just a day as you make your way from ethnic enclaves like Chinatown and Little Tokyo to the Mexican marketplaces of Olvera St and Broadway, and back to the 21st-century America of the Financial District high-rises.

Getting around Downtown is easy; most places of interest are quickly reached by walking, and the weary will welcome the fleet of minibuses – the DASH (25¢ per ride). Avoid horrendous parking fees by using a lot on the Downtown periphery.

Financial District

LA's modern business district extends seven blocks south from the Civic Center to 8th St and from I-110 six blocks east to Hill St. Much of the area is located atop historical Bunker Hill, once a fashionable residential neighborhood flecked with stately Victorian mansions. It deteriorated into a slum after the 1920s and remained in a sorry state until the '60s, when the city opted for razing the

neighborhood and replacing it with a forest of steel-and-glass high-rises. Also here are large condominium complexes and the futuristic **Westin Bonaventure Hotel**, whose five cylindrical glass towers are frequent movie locations (*Terminator*, *In the Line of Fire*).

Grand Ave bisects Bunker Hill's two main complexes: the Wells Fargo Center to the west and California Plaza to the east. On the ground floor of the former is the **Wells Fargo History Museum** (☎ 213-253-7166), with gold rush artifacts such as an original stagecoach and a 2lb gold nugget. Hours are 9 am to 5 pm weekdays; free.

At the north end of California Plaza at 250 S Grand Ave, the acclaimed **Museum of Contemporary Art** (MOCA; ☎ 213-626-6222), designed by Japanese architect Isozaki Arata, presents traveling exhibits, paintings, sculptures and photographs from the 1940s to the present. Hours are 11 am to 5 pm (11 am to 8 pm Thursday), closed Monday; $6/4/4 adults/seniors/students, free after 5 pm Thursday. Tickets are also good for same-day admission to the Geffen Contemporary (see the Little Tokyo section later this chapter).

There are two ways to descend Bunker Hill. The charming **Angels Flight** – 'the shortest railway in the world' – takes just 60 seconds to cover the steep incline between California Plaza and Hill St. Originally opened in 1901, Angels Flight was mothballed in the '60s and resumed rattling in 1996. Another way to descend in style is via the **Bunker Hill Steps**, LA's retort to Rome's Spanish Steps, which lead down to 5th St and the **Library Tower**, the city's tallest building. Immediately opposite is the **Central Library** (☎ 213-228-7000), 630 W 5th St, a repository of nearly 5 million books and historical photographs. It was designed in 1922 by Bertram Goodhue, who, inspired by the discovery of King Tut's tomb the same year, incorporated many Egyptian motifs. On the library's west side is the stylish **Maguire Gardens**, a tranquil park of sinuous walkways, pools and fountains and whimsical artwork.

Civic Center

Extending eight blocks east to west from San Pedro to Figueroa Sts, the Civic Center contains the most important of LA's city, county, state and federal office buildings. The US Federal Courthouse Building, the site of the infamous 1995 OJ Simpson murder trial, is at 312 N Spring St. The area's most distinctive edifice is the 1928 **City Hall**, 200 N Spring St, which served as the 'Daily Planet' building in *Superman* and the police station in *Dragnet*. In spring 1998, a much-needed $235 million renovation began, which will bring the building up to par with earthquake and other safety codes. The building is expected to be closed for several years.

Across Temple St from City Hall is the **LA Children's Museum** (☎ 213-687-8800), 310 N Main St, where kids can enjoy hands-on learning experiences. Regular hours are 10 am to 5 pm weekends year round and also 11:30 am to 5 pm weekdays from late June to early September; $5.

Catty-corner from City Hall, at 202 W 1st St, is the **Los Angeles Times Building** (☎ 213-237-5757), the location of western North America's largest daily newspaper. Free 35-minute tours, offered at 11:15 am weekdays, introduce visitors (10 years and older) to the inner workings of this giant of the print-media world. The entrance is at 145 S Spring St, and there's free parking in the garage at 213 S Spring St.

A short walk southeast is the new **Latino Museum of History, Art & Culture** (☎ 213-626-7600), 112 S Main St, which exhibits the historical and artistic contributions of Latin American artists. Hours are 10 am to 4 pm (closed Sunday and Wednesday; these hours may change, so call ahead); free.

The complex of three theaters – Dorothy Chandler Pavilion, Ahmanson Theatre and Mark Taper Forum – known collectively as the **Music Center of Los Angeles County** (☎ 213-972-7211), 135 N Grand Ave, dominates the west end of the Civic Center mall, between 1st and Temple Sts. Free one-hour guided tours (☎ 213-972-7483) run Tuesday, Thursday, Friday and Saturday, between 10 am and 1:30 pm from May to October (from November to April they run Tuesday to Thursday and Saturday).

By the time you read this, ground should have been broken for the **Walt Disney Concert Hall**, a theater to be located just south of the Music Center, on 1st St. Conceived as the future home of the LA Philharmonic Orchestra, this daring structure by Frank Gehry is scheduled to open in 2001.

El Pueblo de Los Angeles

This 44-acre state historic park north of the Civic Center commemorates the founding site of LA and preserves many of LA's earliest buildings. Fiestas and lively celebrations take place in the pueblo throughout the year.

The park's main attraction is **Olvera St**, a narrow, block-long passageway that's been an open-air Mexican marketplace since 1930. Volunteers lead free two-hour walking tours of El Pueblo Tuesday to Saturday mornings from the visitor center (☎ 213-680-2525) in the 1887 **Sepulveda House**. Also on Olvera St is LA's oldest building, the refurbished **Avila Adobe** (1818), built by a wealthy Mexican ranchero who was LA's mayor in 1810.

Olvera St spills into the Old Plaza, the central square of the original pueblo. West of the plaza is the **Church of Our Lady the Queen of the Angels**, 535 N Main St, originally built of adobe by Franciscan monks and native laborers, between 1818 and 1822.

Southeast of El Pueblo is **Union Station** (☎ 213-683-6875), 800 N Alameda St. The last of the great railroad stations in the US, it was built in 1939. The station's impressive marble-floored waiting room features massive chandeliers dangling above clunky leather armchairs. You may have seen the station in the movies *Bugsy* and *The Way We Were*.

Chinatown

Fewer than 5% of LA's 170,000 Chinese make their home in the 16 sq blocks of Chinatown, but the district north of El Pueblo along Broadway and Hill St is still their social and cultural center. Ask at El Pueblo's visitor center for a walking-tour map of Chinatown ($1.50).

Dozens of restaurants and shops, whose inventories range from cheap kitsch to exquisite silk clothing, inlaid furniture, antique porcelain and intricate religious art, line the streets of Chinatown. In passages like **Bamboo Lane** and **Gin Ling Way**, you'll find traditional acupuncturists and herbalists. At 931 N Broadway is **Kong Chow Temple**, on the 2nd floor, above the East West Bank. To enter, ring the bell and someone will let you in. *Kong Chow*, which translates as 'old temple,' is more than 100 years old and filled with antiques.

Little Tokyo

Immediately south of the Civic Center is Little Tokyo, roughly bounded by 1st and 4th Sts on the north and south, Alameda St on the east and Los Angeles St on the west. This bustling neighborhood was first settled by early Japanese immigrants in the 1880s. During WWII, it was decimated when thousands of US-born Japanese were forced into internment camps. The community took decades to recover. Today, Little Tokyo – or 'J-Town' – is again the social, economic and cultural center for nearly a quarter million Japanese Americans. Along the streets and outdoor shopping centers, you'll find sushi bars, temples and traditional Japanese gardens.

The highlight of the district is the **Japanese American National Museum** (JANM; ☎ 213-625-0414), 369 E 1st St. The museum originally opened in 1992 in the historic Nishi Hongwanji Buddhist temple (1925); in 1998 a new second building opened adjacent to the original. The focus here is on objects of work and worship, photographs and art that relate the history of Japanese emigration to, and life in, the US. Hours are 11 am to 5 pm (Thursdays to 8 pm), closed Monday; $4/3.

Behind the JANM is the **Geffen Contemporary** (☎ 213-626-6222) in a Frank Gehry-designed warehouse at 152 N Central Ave, MOCA's sister museum. It's primarily used for traveling exhibits and large-scale installations. For hours and admission, see MOCA in the Financial District section.

Arts District

In the dilapidated, industrial section on the eastern edge of Downtown, a lively loft arts district has sprung up with plenty of artists' studios and galleries, mostly filled with highly unusual and experimental art. The **Brewery Art Complex** is a self-contained artist colony at 2100 N Main St. Studios are closed to the public except during the twice-annual free Brewery Art Walks (usually in Spring and Fall), though no one will stop you from wandering around to examine the large installations scattered throughout the complex during the rest of the year. The complex also contains two galleries, usually open noon to 4 pm Wednesday to Sunday. Another concentration of galleries and studios is around Traction Ave, just east of Little Tokyo.

Near the Brewery Art Complex is one of LA's best-kept secrets, the **San Antonio Winery** (☎ 213-223-1401), 737 Lamar St, the last remaining winery in the city. It takes vivid imagination to believe that the glass-and-steel towers of Downtown LA stand on land once carpeted with vineyards. In 1917, the year when Italian immigrant Santo Cambianica founded San Antonio Winery, LA had nearly 100 wineries that provided the germ cell for California's fecund wine industry. Today, only owner Steve Riboli and his staff uphold the family tradition, producing prize-winning wines from grapes grown in Northern California. Free tastings are available daily in their tasting room.

South Park

Downtown's South Park district is roughly bordered by I-110 and Hill St to the west and east, respectively, and 9th and I-10 north and south. With the Los Angeles Convention Center as the focal point, the neighborhood is slowly being transformed from sleepy and run-down to vital and spiffed up. Developers hope that the new **Staples Center**, on Figueroa St, will bring added stimulus to the entire Downtown area. Opening in fall 1999, it will be the state-of-the-art home of the LA Lakers and LA Clippers basketball teams and the LA Kings ice hockey team.

East of the center is the **Museum of Neon Art** (MONA; ☎ 213-489-9918), 501 W Olympic Blvd. The only permanent facility of its kind, it showcases artists working in neon, electric and kinetic art. Hours are 11 am to 5 pm Wednesday to Saturday, noon to 5 pm Sunday; $5/3.50.

Southeast of here is LA's **Fashion District**, a 56-block area framed by Broadway and Wall St and 7th St and Pico Blvd. The district forms LA's clothing manufacturing, wholesale and retail center. For details, see the Shopping section later this chapter.

In the 700 block of Wall St is the **Flower Market**, the largest cut-flower market in the country, employing nearly 2000 people and dating back to 1913. Originally off-limits to retail shoppers, the market is now open to the public 8 am to noon Monday, Wednesday and Friday and 6 am to noon Tuesday, Thursday and Saturday. Admission is $2 weekdays, $1 on Saturday.

Nearby, at 1334 S Central Ave, is the 1937 **Coca-Cola Bottling Plant**, whose streamline moderne facade features such design elements as a ship's bridge, porthole windows, ship doors and metal balconies. The corners of an adjacent office building sport two enormous Coke bottles.

EXPOSITION PARK
Exposition Park, which began as a farmers' market in 1872, covers the equivalent of 25 square blocks south of Exposition Blvd and west of Figueroa St. Besides three world-class museums, its grounds contain the Los Angeles Memorial Coliseum, the Memorial Sports Arena and a 7-acre sunken **rose garden** featuring 150 varieties of the noble blossom.

Exposition Park is served from Downtown by DASH buses. The surrounding area, once one of LA's grandest residential districts, is marked by Victorian, Queen Anne and art deco structures.

Natural History Museum of LA County
The wonderful Natural History Museum of LA County (☎ 213-763-3466) is housed in an imposing 1913 Spanish-style structure on the northwestern edge of the park. The museum's vast collections chronicle the earth's evolution and showcase the astonishing diversity of natural life. Two habitat halls present African and North American mammals, but the Dinosaur Hall is the most reliable crowd pleaser. Smaller galleries are dedicated to American history from the pre-Columbian

era to 1914 and to 400 years of California history. The Gem and Mineral Hall dazzles with 2000 specimens, including 300lb of gold. Kids love the Insect Zoo, with its local and exotic creepy crawlies like tarantulas, Madagascan hissing cockroaches and even a giant ant farm. Other exhibits include the Great Bird Hall and the Marine Life Hall. Hours are 9:30 am to 5 pm weekdays, from 10 am weekends; $8/5.50/2 adults/seniors/children.

California Science Center
The California Science Center (☎ 323-724-3623) is a $130-million reinvention of the former Museum of Science and Industry, and a favorite family destination. An interactive, state-of-the-art facility, the museum couches educational experience in a playful, visually delightful environment. Complicated scientific principles are presented accessibly and with a sense of humor.

There are two main exhibition areas. The **World of Life** exhibit, whose highlight is **Bodyworks**, a theater starring a super-sized techno-doll named Tess, which 'comes to life' in a 15-minute multimedia show intended to illustrate homeostasis. Virtual reality games, high-tech simulators, laser animation and other such gadgetry await in the **Creative World** exhibit, whose focus is on human innovations in the fields of communication, transportation and structures. Not to be missed is the **earthquake simulator**, which is enjoyed by out-of-towners but often gives Angelenos visceral flashbacks of the last big jolt. Also fun is the **high wire bicycle** in the central Science Court: junior daredevils, safely strapped into a harness, pedal along the thick cable 43 feet above the floor, counterbalanced by an enormous weight attached to the bicycle.

Museum hours are 10 am to 5 pm daily, except major holidays; free.

Next door is the **IMAX Theater** (☎ 213-744-2014), where movies are screened in 2D, and in a 3D format for which you don polarized, lightweight glasses. Tickets are $8.

California African American Museum
This state-owned museum (☎ 213-744-7432), in the park's northeastern corner, does an

LOS ANGELES

excellent job presenting the complex range of African and African-American art and artifacts in an educational and pleasing environment. Hours are 10 am to 5 pm, closed Monday and major holidays; free.

Los Angeles Memorial Coliseum

This 106,000-seat stadium (☎ 213-748-6131), 3911 S Figueroa St, was built in 1923 and enlarged in 1932. It has hosted not just the 1932 and 1984 Summer Olympic Games, but also the World Series in 1959 and Super Bowls I and VII. One-hour tours run Tuesday, Thursday and Saturday (except on event days) at 10:30 am, noon and 1:30 pm and cost $4/2/1 (call ☎ 213-765-6347 for reservations). Entry is through Gate 33A.

The adjacent **Los Angeles Memorial Sports Arena** (☎ 213-748-6136), 3939 S Figueroa St, dates from 1959 and hosts rock concerts, ice shows, circuses and rodeos.

University of Southern California

Across from Exposition Park at Hoover St and Exposition Blvd, USC, founded in 1880, is one of the oldest private research universities in the American West. Distinguished alumni include George Lucas, John Wayne, Frank Gehry and Neil Armstrong. Free 50-minute campus walking tours are offered 10 am to 3 pm daily; call ☎ 213-740-6605 for reservations.

On campus is the **Fisher Gallery** (☎ 213-740-4561), 823 Exposition Blvd, whose permanent collection includes 19th-century American landscapes, British artists and works from the French Barbizon school. Hours are noon to 5 pm Tuesday to Friday and 11 am to 3 pm Saturday, closed May through August; free.

Just beyond the northeast boundary of the campus looms the 1926 Moorish-style **Shrine Auditorium** (☎ 213-749-5123), 665 W Jefferson Blvd. Besides being the occasional home of the Grammy Awards, the American Music Awards and the Academy Awards, it is also the gathering place and headquarters of the Al-Malaikah Temple, a subdivision of the Arabic Order of Nobles of the Mystic Shrine, aka Shriners.

EAST LOS ANGELES

Driving into East LA – just beyond the LA River east of Downtown – feels a bit like crossing the border from San Diego into Tijuana. With more than 90% of its 1 million residents Latino, this area has the largest concentration of Mexicans outside of Mexico. Though unlikely, the risk of becoming the victim of a crime is greater here than almost anywhere else in LA (with the possible exception of Compton). If you're interested in seeing what life in the barrio is like, come in the daytime. Communication may be easier if you speak at least a few words of Spanish, since not everyone here is bilingual.

Good streets to explore are **Cesar Chavez Ave**, **Mission Rd** and the neon-festooned **Whittier Blvd**, whose section between I-710 and Atlantic Blvd has been dubbed 'East LA's Sunset Strip' for its concentration of clubs, bars and restaurants.

On 3540 N Mission Rd at Valley Blvd is **Plaza de la Raza**, a community arts center that provides free or low-cost after-school classes in theater, dance and the fine arts to underprivileged children in this neighborhood. Another such center is **Self-Help Graphics** (☎ 323-264-1259), 3802 Cesar E Chavez Ave, founded in 1972 by Sister Karen Boccalero, a Franciscan nun with a strong belief in the healing powers of art. Inside are several galleries and a great gift shop. Skip the studio of the arrogant metal worker in the parking lot who seems to have a problem with non-Latino visitors. Instead, check out the beautiful sculpture of the Virgen de Guadalupe, made from tile and glass shards, also in the parking lot.

Mariachi Plaza, at the corner of Boyle Ave and 1st St, is where traditional Mexican musicians wait beneath wall-sized murals to be hired for restaurant performances or social gatherings. Nearby is **El Mercado**, a wonderfully boisterous, sticky and colorful indoor market at 3425 E 1st St, where vendors sell everything from tortilla-making machines to mariachi outfits. At a couple of lively restaurants upstairs, you'll be serenaded with live mariachi music.

SOUTH CENTRAL

Most visitors to LA – and many LA residents – tend to avoid South Central LA, a largely impoverished district that extends south on either side of I-110 from Exposition Park and Martin Luther King Jr Blvd. Many of its neighborhoods were hurt by the 1992 riots, as they were by the Watts riots of 1965. While not a traditional tourist destination, South Central has a culture and history entirely its own. Early LA moguls built grand mansions in South Central, and its culture and arts – especially jazz music – invited comparison to New York's Harlem.

Watts Towers

The Watts area's best-known attraction is the towers of Simon Rodia, at 1765 E 107th St. In 1921, Italian immigrant Rodia, an unskilled laborer, began assembling a free-form sculpture from discarded pipes, steel rods, bed frames and cement embellished with shards of glass, tile, porcelain and seashells. When, in 1954, he decided his work was finished, the assemblage included several towers (the tallest standing almost 100 feet), a gazebo with a circular bench and three birdbaths. It is considered among the world's greatest works of folk art. It's currently under restoration; tours are suspended at least until 2001, though most details can still be appreciated through the fence. The adjacent **Watts Towers Art Center** (☎ 213-485-1795) sponsors free art classes, dance and theater workshops and other programs designed to involve the community and to help locals express themselves artistically.

Watts Labor Community Action Center

This 7-acre complex, simply known as the Center (☎ 323-563-5600), 10950 S Central Ave, was built after the 1992 riots as a symbol of community pride and a place for locals to define themselves through art and

---

To Save & Protect

Guadalupe is beautiful, dark-skinned and wears an innocent smile and flowing robes. She's also the most powerful woman in East LA, a vast neighborhood that's almost entirely Latino. Revered and feared, Guadalupe stops robberies, calls on people to treat each other with respect, protects store owners and keeps taggers from defacing buildings. And she's just about everywhere: you see her around every street corner, gracing stores, apartment buildings and churches.

Her full name is Virgen de Guadalupe and she's a strong spiritual symbol among Mexican Catholics living in neighborhoods where violence and destruction of property are as normal as the sunrise. Her image acts as a deterrent to criminals more effectively than an entire battalion of cops. Shop owners have discovered that having a mural of the Virgen on their facades will keep business out of harm's way. Gang bangers, grandmothers and all the folks in between cross themselves when walking by the paintings.

In an interview with the *LA Times* one tough guy reasoned: 'I don't really trip on her…but I respect her because she's the mother of God. She was pregnant through the spirit.'

In a way it's nothing less than a miracle that it's not prison or even death that scares the bejesus out of these guys. It's a tiny woman in a robe.

LOS ANGELES

The Los Angeles Riots: 1992 & 1965

April 29, 1992: 'Not guilty' – the words cut through the stifling air of a hushed Simi Valley courtroom like a dagger through silk, their gravity unfathomed. More than a year earlier, Simi Valley – a quiet, primarily white desert community on the very northwestern rim of LA County – had been the site of the beating of Rodney King by a cuadrilla of Los Angeles Police Department (LAPD) officers. George Holliday, an amateur photographer, had immortalized the drubbing on a videotape that showed the cops relentlessly kicking, beating and shouting at the African American as he crouched on the asphalt. The images were beamed across the globe ad nauseam.

The verdict that acquitted the officers of all charges unleashed a torrent of fury that would flood the city for three days. Enraged residents of South Central began looting stores in their own community, setting buildings ablaze and assaulting innocent bystanders. As the rioting spread, businesses and schools closed throughout the city and a dusk curfew was imposed, leaving frightened Angelenos huddled in their homes watching events unfold on television. A tearful Rodney King sobbed, 'Can't we all just get along?' an appeal to the rioters as naive as it was futile. The National Guard finally helped restore a semblance of order. The shocking toll: more than 50 dead, 4000 injured, 12,000 arrested and $1 billion in property damage.

The riots of 1992 were eerily reminiscent of the Watts riots a generation earlier. Back in August 1965, a routine traffic stop triggered an angry mob that raged through Watts, determined to pay LA back for decades of oppression, injustice and discrimination. Six days later, as the city began to lick its wounds, then-Governor Pat Brown appointed a commission to study the causes of the riots. The panel found an unemployment rate in South Central double that of the rest of the city, along with overcrowded and underfunded classrooms and housing laws that kept African Americans ghettoized and in substandard homes.

Almost 30 years later, people were once again asking why. Angelenos are split about the root causes of the '92 riots. While most admit that forms of discrimination still exist, others suspect that the riots were not politically motivated but were rather an expression of simple material greed. TV images of laughing hordes hauling everything from sneakers to VCRs from ravaged stores and triumphantly posing with their loot for the cameras have left many thinking that the 'riots' were little more than a free-for-all looting spree. Perhaps the question to ask is, Has LA learned? Or will it burn again a generation from now?

cultural expression. Its highlight is the **Civil Rights Museum**, which has a re-created Mississippi Delta dirt road and an exhibit on Martin Luther King Jr. The museum is open daily; free. The center is primarily a community center, so it does not have set operating hours; call ahead to be sure it's open.

Leimert Park

This neighborhood, south of Martin Luther King Jr Blvd and east of Crenshaw Blvd, is a lovely district with quiet streets canopied by towering trees and lined by gorgeous homes of professional African Americans. In recent years, it's become the hub of cutting-edge

black art and music. The **Museum in Black** (☎ 323-292-9528), 4331 Degnan Blvd, displays masks, fertility and spiritual power figures, instruments, jewelry, beads and other artifacts, mostly imported from Africa, and a collection of American 'Negro' memorabilia – salt shakers, cookie tins and other items portraying exaggerated racial stereotypes of black people. The museum is usually open noon to 6 pm weekdays; free.

Nearby is the **Museum of African American Art** (☎ 323-294-7071), on the 3rd floor of the Robinsons-May department store in the Baldwin Hills Crenshaw Plaza mall at 4005 S Crenshaw Blvd. It's noted for its works of

Palmer Hayden, a leading painter of the Harlem Renaissance. Hours are 11 am to 6 pm Thursday to Saturday, noon to 5 pm Sunday; free.

HOLLYWOOD (MAP 3)

Visitors to Hollywood expecting a dreamworld of celluloid perfection are in for a bummer. Hollywood is all grit and grime; the entire entertainment industry is everywhere *but* here, and you're more as likely to bump into Tom Cruise or Michelle Pfeiffer at Hollywood and Vine as you are to be around for that 9.0 earthquake everybody yacks about. The Queen Anne-style Janes House (☎ 323-461-9520), 6541 Hollywood Blvd, houses a visitor center where you can pick up information and pamphlets about Hollywood and book tours.

Hollywood Sign

This is Hollywood's, and indeed LA's, most recognizable landmark, built in 1923 as an advertising gimmick for a real estate development dubbed 'Hollywoodland.' Each letter is 50 feet tall and made of sheet metal. Hiking up to the sign may seem like a great idea, but it is illegal; for good views, head to **Griffith Park Observatory** or to the top of Beachwood Drive.

Hollywood Blvd

More than 2000 marble-and-bronze stars are embedded in the sidewalk along the **Hollywood Walk of Fame**, stretching east from La Brea Ave to Gower St and south along Vine St between Yucca St and Sunset Blvd. Each star has the celebrity's name engraved and an emblem identifying their artistic field – movies, TV, radio, recording or live theater. Induction ceremonies are held once or twice a month. Call the Hollywood Chamber of Commerce at ☎ 323-489-8311 for the schedule.

At No 7021, the **Hollywood Entertainment Museum** (☎ 323-465-7900) employs state-of-the-art technology for a fun look at the history and mystery of moviemaking – even if it falls short of capturing the glitz and glamour of the art. Hours are 10 am to 6 pm, closed Monday; $7.50/4.50/4 adults/seniors/children.

In the same block, at No 7000, is the 1927 **Hollywood Roosevelt Hotel** (☎ 323-466-7000), which hosted the first Academy Awards ceremony in 1929. It has one of the best historical exhibits about Hollywood on the mezzanine level; free. Catty-corner from the hotel is **Mann's Chinese Theater** (☎ 323-464-8111), at No 6925, the most famous of Hollywood movie palaces (1927). Leaving one's foot or handprints in wet cement in the forecourt has been a special honor since Douglas Fairbanks, Mary Pickford and Norma Talmadge started the tradition. Some celebrities even chose to immortalize other body parts: Jimmy Durante imprinted his nose in the cement, and Betty Grable imprinted her famous legs.

The **El Capitan Theater** (☎ 323-467-7674), at No 6838, has an impressively ornate Spanish Colonial facade and a flamboyant East Indian-inspired interior. Around the corner, at 1666 Highland Ave, is the future home of the **Hollywood Historical Museum**, still under creation at the time of writing.

A trio of well-visited, overpriced tourist traps are **Ripley's Believe it or Not!** (☎ 323-466-6335) at 6780 Hollywood Blvd, where you can examine 300 exhibits of the weird and wild; the **Guinness Book of Records Museum** (☎ 323-462-8860) next door; and the **Hollywood Wax Museum** (☎ 323-462-5991), across the street at No 6767.

A few doors east, at No 6712, is the **Egyptian Theatre**, whose design was inspired by the discovery of King Tut's tomb in 1922. It now houses the American Cinematheque, a nonprofit film organization offering several public screenings daily.

At **Frederick's of Hollywood Lingerie Museum** (☎ 323-466-8506), 6608 Hollywood Blvd, you can admire a tasseled bustier worn by Madonna, Joan Crawford's billowy underskirt and Robert Redford's boxers. You'll also get a not-so-serious look at the evolving shape of bra fashions. Hours are 10 am to 6 pm daily, noon to 5 pm Sunday; free.

The most interesting sight in the vicinity of the fabled intersection of Hollywood and Vine is the **Capitol Records Tower**, 1750 N Vine St, looking very much like a stack of records topped by a stylus.

LOS ANGELES

Hollywood Hills

The rugged ridges above Hollywood are prime real estate for celebrities. An architectural star is the **Freeman House** (☎ 323-851-0671), 1962 Glencoe Way at Hillcrest Rd, designed by Frank Lloyd Wright in 1924. Tours of this experimental Mayan-influenced home run at 2 and 4 pm Saturday ($10/5).

Each summer, some of the world's finest live music wafts upward from the **Hollywood Bowl** (☎ 323-850-2000), 2301 Highland Ave, an outdoor amphitheater that is the summer home of the LA Philharmonic Orchestra. Going to the Bowl with a picnic and a bottle of wine has been a tradition since 1916. For more on its history, visit the Bowl Museum. Nearby is the 1930 **John Anson Ford Theater** (☎ 323-466-1767), 2580 Cahuenga Blvd, whose hillside backdrop of palms and cypress gives it a particularly intimate feeling.

Barnsdall Art Park

Occupying an olive-shrouded hill on Vermont Ave between Hollywood and Sunset Blvds (enter from Hollywood Blvd), Barnsdall Art Park is a city-owned cultural and arts center. Of minor visitor interest are the center's art galleries which showcase contemporary works by students, faculty and community artists.

The park's main attraction is the **Hollyhock House** (☎ 323-913-4157), Frank Lloyd Wright's earliest LA project, built for oil heiress Aline Barnsdall in 1921. Wright's dramatic design extends the interior living space by juxtaposing each room with an outdoor space. Stylized renditions of the hollyhock, Aline's favorite flower, are incorporated throughout.

Earthquakes and time, however, have caused major structural and cosmetic damage to the Hollyhock House. It is under restoration for the foreseeable future, though tours may still be offered occasionally. Call for information.

WEST HOLLYWOOD (MAP 4)

One of LA's hippest neighborhoods, West Hollywood teems with nightclubs, restaurants and elegant hotels. The **Pacific Design Center** and numerous galleries add an artsy touch, and trendy shops cater to fashion slaves from around the world. West Hollywood is also the heart of LA's gay and lesbian community, which accounts for one third of the West Hollywood's 36,000 residents. The Christopher Street Pride Parade in June attracts a quarter million people to Santa Monica Blvd, and the festivities on Halloween are a scream as well.

The West Hollywood Convention & Visitors Bureau (☎ 310-289-2525, 800-368-6020, fax 310-289-2529) is on the mezzanine level in the Pacific Design Center, 8687 Melrose Ave, Suite M26. Hours are 8:30 am to 5:30 pm weekdays.

Gay & Lesbian LA

West Hollywood (WeHo) – or 'Boyz' Town' – is the heart of LA's gay and lesbian scene, and the action in bars, restaurants and clubs along Santa Monica Blvd and its side streets goes on around the clock. Most places cater largely to male homosexuals, though some venues also welcome lesbians.

Vanity reigns supreme in West Hollywood, and the intimidation factor can be high unless you're buffed, bronzed and styled. The scene is more low-key in Silver Lake, cruising heaven for the Levi's, leather and Latino crowd. The beach towns are even more relaxed and have neighborly hangouts; and venues in the San Fernando Valley are altogether more mundane and mainstream gay.

Frontiers Magazine and *Edge* for men, and *Lesbian News* and *LA Girl Guide* for women, are free magazines that have complete updates and entertainment listings. A Different Light Bookstore (☎ 310-854-6601), 8853 Santa Monica Blvd in West Hollywood, is the city's number one gay bookstore. Sisterhood Bookstore (☎ 310-477-7300), at 1351 Westwood Blvd in Westwood, has books, music, jewelry and crafts by women for women, though not exclusively for lesbians.

LOS ANGELES

Celebrity impersonators at Universal Studios

Sand sculptures, Los Angeles

Palisades Park, Santa Monica

Día de los Muertos, Los Angeles

LEE FOSTER

Downtown Los Angeles freeway at night

DAVID PEEVERS

Surfer at Manhattan Beach

DAVID PEEVERS

Teacups at Disneyland

Los Angeles Map Section

LOS ANGELES

MAP 2 DOWNTOWN LO

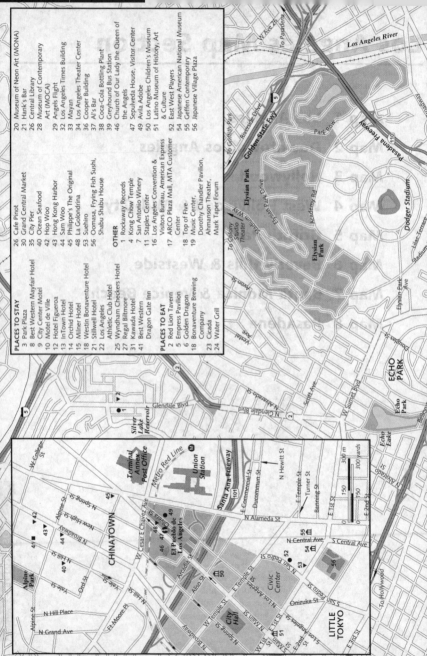

PLACES TO STAY
3 Park Plaza
8 Best Western Mayfair Hotel
9 City Center Motel
10 Motel de Ville
12 Hotel Figueroa
13 InTown Hotel
14 Orchid Hotel
15 Milner Hotel
18 Westin Bonaventure Hotel
21 Stillwell Hotel
22 Los Angeles Athletic Club Hotel
25 Wyndham Checkers Hotel
27 Regal Biltmore
31 Kawada Hotel
41 Best Western Dragon Gate Inn

PLACES TO EAT
5 Red Lion Tavern
6 Empress Pavilion
7 Golden Dragon
18 Bonaventure Brewing Company
23 Cicada
24 Water Grill
26 Cafe Pinot
30 Grand Central Market
35 City Pier
40 Ocean Seafood
42 Hop Woo
43 Hong Kong Harbor
44 Sam Woo
45 Philippe's The Original
48 La Golondrina
53 Suehiro
56 Oomasa, Frying Fish Sushi, Shabu Shabu House

OTHER
1 Rockaway Records
4 Kong Chow Temple
11 San Antonio Winery
16 Staples Center
17 Los Angeles Convention & Visitors Bureau, American Express
17 ARCO Plaza Mall, MTA Customer Center
18 Top of Five
19 Music Center, Dorothy Chandler Pavilion, Ahmanson Theater, Mark Taper Forum
20 Museum of Neon Art (MONA)
21 Hank's Bar
26 Central Library
28 Museum of Contemporary Art (MOCA)
29 Angels Flight
32 Los Angeles Times Building
33 Mayan
34 Los Angeles Theater Center
36 Cooper Building
37 Ali's Bar
38 Coca-Cola Bottling Plant
39 Greyhound Bus Station
46 Church of Our Lady the Queen of the Angels
47 Sepulveda House, Visitor Center
49 Avila Adobe
50 Los Angeles Children's Museum
51 Latino Museum of History, Art & Culture
52 East West Players
54 Japanese American National Museum
55 Geffen Contemporary
56 Japanese Village Plaza

PLACES TO STAY
1 Banana Bungalow Hollywood
4 Highland Gardens Hotel
5 Magic Hotel
12 Orange Drive Manor Hostel
13 Orchid Suites Hotel
14 Hollywood Celebrity Hotel
15 Liberty Hotel
19 Hollywood Roosevelt Hotel
22 Hollywood International Hostel
23 Dunes Sunset Motel
28 Saharan Motor Hotel

PLACES TO EAT
6 Yamashiro
9 Birds
18 Palermo, Fred's 62
20 Hamburger Hamlet
25 Dar Maghreb
31 Cat & Fiddle Pub
34 El Chavo
40 El Floridita
43 Cafe Stella
44 El Conquistador
45 Patina
47 El Siete Mares
50 Musso & Frank Grill
60 Miceli's
61 Les Deux Café

Mt Lee 1680ft ▲

Hollywood Sign

To Universal City

Hollywood Reservoir

Dam

HOLLYWOOD HILLS

Hollywood Bowl

Runyon Canyon Park

Outpost Drive

Wattles Garden Park

Camrose Drive

Sycamore Ave

Hillcrest Rd

Scenic Gardens

Franklin Ave

N Vista St

N Sierra Bonita Ave

Hollywood Franklin Park

Orchid Ave

Hollywood Blvd

Franklin Ave

Yucca St

N Cahuenga Blvd

N Beachwood Drive

Hollywood Freeway

see inset map

CBS Studios

Camino Palmero

N Curson Ave

N La Brea Ave

N Orange Drive

N Highland Ave

W Sunset Blvd

HOLLYWOOD

Wilcox Ave

N Gower St

N Bronson St

N Van Ness St

Delongpre Park

Fountain Ave

Hollywood Recreation Center

Plummer Park

To West Hollywood, Beverly Hills

N Gardner St

N Martel Ave

Warner Hollywood Studios

Poinsettia Recreation Center

N Formosa Ave

N Sycamore Ave

Santa Monica Blvd

Willoughby Ave

Waring Ave

Cole Ave

N Cahuenga Blvd

N Vine St

El Centro Ave

Hollywood Memorial Park

Beth Olam Memorial Park

Paramount Studios

Melrose Ave

N Highland Ave

Las Palmas Ave

Hollywood Blvd

N Cahuenga Blvd

Shrader Blvd

Selma Ave

N Vine St

Rosewood Ave

The Wilshire Country Club

N Rossmore Ave

Beverly Blvd

Robert Burns Park

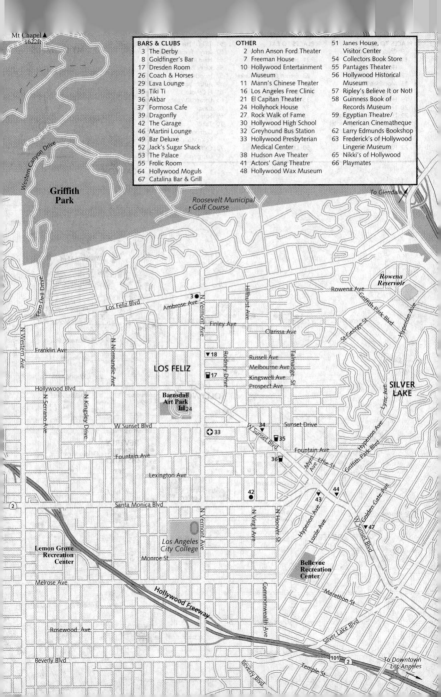

BARS & CLUBS
- 3 The Derby
- 8 Goldfinger's Bar
- 17 Dresden Room
- 26 Coach & Horses
- 29 Lava Lounge
- 35 Tiki Ti
- 36 Akbar
- 37 Formosa Cafe
- 39 Dragonfly
- 42 The Garage
- 46 Martini Lounge
- 49 Bar Deluxe
- 52 Jack's Sugar Shack
- 53 The Palace
- 55 Frolic Room
- 64 Hollywood Moguls
- 67 Catalina Bar & Grill

OTHER
- 2 John Anson Ford Theater
- 7 Freeman House
- 10 Hollywood Entertainment Museum
- 11 Mann's Chinese Theater
- 16 Los Angeles Free Clinic
- 21 El Capitan Theater
- 24 Hollyhock House
- 27 Rock Walk of Fame
- 30 Hollywood High School
- 32 Greyhound Bus Station
- 33 Hollywood Presbyterian Medical Center
- 38 Hudson Ave Theater
- 41 Actors' Gang Theatre
- 48 Hollywood Wax Museum
- 51 Janes House, Visitor Center
- 54 Collectors Book Store
- 55 Pantages Theater
- 56 Hollywood Historical Museum
- 57 Ripley's Believe It or Not!
- 58 Guinness Book of Records Museum
- 59 Egyptian Theatre/ American Cinematheque
- 62 Larry Edmunds Bookshop
- 63 Frederick's of Hollywood Lingerie Museum
- 65 Nikki's of Hollywood
- 66 Playmates

Mt Chapel▲ 1622ft

Western Canyon Drive

Griffith Park

Roosevelt Municipal Golf Course

To Glendale

Fern Dell Drive

Rowena Reservoir

Rowena Ave

Griffith Park Blvd

Hyperion Ave

Los Feliz Blvd

Ambrose Ave

N Vermont Ave

Hillhurst Ave

Finley Ave

Clarissa Ave

St George St

Franklin Ave

N Western Ave

N Normandie Ave

LOS FELIZ

Rodney Drive

Talmadge St

Russell Ave
Melbourne Ave
Kingswell Ave
Prospect Ave

SILVER LAKE

Hollywood Blvd

N Serrano Ave

N Kingsley Drive

Barnsdall Art Park

W Sunset Blvd

Sunset Drive

Fountain Ave

Lyric Ave

Hyperion Ave

Griffith Park Blvd

Fountain Ave

Lexington Ave

N Virgil Ave

N Hoover St

Hollywood Blvd

Santa Monica Blvd

Los Angeles City College

N Vermont Ave

Lucile Ave

Golden Gate Ave

W Sunset Blvd

Bellevue Recreation Center

Lemon Grove Recreation Center

Monroe St

Melrose Ave

Hollywood Freeway

Marathon St

Rosewood Ave

Commonwealth Ave

Silver Lake Blvd

Beverly Blvd

Beverly Blvd

Temple St

To Downtown Los Angeles

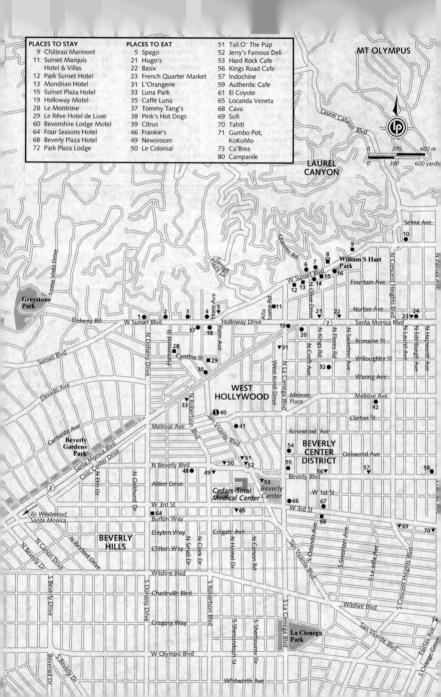

PLACES TO STAY
- 9 Château Marmont
- 11 Sunset Marquis Hotel & Villas
- 12 Park Sunset Hotel
- 13 Mondrian Hotel
- 15 Sunset Plaza Hotel
- 19 Holloway Motel
- 28 Le Montrose
- 29 Le Rêve Hotel de Luxe
- 60 Bevonshire Lodge Motel
- 64 Four Seasons Hotel
- 68 Beverly Plaza Hotel
- 72 Park Plaza Lodge

PLACES TO EAT
- 5 Spago
- 21 Hugo's
- 22 Basix
- 23 French Quarter Market
- 31 L'Orangerie
- 33 Luna Park
- 35 Caffé Luna
- 37 Tommy Tang's
- 38 Pink's Hot Dogs
- 39 Citrus
- 46 Frankie's
- 49 Newsroom
- 50 Le Colonial
- 51 Tail O' The Pup
- 52 Jerry's Famous Deli
- 53 Hard Rock Cafe
- 56 Kings Road Cafe
- 57 Indochine
- 59 Authentic Cafe
- 61 El Coyote
- 65 Locanda Veneta
- 68 Cava
- 69 Sofi
- 70 Tahiti
- 71 Gumbo Pot, KoKoMo
- 73 Ca'Brea
- 80 Campanile

MT OLYMPUS

Laurel Canyon Blvd

LAUREL CANYON

Selma Ave

William S Hart Park

Fountain Ave

Norton Ave

Santa Monica Blvd

Doheny Rd

W Sunset Blvd

Holloway Drive

Romaine St

Willoughby St

Waring Ave

Greystone Park

Sunset Blvd

Cynthia St

WEST HOLLYWOOD

Melrose Ave

Melrose Place

Clinton St

Rosewood Ave

BEVERLY CENTER DISTRICT

Oakwood Ave

Beverly Gardens Park

Santa Monica Blvd

Civic Center Drive

Melrose Ave

N Beverly Blvd

Alden Drive

Beverly Blvd

Cedars-Sinai Medical Center

Beverly Center

W 1st St

W 3rd St

To Westwood, Santa Monica

W 3rd St

Burton Way

Dayton Way

BEVERLY HILLS

Colgate Ave

Clifton Way

Wilshire Blvd

Charleville Blvd

Gregory Way

La Cienega Park

Wilshire Blvd

W Olympic Blvd

Whitworth Ave

ENTERTAINMENT
1 Key Club
2 The Roxy,
   Rainbow Bar & Grill
3 Whisky a Go Go
6 Comedy Store
8 Thunder Roadhouse
10 Laugh Factory
13 Sky Bar
14 House of Blues
17 Viper Room
24 Club 7969
27 Celebration Theater
36 Groundlings Theater
42 The Improv
55 Coronet Theater,
   Coronet Pub
58 Fairfax Cinema
62 New Beverly Cinema
63 Acme Comedy Theater
78 Conga Room

SHOPPING
4 Tower Records
18 Book Soup
20 Dreamdresser
25 Pleasure Chest
30 A Different Light Bookstore
34 Aardvark
36 Off the Wall
41 Daniel Saxon Gallery
43 Scents from Above
44 Slow
45 Wasteland, Wound & Wound
47 Necromance
48 Antiquarius
54 Trashy Lingerie
67 Traveler's Bookcase

OTHER
7 Hyatt Hotel
16 The Argyle
26 Porno Walk of Fame
32 MAK Center for
   Art & Architecture at the
   Schindler House
40 Pacific Design Center,
   West Hollywood Convention
   & Visitors Bureau
66 American Express
74 Petersen Automotive Museum
75 LA County Museum of Art
76 Carole & Barry Kaye
   Museum of Miniature Art
77 La Brea Tar Pits,
   Page Museum of La Brea
   Discoveries
79 MTA Customer Center

MAP 6 BEVERLY HILLS & WESTSIDE

DAVID PEEVERS

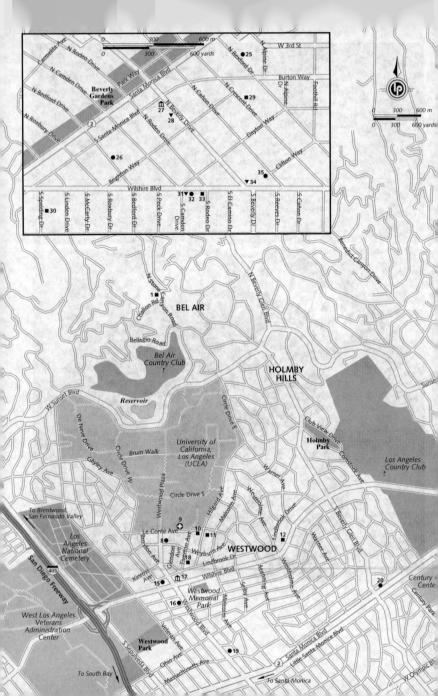

PLACES TO STAY
1 Hotel Bel-Air
3 Beverly Hills Hotel
10 Hilgard House
11 Westwood Marquis Hotel
12 Hotel del Capri
18 Royal Palace Hotel
21 Century Plaza Hotel
29 Crescent Hotel
30 Beverly Hills Inn
33 Regent Beverly Wilshire

PLACES TO EAT
6 Matsuhisa
7 Ed Debevic's
24 Versailles
28 The Farm
31 Planet Hollywood
34 ObaChine

OTHER
2 Greystone Mansion
4 Beverly Hills Post Office
5 American Express
8 STA Travel
9 UCLA Hospital
13 Coconut Club
14 Theatre 40
15 Council Travel
16 Sisterhood Bookstore
17 Armand Hammer Museum
    of Art & Cultural Center
19 Rhino Records
20 Lunaria
22 Shubert Theater
23 Museum of Tolerance
25 Beverly Hills Library
26 Thomas Cook
27 Museum of Television
    & Radio
32 NikeTown
35 Canon Theatre

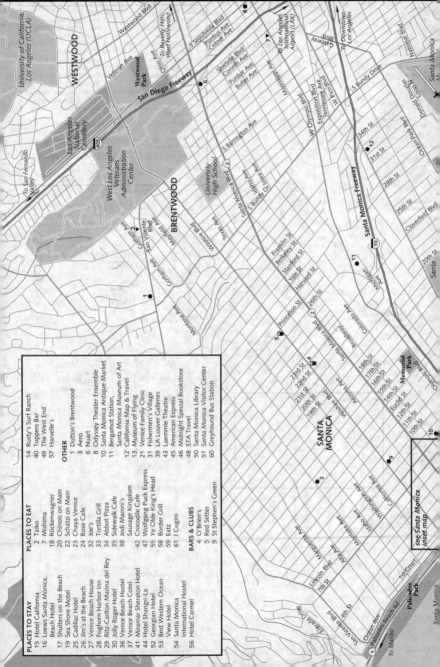

MAP 7 SANTA MONICA

PLACES TO STAY
15 Hotel California
16 Loews Santa Monica Beach Hotel
17 Shutters on the Beach
19 Sea Shore Motel
25 Cadillac Hotel
26 Jim's at the Beach
27 Venice Beach House
28 Foghorn Harbor Inn
29 Ritz-Carlton Marina del Rey
30 Jolly Roger Hotel
36 Venice Beach Hostel
37 Venice Beach Cotel
41 Miramar Sheraton Hotel
44 Hotel Shangri-La
52 Georgian Hotel
53 Best Western Ocean View Hotel
54 Santa Monica International Hostel
56 Hotel Carmel

PLACES TO EAT
2 Taiko
7 Mishima
18 Rockenwagner
20 Chinois on Main
22 Schatzi on Main
23 Chaya Venice
24 Rose Cafe
32 Joe's
33 Tortilla Grill
34 Abbot Pizza
35 Sidewalk Cafe
38 Jodi Maroni's Sausage Kingdom
42 Crocodile Cafe
47 Wolfgang Puck Express
55 Ye Olde King's Head
58 Border Grill
59 Eatz
61 I Cugini

BARS & CLUBS
4 O'Brien's
5 Red Setter
9 St Stephen's Green

14 Rusty's Surf Ranch
40 Toppers Bar
49 The West End
57 Harvelle's

OTHER
1 Dutton's Brentwood
3 Aero
6 Nuart
8 Odyssey Theater Ensemble
10 Santa Monica Antique Market
11 Bergamot Station
12 Santa Monica Museum of Art
13 Museum of Flying
21 Venice Family Clinic
31 Fishermen's Village
39 LA Louver Galleries
43 Laemmle Theatre
45 American Express
46 Midnight Special Bookstore
48 STA Travel
50 Santa Monica Library
51 Santa Monica Visitor Center
60 Greyhound Bus Station

see Santa Monica inset map

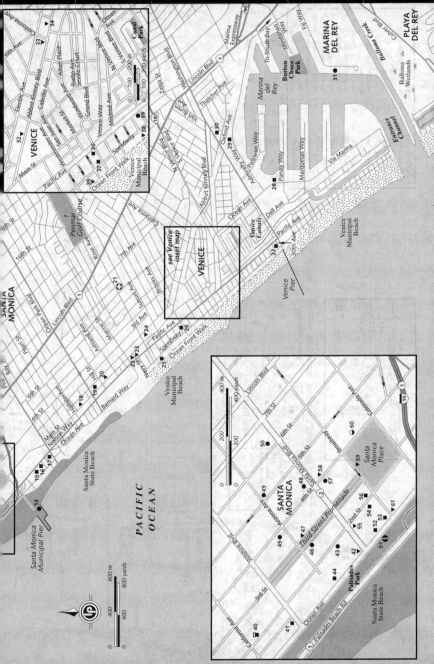

Sunset Strip

The famed Sunset Strip – Sunset Blvd between Laurel Canyon Blvd and Doheny Drive – is renowned as the world's billboard capital, with enormous, and often imaginative, vanity billboards touting new movies, new recordings, new wannabe stars and everybody's favorite 'bad guy' – the Marlboro Man.

Coming from the east, you know you've reached the Strip at the sight of the hulking silhouette of the **Château Marmont** hotel, 8221 Sunset Blvd. Built in 1927, this celebrity hideaway is perhaps best known as the place where comedian John Belushi overdosed. Lodging, dining and entertainment options on the Strip are outlined later in this chapter, but here are a few places worth keeping an eye out for:

The Argyle (1931), 8358 Sunset Blvd
  A glorious monument to art deco, the Argyle is an elegant hotel that is also a frequent movie location (*Pretty Woman*, *The Player*). According to myth, John Wayne once kept a cow in his 12th-floor penthouse.

Thunder Roadhouse, 8371 Sunset Blvd
  Patrick Swayze and Mickey Rourke are rumored to have bought their Harley Davidsons at this cycle shop-cum-biker bar. Its owners include actors Dennis Hopper and Peter Fonda and country singer Dwight Yoakam.

Hyatt Hotel, 8401 Sunset Blvd
  This hotel was a favorite haunt of rock stars in the '70s. Dubbed 'Riot House,' this hotel was wild indeed. Led Zeppelin once rented six floors and rode motorcycles in the hallways, according to Art Fein's *LA Musical History Tour*. Fein also reports that Jim Morrison was once kicked out for hanging out of a window by his fingertips.

Comedy Store, 8433 Sunset Blvd
  David Letterman, Robin Williams and Roseanne Arnold were relative unknowns when they first appeared here. Originally, the club was called Ciro's and was a famous and somewhat shady hangout in the '40s and '50s.

Tower Records, 8801 Sunset Blvd
  To bolster its claim as the world's largest record/compact disc store, Tower added a classical music annex. The store and annex are open until midnight daily.

Viper Room, 8852 Sunset Blvd
  This is the nightclub outside of which River Phoenix died of drug-related complications in 1993. Owned by actor Johnny Depp, this club is a favorite hangout for musicians and others in showbiz.

The next couple of blocks are a page in the book of rock & roll history: the **Whisky a Go Go** at No 8901; the **Roxy** at No 9009; the **Rainbow Bar & Grill** at No 9015; and the Key Club, the former **Gazzarri's**, at No 9039. The Doors, Jimi Hendrix, Bob Marley, Bruce Springsteen and Van Halen are among the many who have performed at these clubs. And if you're into Hollywood history, the Rainbow (then the Villa Nova) was where Marilyn Monroe and baseball star Joe DiMaggio first met on a 'blind' date in 1953. For more on clubs, see Entertainment later this chapter.

LA not only has a Hollywood Walk of Fame, but also a **Rock Walk of Fame**, right in the entrance of the Guitar Center store, 7425 Sunset Blvd. Immortalized in concrete are the hands of legends like BB King, ZZ Top, Steely Dan, the Doobie Brothers and dozens more. And for good measure, there's also the **Porno 'Walk of Fame,'** 7734 Santa Monica Blvd, where hard-core divas and studs like Linda Lovelace and Harry Reems have immortalized their hands and feet (hey, what were *you* thinking?).

Melrose Ave

Until a few years ago, Melrose was LA's epicenter of cool and *the* place for eccentric fashions created by its avant-garde designers. Unfortunately, the cycle of trendiness has moved on, taking some of Melrose's 'edge' with it as mainstream (Gap) and even downscale shops have moved in. This is not to say that Melrose isn't fun anymore. The section between La Brea Blvd and Fairfax Ave, especially, still has lots of fabled restaurants and boutiques just weird enough to confirm every LA cliché ever concocted (see Shopping later this chapter).

Paramount Pictures, 5555 Melrose Ave, is the only movie studio still in Hollywood proper. Two-hour walking tours run weekdays

LOS ANGELES

between 9 am and 2 pm; $15. Children under 10 are not admitted. Call ☎ 323-956-1777 for reservations.

Just north of Paramount Studios, **Hollywood Memorial Park Cemetery** is the final home of legends like Rudolph Valentino, Tyrone Power, Jayne Mansfield, Cecil B DeMille, Edward G Robinson and Douglas Fairbanks. The entrance is at 6000 Santa Monica Blvd between Gower St and Van Ness Blvd. Regular hours are 8 am to 5 pm daily.

Design District
At the heart of a triangle framed by Santa Monica, Beverly and La Cienega Blvds is the Pacific Design Center (☎ 310-657-0800), 8687 Melrose Ave at San Vicente Blvd. This giant glass block, known to locals as the 'Blue Whale,' contains more than 200 showrooms in its 1.2 million sq feet of floor space. Surrounding streets are called the Avenues of Design because of the hundreds of design shops, showrooms and art galleries in the area.

Schindler House
The unusual home of Rudolph Schindler, a leading modernist architect and disciple of Frank Lloyd Wright, is at 835 N Kings Rd. Today, it functions as a think tank for current art and architecture issues but is open for touring 11 am to 6 pm Wednesday to Sunday; $5. Call ☎ 323-651-1510 for information.

MID-CITY (MAP 4)
Mid-City is the area wedged between the Westside and Downtown, north of I-10 but south of Hollywood. **Wilshire Blvd**, which cuts east-west for 16 miles, is the district's principal artery. It passes an eclectic succession of neighborhoods – Koreatown, Hancock Park, the Miracle Mile, the Fairfax District, Beverly Hills, Westwood and finally Santa Monica – before terminating at the Pacific Ocean.

Koreatown
Just east of MacArthur Park is the heart of Koreatown, one of LA's most historic districts. Besides dozens of gorgeous 19th-century churches, the district has the lovely

art deco **Wiltern Theatre** (1931), which gets it name from its location at the southeast corner of *Wil*shire and Wes*tern* Blvds.

The Wiltern has the same turquoise facade as the former 1929 **Bullocks Wilshire Department Store**, a mile east at 3050 Wilshire Blvd. This was the nation's first department store to cater to customers arriving by car. For decades, LA's poshest could be seen capping off successful shopping sprees with afternoon tea in the 5th floor tea room, a tradition that survived until the store closed in 1992. The entire store is now occupied by the Southwestern University School of Law library.

The **Ambassador Hotel** was among LA's grandest hotels when it opened in 1922 but now sits abandoned at 3400 Wilshire Blvd. It was here that Sirhan Sirhan assassinated Democratic presidential nominee Robert F Kennedy in 1968.

Miracle Mile District
The stretch of Wilshire Blvd between La Brea Blvd and Fairfax Ave earned the epithet 'Miracle Mile' after a farseeing entrepreneur, AW Ross, bought previously empty land beside the Rancho La Brea tar pits in 1920 and turned it into a flourishing commercial district by the early 1930s. Today, the strip is also known as 'Museum Row.'

La Brea Tar Pits One of the world's premier paleontological sites, these pits supplied the tar (*brea* in Spanish) used by Native Americans and early settlers to waterproof roofs and boats. In 1906, scientists learned the bubbling black pools had been a unique trap for animal and plant life since the last ice age, beginning 40,000 years ago. Pit excavations yielded more than a million fossilized skeleton parts of such long-extinct mammals as saber-toothed cats, ground sloths, mammoths and mastodons, along with 200 species of birds, reptiles, insects and plant species.

Excavations still continue – usually from July to mid-September – when visitors may observe the process 10 am to 4 pm Wednesday to Sunday; free. For information, call ☎ 323-934-7243.

Page Museum of La Brea Discoveries
Tar pit discoveries are exhibited next door at
the Page Museum (☎ 323-936-2230, www
.tarpits.org), 5801 Wilshire Blvd, where you
also watch scientists in white robes fuss over
an astounding assortment of bones in a glass-
encased paleontology laboratory. Hours are
10 am to 5 pm (closed Monday, daily in
summer); $6/3.50/2 adults/seniors/children,
free the first Tuesday of each month.

LA County Museum of Art Just west of
the tar pits is the Los Angeles County
Museum of Art (LACMA; ☎ 323-857-6000),
5905 Wilshire Blvd, one of the finest art
museums in the US for its size, variety and
staggering permanent collection of art,
sculpture and decorative arts from Asia and
America. The museum is especially strong in
Western European art, from Italy's early
Renaissance to modern masters like Picasso,
Kandinsky, Rothko and David Hockney.

Also on display are 12 centuries of
ancient and Islamic art, with pieces from
Egypt, Greece, Rome, Turkey and Iran. The
museum's assemblage of Southeast Asian
art is comprised of stone and bronze sculpture, painting and decorative arts, and the
Far Eastern section has works from as early
as the Neolithic period (400 to 1800 BC), as
well as bronze, imperial and Song dynasties
and a replica of a Ming-period scholar's
studio. A highlight of the Pavilion for Japanese Art is the collection of rare Shin'enkan
temple paintings. Hours are noon to 8 pm on
Monday, Tuesday and Thursday, to 9 pm on
Friday, 11 am to 8 pm on weekends; $7/5/1.

Museum of Miniature Art The Carole &
Barry Kaye Museum of Miniature Art
(☎ 323-937-6464), 5900 Wilshire Blvd, contains meticulously replicated miniature versions of some 350 palaces, houses, natural
environments, etc, on a scale of 1 to 12.
Thankfully, the kitsch factor has been kept to
a minimum, and most exhibits enchant with
historical detail and superb craftsmanship.
Highlights are Rome's Forum Romanum
and Vatican, and France's Fontainebleau
Palace. Hours are 10 am to 5 pm, from 11 am
Sunday, closed Monday; $7.50/6.50/3.

Petersen Automotive Museum LA's
love affair with the automobile is celebrated
at the Petersen Automotive Museum (☎ 323-
930-2277, www.petersen.org), 6060 Wilshire
Blvd. Even people uninterested in cars will
probably enjoy the mock-streetscape of LA
in the '20s and '30s that chronicle how inven-
tions like gas stations, billboards, mini-malls,
drive-in restaurants and movie theaters were
spawned in LA. Hours are 10 am to 6 pm,
closed Monday; $7/5/3.

Fairfax District
The spine of LA's principal Jewish neighborhood is the section of Fairfax Ave
between Santa Monica and Wilshire Blvds.
It's home to Orthodox and Hassidic Jews,
with lots of yeshivas (gender-segregated
religious day schools) and scores of delis,
kosher butcher shops, furniture stores and
other small businesses.

For visitors, the main point of interest has
nothing to do with Jewish culture; it's the
Farmers Market (☎ 323-933-9211), 6333 W
3rd St. It's as good a place as any to grab a
bite and spend time people-watching. Just
north of the market is **CBS Television City**
(☎ 323-852-2624), 7800 Beverly Blvd.

GRIFFITH PARK (MAP 5)
Spreading across a rugged mountainous
area, Griffith Park is the nation's largest
municipal park. California oak, wild sage
and manzanita blanket much of its 4107
acres. The famous Hollywood sign is atop Mt
Lee, in the park. Within the park's boundaries are an outdoor theater, an observatory,
the city zoo, a major museum, golf courses,
tennis courts, playgrounds, bridle paths and
hiking trails. Park hours are 6 am to 10 pm
daily, but roads and bridle and hiking trails
close at sunset (except the one leading to the
observatory).

**Griffith Observatory
& Planetarium**
On the upper slopes of Mt Hollywood, this
wonderful facility (☎ 323-664-1191), 2800 E
Observatory Rd, has been a local landmark
since 1935. (You may recognize it from
scenes in *Rebel Without a Cause*.) The view

LOS ANGELES

over the city alone is worth making the trip up here.

Housed inside are the **Hall of Science**, a hands-on astronomy museum; two **telescopes** – a 12-inch Zeiss refracting telescope and a solar telescope (not accessible); and the **Planetarium**, with live multimedia presentations several times daily. Its 1964 Zeiss telescope weighs 1 ton and projects about 9000 stars. Take your turn at the telescope any clear night except Monday from 7 to 9:45 pm, or beginning at dusk in summer. The Hall of Science is open in summer 12:30 to 10 pm daily; 2 to 10 pm Tuesday to Sunday the rest of the year. Admission is free except for planetarium shows which are $4/3/2 adults/seniors/children. Show times vary.

Los Angeles Zoo

The LA Zoo (☎ 323-644-6000), 5333 Zoo Drive, may not compare to the renowned San Diego Zoo, but it is well worth a visit, especially for its new Chimpanzees of Mahale Mountains exhibit. Denizens also include 1200 mammals, birds, amphibians and reptiles living in the zoo's re-created natural habitats. There is also an aquatic section, a reptile house, a walk-through aviary and the Adventure Island children's zoo. Zoo hours are 10 am to 5 pm daily; $8.25/5.25/3.25.

Autry Museum of Western Heritage

Anyone interested in the American West should visit this splendid museum (☎ 323-667-2000), 4700 Western Heritage Way, which owes its existence to a generous donation from 'singing cowboy' Gene Autry. Galleries combine scholarship and showmanship to show how the West was discovered again and again, by everyone from prehistoric tribes to Native Americans to missionaries. Special exhibits illustrate what made the West so wild, including an 1880s carved mahogany saloon bar, gaming tables, cheating devices and an impressive Colt collection.

The museum also presents concerts, gallery talks, symposia, panel discussions, film screenings and storytelling sessions for children. Hours are 10 am to 5 pm, closed Monday; $7.50/5/3.50.

Travel Town Museum

Travel Town (☎ 323-662-5874), near the zoo at 5200 N Zoo Drive, is an outdoor transportation museum specializing in pre-WWII railroad antiques. Some 16 steam and diesel locomotives (the oldest from 1864), 10 freight cars and cabooses, and nine passenger cars form part of the collection. On the first Sunday of the month, volunteers run free rides on a caboose pulled by a diesel engine. Trips on a miniature train run daily. Also offered are free docent-led tours of several luxurious, fully restored Union Pacific passenger cars. Museum hours are 10 am to 5 pm weekdays, 10 am to 6 pm weekends, from April to September; closing is one hour earlier the rest of the year; free.

Kid Stuff

Children's attractions, centered in the park's southeast corner, include the historic **Griffith Park Southern Railroad**, which makes a 1-mile loop past pony rides, through an old Western town and a Native American village. Also here is an old-fashioned 1926 **merry-go-round** (11 am to 5 pm daily in summer, weekends only in winter). To get there, follow Crystal Springs Drive up the park's eastern flank.

Forest Lawn Memorial Park – Hollywood Hills

Just west of Griffith Park, at 6300 Forest Lawn Drive, this 340-acre cemetery (☎ 323-254-7251) boasts sculpture, mosaics and artwork, plus a fine catalog of dead celebrities, including Lucille Ball, Liberace, Bette Davis and Stan Laurel. The grounds are open 8 am to 6 pm daily; free.

BEVERLY HILLS (MAP 6)

Throughout the world, mere mention of Beverly Hills conjures images of fame and wealth. TV and film have done their part in reinforcing this image. Stylish and sophisticated, this city-within-a-city is indeed a place where the rich and famous frolic. **Rodeo Drive** is lined with a veritable who's

Famous Alumni

If you want to find out where your favorite celeb studied algebra and French, visit any of the following schools. Except for Immaculate Heart and Harvard-Westlake, all are public schools.

Hollywood High – 1521 Highland Ave
Carol Burnett, Linda Evans, Judy Garland, James Garner, Barbara Hershey, John Ritter, Jason Robards, Mickey Rooney, Charlene Tilton

Beverly Hills High – 241 S Moreno Drive
Corbin Bernson, Albert Brooks, Nicolas Cage, Richard Chamberlain, Jamie Lee Curtis, Richard Dreyfus, Carrie Fisher, Lenny Kravitz, Swoosie Kurtz, Rob Reiner, Pauly Shore

Santa Monica High – 601 Pico Blvd
Glenn Ford, Rob Lowe, Chris Penn, Sean Penn, Charlie Sheen

Westlake School for Girls (now Harvard-Westlake) – 700 N Faring Rd, Bel Air
Candice Bergen, Debby Boone, Bridget Fonda, Tracy Nelson, Sally Ride, Tori Spelling, Shirley Temple

University High – 11800 Texas Ave, West LA
Jeff Bridges, Tone Loc, Randy Newman, Nancy Sinatra, Elizabeth Taylor

Immaculate Heart High –
5515 Franklin Ave, Hollywood
Tyra Banks, Natalie Cole, Mary Tyler Moore

And…Marilyn Monroe, Robert Redford – Van Nuys High; Demi Moore – Redondo Union High; Dustin Hoffman – Los Angeles High; Leonardo DiCaprio – Marshall High; Snoop Doggy Dog – Poly High, Long Beach; Jodie Foster – Le Lycée Français; Myrna Loy – Venice High; Slash of Guns N' Roses – Fairfax High; Quentin Tarantino – Narbonne High, Harbor City; John Wayne – Glendale High

who of fashion designers' shops. Opulent manors face manicured grounds on palm-shaded avenues winding gently uphill on the north side of Santa Monica Blvd. South of Wilshire Blvd are the more simple but no less elegant bungalows of the merely upper class.

You can get maps to the stars' homes at tourist stores or from street-corner vendors, though their maps may not always be current. One of the more intriguing sights is **Greystone Park & Mansion** (☎ 310-550-4654), 905 Loma Vista Drive, where scenes from blockbusters like *The Bodyguard* and *Indecent Proposal* were filmed. Grounds and gardens are open 9 am to 6 pm daily; free. Another landmark is the 1912 **Beverly Hills Hotel & Bungalows** (☎ 310-887-2887), 9641 Sunset Blvd, nicknamed the 'Pink Palace,' whose Polo Lounge is a famous refuge for Industry 'power lunches.'

Museum of Television and Radio

Contrary to its name, the Museum of Television and Radio (MTR; ☎ 310-786-1000), 465 N Beverly Drive, is not a museum but a humongous archive that preserves 90,000 programs spanning 75 years. This dazzling collection is accessible for viewing by museum visitors, in a computerized library. Hours are noon to 5 pm Wednesday to Sunday (noon to 8 pm Thursday); $6/4/3.

Museum of Tolerance

Run by the Simon Wiesenthal Center, this museum (☎ 310-553-9036), 9786 W Pico Blvd, uses the latest interactive technologies to make visitors confront their own closely held beliefs, while teaching them about racism and bigotry. It's an enlightening, frightening and painful experience. The 28,000-sq-foot exhibition has two main thematic sections: the **Tolerancenter**, which focuses on racism and prejudice in America, and the **Holocaust Section**. The only way to experience this museum is on a guided 2½- to three-hour tour, departing continuously 10 am to 4 pm weekdays. On Friday, the last tour starts at 1 pm (3 pm April to October). On Sunday, hours are 11 am to 5 pm. Admission is $8/6/3.

WESTSIDE (MAP 6)

The quiet, affluent neighborhoods of Bel Air and Brentwood and the beautifully landscaped Westwood campus of the University of California, Los Angeles (UCLA) dominate the area of LA flanking I-405 between Beverly Hills and Santa Monica.

Westwood

Built on the site of a former rancho, Westwood Village was once popular as an outdoor walking area filled with cafes, interesting shops and new-release movie theaters. Well, all that's left are the theaters; the crowds have moved on to more fashionable areas like Santa Monica's Third Street Promenade and Old Town Pasadena.

Not even the 35,000 UCLA students infuse the Village with much life. Established in 1919, the 419 nicely landscaped acres of **UCLA** (☎ 310-825-4321) sprawl out north of the commercial center. Four Nobel Prize laureates and seven winners of National Medals of Science sit on its faculty. Research milestones include being the birthplace of the Internet in 1969, and notable alumni are Francis Ford Coppola and Jackie Joyner-Kersee, the late track star. Free student-guided campus tours run 10:30 am and 1:30 pm weekdays (reservations at ☎ 310-825-8764).

Campus highlights are the **Fowler Museum of Cultural History** (☎ 310-825-4361), with its world-class collection of art and artifacts from Latin America, Africa, Asia and the Pacific (open noon to 5 pm Wednesday to Sunday, noon to 8 pm Thursday; $5/3); the tranquil and picturesque **Franklin D Murphy Sculpture Garden**, with 70 works by Rodin, Moore, Calder and other artists; and the **Mildred E Mathias Botanical Garden** with its more than 4000 plant species.

Armand Hammer Museum The UCLA Armand Hammer Museum of Art and Cultural Center (☎ 310-443-7000), 10899 Wilshire Blvd, features changing exhibits and the late industrialist's $450-million personal collection of European and American old masters, impressionist and post-impressionist paintings and drawings done by French caricaturist Honoré Daumier. Hours are 11 am to 7 pm Tuesday to Saturday (11 am to 9 pm Thursday), 11 am to 5 pm Sunday; $4.50/3 adults/seniors. The museum is free Thursday after 6 pm and for children under 17.

Westwood Memorial Park This small, star-studded cemetery is a bit hard to find at 1218 Glendon Ave (from Wilshire Blvd, turn south onto Glendon Ave and look for the driveway immediately to your left). Here you'll find the tombs of Marilyn Monroe, Natalie Wood, Roy Orbison and Frank Zappa (in an unmarked grave).

Getty Center

The new Getty Center (☎ 310-440-7300), 1200 Getty Center Drive, hunkers atop a Brentwood hillside like an impregnable postmodern fortress, but once you arrive within its vast courtyards it's a very welcoming place indeed. It took 14 years of planning and construction and $1 billion to build this stunning Richard Meier-designed 110-acre 'campus.' It unites the art collections that were assembled by oil magnate J Paul Getty – previously displayed at his Roman-style villa in Malibu – with several Getty-sponsored institutes focused on conservation, art research and education.

On view in four two-story pavilions is the museum's permanent collection; a fifth pavilion features changing exhibitions. While the skylit galleries on the upper floors of each building focus on European paintings, the lower floors are given over to sculpture, illuminated manuscripts, drawings, furniture, photography, glass, ceramics and other decorative arts. Tours, lectures and the latest interactive technology make the art accessible to all.

Hours are 11 am to 7 pm Tuesday and Wednesday, 11 am to 9 pm Thursday and Friday and 10 am to 6 pm weekends. Admission is free, but parking reservations ($5) are mandatory; call the center to reserve. When arriving by MTA bus No 561 or the Big Blue Bus No 14, there's no charge besides the bus ride.

Skirball Cultural Center

This cluster of galleries, performance and exhibit spaces (☎ 310-440-4500), 2701 N Sepulveda Blvd, teaches visitors about the history of the Jewish people. It showcases Jewish contributions to the world and to America, often with refreshing irreverence and – unlike most Jewish museums – going far beyond the events of the Holocaust.

Hours are noon to 5 pm daily, 11 am to 5 pm Sunday; $8/6 adults/seniors, children free. There's a free summer outdoor concert series on Thursday evenings and a packed schedule of lectures, concerts and performances (prices vary).

MALIBU

If LA is a 'city on the edge,' Malibu is even more so. Late summer wildfires regularly raze the chaparral-cloaked slopes of the Santa Monica Mountains, often taking with them expensive homes. In denuding the hillsides, the fires also pave the way for the even more damaging mud slides that often follow winter rains. It's not uncommon for Pacific Coast Hwy to be closed by mud slides in winter.

Malibu is best appreciated through its state parks and state beaches. Lining the coast from east to west over a stretch of about 25 miles, the beaches include Las Tunas, Malibu-Surfrider, Pt Dume, Zuma and Leo Carrillo. Along the crest of the Santa Monica Mountains, Mulholland Hwy runs 50 miles from Leo Carrillo Beach to Hwy 101; the panoramic views from the road are simply astounding.

The few cultural sights include the **Adamson House** (☎ 310-456-8432), 23200 Pacific Coast Hwy, a beautiful 1928 Spanish Colonial villa laced with Moorish elements in enchanting surroundings (guided tours only) and the adjacent free **Malibu Lagoon Museum**, a local history museum (open 11 am to 3 pm Wednesday to Saturday). The **J Paul Getty Museum**, 17985 Pacific Coast Hwy, is undergoing extensive remodeling and will reopen in 2002.

SANTA MONICA (MAP 7)

The seaside city of Santa Monica is one of the most agreeable towns in the greater LA area. With its early-20th-century pleasure pier, hotels and restaurants overlooking the Pacific Ocean, pedestrian-friendly downtown and colorful Main St district, Santa Monica is a great place to visit.

Santa Monica's visitor center (☎ 310-393-7593) is in a little kiosk at 1400 Ocean Blvd and is open 10 am to 5 pm daily. The Tide

Shuttle (25¢ per ride) connects major points downtown at 15-minute intervals.

The heart of Santa Monica is the **Third Street Promenade**, a pedestrian mall between Broadway and Wilshire Blvd. Here you'll find street entertainment (especially on weekends), restaurants, bars and movie theaters. The south end of the promenade is anchored by **Santa Monica Place**, a three-story, 150-store, shopping mall designed by Frank Gehry.

Two blocks west of the promenade, Ocean Ave follows **Palisades Park** atop a bluff overlooking the ocean. At the south end of Palisades Park is the famous **Santa Monica Pier**, the West Coast's oldest surviving pleasure pier, with restaurants, bars and shops. Also here is a quaint 1920 **carousel** that starred with Paul Newman and Robert Redford in *The Sting*. Beneath the carousel is the **UCLA Ocean Discovery Center** (☎ 310-393-6149), a teaching facility dedicated to demystifying the oceans for students of all ages, with displays and touch tanks showcasing local marine life. Hours for the center vary; $3. The pier highlight is **Pacific Park**, basically a scaled-down Coney Island with a small roller coaster, a Ferris wheel and a host of smaller kiddie rides and arcade games.

Other Santa Monica areas suitable for strolling, shopping and dining are Montana Ave in the city's northern section and Main St on the south end of town, near the border with Venice Beach.

Bergamot Station

The 30 or so galleries berthed within the sprawling industrial grounds of Bergamot Station (☎ 310-453-7535), 2525 Michigan Ave, have been a nexus of the LA arts scene since the complex opened in 1994. Also here is the **Santa Monica Museum of Art** (☎ 310-586-6488), where you're liable to encounter highly regarded traditional and experimental art forms, including interactive video and photography. Hours are 11 am to 6 pm Wednesday to Sunday; $3.

Museum of Flying

Not only airplane aficionados will enjoy the excellent Museum of Flying (☎ 310-392-8822),

2772 Donald Douglas Loop N at the Santa Monica Municipal Airport (enter from Ocean Park Ave). Housed in an enormous hangar are three floors of exhibits with such legends of flight as the Mitsubishi Zero, the P-51 Mustang, the WWI Fokker and a replica of the *Voyager*, the first aircraft to make a nonstop flight around the world. Hours are 10 am to 5 pm Wednesday to Sunday; $7/5/3 adults/seniors/children.

VENICE BEACH (MAP 7)

A century ago, Venice Beach was just dreary swampland. But then Abbott Kinney, on a quest to build a model community, drained the marsh with a 16-mile network of canals, brought a dozen gondoliers from Europe to pole through his new paradise and attracted scores of new residents and merchants. His 'Playland of the Pacific' had a spectacular grand opening celebration on July 4, 1905. Hollywood soon eclipsed Venice's star, however, and Kinney's vision was taken over by speakeasies and gambling halls in the Prohibition era. Today, only 3 miles of canals survive south of Venice Blvd and east of Pacific Ave, along wee Dell St, where you'll find an enclave of cozy bungalows and four arched Venetian bridges.

The chief attraction of modern Venice, however, is its **Ocean Front Walk** – or, more specifically, the slice of life that hangs out here. Extending from Santa Monica's Ocean Park on the north to the **Venice Pier** at the border with Marina del Rey, this 1-mile stretch must be explored by foot. For the full effect, come on a warm Saturday or Sunday afternoon. You'll encounter jugglers and acrobats, tarot readers and Mad Hatter vendors, jug-band musicians and political types circulating petitions to decriminalize marijuana. Bikini-clad babes watch body builders flex well-oiled biceps at **Muscle Beach**. Basketball courts attract pickup players like the characters in *White Men Can't Jump* (which was filmed here), who will take on all comers.

Venice also has scores of colorful street murals, a reminder of the preponderance of artists (some quite well known, most struggling and bohemian) who live here. Show-cases like the **LA Louver Galleries** (☎ 310-822-4955), 45 N Venice Blvd, and the **Corcoran Gallery** (☎ 310-966-1010), 1633 Electric Ave, exhibit their work.

At the south end of Venice, **Marina del Rey** is home to 6000 private sailboats and motor yachts – the largest artificial small-craft harbor on the earth. The Marina's leading tourist site is **Fishermen's Village**, 13755 Fiji Way, a hokey assemblage intended to resemble a Cape Cod village. You *can* go fishing from here – book a trip with Marina del Rey Sportfishing (☎ 310-822-3625) – but most visitors settle for taking a harbor sightseeing cruise or browsing the diverse novelty and souvenir shops.

SAN PEDRO

About 21 miles south of Downtown LA, San Pedro is a slow-paced harbor community that forms the northern fringe of the **Port of Los Angeles** – Worldport LA – one of the busiest ports in the world.

Sights include the **Maritime Museum** (☎ 310-548-7618), occupying a former ferry terminal on Berth 84 at 6th St. The 75,000-sq-foot facility contains more than 700 intricate ship and boat models, navigational equipment and an operating amateur radio station. Hours are 10 am to 5 pm Tuesday to Sunday; $1 donation requested.

About 1 mile north, at Berth 94, is the **SS Lane Victory** (☎ 310-519-9545), used during WWII to transport cargo to Allied troops. Today, it houses a museum and is open 9 am to 4 pm daily; $3/1.

Just south of the Maritime Museum, **Ports O' Call Village** is a hopeless tourist trap, supposedly evocative of 19th-century New England seaside towns. It's also the main departure point for harbor tours offered several times daily by Spirit Cruises (☎ 310-548-8080) from Berth 77. One-hour narrated tours cost $7.50, 90-minute cruises are $9.

It's a short drive south to the **Cabrillo Marine Aquarium** (☎ 310-548-7562), 3720 Stephen White Drive, a favorite with elementary school kids. Among the 38 tanks displaying colorful fish and other marine life, is a touch tank where visitors are encouraged to pick up starfish, sea urchins, sea cucumbers and other tide-pool denizens. Hours are noon to 5 pm weekdays and 10 am to 5 pm weekends, closed Monday; admission is free, but parking is $6.50.

LONG BEACH

Long Beach is the southernmost city in LA County. It has maintained an easygoing, small-town atmosphere, despite its size. The town center itself is easily explored on foot, but you might want to take the Passport, a free shuttle bus that circulates past most places of interest.

The liveliest street is **Pine Ave**, especially along the three-block stretch between Long Beach Plaza and Ocean Blvd, which has numerous restaurants, nightspots and shops. The visitor center (☎ 562-436-3645, 800-452-7829, fax 562-435-5653) is at 1 World Trade Center, Suite 300, with weekday hours from 8:30 am to 5 pm. On weekends, there's a staffed information kiosk outside the Aquarium of the Pacific (same hours).

Long Beach Aquarium of the Pacific

One of the LA area's major new attractions, the $117-million Aquarium of the Pacific (☎ 562-590-3100, www.aquariumofpacific .org), 100 Aquarium Way, should be on everyone's must-see list. Presented in an imaginative and informative way, the more than 10,000 fish, mammals and birds from 550 species instill a sense of wonder and awe in visitors of all ages. Sound effects, video, models and descriptive panels provide information in an accessible way that does not overwhelm. Seventeen re-created habitats and 30 smaller focus tanks represent three major Pacific Rim regions: Southern California and Baja, Northern Pacific and Tropical Pacific. Hours are 10 am to 6 pm daily; $14.95/11.95/7.95.

Queen Mary Seaport

To casual visitors, Long Beach is best known for the passenger liner *Queen Mary* (☎ 310-435-3511), 1126 Queens Hwy, a major attraction since it was permanently moored here

in 1967. The 81,237-ton ship was launched in 1934 and made 1001 crossings of the Atlantic before being retired in 1964. One of the most luxurious of the luxury liners, it was favored by celebrities and royalty.

Most of the *Queen Mary* can be explored on a self-guided tour, though for a look at the first-class dining hall, indoor swimming pool and other sections, you must join the guided Behind the Scenes Tour ($7 plus admission). Hours are 10 am to 6 pm daily, with extended summer hours; $15/13/9. Parking is an additional $6.

The *Queen Mary*'s new neighbor, the *Scorpion* (☎ 562-435-3511), is a 1973 Russian submarine whose fascinating – if claustrophobic – interior is open for touring (same hours; $10/9/9). Combination tickets with the *Queen Mary* are available.

The huge dome next to the *Queen Mary* housed billionaire aviator Howard Hughes' bizarre flying boat, the *Spruce Goose*, until it was sold to an Oregon museum. The dome is now used by Warner Bros as a soundstage.

Directly across Queensway Bay from the two vessels is **Shoreline Village** (☎ 562-435-2668), a shopping-and-dining complex and departure point for harbor and whale-watching cruises offered by Shoreline Village Cruises (☎ 562-495-5884), 429 Shoreline Village Drive. For deep-sea fishing expeditions – half day to overnight – try Long Beach Sportfishing (☎ 562-432-8993), 555 Pico Ave, Long Beach.

Naples

Alamitos Bay surrounds the isle of Naples, built by Arthur Parson (a chronological and philosophical contemporary of Venice's Abbot Kinney) in the 1920s. Parson's success at community planning was more lasting than Kinney's – the **Rivo Alto Canal** still circles a network of curving lanes built up with garden-shrouded bungalows. See Naples by foot or, better yet, by water.

The authentic boats of **Gondola Getaway** (☎ 562-433-9595), 5437 E Ocean Blvd, will cruise you à la Venice – that's Venice, *Italy* – through the Rivo Alto as you relax. One-hour rides are $55 per couple, by reservation only.

LOS ANGELES

SAN FERNANDO VALLEY

Fully one third of the population of the city of Los Angeles lives in what is known simply as 'The Valley,' a broad, flat 220-sq-mile region that is as well known for its earthquakes as for its seemingly endless commercial strips and tract homes.

Framed by mountain ranges that trap the air, the Valley is usually capped by a thick layer of smog and is about 20°F hotter than Westside and the beach communities. Although living in the Valley is now often mocked by outsiders, it was quite fashionable among early Hollywood moguls, including Walt Disney and John Wayne, who also brought most major studios to the Valley, especially to Burbank. These days, the Valley is also the world capital of the adult film industry.

Glendale

Attractions in Glendale, LA County's third-largest city, include the **Brand Library and Art Galleries** (☎ 818-548-2051), 1601 W Mountain St. Today a repository of some

50,000 books primarily on art and music, the 1904 building was originally the private mansion of Leslie Brand, the 'father of Glendale.' Inspired by the East Indian Pavilion at the 1893 Columbian Expo in Chicago, Brand had his own phantasmagoric 'Taj Mahal' built.

The humongous **Forest Lawn Cemetery** (☎ 818-241-4151), 1712 S Glendale Ave, is often cheekily called the 'country club for the dead.' Besides the tombs of Hollywood legends like Clark Gable, Walt Disney and Carole Lombard, the cemetery also sports copies of Michelangelo's *David* and a stained-glass rendition of da Vinci's *Last Supper*. Despite the obvious kitsch factor, a visit here is fascinating, if only to catch a glimpse of the American death culture so powerfully satirized by Evelyn Waugh's *The Loved One* (1948). Park hours are 9 am to 5 pm daily; free.

Burbank

Burbank got its name from a New Hampshire dentist, Dr David Burbank, and was

---

Valley Secession – The Balkanization of LA

To visitors, Los Angeles is a giant metropolis that sprawls for mile after mile. Few realize that what they're looking at is actually a mosaic of 88 cities, including one called Los Angeles, that collectively make up LA County. Anger and resentment about the way the city of LA is run is so great in some communities that they are striving to secede and become cities of their own. Spearheading the effort is the San Fernando Valley and its 1.3 million residents. Throughout 1998, a group called Valley Voters Organized Towards Empowerment successfully collected the more than 140,000 signatures needed to launch a feasibility study about breaking away from Los Angeles.

As a result, the Local Agency Formation Commission has been conducting a lengthy study on the viability of the new city and the impact secession would have on the remainder of LA. Based on its findings, the agency intends to decide whether to place the issue on the ballot, putting the issue to voters in the next round of elections. A majority of voters in the entire city of LA – not just in the proposed new city – would then have to approve the secession move.

Already waiting in the wings are organizations in other parts of the city ready to move ahead with their own petition drives if the Valley effort proves successful: San Pedro, Wilmington, Westchester, Mar Vista, Playa del Rey, Venice, South Central and West Los Angeles. Planners envision a city of West LA, for instance, to have north-south boundaries from Mulholland Drive in the Santa Monica Mountains to LAX and east-west boundaries from Pacific Palisades to, and including, Hollywood.

the first Valley city to incorporate in 1891, with just 500 residents; today it has 94,000. Besides the movie industry, aircraft manufacturing buttered people's bread after Lockheed set up shop here in the 1930s.

For a rare and realistic glimpse behind the scenes of one of Hollywood's oldest movie and TV production facilities, take the 2¼-hour **Warner Bros Studios Tour** (☎ 818-972-8687), 4000 Warner Blvd. You'll visit the museum, the backlot and its 33 soundstages and several outdoor sets. Tours ($30) run every half-hour between 9 am and 3:30 pm weekdays in summer, hourly 9 am to 3 pm in winter. Reservations are recommended; children under 8 are not allowed.

Nearby, the 70-minute **NBC Studio Tour** (☎ 818-840-3538), 3000 W Alameda Ave, usually takes you to the set of Jay Leno's *Tonight Show* and into such departments as Wardrobe, Makeup, Set Construction, Special Effects and Sound Effects. Tours cost $7/3.75 adults/children and leave regularly 9 am to 3 pm weekdays. Reservations won't hurt.

Universal Studios

Universal Studios Hollywood (☎ 818-508-9600), 100 Universal City Plaza, is the world's largest movie and TV studio, built by Carl Laemmle in 1915 on the site of a former chicken ranch. Formal studio tours began in 1964 and have since been experienced by 90 million visitors.

You'll need to devote a full day to Universal. It gets very busy in summer, so prepare yourself for long waits in stifling heat. Bring a hat, suntan lotion, patience and – if cutting costs is your aim – sandwiches and bottled water. Some rides, including the popular Back to the Future and Jurassic Park, have minimum height requirements (usually 42 or 46 inches).

Universal Studios sprawls across 413 acres, the upper and lower sections connected by a quarter-mile-long escalator. To get your bearings, head straight for the **Backlot Tour**, a 45-minute part educational, part thrill ride behind the scenes of moviemaking. A tram whisks you and about 250 other visitors past the studio's maze of

35 soundstages as your guide showers you with movie trivia. You'll see where parts of *Jurassic Park* and *Apollo 13* were filmed, rumble past outdoor sets like Courthouse Square, best known from *Back to the Future*, and the Bates Hotel featured in Hitchcock's *Psycho*. During the thrill portion of the tour you'll face up to such special-effects crises as an 8.3-magnitude earthquake, a flash flood, a collapsing bridge, volcanic lava, an encounter with a hokey plastic *Jaws* and a roaring, in-yo'-face *King Kong*.

Universal doesn't have as many rides as Disneyland, but that's actually a plus, since it's usually possible to experience them all in a single day. **Back to the Future – The Ride** is popular, with its free falls into volcanic tunnels, plunges down glacial cliffs and collisions with dinosaurs. **The ET Adventure** is a gentle flight aboard a monorailed 'bicycle' through a charming fantasy world. **Backdraft** is a pyrotechnic walking adventure whose climactic conclusion has you engulfed by an inferno roaring through a chemical factory. Top billing goes to **Jurassic Park – The Ride**, a float through a prehistoric jungle past friendly herbivores before coming face to face with vicious velociraptors and a ravenous *T rex*. The ride's end will blow you away.

Universal Studios is open 8 am to 10 pm daily in summer, 9 am to 7 pm the rest of the year (closed Thanksgiving and Christmas). Admission is $38/33/28 adults/seniors/children. Unlimited annual passes are available for $69/59/54. A combined admission ticket to Universal and SeaWorld in San Diego costs $68.95/50.95 adults/children (three to 11). Parking is $7.

Adjacent to Universal Studios is **Universal City Walk**, a controlled fantasy environment of shops, restaurants, cinemas and nightclubs. The best time to visit is after dark, when vibrant neon signs transform the promenade into a miniature Las Vegas-style strip.

Mission San Fernando Rey de España

Founded in 1797, this mission (☎ 818-361-0186), 15151 San Fernando Mission Rd, was the second Spanish mission built in the LA area. The highlight of a visit is the mission's 1822 convent, with 4-foot-thick adobe walls, 21 Roman arches and an elaborate baroque altarpiece from Spain. A museum deals with mission history and displays Native American artifacts. Peacocks strut around the grounds, which are sprinkled with statues and include a 35-bell carillon. Mission hours are 9 am to 4:30 pm daily; $4/3, children under seven free.

PASADENA (MAP 8)

Pasadena was established beneath the lofty San Gabriel Mountains in 1873, by Midwestern settlers who gave it a Chippewa name meaning 'crown of the valley.' The town incorporated in 1886, and before long five commuter trains a day linked it with Downtown LA. Wealthy Easterners, drawn by the temperate climes, made Pasadena a fashionable winter haunt. In the early 20th century, the town became a haven for writers, painters and architects. In 1940, Southern California's first freeway, the Arroyo Seco Pkwy (since designated I-110, the Pasadena Fwy) opened. This connected the city with Downtown LA, and ever more commuters settled in Pasadena. About 139,000 people now call the city home, as do the famed Tournament of Roses (see Special Events), the Rose Bowl and the California Institute of Technology.

Pasadena's visitor center (☎ 626-795-9311, fax 626-795-9656), 171 S Los Robles Ave, is open 8 am to 5 pm weekdays, 10 am to 4 pm Saturday. Free Pasadena ARTS buses regularly shuttle between Old Pasadena, the Pasadena Playhouse District and South Lake Ave.

Old Pasadena

Old Pasadena is a 20-block historic district stretching along Colorado Blvd between Arroyo Pkwy and Pasadena Ave. In the early 1990s, this area underwent a renaissance that left its main streets and alleyways lined with restaurants and coffeehouses, upscale boutiques and bookstores, galleries and antique stores, nightclubs and cinema complexes.

Norton Simon Museum

The Norton Simon Museum (☎ 626-449-6840), 411 W Colorado Blvd, boasts one of the very finest collections of European art from the Renaissance to the 20th century and an exquisite sampling of 2000 years of Asian sculpture from India and Southeast Asia. Boticelli, Cézanne, Degas, Goya, Matisse, Monet, Picasso, Raphael, Rembrandt, Renoir, Rubens, Toulouse-Lautrec and van Gogh are just a few of the big-name artists found here. Hours are noon to 6 pm Thursday to Sunday; $4/2 adults/seniors, free for children.

Wrigley Mansion

South of the Norton Simon Museum along Orange Grove Blvd at No 391 stands the imposing 1914 Wrigley Mansion (☎ 626-449-4100), once owned by chewing gum magnate William Wrigley Jr and now the headquarters of the Tournament of Roses Association. It can be toured for free between 2 and 4 pm on Thursdays from February through August. At all other times only the lush gardens, ablaze with roses and camellias, are open to the public.

Rose Bowl & Arroyo Seco

Among Pasadena's grandest architectural achievements is the 98,636-seat Rose Bowl stadium (☎ 626-577-3106), 1001 Rose Bowl Drive, home of the UCLA Bruins football team, and also the site of the Rose Bowl Game and a monthly flea market. The stadium, built in 1922, sits in the midst of the 61-sq-acre **Brookside Park**, a broadening of Arroyo Seco. Once an orange grove, this gorge is now a recreational center for hikers, bicyclists and horseback riders. Spanning the arroyo is the city's most infamous landmark, the **Colorado St Bridge** (1913). 'Suicide Bridge,' as it has come to be known, became the area's favorite jumping spot for those hard hit by the stock market crash in 1929 and has since remained popular among forlorn souls. It is overlooked by the imposing former **Vista del Arroyo Hotel** (1903), 125 S Grand Ave, restored in the 1980s to house the Ninth

Circuit US Court of Appeals. North of the Rose Bowl is the world-renowned **Art Center College of Design** (☎ 626-396-2200), 1700 Lida St.

The Gamble House

The Gamble House (☎ 626-793-3334), 4 Westmoreland Place, is a 1908 design by Charles and Henry Greene and considered the world's best example of craftsman bungalow architecture. It features terraces, bedroom porches for outdoor sleeping and overhanging eaves to keep out the sun. It starred as the home of mad scientist Doc Brown (Christopher Lloyd) in the three *Back to the Future* movies. Guided one-hour tours depart roughly every 20 minutes noon to 3 pm Thursday through Sunday, except major holidays; $5/4/3 adults seniors/students, children are free. Other Greene & Greene homes are on nearby Grand Ave and Arroyo Terrace, including **Charles Greene's private residence** at 368 Arroyo Terrace.

Pacific Asia Museum

With its upturned roofs, dragon motifs and serene courtyard, the Chinese imperial palace-style museum (☎ 626-449-2742), 46 N Los Robles Ave, is a bit of an architectural oddity. On display is a fine compilation of five millennia of both rare and common art and artifacts. The museum's strength is in Chinese ceramics from several dynasties as well as in Japanese paintings and drawings by Hiroshige and Hokusai. Despite the extraordinary collection, museum curators might give some thought to improving the way objects are presented. Hours are 10 am to 5 pm Wednesday to Sunday; $5/3 adults/seniors, children free.

Nearby is the Pasadena Civic Center, built between 1927 and 1933, where Italian Renaissance and Spanish Colonial architectural styles meet beaux arts. The magnificent Pasadena City Hall, 100 N Garfield Ave, built around a courtyard garden and fountain, is flanked by the Public Library, 285 E Walnut St, and the Civic Auditorium, 300 E Green St.

California Institute of Technology

Twenty-six Nobel laureates and 43 winners of the National Medal of Science are faculty members or alumni of Caltech (☎ 626-395-6327, www.caltech.edu), 551 S Hill Ave, which gives you some idea why it's regarded with awe in academic circles. Free campus tours, conducted at 2 pm weekdays year round (except holidays, rainy days, and during winter break), include a visit to the seismology laboratory. Caltech also operates the **Jet Propulsion Laboratory** (JPL), NASA's main center for robotic exploration of the solar system, in La Cañada just north of Pasadena, though this is not usually open to the public.

Huntington Library, Art Collection & Botanical Gardens

At once a cultural center, a re°search institution and a relaxing place to spend a day, the former estate of railroad tycoon Henry Huntington (☎ 626-405-2141), 1151 Oxford Rd in San Marino, is one LA attraction not to be missed.

The sprawling **botanical gardens**, with some 14,000 species of trees, shrubs, flowering and nonflowering plants, alone are worthy of a visit. Even more impressive is the **library**, with its collection of rare English-language books, maps and manuscripts. Treasures include a Gutenberg Bible, the Ellesmere manuscript of Chaucer's *Canterbury Tales* and Benjamin Franklin's handwritten autobiography.

The Huntington **art gallery**, in the former family mansion, boasts a collection of 18th-century British and French paintings (among them Thomas Gainsborough's *Blue Boy*); European period sculptures, porcelains and tapestries; and American paintings from the 1730s to the 1930s, including works by Mary Cassatt, Edward Hopper and John Singer Sargent.

Hours are 12 to 4:30 pm Tuesday to Friday, from 10:30 am weekends, closed major holidays; $8.50/7/5 adults/seniors/students, free for children and on the first Thursday of each month.

LOS ANGELES

Southwest Museum

Just south of Pasadena, this precious museum (☎ 323-221-2164), 234 Museum Drive, holds one of the most formidable collections of Native American art and artifacts in the US. It's also LA's oldest museum, founded in 1907 by Charles F Lummis. Each of the four halls is dedicated to a native North American culture: the Great Plains, the Northwest Coast, the Southwest and California. The museum owns one of the largest basket collections in the US (11,000 items), as well as some 7000 pieces of pottery and 6600 paintings, textiles, religious icons and decorative and folk art from Latin America. Hours are 11 am to 5 pm, closed Monday; $5/3/2 adults/seniors/children (age seven to 18).

Heritage Square Museum

Eight vintage Victorian buildings dating from 1865 to 1914 were rescued from the wrecking ball and moved to Heritage Square (☎ 626-449-0193), an open-air museum at 3800 Homer St, just off the Ave 43 exit of I-110. Some structures have already been restored; others are still awaiting their face-lifts. Tours are offered 10 am to 3 pm on Friday (free admission). On weekends, hours are 11:30 am to 4:30 pm; admission then is $5/4/2, free under seven.

Mission San Gabriel Arcángel

East of Pasadena, this California mission (☎ 626-457-3048), 537 W Mission Drive, was the fourth in the line of 21. The Franciscans 'persuaded' the local Gabrielino Indians to construct the church from stone, brick and mortar between 1791 and 1805; since then, the church has been destroyed and rebuilt numerous times.

Inside the church is a copper baptismal font, an altar made in Mexico City in 1790 and wooden statues of saints. The cemetery harbors, among many others, 6000 Indians who are honored with a memorial. Also on the grounds are soap and tallow vats, fireplaces, fountains and a replica of a kitchen. The museum contains Bibles, religious robes and Indian artifacts. Hours are 10 am to 5:30 pm daily from June to September and 9 am to 4:30 pm the rest of the year; $4/3/1.

BEACHES

Beaches are LA's major natural asset, and the city's warm, sunny climate is conducive to shore activities year round. Surfing, sailing, swimming, in-line skating, bicycling, sunbathing, volleyball and basketball – or simply strolling through the sand – are all enjoyed by locals and visitors alike.

Water temperatures become tolerable by late spring and are highest (about 70°F, or 21°C) in August and September, but in winter the Pacific is rather chilly. Most beaches provide facilities like showers and rest rooms, lifeguards and snack stands, and are cleaned up regularly.

Hazards are few but shouldn't be ignored. Swimming is usually prohibited for three days after major storms because of dangerously high pollution levels from untreated runoff. Strong currents, often called 'rip tides,' present another danger and can drag swimmers away from the shore.

The beaches in Santa Monica, Venice and Manhattan Beach are the most popular and populated. Other excellent beaches, listed from north to south, include the following: El Pescador, El Matador and La Piedra at the northern edge of the county are secluded and are often used as movie sets. Zuma Beach – probably the best beach in continental America – is a beautiful wide, white sand strip popular with families, teenagers and boogie boarders. It offers great swimming in a wonderfully uncrowded scene. Malibu Lagoon State Beach, aka Surfrider Beach, has some of the best surfing around, and Will Rogers State Beach is a winner with families.

MOUNTAINS

Few LA visitors ever realize that the metropolis actually borders wilderness, in what is the world's largest urban national park, the **Santa Monica Mountains National Recreation Area** (SMMNR). Consisting of more than 150,000 acres, it's a playground cherished by LA residents and an easily accessible way to sample the rugged beauty found throughout California. Even a short hike makes for a refreshing break from urban sightseeing and will increase your appreciation of both the city and its natural surroundings.

Outdoor activities in the park include hiking, mountain biking, horseback riding and bird watching. Almost 600 miles of trails crisscross the area, including the popular 65-mile Backbone Trail. Several canyon roads cut through the mountains, providing easy access to trails.

Spring, when temperatures are moderate and wildflowers are in bloom, is the most pleasant time to visit the park. Avoid midday hikes in summer, when the mercury occasionally climbs to over 100°F (37°C) in the canyons and on exposed mountainsides. Autumn can be nice too, but winter often brings rain that may result in trail closure. In general, most trails are rugged and require sturdy footwear (sneakers or light hiking shoes are OK). Layer your clothing and bring sunscreen, a hat and lots of water. Look out for waxy, glistening leaves that may be poison oak. Other dangers, though rare, come from rattlesnakes and mountain lions (see the Facts about California for details on what to do).

The National Park Service maintains a visitor center (☎ 805-370-2300) at 401 W Hillcrest Drive in Thousand Oaks in the very western San Fernando Valley. They dispense information and sell maps, hiking guides and books between 8 am to 5 pm weekdays, 9 am to 5 pm weekends; closed major holidays.

Guided hikes are offered by the Sierra Club (☎ 213-387-4287, www.edgeinternet.com/angeles/) and the National Park Service (☎ 805-370-2300, www.nps.gov/samo/). Hiking in LA (☎ 818-501-1005) is a company offering educational guided hiking tours in small groups and in several languages. Excellent guidebooks with detailed area hikes are John McKinney's *Day Hiker's Guide to Southern California* and *Walking Los Angeles: Adventures on the Urban Edge*, widely available in city bookstores.

ORGANIZED TOURS

Most LA area tour companies operate year round, with stepped-up schedules in summer and around Christmas. Several companies offer essentially the same types of tours at roughly the same prices, including the popular city tour and a tour of the stars' homes (both around $40). Theme park tours visit Universal Studios, Disneyland, Knott's Berry Farm and Six Flags Magic Mountain

---

Los Angeles Conservancy Tours

Since 1978, the nonprofit LA Conservancy has worked tirelessly – and with increasing success – to raise awareness of and preserve historic buildings in LA. Trained docents conduct a series of themed walking tours through Downtown, which are entertaining and informative. Except where noted, tours meet at 10 am, last two to 2½ hours and cost $5. Following is a listing of the most popular tours. For a complete schedule and reservations (required), call ☎ 213-623-2489.

Art Deco (every Saturday) – spotlights several landmarks built in this jazzy, geometric style in vogue in the 1920s and '30s

Biltmore Hotel (second Saturday at 11 am) – one-hour behind-the-scenes tour of this glamorous hotel, including the health club, kitchen and presidential suite

Broadway Theaters (every Saturday) – takes you inside the Orpheum and other theaters

Pershing Square (every Saturday) – visits the square's landmarks and relates its history

Union Station (third Saturday) – tour of the last great railway station built in the US (in 1939) and a visit to the legendary Fred Harvey restaurant

($60 to $75, admission included). Children's discounts are available.

Tour operators include: Starline Tours of Hollywood (☎ 323-463-3333), LA Tours (☎ 323-962-6793) and GuideLine Tours (☎ 213-465-3004, 800-604-8433). EuroPacific Tours (☎ 800-303-3005) also has an LA by Night tour. Trolleywood Tours (☎ 323-469-8184) offers fun and fact-filled one-hour tours of Hollywood aboard a cute trolley ($16) and two-hour tours of about 60 Beverly Hills celebrity homes in a van ($29).

Grave Line Tours (☎ 323-469-3127), in Hollywood, explores the final resting places of big-screen notables, and the venues of various other deaths, murders and scandals – all in a refurbished hearse.

SPECIAL EVENTS

LA has a packed calendar of special events, with many festivities celebrating the traditions and culture of LA's different ethnic groups. We only have space to list a smattering of what's on, so check the *LA Times* and *LA Weekly* for current information, or call the LA Convention and Visitors Bureau events hotline at ☎ 213-689-8822.

January
Tournament of Roses Parade (☎ 818-419-7673)

February
Chinese New Year (☎ 213-617-0396)

March
LA Marathon & Bike Tour (☎ 310-444-5544)

April
Toyota Grand Prix of Long Beach
  (☎ 800-752-9524)
Blessing of the Animals (☎ 213-628-1274)
Fiesta Broadway (☎ 310-914-0015)

May
Cinco de Mayo Celebration (☎ 213-624-3660)

June
Playboy Jazz Festival (☎ 310-449-4070)
Mariachi USA Festival (☎ 213-848-7717)
Los Angeles Gay & Lesbian Pride Celebration
  (☎ 323-860-0701)

July
Lotus Festival (☎ 213-485-1310)
Malibu Art Festival (☎ 310-456-9025)

August
Central Avenue Jazz Festival (☎ 213-485-2437)
Nisei Week (☎ 213-687-7193)

September
Long Beach Blues Festival (☎ 562-436-7794)
LA County Fair (☎ 909-623-3111)
Oktoberfest (☎ 310-327-4384)
Catalina Island Country Music Festival
  (☎ 619-458-9586)

October
Halloween Party

November
Día de los Muertos (☎ 213-624-3660)
Doo Dah Parade (☎ 818-449-3689)
Hollywood Christmas Parade (☎ 323-469-2337)

December
Holiday Festival of Lights (☎ 323-913-4688)
Christmas Boat Parade (☎ 310-821-7614)
Las Posadas (☎ 213-968-8492)

PLACES TO STAY

Greater Los Angeles has a wide variety of accommodations in all price categories, although finding a cheap bed – especially between Memorial Day (late May) and Labor Day (early September) and around Thanksgiving, Christmas and New Year's – isn't always easy.

Your cheapest lodging options are hostels, which abound in Venice Beach and Hollywood. Santa Monica and San Pedro also have a couple. Budget motels, costing $30 to $70, are abundant in Downtown, Hollywood and Pasadena, though you'll also find plenty along Pacific Coast Hwy, especially in Manhattan Beach and Redondo Beach. Mid-priced hotels range from $70 to $130, and choices are decent in most parts of the city, though perhaps greatest in Downtown, the Marina del Rey/LAX Area and in Santa Monica. The latter also has its share of luxury hotels where the sky's the limit in terms of price. As might be expected, posh abodes abound in Beverly Hills and West Hollywood.

A 'transient occupancy' tax is tacked onto rates listed here (for details, see Taxes earlier this chapter). Free hotel reservation services include the Hotel Reservations Network

(☎ 800-964-6835) and the Central Reservation Service (☎ 800-548-3311).

Camping

LA's campgrounds are open year round. It's wise to make reservations, especially on summer weekends.

In addition to campgrounds mentioned below, the California Department of Parks & Recreation maintains dozens of camping facilities, often in more remote and rural locales. For a complete listing, call the department at ☎ 916-653-6995; for reservations, call ParkNet at ☎ 800-444-7275.

One of these campsites is the kid-friendly *Leo Carrillo State Beach Campground* (☎ 805-488-5223), about 28 miles north of Santa Monica. Charging $18, it has 138 tent or RV sites, a general store, flush toilets and hot pay showers.

Closer to town, *Malibu Beach RV Park* (☎ 310-456-6052, 800-622-6052, fax 310-456-2532, 25801 Pacific Coast Hwy) has 150 sites with full and partial hookups ($25 to $30), plus 52 tent spaces ($17 to $20). Rates include tax.

Dockweiler Beach RV Park (☎ 310-322-4951, 800-950-7275, 12001 Vista Del Mar), in Playa del Rey, is close to LAX, making this quite a noisy, if fairly central, proposition. Catering exclusively to RVs, the park charges $15 to $25 ($12 to $17 in winter).

Hostels

Hollywood The nonsmoking *Orange Drive Manor* (Map 3; ☎ 323-850-0350, fax 323-850-7474, 1764 N Orange Drive) is a rambling 1920s home offering plenty of privacy and a peaceful atmosphere (it's not marked, so just look for the house number). Bunks in four-person dorms with adjacent shower are $20; those with communal facilities are $11.50. Singles/doubles with shared shower cost $29.50/36.50. This one's a winner – make reservations.

A livelier option is the *Hollywood International Hostel* (Map 3; ☎ 323-463-0797, 800-750-6561, fax 323-463-1705, 6820 Hollywood Blvd). It has 42 dorms sleeping three to four each ($12 per bunk) and a few private rooms for $30. Facilities include a

tiny kitchen, gym, laundry room, TV, free coffee and tea and 24-hour check-in. This hostel attracts a rambunctious, sociable, international crowd.

International party animals also love the friendly, popular and noisy *Banana Bungalow Hollywood* (Map 1; ☎ 323-851-1129, 800-446-7835, fax 323-851-1569, 2775 N Cahuenga Blvd). They have 200 dormitory beds in rooms of four, six or 10 ($15 to $18) – each with cable TV, bathroom and lockers. Facilities include free continental breakfast, a bistro, small store, communal kitchen, Internet access, gym, laundry, swimming pool, library and car rental agency. Movies are shown nightly on a large-screen TV, parties thrown throughout the week and free shuttles provided to area attractions.

Coastal Communities Local headquarters for the Hostelling International system, the *Santa Monica International Hostel* (Map 7; ☎ 310-393-9913, 800-909-4776 ext 05, fax 310-393-1769, 1436 2nd St), in Santa Monica, has 238 dorm beds in a huge ivy-covered brick building. A block from Third Street Promenade and the beach, the hostel has a large kitchen, courtyard, library, theater, laundry and a travel store. Beds are $18 to $20, and there is a 2 am curfew. Do book early, especially in summer.

You're best bet in Venice is the *Venice Beach Cotel* (Map 7; ☎ 310-399-7649, fax 310-399-1930, 25 Windward Ave). Amenities include ready-made beds, towels and soap; free boogie boards, volleyball and paddle tennis rentals; a cafe/lounge with free coffee and tea; Internet access; and 24-hour security. Ocean-view bunks are $17 and well worth the extra $4 over those without a view. Private rooms are small but have character, decent furniture – even TVs – and cost $45.50. Americans with passports are OK.

Other options in Venice include nearby *Venice Beach Hostel* (Map 7; ☎ 310-452-3052, 1515 Pacific Ave), which has pretty sparse rooms, though all have their own baths; it's $18 per bed. There's free email and Internet access. Americans with passports are OK. The 45-bed *Jim's at the Beach*

(Map 7; ☎ 310-399-4018, 17 Brooks Ave) has the cluttered, helter-skelter look and feel of a boys' college dorm. Rooms sleep four to six ($20 per bunk); one is set aside for women only. Owner Jim provides the ingredients to make your own breakfast in the communal kitchen and usually throws weekly barbecue parties. International travelers are preferred, but Americans with passports are welcome.

South of Venice in San Pedro, the **HI International Hostel** *(☎ 310-831-8109, 3601 S Gaffey St No 613)*, on a windy bluff overlooking the Pacific, gets the top award for scenery. The hostel recently underwent a complete overhaul, with new decor and upgraded facilities. There's a big kitchen and game and entertainment equipment, plus a volleyball court and free mountain bikes. Bunks in the gender-segregated dorms sleeping three to five cost $12; private rooms are $29.50. Make early reservations for summer.

Downtown (Map 2)

Budget Downtown has lots of affordable accommodations clustered near the convention center and along Wilshire Blvd west of I-110 and in Chinatown. Besides a few motels, low-frills hotels in historic buildings provide a glimpse at the area's faded 1920s grandeur. Prices quoted here may rise considerably when a big convention is in town.

The funky **Stillwell Hotel** *(☎ 213-627-1151, 800-553-4774, fax 213-622-8940, 838 S Grand Ave)* is a recently refurbished property whose 250 rooms with private bath, TV and old-fashioned air-conditioning start at $39/49 single/double.

Side-by-side two blocks west are the spartan **Orchid Hotel** *(☎ 213-624-5855, fax 213-624-8740, 819 S Flower St)*, with rooms priced at $30/35, and the **Milner Hotel** *(☎ 213-627-6981, 800-827-0411, fax 213-623-9751, 813 S Flower St)*, which is a step up in comfort. Their rates of $40 to $65 include a full breakfast.

Motel de Ville *(☎ 213-624-8474, 1123 W 7th St)* has 62 plain but clean rooms for $35 to $45. At the **City Center Motel** *(☎ 213-628-7141, 800-816-6889, fax 213-629-1064,*

1135 W 7th St) you'll pay slightly higher rates; their family rooms for four are $70.

Mid-Range The **Park Plaza** *(☎ 213-384-5281, fax 213-480-1928, 607 S Park View St)* is a 1920s art deco landmark featured in TV shows, commercials and films like *Bugsy* and *The Bodyguard*. Rates range from $50 to $90 and include continental breakfast.

One of the best Downtown hotels in this price range is the **Hotel Figueroa** *(☎ 213-627-8971, 800-421-9092, fax 213-689-0305, 939 S Figueroa St)*. A 1927 classic, its lobby evokes an oversized hacienda. Spacious rooms have all amenities and a price tag from $88/98 single/double. It's very popular, so call ahead. Next door is the less charming but convenient **InTown Hotel** *(☎ 213-628-2222, 800-457-8520, fax 213-687-0566, 913 Figueroa St)*, which charges $60/72.

A good hotel in Chinatown is the family-run Best Western **Dragon Gate Inn** *(☎ 213-617-3077, 800-282-9999, fax 213-680-3753, 818 N Hill St)*. Rooms are large and pleasantly furnished and cost $69 to $100.

The **Kawada Hotel** *(☎ 213-621-4455, 800-752-9232, fax 213-687-4455, 200 S Hill St)* has Japanese ownership, European appeal and room rates of $89 to $119.

Recently renovated, Best Western's **Mayfair Hotel** *(☎ 213-484-9789, 800-528-1234, fax 213-484-2769, 1256 W 7th St)* was a luxury hotel when built in 1928 and maintains a touch of withered elegance. Comfortable rooms range from $105 to $130, including covered parking.

The **Los Angeles Athletic Club Hotel** *(☎ 213-625-2211, 800-421-8777, fax 213-689-1194, 431 W 7th St)* has 72 warmly furnished rooms with all the trappings, including terry robes. Rates of $120 to $150 also buy access to the posh in-house athletic club.

Top End Featured in nearly as many movies as City Hall, the **Westin Bonaventure** *(☎ 213-624-1000, 800-228-3000, fax 213-612-4800, 404 S Figueroa St)* is an LA landmark. Besides 1199 rooms, the complex has 20 restaurants, five bars, 40 retail stores, a swimming pool and a huge fitness deck. Rates start at $159.

Downtown LA's poshest hotel is the **Regal Biltmore** (☎ 213-624-1011, 800-245-8673, fax 213-612-1545, 506 S Grand Ave). Built in 1923, this landmark hotel has the feel of a European palace and has hosted a galaxy of US presidents, celebrities and dignitaries. Rates are $205 to $250.

Across the street is the 1927 **Wyndham Checkers Hotel** (☎ 213-624-0000, 800-996-3426, fax 213-626-9906, 535 S Grand Ave). Marble bathrooms and a rooftop spa are among the elegant touches you'll find in this European-style hotel. Amenities include free newspaper, shoe shine and twice daily limo service within a 2-mile radius. Rooms are $166 to $228.

Hollywood (Map 3)

Budget **Liberty Hotel** (☎ 323-962-1788, 1770 Orchid Ave) is a friendly place with 21 large and bright rooms with private bath costing $40/45 single/double. Rooms with a kitchen are an additional $5. Coffee and parking is free, and there's a guest laundry.

Just as central is the **Highland Gardens Hotel** (☎ 323-850-0535, 800-404-5472, fax 323-850-1712, 7047 Franklin Ave). Comfortable rooms wrap around a leafy, quiet courtyard and cost $60/65. Suites start at $75. The hotel is associated with a bit of Hollywood trivia: Janis Joplin overdosed in room 105 on October 3, 1970.

You can't miss the garish Las Vegas-style sign of the **Saharan Motor Hotel** (☎ 323-874-6700, fax 323-874-5163, 7212 Sunset Blvd). Rooms here have some sense of style and are a good deal at $55 to $65. A couple of strip clubs are nearby, so don't plan on walking around at night. If the hotel's full, you'll find plenty more similarly priced budget properties just east of here, including the nice-looking **Dunes Sunset Motel** (☎ 323-467-5171, 800-443-8637, 5625 Sunset Blvd).

Mid-Range Easily the best value for the money in central Hollywood is the **Magic Hotel** (☎ 323-851-0800, 800-741-4915, fax 323-851-4926, 7025 Franklin Ave). The decor is modern and includes historic magic-themed posters; rates are $69 single and $85 to $125 double. All rooms have kitchens.

In a quiet side street near Mann's Chinese Theater is the **Orchid Suites Hotel** (☎ 323-874-9678, 800-537-3052, fax 323-467-7649, 1753 N Orchid Ave). Don't let the shabby lobby deter you: each of the 36 small apartments are nicely appointed and have kitchens; some also have balconies. Rates range from $75 to $109, less in winter. Two doors down is the **Hollywood Celebrity Hotel** (☎ 323-850-6464, 800-222-7017, fax 323-850-7667, 1775 N Orchid Ave), in a stylish, if slightly neglected, art deco building. Each of the 40 rooms is spacious, quiet and costs around $80. As a special touch, a continental breakfast is brought to your room.

Top End To relive bygone days of glamour and glory, check in at the **Hollywood Roosevelt Hotel** (☎ 323-466-7000, 800-950-7667, fax 323-462-8056, 7000 Hollywood Blvd). This 1927 Spanish Revival-style hotel was the site of the first Academy Awards ceremonies in 1929. Rooms range in price from $109 to $159.

West Hollywood (Map 4)

Mid-Range The **Holloway Motel** (☎ 323-654-2454, 8465 Santa Monica Blvd) can get a bit noisy because of its central location, but it's a friendly place, with cable TV, voice mail and free continental breakfast. Room rates are $70 to $80. **Park Sunset Hotel** (☎ 323-654-6470, 800-821-3660, fax 323-654-5918, 8462 Sunset Blvd), right on the Sunset Strip, is a good value. The rooms are somewhat small, but some have superb views over the city sprawl. Doubles are $84 to $94; two-room suites with kitchen cost $149 to $169.

Nearby, **Sunset Plaza Hotel** (☎ 323-654-0750, 800-421-3652, fax 323-650-6146, 8400 Sunset Blvd) attracts a mixed crowd of families and couples with its high-energy, cosmopolitan flair and reasonable prices. There are 88 nicely decorated and spacious rooms, some with full kitchens, starting at $119.

Top End **Le Rêve Hotel de Luxe** (☎ 310-854-1114, 800-835-7997, fax 310-657-2623, 8822 Cynthia St) is a charming collection of 80 French country-style suites, many with balconies, fireplaces and kitchenettes. Views from the rooftop garden swimming pool are fabulous. Rates start at a reasonable $129 and top off at $205.

The **Beverly Plaza Hotel** (☎ 323-658-6600, 800-624-6835, fax 323-653-3464, 8384 W 3rd St), at La Cienega Blvd, is a trendy boutique hotel where special touches include free taxi rides within a 5-mile radius. The large, lovingly appointed rooms are priced from $121 to $198.

Le Montrose (☎ 310-855-1115, 800-776-0666, fax 310-657-9192, 900 Hammond St) is a cozy hideaway with a $2 million art collection and 120 large suites, each with a sunken living room and fireplace. Views from the rooftop swimming pool, framed by private cabanas, are breathtaking. Rooms cost $175 to $475.

Like the gates to heaven, two giant doors – but no marquee – announce that you have arrived at the **Mondrian** (☎ 323-650-8999, 800-525-8029, fax 323-650-5215, 8440 Sunset Blvd), LA's ultimate place for celeb sightings. Expect to shell out at least $240 for a less-than-standard room and up to $2600 for a suite.

The **Sunset Marquis Hotel & Villas** (☎ 310-657-1333, 800-858-9758, fax 310-652-5300, 1200 N Alta Loma Rd) is a discreet retreat and a favorite among record industry players (it has a $600,000 recording studio on the premises). It's also noted for rolling lawns, its koi pond and tropical gardens. Suites start at $260 and crest at $320.

Get ready for French-flavored indulgences at the **Château Marmont** (☎ 323-656-1010, 800-242-8328, fax 323-655-5311, 8221 Sunset Blvd), modeled after a Norman castle. Its whimsical charm, gorgeous gardens, special services (including complimentary cell phones and newspapers) and legendary discretion make it a favorite celebrity hideaway. Rooms are $195, suites run $250 to $1400.

The **Four Seasons** (☎ 310-273-2222, fax 310-859-3824, 300 S Doheny Drive) is one of those exceptional hotels that dazzles with class, not glitz. Attention to detail is impeccable – even the restaurant bathrooms have fresh flowers. Rates range from $295 to $385; suites start at $450.

Mid-City (Map 4)
Budget The 1924 **Chancellor Hotel** (☎ 213-383-1183, 800-446-4442, 3191 W 7th St) has a sizable population of long-term residents, including international students and senior citizens. Off the huge lobby is a communal area, including a cafeteria where breakfast and dinner are served. Room rates of $49/54 single/double include meals.

The friendly **Park Plaza Lodge** (☎ 323-931-1501, fax 323-931-5863, 6001 W 3rd St), near the Farmers Market, has largish rooms filled with antique-style furniture for $50/55. The decor at the **Bevonshire Lodge Motel** (☎ 323-936-6154, 7575 Beverly Blvd) hasn't changed much since Nixon was president, but who's to complain if charges here are just $39/45.

Mid-Range The Best Western **Mid-Wilshire Plaza Hotel** (☎ 213-385-4444, 800-528-1234, fax 213-380-5413, 603 S New Hampshire Ave), in Koreatown, is not in the most fashionable area, but $60/85 gets a large, friendly room with standard amenities.

Beverly Hills (Map 6)
Mid-Range Moderately priced options are rare in this stronghold of opulence. The contemporary **Crescent Hotel** (☎ 310-247-0505, 800-451-1566, fax 310-247-9053, 403 N Crescent Drive) has smallish rooms for $80 to $95. The **Carlyle Inn** (☎ 310-275-4445, 800-3227-5953, fax 310-859-0496, 1119 S Robertson Blvd) has superb service and rates of $120/130 single/double, which includes breakfast buffet, afternoon tea and cocktails. They offer free shuttle service within a 5-mile radius.

A small gem in this diamond-studded part of town is the cozy **Beverly Hills Inn** (☎ 310-278-0303, 800-463-4466, fax 310-278-1728, 125 S Spalding Drive), which has such amenities as voice mail, a sauna and health center, free parking, buffet breakfast and free newspapers. Room rates range from $130 to $180.

Top End No other hotel dwells in legend as much as the **Beverly Hills Hotel** (☎ 310-887-2887, 800-283-8885, fax 310-281-2905,

9641 Sunset Blvd). A $100 million face-lift in the early '90s – courtesy of current owner the Sultan of Brunei – restored splendor to this venerable château. 'Standard' rooms start at a budget-busting $295.

For a bit of old world flair, check into the **Regent Beverly Wilshire** (☎ *310-275-5200, 800-451-4354, fax 310-274-2851, 9500 Wilshire Blvd)*. Yes, it's the hotel from which Julia Roberts first stumbled, then sashayed, in *Pretty Woman*. Luxury is taken very seriously here, with many of the 285 rooms featuring not one but two bathrooms. Rates start at $265 for standard doubles.

At the **Hotel Bel-Air** (☎ *310-472-1211, 800-648-4097, 701 Stone Canyon Rd)*, the emphasis is on privacy, which is why celebrities love the secluded bungalows, fountain courtyards and gardens. Visit, if only to stroll the grounds or to have a drink. If you want to stay, prepare to drop $240 to $310.

Westwood (Map 6)
Mid-Range The **Royal Palace** (☎ *310-208-6677, 800-631-0100, fax 310-824-3732, 1051 Tilverton Ave)* is no palace, but rooms cost just $66/72 singles/doubles. Assets include free parking (a rare commodity in Westwood), breakfast, cable TV and a two-block walk to UCLA. **Hilgard House** (☎ *310-208-3945, 800-826-3934, fax 310-208-1972, 927 Hilgard Ave)* is a delightful boutique hotel right next to campus. All rooms have antique-style furnishings, and many have spas. Rates start at $109.

The **Hotel del Capri** (☎ *310-474-3511, 800-444-6835, fax 310-470-9999, 10587 Wilshire Blvd)* is a charmer with 36 rooms and 45 suites on four stories surrounding a terrace and swimming pool. Continental breakfast is delivered to your door, and parking is free. Rates run $90 to $110, or $115 to $235 for suites.

Top End The classy **Westwood Marquis Hotel** (☎ *310-208-8765, 800-421-2317, fax 310-824-0355, 930 Hilgard Ave)* is bathed in a sea of flowers and trees. Public areas and rooms ooze sophistication and old-world style, and attention to detail is flawless. Rates in this all-suite property run $260 to $700.

Presidents of countries and corporations have stayed at the **Century Plaza Hotel** (☎ *310-277-2000, 800-937-8461, fax 310-551-3355, 2025 Ave of the Stars)*. Rooms are spacious and appointed with all the usual wonderfully frivolous knickknacks. Rates start at around $200 single/double, though weekend specials are frequent.

Los Angeles International Airport
Budget Apart from inexpensive motels, you'll find numerous other affordable properties in the vicinity of the airport. Most offer free shuttle service to and from Los Angeles International Airport (LAX). The small **Vista Motel** (☎ *310-390-2014, 4900 S Sepulveda Blvd)*, in Culver City, has 22 decent-sized rooms at $37 to $52. Another good choice is the **Skyways Airport Hotel** (☎ *310-670-2900, 800-336-0025, 9250 Airport Blvd)*, whose rooms, some with kitchenette and in-room spas, cost $40 to $60; suites are $60 to $90. The **Sunburst Motel** (☎ *310-398-7523, 3900 Sepulveda Blvd)*, in Culver City, has standard rooms for $59 and small suites for $89.

Mid-Range The 770-room **Furama Hotel** (☎ *310-670-8111, 800-225-8126, fax 310-337-1883, 8601 Lincoln Blvd)* is a pleasant resort-style property. It's right across from a park with tennis courts, golf and a driving range. On the premises are a swimming pool, bowling alley and supermarket. Rates start at $99.

The **Hampton Inn** (☎ *310-337-1000, 800-426-7866, fax 310-645-6925, 10300 La Cienega Blvd)*, in Inglewood, has 148 rooms costing $69 to $95; rates include continental breakfast, newspaper and free local phone calls.

Top End Upscale hotels near LAX cater to business travelers on expense accounts. Rooms range from $119 to $169; suites cost a bit more. They include: **Crowne Plaza LA Airport** (☎ *310-642-7500, 800-255-7606, fax 310-417-3608, 5985 W Century Blvd)*; the 1200-room **Los Angeles Airport Hilton & Towers** (☎ *310-410-4000, 800-445-8667, fax 310-410-6250, 5711 W Century Blvd)*; and the

Los Angeles Airport Marriott (☎ *310-641-5700, 800-228-9290, fax 310-337-5358, 5855 W Century Blvd*).

Malibu

One of the few affordable properties in Malibu is the funky *Topanga Ranch Motel* (☎ *310-456-5486, 18711 Pacific Coast Hwy*), whose 30 trim white cottages across the highway from the beach go for about $60 to $80. Another option is the *Malibu Riviera Motel* (☎ *310-457-9503, 28920 Pacific Coast Hwy*), which has managed to keep prices to $70 during the week and $80 on the weekend.

Lovely *Casa Malibu Inn* (☎ *310-456-2219, 800-831-0858, fax 310-456-5418, 22752 Pacific Coast Hwy*) overlooks a private beach. Some of the 21 rooms have decks, fireplaces and kitchenettes. Rates start at $99 and top out at $199.

The *Malibu Country Inn* (☎ *310-457-9622, 6506 Westward Beach Rd*) offers a quiet retreat. The inn has just 15 rooms, five of them two-bedroom family suites. Rates range from $125 to $190.

The *Malibu Beach Inn* (☎ *310-456-6444, 800-462-5428, fax 310-456-1499, 22878 Pacific Coast Hwy*) is a breezy oceanside getaway near the Malibu Pier. Rooms with partial ocean views range from $149 to $190; those with private outdoor Jacuzzi and suites go for $219 to $275. Rates include continental breakfast.

Santa Monica (Map 7)

Budget Ever since Santa Monica was catapulted onto the trendiness bandwagon, inexpensive accommodations have become elusive. The *Sea Shore Motel* (☎ *310-392-2787, fax 310-392-5167, 2637 Main St*) is well run and has a lot of European influences. Standard rooms cost $65, and suites sleeping up to four cost $95. Ask for special deals when checking in.

Mid-Range The charming *Hotel California* (☎ *310-393-2363, 800-537-8483, fax 310-393-1063, 1670 Ocean Ave*) is only steps from the beach and has largish standard rooms with all the usual amenities for $150 to $170. About $100 more gets a two-

bedroom suite with a pantry kitchen and patio. Parking is free.

The *Hotel Shangri-La* (☎ *310-394-2791, 800-345-7829, fax 310-451-3351, 1301 Ocean Ave*), a swank 1939 art deco building, has long been a sentimental favorite. Rooms – outfitted with retro-style furniture, and some with kitchenettes – start at a very reasonable $130, including continental breakfast and afternoon tea.

Less character but an equally good location is offered by the Best Western *Ocean View Hotel* (☎ *310-458-4888, 800-452-4888, fax 310-458-0848, 1447 Ocean Ave*). Smallish rooms go for $99 to $149 in winter and ratchet up to $139 to $219 in peak season. Just a block inland, *Hotel Carmel* (☎ *310-451-2469, 800-445-8695, fax 310-393-4180, 201 Broadway*) has a lobby with pink ceiling rafters, and newly renovated rooms for $90 to $169.

Top End The *Miramar Sheraton* (☎ *310-576-7777, 800-325-3535, fax 310-458-7912, 101 Wilshire Blvd*) first opened as a hotel in 1889 and was put through a $33 million renovation in 1994. Its 270 guest rooms and 32 bungalows are set amidst semitropical gardens. Rates start at $140, though bungalows are $300.

The 84-room *Georgian Hotel* (☎ *310-395-9945, 800-538-8147, fax 310-451-3374, 1415 Ocean Ave*) has been designated a historic hotel of America, and its blue geometric facade makes it an eye-catching art deco landmark. Standard rooms start at $185; rooms crest at $315.

The beachside *Loews Santa Monica Beach Hotel* (☎ *310-458-6700, 800-235-6397, fax 310-458-2813, 1700 Ocean Ave*) has interior grandeur and a commanding oceanfront perch. Rooms and suites blend rattan and wicker furnishings with a subdued palette of colors. Regular rooms run $250 to $450.

Nearby is *Shutters on the Beach* (☎ *310-458-0030, 800-334-9000, fax 310-458-4589, 1 Pico Blvd*), which has an elegant Cape Cod appearance, two pricey and acclaimed restaurants and plenty of original artwork. Smallish but homey rooms start at $325 and jump to $475 to $525 for ocean views; some rooms have fireplaces, private Jacuzzis and even radios in the showers.

Venice Beach & Marina del Rey (Map 7)

Budget The *Jolly Roger Hotel* (☎ 310-822-2904, 800-822-2904, 2904 Washington Blvd), adjacent to the shore in Marina del Rey, has basic rooms with large baths for $62/72 singles/doubles and motel rooms for $15 less. One of the best bargains in LA is the *Cadillac Hotel* (☎ 310-399-8876, fax 310-399-4536, 8 Dudley Ave), an art deco landmark right on Venice's Ocean Front Walk. Rooms have ocean views, color TV, safe, phone and private bath. There's a gym and sauna, rooftop sun deck and coin laundry. Doubles cost $69 to $99, and there's a triple for $79 and a family room that sleeps four, also for $79. Rates increase by $10 in summer.

Mid-Range The *Foghorn Harbor Inn* (☎ 310-823-4626, fax 310-578-1964, 4140 Via Marina), in Marina del Rey, is right on Mother's Beach, a small inlet favored by parents with splashing kids. The hotel's smallish, plain rooms range from $79 to $149; you can bargain for lower rates.

Draped in ivy, the *Venice Beach House* (☎ 310-823-1966, fax 310-823-1842, 15 30th Ave) is a tasteful, homey retreat. Charlie Chaplin used to stay here when it was the beach house of a local developer. Doubles are $95/120 for shared/private bath.

Romantic touches abound at the *Inn at Playa del Rey* (☎ 310-574-1920, fax 310-574-9920, 435 Culver Blvd). Homemade breakfasts; tea, wine and hors d'oeuvres in the afternoon; and fresh cookies in truly lovely dining and seating areas make this inn well worth the $125 to $175 you'll pay for a standard room.

Top End If you're going to spend big, it might as well be at the classy *Ritz-Carlton Marina del Rey* (☎ 310-823-1700, 800-241-3333, fax 310-823-2403, 4375 Admiralty Way). This lavish property has its own marina with charter yachts, lighted tennis courts, a swimming pool and spa. The 294 palatial rooms start at $280.

Long Beach

Expect plain but clean digs at the *Beach Inn Motel* (☎ 562-437-3464, fax 562-436-4541, 823 E 3rd St), for just $40. Try the Beach Inn only if the *Inn of Long Beach* (☎ 562-435-3791, 800-230-7500, fax 562-436-7510, 185 Atlantic Ave) is full. Costing only slightly more than the Beach Inn, the friendly Inn of Long Beach has rooms (with cable TV and VCR) that face a courtyard with a swimming pool and Jacuzzi.

Since historic B&Bs with rooms under $100 are rare, the *Lord Mayor* (☎ 562-436-0324, 435 Cedar St), a 1904 Edwardian house that was once the home of the city's first mayor, is quite remarkable. Rooms get their character from stylish antique furniture and not from frilly overdecorating; bathrooms have claw-foot tubs, and there's an ample sun deck. Rates range from $85 to $125.

At the *Hotel Queen Mary* (☎ 562-435-3511, 1126 Queens Hwy), you'll stay in the original (refurbished), but somewhat cramped, staterooms of this permanently moored ship. Portholes don't provide much light, but the mood of art deco afloat is unrivaled. Most rooms cost $120 to $160.

San Fernando Valley

Budget The *Chariot Inn Motel* (☎ 818-507-9774, fax 818-507-9774, 1118 E Colorado St), in Glendale, offers free continental breakfasts, refrigerators and movies with its 31 spacious rooms. Singles cost $42 to $52, doubles $50 to $60.

Warner Gardens Motel (☎ 818-992-4426, fax 818-704-1062, 21706 Ventura Blvd), in Woodland Hills, has 42 rooms with refrigerator and microwave at $46 to $54, suites $54 to $65. Rates include continental breakfast, and there's a coffee shop and spa on the premises.

Mid-Range The *Safari Inn* (☎ 818-845-8586, 800-782-4373, fax 818-845-0054, 1911 W Olive Ave), in Burbank, has so much character it's been used as a movie set. The motel has a bar, swimming pool and spa, and its rooms cost $99 single/double year round.

Within walking distance to Universal Studios, just off busy Hwy 101 in Studio City, is the flower-festooned *Universal City Inn* (☎ 818-760-8737, fax 818-762-5159, 10730 Ventura Blvd), whose modern and large rooms have a price tag of $60/80 single/double.

A handsome garden with waterfalls and a swan pond is the centerpiece of the *Sportsmen's Lodge* (☎ 818-769-4700, 800-821-8511, fax 213-877-3898, 12825 Ventura Blvd) in Studio City. Evocative of a British country estate, the lodge's 193 rooms have private patios and are quite reasonably priced at $105 to $133.

Top End Glendale's handsome 19-story *Red Lion Hotel* (☎ 818-956-5466, fax 818-956-5490, 100 W Glenoaks Blvd) is popular with business travelers for its service and facilities, including free shuttles to Burbank Airport. Rooms start at $214, dropping to $139 weekends.

Right on the Universal Studios lot is the 21-story *Sheraton Universal Hotel* (☎ 818-980-1212, 800-325-3535, fax 818-509-0605, 333 Universal Terrace Pkwy). A huge lobby gives access to 417 rooms costing $180 to $250. Similar but slightly less expensive is the Sheraton's 24-story, steel-and-glass neighbor, *Universal City Hilton & Towers* (☎ 818-506-2500, 800-445-8667, 555 Universal Terrace Pkwy).

Pasadena (Map 8)

Budget Pasadena's 'motel row' is along E Colorado Blvd, from Lake Ave all the way to Rosemead Blvd. Literally dozens of budget-priced chain motels line this strip, some in better repair than others, most with rooms around $40. The best bet is the friendly *Westway Inn* (☎ 626-304-9678, fax 626-449-3493, 1599 E Colorado Blvd). Each of the 61 modern rooms have refrigerators, coffeemakers and hair dryers, and cost $53 to $59; Jacuzzi suites are $79. Next door is the *Saga Motor Hotel* (☎ 626-795-0431, 800-793-7242, fax 626-792-0559, 1633 E Colorado Blvd), another above-average motel, which charges $56 to $75 for its recently remodeled rooms.

Mid-Range For charm and a central location, the *Pasadena Hotel* (☎ 626-568-8172,

800-653-8886, fax 626-793-6409, 76 N Fair Oaks Ave) is hard to beat. A B&B housed in a late-eighteenth-century building furnished with Edwardian antiques, it has 12 rooms costing $65 to $100 single, $80 to $150 double. Some have shared baths.

Equally lovely is the tiny *Artists' Inn* (☎ 626-799-5668, 888-799-5668, fax 626-799-3678, 1038 Magnolia St), in a Victorian farmhouse, whose decor recalls various artists and periods. All rooms have private bath and cost $105 to $130. The *Bissell House* (☎ 626-441-3535, 800-441-3530, 201 Orange Grove Ave) is a restored 1887 Victorian villa with leaded glass windows. It has just three rooms, each with bath that has pedestal sinks and claw-foot tubs, costing $100 to $150.

Top End The *Ritz-Carlton Huntington Hotel* (☎ 626-568-3900, 800-241-3333, fax 626-568-1842, 1401 S Oak Knoll Ave) is a sumptuous hostelry surrounded by a magnificent 23-acre garden. Special touches include a covered picture bridge and California's first Olympic-size swimming pool. Rates start at $165 and climb to $500.

Another top property is the modern *Doubletree Hotel* (☎ 626-792-2727, 800-222-8733, fax 626-795-7669, 191 N Los Robles Ave), next to the historic City Hall. Rates are $179 to $299, dropping to $120 to $299 on weekends.

PLACES TO EAT

The folks in San Francisco may disagree, but the fact remains: Los Angeles is the culinary capital of the US West Coast. Why? The number one reason, perhaps, is the willingness to experiment. As a cosmopolitan crossroads, LA attracts people from around the world – and with them comes their food. Creative chefs take bits and pieces from different traditions and combine them in ways that might have been unimaginable only a few years ago.

Innovative cuisine is most commonly found in upscale districts such as West Hollywood, Beverly Hills, Santa Monica, Pasadena and Downtown. Mexican, Chinese, Japanese and other cuisines abound throughout the metropolis, though the best restaurants are usually in the various ethnic districts like Little Tokyo, Chinatown and East LA. Italian and French restaurants are popular everywhere. And there are enough hamburger joints, cafes and hole-in-the-wall diners to suit every pocketbook.

Consider any restaurant where you can dine for less than $10 to be 'budget,' $10 to $20 as 'mid-range,' and over $20 as 'top end.' Although dining is a casual affair in LA, you still should dress according to price. A jacket is appropriate for men at better restaurants. Most mid-range and top-end restaurants take reservations; at the more popular restaurants, in fact, you should call days or even weeks ahead.

Downtown (Map 2)

Broadway & Financial District A dream come true for the cash-strapped is the *Grand Central Market* on Broadway at 4th St. Eating here is super casual; simply pick an eatery and sidle up to the counter. Choices include *Maria's Pescado Frito* in the central aisle for fresh fish tacos and ceviche; *Sarita's Pupuseria* in the right aisle for mouthwatering Salvadoran *pupusas* filled with cheese, pork or beans ($1.50); and *Roast to Go* in the central aisle, with delicious tacos ($1.50) and burritos ($3). *China Cafe*, on the upper level toward the Hill St exit, has steamy and delicious bowls of soup starting at $1.85.

At the *City Pier* (☎ 213-617-2489, 333 S Spring St), popular with *LA Times* reporters, about $6 buys sandwiches bulging with rock shrimp, crawfish or catfish.

The beer garden of the *Bonaventure Brewing Company* (☎ 213-236-0802, 404 S Figueroa St) is a great place for burgers and brews under $10. Other dishes can be too creative for their own good, so stick with the basics.

Cicada (☎ 213-488-9488, 617 S Olive St) is a wonderful restaurant in the glamorous Oviatt Building. The fine food served in the cathedral-like space is of an Italian stripe and a tad overpriced ($20 and up).

For some of LA's most pleasant outdoor dining, head to *Cafe Pinot* (☎ 213-239-6500, 700 W 5th St), set in the quirky Maguire Gardens at the Central Library. The menu is seasonal, though their rotisserie chicken is an ever-popular staple.

The *Water Grill* (☎ 213-891-0900, 544 S Grand Ave) draws kudos for its impeccably fresh gourmet seafood and fish. The Fruits of the Sea platter gives you a sampling from the oyster bar. Maine lobster is about $25 per pound.

Little Tokyo For big bowls of *udon* – thick noodles swimming in an aromatic broth along with anything from egg to beef to shrimp and bamboo shoots – head to *Suehiro* (☎ 213-626-9132, 337 E 1st St). Superb sushi can be found at *Frying Fish* (☎ 213-680-0567) and *Oomasa* (☎ 213-623-9048), both in the Japanese Village Plaza (between San Pedro and S Central Sts and 1st and 2nd Sts). Also here is *Shabu Shabu House* (☎ 213-680-3890), famous for this Japanese-style 'fondue,' which involves briefly dipping wafer-thin slices of beef, and vegetables, into a simmering broth.

El Pueblo & Chinatown *La Golondrina* (☎ 213-628-4349, W-17 Olvera St) is one of LA's oldest Mexican restaurants (1924), and the best on Olvera St. Its prime location translates into main courses costing two or three dollars more than usual ($10 and up), but at least the food and atmosphere are *muy auténtico*. Also in El Pueblo are several casual and inexpensive eateries.

Some of the city's best chefs regularly join the throngs at *Philippe's The Original* (☎ 213-628-3781, 1001 N Alameda St), in business since 1908. Retro-clad 'carvers' prepare juicy roast beef sandwiches dipped into fragrant juice from the roasting pan ($3.95). Coffee is just 9¢ (no misprint).

Chinatown restaurants are divided into two basic types: the more formal banquet hall-type places that are also often dim sum parlors, and casual eateries where you can chow down on chow mein, jumbo shrimp or Mongolian beef at rock-bottom prices.

Top contenders of the former type are *Ocean Seafood* (☎ 213-687-3088, 757 N Hill St), a spacious Hong Kong-style place;

Empress Pavilion (☎ 213-617-9898, 988 N Hill St), on the 3rd floor of Bamboo Plaza; and the slightly less expensive *Golden Dragon* (☎ 213-626-2039, 960 N Broadway).

Simple restaurants abound, but the following are among the best: *Hong Kong Harbor* (☎ 213-617-2983, 845 N Broadway); *Sam Woo* (☎ 213-680-7836, 727 N Broadway); and *Hop Woo* (☎ 213-617-3038, 855 N Broadway).

East Los Angeles

Given its predominantly Mexican population, East LA offers some of the most authentic south-of-the-border food. One restaurant with a huge following is *El Tepeyac Cafe* (☎ 323-268-1960, 812 N Evergreen Ave), whose specialty is bulging, budget-priced burritos smothered in cheese. For an 'excursion' to Mexico, head to El Mercado, 3425 E 1st St, where two restaurants – *El Tarasco* and *El Gallo* – do culinary battle on the cavernous mezzanine level. Pick either, then order a *rica botana* – a plate piled high with fresh seafood and appetizingly served with cocktail sauce. The small *(chica)* plate easily serves two ($24).

South Central

Banish any worries about love handles or clogged arteries when eating at *Phillip's House of Barbecue* (☎ 323-292-7613, 4307 Leimert Blvd), which serves up some of the city's best pork and beef ribs. Sandwich-size portions range from $4.50 to $6.25; dinner-size portions are $6.75 to $11. The classy *Elephant Walk* (☎ 323-299-1765, 4336 Degnan St) is furnished with antiques and original works by local artists and has a seafood dominated mid-priced menu.

Hollywood (Map 3)

Central Hollywood *Hamburger Hamlet* (☎ 323-467-6106, 6914 Hollywood Blvd), across from Mann's Chinese Theater, is perfect for grabbing a quick burger, sandwich, salad or pasta for $6 to $10. *Birds* (☎ 323-465-0175, 5925 Franklin Ave) is a coffee shop that specializes in fowl, including their signature marinated chicken roasted to a light and crispy tan and served

with a choice of tasty dipping sauces, bread and a side dish (less than $10).

Those with a hankering for fish and chips or a ploughman's lunch (around $10) should head to the *Cat & Fiddle Pub* (☎ 323-468-3800, 6530 Sunset Blvd). Lunch on the patio is especially pleasant.

At *Miceli's* (☎ 323-466-3438, 1646 N Las Palmas Ave), Hollywood's oldest Italian haunt, hundreds of (empty) Chianti bottles dangle from the beamed ceiling. The house wine is a steal at $12 a bottle, though the food's mediocre. Not only Cubans give *El Floridita* (☎ 323-871-8612), wedged into a mini-mall at 1253 N Vine St, an enthusiastic thumbs up for its authentic food, energetic atmosphere and vibrant live entertainment. Try the Cuban sandwiches or a dish called *ropa vieja*. Prices hover around $12.

LA's French restaurant 'du jour' is *Les Deux Café* (☎ 323-465-0509, 1638 Las Palmas Ave). The place draws a cool crowd heavy on brass, beauty and power that

Great Celebrity Spotting

Given LA's fickle restaurant scene, what's hot with celebs today may have plunged out of favor by tomorrow. The places listed below are among those that have demonstrated staying power. We can't guarantee you'll see famous faces, but these restaurants are where the stars are known to hang out:

Caffé Luna – Melrose/La Brea
Chinois on Main – Santa Monica
Les Deux Café – Hollywood
Hugo's – West Hollywood
KoKoMo – Fairfax District
I Cugini – Santa Monica
Matsuhisa – Beverly Hills
Musso & Frank Grill – Hollywood
Neptune's Net – Malibu
Pink's Hot Dogs – Melrose/La Brea
Spago – West Hollywood

doesn't care that prices of $20 and up per main course outdistance the chef's skill.

A Hollywood dinosaur is the *Musso & Frank Grill* (☎ 323-467-7788, 6667 Hollywood Blvd), already a hit back in the silent film era. The menu features politically incorrect milk-fed veal cutlet and stick-to-the-ribs fare like steak with gravy, and the martinis are killer. Main dishes start at $15.

Step through the doors of *Dar Maghreb* (☎ 323-876-7651, 7651 Sunset Blvd) and journey from Tinseltown to a setting out of *A Thousand and One Nights*. You'll dine on a seven-course mouthwatering feast fit for a prince ($32) – served family style and eaten without utensils.

A replica Japanese castle, *Yamashiro* (☎ 323-466-5125, 1999 N Sycamore Ave) seductively perches on a southerly slope of the Hollywood Hills, overlooking the sea of glitter that is the city at night. Do what you must to score a window table. The food – served by petite, kimono-clad Japanese waitresses – is mid- to upper-priced and good, though not worth gushing about.

Serious food lovers with deep pockets shouldn't leave LA without worshipping at *Patina* (☎ 323-467-1108, 5955 Melrose Ave), the flagship restaurant of Joachim and Christine Splichal. Joachim digs deep into his bottomless culinary repertory to create a menu that improbably – but successfully – fuses Californian and Germanic flavors.

Silver Lake & Los Feliz On the happening Vermont Ave strip in Los Feliz, you'll find *Fred's 62* (☎ 323-667-0062, 1854 Vermont Ave), which has polyethnic sandwiches, salads, noodles and more dished out around the clock to hungry hipsters on small budgets. Up the street, *Palermo* (☎ 323-663-1178, 1858 Vermont Ave) is an unpretentious, inexpensive neighborhood Italian joint that's as welcoming and comfortable as a hug from an old friend. Pizzas are generously topped and buried under a layer of melted cheese, and the small antipasto salad is enough – as an appetizer – for four.

El Siete Mares (3145 Sunset Blvd) has excellent – and huge – fish tacos and burritos and fresh ceviche tostadas, with nothing on

the menu topping $5. For an eccentric Mexican cantina, head to *El Conquistador* (☎ 323-666-5136, 3701 Sunset Blvd), where great choices include *Sonorense* (chicken sautéed with bacon and vegetables) and jumbo shrimp marinated in tequila sauce (around $8). *El Chavo* (☎ 323-664-0871, 4441 Sunset Blvd), a windowless Mexican classic with kaleidoscopic Christmas lights and a ceiling festooned with fluorescent sombreros, has excellent chicken enchiladas in mole sauce (under $10).

For a slice of France, head to the secluded *Cafe Stella* (☎ 323-666-0265), a friendly and popular cafe in a romantic courtyard at 3932 Sunset Blvd (look for the red star). The bistro-style menu is small and select, with the freshest offerings noted on a chalkboard. Seating spills out onto the courtyard.

For a completely different ethnic experience, head to the *Red Lion Tavern* (Map 2; ☎ 323-662-5337, 2366 Glendale Blvd), where young dirndl-clad waitresses serve the best of German country cooking in a venerable haunt cluttered with Germaniana. The beer garden buzzes in summer.

West Hollywood (Map 4)

Casual California fare is on the menu at *French Quarter Market* (☎ 323-654-0898, 7985 Santa Monica Blvd), especially mountains of fresh, delicious salads. Seating is either on the outdoor patio or the New Orleans-inspired interior decorated with white wrought-iron balustrades and flower boxes.

Down-to-earth *Hugo's* (☎ 323-654-3993, 8401 Santa Monica Blvd), has sidewalk seating, healthy fare like the tantric veggie burger and a huge breakfast menu. Another contender nearby is *Basix* (☎ 323-848-2460, 8333 Santa Monica Blvd), at Flores St, which has an 'Ellis Island' kind of a salad menu (Italian, Greek, Chinese) and interesting pizzas grilled over fruitwood.

Luna Park (☎ 310-652-0611, 665 N Robertson Blvd) offers European sophistication in its restaurant-cum-nightclub-cum-cabaret. The menu is Mediterranean infused with the occasional Asian flavor; there's also a four-course tasting menu for $30 or $55, wine included.

LOS ANGELES

Wolfgang Puck

L'Orangerie (☎ 310-652-9770, 903 N La Cienega Blvd) is a formal French restaurant with pompous Louis XIV-inspired decor. It's a favorite among those who truly know what good food, wine and service is about and are willing – and able – to pay for it.

It's impossible not to mention the original *Spago* (☎ 310-652-4025, 1114 Horn Ave), the place that launched Wolfgang Puck, who helped design 'California' cuisine, as a celebrity chef. Who sits where in this celebrity-heavy haunt is a gauge of current power and popularity. Call at least a week, better two, in advance for a table, or come about 10:30 pm and gawk at the crowd over dessert.

Melrose & La Brea Area At *Caffé Luna* (☎ 323-655-8647, 7463 Melrose Ave), with its secluded flower-festooned courtyard, breakfast is served any time and the rustic Italianate food is delicious and plentiful. A dependable Melrose favorite, *Tommy Tang's* (☎ 323-937-5733, 7313 Melrose Ave), near Fuller Ave, serves updated versions of Thai classics and also has a decent sushi bar. Favorites include the Original Tommy Duck ($14.50), though noodle and rice dishes (around $8) are tasty as well.

For the taste and feel of Little Italy, ex-New Yorkers gravitate to *Frankie's* (☎ 323-937-2801, 7228 Melrose Ave), an airy, uncluttered dining room replete with a shiny baby grand piano. Traditional dishes like seafood chowder and osso buco are good, though lobster aficionados will want to do battle with these spiny creatures, priced at a mere $11.95 per pound.

Citrus (☎ 323-857-0034, 6703 Melrose Ave), which serves California-French cuisine, continues to rank high among LA gourmets. Its four- and five-course dinners are $55/65 and complemented by a premium wine list.

Pink's Hot Dogs (☎ 323-931-4223, 711 La Brea Ave) is a simple stand that's been serving delicious all-beef dogs buried beneath aromatic chili and onions ($2.20) since 1939. The stand is open till 2 am weekdays, 3 am weekends. *Ca'Brea* (☎ 323-938-2863, 346 S La Brea Ave) offers superb Northern Italian selections in a homey, sectioned dining room. Up the street is *Campanile* (☎ 323-938-1447, 624 S La Brea Ave), which has defined 'urban rustic' cooking. Chef Mark Peel comes up with new culinary creations daily, but staples include grilled meats and vegetables.

Fairfax District At the Farmers Market (6333 W 3rd St), you can assemble your own picnic from the cheese, sausage, bread and delicatessen vendors, or grab some takeout and eat it in the central patio. Good bets include the New Orleans-style Gumbo Pot (☎ 323-933-0358), which serves a mean jambalaya, a spicy rice dish with chicken and sausage ($5.95). A good place for huge, hearty breakfasts around $6 is the hip art deco KoKoMo (☎ 323-933-0733), where you belly up to a Formica counter. This place is popular with Industry types from neighboring CBS, as well as the gay crowd.

Beverly Center District One of LA's two branches of the *Hard Rock Cafe* (☎ 310-276-7605) is on the ground floor of the northwest corner of the Beverly Center mall, at 8500 Beverly Blvd. (The other is on the Universal City Walk, ☎ 818-622-7625, next to Universal Studios.) Nearby is one of the last remaining pieces of mimetic archi-

LOS ANGELES

tecture in LA, the hot dog-shaped *Tail O' The Pup* (☎ 310-652-4517, 329 N San Vicente Blvd), in operation since 1938. Its edible, though hardly great, dogs continue to attract a loyal following of showbiz folks.

Jerry's Famous Deli (☎ 310-289-1811, 9701 Beverly Blvd) is a popular 24-hour deli with a menu as long and confusing as a Dostoyevsky novel. For locations of the six other branches, check the Yellow Pages.

With its cool tiled floor, lazy ceiling fans and rattan chairs, *Le Colonial* (☎ 310-289-0660, 8783 Beverly Blvd) makes you feel like you've stepped onto the set of *The Year of Living Dangerously*. The Vietnamese cuisine has complex flavors and can be quite spicy. Dishes are served family style.

More upscale French Vietnamese food is on the menu at *Indochine* (☎ 323-655-4777, 8225 Beverly Blvd), a refined and swank restaurant flaunting exceptional decor and cuisine. Owner Jean-Marc Houmard recreates the lost world of French Indochina with subdued lighting, banana leaf frescos and snug green leather banquettes. Be sure to leave room for the coconut crème brûlée.

Kings Road Cafe (☎ 323-655-9044, 8361 Beverly Blvd) is usually busy, drawing a predominantly young crowd with budget-priced bistro fare. You could make a meal of just soup or salad and the crusty fresh baked country bread served with it. Nearby *Authentic Cafe* (☎ 323-939-4626, 7605 Beverly Blvd) is similar but draws a more diverse clientele, from students to families to suits. The health conscious should be in heaven at *Newsroom* (☎ 310-652-4444, 120 N Robertson Blvd), a breezy, tall-ceilinged cafe whose menu exiles as much fat and sodium as possible. A second branch (☎ 310-319-9100, 530 Wilshire Blvd) is in Santa Monica.

El Coyote (☎ 323-939-2255, 7312 Beverly Blvd) is beloved partly for its bargain-priced basic food, but more so for its stiff margaritas, which at just $2.95, provide a cheap buzz.

At *Locanda Veneta* (☎ 310-274-1893, 8638 W 3rd St), dining takes place in a warmly calibrated dining room of rustic elegance. The upper-priced Northern Italian menu puts substance over culinary pyrotechnics.

Cava (☎ 323-658-8898, 8384 W 3rd St), has Spanish/Latin decor, live music and an inspired menu. Excellent tapas include ceviche served in a half coconut shell ($6.50) and the steamed mussels ($8.50). *Sofi* (☎ 323-651-0346, 8030¾ W 3rd St) delivers the enchantment of a Greek taverna on its shaded, bougainvillea-festooned patio deck. It serves all the staples like *tsatziki*, dolmas, feta and moussaka as a combination appetizer plate. Main courses start at $15.

Tahiti (☎ 323-651-1213, 7910 W 3rd St) has stunning tropical decor and a menu heavy on fish- and meat-based dishes paired with exotic sauces and vegetables.

Beverly Hills & Westside (Map 6)

Beverly Hills *Planet Hollywood* (☎ 310-275-7828, 9560 Wilshire Blvd) has the usual predictable, but fine, burger-salad-sandwich fare, all costing $10 or less. For a flashback to the '50s, try *Ed Debevic's* (☎ 310-659-1952, 134 N La Cienega Blvd), where you can munch on burgers and fries in red Naugahyde booths fitted with miniature jukeboxes on the table. Tourists love this place for the prices (nothing's over $8.95) and the wise-cracking servers.

Owned by Benjamin Ford (Harrison's son), *The Farm* (☎ 310-273-5578, 439 N Beverly Drive) serves creative takes on American favorites, all freshly prepared in an open kitchen and priced around $15. At *ObaChine* (☎ 310-274-4440, 242 N Beverly Drive), Wolfgang Puck takes a journey through several Pacific Rim cultures to bring you such choice morsels as tea air-dried duck and his trademark grilled ahi tuna. There's also a sushi bar and two great-value happy hours.

At *Matsuhisa* (☎ 310-659-9639, 129 N La Cienega Blvd), the chef is as deft with the sushi knife as he is at conceiving creative seafood dishes. The artistic preparation and choice ingredients are unfortunately reflected in the prices (which, incidentally, are not marked) so don't leave home without...you know what.

Elsewhere on the Westside Inside a small mall at 11677 San Vicente Blvd is

LOS ANGELES

Taiko (☎ *310-207-7782*), a prim Japanese noodle house in Brentwood, where generous bowls of succulently flavored *soba* and *udon*, either hot or cold, cost around $7. *Mishima* (☎ *310-473-5297*), in the Olympic Collection mini-mall at 11301 Olympic Blvd in West LA, is its sister restaurant.

For some of the best Cuban food this side of Havana, head to *Versailles* (☎ *310-558-3168, 10319 Venice Blvd*), in Culver City, and try the lip-smacking roast garlic lemon chicken (around $10). The food's also good at the second branch (☎ *310-289-0392, 1415 S La Cienega Blvd*).

Coastal Communities

Malibu *Neptune's Net* (☎ *310-457-3095, 42505 Pacific Coast Hwy*), near the Ventura County line, has such superbly fresh seafood that people from all over LA drive out here. A pound of thick shrimp, freshly cooked and consumed at bare wooden tables, costs about $15.

Most other Malibu restaurants are definitely on the expensive side. Worthwhile splurges include the *Saddle Peak Lodge* (☎ *818-222-3888, 419 Cold Canyon Rd*), a rural oasis with lots of game dishes, including pheasant, venison and buffalo, and a memorable Sunday brunch. The *Inn of the Seventh Ray* (☎ *310-455-1311, 128 Old Topanga Canyon Rd*) is idyllic and permeated with a New Age vibe. The food here is karmically correct, heavy on the tofu and expensive.

Santa Monica Hands-down the best shopping-mall food court is *Eatz* (*Map 7*) inside Santa Monica Place on Broadway. Choices are bewildering, from Chinese stir-fry to kabobs and curries, pizza and croissants. On Third Street Promenade is *Wolfgang Puck Express* (*Map 7;* ☎ *310-576-4770, 1315 Third Street Promenade*), which delivers every time with its delicious Chinese chicken salad ($8, usually enough for two).

A huge ceramic oven that cooks burgers, bakes pizzas and grills chicken over oak flames is the trademark of *Crocodile Cafe* (*Map 7;* ☎ *310-394-4783, 101 Santa Monica Blvd*). The menu is inventive and has many low-fat and healthful options, mostly under

$10. *I Cugini* (*Map 7;* ☎ *310-451-4595, 1501 Ocean Ave*) is an Italian trattoria that makes delicious fresh breads that arrive at your table moments after you sit down. They go especially well with a plate of delectable antipasti, though it's worth leaving some room for the fish and pasta specialties.

Ye Olde King's Head (*Map 7;* ☎ *310-451-1402, 116 Santa Monica Blvd*) is the unofficial headquarters of the Westside's huge British expat community. Bangers and mash or steak and kidney pie go for around $10, but it's the restaurant's fish and chips that are truly 'king.' The *Border Grill* (*Map 7;* ☎ *310-451-1655, 1445 4th St*) has a yuppified but delicious Mexican menu in an environment that looks as though it had been designed by six-year-olds.

Main St in Santa Monica offers a range of upscale dining options, including the loftlike *Röckenwagner* (*Map 7;* ☎ *310-399-6504, 2435 Main St*). Herb-crusted lamb loin and the roasted veal with shiitake mushrooms are almost worth the $21 price tab. *Chinois on Main* (*Map 7;* ☎ *310-392-9025, 2709 Main St*) is another Wolfgang Puck outpost popular with celebrities. Call several days ahead for reservations. Arnold Schwarzenegger's *Schatzi on Main* (*Map 7;* ☎ *310-399-4800, 3110 Main St*) is just down the street. The menu makes frequent forays into the Terminator's Austrian cuisine, like Wiener schnitzel and *Zwiebelröstbraten*.

Venice Beach & Marina del Rey The *Sidewalk Cafe* (*Map 7;* ☎ *310-399-5547, 1401 Ocean Front Walk*) serves big plates of good, old-fashioned American fare (under $10) to a steady stream of locals and tourists. Also on the boardwalk is *Jodi Maroni's Sausage Kingdom* (*Map 7;* ☎ *310-306-1995, 2011 Ocean Front Walk*), whose exotically spiced sausages cost just $4.

The *Rose Cafe* (*Map 7;* ☎ *310-399-0711, 220 Rose Ave*) is an old standby, and its tree-fringed patio is a good place for a leisurely breakfast. *Tortilla Grill* (*Map 7;* ☎ *310-581-9953, 1357 Abbot Kinney Blvd*) serves healthy and delicious, macho-sized burritos and tortas made with lean meats, fresh vegetables and no lard. Practically next door is the excellent *Abbot Pizza (Map 7;* ☎ *310-396-7334, 1407 Abbot Kinney Blvd)*, whose gourmet pies cost $12.50 to $15.95.

Chaya Venice (Map 7; ☎ *310-396-1179, 110 Navy St)* lures regulars back with a surprisingly reasonably priced Asian menu short on trendiness and long on substance. *Joe's (Map 7;* ☎ *310-399-5811, 1023 Abbot Kinney Blvd)* serves up sophisticated French-Californian food from a kitchen the size of most peoples' walk-in closets. Four-course prix-fixe menus are $30 and $40. Reservations are advised.

South Bay The Kettle *(*☎ *310-545-8511, 1138 Highland Ave)*, in Manhattan Beach, has budget-priced, fresh and sizable salads, sandwiches and burgers in an American coffee-shop-style setting. Open 24 hours.

Good Mexican eateries, all serving combinations for around $7 and a la carte items from $2.50, include *El Sombrero (*☎ *310-374-1366, 1005 Manhattan Ave)* in Manhattan Beach; *El Gringo (*☎ *310-376-1381, 2620 Hermosa Ave)* and *La Playita (*☎ *310-376-2148, 37 14th St)*, both in Hermosa Beach.

Great breakfast places are *Uncle Bill's Pancake House (*☎ *310-545-5177, 1305 Highland Ave)* in Manhattan Beach; the *Back Burner Cafe (*☎ *310-372-6973, 87 14th St)* at Hermosa Ave in Hermosa; and the *Beach Hut No 2 (*☎ *310-376-4252)*, across the street. They all close around 2 pm.

Tables at *Buca di Beppo (*☎ *310-540-3246, 1670 S Pacific Coast Hwy)* bend under the huge portions of hearty Southern Italian pasta and pizza. The decor is frantic and definitely part of the experience.

At *Le Beaujolais (*☎ *310-543-5100, 522 S Pacific Coast Hwy)*, you can savor intricately spiced rack of lamb, fresh halibut and other French concoctions in an old-fashioned candlelit dining room. It's pricey, though Sunday brunch offers the best value, with main dishes around $13.

San Pedro & Long Beach Many people make the trip to San Pedro just to indulge in the authentic Greek food served at *Papadakis Taverna (*☎ *310-548-1186, 301 W 6th St)*. Be prepared for some sirtaki

dancing, breaking plates and other supposedly Greek customs.

Long Beach's 'restaurant row' is along Pine Ave, where *Alegria (*☎ *562-436-3388, 115 Pine Ave)* has a trippy, Technicolor mosaic floor, trompe l'oeil murals and tasty entrées. You could make this a budget place by sticking to tapas.

The *Sky Room (*☎ *562-983-2703, 40 S Locust Ave)* is a refurbished art deco supper club on the 15th floor of the historic Breakers Building. Perhaps even better than the continental food is the breathtaking 360-degree view. Leave room for Fred & Ginger, a killer crème brûlée served in a chocolate top hat.

The Valleys

San Fernando Valley Spanish home-cooked meals are served by the De La Cruz family at *El Patio Andaluz (*☎ *818-999-4598, 7257 Topanga Canyon Blvd)*, in Canoga Park, in the western Valley. A plate of shrimp sautéed with choice vegetables and served alongside saffron rice will set you back just $10.

Deeper pockets are required at the *Bistro Garden at Coldwater (*☎ *818-501-0202, 12950 Ventura Blvd)*, in Studio City, which charms with a romantic winter garden setting and sophisticated California cuisine. Entrées start at $20.

There are certainly places that serve better sushi than *Tokyo Delve's (*☎ *818-766-3868, 5239 Lankershim Blvd)*, but the food here is – almost – an afterthought. It's served by insane sushi chefs who…tap dance. There's almost always a line waiting by the roped entrance, so make reservations.

One of the Valley's best restaurants is *Ca' del Sole (*☎ *818-985-4669, 4100 Cahuenga Blvd)*, a slice of Italy in the midst of suburbia, where diners are wowed by tantalizing, flavor-intensive Northern Italian fare consisting mainly of mid-priced pasta dishes.

Burbank A good number of mostly low-key, inexpensive eateries cluster in Burbank Village along San Fernando Blvd, between Olive Ave and Magnolia Blvd. Choices include *Cafe N'Orleans (*☎ *818-563-3569,*

LOS ANGELES

122 N San Fernando Rd) for Cajun offerings, and **Knight** (☎ 818-845-4516, 138 N San Fernando Blvd), a friendly Middle Eastern cafe where you can chow down on budget-priced gyros, falafel and shish kebab. For a genuine slice of Americana, check out **Bob's Big Boy** (☎ 818-843-9334, 4211 Riverside Drive), a classic coffee shop from the late '40s. On Saturday and Sunday between 5 and 8 pm, their car hop service (sans the roller skates) lets you catch that American Graffiti vibe.

Universal City Many restaurants on slick Universal City Walk are clones of immensely popular eateries elsewhere around the city. For a quick snack, **Jodi Maroni's** (☎ 818-622-5639) exotic sausages are your best bet. **Marvel Mania** (☎ 877-362-7835) is a wild and wacky comic book environment serving 'Captain American' hamburgers and the 'She-Hulk Salad.' Most entrées are under $10. **Gladstone's** (☎ 818-622-3485) has fresh seafood and fish, an oyster bar and a salad bar. Sandwiches are $8 to $15, though main dishes cost $20 and up.

Pasadena It's the irresistible aroma of barbecue chicken wafting out from the **Rack Shack** (Map 8; ☎ 626-405-1994, 58 E Colorado Blvd) that pulls people into this tiny restaurant. Choices like the crazy Cajun chicken soaked in mystery spices and the beef back ribs cost $8.95. **Akbar** (Map 8; ☎ 626-577-9916, 44 N Fair Oaks Ave) is an easygoing eatery that has some of the best Indian food in Pasadena. The heat of each dish is classified on a 'chile meter' from one to five. Lunch specials start at $6.25.

The **Twin Palms** (Map 8; ☎ 626-577-2567, 101 W Green St) is a casual California eatery whose menu features lots of seafood prepared with the occasional French touch. The best deal is their two-course express lunch for just $6.95.

At **Yujean Kang's** (Map 8; ☎ 626-585-0855, 67 N Raymond Ave), Chinese dishes are veritable artworks, like soup topped with a meringue featuring a little drawing. There's also a second branch (☎ 310-288-0806, 8826 Melrose Ave). Next door to Yujean's is the equally stylish **Xiomara**

(Map 8; ☎ 626-796-2520), a bistro with a menu where ceviche, foie gras, risotto, goat cheese salad and lamb shank are all comfortable neighbors.

ENTERTAINMENT

To keep your finger on what's hot in LA, your best sources of information are the Calendar section of the daily LA Times (especially the magazinelike Sunday supplement), and the free LA Weekly, available in every neighborhood at restaurants, shops, pubs, etc.

The central ticket source for concerts, sports events, theater, musicals, etc, is Ticketmaster (☎ 213-381-2000). Tickets, plus steep handling fees, are charged to your credit card. Another agency selling tickets by phone is Telecharge (☎ 800-233-3123).

For half-price theater tickets for same-day evening or next-day matinee shows, contact Times Tix (☎ 310-659-3678). Tickets must be bought in person at their office at Jerry's Famous Deli, 8701 Beverly Blvd near the Beverly Center, and are available from noon to 6 pm Thursday to Sunday.

Cinema

Cinemas – usually multiplexes with up to 20 screens – are ubiquitous in the movie capital of the world. First-run films sell out early on Friday and Saturday nights. Shows after 6 pm cost around $7, those before are often discounted. Advance credit card bookings can be made by calling ☎ 213-777-3456 or ☎ 310-777-3456, or by logging on to www.movielink.com; there's no surcharge for this service.

Historic theaters are the Cinerama Dome, the El Capitan and Mann's Chinese Theater in Hollywood, the Warner Grand in San Pedro and the Orpheum in Downtown. One of the largest (and with $8 tickets plus parking the most expensive) is the cinema on Universal City Walk, which has 18 screens. Theaters cluster on Third Street Promenade in Santa Monica, on Colorado Blvd in Old Pasadena and in Westwood Village.

Independent theaters include the **Aero** (Map 7; ☎ 310-395-4990), at 14th St and Montana Ave in Santa Monica, where $6 buys a double bill, and *Fairfax Cinema* (Map 4; ☎ 323-653-3117, 7907 Beverly Blvd), which charges just $2.50 for any ticket, any seat, any time. Revival and art houses include *New Beverly Cinema* (Map 4; ☎ 323-938-4038, 7165 Beverly Blvd); the *Nuart* (Map 7; ☎ 310-478-6379, 11272 Santa Monica Blvd), on the Westside, famous for its Saturday midnight *Rocky Horror Picture Show* screenings; and the fourplex *Laemmle Theatre* (Map 7; ☎ 310-394-9741, 1332 2nd St), which shows highbrow independent US and foreign films.

Theater

Theater has long been a lively and integral part of LA's cultural scene. Choices range from glittery major musicals and plays to ensemble shows and independent fringe theater in unconventional venues. Theaters are great places to catch both the budding stars of tomorrow and see major film and television actors return to their roots as they perform live on stage.

Major Companies The resident troupe at the *Mark Taper Forum* (Map 2; ☎ 213-628-2772), at Downtown's Music Center, 135 N Grand Ave, emphasizes US and world premieres. There's a rush for last-minute $10 tickets at 10 minutes before curtain. In the same complex is the *Ahmanson Theater* (Map 2; ☎ 213-972-0700), a venue for top-notch Broadway musicals and plays. Another place to catch leading musical productions is the *Shubert Theater* (Map 2; ☎ 800-447-7400, 2020 Ave of the Stars), in Century City, or at the historic *Pantages Theater* (Map 3; ☎ 323-468-1770, 6233 Hollywood Blvd), with its stunning lobby.

Small Companies & Venues The *Los Angeles Theater Center* (Map 2; ☎ 213-485-1681, 514 S Spring St) is one of the leading

Getting into a Studio

If you've always dreamed of seeing your favorite TV show in the flesh, your best bet is to watch a taping. Doing so is easy – and tickets are free – but plan well ahead because the most coveted shows, like *Friends*, are usually booked up for months. Production season runs from August through March; shows go on hiatus in the summer. All shows have minimum age requirements (usually 16 or 18). On the day of the taping, come to the studio early to guarantee getting a seat, since tickets are distributed in excess of capacity.

The 'central clearing house' for studio tickets is Audiences Unlimited (☎ 818-753-3483 for recorded information, ☎ 818-753-3470 for tickets), which handles arrangements for most studios and has tickets for shows such as *Friends*, *Everybody Loves Raymond* and *Suddenly Susan*. They also have an in-person office at Universal Studios and a website with schedules and ticket order forms at www.tvtickets.com. Their address is 100 Universal City Plaza, Bldg 153, Universal City, CA 91608.

Another company to try is Hollywood Group Services (☎ 310-914-3400, fax 310-914-3401, www.hollywoodgroups.com). You can also contact some of the major studios directly: CBS Television Center (☎ 323-852-2458), 7800 Beverly Blvd, Los Angeles, CA 90036; Paramount Guest Relations (☎ 323-956-5575 for recorded information, ☎ 323-956-1777 for tickets), 860 N Gower St, Hollywood; NBC Tickets (☎ 818-840-3537 for recorded information, ☎ 818-840-3538 for tickets), 3000 W Alameda Ave, Burbank, CA 91523.

You can also see live filming taking place by obtaining a 'shoot sheet,' a list detailing the locations where movies, TV programs, videos and commercials are being shot that day; it's available free, but only in person, from the Film Permit Office at 7083 Hollywood Blvd, near Mann's Chinese Theater. The list does not reveal which actors are involved in the shoot or whether it's an indoor or outdoor shoot.

theater venues in Downtown. *East West Players* (Map 2; ☎ 213-625-7000, 120 N Judge John Aiso St), in the David Henry Hwang Theater in Little Tokyo, is the leading Asian-American theater company in the US.

Hollywood's 'Theater Row' stretches along Santa Monica Blvd. Standouts include the *Actors' Gang Theatre* (Map 3; ☎ 323-465-0566, 6209 Santa Monica Blvd), one of the most rewarding theatrical experiences in LA. The sophisticated *Hudson Ave Theater* (Map 3; ☎ 323-769-5858, 6539 Santa Monica Blvd) has a checkered schedule of modern stalwarts, ethnic playwrights and crowd pleasers like Neil Simon. *Colony Studio Theatre* (☎ 323-665-3011, 1944 Riverside Drive), in Silver Lake, appeals with quality productions of new plays and revivals of contemporary classics.

As LA's creative hub of art and design, West Hollywood also is rich theater land. *Celebration Theater* (Map 4; ☎ 323-957-1884, 7051-B Santa Monica Blvd) is among the nation's top producers of gay and lesbian plays. Monday night is a great time to check out the *Coronet Theater* (Map 4; ☎ 310-657-7177, 366 N La Cienega Blvd), because that's when the *Playwrights Kitchen Ensemble* (☎ 310-285-8148) holds staged readings of new plays. The work is usually excellent, and big-shot actors sometimes participate in the reading cast. Best of all – it's free!

The Beverly Hills *Canon Theatre* (Map 6; ☎ 310-859-2830, 205 Canon Drive) does primarily crowd-pleasing comedies. *Theatre 40* (Map 6; ☎ 310-277-4221, 241 Moreno Drive), in the Beverly Hills High School, is one of LA's oldest professional companies and has an annual season of classic and modern plays, most of them tried-and-true.

The *Odyssey Theater Ensemble* (Map 7; ☎ 310-477-2055, 2055 S Sepulveda Blvd) is one of LA's top small theater houses, putting on reliably excellent productions under company founder Ron Sossi.

Nestled into Topanga Canyon, in a magical natural outdoor amphitheater, is the *Will Geer Theatricum Botanicum* (☎ 310-455-3723, 1419 N Topanga Canyon Blvd), which does performances of Shakespeare and other classic playwrights. Performance quality can be pretty hippy-dippy, though it's always fun to watch a performance in the shaded canyon.

In the San Fernando Valley, the *Group Repertory Theatre* (☎ 818-769-7529, 10900 Burbank Blvd) offers anything from experimental to modern classics and contemporary works, including those generated in its writers' workshop.

For *A Noise Within* (☎ 323-224-6420), 'classical' has always been equated with 'classy,' which is just what its productions of Elizabethan dramas and Restoration comedies are. Performances take place at the 1150-seat Luckman Fine Arts Complex on the campus of the California State University at Los Angeles, 5151 State University Drive, East LA.

One of LA's top venues is the 1924 *Pasadena Playhouse* (Map 8; ☎ 626-356-7529, 39 S El Molino Ave), where the production quality is often so high that plays are sent on to Broadway.

Comedy

On any given night, comedians may be strengthening their chops in one of LA's many comedy clubs. At the very least, you'll be treated to a hilarious evening with what may well be one of next year's comic sensations: LA is where the funny people come to make it big. Reservations are advised; many clubs have a two-drink minimum in addition to the cover charge.

Clubs abound in West Hollywood. Best of the bunch is the *Groundlings Theater* (Map 4; ☎ 323-934-9700, 7307 Melrose Ave), a repertory improv company whose alumni include Peewee Herman, Jon Lovitz, Julia Sweeney and the late Phil Hartman. Other legendary haunts, which have featured nearly every comic that's gone on to become a household name, include the *Improv* (Map 4; ☎ 323-651-2583, 8162 Melrose Ave); the high-tech *Laugh Factory* (Map 4; ☎ 323-656-1336, 8001 Sunset Blvd); and the *Comedy Store* (Map 4; ☎ 323-656-6225, 8433 Sunset Blvd). *Acme Comedy Theater* (Map 4; ☎ 323-525-0202, 135 N La Brea Ave) is a

LOS ANGELES

smaller venue with sketch and improv comedy on weekends.

Other comedy clubs are peppered throughout the LA area. The *Comedy & Magic Club* (☎ 310-372-1193, 1018 Hermosa Ave), in Hermosa Beach, is where Jay Leno tests out new material for the *Tonight Show*. Pasadena has the *Ice House* (Map 8; ☎ 626-577-1894, 24 N Mentor Ave), which attracts major, professional talents and tomorrow's stars.

Classical Music & Opera

For highbrow music lovers, there's no finer place than the *Dorothy Chandler Pavilion* (Map 2; ☎ 213-972-0700) at the Music Center, 135 N Grand Ave in Downtown. Besides being home to three performing companies, its stages also host Broadway shows, the Academy Awards ceremonies and other large-scale productions.

The *LA Philharmonic Orchestra* (☎ 213-850-2000), under the stewardship of Esa-Pekka Salonen since 1992, has enjoyed a loyal following despite his insisting on programs that often focus on works by obscure composers – or obscure works by famous composers.

The *LA Opera* (☎ 213-972-8001) presents a varied and high-caliber repertory of popular operas like *Carmen* and the *Barber of Seville* but also less mainstream ones like *The Flying Dutchman* and *Werther*, often managing to attract major opera stars, like Placido Domingo, as guest stars.

Los Angeles Master Chorale (☎ 213-626-0624) is a critically acclaimed 120-voice chorus. Founded in 1964, it presents stand-alone recitals and also serves as the chorus for the LA Philharmonics and the LA Opera.

Other notable classical groups include the *Los Angeles Chamber Orchestra* (☎ 213-622-7001), which often performs at UCLA's Royce Hall; the *Hollywood Bowl Orchestra*, led by John Mauceri, the resident orchestra of the Bowl; and the *Beverly Hills Symphony* (☎ 310-859-8075).

Clubs

LA's club scene is one of the liveliest in the country and caters to everyone's tastes and expectations, from pale-faced college-age ravers to designer-chic yuppies and ex-hippie baby boomers. No musical era is off-limits these days, be it '20s jazz, '30s and '40s big band swing, '50s rockabilly, '60s rock & roll, '70s disco, '80s punk and new wave and techno, house, gothic, industrial and trance.

One caveat: one thing constant about the scene is that it changes constantly, so check the local press for up-to-date listings or call the Club Line (☎ 323-258-2546), a free telephone service with information about new and current hot clubs.

Rock & Pop Dark, dank, divey and Downtown, *Al's Bar* (Map 2; ☎ 213-625-9703, 305 S Hewitt St) has cheap drinks and wild and edgy bands. In Hollywood, *Bar Deluxe* (Map 3; ☎ 323-469-1991, 1710 N Las Palmas Ave) has a musical philosophy that runs the gamut from blues to punk, with several, mostly local, bands. *Dragonfly* (Map 3; ☎ 323-466-6111, 6510 Santa Monica Blvd) is a place for moshing and slam dancing.

The *Martini Lounge* (Map 3; ☎ 323-467-4068, 5657 Melrose Ave) serves up good ole rock & roll with its martinis. *Goldfinger's Bar* (Map 3; ☎ 323-769-4329, 6423 Yucca St) has Liberace-style over-the-top decor and caters to hard-core clubbers with its frenzied mix of funk, glam rock and techno.

The warehouse-minimalism of *Hollywood Moguls* (Map 3; ☎ 323-465-7449, 1650 N Schrader Blvd) perfectly matches its schedule of garage and indie bands, but the *Palace* (Map 3; ☎ 323-467-4571, 1735 N Vine St), opposite Capitol Records, is a glamorous art deco landmark dating back to 1924. It presents up-and-coming bands during the week and sizzles with dance tunes on weekends. Nearby is *Jack's Sugar Shack* (Map 3; ☎ 323-466-7005, 1707 N Vine St), a relaxed place that satisfies a wide range of musical tastes, from blues to boogie.

West Hollywood's *Key Club* (Map 4; ☎ 323-274-5800, 9039 Sunset Blvd) is an ultrachic club with galactic decor and top-notch technology, where an eclectic schedule of live acts is followed by DJs. Before making appearances at major arenas, many of tomorrow's top bands play at the **Roxy** (Map 4; ☎ 310-276-2222, 9009 Sunset Blvd), which has also hosted old-time favorites such as Neil Young and Bruce Springsteen. The legendary **Whisky a Go Go** (Map 4; ☎ 310-652-4202, 8901 Sunset Blvd) still showcases all sorts of rock & roll, from national bands to upwardly hopeful locals.

River Phoenix's death outside the Johnny Depp-owned **Viper Room** (Map 4; ☎ 310-358-1880, 8852 Sunset Blvd) propelled this trendy club into the spotlight in 1993. Another celebrity-owned joint is the **House of Blues** (Map 4; ☎ 323-848-5100, 8430 Sunset Blvd), where Dan Akroyd is an investor. It features the customary faux Mississippi Delta decor and top talents of all stripes, not just the blues.

Club 7969 (Map 4; ☎ 323-654-0280, 7969 Santa Monica Blvd) attracts the more bizarre set of LA clubbers with theme nights like drag parties, female topless dance revues, Gothic balls and fetish nights.

Contenders in Silver Lake include the **Garage** (Map 3; ☎ 323-662-6802, 4519 Santa Monica Blvd), the headquarters of Silver Lake's self-styled grungemeisters. Come here for provocatively bizarre bands and wild, wicked clubs run by drag queens with names like Vaginal Davis. Nearby, **Spaceland** (☎ 323-833-2843, 1717 Silver Lake Blvd) is the epicenter of Silver Lake's underground rock scene and the best place to catch emerging bands on their way up.

The Westside has the **Mint** (☎ 323-954-9630, 6010 W Pico Blvd), at Crescent Heights, which has been dishing out live blues, rock and jazz to the faithful in a no-nonsense environment since 1937. On the Santa Monica Pier is **Rusty's Surf Ranch** (Map 7; ☎ 310-393-7437), where bands play to a casual college crowd nightly. Emanating a distinct London vibe, the **West End** (Map 7; ☎ 310-313-3293, 1301 5th St), also in Santa Monica, has lively, partylike dance nights with music from disco to '80s flashbacks, hip hop, reggae and rock.

The **Lighthouse** (☎ 310-372-6911, 30 Pier Ave), in Hermosa Beach, is a timeless, beachside mainstay that's strong on rock and blues. Redondo Beach's **Club Caprice**

(☎ 310-316-1700, 1700 Pacific Coast Hwy) is the number one dance club in the South Bay, with big name live acts most weekends.

Jazz & Blues The best place to see true jazz is the Leimert Park Village in the Crenshaw District. The **World Stage** (☎ 323-293-2451, 4344 Degnan Blvd) is a no-nonsense space run by well-known local drummer Billy Higgins. Around the corner is **Fifth Street Dick's** (☎ 323-296-3970, 3347½ W 43rd Place), a hole-in-the-wall coffeehouse that doubles as a venue for raw and raucous jam sessions held in its rather petite loft. Around the corner again is **Babe & Ricky's** (☎ 323-295-9112, 4339 Leimert Blvd), LA's oldest blues club and a slice of the American South presided over by Mama Laura, aka Laura Gross, for the past 34 years.

LA's top jazz venue, drawing big-name musicians from around the world, is the old-fashioned **Catalina Bar & Grill** (Map 3; ☎ 323-466-2210, 1640 Cahuenga Blvd). One of the revered jazz places in the San Fernando Valley is **Chadney's Lounge** (☎ 818-843-5333, 3000 W Olive Ave), in Burbank, a favorite with musicians from the NBC Studios next door, including Kevin Eubanks and his band from the *Tonight Show*. **BB King's Blues Club** (☎ 818-622-5464), on the Universal City Walk, usually bustles with tourists but also has a schedule of respected musicians. The small **Baked Potato** (☎ 818-980-1615, 3787 Cahuenga Blvd), in North Hollywood, has been dishing out spuds and great jazz for about three decades.

On the Westside you'll find the elegant **Lunaria** (Map 6; ☎ 310-282-8870, 10351 Santa Monica Blvd) in Century City; **Harvelle's** (Map 7; ☎ 310-395-1676, 1432 4th St), a hole-in-the-wall blues joint in Santa Monica; and the nonprofit **Jazz Bakery** (☎ 310-271-9039, 3233 Helms Ave), in Culver City, which showcases major jazz artists, on tour or local, like Billy Higgins, Kenny Burrell and Branford Marsalis.

Swing & Salsa Officially, the swing era may have ended in 1945, but in LA things are just getting started. This isn't a straight retro-scene, either. In typical LA fashion, what you get is a cross between big band, jazz, blues and rockabilly.

LA's most sophisticated swing nightclub is the *Coconut Club (Map 6; ☎ 310-274-7777, 9876 Wilshire Blvd)*, in the Beverly Hilton Hotel. This ballroom-sized venue has theatrical, yet classy, decor that makes you feel like you're in a pre-WWII movie. A small but exquisite supper menu complements a full bar. The *Derby (Map 3; ☎ 323-663-8979, 4500 Los Feliz Blvd)* has been LA 'swing central' since 1993 and was featured in the movie *Swingers*. For those who don't know the first thing about swing dancing, the Derby offers free lessons Sunday to Thursday.

If you're serious about salsa and meringue, *the* place to go Cubano and watch beautiful dancers in action is the exotic *Mayan (Map 2; ☎ 213-746-4287, 1038 S Hill St)* in Downtown. It's housed in a fantastic pre-Columbian-style ex-movie palace from 1927. The chic *Conga Room (Map 4; ☎ 323-549-9765, 5364 Wilshire Blvd)* is a gorgeous venue in Hollywood. A roster of celebs headed by Jimmy Smits and Jennifer Lopez co-owns this super-trendy club where top-notch bands create a sizzling atmosphere. *El Floridita (Map 3; ☎ 323-871-0936, 1253 N Vine St)* is a small Cuban restaurant that's a favorite with Latinos and salsa lovers in general. Monday nights are legendary.

Bars

No matter where you are in LA, you're never far from a bar. Besides the bars mentioned below, many restaurants, hotels and clubs also have bars for sopping up the various LA vibes and observing the scene.

Downtown *Hank's Bar (Map 2; ☎ 213-623-7718, 838 Grand Ave)*, located under the Stillwell Hotel, is a classic dark, tunnel-shaped watering hole where you'll feel like you're in a Raymond Chandler detective novel. *Top of Five (Map 2; ☎ 213-612-4743, 404 S Figueroa St)*, on the top floor of the Westin Bonaventure hotel offers drinks and an eye-popping view.

Hollywood The *Formosa Cafe (Map 3; ☎ 323-850-9050, 7156 Santa Monica Blvd)*, in

Hollywood, in business since 1939, is a dimly lit, casual lounge with a gritty charm, especially in the section built into a 1902 trolley car. A seductive tropical feel pervades the *Lava Lounge (Map 3; ☎ 323-876-6612, 1533 N La Brea Ave)*, with its curvaceous booths, tiny tiki lamps, bamboo and palm fronds and live bands.

Vice still rules at the *Frolic Room (Map 3; ☎ 323-462-5890, 6245 Hollywood Blvd)*, where you can down a few (cheap) stiff ones while blatantly ignoring the smoking ban.

The entrance to celebrity heaven is via the plain white gate of the *Sky Bar (Map 4; ☎ 323-848-6025, 8440 Sunset Blvd)* at the Mondrian Hotel. Should you be famous or attractive – or maybe just plain lucky – enough to get inside, you're likely to rub shoulders with headliners of blockbuster movies and megaconcerts.

Pubs in Hollywood include the *Cat & Fiddle (Map 3; ☎ 323-468-3800, 6530 Sunset Blvd)*; *Coach & Horses (Map 3; ☎ 323-876-6900, 7617 Sunset Blvd)*, which attracts a pretty rough crowd; and the more civilized *Coronet Pub (Map 4; ☎ 310-659-4583, 370 N La Cienega Blvd)*, popular with patrons of the adjacent theater.

Silver Lake *Akbar (Map 3; ☎ 323-665-6810, 4356 W Sunset Blvd)* has Moorish arches and is so dark it'll take a minute or so for your eyes to adjust and focus on the dangling wicker lamps and couches in the back. Smoking is permitted here at *Tiki Ti (Map 3; ☎ 323-669-9381, 4427 Sunset Blvd)*, nearby, which serves tropical drinks and nothing else to showbiz folks, blue-collar types and Silver Lake trendoids. Owner Rae is hard to spot behind the bar's wild assemblage of nautical kitsch and junk.

An institution since the '50s, the *Dresden Room (Map 3; ☎ 323-665-4294, 1760 N Vermont Ave)* has made a comeback after being featured in the movie *Swingers*. The campy singing duo of Marty & Elaine has 'owned' this lounge since 1981 and still pack in an intergenerational crowd of the newly and eternally hip.

For imported German brews on tap, head to the *Red Lion Tavern (Map 2;*

☎ *323-662-5337, 2366 Glendale Blvd)*, in Silver Lake, where you'll be served popular pilsners and Weissbier by a dirndl-clad wait staff.

Westside & Coastal Communities

With its large English and Irish expat population, Santa Monica's pub scene is the best and most authentic. Irish entries are the raucous *Red Setter (Map 7; ☎ 310-449-1811, 2615 Wilshire Blvd)*, *O'Brien's (Map 7; ☎ 310-829-5303)*, at Wilshire Blvd and 23rd St, and *St Stephen's Green (Map 7; ☎ 310-393-6611, 1026 Wilshire Blvd)*. Possibly the best English pub this side of the Thames is *Ye Olde King's Head (Map 7; ☎ 310-451-1402, 116 Santa Monica Blvd)*. The city's best happy hour – with a superb view over the ocean and mountains – is served from 4:30 to 7:30 pm daily at *Toppers (Map 7; ☎ 310-393-8080, 1111 2nd St)*, a lively sports bar on the 17th floor of the Radisson Huntley Hotel.

Of the South Bay beach cities, Hermosa Beach is clearly the one with the craziest, wildest party atmosphere. Its oceanfront walk – the Strand – and the adjacent Pier Plaza are flanked by raucous drinking holes.

Taking the honors for loudest decor and noise level is *Aloha Sharkeez (☎ 310-374-7823, 52 Pier Ave)*, where the objective is to get drunk as fast as possible, which is why mysterious concoctions like Lava Flow and Blue Voodoo come in 48oz pitchers ($14) and 80oz buckets ($22). Another hard-core drinking place is the sweaty and smelly *Poopdeck (☎ 310-376-3223)* on the Strand, which feels like you're crashing a frat party.

In Manhattan Beach is the *Manhattan Beach Brewing Co (☎ 310-798-2744, 124 Manhattan Beach Blvd)*, frequented by the college set. The bar is set against a row of steel brewing vats lined up like organ pipes. San Pedro offers the *Whale & Ale (☎ 310-832-0362, 27 W 7th St)*, a more sedate brass and leather affair. In Long Beach is the *Yard House (☎ 562-628-0455, 401 Shoreline Village Drive)*, where bartenders command an oval bar with some 250 beers on tap.

Pasadena The *Gordon Biersch Brewery (Map 8; ☎ 626-449-0052, 41 Hugus Alley)*, in Pasadena, off Colorado Blvd, is a microbrewery (with a beer garden) working with original German recipes. They churn out respectable smooth-tasting brews, including a crisp pilsner, the slightly sweet Märzen and the full-bodied Dunkles.

SPECTATOR SPORTS
Baseball

The National League's Los Angeles Dodgers play at Dodger Stadium (☎ 323-224-1400 for information; ☎ 323-224-1500 for tickets, www.dodgers.com, 1000 Elysian Park Ave). Tickets, usually available at the box office on game day, start at $6 for seats in the nosebleed section. Better seats cost just $8 to $12; children are half price. Regular season is from April to October.

Football

Both of LA's professional football teams – the Rams and the Raiders – packed up and moved in early 1995, making USC (☎ 213-740-2311) and UCLA (☎ 310-825-2106) the only outdoor games in town.

If indoor ball is your pleasure, the newest kid on the spectator sports block is the LA Avengers, who play arena football at Staples Center (see the Basketball section).

Basketball

Any fan of professional sports won't want to miss attending an event at the brand new Staples Center (☎ 310-287-3950), which opened in October 1999 in the Downtown area at 1830 La Cienega Blvd at 18th St. This state-of-the-art arena, which looks a bit like a spaceship, is home to five sports franchises, among them the city's three professional basketball teams.

The LA Lakers of the National Basketball Association play from October to April, as do the LA Clippers, who are also in the NBA. The Women's National Basketball Association LA Sparks play during the summer. Tickets for all three teams can be purchased through Ticketmaster.

UCLA's basketball team, the Bruins, is one of the best college teams in the US. They play at Pauley Pavilion on the UCLA campus. Call ☎ 310-825-2106 for tickets.

Soccer

The Los Angeles Galaxy (☎ 310-445-1260) has put on an impressive showing since their 1995 launch. They play at the Rose Bowl in Pasadena where tickets cost $10, $15 and $17 and are sold either at the stadium or by calling ☎ 888-657-5425.

Hockey

The Los Angeles Kings of the NHL (☎ 888-546-4752, www.lakings.com), play at the Staples Center in Downtown. Their schedule runs from September to April and they offer individual and group tickets, as well as family night specials.

Horse Racing

Horse racing enthusiasts consider Santa Anita Park (☎ 626-574-7223, 285 W Huntington Drive), in Arcadia east of Pasadena, to be one of the best tracks in America. Admission is $5. The other Los Angeles horse track is Hollywood Park Race Track (☎ 310-419-1500, 1050 S Prairie St), just south of the Great Western Forum in Inglewood. Admission is $6 and includes parking and program. Admission is free to those under 18 and accompanied by an adult.

SHOPPING
Shopping Districts

Most LA residents do their serious shopping in multistory malls, some with upwards of 200 stores. For a more whimsical approach to shopping, head for a handful of streets where the people-watching is as much fun as the window browsing.

Third Street Promenade This pedestrian mall, anchored by the Frank Gehry-designed Santa Monica Place mall on Broadway, is the heart of Santa Monica. Street entertainers keep this strip busy day and night. You'll find the Disneystore, Gap and Banana Republic, novelties and casual clothing at Urban Outfitters, funky fashions at NaNa and more. Other shopping streets in Santa Monica are **Main St** for young designer fashions and antiques, and exclusive **Montana Ave** for gift shops, children's clothing, furniture and elegant women's wear.

Rodeo Drive Known the world over for its up-up-upscale designer boutiques and jewelry stores, art galleries and antique shops, Rodeo Drive provides a tangible definition of Beverly Hills. Start at the Two Rodeo Drive complex on Wilshire Blvd opposite the Regent Beverly Wilshire hotel; from there, follow Rodeo north three blocks, across Dayton Way and Brighton Way, to Little Santa Monica Blvd. Also check out shops on the side streets.

Old Pasadena Colorado Blvd has plenty of bookstores, boutiques, housewares and specialty stores. Highlights include Sur La Table cookware, Restoration home furnishings, Crate & Barrel home accessories and a huge Barnes & Noble bookstore. Also in Pasadena is **South Lake Ave**, notable for its London-esque shopping arcades.

Fashion District Also known as the Garment District, this 56-block area in the southern section of Downtown is the epicenter of LA's clothing manufacturing. The **Cooper Building**, a former warehouse at 9th and Los Angeles Sts, has six floors of outlet stores, mostly for women, including brand-name clothing. Those with a knack for haggling should head to **Santee Alley**, just east of Santee St, between Olympic Blvd and 12th St, an outdoor bazaar where mostly Middle Eastern entrepreneurs hawk designer knockoffs at rock-bottom prices.

Melrose Ave Melrose still has plenty of stores of the 'only in LA' variety, including Off the Wall (☎ 323-930-1185), at No 7325, which specializes in 'antiques and weird stuff' – and they're not kidding. Wound & Wound (☎ 323-653-6703), No 7374, has an incredible assortment of wind-up toys and music boxes. At No 7574, the innocently named Scents from Above sells soaps, oils and aromatherapy in the front, and edible underwear, blow-up dolls, X-rated videos, erotic lingerie and vibrators in the back. Necromance (☎ 323-934-8684), at No 7220, stocks dog skulls, mounted deer heads and insects or mice in formaldehyde, and anything else that might make grave digging obsolete.

Vintage clothing shops include Wasteland (☎ 323-653-3028), at No 7428, Slow (☎ 323-655-3725), at No 7474 (check out their $5 sales rack) and the sentimental favorite, but overpriced, Aardvark (☎ 323-655-6769), at No 7579.

Ocean Front Walk Vendors of all types display their wares along Venice Beach. Among the wacky street life, you may find a bronze dancing Shiva icon or a bronze cowbell from Switzerland. Or perhaps you fancy a spiked leather hat for your dog or a spiked leather bikini for your sister – or vice versa? Whatever it is, this is where you'll find it.

Shopping Malls
Nothing defines shopping in LA more than the mall, a Southern California invention resulting from people's reliance on the car. Much more than a place to shop, malls define and reflect the culture of vanity and commercialism so prevalent here. Be that as it may, LA malls are actually fun and convenient places to shop. Among the favorites are:

Beverly Center (Map 4; ☎ 310-854-0070), 8500 Beverly Blvd at La Cienega Blvd, 160 upscale shops, anchored by Bloomingdale's and Macy's, celebrity-heavy

Century City Shopping Center & Marketplace (☎ 310-553-5300), 10250 Santa Monica Blvd, 140 stores, anchored by Bloomingdale's and Macy's, nice outdoor mall

Westside Pavilion (☎ 310-474-6255), 10800 W Pico Blvd in Westwood, 160 shops, anchored by Nordstrom and Robinsons-May, classy design, horrid parking

Santa Monica Place (☎ 310-394-5451), Broadway & Third Street Promenade, anchored by Robinsons-May and Macy's, great architecture, great cross-section

Fashion Square Sherman Oaks (☎ 818-783-0550), 14006 Riverside Drive in the San Fernando Valley, 135 stores, anchored by Macy's and Bloomingdale's

Glendale Galleria (☎ 818-240-9481), 2148 Glendale Galleria, 260 stores, anchored by Macy's, Robinsons-May, JC Penney, Nordstrom, Mervyn's

Citadel Factory Stores (☎ 213-888-1220), 5675 E Telegraph Rd (right off the I-5 Washington exit), LA's only outlet mall

Antiques
Major antique markets in LA include the Santa Monica Antique Market (Map 7; ☎ 310-314-4899), 1607 Lincoln Blvd, with more than 150 dealers; the Antique Guild (☎ 310-838-3131) in the former Helms Bakery, 3231 Helms Ave, Culver City, covering two acres; and Antiquarius (Map 4; ☎ 310-274-2363), 8840 Beverly Blvd, with 40 shops near West Hollywood's Pacific Design

---

LA's Flea Markets

Flea markets or swap meets: call them what you will, the LA area has plenty. Nourished by a remarkably diverse population with some equally eclectic tastes, these massive gatherings can make for the best bargain shopping around. Whether you're hunting for a Stickley settle or a Hopalong Cassidy pocket knife, you'll seldom find it for a better price (or have half the fun in bargaining). Arrive early, bring along lots of small bills, wear those walking shoes and get ready to haggle.

Pasadena City College Flea Market (☎ 626-585-7906), 1570 E Colorado Blvd, first Sunday of the month 8 am to 3 pm; free

Rose Bowl Flea Market (☎ 213-560-7469), 1001 Rose Bowl Drive, second Sunday of the month 6 am to 4:30 pm; $15 before 7:30 am, $10 until 9 am, $5 thereafter

Long Beach Outdoor Antique & Collectible Market (☎ 213-655-5703), Veteran's Memorial Stadium, Conant St between Lakewood Blvd and Clark Ave, third Sunday of the month 8 am to 3 pm

Santa Monica Outdoor Antique & Collectible Market (☎ 213-933-2511), Airport Ave off Bundy Ave, fourth Sunday of the month 6 am to 3 pm; $4

Melrose Trading Post (☎ 323-932-8155), Fairfax High School parking lot, Melrose and Fairfax Aves, every Sunday 9 am to 5 pm; $2

Burbank Monthly Antique Market (☎ 310-455-2886), Main St and Riverside Drive, every fourth Sunday of the month 8 am to 3 pm; $3

Center. LA's flea and antique markets, held every Sunday in various locales, are other good sources for antiques and collectibles (see 'LA's Flea Markets').

Art Galleries

Art galleries concentrate in several LA neighborhoods, including La Brea Ave in Hollywood, Mid-City, Beverly Hills and Bergamot Station in Santa Monica. Perhaps the single best area for the art lover to explore is the triangle in West Hollywood bounded by Santa Monica, La Cienega and Beverly Blvds.

The heart of the district is the Pacific Design Center, 8687 Melrose Ave at San Vicente Blvd, with cutting-edge furniture and home accessories. It's mainly intended as a wholesale outlet for retailers, but the public is invited to browse. Among three dozen nearby art galleries are the Tobey C Moss Gallery (☎ 323-933-5523), 7321 Beverly Blvd, specializing in California modernism, abstract art and post-surrealism; the Herbert Palmer Gallery, 802 N La Cienega Blvd, displaying 20th-century American and European masters; and the Daniel Saxon Gallery (☎ 310-657-6033), 552 Norwich Drive, for leading Chicano artists working in the media of paintings, prints, glass and sculpture.

The free magazine *Arts Scene* (☎ 213-482-4724, www.artscene.com), with up-to-date information on gallery shows, is available at shops and restaurants.

Lingerie & Erotica

On Hollywood Blvd, between Schrader and Wilcox Aves, are a cluster of seminaughty stores where strippers, exotic dancers, actors, ladies of the night and the merely adventurous get their nocturnal niceties. Among the best of these places is Nikki's of Hollywood (Map 3; ☎ 323-461-8208), 6500 Hollywood Blvd, for footwear and Playmates (Map 3; ☎ 323-464-7636), for non-'professional' lingerie, at No 6438.

The Pleasure Chest (Map 4; ☎ 323-650-1022), 7733 Santa Monica Blvd, is a large sexual hardware store catering to every conceivable fantasy. Dreamdresser (Map 4; ☎ 323-848-3480), 8444 Santa Monica Blvd, is

similar, with lots of wearable vinyl and rubber gadgets, as well as spiky anythings. Finally, there's Trashy Lingerie (Map 4; ☎ 310-652-4543), 402 N La Cienega Blvd, which has custom-made corsets and anything imaginable made from leather, vinyl and lace.

Music

The Sunset Strip Tower Records (Map 4; ☎ 310-657-7300), 8801 W Sunset Blvd, is legendary. Check the Yellow Pages for other branches around the city. A good source for independent labels – including their own, of course – is Rhino Records (Map 6; ☎ 310-474-8685), 1720 Westwood Blvd in West LA.

Rockaway Records (Map 2; ☎ 323-664-3232), 2395 Glendale Blvd, is a warehouse-size place with a superb collection of inexpensive used CDs. Smaller but still a good source is Penny Lane (Map 8; ☎ 626-564-0161), 16 W Colorado Blvd in Old Pasadena, and on Third Street Promenade in Santa Monica.

Sports & Outdoor Gear

One of the best shops for all-around outdoor needs is REI (☎ 310-538-2429), which has a warehouse-size inventory at 405 W Torrance Blvd, just where I-110 and I-405 meet. Another, smaller outfitter on the Westside is Adventure 16 (☎ 310-473-4574), at 11161 W Pico Blvd. A good place for surfing gear is the funky Z-J Boarding House (☎ 310-392-5646), 2619 Main St in Santa Monica. A branch of NikeTown (Map 6; ☎ 310-275-9998) is at 9560 Wilshire Blvd in Beverly Hills.

GETTING THERE & AWAY
Air

If you're flying into Los Angeles, you're most likely to land at Los Angeles International Airport (LAX; ☎ 310-646-5252). Smaller regional airports, mostly for domestic travel, are Burbank-Glendale-Pasadena Airport (☎ 818-840-8847) and Long Beach Airport (☎ 310-421-8293).

LAX has eight terminals, all but one of which are situated around a two-level, central traffic loop that also provides access to short-term parking garages. Ticketing and check-in are on the upper (departure) level,

LOS ANGELES

while baggage claim areas are on the lower (arrival) level. The hub for most international airlines is the Tom Bradley International Terminal (TBIT).

The free Shuttle A travels between terminals and stops outside the lower level, as do hotel courtesy shuttles, door-to-door shuttles and car rental agency vans. For a free minibus equipped with a wheelchair lift for the disabled, call ☎ 310-646-6402.

Bus

Greyhound connects LA with cities all across North America. The 24-hour main terminal (Map 2; ☎ 213-629-8421) is at 1716 E 7th St at Alameda St in Downtown. The area is a bit rough, but the station itself is safe enough inside. Other LA-area Greyhound stations are at 1409 N Vine St, Hollywood (Map 3; ☎ 323-466-6384); on 4th St between Colorado Blvd and Broadway in Santa Monica (Map 7); and at 464 W 3rd St in Long Beach (☎ 562-432-7780).

Greyhound buses to San Diego leave at least hourly, take 2¼ to 3¾ and cost $13/22 one way/roundtrip. Santa Barbara is served a dozen times daily with trips taking 2 to 3 hours; fares are $13/22. Buses to San Francisco depart almost hourly with trips costing $36/69 and taking between 8 and 12 hours.

Green Tortoise (☎ 415-956-7500, 800-867-8647, www.greentortoise.com) has weekly service up and down the West Coast between Seattle and Los Angeles; rides cost $79 each way.

Los Angeles is the gateway for five routes of the USBus and on booth loops of the Ant.

For details on both of these companies, see the Getting Around introductory chapter.

Train

Amtrak (Map 2; ☎ 800-872-7245, www.amtrak.com) arrives and departs from Union Station, 800 N Alameda St in Downtown. Interstate trains stopping in LA are the *Coast Starlight* to Seattle; the *Southwest Chief* with daily departures to Chicago; and the *Sunset Limited* with service thrice weekly to Orlando, Florida. The *San Diegan* regularly connects LA with San Luis Obispo and San Diego. Fares for the latter are $23 each way; the trip takes three hours. Trips to and from Santa Barbara cost $18 each way (2½ hours).

Car & Motorcycle

If you're driving a car or riding a motorcycle into Los Angeles, there are several routes by which you might enter the metropolitan area.

From San Francisco and the Bay Area, the fastest route to LA (about six hours) is via boring I-5. Hwy 101 is slower (about eight hours) but somewhat curvier and far more picturesque. By far the most scenic – and slowest – route is via Pacific Coast Hwy, or Hwy 1 (at least 10 hours).

From San Diego and other points south, I-5 is the obvious route. At Irvine, I-405 branches off I-5 and takes a westerly route to Long Beach and Santa Monica, avoiding Downtown LA entirely and rejoining I-5 near San Fernando. It can be a time-saver if you're headed to the Westside.

If you're going to LA from Las Vegas or the Grand Canyon, take I-15 south to I-10,

then head west. I-10 is the main east-west artery through LA and continues on to Downtown and Santa Monica.

GETTING AROUND

Los Angeles is an enormous metropolis with several forms of public transportation administered by the Metropolitan Transport Authority (MTA), including buses, light rail trains and a subway, although all of these are eclipsed by the car. For shorter trips, especially, it's definitely worth considering public transportation.

To/From LAX

Shuttles Private shuttle vans are a compromise in time and expense between costly taxis and less convenient and slower public transportation. Most operate 24 hours and will drop you off at your accommodations. You may have to wait your turn along the route, because they're dropping off up to a half-dozen other passengers. You'll pay according to how far you're traveling, usually $10 to $20, or at least half the cost of a taxi. All American Shuttle (☎ 310-641-4090 or 800-585-2529), Prime Time (☎ 800-262-7433) and Super Shuttle (☎ 310-450-2377, 800-258-3826) are among the companies that serve the LA and Orange County areas.

Bus The economy-minded approach is to take the free 24-hour Shuttle C bus that stops outside each terminal every 10 to 20 minutes to the LAX Transit Center at 96th St and Vicksburg Ave. Here you can connect to public buses that will take you anywhere in greater LA. For more information, see Bus under Getting There & Away, or call the MTA at ☎ 800-266-6883.

Train LAX is not directly served by train or light rail. The closest station, a 10-minute bus trip on the free Shuttle G, is Aviation on the Metro Green Line (see Metro Rail), which goes south to Redondo Beach and east to Norwalk. On an eastbound train, you can transfer at the Wilmington Station to the Metro Blue Line, which will take you north to Downtown LA or south to Long Beach. The fare is $1.35.

Taxi Curbside taxi dispatchers outside each terminal will summon a cab for you. Average fares are $25 to Santa Monica, $35 to Downtown or Hollywood and up to $80 to Disneyland. A $2.50 airport surcharge will be tacked onto your fare, and there may be additional fees for excess luggage. If there are two or three of you to share the expense, a taxi is the fastest and most convenient way to travel.

Car There are courtesy phones in the arrival areas for making reservations. Car rental offices are located outside the airport, with each company operating free shuttles. Stand outside the terminal and flag down the vehicle of the company with which you made your reservation. For details on renting a car, see Rental under Car & Motorcycle.

To/From Other Airports

If you're flying into or out of one of the other airports that serve Southern California – Burbank (☎ 818-840-8847), Long Beach (☎ 310-421-8293), John Wayne-Orange County (☎ 714-252-5006) or Ontario (☎ 909-983-8282) – you'll find many of the same transportation options available as at LAX, including a wide choice of shuttle services. One exception is that Metro Rail does not serve any airport other than LAX.

Bus

Just 10% of the population of LA County relies upon public transportation to get around the city each day. A network of 208 separate bus routes, operated by several companies, spans the metropolis.

MTA The Metropolitan Transportation Authority (☎ 800-266-6883, www.mta.org) has the largest fleet of buses. Fares are $1.35 for unlimited travel on a single bus or rail line in one direction. Transfers are 25¢ each use. Travel between 9 pm and 5 am is 75¢. Freeway Express buses cost $1.85 to $3.85, depending on the route and distance.

Big Blue Bus Santa Monica's Big Blue Bus (☎ 310-451-5444) is clean, efficient and responsive to customer needs. Its fleet serves much of the Westside, including Westwood,

Pacific Palisades and LAX, as well as Santa Monica and Venice Beach. Bus No 14 goes to the Getty Center. The fare is 50¢; transfers to another Blue Bus are free (those to an MTA or Culver City bus are 25¢.) Express bus No 10 is the fastest way to get to Downtown LA from Santa Monica ($1.25).

DASH Downtown Los Angeles is served by a minibus system – the Downtown Area Short Hop (DASH) – a great way to see the city. Each trip costs 25¢; transfers to another DASH are free. Call ☎ 800-252-7433 or ☎ 808-2273 (no area code required) for more information. Maps are available from this number, at the tourist offices or on each DASH bus.

Train
Long without a viable urban rail system, Los Angeles in recent years has been taking steps toward remedying that deficiency.

Metro Rail Metro Rail (☎ 800-266-6883) has three light rail lines that offer a clean and inexpensive way to travel. The Blue Line operates between Downtown LA's Metro Center station at 7th & Flower Sts and Long Beach. The Red and Blue lines meet at the Metro Center station. The Blue Line connects with the Green Line at the Imperial/Wilmington stop. LA's subway, the Red Line, runs from Union Station through Downtown to Hollywood. The Green Line runs west from Norwalk parallel to I-105. Near LAX, it curves south, terminating at Marine Ave in Redondo Beach. A free bus shuttles between LAX and the Green Line's Aviation Station.

Metrolink Metrolink (☎ 800-371-5465) is a 404-mile system of six commuter train lines, connecting Union Station with the four counties surrounding Los Angeles – Orange, Riverside, San Bernardino and Ventura – as well as with San Diego.

Car & Motorcycle
LA sprawls across such a huge geographical area that unless time is no factor – or money is extremely tight – you're going to want to spend some time behind the wheel. Don't let horror stories about LA freeways (all 1000 miles worth) scare you off. Even if the pretzel-shaped interchanges and access ramps seem daunting at first – and traffic can jam up for miles behind any fender bender – cars are by far the fastest (if not the most environmentally sound) way to get around the city.

Major Freeways

Angelenos live and die by their freeways. Most are known both by their number and their name, which can get confusing. In general, those going east-west have even numbers and those running north-south have odd numbers. There are emergency call boxes with free phones placed every half mile.

LA's major freeways are:

I-5 Golden State Fwy From Downtown northwest to Bakersfield

I-5 Santa Ana Fwy From Downtown southeast to Irvine

I-10 San Bernardino Fwy From Downtown east to San Bernardino

I-10 Santa Monica Fwy From Downtown west to Santa Monica

I-60 Pomona Fwy From I-5 Downtown east to I-10 at Beaumont

I-101 Hollywood Fwy From I-5 and I-10 Downtown northwest to Hwy 170 in North Hollywood

I-101 Ventura Fwy From Hwy 134 in North Hollywood west to Ventura

I-110 Harbor Fwy From I-101 Downtown south to San Pedro

I-110 Pasadena Fwy From I-101 Downtown north to Pasadena

I-210 Foothill Fwy From I-5 in Sylmar east to I-10 in Pomona

I-405 San Diego Fwy From I-5 in San Fernando southeast to I-5 at Irvine

I-605 San Gabriel River Fwy From I-210 in Duarte south to I-405 in Long Beach

I-710 Long Beach Fwy From I-10 in Alhambra south to Long Beach

Parking Santa Monica, Beverly Hills and West Hollywood have public parking garages where the first two hours are usually free and rates are low thereafter. Parking in business districts like Century City or Downtown can cost as much as $3.50 for each 20-minute period. In Downtown, this can easily be avoided by choosing a lot on the area's perimeter, which may charge just $3 all day.

Parking at motels and cheaper hotels is usually free, while fancier hotels charge anywhere from $5 to $20 a day in addition to the room rate. Valet parking at nicer restaurants and hotels is ubiquitous.

Rental Although rental agencies are located throughout the LA area, you may do better at LAX, where the competition is greatest. Costs are highest in summer and during holiday periods and lowest on weekends (when business travel is down) any other time of year. Rental rates for mid-size cars range from $25 to $45 per day, $120 to $200 per week.

Besides the major chains (see the Getting Around introductory chapter for details), some independent agencies that may have lower rates are:

Avon (☎ 310-277-4455), 1100 S Beverly Drive, Beverly Hills

Midway (☎ 800-366-0643), 1901 Ocean Ave, Santa Monica and (☎ 800-643-9294), 4900 W Century Blvd, near LAX

Rapid (☎ 323-467-7368), 6848 W Sunset Blvd, Hollywood

Rent-A-Wreck (☎ 310-478-0676), 12333 W Pico Blvd, West LA

If you're after that 'Easy Rider' feeling, try renting a Harley from Eagle Rider Motorcycle Rental (☎ 800-501-8687), 20917 Western Ave in Torrance, or Rent a Custom Harley-Davidson (☎ 888-434-4473), 4161 Lincoln Blvd, Marina del Rey. Both provide helmets, leather jackets and basic liability insurance. Day rates are $75 to $150.

Taxi
You can't just thrust your arm out and expect to hail a taxi in LA. Except for those lined up outside airports, train stations, bus stations and major hotels, cabbies respond to phone calls. Fares are metered; you pay $2 at flag fall, $1.80 per mile. Companies include Checker (☎ 800-300-5007), Independent (☎ 800-521-8294), United Independent (☎ 800-822-8294), Yellow Cab (☎ 800-200-1085).

Bicycle
Theoretically, cyclists are entitled to their share of LA city streets, though it's generally not a fast way to get from point A to point B. Bicycles are banned from all buses, allowed on Metro Rail trains during nonpeak times provided you have a permit (call ☎ 800-266-6883 for details), and may be taken onto Metrolink trains at no charge any time without a permit.

Around Los Angeles

SANTA CATALINA ISLAND
• population 3000
Santa Catalina – called just Catalina locally – is one of the largest of the Channel Islands, a chain of partially submerged mountains that rise from the floor of the Pacific between Santa Barbara and San Diego.

Discovered by Juan Rodríguez Cabrillo in 1542, the island was left relatively untouched until 1811, when the native seafaring Indians were resettled on the mainland. Most of the island has since been in private ownership. It was purchased in 1919 by chewing gum magnate William Wrigley Jr (1861-1932), who built a mansion and a casino and briefly made Catalina the spring training headquarters for his major league baseball team, the Chicago Cubs.

Even after the Mediterranean-flavored port town of Avalon began attracting tourists in the 1930s, Catalina's interior and most of its coastline remained largely undeveloped. In conjunction with LA County, the nonprofit Santa Catalina Island Conservancy (☎ 310-510-1421) was able to buy 86% of the 8-by-21-mile island from the Wrigley family in 1975, assuring the island's preservation free of future development.

LOS ANGELES

The island's ecosystem has 400 different plants, more than 100 bird species and larger animals such as deer, goat, boar and foxes, as well as several hundred wild American bison descended from those brought here in 1925 for the filming of Zane Grey's *The Vanishing American*.

Catalina's main season is June to September. Rates plunge for midweek travel and during the off-season, though that's also when some activities may not be available.

Avalon

Most of Catalina's 3000 permanent residents (the population quadruples during the summer tourist season) live in tiny Avalon, at Avalon Bay on the southeast shore. Hotels and shops line the shorefront Crescent Ave and its side streets. The visitor bureau (☎ 310-510-1520, www.catalina.com) has a booth open daily on the central pleasure pier – known as Green Pier – with maps, brochures and tour information.

The island's most recognizable landmark is the white, circular, Spanish moderne **Casino** (☎ 310-510-2500), 1 Casino Way, built for Wrigley in 1929. Its top-floor grand ballroom once featured big band dancing; beneath is a gorgeous art deco movie theater with an organ and underwater murals. The theater can be seen during nightly screenings or during a 40-minute tour ($8.50). Also in the building is the **Catalina Island Museum** (☎ 310-510-2414), which explores 7000 years of island history. It's open 10:30 am to 4 pm daily; $1.50.

The **Wrigley Memorial and Botanical Garden** (☎ 310-510-2288), 1400 Avalon Canyon Rd, is about 1½ miles inland. A spiral staircase climbs the 130-foot tower of the memorial, built in 1934 of blue flagstone and decorative glazed tile. The surrounding 38-acre garden has impressive cacti groves, succulents and samples of the eight Catalina endemic species. It's open 8 am to 5 pm daily; $1.

Two Harbors

Besides Avalon, the only development on Catalina is Two Harbors, which occupies an isthmus near the island's northeastern end.

There's a beachfront campground, picnic area, dive shop, general store, restaurant and saloon, and the hilltop **Banning House Lodge** (☎ 310-510-0244), an 11-room B&B that dates from 1910. This remote and pretty area is served by Coastal Shuttle boat from Avalon and the Safari Shuttle Bus (see Getting Around).

Water Sports

People with a love of water sports – above and below sea level – will find plenty to do on Catalina. Most outfitters have shops on Avalon's Green Pier, where you can gather information, rent equipment and book tours.

Swimmers can take to the water from the small beach next to the pier, though a better option is the clublike Descanso Beach just beyond the Casino ($1.50 admission).

Snorkelers should head to Lovers' Cove on the southeastern end of Avalon Bay for a greater density and variety of marine life, including the sunset-colored garibaldi and even the occasional horn or leopard shark (harmless). Snorkeling gear rentals start at $7/12 per hour/day from outfitters set up at the cove and on the pier. Scuba divers will want to head to the spectacular Casino Point Underwater Park right at the Casino. California Divers Supply (☎ 310-510-0330) rents equipment and operates guided dive tours from $65, including all gear.

Kayak rentals are available from Descanso Beach Ocean Sports (☎ 310-510-1226), at Descanso Beach, and at Joe's on the Green Pier (☎ 310-510-0455) for about $10 to $18 per hour.

If you have a sense of adventure and a fat wallet, you'll enjoy taking a sub tour. It's like something out of a Beatles' song – a ride on a yellow submarine in an octopus' garden. You and one other person are seated in a Plexiglas bubble sub attached to a lemon-colored 'sleigh' navigated by a diver who acts as a guide. During the 30-minute tour ($200), he or she points out the amazing diversity of underwater life – moray eels to barracudas to garibaldi – via two-way radio. You may even get to pilot the sub yourself. For information, call ☎ 877-232-6262.

Organized Tours

The easiest way to see Catalina is on an organized tour, offered by several operators, including Santa Catalina Discovery Tours (☎ 310-510-8687) and Catalina Adventure Tours (☎ 310-510-2888). Options include explorations of the protected island interior (from $17) and of Catalina's rich underwater gardens aboard a glass-bottom boat ($9).. There are also scenic tours of Avalon, harbor cruises, night cruises and others. Jeep Eco-Tours (☎ 310-510-2595 ext 0) does two-hour off-road trips for $65.

Places to Stay

Camping in Avalon is at **Hermit Gulch Campground** (☎ 310-510-8368) in beautiful Avalon Canyon. It's $7.50 per person, and tents and camping equipment may also be rented ($10 per day for small tents, $20 for a teepee). It's a 1½ mile hike or ride aboard the Island Hopper bus (see Getting Around) to get to the campground. For information on camping in the island's rugged hinterland, call ☎ 888-510-7979 or check www.catalina.com/twoharbors.

Hostel La Vista (☎ 310-510-0603, 145 Marilla Ave) is a privately run affair that offers bare-bones accommodations at $15 a head, between June and October.

Catalina's hoteliers depend heavily upon summer business, and rates vary widely between seasons. In general, rates mushroom on weekends; sometimes there's a two-night minimum stay.

One of best values is **Hermosa Hotel** (☎ 310-510-1010, 888-592-1313, 131 Metropole St), with cottages costing just $30 in winter and up to $85 in peak season. Family-style accommodations is what you'll find at the contemporary **Seaport Village Inn** (☎ 310-510-0344, 800-222-8254-62). Rooms with a view of the bay range from $100 to $150.

Among Catalina's B&Bs, the **Old Turner Inn** (☎ 310-510-2236) is one of the nicest, with rooms between $90 and $150. For a real retreat, hole up at the 1929 **Zane Grey Pueblo Hotel** (☎ 310-510-0966, 199 Chimes Tower Rd), once the home of its namesake, the Western writer. The 17 rooms have no phones and cost $75 to $145 in peak season,

otherwise $65 to $90. Top of the line is the stuffily stylish and luxurious **Inn on Mt Ada** (☎ 310-510-2030, 398 Wrigley Rd), in the historic Wrigley mansion, which has superb views of the bay. Its six rooms are priced at $250 to $505 in winter and $350 to $630 in summer. Rates include three meals daily and a golf cart, the main means of getting around on this largely car-free island.

Places to Eat

Restaurants in Avalon tend to be pricey. Good choices along waterfront Crescent Ave include the **Blue Parrot** (☎ 310-510-2465) for casual fare like salads and burgers. **Topless Tacos** (☎ 310-510-0100) is casual and has inexpensive Mexican food. Try the **Ristorante Villa Portofino** (☎ 310-510-0508) for top-end Italian, the **Channel House** (☎ 310-510-1617) for upscale seafood and continental cuisine and **Cafe Prego** (☎ 310-510-1218) for pasta.

Huge and satisfying breakfasts are served at the slightly eccentric **Pancake Cottage** (☎ 310-510-0726, 118 Catalina St), just off Crescent Ave. **Casino Dock Cafe** (☎ 310-510-2755), en route to the Casino, is a good place for simple fare and drinks.

Getting There & Away

Cruise boats headed for Avalon depart regularly from Long Beach and San Pedro, Redondo Beach and Newport Beach. The fastest are those of Catalina Channel Express (☎ 310-519-1212) from Long Beach and San Pedro, and Catalina Flyer (☎ 949-673-5245), which departs daily from Newport Beach in Orange County (both $36 roundtrip, 75 minutes). Catalina Cruises (☎ 800-228-2546) is less expensive, with departures from Long Beach, San Pedro and Redondo Beach ($25 roundtrip, 1¾ hour). People in a hurry can take 15-minute helicopter rides offered by Island Express (☎ 310-510-2525) from San Pedro and Long Beach ($66 or $121 roundtrip).

Getting Around

Only 10-year Catalina residents are allowed to have cars on the island. Bicycles and golf carts may be rented for travel around Avalon; if you plan on cycling beyond the

LOS ANGELES

Hail to the Chief

The Ronald Reagan Presidential Library & Museum (☎ 800-410-8354), 40 Presidential Drive, is in Simi Valley on the far northwestern edge of LA County and contains books and interactive computers to help you fathom the thinking behind the 'Reagan revolution.' You can trace the career of the man who would be president from his early days in radio and acting to his stints as president of the Screen Actors Guild and California governor.

The museum features a re-creation of the White House's Oval Office and the Cabinet Room, Reagan family memorabilia, gifts from heads of state and an actual cruise missile. Reflecting Reagan's passion for the Cold War is a graffiti-covered slice of the Berlin Wall.

The museum is open 10 am to 5 pm daily except major holidays. Admission is $4/2 adults/seniors, free for children under 16. To get to the library, take I-405 north to I-118 west, exit at Madera Rd S, turn right on Madera and continue straight for 3 miles to Presidential Drive.

city limits, you'll need to buy a $50 permit (ask at the visitor bureau). The Island Hopper bus provides public transportation around Avalon for $1 per ride. For trips into the interior, including the airport, Little Harbor and Two Harbors, take the Safari Shuttle Bus. In summer, the Catalina Coastal Shuttle boat operates between Avalon and Two Harbors ($13, 45 minutes).

SAN BERNARDINO NATIONAL FOREST

The 1031 sq miles of the San Bernardino National Forest, east of Los Angeles, provide visitors and residents of the metropolitan area with a respite from the urban bustle, and a host of outdoor recreation options. Popular summer activities include hiking, horseback riding, water sports and fishing, and in winter several resorts invite

skiers and snowboarders to their slopes. The forest encompasses half a dozen wilderness areas and just as many peaks above 10,000 feet, including **Mt San Gorgonio** (11,490 feet), Southern California's tallest.

A highlight is a drive along the 107-mile-long **Rim of the World Drive** (Rte 18), a designated national scenic byway, which affords glorious views across the mountain landscape and into the San Gabriel Valley, on its way from the Cajon Pass to Redlands. Towns like Big Bear Lake and Lake Arrowhead make for excellent bases to explore the attractions of the forest, while the San Gorgonio Wilderness offers an opportunity for a complete immersion in nature.

Those exploring the forest by car must obtain a National Forest Adventure Pass from any USFS ranger station in order to use the forest facilities, including hiking trails. For details, see the boxed text in the Activities chapter.

Big Bear Lake
• population 5400 • elevation 6750 feet

The main reason to come to Big Bear Lake (both the name of the lake and the town) in the San Bernardino National Forest is for outdoor recreation. The year-round, family-friendly mountain resort is an easy and popular getaway for people from LA, the deserts and San Diego. In the warmer seasons, the lake itself – 8 miles long and 1 mile across at its widest point – is perfect for swimming, waterskiing, sailing, fishing and other water sports. In winter, downhill skiers and snowboarders are drawn by Southern California's two largest ski areas, Bear Mountain and Snow Summit, which are taken over by mountain bikers after the snow has melted. Big Bear Village is the town's cutesy and touristy center, a vain attempt to capture the atmosphere of a European Alpine village.

Orientation

Finding your way around Big Bear Lake is easy. Most of the town is sandwiched between the lake's southern shore and the mountains and traversed by Hwy 18, here called Big Bear Blvd. Big Bear Village sits right at the center, with most of the cabins and nicer motels located along the highway west of here. East of the village is the more commercial part of town, with a number of motels, fast-food restaurants and a modern shopping center. The lake's northern shore, along Hwy 38 (here North Shore Blvd), is much quieter and the departure point for most hiking trails.

Information

The visitor center (☎ 800-424-4232, fax 909-866-5671, www.bigbearinfo.com), 630 Bartlet Rd in the village, is open 8 am to 5 pm weekdays, 9 am to 5 pm weekends. They can help you with maps, general information and free lodging reservations. Many motels, hotels, shops and restaurants also have racks of information leaflets.

For suggestions on hiking trails, maps and wilderness permits, visit the ranger-staffed Discovery Center (☎ 909-866-3437), on the northern shore (just look for the signs), open 8 am to 6 pm daily, to 4:30 pm in winter. The center also sells the National Adventure Forest Pass.

Skiing

With an 8000-foot ridge rising above the lake's south side, Big Bear Lake usually has snow between mid-December and March or April; cannonlike snowmaking machines produce supplementary snow whenever necessary. The best thing about Big Bear skiing is the weather – sunshine 90% of the time, and shorts and T-shirt temperatures in spring. Basic ski, boot and pole rentals start at $9.50 per day (more for high-performance gear; discounts for weeklong rentals), offered all along Hwy 18 and at ski area lodges.

Big Bear Lake has two main ski mountains, both off Hwy 18: **Snow Summit** (☎ 909-866-5766, www.snowsummit.com), with 12 lifts (including two high-speed quads), 1200 vertical feet and $32 adult lift tickets (less for half-day and night tickets, more during holidays). **Bear Mountain** (☎ 909-585-2519, 800-232-7686 24-hour Snow Phone) has 11 lifts, 1665 vertical feet and $40 tickets. Its Outlaw Snowboard Park is a favorite among young hotdoggers. Although Snow Summit has more terrain, Bear Mountain is a favorite among locals for its steep upper runs.

Smaller areas, good for beginners and low intermediates, are **Snow Forest** (☎ 909-866-8891) and, 11 miles west of Big Bear on Hwy 18, **Snow Valley** (☎ 909-867-2751).

Hiking

In summer, people trade their ski boots for hiking boots and hit the forest trails. The best hiking and most accessible trailheads are on the lake's north shore, off Hwy 38.

One of the nicest trails is Big Bear's portion of the Pacific Crest Trail (PCT), an easy walk along a 2400-foot ridge 2 miles from the highway, which offers great scenery and views. A moderately difficult hike up the Cougar Crest Trail accesses the PCT and has grand views of Big Bear Lake and Holcomb Valley. Popular too is the Woodland Trail, an easy 1½-mile nature trail starting at the lake's eastern end.

Mountain Biking

Mountain biking is big in Big Bear, which hosts several pro and amateur racing competitions. Most popular is the terrain atop Snow Summit, crisscrossed by 40 miles of roads and trails for all levels. A chairlift costing $7 per ride ($19 for an all-day pass) provides easy access to the top. Tickets, guides, maps and bike rentals are available from the Mountain Bike Center (☎ 909-866-4565) at the mountain base. Rentals start at $6.50/32 per hour/day and include helmets. Other popular riding areas include Holcomb Valley, Delamar Mountain and Van Duesen Canyon off Hwy 38. Less aggressive cyclists will enjoy the gentle 2½-mile bike path along the lake's north shore.

Water Sports

In summer, Big Bear Lake is best experienced from the water, which provides a cool respite from the heat. Swim Beach, just east of the village, is the only official swimming area and it's popular with families. The best swimming, however, is on the lake's very western end, in a beautiful secluded bay accented by islands made up of piles of boulders and the privately owned China

Island. There's no access from the street, so the only way to get there is by boat or Jet ski. Jet skis (for one to three people) rent from $45 per hour; speedboats (for four to six) are $60 per hour; pontoon boats (for eight to 10) cost $40 per hour; and sailboats (for two) are $50 per hour. North Shore Landing (☎ 909-878-4386), closest to China Island, at 38573 North Shore Drive, rents them all.

The lake teems with trout, catfish, bass, carp and other fish, though catching them is not always easy. Those bent on success should sign up with the affable John Cantrell (☎ 909-585-4017, 909-593-4309), whose guide service guarantees prospective fisher-folk their catch – or your money back. You'll need a fishing license, available at sporting stores around town, and $40 per hour for the boat. John will provide the poles, bait and expertise.

Other Activities

Guided jeep explorations of the mountainous countryside are offered by **Jeep Tours** (☎ 909-878-5337), 40687 Village Drive. Tours start at $37.95 for a 90-minute outing, though the popular three-hour White Mountain Tour costs $52.95. Another way to see the mountains is on **horseback**. Guided tours are offered by several companies, including Rockin' K Riding Stables (☎ 909-878-4677), 731 Tulip Lane. **Alpine Slide** (☎ 909-866-4626), on Big Bear Blvd just west of the village, involves a placid chairlift ride up Magic Mountain (more a hill, actually), followed by a fun downhill bobsled ride. The complex also includes a water slide, go-cart track and miniature golf. For regular nine-hole or 18-hole **golf**, sign up for tee time at the Bear Mountain Golf Course (☎ 909-585-8002).

Places to Stay

Accommodations in Big Bear Lake run the gamut from snug B&Bs and resort cabins to lodges, hotels, campgrounds and private homes. Rates generally drop during midweek and go up on holiday weekends. The visitor center has a thorough list and makes free reservations.

Camping The most convenient campgrounds are near the lake and have picnic tables, fire rings and potable water. Popular with mountain bikers and close to town, **Pineknot Campground**, at the top of Summit Blvd, has 48 spaces for $15 (open mid-May to late September). On the north shore near the Discovery Center, **Serrano** is the only campground with showers and RV hookups. It has 132 spaces, $15 tent and $24 RV spaces (open May 1 to November 1).

Hanna Flat, 2 miles north of Hwy 38, is remote but still accessible, making it a popular spot with adventurous families. It has 88 spaces and $15 sites (open mid-May to early September). More isolated are the 17 spaces at **Big Pine Flat**, 4 miles past Hanna Flat, and the 19 sites at **Holcomb Valley**, 4 miles north of Hwy 38 (open year round), both costing $10. Pineknot, Serrano and Hanna Flat accept reservations (☎ 800-280-2267); the other campsites are first-come, first-served.

Cabins Renting a cabin is often the most affordable option for groups of four and up. These range from small and shabby to huge and elegant, offering an array of amenities such as kitchens, fireplaces, sun decks and Jacuzzis. Prices vary accordingly, starting at $100 and going up as high as $400. A good option is the lovely **Grey Squirrel Resort** (☎ 909-866-4335, 800-381-5569, 39372 Big Bear Blvd), which also rents beautiful private homes. **Log Cabin Resort Rentals** (☎ 909-866-8708, 800-767-0205, 39976 Big Bear Blvd) has pretty upscale cabins and condos.

Lodges & Hotels Dozens of lodgings, almost all independently owned, are strung up along Big Bear Blvd, most offering standard rooms starting at $70. The best deal in town is the $55 to $75 rooms at **Jensen's Lakefront Lodge** (☎ 909-866-8271), a half mile west of the village on Lakeview Drive. Rooms have that '70s look, but are clean, spacious and quiet, and some have lake views. The friendly **Honey Bear Lodge** (☎ 909-866-7825, 800-628-8714, 40994 Pennsylvania Ave), three blocks from the village, has spacious rooms with TV, microwave, refrigerator and fireplace for $39/89 midweek/weekend; rooms with a lake view are $59/109 and others with Jacuzzi cost $69/139. For a splurge, try the new ***Northwoods Resort*** (☎ *909-866-3121, 800-866-3121, 40650 Village Drive*), where rooms are $99 midweek and $129 to $169 on weekends.

Places to Eat

Breakfast and dinner are the most important meals, since lunch is usually had on a mountain or trail. For self-catering, the ***Vons*** supermarket toward the east end of the lake on Hwy 38 offers the widest choice, with a deli and bakery.

For bear-sized breakfasts, head to the aptly named ***Grizzly Manor Cafe*** (☎ *909-866-6226, 41268 Big Bear Blvd*), a popular local hangout with twisted 'Twin Peak-ish' charm. Owner Jaymie Nordine greets most guests by name, then repairs to the steamy kitchen to produce delicious pancakes the size of catchers' mitts, plus any number of huge plates of food, all costing less than $7. Open till 2 pm.

The closest to gourmet you'll get in Big Bear is ***Mozart's Bistro*** (☎ *909-866-9497, 40701 Village Drive*), which has imaginative crab cakes, juicy filet mignon, huge portions of pork ribs and other upscale hearty fare. Main dishes cost $13 to $25. There's plenty of fine outdoor seating to allow you to enjoy the good mountain air. Across the street, inside the Northwoods Resort, is ***Stillwells*** (☎ *909-866-3121*), which makes large, crisp salads and bulky burgers. Locals like the steaks, prime rib and seafood for around $20 served at the rustic ***Captain's Anchorage*** (☎ *909-866-3997, 42148 Moonridge Way*), in business since 1947. Dinner only.

Getting There & Away

From I-10, take the Hwy 30 exit in Redlands; then follow Hwy 30 to Hwy 330 to Hwy 18. For a more scenic route, exit off I-10 at Orange St N in Redlands and follow the signs to Hwy 38. Mountain Area Regional Transit Authority (MARTA; ☎ 909-584-1111) buses connect Big Bear with San Bernardino's Greyhound Station three times weekdays and twice weekends ($5). Large groups might consider reserving the door-to-door Big Bear Shuttle (☎ 909-585-5514), which costs $150 for one person and $10 per extra person up to

10 people. The shuttle will pick you up anywhere in LA.

Lake Arrowhead

● **population 6200** ● **elevation 5100 feet**

This sophisticated mountain community, about 90 miles east of LA, was one of Southern California's first weekend getaway destinations. Today, a large year-round population lives around the 784-acre lake, which was created in the 19th century. Residents own rights to the lake, making it practically impossible for the general public to get wet. Basically the only way to obtain lake access is by staying at Lake Arrowhead Resort or by renting a cabin or condo with lake access. But people still flock to Arrowhead on weekends to hike the surrounding trails, to shop and to ski at nearby Snow Valley.

About 10 years ago, developers with heaps of economic foresight but little concern for nostalgia razed Arrowhead's rustic old town center and built Arrowhead Village, a spiffy collection of shops and designer outlets on the lake's south shore. This is now Arrowhead's center of activity and home to most services and restaurants. Small communities such as Blue Jay, Crestline and Rimforest provide inexpensive entertainment and places to stay while exploring the area. Arrowhead has also been a movie location for *The American President*, *Space Jam* and *The Parent Trap*.

Orientation & Information Hwy 18 from San Bernardino passes south of the lake and connects with Hwy 330, from Redlands, before heading east to Big Bear. Most small communities lie along this road. To reach the lake and Lake Arrowhead Village, 2 miles north of Hwy 18, turn north on Hwy 189 or 173 (they converge just south of the village).

There are banks, a post office and supermarket in Blue Jay, a mile south of Arrowhead Village. The chamber of commerce (☎ 909-337-3715, fax 909-336-1548), in the village itself, is open 9 am to 5 pm weekdays (closed at lunchtime) and 10 am to 3 pm Saturday. For campground and trail information, maps and wilderness permits, stop by the Arrowhead Ranger Station (☎ 909-337-2444), in Skyforest on Hwy 18, about a quarter mile east of the Hwy 173 turnoff. Hours are 8 am to 4:30 pm Monday to Saturday.

Things to See & Do An example of the worst kind of American tourism, **Lake Arrowhead Village** surrounds a large parking lot with chain stores meant to resemble Bavarian cottages. A sidewalk skirts the lake, and a promontory covered with a small patch of grass is a popular picnic spot. McKenzie Waterski School (☎ 909-337-3814) operates from a dock in front of the village, offering a one-hour lesson or ride for $30. This is also where you can catch the *Arrowhead Queen* (☎ 909-336-6992), a miniature paddle wheeler that makes a 45-minute narrated tour of the lake from 11 am to 5 pm daily ($10/9/6.50 adults/seniors/children). Buy tickets at Leroy's Sports in the village.

Outdoor lovers will probably want to skip the village entirely and head to the hills. **Deep Creek** offers good hiking and mountain biking, with access to the Pacific Crest Trail. To reach the area, take Hwy 173 around the south shore of the lake and turn east on Hook Creek Rd. Two miles past the small town of Cedar Glen, the pavement ends and the country road continues 2 miles to the Splinters Cabin site with a parking lot and marked trailheads.

More tame and accessible is the **Heap's Peak Arboretum Trail**, 2 miles east of the ranger station on Hwy 18. This half-mile trail loops through a lovely garden with views of Lake Arrowhead. Another nice, moderate trail is the **North Shore Recreation Trail** which begins from the North Shore Campground (site No 10), just off Hwy 173 via Hospital Rd on Lake Arrowhead's northeast side.

Blue Jay has a terrific indoor-outdoor ice-skating rink, **Ice Castle** (☎ 909-337-5283), which is also a national training center (Michelle Kwan trains here). The rink is open year round; sessions cost $8/7 and include skate rentals. **Snow Valley** (☎ 909-867-2751, 800-680-7669), east of Arrowhead on Hwy 18, offers mountain biking in summer and skiing and snowboarding in winter. Across from Snow Valley, **Rim Nordic Ski Area** (☎ 909-867-2600) has cross-country skiing,

and **Snow Drift** (☎ 909-867-2640), in the small town of Arrowbear, has sled rentals.

Places to Stay Campgrounds around Arrowhead are run by the USFS, and sites can be reserved through ☎ 800-280-2267. *Dogwood Campground*, off Hwy 18 near the Hwy 189 (Blue Jay) turnoff, is the largest and most popular in the area, with 93 tent/RV sites costing $15 (reservable mid-May through November; otherwise first-come, first-served; closed November to mid-April). A quarter mile (via Hospital Rd) from Hwy 173 on the northwest shore of Lake Arrowhead, *North Shore Campground* has 27 year-round tent/RV sites ($12) surrounded by oak trees and with access to hiking trails.

Staying at the luxurious *Lake Arrowhead Resort* (☎ 909-336-1511, 800-800-6792), next to the village on Hwy 173, makes a trip to the lake worthwhile if you can afford the price tag. Forest-view rooms range from $109 to $179, but a view of the lake requires shelling out $129 to $199. The resort has a beautiful lobby with a large fireplace, as well as a pool, hot tub, fitness center and private beach. Also good and more affordable is the *Tree Top Lodge* (☎ 909-337-2311, 800-358-8733), a half mile from the lake on Hwy 173, which has a pool and access to a private dock. Rustic rooms with refrigerator and TV start at $59 and top out at $164. Ask for a room away from the highway to avoid traffic noise.

A few blocks west on Lake Drive, *Sleepy Hollow Cabins & Motel* (☎ 909-338-2718, 800-909-2718, fax 909-338-4001) has a small pool and rooms and cabins for $50 to $100.

The *Carriage House* (☎ 909-336-1400, 800-526-5070, 472 Emerald Drive) is a snug and romantic New England-style B&B owned by a world-traveling couple. Rates range from $95 to $135 and include elegant breakfast and afternoon appetizers.

Places to Eat The best view in town is from the lakeside patio of *Belgian Waffle Works* (☎ 909-337-5222), right in Arrowhead Village. For fine dining, try *Altitude* (☎ 909-336-2017, 300 S Hwy 173), in the historic Saddleback Inn, which has a contemporary menu with some selections for vegetarians and vegans.

The ***Borderline Family Restaurant*** (☎ 909-336-4363), in Blue Jay, specializes in barbecue and Mexican food (mostly under $10) and has a kids' menu. For a splurge, try the ***Antlers Inn*** (☎ 909-337-4020), on Hwy 189, halfway between Arrowhead Village and Hwy 18. This rustic historic lodge serves exquisite meat-based meals, including buffalo steaks, $15 and up, and has an extensive wine list.

Getting There & Away Lake Arrowhead is directly north of San Bernardino via Hwy 18 (Rim of the World Drive), about 1½ hours from LA. The 40-mile stretch between San Bernardino and the lake is quite beautiful when there is no smog.

MARTA buses (see Getting There & Away under Big Bear Lake) traveling between Big Bear and San Bernardino stop at Lake Arrowhead Village.

San Gorgonio Wilderness
South of Big Bear is the least developed part of the San Bernardino National Forest, including 92 sq miles of trees, lakes and barren slopes designated as the San Gorgonio Wilderness and lorded over by Mt San Gorgonio. Lots of hiking and equestrian trails traverse the area's steep and rugged terrain, which at the low elevations, is arid and hot in the summer and teeming with rattlesnakes. At higher elevations, oak and manzanita are joined by cedar, fir, sugar and lodgepole pines. Black bears, coyote, deer and squirrel are common, and bald eagle sightings are frequent in the Heart Bar Campground area. Backed by Mts San Gorgonio and San Bernardino, Jenks Lake, 2 miles south of Hwy 38, is a scenic spot for picnicking and easy hiking (take the turnoff across from Barton Flats Campground, instead of Jenks Lake Rd, to avoid a long drive).

Hwy 38 runs along the wilderness' northern periphery, giving access to trailheads, campgrounds and the few services in the area. A free wilderness permit, required for day hikes and camping, is available from the Mill Creek Ranger Station (☎ 909-794-1123), 10 miles east of Redlands on Hwy 38, open 8 am to 5 pm weekdays and 6:30 am to 3 pm on Saturday from May to September. They have a wilderness trail map for $3 and USGS quadrangles.

Places to Stay & Eat The campgrounds along Hwy 38 are owned by the USFS and reservable by calling ☎ 800-280-2267. All sites are $9 and there are no hookups. ***Heart Bar Campground*** is the largest in the area, with 94 sites and flush toilets. Sites here are spacious and flat, surrounded by large ponderosa pines that offer beauty but not much privacy. A few miles farther west, ***South Fork Campground*** is the most intimate in the area with secluded, shady sites, but is subject to highway noise. The ***Oso-Lobo***, ***San Gorgonio*** and ***Barton Flats*** campgrounds are all connected by one hiking trail and have similar surroundings of oak and pine. Oso-Lobo gets large groups and has the oldest facilities, but Barton Flats is the most popular and has hot showers.

Noncampers can stay at ***Seven Oaks Mountain Cabins*** (☎ 909-794-1277, 40700 Seven Oaks Rd), west of the campgrounds on Hwy 38, which has charming little no-frills log cabins ($70) beside the Santa Ana River, a volleyball and tennis court and a lodge with games and a big fireplace.

The best place to eat is the ***Oaks Restaurant*** (☎ 909-794-3611, 37676 Hwy 38), in Angelus Oaks, which serves the usual American fare (including vegetarian items) from 6:30 am to 9 pm daily for under $10. The general store next door is a good place to buy supplies.

Orange County

Few visitors realize that there's more to Orange County than Disneyland. While the region needn't be a priority on the itinerary of first-time visitors to California, it does have a wide range of worthwhile attractions beyond the Mouse Park, including excellent beaches (there are 42 miles of coastline), interesting museums and fine entertainment.especially at the Orange County Performing Arts Center in Costa Mesa.

Although a mosaic of 31 separate cities with 2.65 million inhabitants, Orange County identifies itself as a 'county' more than any other in Southern California, with countywide publications such as the daily newspaper *Orange County Register*, and the *Orange County Weekly* for entertainment reviews and listings.

Inland towns have large Latino populations whose ancestors came here when orange crops were the main source of income. Both the demographics and the landscape changed in the 1970s and '80s when several major corporations set up headquarters here, starting a trend that has kept Orange County one of the fastest-growing urban centers in the US. In 1995, mismanagement and corruption forced the county to declare bankruptcy. The resident community, however, remains safely within California's highest per capita income brackets and is characterized by its – occasionally extreme – political conservatism.

Getting There & Away

The Amtrak stations in Fullerton, Anaheim, Santa Ana, Irvine and San Juan Capistrano, all on the Los Angeles-San Diego route, get about eight northbound and 10 southbound trains per day.

Orange County is also home to John Wayne Airport (☎ 949-252-5200), just off I-405 in Irvine. Small and convenient, it is growing in popularity as a viable alternative to Los Angeles International Airport (LAX) for domestic flights. Currently, Alaska,

Highlights

- Crystal Cathedral – a sparkling house of worship by master architect Philip Johnson
- Glen Ivy Hot Springs – fun, clay and sun at Club Mud
- Little Saigon – Confucian statues, commercial bustle and steamy bowls of noodle soup
- Laguna Beach – a breathtakingly beautiful sliver of the California Riviera, with a long tradition in the arts

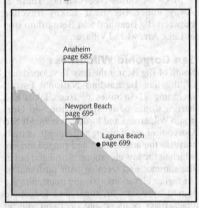

Anaheim
page 687

Newport Beach
page 695

Laguna Beach
● page 699

America West, American, Continental, Delta, Northwest, Reno Air, Southwest, TWA, United and US Airways operate some 300 flights daily.

Getting Around

Orange County Transportation Authority (OCTA; ☎ 714-636-7433) buses serve pretty much all towns and destinations throughout the county; the fare is $1 and transfers are free. An OCTA bus system map and schedule (free) is available at train stations, most chambers of commerce and by calling OCTA.

In addition to OCTA buses, there's also the Orange County Connection (☎ 949-978-8855), a cross between a public and tour bus, which links the county's major towns and attractions. From its main hub at South Coast Plaza in Costa Mesa, three radiating lines serve such communities as Anaheim, Huntington Beach, Newport Beach and Laguna Beach, and destinations such as Disneyland and Fashion Island. Buses leave every two hours; roundtrip fares are $12, 24-hour passes are $20, five-day passes are $30.

Another option is the Airport Bus (☎ 714-938-8900), which charges $10 round-trip to go from Disneyland-Anaheim hotels to Newport Beach several times daily.

ANAHEIM
• **population 301,000** • **elevation 160 feet**
Anaheim, the home of Disneyland and the hub of Orange County, is currently undergoing major growth and transformation. Fueled by the combined financial muscle of the city and Disneyland, Anaheim is being

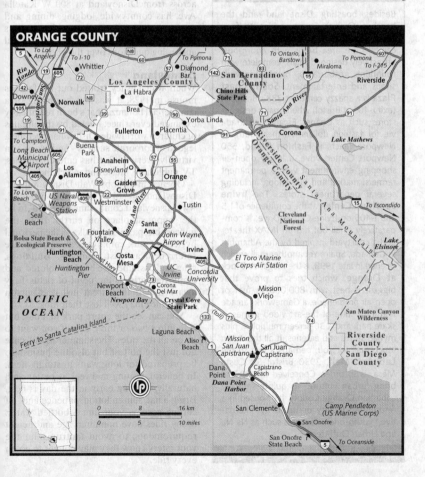

ORANGE COUNTY

'imagineered' (as they say in Disney-speak) into what boosters hope will become the premier destination resort on the West Coast. The revamping is being anchored by the addition of a new theme park – California Adventure – to the existing Disneyland park, an expansion of the convention center and an upgrading of Edison International Field of Anaheim (formerly Anaheim

Stadium, now owned by Disney), home of the Anaheim Angels baseball team. Along the way, the I-5 freeway is being widened and streets and landscaping within the resort area are getting face-lifts. Until the completion of this ambitious project in 2001, visitors to Anaheim will sometimes be aggravated by clogged traffic, dusty streets and construction noise.

The Anaheim/Orange County Convention and Visitor's Bureau (☎ 714-999-8999, fax 714-999-8966, www.anaheimoc.org), across from Disneyland at 800 W Katella Ave, has countywide lodging, dining and transportation information, which staffers will send you for free. They're also helpful answering questions over the phone.

Disneyland

When Walt Disney trotted out his famous mouse in 1928, it was the beginning of a commercial bonanza that's been relentlessly expanded ever since. Fueled by the dreams of children worldwide, Disney has become a legend of corporate success – and excess – in virtually every field it has entered: movies, TV, publishing, music and merchandise.

Opened in 1955 by Walt Disney himself, Disneyland (☎ 714-781-4565, 213-626-8605, www.disneyland.com) is 'imagineered' to be the 'happiest place on earth,' from the impeccable, pastel sidewalks to the personal hygiene of park employees, all of whom are referred to as 'cast members.' Buildings, rides and costumes are brightly colored, and employees grin to the point of rictus, fully aware that if they treat just one person rudely, they may well lose their jobs.

You can see the entire park in a day, but it requires two or three days if you want to go on all the rides. The summer months are not just the hottest but also the busiest, so be prepared for long waits in stifling heat. In general, visiting midweek is better and, naturally, arriving early in the day is best. Bring a hat, suntan lotion, patience and – if cutting costs is your aim – bottled water. Many rides have minimum age and height requirements; to avoid tantrums, let the youngsters know they may not get to go on every ride.

A Shopper's Paradise

Besides boasting Disneyland and the beaches, Orange County prides itself on being Southern California's shopping capital. The area brims with enormous, attractively designed malls, complete with fountains, restaurants, movie theaters, shops and entertainment. **South Coast Plaza** is a snazzy center at 3333 Bristol St (exit I-405 at Bristol) where major designer stores such as Chanel, Escada and Prada vie for fashion dollars. Farther south, in Newport Beach, is **Fashion Island**, 550 Newport Center Drive, a lovely open-air shopping environment with a permanent farmers' market and 200 shops, including several department stores. The **Irvine Spectrum Center**, at the confluence of I-5 and I-405 on Irvine Center Drive, is comparatively small but has an IMAX theater and a courtyard inspired by the Alhambra in Granada, Spain. Yet another mall, which opened in late 1998, is the megasize **Block at Orange**, which tries to prove that biggest is best with 800,000 sq feet of open-air promenade, a Gameworks arcade featuring state-of-the-art video games, a skate park and a 30-screen multiplex, plus myriad stores and eateries. If all this is too much mall for you, perhaps a visit to the **Lab Anti-Mall**, 2930 Bristol St, Costa Mesa, is in order. Conceived in 1993 to bring 'urban culture' to quintessentially suburban Orange County, it's housed in a refurbished factory occupied by 'alternative,' youth-oriented stores such as Na Na and Urban Outfitters.

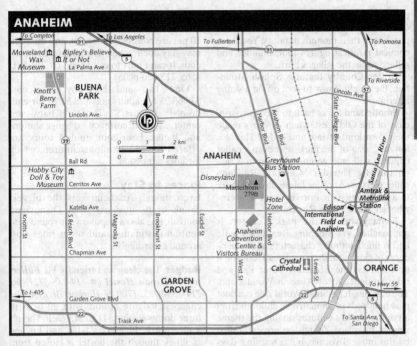

ANAHEIM

You enter Disneyland on **Main Street USA**, which is a cheery re-creation of small-town America circa 1900, with myriad shops and the Candy Palace. Resist the temptation to buy overpriced peanuts, but do stop to have your picture taken with Mickey and Minnie or any of the other jumbo Disney characters that usually hang out around here. Then forge onward to the seven Disney 'lands' centered around Sleeping Beauty's Castle, an architectural confection inspired by Germany's Neuschwanstein palace.

Main Street ends in the Central Plaza. Immediately on your right is **Tomorrowland**, the high-tech showpiece of the park. On the Star Tours ride you're clamped into a Star-Speeder vehicle piloted by a dysfunctional android for a wild and bumpy ride through deep space. Space Mountain will take your head off as you hurtle into complete darkness at a frightening speed – you *will* scream long and loud. On the Rocket Rods, you'll

blast off on a four-minute breakneck journey. Honey, I Shrunk the Audience lets you experience becoming miniature in a world of threatening insects, rodents and reptiles.

In **Adventureland**, to the left of Central Plaza, the highlight is the jungly Indiana Jones Adventure. Enormous HumVee-type vehicles lurch off into the wild for frightening encounters in re-creations of themes and stunts from the famous trilogy. Little ones will love climbing the stairways of the nearby Tarzan's Treehouse and imagining what arboreal life would be like. Also here is the Jungle Cruise, a mellow float through tropical rain forests and some encounters with roaring hippopotami and other jungle denizens.

Just beyond is **New Orleans Square** where offerings include the Haunted Mansion, where you'll be beguiled by hokey frights and sights from the Vincent Price school of horror. Also here is the subterranean float through the tawdry land of the Pirates of the Caribbean, where buccaneers' skeletons perch atop their mounds of booty. You'll see comical piratical figures loot, plunder and pillage while the villages burn.

Critter Country features Splash Mountain, the quickest way to cool off on a sunny afternoon.

Frontierland harks back to the rip-roarin' days of the Old West, when cowboys made their own kind of law and order. This is a low-key area of the park, and even smaller children will emerge unshaken from a ride on the Big Thunder Mountain Railroad roller coaster. Another family favorite here is a churning trip upriver on the sternwheeler Mark Twain Riverboat.

Fantasyland, in the park's center, is approached via Sleeping Beauty's Castle and is filled with the characters and experiences of classic children's stories. Here you'll find Dumbo the Elephant, Peter Pan and rides straight out of Alice in Wonderland. The amazing It's a Small World ride is a float past hundreds of animatronic children from all of the world's cultures singing the theme song of the place. Youngsters are enthralled by this musical voyage, but a warning: days after you've finished picking Disney popcorn out of your teeth, this ear-worm of a song will still be batting around in your head. (The only sure antidote is listening to the entire collection of Led Zeppelin.) A classic ride is the Matterhorn Bobsleds, a roller coaster that's certainly gentle by today's standard, but fun nonetheless.

At the northern edge of the park is **Mickey's Toontown**, another favorite with the elementary school set. This is where Mickey and Minnie make their home (separate ones, of course; this *is* Disney), where Donald keeps his boat, Goofy has a Bounce House, Chip 'n Dale a Treehouse and Roger Rabbit invites you to a Car Toon Spin.

Information Opening hours for Disneyland are quite arbitrary and depend upon the marketing department's projected attendance numbers. In the off-season, the park probably will be open 10 am to 8 pm Monday to Thursday, to 10 pm Friday, to midnight Saturday and to 9 pm Sunday. During summer, weekday hours of 8 am to 10 pm are considered normal, and the park may stay open as late as midnight on weekends. It can't hurt to call ahead (☎ 714-781-4565, 213-626-8605).

One-, two- and three-day passes cost $38/68/95 for adults and $28/51/75 for children. Parking is $7. There's a baby-care center, a kennel, currency exchange stations and banks. Four-hour guided tours are offered for $52/40 adults/children, which includes admission.

Places to Stay

Even though Anaheim gets the biggest chunk of its business from Disneyland tourism, it is also a popular year-round convention destination, and room rates shift around accordingly.

Budget The clean and friendly HI *Fullerton Hacienda Hostel* (☎ 714-738-3721, fax 714-738-0925, 1700 N Harbor Blvd) is the cheapest lodging option, with 20 beds in three dorms costing $11 to $13 each. There's a nice porch, Ping-Pong table and kitchen facilities, though the hostel is closed from 10:30 am to 4 pm and has a midnight curfew and five-night maximum stay. Bus No 47 runs to the hostel from the Greyhound station; from the Anaheim Amtrak station, take bus No 41. Bus No 43A to and from Disneyland stops out front.

Cheap hotels within walking distance of Disneyland include the *Samoa Motel* (☎ 714-776-2815, 425 W Katella Ave), which has island decor and ancient but large rooms costing $30 to $40. Nearby, the *Village Inn Motel* (☎ 714-774-2460, 1750 S Harbor Blvd) makes you feel as if you're at grandma's house, with its brown shag carpet, blue plaid bedspreads and knotty pine walls. Rooms cost around $40.

Mid-Range The area immediately surrounding Disneyland teems with reasonably priced motels, and all major chains – Motel 6, Travelodge, Econo Lodge – are represented. Rooms are reliably clean, have basic amenities and cost $60 or less, sometimes even with continental breakfast thrown in. Most offer shuttle service to Disneyland. Prices may be slightly higher between May and October.

Those willing to spend slightly more should check out the *Castle Inn & Suites* (☎ 714-774-8111, 800-227-8530, fax 714-956-4736, 1734 S Harbor Blvd), which has a pool, a spa, free parking and rooms from $60 to $90. Another good bet with similar prices is across the street, the *Candy Cane Inn* (☎ 714-774-5284, 800-345-7057, fax 714-772-5462, 1747 S Harbor Blvd). Included in the room rate is a satisfying free continental breakfast served in a flower-filled room, as well as shuttle service to the park, a pool, hot tub and impeccable modern rooms.

The *Tropicana Inn* (☎ 714-635-4082, 800-828-4898, fax 714-635-1535, 1540 S Harbor Blvd) offers excellent value, with rooms from $85, a large pool, shuttle service to the park and Amtrak and Greyhound stations, and an in-house car rental service. A few doors down, and run by the same company, the *Park Inn International* (☎ 714-635-7275, 800-828-4898, fax 714-635-7276, 1520 S Harbor Blvd) has similar facilities, plus a complimentary breakfast and refrigerator in every room. Prices are about $20 higher.

Top End Almost rivaling the park in terms of activities and entertainment, the *Disneyland Hotel* (☎ 714-778-6600, fax 714-956-6597, 1150 W Cerritos Ave) and the adjacent *Disneyland Pacific Hotel* (☎ 714-999-0990, fax 714-776-5763, 1717 S West St) may be worthwhile if you plan on staying more than one night. A monorail runs between the hotels and the park, making it easy to go back and forth, and on some days hotel guests get to enter the park 1½ hours before the general public. One-night stands are expensive at $175 to $275, though multiple-night packages (available through ☎ 800-523-9000) might save some money.

A dependable giant both in reputation and size (1580 rooms) is the recently renovated *Anaheim Hilton & Towers* (☎ 714-750-4321, fax 714-740-4460, 777 Convention Way). Besides all the usual amenities, the Hilton has four restaurants, plus (for an additional fee) a state-of-the-art sports and fitness center. Rooms start at $165/185 single/double, though these prices are liable to skyrocket during times of heavy convention business.

Places to Eat

Within Disneyland itself, the nicest restaurant is the *Blue Bayou* (next to the Pirates of the Caribbean), which specializes in fried chicken dinners and sandwiches that don't cost an arm and a leg. The healthiest and spiciest meals – grilled chicken, marinated steak and skewered vegetables (mostly around $5) – are at the *Bengal Barbecue* in Adventureland. Otherwise it's mostly just burgers, fries, ice cream and buckets of popcorn.

Outside the park, pickings are slim for anything other than hotel or chain restaurants. *Tony Roma* (☎ 714-520-0200, 1640 S Harbor Blvd) has good ribs, chicken, beans and onion rings, plus large salads and desserts; lunch is usually less than $10, dinner under $20. The *International House of Pancakes* (☎ 714-635-0933, 1560 S Harbor Blvd) is open 24 hours and has a good kids' menu plus the usual hash-house staples. Inside the Disneyland Pacific Hotel, the *PCH Grill* (☎ 714-999-0990, 1717 S West St) serves California eclectic cuisine and makes an artful presentation of its food, although it's rather pricey. *Hop City Steakhouse* (☎ 714-978-3700, 1939 S State College Blvd) serves Angus steaks from $15 alongside some fine live blues most nights.

Getting There & Away

Anaheim is just off I-5 on Harbor Blvd, about an hour's drive south from Downtown Los Angeles. The most direct (and expensive) transportation is the Airport Bus (☎ 800-772-5299), which runs between Los Angeles International Airport and Anaheim hotels every half-hour; tickets are $14 ($22 roundtrip).

The Greyhound bus station (☎ 714-999-1256) is at 100 W Winston Rd. Buses to and from LA depart often and cost $8. There's also service to San Diego. All San Diego-bound Amtrak trains stop at Anaheim's

Amtrak station on the grounds of Edison International Field of Anaheim. Tickets between Anaheim and LA's Union Station are $7.

AROUND ANAHEIM

People generally avoid interior Orange County – Fullerton, Garden Grove, Orange Santa Ana – which is plagued by smog, traffic and seemingly endless strips of fast-food restaurants, car dealerships and inexpensive housing developments. There are, however, some diamonds in this urban rough.

Knott's Berry Farm

Just 4 miles northwest of Disneyland off of I-5, Knott's Berry Farm is often overlooked and thus is much less crowded. It's a kinder, gentler theme park, with the crush of people and the desperation of the Disneyland crowds noticeably lacking. While most people tackle Knott's as a one-day alternative destination when spending a week near Disneyland, for old-style amusement park fans it warrants a trip in itself.

The park opened in 1932, when Mr Knott's boysenberries (a hybrid of blackberries and raspberries) and Mrs Knott's fried chicken dinners attracted crowds of local farmhands. Mr Knott built an ersatz ghost town to keep them entertained and eventually hired local carnival rides and charged admission. Mrs Knott kept frying the chicken, but the rides and Old West buildings became the main attractions.

The park continues its Old West theme with gold-panning demonstrations, steam train rides and staged gun fights. It also acknowledges pre-gold-rush history with a California missions exhibit; there's even mariachi music in Fiesta Village.

Roller coaster highlights include Montezuma's Revenge, which makes a loop as high as a three-story building, then does it again backward; the Corkscrew, which has a triple upside-down loop; and the six-loop Boomerang. Windjammer is a tandem-style roller-coaster race in which tracks run in side-by-side vertical loops and feature six-story drops that have even the most macho screaming out loud.

The newest scream on the block is Ghost Rider, billed as one of the longest wooden coasters anywhere. It takes passengers on a 4530-foot track – 118 feet tall at its highest point – then drops them 108 feet. Supreme Scream lets you fall 252 feet at 50mph and bounce back upward from the bottom of the ride.

For a tamer adventure, Big Foot Rapids sloshes down a faux white-water river, leaving you absolutely soaked. Camp Snoopy (Peanuts characters – Snoopy, Charlie Brown, Lucy, Linus – are the park's equivalent to Disneyland's Mickey Mouse and Donald Duck) is a kiddy wonderland.

If you pace your day, you might still have enough energy left to enjoy the Edison International Electric Nights multimedia-laser-pyrotechnics show, which is accompanied by water effects.

Information The park (☎ 714-220-5200) is open daily except Christmas. Hours are 9 am to midnight from late May to September; the rest of the year it's open 10 am to 6 pm weekdays, to 10 pm Saturday and to 7 pm Sunday. Admission is $36 for adults, $26 for children and seniors over 60. After 4 pm, admission plummets to $16.95 for all, though this might change; call ahead to confirm. Parking is $7.

Getting There & Away Knott's Berry Farm is at 8039 Beach Blvd, south of I-5 and Hwy 91 in the city of Buena Park. Take the Beach Blvd exit from I-5, I-91, I-22 or I-405. Amtrak's Fullerton Station (☎ 714-992-0530), on the LA-San Diego route, is connected to the park via bus No 99 ($1). MTA bus No 460 connects the park to Downtown LA.

Ripley's Believe It or Not & Movieland Wax Museum

These 'museums' are both truly hokey tourist traps. If you must see one, make it Ripley's (☎ 714-522-7045), 7850 Beach Blvd, just north of Knott's. Robert L Ripley traveled the globe in the 1920s and '30s, collecting weird and exotic artifacts from Africa, Asia and the Pacific Islands. These pieces of folk memorabilia and documentations of human oddities provide some twisted entertainment. Hours are 11 am to 5 pm weekdays, 10 am to 6 pm weekends; $8.95/5.25.

Movieland Wax Museum (☎ 714-522-1154), across the street at 7711 Beach Blvd, is a dizzying maze of wax figures, which can't hold a candle to the people they portray. Maybe the attraction lies in seeing your favorite stars look really bad for once. It's open 10 am to 6 pm weekdays, 9 am to 7 pm weekends; $12.95/$6.95 adults/children. Buying tickets to both these museums gets you a slight discount.

Hobby City Doll & Toy Museum

About 2 miles south of Knott's, at 1238 S Beach Blvd, Hobby City is a group of 20 specialty art and craft shops selling everything from cake decorating equipment to model race car kits. The Doll & Toy Museum (☎ 714-527-2323) here, housed in a half-scale model of the White House, is the best entertainment value around. Along with every type of Barbie doll ever made, the museum has Russian dolls from the 1800s. Its toy replicas of TV, movie and sports personalities, rock stars and presidents present an interesting survey of pop culture in the US over the last 60 years. Unfortunately, the displays themselves – crammed and behind glass – are a bit unimaginative. Museum hours are 10 am to 6 pm daily; $1.

Bowers Museum of Cultural Art

In a gracious 1932 mission-style complex at 2002 N Main St in Santa Ana, this surprising museum (☎ 714-567-3600) has a rich permanent collection of pre-Columbian, African, Oceanic, Asian and Native American art, plus respected changing exhibitions. The building itself, restored in 1994, is an architectural gem surrounding a large courtyard where hands-on crafts demonstrations are held some weekends. The galleries are comfortable, and insightful narration accompanies the various exhibits, which include ritual objects, sculpture, jewelry, costumes and weapons. One block south, the **Bowers Kidseum** keeps youngsters entertained with hands-on exhibits relating to world cultures.

Hours are 10 am to 4 pm (to 9 pm Thursday), closed Monday; the Kidseum is open 10 am to 4 pm weekends; $6/4/2 adults/seniors/children (good for both museums).

The *Topaz Café* (☎ 714-835-2002), in the museum courtyard, has a deservedly high reputation for its creatively presented, razzmatazz California food, though cheap it ain't.

Crystal Cathedral

You needn't agree with televangelist Robert Schuller's teachings or be an 'Hour of Power' fan to appreciate the architecture

Glen Ivy Hot Springs

In Corona, technically just east of Orange County in Riverside County, is this lovely bathing complex (☎ 800-258-2683), nicknamed Club Mud for its main attraction – a red clay mud pool. Like some prehistoric animal wandering into the tar pits, you soak yourself in this muck, then apply what amounts to a full-body mask by grabbing a chunk of clay and smearing it all over yourself before lounging in the sun until it's baked into your skin. Whether this treatment truly has therapeutic effects is debatable, but it's certainly fun. Bring an old swimsuit, though, since the clay stains any cloth it touches.

Besides the mud, there are 15 other pools and spas filled with naturally hot mineral water. It's all surrounded by 10 acres of grounds with abundant bougainvillea, eucalyptus and palm trees. Aqua aerobics classes, massages (extra fee) and a lap pool are part of the deal as well.

The spa is at 25000 Glen Ivy Rd in Corona and open 10 am to 6 pm daily from March 1 to October 31 and till 5 pm the rest of the year. Admission is $19.50 Monday to Thursday and $25 weekends (Friday to Sunday). Children under two are free. To get there, exit I-15 at Temescal Canyon Rd, turn right and drive 1 mile to Glen Ivy Rd, then right again and straight to the end.

of the Crystal Cathedral (☎ 714-971-4000), 12141 Lewis St, in Garden Grove, about 2 miles southeast of Disneyland. Looking like a cross between a modern office complex and a Batman movie set, the cathedral is built in the shape of a four-pointed star and boasts 10,661 windows, seating capacity for 3000 and an organ with 16,000 pipes.

Designed by Cleveland-born Philip Johnson, international-style architect turned postmodernist, the church is part of a campus with additional buildings, gardens, reflecting pool, fountains and sculpture. You can visit it on your own or take a free 30-minute tour (offered hourly). Don't miss the freestanding modern Gothic prayer chapel on the cathedral's north side; its pillars are made of eight different types of Italian marble, and it houses a five-piece lead crystal cross that weighs 200lb.

Schuller's congregation is part of the protestant Reform Church of America (descended from the Dutch Reform Church), formerly worshipped at the Orange County Drive-In movie theater where Schuller preached from atop the snack stand. Schuller's Hour of Power is now broadcast on TV networks around the world. Combined donations from Schuller's various audiences funded the campus' construction, leaving it debt-free at its 1980 dedication.

The church's productions of the Glory of Christmas and the Glory of Easter are its major fund-raisers. They are staged spectacles that reenact these biblical stories using live camels, flying angels and other theatrical gimmicks. For tickets, call ☎ 714-544-5679.

Regular Sunday services, complete with a 110-voice choir and a 20-piece orchestra, are at 9:30 and 11 am and at 6 pm.

Orange
• **population 117,000** • **elevation 187 feet**

The city of Orange, about 6 miles southeast of Disneyland, has the best collection of antiques, collectibles and consignment shops in Orange County. From Disneyland, take OCTA bus No 46 or 50; from coastal communities, take bus No 53.

Originally part of Rancho Santiago de Santa Ana, the land was given to lawyers Alfred Chapman and Andrew Glassell as legal fees in 1869. They laid out a 1-sq-mile town surrounding a plaza (at the intersection of Chapman and Glassell Sts), which is still the center of activity and is known as Old Towne Orange.

In the blocks north and south of the plaza, you'll find serious antique shops such as George II, 114 N Glassell St, which sells French and English furniture. There's also American Heritage, 110 S Glassell St, which hawks Coke memorabilia, vintage gas pumps and old slot machines.

Prices overall are pretty hefty, and unfortunately some dealers try to pass off replicas as antiques, so caveat emptor. Unpretentious stores include the Knot Knew Shop (148-A N Glassell St) and Happiness by the Bushel (128 N Glassell St). Both are sure to be winners with treasure hunters.

The footsore visitor will appreciate a cuppa from either Starbucks or Diedrich Coffee at opposite ends of Plaza Square.

Tricky Dick Library

In Yorba Linda, in northeastern Orange County, is the **Richard Nixon Presidential Library & Birthplace** (☎ 714-993-3393), 18001 Yorba Linda Blvd. Here you can watch a film called *Never Give Up: Richard Nixon in the Arena*, listen to carefully edited White House tapes from the Watergate era, see the pistol given to Nixon by Elvis Presley and view the telephone used to communicate with Apollo 11 astronauts on the moon. There's also a re-creation of the Lincoln Sitting Room, Nixon's favorite White House room. The museum's brochure makes the point that it's the only presidential library built without using taxpayers' money – at a cost of $21 million.

Hours are 10 am to 5 pm daily (from 11 am Sunday); $5.95/3.95, $2 for ages 8 to 11, free if under 8. To get there, exit east on Yorba Linda Blvd from Hwy 57 and continue straight to the museum.

Next to the latter is *Felix's Cafe* (☎ 714-633-5842), an Orange institution and informal eatery serving inexpensive Cuban dishes (under $10). More upscale and pricey, California dining is offered at the postmodern *Citrus City Grille* (☎ 714-639-9600, 122 N Glassell St).

Little Saigon

The city of Westminster, southwest of Anaheim near the junction of I-405 and Hwy 22, is home to a large Vietnamese population, which has carved out its own vibrant commercial district around the intersection of Bolsa and Brookhurst Aves. Its heart is the **Asian Garden Mall**, a behemoth of a structure at 9200 Bolsa Ave. About 400 ethnic boutiques, including herbalists and jade jewelers, invite browsing on two floors. Best among the many casual eateries here is *Pho 79* (☎ 714-893-1883), on the lower level toward the mall's north entrance, which has superb *pho ga* (chicken noodle soup) for only $3.75.

Across the street, the **New Saigon Mall Cultural Court** marries commercialism and spirituality with its impressive display of statues and murals.

Orange County Beaches

The surfers, artists and retirees that inhabit Orange County's beach towns give the coast its own vibe, distinct from the rest of the county. Except for Newport Beach, the small beach communities, strung along Pacific Coast Hwy at roughly 10-mile intervals, are very relaxed despite the area's fast-paced development. Oil rigs sit about a mile offshore all along the coast and are scattered among the houses and businesses inland, giving the landscape a surreal appearance.

Getting Around

The No 1 OCTA bus runs north-south between Long Beach and San Clemente along Pacific Coast Hwy every 20 minutes. It stops in Sunset Beach, Huntington Beach,

Newport Beach, Corona del Mar, Laguna Beach, Dana Point, San Juan Capistrano and San Clemente. The last northbound bus leaves San Clemente at 8:06 pm, and the last southbound bus leaves Long Beach at 8:29 pm. On Saturday, buses are hourly and stop running two hours earlier.

SEAL BEACH
* **population 25,000**

Unlike other towns with their business districts spread out along Pacific Coast Hwy, Seal Beach has a very walkable downtown that lies along a few blocks of Main St, between Ocean Ave, which skirts the beach, and Pacific Coast Hwy. At the end of Main St, the **Seal Beach Pier** extends 1885 feet over the ocean. The current pier, built in 1985, replaced the 1906 original, which was destroyed by the winter storms of 1981-82.

Main St has some interesting antique and consignment clothing stores. The Bay Theater (☎ 562-431-9988), 340 Main St, shows alternative films preceded by live music from the theater's Wurlitzer organ, which once entertained patrons at New York's Paramount theater.

Away from its charming downtown, Seal Beach has a huge naval weapons research station and is home to Leisure World, one of Southern California's first and most exclusive retirement communities.

Bolsa Chica State Beach & Ecological Preserve

The 3-mile stretch of Pacific Coast Hwy between Seal Beach and Huntington Beach is flanked on one side by Bolsa Chica State Beach, and on the other side by the Ecological Preserve of the same name. Less attractive than neighboring beaches, the Bolsa Chica Beach has dark and dusty sand and faces a monstrous oil rig a half mile off shore.

Across Pacific Coast Hwy from the beach, terns, mergansers, pelicans, pintails, grebes and endangered Belding's Savannah sparrows congregate among pickleweed and cordgrass in a restored salt marsh designated as the Bolsa Chica State Ecological Preserve. A 1½-mile loop trail starts from the parking lot on Pacific Coast Hwy.

HUNTINGTON BEACH
• population 189,000 • elevation 28 feet

Huntington was once the least polished and most low-key of Orange County's beaches, but recently has experienced the mushrooming of glitzy chain restaurants and horrendous architecture. Outside of the hub of tourist activity at the corner of Pacific Coast Hwy and Main St (across from the Huntington Pier), Huntington's roots are still intact: surfers outnumber yuppies, 1940s beach cottages house most of the population, and oil derricks are a common lawn adornment.

Ever since Hawaiian-Irish surfing star George Freeth (brought to town by Henry Huntington himself) gave surfing demonstrations here in 1914, Huntington has been one of Southern California's most popular surf destinations, earning the title 'Surf City, USA' from rock & roll surf daddies Jan and Dean. The **Huntington Pier** is site of the Ocean Pacific Pro surf contest – a landmark event held annually in early September – and across from the pier (on Main St) is the Surfing Walk of Fame (like the Hollywood Walk of Fame, only with sand and salt).

Huntington Beach maintains a visitor bureau (☎ 714-969-3492, fax 714-969-5592, www.hbvisit.org) at 101 Main St.

International Surfing Museum

This museum (☎ 714-960-3483), 411 Olive Ave, half a block off Main St, is one of the few of its kind in California and is an entertaining mecca for surf-culture enthusiasts. Exhibits chronicle the sport's history with photos, early surfboards and surfwear, and surf music records by the Beach Boys, Jan and Dean and the Ventures. There is also a good display about women in surfing. Hours are noon to 5 pm daily (closed Monday and Tuesday in winter); $2/1.

Huntington Beach Art Center

Away from the hustle and bustle of downtown, Huntington's Art Center (☎ 714-374-1650) sits at the east end of Main St across from the public library and city hall. The exhibit space is excellent, with high ceilings and concrete floors, which showcase the mostly contemporary installations well. The

art center is open noon to 6 pm Tuesday to Saturday (till 8 pm Thursday) and till 4 pm Sunday; $3/2.

Places to Stay

Huntington Beach is home to the area's only hostel, and it's a real peach: the *Colonial Inn Youth Hostel* (☎ 714-536-3315, 421 8th St) has four-person dorms ($12 per bunk), doubles ($14 per person), a nice kitchen, a living room and backyard, free breakfast, no curfew and is a three-block walk to downtown and the beach.

There are a few budget motels across from the beach, including the *Sun 'n' Sands Motel* (☎ 714-536-2543, 1102 Pacific Coast Hwy), with nice $50 to $80 rooms and a pool. The *Quality Inn* (☎ 714-536-7500, 800 Pacific Coast Hwy), just north of the Huntington Pier, has dependably clean rooms, each with cable TV, refrigerator and at least a partial ocean view. Rates range from $80 to $200.

Fancy accommodations can be had at the *Waterfront Hilton Beach Resort* (☎ 714-960-7873, fax 714-960-2642, 21100 Pacific Coast Hwy), ¼ mile south of the pier. They offer ocean-view rooms starting at $160, $190 in summer, and have a spa, fitness center and a posh restaurant.

Places to Eat

The *Sugar Shack* (☎ 714-536-0355, 213 Main St) is a breakfast and lunch institution, with local artifacts decorating the walls and a restaurant that serves coffee shop food for less than $10 (under $5 for breakfast). Across the street, *Wahoo's Fish Tacos* (☎ 714-536-2050, 120 Main St) serves tacos and burritos with black beans and rice for around $5, and conscientiously lists the caloric and fat content of menu items.

NEWPORT BEACH
• population 72,000 • elevation 5 feet

Newport is the largest and most sophisticated of Orange County's beach towns, with one of the biggest pleasure craft harbors in the US and shopping that rivals Beverly Hills. There is plenty to do both on and off the beach here, but attractions are rather

ORANGE COUNTY

scattered. Pacific Coast Hwy passes through the part of Newport that centers around harbor activity, with boat dealerships, yacht clubs and seafood restaurants clustered in buildings that once served as shipping warehouses for the Irvine Ranch (a large sheep-raising and tenant farming operation that was part of the original Spanish land grant on which Irvine was built). South of Pacific Coast Hwy via Balboa Blvd, the Balboa Peninsula makes a natural 6-mile barrier between Newport Harbor and the ocean. Most tourist activity is located here, including beaches and the Balboa Fun Zone. North of Pacific Coast Hwy, inland Newport is a sprawl of upscale tract homes that house a good chunk of Orange County's corporate workforce. The University of California at Irvine (UCI), northeast of Newport, injects some bohemian flair into this otherwise very bourgeois area.

The week before Christmas brings thousands of spectators to Newport Harbor to watch the nightly Christmas Boat Parade, a tradition begun in 1919. The 2½ hour parade of lighted and decorated boats begins at

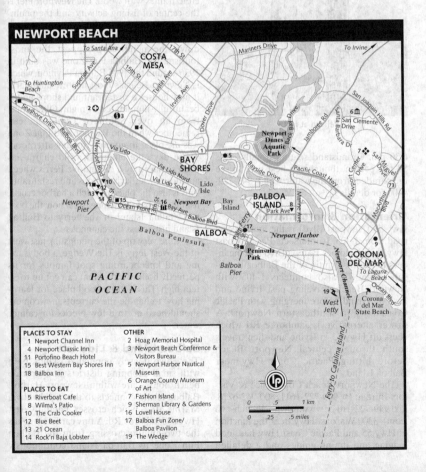

NEWPORT BEACH

PACIFIC OCEAN

PLACES TO STAY
1 Newport Channel Inn
4 Newport Classic Inn
11 Portofino Beach Hotel
15 Best Western Bay Shores Inn
18 Balboa Inn

PLACES TO EAT
5 Riverboat Cafe
8 Wilma's Patio
10 The Crab Cooker
12 Blue Beet
13 21 Ocean
14 Rock'n Baja Lobster

OTHER
2 Hoag Memorial Hospital
3 Newport Beach Conference & Visitors Bureau
5 Newport Harbor Nautical Museum
6 Orange County Museum of Art
7 Fashion Island
9 Sherman Library & Gardens
16 Lovell House
17 Balboa Fun Zone/ Balboa Pavilion
19 The Wedge

0   5   1 km
0   .25   .5 miles

Pelican at rest

6:30 pm. Grandstand seating usually costs $8 per person, though the best way to see the parade is from the water. Call ☎ 949-729-4400 for details.

Orientation & Information

Hwy 55 (Newport Blvd) is the main access road from I-405. It intersects Pacific Coast Hwy, then becomes Balboa Blvd and meanders to the eastern tip of the Balboa Peninsula. Hwy 73 also connects I-405 with Newport Beach, traveling past Irvine and Fashion Island before merging with Pacific Coast Hwy in southeastern Newport. A slower alternative is Jamboree Rd which veers off Hwy 73 in Irvine and then travels south through central Newport Beach before hitting Pacific Coast Hwy near Balboa Island.

The Newport Beach Conference & Visitors Bureau (☎ 949-722-1611, 800-942-6278, fax 949-722-1612, www.newportbeach-cvb.com), 3300 W Coast Hwy, near the junction of Hwy 55 and Pacific Coast Hwy, has good lodging and dining guides and a detailed map. The *Daily Pilot* newspaper has local news and entertainment listings, while *The Log* – available from the visitor bureau and nautical shops – has boating news for all of Southern California.

Balboa Peninsula

This strip of land, about 6 miles long and a ¼ mile wide, has a white sand beach on its ocean side and stylish homes – including Vienna-born architect Rudolph Schindler's 1926 **Lovell House** (on 13th St facing the harbor), which was built using site-cast concrete frames with wood. The **Newport Pier** is the center of fishing activity and the peninsula's most rowdy nightlife, while the **Balboa Fun Zone** and **Balboa Pier** (about halfway down the peninsula) support the most tourism. The Balboa Fun Zone was built in 1936 around the 1905 Balboa Pavilion, which is Newport Beach's most historic landmark; it now houses a restaurant and shops and is beautifully illuminated at night. Older folks from all over Southern California can remember when the Pavilion and Fun Zone was *the* place to go on a Sunday afternoon. These days, the landmark's old charm has been replaced by a diminutive Ferris wheel, arcade games, touristy shops and restaurants. This is also the place to catch a harbor cruise, fishing or whale-watching excursion, the boat to Catalina Island or the ferry to Balboa Island just across the channel.

At the very tip of the peninsula, just west of the West Jetty, is **The Wedge**, a bodysurfing and kneeboarding spot famous for its perfectly hollow waves that can get up to 30 feet high. This is *not* a good place for learning how to handle the currents; newcomers should head north a few blocks for calmer water.

Balboa Island & Lido Isle

These two densely populated islands, both with small shopping districts and upscale beach houses, are within Newport Harbor. Balboa Island connects to the mainland via Marine Ave, which crosses Pacific Coast Hwy as Jamboree Rd. A tiny car ferry makes the two-minute crossing from the Balboa Fun Zone to Balboa Island continuously between 6:30 am and midnight (until 2 am Friday and Saturday). Charges are $1.25 for car and driver, 50¢ per person. The ferry lands at the west end of the island, 11 blocks from the businesses and restaurants on Marine Ave. It's only about 1½ miles around the island, making it a good place to explore on foot or bike.

Lido Isle is connected to the mainland by Via Lido. Streets here are especially narrow, and houses seem to be built one on top of the other. Via Lido wraps around the entire island (about a mile), past upscale beachwear shops and the restored Lido Cinema (☎ 949-673-8350), which shows foreign and nonmainstream films.

Museums

In an obscure location between Jamboree Rd and Fashion Island, the **Orange County Museum of Art** (☎ 949-759-1122), 850 San Clemente Drive, provides both a survey of California art and cutting-edge contemporary exhibits. It's all supplemented by a sculpture garden, gift shop and theater that screens classic, foreign and art-related films. Hours are 11 am to 5 pm, closed Monday; $5/4, children free.

The **Newport Harbor Nautical Museum** (☎ 949-673-7863), housed in a sternwheeler moored at 151 E Coast Hwy, does its best to document and preserve regional maritime heritage through ship models, photographs, paintings and memorabilia. Hours are 10 am to 5 pm, closed Monday; $4/1.

Corona del Mar

A ritzy bedroom community with elegant stores and restaurants, Corona del Mar is spread along Pacific Coast Hwy and hugs the east flank of the Newport Channel. The beach here lies at the foot of rocky cliffs. There are rest rooms and volleyball courts, maintained by the State Park system. Parking costs $5 per vehicle, though there are usually free spaces atop the cliffs behind the beach along Ocean Blvd. Children love the tide pools at Little Corona Beach.

The community's prize attraction is the **Sherman Library & Gardens** (☎ 949-673-2261), housed in a historic, early California-style estate, which occupies an entire block of Pacific Coast Hwy. Begun in 1966, the gardens are lush and well maintained, with profuse orchids and a koi pond and a garden for the visually impaired. The small research library holds a wealth of California historical documents, as well as paintings by early California landscape artists. The gardens are open 10:30 am to 4 pm; $3, free on Mondays.

Places to Stay

A good choice for budget travelers is the **Newport Channel Inn** (☎ 949-642-3030, 800-457-8614, 6030 W Coast Hwy), near the beach, where large but basic rooms cost $59 in winter and from $79 in summer. Closer to the harbor and peninsula, the **Newport Classic Inn** (☎ 949-722-2999, 2300 W Coast Hwy) has rooms for $65 in winter, $76 in summer.

Between the Fun Zone and Balboa Pier, the **Balboa Inn** (☎ 949-675-3412, fax 949-673-4587, 105 Main St) is a lovely hotel with European touches, which was once owned by basketball great Kareem Abdul-Jabbar. Rooms are $109, climbing up to $149 in summer. Rooms with an ocean view are an extra $20. Also on the peninsula, near the Newport Pier, the **Best Western Bay Shores Inn** (☎ 949-675-3463, fax 949-675-4977, 1800 W Balboa Blvd) has standard rooms for $109 to $169 in winter, $139 to $269 in summer, including breakfast, VCR and video rental and use of beach accessories. Perfect for a romantic fling is the classy **Portofino Beach Hotel** (☎ 949-673-7030, 800-571-8749, fax 949-723-4370, 2306 W Oceanfront), whose stately, plush rooms ($130 to $300) have fireplaces, marble bathtubs and views of the Newport Pier.

Places to Eat

The **Crab Cooker** (☎ 949-673-0100, 2200 Newport Blvd) has been dishing out fresh, fishy fare for 46 years. Unfortunately, it's all served on paper plates and with plastic cutlery, making every meal an environmentalist's nightmare. The long wait can be a turnoff too, but the menu and prices – from $7 to $23 depending upon the daily catch – are quite good.

An excellent choice for a romantic gourmet dinner that won't break the bank is the *Riverboat Cafe* (☎ 949-673-3425, *151 E Coast Hwy*), which shares space on a historic sternwheeler with the Newport Harbor Nautical Museum. The salads (under $10) are big enough for two, the filet mignon ($16) melts in your mouth and the desserts delight both eye and palate. Service is young, friendly and impeccable.

McFadden Square at the Newport Pier has a cluster of interesting restaurants, including the funky *Rock'n Baja Lobster* (☎ 949-723-0606, *2104 W Oceanfront*), which serves big buckets of lobster tails, shrimp, chicken and other goodies at $30 for two. Next door, *21 Ocean* (☎ 949-673-2100, *2100 W Oceanfront*) has an overstuffed Victorian dining room with an ocean-view bar and continental entrées costing $20 and up. Around the corner, *Blue Beet* (☎ 949-675-2338, *107 21st Place*), in a 1912 brick building, has reasonably priced steaks and seafood, though it's best known for great jazz and blues, played most nights.

On Balboa Island, *the* place for cholesterol-feast breakfasts is *Wilma's Patio* (☎ 949-675-5542, *225 Marine Ave*), also a good destination for lunch and dinner.

Getting Around

OCTA bus No 53 stops at the corner of Pacific Coast Hwy and Newport Blvd and goes south to the end of the Balboa Peninsula, and north to South Coast Plaza and Old Towne Orange. The No 65 covers the Peninsula, Pacific Coast Hwy from Newport Blvd to MacArthur Blvd, Fashion Island and UCI.

AROUND NEWPORT BEACH
University of California, Irvine

UCI is the up-and-coming University of California campus whose scientific research departments are increasingly well funded, and whose basketball team – the Anteaters – surprised the collegiate world several years ago by beating top-ranked University of Nevada Las Vegas. Although the campus is not too exciting in terms of architecture (most of it was built in the 1970s and '80s), it

occasionally hosts interesting lectures or sporting events. The student union (☎ 949-824-5011), where you'll find a student-staffed information center and a good bookstore, is well marked off Campus Drive, south of I-405 via MacArthur Blvd.

LAGUNA BEACH
• **population 23,200** • **elevation 70 feet**

Secluded beaches, low cliffs, glassy waves, waterfront parks, eucalyptus-covered hillsides and a host of art galleries and boutiques make Laguna Beach one of Southern California's most popular seaside destinations. Home of several renowned arts festivals (see 'Laguna Arts Festivals' boxed text), as well as the highly regarded **Laguna Playhouse** (606 Laguna Canyon Rd), the city draws artists, culture lovers and art collectors from all over the world. Laguna swells with tourists on summer weekends, but away from the Village (the central business district) and Main Beach (where the Village meets the shore), there's plenty of uncrowded sand and water.

History

Laguna's earliest inhabitants, the Ute-Aztecas and Shoshone tribes, called the area 'Lagonas' because of two freshwater lagoons in what is now Laguna Canyon. The name held until 1904, when it was changed to Laguna. At roughly the same time, San Francisco artist Norman St Claire came to Laguna to paint watercolors of the surf, cliffs and hills. His enthusiasm attracted other artists who were influenced by French impressionism and known as the 'plein air' (as in 'outdoors') school. The Laguna Beach Art Association, precursor to the Laguna Art Museum, was founded in 1918, and by the late '20s more than half of the town's 300 residents were artists.

The most lasting development began in Laguna Beach in 1926, when the Pacific Coast Hwy between Newport Beach and Dana Point opened, giving Laguna three access routes. Mary Pickford, Douglas Fairbanks, Mickey Rooney and Bette Davis vacationed here regularly and helped establish the Laguna Playhouse (still in operation)

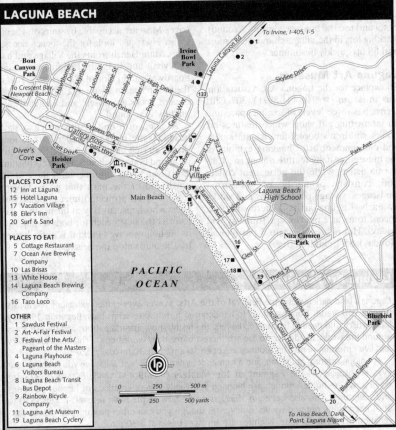

LAGUNA BEACH

PLACES TO STAY
12 Inn at Laguna
17 Hotel Laguna
17 Vacation Village
18 Eiler's Inn
20 Surf & Sand

PLACES TO EAT
5 Cottage Restaurant
7 Ocean Ave Brewing Company
10 Las Brisas
13 White House
14 Laguna Beach Brewing Company
16 Taco Loco

OTHER
1 Sawdust Festival
2 Art-A-Fair Festival
3 Festival of the Arts/ Pageant of the Masters
4 Laguna Playhouse
6 Laguna Beach Visitors Bureau
8 Laguna Beach Transit Bus Depot
9 Rainbow Bicycle Company
11 Laguna Art Museum
19 Laguna Beach Cyclery

PACIFIC OCEAN

and the famous Festival of the Arts, which began in 1932.

Orientation & Information

Though Laguna stretches for about 7 miles along Pacific Coast Hwy, shops, restaurants and bars are concentrated along a quarter-mile stretch in the Village, along three parallel streets (Broadway, Ocean and Forest) and their intersections with Pacific Coast Hwy. Across Pacific Coast Hwy from the Village, Main Beach is the largest public beach in the area. Four miles south, the separate commu-

nity of Laguna Niguel is home to the fancy Ritz-Carlton Hotel, which is on Salt Creek Beach, a favorite with local surfers.

The Laguna Beach Visitors Bureau (☎ 949-497-9229, 800-877-1115, fax 949-376-0558, www.lagunabeachinfo.org) is at 252 Broadway and can make free walk-in lodging reservations. Hours are 9 am to 5 pm weekdays, to 4 pm Saturday, 10 am to 3 pm Sunday (July and August only). The free weekly *Coastline News*, available at the visitors bureau and around town, is a good source for local news and events.

Parking is a perpetual problem. If you're spending the night, leave your car at the hotel and use the bus (see Getting Around). Parking lots in the village charge $6 or more and fill up quickly in summer.

Laguna Art Museum

Showplace for the Laguna Art Association, this museum (☎ 949-494-8971), 307 Cliff Drive, has three levels of exhibit space and an interesting gift shop, which features art books, children's books, jewelry, stationery and consignment art. Changing exhibits in the museum usually feature one or two California artists, while the permanent collection consists primarily of California landscapes, vintage photographs and works by early Laguna artists. There are free docent tours at 2 pm (except Thursday and Friday). Hours are 11 am to 5 pm (closed Monday); $5/4, children free.

Beaches

Laguna Beach has 30 public beaches and coves. Most are accessible by stairs off Pacific Coast Hwy; just look for the 'beach access' signs. Main Beach fronts the Village and has volleyball and basketball courts, a wooden boardwalk and colorful tile benches. This is the best place for swimming, since the water is calm, rocks are absent and lifeguards are on duty year round.

At the north end of this beach, a path heads up the bluff to Heisler Park, a long skinny stretch of grass accented by hibiscus, roses and bougainvillea. Several sets of stairs lead down to the sand, including those at the north end of the park that go to Diver's Cove, a deep protected inlet popular with guess who. Crescent Bay, at the north end of town, is the best beach for bodysurfing with its big hollow waves. Parking is difficult here; try the bluffs atop the beach.

Laguna Art Festivals

Laguna's landmark event is the **Festival of the Arts**, a seven-week juried exhibit of 160 artists whose work varies from paintings to handcrafted furniture to scrimshaw. Begun in 1932 by local artists who needed to drum up buyers, the festival now attracts patrons and tourists from around the world. In addition to the art, there are free daily workshops, a children's art gallery and live entertainment. The grounds are open 10 am to 11:30 pm daily; $5/3.

A unique offering at the fair, and a tremendous experience that will leave you rubbing your eyes in disbelief, is the **Pageant of the Masters** (☎ 949-494-1145, 800-487-3378 for tickets), where human models are blended seamlessly into re-creations of famous paintings and sculptures. This also began in 1932, as a sideshow to the main festival. Tickets ($10 to $50) need to be ordered weeks in advance, though you can often pick up last-minute cancellation tickets at the gate. Nightly performances begin at 8:30 pm.

In the '60s, Laguna Beach artists who did not get into the juried exhibition started their own festival to take advantage of the art seekers passing through town. They set up directly across from the festival (at 935 Laguna Canyon Rd, half a mile from the Village). They mocked the established event's formal atmosphere by scattering sawdust on the ground and thus ended up with the moniker **Sawdust Festival**. Although this alternative show is now juried too, it still has arts and crafts that are utilitarian and quite affordable, so many people actually enjoy this festival more than the main one. Hours are 10 am to 10 pm; $6/1.

A third art happening, the **Art-A-Fair Festival** (☎ 949-494-4514) runs simultaneously. It is a nationally juried show focused mainly on watercolors, pastels and oil paintings, although photography, jewelry, ceramics and other arts and crafts are displayed as well. It is at 777 Laguna Canyon Rd and is open daily to 9 or 10 pm; admission is $3.50/2.50.

Buses (75¢) shuttle continuously between the festivals and the Village from 10 am to midnight.

About 1 mile south of the Village is less-crowded Victoria Beach. Besides volleyball courts, its attraction is the La Tour landmark from 1926, a Rapunzel-tower-like structure that provides private beach access from the house above. Everyone else has to take the stairs down Victoria Drive; there's limited parking on Pacific Coast Hwy. Just south is Aliso Beach, named for the pretty mountain canyon farther inland. It's popular with surfers, and there's also a fishing pier. Parking is fairly plentiful.

Places to Stay

Accommodations get booked far in advance in summer, when prices are hiked considerably and some establishments have a minimum-stay policy of two or three nights. Options include the *Hotel Laguna* (☎ 949-494-1151, 800-524-2927, fax 949-497-2163, 425 S Coast Hwy), right on the beach, which has a pool, spa, sun terrace and a private beach club. Continental breakfast is delivered to the rooms, which cost $100 to $185 ($20 less September to April).

The family-friendly *Vacation Village* (☎ 949-494-8566, 800-843-6895, 647 S Coast Hwy), south of the Village, has 130 units, about half of them with kitchens, plus a pool and spa. Rates start at $80 in summer, $70 in the off-season; a sun-deck suite with ocean view is $288.

Romantics should try to score one of the 11 rooms at *Eiler's Inn* (☎ 949-494-3004, 741 S Coast Hwy), a B&B near Vacation Village. Antique furniture, art nouveau lamps, lots of fluffy pillows and flowery wallpaper are just some of the touches in the rooms, which are set around a central fountain courtyard where wine and cheese are served nightly. Breakfasts are memorable. There's also an ocean-view sun deck. Prices are $120 to $195 in summer ($85 to $160 October to May).

One of Laguna's most elegant establishments is the *Surf & Sand* (☎ 949-497-4477, 800-524-8621, fax 949-494-7653, 1555 S Coast Hwy). Recently renovated, it sports a natural color scheme and luxurious rooms with all the trappings; some have an ocean view. The *Splashes* restaurant serves classy California cuisine right next to the private beach. Room rates range from $225 to $375.

If you're going to splurge, though, your first choice should be the *Inn at Laguna* (☎ 949-497-9722, 800-544-4479, 949-497-9972, 211 N Coast Hwy), perched atop the cliff between Main Beach and Heisler Park. Spacious rooms are appointed with French blinds and lots of special amenities, including a selection of books, CDs and bathrobes. A lavish breakfast is delivered to your room. Rates range from $139 to $209; ocean-view rooms are $219 to $429.

The flashiest hotel in the area is the *Ritz-Carlton Laguna Niguel* (☎ 949-240-2000, 800-241-3333, fax 949-240-0829), west of Pacific Coast Hwy via Ritz-Carlton Drive, which offers lap-of-luxury accommodations in an opulent setting. There are two pools, a full spa, tennis courts, terraced paths to the beach (which happens to be a great surfing spot), a library and smoking lounge and several restaurants. Rooms start at $235. The most affordable experience here is a drink in the Lobby Lounge – a grand place to watch the sunset.

Places to Eat

A Laguna institution with one of the best views, *Las Brisas* (☎ 949-497-5434, 361 Cliff Drive), next to the Laguna Art Museum, serves Mexican seafood dishes (around $20) in the dining room and appetizers and soft tacos ($7) at the patio bar. They also have a lavish breakfast buffet with an omelet chef whisking up your favorites. The *Cottage Restaurant* (☎ 949-494-3023), across the street, is equally popular in the morning. Assets here are the big rustic tables, free newspapers and lip-smacking cranberry orange pancakes ($2.85).

Surfers, the budget-conscious and those wanting a late-night snack flock to *Taco Loco* (☎ 949-497-1635, 640 S Coast Hwy), a sidewalk cafe with a taco bar (from $1.50) as well as quesadillas, nachos and vegetarian choices, all under $5.

A local favorite is *Dizz's As Is* (☎ 949-494-5250, 2794 S Coast Hwy), in a wood-shingled 1920s house with art deco interior. The continental menu changes daily but focuses on seafood and fowl. Complete dinners include pâté, soup or salad and sourdough and range from $16 to $27. Dinner only, closed Monday.

The *White House* (☎ *949-494-8088, 340 S Coast Hwy*) serves contemporary food and turns into a bar and nightclub after dark, often with live music. More entertainment is provided by Laguna's two microbrewery pubs, the *Laguna Beach Brewing Company* (☎ *949-499-2337, 422 S Coast Hwy*) and the *Ocean Ave Brewing Company* (☎ *949-497-3381, 237 Ocean Ave*). Both have indoor and outdoor seating and serve satisfying pub grub.

Getting There & Away
To reach Laguna Beach from I-405, take Laguna Canyon Rd (Hwy 133) west. Laguna is served by the Orange County Connection bus system and by OCTA bus No 1.

Getting Around
Laguna Beach Transit (☎ 949-497-0746) has its central bus depot in the 300 block of Broadway, one block inland from the visitors bureau. It operates three routes at hourly intervals (no service between noon and 1 pm). For visitors, the most important is the Light Blue Line which travels to the hotels and beaches along Pacific Coast Hwy, terminating at the Ritz-Carlton Hotel. Ask for the self-guided bus tour pamphlets at the visitors bureau. Each ride is 75¢.

Several places in town rent bicycles, including Laguna Beach Cyclery (☎ 949-494-1522), 240 Thalia St, and Rainbow Bicycle Co (☎ 949-494-5806), 485 N Coast Hwy. Cost of a 24-hour rental is about $20.

MISSION SAN JUAN CAPISTRANO
This is one of California's most visited and most beautiful missions (☎ 949-248-2048), with a lush garden and graceful arches, located at 31882 Camino Capistrano in San Juan Capistrano. The charming Father Serra Chapel – whitewashed and decorated with colorful symbols – is the only building still standing in which Father Junípero Serra said Mass. Serra founded this mission on

Father Junípero Serra

November 1, 1776, and tended it personally for many years. With access to San Clemente harbor, and as the only development between San Diego and Los Angeles, this was one of the most important missions in the chain. Like most, it was a gathering point for travelers and local land owners, and was largely self-sustaining, with it own mills, granaries, livestock, crops and other small industries.

Plan on spending at least an hour looking at the grounds and exhibits in the mission museum. The bookstore and gift shop both have materials on early California history, and particularly on the missions. The mission is open daily 8:30 am to 5 pm; $5/4.

San Juan Capistrano is also where the legendary swallows return each year – on March 19, the feast of Saint Joseph – after wintering in South America, just as the song says.

Surrounding the mission are converted adobes that now house Mexican restaurants, art galleries and gift shops. Two blocks south, across Via Capistrano, is a historic district with several adobes dating back to the mission's founding.

Getting There & Away
The San Juan Capistrano Amtrak station (☎ 949-240-2972), housed in a converted rail

car one block from the mission at 26701 Verdugo St (behind L'Hirondelle restaurant), gets eight southbound and 10 northbound trains per day en route between Los Angeles and San Diego. OCTA bus No 91 stops in front of the station and goes south to Pacific Coast Hwy, where the No 1 heads north to Orange County beach cities.

San Diego Area

San Diego County covers 4200 sq miles, extending about 60 miles between Orange and Riverside counties to the north and the Mexican border in the south, and about 70 miles from the Pacific seashore over the coastal mountain range to the deserts of Anza-Borrego. The area has a great variety of landscapes, a superb coastline and a near-perfect climate. Its population of more than 2.7 million people is growing at an estimated rate of 11,000 per month.

People looking for a laid-back California lifestyle are often disappointed with the pace and pollution of Los Angeles but find what they want farther south. Comfortable, generally affluent San Diego lacks the high profile and international recognizability of San Francisco or LA, but it's a very pleasant place to visit, especially if you like beaches, water sports or (contrary to the city's sporty image) theater.

The metropolitan part of the county includes the city of San Diego and a number of diverse suburban communities, from La Jolla and Coronado to San Ysidro (for information about the northern and eastern parts of the county and the Mexican city of Tijuana, see the Around San Diego section). Anza-Borrego State Park, actually in San Diego County, is covered in the chapter on the California Deserts.

San Diego

• **population 1.2 million**

HISTORY

As a city San Diego is relatively new. Though human occupation of the area goes back a long time, there are few sites in the county that are genuinely older than a century. The long period of Native American habitation has not left many tangible remains, and despite an abundance of Spanish place names and Spanish-style architecture, only half a dozen structures in

Highlights

• Talk to the animals – the world-class San Diego Zoo

• Balboa Park – museums galore and gardens too

• Cabrillo National Monument – stunning vistas of city and sea

• Like, totally So-Cal – shopping, surfing and caving in La Jolla

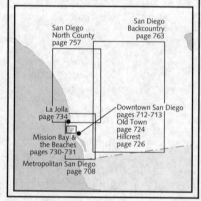

the county actually date from the periods of Spanish and Mexican rule.

Native Peoples

San Diego's coastal area and the periphery of the Salton Sea hold middens (ancient refuse heaps) that date back 20,000 years, making this some of the oldest known human-inhabited land in the US. The Hokan-speaking Kumeyaay had the largest territory, from the coast to the low desert and from south of what's now the Mexican border to near present-day Oceanside. They were mostly dry-land farmers but also traded goods from the Pacific Ocean with tribes from the Colorado River area. The most distinctive artifacts of the Kumeyaay are baskets and nets skillfully woven from sage, tulle, reeds and grasses. In the north, the Ute-Aztecan-speaking Luiseño/Juaneño people lived on the coast and the slopes of Mt Palomar (as some of their descendants still do); they were famed for their sand paintings.

With the arrival of the Spanish, the cultural identity of the various native groups was severely compromised by Catholic missionaries who, as Dolan Eargle Jr (a local Native American author and historian) says, 'were more interested in preserving souls than customs' (see the Facts about California chapter). After various conflicts with these missionaries, most native peoples were put on reservations. There are 12 Kumeyaay reservations in San Diego, including the Viejas and Barona reservations, which are known for their thriving gambling operations. Descendants of the Luiseño and Juaneño peoples still live at the foot of Mt Palomar – on the Pala, Rincon, La Jolla and Pechanga reservations – near the sites of traditional villages. They are said to have experienced less cultural destruction than the Kumeyaay.

The Museum of Man in Balboa Park has excellent exhibits and authentic handicrafts of San Diego's native peoples (see the Balboa Park section in this chapter).

Mission Period

Juan Rodríguez Cabrillo, captain of the first European expedition to come to California, sailed into San Diego Bay in 1542 and claimed the land for Spain. His ships sat out a storm in San Diego Bay, which he named San Miguel, and after six days they continued their northward journey. The next Spaniard to arrive was Sebastián Vizcaíno in 1602. He entered the bay on the feast day of San Diego de Alcalá and could not resist renaming the place San Diego. He and his crew recorded their findings and moved on.

In the 1760s, Spanish interest in Alta (upper) California was reawakened when British, French and Russian rulers started sending scouts to the area. In 1769, under Gaspar de Portolá and Father Junípero Serra, 40 men founded a military outpost and the first of the California missions on the hill now known as the Presidio. Disease struck the settlement from the beginning, and the Kumeyaay made a number of attacks; 19 of the original settlers died in the first six months, and the mission was almost abandoned. The mission eventually achieved some stability at the time of its strongest influence, there were 1500 converted Kumeyaay in the congregation.

Missionary activity spread to the north, and other missions were also established in the San Diego area, including San Luis Rey Francia in 1798, and the *asistencias* (satellite missions) of San Antonio de Pala (1815) and Santa Ysabel (1818).

After Mexico won its independence from Spain in 1821, the grants of land for 'ranchos' and the breakup of the missions (around 1833) displaced the Native Americans. Many of the Kumeyaay fell into poverty and, as means of survival, began raids on isolated ranchos and travelers. The small community of San Diego became a civilian pueblo in 1835, with an alcalde (a combination mayor and magistrate) who had wide powers and dispensed harsh justice to rebellious Indians. Although the ranchos were prosperous, San Diego itself remained a ramshackle village at the base of the Presidio hill, with only a few hundred residents.

Early American Period

The 1849 Gold Rush bypassed San Diego, as did the first rail link to Southern California, and by 1855 the population was still only about 800 and dependent on stagecoaches. In the 1850s William Heath Davis, a former sea captain and San Francisco property speculator, bought 160 acres of bayfront land and erected prefabricated houses, a wharf and warehouses. But the development, dubbed Davis' Folly, was ahead of its time and failed to attract either commercial or government support. In 1867 Alonzo E Horton, another San Francisco speculator and businessman, acquired 960 acres of waterfront land and promoted it as 'New Town.' This time the new subdivision prospered, especially after 1872 when a fire devastated much of the settlement near Presidio hill.

The discovery of gold in the hills east of San Diego in 1869 started a frenetic mining boom that lasted until around 1874 – the town of Julian is one of the few surviving gold-mining settlements. In 1884, the rush brought the railroad to San Diego, but after the gold played out, the population fell from 4000 to 2000. Despite the efforts of the city's boosters, San Diego did not acquire an industrial base in the 19th century – a time when the main economic activity was real estate speculation – and the city saw several cycles of boom and bust.

Panama-California Exposition

To celebrate the completion of the Panama Canal in 1914, San Francisco hosted the Panama-Pacific International Exposition. San Diego, not to be ignored, held its own exposition, which ran for most of 1915 and 1916. In an effort to give the city a distinctive image, the exposition buildings were deliberately designed in a romantic, Spanish-Mexican style. Developers, architects and the public took to this fashion with enthusiasm. San Diego's Mediterranean style, mission-style architecture and Spanish street

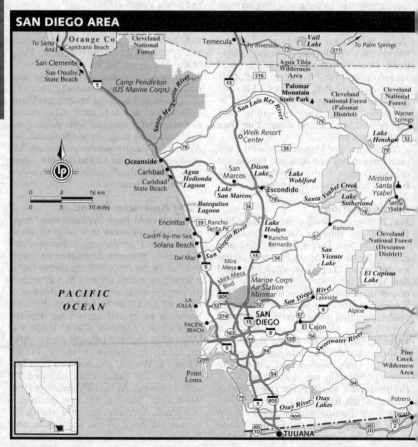

SAN DIEGO AREA

names derive more from this conscious image-building than from the city's actual heritage as a small and remote colonial Spanish outpost.

Modern San Diego

Aviation pioneer Glenn H Curtiss, who operated a flight camp in San Diego during the early part of the 20th century, helped develop ship-based aircraft on San Diego Bay, and the city became a center for US naval aviation. Ryan Airlines built the *Spirit of St Louis* for Lindbergh's transatlantic

SAN DIEGO AREA

Santa Rosa
Mountains
Scenic Area

Salton
Sea

86

Riverside County
San Diego County

To Salton
Sea

Borrego
Springs

S22

S22

S53

S2

78

To Brawley

78

Anza-Borrego
Desert
State Park

Julian

79

Cuyamaca
Rancho
State Park

S1

79   Mt Laguna

Descanso

S2

Pine
Valley

To El
Centro

Lake
Moreno

S1   94

8

Campo

MEX
2

MEXICO

MEX
2

Imperial County

Laguna Mountains

flight in 1927, and Consolidated Aircraft opened its factory in 1931 – San Diego at last had an industry. A steady revenue from naval and military bases helped San Diego weather the Great Depression, along with federal Work Projects Administration (WPA) projects such as the racetrack at Del Mar and San Diego State University. There were, nevertheless, shantytowns of poor immigrants from the Dust Bowl and other depressed areas around the country. In 1935, as the depression eased, San Diego staged another big event, the California-Pacific Exposition, which added even more Hispanic architecture to Balboa Park.

Following the bombing of Pearl Harbor in 1941, the headquarters of the US Pacific Fleet was moved from Hawaii to San Diego. The boom in wartime activity transformed the city: the harbor was dredged and landfill islands were built, vast tracts of instant housing appeared, public spaces were turned into training camps, storage depots and hospitals, and the population doubled in a couple of years. The war, the Marines, the Navy and naval aviators were the subjects of films showcasing San Diego (albeit incidentally) from *Guadalcanal* to the *Sands of Iwo Jima*. Its wartime role, more than anything else, put San Diego on the American map.

Postwar San Diego became a booming city in a booming state. The naval and military presence provided an expanding core of activity, employing up to a quarter of the workforce. The climate and a seafront location have also been major factors in the city's growth. Recreation facilities such as Mission Bay help attract visitors, who now contribute a big slice of the county's income. Education and research (especially in biotechnology) are now major activities too, while the San Diego Padres baseball team and the San Diego Chargers football team have both been positive representatives of the city.

ORIENTATION

San Diego is a pretty easy place to find your way around. The airport, train station and Greyhound terminal are all in or near the downtown area, which is a compact grid east of San Diego Bay. The main north-south

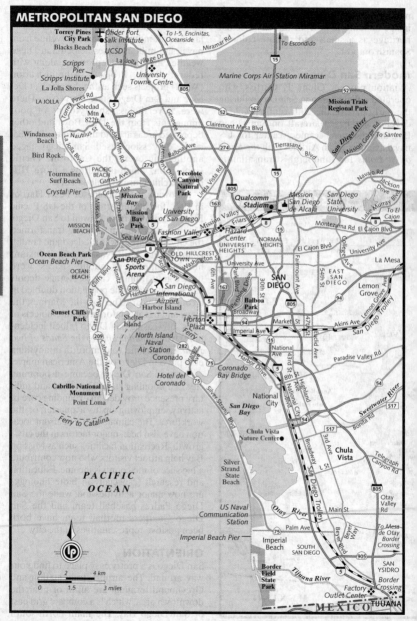

METROPOLITAN SAN DIEGO

freeway is I-5, which parallels the coast from the Camp Pendleton Marine Corps Base in the north to the Mexican border at San Ysidro. Also running north to south, I-805 is a detour from I-5, bypassing the downtown area to the east. Interstate 8 runs east from Ocean Beach, up the valley of the San Diego River (called Mission Valley), past suburbs such as El Cajon and on to the Imperial Valley and Arizona.

It's difficult to appreciate the topography as you cruise the freeways, which often follow the valleys and incorporate steep hillsides into overpasses and interchanges. A close look at a map will reveal lots of places called 'mesa' ('table' in Spanish), which are separated by valleys and canyons such as Carmel Valley, Carrol Canyon, Mission Valley and Telegraph Canyon.

Waterfront attractions along the Embarcadero are just west of the downtown grid. Balboa Park, with its many museums and famous zoo, is in the northeast corner of the city, and Old Town, San Diego's original site, is a couple of miles northwest of downtown. Above Old Town, the Presidio hill overlooks Mission Valley, now a freeway and a commercial corridor, and just to the east is Hillcrest, the center of the city's gay and lesbian community (it's in the heart of Uptown; see the Uptown & Hillcrest section). Coronado, with its well-known 1888-vintage Hotel del Coronado, is across San Diego Bay, accessible by a long bridge or a short ferry ride. At the entrance to the bay, Point Loma offers great views over sea and city from the Cabrillo National Monument. Mission Bay, northwest of downtown, has lagoons, parks and facilities for many recreational activities. The nearby coast – with Ocean Beach, Mission Beach and Pacific Beach – epitomizes the Southern California beach scene, while La Jolla, a little further north, is a more upscale seaside community and the home of the University of California at San Diego (UCSD).

INFORMATION
Tourist Offices
The San Diego Convention & Visitors Bureau (☎ 619-236-1212), 401 B St, will send a complimentary vacation planning guide anywhere in the world and has a good web page (www.sandiego.org). The Greater San Diego Chamber of Commerce (☎ 619-232-0124, www.sdchamber.org) provides lists of accommodations and restaurants.

Downtown, the International Visitors Information Center (☎ 619-236-1212) is on 1st Ave at F St – it's on the side of the Horton Plaza complex, at 11 Horton Plaza. The center has free printed information and a knowledgeable staff. It's open 8:30 am to 5 pm Monday to Saturday, and also 11 am to 5 pm on Sunday in summer. Near the Gaslamp trolley stop at the corner of 6th Ave and L St, the International Information Center (☎ 619-232-8583) is multimedia-based and offers free Internet access, as well as coupons, hotel reservations and custom itineraries. It's open 10 am to 5 pm Tuesday through Sunday (closed Sunday in winter).

Another visitor center (☎ 619-276-8200), at E Mission Bay Drive, off the Clairemont Drive exit of I-15, is convenient and easy to find. The center has tons of brochures, many with discount coupons, but the staffers aren't quite as informative as those in the downtown offices. Hours are 9 am to sunset daily.

There's a Travelers Aid desk at the airport's East Terminal (☎ 619-231-7361) open 8 am to 11 pm daily.

The information office for Balboa Park (☎ 619-239-0512), in the park's House of Hospitality, gives museum hours, prices and current exhibition listings. Coronado's Visitors Bureau (☎ 619-437-8788), 1047 B Ave, focuses on places to stay, eat and be entertained. The Gaslamp Quarter Council (☎ 619-233-5227), 614 5th Ave, suite E, has information, brochures and books about the Gaslamp Quarter.

For information about state parks in San Diego County, go to the Old Town State Historic Park visitor center (☎ 619-220-5427) in the Seely Stables at the end of the plaza at Old Town. It's open 10 am to 5 pm daily.

Money
American Express has a downtown office (☎ 619-234-4455) at 258 Broadway, and a La Jolla branch (☎ 619-459-4161) in downtown

La Jolla at the corner of Girard and Prospect Sts. Thomas Cook has offices on the ground level of Horton Plaza and at 4525 La Jolla Village Drive in the University Towne Centre.

Post & Communications

The downtown post office (☎ 800-275-8777), 815 E St, is open 8:30 am to 5 pm weekdays and 8:30 am to noon on Saturday. General delivery mail goes to the Midway postal station (zip code 92138), which is inconveniently located between downtown and Mission Bay at 2535 Midway Drive, just off Barnett.

Local calls cover only a small area. A pay phone may want a small handful of quarters for a few minutes' call across town – have a credit card ready when you can.

Bookstores

Every shopping mall has at least one bookshop, usually of the large, chain-owned kind. The University of California at San Diego has an excellent bookstore (☎ 619-534-7323) on campus and a branch downtown in the American Plaza opposite the train station. Downtown, Wahrenbrooks Book House (☎ 619-232-0132), 726 Broadway, and William Burgett (☎ 619-238-7323), at the corner of 7th Ave and C St, are the most established stores. La Jolla has DG Wills (☎ 619-456-1800), 7461 Girard Ave, with an outstanding selection of used, rare and out-of-print books.

In the unlikely, touristy setting of Old Town's Bazaar del Mundo, Libros (☎ 619-299-1139) has a good selection of San Diego history books and books in Spanish. Adams Ave Book Row – a concentration of bookstores that excites even the most jaded book hounds – is a great place to browse away an afternoon. Adams Ave is north of I-8 between US 805 and I-15.

There are a number of shops specializing in travel books. Le Travel Store (☎ 619-544-0005), 745 4th Ave in the Gaslamp, has a helpful staff and an excellent selection of maps, travel guides and accessories. Traveler's Depot (☎ 619-483-1421), 1655 Garnet Ave, Pacific Beach, also has a good inventory.

Newspapers & Magazines

The daily *San Diego Union-Tribune* is not a bad daily newspaper, but the *Los Angeles Times* and the *New York Times* are conspicuously available, even from sidewalk vending machines. For information on what's happening in town, and particularly on the active music, art, and theater scene, pick up a free *San Diego Reader* from just about any convenience store or cafe. It comes out every Thursday, but copies can all be gone by the weekend.

A number of free publications have useful information and discount coupons mixed in with the advertisements. The widely available *San Diego This Week,* which actually comes out twice a month, has coupons and listings of events. The *Guide to Downtown* is a similar magazine, which emphasizes downtown eating and entertainment.

Medical Services

Urgent medical attention is available 24 hours a day at Mercy Hospital (☎ 619-294-8111), 4077 5th Ave, and Mission Bay Hospital (☎ 619-274-7721), 3030 Bunker Hill St.

For problems in the ocean or near the shore, contact the nearest lifeguard – look for the bright orange trucks – or go to the nearest lifeguard tower. You can call headquarters (☎ 619-224-2708) for medical inquiries but you should dial 911 for life-threatening emergencies.

Useful Organizations

Gay & Lesbian Travelers The Center (☎ 619-692-2077), at 3916 Normal St, Hillcrest, provides health information and counseling from 9 am to 10 pm daily. Hillcrest is the center of San Diego's gay community, and all sorts of gay-oriented material is available there – look for *Gay & Lesbian Times* published Thursdays.

Automobile Associations The downtown AAA office (☎ 619-233-1000), 815 Date St, has all the AAA maps and tour books. There's another AAA office (☎ 619-483-4960) at 4973 Clairemont Drive, Clairemont, about 9 miles north of downtown, and several others throughout the county.

Disabled Travelers The Access Center (☎ 619-293-3500, TDD 619-293-7757), 1295 University Ave Hillcrest, can refer you to wheelchair-accessible accommodations and wheelchair sale and repair facilities. It's open 9 am to 5 pm weekdays. Accessible San Diego (☎ 619-279-0704), downtown in the Executive Complex Building at 1010 2nd Ave, sells the *Access Guide* ($5) with visitor information on transport, accommodations, attractions and tours. The Metro Transit System has dozens of routes with wheelchair-accessible buses and trolleys. Its information line (☎ 619-233-3004, TTY/TDD 619-234-5005) can give specific information.

Dangers & Annoyances

Areas of interest to visitors are quite well-defined and mostly within easy reach of downtown by foot or by public transportation. San Diego is a fairly safe city, though you should be cautious venturing east of about 6th Ave in downtown, especially after dark. Hostile panhandling is the most common problem.

DOWNTOWN

San Diego's downtown is adjacent to the waterfront in the area first acquired, subdivided and promoted by Alonzo Horton in 1867. Most of the land on the water-side of the trolley line is landfill: until the mid-1920s the south end of 5th Ave was the main unloading dock for cargo boats, and junkets and fishing boats used to be tied where the Convention Center now stands.

In the 1960s, downtown was a combination of uninteresting office developments and creeping inner-urban dereliction. Since then, redevelopment (begun in the '70s) has saved downtown San Diego. Today, a number of pre-1900 'skyscrapers' still stand among their towering mirrored contemporaries. Horton Plaza and the Gaslamp Quarter are the primary hubs for shopping, dining and entertainment, while the Embarcadero is good for a harbor-side stroll. There is enough of interest in these key areas to make a trip downtown worthwhile, but don't expect the traffic, hustle-bustle and cosmopolitan flair of a truly big-city experience.

The main drag is Broadway, which goes east from the waterfront right through the middle of town. It's a functional street, with the Santa Fe train station and the trolley depot at one end, a few cheap hotels, the bus station and a couple of top-end hotels at the other. The large, popular Horton Plaza shopping mall occupies a seven-block area south of Broadway, while the renovated Gaslamp Quarter extends for about eight blocks between 4th and 6th Aves from Broadway south to Harbor Drive and the Embarcadero. East of the Gaslamp is an area that is gradually being redeveloped in anticipation of a new Padres baseball stadium, slated to open in 2002. At the moment, the newly dubbed 'East Village' (possibly so named by civic boosters to make it sound like a potentially prosperous area) is where there are soup kitchens, homeless shelters and the Salvation Army.

In the northwest corner of downtown, Little Italy is a vibrant Italian-American neighborhood and one of the most pleasant places to stay – handy to the freeway, walking distance to the harbor and close to good eats.

Horton Plaza Center

This is the centerpiece of San Diego's downtown redevelopment. Conceived and promoted by mall developer Ernie Hahn, this huge project involved the leveling of seven city blocks and the construction of a five-level complex with 2300 parking spaces. It has a multiscreen cinema, two live theaters, restaurants, cafes and 140 shops lining an open courtyard. It was designed by Jon Jerde, a controversial California-based urban architect, using the 'festival-marketplace' concept of urban renewal, in which a congregation of vendors with separate facades and entrances set up shop in one unified space. It was completed in 1985 at a cost of more than $145 million.

From the outside the plaza is not very inviting (critics say it 'turns its back on downtown' which, at the time of construction, was really run-down). Inside, it has the toy-town arches and balconies typical of postmodernism. A 1907 Jessop Clock (big

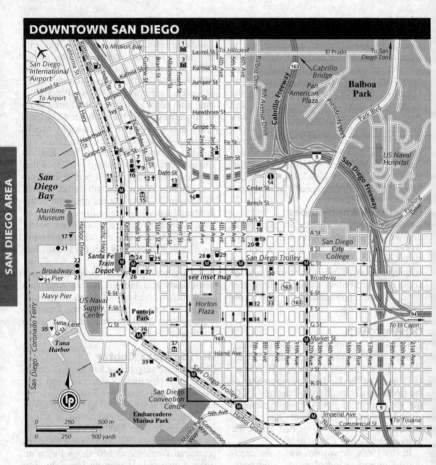

DOWNTOWN SAN DIEGO

and four-sided) provides a touch of nostalgia, and the color scheme is anything but dull. The top-floor food court is not cheap but has inventive signage and is a great place for people-watching. The curved spaces and changes in level can be disorienting – in places it feels as if you're walking through an MC Escher drawing.

The Horton Plaza Center (☎ 619-238-1596) is open 10 am to 9 pm weekdays, 10 am to 7 pm Saturday and 11 am to 6 pm Sunday, though some shops and restaurants have extended hours. The main pedestrian

entrance is on Broadway. Parking is validated with purchase.

Gaslamp Quarter

When Horton first established New Town San Diego in 1867, 5th Ave was its main street and home to its main industries – saloons, gambling joints, bordellos and opium dens. While more respectable businesses grew up along Broadway, the 5th Ave area became known as the Stingaree, a notorious red-light district. By the 1960s it had declined to a skid row of flophouses and

DOWNTOWN SAN DIEGO

PLACES TO STAY
- 5 Corinthian Suites
- 8 La Pensione Hotel
- 11 Econo Lodge
- 16 Pacifica Hotel
- 18 Comfort Inn Downtown
- 19 Marriott Suites
- 27 Inn at the YMCA
- 30 Churchill Hotel
- 32 Maryland Hotel
- 34 Villager Lodge
- 39 Hyatt Regency
- 40 Marriott Hotel & Marina
- 43 Westgate Hotel
- 44 US Grant Hotel
- 46 Westin Horton Plaza
- 51 Ramada Inn
- 62 Grand Pacific Hostel
- 69 San Diego Hostel
- 73 Horton Grand Hotel
- 75 J Street Inn

PLACES TO EAT
- 4 Mona Lisa
- 7 Filippi's Pizza Grotto
- 9 Mimmo's Italian Village
- 17 Anthony's Fish Grotto
- 35 The Fish Market, Top of the Market
- 36 Kansas City Barbeque
- 45 Gyroscope
- 47 Planet Hollywood
- 49 Rubio's
- 50 Dakota Grill
- 52 Croce's Top Hat Bar & Grill
- 54 Fio's Cucina Italiana
- 56 El Indio
- 59 Olé Madrid
- 60 La Provence
- 63 Trattoria La Strada
- 65 The Cheese Shop
- 67 Buffalo Joe's
- 70 Cafe Sevilla
- 74 Royal Thai
- 77 Dick's Last Resort

BARS & CLUBS
- 2 Casbah
- 6 The Waterfront
- 25 Old Columbia Brewery & Grill
- 29 4th & B
- 53 Patrick's II
- 58 The Bitter End
- 78 Hang Ten Brewing Company

OTHER
- 1 Timkin House
- 3 Long-Waterman House
- 10 Caffe Italia
- 12 Our Lady of the Rosary Catholic Church
- 13 New World Coffee
- 14 AAA
- 15 Firehouse Museum
- 20 Copley Symphony Hall
- 21 Cruise Ship Terminal
- 22 Hornblower/Invader Cruises
- 23 San Diego Harbor Excursion
- 24 Museum of Contemporary Art
- 26 UCSD Bookstore
- 28 Civic Theatre
- 31 Ferry Landing
- 33 Post Office
- 37 San Diego Children's Museum
- 38 Seaport Village
- 41 Transit Store
- 42 Spreckels Theater
- 48 Balboa Theatre
- 55 International Visitors Information Center
- 57 Cafe Lulu
- 61 Le Travel Store
- 64 Gaslamp 15
- 66 Old City Hall
- 68 Gaslamp Books & Antiques
- 71 Museum of Death
- 72 William Heath Davis House, Gaslamp Quarter Historical Foundation
- 76 Chinese Mission Building

SAN DIEGO AREA

---

bars, but its seedy atmosphere made it so unattractive to developers that many of its older buildings survived when others around town were being razed. In the early 1980s, when developers started thinking about demolition and rebuilding, local protests and the Gaslamp Quarter Council saved the area.

Wrought-iron streetlamps, in the style of 19th-century gas lamps, were installed, along with trees and brick sidewalks. Restored buildings dating from the 1870s to the 1920s now house restaurants, bars, galleries and

theaters. The 16-block area south of Broadway between 4th and 6th Aves is designated a National Historic District, and development is strictly controlled. There's still a bit of sleaze though, with a few adult entertainment shops and some very downmarket hotels, but they give some character to the area, which might otherwise have become gentrified beyond recognition. An enjoyable time to visit is on a warm evening when people throng the streets and crowd the outdoor tables (see the Places to Eat and Entertainment sections later in this chapter).

To get a feel for Gaslamp Quarter architecture and history, it's better to come and walk around during the day.

To get a full historical picture of the Gaslamp Quarter, take one of the guided walking tours offered by the Gaslamp Quarter Historical Foundation from their headquarters in the **William Heath Davis House**. The 2-hour tour starts at 11 am Saturday and costs $5, students and seniors $3.

The William Heath Davis House is at the corner of Island and 4th Sts. It is one of 14 prefabricated houses that Davis brought from Maine in 1850, though he never actually lived in this one. The building is very plain, of a type frankly called a 'saltbox,' and contains a small museum with 19th-century furnishings. You can call the Gaslamp Quarter Historical Foundation (☎ 619-233-4692) for museum hours and tour information.

At 413 Market St is **Gaslamp Books & Antiques**, which doubles as a museum, since the owner displays all sorts of memorabilia that he's collected during his 50-plus years in San Diego. It's worth a look and is free. At the 5th Ave and G St intersection, the Italianate building on the southwest corner is the Old City Hall (1874). In the faux-casket-style basement (the walls are quilted with satiny coffin-lining material) of the Marin Building (1870) at 548 5th Ave, the **Museum of Death** (☎ 619-338-8153), has a collection of gruesome, real-life road kill pictures, various execution devices and art by infamous American murderers such as Charles Manson. It's an odd place and probably worth the $3 admission, unless it makes you lose your $4 lunch. It's open noon to midnight Friday and Saturday and noon to 10 pm the rest of the week.

The heart of San Diego's China Town has always been on 3rd Ave (although it has spread out considerably in recent years). At the corner of J St, the **Chinese Mission Building** was designed by Louis J Gill (minimalist San Diego architect Irving Gill's nephew) and houses the San Diego Chinese Historical Museum (☎ 619-338-9888). Built in the 1920s, it's a small, stucco building with red tiles decorating the roofline, hardwood floors and a nice backyard. Hours are 10:30 am to 4 pm Tuesday to Saturday, noon to 4 pm Sunday.

Museum of Contemporary Art

Opposite the train station and adjacent to the San Diego Trolley stop at 1001 Kettner Blvd, the MCA (☎ 619-234-1001) is the downtown branch of the La Jolla-based institution that has shown innovative artwork to San Diegans since the 1960s. The ever-changing exhibits of painting and sculpture are publicized widely (see the *Reader* or call the gallery). The museum is open 10:30 am to 5:30 pm Tuesday to Sunday; $2, $1 students and seniors, free the first Sunday and first Tuesday of every month.

San Diego Children's Museum

Young children enjoy this interactive place. There are giant construction toys, spaces for painting and modeling, a stage with costumes for impromptu theater, as well as storytelling, music, activities and changing exhibits. The museum (☎ 619-233-8792), 200 Island Ave, is open 10 am to 3 pm Tuesday to Friday and 10 am to 4 pm weekends (closed Monday); $6 for ages two and up.

Little Italy

Between Hawthorn and Ash Sts on the north and south, and Front St and the waterfront on the east and west, is San Diego's Little Italy. The area was settled in the mid-19th century by Italian immigrants, mostly fishermen and their families, who created a cohesive and thriving community. They enjoyed a booming fish industry and whiskey trade (which some claim was backed by local Mafia).

When I-5 was completed in 1962, the heart (and, many say, soul) of the area was destroyed. Buildings were condemned and entire blocks were demolished for the freeway's construction. After its completion, increased traffic turned pedestrian streets and harbor access routes into busy thoroughfares. Still, the area (especially along India St) is a good place to find imported foods (see the Places to Eat section), Italian newspapers and people who speak with their hands as much as with their mouths. There are also some furniture and art stores that cater to the architects who have recently found the neighborhood interesting. Check out the newish live-work lofts on Kettner Blvd between Fir and Grape Sts designed collectively by four architecture firms that won a competition to build on the space after it was abandoned by a major supermarket chain.

Built in 1925, **Our Lady of the Rosary Catholic Church**, at the corner of State and Date Sts, is still a hub of Little Italy activity. Its rich ceiling murals, painted by an Italian who was flown over to do the work, are among San Diego's best pieces of religious art. Across the street in Amici Park, locals play *boccia*, a leisurely form of outdoor bowling.

The **Firehouse Museum** (☎ 619-232-3473), 1572 Columbia St at Cedar St, preserves a historical collection of fire-fighting equipment and has exhibits depicting some of San Diego's 'hottest' moments. Hours are 10 am to 2 pm Thursday and Friday, 10 am to 4 pm weekends; $2.

EMBARCADERO

San Diego's waterfront, built almost entirely on landfill, is about 500 yards wider than it was in the late 1800s. The result is a well-manicured area to the west of downtown that is clean and attractive. Since most of the shipyards and naval facilities are farther southeast (near the Coronado Bay Bridge) and down at National City (see the South Bay & Chula Vista section), this area is geared toward pedestrian pleasure seekers. You can take a pleasant walk along the Embarcadero from the Maritime Museum, past ships and seafood restaurants, to Seaport Village and the San Diego Convention Center.

Maritime Museum

The Maritime Museum (☎ 619-234-9153) consists of three restored vessels moored at 1306 N Harbor Drive, just north of the Ash St corner. It's not hard to find the museum, as the masts of the square-rigger *Star of India*, more than 100 feet high, make a good landmark. Built on the Isle of Man and launched in 1863, the tall ship plied the England-India trade route, carried immigrants to New Zealand, became a trading ship based in Hawaii and, finally, worked the Alaskan salmon fisheries. It's a handsome ship, but don't expect anything romantic or glamorous on board; this is an old workhorse, not the Love Boat. Also moored here are tall ships the *Berkeley* and the *Medea*.

The museum is open 9 am to 8 pm daily, and the $5 ticket buys admission to all three vessels; $4 seniors and teens, $2 children.

Seaport Village

Neither a port nor a real village, this collection of novelty shops, restaurants and snack outlets has an unconvincing maritime theme with ersatz turn-of-the-century seafront architecture. It's touristy and twee, but not a bad place to look for souvenirs and have a bite to eat. Seaport Village (☎ 619-235-4014) is open 10 am to 9 pm daily (to 10 pm in summer), and there are two hours of free validated parking with any purchase.

San Diego Convention Center

Built in a successful attempt to promote the city as a site for major conventions, this unusual-looking complex opened in 1989 and is booked solid more than 5 years into the 21st century. There's a plan to double its size in the not-too-distant future. The design, by Canadian avant-garde architect Arthur Erickson, was said to have been inspired by an ocean liner. It features large cylindrical windows (portholes?) and a roof space sheltered by white Teflon 'sails.' The convention center (☎ 619-525-5000) sometimes offers tours and is open most days if you want to have a look inside.

Look past the masts in the nearby Marriott's marina for **Embarcadero Marina Park**, where there's a public fishing pier and an open-air amphitheater, which presents free concerts on summer evenings.

BALBOA PARK

Maps dating from 1868 that show Alonzo Horton's planned additions to San Diego included a 1400-acre City Park at the northeast corner of what was to become the

SAN DIEGO AREA

SAN DIEGO AREA

downtown area. The decision to provide for such a large park is usually attributed to far-sighted civic leaders, but it was probably also consistent with the short-term interests of the shrewd Mr Horton. By restricting the areas available for future development, the value of the land in his subdivision would be enhanced. Though the expansive park looked good on the map, it was still bare hill-tops, chaparral and steep-sided arroyos (water-carved gullies) until 1892 when Kate Sessions started her nursery on the site, paying rent to the city in trees (100 per year; see the boxed text later in this chapter).

By the turn of the century, Balboa Park had became a well-loved part of San Diego, and a contest was held to find a suitable name. The winning entry honored Vasco Núñez de Balboa, a Spanish conquistador and the first European to sight the Pacific Ocean.

The 1915-16 Panama-California Exposition developed the Spanish colonial theme even further. Irving Gill's modern, minimalist architecture was rejected in favor of the beaux arts style and baroque decoration of New Yorkers Bertram Goodhue and Carlton Winslow. The exposition buildings were meant to be temporary and were constructed largely of stucco, chicken wire, plaster, hemp and horsehair. They were so popular, however, that many continued to be used. As the originals deteriorated, they were replaced with durable concrete structures. These buildings now house the museums along El Prado, the main pedestrian thoroughfare in the park.

The Pacific-California Exposition was staged in Balboa Park in 1935, with new buildings erected southwest of El Prado around the Pan-American Plaza. Architecturally, the Spanish colonial theme was expanded to include the whole New World, from indigenous styles (some of the buildings had Pueblo Indian and even Mayan influences) through the 20th century. Most of these have been preserved too and now house other exhibits, museums and theaters.

The San Diego Zoo occupies 200 acres in the north of the park, and the eastern third is occupied by the sports facilities of Morley Field, with tennis courts, a swimming pool, a velodrome, nine- and 18-hole golf courses, and even a golf course designed for playing with Frisbees. About a quarter of the original 1400 acres has been given over to the Cabrillo Freeway, the US Naval Hospital and other non-park uses.

But Balboa Park retains extensive and beautiful green areas and a large assortment of things to see and do.

Orientation & Information

If you just want to enjoy the gardens and the atmosphere, you can visit Balboa Park any time and just stroll around, but be cautious after dark. To visit all the museums and attractions would take days, so it's a good idea to plan your visit. Note that many museums are closed Monday and several per week (on a rotating basis) are free Tuesday.

The Balboa Passport (available at the Information Center) costs $21 and is good for a single entry to 12 of the park's museums for one week. If you come on Tuesday, or only want to see a couple of the museums, the passport is not such a good deal. Most of the museums are open from about 10 am to 4:30 pm. The Balboa Park Information Center (☎ 619-239-0512), open 9 am to 4 pm daily, is in the House of Hospitality at 1549 El Prado and has a helpful staff and a good park map.

Balboa Park is easily reached from downtown on a buses No 7, 7A or 7B along Park Blvd. By car, Park Blvd provides easy access to free parking areas near most of the exhibits, but the most scenic approach is over the Cabrillo Bridge. From the west, El Prado is an extension of Laurel St, which crosses Cabrillo Bridge with the Cabrillo Freeway 120 feet below. Make a point of driving this stretch of freeway (State Hwy 163) – the steep roadsides, lush with hanging greenery, look like a rain-forest gorge.

The free Balboa Park Tram stops at various points on a continuous loop through the main areas of the park. (It's actually a bus rather than a tram and is not to be confused with the Old Town Trolley tour bus.) For the most part, however, it's more enjoyable to walk between the attractions.

A tip for winter visitors: the first Friday and Saturday in December, Christmas on the Prado brings free entrance to most museums and turns El Prado into a showcase of performance art, crafts and international food.

California Building & Museum of Man

El Prado passes under an archway and into an area called the California Quadrangle, with the **Museum of Man** (done in the classical revival style) on its north side. Figures on either side of the arch represent the Atlantic and Pacific Oceans, while the decoration of the arch itself symbolizes the Panama Canal linking the two. This was the main entrance for the 1915 exposition, and the building was one of Goodhue's most ornate Spanish colonial revival creations, said to be inspired by the churrigueresque church of Tepotzotlán near Mexico City. Its single **Tower of California**, richly decorated with blue and yellow tiles, is an architectural landmark of San Diego.

Originally, the building displayed more than 5000 ethnographic artifacts, including some that were specially made for the exposition – the cast concrete reproductions of Mayan carvings are still on display. The museum now specializes in Indian artifacts from the American Southwest and has an excellent display of baskets and pottery from the San Diego area. The museum store sells good handicrafts from Central America and elsewhere. The Museum of Man (☎ 619-239-2001) is open 10 am to 4:30 pm daily, $5/3, adults/children 6-17, free on the third Tuesday of each month.

Simon Edison Centre for the Performing Arts

This complex includes three theaters. Best known is **The Old Globe**, where visitors to the 1935-36 exposition enjoyed 40-minute renditions of Shakespeare's greatest hits. Saved from demolition in 1937, the theater became home to a popular summer series of Shakespeare plays, which were performed in full. In 1978 the whole complex was destroyed by an arson fire, but was rebuilt in the style of the original 17th-century Old Globe in England. It reopened in 1982, winning a Tony award in 1984 for its ongoing contribution to theater arts. The Old Globe, plus the **Cassius Carter Stage** and the outdoor **Lowell Davies Festival Theater**, are at the heart of San Diego's live-theater scene. There are performances most evenings and matinees on weekends (☎ 619-239-2255). Guided tours run on some weekends (☎ 619-231-1941).

Plaza de Panama

This space, in the middle of El Prado, was at the center of the Panama-California Exposition. The equestrian statue on the south side is of **El Cid**, who led the Spanish revolt against the Moors in the 11th century. On the plaza's southwest corner, next to a rare New Zealand agathis tree (a small, fragrant evergreen with flat leaves), the **House of Charm** was the Indian Arts building for the Panama exposition, but got its present name during the 1935 fair as a souvenir market. It was recently rebuilt to its original form and now houses the **Mingei Museum of Folk Art** (☎ 619-239-0003), which has an excellent permanent collection of costumes, toys, jewelry, utensils and other handmade objects from traditional cultures around the world. It's open 11 am to 4 pm Tuesday to Sunday; $5 ($2 for students).

San Diego Museum of Art

This 1924 building was designed by San Diego architect William Templeton Johnson in the 16th-century Spanish plateresque style, so named because it features heavy ornamentation resembling decorated silverwork. The facade is particularly ornate, with sculptures depicting Spanish artists (most of whom have pieces inside the museum). Important traveling exhibits are shown here with increasing frequency. The permanent collection has a number of fine European paintings (though no really famous works), some worthwhile American landscape paintings and some very interesting pieces in the Asian galleries. The **Sculpture Garden**, behind the cafe to the west of the main museum building, has pieces by Alexander

Calder and Henry Moore. The museum (☎ 619-232-7931) is open 10 am to 4:30 pm Tuesday to Sunday; $8/6 adults/seniors and ages 18-24, $3 for children ages 6-17.

Timken Museum of Art

Distinctive for *not* being in imitation Spanish style, this 1965 building at 1500 El Prado houses the Putnam collection. The small but impressive group of paintings includes works by Rembrandt, Rubens, El Greco, Cézanne and Pissarro. There's also a wonderful selection of Russian icons, which will appeal even to those who are not fans of this art form. Don't miss the Timken (☎ 619-239-5548), which is free. Closed Monday, Sunday morning and the entire month of September.

Botanical Building

This building looks just lovely from El Prado, reflected in a large lily pond that was used for hydrotherapy in WWII when the Navy took over most of the park. The building's central dome and two wings are covered with redwood lathes, which let filtered sunlight into the collection of tropical plants and ferns. It's free, and the planting changes every season (there's a great poinsettia display in December). It's closed Thursdays.

Casa del Prado

This is one of the handsomest buildings along El Prado, but there is little to draw the visitor inside. It was built as a temporary structure for the 1915 exposition, but an earthquake in 1968 caused so much damage that the building was condemned. It was rebuilt with the support of community arts groups, who now use it for theater and dance performances.

Casa de Balboa

The House of Commerce & Industry was designed by Goodhue in the imitation Spanish colonial style for the 1915 exposition and later used for a variety of purposes until it burned down in 1978. The original building was faithfully reconstructed, including concrete decorations cast from pieces of the original. It now houses three museums, each with its own museum shop and a small cafe. Admission to each museum is $4.

The highlight here is definitely the **Museum of Photographic Arts** (☎ 619-238-7559), expanded fairly recently by La Jolla architect David Singer. International exhibits range from wildlife shots to 'what the heck is that' art pieces. MoPA is open until 5 pm daily and is free the second Tuesday of the month.

The **Museum of San Diego History** (☎ 619-232-6203) covers mainly the American period from about 1848. It's open 10 am to 4:30 pm Tuesday to Sunday. Admission is $5 for adults (free the second Tuesday of each month).

Downstairs, the **Model Railroad Museum** (☎ 619-696-0199) has working models of actual railroads in Southern California, both historical and contemporary. It's open 11 am to 4 pm Tuesday to Friday, to 5 pm on weekends. It's always free for children under 15, and for everyone else on the first Tuesday of the month.

Reuben H Fleet Space Theater & Science Center

One of Balboa Park's most publicized venues, this one features a hands-on science museum and a huge-screen Omnimax theater. The hemispherical, wrap-around screen and 152-speaker sound system create sensations that range from fantastic to OK, depending on what film is showing. The interactive science display was very innovative when this center opened in 1973, but that type of thing has since been done often and better. The theater (☎ 619-238-1233) has shows from 9:30 am to 9 or 11 pm daily and costs $9/7.20 general/students. The Science Center (☎ 619-238-1233) is included in the theater price but can be visited by itself for $6.50/5 adults/children.

Natural History Museum

This 1933 William Templeton Johnson building at the east end of El Prado houses lots of rocks, fossils and stuffed animals, as well as an impressive dinosaur skeleton and a California fault-line exhibit. Special children's programs are held most weekends. The museum (☎ 619-232-3821) is open from 9:30 am to 4:30 pm daily. Admission is $3 for regular exhibits, $12 for special exhibits, free on the first Tuesday of the month. The museum also arranges field trips and nature hikes in Balboa Park and farther afield.

Spanish Village Area

Behind the Natural History Museum is a grassy square with a magnificent Moreton Bay fig tree (sorry, no climbing). Opposite is a group of small tiled cottages, billed by park authorities as 'an authentic reproduction of an ancient village in Spain,' which are rented out as artists' studios. You can watch potters, jewelers, glass blowers, painters and sculptors churn out pricey decorative items, 11 am to 4 pm daily. North of the Spanish Village is a 1924 **Carousel** and a **Miniature Railroad**; both operate from 11 am to 4:30 pm on weekends and holidays (daily in summer) and charge $1 per ride.

Spreckels Organ Pavilion

Going south from Plaza de Panama, you can't miss the circle of seating and the curved colonnade in front of this organ, said to be the largest outdoor musical instrument in the world. Donated by the Spreckels family of sugar fortune and fame, the organ came with the stipulation that San Diego must have an official organist. Free concerts are held at 2 pm every Sunday, and at 8 pm on Mondays during July and August.

Pan-American Plaza

This plaza is now just a large parking lot southwest of the Spreckels Organ. As you approach it, the **United Nations Building** is on your right. The UNICEF International Gift Shop here, open daily, has a good selection of stationery, jewelry and candy, and gives most of its proceeds back to the artists. Nearby, the **House of Pacific Relations** (☎ 619-292-8592) is actually 15 cottages from the 1915 exposition, inside which you will find furnishings and displays from many countries. The

cottages are open free of charge on Sunday afternoons and often have crafts and food for sale.

Also of interest are the Palisades Building with the **Marie Hitchcock Puppet Theater** (☎ 619-685-5045); the **San Diego Automotive Museum** (☎ 619-231-2886), which has a varied collection of more than 60 cars and motorcycles, perfectly restored and well displayed, with helpful staff and classic cars and motorcycles such as a 1933 Duesenberg Roadster and a classic motorcycle by Indian.

The round building at the south end of the plaza houses the excellent **Aerospace Museum** (☎ 619-234-8291), with an extensive display of aircraft – originals, replicas, models and a lot of Charles Lindbergh memorabilia. Don't miss the planes out front, or the courtyard, where a Phantom jet pursues an Russian MiG-17 between art deco lamp standards.

At the adjacent **Starlight Bowl**, the Starlight Opera (☎ 619-544-7800) presents a summer season of musicals and light opera.

The Federal Building was built for the 1935 exposition but was recently renovated to hold the **San Diego Hall of Champions Sports Museum** (☎ 619-234-2544), which has exhibits on San Diego sports figures (baseballer Ted Williams and Olympic diver Greg Louganis are perhaps the best known), a rock-climbing wall and a 'Center Court' where you might see a mini-Chargers training camp at which actual Charger team members strut their stuff. The museum is open daily and costs $6.

Classic motorcycle made by Indian

SAN DIEGO AREA

Centro Cultural de la Raza

This center for exhibitions of Mexican and Native American art is way out on the fringe of the main museum area (easiest access is from Park Blvd). The round, steel building is actually a converted water tank. Inside, the temporary exhibits of contemporary indigenous artwork can be very powerful. The Centro Cultural de la Raza (☎ 619-235-6135) is open noon to 5 pm Thursday to Sunday; free ($3 donation suggested).

Marston House

In the far northwest corner of Balboa Park is the former home of George Marston, philanthropist and founder of the San Diego Historical Society. The house was designed in 1904 by noted San Diego architects William Hebbard and Irving Gill and is a fine example of the American Arts and Crafts style. The society is currently restoring the interior as a showplace for Arts and Crafts furnishings and decorative objects. The Marston House (☎ 619-298-3142) is at 3525 7th Ave. The Historical Society (☎ 619-232-6203) conducts tours of the house ($4)

and the gardens ($1 extra) from 10 am to 4:30 pm Friday, Saturday and Sunday.

Gardens of Balboa Park

Balboa Park includes a number of quite distinct garden areas, reflecting different horticultural styles and different environments. A way to learn more about the gardens is to take one of the free weekly Offshoot Tours, conducted by park horticulturists from mid-January to Thanksgiving. The Park & Recreation Department (☎ 619-235-1114) has more information, but reservations are not required – just be at the front of the Botanical Building by 10 am.

If you're exploring on your own, visit the **Alcazar Garden**, a formal, Spanish-style garden; **Palm Canyon**, which has more than 50 species of palms; the **Japanese Friendship Garden**, open on Tuesday and Friday to Sunday for $2, and the third Tuesday of the month for free; the **Australian Garden**; the **Rose Garden**; the **Desert Garden**, which is best in spring; and **Florida Canyon**, which gives an idea of the San Diego landscape before the Spanish settlement. The Natural

---

The Legacy of Kate Sessions

Kate O Sessions graduated with a degree in botany from the University of California at Berkeley in 1881, a time when few women attended college and even fewer studied the natural sciences. She came to San Diego as a schoolteacher but soon began working as a horticulturist, establishing gardens for the fashionable homes of the city's emerging elite. In 1892, in need of space for a nursery, she proposed an unusual deal to city officials: she would have the use of 30 acres of city-owned Balboa Park for her nursery in return for planting 100 trees a year and donating 300 others for placement throughout San Diego. The city agreed to the arrangement, and Kate Sessions more than fulfilled her side of the bargain. Within 10 years, Balboa Park had shade trees, lawns, paths and flower beds. Over a 35-year period she planted some 10,000 trees and shrubs. Grateful San Diegans soon began referring to her as 'The Mother of Balboa Park.'

In 1910 she moved her nursery to the newly developing suburb of Mission Hills, where she persuaded developers to leave some of the canyons in their natural state and to lay out some streets following the contours of the land rather than in an arbitrary rectangular grid. She later moved to Pacific Beach, where her memory has been honored by the creation of Kate Sessions Park. She was an active horticulturist up to the 1930s, working on gardens from Coronado to La Jolla. Her work surrounds the houses of some of San Diego's best-known architects. The trademarks of her style – shady arbors hung with bougainvillea and informal plantings softening steep hillsides – define much of what is lovely today in San Diego landscaping.

History Museum (☎ 619-232-3821) conducts guided walks in the canyon.

San Diego Zoo

The zoo is one of San Diego's biggest attractions, and anyone at all interested in the natural world should allow a full day to see it. More than 3000 animals, representing more than 800 species, are exhibited in a beautifully landscaped setting, typically in enclosures that replicate their natural habitats.

History The origins of the San Diego Zoo can be traced to the 1915 Panama-California Exposition and the enthusiasm of one local man, Dr Harry Wegeforth. The exposition featured an assortment of animals in cages along Park Blvd. It's now San Diego folklore that Wegeforth, hearing the roar of one of the caged lions, exclaimed, 'Wouldn't it be wonderful to have a zoo in San Diego? I believe I'll build one.' He started his campaign in 1916 in the newspaper and soon formed the Zoological Society of San Diego. By pulling a few strings, Dr Wegeforth then ensured that quarantine requirements made it almost impossible to remove exotic animals from the county, so the society was able to acquire much of the menagerie left over from the exposition.

As a private organization, the Zoological Society could not be given a site on public land, but in 1921 a nice compromise was reached. The society donated all the animals and facilities to the city, and the city provided 200 acres of Balboa Park to use as a zoo, which would then be administered by the society. Though the site is bisected by canyons and largely barren, these problems were turned to advantage: canyons provided a means of separating different groups of animals to prevent the spread of disease, and they could be individually landscaped to simulate appropriate natural settings.

Wegeforth had a talent for extracting money from wealthy benefactors – John Spreckels, the millionaire sugar king, warned that the wily surgeon would 'cut you off at the pockets.' One of the first big donations was from journalist Ellen Browning Scripps

(founder of Scripps College in Claremont, California), who paid for a perimeter fence, which was to enforce the payment of admission fees as much as to keep the animals in.

Local support for the zoo meant that unorthodox ways were often found to add to its collection. San Diegans brought in various finds, such as seals and snakes, which were never refused – rattlesnakes caught in Balboa Park were often profitably traded for animals from other zoos. In one exchange, the zoo provided fleas for a New York flea circus. The US Navy unofficially contributed an assortment of animals that had been adopted as mascots but could no longer be kept on ships. US Marines landing in Nicaragua were offered prizes if they captured beasts for Dr Wegeforth. During the 1930s Wegeforth himself traveled the world, collecting jaguars from Venezuela, orangutans from Borneo and marsupials from Australia. On a trip to India, Wegeforth contracted pneumonia and malaria; he died in 1941. His final contributions to the zoo were three elephants, which arrived in San Diego two months after his death.

By the end of WWII, the San Diego Zoo had a worldwide reputation, and it helped to rebuild the collections of European zoos that had been devastated by the war. The Zoological Society continued at the forefront of zoo management with the introduction of 'bioclimatic' habitats, which allowed a number of different types of animals to share a simulated natural environment. In the 1960s the society started work on an 1800-acre Wild Animal Park, 32 miles north of the city (see the Escondido section), which now provides free-range areas for many large animals.

Information The zoo (☎ 619-234-3153) is in the northern part of Balboa Park and has a large free parking lot off of Park Blvd. The No 7 bus will get you there from downtown. Visitors should call for current hours, as they vary according to the time of year. The information booth is just to the left of the entrance as you come in – if you would like to leave the zoo and return, they'll stamp your hand.

The regular daily admission price is $16/7 adults/children. The 'deluxe admission package' costs $24/13 and includes a 40-minute guided bus tour ($3/2.50) as well as a round-trip aerial tram ride. Discount coupons for the zoo are widely available. A combined ticket to visit both the San Diego Zoo and the Wild Animal Park within a five-day period costs $34/19.95.

It's wise to arrive early, as many of the animals are most active in the morning. You might start with a tour in a double-decker bus, which gives a good overview of the zoo and includes an informative commentary. Animal shows are held in the two amphitheaters (no extra charge), and they're usually entertaining, especially for kids who might need a rest anyway. The Skyfari cable car goes right across the park and can save you some walking time, though you might have to wait in line to get on it.

Facilities are provided for disabled visitors; call the zoo (☎ 619-231-1515 ext 4526) for specific information.

Highlights The zoo and the Wild Animal Park share an active program of breeding endangered species in captivity for reintroduction into their natural habitats. This has been done with a number of species, including the Arabian oryx, the Bali starling and the California condor.

The zoo gardens are well-known. They now include some plants that are used for the specialized food requirements of particular animals.

The zoo has also expanded its entertainment and educational role in the community with the opening of a children's zoo exhibit (where youngsters can pet small critters) and of outdoor theaters for animal shows. Both children and adults will enjoy the animal nursery, where you can see the zoo's newest arrivals.

Most visitors will have their own favorites. The koalas are so popular that Australians may be surprised to find them a sort of unofficial symbol of San Diego. The Komodo dragon, an Indonesian lizard that can grow up to 10 feet long, not only looks fearsome, but strides around the reptile house in a very menacing manner.

The Komodo dragon can grow to be 10 feet long.

Tiger River, a realistic, re-created Asian rain forest, is one of the newer bioclimatic exhibits. Gorilla Tropics is an African rain forest. A third bioclimatic environment is the Sun Bear Forest, where the Asian bears are famously playful.

The large Scripps Aviary and Rainforest Aviary are both impressive structures where carefully placed feeders allow some close-up viewing. Finally, don't miss the African Rock Kopje (outcrop), where klipspringers (small antelopes) demonstrate their rock-climbing abilities.

MISSION VALLEY

Although it would often dry up in late summer, the San Diego River was still the most reliable source of freshwater for the crops and the livestock of the early missions. The river valley, now called Mission Valley, was frequently flooded until, in the mid-1950s, dams were completed upstream. In the 1950s and '60s there was disagreement over the valley's development, but I-8 now runs its length and is dotted with hotels and shopping centers. Some green, open space remains, but much of it is golf courses and country clubs. The restored Mission San Diego de Alcalá is definitely worth a visit, but Mission Valley's most touted feature now is its triad of shopping centers: Fashion Valley, the Hazard Center and Mission Valley Center.

The San Diego Trolley runs the length of the valley, from downtown to the mission, with stops at Qualcomm Stadium and all the shopping centers. The trolley's route cuts through a scenic corridor of riparian land (and golf courses) not seen from the freeway. You could make a day of trolley-shopping, getting off at each of the big centers. Fashion Valley has specialty stores such as Tiffany & Co, Enzo Antolini and Restoration Hardware, as well as biggies such as Saks Fifth Ave, Macy's and Nordstrom; most are open until 10 pm. Mission Valley Center is known for its upscale discount outlets, which include the Nordstrom Rack and Saks Off Fifth Ave; both malls have some good restaurants and multiplex movie theaters.

Mission San Diego de Alcalá

Though the first California mission was established on Presidio hill, Padre Junípero Serra decided in 1773 to move it a few miles upriver, closer to a better water supply and more arable land.

In 1784 the missionaries built a solid adobe and timber church, but it was destroyed by an earthquake in 1803. The church was promptly rebuilt, and at least some of it still stands on a slope overlooking Mission Valley. With the end of the mission system in the 1830s, the buildings were turned over to the Mexican government and fell into disrepair. Some accounts say that they were reduced to a facade and a few crumbling walls by the 1920s.

Extensive restoration began in 1931, with financial support from local citizens and the Hearst Foundation, a philanthropic organization funded by one of California's most influential families (see the Hearst Castle section in the Central Coast chapter of this book). The pretty white church and the buildings you see now are probably about 95% restoration.

The visitor center (☎ 619-281-8449) has a friendly and informative staff, some good books and some tacky souvenirs. The mission is open 9 am to 5 pm daily; $3/2 adults/children. It's on Friars Rd (two blocks north of I-8), between I-15 and Mission Gorge Rd; from the Mission trolley stop, walk two blocks north and turn right onto Friars Rd.

Conversion & Revenge

The first missionaries visited Indian settlements with gifts and promises, and their first converts – whom they called 'neophytes' – were encouraged to move into the mission compound on the Presidio, where they lived and worked and contracted European diseases.

The Spanish soldiers in the Presidio garrison abused the mission neophytes and also raided Indian villages. According to Padre Serra's reports, soldiers would chase their victims on horseback and 'catch an Indian woman with their lassos, to become prey for their unbridled lusts.' So, in 1774, the priests left the Presidio and started their new mission near a large Kumeyaay village, well away from the bad influence of the military.

Unfortunately, they were also away from the protection of the military, and in November 1775 the increasingly resentful Kumeyaay made a concerted attack on the mission and burned it to the ground. One of the priests, Luis Jayme, appealed to the attackers with arms outstretched, crying 'Love God, my children!' He was dragged away and beaten to death, becoming California's first martyr. The survivors retreated to the Presidio, and the Spanish authorities captured, flogged and executed the leaders of the attack. After a few months, the missionaries returned to their site in the valley and built a second mission, with a tiled roof to resist the flaming arrows of Indian attacks – this type of roof became a standard feature of mission architecture.

OLD TOWN

Under the Mexican government, which took power in 1821, any settlement with a population of 500 or more was entitled to become a 'pueblo.' Since the Presidio's population was about 600, soldiers from the garrison were able to cultivate and partition the land below Presidio hill and to make it the first

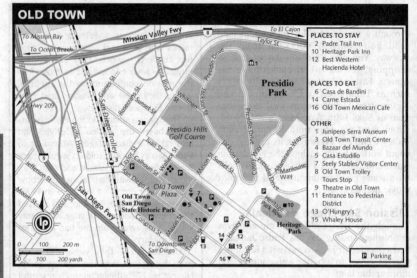

OLD TOWN

PLACES TO STAY
2 Padre Trail Inn
10 Heritage Park Inn
12 Best Western
    Hacienda Hotel

PLACES TO EAT
6 Casa de Bandini
14 Carne Estrada
16 Old Town Mexican Cafe

OTHER
1 Junipero Serra Museum
3 Old Town Transit Center
4 Bazaar del Mundo
5 Casa Estudillo
7 Seely Stables/Visitor Center
8 Old Town Trolley
    Tours Stop
9 Theatre in Old Town
11 Entrance to Pedestrian
    District
13 O'Hungry's
15 Whaley House

P Parking

SAN DIEGO AREA

official civilian Spanish settlement in California – the Pueblo de San Diego. A plaza was laid out around Casa Estudillo, home of the pueblo's commandant, and within 10 years it was surrounded by about 40 huts and a few larger, whitewashed houses. This square mile of land (roughly 10 times what is there today) was also the center of American San Diego until the fire of 1872, after which the city's focus moved to the new Horton subdivision.

John Spreckels built a trolley line from Horton's New Town to Old Town in the 1920s and, to attract passengers, began restoring the old district. In 1968 the area became Old Town State Historic Park, archaeological work began and the few surviving original buildings were restored. Other structures were rebuilt, and the area is now a pedestrian district (there are parking lots around the edges) with shade trees, a large open plaza and a cluster of shops and restaurants.

In an attempt to emphasize Old Town's historical significance – it had become primarily a shopping and eating destination – the Park Service has hired interpretive rangers to give tours and has expanded the visitor center to include an excellent American-period museum (Indian pieces are in the Museum of Man at Balboa Park). The visitor center (☎ 619-220-5427) is in the Seely Stables at the south end of the plaza and is open 10 am to 5 pm daily. The center has a California history slide show, a good collection of stagecoach and *vaquero* (Mexican cowboy) memorabilia and an informative staff.

If you're particularly interested in the historical background, pick up a copy of the *Old Town San Diego State Historic Park Tour Guide & Brief History* ($2), or take a guided tour, which leaves the visitor center at 2 pm daily (there's also an 11 am tour if enough people show up).

Across from the center is **La Casa de Estudillo**, a restored adobe home furnished with original furniture. It's worth a look and has a self-guided tour map, available from a docent at the house's northwest entrance. On the opposite side of the plaza, the Robinson-Rose building has some good history books for sale and a diorama depicting the original pueblo.

The **Bazaar del Mundo**, just off the plaza's northwest corner, is a colorful collection of import shops and restaurants that are open late and definitely worth passing through. Along San Diego Ave, on the south side of the plaza, is a row of small, historical-looking buildings (only one is authentically old), some of which house souvenir and gift shops. At 2482 San Diego Ave, two blocks from the Old Town perimeter, the **Whaley House** has fairly plain architecture but is the original – and supposedly haunted – 1856 home of Thomas Whaley, who moved to San Diego in 1851 and prospered as a merchant. There is an excellent collection of period furniture and clothing on display. The home (☎ 619-298-2482) is open 10 am to 4:30 pm daily (closed Tuesday in winter); $4.

Just north of Old Town, the **Casa de Carrillo** dates from about 1820 and is the oldest house in San Diego. It is now the pro shop for the public Presidio Hills Golf Course (☎ 619-295-9476).

The Old Town Transit Center, on the trolley line at Taylor St at the northwest edge of Old Town, is a stop for the *Coaster* commuter train, the San Diego Trolley (red line) and buses No 4 and 5 from downtown; Old Town Trolley tours stop southeast of the plaza on Twiggs St.

Presidio Hill

In 1769 Junípero Serra and Gaspar de Portolá established the first Spanish settlement in California on Presidio hill, overlooking the valley of the San Diego River. You can walk up from Old Town along Mason St and get excellent views of San Diego Bay and Mission Valley. Atop the hill, **Presidio Park** has a few walking trails and shaded benches. A large cross, constructed with tiles from the original mission, commemorates Padre Serra.

American forces occupied the hill in 1846, during the Mexican-American War, and named it Fort Stockton, for American commander Robert Stockton. A flagpole, cannon, some plaques and earth walls now comprise the **Fort Stockton Memorial**. The nearby **El Charro Statue**, a bicentennial gift to the city from Mexico, depicts a Mexican cowboy on horseback. Nothing remains of the original Presidio structures, but there are archaeological digs under way to unearth the past.

It would be easy to believe that the **Junípero Serra Museum** is a well preserved Spanish colonial–style structure, but in fact it was designed by William Templeton Johnson in 1929. The museum has a small but interesting collection of artifacts and pictures from the Mission and rancho periods, and gives a good feel for the earliest days of European settlement. Call the museum (☎ 619-297-3258) for current hours, as they vary with the season. Admission is $5/2.

UPTOWN & HILLCREST

Without being too precise, Uptown is a triangle north of downtown, east of Old Town and south of Mission Valley. In the late 19th century it was fashionable to live in the hills north of downtown – only those who owned a horse-drawn carriage could afford it. Called Bankers Hill after some of the wealthy residents – or Pill Hill, because of the many doctors – these upscale heights had unobstructed views of the bay and Point Loma before I-5 was built. A few of the ornate Victorian mansions survive, most notably the 1889 **Long-Waterman House**, 2408 1st Ave. Easily recognized by its towers, gables, bay windows and veranda, it was once the home of former California governor Robert Waterman. Also notable is the **Timkin House**, one block to the north.

A favorite pastime of residents old and new is crossing the 375-foot long **Spruce Street Footbridge** that hangs over a deep canyon between Front and Brant Sts. The **Quince Street Bridge**, between 4th and 3rd Aves, is a wood-trestle bridge built in 1905 and refurbished in 1988 after its slated demolition was vigorously protested by community activists.

At the corner of Washington and India Sts is a shingled complex once known as the India Street Art Colony. Opened in the 1970s by architect and artist Raoul Marquis, the art studios, import shops and theaters that originally occupied it are gone. They have been replaced by an excellent cafe and

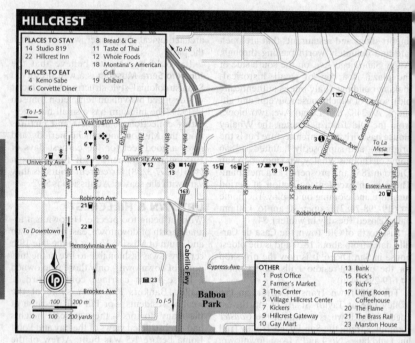

HILLCREST

PLACES TO STAY
14 Studio 819
22 Hillcrest Inn

PLACES TO EAT
4 Kemo Sabe
6 Corvette Diner

8 Bread & Cie
11 Taste of Thai
12 Whole Foods
18 Montana's American
   Grill
19 Ichiban

OTHER
1 Post Office
2 Farmer's Market
3 The Center
5 Village Hillcrest Center
7 Kickers
9 Hillcrest Gateway
10 Gay Mart

13 Bank
15 Flick's
16 Rich's
17 Living Room
   Coffeehouse
20 The Flame
21 The Brass Rail
23 Marston House

some first-rate inexpensive eateries (see the Places to Eat section). Across I-5 on Washington St, the **Mission Brewery Plaza** brewed Bavarian beer from 1913 to 1918 – it was closed during Prohibition – then processed seaweed (for food use as a thickening and coloring agent) for American Agar until 1987. In 1989 the original chimney, tile roof and cupola, which were exempted from coastal height limitations, were restored and the plaza was put on the National Register of Historic Places. It's now used as a business complex and is mostly just interesting from afar.

At the heart of the Uptown is **Hillcrest**, the first suburban real estate development in San Diego. It is close to the greenery of Balboa Park and linked to downtown by a trolley line up Bankers Hill. If you drive around, you'll see the work of many of San Diego's best-known architects from the early 20th century, including Irving Gill and

William Templeton Johnson. The Mediterranean and Spanish mission styles, and the influence of the Arts and Crafts movement, make an interesting contrast with the Victorian houses from an earlier era.

Hillcrest is now one of San Diego's liveliest areas and is the center of San Diego's gay and lesbian community. To look around, start at the Hillcrest Gateway, which arches over University Ave at 5th Ave. Go north and check out the retro '50s style of the Corvette Diner at 3946 5th Ave, and the fashionable menswear shops and Gay Mart at the corner of University and 6th Aves. Not far away, on 5th Ave between University Ave and Washington St, is the Village Hillcrest Center, with its colorful postmodern architecture. There you will find a multiplex cinema (☎ 619-299-2100) and restaurants and shops, as well as News Etc, a newsstand with a great selection. Go east on University Ave to see the 1928 Kahn Building at No 535; it is an original

Hillcrest commercial building with architectural elements that border on kitsch. Go south on 5th Ave, to find a variety of bookstores, many with a good selection of non-mainstream publications.

From 9 am to noon on Sunday, Hillcrest's Farmers' Market, corner of Normal and Lincoln Sts, is a fun place to people-watch and buy fresh produce.

POINT LOMA & OCEAN BEACH

Point Loma is the peninsula that seems to hang down across the entrance to San Diego Bay, protecting it from the Pacific Ocean. At Cabrillo National Monument, on the southern tip (from where there are stunning panoramas over San Diego Bay and out to sea), you will find excellent exhibits on Point Loma's history and on the environment there. This is the best place in San Diego to see the gray whale migration (January to March) from land. The whales used to birth their young in San Diego Bay, but, because of the high level of human activity there, they now go to Baja.

San Diego's first fishing boats were based at Point Loma, and in the 19th century whalers dragged carcasses onto its shores to extract the whale oil. Chinese fishermen settled on the harbor side of the point in the 1860s but were forced off in 1888 when the US Congress passed Scott Act prohibiting anyone without citizenship papers from entering the area. Coming home from a normal day's run outside the international waters boundary (30 miles offshore), the Chinese were met by officials who prohibited them from re-entering the harbor. Portuguese fishing families came about 50 years later – around the same time that Italian immigrants settled on the other side of the harbor – and established a permanent community. The Portuguese Hall is still a hub of activity and many people living on Point Loma are of Portuguese descent.

Given the strategic location, it's not surprising that the US military occupies much of Point Loma's land, though the biggest site is actually Fort Rosecrans National Cemetery, established in 1899. At the **Marine Corps Recruit Depot Command Museum**

(☎ 619-524-6719, 619-524-4426) are exhibits that cover US Marines history from the Mexican-American War to the Gulf War. It's off Pacific Hwy at Barnett Ave; look for the signs and enter at Gate 4.

The tidal flats of Loma Portal, where Point Loma joins the mainland, were used as an airstrip in 1927 by Charles Lindbergh for flight testing the *Spirit of St Louis*. The following year a functioning airport was established; it was named Lindbergh Field. It has expanded considerably and is now known as San Diego International Airport.

Cabrillo National Monument

Among the best places to visit in San Diego, this monument commemorates Portuguese explorer Juan Rodríguez Cabrillo, who led the first Spanish exploration of the West Coast. The visitor center (☎ 619-557-5450) has an excellent presentation on Cabrillo's exploration and very good exhibits on the native inhabitants and the area's natural history (open 9 am to 5:15 pm daily). The nearby lookout area has an imposing statue of Cabrillo and a great view over Coronado Island, the bay and the city. For whale watching, see the Activities section.

A short and scenic walk brings you to the 1854 **Old Point Loma Lighthouse** on the top of the point. It closed in 1891 and, in 1913, was declared a national monument. It's now furnished with typical lighthouse furniture from the late 19th century, including lamps and picture frames hand-covered with hundreds of shells – testimony to the long, lonely nights endured by lighthouse keepers.

On the ocean side of the point, you can drive or walk down to the **tide pools**, which are most interesting at low tide. Look for anemones, starfish, crabs, limpets and dead man's fingers (thin, tubular seaweed), but don't damage or remove anything – it's all protected by law.

Reach the monument via Catalina Blvd, which connects to Nimitz Blvd and Hwy 209. The entrance fee – payable at the gate and good for one week – is $5 per car, $2 if you're on a bike or a bus (No 26 from downtown). The monument is open 9 am to 5:15 pm daily.

Ocean Beach

San Diego's most bohemian seaside community once had a somewhat sleazy reputation, but OB (as it's commonly called) has moved slightly upscale. It's still a long way from pretentious – there's not even a Starbucks Coffee – and is more compact than San Diego's other beach towns, making it enjoyable for strolling. Newport Ave, the main drag, is well stocked with surf shops, music stores, used-clothing stores and, in the 4800 and 4900 blocks, antiques consignment stores.

The street performers and food vendors that frequent the OB Farmers' Market, from 4 to 7 pm Wednesday (until 8 pm from June to September), make it one of San Diego's most enjoyable.

The half-mile-long Ocean Beach Pier is good for fishing and for a breath of fresh air. Just north of the pier, near the end of Newport Ave, is the beach scene headquarters, with volleyball courts and sunset barbecues. It can get crowded all the way up to near Voltaire St. North of here is Dog Beach, where dogs can run unleashed and chase birds around the marshy area where the San Diego River meets the sea. A few blocks south of the pier is Sunset Cliffs Park, where watching surfers and the sunset is the big attraction.

There are good surf breaks at the cliffs and, to the south, off Point Loma. Under the pier, hot surfers slalom the pilings. Those who are not so hot need to beware of the rips and currents, which can be deadly.

Harbor Island & Shelter Island

Soil dredged from the bottom of the harbor was used to build Shelter Island (1950) and Harbor Island (1969), which are not really islands, but T-shaped peninsulas joined to the mainland by causeways. They now provide moorings for a huge flotilla of pleasure boats and are covered with hotels, restaurants, boatyards and parking lots. There's a classic view of San Diego from here, across the bay through a forest of masts. The pointy building on Shelter Island, which resembles the tower of the Hotel del Coronado, is the clubhouse of the San Diego Yacht Club, which held the America's Cup yachting trophy from 1987 to 1995.

CORONADO

The community of Coronado, with a population of 28,500, is right across the bay from downtown San Diego and is a combination of middle-class suburbia, retirement village and upscale seaside resort. Administratively, it is a separate city from San Diego, a city known for closely guarding its ambience and environmental quality.

Coronado is joined to the mainland by a spectacular 2.12-mile bridge (opened in 1969), which arches over the bay, and by a long, narrow sand spit, the Silver Strand, which runs south to Imperial Beach. Nevertheless, it's often referred to as Coronado Island, and the locals like to call it 'the Village.' The large North Island Naval Air Station occupies a big chunk of land, which was once an island.

In 1888 Elisha Babcock and Hampton Story opened the Hotel del Coronado, the showy centerpiece of a new resort, and by 1900 they were broke. John D Spreckels, the millionaire who bankrolled the first rail line to San Diego, took over Coronado and turned the whole island into one of the most fashionable getaways on the West Coast.

Information

The Coronado Visitors Bureau (☎ 619-437-8788), 1047 B Ave, is open 9 am to 5 pm weekdays, 10 am to 5 pm Saturday and 11 am to 4 pm Sunday. For some insight into Coronado history, try a guided Historical Walking Tour ($6), starting from the Glorietta Bay Inn (☎ 935-435-3101) at 1630 Glorietta Blvd near Silver Strand Blvd. Tours are at 11 am Tuesday, Thursday and Saturday. The 90-minute route takes in many of Coronado's most interesting sights. There's also a self-guided walking tour that starts at the Coronado Historical Museum, 1126 Loma Ave, for $2. The free and semi-interesting museum is open 10 am to 4 pm Wednesday to Sunday.

There's a $1 toll for cars coming over the bridge to Coronado, but it's free for vehicles with passengers. Buses No 901, 902 and 903 from downtown run the length of Orange

Ave to the Hotel del Coronado. Or you can come across on the ferry from Broadway Pier ($2) and use a rented bike or the Coronado Electric Shuttle to get around. The beach can have good surf in summer, with a south swell and a north wind.

Hotel del Coronado

Commonly known as the Hotel Del (☎ 619-435-6611), this place is a much-loved San Diego institution. Architecturally, it's pretty quirky, with its conical towers, cupolas, turrets, balconies and dormer windows. It's an all-timber building, and the cavernous public spaces reflect the background of railroad depot-designing architects James and Merritt Reed. The acres of polished wood do give the interior a warm, old-fashioned feel.

The Del was where Edward (then Prince of Wales) first met Mrs Simpson (then Mrs Spenser) in 1920, though the two did not become an item until some years later. Other hotel guests have included many US presidents and other dignitaries – pictures and mementos are displayed in the hotel's History Gallery. Hotel Del achieved its widest exposure in the 1959 movie *Some Like It Hot*, which earned it a lasting association with Marilyn Monroe. Take a cassette-guided tour ($3) from the Lobby Shop or one of the personally guided tours ($10 hotel guests, $15 for non-guests), which start at 10 am, 11 am and 1 pm daily except Sunday. There's an interesting resident ghost story too – something about a woman suffering from unrequited love who silently appears on a TV screen in the room where she had her heart broken.

See the sections on Places to Stay and Places to Eat for more details.

Bicycling

The best way to spend a day in Coronado is to come across by ferry and cruise by bike. You can rent one at the Ferry Landing Marketplace for about $5/hour or bring one on the ferry for 55¢. The main drag across Coronado is Orange Ave, which passes through the well-clipped Spreckels Park and then swings south toward the Hotel del Coronado. There are some designated bicycle routes, which avoid Orange Ave because it can be busy (be sure to get a map when you rent your bike).

MISSION BAY

In the 18th century, the mouth of the San Diego River formed a shallow bay when the river flowed, and a marshy swamp when it didn't – the Spanish called it False Bay. After WWII, a fine combination of civic vision and coastal engineering turned the swamp into a 7-sq-mile playground, with 27 miles of shoreline and 90 acres of public park. With financing from public bonds and expertise from the Army Corps of Engineers, the river was channeled to the sea, the bay was dredged and millions of tons of sludge were used to build islands, coves and peninsulas. A quarter of the land created has been leased to hotels, boatyards and other businesses, repaying the bonds and providing ongoing revenue for the city.

The attractions of Mission Bay run the gamut from luxurious resort hotels to free outdoor activities. Kite flying is popular in Mission Bay Park, and there's delightful cycling and in-line skating on the miles of smooth bike paths. You can rent equipment just off East Mission Bay Drive, opposite the Hilton, or at the Catamaran Resort Hotel in Mission Beach. Beach volleyball is big on Fiesta Island.

The waters around Fiesta Island are used by power boats and water-skiers; the Hilton Beach Resort (☎ 619-276-4010) rents the necessary equipment. Overpowered 'thunderboats' race on the bay during the third weekend of September. Sailing, windsurfing and kayaking dominate the waters in northwest Mission Bay. Boats and boards can be rented from Mission Bay Sportcenter (☎ 619-488-1004), at 1010 Santa Clara Place, or CP Watersports, located at the Hilton (☎ 619-275-8945).

The *Bahia Belle* (☎ 619-488-0551) is a floating bar disguised as a stern-wheeler paddleboat. It cruises between two resort hotels, the Catamaran and the Bahia. Call for times, which vary depending on the season. It's a beautiful way to see the bay and costs $6, plus drinks.

MISSION BAY & THE BEACHES

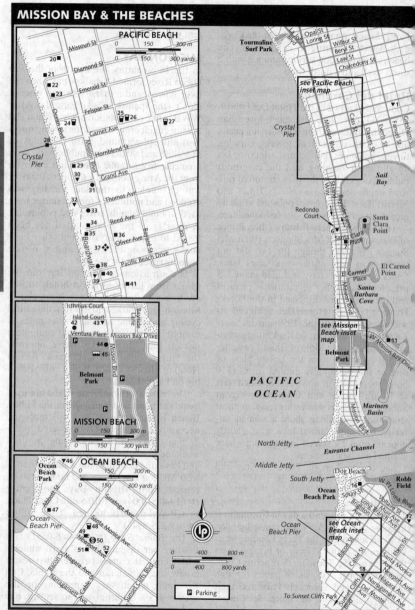

PACIFIC BEACH

0   150   300 m
0   150   300 yards

Missouri St
20
21
22
23
Diamond St
Emerald St
Felspar St
25
26
24
27
Garnet Ave
28
Hornblend St
Crystal Pier
29
30
31
Grand Ave
Thomas Ave
32
33
34
Reed Ave
35
36
37
Oliver Ave
38
40
39
41
Ocean Blvd
Mission Blvd
Boardwalk
Bayard St
Cass St

MISSION BEACH

Isthmus Court
Island Court
42   43
Ventura Place
44
45
Belmont Park
Bayside Lane
Mission Bay Drive
Mission Blvd

0   150   300 m
0   150   300 yards

OCEAN BEACH

Ocean Beach Park
46
Abbott St
47
Ocean Beach Pier
Saratoga Ave
48
49
50
51   52
Santa Monica Ave
Newport Ave
Bacon St
Niagara Ave
Narragansett Ave
Cable St
Sunset Cliffs Blvd

0   150   300 m
0   150   300 yards

Tourmaline
Surf Park
La Jolla Blvd
Opal St
Loring St
Wilbur St
Beryl St
Law St
Chalcedony St

see Pacific Beach
inset map

Crystal
Pier
1
Mission Blvd
Cass St
Everts St
Dawes St
Gresham St
Fanuel St

Sail
Bay

Redondo
Court
Bayside Walk
Strand Way
Bayside Lane
Santa Clara
Point
8
6
Santa Clara
7   Place
El Carmel
Place
El Carmel
Point
Santa
Barbara
Cove
Mission Blvd

see Mission
Beach inset
map

Belmont
Park
11
W Mission Bay Drive

PACIFIC
OCEAN

Mariners
Basin
Mission Blvd

North Jetty
Middle Jetty
South Jetty
Entrance Channel

Dog Beach
Robb
Field
W Pt Loma Blvd
16
Ocean
Beach Park
Spray St
Voltaire St
Long Branch Ave
Brighton
Muir Ave

Ocean
Beach Pier

see Ocean
Beach inset
map

Bacon St
Cable St
18
Sunset Cliffs Blvd
Del Monte Ave
Santa Monica Ave
Newport Ave
Niagara Ave
Narragansett Ave

To Sunset Cliffs Park

0   400   800 m
0   400   800 yards

P Parking

SAN DIEGO AREA

MISSION BAY & THE BEACHES

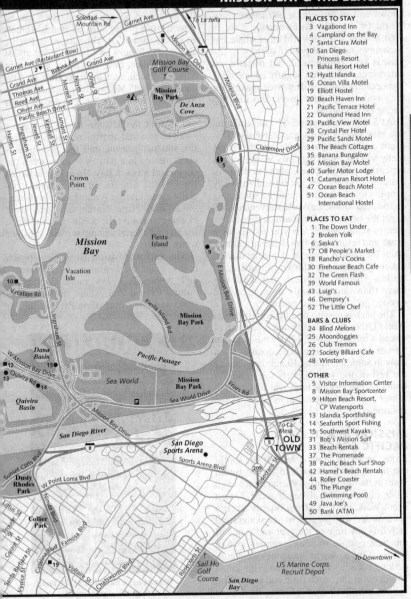

PLACES TO STAY
- 3 Vagabond Inn
- 4 Campland on the Bay
- 7 Santa Clara Motel
- 10 San Diego Princess Resort
- 11 Bahia Resort Hotel
- 12 Hyatt Islandia
- 16 Ocean Villa Motel
- 19 Elliott Hostel
- 20 Beach Haven Inn
- 21 Pacific Terrace Hotel
- 22 Diamond Head Inn
- 23 Pacific View Motel
- 28 Crystal Pier Hotel
- 29 Pacific Sands Motel
- 34 The Beach Cottages
- 35 Banana Bungalow
- 36 Mission Bay Motel
- 40 Surfer Motor Lodge
- 41 Catamaran Resort Hotel
- 47 Ocean Beach Motel
- 51 Ocean Beach International Hostel

PLACES TO EAT
- 1 The Down Under
- 2 Broken Yolk
- 6 Saska's
- 17 OB People's Market
- 18 Rancho's Cocina
- 30 Firehouse Beach Cafe
- 32 The Green Flash
- 39 World Famous
- 43 Luigi's
- 46 Dempsey's
- 52 The Little Chef

BARS & CLUBS
- 24 Blind Melons
- 25 Moondoggies
- 26 Club Tremors
- 27 Society Billiard Cafe
- 48 Winston's

OTHER
- 5 Visitor Information Center
- 8 Mission Bay Sportcenter
- 9 Hilton Beach Resort, CP Watersports
- 13 Islandia Sportfishing
- 14 Seaforth Sport Fishing
- 15 Southwest Kayaks
- 31 Bob's Mission Surf
- 33 Beach Rentals
- 37 The Promenade
- 38 Pacific Beach Surf Shop
- 42 Hamel's Beach Rentals
- 44 Roller Coaster
- 45 The Plunge (Swimming Pool)
- 49 Java Joe's
- 50 Bank (ATM)

SAN DIEGO AREA

SeaWorld

Undoubtedly one of San Diego's best known and most popular attractions, Sea-World (☎ 619-226-3901) opened here in 1964. Shamu, the SeaWorld killer whale, has become an unofficial symbol of the city. The park is very commercial, but nonetheless entertaining and even slightly educational. Its popularity can be a drawback, making for long waits for some shows and exhibits during peak seasons.

At $38 for adults and $29 for children, you may have a pretty expensive day. Discount coupons are available, but the extras really add up – parking costs $6, the food is expensive (use the picnic areas at the park entrance to save a few bucks) and not many people escape without spending something on the ubiquitous SeaWorld souvenirs. Ways to get the best value for your ticket include a reentry stamp, which lets you go out for a break and return later (good during summer when the park is open late); a combination ticket that's also good for Universal Studios (in Los Angeles); and deals that admit you more than once (usually on consecutive days) at greatly reduced prices.

The park is easy to find by car – take Sea World Drive off I-5 less than a mile north of where it intersects with I-8. By bus, take No 9 from downtown. The gates open at 9 am daily in summer, and at 10 am daily during the rest of the year. Tickets sales end 1½ hours before closing time, which is around sunset most of the year, but as late as 11 pm in summer.

MISSION BEACH & PACIFIC BEACH

From the South Mission Jetty at the southern tip of Mission Beach to Pacific Beach Point at the north end of Pacific Beach are 3 miles of solid So-Cal beach scene. Ocean Front Walk, the beachfront boardwalk, can get crowded with joggers, in-line skaters and bicyclists any time of the year and is one of the best people-watching venues in San Diego. On a warm summer weekend, parking becomes impossible and suntanned bodies cover the beach from end to end. The main north-south road, Mission Blvd, is so crowded that the police often just close it down. A bike or in-line skates are probably the best ways to get around. Both can be rented from places such as Beach Rentals near the beach at Thomas Ave, Pacific Beach, or Hamel's (☎ 619-488-5050) at 704 Ventura Place, near the roller coaster in Mission Beach, or Cheep Rentals (☎ 619-488-9070), 3685 Mission Blvd at Santa Clara St, which has low prices and decent bikes and rollerblades.

Down at the Mission Beach end, many small houses and apartments are rented for the summer season, and the hedonism is concentrated in a narrow strip between the ocean and Mission Bay. Up in Pacific Beach (or PB) the activity spreads inland, especially along Garnet Ave, which is well supplied with bars, restaurants and used clothing stores. At the ocean end of Garnet, the Crystal Pier is a popular place to fish or watch surfers.

The surf at Mission Beach is a beach break, good for beginners, bodyboarders and bodysurfers. It's more demanding around Crystal Pier, where the waves are steep and fast. Tourmaline Park, at the far

You can have more fun at the beach than the sign suggests.

north end of the beach, is particularly popular with longboarders. There are many surfboard rental places, such as Bob's Mission Surf (☎ 619-483-8837), 4320 Mission Blvd near Grand and the Pacific Beach Surf Shop (☎ 619-488-9575), 747 Pacific Beach Drive. Prices are $3 to $8/hour for bodyboards and surfboards, $3 for wet suits.

Belmont Park
This family-style amusement park in the middle of Mission Beach has been here since 1925. When it was threatened with demolition in the mid-'90s, concerted community action saved the classic wooden roller coaster and the large indoor pool known as the Plunge. More modern attractions include the Pirates Cove children's play zone and Venturer II, which features amusement machines that combine video games with virtual reality technology. There are also beachwear boutiques, a bar and some places to eat. It's free to enter Belmont Park; you pay separately for the attractions – the roller coaster is $2.50 and opens at 11 am daily.

LA JOLLA
La Jolla is the suburban next-door neighbor to the north of Pacific Beach, but a substantial distance away in socio-economic status. La Jolla is often translated from Spanish as 'the jewel,' though Indians who inhabited the area from 10,000 years ago to the mid-19th century called the place 'mut la Hoya, la Hoya' – the place of many caves. In any case, it's pronounced la HOY-ya.

The area was subdivided in the 1880s but started developing with purpose when Ellen Browning Scripps moved here in 1897. The newspaper heiress acquired much of the land along Prospect St, which she subsequently donated to various community uses. Not only did she support local institutions such as the Bishop's School (at the corner of Prospect St and La Jolla Blvd) and the La Jolla Woman's Club (715 Silverado St), she had them designed by Irving Gill, who set the architectural tone of the community – an unadorned Mediterranean style characterized by arches, colonnades, palm trees, red-tile roofs and pale stucco.

The surrounding area is home to UCSD, several renowned research institutes and a new-money residential area called the Golden Triangle, bounded by I-5, I-805 and Hwy 52. The space-age church in this area that you see from I-5 is a Mormon Temple, completed in 1993.

Downtown La Jolla
The compact town sits atop cliffs surrounded on three sides by the ocean. Distant views of Pacific blue are glimpsed through windows and from between buildings, but there is little interaction between the heart of downtown and the sea. The main thoroughfares, Prospect St and Girard Ave, are known for the 'three Rs' – restaurants, rugs and real estate – making La Jolla San Diego's best place to go for high-class shopping. Galleries sell paintings, sculpture and decorative items, and small boutiques fill in the spaces between Banana Republic, Armani Exchange and Saks Fifth Avenue, which is on Wall St near Herschel Ave. Alternative health guru Deepak Chopra's Center for Well Being (☎ 619-551-7788), 7630 Fay Ave, attracts wellness-conscious people from around the globe.

For a bit of old La Jolla, head northwest along Prospect St. John Cole's Bookshop (☎ 619-454-4766), at 780 Prospect St, is in a cottage once owned by Ellen Browning Scripps and renovated to Irving Gill's design. Around the corner on Eads Ave, the La Jolla Historical Society (☎ 619-459-5335) has vintage photos and beach memorabilia – think old bathing costumes, lifeguard buoys and the like; open noon to 4:30 pm Tuesday and Thursday. Farther northwest on Prospect, you will find St James Episcopal Church, the La Jolla Recreation Center and the Bishop's School, which were all were all built in the early 20th century.

The **Museum of Contemporary Art** (☎ 619-454-3541), at 700 Prospect St, has been a center for La Jolla culture since 1941. Originally designed by Gill in 1916 as the home of Ellen Browning Scripps, the building has been recently renovated by Philadelphia-born postmodern architect Robert Venturi and has one of Jonathan Borofsky's

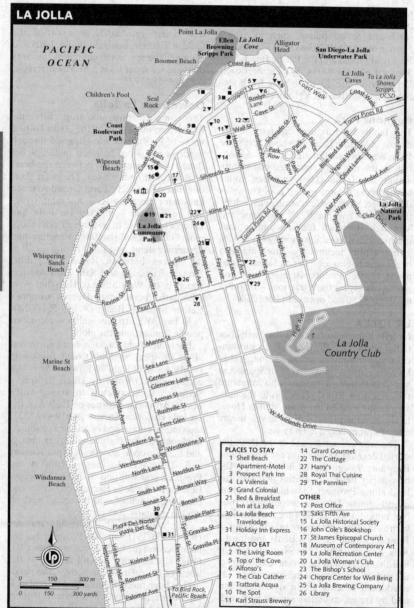

LA JOLLA

PLACES TO STAY
1 Shell Beach Apartment-Motel
3 Prospect Park Inn
4 La Valencia
9 Grand Colonial
21 Bed & Breakfast Inn at La Jolla
30 La Jolla Beach Travelodge
31 Holiday Inn Express

PLACES TO EAT
2 The Living Room
5 Top o' the Cove
6 Alfonso's
7 The Crab Catcher
8 Trattoria Acqua
10 The Spot
11 Karl Strauss Brewery
14 Girard Gourmet
22 The Cottage
27 Harry's
28 Royal Thai Cuisine
29 The Pannikin

OTHER
12 Post Office
13 Saks Fifth Ave
15 La Jolla Historical Society
16 John Cole's Bookshop
17 St James Episcopal Church
18 Museum of Contemporary Art
19 La Jolla Recreation Center
20 La Jolla Woman's Club
23 The Bishop's School
24 Chopra Center for Well Being
25 La Jolla Brewing Company
26 Library

Hammering Man sculptures out front. It's open 10 am to 5 pm Tuesday to Saturday, until 8 pm Wednesday, from noon to 5 pm Sunday; $4, free the first Tuesday and Sunday of each month.

The Coast

Downhill from downtown, the La Jolla coastline is rugged and invigorating. Private properties going right down to the beach restrict access, and parking is very limited at some points, but there is a wonderful walking path that skirts the shoreline for a half-mile. The path's west end begins at the **Children's Pool**, where a jetty (funded by – you guessed it – Ellen Browning Scripps) protects the beach from big waves. Originally intended to give La Jolla's youth a safe place to frolic, the beach is now more popular with sea lions and is a great place to view them up close as they lounge on the shore. East of the Children's Pool, La Jolla's only 'skyscraper' – the infamous mid-'60s-vintage 939 Coast Building – created the impetus for current city codes, which limit new structures west of I-5 to a height of 30 feet. Atop Point La Jolla, at the path's east end, **Ellen Browning Scripps Park** is a tidy expanse of green lawns and palm trees overlooking La Jolla Cove to the north. The cove's lovely little beach offers some of the best snorkeling around and is popular with rough-water swimmers.

The offshore area from Point La Jolla north to Scripps Pier (visible to the north), marked by white buoys, is the **San Diego–La Jolla Underwater Park**, a protected zone with a variety of marine life, some kelp forest and interesting reefs and canyons (see Scuba Diving in the Activities section).

Waves have carved a series of caves in the sandstone cliffs east of the cove. The largest is called Sunny Jim Cave.

The best place to surf and see surfers is 2 miles south of downtown (take La Jolla Blvd south and turn west on Nautilus St) at Windansea beach. The surf's consistent peak (a powerful reef break, not for beginners) works best at medium to low tide. Immediately south, at the foot of Palomar St, Big Rock is California's version of Hawaii's Pipeline with steep, hollow, gnarly tubes. The

name comes from the large chunk of reef protruding from just off shore – a great spot for tide-pooling at low tide.

La Jolla Shores

Called 'the Shores,' this area northeast of La Jolla Cove is where La Jolla's cliffs meet the wide, sandy beaches that stretch north to Del Mar (see the North County Coast section in Around San Diego). Primarily residential, the Shores is home to the members-only La Jolla Beach and Tennis Club (its orange tile roof is visible from La Jolla Cove) and Kellogg City Park, whose beachside playground is good for families with children. To reach the beach, take La Jolla Shores Drive north from Torrey Pines Rd and go west at the first stoplight. The waves here are gentle enough for beginning surfers, and kayakers can launch from the shore without much problem.

Some of the best beaches in the county are north of the Shores in **Torrey Pines City Park**, which covers the coastline from the Salk Institute up to the Torrey Pines State Reserve. At extreme low tides (about twice a year), you can walk from the Shores north to Del Mar along the beach. The **Torrey Pines Glider Port**, at the end of Torrey Pines Scenic Drive, is the place for hang-gliders and paragliders to launch themselves into the sea breezes that rise over the cliffs. It's a beautiful sight – tandem flights are available if you can't resist trying it. Down below is **Blacks Beach**, where bathing suits are technically required but practically absent. This is a popular hangout for gay men.

Scripps Institution of Oceanography

Marine scientists were working here as early as 1910 and, helped by donations from the ever-generous Scripps family, it has grown to one of the world's largest marine research institutions. It is now part of UCSD, and its pier is a landmark on the La Jolla coast.

A public education project of SIO, the **Stephen Birch Aquarium-Museum** replaces the old Scripps Aquarium and has brilliant displays on the marine sciences and of marine life. The Hall of Fishes has more than

30 fish tanks, simulating marine environments from the Pacific Northwest to tropical seas. The aquarium (☎ 619-534-3474), at 2300 Exhibition Way off N Torrey Pines Rd, is open 9 am to 5 pm daily; general admission $7.50, with special rates for students and children.

The SIO is not to be confused with the Scripps Research Institute (10550 Torrey Pines Rd), a private, nonprofit biomedical research organization.

Salk Institute

This institution for biological and biomedical research was founded by Jonas Salk, the polio prevention pioneer, in 1960. San Diego County donated 27 acres of land, the March of Dimes provided financial support, and Louis Kahn designed the building. Completed in 1965, it is regarded as a modern masterpiece, with its classically proportioned travertine marble plaza and cubist, mirror-glass laboratory blocks framing a

JAMES LYON

The Salk Institute

perfect view of the Pacific. The Salk Institute attracts the best scientists to work in a research-only environment. The facilities were recently expanded, with new laboratories designed by Jack McAllister, a follower of Kahn's work. The Salk Institute (☎ 619-453-4100 ext 1200) is at 10010 N Torrey Pines Rd, and you can tour the building with a volunteer guide at 11 am and noon Monday to Friday. Buses No 41 and 301 go along N Torrey Pines Rd.

Torrey Pines State Reserve

Encompassing the land between N Torrey Pines Rd and the ocean from the Torrey Pines Glider Port to Del Mar, this reserve preserves the last mainland stands of the Torrey pine *(Pinus torreyana)*, a species adapted to sparse rainfall and sandy, stony soils. Steep sandstone gullies are eroded into wonderfully textured surfaces, and the views over the ocean and north to Oceanside are superb, especially at sunset.

The main access road, off N Torrey Pines Rd at the reserve's north end, leads to a simple adobe – built as a lodge in 1922 by (drum roll, please) Ellen Browning Scripps – which now acts as a visitor center with good displays on the local flora and fauna. Entry and parking is $4 per car – if the ticket office is closed, get a permit from the yellow machine in the lower parking lot – or free if you walk in. Several walking trails wind through the reserve and down to the beach. If you want to hike, park near the driving range on N Torrey Pines Rd and take the paved path northwest until you reach a box of trail maps at the beginning of the Broken Arrow Trail. The reserve (☎ 619-755-2063) is open from 9 am till sunset daily.

University of California, San Diego

A campus of the University of California, UCSD was established in 1960 and now has more than 18,000 students and an excellent academic reputation, particularly for its math and science programs. It lies on rolling coastal hills in a park like setting, with many tall and fragrant eucalyptus trees. Its most distinctive structure is the Geisel Library (formerly the Central Library), an upside-down pyramid of glass and concrete whose namesake, children's author Theodor Seuss Geisel, is better known as Dr Seuss, creator of the *Cat in the Hat*. He and his wife have contributed substantially to the library, and there is a collection of his drawings and books on the ground level.

From the east side of the library's second level, an allegorical snake created by artist Alexis Smith winds down a native California plant garden past an enormous marble copy of John Milton's *Paradise Lost*. The piece is part of the **Stuart Collection** of outdoor sculptures spread around campus. Other works include Niki de Saint Phalle's *Sun God*, Bruce Nauman's *Vices & Virtues* (which spells out seven of each in huge neon letters), Robert Irwin's very blue *Fence*, and a forest of talking trees. Most installations are near the Geisel Library, and details are available from the Visual Arts Building or the Price Center, where the UCSD bookstore (☎ 619-534-7323) has an excellent stock and a helpful staff. In the Mandell Weiss Center for the Performing Arts is the **La Jolla Playhouse** (☎ 619-550-1010), known for its high-quality productions.

The best access to campus is off of La Jolla Village Drive or N Torrey Pines Rd; parking is free on weekends.

University Towne Centre

If you can ignore the pretentious spelling, you may decide UTC (☎ 619-546-8858) is the best shopping mall in the classy northern suburbs. Its 160 stores, which include Macy's, Nordstrom, Crate & Barrel and numerous specialty outlets, open to an outdoor corridor lined with fountains in which bronze dolphins swim and spout. There's also a food court, an Olympic-size ice-skating rink, six-screen movie theater, video arcade and child-care center.

Soledad Mountain

For a 360-degree view of La Jolla, take Nautilus St east from La Jolla Blvd, turn left on La Jolla Scenic Drive and follow it to Soledad Mountain Park. The large cross on top was the subject of an unsuccessful law-suit in the late 1960s – residents objected to the sectarian religious symbol on publicly owned land.

SOUTH BAY & CHULA VISTA

Between downtown and the Mexican border, the South Bay area is the least affluent part of San Diego. It is interesting to see that San Diego does have a gritty side. If you take the San Diego trolley to the San Ysidro border crossing, you'll see a reasonable cross section.

A city of 60,000 within San Diego County, **National City** is a compact square just south of downtown San Diego. It was first developed in the 1870s and still has several Victorian homes. In WWII, the city gave all the land fronting San Diego Bay to the US Navy. It remains the home of the US Pacific Fleet, a major San Diego employer.

The city of **Chula Vista** extends from the bay to the hills, and, despite being a sprawling suburb, it still has some of the citrus orchards for which it was once renowned.

The Sweetwater Marsh National Wildlife Refuge, one of the few areas of salt marsh left on the Pacific Coast, occupies much of Chula Vista's waterfront. Some 210 bird species inhabit the refuge, several of them rare or endangered. The **Chula Vista Nature Center** (☎ 619-422-2473) has some good exhibits. To get there by car, take the E St exit from I-5 and go west to the parking lot, from which a shuttle runs to the nature center every 25 minutes or so until 4 pm. The shuttle also picks up from the E St trolley station. The center is open 10 am to 5 pm daily in summer, but closes on Mondays and public holidays for the rest of the year. Interpretive tours are given at 2 pm Wednesday, Saturday and Sunday; \$3.50/1 adults/children.

Imperial Beach was once a popular holiday spot for visitors from the Imperial Valley (see the California Deserts chapter). Its long stretch of sandy beach is the site of the US Open Sandcastle contest every July. The water is sometimes unsafe for swimming because of pollution from the Tijuana River – the Border Environment Cooperation Commission is attempting to deal with the problem. **Border Field State Park**, a coastal reserve accessible from I-5, goes right to the Mexican border. It's open 9:30 am to sunset daily; entry is $4 per vehicle.

One of the busiest international border crossings in the world, **San Ysidro** –'Gateway to Mexico' – is largely populated by Mexican Americans and well supplied with Mexican restaurants, money changers and sellers of Mexican auto insurance, particularly along San Ysidro Blvd.

ACTIVITIES
Surfing
Surfing is popular along the San Diego coast, and the surf can get crowded. Fall offers the best chance to find strong swells and offshore Santa Ana winds. In summer, swells come from the south and southwest, and in winter, from the west and northwest. Spring brings more frequent onshore winds, but the surfing can still be good. For the latest beach, weather and surf reports, call City Lifeguard at ☎ 619-221-8824. Beginners looking to rent equipment should head to Mission Beach or Pacific Beach, where the waves are gentle. Places such as Bob's Mission Surf (☎ 619-483-8837), 4320 Mission Blvd near Grand, and the Pacific Beach Surf Shop (☎ 619-488-9575), 747 Pacific Beach Drive, rent boards ($5 to $8/hour) and wet suits ($3).

The best surf breaks, from south to north, are at Imperial Beach (especially in winter), Point Loma (reef breaks which are less accessible, but therefore less crowded; best in winter), Sunset Cliffs in Ocean Beach, Pacific Beach, Big Rock (California's Pipeline), Windansea (hot reef break, best at medium to low tide, but crowded), La Jolla Shores (beach break best in winter) and Blacks Beach (a fast, powerful wave). Farther up, in North County, there are breaks at Cardiff State Beach, San Elijo State Beach, Swami's, Carlsbad State Beach and Oceanside.

Body surfing is good at Coronado, Pacific Beach, Boomer Beach near La Jolla Cove (for the experienced only; best with a big swell) and La Jolla Shores. To get into the whomp (the forceful tubes that break directly on shore), know what you're doing

and head to Windansea or the beach at the end of Sea Lane (both in La Jolla).

For a glossary of surfing terms, see the Outdoor Activities chapter.

Scuba Diving
There are dive sites all along the coast of San Diego County, with some of California's best diving in the San Diego–La Jolla Underwater Park Ecological Reserve. The 6000 acres of look-but-don't-touch underwater real estate is accessible from the La Jolla Cove. The depth of the reserve averages 10 to 30 feet, which, on good-visibility days, makes it great for snorkeling as well. Ever-present are the spectacular, bright orange Garibaldi fish – California's official state fish and a protected species (there's a $500 fine for hooking one of these). Farther out are forests of giant Californian kelp, one of the world's fastest growing plants, which can increase its length by up to 3 feet per day. Islands off the Baja California coast also offer noteworthy diving.

Beginning divers train off Mission Beach, Kellogg Park (in La Jolla Shores) and La Jolla Cove. Other dive sites, including the 100-foot-deep La Jolla Canyon (part of the Underwater Park), are for more experienced divers.

Quite a few commercial operators conduct scuba courses, sell or rent equipment, fill tanks and arrange trips; prices are $90 to $210 per person, per day. Try OE Express (☎ 619-454-6195), 2158 Avenida de la Playa, in La Jolla; Ocean Enterprises (☎ 619-792-1903) in Del Mar; or the Sport Chalet (☎ 619-453-5656) at University Towne Centre. Islandia Sportfishing (☎ 619-222-1164), 1551 Quivira Rd, is a charter operation that takes people on dive trips.

Fishing
A state fishing license is required for people over 16 years old (see the Outdoor Activities chapter). A recorded service (☎ 619-465-3474) provides fishing information.

The most popular public fishing piers are Imperial Beach Municipal Pier, Embarcadero Fishing Pier, Shelter Island Fishing Pier, Ocean Beach Pier and Crystal Pier at

Pacific Beach. The best time of year for pier fishing is from about April to October. Offshore catches can include barracuda, bass and yellowtail. In summer, albacore is a special attraction.

Many firms run full-day and half-day charter fishing trips. Large parties prepared to pay $1200 to $2000 for a 20-hour trip can contact Islandia Sportfishing (☎ 619-222-1164), Fisherman's Landing (☎ 619-222-0391) and Fish n' Cruise Charter Association (☎ 619-224-2464). The less dedicated can buy a ticket on a half- or full-day excursion with H&M Landing (☎ 619-222-1144) on Shelter Island, Seaforth Sport Fishing (☎ 619-224-3383) in Quivira Basin on Mission Bay, or Point Loma Sport Fishing (☎ 619-223-1627); average prices for all companies run about $25/half-day, $75 to $108/day ($12 more if you need a license and equipment).

Boating

Power and sailboats, rowboats, kayaks and canoes can be rented on Mission Bay – try Mission Bay Sportcenter (☎ 619-488-1004) at 1010 Santa Clara Place; CP Watersports at the Hilton (☎ 619-275-8945) and Dana Inn (☎ 619-226-8611); or Seaforth Boat Rentals (☎ 619-223-1681), 1641 Quivira Rd.

Ocean kayaking is a good way to see sea life and explore cliffs and caves inaccessible from land. Southwest Kayaks (☎ 619-222-3616), near SeaWorld at the Dana Landing, has guided trips and classes starting at $35. OE Express (☎ 619-454-6195), 2158 Avenida de la Playa in La Jolla, rents kayaks for $35 for two hours.

Experienced sailors can charter yachts for trips on San Diego Bay and out into the Pacific. Quite a few charter companies are based around Shelter Island, including Shelter Cove Marina (☎ 619-224-2471), 2240 Shelter Island Drive; San Diego Yacht Charters (☎ 619-297-4555), 1880 Harbor Island Drive; and Harbor Sailboats (☎ 619-291-9568), 2040 Harbor Island Drive, suite 104.

Whale Watching

Gray whales pass San Diego from mid-December to late February on their way south to Baja and again in mid-March on their way back up to Alaskan waters. Their 12,000-mile roundtrip journey is the longest migration of any mammal on earth.

Cabrillo National Monument is the best place to see the whales from land (Torrey Pines State Reserve and La Jolla Cove are also good spots) and has exhibits, whale-related ranger programs and a shelter from which to watch for the whales' spouts (bring binoculars).

Hang Gliding & Skydiving

Glider riders hang at Torrey Pines Gliderpark (☎ 619-452-9858), 2800 Torrey Pines Scenic Drive, La Jolla, which is famous as a gliding location. Tandem flights in a hang-glider are $125 for 15 to 30 minutes.

Experienced pilots can join in if they have a USHGA Hang 4 rating and take out an associate membership of the Torrey Pines Hang Glider Association.

Hot-Air Ballooning

Brightly colored hot-air balloons are a trademark of the skies above Del Mar, on the northern fringe of the metropolitan area. For pleasure flights, contact Skysurfer Balloon Company (☎ 760-481-6800), 1221 Camino del Mar.

The *Reader* carries other balloon company listings and frequently contains hot-air excursion discount coupons. Flights are usually at sunrise or sunset. They last an hour (though up to 3 hours may be required for instruction and transportation) and cost around $130 on weekdays, $150 weekends.

ORGANIZED TOURS

Several companies run narrated tours of the city and surrounding attractions. Grayline (☎ 619-491-0011) has four-hour city tours twice daily in summer (once daily in winter) for $25/11 for adults/children, and trips to Wild Animal Park, La Jolla, Coronado and other destinations. San Diego Scenic Tours (☎ 619-273-8687) covers the city for similar prices. Both companies offer four-hour trips to Tijuana for $26, and San Diego Scenic offers an eight-hour shopping trip to Tijuana for the same price.

Old Town Trolley

Not to be confused with the Metropolitan Transit System's trolleys, which run on rails, the Old Town Trolley is a green and orange bus done up to resemble an old-fashioned streetcar. Old Town Trolley Tours (☎ 619-298-8687) do a loop around the main attractions near downtown and in Coronado, and you can get on or off at any number of stops, staying to look around as long as you wish. They start at 9 am and run every 30 minutes or so until 7 pm. You can start at any trolley stop (they are well marked with orange and are usually next to a regular San Diego Transit bus stop), though the official trolley stand is in Old Town (which is convenient for parking) on Twiggs St. The tours make quite a good introduction to the city, and the commentary is entertaining. The cost is $24/12.

Pedicabs

San Diego's version of a rickshaw is the pedicab – a carriage pulled behind a bicycle that takes up to four people. These are a fun way to get from place to place and a good way to see downtown. The drivers (pedalers?) often have tips on what's happening around town. You can flag an empty pedicab, or call Bikecabs (☎ 888-245-3222) and they'll pick you up. They operate 10 am to midnight daily, until 3 am on weekends. It costs $4 per person to get from the Embarcadero to Horton Plaza.

Naval & Military Bases

The Old Town Trolley also gives tours of some of the military bases, including the Diego Naval Station, North Island Naval Air Station, ships in port and other military facilities ($22/8 for adults/children). Call ☎ 619-298-8687 for information. On weekends, the Navy itself often conducts free tours of ships in port – call ☎ 619-437-2735 to find out if any are open.

Harbor Cruises

Both Hornblower/Invader Cruises (☎ 619-234-8687) and Harbor Excursions (☎ 619-234-4111) depart from the Embarcadero (near the *Star of India*) for one- and two-hour sightseeing tours. There are around six departures per day and prices are $12 and $17. Hornblower also has nightly dinner-dance cruises for $49 per person ($54 on Saturday).

SPECIAL EVENTS

The calendar is full of community, cultural and sporting events. Some of the most interesting and unusual are listed below. A more detailed list with up-to-date information can be obtained from the San Diego Convention & Visitors Bureau (☎ 619-236-1212).

January

Penguin Day Ski Fest – people doing things without wet suits, on waterskis and blocks of ice

February

Chinese New Year – Chinese food, culture and martial arts, at Del Mar Fairgrounds (☎ 619-234-4447)

March

Ocean Beach Kite Festival – kite making, decorating, flying and competitions, at Ocean Beach (☎ 619-531-1527)

Saint Patrick's Day Parade – 6th Ave (☎ 619-299-7812, 619-268-9111)

April

San Diego Crew Classic – national college rowing regatta, Crown Point Shores

San Diego Earth Fair – an Earth Day parade and environmental displays, in Balboa Park

May

Cinco de Mayo – the Mexican national day, celebrated with gusto in Old Town and elsewhere in the county (☎ 619-296-3161)

American Indian Cultural Days – Native American dancing, music and arts displays, in Balboa Park (☎ 619-281-8964)

Pacific Beach Block Party – lots of music and fun, on Garnet Ave (☎ 619-483-6666)

June

Indian Fair – Native American cultural exhibition, at the Museum of Man in Balboa Park (☎ 619-293-2001)

Ocean Beach Street Fair & Chili Cook-Off – popular two-day street party (☎ 619-224-4906)

SAN DIEGO AREA

Del Mar Fair – from June 15 to July 4, a huge county fair with headline acts and hundreds of carnival rides and shows, at the Del Mar Fairgrounds (☎ 619-755-1161)

July

Fourth of July – in Coronado, one of the most popular parades (☎ 619-437-8068)

Sand Castle Days – amazing sand castle-building competition, at Imperial Beach (☎ 619-424-6663)

Old Globe Festival – renowned Shakespearean festival, at the Old Globe Theatre in Balboa Park (☎ 619-239-2255)

Over-the-Line Tournament – lots of over-the-top teams in this very local variant of beach softball, on Fiesta Island (☎ 619-688-0817)

August

Hillcrest City Fest – street fair in one of San Diego's liveliest districts (☎ 619-299-3330)

Air Show – the right stuff, shown off by the Blue Angels and Top Guns, at the Marine Corps Air Station Miramar

Summerfest Chamber Music Festival – a two-week series with international performers (☎ 619-459-3728)

September

San Diego Street Scene – street festival with music on outdoor stages and plenty of food, in the Gaslamp Quarter

Thunderboat Races – unlimited hydroplane championship, on Mission Bay

October

Halloween – featuring an underwater pumpkin carving contest for scuba divers, at La Jolla (☎ 619-565-6054)

November

Thanksgiving Dixieland Jazz Festival – Dixieland bands converging on the Town & Country Hotel (☎ 619-297-5277)

December

Christmas on El Prado – crafts, carols and candlelight parade, in Balboa Park (☎ 619-239-0512)

Harbor Parade of Lights – dozens of decorated, illuminated boats, afloat in procession, on the harbor

Old Town Posadas – a traditional Latin Christmas celebration, in Old Town

PLACES TO STAY

Tourism is a major industry in San Diego, and there are more than 45,000 hotel rooms in the county. In the summer season (roughly Memorial Day to Labor Day), accommodations, particularly near the beaches, are heavily booked and prices are higher. **Sights of San Diego** (☎ 800-434-7894) books rooms at numerous hotels at discounted rates for no service charge. Taxes in San Diego County add 10.5% to the bill.

Apart from what's listed below, there is a wealth of summer rentals in the beach areas. If you have a group of friends or family, and you want to stay for more than a few days, renting a place can be an excellent value. Try calling agents such as **Mission Bay Vacations** (☎ 619-488-6773, 800-882-8626) or **Penny Realty** (☎ 619-272-3900, 800-748-6704), but call early.

Places to Stay – Budget

Camping There are several campgrounds around San Diego, but only two allow tent camping. **Campland on the Bay** (☎ 619-581-4260, 800-422-9386, 2211 Pacific Beach Drive) has more than 40 acres fronting Mission Bay. There's a restaurant, pool, boating facilities and full RV hookups. Sites cost $27 to $100 in winter, $25 to $150 in summer, depending on proximity to the water. The location is great, but the tent area is not very attractive (too many RVs, not enough trees) and can be crowded. Reservations are a good idea in the warmer months. The **KOA** (☎ 619-427-3601, 111 N 2nd Ave), in Chula Vista, is about 5 miles southeast of downtown San Diego and charges $28 for tent sites, $36 for RV sites, and has cabins from $39 to $47.

Hostels The HI **San Diego Hostel** (☎ 619-525-1531, 521 Market St) is centrally located in the Gaslamp Quarter, handy to public transportation and nightlife. It offers basic dorm rooms for $16 per night, or $19 for non-members, and has nice kitchen facilities. It's open 7 am to midnight. HI's **Elliott Hostel** (☎ 619-223-4778, 3790 Udall St), in Loma Portal (near Voltaire St), is tricky to find if you're driving and not convenient without a car. It's close to the beaches, has a good atmosphere and charges $13/16. The *Inn at the YMCA* (☎ 619-234-5252, 500 W Broadway) is handy to the Amtrak and Greyhound stations and to the trolley to Tijuana. It has rooms with shared bathroom for $30, which are quite OK as a money-saving option.

Several private hostels offer basic budget backpacker accommodations for international travelers (Americans are often allowed with proof of out-of-state residency). Downtown, the *Grand Pacific Hostel* (☎ 619-232-3100, 800-438-8622, 726 5th Ave), above Asti's Ristorante, is a Victorian-era hotel refitted with six-bed dorms ($17 per bed) and some double rooms ($38). The price includes breakfast cereal and coffee, free shuttles to most attractions, transportation to/from the airport, day tours, in-house parties and a beach barbecue on Sunday. They also sometimes run a summertime shuttle to Venice Beach, in Los Angeles, twice weekly (check with the hostel for availability). The lounge and kitchen areas are large and well kept. It's right in the Gaslamp Quarter, so can be a bit noisy, but the young crowd here doesn't seem to mind.

Only a couple of blocks from the ocean, *Ocean Beach International Hostel* (☎ 619-223-7873, 800-339-7263, 4961 Newport Ave) charges $17 for a bed in a dorm with three others. It's a friendly, fun place – popular with European travelers – with a helpful staff. Bus No 35 from downtown passes Newport Ave a block east of the hostel. Right on Mission Beach, *Banana Bungalow* (☎ 619-273-3060, 707 Reed Ave) has a top location, a beach-party atmosphere and is reasonably clean, but it's pretty basic and can get crowded. They have dorm beds, breakfast included, for $18. The communal area is a patio, which fronts right on the boardwalk and is a great place for people-watching and beer-drinking.

Downtown Note that some of the cheapest downtown hotels provide what is sometimes called SRO (single room occupancy); they rent basic rooms, by the day, week or month,

to people who might otherwise be homeless. Low-budget travelers often stay in these places and find them quite tolerable, though some regular guests can be, well, colorful characters. There are developers who would like to get rid of SROs, especially in the 'improving' areas such as the Gaslamp Quarter, but they serve a useful social function and are a relief from total gentrification. Rates are cheaper by the week, but there is typically a key deposit. In the cheapest rooms, you share a hall bathroom.

A good choice near the Gaslamp Quarter is the postmodern, rather hip *J Street Inn* (☎ 619-696-6922, 222 J St), where single-person units with kitchenettes start at $40. Also near the Gaslamp are the restored *Maryland Hotel* (☎ 619-239-9243, 630 F St), with very basic rooms from $35/44, and the *Villager Lodge* (☎ 619-238-4100, 660 G St) at 7th Ave, with units from $50.

For something different, try the *Churchill Hotel* (☎ 619-234-5186, 827 C St). It looks like a medieval castle and has bizarre theme rooms (Wild West, Jungle Safari, Chrome-a-Rama) from $45 to $55, but ordinary rooms, some with shared bath, cost around $35 to $40.

The *Pacifica Hotel* (☎ 619-235-9240), 1546 2nd Ave, is a budget hotel, very clean and well designed and only five blocks from the center of town. The rooms have basic cooking facilities, and there's a laundry, market and deli on the premises. Singles/doubles cost from $30/40 to $50/60. Its sister hotel, *La Pensione Hotel* (☎ 619-236-8000, 800-232-4683, 1700 India St) has the same ownership, the same high-quality rooms and the same low prices, and is in the heart of Little Italy. Rooms run from $59 to $79 in the summer ($10 less in winter).

Near Downtown The *E-Z 8 Motel* chain has about seven establishments around San Diego, and they all have budget-priced rooms that are clean and comfortable. The most central are near Old Town (☎ 619-294-2512, 4747 Pacific Hwy) and near the Sports Arena (☎ 619-223-9500, 3333 Channel Way). Prices vary depending on the location and the season – around $40 to $60.

Corinthian Suites (☎ *619-236-1600, 1840 4th Ave*) between downtown and Hillcrest, has rooms with kitchenettes from only $45 to $65. *Padre Trail Inn* (☎ *619-297-3291, 4200 Taylor St*) right by Old Town, is pretty cheap and conveniently located. There's a pool, bar and restaurant, and air-conditioned rooms with one/two beds cost $69/79 in summer, or $49/59 at other times. *Old Town Inn* (☎ *619-260-8024, 800-643-3025, 4444 Pacific Hwy*) has rooms from $45 to $90 (higher in the summer).

Hillcrest *Studio 819* (☎ *619-542-0819, 819 University Ave*) has nice, modern, little rooms with a bathroom, kitchenette and phone, starting at $39 – bigger rooms cost up to $50/53, but they're all cheaper by the week.

Point Loma There are budget motels on Rosecrans St, the main commercial road going to Point Loma. The cheapest places include the *Howard Johnson Inn* (☎ *619-224-8266, 800-742-4627, 3330 Rosecrans St*) and *Loma Lodge* (☎ *619-222-0511, 800-266-0511, 3202 Rosecrans St*), both with pools. Rooms start at less than $40.

Mission Bay The *Vagabond Inn* (☎ *619-274-7888, 4540 Mission Bay Drive*) is not on the beach, but it's handy to I-5. Rooms start at $65 to $79 in the summer and are $10 to $15 less in the off-season.

Pacific Beach Motels near the beach can be a pretty good value at the off-season prices quoted here, but in summer (mid-June to mid-September) prices increase by 30% or more, and rooms can be scarce. *Pacific View Motel* (☎ *619-483-6117, 610 Emerald St*) is classic '60s in appearance and close to the beach, and starts at $40/46 for singles/doubles during the off-season. *Pacific Sands Motel* (☎ *619-483-7555, 4449 Ocean Blvd*) is also well positioned and well worn, with rooms from $40 to $60. Rooms at *Mission Bay Motel* (☎ *619-483-6440, 4221 Mission Blvd*) overlook a parking lot and a busy street, but they cost only $45/65 in the off-season ($75/125 in summer) and are close to the beach and to Garnet Ave.

Places to Stay – Mid-Range

Downtown In the Gaslamp Quarter, the *Ramada Inn* (☎ *619-234-0155, 830 6th Ave*) is in the old Hotel St James (built in 1913) but has been thoroughly modernized. Rooms start at $119 year round.

The *Comfort Inn Downtown* (☎ *619-232-2525, 719 Ash St*) is a nicer-than-average budget motel that has a free shuttle to the airport and to the train station (hourly, 24 hours per day) and rooms starting at $70 (winter) and $80 (summer).

There's another group of budget motels such as the *Days Inn* and *Econo Lodge* along Pacific Hwy as you approach the downtown area from the north. These are near the Embarcadero and within walking distance of Little Italy.

Mission Valley Hotel Circle North and Hotel Circle South on either side of I-8 have a dozen or so mid-range motels, handy to Old Town, shopping centers and the San Diego Trolley line. The cheapest are *Vagabond Inn* (☎ *619-297-1691, 800-522-1555, 625 Hotel Circle S*), from $45 to $105, and *Comfort Inn Suites* (☎ *619-291-7700, 800-647-1903, 2485 Hotel Circle Place*), from $69/79, more in summer. More expensive places, with recreational facilities, include *Handlery Hotel & Resort* (☎ *619-298-0511, 950 Hotel Circle N*); the *Town & Country Hotel* (☎ *619-291-7131, 500 Hotel Circle N*); and the *Hanalei Hotel* (☎ *619-297-1101, 2270 Hotel Circle N*).

Hillcrest In the heart of the area, *Hillcrest Inn* (☎ *619-293-7078, 3754 5th Ave*) welcomes straight and gay guests (no children), has a friendly atmosphere and is quite a good value, with rooms starting at $55. *Inn Suites* (☎ *619-296-2101, 2223 El Cajon Blvd*) has a large pool and a bit more character than most chain motels, with rooms from $79, $20 more in summer. *Embassy Hotel* (☎ *619-296-3141, 3645 Park Blvd*) is in a quiet location and well priced at around $45/54.

Point Loma, Harbor & Shelter Islands Hotels here tend to be expensive and to cater to conventioneers and yachters, but the

SAN DIEGO AREA

area is close to the airport and has good views across the bay to the city. The more economical places are in Point Loma, near the Shelter Island Marina. A good choice is the *Vagabond Inn* (☎ 619-224-3371, *1325 Scott St)*, with rooms from $59 to $75.

Ocean Beach Right by the beach, the *Ocean Beach Motel* (☎ *619-223-7191, 5080 Newport Ave)* has rooms with ocean views starting at $55 per night. Farther north, also close to the sea, the *Ocean Villa Motel* (☎ *619-224-3481, 5142 W Point Loma Blvd)* is a family place ('no pets, no parties'), clean and well run, with a pool and a variety of rooms from $50 in summer, or from $55 with kitchenette.

Mission Beach An ordinary motel with a great location, within a couple of blocks of both ocean and bay beaches, the *Santa Clara Motel* (☎ *619-488-1193, 839 Santa Clara Place)* is not especially cheap, from around $95 in summer, but they may give you a good deal out of season.

Pacific Beach One of the most interesting places to stay in all San Diego is the *Crystal Pier Hotel* (☎ *619-483-6983, 800-748-5894)* – the address is 4500 Ocean Blvd, but the rooms are actually cottages on the pier itself, right above the beach and the ocean. Dating from 1927, the distinctive arched entrance to the pier is a landmark at the end of Garnet Ave. Winter prices range from $125 for the original cottages (which sleep one to four people), up to $250 for newer and larger cottages (some of which sleep up to eight people), with a two-night minimum stay. Summer rates range from $120 to $305, with a three-night minimum.

Just north of the pier, *Diamond Head Inn* (☎ *619-273-1900, 605 Diamond St)* has rooms with kitchens from $115 year round, and the best rooms face the sea. *Beach Haven Inn* (☎ *619-272-3812, 800-831-6323, 4740 Mission Blvd)* is a block from the beach, with quite good rooms from about $65 to $155. A bigger place is *Surfer Motor Lodge* (☎ *619-483-7070, 711 Pacific Beach Drive)*, right on the beach with a pool and a restaurant. They

have a variety of rooms, all with refrigerator, phone and TV, from $70 ($87 for family units); summer prices start at $83.

The *Beach Cottages* (☎ *619-483-7440, 4255 Ocean Blvd)* has motel rooms, apartments and beachfront cottages, priced from $55 in winter and $95 in summer. It's a well-run place, and you have to book early.

La Jolla In the town itself, it's hard to find a room for under $100. Try the *Shell Beach Apartment-Motel* (☎ *619-459-4306, 981 Coast Blvd)*, across from La Jolla Cove, where studios start at $65, one-bedroom suites at $98 ($20 more for an ocean view). Also downtown, the *Prospect Park Inn* (☎ *619-454-0133, 1110 Prospect St)* has very nice rooms for $140 year round.

Additional reasonably priced lodgings can be found on La Jolla Blvd south of town. Near Windansea beach, the *La Jolla Beach Travelodge* (☎ *619-454-0716, 6750 La Jolla Blvd)* and *Holiday Inn Express* (☎ *619-454-7101)*, across the street, have rooms starting at around $89 ($139 in summer). Farther south, in the area close to the rocky surfers' beach known as Bird Rock (near restaurants and the water but not near a swimming beach), are a few oldies but goodies including *The Inn at La Jolla* (☎ *619-454-6121, 5440 La Jolla Blvd)*, the *La Jolla Biltmore Motel* (☎ *619-459-6446, 5385 La Jolla Blvd)* and the *Sands of La Jolla* (☎ *619-459-3336, 5417 La Jolla Blvd)*, all with rooms from $69/79.

Places to Stay – Top End
Downtown The classiest and most historic downtown hotel is the *US Grant Hotel* (☎ *619-232-3121, fax 619-232-3626, 326 Broadway)*. It's not very old (1910), but it was built by Ulysses S Grant Jr and named for his father, and it has housed a host of famous guests, including Charles Lindbergh, Albert Einstein and Harry S Truman. It was handsomely renovated in the 1980s and is beautifully appointed with antique-style furnishings. Year-round rates are from $135/155 to $165/185; suites from $295. Special packages can be substantially cheaper, so it's worth calling.

The **Horton Grand Hotel** (☎ 619-544-1886, 800-542-1886, 311 Island Ave), reconstructed on this site from two 19th-century hotels, is more nostalgic than historic, but lots of people seem happy to pay $130 and up for a room with lace curtains and a gas-fueled fireplace. Ask about special rates before you book.

Part of Horton Plaza itself, the upscale **Westin Horton Plaza** (☎ 619-239-2200, 800-228-3000, 910 Broadway Circle) has distinctive architecture, tennis courts and a pool; from $99 (off-season) to $199 and up per night.

Other large, elegant hotels downtown include the **Hyatt Regency** (☎ 619-232-1234, 1 Market Place) and the **Marriott Hotel & Marina** (☎ 619-234-1500, 333 W Harbor Drive), both near the harbor and Convention Center; the **Marriott Suites** (☎ 619-696-9800, 701 A St), above the Symphony Hall; and the **Westgate Hotel** (☎ 619-238-1818, 1055 2nd Ave), opposite Horton Plaza.

Old Town On a quiet street near Old Town, the **Heritage Park Inn** (☎ 619-234-2926, 2470 Heritage Park Row) is a B&B in a Queen Anne-style mansion. It has 10 guest rooms starting at $100 for a double.

Handy to the San Diego Trolley and Old Town's shops and restaurants, the **Best Western Hacienda Hotel** (☎ 619-298-4707, 800-888-1991, 4041 Harney St) has suites (and only suites) with basic kitchens from $125 to $145. It also has a pool, a workout room and a Jacuzzi.

Coronado Obviously, the top-end place to stay is the **Hotel del Coronado** (☎ 619-435-6611, 800-468-3533, 1500 Orange Ave) Apart from the historical ambience, there are tennis courts, a pool, a spa, shops, restaurants and the Pacific Ocean out back. Remember that nearly half the accommodations are not in the main hotel but in an adjacent seven-story modern building with no historical feel at all. Even the rooms that are in the original building are pretty ordinary. Prices run from $205 to $595 and up.

Coronado Victorian House (☎ 619-435-2200, 1000 8th St) was built in 1894 and was recently restored. It is a B&B with eight units, all with private bathrooms. Gourmet lunches and dinners (not available to the general public) can be purchased, and guests can take dancing lessons and fitness classes, go on local tours and participate in murder-mystery theme nights. Prices run from $250 to $500.

Harbor Island & Shelter Island If you like yachts and harbor views, then you might want to stay on one of these landscaped breakwaters. The **Sheraton Harbor Island** (☎ 619-291-2900, 1380 Harbor Island Drive) offers the complete luxury experience for around $150. On Shelter Island, **Humphrey's Half Moon Inn** (☎ 619-224-3411, 800-542-7400, 2303 Shelter Island Drive) has a tropical island atmosphere and a good jazz club; rooms start at $149 in the off-season and $159 in the summer. The **Best Western Island Palms Hotel** (☎ 619-222-0561, 2051 Shelter Island Drive) is less fancy and usually around $10 cheaper, while the **Shelter Point Hotel & Marina** (☎ 619-221-8000, 1551 Shelter Island Drive) is newly renovated. Prices run from $99 to $109 in the low season and $139 to $149 in the summer.

Mission Bay The best places on Mission Bay are like tropical resorts, with lush gardens and private beaches. One of the first and finest of these developments, in the center of Mission Bay on Vacation Isle, is the **San Diego Princess Resort** (☎ 619-274-4630, 1404 W Vacation Rd), where there are several bars, restaurants and pools, plus boat, bike and skate rentals. High-season rates start at about $175. Other resort hotels, with slightly cheaper rates, include the **Bahia Resort Hotel** (☎ 619-488-0551, 998 W Mission Bay Drive); **Catamaran Resort Hotel** (☎ 619-488-1081, 3999 Mission Blvd); and **Hyatt Islandia** (☎ 619-224-1234), 1441 Quivira Rd.

Pacific Beach For comfort in an area with character, consider the **Pacific Terrace Hotel** (☎ 619-581-3500, 800-344-3370, 610 Diamond St) right on the beach. It's new and well appointed, and rates range from $215 to $280 for rooms with ocean views; $310 to $615 for suites with 'spectacular' ocean views.

La Jolla There are a number of top-end places to stay here, many of them with old-fashioned charm. Most famous is *La Valencia* (☎ 619-454-0771, 1132 Prospect St), with great views, pink walls, palm trees and Mediterranean-style architecture, and year-round room prices ranging from $225 on the low end to $1200 for the best suite. Designed by William Templeton Johnson, it has attracted movie stars and millionaires since it opened in the 1920s.

Recently renovated, the older and smaller *Grand Colonial* (☎ 619-454-2181, 910 Prospect St) dates from 1913 and maintains a refined atmosphere, with rooms from $174 to $390, but less in winter. For luxury and style right on the beach, check out the *Sea Lodge* (☎ 619-459-8271), 8110 Camino del Oro, where most rooms have a seafront balcony or patio and cost from $149 in winter up to $479 for the best rooms in summer.

Farther north, the *Hilton La Jolla Torrey Pines* (☎ 619-558-1500, 10950 N Torrey Pines Road) is a modern luxury hotel, which boasts a butler on every floor. Prices start at $250/280 single/double.

Also to the north, the *Bed & Breakfast Inn at La Jolla* (☎ 619-456-2066, 7753 Draper Ave) is a 1913 Irving Gill house with a Kate Sessions garden – surely a San Diego classic. Sixteen rooms range in price from $129 to $329 year round and all include little extras such as fresh flowers. Also, the location is unbeatable – walking distance to most La Jolla sights.

PLACES TO EAT
Downtown
There are cheap, uninteresting eateries on Broadway including the *Grand Central Café* (☎ 619-234-2233, 500 Broadway) in the YMCA building, with $4 breakfasts and $5 to $6 lunches, and the *New Peking* (☎ 619-235-6900, 638 Broadway), which does an all-you-can-eat lunch and dinner for less than $5. In the US Grant Hotel, the *Grant Grill* (☎ 619-239-6806, 619-232-3121) has live jazz most nights and is excellent but expensive.

Horton Plaza has a variety of eateries, scattered through the complex. The top floor has a food court with lots of high-quality choices and the upscale *California Cafe Bar & Grill* (☎ 619-238-5440), with indoor and outdoor dining, a brilliant view and Sunday brunch; meals are around $8. *Planet Hollywood* (☎ 619-702-7827), facing the Horton Plaza park, is a fun place, with a movie memorabilia theme.

In the southwest corner of downtown, *Kansas City Barbeque* (☎ 619-231-9680), at the corner of Columbia and Market Sts, is a popular place for ribs, onion rings and fried chicken, and slightly famous as the locale for the sleazy bar scene in *Top Gun*.

Gaslamp Quarter More than 65 places here offer everything from a quick breakfast to a gourmet dinner, with quite a range of prices. Some eateries are mainly daytime operations, while others offer entertainment well into the night (see the Entertainment section). Many change their character and clientele as the day progresses, serving lunch to businesspeople, light dinner to the theater set and cocktails to a late-night crowd. It's a great area to walk around and choose a place you like – many have a menu posted out in front.

For quick, cheap and good, try the Baja-style Mexican food at *Rubio's* (☎ 619-231-7731, 901 4th Ave), or more traditional Mexican dishes (their tamales are famous) at *El Indio* (☎ 619-239-8151), at the corner of 4th Ave and F St; both are under $7. At 926 5th Ave, *Gyroscope* (☎ 619-235-4635) has a good selection of Greek dishes at around $10.

With breezy cafe decor and an outside terrace, *Cafe Lulu* (☎ 619-238-0114, 419 F St) is a good spot for coffee and light meals ($4 to $8) till 4 am. Next door, the *Star of India* (☎ 619-544-9891, 423 F St) is a first-class restaurant with north Indian food for $7 to $12.

At the corner of 4th Ave and G St, *The Cheese Shop* (☎ 619-232-2303) is a daytime deli much loved by locals for its great sandwiches and coffee. On the opposite corner of the same intersection is cozy, *La Provence*

(☎ 619-544-0661), which serves coastal French specialties for $6 to $13.

Olé Madrid (☎ 619-557-0146, 751 5th Ave) and **Café Sevilla** (☎ 619-233-5979, 555 4th Ave) are both Spanish tapas restaurants where the tab can add up to a hefty total (figure $20 per person), especially if you stay around to enjoy the sangria (around $14 a pitcher) and live music. Both places stay open till 2 am and have dancing.

For a more casual atmosphere, try the legendary **Dick's Last Resort** (☎ 619-231-9100 345 4th Ave), which serves buckets of beer and heaping helpings of fried food ($5 to $9) and has a large patio. The building at the corner of 5th Ave and Island St has been an Asian restaurant since it opened its doors as Nanking Cafe in 1912; it's now the excellent, elegant **Royal Thai** (☎ 619-230-8424), with $5 to $11 dishes and $6 lunch specials. It has another location in La Jolla (☎ 858-551-8424, 757 Pearl St).

On 5th Ave just north of G St is a group of quality Italian restaurants, including **Trattoria La Strada** (☎ 619-239-3400, 702 5th Ave), which specializes in Northern Italian food and has dishes for a wide range of prices. A block north, the Croce family runs **Croce's Restaurant & Jazz Bar** (☎ 619-233-4355, 802 5th Ave) and **Croce's Top Hat Bar & Grill** (☎ 619-232-4338). Both have live music and serve good salads, pastas and American fare for $8 to $15.

One of the most fashionable places in town is **Fio's Cucina Italiana** (☎ 619-234-3467, 801 5th Ave), a modern Italian place with a piano bar (main courses are $10 to $20). The food is very good and the wine list is extensive. One block north is a place to see and to be seen in, the **Dakota Grill** (☎ 619-234-5554, 901 5th Ave) at the corner of E St. It serves first-rate California/Western cuisine. Appetizers are $5 to $10, salads $3 to $9 and main courses $13 to $25. In addition to its extensive food menu, the Dakota features its own microbrewed beers and a large wine list. In true California style, it also has an open kitchen where you can watch the chef in action, and an atmosphere the manager has been heard to call 'casual but elegant.'

Embarcadero

One of the liveliest places for seafood is the market-cum-deli at **Point Loma Seafoods** (☎ 619-223-1109, 2805 Emerson St) in the Shelter Island Marina. Sushi, sandwiches and seafood platters ($4 to $8) are made with the freshest fish available, and they sell fresh bread, beer and wine to go with it.

On the Embarcadero itself, the various Anthony's outlets have been serving up seafood for decades. Their classiest, and costliest, place is **Star of the Sea** (☎ 619-232-7408), built over the water at the end of Ash St. You can eat virtually the same seafood in simpler surroundings and for less money at **Anthony's Fish Grotto** (☎ 619-232-5103) right next door – main dishes cost from $7 to $26. Cheapest of all is **Anthony's Fishette**, on a veranda south of the Grotto, where excellent fish-and-chips with coleslaw cost around $5 and you can still enjoy the same view over the harbor.

A little farther south, the building at the tuna harbor has two seafood places. Downstairs is **The Fish Market** (☎ 619-232-3474), an oyster and sushi bar where a meal will cost about $6 to $15. Upstairs, the **Top of the Market** (☎ 619-234-4867) is more elegant and quite expensive.

To eat right on the harbor, take a brunch or dinner cruise with **Hornblower/Invader** (☎ 619-234-8687), departing from 1066 N Harbor Drive. A dinner cruise costs $40 for adults (more on Saturday), half-price for children, plus drinks, tax and tips. On weekends, a buffet brunch costs $35.50, and they throw in the champagne.

Little Italy

In the northwest corner of downtown, along India St, you can find authentic Italian markets and restaurants. **Filippi's Pizza Grotto** (☎ 619-232-5094, 1747 India St) is about the oldest pizza place in town and still one of the best, with inexpensive pies to eat in or take out. The **Mona Lisa** (☎ 619-234-4893, 2061 India St) has hearty meals for $6 to $11, and **Mimmo's Italian Village** (☎ 619-239-3710, 1743 India St) has terrific hot and cold sandwiches and pasta salads from $3; both double as markets

SAN DIEGO AREA

and offer a variety of imported and fresh food items.

Farther north on India St, where it meets Washington St, is a block of well-known casual eateries. *Saffron* (☎ 619-574-0177, *373 India St*) is a shoe-box-sized take-away joint that serves Asian basics – roasted chicken, rice, cabbage salad – with a variety of excellent home-made sauces for around $5; you can eat outside on the adjacent terrace. Next door, the original *El Indio* (☎ 619-299-0394) is known for its tacos ($1.50) and tamales ($2) but has a large menu and excellent breakfast burritos ($3). The *Shakespeare Pub & Grille* (☎ 619-299-0230) is one of the most authentic English ale houses in town with darts, a large selection of beers on tap and pub grub such as fish and chips, beef stew, and bangers and mash for around $6. San Diego's best Italian-style ice cream comes from *Gelato Verro Caffe* (☎ 619-295-9269) at the corner of Washington and India Sts, which is open late and displays local artists' work.

Old Town

Mexican and Southwestern flavors predominate in most Old Town eateries. They tend to go for contrived Mexican atmosphere (lots of margaritas, and mariachi bands cruising the tables), but the food can be good, outdoor tables are popular, and it all can make for a pleasant evening. *Casa de Bandini* (☎ 619-297-8211, *2660 Calhoun St*) is one of the most established places, serving reasonably priced meals such as *pollo asado* ($10.50) or enchiladas ($8).

Bazaar del Mundo, at the northwestern corner of the Old Town Plaza, has three restaurants with a lively atmosphere and mediocre food (meals are $5 to $11, appetizers around $4) – good, though, for drinks and for people-watching. Also here, *La Panaderia* is a Mexican bakery where you can grab a quick *churro* (a crispy stick of crenellated dough that's been deep-fried and rolled in sugar).

One of the least expensive but most authentic places is *Carne Estrada* (☎ 619-296-1112), a take-out taquería at the corner of San Diego Ave and Harney St, where

items cost less than $5. A favorite among locals is the *Old Town Mexican Cafe* (☎ 619-297-4330, *2489 San Diego Ave*). It has a big bar and dining room as well as excellent food for around $8; their *machacas* (shredded pork with onions and peppers) are famous in San Diego. You can watch tortillas being made as you wait to be seated.

Hillcrest

There are more than 80 places to eat here. Many are well out of the ordinary, and most are competitively priced. Tuesday night specials are offered at many eateries (from 5 to 8 pm) and can range from a free appetizer to a buy-one-meal-get-one-free. It's a great place to look around, which is all you may get to do since parking is often difficult (tickets for violations cost $72).

A classic is *The Corvette Diner* (☎ 619-542-1001, *3946 5th Ave*), with its riotous '50s-theme decor and an all-American menu with most items around $6. More contemporary is its neighbor *Kemo Sabe* (☎ 619-220-6802, *3958 5th Ave*), elegantly decorated, featuring Asian-influenced cuisine starting at $6 for lunch, $10 for dinner.

Numerous ethnic restaurants serve every kind of fare, from Sicilian to Szechwan. Two long-standing favorites are *Taste of Thai* (☎ 619-291-7525, *527 University Ave*), whose dishes ($6 to $9) can be made with or without meat and to suit any level of spice tolerance, and the less atmospheric *Ichiban* (☎ 619-299-7203, *1449 University Ave*), whose sushi and bento box specials are a bargain at around $5.

Montana's American Grill (☎ 619-297-0722, *1421 University Ave*) is a classy lunch or dinner destination. It has a full bar, extensive wine list, pastas ($8 to $13), grilled fish and meat ($9 to $22) and live jazz most weekend nights.

For the cafe society experience, hang at the comfy *Living Room Coffeehouse* (☎ 619-295-7911, *1417 University Ave*), which is open late. Grab-and-go goods are best from *Whole Foods* (☎ 619-294-2800, *711 University Ave*), a huge and high-quality health-oriented market which also has a cafe, and *Bread & Cie* (☎ 619-683-9322, *350 University Ave*), where handcrafted bread can be made into a sandwich or eaten as a meal in itself.

Coronado

Definitive Coronado dining is at the Hotel del Coronado (☎ 619-522-8496), where the Sunday brunch in the **Crown Room** is an institution for $26, often crowded and maybe overrated. The upscale restaurant in the famous **Prince of Wales** room has recently been renovated; you can also try the **Ocean Terrace Lounge**, where main courses cost from $10 to $15. Less extravagant and more swank is the **Rhinoceros Cafe & Grill** (☎ 619-435-2121, 1166 Orange Ave), which has pastas, sandwiches, salads and daily specials for $9 to $14. The **Coronado Brewing Co** (☎ 619-437-4452, 170 Orange Ave) has a patio, nice pub food and home brew for under $10.

The Beaches

Many places along the beach offer inexpensive food and a young, local scene. Garnet Ave has a wide variety of cuisines and numerous bars that will feed you between drinks. The **Down Under** (☎ 619-581-1103), on Garnet between Gresham and Fanuel Sts, has excellent burgers and meat pies ($4 to $7). For breakfast, try one of the 47 omelette specials at the **Broken Yolk** (☎ 619-270-9655, 1851 Garnet Ave), or wait in line at **Kono's Surf Club Cafe** (☎ 619-483-1669, 1815 Garnet Ave), across from the Crystal Pier, for $4 breakfast burritos and blueberry pancakes.

Slightly upscale, the **Firehouse Beach Cafe** (☎ 619-272-1999, 722 Grand Ave), overlooking the beach, has good lunch and seafood dinners, as does **The Green Flash** (☎ 619-270-7715) on the boardwalk at the west end of Thomas Ave. Also on the boardwalk, three blocks south at the end of Pacific Beach Drive, **World Famous** (☎ 619-272-3100) has good burgers and fish sandwiches for $6 and a boisterous bar.

Farther south, in Mission Beach, **The Mission Cafe** (3795 Mission Blvd) serves light breakfasts, excellent salads and sandwiches ($4 to $7), dinner specials (around $8) and famously good coffee. **Saska's**

(☎ 619-488-7311, 3768 Mission Blvd) has steak and seafood from $9 to $19. **Luigi's** (☎ 619-488-2818, 3210 Mission Blvd) is an economical pizza and pasta place, with main courses around $6.

In Ocean Beach, there are good eating options on Newport Ave. **The Little Chef** (☎ 619-222-3255, 4902 Newport Ave) is good for breakfast and has a multicultural selection of dishes, burgers and sandwiches for lunch and dinner, all around $5. **Rancho's Cocina** (☎ 619-226-7619, 1830 Sunset Cliffs Blvd), two blocks south of Newport Ave, serves healthful Mexican food and has an outdoor patio. Many of their tasty dishes are under $5. On the beach at the end of Saratoga Ave, **Dempsey's** (☎ 619-222-7740) looks like a shack but serves excellent breakfasts and lunches ($4 to $7). The **OB People's Market** (☎ 619-224-1387), on Voltaire at Sunset Cliffs Blvd, is an organic cooperative with bulk foods and an excellent delicatessen.

La Jolla

There are many top restaurants here, and most of them charge top dollar. An excellent exception is **Don Carlos Taco Shop** (☎ 858-456-0462, 737 Pearl St), where $4 buys anything on the menu – the fish potato burrito and rolled beef tacos are recommended. Good medium-priced restaurants are **Alfonso's** (☎ 619-454-2232, 1251 Prospect St), which serves wicked margaritas and good-sized Mexican dishes from about $8, and the **Spot** (☎ 619-459-0800, 1005 Prospect St), serving steaks, seafood and Chicago-style pizzas. Both have bars and are open late. **Karl Strauss Brewery** (☎ 858-551-2739), at the corner of Wall St and Herschel Ave, is an upscale place with excellent beer and good food – especially appetizers which are $1 off from 4 to 7 pm (when pints are $2).

For breakfast or lunch, try the **Cottage** (☎ 619-454-8409, 7702 Fay Ave) or **Harry's** (☎ 619-454-7381, 7545 Girard Ave), a veritable institution that's a favorite with professional athletes and has been reviewed in the *New York Times*; breakfast at either one is around $7. The **Girard Gourmet** (☎ 858-454-3321, 7837 Girard Ave) is a quality deli

SAN DIEGO AREA

with heaped-up sandwiches, hot lunch specials and irresistible pastries for less than $5.

If money is no object and you want a good view, make a reservation, dress up and go to the *Crab Catcher* (☎ 619-454-9587, *1298 Prospect St)*, in the Coast Walk complex, for excellent seafood ($15 to $30); *Trattoria Acqua* (☎ 619-454-0709), next to the Crab Catcher, for first-rate Northern Italian cuisine ($11 to $17); or the *Top o' the Cove* (☎ 619-454-7779, 1216 Prospect St).

Two La Jolla standbys are the *Pannikin* (☎ 619-454-5453, 7467 Girard Ave), which has been 'wakin' up San Diego since 1964,' and *The Living Room* (1010 Prospect St), which gets an international student crowd from the adjacent language school; both serve meals for less than $10 and are open late.

ENTERTAINMENT

There's a lot going on in San Diego, and you'll need some local information. The free weekly *San Diego Reader* and *San Diego Union Tribune*'s Night & Day section hit the stands on Thursdays – both have comprehensive listings and reviews of movies, theater, galleries and gigs. The *Performing Arts Guide*, available from the International Visitors Center, covers theater, music and dance offerings over a two-month period.

Call Ticketmaster for event information and to book tickets (☎ 619-220-8497). Times Arts Tix (☎ 619-497-5000), in the little Horton Plaza park on Broadway, sells half-price theater tickets on the day of a performance, as well as full-price tickets to most major events in the area.

Bars & Clubs

San Diego's first liquor license was granted in the 1930s and is still held by its original owner, the *Waterfront* (☎ 619-232-9656, 2044 Kettner Blvd) – which actually was on the waterfront until the harbor was filled and the airport built. The bar is still going strong and, besides being full of historic 'stuff,' is one of the best places to spend the afternoon or evening – there's a big window that opens onto the street, $5 bar food and live music on weekends.

The Shame of the Gaslamp

You can't ignore *Dick's Last Resort* (☎ 619-231-9100, 345 4th Ave), a venue that thrives on its own negative publicity. The self-proclaimed 'Party from Hell Place' is a beer barn that advertises 'no ferns, no fine art, no elite atmosphere, and no class, ever.' Instead of happy hour, they have a weekday 'decompression deal' for the 'working stiff,' which features a 2½-hour 'supervisor slam-o-rama,' $1 draft beer and $2 margaritas. Their 'worthless eats' are served not on plates but in plastic buckets. After 8 pm, they have live rock and jazz bands, which get a rowdy reception. I had heard they had some particularly tacky decor, and deliberately rude staff, so I went to check it out.

The waitress was very friendly and politely offered to take a drink order. I asked her if it was true that the staff at Dick's were rude. She replied, somewhat apologetically, that they usually were but that she just didn't feel like it that evening. I walked past the bar, which was festooned with underwear, and suddenly I heard someone yelling. It was the bartender – 'Hey, you! What are you looking at? You look like a fucking tourist! Sit down, have a drink, and for Chrissake get yourself an *attitude*!'

– James Lyon

If you like buying your beer at the source, San Diego has a number of microbreweries. Karl Strauss beer, for instance, is available at many bars but made at the *Old Columbia Brewery & Grill* (☎ 619-234-2739, 1157 Columbia St).

Gaslamp Quarter The distinction between eating and entertainment venues can be fuzzy in this lively area, as it seems to be in the places run by the family of the late bluesman Jim Croce. The bar at *Croce's Restaurant & Jazz Bar* (☎ 619-233-4355, 802 5th Ave) is regularly packed with jazz fans, while *Croce's Top Hat Bar & Grill* (☎ 619-232-4338), next door, is more of a blues and R&B venue.

Patrick's II (☎ 619-233-3077) on F St is a popular R&B bar. *Buffalo Joe's* (☎ 619-236-1616, 600 5th Ave) has a variety of live bands, as does *Dick's Last Resort* (☎ 619-231-9100, 345 4th Ave), which also has pool, darts and a big patio. *4th & B* (☎ 619-231-4343), at – you guessed it – the corner of 4th Ave and B St, gets semi-famous contemporary groups and the occasional swing band. If nothing else looks appealing, head to *The Bitter End* (☎ 619-338-9300, 770 5th Ave), where an old brothel has been turned into an atmospheric watering hole.

Also in the Gaslamp, the *Hang Ten Brewing Company*, at 5th Ave and K St, brews several types of beer, which it serves up along with good food and sports on TV.

Other interesting downtown venues include *Cafe Sevilla* (☎ 619-233-5979, 555 4th Ave), which has live Latin American music and dancing most nights; *La Gran Tapa* (☎ 619-234-8272, 611 B St); and *Olé Madrid* (☎ 619-557-0146, 751 5th Ave), which often features DJs spinning funk and acid jazz.

Near Little Italy, the *Casbah* (☎ 619-232-4355, 2501 Kettner Blvd) is a fun place to see alternative rock bands. It has couches, pinball machines and dimly lit alcoves if you don't feel like dancing.

Old Town Despite the name, *O'Hungry's* (☎ 619-298-0133, 2547 San Diego Ave) is more for drinking than for eating. They serve beer by the yard, and sometimes have live music – it can be a fun place.

Hillcrest Nearly all the bars cater to a mainly gay and lesbian clientele. Some of the most popular are *Kickers* (☎ 619-491-0400, 308 University Ave), *The Brass Rail* (☎ 619-298-2233, 3796 5th Ave), *Flick's* (☎ 619-297-2056, 1017 University Ave) and *Rich's* (☎ 619-295-0750, 1051 University Ave). A few blocks east of Hillcrest, *Pecs* (☎ 619-296-0889, 2046 University Ave) is a heavy leather scene, while to the west across I-5, *West Coast Production Company*

(☎ 619-295-3724, 2028 Hancock St) has loud disco music and a reputation as a meat market. *The Flame* (☎ 619-295-4163, 3780 Park Blvd), where the lesbian scene is lively, features bands most nights.

The Beaches In Pacific Beach, there are a number of bars and clubs on and around Garnet Ave and near the beach – most of them pretty down-to-earth. *Blind Melons* (☎ 619-483-7844, 710 Garnet Ave) has mainly blues performers and some rock. A dance club popular with a young crowd, *Club Tremors* (☎ 858-272-7278, 860 Garnet Ave), has a low cover charge and cheap snacks. *Moondoggies* (☎ 858-483-6550, 832 Garnet Ave), next door to Club Tremors, has a large patio, big-screen TVs, pool tables, good food and an extensive tap selection. The *Society Billiard Cafe* (☎ 619-272-7665, 1051 Garnet Ave) is billed as San Diego's plushest; it offers 15 full-size tables, snacks and a bar, which is open from 11 am to 2 am daily. The *Cannibal Bar* (☎ 619-539-8650, 3999 Mission Blvd), in the Catamaran Resort Hotel, is an intimate tropical place that books reggae, Latin and acid-jazz bands.

In Ocean Beach, *Winston's* (☎ 619-222-6822, 1921 Bacon St) features live reggae most nights.

La Jolla Jazz is the thing in La Jolla, and there's plenty of it at *Milligan's* (☎ 619-459-7311, 5786 La Jolla Blvd), in the Bird Rock area of La Jolla, starting at 8 pm Thursday through Sunday. Fittingly, Milligan's also makes one of San Diego's best martinis. Other jazz venues include the *Crescent Shores Grill* (☎ 619-459-0541, 7955 La Jolla Shores Drive) atop Hotel La Jolla, and the *Torreyana Grille* (☎ 619-450-4571, 10950 Torrey Pines Rd) in the Hilton Torrey Pines.

On the microbrewery scene, try *La Jolla Brewing Company* (☎ 619-456-2739, 7536 Fay Ave). If you didn't get to the Old Columbia Brewery for your Karl Strauss beer, you can also find it being made at the *Karl Strauss Brewery* (☎ 858-551-2739) at the corner of Wall St and Herschel Ave, where pints are $2 from 4 to 7 pm weekdays.

SAN DIEGO AREA

And just for laughs, try one of the area's most established comedy venues, **The Comedy Store** (☎ 619-454-9176, 916 Pearl St) in La Jolla. It is open nightly, serving meals, drinks and chuckles. There's often a cover charge ($6 to $12 on weekends with a two-drink minimum).

Coffeehouses

Coffeehouses in San Diego are popular hangouts as well as nighttime venues; often they have live music. Try **Cafe Lulu** (☎ 619-238-0114, 419 F St) in the Gaslamp Quarter; **New World Coffee** (☎ 619-702-5436, 1602 Front St) downtown; Little Italy's **Caffe Italia** (1704 India St); **Java Joe's** (☎ 619-523-0356, 4994 Newport Ave) in Ocean Beach; **Zanzibar**, Garnet Ave, Pacific Beach; and **The Pannikin** (☎ 858-454-6365, 7458 Girard Ave) in La Jolla.

Theater

Theater thrives in San Diego and is one of the city's greatest cultural attractions. Book tickets from the theater or with one of the agencies listed in the introduction to this section. Venues include:

Civic Theatre (☎ 570-1100, 202 3rd Ave) – in the Community Concourse, at B St

Grand Theatre Horton (☎ 619-234-9583, 444 4th Ave)

La Jolla Playhouse (☎ 619-550-1010) – at UCSD

Old Globe Theater (☎ 619-239-2255) – one of three theaters in the Simon Edison Centre in Balboa Park

San Diego Junior Theatre (☎ 619-239-8355) – Casa del Prado, Balboa Park

San Diego Repertory Theatre (☎ 619-231-3586, 79 Horton Plaza)

Spreckels Theater (☎ 619-235-9500, 121 Broadway)

Theatre in Old Town (☎ 619-688-2494, 4040 Twiggs St)

Lamb's Players Theater (☎ 619-437-0600, 1142 Orange Ave) – Coronado

Cinema

The main downtown cinemas are the **UA** complex at Horton Plaza (☎ 619-234-4661)

Garden Cabaret

Modeled after Italian outdoor cinemas but updated with heat lamps, table seating and whimsical decor, San Diego's **Garden Cabaret** (☎ 619-295-4221, 4040 Goldfinch St), off Washington Ave in Hillcrest, is an extremely enjoyable place to see a movie. The program is usually heavy on Hollywood classics – think *Some Like It Hot*, *Rear Window*, *Roman Holiday* – and films with contemporary historical significance (a slew of Kubrick films were shown after he died). All shows are preceded by a few cartoons, just like in the early years of Hollywood cinema. Sunday night shows are based on a theme that runs the length of the season, which lasts from June to August. All shows are at 8:30 pm and cost $8; starting at noon the same day you can reserve a table for $2 extra. Coffee, tea, designer sodas, decadent deserts and (of course) popcorn are sold. Call the box office or stop by the theater for current show information.

and Pacific Theater's elegant new **Gaslamp 15** (☎ 619-232-0400) at 5th and G Sts; both show current release movies. The **Village Hillcrest** (☎ 619-299-2100), on 5th Ave in Hillcrest, **The Ken** (☎ 619-283-5909, 4061 Adams Ave), in Kensington, and **The Cove** (☎ 619-459-5404, 7730 Girard Ave), in La Jolla, show some European and classic movies, as well as current releases.

Opera

Conducted by Karen Keltner, the **San Diego Opera** (☎ 619-570-1100) is known to rival its Los Angeles counterpart for high-quality, eclectic programming. It has hosted such stars as Placido Domingo, José Carreras and Cecilia Bartoli. Its season runs from January to May, with performances at the Civic Theatre. Tickets cost from $35 to $115. Discount tickets are sometimes available from Times Arts Tix, and standing-room tickets ($18) are available from the theater just before a performance (arrive an hour early to ensure getting a place). With a standing-room ticket you are allowed to take any empty seat once the lights go down.

Symphony

The Fox Theatre, a heavily decorated Spanish-rococo structure, originally opened as a cinema in 1929. In the 1980s the block it sits on, bounded by A and B Sts and 7th and 8th Aves, was redeveloped, but fortunately the theater was spared. San Diego lost its symphony several years ago, but the theater, renamed *Copley Symphony Hall*, hosts guest orchestras; check the *Reader* for current performances. The *La Jolla Symphony* (☎ 619-534-4637) is of very good quality and holds concerts at UCSD's Mandeville Auditorium from November to May.

SPECTATOR SPORTS

San Diego-Jack Murphy Stadium, now called Qualcomm Stadium (☎ 619-283-4494) as a result of a controversial name change in the '90s, is San Diego's big sports venue, at 9449 Friars Rd in Mission Valley (there's a San Diego Trolley stop right in front). It was originally named for sports journalist Jack Murphy, who was instrumental in getting the park built. He also worked to bring the Chargers football team to town in 1961 and the Padres baseball team in 1968. Both of these professional teams are well supported, so book in advance for big games. Padres tickets are usually available at the gate unless it's a game crucial to the standings or they are playing the LA Dodgers on a Friday or Saturday night.

The Sports Arena (☎ 619-224-4176), 3500 Sports Arena Blvd, is where the San Diego Sockers play soccer and the San Diego Gulls play ice hockey. It's also the venue for any big rock concerts visiting town. Be aware that the neighborhood may be a little rough after dark.

SHOPPING

Every museum and visitor attraction has a gift shop, so souvenir hunters might find a stuffed Shamu at SeaWorld, a realistic rubber snake at the zoo or an old photo at the Museum of San Diego History. The Spanish Village area of Balboa Park is a good place to find paintings (mostly water-colors) of the San Diego area. A uniquely San Diegan gift would be anything emblazoned with the logo of a local surf shop. If you make a trip into the Backcountry (see the Backcountry section in this chapter), locally-grown dates, avocados, citrus fruit and wine can be had at reasonable prices.

The most expensive shops are in Horton Plaza and downtown La Jolla, while big department stores – Macy's, Nordstrom, Robinsons-May, etc – are in Fashion Valley and the University Towne Centre mall. There are numerous other shopping malls in the suburbs.

The Factory Outlet Center (☎ 619-690-2999), just west of I-5 in San Ysidro, has discount outlets for Nike, Levi's and other big names. There's also the North County Factory Outlet Center (☎ 619-595-5222), 1050 Los Vallecitos Blvd, San Marcos. For really cheap stuff, try Kobey's Swap Meet (☎ 619-226-0650), a massive flea market in the parking lot of the Sports Arena, from 7 am to 3 pm Thursday to Sunday. Shopping in Tijuana can be cheap, but you must shop around for good-quality silver, baskets and blankets.

GETTING THERE & AWAY
Air

San Diego is quickly becoming a major gateway. If you're flying in from abroad, however, you will most likely come via Los Angeles, and it's hardly worth getting a connecting flight to San Diego (the standard one-way fare is about $75). The flight from LA takes only about 35 minutes, but it's almost as quick to drive down if there's no traffic on the freeway, and it's just as cheap to rent a car in LA as in San Diego.

If you're flying to or from other US cities, it's almost as cheap to fly to or from San Diego as it is to LA. It's worth shopping around for inexpensive fares and allowing about three weeks for advance purchase. Airlines serving San Diego's Lindbergh Field (☎ 619-231-2100) include Aeromexico, America West (worth checking for cheap fares), American, Continental, Delta, Northwest, Southwest and US Airways.

Bus

The Greyhound station (☎ 619-239-8082), at 120 W Broadway, has luggage lockers ($2 for 6 hours) and telephones and is generally user-friendly. Daily bus routes include:

destination	price	duration	buses per day
Los Angeles	$13	2½ hours	20
Oceanside	$5	1 hour	11
El Centro	$11	2½ hours	9
			(3 continue to Phoenix, Tucson and El Paso)
San Ysidro/ Mexican border	$4	½ hour	19
Las Vegas	$42/45	8 hours	5 weekdays/ weekends
San Francisco	$41/44	11 hours	4

Train

The Santa Fe depot is one of the Spanish colonial-style structures built at the time of the 1915 exposition. Colonnaded, clean and spacious, but not overdone, it is almost definitive San Diego architecture. It's easy to find, at 1050 Kettner Blvd at the west end of C St.

Amtrak's only services to and from San Diego are along the coast. From the Santa Fe depot, the *San Diegan* goes to Los Angeles nine times daily, with stops at six stations in between. Three of these trains continue to Santa Barbara. The first train leaves at 5 am, and the last at 8:45 pm, and it takes about three hours to reach LA. Services into San Diego from the north are similar, with incoming trains arriving between 7:50 am and noon. There's some nice coastal scenery along the way. Contact Amtrak for reservations and information.

GETTING AROUND

Many people get around San Diego by car, but you can reach most places fairly easily on public transport. Metropolitan buses and the trolley lines are run by Metropolitan Transit Service (MTS), and several other bus companies serve surrounding areas. All sorts of local public transport tickets, maps and information are available from the Transit Store (☎ 619-234-1060), 102 Broadway at 1st Ave, open 8:30 am to 5:30 pm weekdays, noon to 4 pm weekends. They sell the Day Tripper Transit Pass, which is good for unlimited travel on local buses, the trolley and bay ferry. It costs $5 for one day and $12 for four consecutive days.

To/From the Airport

San Diego International Airport at Lindbergh Field is quite close to downtown and easily reached by bus No 992 ($2). Various shuttle services go to and from the airport, including Cloud Nine (☎ 800-974-8885). The ride from the airport to downtown costs about $8. The Grand Pacific Hostel (see the Places to Stay section) and many top-end hotels offer a free shuttle for their guests.

Bus

MTS covers most of the metropolitan area, North County, La Jolla and the beaches and is most convenient if you're going to or from downtown and not staying out late at night. Get the free *Regional Transit Map* from the Transit Store (see the Getting Around section), or call for taped information (☎ 619-685-4900) to find out individual schedules. Fares are $1.75 for most trips, including a transfer that is good for at least an hour; on express routes it's $2: exact fare is required.

Trolley

Two trolley lines run to and from the downtown terminal near the Santa Fe train depot. The blue line goes south to the Mexican border at San Ysidro and north to Old Town, then east through Mission Valley. The orange line goes east, past the Convention Center to El Cajon. Trolleys run every 15 minutes during the day (from 5 am), and every 30 minutes in the evening (the last trolley leaves the city about 12:15 am). Fares vary with distance, up to $2.

Train

A commuter rail service, the *Coaster*, operates up the coast to North County with stops in Solana Beach, Encinitas, Carlsbad and Oceanside. In the metropolitan area, it stops at the Sorrento Valley station (where there's a connecting shuttle to UCSD), Old Town and the Santa Fe depot. Tickets cost from $3 to $3.75 depending on the distance traveled. The *Coaster* accommodates bicycles; racks can be found by entering through one of the doors marked with a bike emblem. There are nine trains in each direction per day weekdays, with two added on Friday night to extend service to around 11 pm (otherwise it stops around 6:30 pm). There are four trains on Saturday, none on Sunday. For information call Regional Transit (☎ 619-685-4900).

Car

The big-name rental companies have desks at the airport, but the lesser-known ones can be cheaper. It's definitely worth shopping around and haggling – prices vary widely, even from day to day within the same company. The west terminal at the airport has free direct phones to a number of car-rental companies – you can call several and then get a courtesy bus to the company of your choice. Also, car rentals are as cheap or cheaper in LA, so it might be preferable to get one there.

Thrifty (☎ 619-233-9333) rents compact cars from $140 per week with unlimited miles (can be less in off season or with special deals). West Coast (☎ 619-544-0606) has cars from $24 per day. Tropical (☎ 619-239-9017) is also cheap, at $20/day, $99/week, but they don't allow you to go outside San Diego County. Others to try include Admiral (☎ 619-696-9900), Getaway (☎ 619-233-3777), National (☎ 619-497-6777), Avis (☎ 619-231-7171) and Dollar (☎ 619-234-3388).

Taxi

Established companies include American Cab (☎ 619-292-1111), Orange Cab (☎ 619-291-3333), Silver Cab (☎ 619-280-5555) and Yellow Cab (☎ 619-234-6161). Fares are around $1.80 to start and then about $1.90 per mile.

Bicycle

Some areas around San Diego are great for cycling, particularly Pacific Beach, Mission Beach, Mission Bay and Coronado. MTS buses on some routes have a bike rack, and bikes can be transported without extra charge. These routes include bus No 34 between downtown and La Jolla (via Ocean Beach, Mission Bay, Mission Beach and Pacific Beach), No 41 between Fashion Valley Center and UCSD, No 150 between downtown and University Towne Centre, No 301 between University Towne Centre and Oceanside, and No 902 between downtown and Coronado. The bike-rack routes are indicated by a bicycle symbol on the bus stop signs. For more information call ☎ 619-685-4900. You'll need a permit to take a bike on the San Diego Trolley, obtainable from the Transit Store.

Bike rentals are available at Coronado, Mission Bay and the beaches (see the Activities section). Rent-a-Bike (☎ 619-232-4700), at 523 Island St, has a variety of mountain bikes, road bikes, kids' bikes and cruisers, and will deliver one to you, seven days a week.

Boat

A regular ferry ($1.50) goes between Broadway Pier and Coronado. Water Taxi (☎ 619-235-8294) makes a regular connection between Seaport Village and Coronado, where it stops at the Ferry Landing Marketplace and Glorietta Bay. It also makes on-call trips to Shelter Island, Harbor Island, Chula Vista and South Bay. The cost is $5 per person.

Around San Diego

NORTH COUNTY COAST

The North County extends up the coast from the petty seaside town of Del Mar to the Camp Pendleton Marine Base. This continuous string of beach-side suburban communities resembles the San Diego of 30 years ago, though more and more development (especially east of I-5) is turning North County into a giant bedroom community for San Diego and Orange County. Still, the beaches here are terrific, and the small seaside towns are good places to stay for a few days if, more than sightseeing, you want to soak up the laid-back Southern California scene.

From the south, N Torrey Pines Rd is the most scenic approach to Del Mar, and you can continue along the coast on S-21 (which changes its name from Camino del Mar to Pacific Coast Hwy to Old Hwy 101, going north). A quicker route is I-5, which continues to Los Angeles and beyond. Bus No 301, which allows bikes, departs from University Towne Centre and follows the coast road to Oceanside, while No 800 is a peak hour express service; for information call the North County Transit District (☎ 760-722-6283). Greyhound buses stop at Del Mar, Solana Beach, Encinitas and Oceanside. The *Coaster* commuter train stops at convenient locations in Solana Beach, Encinitas, Carlsbad and Oceanside.

Del Mar

This is the ritziest of North County's seaside suburbs. It has excellent (if pricey) restaurants, unique galleries, high-end boutiques and a horse-racing track, which is the site of the annual county fair. Downtown Del Mar (sometimes called 'the village,' as is the upscale Coronado) extends for about a mile along Camino del Mar. At its hub, where 15th St crosses Camino del Mar, the very tasteful **Del Mar Plaza** – designed by Jon Jerde of Horton Plaza fame – overlooks the water with terraces, restaurants and quality boutiques. Esmeralda's Books & Coffee (☎ 858-755-2707), at the top of the plaza near Il Fornaio, has colorful artwork and often gets well-known authors for its weekly readings. At the beach end of 15th St, **Seagrove Park** overlooks the ocean. This little chunk of well-groomed beachfront is a community hub frequented by locals.

Hot-air balloons are a common and colorful sight over Del Mar, especially at sunset (see the Activities section earlier in this chapter).

Del Mar Racetrack & Fairgrounds The Del Mar Racetrack (☎ 619-755-1141) was started in 1937 by a group including Bing Crosby and Jimmy Durante, and its lush gardens and pink, Mediterranean-style architecture are delightful. The thoroughbred racing season runs from mid-July to mid-September, and track admission is $3.

From mid-June to July 4, the **Del Mar Fair** (☎ 619-755-1161) is a major event, with livestock exhibits, carnival shows, rides and big-name performers every night. Admission is $8 for adults.

Places to Stay & Eat Staying near the beach in Del Mar is nice, and there are plenty of hotels, but it's not cheap. The **Del Mar Motel** (☎ 619-755-1534, 800-223-8449, 1702 Coast Blvd) is right on the beach and costs from $80/120 in winter to $120/170 in summer.

The patio and restaurants atop Del Mar Plaza have one of San Diego's best vantage points – if you can't afford a meal at one of these places at least go have a look. If you do want to splurge, **Pacifica Del Mar** (☎ 619-792-0476) has excellent California cuisine and fresh fish ($15 to $20), **Epazote** (☎ 619-259-9966) has an interesting Southwest-style menu ($6 to $22) and **Il Fornaio** (☎ 619-755-8876) does upscale Italian (up to $27 for dinner). Cheaper options are the deli at the **Good Nature Market** (☎ 858-481-1260) and Il Fornaio's **Enoteca**, which serves grappa, wine and light meals.

Solana Beach

Solana Beach is the next town north, not quite so posh, but with good beaches and the recently dubbed **Design District** along Cedros Ave, which has unique art and architecture studios, antiques stores and handcrafted clothing boutiques. One of the first businesses here was the **Belly Up Tavern** (☎ 619-481-2282, 619-481-8140, 143 S Cedros Ave), a converted warehouse that is still a popular music venue and regularly gets great bands. Cover charge is $4 to $7, or even $10 for top attractions. The **Wild Note Cafe** (☎ 619-259-7310), a new part of the Belly Up, is a good spot for lunch or dinner with prices starting at $6.

Two long-standing Mexican restaurants are worth looking up – **Fidel's** (☎ 619-755-5292, 607 Valley Ave) and **Tony's Jacal** (☎ 619-755-2274, 621 Valley Ave). Valley Ave

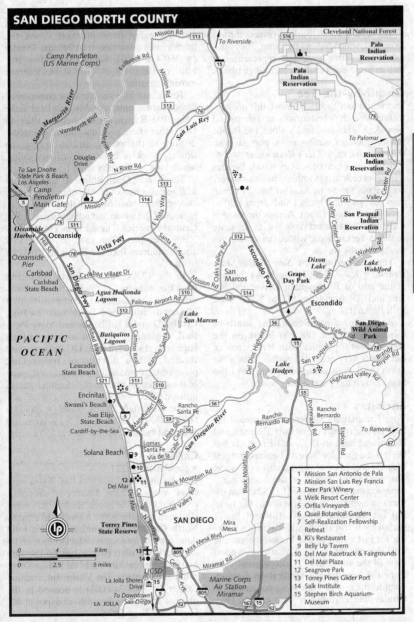

SAN DIEGO NORTH COUNTY

1   Mission San Antonio de Pala
2   Mission San Luis Rey Francia
3   Deer Park Winery
4   Welk Resort Center
5   Orfila Vineyards
6   Quail Botanical Gardens
7   Self-Realization Fellowship Retreat
8   Ki's Restaurant
9   Belly Up Tavern
10 Del Mar Racetrack & Fairgrounds
11 Del Mar Plaza
12 Seagrove Park
13 Torrey Pines Glider Port
14 Salk Institute
15 Stephen Birch Aquarium-Museum

goes north of Via de la Valle, just west of I-5. Both places offer meals for less than $10.

There are some budget-priced motels along S21, which follows the coast. They are a mixed bag, with a few chains represented as well as some independent, mid-range places.

Cardiff-by-the-Sea

Shortened to 'Cardiff' by most, this noncentralized stretch of restaurants, surf shops and New Age–style businesses along the Pacific Hwy is good for surfing and is popular with the laid-back crowd. *Ki's Restaurant* (☎ 760-436-5236) is a hub of activity which, besides having excellent smoothies, health-burgers and salads for $4 to $8, also has an ocean view and jazz and blues bands from 8:30 to 11:30 pm Fridays (free). Across the road is Cardiff's 'restaurant row,' with upscale seafood restaurants whose windows get washed by the waves.

The campground at *San Elijo State Beach* (☎ 760-753-5091) overlooks the surf at the end of Birmingham Drive, and has tent and RV sites from $17 to $22 – book with Parknet.

At Cardiff State Beach, just south of Cardiff-by-the-Sea, the surf break on the reef is mostly popular with longboarders, but it gets very good at low tide with a big north swell. A little farther north, San Elijo State Beach has good winter waves.

Encinitas

Yogi Paramahansa Yoganada founded his Self-Realization Fellowship Retreat and Hermitage here in 1937, and Encinitas has been a magnet for holistic healers, natural lifestyle seekers and vegetarians ever since. The gold lotus domes of the hermitage – conspicuous on Old Hwy 101 (S21) – mark the southern end of Encinitas and the turnout for **Swami's**, a powerful reef break surfed by territorial locals. There's a parking lot just south of the hermitage, on the west side of Old Hwy 101, that gives a good view of the surf. There is also a great vista from the hermitage's **Meditation Garden**, open to the public 9 am to 5 pm Tuesday to Sunday; the entrance is west of Old Hwy 101 at 215 K St.

The heart of Encinitas is north of the hermitage between E and D Sts. Besides outdoor cafes, bars and surf shops, the town's main attraction is **La Paloma Theater** (☎ 760-436-7469), 471 S Coast Hwy 101, built in 1928. La Paloma shows current movies nightly.

The inland hills are used for commercial flower farms, most notably the Paul Ecke Poinsettia Ranch, established in 1928. In December there's an enormous poinsettia display at the ranch, and in spring the flowers grow in bands of brilliant color, which look spectacular from I-5.

The 30-acre **Quail Botanical Gardens** has a large collection of California native plants and sections planted with flora of various regions of the world, including Australia and Central America. The gardens (☎ 760-436-3036) are open 9 am to 5 pm daily; $5/2 adults/children. Take the Encinitas Blvd exit from I-5.

In the 1920s, **Rancho Santa Fe**, inland from Encinitas on County Road S9, was subdivided as a residential community that attracted Hollywood types such as Bing Crosby, Douglas Fairbanks and Mary Pickford. National City–born architect Lilian Rice, who graduated from UC Berkeley and studied with a disciple of Irving Gill, planned the community and designed many of the original homes in the elegant Spanish mission style.

The *Moonlight Beach Motel* (☎ 760-753-0623, 800-323-1259, 233 2nd St) is large and in a good location; rooms start at $50 a night.

Carlsbad

- population 68,221

Carlsbad is a good place to stay if you want to be within walking distance of shopping, restaurants and the beach. Rather than being stretched out along the highway like many North County communities, it has a solid downtown of four square blocks between I-5 and Carlsbad Blvd (which run north-south and are connected by Carlsbad Village Drive running east-west). The Visitor Information Center (☎ 760-434-6093) is housed in the original 1887 Santa Fe railroad depot at 400 Carlsbad Village Drive.

The town came into being when the railroad came through in the 1880s. John Frazier, an early homesteader, former sailor and ship's captain, sank a well and found water that had a high mineral content, supposedly the identical mineral content of spa water in Karlsbad (hence the town's name), Bohemia (now the Czech Republic). He capitalized on the aquatic similarities of the two places and built a grand spa hotel, which prospered until the 1930s. The Queen Anne–style building that was the hotel is now *Neiman's Restaurant* (☎ 760-729-4131, 2978 Carlsbad Blvd), a place where the atmosphere is appreciably better than the overpriced food.

A private investment company built a day spa in 1994, but the attempt to revitalize the spa industry was short-lived. The real success story in the North County is the fairly recent emergence of a thriving wine business. Witch Creek Winery (☎ 760-720-7499), 2906 Carlsbad Blvd, has a tasting room downtown where you can sample six wines for $3 and take home the glass. East of I-5, off the Palomar Airport Rd exit, Belle-fleur Winery (☎ 760-603-1919) at 5610 Paseo del Norte has lovely gardens, a tasting room and a high-end restaurant.

The long, sandy beaches of Carlsbad are great for walking and seashell hunting. Good access is from Carlsbad Blvd, two blocks south of Carlsbad Village Drive, where there's a boardwalk, rest rooms and free parking.

Places to Stay & Eat You can camp at *South Carlsbad State Park* (☎ 760-438-3143), where sites cost from $17 to $22 ($1 more on Saturday nights) and can be booked through Parknet (☎ 800-444-7275). There are plenty of other accommodations, but they tend to be expensive, especially in summer. Best value is probably the *Motel 6* (☎ 760-434-7135, 1006 Carlsbad Village Drive) for $39/44, or one of the other chain-operated motels in the area. Top-end options include the *Carlsbad Inn* (☎ 760-434-7020, 800-235-393, 3075 Carlsbad Blvd), on the beachfront, with rooms starting at $169, and *La Costa Resort & Spa* (☎ 760-438-9111), on Costa Del Mar Rd, 2 miles east of I-5, with acres of grounds, all sorts of recreational facilities and rooms from $315 to $500 and up (cheaper by the month).

There are plenty of eateries downtown, west of I-5. Locals often choose *The Armenian Cafe* (☎760-720-2233) on Carlsbad Blvd two blocks south of Carlsbad Village Drive for $5-to-$9 Middle Eastern food; and *Pizza Port* (☎ 760-720-7007, 571 Carlsbad Village Drive) for salads ($3), pizza (around $15 for a large) and locally brewed beer.

Legoland

Local citizens, fearing traffic congestion and the other effects of rampant tourism, nearly quashed the opening of the new US Legoland (the original is in Denmark), which is in Carlsbad, 50 miles north of downtown San Diego. But despite community fears, the traffic now slips smoothly off I-5, directed by large freeway signs that mark the way to the attraction. And the overall appearance of the place is far less touristy than, say, SeaWorld. In fact, people now seem quite proud of the town's newest point of interest, which is exceeded in size and popularity only by the beach. Legoland publicity may lead you to believe this place is most interesting to children, but people of all ages seem to enjoy the historic cities, monuments and mountain ranges – all made of little plastic bricks. There are bicycles to ride around the grounds, a boat tour of some exhibits, and many opportunities to build (and buy) your own Lego structures.

To get to Legoland California (☎ 760-918-5346, www.legolandca.com), take the Legoland/Cannon Rd exit off I-5 and follow the signs. From downtown San Diego, take the *Coaster* train to the Poinsettia Station, then North County Transit (☎ 800-266-6883) bus No 344 to the park; park hours are 9 am to 9 pm daily. It ain't cheap: tickets are $32/25 adults/children and parking is an extra $6.

Oceanside
• **population 72,512**

Oceanside is home base for many of the employees who work on, or for, the big Camp Pendleton Marine Base on the town's northern border. Most attractions of interest to visitors will be found along the coast, unless you're in the market for automotive parts or a military-style jacket. The main thing to look at is the wooden **Oceanside Municipal Pier**, extending more than 1900 feet out to sea. It's so long that there's a little golf buggy to transport people to the end (25¢). There are bait and tackle shops, with poles to rent and lights for night fishing, as well as snack bars and the mid-priced, '50s-style **Ruby's** (☎ 760-433-7829), which, in addition to good burgers and milkshakes, has a full bar. Two major surf competitions – the West Coast Pro-Am and the National Scholastic Surf Association (NSSA) – take place near the pier in June.

A history of these contests, plus photos, old boards and memorabilia of Duke Kahanamoku (the Olympic gold medal swimmer and surfing pioneer who died in 1968) is on display at the **California Surf Museum** (☎ 760-721-6876) at 223 N Coast Hwy. It's free and open weekdays; call for hours.

Very few buildings remain from the 1880s, when the new Santa Fe coastal railway came through Oceanside, but there are still a few left that were designed by Irving Gill and Julia Morgan. The Oceanside Visitor Information Center (☎ 760-721-1101), at 928 N Coast Hwy, has a pamphlet describing a self-guided history walk.

Oceanside Harbor At the northern end of the waterfront, the extensive Oceanside Harbor provides slips for hundreds of boats. Helgren's (☎ 760-722-2133), 315 Harbor Drive S, offers a variety of charter trips for sportfishing ($22 to $32) and whale watching ($14). At the south end of the harbor, Cape Cod Village, a group of shops and restaurants, has a distinctly nautical flavor.

Mission San Luis Rey Francia Founded in 1798, this was the largest California mission and the most successful in recruiting Indian converts. It was known as the 'king of the missions,' and at one time some 3000 neophytes lived and worked here. After the Mexican government secularized the missions, San Luis fell into ruin – the adobe walls of the church, from 1811, are the only original parts remaining. Inside there are displays on work and life in the mission, with some original religious art and artifacts. The mission (☎ 760-757-3651) is 4 miles inland at 4050 Mission Ave (Hwy 76) and costs $4. Call for hours.

Places to Stay Budget motels are not hard to find but may fill up on weekends and in summer. The **Bridge Motor Inn** (☎ 760-722-1904), close to I-5 off the Coast Hwy exit, is an old standby with a restaurant and harbor view; rooms start at $65. There's also the **Days Inn** (☎ 760-722-7661), near the Oceanside Harbor Drive exit, with $57/65 rooms.

Getting There & Away The Oceanside Transit Center, 235 S Tremont St, is the station for Metropolitan Transit System buses, Amtrak (☎ 760-722-4622) and Greyhound (☎ 760-722-1587), which has 14 buses to San Diego ($5, 45 minutes) and 16 to Los Angeles ($10, two hours) daily.

Camp Pendleton

Driving through on I-5, you can often see Marines making amphibious 'attacks' on the beaches. For a closer look, you can do a free driving tour of Camp Pendleton (☎ 760-725-5569), but there's not much to see except the **Landing Vehicle Museum**.

The base is often closed to outside visitors because of the training or combat-preparation procedures taking place there. The main gate is off I-5 just north of Oceanside, and you need to show your driver's license and vehicle registration.

San Onofre State Beach

A long and largely undeveloped beach area north of Oceanside, San Onofre is well known to longboarders. It is often called 'old man's' because the older generation likes the gentle waves here. The younger, more aggressive set surfs Trestles, a fast, hollow wave at the north end of the beach. Access to San Onofre is off I-5, via Basilone Rd, north of a highly conspicuous nuclear power plant (which is reputed to make the water warmer here). There are campsites on the bluffs above the beach, which cost $16 in summer, $14 the rest of the year – reserve through Parknet.

NORTH COUNTY INLAND

I-15 heads north from San Diego, through Rancho Bernardo (a residential community with miles of mission-style houses) and Escondido to the Riverside County line. The number-one attraction is the Wild Animal Park near Escondido, but there are also some interesting historical sites, and the area provides access to the scenic backcountry around Palomar (see the Backcountry section). You can get out to Escondido by bus – call the North County Transit District (☎ 760-743-6283, 760-722-6283) for information.

Escondido

Many people retire to this quiet satellite city. Heritage Walk (☎ 760-743-8207), in Grape Day Park, is a collection of retired Victorian buildings that have been moved here. Hours are Thursday to Saturday 1 to 4 pm. The chamber of commerce (☎ 760-745-2125), 720 N Broadway, has information about all of North San Diego County; their hot line (☎ 800-848-3336) is accessible 24 hours, or call ☎ 760-754-4741.

There are plenty of places to stay; the chain motels are near I-15, including *Motel 6* (☎ 760-745-9252, 900 N Quince St), *Best Western Inn* (☎ 760-740-1700, 1700 Seven Oakes Rd), *Comfort Inn* (☎ 760-489-1010, 1290 W Valley Pkwy), plus *Howard Johnson, Holiday Inn, Super 7* and *Rodeway Inn*.

Wineries Spanish missionaries planted some of California's first grapevines around Escondido. Orfila Vineyards, formerly Thomas Jaeger Winery (☎ 760-738-6500), at 13455 San Pasqual Rd, is open 10 am to 6 pm daily (until 5 pm in the winter), with guided tours at 2 pm. **Deer Park Winery and Auto Museum** (☎ 760-749-1666), 29013

Welk Resort Center

The Welk Resort Center (☎ 760-749-3000, 800-932-9355), 8860 Lawrence Welk Drive, is about 7 miles north of Escondido. It incorporates the Lawrence Welk Dinner Theater (☎ 760-749-3448), which runs a summer season of light musicals, and the Lawrence Welk Museum, open from 10 am daily, which has memorabilia of Lawrence Welk's life and work.

Welk, also known as 'Mr Bubbles,' was the man responsible for 'champagne music,' and he hosted the 'wunnerful, wunnerful' Lawrence Welk Show in the 1940s and '50s – it was the longest-running music program in TV history. The Lawrence Welk restaurant has a $10 buffet lunch, which is a good value if you're hungry.

SAN DIEGO AREA

Champagne Blvd just north of the Welk Resort Center, open 10 am to 5 pm, is touted as the world's only combination winery and car museum – it specializes in convertibles, and has more than 100 on display.

Getting There & Away North County Transit (☎ 760-743-6283) bus No 20 runs Monday to Saturday between downtown

San Diego and the Escondido Transit Center at 700 W Valley Parkway; bus No 810 is a peak-hour commuter service that runs Monday to Friday in the late afternoon. Greyhound (☎ 760-722-1587) buses use the same stop.

Wild Animal Park

Since the early 1960s, the San Diego Zoological Society has been developing this 1800-acre, free-range animal park. The main attractions at Wild Animal Park (☎ 760-747-8702) are herds of giraffes, zebras, rhino and other animals roaming the open valley floor. Visitors take a 50-minute ride around the animal preserves on the Wgasa Bush monorail (actually an electric tram), which gives great views of the animals and includes an interesting commentary. The animals look wonderful in the wide open spaces, though often you can't get as close to them as you can in a regular zoo.

At the Petting Kraal you can often touch some of the youngest animals in the park. Animal shows are held in a number of areas, starting between 11 am and 4:30 pm. Get a map and a schedule as you enter.

The park has a full range of services, souvenir shops and places to eat. It is just north of Hwy 78, 5 miles east of I-15 from the Via Rancho Parkway exit. Bus No 307 will get you there from the Escondido Transit Center, Monday to Saturday, but it's a long, involved process getting back, so you may be better off going by car.

The gates are open 9 am to 6 pm daily in summer, to 4 pm for the rest of the year; you can stay in the park an hour after the gates close. Admission costs $19.95 for adults, $17.95 seniors and $12.95 for children 3 to 11 years old, including the monorail ride and all animal shows. Discount coupons are widely available. A combined ticket to visit both the San Diego Zoo and the Wild Animal Park within a five-day period costs $35.50/25.75. Parking is $3 extra. For a real safari experience, photo caravan tours go right in among the animals, but they're quite expensive, and reservations are required – call the main number and ask for guest relations. Facilities are available for disabled visitors; call ☎ 760-738-5067 for information.

Mission San Antonio de Pala

Built in 1810 as an *asistencia* to Mission San Luis del Rey, this was to have been one of a chain of inland missions, but the plan was abandoned, as was the whole mission system a few years later. This mission – on Hwy 76, 7 miles east of I-15 – is largely reconstructed and has a small museum (☎ 760-742-3317), open 10 am to 4 pm daily except Monday; $2. It's on the Pala Indian reservation in a quiet, rural area and makes for a pleasant stop along Hwy 76, but it's not much of a destination.

THE BACKCOUNTRY

Going inland from San Diego, you quickly get into sparsely populated rural areas a world away from the highly developed coast. Much of San Diego County's backcountry is occupied by the Cleveland National Forest, which offers camping, hiking and mountain biking. An excellent book for the trail – or for finding a trail – is Jerry Schad's *Afoot and Afield in San Diego County*, widely available for around $12.

If you are exploring the Cleveland National Forest by car, you must obtain a National Forest Adventure Pass in order to use forest facilities, including hiking trails (see the boxed text in the Outdoor Activities chapter for details).

Highway 79 is a scenic route through the backcountry, from the wine- producing area near Temecula (in Riverside County), south via Warner Springs and the old gold-mining area of Julian, to Cuyamaca Rancho State Park and I-8. To explore the backcountry, you can go by car, though you can get to most places by buses, which run infrequently but are cheap – call Northeast Rural Bus System (☎ 760-767-4287) at least a day ahead.

Palomar Mountain

At 5535 feet, Palomar Mountain is the centerpiece of three promontories that make up the 25-mile-long Palomar Range. It is densely forested with pine, oak, fir and

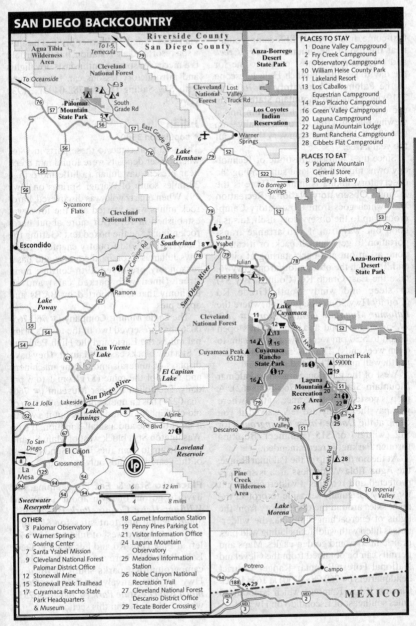

SAN DIEGO BACKCOUNTRY

PLACES TO STAY
1 Doane Valley Campground
2 Fry Creek Campground
4 Observatory Campground
10 William Heise County Park
11 Lakeland Resort
13 Los Caballos
  Equestrian Campground
14 Paso Picacho Campground
16 Green Valley Campground
20 Laguna Campground
22 Laguna Mountain Lodge
23 Burnt Rancheria Campground
28 Cibbets Flat Campground

PLACES TO EAT
5 Palomar Mountain
  General Store
8 Dudley's Bakery

SAN DIEGO AREA

OTHER
3 Palomar Observatory
6 Warner Springs
  Soaring Center
7 Santa Ysabel Mission
9 Cleveland National Forest
  Palomar District Office
12 Stonewall Mine
15 Stonewall Peak Trailhead
17 Cuyamaca Rancho State
  Park Headquarters
  & Museum
18 Garnet Information Station
19 Penny Pines Parking Lot
21 Visitor Information Office
24 Laguna Mountain
  Observatory
25 Meadows Information
  Station
26 Noble Canyon National
  Recreation Trail
27 Cleveland National Forest
  Descanso District Office
29 Tecate Border Crossing

SAN DIEGO AREA

cedar and receives several feet of snow a year. Although there are two self-register, first-come, first-served USFS campgrounds near the top of the mountain – *Fry Creek* and *Observatory* – most people come for the day to see the 200-inch Hale telescope at the **Palomar Observatory** (☎ 760-742-2119) near **Palomar Mountain State Park**, in use since 1948. There's a museum and a viewing platform that are open usually 9 am to 4:30 pm daily (hours can vary throughout the year); free.

Since the California Institute of Technology owns most of the land surrounding the observatory, hiking is limited. There is the 2.2-mile **Observatory National Recreation Trail**, which goes from Observatory Campground up to the observatory itself; this is a good one-way trail if you arrange transportation to get yourself back, or it can be done as an out-and-back starting at either end. To reach the observatory from Hwy 76, take the East Grade Rd (County Hwy S7) or steep and windy South Grade Rd (County Hwy S6) to the junction, where the *Palomar Mountain General Store* (☎ 760-742-3496) has food and supplies (it's open 11 am to 5:30 pm weekdays and 8:30 am to 6 pm weekends). The observatory is 5 miles north, well marked by road signs.

West of the junction, S7 goes to **Palomar Mountain State Park** (☎ 760-742-3462). A map is posted at the entrance station, where you pay the $5 day-use fee, waived if you camp at the *Doane Valley Campground* for $12 (winter) or $15 (summer). Booking through Parknet is recommended.

At the northern tip of the Palomar Range, the **Agua Tibia Wilderness** area is specially protected and requires a wilderness permit for entry. Originally set aside to protect the night skies around the observatory from the lights of encroaching suburbia, the wilderness is filled with wildlife, including wild pigs, prairie falcons and golden eagles. Maps and permits can be obtained from the Cleveland National Forest Palomar Ranger District headquarters (☎ 760-788-0250) at 1634 Black Canyon Rd in Ramona, which is about 15 miles southeast of Escondido on Hwy 78.

Warner Springs

Some 30 miles east of Palomar Mountain via Hwys 76 and 79, Warner Springs has just a spa resort and a gas station, but the airfield is a mecca for soaring enthusiasts. Joy flights and introductory lessons can be arranged with Sky Sailing (☎ 760-782-0404), 31930 Hwy 79.

Julian

• **population 3500**

The gold rush came to these parts in 1869, when placer deposits were found in a creek near present-day Julian (a little more than 20 miles south of Warner Springs on Hwy 79). When quartz gold was discovered, hard-rock mines were started and the town was established in 1870 (for more about hard-rock mining, see the boxed text 'Getting the Gold' in the Gold Country chapter). These days Julian is in orchard country and has a reasonably preserved 19th-century main street (lined with parked cars) and an economy that is supported by B&Bs and apple pies.

The **Eagle Mining Company** (☎ 760-765-0036) has preserved two of the town's original mines, the Eagle and the High Peak, up C St a few blocks east of Main St. They have displays of minerals and mining machinery and tours of the mine ($7) from 1 to 3 pm daily. The **Julian Pioneer Museum** (☎ 760-765-0227) has an unexceptional collection of old clothing, tools and photos, but it's worth a short browse and a small donation. It's on Washington St, a block west of Main St, and open 10 am to 4 pm Tuesday to Sunday most of the year; weekends only in winter.

Places to Stay & Eat   For camping, you have to go out of town about 3 miles to *William Heise County Park* (☎ 760-565-3600), which has tent sites for $14 in a pretty setting. Go west of Julian on Hwy 78, left at Pine Hills Rd and left again at Deer Lake Park Rd. There are also a few private campground-RV parks south of town on Hwy 79. Alternatively, go down to *Cuyamaca Rancho State Park* (☎ 760-765-0755), which is described in this section.

Accommodations in Julian are mostly pricey B&Bs. Places fill up on weekends and holidays, and many have a two-night minimum stay. The chamber of commerce (☎ 760-765-1857), 2129 Main St, has information about many of them. About the most appealing is the *Julian Hotel* (☎ 760-765-0201, 2032 Main St), which dates from 1897. Most of the rooms don't have bathrooms, and it's not a great value at $82 ($105 on weekends).

Many of the restaurants and cafes on Main St sell lunches and apple pies. For something different, try *Bailey's BBQ Pit* (☎ 760-765-9957) at the corner of Main and A Sts at the north end of town. They have a reputation for good food ($5 to $8); there's live music on weekends.

Near the town of Santa Ysabel, northwest of Julian on Hwy 78, *Dudley's Bakery* (☎ 760-765-0488) is enormously popular with San Diegans for homemade bread, cakes and pastries. They're closed Monday and Tuesday.

Cuyamaca Rancho State Park
Delightful for the variety of its landscapes, Cuyamaca Rancho is a lush, cool contrast to both the coastal areas and the deserts. Situated 6 miles north of I-8 on Hwy 79, its 33 sq miles embrace meadows with spring wildflowers, forests of oak, willow, sycamore and pine, and wild animals such as deer, raccoons, bobcats and squirrels; there's also rich bird life.

The genesis of the park was in 1870 when gold was discovered just south of Cuyamaca Lake. By 1872 the town of Cuyamaca had grown up around the Stonewall Mine, and from 1887 to 1891 California governor Robert Waterman developed the area with gusto. When the ore – and Waterman's interest in the mine – petered out, homesteaders tried to make the area into a resort. A Mr Dyars, who was a descendant of a gold rush '49er, bought the rancho in 1923 and 10 years later helped create the state park. The Dyars' former home is now the park headquarters (☎ 760-765-0755), open 8:30 am to 4:30 pm weekdays, and a museum with a good display on local Native Americans (open daily; free).

The park is popular with hikers, mountain bikers and equestrians and has miles of well-defined trails that start from trailhead parking lots along Hwy 79; maps are posted at each trailhead. Two recommended hikes are the 5½ mile (round-trip) climb to Cuyamaca Peak (6512 feet), offering a panoramic view, and the 4½ mile hike up Stonewall Peak (5730 feet) to look over the old mine site. You can also drive to the mine site: turn east off Hwy 79 at the 'Los Caballos Campground' sign, 1 mile north of Paso Picacho Campground.

There are two drive-in campgrounds in the park, *Green Valley* and *Paso Picacho*, both charging $12 per site ($14 in summer); Paso Picacho also has very basic cabins for $22. Call Parknet for reservations. There are two undeveloped, walk-in campsites – *Arroyo Seco* and *Granite Springs* – as well as *Los Caballos*, an equestrian campground equipped with corrals (reservations for these three can also be made through Parknet). *Lakeland Resort* (☎ 760-765-0736, 14916 Hwy 79), opposite the lake just outside the park's northern boundary, has cabins for $40 to $45.

Holidays on Horseback (☎ 619-445-3997), in Descanso, near the south entrance to the park, will arrange trail rides in the park for $35 to $75.

Highway 79, which can be approached from the north, via Julian, or the south, off I-8, goes right through the park. Coming from the south, there's a shop, pay phone and a place to eat (closed Tuesday) at Descanso. There's also a shop, bar and restaurant at Lake Cuyamaca, on the north side of the park. For maps and information, stop at one of the campground entrance kiosks or (in winter) at the office upstairs in the park headquarters. There's a $5 day-use fee, which you need to put in an envelope when you park.

Laguna Mountains
The Laguna crest lies at the eastern edge of the Cleveland National Forest. From the

crest there is a 6000-foot drop to the Anza-Borrego Desert below – you can often see the Salton Sea, 60 miles away, and the San Jacinto range, which is 2000 feet higher than the sea and often snow-covered. The Lagunas are slightly lower and drier than the Cuyamacas – which lie 11 miles west – but they support a wonderful array of plant life, including Jeffery and Coulter pines and the rare Laguna aster (*Machaeranthera asteroides lagunesis*), which blooms in August and September. Coyotes, mountain lions and foxes are among the four-footed creatures you might see.

The Sunrise Hwy (County Road S1) runs along the highest part of the range, which is designated as the Laguna Mountain Recreation Area from I-8 in the south to Hwy 79 in the north. There are self-service information booths at both ends of the highway, and a Visitor Information Office (☎ 619-473-8547) that is open weekends in the small community of Mount Laguna, about halfway between I-8 and Hwy 79 on County Road S1. There's also information at the Cleveland National Forest Descanso Ranger District headquarters (☎ 619-445-6235), off I-8 east of Alpine.

At the south end of the Laguna Mountain Recreation Area, off the Sunrise Highway, is the **Mount Laguna Obervatory** (☎ 619-594-6182), operated by San Diego State University, where there is a summer visitor program. It generally runs from Memorial Day through Labor Day, when the Buller 21-inch visitor's telescope and the visitor center are open from 7:30 to 9:30 pm Friday and Saturday nights.

The *Laguna Mountain Lodge* (☎ 619-445-2342), in Mt Laguna township, has a good selection of maps, books and groceries, and rents cabins starting at $55 midweek. Campgrounds (☎ 877-444-6777), such as *Laguna Campground* and *Burnt Rancheria Campground* along Sunrise Hwy and *Cibbets Flat Campground* on Kitchen Creek Rd, are half by reservation, half first-come, first-served and cost $14 per site; reservations are a good idea on weekends and holidays.

Hiking This area has a number of hiking trails, including a 37-mile section of the Pacific Crest Trail and the 10-mile Noble Canyon National Recreation Trail. The Penny Pines parking lot, 4 miles north of Laguna Mountain Lodge, is a good starting point for several hikes. A 2-mile jaunt (on the Pacific Coast Trail) up to Garnet Peak is worthwhile on a clear day – the views are dizzying. West, across Sunrise Hwy from Penny Pines, the trail to Big Laguna Lake leads through stands of Jeffery pine and a large open meadow. You can also hike over to the Cuyamacas by way of the Indian Creek trail.

A good little *Hiking Trails* booklet, published by the Laguna Mountain Volunteer Association, is available for $2 at the Descanso ranger station and the Visitor Information Office.

Tijuana, Mexico

Visiting Tijuana is a real experience. As a Mexican city, Tijuana is neither typical nor attractive, but as border towns go, it is almost an archetype, with gaudy souvenir shops, noisy bars and sleazy backstreets. Though more respectable than it once was, it has never completely overcome the 'sin city' image it acquired during US Prohibition. It still attracts young Americans who can get legally drunk at age 18, but these days most people can feel comfortable in the main shopping streets, at least until sunset.

Tijuana (pronounced tee-HWAH-na and sometimes called TJ) has a population unofficially estimated at around 1 million. Just across the US border from San Diego's southern suburbs, it's a significant city in its own right, though in some ways the two cities are so interdependent that they can almost be regarded as a single urban area. About 70% of Tijuana's economy is based on 'frontier transactions' such as tourism, and another 15% is from *maquiladoras* (factories assembling products for the US market). Tijuana is one of the wealthiest cities in Mexico.

Meanwhile, San Diego promotes Tijuana as one of its own tourist attractions and depends on the border town for a supply of cheap labor. But beyond the shopping and entertainment precincts, Tijuana does have its own life, with office buildings, factories and housing developments, as well as two universities.

ORIENTATION

Tijuana's central grid consists of north-south *avenidas* (avenues) and east-west *calles* (streets). Most of the calles have names as well as numbers, but are usually known by the number. South of Calle 1A, Avenida Revolución is the main commercial thoroughfare. To the east, the 'new' commercial center straddles the Río Tijuana. Mesa de Otay, to the northeast, contains the airport, maquiladoras, residential neighborhoods and shopping areas.

The farther from the border you go, the less touristy Tijuana becomes. Atop the hill at the south end of Avenida Constitución is a shady square, the Parque 18 de marzo, where people play basketball and everyday life in TJ can be observed.

INFORMATION

For those venturing farther down the Baja California peninsula, the book *Baja California*, published by Lonely Planet, is highly recommended.

Tourist Offices

There's a Tijuana city tourist office just south of the pedestrian border crossing, open 9 am to 7 pm Monday to Saturday, until 2 pm Sunday. The Tijuana Secretary of Tourism (☎ 66-85-05-55, 66-88-16-85), on Calle 1A at the corner of Revolución, is open 24 hours.

Consulates

The US consulate (☎ 66-81-74-00) is at Tapachula 96, just behind the Club Campestre Tijuana (Tijuana Country Club). There are also consulates for Great Britain (☎ 66-81-73-23) and Canada (☎ 66-84-04-61), as well as for France and Germany.

Visas & Immigration

If you're not going past the border zone (beyond Ensenada), or staying more than 72 hours, you don't need a visa or even a passport to enter Tijuana, but you should have some form of identification, with your photo on it. Returning to the US, non-Americans can be subject to a full immigration interrogation, so bring your passport with a US visa (if you have one). If your immigration card still has plenty of time on it, you will probably be able to reenter with the same one; but if it has nearly expired, you will have to apply for a new one, and they may want to see that you have an onward air ticket and sufficient funds.

Money

Everyone accepts (even prefers) US dollars, and tourist prices are usually quoted in dollars. There are lots of *casas de cambio*, which will change money and traveler's checks at almost any hour. The Terminal Turistica Tijuana, at 1025 Av Revolución, has an ATM that gives dollars. Bring small bills and coins, or you may have to accept change in pesos at very low rates. At most souvenir stalls and shops, prices are not marked and haggling is expected.

Post & Communications

Tijuana's central post office, at Av Negrete and Calle 11A, is open from 8 am to 4 pm weekdays.

Tijuana has many public telephones and long-distance offices. The Central Camionera has several *cabinas* (Spanish for 'telephone booths') with operators and public fax machines. To call Tijuana from the US, dial 011 (for international calls) + 52 (for Mexico) + 66 (for Tijuana) + the number. To call the US from a pay phone, get a Ladatel phone card from a pharmacy or market, and dial 95 + the area code (eg, 619 for San Diego), then the number. For collect or person-to-person calls to the US, dial 001, then the area code and number. Private telephone offices in Tijuana offer special deals, which are often cheaper than the standard rates.

SAN DIEGO AREA

Speaking Spanish

It's easy to get around Tijuana without speaking much Spanish, but knowing just a bit will definitely help you, and is also appreciated by the locals. Here are some of the basics:

yes	*sí*
no	*no*
thank you	*gracias*
you're welcome	*de nada*
hello	*hola*
good morning	*buenos días*
good afternoon	*buenas tardes*
good evening/night	*buenas noches*
goodbye	*adiós*
I don't speak Spanish	*No hablo español*
I understand	*Entiendo*
Where?	*¿Dónde?*
Where is . . . ?	*¿Dónde está . . . ?*
Where are . . . ?	*¿Dónde están . . .?*
How much?	*¿Cuanto?*
How many?	*¿Cuantos?*
How much does it cost?	*¿Cuanto cuesta?*
It's very expensive	*Es muy caro*
When?	*¿Cuando?*
How?	*¿Cómo?*
Why?	*¿Por qué?*
Is there . . . ? Are there . . . ?	*¿Hay?*
I want/would like	*Quiero/Quisiera*
I have	*Tengo*
I like . . .	*Me gusta . . .*
Do you have?	*¿Tiene?*

To make a verb negative, add *no* before the verb; I don't have is *No tengo*, I don't like is *No me gusta*.

and	*y*
to/at	*a*
for	*por, para*
of/from	*de, desde*
in	*en*
with	*con*
without	*sin*
before	*antes*
after	*después*
soon	*pronto*
now	*ahora*

here	*aquí*
there	*allí or allá*
coffee	*café*
tea	*té*
beer	*cerveza*

Numbers

1	*uno*
2	*dos*
3	*tres*
4	*cuatro*
5	*cinco*
6	*seis*
7	*siete*
8	*ocho*
9	*nueve*
10	*diez*
20	*veinte*
30	*treinta*

Time

What time is it?	*¿Qué hora es?*
At what time does it open/close?	*¿A qué hora se abre/se cierra?*

Telling time is fairly straightforward. Eight o'clock is *las ocho*; 8:30 is *las ocho y treinta* or *las ocho y media* (eight and a half). However, 7:45 is *las ocho menos quince* (eight minus fifteen) or *las ocho menos cuarto* (eight minus one quarter). Times are modified by morning (*de la mañana*) or afternoon (*de la tarde*) instead of am or pm.

Days of the Week

Monday	*lunes*
Tuesday	*martes*
Wednesday	*miércoles*
Thursday	*jueves*
Friday	*viernes*
Saturday	*sábado*
Sunday	*domingo*

Medical Services

The Cruz Roja (Red Cross) is on Vía Oriente in the Zona Rosa (☎ 66-132). The Hospital General (☎ 66-84-09-22) is north of the river on Av Padre Kino, west of Rodríguez. There are also many clinics that cater to US visitors.

Dangers & Annoyances

'Coyotes' and *polleros* – human smugglers – and their clients congregate along the river, west of the San Ysidro crossing. After dark, avoid this area and Colonia Libertad, east of the crossing. The Zona Norte, a seedy red-light area, north of Calle 1A and west of Constitución, can also be dangerous, especially at night. Theft and pickpocketing are not uncommon in Tijuana. The state government has a tourist protection service (☎ 66-88-05-55). For police, call ☎ 66-134.

Avenida Revolución

South of Calle 1A, Avenida Revolución (La Revo) is Tijuana's tourist heart. Most visitors brave at least a brief stroll up this raucous avenue of seedy bars and restaurants, brash taxi drivers, tacky souvenir shops, funky dance clubs and street photographers with zebra-striped *burros*.

Frontón Palacio Jai Alai

Fast-moving jai alai matches at the Frontón Palacio Jai Alai (☎ 66-38-43-08), on Revolución between Calles 7A and 8A, resemble a hybrid of tennis and handball. Frontón staff will explain details to neophyte bettors, and the bilingual narration is also helpful. Stop by the ticket office on the north side of the building for current schedules and ticket information.

Centro Cultural Tijuana

This modern cultural center, called CECUT (☎ 66-84-11-11), at Paseo de Los Héroes and Av Independencia, is conspicuous for its spherical **Cine Planetario** (locally known as La Bola – The Ball – designed by Pedro Ramierez Vazquez and Manuel Rosen Morrison), which shows a variety of films on a 180° screen ($3.25).

The building behind La Bola formerly housed the Museo de las Identidades Mexicanas and now has rotating exhibitions on Mexican painting, sculpture and architecture, which can be excellent; free. There's also a bookshop, live performance theater and restaurant. Hours are 10 am to 9 pm Tuesday through Sunday.

Plaza Fiesta Mall

Also at the junction of Av Paseo de Los Héroes and Av Independencia, across the traffic circle from CECUT, this shopping center is an imitation Mexican village, which somehow avoids being total kitsch. Across Av Paseo de los Héroes, the Plaza Rio Tijuana is the Mexican equivalent of an American shopping mall, where locals browse and school children hang out and eat ice cream.

Mercado Hidalgo

This is where locals come to buy spices, dried chilies, exotic produce, fresh tortillas and seasonal specialties made from Aztec grains. The partially covered stalls open on to a main square – usually filled with delivery trucks – which takes up several blocks that are bounded Av Paseo de los Héroes, Av Independencia and Av Sanchez Taboada. The easiest way to find the market is to walk east from Av Revolución on Calle 9A (called via Zaragoza) until you reach Av Sanchez Taboada, cross the street and continue down Av Javier Mina; the market is on the right.

On Calle 9A between Av Pio Pico and Av Sanchez Taboada, tiny **La Tortilleria las 4 Milpas** is a good place to see tortillas being made in the traditional way.

Bullfights

On Sundays from April to October, *corridas de toros* take place at two bullrings: the famous Plaza Monumental near the beach (follow the road signs to Playas, or take a taxi for around $8), and the less spectacular El Toreo de Tijuana, Blvd Agua Caliente 100. Phone ☎ 66-86-15-10 or 66-86-12-19 for reservations. Tickets cost from $4 to $16.

SAN DIEGO AREA

Places to Stay

Most visitors just come to Tijuana for the day, but if you stay too late to get back, there are plenty of accommodations available. Many places are much cheaper and rougher than anything you'll find in San Diego, but mid-range hotels are quite accommodating and less expensive than equivalent lodgings on the other side of the border. The really cheap hotels in the Zona Norte should definitely be avoided, however.

Try the **Hotel Nelson** (☎ 66-85-43-03, Revolución 721), a longtime favorite for its central location, respectable owner and tidy rooms. Windowless singles or doubles with telephone and spotless toilets cost $42 and up. The three-star **Hotel Villa de Zaragoza** (☎ 66-85-18-32), on Av Madero east of the Frontón, has clean, well-equipped rooms with air-conditioning for $39.

Places to Eat

There's a taco stand (or two) on nearly every corner and carts that sell roasted corn, fresh fruit and fresh seafood. The tastiest stuff usually comes from the place that's most crowded. If you want to avoid the Tijuana trots, stick to one of the established places listed in this section. Except for gringo hangouts, it's difficult to pay more than $5 for a meal in TJ.

The coffee shop on the ground level of the Hotel Nelson has reasonably priced Mexican food and good breakfasts. On the street behind the Hotel Nelson, which starts at the corner of Av Revolución and Calle 1A, the **Boy'z Huaraches** is popular with locals and is far quieter than the average La Revo eatery.

Tía Juana Tilly's is a moderately expensive gringo hangout, next to the Frontón, while **Tilly's Fifth Avenue**, at Revolución and Calle 5A, is more of a nightspot. At Revolución and Calle 8A, **Sanborns** (☎ 66-88-14-62) has both a bar and an upscale restaurant. For generous portions of reasonably priced pizza and pasta, try **Vittorio's** (Revolución 1269), at the corner of Calle 9A. Italian chef Caesar Cardini supposedly created the Caesar salad in 1924 at **Hotel**

Caesar, on Av Revolución between Calles 4 and 5. It's a calm spot, with high ceilings, bit-leather chairs and mariachi music – and not a bad place to eat, even if you don't have the $4 salad.

Several restaurants at the Plaza Fiesta and Rio Tijuana malls, at Los Héroes and Independencia, are worth a try – **California Restaurantes**, open 24 hrs, has air-conditioning and a large buffet, while **Taberna Española** (☎ 66-84-75-62) is good for Spanish tapas. For a healthy bite to go, try **Panaderia Integrale La Sonrisa** which makes sweets and sandwiches from natural ingredients.

Entertainment

The rowdy Av Revolución is the place to go for ear-splitting live and recorded music at bars and clubs such as **Margarita's Village**, **Club A**, **Escape**, **Hard Rock Café**, and many others.

Fancier discos and dance clubs are in the Zona Río, such as the kitschy **Baby Rock** at Diego Rivera 1482 near Los Héroes. Patrons dress well and start arriving late.

Shopping

Many Americans make regular trips across the border to purchase prescription drugs and pharmaceutical items, which are significantly cheaper here. Other popular buys are vanilla, Kahlua, tequila and turtle oil lotion.

Jewelry, wrought-iron furniture, baskets, silver, blown glass, blankets, pottery, leather goods and Mexicana of every description are available on Revolución and Constitución, at the municipal market on Niños Héroes between Calles 1A and 2A, and at the sprawling Mercado de Artesanías at Calle 1A and Ocampo. Auto-body and upholstery shops along Ocampo offer real bargains.

Each person returning to the US is allowed to bring $400 worth of goods duty-free back across the border. The symbol 'CH' behind 10k or 14k on a gold product means that it's gold-plated or gold-filled. Real silver products must be stamped .925, and *alpaca* means silver-plated.

Getting There & Away

The San Ysidro crossing is open 24 hours. Mesa de Otay, about 6 miles east of Tijuana, is open from 6 am to 10 pm and is much less congested.

Air Flights to other Mexican cities can be substantially cheaper from Tijuana than from San Diego, LA or other US cities, but this depends on the exchange rate. To US cities, it would be better to fly from San Diego, since it is generally cheaper and there are more flights. Also, of course, there are no customs to go through when you arrive at your destination.

Bus Only ABC local buses and the US-based Greyhound use the handy but dilapidated downtown terminal at Av Madero and Calle 1A. From the Plaza Viva Tijuana, near the border, ABC and Autotransportes Aragón go to Ensenada.

Both ABC and Greyhound (☎ 66-21-29-82, 66-21-29-85) also use the Central Camionera, about 5km southeast of downtown. From Calle 2A, east of Constitución, take any Buena Vista, Centro, or Central Camionera bus. The gold-and-white cabs, which run to and from Mesa de Otay and can be picked up on Av Madero between Calles 2A and 3A, are quicker and more convenient, and still cheap.

Buses from San Diego's Greyhound station ($4) depart almost hourly between about 5:30 am and 12:30 am. Greyhound buses to San Diego from the Central Camionera also have connections to Los Angeles ($18). Mexicoach runs buses from the Terminal Turistica Tijuana, 1025 Av Revolución, to the US side of the San Ysidro border crossing every half-hour ($1).

Trolley The trolley runs from downtown San Diego to San Ysidro every 15 minutes from about 5 am to midnight. From the San Ysidro stop, take the pedestrian bridge over the road and go through the turnstile into Mexico. You don't need a taxi to get to the middle of town – just follow the footpath to the right and walk through the largely deserted tourist trap of Plaza Viva Tijuana, take another pedestrian bridge across the Río Tijuana and walk another couple of blocks to the north end of Av Revolución.

Car If you're going to Tijuana for just a day, don't drive your car – the traffic is frenetic, parking is a pain and there may be a long wait to cross back into the US. It's better to take the trolley or drive to San Ysidro (exit I-5 at the last exit before the border), leave your car in a day parking lot (about $6) and walk across the border. If you want to go farther down into Baja, a car is useful. It's much cheaper to rent a car in San Diego than in Tijuana, but make sure the rental company will let you take it across the border.

If you do drive into Mexico, you'll need supplemental Mexican insurance for your vehicle. Policies cost about $6 to $17 for one day of full coverage, about half that if you buy only liability coverage. Policies are readily available in all border towns from such agencies as Sanborn's Insurance (☎ 800-222-0158, www.sanbornsinsurance.com), which has offices in most border communities, or AAA. Many rental-car companies do not allow their vehicles to enter Mexico, so check your agency's policy before reserving.

If you plan to drive beyond the border area, you'll also need to get a car permit, which may be obtained at the border after the tourist card is stamped by Mexican authorities. Auto permits are good for 180 days; they cost about $10 and must be paid for with a bank-issued credit card or by posting a bond. Permits are good for multiple entries into Mexico, but they must be surrendered before expiration.

Whenever you drive into Mexico, one important thing to remember is who can actually operate the car. Legally, the car must be driven only by the person whose name is on the title and by no one else. If, for example, a married couple enters Mexico and only the wife's name is on the title, the husband may not drive – and if he does and is involved in an accident, the insurance company can refuse to pay.

For rental cars, company cars or cars on which you're making payments (whether you own or lease the vehicle), you must carry a notarized letter of permission from the rental company, business or bank holding title to the car.

Getting Around

Local buses go everywhere for 2.50 pesos (about 40¢), but more expensive 'route taxis' are much quicker. Tijuana taxis lack meters – most rides cost 10 to 25 pesos (around $1.60 to $4). Beware of being overcharged.

California Deserts

Forget about green. After a while, the starkness of the desert landscape, the clarity of the light and the spaciousness are beautiful in their own way. The desert climate is easy to appreciate. Sometimes intensely hot, but rarely oppressive, it has long been regarded as healthy, especially by those from colder, wetter and greener places.

California's deserts are sparsely populated, except for the resort cities around Palm Springs and the irrigated agricultural area of the Imperial Valley. Even the most spectacular areas – Death Valley National Park, Joshua Tree National Park and Anza-Borrego Desert State Park – are not crowded for most of the year. At lesser known or less accessible places, such as the Trona Pinnacles or the Algodones Dunes, and the long stretches of road between them, solitude is likely to be a real attraction. The harshness and the isolation of the desert can also present real dangers. Visitors should be well prepared and take proper precautions.

Anyone looking to do some hiking should pick up *Hiking California's Desert Parks*, by Bill Cunningham and Polly Burke, or John Krist's *50 Best Short Hikes in California Deserts*, both widely available at visitor centers and bookstores in the San Diego area.

History

Since prehistoric times people have lived in those corners of the desert where springs, streams or lakes can sustain them. Signs of this ancient occupation are found at several desert sites. For early European explorers, such as Juan Bautista de Anza and Jedediah Smith, the desert was a barrier between the habitable West Coast and the settled areas to the south and east. The trails they pioneered, such as the De Anza Trail and the Spanish Trail, can still be traced. Miners also came and went, establishing towns that died as the minerals played out, leaving their scattered, spooky skeletons in the desert.

Highlights

- Joshua Tree National Park – funky trees and fun climbing

- Death Valley – salt flats, sand dunes, spectacular sunrises and sunsets

- Palm Springs Aerial Tramway – hot desert to cool pine forest in 14 minutes

- Anza-Borrego Desert State Park – palm oases, deep canyons and wide open spaces

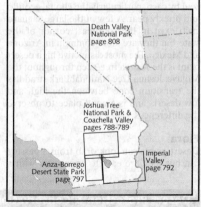

Death Valley National Park page 808

Joshua Tree National Park & Coachella Valley pages 788–789

Imperial Valley page 792

Anza-Borrego Desert State Park page 797

Permanent European settlements came only with dependable water supplies, first with agricultural communities in the Imperial Valley and Coachella Valley, followed by the health and holiday resorts of Palm Springs. The military took over huge areas for training in WWII and still has 3 million acres of weapons test sites, desert training centers, gunnery ranges, live bombing areas and the large Edwards Air Force Base, which is used for aircraft testing and space shuttle landings.

Geography

About one quarter of California is desert. The area roughly south and east of Palm Springs is the 'low desert,' called the Colorado Desert since it's the area around the valley of the

Colorado River. It is actually part of the great Sonora Desert, most of which lies in Arizona and Mexico. The area roughly north of Palm Springs, south of Sierra Nevada, and east of Bakersfield is the 'high desert.' Named the Mojave Desert, it extends into northwest Arizona, southern Nevada and the southeast corner of Utah. The low desert is mostly less than 600 feet above sea level (though there are a few peaks over 1000 feet), while the high desert averages about 2000 feet (though Death Valley, in the middle of the high desert, drops below sea level to the lowest point in the US).

The distinction between the two is really one of ecology. The low desert is character-ized by cacti, particularly the cholla, ocotillo and prickly pear. A few of the large saguaro cacti exist in the southeast corner of the state, but they are more common in Arizona and Mexico. The most distinctive high desert plant is the Joshua tree, seen throughout the Mojave. Joshua Tree National Park straddles the transition zone between the high and low deserts and is a good place to observe the differences.

Flora

Desert plants can look drab from a passing car, but they are easy to appreciate with a closer look. Adaptations to the arid climate include thin, spiny 'leaves,' which resist moisture loss and deter grazing animals. Many plants have the ability to produce flowers and seed during brief periods of moisture, then become almost inert for the rest of the year. The best times to see the flowers blooming are in February and March in the low desert, extending into April and May at the higher elevations.

Small streams run down from the moun-tains in valleys and gorges that support tiny oasis ecosystems, shaded by palm trees. Though palm trees are emblematic of Southern California, only one variety is native – the California fan palm (*Washing-tonia filifera*), which grows in desert oases. It's a handsome tree and produces stalks of small black berries that are quite tasty. The soils of the low desert are actually very fertile. With irrigation they grow a variety of hot-weather crops such as dates, grapes, cotton and citrus trees.

Visitor centers at the various desert parks and reserves have excellent displays and information on desert plants and the envi-ronment and usually sell quality reference books. For descriptions of some desert plants, see the Flora section in the Facts about California chapter.

Desert Protection & Conservation

In October 1994, the California Desert Protection Act was passed by Congress, giving addi-tional environmental protection to millions of acres of California deserts. Death Valley and Joshua Tree were upgraded from national monuments to national parks, and 2031 sq miles were added to the protected area of Death Valley. The act also created the East Mojave National Preserve, which transferred the management of the former East Mojave National Scenic Area from the Bureau of Land Management (BLM) to the National Park Service (NPS).

Though generally welcomed by conservationists, these changes had some controversial features. Existing mining activities were allowed to continue in the extended areas of Death Valley National Park, which was seen as an erosion of the level of protection offered by national park status. Hunting was permitted in the East Mojave National Preserve, though it is not exactly a preservation activity. Then there was the question of funding the land man-agement – the Republican Congress allocated the NPS an additional $1 (yes, just one dollar) per year to manage the 2188-sq-mile East Mojave National Preserve.

Most of California's deserts are recognized as being of international environmental signifi-cance. They form part of the UN-designated Mojave & Colorado Deserts Biosphere Preserve.

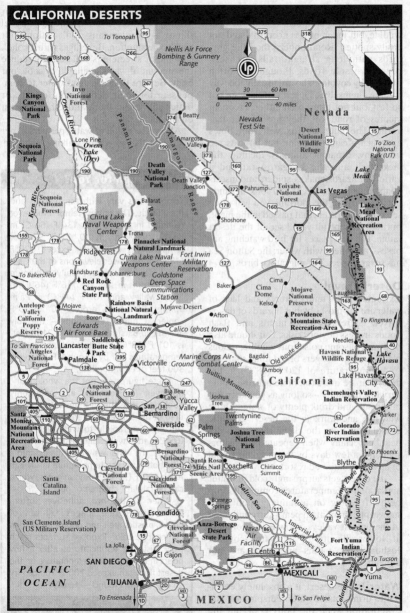

CALIFORNIA DESERTS

Fauna

The desert also supports a good deal of wildlife, but much of it is nocturnal and not easily spotted. Roadrunners, the little gray birds with long straight tails, are seen running beside roads, though not often pursued by coyotes, who are usually too wily to show themselves. Desert tortoises are not so fast, but not often seen either: Frequent victims of road kill, they are now endangered. The cute kit fox will sometimes approach a camp at night, but bobcats are very shy. Smaller animals include the jackrabbit and the kangaroo rat and a variety of lizards, snakes, spiders and insects adapted to desert life. If you look in sandy patches early in the morning you will often see tracks of critters that passed in the night, but that may be all you'll see of the desert fauna. The best places for bird watching are oases – anywhere with water; the Salton Sea has several species of migratory birds.

Desert Travel

Extremely high temperatures and lack of water are the most obvious hazards of desert travel. Extremely cold nights and flash floods are less obvious risks. You should also be aware of some poisonous wildlife, vicious plants and the dangers of old mine shafts.

A temperature of 120°F (48°C) in the desert can be quite tolerable because of the very low humidity – so long as you keep out of the sun and drink plenty of water. Those who live and work in the desert get little consolation from the cliché that 'it's a dry heat,' especially when repeated by visitors spending a few days by the swimming pool of an air-conditioned resort.

The desert gets surprisingly cold in winter and at night. Temperatures commonly drop below freezing on a January night, and snowcapped mountain peaks surround some of the hottest valleys. Snow is less common at lower elevations, but snow-covered Joshua trees, palms and cacti are not unheard of.

Water In the desert, it's absolutely essential to drink lots of water. Perspiration and evaporation keep the body cool, but the rate of moisture loss is high. Take regular drinks of water even if you don't feel thirsty – by all means don't ration your water consumption. Beverages with alcohol, caffeine or sweeteners will actually reduce the amount of water available to cool your body. Be sure to drink extra water to compensate for their dehydrating effects, or better still, avoid them altogether, at least during the day.

Allow one gallon of water per person per day, twice that if you're walking, climbing,

Hot Enough for You?

Temperatures vary with the seasons and the altitude. The hottest temperature ever recorded in the US was 134°F (56°C) in Death Valley on July 10, 1913. Summer temperatures commonly exceed 120°F (48°C) in the lower elevations of the California deserts. Average daily maximum temperatures in July are 116°F (46°C) in Death Valley and 107°F (41°C) in Palm Springs. It's usually around 10° to 15°F cooler at higher elevations – the July average in Barstow, which is at 2100 feet, is 101°F (38°C). A rule of thumb is that temperatures fall by about 1°F for every 300 feet of elevation loss.

These figures are not the whole story, however. The reported and commonly quoted figure is the air temperature measured in the shade – a thermometer in the sun can rise rapidly to well over 150°F (65°C) and may literally burst. Sun blazing through the windows will turn a car into a little hothouse; the temperature inside can reach 160°F (70°C) within minutes, which can be fatal for children or pets.

When it's this hot, adhesives soften, boxes disintegrate, pages fall out of books, plastics melt and photographic film can change color. Exposed surfaces reach truly blistering temperatures after a few hours in the sun – the temperature on the desert floor can exceed 200°F. You can fry an egg on the ground – literally!

cycling or engaging in any other outdoor activity. Carry an extra gallon of water per person in case you get stuck, as well as a few gallons of radiator water for your car. Always carry water in non-breakable containers.

There are natural springs in the deserts, but don't rely on them as a water source: their flows change from year to year and the water is usually not potable without purification.

Clothing Wear a hat that shades the head and neck. It's best to wear loose, light-colored clothing that covers most of the body. Shorts, sandals and tank tops leave too much skin exposed to the heating effects of the sun. Thick-soled shoes are necessary to protect your feet from the hot ground. Bring warmer clothing for night wear – at least a sweater, hat and windbreaker – plus extra layers in winter.

Sunburn (caused by UV radiation) is a separate problem, distinct from the heating effects of the sun (which is infrared radiation). To protect against sunburn, use a high SPF sunscreen (don't forget to put it on your ears!), lip balm and quality sunglasses. Small communities and visitor centers often sell these items at higher prices; it's best to pack them with you.

Desert Survival The biggest danger is being stranded in the desert without adequate supplies of water. An interesting back-road drive can become a disaster if a car breaks down or gets stuck in sand. Even a short walk can turn fatal if you get lost or injured.

Sparse vegetation beckons cross-country travel, but natural markers on the landscape are few and often look similar to each other: remember that harsh light and wide open spaces can play tricks on your vision. To avoid getting stuck, take a map and compass and know where you're going. Be sure that your vehicle is in good condition, and don't push it beyond its limits. Never venture alone into remote areas. Always tell someone where you're going and when you'll be back.

If you do get stuck, stay with your vehicle and wait for rescue. A car is easier to spot from a distance than a lone walker. If you

become hopelessly lost while walking, seek the closest shady spot and stay put. People walking around in the desert can become exhausted and/or dehydrated very quickly.

A few basic emergency supplies can greatly prolong desert survival. Have at least a gallon of water per person in reserve. Take a mirror, matches and maybe some flares so you can signal for help. A tent or ground-sheet can provide vital sun protection as well as increase your visibility. A flashlight, pocketknife, first aid kit and extra food may also be useful.

Flash Floods Flooding can occur after heavy rains, even if the downpour is many miles away. It is unwise to camp or park in streambeds or washes if there is even the slightest chance of rain in any upstream area.

Poisonous Animals Black widows, scorpions, rattlesnakes and centipedes are venomous but unlikely to attack. See the Facts for the Visitor chapter for more information.

Pointy Plants Obviously, cacti have spikes. Less obvious are the tiny barbs, which make the spikes difficult to pull out of your skin. Bring strong tweezers or pliers to extract them, and avoid hiking in shorts.

Mines There are hundreds, perhaps thousands, of abandoned mineral mines in the California deserts. Watch out for holes or shafts, which can be hard to see and easy to fall into. Old shafts are very dangerous as the supporting timbers have usually deteriorated and the air may contain poisonous gases. Never enter old mines.

Railroads Old rail lines may appear to be abandoned but are often still in use – by mineral extraction companies or private railroad enthusiasts. Never walk on railroad tracks where there is no escape route or where you can't see a half-mile in both directions.

Explosives Much of the desert has been used for military training and testing. Though this is done mostly in well-defined

CALIFORNIA DESERTS

areas, unexploded bombs and shells have turned up in many places and should never be touched. It is unwise to enter any area marked as a live bombing range or to venture off on any unmapped side roads.

Getting Around

The main desert towns are reachable by bus, and some by rail as well, but to get out into the desert itself you really need your own transportation. You can rent cars in the desert towns, but rentals are usually cheaper in the coastal cities. Don't even think about hitchhiking – you could die from the heat just waiting for a lift.

Car Much of California's desert is accessible on paved roads and requires no more than a regular car, driven with care. Many car rental contracts do not allow the vehicle to be driven off normally trafficked roads.

As you travel into more remote areas, it's increasingly important to make sure the car is in good condition and that you have spare gasoline, oil and coolant. You might also carry a tire pump, a shovel to dig your wheels out and a board or traction mats in case you get stuck in loose sand. For really rough roads a 4WD vehicle is best, but regular cars can travel most unpaved roads if the clearance between the underside of the car and the ground is adequate. Visitor centers usually post current road conditions that tell which roads require 4WD. Off-road driving is prohibited on all public land, except in areas designated for off-road vehicle use.

When your car is parked, use cardboard, plastic sunshields or towels to cover the steering wheel, dashboard and seats. Even a few minutes parked in the sun can leave the interior too hot to touch. Perishable food should be stored in the trunk.

Check tires before you start a day's hot-weather driving and make sure they are at full pressure – an under-inflated tire can overheat very quickly. Never deflate a tire that has become hot after driving.

Watch the temperature gauge of your car. If it starts to heat up, turn off the air-conditioning. If it continues to get hotter,

pull over, face the front of the car into the wind, keep the engine running and dribble water over the front of the radiator (*not* over the engine or fan). Turning the car heater on to the max can also help.

Bicycle In winter, bike touring can be wonderful if you are prepared: Bring extra tires and inner tubes, several gallons of water per day and cold-weather gear for the night. Start early in the morning, rest during the hottest part of the day and start up again when the sun is getting low. The best places for this are where visitor facilities are close together: Anza-Borrego, Death Valley and Palm Springs. You can rent mountain bikes in most desert towns for one-day trips.

Note: bikes must stay on designated roads because their continuous tire-track acts as a waterway, causing more damage than isolated footprints.

Organized Tours An alternative to driving may be an organized tour from the nearest city. For tours to Joshua Tree National Park, look for an operator in Palm Springs; for Anza-Borrego, check operators in San Diego; for Death Valley, try Las Vegas.

Palm Springs & Coachella Valley

The so-called resort cities extend the length of the Coachella Valley, forming an almost continuous sprawl of suburbs and golf courses. Palm Springs, with a population of around 54,000, is the original, best-known and most visited area. It's famous as a winter retreat for Hollywood stars, but it has increasingly become a well-scrubbed retirement community for the moderately rich. Going southeast down the valley, Cathedral City, Rancho Mirage and Palm Desert take turns at being the 'in' place, though Palm Desert's El Paseo shopping district (the Rodeo Drive of the desert) distinguishes it from the others. At the far southern end of the valley, Indio originally serviced the railroad and the surrounding agricultural areas and is still home to the valley's service industry employees (greens keepers, gardeners, hotel maids) and restaurant workers.

To put things in perspective, the valley has about 250,000 residents, 10,000 swimming pools, 85 golf courses and more plastic surgeons per head than anywhere else in the US.

Most visitors (about 3.5 million per year) come in the cooler months to play golf or just enjoy the desert climate. There's a growing gay scene in Palm Springs and Cathedral City, and thousands of college kids descend on the town for spring break. In the midday heat, there's not much to do except hang around a pool, get up into the mountains via the aerial tramway or head into an air-conditioned place like a museum or shopping center (from which there are plenty to choose).

History

Cahuilla people occupied the canyons on the southwest side of the Coachella Valley, where permanent streams flowed from the San Jacinto Mountains. They also used the hot springs where the city of Palm Springs now stands. The early Spanish explorers gave the Cahuilla the name Agua Caliente, meaning 'hot water.'

In 1851, the Cahuilla staged a revolt against American authorities and, though it was put down, their land rights were recognized in the 1852 Treaty of Temecula. However, the treaty was not ratified by Congress and was superseded by a new arrangement in 1876.

In order to promote the construction of a railroad from Los Angeles to Yuma, Arizona, the valley was divided into a checkerboard of square-mile sections. The odd-numbered sections were granted to the Southern Pacific Railroad, while the even-numbered sections were given to the Agua Caliente as their reservation. After the railroad was built, the company sold most of its land and the whole valley was developed first as farmland, and later with health spas, hotels and resorts.

It was not until the 1940s that surveys established the exact boundaries of the sections, and by then much of the Native American land had been built on. Though they

Palm Springs Celebrities

A long list of Hollywood stars have lived or stayed in Palm Springs, including Jean Harlow, Al Jolson, Nat King Cole, Liberace, Dean Martin, Jack Warner, Liz Taylor, Spencer Tracy, Bing Crosby, Lawrence Olivier, Goldie Hawn and Kirk Douglas. Name-dropping comes easy in a place with streets like Dinah Shore Drive and Gene Autry Trail. Former president Gerald Ford makes frequent golfing forays to the valley and also has a drive named after him.

The town is also associated with some well-known scandals, romances and marriages – Clark Gable and Carole Lombard, Frank Sinatra and Ava Gardner, Elvis and Priscilla Presley (who honeymooned here), Bob and Dolores Hope (Dolores is much more popular in Palm Springs than Bob), the former evangelical team of Jim and Tammy Faye Bakker, and Zsa Zsa Gabor (plus six or eight of her husbands).

Sonny Bono, late of Sonny and Cher, owned a fashionable restaurant here and was once mayor of Palm Springs. His accidental, premature death was cause for mourning and flags flying at half-mast throughout the city.

couldn't sell the land, the Indians were able to charge rent. As the valley has grown more affluent, the several hundred Indians who have established tribal membership have become very wealthy.

At the southern end of the valley, Indio was a construction camp for the railway in the 1870s, and its artesian water was tapped to irrigate the first crops. Date palms from Algeria were introduced in 1890 and have become the major fruit crop of the valley, along with citrus fruits and table grapes. Later, water was brought all the way from the Colorado River.

In Palm Springs, the first hotels were for those who sought the health benefits of the natural hot springs and a desert climate. From the late 1920s it became popular as a resort area and as a winter getaway for Hollywood stars. One of the city's first councilwomen, Ruth Hardy, was responsible for many of the restrictive ordinances that saved Palm Springs from the excesses of uncontrolled development, including bans on two-story houses and large outdoor advertisements.

Orientation

The resort cities extend more than 25 miles from Palm Springs to Indio, with most of the communities along Hwy 111, south of I-10. Going up and down the valley, it's often quicker to take the interstate than to follow Hwy 111 through miles of suburbs and dozens of traffic lights.

Palm Springs has a reasonably compact downtown area, centered on about four blocks of Palm Canyon Drive, with shops, banks, restaurants and a few sights. In this area, traffic goes south on Palm Canyon Drive and north on Indian Canyon Drive. Tahquitz Canyon Way divides these streets into north and south. The ritziest residential area is Little Tuscany on the slopes to the west of N Palm Canyon Drive. Head to the top of Chino Canyon Rd for a view over town.

Restaurants and chain motels are spread out along E Palm Canyon Drive and Hwy 111 from Palm Springs to Cathedral City. Some of the main attractions are just outside of Palm Springs, particularly the aerial tramway that ascends the San Jacinto Mountains to the west, and the Indian Canyons, which are now part of the Agua Caliente Indian Reservation, to the south.

Information

The Palm Springs Visitor Center (☎ 760-778-8418), 2781 N Palm Canyon Drive, near the turnoff to the aerial tram, has a helpful staff that can give you information about local hotels and attractions. Hotel referrals and bookings (☎ 800-347-7746) are available 9 am to 5 pm weekdays daily (until 7 pm Friday).

Free publications with visitor information include *Desert Key* magazine and *Desert Guide. Lifestyle Magazine* has information for the gay community.

The Palm Springs post office (☎ 800-275-8777) is at 333 Amado Rd. Desert Hospital

(☎ 760-323-6511), 1150 N Indian Canyon Drive, is the place to get 24-hour emergency care.

Palm Springs Desert Museum

Some of the most interesting exhibits in this museum (☎ 760-325-0189), 101 Museum Drive, west of Palm Canyon Drive behind Desert Fashion Plaza, are the large dioramas and displays of desert plants and wildlife – they're informative and very well done. There are also some excellent Cahuilla baskets, temporary and permanent exhibitions of Western American art and a fine sculpture collection. Be sure to pick up a museum guide when you enter, as all the wings and galleries are identified only by the names of museum benefactors. While this must be gratifying for the donors, it is not very helpful for visitors.

The museum hours are 10 am to 5 pm Tuesday to Saturday, from noon Sunday; $7.50/3.50 adults/children, free on the first Tuesday of the month.

Village Green Heritage Center

This grassy little square in the heart of downtown at 221 S Palm Canyon Drive has some 'heritage' attractions, though most people use it as a place to sit and eat ice cream and fudge (which you can buy at the sweets store next door). Most interesting is probably the Agua Caliente Cultural Museum (☎ 760-323-0151), which has pictures and artifacts on the tribe's history; closed Monday and Tuesday. Ruddy's General Store, a reproduction of a 1930s general store, is also worth a look for its authentic period fittings and goods in their original packages; it's open Thursday to Sunday from October to June, weekends only in summer.

The 1884 McCallum Adobe, said to be the home of Palm Springs' first white settler, has been reconstructed on this site and has a collection of old pictures and artifacts. The Cornelia White House (☎ 760-323-8297), next door, is another relocated pioneer house, made of old railroad ties. Tours of the houses are given from October to May; call for times.

Hot Springs

The original hot springs have been part of the Indian-owned Spa Hotel & Casino (☎ 760-325-1461), 100 N Indian Canyon Drive, for over 30 years. Day visitors can use the spa for $15.

Oasis Water Park

With 12 water slides, a large wave pool and an indoor rock-climbing center, Oasis Water Park (☎ 760-325-7873), 1500 Gene Autry Trail, is a lot of fun in the hotter months. The park charges by height: $18.95 if you're taller than 60 inches, free if you're under 36 inches, and $11.95 if you're somewhere in between. Discounts and coupons are available. Hours are 11 am to 6 pm; closed November to April.

Moorten Botanic Gardens

If you're really interested in desert plants, you might find the gardens (☎ 760-327-6555), 1701 S Palm Canyon Drive, worth a visit, though they're not very attractively laid out and there's little in the way of informative signs or pamphlets. The gardens are open daily; $2.

Aerial Tramway

A real highlight of a visit to Palm Springs is a trip in this cable car (☎ 760-325-1391), which climbs nearly 6000 vertical feet, from the desert floor up to the San Jacinto Mountains, in about 14 minutes. You ascend through visibly different vegetation zones from the Valley Station (2643 feet) to the Mountain Station (8516 feet). It's 30° to 40°F cooler as you step out into pine forest at the top, so bring some warm clothing – the trip up is said to be the equivalent of driving from Mexico to Canada.

The Mountain Station at the top of the tram has a bar, cafeteria, observation area and a theater showing a short film on the tramway. The views over the valley are brilliant.

It's worth allowing some time (a day or two if you're a backcountry enthusiast) at the top to enjoy the San Jacinto Wilderness State Park. There are miles of trails, including a nontechnical route up to San Jacinto peak (9879 feet), used for hiking in summer, snowshoeing and skiing in winter. There are also several primitive campgrounds, which are free. Everyone going into the backcountry (even for a few hours) must register at the ranger kiosk for rescue purposes. Maps are available ($1 to $7) at the kiosk and, better yet, at the State Park Visitor Information Center at the Mountain Station. At the visitor center, ask about the cross-country ski center, which operates when there's ample snow. You can rent skis, sleds and snowshoes for around $7 an hour, $15 a day. The staff is knowledgeable about snow conditions and backcountry routes.

Tramway hours are 10 am to 8 pm weekdays, from 8 am weekends and holidays. During daylight saving time, the last car goes up at 9 pm and comes down at 10:45 pm. It costs $17 roundtrip, and various discounts are available. A Ride 'n' Dine combination, which includes a buffet dinner at the top, is available after 4 pm for $22/15. It's not a bad dinner for $5, but the deal may not allow enough time for a leisurely look around at the top.

It's also possible to hike to the top of the tram via the Skyline Trail, which starts near the Palm Springs Desert Museum. This is an *extremely* challenging hike, suggested only for the very fit who have a whole day to spend and leave no later than 7 am. The reward, besides stellar views and multiple climatic zones, is a free tram ride down.

Indian Canyons

Streams flowing from the San Jacinto Mountains sustain a rich variety of plants in the canyons around Palm Springs. The canyons were home to Indian communities for hundreds of years and are now part of the Agua Caliente Indian Reservation. A walk up these canyon oases, shaded by fan palms and surrounded by towering cliffs, is a real delight. From downtown, go south on Palm Canyon Drive for about 2 miles to the reservation entrance. Hours are 8 am to 5 pm in fall and winter, until 6 pm in spring and summer; $5.

Closest to town is Andreas Canyon, where there's a pleasant picnic area. Nearby are imposing rock formations where you can find Indian mortar holes, used for grinding seeds, and some rock art (see Prehistory and California's Indians in Facts about California). The trail up the canyon is an easy walk.

About a 20-minute walk south from Andreas Canyon is **Murray Canyon**, which can't be reached by road and is therefore less visited. It's a good place for bird watching, and bighorn sheep might be seen on the slopes above the canyon.

Following the winding access road to the end brings you to **Palm Canyon**, which is the most extensive of the canyons, some 15 miles long, with good trails and a store selling snacks and souvenirs. In the morning, look for animal tracks in the sandy patches.

Another canyon just west of town, **Tahquitz Canyon**, is currently closed to visitors, though you may be able to see it with one of the hiking groups listed under Hiking. The Trail Discovery Outdoor Guide Service and the Coachella Valley Hiking Club both do trips into Tahquitz Canyon. It is noted for its waterfalls and swimming holes, and it once supported a large Native American population.

The Living Desert

The desert is living all around – a fact that is sometimes hard to remember with pavement and golf greens stretching in all directions. For guaranteed wildlife sightings and interpretive plaques, pay $7.50/3.50 and visit this outdoor museum and botanical garden (☎ 760-346-5694), 47-900 Portola Ave, south of Hwy 111, Palm Desert. It has a wide variety of desert plants and animals, plus wonderful exhibits on desert geology and Indian culture. The Living Desert is open year round (9 am to 4:30 pm September to June, 8 am to 1:30 pm in summer). Between Thanksgiving and January 1, from 6 to 9 pm, the museum also presents its WildLights show, a light festival featuring lights on the trees and special animal shapes, for an additional $4. Discounts are available.

Other Museums

There are quite a few other attractions in and around the valley, which may be worth a visit if you have the time and a particular interest. One of the weirdest is **Cabot's Old Indian Pueblo Museum** (☎ 760-329-7610), 67616 E Desert View Ave, Desert Hot Springs. It's a ramshackle, junk-filled old house built by a rich East Coaster who gave up his fortune to become a desert-loving recluse. It's closed from late May to mid-September, but it opens weekends and most other days during the rest of the year; $2.50.

At the Eisenhower Medical Center, the **Museum of the Heart** (☎ 760-324-3278), 39-600 Bob Hope Drive, Rancho Mirage, explains all about heart attacks and how to avoid them, while giving you a chance to step inside a giant aorta. The suggested donation is $2, but if you're about to pay for a coronary bypass, they may overlook it.

Golf

Golf is huge here, with more than 80 public, semiprivate, private and resort courses, and a total of 1553 holes. It takes 1 million gallons of water per day to irrigate the golf courses. There are several big tournaments annually, and the College of the Desert even has a School of Golf Management. Greens fees run from $26 to $215, depending on the course, the season and the day of the week. Most hotels can make arrangements for their guests to play on at least one local course. You can receive substantial savings through Stand-by Golf (☎ 760-321-2665), which can provide guaranteed tee times, at a discount, for same-day or next-day play at 20 courses; open 6:30 am to 9 pm daily.

Hiking

There are lots of enthusiastic local hikers, and it's a great way to see the desert. Most hiking is in the canyons and in the San Jacinto and Santa Rosa mountains. Some of the most easily accessed trails are from the top of the aerial tramway (see Aerial Tramway earlier in this chapter). Trail Discovery Outdoor Guide Service (☎ 760-325-4453) offers guided hiking and running trips locally and in Joshua Tree National Park. They don't operate during the hottest times of year, so call for availability and prices.

The Palm Springs Desert Museum (☎ 760-325-0189), at 101 Museum Drive, conducts short hikes on Friday and Saturday, and visitors may be able to join in; call for information. Visitors may also be able to join trips run by the Coachella Valley Hiking Club (☎ 760-345-6234); call during regular business hours for information.

Bicycling
Palm Springs and the valley have several bike paths. Bighorn Bike Adventures (☎ 760-325-3367), downtown at the corner of Palm Canyon Drive and Amado St, rents bikes ($7/25/75 per hour/day/week) and leads daily tours of the Indian Canyons. They are a good general resource for biking information; open 9 am to 5 pm daily.

Horseback Riding
Smoketree Stables (☎ 760-327-1372), 2500 Toledo Ave, Palm Springs, arranges trail rides, from a one-hour outing to an all-day trek. The cost is about $25/hour and they take novice or experienced riders. Rides leave on the hour, but it's suggested you arrive 20 minutes early to get a spot.

Hot-Air Ballooning
Several operators do hot-air balloon flights, including Fantasy Balloon Flights (☎ 760-568-0997). Flights are usually around sunrise or sunset and last about three hours.

Organized Tours
Celebrity Tours About the best way to pick up on the gossip and glamour of Palm Springs is to take a trip with Celebrity Tours (☎ 760-770-2700), based at Rimrock Plaza Shopping Center, 4751 E Palm Canyon Drive. You can do it yourself with a map of the stars' homes from the visitor center ($5!), but you'll miss out on the amusing commentary and all the juicy gossip. Tours cost $15 for an hour, $20 for the deluxe, 2½-hour run.

Desert Adventures This very professional operation runs guided jeep tours to the Indian Canyons, Santa Rosa Mountains, around the Bighorn Sheep Preserve and to other areas that can be hard to get to, even with your own 4WD. The driver/guides are full of information about the natural environment and Indian lore. Tours cost about $25/hour; $70/half-day. Make a booking by calling ☎ 760-324-5337 or ☎ 888-440-5337.

Covered Wagon Tours This leisurely two-hour tour of the Coachella Valley Preserve in a mule-drawn covered wagon (☎ 760-347-2161) follows the San Andreas Fault. Guides describe many of the plants and how they were used by the Agua Caliente people. At the end of the trip there's an optional cowboy cookout from the chuck wagon and a country music sing-along. It's $30 for the tour, $55 with dinner, and half-price for kids. Reservations are required.

Special Events
Dinah 'Shaw' Weekend This event marks the biggest lesbian happening in the US, when 25,000 women descend upon Palm Springs during the Dinah Shore Golf Tournament (which is renamed with a Southern accent, just for fun!) in March. While some women actually watch golf, most go just for the pool parties and events.

The weekend used to be a Southern California affair but in recent years it has developed an international flavor, with lesbians arriving from all over the globe. Book your room early, as accommodations are likely to fill. For a complete listing of the weekend's events, pick up the *Lesbian News* or *Female FYI*. Call ☎ 760-324-4546 for information and tickets.

Villagefest Every Thursday from 6 to 10 pm the downtown blocks of N Palm Canyon Drive are closed to traffic for Villagefest, where dozens of street vendors sell handicrafts, souvenirs, snacks and produce. There is often live music as well, making this a fun place to spend a balmy desert evening.

Places to Stay
Many of the accommodations in and around Palm Springs are in expensive resort-style hotels, but there are some budget places around, all with swimming pools and air-conditioning. Palm Springs has a problem with the word 'motel,' so there are lots of

CALIFORNIA DESERTS

inns and lodges. Peak season is January and February, when prices really go up and rooms can be hard to find. Taxes add another 10% to 11% to these prices.

Places to Stay – Budget

Camping There are several RV parks, but the only place for tent camping is way down in La Quinta at the *Lake Cahuilla County Park*, at the west end of 58th Ave. There are 150 tent and RV sites from $9 to $14. Reservations (☎ 760-564-4712) are recommended in the winter holiday season. Better spots for camping are Joshua Tree National Park (see that section later in this chapter), which is only an hour away by car, and San Jacinto Wilderness State Park, which has primitive sites, at the top of the aerial tramway (see Aerial Tramway earlier in this chapter).

Motels About the cheapest night's stay is the *Pepper Tree Inn* (☎ 760-320-8774, *645 N Indian Canyon Drive*). You won't be overwhelmed by the service, but you'll pay only about $30/35 for singles/doubles in summer and not much more in winter. Other cheap sleeps are in chain motels spread along Palm Canyon Drive. On E Palm Canyon Drive is a *Travelodge* (☎ 760-327-1211, *333 E Palm Canyon Drive*), with spacious rooms starting at $39 in the summer (more in winter); *Motel 6* (☎ 760-325-6129, *595 E Palm Canyon Drive*), which, at around $48, is a bargain for Palm Springs; and *Quality Inn* (☎ 760-323-2775, *1269 E Palm Canyon Drive*) with $85 rooms.

On S Palm Canyon Drive, you'll find a *Budget Host Inn* (☎ 760-325-5574, *800-829-8099, 1277 S Palm Canyon Drive*), with rooms from $50 (up to $90 in peak season), and a *Motel 6* (☎ 760-327-4200, *660 S Palm Canyon Drive*) with similar rates. On N Palm Canyon Drive, there's a good *Super 8 Lodge* (☎ 760-322-3757, *1900 N Palm Canyon Drive*), with rooms from $58 (slightly lower in summer).

Places to Stay – Mid-Range

Accommodations in the mid-range category include the better-quality chain motels and moderately priced places with a bit of character. One block away from the action on Palm Canyon Drive and in the shadow of the San Jacinto Mountains are several charming old hotels with very reasonable prices and beautiful decor. Cheapest in this area is the *Historic Oasis Hotel* (☎ 760-320-7205, *177 W Tahquitz Canyon Way*), whose rooms ($69) have housed movie stars since the 1930s. The *Orchid Tree Inn* (☎ 760-325-2791, *800-733-3435, 261 S Belardo Rd*) and *Estrella Inn* (☎ 760-320-4117, 800-237-3687, 415 S Belardo Rd*) each have a pool and gardens; their prices fluctuate, so it is best to check before booking. The *San Marino Hotel* (☎ 760-325-6902, *225 W Baristo Rd*) was designed in 1947 and has 16 rooms for $59 to $159. The *Ingleside Inn* (☎ 760-325-0046, *200 W Ramon Rd*) is another venerable, classy Palm Springs institution, with rooms from $76 to $310 in summer, $95 to $395 in winter.

Also well located, the *Spa Hotel & Casino* (☎ 760-325-1461, *100 N Indian Canyon Drive*) is on the site of the original Agua Caliente Indians' mineral springs, and the hotel is still owned by the Indian community. Rooms cost $69 to $149 in the summer and $159 to $279 in winter.

Gay Lodging In the Warm Sands area, south of Hwy 111 via Warm Sands Drive, are some places that cater expressly to gay clientele. Some allow women, others do not, but all are lovely and well run. *Inntimate* (☎ 760-778-8334, *556 Warm Sands Drive*) has rooms from $89 in winter, $69 in summer. *Inntrigue* (☎ 760-323-7505, *800-798-8781, 526 Warm Sands Drive*) is similarly priced. The *Inn Exile Hotel* (☎ 760-327-6413, *800-962-0186, 545 Warm Sands Drive*) is male only and has rooms from $85 to $115 year round. *Marquis* (☎ 760-322-2121, *150 S Indian Canyon Drive*) welcomes gays and lesbians; rooms go for around $105 (summer) to $155 (winter).

Places to Stay – Top End

There's no shortage of luxury in Palm Springs. *La Mancha Resort* (☎ 760-323-1773, *800-647-7482, 800-255-1773, 444*

Avenida Caballeros) prides itself on absolute discretion. Double rooms, units and villas cost between $185 and $1150, and they won't breathe a word to anyone.

Other top-end resorts are in Desert Springs and Rancho Mirage. Most expensive is *Marriott's Desert Springs Resort & Spa* (☎ 760-341-2211, 74855 Country Club Drive), in Desert Springs, where small boats take you across an artificial lake to the restaurant. Rooms and suites cost from $235 to $2100 in winter, but less than half of that in summer. The luxurious *Ritz-Carlton* (☎ 760-321-8282, 68-900 Frank Sinatra Drive), Rancho Mirage, has rooms from $365 in winter, but in summer they go for $119.

Places to Eat

Many restaurants in and around Palm Springs are pretentious and overpriced. Most Palm Springs places are on Palm Canyon Drive. There's also a good selection along El Paseo in Palm Desert. The usual fast-food franchises are less in evidence – the size and placement of their familiar signs is severely restricted – but you'll find some of them along Palm Canyon Drive north or south of the center of town. Outdoor eating areas are sometimes sprayed with a fine mist of water to keep them cool, which is a nice touch. One 'must-have' while visiting here is a date milkshake from Shields (see the Shopping section later on).

An old local favorite is the original *Las Casuelas* (☎ 760-325-3213, 368 N Palm Canyon Drive), with fine Mexican main courses for $7 to $12. Its offshoot, *Las Casuelas Terraza* (☎ 760-325-2794, 222 S Palm Canyon Drive) is in a great-looking Mexican-style building and has a menu and prices similar to the original. *Trilussa* (☎ 760-323-4255, 123 N Palm Canyon Drive) does excellent Italian food for $7 to $13. *Cafe St James* (☎ 760-320-8041, 254 N Palm Canyon Drive) is an upscale restaurant and bar with an international menu, including some good vegetarian dishes. Lunch costs $6 to $11, dinner $9 to $15.

Several places offer English cooking. Among them, *Churchill's Fish & Chips* (☎ 760-325-3716, 665 S Palm Canyon Drive)

has a British pub atmosphere and serves jolly good fish-and-chips for $7.50. They also have shrimp, scallops and clams, as well as Guinness on tap for $2.75. At breakfast time, the line extends out the door at *Louise's Pantry* (☎ 760-34-1315, 44491 Town Center Way, off Fred Waring Dr), Palm Desert, but the food is mediocre and overpriced.

Mario's (☎ 760-346-0584, 73399 El Paseo), Palm Desert, has two seatings nightly for its operatic Italian dinners. For $20 per person, you get a good four-course meal and waiters and waitresses who sing as well as serve; reservations are recommended.

Other top-end restaurants have excellent food, elegant surroundings and also offer the hope of seeing a celebrity (though now that Frank Sinatra is gone, it's not nearly as exciting). Two of the best prospects, in the right season, are *Melvyn's* (☎ 760-325-2323, 200 W Ramon Rd), at the Ingleside Inn, which was featured on *Lifestyles of the Rich & Famous*, and *Le Vallauris* (☎ 760-325-5059, 385 W Tahquitz Canyon Way), 'where the stars entertain their friends.' A star might expect to pay around $30 for a friend's main course at either restaurant. Nonstars should make reservations and dress up.

Entertainment

Palm Springs Follies This Ziegfeld Follies-style review includes music, dancing, showgirls and comedy and is presented at the historic 1936 *Plaza Theater* (☎ 760-327-0225, 128 S Palm Canyon Drive). The twist is that many of the performers are as old as the theater – all are over 50, some up to 80. But this is not the amateur hour. Palm Springs can pull some big names out of its celebrity closet, and the show has been known to feature such stars as Bing Crosby, Doris Day and Jack Benny. At $25 to $60, it's not cheap, but the cast from the past can turn in a great performance. They perform evening shows and matinees from November to May; reservations are recommended.

Theater The *Annenberg Theater* (☎ 760-325-4490, 101 Museum Drive), in the Palm Springs Desert Museum, has regular music performances, theater and dance.

Casinos Legal gambling is possible on Indian reservations, at the *Spa Hotel & Casino* (☎ 800-258-2946, 100 N Indian Canyon Drive) – the casino entrance is at 140 N Indian Canyon Drive – and, near Indio, at the *Fantasy Springs Casino* (☎ 800-827-2946, 84245 Indio Springs Drive), which has entertainers and 24-hour gambling.

Clubs *Zelda's Nightclub & Beachclub* (☎ 760-325-2375, 169 N Indian Canyon Drive) is a long-standing popular place, attracting a mixed crowd for drinking and dancing ($6 cover charge, higher on weekends). The *Village Pub* (☎ 760-323-3265, 262 S Palm Canyon Drive) is a casual place with live music, darts and good beer on tap. In Palm Springs, the *Toolshed* (☎ 760-320-3299, 600 E Sunny Dunes Rd) is a popular gay bar.

Coffeehouses *LaLaJava* (☎ 760-325-3494, 300 N Palm Canyon Drive) makes a good cup, but *Peabody's* (☎ 760-322-1877, 134 S Palm Canyon Drive) is the local favorite, with live jazz on weekends.

Shopping

There are quite a few art galleries and antique stores, but unless you have a mega-budget, you'll be looking more than buying. Coffman's Fine Art (☎ 760-325-0676), 457 N Palm Canyon Drive, has a good selection of American Indian and Western arts and crafts. Adagio Galleries (☎ 760-320-2230), 193 S Palm Canyon Drive, exhibit and sell contemporary paintings and sculpture, B Lewin Galleries (☎ 760-323-0686), 210 S Palm Canyon Drive, has an extensive collection of paintings by the best Mexican artists.

The Desert Fashion Plaza (☎ 760-320-8282), 123 N Palm Canyon Drive, has a number of upscale fashion outlets. Lots of stores in downtown Palm Springs sell 'resort wear,' a typical Palm Springs purchase. Another local specialty is dates – the Coachella Valley produces 90% of the US supply. Since 1924, Shields (☎ 760-347-0996), 80-225 Hwy 111, on the east edge of Palm Desert, has shown its visitors a film on 'The

Romance and Sex Life of the Date.' They have gift boxes, date cakes and date milkshakes for sale.

Getting There & Away

Air Palm Springs Regional Airport (☎ 760-323-8161) is served by Alaska Airlines, American Airlines, America West, Delta Air Lines/SkyWest, United Airlines and US Airways Express.

Bus The Greyhound bus station (☎ 760-325-2053) is at 311 N Indian Canyon Drive. There are seven buses between 6 am and 9 pm daily that go to Los Angeles ($16, three hours). Amtrak buses go to Bakersfield, Stockton, Fresno and Oakland.

Car & Motorcycle I-10 from Los Angeles (about a two-hour drive) is the main route into and through the Coachella Valley, but Hwy 74, the Palms to Pines Hwy, is the more scenic route and worth a detour.

Car rental companies include Alamo, Avis, Dollar, Hertz, Thrifty (see the Toll-Free Number appendix for phone numbers).

Getting Around

To/From the Airport Buses on Line 21 (see the Bus section) run hourly between the airport and downtown Palm Springs. Taking a taxi to/from the airport costs about $15.

Bus Sunline (☎ 760-343-3451), the local bus service, covers the whole valley from about 6 am to 10 pm. The air-conditioned buses are clean, comfortable and run every 20 to 30 minutes along the main routes, but they're not a fast way to get around. Line 111 follows Hwy 111 between Palm Springs and Indio (about 1½ hours). You can transfer to other lines that loop through the various communities. The standard fare is 75¢ (exact change required), plus 25¢ for a transfer. All the buses have wheelchair lifts and a rack for two bicycles.

Taxi Ace Taxi (☎ 760-835-2445) provides 24-hour taxi service. Prime Time Shuttle (☎ 760-341-2221) has good rates to the airport and for trips between Palm Springs and Palm Desert.

Joshua Tree National Park

Joshua Tree National Park straddles the transition zone between the high and low deserts and has a variety of plant life, but is famous for its amazing concentration of distinctive Joshua trees that look like something out of Dr Seuss. Wonderfully shaped rock outcrops (mostly of quartz monzonite) are popular with rock climbers who generally consider 'J-Tree' the best place to climb in California. Backpackers are less enthusiastic about the park since there is no natural water flow, but day hikers and campers enjoy the array of subtle desert colors and the profusion of wildflowers in spring.

The biggest trees are near Covington Flats. To see the transition from the high Colorado Desert/Sonora Desert to the low Mojave, drive the Pinto Basin Rd, which drops from the Twentynine Palms area into the Pinto Basin.

Information
The park headquarters is at the Oasis Visitor Center (☎ 760-367-5522, 760-367-5500, www.nps.gov/jotr), National Monument Drive in Twentynine Palms, just outside the park's northern boundary. It's open 8 am to 5 pm daily (until 6 pm in winter) and has useful information, books and maps. The smaller Cottonwood Visitor Center is a few miles inside the park's southern entrance. Vehicle entry, good for seven days, costs $10; walkers, cyclists and bus passengers are charged $3. For emergency assistance, call ☎ 909-383-5651.

Hiking
You really need to get away from your car to appreciate Joshua Tree's eerie landscapes and intriguing details. The visitor centers will give you maps and advice about the following short, marked trails that focus on differ-

ent features of the park: Fortynine Palms Oasis, Hidden Valley, Lost Horse Mine, Keys View & Inspiration Point, Ryan Mountain, Cholla Cactus Garden and Lost Palm Oasis. The 1.7-mile Skull Rock Loop is an easy, well-marked trail with interpretive panels along the way.

Overnight Hikes Longer hikes are possible, but are a real challenge because of the need to carry water – at least two gallons per person per day. Anyone going overnight into the backcountry must fill out a registration card (to aid in census-taking and rescue efforts) and deposit the stub at one of 12 backcountry boards in parking lots throughout the park. Cars left overnight not identified on a registration card may be cited or towed away.

The well-traveled, 16-mile Boy Scout Trail, on the west side of the park, starts from either the Indian Cove or Keys West backcountry board.

Rock Climbing
From boulders to cracks to multi-pitch faces, there are possibly more routes here than anywhere else in the US. The longest climbs are not much more than a 100 feet or so, but there are many challenging technical routes, and most can be easily top-roped for training. Some of the most popular climbs are in the Hidden Valley area.

A specialized climbing book, such as *Joshua Tree Rock Climbing Guide* by Randy Vogel, is a must. There are many climbing schools and guide services in the area, including First Ascent Climbing Services (☎ 800-325-5462), Joshua Tree Rock Climbing School (☎ 800-890-4745) and the Boojum Institute (☎ 909-659 6250). Nomad Ventures (☎ 760-366-4684), in the town of Joshua Tree, is the only climbing store around and is a good resource for equipment and information. It's open 8 am to 6 pm daily (later on weekends during winter).

Bicycling
Joshua Tree is popular for cycling, though bikes must stay on the roads and trails.

CALIFORNIA DESERTS

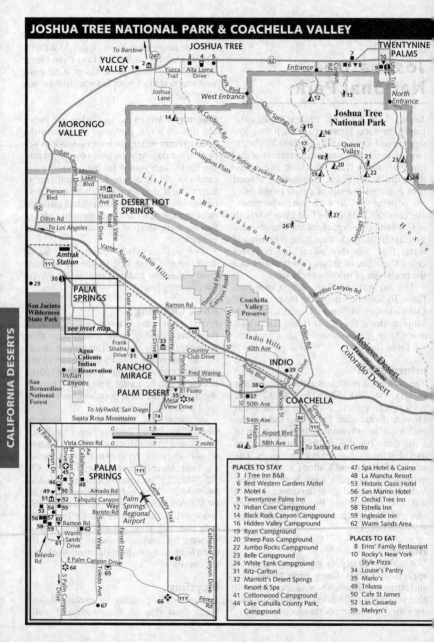

JOSHUA TREE NATIONAL PARK & COACHELLA VALLEY

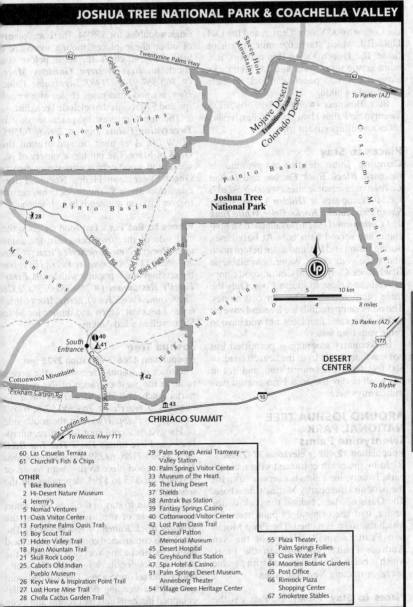

JOSHUA TREE NATIONAL PARK & COACHELLA VALLEY

Joshua Tree
National Park

To Parker (AZ)

To Parker (AZ)

DESERT
CENTER

To Blythe

CHIRIACO SUMMIT

To Mecca, Hwy 111

CALIFORNIA DESERTS

Two favorite bicycle routes are the challenging Pinkham Canyon Rd, which begins at the Cottonwood Visitor Center, and the Old Dale Rd, which starts 6½ miles north of there. The Queen Valley Rds network is a more gentle set of trails and has bike racks along the way so people can lock up their bikes and go hiking.

Bike Business (☎ 760-365-1078), 56778 Twentynine Palms Hwy, Yucca Valley, repairs bikes and offers guided trips.

Places to Stay

Camping There are nine campgrounds in the park. ***Black Rock Canyon*** and ***Indian Cove*** have reservable sites (☎ 800-365-2267) for $10; campsites at ***Hidden Valley***, ***Ryan***, ***Sheep Pass***, ***Jumbo Rocks***, ***Belle***, ***White Tank*** and ***Cottonwood*** ($8) are available on a first-come, first-served basis only. At busy times, during spring and fall, find a site before noon and stake your claim. Water is available at Black Rock Canyon and Cottonwood campgrounds, and close to Indian Cove. Only the three campgrounds with water cost money. The other campgrounds are free and have pit toilets, tables and fireplaces, but you have to bring your own water.

Backcountry camping is permitted but not less than a mile from the nearest road, or 500 feet from the nearest trail, and not in any wash or day-use area. Fires are not permitted anywhere.

AROUND JOSHUA TREE NATIONAL PARK
Twentynine Palms
• population 12,402 • elevation 3242 feet
Right by the north entrance to the national park, Twentynine Palms is a service town for the park and the nearby Marine Corps base. The Oasis of Mara, behind the park visitor center, had the original 29 palm trees for which the town is named. The Pinto Mountain Fault (a small relative of the San Andreas Fault) runs through the oasis, which is believed to be charged with psychic energy, attracting New Age types.

Places to Stay Twentynine Palms is the best for accommodations near the national

park. ***Motel 6*** (☎ 760-367-2833, 72562 Twentynine Palms Hwy) is nice and clean and ha singles/doubles for $38/44. There are plenty of other cheap places, though some are a little seedy, so check the room before you check in. ***Best Western Gardens Mote*** (☎ 760-367-9141, 71487 Twentynine Palm Hwy) is a good mid-range choice with a pool spa and $70 rooms that include breakfast.

The most interesting place to stay is ***Twentynine Palms Inn*** (☎ 760-367-3505, 73950 Inn Ave) built on and around the Oasis of Mara. The inn has a variety of old adobe and wood cabins with names such as Ghost Flower and Hedge Needle. Prices range from about $70 midweek in low season to over $100 on weekends in high season.

Places to Eat For a fast-food fix, go to the east side of the town center. In the same area, ***Rocky's New York Style Pizza*** (☎ 760-367-9525, 73737 Twentynine Palms Hwy) has big servings and is popular with locals. ***Erins Family Restaurant*** (☎ 760-376-0138, 72576 Twentynine Palms Hwy), across from Motel 6, has breakfast, lunch and dinner for $4 to $8, as well as a kids' menu.

Joshua Tree
• population 4286 • elevation 2728 feet
The town of Joshua Tree, where the access road to the west entrance of the national park branches off Hwy 62, attracts the area's climbers. ***Jeremy's*** (☎ 760-366-9799, 61597 Twentynine Palms Hwy), on the south side of Hwy 62, is a cool spot for coffee, microbrews and live music. The ***J Tree Inn B&B*** (☎ 760-366-1188, 61259 Twentynine Palms Hwy) is a good place to stay, with rooms or cottages for $75 to $195, depending on the season.

If you plan to stay in the area for a while, consider one of the lovely cabins at the ***Mohave Rock Ranch*** (☎ 760-366-8455). The ranch was constructed completely from local materials (including recycled relics of the past – rocks, fossils, wagon wheels, shells, bones) and set on 55 acres. The two-bedroom cabins have sleeping porches, patios, fully-equipped kitchens and bathrooms and sleep one to four people for $175 and up.

Yucca Valley
• population 15,844 • elevation 3279 feet
To the west, the town of Joshua Tree merges into the town of Yucca Valley, with Hwy 62 (here called Twentynine Palms Hwy) lined with unattractive commercial developments and the Institute of Mental Physics, a 'spiritual center.' The **Hi-Desert Nature Museum** (☎ 760-369-7212), 57116 Twentynine Palms Hwy, has a few interesting exhibits on desert flora and fauna – the spring wildflower displays can be good and the scorpions are impressive. It's open 10 am to 5 pm Tuesday to Sunday; free (donations requested).

Along or near Twentynine Palms Hwy you'll find several motels, including a **Super 8** (☎ 760-228-1773, *570962 Twentynine Palms Hwy*) and the **Desert View** (☎ 760-365-9706, *57471 Primrose Drive*), as well as several fast-food outlets. Twenty-nine Palms Hwy continues west, then turns south to meet I-10 near Palm Springs.

Chiriaco Summit
• population 1363 • elevation 1710 feet
This highway stop has a motel with standard air-conditioning rooms for $28 and a diner serving grilled food, including burgers such as the $5.25 Desert Training Center Burger, which is made with Spam. (The Desert Training Center was a WWII training ground that covered 18,000 sq miles of the surrounding desert – the largest military training ground in history.)

General Patton Memorial Museum
This museum (☎ 760-227-3483) has a large but poorly explained collection of war junk recalling General George S 'Blood 'n' Guts' Patton's career, with an archive, library and publications on sale. Patton established the Desert Training Center to prepare US troops for the North African campaign in WWII. Patton said of the harsh desert environment that 'if you can work in this country, it will be no difficulty at all to kill the assorted sons of bitches you will meet in any other country.' The museum is open 9:30 am to 4:30 pm daily; $4.

An interesting nonmilitary exhibit is **The Big Map**, a 5½-ton relief map of Southern California used to plan the 242-mile aqueduct that brings water from the Colorado River to LA. The museum is open 9 am to 5 pm daily; $3. The old tanks outside can be seen for free.

The Low Desert

The rich agricultural district of the Imperial Valley is a monument to vision and pioneering enterprise, but only those with an interest in irrigation and agribusiness will find much to see. The Salton Sea looks intriguing on a map but is uninspiring in reality, though it does attract many waterbird species. The most interesting parts for desert lovers are the remote Algodones Dunes, where thousands of people spend the whole winter in colonies of motor homes – a bizarre sight.

IMPERIAL VALLEY
The soil of the Imperial Valley is rich in alluvial deposits from the ancient course of the Colorado River, and its agricultural potential was recognized as early as the 1850s. Because the area is actually below sea level, water flowing down the Colorado River to the Gulf of Mexico was able to be channeled via the Alamo watercourse, through Mexican territory, then back north into the Imperial Valley. This ambitious plan was realized by CR Rockwood, George Chaffey and their California Development Company, and was bankrolled by the sale of water rights to local water companies. The first water flowed in 1901. By 1905 the valley had 67,000 acres irrigated and a population of 12,000. An agreement with the Mexican government in 1904 stipulated that half the diverted water be supplied to Mexico, where much of it was used to grow cotton in the Mexicali valley by a US company using imported Chinese laborers.

In 1905, the Colorado River flooded, its water flowing uncontrolled through the canals and into the Imperial Valley. The disaster provided impetus for a more effective and centralized water management system. Local water companies amalgamated to form the Imperial Irrigation District (IID),

CALIFORNIA DESERTS

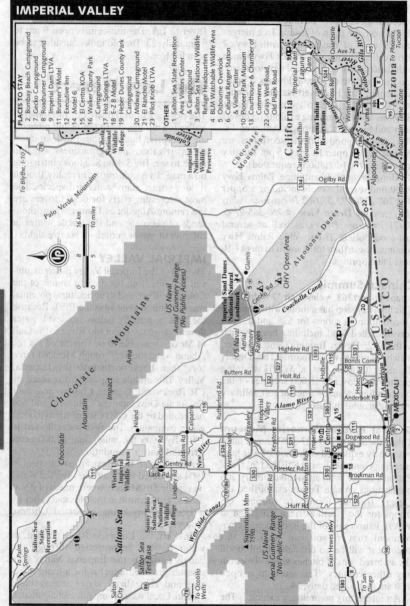

IMPERIAL VALLEY

PLACES TO STAY
2 Bombay Beach Campground
7 Gecko Campground
8 Roadrunner Campground
9 Imperial Dam LTVA
11 Brunner's Motel
12 Executive Inn
14 Motel 6
15 El Centro KOA
16 Walker County Park Campground
17 Hot Springs LTVA
18 E-Z 8 Motel
19 Heber Dunes County Park Campground
20 Midway Campground
21 El Rancho Motel
23 Pilot Knob LTVA

OTHER
1 Salton Sea State Recreation Area Visitors Center & Campground
3 Salton Sea National Wildlife Refuge Headquarters
4 BLM Watchable Wildlife Area
5 Osbourne Overlook
6 Cahuilla Ranger Station & Visitor Center
10 Pioneer Park Museum
13 Courthouse & Chamber of Commerce
22 Grays Well Road, Old Plank Road

which initiated US congressional support for large-scale management of the Colorado River. This resulted in the construction of the 80-mile-long All-American Canal, which diverts water from the Colorado River at the Imperial Dam and carries it to Calexico, without passing through Mexico, as did the Inter-California Canal that it replaced.

IID water now irrigates more than 500,000 acres. An orderly patchwork of fields produces cattle feed, cotton, tomatoes, sugar beets, melons, strawberries, lettuce and other crops. Some fruits and vegetables are grown in winter to take advantage of higher out-of-season prices. An interesting environmental discussion about agriculture in the Imperial Valley is found in Marc Reisner's *Cadillac Desert: The American West and Its Disappearing Water*.

El Centro

• population 33,960 • elevation 42 feet

The Imperial Valley county seat, El Centro has a moderately imposing courthouse, three shopping centers, the standard range of restaurants and motels and a pretty good museum.

Pioneers Park Museum This museum (☎ 760-352-1165), 373 E Aten Rd, at the corner of Hwy 111, is a cut above the average local historical society effort and is well worth a stop. It tells the story of irrigation, inundation and immigration in the Imperial Valley. Particularly interesting are individual exhibits on a dozen different ethnic groups who settled the valley in the early 20th century. Displays of the artifacts and traditions they brought to the valley, plus photos of family life and work, reveal much of their sacrifice, hope and determination. The museum is open 10 am to 4 pm Tuesday to Sunday; $2 donation.

Places to Stay Walker County Park and Heber Dunes County Park both have free campgrounds.

A number of inexpensive motels can be found near the Hwy 86/4th St exit from I-8. *Motel 6* (☎ 760-353-6766, 395 Smoketree Drive), just north of the interstate, and *Executive Inn* (☎ 760-352-8500, 725 State St), about a mile farther north, both cost around $35/44 singles/doubles. South of the interstate, *E-Z 8 Motel* (☎ 760-352-6620, 455 Wake Ave) costs $33/39. The best place is probably *Brunner's Motel* (☎ 760-352-6431, 215 N Imperial Ave), with a selection of rooms starting at $65/69.

Calexico

• population 23,800 • elevation 1 foot

On the border of California and Mexico, Calexico (get it?) was founded in 1900 as a work camp and construction headquarters for the builders of the Imperial Canal. It thrived during Prohibition as a base for cross-border binges but fell from fashion when booze was legalized in the US. It's still a major gateway from Mexico into the US. It has better value accommodations than Mexicali, but there's no other reason to stop here.

Places to Stay There's a selection of inexpensive motels on E 4th St, just east of Imperial Ave, all with small pools, air-conditioning and similar prices. The *El Rancho Motel* (☎ 760-357-2468, 341 E 4th St) is typical with single/double rooms for around $30/35. Others nearby on this street include the *Border Motel* (☎ 760-357-2707, 120 E 4th St) and *Don Juan Motel* (☎ 760-357-3231, 344 E 4th St). A step up is the *Quality Inn* (☎ 760-357-3271, 801 E 4th St), which has a pool, restaurant and lounge.

Getting There & Away Greyhound (☎ 760-357-1895), 123 E 1st St, near the border crossing, has daily buses to and from Los Angeles ($27, 4½ hours) and San Diego ($18, 1¾ hours).

Mexicali, Mexico

• population 900,000 • elevation sea level

Much larger than its counterpart across the border, Mexicali is the capital of the Mexican state of Baja California, an educational center and the terminus of Mexico's main northern railroad. It's a modern city with some grandiose monuments but not much to see. Most tourists head straight through to mainland Mexico, Baja California or the beaches of San Felipe.

The blocks near the border have lots of souvenir shops and touristy restaurants. Farther south is La Chinesca, Mexicali's Chinatown, around the intersection of Avenida Juárez and Calle Altamirano. The Centro Cívico-Comercial (Civic & Commercial Center), about 2 miles southeast of the border post, is a modern complex with government offices, a medical school, bullring, cinemas, bus station, hospitals and restaurants. Just south of there is the Zona Rosa, an area of fancy hotels and restaurants.

Visas & Immigration The border is open 24 hours. You don't need a visa or a passport to cross into Mexicali, but you should have some form of photo identification. Returning to the US, non-Americans need to show a passport. If you're going east into Sonora or south past San Felipe, or are staying more than 72 hours, you'll need a Mexican tourist card.

Places to Stay & Eat The respectable *Hotel Plaza* (☎ 011-52-65-52-97-57, *Madero 366*) charges around $32 for a double. If you can afford more than $25, you'll get better accommodations on the US side.

It's worth coming over to Mexicali for Mexican food and the big selection of Chinese restaurants. Quite a few restaurants are along Avenida Reforma, two blocks south and parallel to the border. It's hard to pay over $10 for a meal. An above-average place in price and quality is *La Villa del Seri* (☎ 011-52-65-53-55-03), at Avenida Reforma and Calle D, which specializes in Sonoran beef, but also has excellent seafood and *antojitos*. Only three blocks southeast of the border crossing, the inexpensive *Alley 19*, Avenida Juárez 8 near Azueta, is Mexicali's oldest Chinese restaurant, opened in 1928.

SALTON SEA

The largest lake in California, the Salton Sea is surprisingly unattractive. Filled with water in the 1905 flood, it was stocked with fish and soon attracted colonies of migratory birds. The Salton Sea State Recreation Area, on the eastern shore, has a visitor center (☎ 760-393-3052), at Bombay Beach, with information about local fishing and bird watching. It's open daily from October to May. There are some failed lakeside resorts on the western shore, of which Salton City is the biggest and most depressing.

The Sonny Bono Salton Sea National Wildlife Refuge provides a habitat for migrating and endangered birds, including snow geese, mallard, brown pelicans, bald eagles and peregrine falcons. Its headquarters (☎ 760-348-5278), 906 W Sinclair Rd, off Hwy 111 between Niland and Calipatria, is open 7 am to 3:30 pm weekdays, but the refuge is open dawn to dusk.

Fishing has been adversely affected by increasing salinity, but it's still popular. The best fishing is for croaker, sargo, tilapia and especially orangemouth corvina. Eating the fish is not recommended because of the high concentration of selenium. There are three boat launching ramps, and small boats may be launched anywhere round the shoreline.

Swimming is not pleasant – the water is murky with plankton and the salt stings the eyes – nor is it recommended at the south end of the sea because of pollution.

Places to Stay

Camping The Salton Sea State Recreation Area has several campgrounds, with tent and RV spaces ranging from $7 for a primitive site to $19 for one with electricity and water. The best and most popular campground is the *Bombay Beach Campground*, south of the visitor center on the east shore.

ALGODONES DUNES

Up to 300 feet high, these sand dunes along the eastern edge of the Imperial Valley were once beaches on Lake Cahuilla. The shifting sands were an obstacle for early European explorers and the builders of canals and roads.

When the dunes buried the first trails between the Imperial Valley and Yuma, a wooden road was tried. Sections of heavy timber planks, bound together with steel

CALIFORNIA DESERTS

Now You Sea It, Now You Don't

Fifteen million years ago, the area that is now the Imperial Valley and the Salton Sea was under the Pacific Ocean. Uplifts in the earth's crust created the mountains that now form Southern California's coastal range and the spine of Baja California. The ancient seabed was raised, lifting marine fossil beds hundreds of feet above sea level. Then, starting 12 million years ago, tectonic movements separated Baja California from the mainland, creating the elongated trough we call the Gulf of California. The gulf extended much farther north than it does now – all the way to the San Gorgonio Pass, beyond Palm Springs. The area of the Imperial Valley and the Salton Sea was under water again.

The Colorado River, flowing somewhat west of its present course, carried huge quantities of sediment into the northern end of this gulf – all the material eroded from the Grand Canyon ended up here. The sediment progressively built up until it formed a gigantic levee that separated the Imperial Valley from the Gulf of California. The course of the Colorado shifted eastward, flowing directly into the gulf, and the water in the Imperial Valley began to evaporate, leaving a dry, empty basin.

Sometime later the river shifted again, perhaps in a large flood, filling the valley with fresh water to a height some 30 feet above sea level. This water line is clearly visible on the mountainside at Travertine Point, south of Indio, and it corresponds to the height at which the water would overflow the valley and run south to the gulf. This cycle was probably repeated many times, with the Colorado changing its course, filling the lake, clogging itself with silt, and then swinging back to the gulf, allowing the lake to become dry again.

Shells and mineral deposits indicate that there was a freshwater lake here around 3000 years ago. There are many sites that show that people lived on its shores, trapping fish and making extensive use of lakeside plants. Around five or six hundred years ago, the Colorado River changed its course again, the lake started to dry up, and these lakeside dwellers moved away. When white settlers first arrived, the whole Imperial Valley was dry, and its deepest part was a salty depression that was dubbed the Salton Sink. A US Army survey in 1852 found traces of the old lake, which they called Lake Cahuilla after the Cahuilla Indians who lived in the area at that time. (In fact, the Indians living along the shores of the ancient lake were probably not ancestors of the Cahuilla. More likely they were Yumans, whose descendants lived in the San Diego area and on the banks of the Colorado River when European explorers arrived.)

In 1905, the Colorado River again flooded and overflowed into irrigation channels, nearly inundating the entire valley once more. It took 18 months, 1500 workers, $12 million, and half a million tons of rock to put the Colorado River back on its course to the Gulf of Mexico. The previously dry Salton Sink had again become a lake, 45 miles long and 17 miles wide. It had no natural outlet and, as evaporation reduced its size, the natural salt levels became more concentrated. The Salton became an inland sea, with its surface actually 228 feet below the level of the sea in the Gulf of California.

Colorado River water continued to flow into the Imperial Valley via irrigation canals and pipelines, but years of irrigation have caused salt to percolate to the surface of farmland. This problem is being relieved by periodically flooding the land and flushing off the excess salt. Each year, this adds another 4½ million tons of salt to the Salton Sea, which now has 1½ times the salinity of seawater. Fewer types of fish can survive in the Salton Sea now, the number of waterbirds is thought to be declining, and the salt concentration continues to rise. Unless this problem is solved, the Salton Sea will become a Dead Sea.

straps, formed the road's surface. When sand covered a section, it could be dragged to a new position by a mule team. The 'plank road,' continually being moved with the dunes, provided the only link across this strip of desert from 1916 to 1926 when a surfaced highway was built. Remnants of the plank road may be seen from Grays Well Rd, south of I-8, and there's a section in the Pioneer Park Museum near El Centro.

Much of the dunes area is open to off-road vehicles or off-highway vehicles, but there's also a designated wilderness area near the town of Glamis. If you want to see some undisturbed dune country, try the Imperial Sand Dunes National Natural Landmark, north of Hwy 78 and west of Glamis. It's a preserve for desert plants and animals, closed to vehicles, but open for walkers. For a good view of the area, try the Osbourne Overlook, off Hwy 78 about 4 miles west of Glamis. For hiking, head north from Glamis on Ted Kips Rd (at the Glamis Store, immediately west of the railroad tracks) and go 2 miles to the BLM Watchable Wildlife area.

The El Centro Field Office (☎ 760-337-4400), 1661 S 4th St, El Centro (open weekdays), and the Cahuilla Ranger Station & Visitor Center (☎ 760-344-3919), Gecko Rd south of Hwy 78 (open weekends), have maps and information. Phones, food and gas are available in Glamis on Hwy 78. Otherwise, there are virtually no facilities at all between the Imperial Valley and the Colorado River.

Rattlesnakes abound in California's deserts.

Places to Stay

Camping The BLM operates free camping at Midway, Gecko and Roadrunner campgrounds. They have toilets, but no water or other facilities. You can camp anywhere on undeveloped public land for up to 14 days. Long-term visitor areas (LTVAs) have been established for those who spend the whole winter in motor homes in undeveloped desert areas.

Anza-Borrego Desert

This desert – which contains the 600,000-acre Anza-Borrego Desert State Park – has some of the most spectacular and accessible desert scenery you'll find anywhere. The human history goes back 10,000 years, recorded in ancient Native American pictographs. Spanish explorer Juan Bautista de Anza passed through in 1774, pioneering an immigrant trail from Mexico. The Mormon Battalion came this way to fight the Californios, and the Southern Emigrant Trail and the Butterfield Stageline followed a route along the Vallecito Valley in the southern part of the park.

ANZA-BORREGO DESERT STATE PARK

There are three different sections to Anza-Borrego Desert State Park, each near a major travel artery; you really need a car to get around it and to access the many points of interest.

The area around Borrego Springs is the most visited and can get crowded on weekends, especially during the wildflower bloom in February and March. It's a good destination for first timers and day-trippers, since it's home to the excellent Anza-Borrego Desert State Park Visitors Center. A number of easy-to-reach sights, including Font's Point and Borrego Palm Canyon, lie to the south, near Ocotillo Wells. The Fish Creek area is popular with off-road vehicles, but also contains interesting geology and spectacular wind caves. The desert's southernmost region, near Ocotillo, is the least visited and has few developed trails and facilities. Attractions here,

CALIFORNIA DESERTS

ANZA-BORREGO DESERT STATE PARK

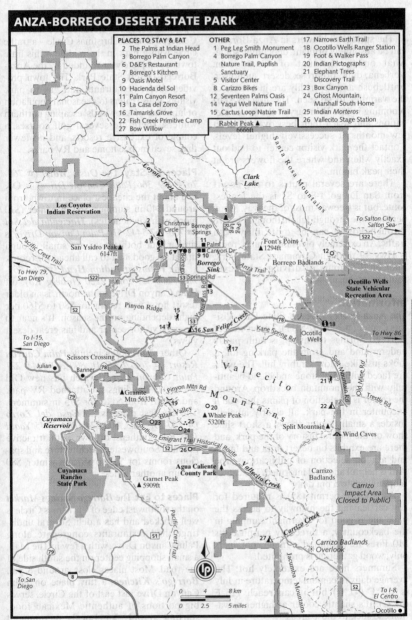

PLACES TO STAY & EAT
2 The Palms at Indian Head
3 Borrego Palm Canyon
6 D&E's Restaurant
7 Borrego's Kitchen
9 Oasis Motel
10 Hacienda del Sol
11 Palm Canyon Resort
13 La Casa del Zorro
16 Tamarisk Grove
22 Fish Creek Primitive Camp
27 Bow Willow

OTHER
1 Peg Leg Smith Monument
4 Borrego Palm Canyon
    Nature Trail, Pupfish
    Sanctuary
5 Visitor Center
8 Carrizo Bikes
12 Seventeen Palms Oasis
14 Yaqui Well Nature Trail
15 Cactus Loop Nature Trail

17 Narrows Earth Trail
18 Ocotillo Wells Ranger Station
19 Foot & Walker Pass
20 Indian Pictographs
21 Elephant Trees
    Discovery Trail
23 Box Canyon
24 Ghost Mountain,
    Marshall South Home
25 Indian *Morteros*
26 Vallecito Stage Station

Rabbit Peak ▲
6666ft

Santa Rosa Mountains

Coyote Creek

Clark
Lake

Los Coyotes
Indian Reservation

Pacific Crest Trail

San Ysidro Peak ▲
6147ft

Christmas
Circle

Borrego
Springs

Palm
Canyon Dr

To Salton City,
Salton Sea
S22

Font's Point
▲1294ft

Borrego Badlands

12

Ocotillo Wells
State Vehicular
Recreation Area

*Borrego
Sink*

Anza Trail

To Hwy 79,
San Diego

S22

S2

Pinyon Ridge

Yaqui Pass Rd

Borrego
Springs Rd

53

15

16 San Felipe Creek

Kane Spring Rd

78

Ocotillo
Wells

18

To Hwy 86

Split Mountain Rd

Old Mine Rd

Trestle Rd

To I-15,
San Diego

14

17

V a l l e c i t o

21

22

Julian

Scissors Crossing

Banner   78

Pinyon Mtn Rd

M o u n t a i n s

20

▲Whale Peak
5320ft

Split Mountain ▲

Wind Caves

Cuyamaca
Reservoir

▲Granite
Mtn 5633ft

19

Blair Valley

23

25

24

Split Mountain Rd

Southern Emigrant Trail Historical Route

S2   26

V a l l e c i t o

Carrizo
Badlands

Cuyamaca
Rancho
State Park

Garnet Peak
▲5909ft

Agua Caliente
County Park

Vallecito Creek

Carrizo
Impact Area
(Closed to Public)

S1

Pacific Crest Trail

To San
Diego

79

Carrizo Creek

27

Carrizo Badlands
Overlook

Jacumba Mountains

To I-8,
El Centro

S2

8

79

Julian

To San
Diego

0   4   8 km
0   2.5   5 miles

LP

Ocotillo

CALIFORNIA DESERTS

CALIFORNIA DESERTS

besides the solitude, include Goat Trestle and the Carrizo Badlands.

The spring wildflowers in Anza-Borrego can be absolutely brilliant, depending somewhat on the amount of winter rain. Verbena, dune primrose, desert sunflower, brittlebush and desert lily are just some of the varieties to be seen. The flowers start blooming in late February at the lower elevations and reach their best over the next few months at successively higher levels. Contact the park visitor center to find out exactly when and where the flowers are at their peak bloom.

There are several routes to the desert from San Diego: I-8 to S2 is the longest route, but is freeway most of the way. Many people come through Julian, though Hwy 78 through Poway can be quite busy with traffic. An extremely pleasant, if curvy, route is Hwy 79 through Cuyamaca State Park. Plan on 2½ hours of driving, whichever route you take.

Information

The Anza-Borrego Desert State Park Visitors Center (☎ 760-767-5311), 2 miles west of Borrego Springs township, is built partly underground and, from the parking lot, it looks just like a low scrubby hill. The walls are faced with local stone and blend beautifully with the mountain backdrop. Around the center is a selection of plants that you'll encounter in the park, all clearly labeled. Inside, a small theater shows a short slide show on the natural history of the park, and there are exhibits on desert flora and fauna and a good selection of publications. The staff is helpful and well informed. The center is open 9 am to 5 pm daily.

A park-use permit ($5) is required for any car leaving the highway to access the park and is good for overnight camping in the backcountry; a three-day permit costs $10. Fires are permitted in metal containers only; wood gathering is prohibited.

Summers here are extremely hot. The average daily maximum temperature in July is 107°F (41°C) but it can reach 125°F (51°C). It's slightly cooler at higher elevations, so stick to those areas.

Borrego Springs
• population 2989 • elevation 590 feet

Centered around Christmas Circle – a traffic circle with a park in the middle – this little town is completely surrounded by the Anza-Borrego Desert State Park. The town provides shops, restaurants and gas to park visitors. It also caters to a seasonal population of hundreds of 'snowbirds' escaping northern winters. There are several golf courses, a couple of expensive resorts, and no fewer than seven mobile home and RV parks.

Places to Stay The *Oasis Motel* (☎ 760-767-5409, 366 Palm Canyon Drive) is OK and about the cheapest place in town, from around $40 in summer, $60 in winter ($10 more with kitchenettes). *Hacienda del Sol* (☎ 760-767-5442, 610 Palm Canyon Drive) is similar, but both places are small enough that it's a good idea to call ahead for rooms.

The Palms at Indian Head (☎ 760-767-7788, 800-519-2624, 2220 Hoberg Rd), off Palm Canyon Drive to the north, is an older resort hotel with rooms for $80 to $160 per night depending on the season. It's near to the park visitor center and has great desert views.

Other resort hotels include *Palm Canyon Resort* (☎ 760-767-5341, 800-242-0044, 221 Palm Canyon Drive), which has new Old West-style buildings, an attached RV park and rooms from $115 (or $75 in summer). The classiest place is *La Casa del Zorro* (☎ 760-767-5323, 800-824-1884, 3845 Yaqui Pass Rd), southeast of town, with attractive grounds, Southwestern architecture and spacious rooms for $95 to $875 in winter, $80 and up at other times.

Places to Eat The *Borrego Springs Market* on the southwest edge of Christmas Circle is well stocked and has a deli. Several undistinguished restaurants congregate along Palm Canyon Drive, with a few in The Mall, a small shopping center on the south side of the road. Most places close around 8 pm. *Borrego's Kitchen*, a tiny place on Palm Canyon Drive just east of the Circle, serves big portions of authentic Mexican food, starting at only $6. Locals recommend

D&E's Restaurant (☎ 760-767-4954, 818 Palm Canyon Drive) for Italian food (main courses are around $8) and the restaurant at *La Casa del Zorro* (☎ 760-767-5323, 800-824-1884, 3845 Yaqui Pass Rd), if you want to go gourmet, for around $15 per person.

Peg Leg Smith Monument & Liars Contest

Northeast of Borrego Springs, where S22 takes a 90° turn to the east, there's a pile of rocks just north of the road. This is a monument to Thomas Long 'Peg Leg' Smith – mountain man, fur trapper, Indian fighter, horse thief, liar and Wild West legend. Around 1829, Peg Leg passed through Borrego Springs on his way to Los Angeles and supposedly picked up some rocks that were later found to be pure gold. Strangely, he didn't return to the area until the 1850s, when he was unable to find the lode. Nevertheless, he told lots of people about it (often in exchange for a few drinks), and many came to search for the gold and add to the myths.

On the first Saturday of April, the Peg Leg Liars Contest is a hilarious event in which amateur liars compete in the western tradition of telling tall tales. Anyone can enter, so long as the story is about gold and mining in the Southwest, is less than five minutes long and is anything but the truth.

Pupfish Sanctuaries

The desert pupfish (*Cyprinodon macularius*) is an Ice Age remnant species, now very rare and on the endangered list. Adapted to life in desert water holes and intermittent streams, the pupfish can live in freshwater or salt water from near the freezing point to over 100°F (37°C). Two ponds, one near the visitor center and one at the start of the Borrego Palm Canyon Nature Trail, are sanctuaries for this unique creature.

Font's Point

A 4-mile dirt road, usually passable without 4WD (check with the visitor center) goes south of S22 to Font's Point, which offers a spectacular panorama over the Borrego Valley to the west and the Borrego Badlands to the south. Walking the 4 miles to the point is a

good way to *really* be amazed when the desert seemingly drops from beneath your feet.

Split Mountain

Going south from Hwy 78 at Ocotillo Wells, paved Split Mountain Rd leads to a dirt-road turnoff for Fish Creek Primitive Camp and Split Mountain. The road – very popular with off-road vehicles – goes right through Split Mountain between 600-foot-high walls created by earthquakes and erosion. The gorge is about 2 miles long from north to south. At the south end, several steep trails lead up to delicate caves carved into the sandstone outcroppings by the wind. On Split Mountain Rd you pass the Elephant Trees Discovery Trail, one of the few places to see a herd of the unusual elephant trees, and a small ranger station.

Blair Valley

This area, near S2 some 5 miles southeast of Scissors Crossing, has pleasant campsites and some attractive walks, but is also of particular archaeological interest. Short trails lead to sites with Indian pictographs and *morteros* (hollows in rocks used for grinding seeds).

A monument at Foot and Walker Pass marks a difficult spot on the Butterfield Overland Stage Route, and in Box Canyon you can still see the marks of wagons on the Emigrant Trail. A steep 1-mile climb leads to Ghost Mountain and the remains of a house occupied by the family of desert recluse Marshall South.

Vallecito Stage Station

Going west, both the Southern Emigrant Trail and the Butterfield Overland Stage Route crossed the fiercely hot and dry Imperial Valley then followed the Vallecito Creek up into the mountains for the final part of the journey to the coast. The Vallecito station was built in 1852 as a major stop on the route, though the present building is a 1934 reconstruction.

Hiking

The **Borrego Palm Canyon Nature Trail** is a popular self-guiding loop trail that goes northeast from the Borrego Palm Canyon Campground, climbing 350 feet in 3 miles past a palm grove and waterfall, which make a delightful oasis in the dry rocky countryside.

A variety of other short trails have been laid out, many of them with informative little signs or self-guiding brochures – different trails highlight different features. The 1-mile Cactus Loop Nature Trail is a good place to see a variety of cacti. Nearby, the 2-mile Yaqui Well Nature Trail has many labeled desert plants and passes a natural water hole that attracts a rich variety of bird life as well as the occasional bighorn sheep in winter. The Narrows Earth Trail, 2 miles east of Tamarisk Grove, is a short trail that highlights the local geology but also has some unusual chuparosa shrubs, which attract hummingbirds.

A dirt road, which may require 4WD, goes 3 miles off S22 to within a few hundred yards of Seventeen Palms Oasis, which is a permanent water source and a great place to spot wildlife.

Mountain Biking
Both primitive roads and paved roads are open to bikes. Popular routes are Grapevine Canyon, Oriflamme Canyon and Canyon Sin Nombre. The visitor center has a free mountain bike guide. Carizzo Bikes (☎ 760-767-3872), 648 Palm Canyon Drive in Borrego Springs, rents bikes for $7 per hour or $29 for 24 hours, and also leads guided rides.

Places to Stay
Camping *Borrego Palm Canyon Campground* (☎ 800-444-7275 for reservations), 2 miles west of Borrego Springs, has tent sites with all the amenities for $16, but don't expect a shady haven. *Tamarisk Grove Campground* (☎ 800-444-7275 for reservations), on S3, 12 miles south of Borrego Springs near Hwy 78, is smaller but has more shelter and similar facilities for the same price.

Bow Willow Campground, off S2 in the southern part of the park, has only 14 sites, with water, toilets, tables and fire pits, for $9. There are several other campsites in the park – Culp Valley, Arroyo Seco, Yaqui Well,

Yaqui Pass, Fish Creek and Mountain Palm Springs – which are free but have no water and only minimal facilities. Camping is permitted just about everywhere, though not within 200 yards of any water source; a required backcountry camping permit ($5) can be purchased at the visitor center. You can't light a fire on the ground, and gathering vegetation (dead or alive) is prohibited.

OCOTILLO WELLS STATE VEHICULAR RECREATION AREA
The town of Ocotillo Wells is on Hwy 78, just outside the eastern edge of the state park. On the north side of the highway is the Ocotillo Wells State Vehicular Recreation Area (☎ 760-767-5391), where 40,000 acres of dunes and dry washes have been sacrificed to meet the needs of off-road vehicles. Dune buggies and dirt bikes race around in a storm of dust and engine noise, but though it looks like anarchy on wheels, there is actually a long list of regulations and restrictions. Camping is permitted anywhere in the recreation area, but there are no established campgrounds and no water is available. Gas, food and phones are available in Ocotillo Wells.

The Mojave

The Mojave Desert covers a vast region, from urban areas on the northern edge of LA County to the remote, sparsely populated country of the Mojave National Preserve. Most people just pass through the desert on their way to the Eastern Sierra, Death Valley or Las Vegas, but those with the time will find a lot worth stopping for. It's not really feasible to explore the Mojave without your own vehicle.

ANTELOPE VALLEY
Palmdale & Lancaster
This area is dead flat, and it's difficult to see a valley, much less an antelope. The two main towns have a combined population of about 174,000 and dormitory suburbs that seem to go on forever. A few things worth

Point Loma, San Diego

San Diego skyline

Geisel Library, UC San Diego

Star of India, San Diego

Botanical Building at Balboa Park, San Diego

Giraffe, San Diego Zoo

Coyote, Joshua Tree National Park

Mojave National Preserve

JOHN ELK III

LEE FOSTER

SCOTT MCNEELY

JOHN ELK III

Hidden Valley, Joshua Tree National Park

Antelope Valley California Poppy Reserve

Ward Charcoal Ovens, Ely, Nevada

JAMES LYON

The Luxor, Las Vegas, Nevada

DAVID PEEVERS

Virginia St, Reno, Nevada

JOHN ELK III

Wheeler Peak and bristlecone pine, Great Basin National Park

JOHN ELK III

Lonely Hwy 50, Nevada

seeing are miles away from the urban area. If you need to stay here, you'll find motels off Hwy 14 at Palmdale Blvd and on Avenue K in Lancaster.

Antelope Valley California Poppy Reserve

From mid-March to mid-May, the hills are covered with wildflowers, particularly California's state flower, the golden poppy, and there are easy hiking trails. The interpretive center (☎ 661-724-1180) has more information. To get here, take the W Avenue I exit from Hwy 14 and continue west for about 13 miles. It's open daily in the blooming season; entry costs $5 per car.

Antelope Valley Indian Museum

Incongruously housed in a Swiss chalet, this museum (☎ 805-942-0662) has a very good collection of Indian artifacts from California and the Southwest. Official hours are 11 am to 4 pm on weekends from mid-September to June, but call first to be sure. From Hwy 14 take the E Avenue I exit and go east about 8 miles south to Avenue J. Then head east another 9 miles to 150th St, south to Avenue M, and lastly east until you see the chalet up among the boulders on your left. It's free, but worth a donation.

Saddleback Butte State Park

Rising 1000 feet above the desert floor, this granite butte has a great view if you make it to the top (and if it's a clear day). The park (☎ 805-942-0662) also has a good selection of desert plants and wildlife and a *campground* with flush toilets and first-come, first-served sites for $10. From Hwy 14 take the E Avenue I exit, go east about 8 miles, south to Avenue J, then east another 10 miles. The park is on the right after 170th St.

VICTOR VALLEY

Victor Valley includes the residential communities of Victorville, Hesperia and Apple Valley, with a total population of more than 150,000. Many residents are retirees. Victor Valley was also home to Roy Rogers and Dale Evans, until Roy's death in 1998.

Roy Rogers – Dale Evans Museum

Roy Rogers ('King of the Cowboys') made more than 80 movies for the Republic studio between 1938 and 1952, as well as more than 100 half-hour TV shows and a comeback movie in 1976. Many also featured his wife, Dale Evans ('Queen of the West'), and his horse Trigger ('The Smartest Horse in the Movies').

This museum (☎ 760-243-4547), housed in a building resembling a fort from the Old West, has a mind-boggling collection of souvenirs, awards, testimonials, photographs and mementos. There are Roy's favorite cars and boats; autographed baseballs; dozens of guns; ornate saddles; the stuffed heads of animals killed on hunting trips to Africa, Asia and Alaska; and a framed invitation to Ronald Reagan's inauguration. Trigger himself is here, stuffed and saddled. The museum was established by Roy and Dale, and taken as a whole (including its visitors) is well worth visiting as an authentic and not terribly self-conscious piece of mid-20th-century Americana.

To get here, exit I-15 at Roy Rogers Drive in Victorville and go west. Then take the first left and look for the giant statue of Trigger at the end of Civic Drive. The museum, open 9 am to 5 pm daily, costs $7; discounts for seniors, children and AAA members.

UPPER MOJAVE

About 70 miles north of LA you cross the LA county line and really feel like you are out of the city. The Upper Mojave is harsh, inhospitable country, with sporadic mining settlements and vast areas set aside for weapons and aerospace testing.

Mojave

• **population 4297** • **elevation 2757 feet**

The town of Mojave has Hwy 14, or the Sierra Hwy, as its main street, with the railroad on its west side and a commercial strip of motels, shops and eateries on the east side. Tourist information is available, sometimes, in the old red railroad caboose in the lot next to Mike's Family Restaurant. Driving through, you might think this town has a

Prickly pear cactus

huge international airport, but all those airliners are actually in storage, where deterioration is minimal in the dry desert air.

Places to Stay The *Best Motel* (☎ 661-824-4523, 15620 Sierra Hwy) is a pretty comfortable place to stay, with a pool, cable TV and singles/doubles for $23/30. *White's Motel* (☎ 800-782-4596, 16100 Sierra Hwy) is also OK at $34/40 and has a big, red neon arrow that makes it easy to find.

Around Mojave

Edwards Air Force Base Southeast of town, this 301,000-acre base (formerly called Muroc) is a flight test facility for the US Air Force, NASA and civilian aircraft, and a training school for test pilots with the 'right stuff.' It was here that Chuck Yeager flew the Bell X-1 on the world's first supersonic flight, and the first shuttles glided in after their space missions (they still land here when the weather is bad at Cape Canaveral). Free 90-minute tours of the air force base are available at 10 am on most Fridays by appointment only (☎ 805-277-3517). Most people take this tour, have lunch at the NASA cafeteria, then catch the 1:15 pm tour (also 90 minutes) of the **NASA-**

Dryden Flight Research Facility (☎ 805-258-3446). The NASA facility has tours at 10:15 am and 1:15 pm weekdays.

Boron Thirty miles east of Mojave, Boron is the site of a huge open-cut borax mine. North of Boron, visible from Hwy 395, is a vast array of solar collectors, part of the Luz Corporation's electricity generating system.

Red Rock Canyon State Park This small park (☎ 805-942-0662) straddles Hwy 14 about 20 miles north of Mojave. Its very striking sandstone cliffs have eroded into weird formations that present a spectacular range of colors at sunrise and sunset; you may recognize it from the opening scenes of *Jurassic Park*. There are some marked hiking trails, where you'll see Indian grinding holes and a variety of desert plants. The *campground* has 50 tent sites and toilets but no other facilities. Camping is on a first-come, first-served basis and costs $10. The visitor center is open on weekends (closed in summer). There's a day-use fee of $5.

Rand Mining District

Gold and silver ores discovered here in the 1890s were thought to resemble those found in the Rand district of South Africa, hence the town names of Randsburg and Johannesburg. In 1900, thousands of people were working in mines here. Today, it's almost deserted and quite picturesque. There's a lot of old mining junk around – in the hills, on private property, as well as in the Desert Museum on Butte Ave in Randsburg, open most weekends. The area hasn't been made pretty or touristified yet, but there are a couple of places to stay.

Places to Stay & Eat In Johannesburg is the euphemistically named *HI Death Valley Hostel* (☎ 760-374-2323), located 27 miles north of Hwy 58 on US 395, about a two hours' drive from Death Valley's Furnace Creek. It is, however, a comfortable hostel (set up as a home; it runs on the honor system) with a kitchen, in-house food store, mountain bike rental and friendly staff that arranges free tours of the Trona Pinnacles

CALIFORNIA DESERTS

and petroglyphs, Fossil Falls, Red Rock Canyon and more. Beds are $12 for HI members, $15 for nonmembers. The hostel opens from 7 to 9 am and 6 to 9 pm.

The *Cottage Hotel* (☎ 760-374-2285, 130 Butte Ave) has rooms from $60, including breakfast, wine and cheese in the afternoons and an indoor spa. Three miles away, on Hwy 395, the *Old Owl Inn* (☎ 760-374-2235, 701 Hwy 395) in Red Mountain is another ex-bar-and-brothel that is now an antique shop and has two cottages with kitchenettes for $45 per night ($55 with food) for two people. In Randsburg, the *Whitehouse Saloon & Floozy House* (☎ 760-374-2464) was originally the mine owner's house, later a brothel and will now provide you with a beer or a burger and lively conversation.

Ridgecrest
• population 28,222 • elevation 2289 feet

This is the last sizable town before Death Valley, and not a bad place to stock up on water, gas and supplies or to spend a night in reasonably priced accommodations. The town is here because of the China Lake Naval Weapons Center on its eastern edge; you can see what this facility does by looking at the China Lake Exhibit Center (☎ 760-939-3454, 760-939-8645) from 7:30 am to 4:30 pm on weekdays.

It's also worth looking at the Maturango Museum (☎ 760-375-6900), which has good exhibits on Native American art and archaeology and a nice gift shop. It's on the corner of China Lake Blvd and Las Flores Ave and is open 10 am to 5 pm daily; $2. They also conduct tours of Little Petroglyph Canyon every Saturday from mid-September to mid-December. The fee is $25 per person; meet at the museum at 8 am (you'll return around 4 pm) and bring your own food and water. Be sure to call ahead, as the tours usually get booked solid by early September.

Places to Stay & Eat There are several budget motels south of town along S China Lake Blvd, including a *Quality Inn* (☎ 760-375-9731, 507 S China Lake Blvd) at $35 to $50 and a *Motel 6* (☎ 760-375-6866, 535 S China Lake Blvd) at $33/40. China Lake

Blvd has an almost complete set of the most popular fast-food franchises.

Around Ridgecrest
Little Petroglyph Canyon The rock walls here have a huge number of ancient petroglyphs, but the canyon is on the Naval Weapons Center Reserve and not open to the public. You may be able to see the petroglyphs on one of the tours conducted by the Maturango Museum on weekends during spring and autumn.

Pinnacles National Natural Landmark This strange group of rock pinnacles, up to 150 feet tall, are in stark and lonely desert country about 20 miles east of Ridgecrest. The pinnacles were formed when calcium-laden springs bubbled into the carbon-rich waters of an ancient lake, forming tufa spires of calcium-carbonate. This is the same process that created the spires in Mono Lake, 175 miles to the northwest, but here the lake has long since dried up, leaving the spires standing like a ruined city. The area is completely undeveloped, but camping is permitted. The pinnacles are 3 miles down a dirt road, south of Hwy 178.

Trona An industrial complex here processes chemicals extracted from the dry bed of Searles Lake, which contains quantities of just about every useful mineral known to science. A strong, sulfurous smell hangs in the air for miles around.

Ballarat A few ruins on the edge of a shining salt flat are all that remain of the mining camp of Ballarat, presumably named after a city in the Australian gold fields. It's probably the only place in America with an Australian Aboriginal name.

BARSTOW
• population 22,000 • elevation 2106 feet

At the junction of I-40 and I-15, Barstow is about halfway between Los Angeles and Las Vegas, and lots of travelers break their journey here. They're not looking for charm, nor will they find any. In fact, this area has been a crossroads for desert travelers for

CALIFORNIA DESERTS

Alternative Energy

California is a massive consumer of fossil fuels, but it has also established some full-scale projects to exploit alternative sources of energy. The desert regions offer not just an abundant source of strong sunshine, but also excellent sites for wind generators and areas where geothermal energy can be tapped.

One of the first large solar energy power plants is near Daggett, east of Barstow. A field of pivoting mirrors tracks the sun and reflects its light onto a cylindrical collector at the top of a 60-foot tower, where a boiler produces water to drive a steam-powered generator. Nearby is a newer type of plant, where curved mirrors focus the sun onto horizontal pipes in which water is heated to power the generators. The mirrors rotate on a horizontal axis to follow the sun from east to west. The concept is simple, but the scale can be impressive; at the site near Boron these mirrors cover hundreds of acres of the desert floor.

More spectacular are the wind generators, with blades the size of airplane wings, rotating on top of 80-foot towers that turn to face the prevailing wind. Thousands of these towers are lined up at locations like the San Gorgonio Pass near Palm Springs and the Tehachapi Pass west of Mojave, where geographical conditions reliably produce strong winds. As air in the desert heats and rises during the day, cooler air is drawn in from the coastal areas, accelerating as it goes through the narrow passes (the average wind speed in the San Gorgonio Pass is 15 to 20 mph). The older generators (many imported from Denmark) have a capacity of around 40 to 50kW. But with technology rapidly developing, the newer turbines are much larger and have a capacity of around 500kW. For more information, call the Desert Wind Energy Association at ☎ 760-329-1799.

The potential for geothermal energy also results from geographical circumstances. The Salton Trough, extending from the Gulf of California through the Imperial and Coachella valleys, was created by massive sections of the earth's crust moving apart. This movement creates fractures and stress points. These not only cause earthquakes but also allow molten magma to work its way close to the earth's surface, heating the groundwater. In some places, this creates natural hot springs, but the heat can also be tapped to provide steam to power generators. Geothermal power plants operate at a number of sites near the Salton Sea, which is the deepest part of the trough, and the thinnest part of the earth's crust.

centuries. The Spanish priest Francisco Garcés came through in 1776, and the Old Spanish Trail passed nearby. By the 1860s, settlers on the Mojave River were selling supplies, mostly liquor, to California immigrants. Mines were established in the surrounding hills, but Barstow really got going as a railroad junction after 1886. It still has a big rail freight business and serves a couple of military bases, as well as being the unofficial capital of the Mojave.

Information

The Barstow Rd exit, heading north from I-15, takes you right past the California Desert Information Center (☎ 760-252-6060), which has some pretty good exhibits on desert environments and history, plus lots of tourist information on Barstow and the Mojave. It's open 9 am to 5 pm daily (closed for lunch).

Mojave River Valley Museum

On Barstow Rd, two blocks north of I-15, this small museum (☎ 760-256-5452) concentrates on local history and has some artifacts from the Calico Early Man Archaeological Site (see the Around Barstow section later in this chapter). It's open 11 am to 4 pm daily; free.

Places to Stay

Budget motels on E Main St have rooms from $28/30 for a single/double and include *Stardust Inn (☎ 760-256-7116, 901 E Main*

St), **Desert Inn** (☎ 760-256-2146, 1100 E Main St) and **Executive Inn** (☎ 760-256-7581, 1261 E Main St).

For a slightly more expensive place, try the **Quality Inn** (☎ 760-256-6891, 1520 E Main St) for $49/58 or the **Best Western Desert Villa** (☎ 760-256-1781, 800-528-1234, 1984 E Main St), where rooms start at $70, including breakfast. The most comfortable accommodations are probably at the **Holiday Inn** (☎ 760-256-5673, 1511 E Main St), with $90 rooms, a pool, a spa and a restaurant.

Places to Eat

Apart from the standard, big-name places like **Carrows** and **International House of Pancakes**, both on E Main St, there are some local places of good value. The **Golden Dragon** (☎ 760-256-1890, 1231 E Main St) serves substantial Chinese or Thai dishes for $6 to $8 and has good dinner specials. For similarly priced Mexican food, go a mile or so from the main strip to **Rosita's** (☎ 760-256-1058, 540 W Main St). On the way you'll pass a few of Barstow's bars. The **McDonald's** (1611 E Main St) on E Main St is said to be the chain's busiest US outlet. It's in an old railway carriage, along with a couple of other food shops and the tackiest selection of souvenirs you'll see anywhere.

Shopping

Factory Merchants (☎ 760-253-7342), at the Lenwood Rd exit off of I-15, just south of town, is a factory outlet center with more than 50 stores selling fashions, footwear and household goods. It's open 9 am to 8 pm daily.

Getting There & Away

Buses and trains both arrive and depart from the historic railroad station, the Casa del Desierto, north of Main St. You'll really need a car to get around Barstow and the surrounding area.

Bus Greyhound (☎ 760-256-8757) has 10 buses a day to Los Angeles ($21, 2½ to four hours) and San Diego ($37, four hours). Two buses per day go east to Las Vegas ($28, 3½ hours) and on to Denver. The station is open

9 am to 2 pm and 3 pm to 6 pm. Amtrak has two motorcoaches per day headed for Mojave, Bakersfield and Oakland.

Train Amtrak has two trains stopping at Barstow: the *Desert Wind* going on to Las Vegas, and the *Southwest Chief* from LA to Chicago. Buy tickets on board.

Car Enterprise Rent-a-Car (☎ 760-256-0761), 620 W Main St, rents compact cars from about $30 per day, plus tax, with unlimited mileage.

AROUND BARSTOW
Rainbow Basin
National Natural Landmark

Amazingly colorful layers of sedimentary rock can be seen here, folded and distorted into interesting formations. There's a scenic drive and several short hiking trails. Many mammal fossils, from 12 to 16 million years old, have been found at the site. The nearby **Owl Canyon Campground** is OK at $6 a night but doesn't have water. To get to Rainbow Basin and the campground, take Fort Irwin Rd north of Barstow for 6 miles, then take Fossil Bed Rd west for 2 miles.

Calico Ghost Town

The mines around here produced millions of dollars worth of silver and borax, but as the ore played out and the price of silver fell, the town died and was virtually abandoned by 1907. There was little left but foundations in 1951 when Walter Knott (of Knott's Berry Farm fame) began to rebuild it. Calico Ghost Town (☎ 760-254-2122) is now a tourist attraction, only marginally more authentic than Frontierland and just as commercial. Entry is $6/3, and you pay extra to go gold panning, tour the Maggie Mine, ride a little steam railway, see the 'mystery shack,' or catch a show at the Calikage playhouse; these attractions are about $2.25 each. Calico Ghost Town is off I-15 about 10 miles north of Barstow and is open 9 am to 5 pm daily.

The Calico *campground* is a red earth parking lot adjacent to the ghost town, with sites for $22 with hookups, $18 without. The

CALIFORNIA DESERTS

KOA (☎ 760-254-2311), near the interstate, has the same prices and is better. The **Calico Motel** (☎ 760-254-2419), on the south side of I-15, looks like it hasn't changed since the 1950s, but it's kind of cute and costs only $24/33.

Calico Early Man Archaeological Site

Artifacts found at the 'Calico Dig' have been dated to 200,000 years, which doesn't fit with the theory that the first Americans came from Asia some 20,000 years ago. But are these stones really human tools? Some of them just look like rocks with chips in them, and no human bones have yet been found at the site. See for yourself on one of the site tours offered at 1:30 and 3 pm Wednesday and from 9:30 am to 4:30 pm Thursday to Sunday. The site is north of I-15, 15 miles east of Barstow.

EASTERN MOJAVE

I-15 and I-40 traverse the eastern Mojave, and most travelers never veer off them. But to pass up at least a brief exploration of the eastern Mojave would be a mistake. Smaller roads crisscross the desert between the interstates, giving access to a number of interesting and uncrowded desert features. Some of these roads are unpaved, but most can be traveled by cars. Those who really want to explore the area will find useful information in *Walking the East Mojave* by John McKinney and Cheri Rae.

Afton Canyon

A permanent watercourse flows through this canyon, making it a mecca for wildlife. The *campground* has primitive sites for $6. Afton Canyon Natural Area is 3 miles south of I-15, 38 miles east of Barstow.

Mojave National Preserve

As a national scenic area, this large preserve (more than 2000 sq miles) is jointly managed by the NPS and the BLM; the latter published a series of 22 *Desert Access Guides* with detailed information about many places of interest in the Mojave. For more information, call the Hole-in-the-Wall Visitor Center at ☎ 760-255-8800.

Kelso The old Kelso railroad depot is a handsome Spanish-style building. Two miles from town, the isolated Kelso Dunes, also called the Devils Playground, are delicately colored and beautifully shaped. They frequently produce a booming or singing noise as sand shifts down the 'slip-face' of the dunes.

Cima Dome Visible from Cima Rd, this perfectly formed, 1500-foot batholith is covered with a unique type of Joshua tree.

Hole-in-the-Wall Hiking trails lead through diverse plant communities and past interesting rock formations. There are pleasant *campgrounds* here (at 4200 feet), and nearby at Mid Hills (5600 feet). There's also a Hole-in-the-Wall Visitor Center (☎ 760-255-8800).

Providence Mountains SRA This is a state park (☎ 805-942-0662), accessed from Essex Rd. There are six primitive campsites ($10), but be well prepared – at 4300 feet it's hot in summer, cold in winter, wet in spring and fall, and can be windy at any time. There's a native botanical garden, and the 1¼-mile, self-guiding Mary Beale Nature Trail. Within the recreation area, the **Mitchell Caverns Natural Preserve** is a limestone cave that you can see only on a $6 guided tour on weekends at 1:30 pm.

Old Route 66

Nostalgia buffs like to explore this old highway, sometimes called 'The Mother Road.' Old 66 went from Chicago to LA – in California it crossed the Mojave from Needles to Barstow. The old route swings south of I-40 through Amboy, where there's an impressive volcanic crater, and Bagdad, where there used to be a cafe.

Death Valley

The name itself evokes all that is harsh, hot and hellish in the deserts of the imagination, a punishing, barren and lifeless place of Old Testament severity. Historically, though, the valley has not been as deadly as other parts of California, and naturalists are keen to point out that many plants and animals thrive here. Still, the average visitor expecting blazing sunlight, stark scenery and inhuman scale will not be disappointed.

DEATH VALLEY NATIONAL PARK

The actual valley is about 100 miles north to south and 5 to 15 miles wide, with the Panamint Range on its west side and the Amargosa Range on its east side. Death Valley National Park covers a much larger area – more than 5000 sq miles – which includes several other ranges and valleys to the north. Created as part of the 1994 California Desert Protection Act, the park's primary reason for being is protection, not tourism. You won't find the barrage of services, ranger programs and developed sights common to California's other national parks, and sometimes you'll have to make a concerted effort to pay the $10 entrance fee (especially from April to October).

History

Native Americans The Timbisha Shoshone lived in the Panamint Range for centuries, visiting the valley from winter to early summer every year to hunt and gather food, particularly mesquite beans. They also hunted waterfowl, caught pupfish in marshes and cultivated small areas of corn, squash and beans. Encroachments made by mining and tourism interests saw the Shoshone become more sedentary, with many taking on paid work, some making baskets for the tourist market. In 1933, the tribe was allocated a village site near Furnace Creek, which they still occupy.

Mining The fractured geology of Death Valley left many accessible minerals. The earliest miners here, in the 1860s, sought gold, silver, copper and lead. A dozen mines were started in the surrounding mountains, each closing as the ore played out. The most sustained mining operation was the Harmony Borax Works, which extracted borate, an alkaline mineral used to make detergents and other products. The stuff was

Death in the Valley

A small party of forty-niners wandered into the valley when they separated from a larger emigrant group crossing western Nevada. Taking what they hoped would be a shortcut to the California gold fields, they entered the valley from the east in December 1849. They crossed the valley floor, but could not get their wagons over the Panamint Range. While most of the party sheltered near a water hole, two young men, Lewis Manly and John Rogers, were sent to scout for a route west over the mountains. The captain of the group explored to the south, but after some days of walking he turned back, dying before he reached the water hole again.

The remainder of the party split up, with one group eventually making their way out over Towne Pass. The others, members of the Bennett and Arcan families, including women and children, waited for the two scouts. Manly and Rogers eventually returned, after 26 days and 600 miles in the wilderness, and guided the survivors out of the valley along the route now called Emigrant Canyon. As they left the valley, Ms Bennett reputedly looked back and uttered the words 'Good-bye, death valley.' It's not surprising the name stuck; more remarkable is the fact that 24 of the 25 emigrants actually survived the ordeal.

shipped out in wagons pulled by 20-mule teams and hauled 160 miles to a railhead at Mojave. By the late 1920s, most of the mining had ceased, though there was a brief resurgence during WWII when minerals like manganese, tungsten and lead were needed for wartime production.

Tourism Tents at Stovepipe Wells in the 1920s were the first tourist accommodations, followed by converted workers' quarters at Furnace Creek. In 1933, the area was designated a national monument, and for the next 11 years units of the Civilian Conservation

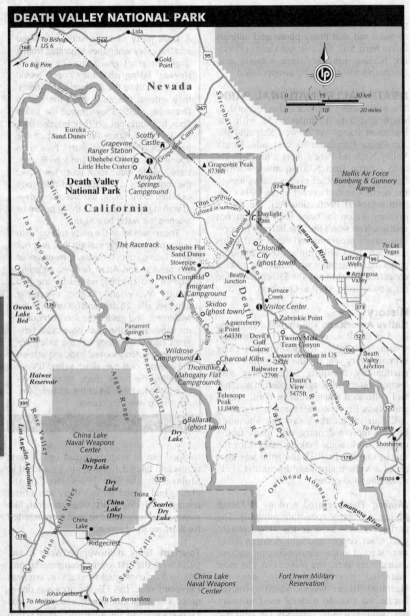

DEATH VALLEY NATIONAL PARK

To Bishop US 6
To Big Pine
Lida
266
168
Gold Point
95
Nevada
267
Sarcobatus Flat
Eureka Sand Dunes
Scotty's Castle
Grapevine Ranger Station
Ubehebe Crater
Little Hebe Crater
Grapevine Peak 8738ft
374
Beatty
Nellis Air Force Bombing & Gunnery Range
Saline Valley
Death Valley National Park
Mesquite Springs Campground
Titus Canyon (closed in summer)
Daylight Pass
Mud Canyon
California
Amargosa River
To Las Vegas
Inyo Mountains
The Racetrack
Mesquite Flat Sand Dunes
Stovepipe Wells
Chloride City (ghost town)
Lathrop Wells
95
Amargosa Valley
Owens Valley
136
Devil's Cornfield
Skidoo (ghost town)
Beatty Junction
Furnace Creek
Visitor Center
373
Panamint Springs
190
Emigrant Campground
Aguereberry Point 6433ft
Zabriskie Point
127
Owens Lake Bed
395
Twenty Mule Team Canyon
Death Valley Junction
Wildrose Campground
Devil's Golf Course
Dante's View 5475ft
190
Charcoal Kilns
Lowest elevation in US -282ft
Badwater -279ft
Haiwee Reservoir
Argus Range
Thorndike, Mahogany Flat Campgrounds
Greenwater Valley
To Pahrump
Telescope Peak 11,049ft
127
Rose Valley
Ballarat (ghost town)
Dry Lake
Shoshone
China Lake Naval Weapons Center
Airport Dry Lake
178
Los Angeles Aqueduct
Dry Lake
Panamint Valley
Owlshead Mountains
Tecopa
Amargosa River
Trona
Searles Dry Lake
China Lake (Dry)
China Lake
178
Ridgecrest
14
Indian Wells Valley
Searles Valley
China Lake Naval Weapons Center
Fort Irwin Military Reservation
Johannesburg
To Mojave
To San Bernardino
395

0   15   30 km
0   10   20 miles

Corps constructed roads, ranger stations, campgrounds and entrance gates. The area under protection was increased in 1994 when Death Valley was designated a national park, becoming the largest national park in the continental US.

Geology

The rock formations you see today were created by geological events that occurred as long as 500 million years ago. Extensive faulting and fracturing allows some of the oldest rocks to be visible on the earth's surface, when normally they would be hidden deep underground.

Limestone and sandstone from the earliest period, seen in the Panamint and Funeral mountains, were formed on an ancient seabed and slowly lifted by movement in the earth's crust. From 70 million to 250 million years ago, the rock strata were bent, folded and cracked as converging tectonic plates pushed up mountain ranges. These stresses weakened the earth's crust, leading to a period of volcanic activity, distributing ash and cinders that provided much of the rich coloring seen in the valley.

About 3 million years ago, the tectonic plates began to move apart, causing major faults. One of these faults formed on the eastern side of what is now Death Valley, and another formed on the west side of the Panamint Range. The valley floor and the mountain range together form a single geological structure, which is slowly rotating – the valley floor is subsiding while the range is being lifted. At the same time, erosion is carrying material down the mountains and depositing it in the valley. Much of this erosion occurred between 2000 and 10,000 years ago, when the climate was much wetter than at present, so the valley was filling with sediment even as its floor subsided. At Badwater, the lowest part of the valley, the sediment layer is some 9000 feet deep.

When to Visit

Winter is the peak season, when accommodations can be booked solid, campgrounds are filled before 11 am and people wait in line for hours to see Scotty's Castle. Autumn is less crowded, while spring is the best time for wildflowers. Death Valley used to be practically empty in summer, but it has become more popular in recent years, especially with European visitors who are keen to experience 120°F (48°C) temperatures. With an air-conditioned car, a summer trip is quite feasible, especially if you do your sightseeing in the early morning and late evening, spending the hottest part of the day by a pool or at the significantly cooler higher elevations.

Orientation

It's not hard to find your way around the valley by car. There are only a few main roads and they're all well marked. Furnace Creek, toward the southern end of the valley, has most of the facilities for visitors, including a well-stocked general store (open 7 am to 10 pm), a post office, gas station, campground, restaurants and accommodations. There's also a smaller store, accommodations and a campground at Stovepipe Wells. Supplies and gas are expensive in the valley. Food and water are available, and gas is cheaper in the north end of the valley at Scotty's Castle.

Information

The entrance fee of $10 per vehicle is valid for multiple entries over seven days and includes a good map of the park. Not all entrances have a fee collection station open at all times, but you are still expected to pay at one of the ranger stations. Make a point of doing so – the rangers have better things to do than chase fee dodgers and the NPS needs the funding.

The excellent Furnace Creek Visitor Center (☎ 760-786-2331) has a small museum on the natural and human history of the valley, a good selection of books, maps and information, and a moderately interesting slide show every half-hour. The center is open 8 am to 6 pm daily.

For 24-hour ranger assistance, call ☎ 760-786-2330. For other emergencies, dial ☎ 911.

Driving Tour

This tour goes from south to north and back. Even starting outside the valley, you could

CALIFORNIA DESERTS

do it all in a single day if you started very early, which is always a good thing to do in the desert. If you have more time, take one of the side trips listed later.

Start by driving up to **Dante's View** (5475 feet), which offers one of the best overall views of the valley at any time, but the view is absolutely brilliant if you can make it for sunrise or sunset. Heading down toward the central valley, take a short walk out to **Zabriskie Point**, which is a great place to see lava-capped formations and eroded badlands; you'll have plenty of company on the paved trail leading to the viewing platform. The hiking trail, which is 50 yards to the right of the paved trail and skirts the base of the formations, is usually empty. Then, get in your car and backtrack about 3 miles, to go through **Twenty Mule Team Canyon**, a windy one-way loop through an ancient lake bed – it will make you feel like an ant in a quarry.

Continue north to Furnace Creek, where you can have breakfast, take a break and sit in some shade. The **Borax Museum** on the Furnace Creek Ranch will tell you all about the stuff, and there's a big collection of old coaches and wagons out back. The National Park Visitor Center is just up the road, and you should see its exhibits on Death Valley. Farther north again is a not-so-interesting interpretive trail through the ruins of the Harmony Borax Works.

From Furnace Creek you can drive 50 miles straight through to the north end of the valley or stop for sightseeing on the way. If it's getting hot, go straight through and see the sights on the way back. When you get to the Grapevine ranger station you'll have to pay the entry fee if you haven't done so yet (keep your ticket). A few hundred yards after the gate, turn right to Scotty's Castle, which is nearly 3000 feet above sea level and noticeably cooler. The large palm-shaded lawn here is one of the most enjoyable places to be in the heat of midday. You can get food here, though it's better to bring a picnic.

Going west after the Grapevine ranger station brings you to **Ubehebe Crater**, a ½-mile-wide hole caused by the explosive meeting of superheated volcanic lava with cool groundwater. You can take a 1-mile

walk around its rim, and a ½-mile walk up to the younger and smaller **Little Hebe Crater**.

Head back down the valley, and by the time you get to the scenic loop of the **Mesquite Flat Sand Dunes** the temperature should be more bearable, and the sun will be lower in the sky, making the dunes more photogenic. This is another good place to spend some time out of the car. Near the road, an old pump marks the site of the original **Stovepipe Wells**, which were tapped by pounding old stovepipes into the sand at a dried-up water hole. Opposite the end of the loop, look for the field of arrow weed clumps called the **Devil's Cornfield**. Nearby is Stovepipe Wells Village, with a ranger station, a store and a pool you can use for $2.

Return to Hwy 190, drive back south through Furnace Creek and branch right at the next junction. Two miles south is **Golden Canyon**, which really glows in the late afternoon. Six miles farther is the turnoff for the **Artists Drive** scenic loop, which is also at its best around sunset – the spot called **Artists Palette** is particularly colorful. Across to the west, the valley floor is filled with lumps of crystallized salt in what is called the **Devil's Golf Course**; in the middle of this salt pan is the deepest part of the valley. The lowest point accessible by road is **Badwater** (282 feet below sea level), a little farther south. It's a pool of salty, mineralized water that is the only habitat of the soft-bodied Death Valley snail.

Scotty's Castle
This Spanish-Moorish pile was built in the 1920s for Chicago insurance magnate Albert Johnson. Walter E Scott, alias 'Death Valley Scotty,' had for years persuaded Johnson to bankroll his seldom-successful gold prospecting; eventually, after Johnson's doctor recommended he move to a warm, dry climate, Scotty convinced him to fund this elaborate vacation home. Scotty seems to have been something of a liar and a freeloader, and after supervising the construction of the house, and being a frequent long-term guest and caretaker, he began claiming it was his own.

When Johnson died in 1948, the house was willed to a charity, but Scotty was allowed to stay on until he died in 1954. The gardens were never finished, but part of the grand swimming pool can be seen outside. Inside are furnishings imported from Europe, handmade tiles, carved timber and elaborate wrought iron made especially for the house.

To get the full story on Scotty's Castle (☎ 760-786-2392), take one of the guided tours, which leave on the hour between 9 am and 5 pm. They cost $8, and there can be a long wait (or they can sell out completely); call ahead to find out.

Side Trips

There are many interesting side trips along the edges of the valley and in the surrounding ranges. Detailed information is available from the Furnace Creek Visitor Center (☎ 760-786-2331). It's wise to check with the center first for information, maps and an update on road conditions.

Emigrant Canyon Rd A scenic road climbs steeply up this canyon to Emigrant Pass (5318 feet). On the way, dirt roads turn off to Skidoo ghost town and Aguereberry Point, which has superb views over Death Valley. Continue up Emigrant Canyon Rd and turn left up Wildrose Canyon to reach the Charcoal Kilns, a line of large, stone, beehive-shaped structures used to make charcoal for smelting silver ore.

The landscape here is sub-alpine, with forests of piñon pine and juniper, and can be covered with snow in winter. You may need a 4WD to reach the end of the road at Mahogany Flat (8133 feet). A trail goes from there to Telescope Peak (see Hiking later in this section).

The Racetrack Large rocks appear to be moving across this mud flat, making long, faint tracks in the sun-baked surface. One theory is that winds push the rocks along when the valley is wet or icy. The Racetrack is 20 miles south of Ubehebe Crater, via a dirt road that sometimes requires 4WD.

Daylight Pass The Daylight Pass Rd (Hwy 374 to Beatty, Nevada) goes east of the

valley, past a rough road to the ghost town Chloride City. Off the Daylight Pass Cutoff, another rough road leads to the ruins of the Keane Wonder Mine.

Titus Canyon A 25-mile, one-way scenic road goes from the Daylight Pass Rd through this dramatic canyon to the floor of Death Valley. It's usually closed in summer, and may only be passable for 4WD vehicles.

Eureka Sand Dunes Rising up to 680 feet from a dry lake bed, these are perhaps the tallest dunes in the country. From the north end of the valley, near Ubehebe Crater, 44 miles of dirt road leads to the dunes. Unless there has been wet weather, the road can be traveled by a regular car.

Hiking

The Furnace Creek Visitor Center (☎ 760-786-2392) has good maps and hiking information, and will encourage you to fill out a backcountry registration form. Rangers regularly conduct guided hikes, except during summer.

In the valley, the most popular hikes are the ones that let you explore the numerous side canyons, such as Mosaic Canyon, Golden Canyon, Natural Bridge Canyon and Titus Canyon Narrows. At higher (and cooler) elevations, hiking trails skirt some of the old mining areas, such as the Keane Wonder Mine and Chloride City. The hike to Wildrose Peak (9064 feet) from the charcoal kilns is 8½ miles roundtrip, with a healthy climb of nearly 3000 feet.

The most demanding hiking trail climbs 7 miles and 3000 feet from Mahogany Flat to the summit of **Telescope Peak** (11,049 feet). From here it's possible to see both the highest and the lowest points in the continental US, Mt Whitney and Badwater. Allow six to nine hours for the roundtrip, and don't attempt it in winter unless you're equipped for snow and ice climbing. The last 2 miles to the trailhead might be too rough for a regular car, so you may have to start walking from the charcoal kilns – this will add about 4 miles, and 2000 feet, to the trip.

Bicycling

Bikes are only allowed on roads open to vehicle traffic – not on hiking trails. The visitor center has a list of suggested bike routes.

Horseback Riding

Furnace Creek Ranch (☎ 760-786-2345) arranges one- and two-hour trail and carriage rides, except during summer. Prices at this writing were $25 for one hour and $40 for two, but were expected to go up.

Places to Stay

Apart from the campgrounds, all accommodations in the valley are overpriced, with minimal standards of service. If you want a roof over your head, you get much better value in one of the towns around Death Valley. Beatty, Nevada, is the most convenient, while Johannesburg in California has an HI hostel (see Places to Stay in the Rand Mining District section earlier in this chapter).

Camping As well as saving money, camping is a great way to experience the Death Valley environment. The campgrounds are not particularly appealing (some are like gravel parking lots with a toilet block), but the attraction is just being out here for the sunset, the stars, the sunrise and the silence. In summer, camping at the lower levels is not really feasible – it's just too hot. Only three campgrounds are open year round: Furnace Creek, Mesquite Spring and Wildrose. Call ☎ 800-365-2267 to book a site at any one of these campgrounds (booking is possible only from October to April, not during the hot summer months).

Furnace Creek Campground, with its entrance just north of the visitor center, has 136 sites for $16 ($10 from October to April) and is close to the facilities at Furnace Creek. It fills up early during busy times and has very little shade. Nearby, *Texas Springs* has a little more shade and costs $10, but it's open only from October to April. The large *Sunset Campground*, also closed May to September, is mainly for RVs ($10). *Furnace Creek Ranch* operates a trailer park that costs $20.

The *Stovepipe Wells Campground*, open October to April, has very little shade and lots of RVs ($10). There's also a 14-site RV park next to the general store, run by *Stovepipe Wells Village*.

The small *Emigrant Campground*, 9 miles south of Stovepipe Wells, is free and open from April to October. At 2100 feet, it should be a little cooler, though it doesn't have any shade at all. Toward the north end of the valley, *Mesquite Springs*, at 1800 feet, is one of the more attractive campgrounds, open all year for $10.

In the Panamint Mountains, approaching Telegraph Peak, are three free campgrounds that have mild weather in summer. *Wildrose* (4100 feet) is open all year (unless it's snowed in), and water should be available in summer. *Thorndike* (7500 feet) and *Mahogany Flat* (8200 feet) are small sites, open March to November. You may need a 4WD to reach them.

By going into the backcountry, you can camp for nothing in most parts of the national park, so long as you're at least 1 mile from the nearest road and ¼ mile from any water source. The old mining areas are for day-use only; they don't want people in them after dark. It's a good idea to check with the visitor center first and to fill out a backcountry registration form.

Hotels Run by Amfac, the *Furnace Creek Ranch* (☎ 760-786-2345), a quarter mile south of the Furnace Creek Visitor Center, has pretty ordinary cabins at $94 for one or two people and motel rooms starting at $119. Extra adults cost $15. Facilities include a large swimming pool, tennis courts and a golf course (greens fees are $50 in winter, $25 in summer). Up the hill from the ranch is the top-end *Furnace Creek Inn* (☎ 760-786-2345), also run by Amfac, which has elegant, Spanish-style stone buildings dating from 1927; an attractive, chemical-free, springwater-fed, solar swimming pool; tennis courts; and palm-shaded grounds. It's open year round with prices starting at $230 (dropping $100 in mid-May).

Stovepipe Wells – a pretty unattractive place except for a few trees and pool – has accommodations at **Stovepipe Wells Village** (☎ 760-786-2387). Standard rooms cost $58 and 'deluxe' rooms are $80. They also have 'patio rooms' for $38, but they won't tell you about these unless you ask, but even then they are reluctant to rent them. Rooms are small, a bit worn and the air-conditioning is noisy, but they're definitely the cheapest rooms in the valley.

Places to Eat

You can find grocery items at Stovepipe Wells and, better yet, Furnace Creek. Restaurants at the Furnace Creek Ranch include the **Forty Niner Cafe**, which has breakfast and lunch for $6 to $8, dinner for around $10; and the **Wrangler Steak House**, which has a buffet at breakfast ($6) and lunch ($9), and steak and/or seafood dishes ($13 to $21) for dinner. The **Furnace Creek Inn** has two pricey restaurants, one of which boasts a dress code. The **Corkscrew Saloon** is the only night life, and it's not a bad place for a drink.

The dining room at **Stovepipe Wells Village** (☎ 760-786-2387) serves breakfast, lunch and dinner for under $10 and has a full bar that is OK for the whole family.

Getting There & Away

Bus There is no regular scheduled service to Death Valley, though some charter buses and tours operate from Las Vegas.

Car & Motorcycle Good roads come into Death Valley from every direction, and all of them offer some spectacular views. Given the cost of rooms inside the national park, you may want to plan your route so you can spend a night nearby (see Around Death Valley). Gas is expensive in the park too, so fill up before you enter.

AROUND DEATH VALLEY
Beatty, Nevada
• population 1623 • elevation 3308 feet
This little Nevada town is the best bet for cheap accommodations near Death Valley, only 40 miles from Furnace Creek. **El Portal Motel** (☎/fax 775-553-2912, 301 Main St) is a well-run little place on the road to the

national park and a good value at $30 to $60. **Stagecoach Hotel & Casino** (☎ 775-553-2419, 800-424-4946, fax 775-553-2548), on Main St north of town, looks like a tawdry gambling joint, but the rooms are quite good for $35 to $45. Other options include the **Phoenix Inn** (☎ 775-553-2250, 800-845-7401, fax 775-553-2260), with rooms from $35 to $46, and the slightly upscale **Exchange Club Motel & Casino** (☎ 775-553-2333, fax 553-9348), from $38 to $68.

Amargosa Valley

Straddling the California-Nevada border on Hwy 373, the **Longstreet Inn & Casino** (☎ 775-372-1777, 800-508-9493, fax 775-372-1280) is a very lively place and a good choice for people who want to spend some idle time outside the park. There's a laundry, store, two OK restaurants, gambling, a pool (with a mini-waterfall), a whirlpool and a nine-hole golf course. Rooms start at $60 and RV sites are $16.

Death Valley Junction
• population 8 • elevation 2040 feet
The junction of Hwys 127 and 190, 12 miles east of the park boundary, is famous for the **Amargosa Hotel & Opera House** (☎ 760-852-4441), a creation of the multitalented

The roadrunner, a swift desert denizen

Marta Becket. Marta does a season of solo dance and mime performances in which she presents a varied and entertaining cast of characters. Performances run October to May, and tickets are $10/8. Call first to book and confirm show times (there are no shows June through September).

The theater space has been fancifully decorated with an audience of renaissance figures painted by Marta herself. The 12 hotel rooms are $45 with one bed and shower or $55 with two beds and bath (less in summer).

Shoshone
• population 70 • elevation 1569 feet
The small town of Shoshone gives good access to Death Valley by a choice of two scenic routes. It's 57 miles via the shorter, northern route from Furnace Creek. The **Shoshone Inn** (☎ 760-852-4335) is the only place to stay and not bad at $36/54. Price includes access to an old but clean and very relaxing natural hot springs pool.

You'll have a few more choices at Baker, but it's 58 miles farther south from Death Valley. Do stop in Baker to see the world's largest thermometer and have a bite to eat ($4 to $7) at the very good **Greek Restaurant** at the Hwy 127/I-15 junction.

Pahrump, Nevada
• population 7424 • elevation 2690 feet
This Nevada town, 60 miles from Furnace Creek, has two motels on Hwy 160, including a **Days Inn** (☎ 775-727-5100, 2021 E Loop Rd) charging $47 to $80. For more on Pahrump, see the Las Vegas & Canyon Country chapter.

Lake Havasu & Colorado River

Straddling the California-Arizona border, 46-mile-long Lake Havasu was created in 1938 with the completion of Parker Dam.

The area encompasses pockets of breathtaking beauty, but during spring break (around mid-April) – when college students come in force to delight in warm weather, water sports and each other – it can be a sloppy, bacchanalian scene.

HAVASU NATIONAL WILDLIFE REFUGE
This is one of a string of protected areas along the lower Colorado River. Habitats include marshes, dunes, desert and the river itself. Wintering geese, ducks and cranes are found in profusion and, after their departure, herons and egrets nest here in large numbers. Bald eagles and ospreys are often sighted in winter, bighorn sheep are sometimes seen and the elusive bobcat is also present. You can also see common desert mammals such as coyotes, rabbits and pack rats.

Orientation & Information
The section of the refuge north of I-40 is the Topock Marsh. South of I-40, the Colorado flows through Topock Gorge. The southern boundary of the reserve abuts the northern boundary of Lake Havasu State Park, about 3 miles north of the famous (and still-standing) London Bridge.

The Havasu National Wildlife Refuge headquarters (☎ 760-326-3853), 317 Mesquite Ave, Needles, is open 8 am to 4 pm weekdays for maps, bird lists and other information.

Boating
The Jerkwater Canoe & Kayak Company (☎ 520-768-7753, 800-421-7803) in Topock offers canoe rentals and guided day trips ($35 per person) through Topock Gorge, as well as overnight excursions along the river, where you may see bighorn sheep. Trips start at Park Moabi Campground (☎ 760-326-3831) in Needles just north of where I-40 crosses the Colorado River, where there's a lagoon for people to practice their canoeing skills. Nearby, the Topack Gorge Marina (☎ 520-768-2325) has a bar and restaurant popular with the boating crowd – a good place to find information if you have your own boat. Allow about seven hours for the float through the gorge.

Jet boat tours from Lake Havasu City are operated by Bluewater Charters (see Boating under Lake Havasu City).

Places to Stay

Camping Camping is not allowed in Topock Gorge. Camping is permitted on the Arizona side of the river, south of the gorge, everywhere except Mesquite Bay. Tent and RV camping ($8, no hookups) is available at *Five Mile Landing* (☎ 520-768-2350), on the Arizona side of Topock Marsh, about 6 miles north of I-40 on Hwy 95.

LAKE HAVASU CITY, ARIZONA

• population 42,000 • elevation 456 feet
Parker Dam, finished in 1938, created 46-mile-long Lake Havasu. Until 1963, there was no town along the lake. Developer Robert McCullouch planned Lake Havasu City as a center for water sports and light industry/business. Both he and the area received a huge amount of publicity when McCullouch bought London Bridge for $2,460,000, disassembled it into 10,276 granite slabs and reassembled it at Lake Havasu City. The bridge, originally opened in London, England, in 1831, was rededicated in 1971 and has become the focus of the city's English Village – a complex of English-style restaurants, hotels and shops.

The move was a huge success and today Lake Havasu City is host to millions of visitors coming not just to see the strange sight of London Bridge in the desert, but to enjoy water sports, boat tours, shopping, golf and tennis.

Orientation & Information

Highway 95, the main drag through town, runs north-south. McCullouch Blvd is the main east-west street and goes over London Bridge. Note that you can't turn from Hwy 95 onto McCullouch Blvd – you have to turn a block before or after and reach McCullouch via Lake Havasu Ave.

The chamber of commerce (☎ 520-855-4115, 800-242-8278), 314 London Bridge Rd, is open 8 am to 5 pm weekdays. A visitor center at the English Village (☎ 520-855-5655) is open 9 am to 5 pm daily. The post office (☎ 520-855-2361) is at 1750 McCullouch Blvd. The Havasu Samaritan Regional Hospital (☎ 520-855-8185) is at 101 Civic Center Lane.

Boating

Many companies offer **boat tours** of the lake region, most departing from under London Bridge. Narrated day and sunset tours cost about $15 on the *Dixie Belle* (☎ 520-453-6776). Bluewater Charters (☎ 520-855-7171) has jet boat tours that cover 60 miles in three hours. Fares are $35/17.50 adults/children, free for kids under six. A cheap, quick cruise can be taken on the *Dream Catcher* ferry operated by the Chemehuevi Indians. Cruises leave from English Village several times daily, heading for the Havasu Landing Resort operated by the tribe on their California reservation. Fares are $3/1.50.

Boats for fishing, waterskiing or sightseeing can be rented from Resort Boat Rentals (☎ 520-453-9613) in the English Village; or the Havasu Landing Resort (☎ 800-307-3610). Boat rentals vary from about $40 per day for a four-person fishing boat to as much as $300 per day for a ski boat. Jet Skis, wave runners and parasailing are available from the Water Sports Center at the Nautical Inn (☎ 520-855-2141 ext 429).

Other Activities

Outback Off-Road Adventures (☎ 520-680-6151), 2169 Swanson Ave, offers 4WD desert tours for $65/half-day; the $130 full-day trip, which includes lunch, is only available at certain times. Groups of four or more, seniors and children get discounts.

Places to Stay

The winter season sees the lowest hotel prices; costs rise in summer, which in Lake Havasu City stretches from March to November. Reservations are a good idea for summer weekends and holidays.

Places to Stay – Budget

Camping Lake Havasu State Park has two campgrounds, both operate on a first-come, first-served basis. The *Windsor Beach Campground* (☎ 520-855-2784), 2 miles north of McCullouch Blvd on London Bridge Rd, and *Cattail Cove* (☎ 520-855-1223), 15 miles south on Hwy 95, both offer showers, boat launch and tent camping for $10 per day. Cattail Cove also has 40 RV sites with hookups for $15. There are other camping areas near Parker Dam and also on the California side of the lake.

Motels The cheapest places, with doubles around $45 midweek in winter but rising to over $59 during summer/holiday weekends, cluster along Acoma and London Bridge Rds. These include the *E-Z 8 Motel* (☎ 520-855-4023, 41 Acoma Blvd) and the *Windsor Inn* (☎ 520-855-4135, 451 London Bridge Rd), with a pool and spa. Both have kitchenettes.

Places to Stay – Mid-Range

The *Havasu Travelodge* (☎ 520-680-9202, 480 London Bridge Rd) has a spa and exercise room and charges about $50/60 for singles/doubles midweek or $60/70 weekends, including continental breakfast. For about $10 more, the *Ramada Inn* (☎ 520-855-1111, 271 S Lake Havasu Ave) has a pool, spa, laundry room, as well as a restaurant and bar.

Places to Stay – Top End

The *Holiday Inn* (☎ 520-855-4071, 245 London Bridge Rd) has rooms starting at around $60 ($10 more for lake views), but the rooms are better than most for this price. Many rooms come with a refrigerator and a balcony. The hotel offers a pool and spa, bar and restaurant, and entertainment (music with dancing) most nights. There is also a coin laundry. The *Nautical Inn* (☎ 520-855-2141, 800-892-2141, 1000 McCullouch Blvd) was the first of Lake Havasu's resort hotels; fishing, boating, waterskiing, Jet Skiing and parasailing are available. The inn also has a pool, spa and golf and tennis facilities. Rooms cost $90 to $159 on summer weekends, but can drop to as low as $75 to $119 midweek.

Places to Eat

You'll find a variety of restaurants around the half-mile of McCullouch Blvd between Smoketree Ave and Acoma Blvd.

Shugrues (☎ 520-453-1400, 1425 McCullouch Blvd) is considered by many to be the best restaurant in town, with fine seafood and steak dinners. Dinner prices are $13 to $25 and reservations are advised. Other good restaurants are found in the better hotels: the *Captain's Table* (☎ 520-855-2141, 1000 McCullouch Blvd), at the Nautical Inn, the *King's Retreat* (☎ 520-855-0888, 1477 Queens Bay), at the London Bridge Resort, and the *Bridge-Room* (☎ 520-855-4071, 245 London Bridge Rd), at the Holiday Inn, all serve breakfast, lunch and dinner for $6 to $11. For Mexican food, *Casa de Miguel* (☎ 520-453-1550, 1550 S Palo Verde Blvd) is a popular spot, especially with the party-minded crowd. Most items are under $10.

Entertainment

Several of the hotels and restaurants mentioned above have lively nightlife. *Kokomo's* at the London Bridge Resort is probably the most happenin' bar in town and a good spot for tropical sunset drinks. *Hussongs*, adjoining Casa de Miguel, is one of the most popular dance spots for the college-age crowd. Slightly more sedate dancing is found in the *Reflections Lounge* (☎ 520-855-4071, 245 London Bridge Rd), at the Holiday Inn, and the *Captain's Cove* (☎ 520-855-2141, 1000 McCullouch Blvd), at the Nautical Inn.

Getting There & Away

The KT Services bus (☎ 520-764-4010) departs daily for Phoenix ($33, five hours) and Las Vegas ($35, 3½ hours) from inside the Texaco station at 3201 Hwy 95. The Havasu-Vegas Express (☎ 800-459-4884) embarks on the three-hour journey ($49) to Las Vegas between 6 and 7 am and leaves Las Vegas for Havasu City around 2 pm. They'll pick up and drop off at most motels and the Las Vegas airport.

Nevada

JAMES LYON

Facts about Nevada

HISTORY

Archaeological evidence of human habitation in Nevada goes back many thousands of years. Remains found at Nevada sites include stone tools, arrow and spear points and bones as old as any in the Americas. The Lost City Museum, at Overton, displays adobe and pit dwellings and artifacts from several cultures dating back 10,000 years. The ancient Lake Lahontan, which covered much of western Nevada until about 5000 years ago, was home to communities who fished and hunted on its shores. Among the more interesting artifacts found in the region are fishhooks, baskets and duck decoys made from tule reeds (the Nevada State Museum in Carson City has good exhibits on these ancient societies). After the lake dried up, the region was inhabited by northern Paiute people, who were adapted to life in the desert and lived by hunting small animals and gathering food from the wild.

Other ancient cultures waxed and waned in what is now the southeastern part of Nevada. From around 4000 years ago, small nomadic groups lived by hunting bighorn sheep, using spears and the *atlatl*, a notched stick used to throw a spear with greater power than a hunter could by hand. This is clearly depicted in petroglyphs in the Valley of Fire State Park. At some point, the bow and arrow replaced the atlatl as the weapon of choice for nomadic hunters. Around 2500 years ago, a new group of people arrived, the Anasazi, who also inhabited areas to the east and south. Living in extended families, they cultivated corn, squash and beans, hunted small game, and lived in pit dwellings. Later they learned to make earthenware pots and constructed groups of adobe buildings similar to the pueblos built by their cousins in Utah, Arizona and New Mexico.

Around 900 years ago, the Anasazi left southern Nevada for reasons still not clear; one theory is that a prolonged drought forced them to migrate to more fertile lands. Southern Paiute hunter-gatherers, with whom the Anasazi had long coexisted, now had the area to themselves for a few centuries.

When the first Europeans arrived, four main Indian groups existed in Nevada. Northern Paiute tribes occupied much of the northwest, while the Lake Tahoe area and the eastern foothills of the Sierra Nevada were Washo country. Southern Paiute inhabited most of the Mojave region, from around Las Vegas on into southern Utah, and Shoshone tribes lived in eastern Nevada and western Utah. Most of these Native Americans lived in bands of a few dozen people and made seasonal migrations between mountains and valley areas. Each band required a substantial area of land, and consequently the total Native American population was quite low, probably under 100,000.

European Exploration

By the early 1800s Europeans had been through most of the West: Spanish outposts were established in California and New Mexico, and Spanish explorers had ventured into Utah (see Facts about California for details). Lewis and Clark had crossed the continent to the north of Nevada, but the area of modern Nevada had scarcely been touched by European explorers. As Mexico struggled for independence from Spain, it agreed with the US that the 42nd parallel (now Nevada's northern border) would be the northern limit of Mexican territory. After independence, the Mexican government was not as strict about trespassing as the Spanish had been, and during the 1820s American and British trappers started to venture even farther south, into the Humboldt River valley.

Jedediah Smith, an American trader from St Louis, traversed southern Nevada in 1826, causing consternation among the Mexicans when he turned up in San Diego. In 1827, returning east, Smith became the first white American to cross the Sierra Nevada and

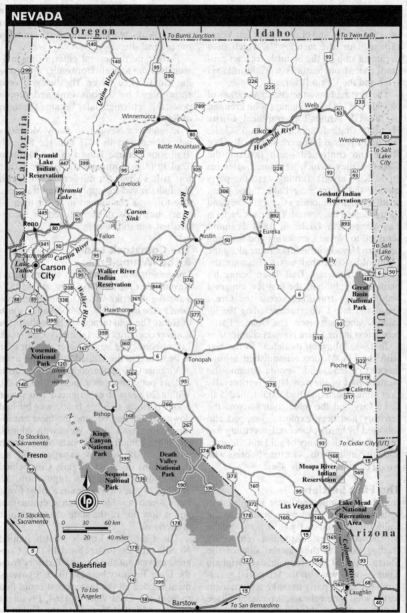

NEVADA

Oregon · To Burns Junction · Idaho · To Twin Falls

California

Pyramid Lake Indian Reservation

Pyramid Lake

Reno

Carson City

Lake Tahoe

To Sacramento

Walker River Indian Reservation

Winnemucca

Battle Mountain

Lovelock

Carson Sink

Fallon

Austin

Quinn River

Reese River

Humboldt River

Wells

Elko

Wendover

To Salt Lake City

Goshute Indian Reservation

Eureka

Ely

Great Basin National Park

To Salt Lake City

Hawthorne

Yosemite National Park
(closed in winter)

To Stockton, Sacramento

Fresno

To Stockton, Sacramento

Kings Canyon National Park

Sequoia National Park

Tonopah

Pioche

Caliente

Bishop

Death Valley National Park

Beatty

To Cedar City (UT)

Moapa River Indian Reservation

Las Vegas

Lake Mead National Recreation Area

Arizona

Bakersfield

Colorado River

Laughlin

To Los Angeles

To San Bernardino

0   30   60 km
0   20   40 miles

FACTS ABOUT NEVADA

the Great Basin (see Geography). At about the same time, a Spanish expedition discovered the springs and grasslands of Las Vegas (Spanish for 'the meadows'), which then became a stop on the Spanish Trail, an emigrant route from Santa Fe to California via Utah and the Virgin River.

The first really systematic exploration of Nevada was led by Lieutenant John Frémont of the US Army Topographical Corps. Heading south from Oregon in 1843, he admired Pyramid Lake, crossed the Truckee River and continued south through the Carson Valley (which he named after his guide, Kit Carson). Turning west, the party crossed the Sierra near Lake Tahoe, went south through California's Central Valley, and then followed the Spanish Trail back east, via Las Vegas and Utah. In 1844 Frémont returned to Nevada, exploring and mapping northern Nevada, including a route along the Humboldt River that was to become the Humboldt Emigrant Trail. Even before his maps were published, the first few emigrant wagons were trundling across the Great Basin and into California, including the ill-fated Donner party (see 'The Donner Party' boxed text in the Sierra Nevada chapter).

In 1848, following its defeat in the war with the US, Mexico relinquished a huge amount of land, and Nevada became the western part of the new Utah Territory. By that time Mormons had established Salt Lake City and the main routes across the territory had been explored, mapped and followed by hardy pioneers. Everything was ready for the discovery of gold in California and the coming rush of fortune hunters who would become known as '49ers.

The First Settlers

Initially, few emigrants were interested in settling Nevada. Most were heading to the California gold fields. By 1850, however, the Mormons had established a temporary trading post on the eastern side of the Sierra. In 1851, Mormon leader Brigham Young – who was also the territorial governor – ordered a party to make a permanent fort in what is now the small, pleasant village of Genoa, Nevada. Mormons do not engage in mining, but they had no problem selling food, equipment, timber or other supplies to miners. A re-creation of the fort stands on the original site.

Farther north, several enterprising individuals set up to profit from emigrants crossing the Truckee River. The bridges were soon joined by saloons, inns and supply posts; this settlement later became the town of Reno.

In southern Nevada, so many Mormons were going west in 1847 that the Spanish Trail soon became known as the Mormon Trail. In 1855, Mormons established another fort at Las Vegas, for missionary work with the Indians and to supply passing travelers. The fort was abandoned in fewer than 10 years, but parts of it, restored or reconstructed, can still be seen.

The Comstock Lode & the Mining Era

Immigrants and prospectors swarmed into Nevada over the eastern Sierra, and in 1859 a small gold strike was made in the mountains to the east of the Washoe Valley, south of Reno. The gold turned out to be the tip of a silver iceberg; the fabulous Comstock Lode became the largest silver deposit ever to be mined in the United States. The town of Virginia City appeared almost overnight, and its population soon peaked at 30,000. Within 20 years it experienced two major boom periods, two big busts, was burned down, rebuilt, and became the most notorious mining town in the West, with saloons, gunfights, gambling and vice. Mark Twain wrote for the local newspaper, and his descriptions of life in Virginia City helped immortalize the town's reputation. In another 20 years it was almost a ghost town, but it found new life as a tourist destination and is now one of the state's most popular attractions.

The Comstock Lode's wealth helped Nevada progress to statehood. In 1861, Congress carved out the Nevada Territory from the Utah Territory because the US government needed all the resources it could find to fight the Civil War. In 1864, President Lincoln admitted Nevada to the Union as the 36th state, thus gaining the one extra vote needed to ratify the 13th Amendment, abolishing slavery. The state nickname, 'The Battle Born State,' thus refers to the financing and politics of the Civil War, not to any battles fought on Nevada soil.

The frenetic mining of the Comstock stimulated activity elsewhere, from agriculture in the Washoe Valley and lumbering in the Sierra to stock speculation and scandal in San Francisco, where greedy investors and bankers – among them William Ralston and James Crocker, founders of the Bank of California; George Hearst, father of William Randolph; Adolph Sutro and Leland Stanford – sold and traded stocks and bonds many times over the actual value of the mined gold and silver. While their quick-money mentality made these entrepreneurs balk at financing a transcontinental railroad, from which they would reap no immediate profit, the prospects for a rail link across the Sierra to Comstock country offered sufficient incentive for them to finance the most difficult part of the whole project.

By 1880, the Comstock Lode had played out, along with other, smaller finds throughout the state. Nevada's population plunged from 62,000 in 1880 to 47,000 in 1890. It took 20 years for the population to get back to boom-time levels. The cattle industry had grown with the arrival of railroads in northern Nevada, but suffered during severe winters in the 1880s. In the early 20th century, new mineral discoveries revived the state's fortunes, with silver at Tonopah, copper near Ely and gold at Goldfield.

Native Americans

The Indian populations were in trouble even before mining and railways made a major impact. The first few emigrants brought enough cattle to damage the grasses that the Indians and the game they hunted depended on, and the settlers' guns took a disproportionate share of the wildlife. If the Indians resisted, they were subject to brutal attacks and reprisals; there were several battles in the 1860s. The mining industry devastated the rest of the natural resources on which the Indians depended, especially the piñon

pine, which was clear-cut along with most of the other trees around the mining areas and used for fuel, construction and shoring up the mines. By 1890, most of the Indians lived on poorly run reservations that provided little chance of economic survival, forcing them into dependency on government assistance programs.

Economic Diversification

The second mining period saw some diversification. Railroads built branch lines, which stimulated a revival of the cattle industry, and WWI saw a strong demand for beef. Irrigation projects turned the Carson and Washoe valleys into productive agricultural areas, while motor vehicles and new roads made more of the state accessible for tourism, commerce and new settlement. The Great Depression hit hard in Nevada, bringing a collapse in mineral and crop prices and the failure of most of the state's banks. In 1931 the state government officially legalized gambling and created agencies to tax it, turning an illegal underground industry into a major tourist attraction and revenue source. At the same time, Nevada reduced the period of residency required to get a divorce, creating one of the most bizarre industries ever (see 'The Business of Divorce' boxed text in the Western Nevada chapter).

Construction of Hoover Dam was a depression-era project, started in 1931 and finished in 1935, two years ahead of schedule. It provided much-needed work and income for southern Nevada and created the water and electricity supply that enabled Las Vegas to grow into a major city. WWII brought a number of military bases to Nevada. New industries, like the extraction and processing of magnesium to meet the needs of the aircraft industry, made Henderson (near Las Vegas) the first industrial area in southern Nevada.

Reno was the first city to make an industry out of gambling, but Las Vegas caught up and surpassed it in the 1940s and '50s, with gangsters like Benjamin 'Bugsy' Siegel providing and generating plenty of investment funds and big-name entertainers to draw people to the casinos. The rest of the country, including the FBI, was less than impressed with Nevada's criminal connections and sleaze industries, but the state continued with its unconventional sources of revenue and actually managed to impose some measure of control over the gaming industry. Billionaire Howard Hughes brought legitimate money to invest in Las Vegas, displacing some of the underworld casino owners and bringing a semblance of respectability to the industry. Not too much respectability though, as Hughes himself was decidedly weird. A little wickedness remains part of the Las Vegas attraction.

One attraction that has lost its appeal is nuclear testing. In the 1950s Nevada welcomed the nuclear test facility northwest of Las Vegas. Locals even held all-night parties that climaxed with a rooftop view of the big blast at dawn, and travel agents sold special packages for tourists to witness the explosions. The testing went underground in the 1960s and has now stopped, but the US Department of Energy has proposed making the Nevada Test Site a long-term nuclear waste dump. (See Ecology & Environment, later this chapter, and Yucca Mountain, in the Great Basin chapter.)

The federal government's grip on Nevada's public lands (it owns 87%, most of it under the jurisdiction of the Bureau of Land Management) was fiercely contested during the so-called Sagebrush Rebellion of the late 1970s and early '80s. Several

Western states, Nevada among them, banded together to try to force the federal government to relinquish control of all public lands within their borders. The movement's advocates decried federal ownership of those lands as unconstitutional, arguing that sovereign states by definition ought to be in control of their own destiny, and they could not be if they had no control over their own land. The rebellion was ultimately unsuccessful; in 1998, a group called the Nevada Freedom Coalition tried to rekindle the protest, but its efforts also failed.

It may feel hamstrung by the feds on land issues, but Nevada still manages to live up to its reputation as a freewheeling state. Besides gambling, there's prostitution, which is neither legal nor banned by the state government; instead, it's left up to the county administrations. Illegal in the two largest counties (Clark County, which includes Las Vegas, and Washoe County, which includes Reno), prostitution is tolerated in many of the small counties, which see no reason to stifle an activity that has gone unfettered since the mining days and that brings in much needed local taxes.

Another sign that things are tolerated in Nevada that wouldn't be elsewhere is the 1999 election of Oscar Goodman, a former lawyer for the Mafia, as mayor of Las Vegas. In 30 years of legal practice, Goodman represented such legendary mob figures as financier Meyer Lansky and Anthony 'the Ant' Spilotro, who was accused of more than 20 murders. Recent nonmob clients have included Mike Tyson and LaToya Jackson. Goodman, who had never run for office before, sailed to victory with such promises as making casino developers help pay for cleaning up neglected neighborhoods.

A possibly more respectable aspect of Nevada society is reflected in its role as a corporate and financial center: low state taxes and light government regulation make the state attractive to business. Already Nevada has done well with its Freeport Law, which makes warehousing free of taxes; storage, distribution and light manufacturing operations have boomed in Sparks ever since this law was imposed. And because gambling taxes provide so much of the state's revenue, Nevada has no income tax or tax on corporate profits. Red tape is kept to a minimum, and the requirements that a corporation's primary business be conducted in the state – or that its officials even be residents of Nevada – have been abolished.

Despite rapid growth, the state is still sparsely populated, and its potential for more outdoor adventure activities and eco-tourism is enormous and largely untapped. In fact, most of the state's development has been at the cost of the environment. Recent developments have focused on adding and expanding hotels and casinos, especially in Las Vegas and in newer gambling boom-towns such as Mesquite and Wendover. Furthermore, the current golfing craze has led to the opening of several nine- and 18-hole golf courses, an environmental travesty in this parched desert state.

GEOGRAPHY & GEOLOGY

Roughly three quarters of Nevada is in the Great Basin, a high desert region of rugged ranges and broad valleys that extends into Utah, California and Oregon. It's called a 'basin' because its rivers drain to inland lakes and sinks and do not flow to the sea. It's more descriptively known as the Basin and Range country – dozens of jagged, north-south mountain ranges cross the state, dividing up the bottom of the so-called basin.

Many of these mountain ranges, known as 'fault-block ranges,' were created when sections of the earth's crust were lifted above the surrounding land by the collision of the Pacific and North American tectonic plates. Small earthquakes are still common in western Nevada, an indication that mountain building is still occurring. Nevada's southern corner, around Las Vegas and the Colorado River, is part of the Mojave Desert, another high desert, which extends from California. The western corner of the state, around Lake Tahoe, is geographically on the fringe of the Sierra Nevada. Volcanic activity created many of the ranges in western Nevada – like the Virginia Range. A small area in northern Nevada is on the edge of the Columbia Plateau, an area covering about 100,000 sq miles, primarily in Washington, Oregon and Idaho.

CLIMATE

Nevada is generally quite dry; most moisture from the Pacific's prevailing winds is lost as precipitation over California's mountains. Nevada's high elevations and inland location make for wide variations in temperature over the course of the day and the year.

The Great Basin areas get about 8 inches of precipitation per year, much of it falling as winter snow (*nevada* means 'snowfall' or 'snow-covered' in Spanish). Summer days are hot, averaging around 90°F (32°C), while winter days range from cool to cold – around 35°F (2°C) in the valleys, and colder in the mountains. Nights are very cold, even dropping below freezing for seven months of the year.

The Mojave region is even drier than the Great Basin, with fewer than 4 inches of precipitation per year. Temperatures are hot in summer and mild in winter – Las Vegas averages around 100°F (37°C) from June to September, around 55°F (13°C) in December and January. Winter nights are cool, but not often below freezing. Occasional heavy thunderstorms, most common in summer, can deluge an area within an hour and create dangerous flash floods.

Avoid traveling in the Great Basin in midwinter and the southern desert areas in midsummer; any time outside those extreme periods is fine for visiting Nevada, especially for those spending most of their time in climate-controlled casinos.

ECOLOGY & ENVIRONMENT

With an absence of polluting industries and a low population density, Nevada has fewer obvious environmental problems than neighboring California. Though recent growth has been very rapid, it seems to be testing only one major environmental constraint: the water supply. Nevada draws most of its water from precipitation in the Sierra Nevada and from the Colorado River. Large aquifers lie below the desert, but they rely on natural precipitation to replenish them. If water is extracted beyond the rate of natural

GEOGRAPHY OF NEVADA

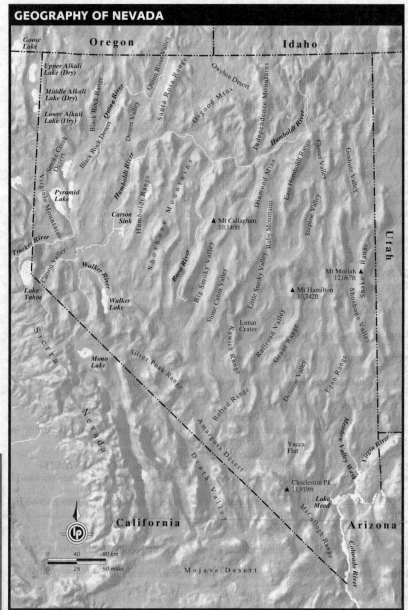

replenishment, the resource will be depleted, as has happened in Las Vegas. Conservationists critically refer to excessive pumping from aquifers, which is obviously unsustainable, as 'mining water.'

A drought in the early 1990s severely reduced the available water, lake levels dropped and the sustainability of urban growth was questioned. With the end of the drought, the water issue is commonly seen as a political rather than environmental problem – a matter of negotiating an adequate share of the available water from the other states with claims on the Colorado River and Sierra runoff. However, those other states – California, Arizona, New Mexico and Baja California (in Mexico) – are also experiencing significant growth rates; it's likely that the issue will be hotly contested in coming years.

Another contentious environmental issue is nuclear waste. Nevada was used as a nuclear test site for years, but with the end of testing, the US Department of Energy (DOE) has proposed that the location be used as a nuclear waste dump to provide a badly needed alternative to the present 'temporary' storage of waste at nuclear power plants around the country. A feasibility study of the Nevada site is ongoing, but many Nevadans fear that its results will prove a foregone conclusion – and with good reason. In 1999, Republican members of Congress introduced legislation that would force the DOE to use the Nevada Test Site for interim storage of nuclear waste. It was expected that President Bill Clinton would veto it, preferring to wait at least until the results of the feasibility study were in. Meanwhile, with all the attention focused on Nevada, the government quietly inaugurated another nuclear repository: on March 22, 1999, the first shipment of radioactive waste from the research and production of nuclear weapons arrived at the Waste Isolation Pilot Project, near Carlsbad, New Mexico. See Yucca Mountain, in the Great Basin chapter, for more information.

Altitude & Life Zones

An interesting feature of the Great Basin is the change in plant and animal habitats as you climb into the mountain ranges, which have been described as islands in a sea of sagebrush. A very rough rule of thumb is that gaining 1000 feet in elevation is equivalent to traveling several hundred miles north, so the vegetation of the highest mountains is comparable to that of Canada. Biologists divide the elevations of the mountains into a series of 'life zones,' which are useful in categorizing the changes you see, though the actual altitudes are somewhat generalized:

4500 to 6500 feet
Desert vegetation of cacti, agaves, yuccas, creosote and sagebrush gives way to evergreen trees, first small junipers and then piñon pine (pine nuts were a dietary staple of Native Americans).

6500 to 8000 feet
Stands of ponderosa pine are here, as well as oak, cottonwood and aspen. Squirrels and chipmunks are common, as are mule deer and the occasional mountain lion.

8000 to 9500 feet
The predominant trees are sugar pine, Douglas fir and aspen, with a few shrubs in the shaded understory.

9500 to 11,500 feet
Spruce and fir trees dominate, with bristlecone pines growing right up to the tree line.

Above 11,500 feet
The tree line is around this level, above which there are mosses, lichens and small tundra-variety plants.

FLORA & FAUNA
Great Basin

The Great Basin is a high desert, with most of the basins at over 4000 feet and most of the ranges up to and over 10,000 feet. There are few trees or cacti; the dominant plant, sagebrush, amounts to about 70% of the ground cover and is Nevada's official state flower. Sage can grow to more than 10 feet high, but in Nevada's basins it is usually low to the ground. It was used by Indians for smudge sticks and medicines, and the young shoots are edible for cattle; otherwise sage has little commercial value. Many types of wildflowers bloom in the Great Basin after spring rains, including primroses, buttercups, phlox, paintbrush and coral mallow.

The sagebrush provides a habitat for many small animals, including rabbits, squirrels, snakes, lizards and sage grouse, one of the few species which can survive by eating the sage. The male sage grouse makes a resonant booming call and dances in a specific place, called a 'lek,' to attract females during the spring breeding season, which is the best time to observe these birds. The Great Basin rattlesnake and the Great Basin gopher snake are the most common serpents in the area. A common lizard is the Great Basin whiptail, identifiable by its long thin tail. Larger animals include the coyote, pronghorn antelope and mountain lion, as well as feral horses and burros.

Bristlecone pines are Nevada's most interesting trees, capable of surviving in the highest, coldest, harshest environments. They are also the oldest living things on earth. The oldest documented specimen was 4900 years old. The harsher the environment, the longer they live. The best place to see bristlecone pines is Great Basin National Park.

Birds of this region include the small and elusive sage sparrow and sage thrasher and larger raptors, like eagles, hawks and falcons. Nevada's Great Basin is on a migratory flyway, and thousands of birds fly over in spring and fall from the Pacific Northwest, Canada and Alaska to summer sites in Texas, Mexico and beyond. The Ruby Lake National Wildlife Refuge (near Elko) and the Stillwater Wildlife Management Area (near Fallon) are two of the best places for bird watching. Pelican colonies can be seen at Pyramid Lake.

Mojave Desert

The Mojave Desert – the smallest, driest and hottest of the country's deserts – covers parts of southern Nevada, southeastern California, northwestern Arizona and the extreme southeast of Utah. The Mojave is something of a transition zone between the Colorado and Sonoran deserts and the Great Basin, with altitudes as low as 282 feet below sea level in Death Valley, but typically from 1000 to 2000 feet. The lowest areas are usually the hottest and driest, characterized by widely spread, shrubby vegetation, or empty sand dunes and dry lake beds.

At the higher elevations, the eerie Joshua trees grow up to 40 feet high and are believed to live as long as a thousand years. Other members of the same family include the Utah yucca and the Mojave yucca, also called Spanish bayonet.

If there are sufficient winter rains, spring can carpet the desert with around 250 species of wildflowers, of which 80% are endemic to the Mojave. The indigo bush, desert primrose, paper flower, desert holly and the catclaw will produce flowers in the right conditions. Creosote bushes are the most common – and the most aromatic – of Mojave plants, often growing together with bursage, the favorite forage plant of burros. Small cacti, like the cholla and beavertail, are also common.

Large numbers of lizards and desert birds are present. The most interesting lizard is the colorfully patterned, venomous, but elusive Gila monster; the most common is the chuckwalla, a large lizard, frequently more than a foot long. The desert tortoise (Nevada's state reptile) is an endangered species, with preservation programs under way near Las Vegas and in California. There are several types of rattlesnakes, of which the Western diamondback and the Mojave rattler are the largest and most distinctive, not to mention the country's deadliest. Desert mammals include the coyote and the kit fox.

The bighorn sheep, Nevada's state animal, is a handsome creature that has long been hunted in the Mojave; it is clearly recognizable in ancient petroglyphs in the Valley of Fire State Park. Well adapted to desert life, the bighorn eats more varieties of plant than any other hoofed animal. The Desert National Wildlife Range, just north of Las Vegas, is a protected habitat for bighorn sheep.

For more information about the desert environment and desert travel, see the California Deserts chapter.

NATIONAL & STATE PARKS

Nevada has one national park, the highly recommended Great Basin National Park, and also the Lake Mead National Recreation Area. See the Las Vegas and Great Basin chapters for details. In addition there are two national forests, the Humboldt and the Toiyabe, which between them include a dozen separate forest areas and 22 state parks. Their joint headquarters are in Sparks (☎ 775-331-6444), 1200 Franklin Way, Sparks, NV 89431.

The Humboldt National Forest has two units in the northern reaches of the state. Areas in the forest of particular interest to visitors with an outdoor bent are the Santa Rosa Mountains, north of Winnemucca; the Jarbidge Wilderness Area, north of Elko; and the Ruby Mountains, south of Elko. See the Great Basin chapter for more information.

The Toiyabe National Forest has four units in the central and western parts of the state, some of them straddling the California border. The most interesting features are the Toiyabe Crest National Recreation Trail and the Arc Dome Wilderness, both south of Austin in the Great Basin, and the Mt Charleston area near Las Vegas.

Of the state parks, the following are of particular interest and are described in more detail in the text:

Valley of Fire State Park offers stunning desert scenery, rock formations and ancient rock art; it's about 55 miles northeast of Las Vegas (see the Las Vegas chapter).

Spring Mountain Ranch State Park is a green and picturesque old ranch, just west of Las Vegas (see the Las Vegas chapter).

Berlin-Ichthyosaur State Park, about 60 miles south of Austin, is an old ghost town and ancient dinosaur fossil site (see the Great Basin chapter).

Fort Churchill State Historic Park has evocative ruins of an 1860s army outpost; it's about 45 miles east of Carson City.

Cathedral Gorge State Park is a spectacularly eroded canyon in the eastern part of the state, 110 miles south of Ely (see the Great Basin chapter).

Lake Tahoe Nevada State Park is a great place for hiking, mountain biking, water sports and cross-country skiing (see the Sierra Nevada chapter).

GOVERNMENT & POLITICS

Nevada has a bicameral legislature, with a 20-member senate elected to four-year terms and a 40-member assembly elected to two-year terms. The state judicial arm comprises a supreme court and a number of district courts. There are 16 counties, some with populations of only a few thousand. The Nevada Gaming Commission, one of the most important state bureaucracies, regulates the gaming industry and collects the 'amusement tax,' a principal source of state revenue.

ECONOMY

Tourism and gaming, together, are the state's biggest industries, employing a third of the workforce and generating more income than all other industries combined. Within this total, about 40% is gambling revenues and 60% is revenue from accommodations, food, drink, entertainment, transportation and all other tourist services. (This means that the average visitor who spends $100 for accommodations and food on a trip to Nevada will also lose an average of about $67 gambling.)

Retail is the second-biggest income earner, accounting for nearly 100,000 jobs, followed by construction (41,000 jobs) and manufacturing (27,500). Mining, a traditional Nevada industry, experienced a recent resurgence but doesn't weigh in heavily, employing only about 3% of the workforce – partly because mining revenues fluctuate with mineral prices, the opening of new mines and the closure of old ones. Still, Nevada is the major US producer of gold, silver and other precious metals. Other mineral products include mercury, barite, sand, gravel, gypsum, manganese and copper. The big Carlin County mine, opened in 1965, was the first new US gold mine in 30 years, and it now produces over one quarter of Nevada's gold.

Agricultural output is significant, with livestock its most important component; cattle are grazed on the vast acreage of the Great Basin and often sent elsewhere for fattening and sale. The main crops are alfalfa, grains, potatoes, fruit, cotton, figs and grapes, grown mostly in the western and southern corners of the state.

POPULATION & PEOPLE

Nevada's population grew by 39.5% between 1990 and 1997 and is projected to hit 1.87 million in 2000, making it the fastest-growing state in the country. This growth is the result of migration and immigration, not fecundity – only a quarter of the current residents were born in Nevada. The vast majority of people, nearly 90%, live in urban areas. Las Vegas, by far the biggest city, had 1.1 million people in 1997, having posted a growth of nearly 50% since 1990. Nearly three in four Nevadans live here. With such a big land area, and the small population clustered in a few towns and cities, it's no wonder that much of the state seems so empty.

Nevada's ethnic breakdown is as follows: 1,448,210 whites, 253,329 Latinos, 125,346 blacks, 73,611 Asians and Pacific Islanders and 29,642 Native Americans. The median age is 35.

Ethnically, the population is 95% American born, though there is greater diversity in Las Vegas. Nevada has several Native American communities, but they form only a tiny percentage of the population. Around 20,000 people, mainly in the north of the state, are of Basque ancestry, descended from 19th-century immigrant sheepherders.

CULTURE & SOCIETY

No one expects a big cultural scene in Nevada, given its short history and small population. The Nevada Arts Council, however, was established in 1967, and Las Vegas and Reno have art galleries, public libraries, orchestras and live theater.

The culture of the cowboy and the American West is still alive and kicking in Nevada. It's most diligently cultivated in Elko, where the Western Folklife Center organizes a Cowboy Poetry Gathering every January. Away from the tourist haunts and casinos, it's easy to find a bar with country & western music and, quite likely, some country dancing. Rodeo is a popular spectator sport, though the average cowboy these days does

his riding in a pickup truck. In rural areas, the dress code for men is most likely to include cowboy boots, checkered shirts, Stetson hats and big belt buckles.

Elko is also the capital of the Basques, people who descended from the sheepherders who migrated here in the 19th century from their country, which straddles the Pyrenees mountain range in today's Spain. Their traditional costumes, dance and cuisine are celebrated during the National Basque Festival in early July. Winnemucca, another Basque center, holds a festival a month earlier. The Northeastern Nevada Museum in Elko has a good exhibit on Basque culture.

Naturally, long before there were cowboys and Basques, there were Indians, and Native American culture has left its mark throughout Nevada. For centuries, five main tribes have called the area of today's state home: the northern Paiute (Pyramid Lake near Reno, Walker Lake near Hawthorne and other parts of the Great Basin), the southern Paiute (southern Nevada, including Las Vegas), the Washo (Lake Tahoe), the Goshute (near the Nevada-Utah border) and the Shoshone (the Ruby Mountains near Elko).

Excellent museums to visit to study Native American art, artifacts and traditions include the Stewart Indian Museum in Carson City (see the Western Nevada chapter), the Lost City Museum in Overton and the Nevada State Museum in Las Vegas (see that chapter). The Carson City Branch of the Nevada State Museum has an exceptional collection of willow baskets by Washo master weaver Dat-So-La-Lee. The Valley of Fire is one of the best sites to see ancient petroglyphs, and Pyramid Lake is still on reservation land and has great spiritual significance to the local Paiute people.

Indian reservations are scattered throughout the state. Many hold powwows, festive celebrations with dance competitions, food and drink and tribal members dressed in traditional garb. Most of the celebrations are open to the public. For dates and locations check with the Nevada Commission on Tourism.

Gambling

Except for poker, all gambling pits the player against the house, and the house nearly always has a statistical edge. The minimum age to enter the gambling pit is 18, but you must be at least 21 years old in order to play. The standard advice to gamblers is

• Understand the game you are playing.

• Don't bet more than you can afford to lose.

• Quit while you're ahead.

Casinos offer several basic gambling options: machines, table games, keno and the sports books. In terms of player numbers, machines are by far the most popular choice, largely because they require a minimal skill level and can be played with little money. Many casinos, especially in small towns, will offer little more than a few blackjack tables, dozens of slot machines and flat-top video poker games.

Machines

Slot Machines

The 'slots' are mind-numbingly simple – you put in a coin and push a button or pull the handle. Most machines take quarters, some take nickels and dimes, and a few take tokens of $1, $5 or more. There are several variants on the number of spinning wheels and what combinations pay out, but once you've put in the money it's out of your hands. The probability of a win, and the size of the payout, is programmed into the machine.

The only important decisions a gambler must make when playing the slots are which machine to play and when to stop. Some machines pay back a higher proportion of the money deposited than others. Those

 that return a lot to the player, as much as 97%, are called 'loose' – hence the signs advertising 'the loosest slots in town.' Loose slots are more likely to be found in the main gaming areas of big casinos. Slots with a lower return, down to 84% or even less, are more common in impulse gambling locations such as waiting rooms, bars, bathrooms, and supermarkets. But most players are gambling with a limited sum of money and keep playing until they've lost every last nickel they brought with them. If they play a loose machine, it just takes them a little longer to lose their stake.

'Progressive slots' offer a jackpot that accumulates, and many slots are now linked in networks to generate bigger jackpots. Often these pay off in the form of a new car, which is prominently displayed in the casino. The jackpots are factored into the payout percentage, so there's no extra statistical advantage to the player, except that a payout of a few thousand dollars may induce some to quit while they're ahead, instead of putting all the winnings back into the slot.

Video Poker

Increasingly popular, video poker games are often built into bars. For a quarter, they deal you five electronic cards, let you hold or draw, and pay off if you get a pair of jacks or better. They don't pay well, though; a royal flush will pay 250 times the amount bet, but the odds against getting a royal flush are just over one in a million.

Table Games

The table games can involve complicated betting options and even more complicated payout levels, so it can be hard to figure out the house's statistical edge. All table games are played with chips, which can be bought from the dealer. Dealers expect to be tipped (or 'toked') by winning players, maybe 10% of a good win, or with a side bet that the dealer collects if it wins. If you have any left when you finish playing, go to the cashier to 'cash in your chips.'

Blackjack

Basically the same as twenty-one, blackjack is the most popular table game in Nevada. Players bet against the dealer, with the object being to draw cards that total as close to 21 as possible without going over. Jacks, queens and kings count as 10, an ace is worth either 11 or 1 (the player's choice), and other cards are counted at face value. The player places a bet and is dealt two cards. The dealer then gets two cards, one facing up and the other concealed. The player can 'stand' on the cards dealt, or 'hit' (take more cards from the dealer, one at a time). Variants are to 'double down,' which means doubling your bet and taking one more card; or to 'split' a hand, if it has two cards of the same value, by matching the original bet and playing the cards as two separate hands.

Players draw cards until they stand on their total or 'bust' (go over 21 and lose). The dealer then draws cards and, by house rules, must hit on any total of 16 or less or stand on any total of 17 or more. The player must score higher than the dealer to win. Most wins are paid at even money, except if a player is dealt blackjack (an ace plus a card valued at 10), which pays 3 to 2 ($3 for every $2 bet).

The skill is in knowing when to stand, draw, double down or split to maximize your chances of beating the dealer. Some gambling books publish charts that show the best move to make for every dealt hand and every up card the dealer may have. If you follow these exactly, your chances of winning an even-money payout are slightly less than 50%. Professional gamblers count the cards as they are dealt (even though more than one deck is used), and by knowing the probability of drawing a given card, they can sometimes beat the odds. But card counting is regarded as cheating in Nevada, and you won't be allowed to do it in any visible way.

Craps

If you throw two dice, the top faces will add up to a number from 2 to 12. Craps has some very complicated ways of betting on this outcome. The possible bets are marked on the green felt of the playing table, but they're far from self-explanatory. A 'pass line' bet wagers that on the first roll (the 'come out' roll) the dice will total 7 or 11. If the dice total 2, 3 or 12 (called 'craps'), the player loses. Any other number is a 'point,' and the dice are rolled again until either a 7 or the point number comes up. If a 7 comes up first, the player loses; if the point comes up, the player wins.

A 'don't pass' bet is basically the reverse – if the come-out roll totals 7 or 11, the player loses; if it's 2 or 3 the player wins, while the 12 is a tie. If a point is established, the don't-pass bettor wins on a 7 and loses if the point is rolled again. All these bets pay even money, and the player's statistical chance of winning is just under 50%.

'Come' bets are placed after a point is established; 7 and 11 win, while 2, 3, or 12 lose. If it's none of these, the dice are thrown again until the point is thrown, and the player wins, or an even is thrown and the player loses. The don't-come bet is the reverse, except that 12 is a draw, not a win for the player. Come and don't-come bets pay even money, and again the odds of winning are just under 50%.

If you've already made a pass or come bet, and a point has been estab-lished, you can bet that the point will come up before a 7 is thrown. These bets pay off at a rate equal to the statistical chance of a win, so the house has no edge – this is called a 'free-odds' bet (or just an 'odds' bet), and it is the best chance you'll get in a casino. You don't have an advantage against the house, but at least the odds aren't against you, except that you have to place one of the less-favorable bets first.

Other options include a 'place bet' (that a 4, 5, 6, 8, 9, or 10 will be rolled before a 7) or a 'field bet' (that the next roll will be a 2, 3, 4, 9, 10, 11, or 12). The house has an edge of between 1.5% and 6.7% on these bets. 'One-roll' bets offer a chance to bet on various outcomes for a single roll, and the house edge is between 9% and 17% – pretty bad for the bettor.

In short, some craps bets are much better than others, but even on the best of them, with an optimum playing strategy, the odds are still against the player. The game is fast and complicated, so if you want to maximize your chances, take a lesson, watch some games and don't expect to win in the long run.

Roulette

This is the easiest game to understand, and the one that most clearly demonstrates the house edge. The roulette wheel has 38 numbers – from 1 to 36, plus 0 and 00. Half the numbers are colored red, half are black and the two zeros are green. The table is marked with the numbers and the various combinations that can be bet.

You can bet that a result will be odd or even, red or black, high (19 to 36) or low (1 to 18). All these bets pay off at even money, but the chances of a win are less than 50% because the 0 and 00 don't count as odds or evens, red or black, high or low. Your chances of winning are 18 in 38 (47.37%), not 18 in 36.

You can bet on a single number (including the 0 and 00), which will pay at 35 to 1, though there are 38 possible outcomes. You can also bet on pairs of numbers, or groups of four, five, six or 12 numbers, and they all pay off at a level that gives the house a 5.26% advantage (except for the five-number bet, which is slightly worse).

Baccarat

This game is offered in some Las Vegas casinos, but it's not very popular, partly because it requires a minimum bet of $20 or $25. Bets are placed, and the player and the banker are dealt two cards; the hand closest to 9 points wins. Aces through 9s count at face value; face cards are worth zero. If the cards exceed 10 points, only the second digit is counted. Hands totaling 8 or 9 are instant winners. The rules are quite fixed, and the house edge is low (1.17% betting for the banker and 1.36% for the betting player), but there are no decisions for the player to make except the size of the initial bet. The winning hand is paid even money (1 to 1).

Poker

This is an unusual casino game, because players bet directly against each other rather than the house. The house provides the table, the cards and the dealer, who sells the chips, deals the hands and collects a 'rake' from each pot. If you're not already a good poker player, don't even think about getting involved in a casino game in Nevada. In any case, few casinos offer public poker games, though the big places usually run semiprivate games in back rooms for high rollers.

Wheel of Fortune

You sometimes see these wheels near the slot machine area of a casino. You place your bet, spin the wheel and in most cases lose your money. They don't offer good odds.

Keno

Keno is like lotto. There are 80 numbered squares on a card; a player picks from one to 15 numbers and bets $1 or so per number. At the draw, the casino randomly selects 20 of the numbers, and winners are paid off according to how many of the winning numbers they chose, as shown on a 'payoff chart.' Payoffs range from $3 to $100,000. The amount paid off is distinctly less than the probability of selecting the numbers by chance, so the odds favor the house by over 20%.

Sports Betting

Some of the bigger casinos have 'sports book' rooms, where sports events from around the country are displayed on video screens covering an entire wall. Players can bet on just about any ball game, boxing match, horse race or hockey game in the country, except for events taking place in Nevada.

Las Vegas & Canyon Country

The triangle of southern Nevada is part of the Mojave Desert, which extends into California, northwestern Arizona and southern Utah. The main city is, of course, Las Vegas, the sprawling, world-renowned gambling mecca that everyone should see at least once.

Las Vegas also forms an excellent base for exploring other regional attractions. Dramatically beautiful Red Rock Canyon is just beyond the city limits, and the forests and snow fields of Charleston Peak are less than an hour away. Also close are imposing Hoover Dam, Lake Mead, the gambling gulch of Laughlin and the brilliant Valley of Fire. California's Death Valley is a few hours' drive away, and driving a few hours in the other direction brings you to the Grand Canyon, Arizona's Navajo reservation and the national parks of Zion and Bryce Canyon in Utah.

Las Vegas

- **population 881,000** - **elevation 2174 feet**

Most people are dazzled by their first sight of the bright lights in Glitter Gulch and the Strip and staggered by the scale and extravagance of it all. Las Vegas is an exciting place for a brief visit, and if you like gambling and glitter, you'll love it – at least until your money disappears or the incessant ding-ding-ding of slot machines and the haggard countenances of down-and-out gamblers wear you down. Kids love Las Vegas. There are so many things here just for fun. Budget backpackers love it; they can get great meals for a few bucks and great entertainment free. But to anyone with cultural pretensions, Las Vegas is tasteless, gaudy, and commercial – a giant coliseum of kitsch. It's a place people love to hate.

Despite what one might feel about Las Vegas, it is truly remarkable. In 90 years it has grown from nothing to nearly a million people. In 1997, it was the fastest-growing

Highlights

- Las Vegas – glitz, glamour, gambling: love it, hate it, but don't miss it

- Bryce Canyon – technicolor nature better than Disney could draw it

- Zion – muscular beauty, awe-inspiring vistas & the Narrows (not for the claustrophobic)

- Grand Canyon – playground of the giants: surreal, serene & sublime

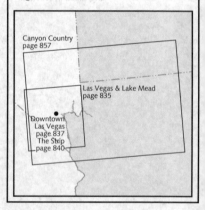

Canyon Country
page 857

Las Vegas & Lake Mead
page 835

Downtown
Las Vegas
page 837
The Strip
page 840

city in the USA, with greater name recognition than many cities twice its size. In fact, in terms of visitor numbers (about 30 million a year), Vegas is the biggest single destination in the country. Amazingly, all this has been achieved in an isolated location in the middle of a desert that's almost entirely devoid of natural resources. Las Vegas has made an industry of providing the whole country with something it wants: budget-priced glamour for mass consumption and the delusional hope of instant wealth.

History

The only natural feature to account for the emergence of Las Vegas is a spring north of downtown once used by Paiute Indians on seasonal visits to the area. In 1829 Rafael Rivera, a scout for a Mexican trading expedition, discovered the spring, after which the area became known to overland travelers as *las vegas* (the meadows), a place with reliable water and feed for horses. Explorer John Frémont literally put the place on the map in 1844. Las Vegas became a regular stop on the Spanish Trail. Mormons built the first structure in the 1850s, a small mission and fort abandoned by 1858. There was little development until 1902, when much of the land was sold to the San Pedro, Los Angeles

and Salt Lake Railroad, later absorbed by its parent, the Union Pacific. Work on the railroad connecting Las Vegas with California began in the summer of 1904, with train operation kicking off in January 1905.

Union Pacific subdivided what is now downtown Las Vegas was subdivided, and 1200 lots were auctioned off in a single day, May 15, 1905, now celebrated as the city's birthday.

As a railroad town, Las Vegas had machine shops, an ice works and its share of hotels, saloons and gambling houses. In 1920

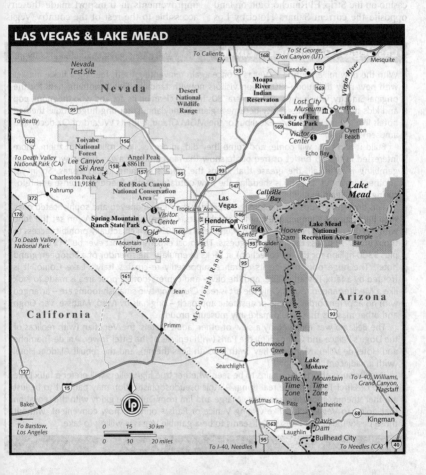

LAS VEGAS & LAKE MEAD

the population was 2300. The railroad laid off hundreds in the mid-1920s, but one depression-era development infused new life into the city: the building of Hoover Dam. This huge project, begun in 1931, provided jobs and growth in the short term, and the water and power necessary for the city's long-term growth.

In 1931, Nevada legalized gambling and simplified its divorce laws, but Las Vegas, dominated by conservative Mormon politics, was not quick to capitalize on these changes as Reno had been. The first big casino on the Strip, El Rancho, built on land opposite the current Sahara Hotel by Los Angeles developers, opened in 1941. The next wave of investors, also from out of town, were mobsters like 'Bugsy' Siegel, cocreator of the Flamingo in 1946. The Flamingo set the tone for the new casinos – big and flashy, with lavish entertainment to attract the high rollers. The underworld connections, if anything, added to the city's burgeoning mystique.

The glitter that brought in the high rollers also attracted large numbers of smaller fish. Southern California provided a growing market for Las Vegas entertainment, and improvements in transport made the city accessible to the rest of the country. Vegas

Las Vegas: Gambling on Luxury

With the new millennium, Las Vegas is once again reinventing itself, feeding a fickle market with new new titillation – 30 million visitors notwithstanding. This is nothing new for the original Sin City, which in the Reagan-era '80s tried to clean up its act and woo the mom, pop and kids market. The desert city became a giant Disneyland, sprouting huge kiddie-themed hotels like the medieval-style Excalibur or the MGM Grand, with its Wizard of Oz decor and amusement park.

Build it and they will come, and come they did, in droves, low rollers all of them, more interested in the $5 buffet or free pirate show than in gambling away their paychecks. But gambling is, after all, the grease that keeps the wheels spinning in Las Vegas. So in yet another turnabout, the city is shedding the now outdated family-friendly pretense and refocusing once again.

This time grown-ups are the target – especially the more moneyed and sophisticated ones who have largely shunned the city in recent years. Casino mogul Steve Wynn set the tone with the opening of the 2900-room Bellagio resort in 1998, which actually prohibits access to those under 18 unless they are hotel guests. The most expensive resort ever built ($1.6 billion plus $300 million for the art collection), it seeks to emulate the splendor of a European grand hotel. The huge pool outside its entrance supposedly re-creates Italy's Lake Como. It is fronted by a faux Tuscan village, and the olive- and cypress-dotted pool area is made to look like a Mediterranean resort. Only the art is real. Cluttering two smallish rooms are – arranged with no apparent order, theme or aesthetic approach – originals by Miró, Matisse, van Gogh and other masters that would make any museum proud.

The Bellagio was followed by a slew of other 'adult' hotels: the Venetian (with replicas of the Doge's Palace and Campanile), the Paris (with replicas of the Eiffel Tower, Arc de Triomphe and Hotel de Ville), Mandalay Bay (with a South Seas theme), and the rebuilt Aladdin Hotel (with an adjacent 'music hotel').

Despite such efforts, it remains to be seen whether true high rollers will prefer a faux Lake Como or Eiffel Tower to the real thing. All this pseudosophistication may pan out to be just another 'theme,' more likely to make Marge and Jim from Dubuque giddy with the sensation that going to Vegas is just like visiting Venice or Paris – only, oh how convenient, without those pesky Italians or Parisians. It seems to be a gamble Vegas is willing to take.

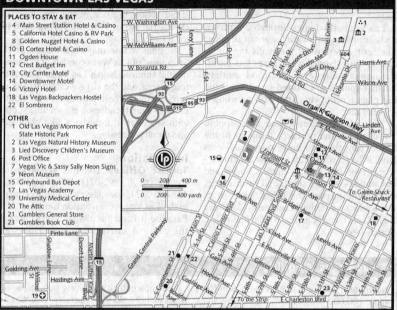

DOWNTOWN LAS VEGAS

PLACES TO STAY & EAT
4 Main Street Station Hotel & Casino
5 California Hotel Casino & RV Park
8 Golden Nugget Hotel & Casino
10 El Cortez Hotel & Casino
11 Ogden House
12 Crest Budget Inn
13 City Center Motel
14 Downtowner Motel
16 Victory Hotel
18 Las Vegas Backpackers Hostel
22 El Sombrero

OTHER
1 Old Las Vegas Mormon Fort
  State Historic Park
2 Las Vegas Natural History Museum
3 Lied Discovery Children's Museum
6 Post Office
7 Vegas Vic & Sassy Sally Neon Signs
9 Neon Museum
15 Greyhound Bus Depot
17 Las Vegas Academy
19 University Medical Center
20 The Attic
21 Gamblers General Store
23 Gamblers Book Shop

soon evolved into a mass tourism destination. Most of its phenomenal development occurred after WWII, when innovations like air-conditioning and reliable water supplies made life in the desert not just bearable, but desirable.

In the 1950s, a slew of huge resorts began giving shape to the Las Vegas Strip. Of these, only a few still exist today, including the Desert Inn, the Sahara and the Riviera, although all have since undergone multiple face-lifts.

To keep hotel beds filled during lulls in the tourist season, Las Vegas also got into the convention business, with the first center opening in April 1959; the newest incarnation dates to 1998. In 1997, 3750 conventions took place in Las Vegas, flooding the city with some 3.5 million conventioneers. Tourism in general generated $25 billion that year, including nearly $5 billion from gambling alone.

Orientation

Two main highways come into Las Vegas, I-15 and Hwy 95. For downtown, exit Hwy 95 at Las Vegas Blvd or I-15 at Charleston. I-15 parallels the Strip – a 3-mile stretch of Las Vegas Blvd – so work out which cross street will bring you closest to your destination. If it's your first time in Vegas and you're not in a hurry, get off I-15 at Blue Diamond Rd (exit 33) and cruise the length of the Strip from south to north, right up to downtown.

Downtown Las Vegas, the original town center, is a compact grid. Its main artery, Fremont St, is now a covered pedestrian mall lined with older, smaller and more low-key casinos and hotels. Public buildings, like the post office and city hall, are a few blocks north. There's virtually no shopping, except for souvenirs.

The blocks around the intersection of Main St and Fremont St are known as

'Glitter Gulch' and feature those longtime grinning neon icons, Vegas Vic and Sassy Sally.

Las Vegas Blvd goes through downtown and continues southward for about 10 miles. The Strip has most of the really big hotel-casinos, interspersed with vacant lots, garish shopping malls and fast-food outlets. Smaller motels are slotted in between the big places, occupying sites still awaiting a grander fate.

The colossal, three-legged Stratosphere Tower marks the northern terminus of the Strip. From there to downtown, Las Vegas Blvd is lined with tatty looking buildings – cheap motels, wedding chapels, shops and gas stations. At the south end of the Strip, toward the airport, the bright lights peter out a block past the brand-new Mandalay Bay Resort and Casino, which opened in March 1999.

Traffic is heavy on the Strip around the clock. Unless you want to be part of the street action, use one of the parallel roads (Industrial Rd or Paradise Rd) or take the local buses .

Besides a few major casinos near the Strip, most of Las Vegas consists of plain residential suburbs. North Las Vegas is a pretty tough area, and the city's western fringe has some of the biggest, fanciest houses. Southeast of Vegas, Henderson is a satellite suburb with some 'real' industries, like chemicals and metal processing.

Information

Tourist Offices The Las Vegas Visitor Center (☎ 702-892-0711, 800-332-5333, fax 702-892-2824, www.lasvegas24hours.com) is in the Las Vegas Convention Center at 3150 Paradise Rd and has plenty of brochures on the city and surrounding area. Hours are

A Las Vegas Wedding

Nowhere is getting married as easy as in Nevada. And apparently it's also very popular, with some 100,000 couples exchanging vows in Las Vegas in 1997 alone. Predictably, Valentine's Day (February 14) is the most popular wedding date: more than 3000 licenses were issued by the Clark County Courthouse on that day alone.

Part of the appeal is that, in Nevada, you can get hitched in a flash. Other states require residency periods, blood tests and other such time-consuming formalities. But here, all you need is to be over 18, have proof of identity and date of birth and $35 in cash for the marriage license.

The license may be picked up from any county courthouse, most of which keep convenient hours: the courthouse in Las Vegas (☎ 702-455-4416 or 702-455-4415), 200 S 3rd St, is open around the clock on weekends and holidays. If either party has been previously married, the divorce must be final in the state or country where it was granted, and you'll need to give the date and the location of the decree. People from ages 16 to 18 may be married with the written consent of a parent or legal guardian. With special consent of the Nevada District Court, it is even possible to marry under the age of 16.

With license in hand, you can then shell out another $35 to get married right at the courthouse or find yourself a wedding chapel, complete with a minister, for just a little more money ($100). Don't expect much ceremony, though. Some of these 'marriage factories' go through a hundred weddings in a 24-hour period. For those really in a hurry, the Little White Chapel (where Joan Collins got married), 1301 Las Vegas Blvd S, features a 24-hour drive-through window!

Other famous people who have exchanged vows in Vegas include Elvis and Priscilla Presley, Frank Sinatra and Mia Farrow, Bruce Willis and Demi Moore and, of course, Dennis Rodman and Carmen Elektra.

weekdays 8 am to 6 pm, weekends 8 am to 5 pm. Another useful website is by the *Insider* magazine, at www.insidervlv.com.

Businesses along the Strip advertising themselves as 'tourist offices' are basically travel agents, though they may have some maps, brochures and discount books.

The Las Vegas office of AAA (☎ 702-870-9171) is at 3312 W Charleston Blvd and open weekdays 8:30 am to 5:30 pm.

The Gay & Lesbian Community Center (☎ 702-733-9800), 912 E Sahara Ave at Maryland Parkway, gives referrals to gay-friendly hotels, clubs and the like. (Like most of Nevada, Las Vegas is not particularly gay friendly.)

Money Casino cashiers, open 24 hours, exchange traveler's checks and major foreign currencies, but banks will give a better rate. Along the Strip, ATMs are practically nonexistent outside the casinos, where you may be charged higher transaction fees than when withdrawing money from a bank ATM.

Tipping Las Vegas is one of *the* service job capitals of the world, and most of the staff depend on tips to supplement their meager wages. Drinks are usually complimentary while you're playing the tables, but tip the waitress $1 or so for a round. Dealers expect to be tipped (or 'toked') only by winning players, maybe 10% of a win or with a side bet that the dealer collects if the bet wins. Buffet meals are self-serve, but it's nice to leave a small tip for the person who brings you a drink or cleans your table. Maids appreciate $1 a day, and it's customary to tip parking valets a dollar or two.

Post The downtown post office is at 301 Stewart Ave. General delivery mail comes here and can be collected, with photo ID, between 9 am and 3 pm weekdays.

Bookstores There's a Waldenbooks (☎ 702-733-1049) in Fashion Show Mall, at 3200 Las Vegas Blvd. The Gamblers Book Club (☎ 702-382-7555), at 630 S 11th St, has books on every aspect of gambling.

Medical Services University Medical Center (☎ 702-383-2000), 1800 W Charleston Blvd, has 24-hour emergency service. Gamanon (Gamblers Anonymous; ☎ 702-731-0905) is at 900 Karen Ave. One of the best places for the treatment of problem gambling is the counseling center at the Charter Behavioral Health Hospital (☎ 702-876-4357), 7000 Spring Mountain Rd.

Dangers & Annoyances Most tourist areas are well lit, populated and pretty safe. North Las Vegas is reputed to be an unsafe area, but there's not much reason to go there anyway. The stretch of Las Vegas Blvd between downtown and the Stratosphere Tower is rather unsavory and may feel a bit threatening.

The words 'smoke-free' and 'Las Vegas' are never in the same sentence: there are ashtrays at every telephone, elevator, pool and shower, in toilets, taxis and at the movies.

Casinos

Casinos make money if they can get the punters through the doors, and in Las Vegas the competition is so intense that casinos go to extraordinary lengths to lure their marks. Cheap booze, food and entertainment are still the prime draws, but several casinos also offer 'family-friendly' theme-park-style amusements (although family entertainment may soon be a thing of the past; see 'Gambling on Luxury' earlier in this chapter).

With minor variations, casinos offer the same range of gambling options (see Gambling in the Facts about Nevada chapter). For novices, many offer free lessons – see *Today in Las Vegas,* a free paper available around town, for a current list of times. For information about the Las Vegas shows, see Entertainment.

On the inside, casinos are gaudy, noisy and deliberately disorienting. Long rows of slot machines are surrounded by mirrors, lights, and more slot machines, all beeping and ringing like demented computer games and rattling the occasional win into a metal trough with as much noise as possible. You

THE STRIP

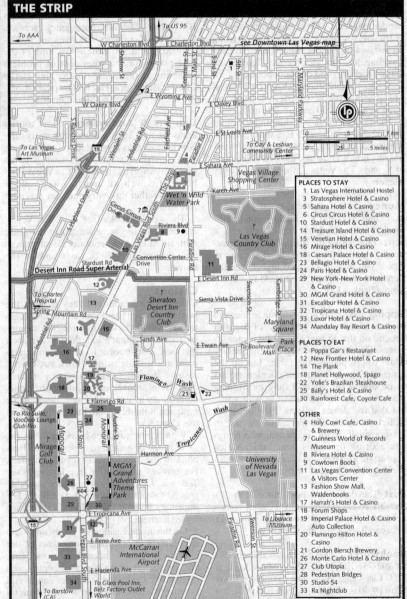

To AAA

To US 95

W Charleston Blvd   E Charleston Blvd   see Downtown Las Vegas map

E Wyoming Ave

W Oakey Blvd   E Oakey Blvd

E St Louis Ave

To Gay & Lesbian
Community Center

E Sahara Ave

Vegas Village
Shopping Center

Karen Ave

Wet 'n Wild
Water Park

Circus Circus
Drive

Riviera Blvd

Las Vegas
Country Club

Convention Center
Drive

Stardust Rd

Desert Inn Road Super Arterial

E Desert Inn Rd

To Charter
Hospital

Sierra Vista Drive

Spring Mountain Rd

Sheraton
Desert Inn
Country Club

Maryland
Square

Sands Ave

Park
Place

E Twain Ave   To Boulevard
Mall

Flamingo   Wash

To Rio Suite,
VooDoo Lounge,
Club Rio

E Flamingo Rd

Wash

Tropicana

Mirage
Golf Club

University
of Nevada
Las Vegas

MGM
Grand
Adventures
Theme
Park

Harmon Ave

To Liberace
Museum

E Tropicana Ave

E Reno Ave

McCarran
International
Airport

E Hacienda Ave

To Glass Pool Inn,
Belz Factory Outlet
World

To Barstow
(CA)

PLACES TO STAY
1   Las Vegas International Hostel
3   Stratosphere Hotel & Casino
5   Sahara Hotel & Casino
6   Circus Circus Hotel & Casino
10 Stardust Hotel & Casino
15 Treasure Island Hotel & Casino
15 Venetian Hotel & Casino
16 Mirage Hotel & Casino
18 Caesars Palace Hotel & Casino
23 Bellagio Hotel & Casino
24 Paris Hotel & Casino
29 New York-New York Hotel
    & Casino
30 MGM Grand Hotel & Casino
31 Excalibur Hotel & Casino
32 Tropicana Hotel & Casino
33 Luxor Hotel & Casino
34 Mandalay Bay Resort & Casino

PLACES TO EAT
2   Poppa Gar's Restaurant
12 New Frontier Hotel & Casino
14 The Plank
18 Planet Hollywood, Spago
22 Yolie's Brazilian Steakhouse
25 Bally's Hotel & Casino
30 Rainforest Cafe, Coyote Cafe

OTHER
4   Holy Cow! Cafe, Casino
    & Brewery
7   Guinness World of Records
    Museum
8   Riviera Hotel & Casino
9   Cowtown Boots
11 Las Vegas Convention Center
    & Visitors Center
13 Fashion Show Mall,
    Waldenbooks
17 Harrah's Hotel & Casino
18 Forum Shops
19 Imperial Palace Hotel & Casino
    Auto Collection
20 Flamingo Hilton Hotel &
    Casino
21 Gordon Biersch Brewery
26 Monte Carlo Hotel & Casino
27 Club Utopia
28 Pedestrian Bridges
30 Studio 54
33 Ra Nightclub

have to pass hundreds of these things to get to the bar, bathroom, restaurant or registration desk of most big casinos. The tables for blackjack, craps and roulette are less raucous and slightly more classy, but by the time you've found them you won't be able to see the exit.

Black globes in the ceiling with hidden cameras survey the scene constantly, while the cocktail waitresses cruise among the customers, dressed in fishnet stockings, togas, cowboy boots, grass skirts, or other outfits contrived to match the casino theme. Most of the customers are dressed somewhere between casual and sloppy. In special rooms for the real high rollers, the stakes are higher, and the people flaunt their wealth by losing hundreds or thousands without flinching.

You can drive around back to the free parking lot or multistory garage, if you choose. But we recommend that you leave your car with a parking valet; the $1 tip will spare you a walk of as much as a quarter mile. The big casinos on the Strip are set way back from the street. You may ride in on a moving footpath or an escalator, but when you want to leave, you'll be walking all the way.

Downtown casinos are less gimmicky and concentrate on gambling. The casinos listed here, all on the Strip and ordered from north to south, are worth visiting as attractions in themselves. Getting in is free, as are some of the attractions, though not the rides or special exhibits.

Stratosphere Opened on the Strip in 1996, this hotel-casino (☎ 800-998-6937), at 2000 Las Vegas Blvd S, features a landmark 1149-foot tower, on top of which are a couple of thrill rides: High Roller ($5), a fairly harmless and short roller coaster and Big Shot ($6), which catapults you 160 feet into the sky with rocket acceleration and then drops you in a terrifying free fall that causes a rush like a brush with death.

Circus Circus One of the original casino-cum-theme parks, Circus Circus has a variety of free circus acts in the tentlike interior, a 'midway' with carnival attractions and a room of video games. Under the 'Adventuredome' are a double-loop roller coaster and 15 other rides. This casino was hilariously immortalized in the surreal *Fear and Loathing in Las Vegas* by Hunter S Thompson.

Treasure Island From the street you'll notice the pirate ship and man-o'-war parked in 'Bucaneer Bay', a manmade lagoon fronting this pirate-themed hotel. Here, every 90 minutes from 4:30 pm to midnight, the hotel stages a pyrotechnic sea battle with lots of noise, smoke and drama (free). Kids love it.

Mirage A fake volcano erupts outside the hotel at least every half hour after dusk, with lots of smoke, noise and flames. Inside is a re-created tropical rain forest and the white tigers of the Siegfried & Roy stage show. A 2½ million-gallon tank holds five dolphins, which you can see, from above and below the water, for $3.

Caesars Palace A moving footpath, drawing you past 'classical' columns and 'ancient' statues, takes you into the gaming rooms and to the Forum Shops (see Shopping). The main attractions here are Atlantis: The Ride, a 3-D motion ride ($9.50) and two free shows: a fire-and-smoke battle in the Great Hall, which which also features a 50,000 gallon aquarium filled with exotic fish, and the Festival Fountain Show, starring animatronic Roman 'gods' in a campy show of special effects.

Bellagio Catering to upscale tastes and fat wallets, Bellagio offers lovely architecture and decor in its public areas; a small art gallery with a $300 million collection of paintings

Stratosphere Tower

by Matisse, van Gogh and others ($10 admission); 17 restaurants; and an impressive free show of 1200 water jets erupting in a spectacle of water, lights and music.

MGM Grand With over 5000 rooms, this massive, green-striped structure is one of the world's largest hotels. Its glowing green facade conjures up the Emerald City from *The Wizard of Oz*, the hotel's former theme. A $1 billion expansion was scheduled for completion in 1999 and intended to give the place a more generic 'City of Entertainment' theme.

Excalibur This huge hotel (4000 rooms) is made to look like a medieval castle and has an Arthurian theme. One of the few features that doesn't try to mimic olde England is the collection of Magic Motion Machines ($3 per ride), rides which create the illusion that you're doing something exciting. On the 2nd floor is a faux medieval village where strolling magicians, jugglers and singers keep the crowds entertained.

New York-New York This hotel's facade re-creates the Manhattan skyline, with replicas of the Statue of Liberty, Brooklyn Bridge and more. Roller coaster fans won't want to miss the Manhattan Express, which plunges, twists and loops above the Strip in what is a *major* rush ($7).

Luxor This remarkable steel-and-glass, pyramid-shaped hotel is a sight in itself, as are the sphinx and the obelisk out front. A beam of light pointing up from the pyramid's apex can be seen for miles. The Egyptian theme continues inside the huge, but fairly classy, atrium lobby and throughout the hotel. Attractions include motion simulator rides ($5), an IMAX theater ($8) and King Tut's Museum ($5), a not-too-tacky replica of the famous pharaoh's tomb.

Fremont Street Experience
In an effort to inject new life into Las Vegas' formerly grungy downtown, a $70 million canopy now covers a four-block section of casino-lined Fremont Street, now a pedes-

trian mall. After dark, the canopy regularly erupts in a dizzying, free six-minute light and music extravaganza that uses more than 2 million lightbulbs and 540,000 watts of sound.

Just east of here is the new **Neon Museum** (☎ 702-229-4872), an outdoor exhibit that showcases neon signs retrieved from recently leveled hotels like the Hacienda and the old Aladdin. Look for the gaucho on horseback, Aladdin's lamp and the Chief Hotel Court sign.

Wet 'n Wild
Right on the strip, this water park (☎ 702-734-0088), 2601 Las Vegas Blvd S, has some great water slides, like the High Roller and the Bomb Bay, a wave pool and a river ride. It's open daily 10 am to 6 pm May to September, with extended hours in the hottest months; $24/18 adults/children (three to nine). Children under three get in free, and discounts are available.

Imperial Palace Antique & Classic Auto Collection
A highlight for car buffs, this excellent museum (☎ 702-331-3311) includes a dozen Duesenbergs and lots of unique vehicles. There's a 1914 Rolls-Royce owned by Czar Nicholas II, a 1935 Packard limo owned by

Japan's Emperor Hirohito, a 1939 Mercedes used by Adolf Hitler (look for the marks where he tested the bullet-proofing), Khrushchev's 1962 Chaika and Howard Hughes' 1954 Chrysler (the air purifier cost more than the car). The collection of US presidents' cars alone is an automotive history. Besides these permanent displays, about 200 vehicles (from a selection of over 800) are displayed on a monthly rotating basis. The museum is on the 5th floor of the Imperial Palace casino, 3535 Las Vegas Blvd S and open daily 9:30 am to 11:30 pm; $7/3 adults/children. Look for coupons and freebies while at the visitor center.

Guinness World of Records Museum

If you enjoy the detail, diversity and authenticity of the *Guinness Book of World Records,* you'll be disappointed by this museum (☎ 702-792-3766), 2780 Las Vegas Blvd S. Its exhibits include an unrealistic mannequin of the world's tallest man, a grainy video clip of someone riding the world's smallest bicycle, and computers displaying sporting records almost as quickly as you could look them up in the book. Hours are daily 9 am to 6 pm; $5/4/3 adults/seniors/children.

Liberace Museum

For the lowdown on high camp, the museum (☎ 702-798-5595), 1775 E Tropicana, dedicated to the pianist Wladziu Valentino Liberace (1919-87) is the one to see. Memorabilia from his life, including the world's largest rhinestone and his glittery outfits and pianos, are of interest, as is a quiet acknowledgment of his long-term gay orientation. Hours are 10 am to 5 pm (Sunday from 1 pm); $7/5 adults/seniors; free for children. Proceeds go to the Liberace Foundation, which sponsors the musical education of talented young people.

Lied Discovery Children's Museum

This hands-on science museum (☎ 702-382-3445), 833 Las Vegas Blvd N, has exhibits that allow kids to make giant bubbles, be a radio disc jockey or pilot a space shuttle simulator. The museum is in the same building as the Las Vegas Library (an interesting piece of architecture), about half a mile north of Hwy 95. Hours are 10 am to 5 pm Tuesday to Saturday, noon to 5 pm Sunday. The museum is closed Monday in the summer and Monday and Tuesday during the school year; $5/4/3.

Las Vegas Natural History Museum

The most interesting exhibits here are the full-size dinosaur models and the diorama showing plants and animals of Nevada's deserts. The museum (☎ 702-384-3466) is in a factory-like building at 900 Las Vegas Blvd N. Hours are daily 9 am to 4 pm; $5/4/2.50 adults/seniors/children.

Nevada State Museum & Historical Society

This museum (☎ 702-486-5205), 700 Twin Lakes Drive in Lorenzi Park, provides a survey of the state's history and an introduction to its flora and fauna (there's even a mammoth skeleton). More interesting, though, is the section that examines the role of the mob in turning the old railroad town into a gambling resort (with a special exhibit on the Flamingo Hotel). Also look for the displays on atomic testing that went on in the state and marvel at the fact that being near an explosion was once touted as a tourist attraction. Open daily 9 am to 5 pm; $2, free for kids under 18.

Old Las Vegas Mormon Fort State Historic Park

The remains of the Las Vegas Mormon Fort (☎ 702-486-3511), 908 Las Vegas Blvd N, are fairly unspectacular, but this is where it all started in the 1850s. An adobe quadrangle provided a refuge for travelers along the Mormon Trail between Salt Lake City and San Bernardino. Some of the original walls still stand, and a three-room display shows artifacts and photos from the early days. Outside are sample fields of the first crops grown here and an archaeological dig. The fort is a mile north of downtown, next to the

Cashman Field sports center and surrounded by a wire fence. It is open daily 8:30 am to 3:30 pm (you may have to ring the bell for the attendant); free.

Historic Buildings

Unsurprisingly, there aren't many. Not only is this a new city, but many of the original buildings have long since been demolished or rebuilt. Even on the Strip, landmarks like the fortresslike 'Bugsy Suite' – with its false stairways and the gangster's bulletproof office – in the back of the Flamingo Hotel have been razed to make way for newer attractions. Downtown has a few survivors, like the Victory Hotel, 307 S Main St, the oldest hotel in town (1910), fronted by an arcade to provide shade from the fierce sun. The 600 block of 3rd St still has some of the railroad company houses from the same period. The 1930 Las Vegas Academy, 315 S 7th St, has art deco detailing, while nearby, some substantial residences of the same era are built in Spanish mission style.

Organized Tours

Gray Line (☎ 702-384-1234, 800-634-6579) does tours of the city as well as of the Lake Mead National Recreation Area, Hoover Dam and national parks farther afield. See Organized Tours in the Canyon Country section for company listings.

Special Events

Las Vegas hosts a huge number of conventions, trade shows and major sporting events. The big ones fill hotel rooms and raise prices all over town. Many casinos have 'gaming tournaments,' which try to turn slot machine playing, keno, or blackjack into a competitive event. For a list of upcoming events, call the Las Vegas Convention and Visitor Center.

Places to Stay

With nearly 130,000 hotel rooms – and counting – finding a place to stay in Las Vegas is usually not a problem – except when one or two big conventions are in town (the Comdex computer show in November is a good example). During those times, prices are hiked enormously and finding a roof

Conservation, Vegas-Style

Las Vegas is a byword for extravagance and consumption, where elaborate fountains and lakes evaporate into the desert air, acres of colored neon blaze all night long, and a typical hotel uses as much electricity as a town of 6000 people. It was therefore surprising to find, in the bathroom of a large casino-hotel, a card with the headline 'A Commitment to the Environment.'

The card said that the place is run by an 'environmentally aware company with a sincere commitment to recycling and energy conservation programs' and went on to request that guests turn off the lights when they leave their rooms and turn off the air-conditioning and heating when they aren't needed. It also advised that 'in the interests of energy conservation' bed linen would be changed only every other day. This was in a 20-story building completely covered with colored lights burning from dusk to dawn, visible from 10 miles away.

It's easy to be skeptical about this, but it does raise a serious question of how to reconcile conservation with self-indulgence. Certainly, some newer hotels are being built with systems to recycle wastewater, and changing bed linen every other day may well be a major saving in power and water without compromising the glamour of the visitor's experience. It's also true that the casinos use only a small proportion of the water and energy consumed in Las Vegas. But if it were simply a question of turning off the lights when they weren't needed, a hard-core conservationist could well suggest pulling the plug on the whole city.

over your head can be nearly impossible unless you're willing to part with hundreds of dollars. The obverse is true during lulls in convention activity, in summer and around the Christmas holidays, when the same rooms go for rock-bottom rates.

In general, prices are considerably lower Sunday to Thursday, when even the big hotel-casinos try to lure you with deals of $30 or $40, a rate that may shoot up to $129 or more on the weekend.

It's a very competitive market, and deals come and go by the hour. Call the hotels before you arrive and try some of the hotel booking services as well. National Reservation (☎ 800-732-1194) enjoys a good reputation, as does Las Vegas Reservation Systems (☎ 800-233-5594).

Motel prices are less variable, but they still tend to be higher on Friday and Saturday nights and may have a two-night minimum.

Budget
Camping Some of the hotel-casinos on the Strip – including Circus Circus and the Stardust – have RV parks with spaces costing around $15. These parking lots are not suitable for tent camping, but they do include use of hotel facilities. *KOA* (☎ 702-451-5527, 800-562-7782, 4315 Boulder Hwy), a few miles south of town, has tent and RV sites ($24 for two people) and a swimming pool. Other options for tent campers are outside of town at Lake Mead or Mt Charleston.

Hostels The no-frills *Las Vegas International Hostel* (☎ 702-385-9955, 1208 Las Vegas Blvd) is popular with international backpackers. There's a small kitchen, lounge, laundry and free tea and coffee. It's pretty clean and well run but can get crowded, so check in early if you can (no reservations). They also run inexpensive tours to the Grand Canyon, Bryce Canyon and Zion national parks. Space in four-bed dorms is $12 to $14. Private rooms are $28.

Las Vegas Backpackers Hostel (☎ 702-385-1150, fax 702-385-4940, 1322 Fremont St) is in a not-so-nice area of eastern downtown, but the facilities (including a pool and Jacuzzi) are top notch. Dorm beds are $12 ($15 on weekends); private rooms are $30 on weekdays, $35 on weekends. Call for free pickup from the Greyhound station.

Motels Inexpensive motels abound; usually they aren't as good a value as a casino special, but are usually cheaper than a casino on weekends. One distinct advantage of a motel is that there's no walking for 'miles' between the parking lot and your room, as is inevitable in the mega-hotel-casinos. Most hotels listed here are downtown.

The ultracheap *Ogden House* (☎ 702-385-5200, 800-634-6703, 651 E Ogden Ave) is managed by El Cortez (see Mid-Range) and has no-frills rooms starting at $18. The *Victory Hotel* (☎ 702-387-9257, 307 S Main St) is only a block from the Greyhound station and has 32 rooms ranging from $24 to $45. As you might guess, it's very basic, but it has the distinction of being the city's oldest hotel (1910). The 200-room *Crest Budget Inn* (☎ 702-382-5642, 800-777-1817, fax 702-382-8038, 207 N 6th St) starts at just $25 but also has some decidedly nonbudget rooms for $175. Near Ogden House, the *Downtowner Motel* (☎ 702-384-1441, 800-777-2566, fax 702-384-2308, 129 N 8th St) is also OK, with rooms starting at $25. The *City Center Motel* (☎ 702-382-4766, fax 702-310-0286, 700 Fremont St), although nothing special, is close enough to the action and has rooms costing $32 to $129.

A good choice at the south end of the Strip, near the airport, is the *Glass Pool Inn* (☎ 702-739-6800, 800-527-7118, 4611 Las Vegas Blvd S), famous for its swimming pool with big, round windows that allow you to see the pool from below the waterline. Double rooms begin at $39, crest at $109.

Mid-Range & Top End
Casinos – Downtown When built in 1941, *El Cortez Hotel & Casino* (☎ 702-385-5200, 800-634-6703, fax 702-385-9765, 600 Fremont St) was the first hotel-casino to be owned by an East Coast organized crime syndicate. The hotel has gone legit since then. Now rooms cost $23 to $40. *California Hotel Casino & RV Park* (☎ 702-385-1222, 800-634-6255, fax 702-388-2660, 12 Ogden St) has inoffensive tropical decor and rooms ranging from $40 to $100.

Golden Nugget (☎ 702-385-7111, 800-634-3454, fax 702-386-8364, 129 Fremont St) is the best of the downtown hotel-casinos; its least expensive rooms are $49, which is a great value for a place like this. More up-scale, but still a good deal, is the *Main Street Station* (☎ 702-387-1896, 800-634-6255, fax 702-388-2660, 300 N Main St), which has tastefully done Victorian-style decor and about 400 rooms costing $45 to $65.

Casinos – The Strip *Circus Circus* (☎ 702-734-0410, 800-634-3450, fax 702-734-2268, 2880 Las Vegas Blvd S) is a big, family-friendly budget place; rates begin at $29, though a family of four may pay up to $99. *Sahara* (☎ 702-737-2111, 800-634-6666, fax 702-737-1017, 2535 Las Vegas Blvd S) is an older hotel with no special gimmick or theme; it's very comfortable and has great specials, starting at $45. The *Stardust* (☎ 702-732-6111, 800-634-6757, fax 702-732-6257, 3000 Las Vegas Blvd S) is a 1950s hotel, renovated in the '90s. Rates start at around $36, though that may put you in the barrack-like motel blocks out back.

Caesars Palace (☎ 702-731-7110, 800-634-6661, fax 702-731-6636, 3570 Las Vegas Blvd S) is one of the ritziest places on the Strip, with large, luxurious rooms starting at $59, though you're more likely to pay double that. Suites crest at $500.

One of the newest entries on the Strip, *Bellagio* (☎ 702-693-7111, 888-987-6667, fax 702-693-8546, 3600 Las Vegas Blvd S) does come with a steep price tag designed to keep riffraff out. Rooms, however, are not nearly as luxurious as one might expect. Official rates start at $159, though you might get lucky and get a $99 special on a slow night.

New York-New York (☎ 702-740-6969, 800-693-6763, fax 702-740-6810, 3790 Las Vegas Blvd) replicates the Big Apple skyline and charges $79 to $229. Across the Strip, the *MGM Grand* (☎ 702-891-1111, 800-929-1111, fax 702-891-1030, 3799 Las Vegas Blvd S) has 5005-rooms, child care, a theme park and rates from $69 to $269. At the same intersection, the turrets and towers of *Excalibur* (☎ 702-597-7777, 800-937-7777, fax 702-597-7040, 3850 Las Vegas Blvd S) loom over the Strip. Rooms are spacious and cost $59 to $159.

Next door is *Luxor* (☎ 702-262-4000, 800-288-1000, fax 702-262-4454, 3900 Las Vegas

Blvd S), a glass pyramid with an ancient-Egyptian theme; rooms start at $69 and top off at $259.

Places to Eat

All the casinos have restaurants, and the bigger casinos can have four or more, serving different styles of food for all budgets; most have an all-you-can-eat buffet and special meal deals (see 'How to "Do" Buffets' in this chapter). All major fast-food franchises have one or more outlets on the Strip. Most visitors will find that the casinos offer more than enough variety and value, but the locals do have a life, and an appetite, away from the Strip – good restaurants are out there.

Casino Buffets & Specials The all-you-can-eat buffet is a Nevada dining institution, and one that can get pretty gross as greedy diners pile their plates with mountains of schlock – as if eating $30 worth of food at a $5 buffet will recoup the $25 they've just lost in the slots. Prices have recently gone up by a dollar or two, though the quality has generally stayed the same.

Cheapest is the *Circus Circus* (☎ 702-734-0410, 2880 Las Vegas Blvd S) buffet, at $4.50 for breakfast, $5.50 for lunch and $7 for dinner; it's a truly lowbrow dining experience. *Excalibur's* (☎ 702-597-7777, 3850 Las Vegas Blvd S) Round Table Buffet is huge but of average quality, with prices of $5/6/8 breakfast/lunch/dinner.

The best buffet is a subject of local debate, but you can't go wrong with the Carnival World Buffet at the *Rio Suite Hotel and Casino* (☎ 702-252-7777, 3700 W Flamingo Rd), with several food stations where dishes are prepared to order ($8/10/12). Also good is the Grand Buffet at *MGM Grand* (☎ 702-891-1111, 3799 Las Vegas Blvd S), which often features all-you-can-eat shrimp. They only do brunch ($8, served 7 am to 2:30 pm) and dinner ($13, from 4 pm). Other buffets commonly given high ratings are the *Golden Nugget* (☎ 702-385-7111, 129 Fremont St) with meals for $3.50/5/7, the Big Kitchen Buffet at *Bally's* (☎ 702-739-4111, 3645 Las Vegas Blvd S) for $9/10/14 and the Palatium Buffet at *Caesars*

Palace (☎ 702-731-7110, *3570 Las Vegas Blvd S*) for $7.35/9.25/14.

Most casinos also advertise special bargain-priced meals; the 12-ounce prime rib special ($4) at the ***New Frontier Hotel*** (☎ 702-794-8200, *3120 Las Vegas Blvd S*), served from 11 am to 11 pm, is a good deal.

Casino Restaurants If you're not after buffets or bargains, the best approach is to get a copy of *Today in Las Vegas*, which lists dozens of casino restaurants according to the kind of cuisine they offer and gives an indication of the price for a meal.

A successful marriage of design and food is the ***Rainforest Cafe*** (☎ 702-891-8580, *3799 Las Vegas Blvd S*) in the MGM Grand, which feeds you burgers and salads in a lush jungle environment. Another worthwhile theme restaurant is ***Planet Hollywood*** (☎ 702-791-78277, *3570 Las Vegas Blvd S*) at Caesars Palace, which has moderately expensive pastas, pizzas, grills, salads and vegetarian dishes served amid a collection of Hollywood props. The ***VooDoo Cafe*** (☎ 702-247-7800, *3700 W Flamingo Rd*) at the Rio has 21st-century fusion food that perhaps outdistances the chef's skills and is vastly overpriced at that, though the view over the city is an asset.

For better value, visit the ***Plank*** (☎ 702-894-7351, *3300 Las Vegas Blvd S*) at Treasure

How to 'Do' Buffets

Most large hotel-casinos in Nevada operate buffets offering a bonanza of food at excellent value. As anyone who has ever 'done' a buffet knows, they can be both a blessing and a curse, leaving you feeling as puffed up as Winnie-the-Pooh in a honey factory but as sluggish as a bear in winter – unless you observe a few crucial rules. So here are some insights – gained the hard way – on buffet etiquette.

- Look before you buy. Not all buffets are created equal, but you always have to pay up front. No host should stop you from perusing the offerings before putting down your money.

- Look again before you choose. It may all look good and appetizing, but resist the temptation to fill up your plate right away. Take a stroll and make mental notes about what looks best; then go back.

- Be choosy. Buffet designers try to entice you to load up on the less expensive – but filling – fare (potatoes, rice, pasta, gravy, etc) by strategically placing them up front or closer to the tables. Bypass those to get to the good stuff – shrimp, ribs, beef, etc.

- Don't pile it on. Buffets are all you can eat, so there's no need to jam your plate the first time around. Or would you serve salmon on the same plate with beef bourguignonne at home?

- Chew. This piece of advice may be self-evident, but believe us, many people forget this most basic of eating motions when faced with endless amounts of food.

  Bon appetit.

Island, an upscale eatery with classy decor, crisp table linens, heavy silverware and a well-trained wait staff. An entire meal can be made out of salad and appetizers for around $12 per person.

For a pricey but reliably good meal, make reservations at **Spago** (☎ 702-369-6300, 3570 Las Vegas Blvd S) at the Forum Shops in Caesars Palace (innovative California cuisine) or at the **Coyote Cafe** (☎ 702-891-7349, 3799 Las Vegas Blvd S) at the MGM Grand (nouvelle Southwestern).

Other Restaurants Favorite local haunts include the **Green Shack** (☎ 702-383-0007, 2504 Fremont St), a relic by Las Vegas standards, having already served its pan-fried chicken to Hoover Dam laborers in the 1930s. Still popular today, the shack has an old-fashioned dining room, chicken dishes for around $10 and a cool lounge with Naugahyde booths.

Another old-timey, unassuming eatery – in business since 1951 – is **El Sombrero** (☎ 702-382-9234, 807 S Main St), a basic Mexican place that serves huge portions of delicious fare, none costing more than $10. Another favorite, especially for breakfast, is **Poppa Gar's** (☎ 702-384-4513, 1624 W Oakey Blvd). For good marinated steaks, head to **Yolie's Brazilian Steakhouse** (☎ 702-794-0700, 3900 Paradise Rd), a restaurant with prix fixe dinners around $25.

Insiders drive miles to buy their doughnuts at **Krispy Kreme**, 7015 W Spring Mountain Rd, a chain that's taken Sin City by storm since migrating here from the South. A dozen of these mouthwatering guilty pleasures costs $5.

Entertainment

Free papers like *Today in Las Vegas* and *What's On*, available around town, provide thorough listings of mainstream current happenings. Alternatives to the casino scene, and local gossip, are covered in the *Las Vegas Weekly* and *New Times*.

Casinos The major casinos offer several types of entertainment. The 'big room' shows can be concerts by famous artists,

Broadway musicals or Vegas-style productions. These typically cost $30 to $50, which may include dinner, drinks, tax or tip. Lounge acts are less elaborate shows in smaller venues. The cost ranges from free to around $20; lounge acts can be entertaining, but are often quite tacky. If two shows are scheduled nightly, there will be more skin in the later one.

Often seats cannot be reserved and are allocated on a first-come, first-served (or tip-the-usher) basis. For dinnertime performances, arrive two hours before show time to ensure good seats. The most popular shows often sell out, so try making advance reservations, especially if your visit is on a weekend. Below is a sample of the entertainment offered in some of the best-known venues.

Bally's (☎ 702-739-4567, 3645 Las Vegas Blvd S) books big-name acts in its Celebrity Room ($28 to $39); its long-running *Jubilee* ($50 to $66) is a magic show that features the *Titanic* sinking on stage.

Bellagio (☎ 702-693-7722, 3600 Las Vegas Blvd S) has the best – and most expensive – show in town: the awe-inspiring *O*, which features the Cirque du Soleil in its first-ever aquatic production ($90 and $100).

Caesars Palace (☎ 702-731-7333, 3570 Las Vegas Blvd S) has big-name acts appearing at Circus Maximus ($50 to $80), though as of yet, no gladiators (unless you count boxing).

Excalibur (☎ 702-597-7600, 3850 Las Vegas Blvd S) has the *Tournament of Kings*, featuring jousting, jesters, wizards, invading armies and dragons in combat, while spectators feast on a medieval banquet ($30).

Flamingo Hilton (☎ 702-733-3333, 3555 Las Vegas Blvd S) has the *Great Radio City Spectacular*, featuring the Rockettes; the dinner show costs $52.50 and up, the cocktail show, at 10:30 pm, is $42.50); Bugsy's Celebrity Theater features smaller shows like the long-running *Forever Plaid* ($20).

Golden Nugget (☎ 702-386-8100, 129 Fremont Street), in keeping with Vegas' regained lasciviousness, presents the *History of Sex*, a 21-and-over musical revue for $30.

Harrah's (☎ 702-369-5222, 3475 Las Vegas Blvd S) big production is *Spellbound*, which you can see for $35; comedy acts appear at the **Improv** (☎ 702-369-5223) for $17.

Luxor (☎ *702-262-4400, 3900 Las Vegas Blvd S*) offers sort of a poor man's version of Cirque du Soleil, *Imagine*, which features magic, dance and aerial acts for $40.

MGM Grand (☎ *702-891-7777, 3799 Las Vegas Blvd S*) has *EFX*, an over-the-top extravaganza with more than 250 special effects ($52 and $72).

Mirage (☎ *702-792-7777, 3400 Las Vegas Blvd S*) is host to the very popular and long-running magic show by Siegfried & Roy, complete with white tigers, whose dinner you'll help finance at $90 a ticket.

Monte Carlo (☎ *702-730-7777, 3770 Las Vegas Blvd S*) is the home of magician Lance Burton, since the demise of the Hacienda Hotel, with shows costing $35 and $40.

Riviera (☎ *702-794-9433, 3901 Las Vegas Blvd S*) runs several shows including the latest version of the long-running *Splash* with a topless show at 10:30 ($40 to $50); *Crazy Girls*, another topless revue, costs $19; *La Cage* with female impersonators is $22; and comedy shows are $15.

Treasure Island (☎ *702-894-7722, 3300 Las Vegas Blvd S*) presents *Mystère*, featuring Cirque du Soleil, for $63.50.

Tropicana (☎ *702-739-2411, 3801 Las Vegas Blvd S*) has been running its classic production *Folies Bergère* for years ($50 and $60).

Bars & Clubs A popular dance spot among visitors and locals is **Club Utopia** (☎ *702-740-4646, 3765 Las Vegas Blvd S*), across from the Monte Carlo Hotel-Casino, which plays techno-pop, hip-hop, alternative and Top 40 music ($10 cover on weekends). Note that many dance clubs, including this one, have specific dress codes (no jeans or sports attire).

Inside the Luxor, at 3900 Las Vegas Blvd, is the super-trendy **Ra** (☎ *702-262-4400*), with gigantic statues of the Egyptian sun god lording over the dance floor. The atmosphere is upscale but sexy, with skimpily clad go-go dancers and the occasional live show. MGM Grand, at 3799 Las Vegas Blvd S, offers up its version of **Studio 54** (☎ *702-891-7254*), a vibrant dance club with three floors and four bars.

The Rio, at 3700 W Flamingo Rd has **Club Rio** (☎ *702-252-7977*) with '70s and Top 40 nights, though locals seem to flock to the hotel's **VooDoo Lounge** (☎ *702-252-7777*), upstairs from the overpriced cafe of the same

It's Show Time

The Las Vegas production show is a local institution, typically featuring a large cast in elaborate costumes, performing in a music and dance spectacular full of sound and color, signifying not very much. These are sometimes called 'continental' production shows, or 'European-style' revues, though this style of entertainment is largely extinct in Europe.

Maybe 50 years ago the sight of a semi-naked female was so risqué that the whole performance had to be lavishly dressed up so that no one could call it sleazy. To judge by the promotional pictures, which usually feature the fabled Las Vegas showgirls, titillation is still their main attraction, along with images of glamour and extravagance.

To avoid being considered a dated art form, many productions have recently been 'sexified,' another sign that Vegas is definitely no longer courting the family market. (See 'Las Vegas Gambling on Luxury'). The Tropicana recently made its long-running *Folies Bergère* show 'sexier than ever,' while the Riviera requires the women of its *Crazy Girls* and *Splash* extravaganzas to go topless. The Golden Nugget, meanwhile, gives its babe show an 'educational' component by calling it the *History of Sex*, though it admits to being 'a fresh new adult musical revue.'

Lots of visitors see these shows, perhaps because it's part of their package, or perhaps they're enticed by a $2 discount coupon. Many seem pretty bemused after watching for an hour or so, and walk out wondering what it was all about.

name and overlooking the glittering city from its top-floor perch. The **Gordon Biersch Brewery** (☎ *702-312-5247, 3987 Paradise Rd*), in the Howard Hughes Center, is one of the city's microbreweries. Their delicious lagers are brewed according to old German recipes, and there's frequent live music.

At the corner of Sahara Ave and the Strip, the *Holy Cow! Cafe, Casino & Brewery* (☎ 702-732-2697, *2423 Las Vegas Blvd S*) has some fine beers and a fun atmosphere. You'll recognize it by the large plastic cow outside.

Shopping

Downtown is remarkably devoid of shops. Fashion Show Mall (☎ 702-369-8382), 3200 Las Vegas Blvd S next to Treasure Island, has 140 mostly upscale stores, including Neiman-Marcus, Saks Fifth Avenue and Robinsons-May. Two of the largest suburban shopping centers are Boulevard Mall (☎ 702-732-8949), 3528 Maryland Pkwy, east of the Strip between the Desert Inn and Twain Ave, and Meadows Mall (☎ 702-878-3331), 4300 Meadows Lane, off Hwy 95 west of downtown.

For outlet shopping, the Belz Factory Outlet World (☎ 702-896-5599), 7400 Las Vegas Blvd S at Warm Springs Rd, has some 160 stores selling name brands at up to 75% off.

For a truly distinctive and entertaining Las Vegas-style experience, go to the Forum Shops (☎ 702-893-4800) at Caesars Palace. This indoor imitation of a Roman street has a painted sky that changes from dawn to dusk every three hours and a fountain where marble statues come to life and deliver homages to self-indulgence. Besides the major retail chains like Gap and the Body Shop, there's a Disney store, a NikeTown and the famous toy store FAO Schwarz, which is entered through a three-story tall 'Trojan Horse.'

At the Gamblers General Store (☎ 702-382-9903), 800 S Main St, you can buy your own slot machine (they'll ship it), personalized poker chips and anything else you need to start a casino. At Cowtown Boots (☎ 702-737-8469), 2989 Paradise Rd across from the Las Vegas Hilton, you can put together an entire Western outfit, leather hat to ostrich footwear. For a surreal collection of vintage clothing, head to the Attic (☎ 702-388-4088), 1018 S Main St, though the owner is notorious for overpricing his stuff.

Opportunists might find some real bargains in Las Vegas pawn shops, where less-fortunate gamblers hock their jewelry, cameras and musical instruments. You have to know what you're buying though – there are no guarantees.

Getting There & Away

Air McCarran International Airport (☎ 702-261-5743, www.mccarran.com) has direct flights from most US cities and a few from Canada and Europe. Airlines flying to Las Vegas include America West, American, Continental, Delta, Hawaiian, Northwest, Southwest, United and US Airways. Coming to Las Vegas on a special package including airfare and hotel may be the best deal. Check with a travel agent.

Bus The Greyhound bus station (☎ 702-382-2292), 200 S Main St downtown, has regular buses to and from Los Angeles ($31) and San Diego ($38), plus connections to San Francisco via Reno. Package tours to Las Vegas often include bus transportation for little more than the usual cost of accommodations. Other agencies offering bus service to Las Vegas are the USBus and the ANT (see the Getting Around chapter).

Train For the time being, direct Amtrak (☎ 800-872-7245) service to Las Vegas has been canceled, though trains have been replaced by buses. Express bus service from Los Angeles to the Las Vegas Greyhound depot, for instance, is $34 roundtrip.

Car Car rental agencies abound and competition keeps prices fairly low, except during peak times. Besides all the major agencies like Budget and Hertz, there are Brooks (☎ 702-735-3344), Fairway (☎ 702-369-0308), Sav-Mor (☎ 702-736-1234) and Value (☎ 702-733-8886).

Getting Around

To/From the Airport The airport is close to the south end of the Strip. Bell Trans (☎ 702-739-7990) and Gray Line (☎ 702-384-1234) provide airport shuttle service ($3.50 to $5 per person). Taxi fares to a Strip hotel range from $7 to $10; to downtown, expect to pay between $10 and $18 .

Bus Local bus service is provided by Citizens Area Transport (CAT, ☎ 702-228-7433); bus No 301 runs up and down the Strip, 24 hours a day, all the way to downtown. Fares are a flat $1.50. Exact change is required, but they do accept dollar bills.

The Strip Trolley (☎ 702-382-1404) operates a loop from the Luxor to the Stratosphere, stopping at every major hotel, every 25 minutes until 2 am ($1.30).

Monorail A short, free monorail runs between Bally's and the MGM Grand, but you could almost walk it in the time you spend finding the monorail station, waiting for a train and trundling along the track. Another monorail connecting Bellagio with the Monte Carlo covers a greater distance and saves you from walking along a desolate stretch of the Strip.

Limousine If you want to travel in style, limousines are available for rent starting at $35 per hour from Ambassador Limo (☎ 702-362-6200) and LV Limo (☎ 702-739-8414), among others.

Taxi Standard base fares are $2.20 for the first mile, plus $1.50 each additional mile, plus 35¢ a minute for traffic light wait time. Companies include Whittlesea (☎ 702-384-6111), Star Cab (☎ 702-873-2000) and Yellow Cab (☎ 702-873-2000).

Around Las Vegas

WEST OF LAS VEGAS
Red Rock Canyon

The contrast between the artificial brightness of Las Vegas and the natural splendor of Red Rock Canyon Conservation Area, a 20-mile drive west of the Strip, couldn't be greater. The canyon is actually more like a valley, with the steep, rugged Red Rock escarpment rising 3000 feet on its western edge. It was created around 65 million years ago, when tectonic plates collided along the Keystone Thrust fault line, pushing a plate of gray limestone up and over another plate of younger red sandstone. In 1994, President Clinton doubled the conservation area to almost 312 sq miles. Red Rock should be on the must-see list of every visitor to Las Vegas but – perhaps fortunately – it usually isn't.

The canyon rocks make for some of the finest rock climbing in the nation, though not for the inexperienced. Jackson Hole Climbing School (☎ 702-223-2176) offers basic climbing courses for $65 and guided climbs starting at $80.

Orientation & Information To get to the canyon from Las Vegas, go west on Charleston Blvd, which turns into SR 159, for about 30 minutes. At the canyon, a 13-mile, one-way scenic loop allows you to drive past some of the most striking features and access the hiking trails.

The excellent visitor center (☎ 702-363-1921) has maps and information about several short hikes in the area and is open daily 8:30 am to 4:30 pm. The scenic loop drive is open 8 am to dusk (sunset and sunrise are the best times for viewing). The park day-use fee is $5. First-come, first-served camping at the Oak Creek site is available year round.

Spring Mountain Ranch State Park

South of the scenic loop drive, a side road goes off to the west, to Spring Mountain Ranch, underneath the steep Wilson Cliffs. The ranch was established in the 1860s and owned by the Wilson family for over 70 years. Then it had various owners, including Vera Krupp (of the German industrialist family) and Howard Hughes, before the state bought it in 1974. It's amazingly green and lush, with white fences and an old red ranch house, like a farm home from back East. The park is open for visits and picnics 8 am to dusk daily ($3 day-use fee), and you can tour the ranch house on Fridays and weekends.

Bonnie Springs Old Nevada

At the southern end of Red Rock Canyon, Old Nevada (☎ 702-875-4191) is a tourist-trap reproduction of an 1880s mining town, with wooden sidewalks, staged gunfights and hangings and a Boot Hill cemetery. It also has a restaurant, ice cream parlor, saloon and motel. The adjacent Bonnie Springs Ranch has various types of farm animals, a petting zoo and guided horseback riding trips. Hours are daily 10:30 am to 6 pm; $6.50/5.50/4 adults/seniors/children.

Toiyabe National Forest
The Spring Mountains form the western boundary of the Las Vegas Valley, with the highest point, Charleston Peak, 11,918 feet above sea level. It's an area of pine forests, higher rainfall and lower temperatures, and it's extremely popular on weekends. As an isolated mountain range surrounded by desert, Toiyabe has evolved some distinct plant species endemic to the area.

Sixteen miles north of Las Vegas, Hwy 157 follows Kyle Canyon up to the village of **Mt Charleston,** which has a USFS district office (☎ 702-873-8800). The trailhead at the end of the road provides access to several hikes, including the demanding 9-mile trail to Charleston Peak.

Campgrounds, open from about May to October, are $7. Reservations can be made through the National Recreation Reservation Service at ☎ 800-280-2267 or at their website at www.reserve.usa.com. The *Mt Charleston Hotel* (☎ 702-872-5500, 800-794-3456, fax 702-872-5685) on Kyle Canyon Rd is a comfortable place, with a mountain lodge atmosphere. Rooms cost about $50 most nights, though prices can climb up to $140. Also here is the even more rustic *Mt Charleston Lodge* (☎ 702-872-5408, 800-955-1314, fax 702-872-5403). A lovely cabin with a fireplace, double whirlpools and private deck costs $125 midweek and $180 weekends.

About 30 miles north of Las Vegas, Hwy 156 turns southwest from Hwy 95 and goes to **Lee Canyon Ski Area** (☎ 702-645-2754). It's a small, mostly intermediate ski area (1000-foot vertical drop) that is busy on weekends, with good scenery and a season from late November to April. Lift tickets are $27. Call to find out if the bus service is running from Las Vegas. A couple of nearby campgrounds are open in the warmer months.

Hwy 156 and Hwy 157 are connected by scenic, 12-mile Hwy 158; driving the loop is possible unless the roads are closed by snow.

Pahrump
• **population 28,000** • **elevation 2695 feet**
It might not look like it, but the real estate tracts spreading out along this valley, between the Spring Mountains and the California state line, constitute one of the fastest-growing areas in Nevada. Pahrump is home to Pahrump Valley Winery (☎ 702-727-6900), the state's only winery, which produces white and rosé wines and offers free tours and tastings, as well as lunch and dinner.

Two casinos, Saddle West and Mountain View, draw business from the California side of the border, but it's fair to say that a high proportion of short-term visitors are here for something else. Pahrump is in Nye County, which has the closest legal brothels to Las Vegas, 70 miles away. Well-publicized in Sin City, these establishments provide limos, even light planes, to bring in their customers. The most famous brothel is the **Chicken Ranch**, which survived for more than 130 years in La Grange, Texas, before being reopened here in 1976, much to the consternation of many residents of Pahrump.

Primm & Jean
For those who just can't wait to start gambling, casinos have sprung up along I-15 on the 45 miles between the California state line and Las Vegas. Right on the border, in Primm, three casinos – Primadonna, Whiskey Pete's and Buffalo Bill's – face each other across the freeway, each with bizarre theme-park gimmicks. Primm gets its name from the family that owns most of the land and the casinos. Until recently, Primm was simply called Stateline, but it had to be renamed because there was already a town by that name near Lake Tahoe. A must for roller coaster fans is a ride on the Desperado ($5) at Buffalo Bill's, advertised as the highest and the fastest roller coaster in the world. Primm also has are two 18-hole golf courses.

About 15 miles from the border, exit 12 will leave you in Jean, where the big and garish Gold Strike Hotel and Casino looms on one side of the road and the big and garish Nevada Landing sits on the other. Both have 19th-century decor. The Jean Visitor Center (☎ 702-874-1360) can also give you lots of information about Las Vegas. The small Jean airport doubles the base of the Las Vegas Skydiving Center (☎ 702-877-1010), which offers tandem jumps for $179, accelerated freefall jumps for $300 and static-line jumps $195 year round.

EAST OF LAS VEGAS
Boulder City
• population 13,000 • elevation 2500 feet

About 30 miles southeast of Las Vegas, this pretty town was founded in 1931 as a residential community for Hoover Dam workers. Still the main gateway to Hoover Dam, Boulder City is unique in Nevada because it has never allowed gambling. Back in 1931, when gambling was legalized throughout the state, it was felt that only a strict moral code would ensure the dam workers' productivity.

With its grassy parks, trees and quiet streets, Boulder City is a lovely piece of old-fashioned, small-town America, and a complete contrast with Las Vegas. A few of the original buildings, including the Boulder Dam Hotel, frame Hotel Plaza. The **Hoover Dam Museum** (☎ 702-294-1988), 444 Hotel Plaza, preserves artifacts and records from the early days of the dam's construction and the town. Hours are 10 am to 4 pm daily; donation requested. The visitor center (☎ 702-294-1252) is at 100 Nevada Hwy.

The historic *Boulder Dam Hotel (☎ 702-293-3510, 1305 Arizona St)* was set to reopen in July 2001, after restoration, and is the most interesting hotel in town. The *Sands Motel (☎ 702-293-2589, 809 Nevada Hwy)* has some of the cheapest rooms, from $37 to $52. A bit nicer is *El Rancho Boulder Motel (☎ 702-293-1085, 725 Nevada Hwy)*, which charges from $60 to $150. The *Happy Days Diner (☎ 702-293-4637 or 702-294-2653, 512 Nevada Hwy)* is a nifty '50s place with tasty, low-priced American fare.

Lake Mead National Recreation Area

It's less than an hour's drive down Hwy 95/93 from Las Vegas to Lake Mead and Hoover Dam. They are the most-visited sites within the 2337-sq-mile Lake Mead National Recreation Area (☎ 702-293-8907), which encompasses 110-mile-long Lake Mead, 67-mile-long Lake Mohave and many miles of desert around the lakes. Despite the high volume of visitors, motels, campgrounds, restaurants, marinas, grocery stores and gas stations are sparse in this area.

Boulder Dam (later renamed Hoover Dam) was built between 1931 and '35 and was the world's largest dam at the time. It backed up the Colorado River to form Lake Mead, flooding canyons, archaeological sites, wilderness areas and communities. In 1953, the smaller Davis Dam was completed, forming Lake Mohave. The Colorado River and the two lakes form a border with Arizona to the east.

Hwy 93, which connects Kingman, Arizona with Las Vegas, crosses the dam, passing the main visitor center. Another important road is Hwy 68, which runs between Kingman and Laughlin, at the southern tip of the recreation area.

Lake Mead Lake Mead has 500 miles of shoreline and a capacity of 9.2 trillion gallons, equal to two years of the normal flow of the Colorado River. Popular activities include swimming, fishing, boating, water-skiing and even scuba diving. The lake is surrounded by beautiful scenery, most of which is protected as part of the recreation area.

The Alan Bible Visitor Center (☎ 702-293-8990), on Hwy 93 about 26 miles east of Las Vegas, has information on recreational options, camping and natural history and is open daily from 8:30 am to 5 pm (4:30 pm in winter). Don't miss the free documentary on the history of Hoover Dam.

The usual scenic drive is along N Shore Road, which starts near the visitor center and leads up from there to Valley of Fire State Park and Overton. Lake Mead Cruises

(☎ 702-293-6180) operates sightseeing trips ($14.50) and a variety of cruises from the Lake Mead Resort Marina.

Shoreside campgrounds are at Boulder Beach, Las Vegas Wash, Callville Bay, Echo Bay and Temple Bar (in Arizona). Accommodations, starting around $70, are available at *Echo Bay Resort* (☎ 702-394-4000) near Overton, which has a restaurant, bar and store, and at *Lake Mead Resort & Marina* (☎ 702-293-2074) near Boulder Beach. The toll-free number for both is ☎ 800-752-9669.

Hoover Dam At 726 feet high, the concrete Hoover Dam is one of the tallest in the world. It has a striking beauty, with its imposing, graceful curve filling a dramatic red rock canyon, backed by the brilliant blue waters of Lake Mead. Its simple form and art deco embellishments and design sit beautifully within the stark landscape. Its construction in the 1930s provided needed employment as the country struggled through the Great Depression. The dam opened in 1936, ahead of schedule by two years and under budget by $14 million (total cost: $165 million).

Flood control, irrigation, hydroelectric power and a regulated water supply were the main purposes for Hoover Dam's construction, and they remain the dam's primary functions today. The waters of the lower Colorado irrigate about 1500 sq miles of land in the US and almost 800 sq miles in Mexico; provide water to 25 million people primarily in Las Vegas, Los Angeles, San Diego, Phoenix and Tucson; and generate 4 billion kilowatt hours a year for Southern California, Arizona and Nevada.

Two types of tours leave from the visitor center (☎ 702-294-3524) atop the dam. The 35-minute basic tour takes you down into the power plant at the bottom of the dam wall, opening up a truly magnificent view of the dam and the canyon from below. Tours leave continuously between 9 am and 6 pm; $8/7 and $2 for children under 16. In summer, long waits are common. The 75-minute 'Hard Hat Tour' providing a more in-depth look, operates daily between 9:30 am and 4 pm and costs $25.

The visitor center itself provides very little free background information and functions primarily as a ticket office. The Hoover Dam film, which is also shown at the Alan Bible Visitor Center, is open to tour ticket holders only. Perhaps all this would be less vexing if it hadn't taken $125 million tax dollars to build this facility, a fourfold cost overrun and, incidentally, only $40 million less than the price tag of Hoover Dam.

If you come by car, leave it in the multi-floor parking lot *before* you reach the dam. Bus tours from Vegas are a good deal (about $20) and guarantee tickets to the basic tour. The *Snacketeria* at the Nevada spillway on the north side of the dam wall sells food, film, books and souvenirs.

Lake Mohave South of Hoover Dam, the Colorado River is impeded by the Davis Dam, near Laughlin, creating the narrow, 67-mile-long Lake Mohave. Access to the lake is from side roads off Hwy 95, one of which (SR 164) goes to Cottonwood Cove, which has a campground and boat rentals. Farther south, a rough road travels east over Christmas Tree Pass then south past Grapevine Canyon. A pleasant half-mile walk from the parking lot leads to a small canyon brimming with petroglyphs.

The Katherine Landing Visitor Center (☎ 520-754-3272) is in Arizona – reached via SR 163 – 3 miles north of Davis Dam and is open daily 8 am to 4 pm (Arizona is on Mountain Time; add one hour). Information is also available from ranger stations throughout the area. Call ☎ 702-293-8906 for advance information.

Valley of Fire State Park

Near the north end of Lake Mead National Recreation Area, Valley of Fire State Park is a masterpiece of desert scenery – a fantasy of wonderful shapes carved in psychedelic sandstone. It's similar, in appearance and geology, to the desert landscapes of Utah, Arizona and New Mexico, but easily accessible from Las Vegas and not crowded with tourists.

Early residents included a tribe called the Basket Makers or Anasazi Indians. Several petroglyphs survive throughout the park as a reminder of this early native civilization.

The visitor center (☎ 702-397-2088) is just off SR 169, which runs through the park. Open daily 8:30 am to 4:30 pm, it has excellent exhibits, general information and hiking suggestions. Some of the most interesting rock formations are **Elephant Rock**, the **Seven Sisters** and **Rainbow Vista**. The winding side road to **White Domes** is especially scenic, and **Atlatl Rock** has some very distinct and artistic petroglyphs. There's a $5 day-use fee per vehicle.

The valley is at its most fiery at dawn and dusk, so staying in one of the two campgrounds ($7 for tent sites) is a good option. Nearby Overton also has accommodations, and Las Vegas is only 55 miles away. The quickest route from Las Vegas is via I-15 and SR 169, though the drive along Lake Mead's Northshore Rd and SR 169 is more scenic and hooks up with Hwy 95 near Henderson, south of Vegas.

Overton
• population 1800 • elevation 1250 feet
Over 1000 years ago, a community of Anasazi Indians farmed here and built structures, found nowhere else in Nevada, resembling the pueblos of the Southwest. For some unknown reason, the Anasazi left the area, which was later occupied by Paiute people. Mormons settled the Muddy (or Moapa) River in 1864, but after seven years they also moved on, and it wasn't until 1880 that new settlers came and stayed. Today Overton is a small agricultural town with a couple of motels, bars and other businesses along the dusty main street.

The foundations of the original Pueblo Grande de Nevada were noted by Jedediah Smith in the 1820s. Outside the **Lost City Museum** (☎ 702-397-2193), 721 S Moapa Valley Blvd, some adobe dwellings reconstructed on the original foundations provide an idea of what the original settlement looked like. Inside is a collection of artifacts going back 10,000 years, information on the original inhabitants and early European settlers and photos of archaeological excavations. Hours are daily 8:30 am to 4:30 pm; $2.

Mesquite
• population 10,091 • elevevation 1597 feet
Northeast of the Lake Mead recreation area, Mesquite is typical of a Nevada-style boomtown, becoming a tourist destination only in the 1980s, with the construction of the Peppermill Hotel-Casino. Now metamorphosed into *Si Redd's Oasis Hotel* (*☎ 702-346-5232, 800-216-2747, fax 702-346-5722, 1137 Mesquite Blvd*), it has rooms ranging from $39 to $69 and two 18-hole Arnold Palmer golf courses. The hotel has since been joined by four other hotel-casinos accounting for about 2500 rooms, and no end to the boom is in sight.

The **Desert Valley Museum** (☎ 702-346-5705; closed Sunday), 35 Mesquite Blvd, documents area history with pioneer and Native American artifacts. Mesquite is 70 miles from Vegas and a good base for exploring Zion and Bryce Canyon national parks in Utah, though the resort really seems to be banking on entertainment-starved visitors from Utah and Arizona. The visitor center (☎ 702-346-2702) is at 460 N Sandhill.

LAUGHLIN
• population 8000 • elevation 510 feet
About 80 miles south of Las Vegas is the booming gambling resort town of Laughlin. In 1966, Don Laughlin bought land along the Colorado River and started a gambling operation in a dilapidated hotel catering primarily to Arizonans hungry for their turn at blackjack and poker.

A dozen large hotel-casinos now line the west bank of the Colorado River, which is thick with power boats and Jet Skis. The casinos are almost as glittery as those in Las Vegas, but without as many gimmicks... yet. Entertainment tends toward country music and golden oldies. Comfortable casino accommodations are cheap here, and swimming in the lake is an option in summer. There is, however, no other reason to come here unless you want to gamble and you can't stand Las Vegas.

The visitor bureau (☎ 702-298-3022, 800-452-8445, fax 702-298-0013), 1555 S Casino Drive, is open daily 8 am to 5 pm. A fun way of getting around Laughlin is via water taxis, which shuttle between hotels and also cruise the river at sunset ($3/2 roundtrip/ one way).

Places to Stay

Riverside Resort Hotel & Casino (☎ 702-298-2535, 800-227-3849, fax 702-298-2614, 1650 S Casino Drive) is one of the original Laughlin casinos, with lots of slots, restaurants and an entertainment venue called the Losers' Bar. Room rates are $17 to $109. The *Ramada Express Hotel & Casino* (☎ 702-298-4200, 800-243-6846, fax 702-298-6403, 2121 S Casino Drive) is done up with a railroad theme; their locomotive-shaped swimming pool and a train ride around the parking lot should amuse the kids. Rooms are $16 to $49. The *Colorado Belle Hotel & Casino* (☎ 702-298-4000, 800-477-4837, fax 702-298-5822, 2100 S Casino Drive) is a big place pretending to be a Mississippi riverboat. Rooms are $18 to $75. For a list of houseboating outfits, which offer a place to stay and way to tour the lake, see Accommodations in the Facts for the Visitor chapter.

Canyon Country

Las Vegas is the antithesis of a naturalist's vision of America, but it is surprisingly near some of the Southwest's most spectacular attractions. Lonely Planet's *Southwest USA* extensively covers outdoor recreation in Arizona, Utah and New Mexico, but for travelers with more interest than time to spare, the following section provides basic information for several easily accessible tours.

The information is organized as a loop itinerary, beginning east of the Lake Mead National Recreation Area, continuing to the Grand Canyon South Rim in Arizona, then northeast through Navajo country, and across the Colorado River and Lake Powell near the Utah border. From there, it's either northwest to Bryce Canyon and Zion national parks in Utah or southwest to the

North Rim of the Grand Canyon, again, in Arizona.

Summer travelers and those most interested in the national parks should consider skipping the South Rim of the Grand Canyon and head straight to St George, Utah, 120 miles northeast of Las Vegas, via I-15. From St George, Zion, Bryce Canyon, and the North Rim of the Grand Canyon are all within a few hours' drive. The entire loop can be done in three or four days, allowing just enough time to get a glimpse of each area, or you can take several weeks and fully explore each national park.

Note that Arizona and Utah are on Mountain Time, which is seven hours behind Greenwich mean time and one hour ahead of California and Nevada time. However, with the exception of the Navajo Indian reservation, Arizona does *not* use daylight saving time (in effect from the first Sunday in April to the last Sunday in October). During that period, Arizona time is the same as in California and Nevada.

Organized Tours

The vast majority of the many tours offered out of Las Vegas go to Canyon Country areas. The most heavily promoted are air tours over the Grand Canyon. The main option is a flight over Hoover Dam, Lake Mead and the western portion of the Grand Canyon, for about $75. An air and ground tour, which involves a similar flight but also lands at Grand Canyon Airport and includes sightseeing at the South Rim, starts at around $130.

Overnight trips, some of them with hiking or rafting options, cost around $200 to $300. You might save a few dollars by shopping around. Some operators to try include Air Nevada (☎ 702-736-8900, 800-634-6377), Vision Air (☎ 702-261-3850) and Scenic Airlines (☎ 702-638-3200).

One-day bus tours from Las Vegas are available to the Grand Canyon, Bryce Canyon, Zion or Death Valley; they usually take about 10 hours and cost about $90. One large bus operator is Gray Line (☎ 702-384-1234).

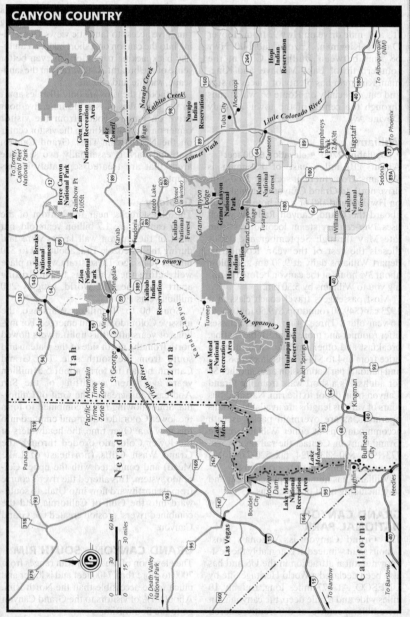

CANYON COUNTRY

LAKE MEAD TO GRAND CANYON NATIONAL PARK

It's a 71-mile drive on Hwy 93 from Hoover Dam to Kingman, Arizona and I-40. Hwy 68 runs between Bullhead City, at the southern tip of Lake Mohave, and Kingman. Kingman has plenty of places to stay and eat, especially on Route 66, which runs through the center of the town as Andy Devine Ave.

Williams

- **population 2700** • **elevation 6700 feet**

About 110 miles east of Kingman is Williams; from there it's either a 60-mile drive north to Grand Canyon National Park on Hwys 64 and 180 or a 2¼ hour train ride aboard the **Grand Canyon Railway,** which uses 19th-century steam locomotives from late May through September and 1950s diesels the rest of the year. Roundtrips depart Williams daily at 9:30 am and allow about 3½ hours at the canyon before returning you to Williams by 5:30 pm.

Most passengers travel coach class in a 1923 car ($49.50 roundtrip, $19.50 for two- to 16-year-olds). Three other, fancier, classes offer roomier and more comfortable seating, breakfast and other amenities and range in price from $64 to $114. Tax is an extra 8.8%, and national park admission adds another $6 for adults. It's a short walk from the Grand Canyon train depot to the rim. Narrated bus tours of various lengths are available various operators, as are overnight packages with accommodations at either Williams or the Grand Canyon. Contact the railway (☎ 520-773-1976, 800-843-8724, fax 520-773-1610) for more information or reservations.

Williams has numerous places to eat and stay, including most of the chains.

GRAND CANYON NATIONAL PARK

The Grand Canyon is Arizona's most famous sight – indeed, it is arguably the best-known natural attraction in the US and has also been declared a World Heritage Site by UNESCO. At 277 miles long, roughly 10 miles wide and a mile deep, the canyon is an incredible spectacle of differently colored rock strata. The many buttes and peaks within the canyon itself and its meandering rims give access to fantastic views. Descending into the canyon on a short hike or a multi-day backpacking trip offers an even better sense of the breathtaking variety in the landscape, wildlife and climate.

Although the rims are only 10 miles apart as the crow flies, it is a 215-mile, five-hour drive on narrow roads from the visitor center on the South Rim to the visitor center on the North Rim. Thus, Grand Canyon National Park is essentially two separate areas that are treated separately in this chapter.

Geology

The oldest rocks, near the bottom of the inner canyon, are 1.7 billion years old, but most of the canyon wall layers were laid during the Paleozoic Era, about 250 to 570 million years ago. These strata were in place well before the Americas began drifting apart from the Old World, roughly 200 million years ago.

Some 60 to 70 million years ago, the massive Colorado Plateau emerged. For millions of years after this uplift, rivers flowed north from the north side of the plateau and south from the south side. The Grand Canyon began to form about 5.5 million years ago when a shifting of the San Andreas Fault created the Gulf of California. South-flowing rivers combined to form the lower Colorado River and emptied into this new sea. Over time, the headwaters of the lower Colorado eroded through the Grand Wash Cliffs (northeast of Lake Mead) and connected with the upper Colorado system. This altered the river's course from its northward flow into Utah, to southward into the Gulf of California, and the combined rivers' erosion created the Grand Canyon.

GRAND CANYON – SOUTH RIM

The elevation of the South Rim ranges from 7000 to more than 7400 feet and is lower and much more accessible than the North Rim. About 90% of visitors to the Grand Canyon go to the South Rim.

The foremost attraction is the rim itself, paralleled by a 33-mile scenic drive with numerous parking areas, scenic views and trailheads. However, this drive has become overcrowded and, by 2002, a light railroad is planned to take visitors from the gateway community of Tusayan, 4 miles south of South Entrance Station, to the South Rim (see 'The Grand Canyon in the 21st Century').

Another attraction is Grand Canyon Village, with both early-20th-century hotels and modern amenities. The canyon itself is accessed by numerous hiking trails (some are detailed in this section). If you'd rather get away from the topside traffic, hike down to the canyon bottom and stay at Phantom Ranch or at one of several campgrounds, although advance reservations are definitely necessary. Other activities, including mule rides, river running and backcountry backpacking, also require advance planning.

Orientation

At Grand Canyon Village, Hwy 64 from Williams turns east and becomes Rim Drive. As it exits the park, Hwy 64 continues east through the Kaibab National Forest and Navajo reservation to Cameron. It's 53 miles from Grand Canyon Village to Cameron, and a further 51 miles south on Hwy 89 to Flagstaff. Entering the park from the east is preferable, particularly in the morning, since this gives easier access to the Rim Drive pullouts.

Information

When to Go The peak season ranges from about April to November, and the park is busiest from Memorial Day to Labor Day,

The Grand Canyon in the 21st Century

Grand Canyon National Park is by far the most heavily visited of all the national parks in the Southwest. For years, annual visitation has been close to 5 million, which has influenced and strained many aspects of the park.

During the busy summer season, hotels and campgrounds are booked up months in advance and parking lots are often filled to capacity. Drivers may have to wait just to park. People come for terrific views and instead get traffic jams. Clearly, overcrowding is a major concern.

Various solutions have been proposed and considered. The Park Service wants everyone to be able to enjoy the canyon (after all, this is why the national park was created), so limiting the number of visitors is not an option. Instead, a plan is being implemented to limit the number of cars in the park.

In November 1997 the US government approved a $67 million program that will change the way most people visit the Grand Canyon. By the year 2002, visitors will leave their cars in a huge parking lot (with more than 3000 spaces) in Tusayan, about 4 miles outside the south entrance of the park, and use a light-rail system capable of carrying 47,000 passengers a day to the rim of the canyon. Mather Point is proposed as the rail terminal point.

Once at the rim, visitors will be able to continue by foot, bicycle or by an alternative fuel shuttle bus. The current free shuttle route, which runs along the West Rim from about March through October, will be expanded to run year round and include the East Rim all the way to Desert View.

Cars will not be banned, however. Visitors with overnight reservations will be able to drive up to their motel room or campground. Drivers will still be able to enter via the longer route from the east, though there may be restrictions on this eventually. But the busiest route, the short drive from Tusayan through the south entrance to Grand Canyon Village, will become a short railway trip all the way to the edge of the canyon – and the 21st century.

– Rob Rachowiecki

so it's best to avoid that time if possible. On average, temperatures are 20°F cooler on the South Rim than at the bottom of the canyon. In summer, expect rim highs in the 80s and lows around 50°F.

June is the driest month, and summer thunderstorms make July and August the wettest. Weather is cooler and changeable in fall, and snow and freezing overnight temperatures are likely by November. Winter weather can be beautifully clear, but be prepared for occasional fierce storms and extreme cold.

Visitor Centers The main visitor center is in Grand Canyon Village, about 6 miles north of the south entrance. A large bulletin board provides information on lodging, weather, tours, talks and a host of other things. If you can't find the information you need, rangers are available to assist you between 8 am and 5 pm, with longer hours added from April to November. Park maps and the *Guide* newspaper, with up-to-date park information, are available free.

A smaller visitor center at Desert View, near the east entrance of the park, is open daily in summer and is usually closed in winter. You'll also get assistance at ranger stations near the Grand Canyon Railway depot, Indian Garden below the South Rim, the River ranger station and Phantom Ranch at the canyon's bottom, and Cottonwood Campground below the North Rim.

Call ☎ 520-638-7888 for recorded information on everything from weather conditions to applying for a river-running permit. The park's home page is at www.thecanyon.com/nps.

Fees & Permits Entrance to the park is $20 per private vehicle or $10 for bicyclists and pedestrians. Tickets are valid for seven days and can be used at any entrance point. Golden Access, Age and Eagle Passports (see Facts for the Visitor) are honored. Bus and train passengers either pay a lesser fee or may have the fee included in the tour. Note that fees may change in 2002 when the light rail shuttle to the rim is expected to be fully implemented.

Backcountry Permits Permits for any backcountry campgrounds, including the popular Cottonwood, Bright Angel, North Rim and Indian Garden, must be applied for in writing as far in advance as possible with the Backcountry Office, PO Box 129, Grand Canyon, AZ 86023 (fax 520-638-2125). A permit costs $20, plus $4 per person per night. This fee is nonrefundable.

If you don't have an advance reservation, go to the Backcountry Office; there are branches at the Maswik Transportation Center at the South Rim and at the North Rim ranger station (see that section for details), as soon as you arrive. Both are open daily in season from 8 am to noon and 1 to 5 pm. Most likely, you will have to put your name on a waiting list and hope for cancellations. Your chances of getting a permit for Cottonwood or Bright Angel for the next day are slim; however, if you can wait two to four days, you'll probably get one. The Backcountry Offices can also advise you of other, more remote backcountry campgrounds, most of which require a long drive on dirt roads followed by a hike on unmaintained trails below the rim. For a complete listing of campgrounds and backcountry trip planner, fax or write to the Backcountry Office address listed above.

Services Grand Canyon Village has the most visitor services, but prices are not cheap and lines can be long. Services available include hotels, restaurants, campgrounds, coin laundry and showers, gift shops and transportation services. Car towing and mechanics (☎ 520-638-2631) are available 8 am to 5 pm and for 24-hour emergency service. A gas station is open daily. A medical clinic (☎ 520-638-2551, 520-638-2469) is open weekdays 8 am to 5:30 pm, on Saturday 9 am to noon.

Ranger-Led Activities

Call the park's information service (☎ 520-638-7888) or ask at a visitor center about free ranger-led activities. Programs include talks (including slide shows) and guided walks from a few hundred flat yards (40 minutes) to 3 miles below the rim (three to four hours). In summer there are Junior Ranger activities for children four to 12.

Rim Trail

The paved Rim Trail skirts the rim for about 3 miles from **Yavapai Point** to **Maricopa Point**. It extends unpaved almost 7 miles farther west past several viewpoints to Hermits Rest. The Rim Trail is the park's most popular walk and visitors can hike as far as they feel comfortable. The rewards are beautiful views with many interpretive signs. Only foot and wheelchair traffic are allowed – no bicycles. During winter, snow or ice may temporarily cover the trail.

East & West Rim Drives

The West Rim is accessible by road for 8 miles west of Grand Canyon Village (and by the Rim Trail). At the end of the drive and trail is **Hermits Rest,** with a snack bar and the Hermit Trailhead leading down into the canyon; if you don't descend, you have to return the way you came.

Cycling along the road is permitted year round, though cars are banned from about mid-March to mid-October; free shuttles operate every 10 minutes. In winter you can make this drive in your own car, although planned shuttle services may change this. Narrated bus tours are also available (see Organized Tours later in this chapter).

The East Rim is longer and a little less crowded than the West Rim, but offers equally spectacular views. At this time, there are no free shuttle buses or walking trails, but you can drive, bike or take a narrated bus tour. The planned shuttle service will provide access to the East Rim as well as the West Rim.

East Rim Drive ends at **Desert View**, about 25 miles east of Grand Canyon Village and is the highest point on the South Rim. The road then leaves the national park through the Navajo reservation to Cameron.

Hiking & Backpacking

The easiest walks are along the Rim Trail. Hikes below the rim are strenuous and some visitors prefer to use mules (see Organized Tours in the North Rim section). Mule riders

have the right of way. Hikers meeting a mule train should stand quietly on the upper side of the trail until the animals have passed.

Keep this in mind when hiking into the canyon: First, it's easy to stride down the trail for a few hours, but the steep uphill return during the heat of the day when you are tired is much more demanding. Allow at least two hours to return uphill for every hour of hiking downhill. Second, it's a lot hotter inside the gorge than at the rim and water is scarce. Carry plenty of water, at least a gallon per person, and sun protection. In summer, temperatures can exceed 110°F (43°C) in the inner gorge.

The two most popular below-the-rim trails are the Bright Angel Trail and the South Kaibab Trail. Both are well maintained and suitable for either day hikes or, with a backcountry permit and advance reservation, overnight backpacking trips (see Backcountry Permits earlier this section). No permit is necessary for a day trip. Mule riders also use these trails. Though steep and strenuous, they are considered the easiest rim-to-river trails in the canyon, and even a partial descent will completely alter your perspective. Day hikers should not expect to reach the river and return in one day.

Bright Angel Trail Bright Angel Trail leaves the Rim Trail a few yards west of Bright Angel Lodge in Grand Canyon Village. From the trailhead at about 6900 feet, the trail drops to Indian Garden, 4.6 miles away at about 3800 feet, where there's a ranger station, campground, rest rooms and water. From Indian Garden, an almost flat trail goes 1½ miles to Plateau Point, with its exceptional views into the inner gorge. The 12.2-mile roundtrip from the rim to Plateau Point is a strenuous all-day hike. There are rest houses after 1½ miles (1130-foot elevation drop) and 3 miles (2110-foot elevation drop). The 1½ mile rest house has rest rooms; both have water in summer only.

From Indian Garden, the Bright Angel Trail continues down to the Colorado River (2450 feet elevation), which is crossed by a suspension bridge – the only bridge within the park. The Bright Angel Campground is a short jaunt north of the bridge and 9½ miles from the South Rim. Just beyond is Phantom Ranch, with its welcome water, food, accommodations and a ranger station.

South Kaibab Trail This trail leaves the South Rim near Yaki Point, about 4½ miles east of Grand Canyon Village. From the trailhead, at 7262 feet, it's a 4800-foot descent to the river and Bright Angel Campground, but the distance is only 6.7 miles. Clearly, this makes South Kaibab a much steeper trail than Bright Angel, but it follows a ridge with glorious views. The first 1½ miles drop 1300 feet to Cedar Ridge, making a good short half-day hike.

North Kaibab Trail From the Bright Angel Campground on the north side of the river, the North Kaibab Trail climbs to the North Rim, at 8200 feet, in 14 miles – allowing a rim-to-rim crossing of the canyon. Descending from the South Rim to the river and returning – or making a rim-to-rim crossing in one long day – is discouraged, especially for inexperienced hikers.

River Running

Well over 20,000 visitors a year run the river, almost all of them with commercial operators. These trips aren't cheap – expect to pay up to $200 per person per day. Companies authorized to run the Colorado River through the national park include Arizona Raft Adventures (☎ 520-526-8200, 800-786-7238), Grand Canyon Expeditions Co (☎ 801-644-2691, 800-544-2691) and OARS/Grand Canyon Dories (☎ 209-736-0805, 800-346-6277). Trips fill up several months (even a year) in advance, so plan ahead.

Organized Tours

Within the park, most tours are run by a company called Amfac (☎ 303-297-2757, fax 303-297-3175), which has a transportation desk at the Bright Angel Lodge (☎ 520-638-2631) and information desks at the visitor centers. Narrated bus tours leave from lodges in Grand Canyon Village. These include a two-hour West Rim tour, a 3¾

hour East Rim tour, or a combination of both. Both leave twice daily year round and cost $12 and $19. Sunset tours ($8) are offered in summer. Reservations are advised in summer, though it's usually not a problem getting on a tour the same or next day.

Places to Stay

Reservations are essential in summer and are a good idea in winter. Cancellations provide a lucky few with last-minute rooms. If you can't find accommodations in the national park, try Tusayan (4 miles south of the South Entrance Station), Valle (31 miles south), Cameron (53 miles east), Williams (60 miles south) and Flagstaff (about 80 miles south).

Camping Campers should be prepared for freezing winter nights. Backcountry camping is available by reservation and permit only (see earlier this section). In Grand Canyon Village, *Mather Campground* has 320 sites (no hookups) for $12 to $15. Reservations are accepted – up to five months in advance – from March 1 to November 30, either on the Internet at http://reservations.nps.gov or by calling ☎ 301-722-1257, 800-365-2267. Otherwise it's first-come, first-served and $10 per site.

The *Desert View Campground* near the east entrance has 75 campsites on a first-come, first-served basis from April to October, though they're often full by early morning. There is water but no showers or RV hookups, and fees are $10.

Below the canyon rim, *Bright Angel Campground* and the campground at *Indian Garden* are available for campers with reservations and a backcountry permit.

Lodges About 1000 rooms are available on the South Rim in several lodges run by *Amfac Grand Canyon National Park Lodges* (☎ 520-638-2631 for same-day information, 303-297-2757, fax 303-297-3175 for advance reservations). Grand Canyon Village has six lodges. Prices range from $120 to $180 for stays at historic *El Tovar Hotel* to simple lodge rooms at the 1935 *Bright Angel Lodge* costing $40 to $60.

Phantom Ranch at the bottom of the canyon has basic cabins sleeping four to 10 people and segregated dorms sleeping 10 people in bunk beds. Dorm rates are $21 per person, including bedding, soap and towels. Meals are available by advance reservation only. If you lack a reservation, try showing up at the Bright Angel Lodge transportation desk at 6 am to snag a canceled bunk (some folks show up even earlier and wait). Snacks, limited supplies, beer and wine are also sold.

Places to Eat

In Grand Canyon Village, by far the best place for quality food in an elegant and historic setting is *El Tovar Dining Room,* which has main courses in the $15 to $25 range; dinner reservations are recommended. More moderate prices and an American menu are available all day at the *Bright Angel Restaurant* in the Bright Angel Lodge. Next door, the *Arizona Steakhouse* serves steaks and seafood from 5 to 10 pm, from March through December. Canyonside snacks and sandwiches are sold from 8 am to 4 pm at the *Bright Angel Fountain* near the Bright Angel trailhead, from March to October. Self-service dining is available at the *Maswik Cafeteria* and at the *Yavapai Cafeteria and Grill* from March through December. *Babbitt's Deli*, in the shopping center opposite the visitor center, has a dining area and carry-out food from 8 am to 6 pm.

Hermits Rest Snack Bar, at the end of the West Rim Drive, and *Desert View Fountain* near the east entrance, are both open daily for snacks and fast food; hours vary by season.

Getting Around

Free shuttles operate along three routes from mid-March to mid-October (dates may be extended in 2002). The Village Loop goes around Grand Canyon Village, stopping at lodges, campgrounds, the visitor center the Maswik Transportation Center with the Backcountry Office, Yavapai Lodge and other points. Buses leave every 10 minutes from 6:30 am to 10:30 pm (every half hour

from one hour before sunrise to 6:30 am and for one hour after sunset) and take 50 minutes for the entire loop.

The Village Loop bus connects with the West Rim shuttle at the Bright Angel trailhead (called the West Rim Interchange Stop). The West Rim shuttle operates every 15 minutes from 7:30 am to sunset, stops at eight scenic points and takes 90 minutes roundtrip.

Shuttles also run every 30 minutes to Yaki Point and the South Kaibab Trailhead, with pickups at the Backcountry Office in the Maswik Transportation Center, Yavapai Lodge and Bright Angel Lodge. Operating from one hour before sunrise to one hour after sunset, this shuttle is especially useful to hikers on the South Kaibab Trail.

NAVAJO INDIAN RESERVATION

Driving from Grand Canyon Village along East Rim Drive/Hwy 64 offers many spectacular views. East Rim Drive ends at Desert View, then proceeds as Hwy 64 through the Navajo reservation to Cameron. Along the way is the Little Colorado River Gorge Navajo Tribal Park, with a scenic overlook worth a stop.

From Cameron, heading north, Hwy 89 leads through the vast countryside of the Navajo reservation, which covers about 25,000 sq miles – the entire northeast corner of Arizona. Other highways crossing the reservation are Hwy 160, which forks off Hwy 89 about 20 miles north of Cameron then cuts northeast towards Utah and Colorado; Hwy 264, which cuts west-east from Tuba City/Moenkopi to Window Rock near the New Mexico border; and I-40, which roughly forms the southern boundary of the reservation.

As befits the nation's largest tribe (about one in seven Native Americans is Navajo), this is the largest reservation in the USA. About 75% is high desert and the remainder is forest. Today, over half of the approximately 250,000 members of the Navajo Nation live here.

Please note that, unlike the rest of Arizona, daylight saving time is in effect on the Navajo Indian reservation.

Information Information about the entire reservation is available from Navajo Nation Tourism Department (☎ 520-871-6436, 520-871-7371, fax 520-871-7381) in Window Rock. Its offices are in a trailer 2 miles west of town on Hwy 264, at the intersection of Hwys 264 and 12.

Photography is permitted almost anywhere on the reservation where there's tourism. Taking photographs of people, however, is not appropriate unless you ask for – and receive – permission from the individual involved. A tip is usually expected.

Alcohol and drugs are strictly prohibited throughout the reservation. It is a violation of federal, state and tribal laws to disturb, destroy, injure, deface or remove any natural feature or prehistoric object.

Shopping
At numerous stands along Hwy 89, Navajo craftspeople offer their wares, including hand-woven rugs, traditional silverwork (often with turquoise and coral), jewelry, blankets, etc. There are also 'official' stores run by the tribe, called 'trading posts.' Buying at a trading post does not guarantee that the quality of items will be any better than those at the roadside stalls. When you buy direct, you may find that you pay less, and the sellers may still make more than if they had sold their wares through the official merchants.

GRAND CANYON – NORTH RIM
The main differences between the North and South rims of the Grand Canyon are elevation and accessibility. The North Rim is more than 8000 feet above sea level. There is only one road in, so visitors must backtrack more than 60 miles after their visit. Winters are colder, the climate is wetter and the spruce and fir forest above the rim is much thicker than at the South Rim. Winter snows close the roads to car traffic from December 1 (earlier if there's heavy snow) until mid-May.

Because it's such a long drive from any major city or airport, only 10% of Grand Canyon visitors come to the North Rim (though for visitors from Las Vegas this is

the more accessible area). But the views here are spectacular. North Rim visitors are drawn by the lack of huge crowds and the desire for a more peaceful, if more spartan, experience of the canyon's majesty.

Orientation
Hwy 89 splits a few miles before crossing the Colorado River, with Hwy 89 continuing north to Page and the Glen Canyon and Lake Powell region. Alt Hwy 89 heads northwest and crosses the Colorado by the Navajo Bridge at Marble Canyon. It's 44 miles south on Hwy 67 from Alt Hwy 89 to the Grand Canyon Lodge. Almost 30 miles of paved roads lead to various overlooks to the east.

Information
The visitor center (☎ 520-638-7864) is in the Grand Canyon Lodge (the North Rim's only hotel) and is open 8 am to 8 pm from mid-May through mid-October.

The Backcountry Office (for backpackers) is in the ranger station near the campground, 1½ miles north of the lodge. Other services available at the North Rim (in season) are a restaurant, gas station, post office, bookstore, general store, coin laundry and showers, medical clinic and tours. After October 15, all services are closed except the campground, which remains open, weather permitting. After December 1, everything is closed.

Park headquarters are at the South Rim. See that section earlier in this chapter for entrance fees. The park's automated telephone system (☎ 520-638-7888) has both South Rim and North Rim information.

When to Go North Rim overnight temperatures drop below freezing as late as May and as early as October. The hottest month, July, sees average highs near 80°F (26°C) and lows in the mid-40s. The North Rim is wetter than the South Rim although the rain pattern is similar. Snowfall is heaviest from late December to early March, when overnight temperatures normally fall into the teens and sometimes below.

North Rim Drives

The drive on Hwy 67 across the Kaibab Plateau to Bright Angel Point takes you through thick forest. There are excellent canyon views from the point, but to reach other overlooks you need to drive north for almost 3 miles and take the signed turn east to **Point Imperial** and **Cape Royal**. It is 9 miles to Point Imperial (8803 feet), the park's highest overlook.

One of the most spectacular of these remote overlooks is the **Toroweap Overlook** at **Tuweep**, far to the west of the main park facilities. An unpaved road, usually navigable for cars, leaves Hwy 389 about 9 miles west of Fredonia and heads 55 miles to the Tuweep Ranger Station, which is staffed year round. It is another 5 miles to the overlook, which has primitive camping (no water).

Hiking & Backpacking

The most popular quick hike is the paved half-mile trail from the Grand Canyon Lodge south to the extreme tip of **Bright Angel Point**, which offers great views at sunset. The 1½ mile **Transept Trail** goes north from the lodge through forest to the North Rim Campground.

Two trailheads are at a parking lot 2 miles north of the lodge. The **Ken Patrick Trail** travels through rolling forested country northeast to Point Imperial, about 10 miles away. This trail may be overgrown and can require route-finding skills. About a mile along this trail, a fork to the right (east) becomes the Uncle Jim Trail, a fairly rugged 5-mile loop offering fine views.

The **North Kaibab Trail** plunges from the parking lot down to Phantom Ranch at the Colorado River, 5750 feet below and 14 miles away. This is the only maintained rim-to-river trail from the North Rim, and it connects with trails to the South Rim. The first 4.7 miles are the steepest, dropping well over 3000 feet to **Roaring Springs** – a popular all-day hike and mule-ride destination. Drinking water is available at Roaring Springs from May to September only. If you prefer a shorter day hike below the rim, you can walk just ¾ of a mile down to **Coconino Overlook** or 1 mile to

the **Supai Tunnel**, 1400 feet below the rim, to get a flavor of steep, inner-canyon hiking.

Cottonwood Campground is 7 miles and 4200 feet below the rim and is the only campground between the North Rim and the river. Phantom Lodge and the Bright Angel Campground are 7 and 7½ miles, respectively, below Cottonwood (see Places to Stay in the South Rim section).

In winter, the trails of the North Rim are regarded as backcountry use areas (see Backcountry Permits in the South Rim section), as snow can be 5 feet deep. The North Rim Campground (see Places to Stay) is still open for backcountry use, however there are only two ways to get to the campground in winter – either by hiking from the South Rim up to the North Rim via the North Kaibab Trail (only for the truly Nordic) or cross-country skiing 52 miles from the town of Jacob Lake, a route that takes three days.

Organized Tours

In season, daily three-hour narrated tours to Point Imperial and Cape Royal leave from the Grand Canyon Lodge and cost $20/10 adults/children. A schedule is posted in the lobby.

Trail Rides (☎ 520-638-9875 in season, 801-679-8665 otherwise), offers mule rides for $15 an hour (minimum age is six), $35 a half day (minimum age is eight) and $85 for an all-day tour into the Grand Canyon, including lunch (minimum age is 12). Advance reservations are recommended, or stop by their desk (open 7 am to 7 pm) in the Grand Canyon Lodge to see what is available.

Places to Stay & Eat

The *North Rim Campground*, 1½ miles north of the Grand Canyon Lodge, has 82 sites costing $12. The campground has water, a store, a snack bar and coin-operated showers and laundry, but no hookups. Make free reservations, up to five months in advance, by calling ☎ 301-722-1257, 800-365-2267, or online at http://reservations.nps.gov. Without a reservation, show up before 10 am and hope for the best. All other campgrounds require a backcountry permit.

The historic **Grand Canyon Lodge** (*☎ 520-638-2611 in season, 303-297-2757, fax 303-297-3175 year round for reservations*) is usually full, and reservations should be made as far in advance as possible. It has about 200 units, both motel rooms and cabins sleeping up to five people, all with private baths. Rates vary from $55 to $95 for a double and $70 to $110 for five people. There's a snack bar, restaurant and bar at the lodge.

BRYCE CANYON NATIONAL PARK

North of Kanab, Utah, Hwy 89 intersects with Hwy 12 heading east through Bryce Canyon, past three state parks, and terminates at Torrey on Hwy 24, about 4 miles from Capitol Reef National Park. The 122-mile long Hwy 12 is one of the most scenic roads in Utah.

The Grand Staircase – a series of steplike uplifted rock layers stretching north from the Grand Canyon – culminates in the Pink Cliffs formation at Bryce Canyon. These cliffs were deposited as 2000-foot-deep sediment in a huge prehistoric lake some 50 to 60 million years ago, slowly lifted up to over 7000 and 9000 feet above sea level, and then eroded into wondrous ranks of pinnacles and points, steeples and spires, cliffs and crevices. And then there are the wondrous 'hoodoos.' These are phalanxes of oddly luminous stone towers that line up as if awaiting some kind of blessing. It's like Stonehenge rendered in a roseate stone that's incredibly variable in hue; a shaft of sunlight can suddenly transform the view from merely magnificent to otherworldly.

Orientation

Scenic Hwy 12 is the main paved road to Bryce Canyon and cuts across its northern portion. (There is no entrance fee for driving through this northern corner.) From Hwy 12 (14 miles east of Hwy 89) Hwy 63 heads south to the official park entrance, about 3 miles away. From here, an 18-mile dead-end drive continues along the rim of the canyon. Rim Rd climbs slowly past turnoffs to the

visitor center (at almost 8000 feet), the lodge, campgrounds, scenic viewpoints and trailheads, ending at Rainbow Point, 9115 feet above sea level. Trailers are allowed only as far as Sunset Campground, about 3 miles south of the entrance. Vehicles over 25 feet in length have access restrictions to Paria View in summer. Plans are in the works for a new shuttle system to cut down on parking and driving problems.

Information

The visitor center (*☎ 435-834-5322, fax 435-834-4102*) is the first main building along Hwy 63 after you officially enter the park. It is open 8 am to 4:30 pm daily (except New Year's Day, Thanksgiving and Christmas), with extended hours from late spring to early fall. Entrance to the park is $5 per person or $10 per private vehicle. Tickets are valid for seven days, and Golden Age, Eagle and Access Passports (see Facts for the Visitor) are honored. The entrance station and the visitor center provide free park maps and informative brochures.

When to Go The park is open year round, with the period of May to September seeing about 75% of the approximately 1.6 million annual visitors. Summer high temperatures at the 8000- to 9000-foot elevation of the rim may reach 80°F (26°C) – and even hotter below the rim – so carry water and sun protection. Summer nights have temperatures in the 40s. June is relatively dry, but July and August see sudden, but usually brief, torrential storms.

Snow blankets the ground from about November to April, but most of the park's roads remain open. A few are unplowed and designated for cross-country skiing or snowshoeing. The main Rim Rd is occasionally closed after heavy snow, but only until the plows have done their job. January is the slowest month.

Scenic Drives

Almost all visitors take all or part of the Rim Rd drive, normally in their own cars, although a shuttle system may be implemented soon.

Near the visitor center, short side roads go to several popular viewpoints overlooking the Bryce Amphitheater. Beyond, the Rim Rd passes half a dozen small parking areas and viewpoints on its way to Rainbow Point – all are worth a look.

Hiking & Backpacking

Views from the rim are superb, but you gain a completely different perspective during a hike, either along the rim or, better still, below it. Hikes below the rim descend for quite a way and the uphill return can be strenuous, so allow enough time and carry extra water. Also remember that most trails skirt steep drop-offs; if you suffer from fear of heights, these trails are not for you. During the July-August thunderstorm season, early morning departures are a good way to avoid the storms, which usually occur in the afternoon.

The easiest hike is along the **Rim Trail**, which is 5½ miles long (one way) and skirts the Bryce Amphitheater. It passes several viewpoints near the visitor center, so shorter sections can be hiked. The 1-mile section between the North Campground and Sunset Point is the most level.

One of the most popular trails below the rim is the ¾-mile trail from Sunrise Point, at 8000 feet, down to the **Queen's Garden**, 320 feet below. From here, you can either return the way you came or continue descending farther, connecting with the **Navajo Trail** for a more strenuous hike. These trails tend to be heavily used in summer and are among the few that may remain open even in winter.

One trail suitable even for those with a fear of heights is the mile-long **Whiteman Connecting Trail**, which leaves Rim Rd about 9 miles south of the visitor center. This trail follows an old dirt road that connects with the Under-the-Rim Trail; the descent is about 500 feet, and you return the way you came.

If you really want to get away from the crowds, shoulder a pack and get down below the rim for a night or two. There are 10 designated campsites, and most can accommodate up to six backpackers. Permits are $5. Backpackers must register at the visitor center. Park rangers will issue your permit, discuss your route, tell you where to find water and where camping is permitted. Note that campgrounds are primitive, without facilities – all water below the rim must be purified, no fires are allowed, and you must carry out *all* your trash.

From November to April, backcountry camping may be difficult because many trails are snow-covered and hard to find. But one or two campsites should be accessible even then – the rangers will know.

Organized Tours

Canyon Trail Rides (☎ 435-679-8665), PO Box 128, Tropic, UT 84776, operates horse or mule tours into the backcountry. Two-hour rides to the canyon floor are $25, half-day loop tours are $35. Bus tours along the park roads start at around $10. The Bryce Canyon Lodge (see Places to Stay & Eat) also has information – the tours start there. Comparably priced trail rides are offered by lodges outside the park.

Places to Stay & Eat

Inside the Park The Park Service operates *North Campground* near the visitor center and *Sunset Campground* about 1 mile south, both with toilets and drinking water. Sites are $10 and often fill up by noon in summer. Between the two campgrounds is a *General Store* for basic food, camping supplies – and coin-operated showers and laundry in summer. (See Outside the Park for places to shower in winter.)

The 1924 *Bryce Canyon Lodge* (☎ 435-834-5361, fax 435-834-5464), near the visitor center, is open April through October, with 120 units, a restaurant, coin laundry and rates from $80 to $115. Reservations (☎ 303-297-2757) are essential.

Outside the Park Bryce Central Reservations (☎ 800-462-7923) can find places to stay in the whole area.

The *Best Western Ruby's Inn & Campground* (☎ 435-834-5341, fax 435-834-5265) is a huge, popular and unrelentingly Western complex on Hwy 63, about 1 mile north of the park entrance. Facilities include a pool, spa, post office and coin laundry. Horse, bike and ski rentals are available. Open from April to October, the campground has 200 sites costing $14 (tents) and $22 (hookups) – its coin showers and laundry stay open all year. Pleasant rooms at the motel are $90 to $110 in summer (make reservations early), dropping to half that from January to March.

Pink Cliffs Village (☎ *435-834-5351, 800-834-0043, fax 435-834-5256)* is near the junction of Hwys 12 and 63, about 3 miles north of the park. It has an RV park, about 70 rooms, coin laundry, a pool and a restaurant and bar at prices a little lower than Ruby's Inn, but the facilities are much more modest. Dorm beds start at $15.

Other places to try are *Foster's Motel & Restaurant* (☎ *435-834-5227, fax 435-834-5304)*, on Hwy 12 a couple of miles west of the junction with Hwy 63, with simple but clean rooms and *Bryce Canyon Pines Motel & Campground* (☎ *435-834-5441, fax 435-834-5330)*, on Hwy 12 about 3 miles west of Hwy 63. Each has a restaurant and charges about $60 per room in summer, less in winter.

ZION NATIONAL PARK

Northeast of Kanab, Hwy 89 intersects with Hwy 9, which heads west into Zion National Park, where the white, pink and red rocks are so huge, overpowering and magnificent that they are at once a photographer's dream and despair. Few photos can do justice to the magnificent scenery found in this, the first national park established in Utah.

The highlight is Zion Canyon, a half-mile-deep slash formed by the Virgin River cutting through the sandstone. Tourists drive down the narrow paved road at the bottom, straining their necks to see the colorful vistas of looming cliffs, domes and mountains. So popular is this route that it has become severely overcrowded with vehicles, and the NPS is implementing a shuttle service in May 2000 to mitigate this problem, closing the scenic drive to motor vehicles in the summer months. Other scenic drives are less crowded and just as magnificent. If you have the time and energy, day and overnight hikes can take you into spectacularly wild country.

Orientation

Three roads enter the park. Hiking trails depart from all three, leading you farther into the splendor. At the southern end, the paved Zion-Mt Carmel Hwy (Hwy 9 between Mt Carmel Junction and Springdale) is the most popular route and leads past the entrance of Zion Canyon. This road has fine views, but it is also exceptionally steep, twisting and narrow. A mile-long tunnel on the east side of Zion Canyon is so narrow that RVs and other large vehicles must be escorted. A fee of $10 for the escort is collected as you enter the park where personnel will also arrange for a ranger to meet you. Most passenger cars do not require an escort. Bicycles are prohibited in the tunnel unless transported on a vehicle.

The main visitor center and campgrounds lie at the mouth of Zion Canyon; lodging is nearby, either in the canyon or Springdale. The elevation in Zion Canyon is about 4000 feet, and at the east entrance, 5700 feet.

For the middle of the park, paved **Kolob Terrace Rd** leaves Hwy 9 at the village of Virgin, about 30 miles west of the south entrance, climbs north to the Kolob Plateau for about 9 miles and then becomes gravel for a few more miles to Lava Point, where there is a ranger station and primitive campground. This road (closed by snow from about November to May) continues as a dirt road that becomes impassable after rain out of the park past Kolob Reservoir, to Hwy 14 and Cedar City.

At the north end, paved **Kolob Canyons Rd** leaves I-15 at exit 40 and extends 5 miles into the park. There is a visitor center (☎ 435-772-3256) at the beginning of the road, but no camping. The road climbs to more than 5000 feet, is open all year, and has several scenic lookouts over the Finger Canyon formations.

Information

The main visitor center (☎ 435-772-3256) is on Hwy 9 near the mouth of Zion Canyon, less than a mile from the south entrance near Springdale. A new visitor center near the south entrance of the park is scheduled for completion in May 2000. The smaller

Kolob Canyons Visitor Center (☎ 435-586-9548) is at the beginning of Kolob Canyons Rd. Both are open 8 am to 4:30 pm, with extended hours to 7 pm between Memorial Day and Labor Day.

Entrance to the park is $5 per person or $10 per private vehicle. Tickets are valid for seven days, and Golden Age, Eagle and Access Passports (see Facts for the Visitor) are accepted. The south and east entrance stations (at either end of the Zion-Mt Carmel Hwy) and the visitor centers provide park maps and informative brochures.

Starting in May 2000, Zion Canyon will only be accessible by a new shuttle bus service. The NPS also plans to extend the shuttle route through Springdale, enabling hotel guests to leave their cars at the hotel and ride all the way into the canyon.

When to Go From as early as March to as late as November, campgrounds may fill to capacity, often by late morning in high season. Almost half of the park's annual visitors arrive in the Memorial Day to Labor Day period, while only about 7% come between December and February.

Summer weather is hot (well over 100°F is common), so bring plenty of water and sun protection. Temperatures may drop to 60°F (15°C) at night, even in midsummer. Summers are generally dry, but from late July to early September, when the so-called monsoons – short but heavy rainstorms – occur.

There is snow in winter, but the main roads are plowed. Though it may freeze at night, daytime temperatures usually rise to about 50°F (10°C). Hikers climbing up from the roads will find colder and more wintry (snow and ice) conditions.

Spring weather is hard to predict – rainstorms and hot sunny spells are both likely. May is the peak of the wildflower blooming. Spring (and early summer) is also the peak of the bug season – bring insect repellent.

Fall is magnificent, with beautiful foliage colors peaking in September on the Kolob Plateau and October in Zion Canyon. By then, daytime weather is pleasantly hot and nights are in the 40s and 50s.

Zion Canyon

From the visitor center, it's 7 miles to the north end of the canyon. The narrow road follows the Virgin River, and the only places to stop are at nine parking areas; most have signed trailheads. In order of increasing difficulty, the best trails accessible from the Zion Canyon road are outlined in the following paragraphs. All have superb views. Distances listed below are one-way.

You can stroll along the paved **Pairus Trail**, which parallels the road for almost 2 miles from the Watchman Campground to the main park junction. Take an easy walk near the canyon's end along the paved and popular **Riverside Walk**, about a mile long, fairly flat and partly wheelchair-accessible. (You can continue farther along into the Narrows – see Backpacking.) The quarter-mile-long **Weeping Rock Trail** climbs 100 feet to a lovely area of moist hanging gardens. **Emerald Pools** can be reached by a mile-long paved trail or a shorter unpaved one climbing 200 feet to the lower pool; a shorter trail scrambles another 200 feet up to the upper pool. Swimming is not allowed here.

Hidden Canyon Trail has a few long drop-offs and climbs 750 feet in just over a mile to a narrow and shady canyon. **Angels Landing Trail** is 2½ miles with a 1500-foot elevation gain. Allow three to four hours roundtrip. There are steep and exposed drop-offs with chains to hold on to for security. Views are superb, but don't go if you're afraid of heights. **Observation Point Trail** is almost 4 miles long, with a 2150-foot elevation gain; it's less exposed than Angels Landing and offers great views too.

Note that all these trails can be slippery with snow or ice in winter or after heavy rain, so hike carefully in those conditions and ask park rangers for advice if you are unsure.

Zion-Mt Carmel Hwy

The road east of Zion Canyon is somewhat of an engineering feat, with switchbacks and a long tunnel (check the Orientation section for vehicle restrictions). East of the tunnel, the geology changes into slickrock, smooth gypsum with many carved and etched formations of which the mountainous Checkerboard Mesa is a memorable example. The road travels for about 10 miles from the Zion Canyon turnoff to the east exit of the park, with several parking areas along the road. Only one, just east of the mile-long tunnel, has a marked trail – the half-mile-long **Canyon Overlook Trail**, which climbs more than 100 feet and gives fine views into Zion Canyon, 1000 feet lower.

Backpacking

You can backpack and wilderness camp along the over 100 miles of trails in Zion. Starting from Lee Pass on the Kolob Canyons Rd in the north, you could backpack along a number of connected trails emerging at the east entrance of the park. This entire traverse of the park is about 50 miles. Park rangers can suggest a variety of shorter backpacking options.

The most famous backpacking trip is through the **Narrows** (also called the Zion Narrows) – a 16-mile journey through canyons along the North Fork of the Virgin River. In places, the canyon walls are only 20 feet apart and tower hundreds of feet above you. The hike requires wading (sometimes swimming) the river many times. The hike is usually done from Chamberlain's Ranch (on North Fork Road, which intersects Hwy 9 outside the east entrance to the park) to the Riverside Walk Trail at the north end of Zion Canyon, to allow hikers to move with the river current. The trip takes about 12 hours and camping for a night is recommended. This hike is limited to June to October and may be closed from late July to early September because of flash flood danger. The few miles at the north end of Zion Canyon can get crowded with hundreds of day hikers.

Backpackers require a permit ($5 per person per night) from either visitor center. Normally, these are issued the day before or the morning of the trip; problems with selecting a route are rare (although there may be a day or two wait for the Narrows). Camping is allowed except in restricted areas; ask a park ranger. Zion's springs and rivers flow year round but their water must be boiled or treated before drinking. Day hikers do not require a permit, with the exception of people venturing into the Narrows in one day.

Campfires are not allowed, so carry a camping stove or food that doesn't need to be cooked. Sun protection is essential – sunblock, hat, dark glasses and long sleeves. Insect repellent is priceless in spring and early summer.

Many backpacking trips require either retracing your footsteps or leaving a vehicle at either end of the trip. If you don't have two vehicles, a ride board at the main visitor center in Zion Canyon can connect you with other backpackers. Also, Zion Lodge (☎ 435-772-3213) has a shuttle desk and will arrange a ride for a fee.

Places to Stay & Eat

Between the south entrance and the main visitor center are two NPS campgrounds, **Watchman** (year round) and **South** (March to October) with water and toilets, but no showers. Sites are $10 (tents) and $14 (hookups) and may be reserved at ☎ 800-365-2267 or online at http://reservations .nps.gov. Some are available first come, first served and usually all are claimed by the afternoon.

Zion Lodge (☎ 435-772-3213, reservations at 303-297-2757, fax 435-772-2001), halfway up Zion Canyon, has motel rooms ($80 to $95) and cabins ($75 to $95), most with excellent views and porches. Book early – summer dates may fill up months ahead. The lodge's restaurants serve breakfast, lunch and dinner.

Outside the east entrance and 5 miles north from Hwy 9 on North Fork County Rd is the new **Zion Ponderosa Ranch Resort** (☎ 435-648-2700, 800-293-5444), with pool, hot tub, restaurant and a cornucopia of activities, including horseback riding, mountain biking and a climbing wall. Tent sites are $45 to $49; cowboy cabins with shared bath cost $49 to $89; and log cabins with private bath are $79 to $139. All rates are per person and include most activities. Spring and fall rates are lower. The resort is closed in January and February.

ZION NP TO LAS VEGAS

Twenty-eight miles after leaving the west entrance of Zion National Park, Hwy 9 intersects I-15. Heading south, I-15 leads to St George and, 8 miles farther, to the Arizona state line. Here, through an area known as the Arizona Strip, I-15 winds through some breathtaking canyons chiseled deep into red-rock slopes, taking you back to Las Vegas in about two hours.

Western Nevada

The western corner of the state is the birth-place of modern Nevada. It was the site of the first trading post, the first farms and the fabulous Comstock Lode, which spawned towns, financed the Union side in the Civil War and earned Nevada its statehood. This chapter covers the main towns of the area. Reno, and its neighbor Sparks, started as way stations for emigrants and grew to become centers of rail transport, entertainment, services and education. Virginia City was the scene of the big mining bonanza when the Comstock Lode was discovered. Carson City, the state capital, emerged from the orderly farming communities of the Carson Valley.

This part of Nevada is more densely settled than most of the state, and these days it seems more settled in character as well. Reno has not experienced the boomtown mentality of Las Vegas; Virginia City stopped booming a long time ago; and the other communities in Western Nevada have none of the Wild West rawness still extant in the towns of the Great Basin.

RENO
• population 164,000 • elevation 4500 feet

It's hard not to think of Reno as a little Las Vegas, although Reno has preserved a certain small-town charm. You can see people fishing in the city's Truckee River, and the university campus is positively serene. Reno repeatedly reminds you that it's 'The Biggest Little City in the World.' What they really mean is that it's a large country town with some big city characteristics.

The proliferation of gambling throughout the country has cost Reno some visitors in recent years. Its downtown casinos on Virginia St have lost some of their luster, and some have even been forced to close, making the street more like a Glowing Gully than a Glitter Gulch. To stem the tide, the city is completing an ambitious downtown redevelopment program with a state-of-the-art entertainment complex with a multiplex

Highlights

- National Automobile Museum in Reno – Dymaxion, Phantom Corsair, Beatnik Bandit and other quirky cars

- Genoa – Nevada's first European settlement, with a fascinating museum and soothing hot springs

- Virginia City – home of Mark Twain, the Comstock Lode and eccentric old-timey saloons

- Pyramid Lake – a gem in the desert, alive with cutthroat trout

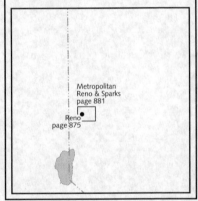

Metropolitan
Reno & Sparks
page 881

Reno
page 875

cinema, shops, galleries and restaurants built along the river.

If you want to gamble, the games inside the casinos are exactly the same as the ones in Las Vegas, and you're just as likely to lose your money. Reno is also a good base for trips into the scenic surrounding areas.

History

In the 1850s, travelers on the Humboldt Trail to California crossed the Truckee River at Truckee Meadows (where Reno now stands), followed the river up into the mountains north of Lake Tahoe and crossed the Sierra at Donner Pass – basically the route of today's

I-80. Several people established river crossings and charged tolls; the most enterprising of them, Myron Lake, also built a hotel, saloon and several miles of road to steer people to his bridge. When the mining boom started in Virginia City, Lake's crossing became a busy thoroughfare, and Lake became rich, acquiring most of the surrounding land.

When the Central Pacific Railroad came through, Lake offered to donate land for a town if the company would establish a passenger and freight depot. A deal was struck and, in May of 1868, lots were auctioned in a new town named after Jesse Reno, a Union general killed in the Civil War. In 1870, Reno became the seat of Washoe County, and in 1872 the Virginia & Truckee Railroad linked it to the boomtowns of the Comstock Lode. By 1900 Reno was a rough railroad town of 4500 people, though it had acquired a university, thanks to some generous mining magnates.

As the mining boom played out and most of Nevada stagnated, Reno made an economic virtue of social vices. Gambling and prostitution were frontier traditions that became attractions in Reno as they were suppressed in increasingly respectable California. During Prohibition, Reno not only tolerated the speakeasies, but became a place for mobsters to launder their money. The other major 'industry' was that of divorce, easily finalized after a short six-week residency requirement (see 'The Business of Divorce').

Irrigation in the Carson Valley, agriculture, light industry and warehousing have since helped to diversify the economy, along with tourism based on gambling and the attractions of Lake Tahoe and the region's history.

Orientation

The main highway to and from Reno is I-80, which heads west to Truckee (32 miles) and San Francisco and east to Salt Lake City. Hwy 395 heads south through Carson City (30 miles) and Bishop to Southern California. Carry snow chains during winter, especially if you're thinking of driving through the Sierra. For road conditions, call the Nevada Department of Transportation (☎ 775-793-1313).

Reno's main drag, with most of the casinos, is N Virginia St, north of the Truckee River. The landmark Reno Arch crosses Virginia St at Commercial Row, with the railroad tracks cutting through the town behind it. The sight of a giant freight train lumbering across the glittery stretch of casinos is one of Reno's wonderful incongruities (though you may not care for the air horns blasting throughout the night). S Virginia St runs several miles south of the river and has motels, malls, casinos and the Reno-Sparks Convention Center. I-80 cuts across the

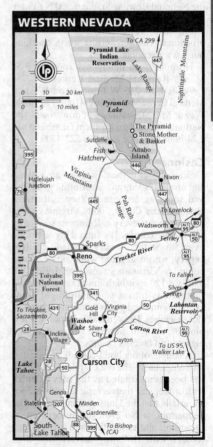

WESTERN NEVADA

To CA 299
Pyramid Lake Indian Reservation
Lake Range
Nightingale Mountains
447

0   10   20 km
0   5   10 miles

Pyramid Lake

The Pyramid
Stone Mother & Basket

Sutcliffe
Fish Hatchery
Anaho Island
446

Nixon
447

395

Virginia Mountains

Hallelujah Junction
70

445

Pah Rah Range

To Lovelock

Wadsworth
ALT 80
ALT 95

California

80
Sparks
Reno
Truckee River
Fernley
ALT 50
ALT 95

Toiyabe National Forest
395
341

To Fallon
Silver Springs
Lahontan Reservoir

To Truckee, Sacramento
431
Gold Hill
Virginia City
50
Carson River
ALT 95

28
Washoe Lake
Silver City
Dayton

Incline Village

To US 95, Walker Lake

Lake Tahoe
28
50
Carson City

Genoa

Stateline
207
Minden
Gardnerville

South Lake Tahoe
88
395
To Bishop (CA)

north side of the downtown area, heading east to Sparks. The University of Nevada campus is just north of the interstate.

One pleasant downtown feature is Riverwalk, a pedestrian path that follows the Truckee River the whole width of downtown, from the National Automobile Museum in the east to beyond Idlewild Park in the west.

Information

Reno's downtown visitor center (☎ 775-827-7366, 800-367-7366, fax 775-827-7713, www.playreno.com) is a desk in the lobby of the National Bowling Stadium, 300 N Center St. It's open 9 am to 5 pm daily and has an enthusiastic volunteer staff and lots of brochures. Another website worth checking out is www.renotahoe.com.

Hospitals with emergency rooms are St Mary's Regional Medical Center (☎ 775-789-3060), at 235 W 6th St, and Washoe Medical Center (☎ 775-982-4100), 77 Pringle Way at Mill St, southeast of downtown. The National Council on Problem Gambling has a 24-hour help line at ☎ 800-522-4700.

Casinos

Casinos cluster in the downtown area, along and around N Virginia St, offering gambling and some entertainment (see Entertainment). **Circus Circus**, 500 N Virginia St, has free circus acts every half-hour or so, like its Las Vegas cousin. It's linked by a bridge over 5th St to the very Vegas-like **Silver Legacy**, whose gigantic white dome looms behind a Victorian streetscape. Inside the ball is a 120-foot-high imitation mining rig that erupts into a sound-and-light show every 2 hours and pours coins into a bank of slot machines. The venerable **Harrah's**, a few blocks south of here, is still one of the biggest and fanciest casinos.

A couple of big hotel-casinos are located on S Virginia St. The old Clarion, at No 3800, has been reincarnated as the ritzy **Atlantis**, with a tropical theme replete with indoor waterfalls, thatched huts and palm trees. The **Peppermill**, at No 2707, just underwent an expansion and renovation and attracts customers with titillating advertising, then

blows them away with psychedelic decor. Two new restaurants here were designed by the team that worked on the *X-Files* and *Godzilla*.

Some 7 miles west on I-80 is **Boomtown**, a hotel-casino that began as a humble truck stop in 1954 and may yet grow into the area's newest megacomplex. Groundbreaking for a 2000-room tower is set for 2000. For now, Boomtown caters primarily to families with its Western theme and huge 'fun center' of arcade games and motion simulator rides. The Reno-Tahoe Gaming Academy (☎ 775-329-5665), 300 E 1st St, offers a two-hour inside view at the gambling business, with an introduction to the main casino games for $15.

National Automobile Museum

For anyone even slightly into cars, or social history, this museum is a must. A great number and variety of perfectly restored vehicles are on display, informatively labeled and shown in settings that convey something of their era and social context. The collection includes some one-of-a-kind, custom-built and experimental vehicles, such as Buckminster Fuller's 1934 Dymaxion, a 1938 Phantom Corsair that looks like a Batmobile prototype, and Ed Roth's 1961 Beatnik Bandit. Old advertisements, fashions, touring maps and other automotive memorabilia help fill out the picture. You can even dress up in 1930s gear and be photographed behind the wheel of an old

Ed Roth's Beatnik Bandit

classic. There's also a multimedia presentation, though we advise skipping it if you don't have much time.

The museum (☎ 775-333-9300) is at 10 Lake St, on the south bank of the Truckee River, an easy walk from downtown. Hours are 9:30 am to 5:30 pm daily (Sunday 10 am to 4 pm); $7.50/2.50 adults/children (ages six to 18).

National Bowling Stadium

Pundits have called it the 'Taj Mahal of Tenpins,' and to bowling aficionados, Reno's

National Bowling Stadium (☎ 775-334-2695), 300 N Center St, is definitely worth a pilgrimage. One of Reno's most recent downtown developments, this blue-collar palace hosts major televised pro and amateur bowling competitions, although there's no public play. The 363,000-sq-foot facility has 78 lanes and a small spectator stage. The Reno visitor center is in the complex lobby, and the dome houses a four-story IMAX-style theater with movies costing $6 for adults, $4 for children 12 and under and seniors over 60.

WESTERN NEVADA

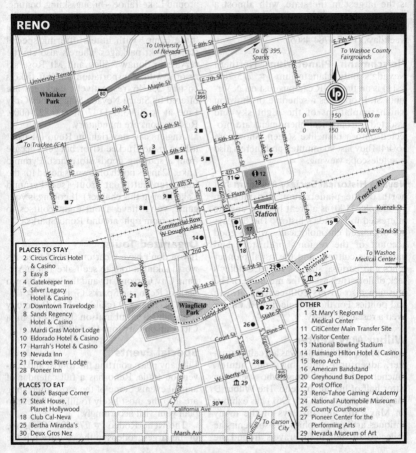

RENO

PLACES TO STAY
2   Circus Circus Hotel & Casino
3   Easy 8
4   Gatekeeper Inn
5   Silver Legacy Hotel & Casino
7   Downtown Travelodge
8   Sands Regency Hotel & Casino
9   Mardi Gras Motor Lodge
10 Eldorado Hotel & Casino
17 Harrah's Hotel & Casino
19 Nevada Inn
21 Truckee River Lodge
28 Pioneer Inn

PLACES TO EAT
6   Louis' Basque Corner
17 Steak House, Planet Hollywood
18 Club Cal-Neva
25 Bertha Miranda's
30 Deux Gros Nez

OTHER
1   St Mary's Regional Medical Center
11 CitiCenter Main Transfer Site
12 Visitor Center
13 National Bowling Stadium
14 Flamingo Hilton Hotel & Casino
15 Reno Arch
16 American Bandstand
20 Greyhound Bus Depot
22 Post Office
23 Reno-Tahoe Gaming Academy
24 National Automobile Museum
26 County Courthouse
27 Pioneer Center for the Performing Arts
29 Nevada Museum of Art

Nevada Museum of Art

You'll find contemporary works, Native American baskets and temporary exhibitions at this museum (☎ 775-329-3333), 160 W Liberty St. It's open 10 am to 4 pm Tuesday, Wednesday, Friday; 10 am to 7 pm Thursday; and noon to 4 pm weekends; $3/1.50, free on Friday.

University of Nevada, Reno

Founded in 1874, the University of Nevada at Reno (UNR) has some 12,500 students enrolled in 10 schools and colleges, including the Mackay School of Mines. UNR's library is the largest in the state, with almost a million volumes. Tours of the sprawling campus are offered at 10 am, noon and 3 pm weekdays (☎ 775-784-4865).

Fleischmann Planetarium Northern Nevada's only planetarium (☎ 775-784-4811) is on the UNR campus, just off N Virginia St. It operates a schedule of shows in which simulations of the night sky and assorted astronomical phenomena are projected onto a domelike screen. Shows are $6/4/4. They last 90 minutes, and there's also free telescope viewing.

Nevada Historical Society Museum Just north of the planetarium, this museum (☎ 775-688-1190) is a great find for anyone interested in Nevada's history. The displays are organized chronologically, with a good account of the region's prehistory and indigenous cultures, and the usual pioneer relics and curiosa, such as Reuel Gridley's sack of flour (just ask at the museum...). The museum also covers 20th-century growth and politics. For the truly dedicated, there's even a research library.

Wilbur May Center

Wilbur May (1898-1982) was a wealthy traveler, adventurer, pilot, big game hunter, rancher and philanthropist who spent the latter half of his life in Reno. The **Wilbur D May Museum** (☎ 775-785-5961) has exhibits on May's life and displays of the many antiques, artifacts, trophies and souvenirs he collected, or shot, in his travels around the world. It's great if you have a taste for the eclectic and aren't turned off by taxidermy. Nearby, the **arboretum** has outdoor gardens, with a collection of Great Basin desert plants and an indoor tropical garden. The **Great Basin Adventure** is a children's fun park with log rides and a petting zoo. The center is located in Rancho San Rafael Park and is open 10 am to 5 pm Tuesday to Saturday (Wednesday to Saturday in winter) and from noon on Sunday; $4/3.

Activities

For details on outdoor activities on and around Lake Tahoe – hiking, skiing, boating, fishing, etc – see the Sierra Nevada chapter. Reno is heavily promoting itself as a skiing 'base camp,' with hotels offering special stay-and-ski packages. There's also shuttle service to Squaw Valley and Mt Rose ski resorts, with transportation and lift tickets costing $53/46, respectively. Packages are offered by Sierra Nevada Stage Lines/Gray Line at ☎ 702-331-1147 or 800-822-6009. Reservations are mandatory.

Anglers can stay right in Reno for trout fishing in the Truckee River, but get a license from a sporting goods store first. Pyramid Lake, 32 miles north of town, is noted for the Lahontan cutthroat trout (see Pyramid Lake later in this chapter). If golfing is your game, you'll have about eight courses to choose from right around Reno/Sparks.

Organized Tours

If you don't have a car or a lot of time, it's worth taking a tour to see Lake Tahoe, Virginia City, Carson City and the lesser known parts of Reno and Sparks. Gray Line (☎ 775-331-1147) has $30 (children $15) Reno city tours and a combination Tahoe-Virginia City-Carson City tour for $49/39.

Special Events

Like any place courting the tourist and convention trade, Reno has a full calendar of annual events. Some of the most interesting are also the most likely to fill the hotels, so plan your visit accordingly.

The Reno Rodeo (☎ 775-329-3877), one of the largest rodeos in the country, fills the

Livestock Events Center every June with bucking broncos and bruised cowpokes. Hot August Nights (☎ 775-356-1946) is the summer's next big happening, with parades and concerts celebrating the cars and music of the 1950s and '60s. The Livestock Events Center again heats up in late August as the Nevada State Fair (☎ 775-688-5767) brings back that good old country fair fun, with rides, games and livestock events. In mid-September, the National Championship Air Races (☎ 775-972-6663) – the world's longest running air race – rounds out Reno's events season with races in four classes, aerobatics and military jet displays. It all happens at the Stead Airport, northwest of downtown.

Places to Stay

Bargains in quality accommodations are often available in Reno, though not on weekends and not during major events. Book ahead if you can; the visitor center gives referrals and advice. A notice board at the Greyhound bus station advertises cheaper rates than the hotels offer at the front desk. There's a free phone connection in the station, and the hotel might even send someone to get you.

Camping Just 1 mile west of downtown, ***Keystone RV Park*** *(☎ 775-324-5000, 1455 W 4th St)* is the most convenient. It has 101 sites and is next to a large shopping center. The next nearest campgrounds are all about 20 miles away. ***Davis Creek Park*** *(☎ 775-849-0684)* is south on Hwy 395 and has 63 tent and trailer sites. ***Mt Rose Campground*** *(☎ 800-280-2267)*, southeast of town on SR 431, is open July to mid-September only.

Hotels & Motels Many downtown motels, such as the Mizpah Hotel and Windsor Hotel, though cheap, rent rooms by the week or month to transients and unsavory characters and should generally be avoided. One of the cheapest places that offers both clean rooms and overall safety is the ***Gatekeeper Inn*** *(☎ 775-786-3500, 800-822-3504, 221 5th St)*, where $28 buys the proverbial roof over the head. Another option, with rates starting at

The Business of Divorce

When times are tough, morality goes out the window. That was certainly the case in 1931 when Nevada lawmakers – trying to ride out the aftermath of the Great Depression – laid the groundwork for a new, most bizarre 'industry': divorce. Nevada had always had liberal divorce laws, but in 1931 residency requirements plunged to an unprecedented six weeks. This met a definite demand among residents of other states and, seemingly overnight, divorce became big business. In the first year alone, about 5000 couples came to take the 'six-week cure.' Reno, especially, captured front pages and gossip columns nationwide with dozens of scandalous celebrity divorces.

It was common for the unhappily married couple to arrange a six-week 'holiday' in Nevada, filling hotels with would-be divorcees, often with their new partners staying in the same place. Some hotels and resorts specialized in the divorce trade, like the Floyd Lamb Ranch near Las Vegas and the Riverside Hotel in Reno. They provided not only comfortable accommodations and plenty of diversions, but also enough discretion to leave everything to the fertile imagination of the gossip columnists.

$30, is the 30-room ***Mardi Gras Motor Lodge*** *(☎ 775-329-7470, 200 W 4th St)*. The riverside ***Nevada Inn*** *(☎ 775-323-1005, 800-999-9686, 330 E 2nd St)* even has a small pool and charges $30 to $80 for a room. Nonsmokers will prefer the ***Truckee River Lodge*** *(☎ 775-786-8888, 800-635-8950, fax 775-348-4769, 501 W 1st St)*, which also offers bike rentals ($20 per day); rooms start at $34.

There are plenty of chain motels too, including five ***Motel 6*** branches, the ***Easy 8 Motel*** *(☎ 775-322-4588, 255 W 5th St)*, ***Days Inn*** *(☎ 775-786-4070, 701 E 7th St)* and the ***Downtown Travelodge*** *(☎ 775-329-3451, 655 W 4th St)*. Expect to pay $40 or less for a room at any these places, though the Downtown Travelodge may occasionally charge up to $60.

If you can afford to spend more, one hotel getting kudos from locals is the *University Inn* (☎ 775-323-0321, fax 775-323-2929, 570 N Virginia St), west of UNR. It's quiet, friendly and has newly renovated rooms costing $60 to $125, with all the standard amenities.

Casinos Rates at the big hotel-casinos fluctuate with demand. It may pay off to call the visitor center or some establishments directly.

Next to the county courthouse, the *Pioneer Inn* (☎ 775-324-7777, 800-648-5468, fax 775-323-5343, 221 S Virginia St) is a smaller property with 253 rooms costing from $38 to $65.

South of downtown, near the convention center, is *Atlantis* (☎ 775-825-4700, 800-723-6500, fax 775-825-1170, 3800 S Virginia St) which offers free 24-hour valet service, an outdoor pool, health club, spa and sundeck. Rooms, 1000 in all, start at $49, with suites costing as much as $159.

Nearby is the *Peppermill* (☎ 775-826-2121, 800-648-6992, fax 775-826-5205, 2707 S Virginia St), which has a neat outdoor pool with a faux mountainscape and a waterfall. Rates here start at $49, though the top suite costs $500.

Back in downtown, the *Sands Regency* (☎ 775-348-2200, 800-648-3553, fax 775-348-2226, 345 N Arlington Ave) counts a penthouse health club among its features and also has rooms from $49.

The gigantic *Circus Circus* (☎ 775-329-0711, 800-648-5010, fax 775-329-0599, 500 N Sierra St) has been a Reno institution for more than two decades and recently traded its garish pink facade for a more subdued gold, green and maroon look. Each of the rooms reflects the place's turn-of-the-century circus theme and features coffeemakers and data ports among its amenities. Rates start at $59.

The *Eldorado* (☎ 775-786-5700, 800-648-5966, fax 775-348-7513, 345 N Virginia St), a 836-room tower with eight restaurants, is

family-owned and operated. The mezzanine level features ceiling murals, arched walkways, columns and the Fountain of Fortune, a bronze-and-marble kitsch fantasy. Rooms may occasionally be available for $40, though you're more likely to pay $60 to $80.

One of the most entertaining places in town is the *Silver Legacy* (☎ 775-329-4777, 800-687-8733, fax 775-325-7177, 407 N Virginia St), built atop an actual silver mine discovered by Sam Fairchild in the 1850s. Rooms range from a reasonable $49 to $119.

The top place in town is *Harrah's* (☎ 775-786-3232, 800-427-7247, fax 775-788-2644, 219 N Center St), in business since 1937. Signature amenities include a big health club and rooms with coffeemakers, irons, ironing boards and Nintendo; 50% are nonsmoking. Rates start at $79.

Fantasy Motels Maybe it's an extension of the wedding and divorce industries, but several motels in Reno specialize in 'exotic' rooms with themes, such as the Roman room, bordello room, Oriental suite or luxury cave. If you've ever fancied experiencing *it* on a zebra-skin rug, circular bed, heart-shaped spa or in the back seat of a 1958 Chevrolet, this might be your chance. Try the *Romance Inn* (☎ 775-826-1515, 800-662-8812, fax 775-826-4114, 2905 S Virginia St), where rooms cost $69 to $140 weekdays, $110 to $180 weekends. Farther south is the *Adventure Inn* (☎ 775-828-9000, 800-937-1436, fax 775-825-8333, 3575 S Virginia St), which charges from $59 weekdays for the jungle room to $235 for a Saturday night in the Super Ocean Suite, waterfall included.

Places to Eat

Reno has lots of good eateries, though people looking for cutting-edge cuisine and top-notch chefs may have to go elsewhere. Budget-minded travelers, though, have plenty to choose from, including the casinos' all-you-can-eat buffets, which are a good deal, especially if you're really hungry. *Circus Circus* (☎ 775-329-0711, 500 N Sierra St) has the least expensive buffet, though it's worth spending a little more for the better quality and selection offered at the *Eldorado* (☎ 775-786-5700, *345 N Virginia St*), *Silver Legacy* (☎ 775-329-4777, *407 N Virginia St*) and *Peppermill* (☎ 775-826-2121, *2707 S Virginia St*).

The *Club Cal-Neva* (☎ 775-323-1046), Virginia at 2nd St, has a 99¢ breakfast, an all-night food court and steak specials in between. *Twisted Chimney* (☎ 775-323-2277, *1305 N Virginia St*) is a popular student hangout just west of the campus, on N Virginia St at College. Also popular with young people for its pizza and beer is *Breakaway* (☎ 775-324-6200, *10 E 9th St*).

The *Blue Heron* (☎ 775-786-4110, *1091 S Virginia*) is a reasonably priced vegetarian and health food restaurant, with substantial servings. *Einstein's Quantum Cafe* (☎ 775-825-6611, *6135 Lakeside Drive*) is another welcome addition to Reno's vegetarian circuit.

Deux Gros Nez (☎ 775-786-9400), French for 'two big noses,' is a Reno institution, a uniquely decorated coffeehouse, upstairs at 249 California Ave. Another winner is *Louis' Basque Corner* (☎ 775-323-7203, *301 E 4th St*), where you need a huge appetite but not a huge wallet. About $16 buys a full dinner, with soup, salad, two courses and side dishes, one glass of wine or nonalcoholic drink and ice cream. For the alcoholic equivalent of crack cocaine, order a 'picon.' But stand up frequently to check your mobility between rounds and *do not* start talking about politics or religion.

Fans of megaportions should also try the family-owned *Bertha Miranda's* (☎ 775-786-9697, *336 Mill St*), across from the National Automobile Museum, for terrific Mexican food in authentic surroundings at budget prices.

Some of Reno's better eateries are at the casinos. Peppermill has the *White Orchid* (☎ 775-826-2121), distinguished by an extensive wine list and a sophisticated menu of fine continental dishes, many priced under $20. If you like a clubby atmosphere, excellent service and food – and are willing and able to pay for it – head to the *Steak House* (☎ 775-786-3232) at Harrah's, a classy dining establishment favored by Reno's old money.

Reservations are recommended. For those preferring more jazzy surroundings, there's always *Planet Hollywood* (☎ 775-323-7837), also at Harrah's.

Entertainment

Reno doesn't have the excessively slick glitz of Las Vegas, but there's plenty here to keep you entertained. Free papers such as *Reno/Tahoe Showtime* and *Best Bets* list current schedules.

Major casino showrooms include that of *Harrah's* (☎ 775-788-3773, *219 N Center St*), which has Sammy's Showroom, named in honor of Sammy Davis Jr, who performed here 40 times between 1967 and 1989. It hosts theme shows (*Cirque Berserk,* a spoof on traditional circus acts, is a recent example), as well as *Skintight,* Reno's only adult revue ($21.95).

The *Reno Hilton* (☎ 775-789-2285, *2500 E 2nd St*) hosts variety shows at its Hilton Showroom (average entry $25), headliners at its Outdoor Amphitheatre (from $30) and stand-up comedians at its Improv Comedy Club ($15.35 to $17.55).

In Sparks, *John Ascuaga's Nugget* (☎ 775-356-3304, *1100 Nugget Ave*) is a behemoth anchoring the south side of Victoria Square. Big headliners like Tony Bennett appear at its 2000-seat Rose Ballroom; lesser stars have to make do with the Celebrity Showroom (800 seats).

Other major showrooms are at the *Flamingo Hilton* (☎ 775-322-1111, *225 N Sierra St*) and the *Eldorado* (☎ 775-786-5700, *345 N Virginia St*).

Nightclubbers could check the fairly classy dance scene at *Atlantis Casino* (☎ 775-825-4700). *Hacienda Restaurant & Bar* (☎ 775-746-2228, *10580 N McCarran*) has good live music, as does the *Great Basin Brewing Company* (☎ 775-355-7711, *846 Victorian Ave*) in Sparks.

Reno also has seasons of ballet, orchestral music, opera, jazz and theater. Most performances take place at the Pioneer Center for the Performing Arts, at the corner of S Virginia and Court Sts. Call the Sierra Arts Foundation (☎ 775-329-1324) to find out what's on.

Getting There & Away

Air Reno-Tahoe International Airport (☎ 775-328-6400) is 5 miles southeast of downtown. Direct flights go mostly to the West Coast, but also to Dallas, Denver and Chicago. The cheapest airlines serving Reno-Tahoe are Reno Air and Southwest, though special flight/hotel packages may offer the best deals.

Other airlines serving Reno are Alaska, America West, American, Canadian Air, Delta, Northwest, Skywest, TWA and United.

For details about the airport at South Lake Tahoe, see the Sierra Nevada chapter.

Bus The Greyhound station (☎ 775-322-2970) is at 155 Stevenson St and has regular departures to Sacramento ($20) and San Francisco ($32). A direct bus leaves for Los Angeles ($50) once daily. Buses also go to and from Las Vegas and Salt Lake City.

Train The Amtrak station (☎ 775-329-8638) is at 135 E Commercial Row. Trains headed for Sacramento ($52) and San Francisco ($58) depart daily in the afternoon.

Getting Around

To/From the Airport RTC bus No 24 runs between Reno-Tahoe airport and downtown. The larger hotels offer free shuttle service. The Tahoe Casino Express is a regular shuttle service (☎ 800-446-6128) to the South Lake Tahoe airport.

Bus The RTC Citifare bus system (☎ 775-348-7433) covers most of the metropolitan area. Routes generally converge at the Citi-Center Main Transfer Site downtown, which also has an information booth. Fares are $1.25 (exact change required) and transfers are free. Some routes operate Monday to Saturday 7 am to 7 pm, but others have more restricted hours. Useful routes include No 7 (for the university), No 19 (for the Greyhound station) and No 24 (for the airport).

Car All the main rental agencies are here, including Alamo, Budget, Dollar, Enterprise, Hertz and Thrifty. Most are based at the airport.

AROUND RENO
Sparks

• **population 61,400** • **elevation 4500 feet**

Though Reno and Sparks are now virtually a continuous urban area, Sparks is actually a separate city. It was established in 1901 as a railroad maintenance depot and switching yard and resisted Reno-style casinos and vice...at least until the 1950s when the railroad pulled out. Sparks grew quickly in the 1960s and '70s as a warehousing and light industrial center, with gambling as a minor attraction.

Serious efforts to attract visitors are quite recent and have focused on the development of **Victorian Square**. This four-block strip in the center of Sparks, next to I-80, has been remodeled in a pseudo-Victorian style. It has casinos, restaurants, shops and plenty of parking. Interesting at night for its colored lights, it feels more like a shopping mall parking lot in the daytime. In 1998 a 14-screen multiplex cinema was added, as were more stores and restaurants. Another feature is a 30-foot fountain with water shows choreographed to music daily from 11 am to 11 pm.

The **Sparks Museum** (☎ 775-355-1144), 820 Victorian Ave, has exhibits from the early 20th century, including a replica barber shop, vintage model trains and farm and ranch equipment.

Sparks' biggest summer attraction is the **Wild Island** water park (☎ 775-331-9453), north on Sparks Blvd off I-80, east of town. It's open 11 am to 7 pm daily; $15/11 adults/children. Airplane buffs might enjoy the **National Air Race Museum**, 1570 Hymer St, with some full-size planes and lots of models.

Pyramid Lake

A beautiful blue expanse in the high desert, about 30 miles north of Reno, Pyramid Lake is popular for recreation and fishing. The lakeshore was inhabited as early as 11,000 years ago, and the seminomadic Paiute tribe visited the lake annually to powwow and to harvest fish congregating for their spawning run up the Truckee River. In 1843, explorer John Frémont

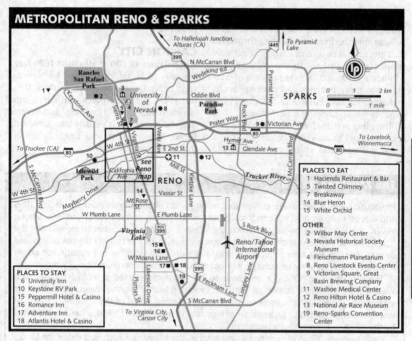

METROPOLITAN RENO & SPARKS

To Hallelujah Junction, Alturas (CA)

To Pyramid Lake

N McCarran Blvd

Wedekind Rd

SPARKS

Rancho San Rafael Park

University of Nevada

Oddie Blvd

Paradise Park

Prater Way

Victorian Ave

To Lovelock, Winnemucca

To Truckee (CA)

Idlewild Park

Hymer Ave

Glendale Ave

RENO

Mayberry Drive

W Plumb Lane

E Plumb Lane

Mt Rose St

Vassar St

Virginia Lake

Reno/Tahoe International Airport

W Moana Lane

To Virginia City, Carson City

PLACES TO STAY
6 University Inn
10 Keystone RV Park
15 Peppermill Hotel & Casino
16 Romance Inn
17 Adventure Inn
18 Atlantis Hotel & Casino

PLACES TO EAT
1 Hacienda Restaurant & Bar
5 Twisted Chimney
7 Breakaway
14 Blue Heron
15 White Orchid

OTHER
2 Wilbur May Center
3 Nevada Historical Society Museum
4 Fleischmann Planetarium
8 Reno Livestock Events Center
9 Victorian Square, Great Basin Brewing Company
11 Washoe Medical Center
12 Reno Hilton Hotel & Casino
13 National Air Race Museum
19 Reno-Sparks Convention Center

WESTERN NEVADA

---

named the lake for the small island he thought resembled the Pyramid of Cheops.

The great Paiute chief Winnemucca negotiated treaties with the European settlers as early as 1855, but two bloody conflicts occurred in 1860. In 1874, Pyramid Lake and the surrounding lands were declared an Indian reservation, though settlers and the railroad companies still managed to acquire portions of the best land. Truckee River water, which had always replenished the lake, was also siphoned off for irrigation, lowering the water level by more than 100 feet.

For modern anglers, the most prized catch is the Lahontan cutthroat trout (in fact, a type of salmon), which can grow up to 40 pounds and has the honor of being Nevada's state fish. Along with the endemic cui-cui, another remnant from ancient Lake Lahontan, the cutthroat trout has suffered a disastrous decline in numbers because of environmental changes, such as dams interfering with their spawning runs. Since the 1970s, efforts have been made to restore the environment of the lake and to stock it with fish spawned in hatcheries. The number and size of the fish have been improving.

The usual entry to the Pyramid Lake Paiute Indian Reservation is off Hwy 445 from Sparks; the boundary is near the Pyramid Lake Store, 23 miles from Sparks. Some 5 miles farther north is **Sutcliffe**, where you can get supplies, and permits for camping, fishing and boating from the ranger station/visitor center (☎ 775-476-1155/56). You can stay at **Crosby's Lodge** (☎ 775-476-0400), which has nine rooms costing $30 to $80. There's a developed campground, with facilities, next to the ranger station in the Sutcliffe marina, but camping is allowed in most places around the lake. Pick up a permit ($5 per person, per night) from the ranger station. Visit the **fish hatchery** to see exhibits about the lake and the Paiute fish-breeding program. Across the lake, you can see Anaho Island, a sanctuary for the American white pelican, and the Pyramid, the tufa formation that gives the lake its name. The distinctively shaped rocks just south are called Stone Mother and Basket. The area north of Sutcliffe has more beaches and camping areas, including Pelican Point and Warrior Point, beaches where camping is permitted.

Traveling south along the lakeshore will take you past more sandy beaches and to a tribal museum and visitor center near the village of **Nixon**, the site of the Paiute tribal headquarters.

CARSON CITY
• **population 43,600** • **elevation 4600 feet**
It's easy to be underwhelmed by Nevada's state capital, some 30 miles south of Reno, but it's a pleasant place, with tree-lined streets, handsome old buildings and a couple of good museums. It's easily accessible from Reno, Virginia City and Lake Tahoe and makes a good day trip.

WESTERN NEVADA

The Mustang Ranch

Prostitution was a fact of life in Nevada's mining and railroad camps from the earliest days and was officially ignored in Reno throughout the notoriously corrupt 1920s and '30s. During WWII, the War Department compelled the Washoe County authorities to close down the 'cribs' in Reno's Lake St and Riverside red-light districts, mainly to counter the risk of venereal disease. For the first time prostitution was made officially illegal in the county, but not in response to any local moral outrage, nor out of concern for the exploitation of women.

Then, in the mid-1950s, a man named Joe Conforte started a mobile brothel near Wadsworth, where the corners of Washoe, Lyon and Storey counties meet. He shifted the establishment between the three counties, always staying ahead of the authorities (some of whom were persuaded to be less than enthusiastic in pursuit) until 1960, when he was jailed by the Washoe County district attorney.

On his release, Conforte opened a new brothel, the Mustang Ranch, just inside the Storey County line. He paid his local taxes, paid off the authorities and campaigned for changes in the law. By 1971 the Mustang Ranch was the biggest taxpayer in Storey County, and the county commissioners passed an ordinance making brothels (or at least Conforte's brothel) legal. It was the first such ordinance in the US.

After several years of legal and lucrative operation, Conforte acquired a new enemy. The IRS pursued him for over a decade on charges of income tax evasion. In 1990, with Conforte owing over $10 million in back taxes, the brothel was declared bankrupt. Conforte fled to South America; the IRS seized the brothel and put it up for auction: a 300-acre ranch, with offices, living quarters, catering facilities, a fancy lobby, large bar and 100 bedrooms, each with bathroom, bidet and fancy decor. It was acquired for the bargain price of $2.5 million by a consortium that – unbeknownst to the government – consisted of several FOCs (Friends of Conforte), who promptly appointed Conforte as manager in absentia.

Keeping Conforte fed and happy in South America apparently required some 'official' help. It came in the person of Shirley Colletti, a former county commissioner who, for years, collaborated with the consortium to pump prostitutes' proceeds to Conforte at his hideout. In July 1999, a federal jury found her guilty of 12 charges, including two counts of racketeering. Ms Colletti's political future is an uncertain one: most probably it will include her being the guest of the federal government in *very* secure surroundings for years to come.

Meanwhile, the feds are once again the landlords of Nevada's most notorious whorehouse, closing it down in late summer of 1999. The locals, though, aren't betting that the Mustang Ranch will remain that way. Stay tuned!

History

Carson City was created almost solely by the initiative of New York businessman Abe Curry, who envisioned the site as a state capital before Nevada was even a state. With a mixture of vision, business acumen and civic generosity, he acquired the land in 1858, had the town site plotted and set aside four blocks for a capitol building. The city was named after frontiersman Kit Carson, or perhaps for the Carson Valley (which, in any case, was named after Kit Carson, the scout for John Frémont's 1844 expedition).

With the discovery of gold and silver in the nearby hills, Carson City became a busy way station on the route to the mines, growing to more than 500 people within two years. In 1861, it was selected as the capital of the Nevada Territory, and Curry provided, free of charge, a building in which the territorial assembly could meet. When Nevada gained statehood in 1864, Carson City became its capital. A short railway line to the mining boomtown Virginia City was completed in 1869 and soon extended to Reno, giving Carson City a small industrial base and a rail link to the rest of the country.

The rail link enabled Carson City to benefit from the mining booms at Tonopah and Goldfield, and the government bureaucracy provided an ongoing economic base. Nevertheless, Carson City stagnated with the rest of the state as the mining booms played out. Its population plunged to 2000 during the Great Depression, but benefiting from the liberalization of gambling and divorce laws, Carson City grew again in the 1930s and '40s. It recovered strongly after WWII, because of burgeoning government services and growth in the Carson Valley and Lake Tahoe regions.

Orientation

Carson City straddles Hwy 395, the main road to and from Reno in the north. It's also the town's main drag, called Carson St within city boundaries. Hwy 50 from Virginia City comes into town as Williams St. The street layout is a straightforward grid, and most of the motels, restaurants, casinos and public buildings are along Carson St, south of Williams.

Information

The Carson City Chamber of Commerce (☎ 775-882-1565, fax 775-882-4179), 1900 S Carson St, is open 8 am to 5 pm weekdays and 10 am to 3 pm weekends. The Convention & Visitors' Bureau (☎ 775-687-7410, 800-638-2321, fax 775-687-7416, www.carson-city.org) is at 1900 S Carson St, Suite 200. Both offices have a free map of town that plots a 2½-mile walking tour past historic buildings. For more in-depth information, pick up the *Kit Carson Trail Map* ($2.50), a full-color, illustrated historical guide. In summer, guided tours leave Saturday at 10 am from the Nevada State Museum.

Carson City also has a 'Talking Houses' program, in which about two dozen of the historic structures broadcast information about their past over AM radio; simply tune in to the frequency posted outside each house.

Capitol Building & Museum

The Nevada State Capitol was built in 1857, complete with a silver-covered dome symbolizing its 'Silver State' status. New legislative chambers were completed in 1913, and the original senate chamber now houses a museum of Nevada's state souvenirs. The old assembly chamber has an exhibit on the USS *Nevada* battleship. Both the capitol and the museum (☎ 775-687-4810), 101 N Carson St, are open 8 am to 5 pm daily; free. The modern structures just south of here house the state assembly and the state supreme court. The state archive building is also here.

Nevada State Museum

Built in 1869 as a branch of the US Mint, this sandstone building looks suitably solid. It closed as a mint in 1893 and reopened as a museum in 1941. Its galleries have fine exhibits on many aspects of the state, as well as the coin press from the original mint and examples of every coin it ever produced.

The Earth Science Gallery explores the area's geologic history and recreates in miniature the Devonian sea that once covered much of Nevada. The museum is especially proud of its basket collection by Washo master weaver Dat-So-La-Lee. Other highlights include a gigantic imperial mammoth and the silver service from the USS *Nevada*, made from locally mined silver. Also worth a closer look are the Ethnology and Archaeology galleries, with dioramas depicting Indian life in the Great Basin, though you haven't seen it all until you've checked out the mummified cat, one of the museum's more bizarre exhibits.

The excellent museum bookstore has tomes on everything from Paiute culture to nuclear politics. The museum (☎ 775-687-4810), 600 N Carson St, is open 8:30 am to 4:30 pm daily; $3, free if under 18.

Nevada State Railroad Museum

The Virginia & Truckee Railroad endures at this museum (☎ 775-687-6953), 2180 S Carson St, with three perfectly restored steam locomotives, antique passenger carriages and interesting exhibits about this historic short railroad. Built in a single year, the railroad climbed 1600 feet from the Carson Valley to Virginia City. From 1869 to 1948 it hauled massive quantities of timber, supplies and everything else up to the mines, carrying back huge loads of ore. The trains were also featured in Hollywood Westerns from the 1930s to the '50s. Hours are 8:30 am to 4:30 pm daily; $2, free if under 18 (buy tickets at the Wabuska Station, at the north end of the parking lot).

Stewart Indian Museum

In the 1880s, Senator William Stewart convinced the federal government to fund a school for Indian children, with the aim of teaching them trade skills to help them integrate into society. It took many years before the school, and society, accepted that the Native American culture was not extinct and began incorporating elements of the traditional heritage into the school program. The school was closed in 1980 by the US Bureau of Indian Affairs, but the campus is still used by the Native American community. The school is very pretty, with big trees and rustic stone buildings from the 1930s.

The museum has some accomplished baskets and pottery, an arrowhead collection and old photographs of the school and its students, though it falls short of putting them into the context of the history or culture of Nevada's native people. The excellent photogravures by Edward E Curtis, one of the earliest acknowledged masters of Old West photography, are worth seeing. The museum (☎ 775-882-1808) is at 5366 Snyder Ave, which branches off Hwy 395 about 3 miles south of town, and is open 9 am to 4 pm daily; donation requested.

Casinos

Compared to Las Vegas and Reno, Carson City has just a few, fairly unspectacular, casinos. **Ormsby House** (☎ 775-882-1890), 600 S Carson St, is the oldest and largest. The **Best Western Carson Station Hotel & Casino** (☎ 775-883-0900), 900 S Carson St, is popular and is the most likely spot for finding entertainment.

Places to Stay

Motels line Carson St, but they can fill up on a Friday or Saturday night and aren't such a good value anyway. Among the cheapest is the *Forty-Niner Motel* (☎ 775-882-1123, 2450 N Carson St), which has a pool and rooms for $30 to $90. The *Frontier Motel* (☎ 775-882-1377, fax 775-882-9579, 1718 N Carson St) actually has rooms for $23, though you're more likely to pay around $40 and up. You might also try the *Downtowner Motor Inn* (☎ 775-882-1333, 800-364-4908, 801 N Carson St), where rooms start at $32, topping out at $99.

Carson City's chain motels might present a better value; try *Motel 6* (☎ 775-885-7710, 2749 S Carson), with rooms for $28 to $40, or the mid-range *Days Inn* (☎ 775-883-3343, 3103 N Carson St), with rates of $36 to $100. The *St Charles Hotel Executive Suites* (☎ 775-882-1887, 310 S Carson St), is an old place, renovated, but with a bit of character. Its 24 rooms go for $49 to $129.

Places to Eat

Most of the restaurants, more than 20 of them, are on Carson St. A popular, casual place serving American food is *Scotty's* (☎ 775-882-2982, *1480 Carson St*), with big, inexpensive lunches and dinners. International restaurants include *Szechuan Express* (☎ 775-884-2666, *3697 Carson St*), with mid-priced specials, and *El Charro Avitia* (☎ 775-883-6261, *4389 Carson St*) for excellent and inexpensive Mexican food. Casino meals can be a good value, especially the buffet at the *Nugget* (☎ 775-882-7711, *651 N Stewart St*), which spotlights a different cuisine nightly. The best and priciest restaurant is *Adele's* (☎ 775-882-3353, *1112 Carson St*), with a first-class continental menu and an elegant atmosphere.

Getting There & Away
Greyhound buses (☎ 775-782-4544) stop at 111 E Telegraph Ave and at the Frontier Motel. There are connections to Reno twice daily ($9), daily to Las Vegas ($72) and to Los Angeles ($71).

AROUND CARSON CITY
Genoa
• population 200 • elevation 4788 feet
This pretty village at the edge of Carson Valley, beneath the Sierra, was the first European settlement in Nevada, at that time the western edge of the Utah Territory. After establishing temporary camps in 1849 and 1850, a group of Mormons established a trading post here in 1851 and ran a good business, provisioning emigrant groups for the final leg of the trip to California. Later, Genoa provided food for Virginia City miners and timber for their mines; big trees were cleared from the mountains and transported to the valley via timber flumes down Jacks Valley and Clear Creek. The **Genoa Saloon** claims to be the oldest bar in the state (since 1863), and it looks the part. Very atmospheric, it's a good place to hunker down with a drink.

Genoa Courthouse Museum The old Douglas County Courthouse, a well-proportioned red brick building from 1865, has good exhibits on local history and contains the original jail, a blacksmith shop, kitchen parlor and schoolroom. You'll also find here

the origins of surprising tales, such as the one about George Ferris, a local engineer who – inspired by the giant waterwheels in Carson Valley – came up with a new type of attraction for the Chicago World's Fair: the Ferris wheel. Another remarkable tale concerns 'Snowshoe' Thompson, a Norwegian who carried mail between Genoa and Placerville, California, from 1856 to 1876. All through winter, twice per month, with 60- to 80-pound loads, he traveled the route on skis, taking two days to reach Placerville and three days to return. The museum (☎ 775-782-4325) is open mid-May through October 10 am to 4:30 pm daily; donation requested.

Mormon Station State Historic Park The wooden stockade across from the courthouse is a reproduction of the original Mormon trading post fort and is also a good place for a picnic. There's a small museum with artifacts from the pioneer era open 10 am to 5 pm; free.

Walley's Hot Springs A trip to this lovely hot springs resort (☎ 775-782-8155, 800-628-7831) makes for a wonderful respite from traveling Nevada's dusty roads. There's been a hotel here since 1862. It was rebuilt – true to the original – in the 1980s and is now a luxurious resort surrounded by beautiful landscaping. A mile south of Genoa off Hwy 208, the springs are open to day visitors year round 7 am to 10 pm weekdays and 8 am to 10 pm weekends. Those fancying a workout can make use of the swimming pool, saunas and fitness equipment. If you want to stay, cabins are $92 to $130 and sleep up to four. The rustic restaurant serves upper-mid-priced American food.

VIRGINIA CITY
• population 1500 • elevation 6220 feet
If you're interested in history and can turn a cold eye on flagrant commercialization, you'll enjoy a day in Virginia City, about 23 miles south of Reno. The greatest mining boomtown of the late 19th century, it's also a National Historic Landmark and the site of the **Comstock Lode**. It's a touristy town, overrun in the summer, with a main street of

old buildings housing souvenir shops, saloons, restaurants and some pretty hokey 'museums.' Nonetheless, Virginia City is picturesque and considerably more authentic than many other overly restored and reconstructed 'historic' towns. The drive via Hwy 341, which offers great views of the mountains and passes Geiger Grade summit at 6799 feet, is an experience in itself.

History

The exploitation of the Comstock Lode is a tale of luck, greed and trickery. In the late 1840s, two brothers, Ethan Allen and Hosea Ballon Grosh, began panning for gold in Six Mile Canyon near today's Virginia City, finally striking a body of ore in 1857. Soon thereafter, they both died under tragic circumstances before their claims could be registered. A friend of theirs, Henry Comstock, then foraged through their cabin, finding maps marking the sites, and claimed the findings for himself.

At about the same time, two Irish prospectors, Pat McLaughlin and Peter O'Reilly, also discovered quartz ore in the same general area. Comstock also got wind of this and fraudulently claimed that the dig was on his land, conning the men into giving him a large chunk of pay dirt.

It is, perhaps, appropriate that the Comstock Lode was named after a con man, for though it yielded perhaps $400 million in precious metals (the estimates vary from under $300 million to over $700 million), several times this amount was traded in mining stocks and bonds by investors and speculators in San Francisco and elsewhere.

The initial digging for surface gold was impeded by heavy gray mud, which was soon found to contain, in addition to the gold, as much as $3000 of silver per ton. The ore body dipped steeply into the mountainside, so when the first finds were exhausted, deep mining operations were required. This meant major capital investments, the floating of shares, stock certificates and wild speculation. With rich deposits deep underground and claims on the surface inaccurately recorded, the Comstock became a patchwork of overlapping lots on top of a labyrinth of shafts, contested by crooked lawyers in interminable cases that clogged the corrupt courts. The total area claimed was three or four times the actual acreage above the lode.

Nevertheless, the first five years of frenetic activity saw the development of new mines deep in the unstable ground, dozens of stamp mills to process the ore and the completion of a toll road from the Carson Valley. The new town gained gas lines, a sewer system and a population of 15,000. It also got a newspaper on which Samuel Clemens (before adopting his pen name, Mark Twain) worked from 1862 to 1864. Nevada was admitted to the Union in 1864, and federal judges succeeded at sorting out the mess of conflicting claims. Then the main mines hit the bottom of the lode, stock prices crashed and the population slumped to 4000.

The crash allowed big investors such as William Ralston and James Crocker, founders of the Bank of California, and their associates to consolidate control of the mines, the stamp mills and the new railway to Carson City. The town grew again as new mines went down to deeper parts of the lode, then declined again in 1870. In 1873, John Mackay, a rival of Ralston, struck it really rich when his Consolidated Virginia mine hit the 'Big Bonanza' ore body, 1200 feet down in the Comstock Lode. Virginia City boomed again, with 30,000 people by 1874. The following year a fire destroyed most of the town, but such was the new wealth that the town was nearly all rebuilt within a year. Most of today's structures date from this reconstruction.

By 1878, even the Big Bonanza was played out, and the town barely survived, though there was an unspectacular industry of reprocessing the tailings with new cyanide mineral extraction techniques. By the 1930s Virginia City was down to 500 people and would have disappeared altogether without its appeal as a tourist destination.

Orientation

Virginia City is built on a hillside, with pleasing views of the old mines and the hills and vast valleys to the east. The main street is C St, flanked by old buildings and verandas containing most of the tourist attractions. B St, parallel to C St and one block up the hill, is also of interest for its historic architecture. Go downhill to the railroad station, between D and F Sts, then see the Mackay Mansion on D St and, further south, the Chollar mine. It's best to park your car and walk around the town; parking lots are on D St, at the north end of town, and in the middle of C St.

A Brief History of the 'Humped' in Nevada

No, this isn't a history of prostitution in Nevada. It is, rather, a brief chronicle of a strange species, no less exotic than Nevada's 'working girls.' Thanks to military intelligence – that most wonderful of oxymorons – the camel made its improbable arrival in the US. In 1856-57, the War Department brought 72 disoriented camels ashore in Texas, thinking they'd be ideal in supplying far-flung military outposts throughout the Southwest's deserts. And indeed, both dromedaries (one-humpers) and Bactrians (two-humpers) proved enormously sure-footed and capable of lugging much larger loads than mules and horses.

Unfortunately, there were problems from the get-go. The mules and horses (probably fearing competition) went berserk whenever their humped cousins were within sniffing distance. The US Camel Corps was disbanded in 1863, and all animals were auctioned off, only to resume their careers soon thereafter hauling freight between the mining towns of the Comstock.

Meanwhile, however, a vicious, puritanical anti-humper lobby had formed, which in 1875, forced the Nevada legislature to pass a bill entitled 'An Act to Prohibit Camels and Dromedaries from Running at Large on or About the Public Highways of the State of Nevada.' Soon thereafter, the humped ones were banished into the deserts of Arizona or shipped to that other paradise where the quirky and unloved have always prospered, Australia. The last wild camel was spotted in Nevada in 1936.

The next chapter in Nevada's humped history begins in the mid-1950s, with Bob Richards, editor of Virginia City's *Territorial Enterprise*. Bored by an acute lack of news or gossip, Richards announced in his paper the upcoming reenactment of a famous camel race that had allegedly taken place in 1866. There was just one problem: there were no contestants, and no camels showed up – at least not until August 26, 1960. On that date, the *Enterprise* banner headline screamed: 'The Camels Are Coming!' Famed movie director John Huston was in the area filming *The Misfits*, and he and his sidekick, former jockey Billy Pearson, agreed to race. Everybody thought this was just a joke until, on September 2, a truck drew up and two camels (one Bactrian and one dromedary, on loan from the San Francisco Zoo) staggered into the bright Nevada sunlight. The local tennis net was procured as a saddle for Pearson, but Huston swept to victory by 17 snarling and spitting lengths. A third, last-minute, entrant disappeared up the stairs of a saloon.

Since 1969, the IOCJ (International Order of Camel Jockeys) has honored Virginia City as the site of their annual premier event with contestants flying in from such countries as Germany, France and Saudi Arabia. The camel (one hump, or two) will forever be part of Nevada myth.

Information

The chamber of commerce (☎ 775-847-0311) is in an old railroad car at 131 South C St, open 10 am to 5 pm weekdays, 10 am to 4 pm weekends. In season, hours are 9 am to 5 pm daily. The Mark Twain Bookstore (☎ 775-847-0454), owned by the affable Joe and Ellie Curtis, is a treasure trove of books about the town, regional history and, of course, Mark Twain. They also have a neat collection of antique and out-of-print tomes.

The Way It Was Museum

If you're only going to see one museum in Virginia City, make it this one, which looks at the Comstock's history from several angles. A 15-minute video provides background on the town's trio of main attractions: its mines, the Piper Opera House and Mark Twain. The models of the mines show how extensive the tunnels beneath your feet truly are – all 750 miles of them. Some of the quirkiest exhibits are actually the most fun, such as the ones about the 'ancient' telephones, old-timey pharmaceuticals and 'a short history of barbed wire.' The museum, 66 North C St, is open daily 10 am to 6 pm year round; $2.50, free for kids under 11.

The Castle

Mine engineer Robert Graves had this house built for his family in 1868. Surviving largely intact, it's notable for its lavish interior and expensive furnishings. Bohemian crystal chandeliers, French wallpaper and Italian marble fireplaces were all shipped from Europe, around Cape Horn to San Francisco and hauled over the Sierra by wagon. The exhibit gives a great insight into the lives of the elite in what was a very stratified society. The Castle (☎ 775-847-0275) is at 70 South B St and can be seen by guided tour daily from May to October; $3.

Mackay Mansion

The Mackay Mansion is not quite as lavish or as original as the Castle, but you can see all the rooms, including the utility rooms, and it looks more lived in. The main interest here is the life of its one-time owner, John Mackay, an Irish miner who arrived at the Comstock with empty pockets in 1860. Through hard work, diligent study and well-calculated risk, he became one of the 'silver kings' and successfully challenged the big-money bankers from San Francisco. He was also noted for his personal charm, civic leadership and generous endowment of the University of Nevada. The mansion (☎ 775-847-0173) is at 129 South D St, and open 10 am to 6 pm daily in summer; $3.

Piper's Opera House

Often considered the first theater in the West, the current opera house (☎ 775-847-0433) was built by John Piper in 1885, after its two predecessors burned down. The theater, which staged raucous melodramas, proved hugely popular because it offered a way to escape the harsh realities of everyday life on the frontier. Ingeniously designed, it has a raked stage and a wooden floor 'sprung' on railroad springs, to give dancers an extra bounce. It's still in operation today and may be visited noon to 4 pm daily, May to September only; $2.

Chollar Mine

A 30-minute underground tour (☎ 775-847-0155) will show you how the other half lived on the Comstock. The most significant feature is the use of 'square-set' timbering, developed in the local mines. It enabled large ore bodies to be mined at great depths, even in unstable ground. The system was invented by Phillip Deidesheimer, an engineer from Germany, in 1861. He did not patent it, but actively encouraged its use in the Comstock because it was so much safer than earlier techniques. The mine is at the south end of F St, and tours run every afternoon between May and September; $4.

St Mary in the Mountains Church

Of Virginia City's many churches, St Mary is the most impressive. Luminous stained-glass windows bathe the church with muted light, highlighting its soaring Gothic-style ceilings, with their unusual beam-supporting rafters.

Museum Madness

It will take the better part of a day to see Virginia City's staple attractions, but there are dozens. Some are of very limited interest, others are pretty good. The following are listed from north to south via C St.

Mark Twain Museum (☎ 775-847-0525), inside a knickknack store on C St at Taylor, has old printing technology, Twain's writing desk and an overdone recorded commentary; $1.

Red Light Museum (☎ 775-847-9394), 5 South C St under the Julia C Bulette Saloon, is home to an unarousing collection of medical instruments, opium pipes, French postcards, letters and so forth; $1.

Marshall Mint & Museum (☎ 775-847-0777), North C St at Sutton St, displays gold, silver, precious stones, minerals, coins, etc, and you can pan for gold; $4.

Ponderosa Saloon Underground Mine Tours (☎ 775-847-0757), South C St, raises the question: 'Why shouldn't you have a mine shaft in the back of a saloon?' This one shows most of the mine features you'll see at the Chollar mine and has a good commentary; $3.50/1.50 adults/children.

Nevada Gambling Museum (☎ 775-847-9022), 22 South C St, has all kinds of gambling artifacts, though most people seem to be most interested in its collection of cheating devices; $1.50.

Comstock Firemen's Museum (☎ 775-847-0717), 51 South C St, has some beautifully restored fire-fighting equipment. Open May to November; donation requested.

Fourth Ward School Museum (☎ 775-847-0975), South C St, is an impressive old building with period classrooms and displays on the history of mining and Virginia City. The last class graduated in 1936. Open May to October; donation requested.

Radio Museum (☎ 775-847-9047), on F St at Taylor, has about 100 wireless sets and radios from 1915 to 1950. Open weekends, daily April to November.

Though the fire of 1875 burned down the original church, most of what you see today is still more than a century old. Also note the altar and bronze baptismal font in the left nave.

Virginia & Truckee Railroad

This railroad was built in 1869 and ran to Carson Valley via Gold Hill and Silver City. Most of the track has been removed, but a narrated 35-minute trip takes you through the old mining areas and a tunnel to Gold Hill and back, behind a vintage steam locomotive. The train runs from late May through mid-October and costs $4.75/2.50 roundtrip, or $9.50 for an all-day pass. For information, call ☎ 775-847-0380.

Places to Stay

It's feasible to commute from Reno, Carson City or even Tahoe, but staying overnight lets you see Virginia City with fewer tourists, less traffic and more character.

The *RV Park* (☎ 775-847-0999, 800-889-1240, 355 North F St) is pretty good and takes tent campers from $5 per person. RV sites with hookups cost up to $20.

The hotels in town aren't cheap, but check the *Comstock Lodge* (☎ 775-847-0233, fax 775-847-9392, 875 South C St), which has a bunch of new cottages with old-style furnishings for $45 to $68. The *Sugar Loaf Motel* (☎/fax 775-847-0551, 430 South C St) is similar, with rooms from $45 to $55.

A mile south of town, the *Gold Hill Hotel* (☎ 775-847-0111, *1540 Main St*) claims to be Nevada's oldest (established 1859) and makes for an interesting and historic stay. Nicely furnished rooms in the old part of the building start at $40, and newer, more comfortable ones can cost as much as $135. Rates include continental breakfast, and there's a good French restaurant on the premises.

Places to Eat

Most visitors are here for lunch, but it's nice to stay for dinner, when the commercial hype subsides. One of the best values – and popular with the locals – is the *Wagon Wheel* (☎ 775-847-0500, *171 South C St*), an unpretentious coffee shop with enormous breakfasts and lunches at good prices. The *Delta Saloon* (☎ 775-847-0789, *18 South C St*) serves inexpensive American fare and also stays open for dinner. The *Julia C Bulette Saloon* (☎ 775-847-9394, *5 South C St*) does an OK lunch and snacks, but closes early in the evening.

Saloons

Saloons – in the true Wild West sense – were common in old Virginia City, and a number of fine examples survive on C St, although some are packed with slot machines that do nothing for the historical ambiance. The *Old Washoe Club* has a fine bar, and the local Millionaires' Club used to meet upstairs. The *Silver Queen* is another great watering hole, with a wall-sized portrait of a woman portrayed, largely, in silver coins. The *Delta Saloon* is the location of the much-touted 'suicide table' (go in and read the story), though its main business is slot machines. On the other side of the street, the *Bucket of Blood* has honky-tonk entertainment and a panoramic window looking down the valley.

Getting There & Away

Gray Line Tours offers day excursions from Reno and Tahoe that take in Virginia City as well. For details, see the Reno section earlier in this chapter.

Nevada Great Basin

Geographically, nearly all of Nevada is in the Great Basin – a high desert characterized by a series of rugged mountain ranges and broad valleys that also extends into Utah, California and Oregon. It's a basin in the sense that water does not drain out of it to the ocean but into shallow salt lakes, marshes and mud flats, where it disappears underground or just evaporates. The mountain ranges, some remote and sparsely populated, are of great interest to outdoor enthusiasts, with wonderful opportunities for hiking in summer and skiing in winter. Most are part of either the Toiyabe National Forest or the Humboldt National Forest. USFS offices have excellent maps and information; another in-depth source is *Hiking the Great Basin* by John Hart.

Most travelers pass the Great Basin on one of several main highways cutting across the state. This chapter describes each of those routes, the places along the way and some interesting detours.

History

The Shoshone and Paiute lived here for at least 700 years, gathering piñon nuts in the mountains in the warmer months and hunting rabbits, antelope and fowl in the valleys during winter. Their culture, way of life and very existence were almost totally wiped out by European settlement. This was not so much through direct conflict – though there was plenty of that – but because cattle grazing, mining and logging destroyed the natural resources on which the Indians depended.

Reservations were established early in the process of European settlement, often as a part of treaties in which Indians lost access to large areas of their traditional lands. In many cases, the reservations were poorly managed and did little or nothing to preserve Indian culture or foster self-reliance. The main enterprises a visitor will see on reservations today are smoke shops in which tobacco products are sold free of

Highlights

- Elko – capital of cowboy culture, Basque traditions and gateway to the Ruby Mountains

- Angel Lake Road & Lamoille Canyon Road – two winding scenic byways with access to backcountry hiking

- Pioche – where the West is still wild

- Great Basin National Park – great hikes, spectacular vistas and the subterranean charms of the Lehman Caves

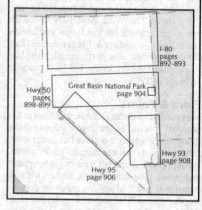

local taxes. These have actually been quite successful in earning income for Indian communities.

Though the Great Basin was part of Mexico until 1848, American and British explorers ventured into the area much earlier. The first were fur trappers who pioneered the trails along the Humboldt River. American frontiersman Jedediah Smith first crossed the Great Basin in 1827. A decade and a half later, the army sent Lieutenant John Frémont to explore and map the region, and he spent most of 1843 doing so, searching for the mythical San Buenaventura River, believed to flow west to the Pacific. Finally convinced that the river did not exist, Frémont dubbed the area the 'Great Basin.'

In the years of the California gold rush, well-worn emigrant trails were established along the routes of trappers and explorers. This remote area was the last great barrier before crossing the Sierra to the promised land of California. Hundreds of thousands of emigrants passed through what was then the Utah Territory; only a few settled here. The area's history is largely that of developing ways to bridge the distance: trails and roads, the Pony Express and the telegraph, the railroad and the highway. Mining towns mushroomed when gold, silver and other minerals were discovered, though most died after their lodes played out. Cattle ranching followed the railroad and expanded to feed the miners. The Wild West period – with free-range grazing, lawless towns and Indian skirmishes – endured longer here than almost anywhere else in the country: the last stagecoach robbery in the US took place in Jarbidge in 1916.

Flora & Fauna

Many visitors wonder at the lack of trees in the national forests, as the lower slopes of the mountain ranges have nothing but desert vegetation, mainly sagebrush, to cover them. Above 6000 feet, juniper trees begin to appear and piñon pine trees a little higher, with an occasional patch of willow, aspen or cottonwood. Around 8000 feet and up, higher rainfall and cooler temperatures favor the pine and fir trees, with the really tall spruces occurring up to 10,000 feet and the ancient bristlecone pine at the upper limits of survival.

Different plant communities support different animal species, and it's a real delight to see changes in the various 'life zones' as you climb into the higher ranges. Because the ranges are separated by broad, hot, dry valleys, many ranges are like ecological islands, where species endemic to the area are found.

ALONG I-80

The fur trappers' route followed the Humboldt River from northeastern Nevada to

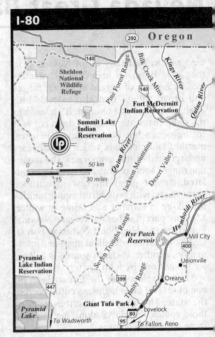

where it peters out in the Humboldt Sink, near Lovelock. By traveling southwest, it was possible to find the Truckee River and follow it up into the Sierra north of Lake Tahoe. This route was one of the earliest emigrant trails to Northern California and was called the Humboldt Trail or the Emigrant Trail. Though not the most direct route across Nevada, it became the route of the Central Pacific Railroad because it skirted many of the Great Basin's steep north-south ranges. Transcontinental railroad tracks from the West reached Reno in May 1868 and crossed the state within a year.

By the 1920s, a new automobile road, Hwy 40 – the Victory Highway – followed the same route. This was upgraded as part of the federal interstate highway program and is now a section of the transcontinental I-80. It was one of the last sections of I-80 to be completed.

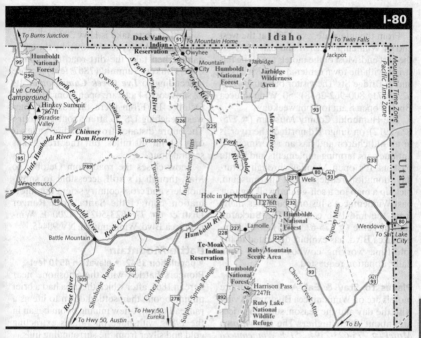

I-80

NEVADA GREAT BASIN

Lovelock

• population 2143 • elevation 3975 feet

Founded in the 1860s, this small town is the county seat of Pershing County, providing services to the surrounding farmlands and to travelers on the interstate. Two freeway exits, 105 and 107, lead to Cornell Ave, which has plenty of motels and places to eat. For visitor information, go to the chamber of commerce (☎ 775-273-7213), close to exit 105. The nearby **Marzen House** (1876) houses the county museum, which has displays of mining equipment and artifacts from the so-called red-headed giants, a tribe that originally lived in the area. The museum is closed Monday. The **Pershing County Courthouse** (1919) on Main St is said to be the only round courthouse in the country and is open 10 am to 4 pm weekdays; free. A pleasant, shady park and a public swimming pool are nearby.

Seven miles west of town, **Giant Tufa Park** sports a group of calcium carbonate spires that grew in the ancient Lake Lahontan. To get there from the town center, drive north on Central Ave for 1½ miles, then turn west (left) on Pitt Rd for about 2½ miles. Look for an unmarked gravel road on your right and follow it for about 1 mile.

Winnemucca

• population 6100 • elevation 4324 feet

The biggest town on this stretch of I-80, Winnemucca has been a travelers' stop since the days of the Emigrant Trail, when many of the emigrants forded the Humboldt River here to take a cutoff trail to Northern California and Oregon. With the arrival of the railroad in 1865, the town was named after the famous Paiute chief. In the past decade it has grown rapidly because of large mining operations in the Osgood Mountains east of town. It's also a center of Nevada's Basque community.

From the interstate, exit 176 is at the west end of Winnemucca Blvd and exit 178 is at the east end. Most of the motels are along this street, with the town center around Melarkey and N Bridge Sts. The visitor bureau (☎ 775-623-5071, 800-962-2638), 50 Winnemucca Blvd, is open 8 am to 5 pm weekdays.

The **Humboldt County Museum** (☎ 775-623-2912), on Jungo Rd north of the river, is in an old church and has an assortment of antique cars, farming implements and Paiute baskets. It's open Monday through Saturday; donation requested. At the museum, pick up a map for a self-guided walking tour past Winnemucca's historic buildings, many from the mid-19th century. The **Buckaroo Hall of Fame** (☎ 775-623-2225), 30 W Winnemucca Blvd, has exhibits dedicated to the 'old-time working cowboy' and is open daily; donation requested.

Places to Stay & Eat A dozen or more motels are on Winnemucca Blvd; prices vary with the day and the season; summer prices are about 25% higher. The *Downtown Motel* (☎ 775-623-2394, 251 E Winnemucca Blvd) is one of the cheapest, with rooms for $32 to $40. *Motel 6* (☎ 775-623-1180, 1600 W Winnemucca Blvd) charges $30 to $44. For more comfort, try the *Red Lion Inn & Casino* (☎ 775-623-2565, 800-633-6435, fax 775-623-5702, 741 W Winnemucca Blvd), which counts a restaurant and pool among its facilities and charges $59 to $130.

The buffet at *Pete's Coffee Shop* at Winners Hotel & Casino (☎ 775-623-2511, 185 W Winnemucca Blvd) is a great value; they also do barbecue on Saturdays. Other good eateries include the *Griddle* (☎ 775-623-2977, 460 W Winnemucca Blvd) for breakfast and *Grandma's Diner* (☎ 775-623-2511, 185 W Winnemucca Blvd) for fairly upscale dinners. Excellent Basque food is available at *Martin's* (☎ 775-623-3197) at Melarkey and W Railroad Sts.

Around Winnemucca

About 50 miles north of Winnemucca, the Santa Rosa Mountains lie within the **Humboldt National Forest**, a far-off, handsome wilderness area with abundant hiking trails. A good drive to take is Hwy 290 up beautiful Paradise Valley to the town by the same name. Then take the dirt road that climbs over Hinkey Summit (7867 feet) before descending to *Lye Creek Campground*. Its 12 sites cost $4 and are open from June 1 to October 15. From there the road rumbles west, reaching US 95 after about 1½ hours. The entire distance from Paradise Valley is only about 40 miles, but the trek takes several hours.

Snow closes the road from October to May, though it's still accessible to snowmobilers and cross-country skiers. For information, contact the Santa Rosa Ranger District (☎ 775-623-5025), 1200 E Winnemucca Blvd, Winnemucca, NV 98445.

Battle Mountain
- population 3542 • elevation 4510 feet

Pioneers battled with the Shoshone near here in 1861, after which the area had a brief mining boom, then settled down to life as a railroad town. A new mining boom began in the 1980s, with huge operations extracting gold and silver from the surrounding hills.

Exits 229 and 233 go to Front St, which has motels, restaurants and casinos on one side and rail yards on the other. It's not a great place to stop; accommodations are often filled with mine workers, and prices tend to be high.

South of Battle Mountain, Hwy 305 goes to Austin, 89 miles away. The road follows the Reese River between two mountain ranges. It's picturesque in a bleak, lonely, wide-open-spaces kind of way.

Elko
- population 15,000 • elevation 5067 feet

Though small, Elko is the largest town in rural Nevada and a center of cowboy culture, with a calendar of Western cultural events and a museum big on buckaroos, stagecoaches and the Pony Express. The other cultural influence is Basque; in fact, Basque sheepherders and Old West cattlemen had some violent conflicts over grazing rights in the late 19th century.

Elko's history is typical of towns along I-80, with the Emigrant Trail, the mining booms and the arrival of the railroad in 1868. Stage lines extended north and south of Elko's railroad, and Elko became a marketing and livestock center in the 1870s and '80s, the era of the 'cattle kings.' It became a county seat and was the first home to the University of Nevada, later moved to Reno.

A recent resurgence in gold mining has fed Elko's prosperity, and gambling, ranching and tourism continue to be the other major slices of the local economy. It's a popular stop for truckers and travelers, and visitors flock in for several well-promoted annual events, casinos with quality entertainment and more brothels than you'd think they'd have use for in a town of this size. Elko is also a good base from which to explore the superb, scenic country to the north and south.

Orientation & Information Idaho St is the main drag; from I-80, exit 301 leads to its west end, exit 303 to the east. Visitor information (☎ 775-738-7135, 800-428-7143, fax 775-738-7136) is available at 1601 Idaho St from 9 am to 5 pm weekdays. For maps and backcountry information, visit the USFS office (☎ 775-738-5171), 976 Mountain City Hwy, between exit 301 and downtown, open 7:30 am to 4:30 pm weekdays.

Northeastern Nevada Museum This modern museum has excellent displays on everything from pioneer life to the Basque settlers, wildlife to the latest gold mining techniques. Exhibits include Indian artifacts, an original stagecoach, faded photographs and an old Pony Express cabin. The attachable cow hooves once worn by Crazy Tex, a cattle thief who repeatedly fooled law enforcers in the 1920s, are a curious highlight. The museum (☎ 775-738-3418), 1515 Idaho Ave, is open 9 am to 5 pm Monday to Saturday, 1 to 5 pm Sunday; free.

Western Folklife Center The historic Pioneer Saloon, at the corner of 5th and Railroad Sts, now houses this organization (☎ 775-738-7508, 800-748-4466). There are exhibitions of Western art and a folk art shop. Hours are 10 am to 5:30 pm Tuesday to Saturday.

Special Events The Western Folklife Center organizes the Cowboy Poetry Gathering that brings about 8000 fans to Elko in late January; phone ahead for information and tickets. The National Basque Festival (☎ 775-738-7991), the biggest in the country, is held in Elko every year around the Fourth of July.

Places to Stay Elko's not a super-cheap place to spend a night, especially in summer. The largest selection of motels, mostly chains, is on Idaho St, east of the town center. The cheapest of them is the *Elko Motel* (☎ 775-738-4433, 1243 Idaho), with rooms costing $32 to $95. *Motel 6* (☎ 775-738-4337, 3021 Idaho St), east of the turnoff to I-80, charges around $40. Similarly priced but closer to town is the *Holiday Motel* (☎ 775-738-7187, 1276 Idaho St). The *Centre Motel* (☎ 775-738-3226, 475 3rd St), in the middle of town, doesn't look pretty, but it's OK for $30; some of the newer rooms cost up to $62. All these places have small heated pools.

Park View Inn (☎ 775-753-7747, fax 775-753-7347, 1785 Idaho St) is comfortable and charges $40 to $60 year round. The best places to stay are either the *Best Western Ameritel Inn* (☎ 775-738-8787, fax 775-753-7910, 1930 Idaho St), at $67 to $150, or the *Red Lion Inn & Casino* (☎ 775-738-2111, 800-545-0044, fax 775-753-9859, 2065 Idaho St), with rooms ranging from $79 to $259.

Places to Eat Fast-food franchises are strung along Idaho St, but other eating options abound, though predictably most are rather meat-intensive. Vegetarians are most likely to find choices at the *Red Lion Inn & Casino* buffet, definitely a good value. For Basque food, try the *Star* (☎ 775-753-8696, 246 Silver St) or the *Nevada Dinner House* (☎ 775-738-8485, 351 Silver St); a full meal will run about $15 to $20.

Around Elko
Humboldt National Forest Humboldt National Forest measures nearly 3900 sq miles scattered across north-central

Nevada. Named for Alexander Humboldt, a German naturalist, it offers a landscape that ranges from lowlands covered with sagebrush to alpine meadows, snow-dusted peaks and crystalline streams. Mountain goats, bighorn sheep and a wide range of birds, including sage grouse and partridge, make the forest their home.

Hwy 225 north of Elko is a paved road going into the forest to Mountain City, then continuing through the Duck Valley Indian Reservation into Idaho. Mountain City has two motels with rooms starting at $30, there are quite a few campgrounds in the area as well. One of the most remote towns in this part of the state (the first phone arrived in 1984), **Jarbidge** is another old mining town, with maybe 50 residents. Getting there means rattling along on a gravel road for 50 miles; the turnoff is just south of the Wild Horse State Recreation Site. Jarbidge has gas, food, accommodations and campgrounds and provides the closest access to the **Jarbidge Wilderness**. If you want to explore this rugged, pristine and nearly inaccessible area, first get information from the USFS in Elko or from the Trading Post (☎ 775-488-2315) in Jarbidge.

Ruby Mountains This beautiful, fairly verdant mountain range is like a jagged saw running south from Wells. The best access is from Elko. Hwy 227 leads 20 miles to the picture-perfect village of **Lamoille**, where food and lodging are available at *Pine Lodge* (☎ 775-753-6363) on Main St, with rooms for $55 to $75.

Just before the village, Lamoille Canyon Rd – a designated Scenic Byway – branches south, following the forested canyon for 12 miles past cliffs, waterfalls and other glacial sculptures. At the end of the road is a trailhead for the 2-mile trail to Island Lake and the 40-mile Ruby Crest Trail.

The Ruby Mountains are a declared wilderness area, with prominent peaks, glacial lakes and alpine vegetation. It's brilliant terrain, but the hiking season is short – from about mid-June to mid-September. Other activities include heli-skiing with Ruby Mountain Heli-Ski (☎ 775-753-6867). On the

east side of the range, **Ruby Lake National Wildlife Refuge** is a rest stop for migrating waterbirds and is also good for fishing.

In summer you can drive across the southern end of the range via the 7250-foot Harrison Pass, at the southern end of the Ruby Crest Trail. Camping is possible at *Ruby Marsh Campground*, a Bureau of Land Management site, for $2 (first-come, first-served), and *Thomas Canyon Campground*, halfway up Lamoille Canyon Rd, for $10 to $16. Both are open from around late May to early September; sites at the latter may be reserved through National Recreation Reservation Service at ☎ 877-444-6777.

Wells
* population 1300 * elevation 5630 feet

Wells, at the junction of Hwy 93 and I-80, has gas, food and cheaper lodging than other towns along the interstate. Most of the motels are on 6th St. For trivia buffs, let it be known that Jack Dempsey started his boxing career here – as a bouncer in the local bars.

Angel Lake Road – or Hwy 231, also a scenic byway – heads into the mountains southwest of town, past sagebrush, piñon pine and aspen. After about 12 miles, the road terminates at cobalt-blue Angel Lake, a glacial cirque embedded in the East Humboldt Range at 8300 feet. *Angel Lake Campground* is right here and open from mid-June to early September with sites costing $10 to $18. *Angel Creek Campground* is en route, about 8 miles from the Angel Lake Road turnoff, and beautifully located in a ravine. It's open from mid-May to early September and has sites costing $9 to $16. For reservations at either campground, call NRRS at ☎ 877-444-6777 or go to the Web at www.reserveusa.com. From Hwy 232, south of Wells, you can see the large natural window near the top of 11,300-foot Hole in the Mountain Peak. Southwest of Wells, the **Ruby Marshes** offer some of the best fishing around.

Wendover
* population 2650 * elevation 4450 feet

Wendover is a gambling boomtown. Motels and casinos line Wendover Blvd, the main drag, which continues into Utah. The state line is painted across the road, at the large cowboy statue of Wendover Will.

On the Nevada side, the Welcome Center (☎ 775-664-3414, 800-426-6862, fax 775-664-2316), 735 Wendover Blvd, has displays on local and regional history as well as the WWII-era goings-on at Wendover Air Force Base, which prepared the *Enola Gay* crew for dropping atomic bombs. On the Utah side, the Bonneville Speed Museum (☎ 801-665-7721) documents attempts to set land speed records on the nearby Bonneville Salt Flats.

Accommodations in Wendover tend to be expensive, especially on weekends. The *Super 8 (☎ 775-664-2888, 800-800-8000, 1325 Wendover Blvd)* is about the cheapest motel, with rooms starting at $35, but you might find a better value on the Utah side. For food, the buffets at the *Peppermill Hotel-Casino (☎ 775-664-2255, 800-648-9660, 680 Wendover Blvd)* and the *Rainbow Hotel-Casino (☎ 800-217-0049, 1045 W Wendover Blvd)* present the best value.

There's a *KOA Campground (☎ 775-664-3221, 800-562-8552, fax 775-664-3712, 1250 N Camper Drive)* at exit 410 with 150 sites.

ALONG HWY 50

This road is often described as the 'loneliest road in America,' a slogan usually attributed to a story in *Life* magazine. Local publicists figured that any superlative was good advertising and used it as a tourism promotion theme. Tourist offices will give you passports that you can get stamped along the way and bumper stickers boasting, 'I survived the loneliest road in America.'

In fact it's no great ordeal to cross Nevada on Hwy 50. It is about a two hours' drive (hardly exceeding the speed limit at all) from Fallon to Austin, a longish hour to the historic mining town of Eureka, and about 1½ hours more to Ely. From Ely, it's another hour to Great Basin National Park near the Utah border, which on its own is worth the whole trip.

The route cuts across the natural grain of the country – repeatedly you climb up the side of a range, go through a mountain pass,

roll down the other side, cross a broad valley and climb up the next range. This is basin-and-range terrain. It must have been heartbreaking in a pioneer's covered wagon, but in a car it's a lot more interesting than a long, straight, flat freeway. Detours north or south of Hwy 50, typically along valleys between the ranges, provide access to an amazing range of natural and historic sites, including an ancient lake, Indian petroglyphs, a giant sand dune and mountains peaking at over 13,000 feet.

West of Austin, Hwy 50 follows the route of the Overland stagecoach lines and the Pony Express. The first transcontinental telegraph line also took a central route across Nevada – via Ely, Eureka, Austin and Fallon – putting the Pony Express out of business even as the railroad across the north made the stagecoach line obsolete.

As road traffic became more important, the Lincoln Highway (Hwy 50) was established almost exactly along the route of the telegraph line, but the northern route, the Victory Highway (Hwy 40), attracted federal funding and became I-80. The 'lonely' Lincoln was left to be a tourist attraction.

Silver Springs
• population 2250 • elevation 4209 feet
There's not much at this crossroads of Hwy 50 and Alt US 95, but Silver Springs is the gateway to the **Lahontan State Recreation Area** (☎ 775-867-3500 or 775-577-2226), which wraps around a 16-mile-long reservoir bordered by sandy beaches and good for swimming, fishing and water sports.

Eight miles south on Alt US 95 is the turnoff to **Fort Churchill State Historic Park**. Built in 1860, the fort was partly established to protect the Pony Express and Overland stagecoach lines. Its other functions were to deter Indian attacks on the mining settlements and, more importantly, to help ensure that both California and Nevada remained decidedly pro-Union in the Civil War.

The fort has been abandoned since 1870, leaving only a few adobe ruins. It's still worth seeing. The fort's main quadrangle is quite discernible, and excellent interpretive

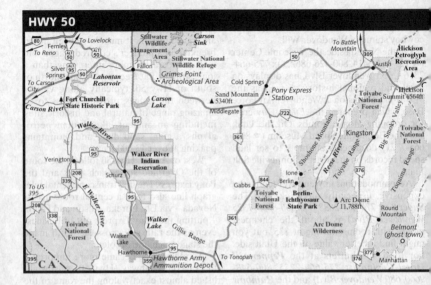

HWY 50

NEVADA GREAT BASIN

signs make it easy to imagine the place filled with parading soldiers and cavalry horses. Incidentally, the fort was named after Sylvester Churchill, inspector general of the US Army.

The visitor center (☎ 775-577-2345) has engaging exhibits on life in the fort and is open 8:30 am to 4 pm daily. Nearby *Buckland Campground* has beautiful shaded sites for $6 per vehicle.

Fallon
• population 7400 • elevation 3963 feet

The seat of Churchill County and the self-proclaimed 'oasis of Nevada,' Fallon is the heart of an irrigated agricultural area whose main products are alfalfa and cantaloupes. Look into the sky and you might spot an F-16 heading out from the **Fallon Naval Air Station**, home of the fighter-pilot school featured in the Tom Cruise movie *Top Gun*.

The town has a good museum and three small casinos, but there's no real reason to spend the night. If you must, the cheapest place is probably *Fallon Motel (☎ 775-423-4648, 390 W Williams Ave)*, which charges $29 to $55. More motels are farther along on the western edge of town. The visitor bureau (☎ 775-423-4556, 800-874-0903, fax 775-423-8926, www.fallon.net) is at 100 Campus Way.

For a slice of Nevada, stop by *Bob's Root Beer Drive-in (☎ 775-867-2769)*, on Hwy 50 about three miles west of Fallon, where they've been dishing out honest burgers, fries and homemade root beer since 1962. Carhops will come to your car, and on Tuesday burgers cost just 69¢. It's closed December through March.

Churchill County Museum It's worth stopping in Fallon to see this museum, which has good displays of Paiute artifacts, including a traditional dome-shaped shelter made from tule reeds. The tule duck decoys are whimsical and well done. Some of the artifacts are from Hidden Cave, an important archaeological site, which can be visited on museum-led tours at 9:30 am on the second and fourth Saturday of the month. Better-than-usual displays feature early clothing, furniture and household goods, including some very fine hand-stitched quilts. The

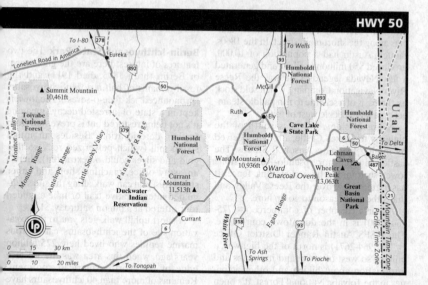

NEVADA GREAT BASIN

museum (☎ 775-423-3677), 1050 S Maine St, is open 10 am to 5 pm daily (10 am to 4 pm, closed Thursday, in winter); donation requested.

Around Fallon

Grimes Point Archaeological Area On the northeast side of the highway, about 8 miles east of Fallon, you'll see signs pointing to this area. A marked trail leads past scores of boulders covered in ancient petroglyphs. Thought to date from 400 to 7000 years ago, the pictures are believed to have been made by shamans as part of rituals to ensure a successful hunt. But in fact their significance and age are not known for certain. **Hidden Cave** is in the same general area (see Churchill County Museum in the Fallon section), as is the **Stillwater Wildlife Refuge**, popular with geese and ducks as a stop on their annual migration.

Sand Mountain About 25 miles southeast of Fallon, near Sand Mountain itself, Sand Mountain Recreation Area is a 2-mile-long, 600-foot-high sweep of sand dunes that occasionally produces a low-pitched hum caused by the vibration of wind-blown sand crystals. The best time to hear the sound is on a hot, dry evening when the dune is not covered with screeching off-road vehicles. Nearby, the ruins of an old Pony Express station have been excavated from the sand.

Middlegate At the junction of Hwys 50 and 361, the Old Middlegate Station sells gas, burgers, beer and hot dogs. Highway 361 goes south to the turnoff for Berlin-Ichthyosaurus State Park (see that section later in this chapter) and Gabbs.

Cold Springs About 52 miles east of Fallon (47 miles west of Austin) there's a historical marker and 1½-mile self-guided trail around the ruins of the Cold Springs Pony Express Station. It makes for a good place to stop and stretch your legs.

Austin

• **population 370** • **elevation 6577 feet**
It might look interesting after an hour or so of uninterrupted basin and range, but

there's not much to see in Austin – just a few pleasantly old, almost decrepit, frontier buildings along the short main street. In the 1860s, though, Austin had a population of 10,000, produced $50 million in silver and generated a few Nevada legends. One was the Reese River Navigation Company, which sold stock on the basis of a scheme to run paddle steamers on a large trickle west of town.

A gravel side road goes south of the highway to **Stokes Castle**, a folly conceived by mining magnate Anson P Stokes. The castle is a three-story, pseudo-Roman stone tower surrounded by a chain-link fence. It has a great view over the Reese Valley, and that's the best reason to go up here.

Austin's chamber of commerce (☎ 775-964-2200) is in the downtown courthouse. The USFS Austin Ranger District Office (☎ 775-964-2671) is north of the highway, a mile or so west of town, and has maps and information about hiking and other activities in the Toiyabe National Forest. It's open 7:45 am to 4:30 pm on weekdays.

Places to Stay & Eat Three undistinguished motels on the south side of the main street have rooms for $30 to $50. The *Pony Canyon Motel* (☎ 775-964-2605) looks to be the best of them. The *International Hotel* is now a restaurant, with OK food at basic prices. It was moved here in pieces from Virginia City in 1863 and is one of the oldest buildings in the state.

Around Austin

Toiyabe National Forest This national forest covers five separate mountain ranges in central Nevada, the most impressive of which is Toiyabe Range, extending south from Austin. A highlight is the demanding 73-mile Toiyabe Crest National Recreation Trail, which requires about five days to hike; intermediate trailheads give access to shorter sections. The **Arc Dome Wilderness** in the southern part of the range is the largest wilderness area in the state. There are four designated campgrounds with toilet facilities ($2). Pretty *Big Creek Campground* is the most accessible, 13 miles southwest of Austin. Stop by the USFS

station in Austin for driving recommendations and other information.

Berlin-Ichthyosaur State Park The two features of interest here are the ghost town of Berlin (born 1895, died 1911) and the fossil remains of half a dozen ichthyosaurs (pronounced 'ick-thee-o-sores'). The town is kept in a state of 'arrested decay,' meaning it's not being restored but is prevented from further deterioration. Besides an intact stamp mill (which pulverized rock so that gold and silver could be extracted), there's an assay office, machine shop and other structures. You can walk along the site's self-guided interpretative trail or take a guided tour offered at 3 pm on Saturday; $1.

A short uphill walk gets you to the excavation site of the ichthyosaurs, carnivorous marine reptiles who lived here 225 million years ago, when this area was the western edge of the North American continent. Remains of more than 40 ichthyosaurs have been discovered, including six specimens apparently trapped together in a muddy pool. This site was excavated in 1954 and is now protected by an A-frame shelter. Tours of the fossil site are given at 10 am, 2 and 4 pm or by request on weekends; $4. Call ☎ 775-964-2440 for details. Camping is available nearby for $7.

To get to the park, follow the picturesque Reese Valley on a dirt road southwest from Austin and cross the Shoshone Mountains via Ione. Alternatively, head south from Middlegate on Hwy 361 and go east over the Paradise Range on Hwy 844, just north of Gabbs.

Hickison Petroglyph Recreation Area North of Hwy 50, 22 miles east of Austin, Hickison Summit has a rest stop, BLM campground and a self-guided trail for viewing the petroglyphs. A couple of lookout points provide panoramic views. More petroglyphs are at the Toquima Caves, 6 miles farther east.

Big Smoky Valley A truly scenic drive follows Hwy 376 about 100 miles from Hwy 50 south to Tonopah along the Big Smoky Valley. On the way, there are interesting stops and side trips to Kingston Canyon and the old mining towns of Round Mountain and Manhattan. A rough road crosses the Toquima Range to the ghost town of Belmont.

Eureka
• **population 800** • **elevation 6937 feet**

Don't call Eureka a ghost town; it may have shrunk some from its peak population of 11,000, but it is still the seat of Eureka County. Between 1875 and 1890, $40 million worth of silver was extracted from lead-rich ore in this area. Hills were stripped of trees to make charcoal, and smelters belched lead-laden smoke, poisoning plants and people for miles around. In recent years, Eureka has been experiencing a second, smaller, boom, thanks to a nearby gold strike.

After a fire in 1879, a number of large brick buildings were built, many of which have survived to this day. They can easily be seen on a short walk around town; pick up a historic walking brochure from the chamber of commerce (☎ 775-237-5484).

Pride of place goes to the handsome brick **county courthouse** at Main and Bateman Sts, completed in 1880. Still in use, it features unusual pressed-tin ceilings and walk-in vaults and is usually open to visitors 8 am to 5 pm weekdays; free. The **Eureka Sentinel Museum** (☎ 775-237-5010), at Monroe and Bateman Sts, displays late-19th-century newspaper technology and colorful examples of period reportage. It's open daily in summer and closed Sunday and Monday otherwise; free. The chamber of commerce is in the same building. Stroll past other old buildings along Main St to the 1880 **Eureka Opera House** (☎ 775-237-6006), which was restored in 1984, garnering an award from the National Trust for Historic Preservation. It's open 8 am to 5 pm weekdays; free.

Lake Lahontan: The Giant That Disappeared

The Lahontan Reservoir, west of Fallon, is a mere puddle compared to the giant ancient Lake Lahontan that once blanketed a large triangular area between McDermitt (on the Nevada-Oregon border) in the north, Susanville, California, to the west, and Mono Lake, California, to the south.

Starting around 21,000 years ago – at a time when the climate in the Great Basin was significantly wetter than today – the water level in seven sub-basins rose rapidly to eventually form a huge combined lake. Lake Lahontan reached its highest water level about 13,000 years ago, with a surface area of 8500 sq miles and a maximum depth of 886 feet. About 12,500 years ago, the lake level began to decrease, leaving all the sub-basins but Pyramid Lake and Walker Lake dried up by about 5000 years ago. Geologists refer to these types of lakes with such dramatic water-level fluctuations as pluvial lakes.

The lakeshore was home to prehistoric peoples as early as 11,000 years ago, when woolly mammoths, mastodons, bison and caribou roamed the area. As Lake Lahontan started to dry up, much of the population disappeared. Paiute people – having adapted to life in the desert – inhabited the area when British and American explorers arrived. Petroglyphs indicate they'd been in the area a long time, but it's not clear whether they were descendants of the Lahontan people, displaced them or came here some time after the Lahontans had left.

Besides Pyramid Lake and Walker Lake, other geological remnants of the once enormous Lake Lahontan include the salt pan at Eightmile Flats and the tufa spires near Lovelock. Another Lahontan survivor is the cui-cui fish, which existed in the ancient lake and, until recently, thrived in Pyramid Lake. Once an important food source for the Paiute, cui-cui are now an endangered species, partly because the dam at the mouth of the Truckee River has blocked the natural access to their spawning areas. Efforts are under way to spawn them in hatcheries.

Places to Stay Eureka has three simple motels, all on Main St, with rooms for $25 to around $40: the ***Colonnade Hotel*** (☎ 775-237-9988), the ***Ruby Hill Motel*** (☎ 775-237-5339) and the ***Sundown Lodge*** (☎ 775-237-5334). For a special treat, check in with the ***Parsonage House Cottage*** (☎ 775-237-5756), at the corner of Spring and Bateman Sts. Owner Frank Bleuss created this cute B&B from a 19th-century miner's shack; the single room rents for $54. ***Jackson House B&B*** (☎ 775-237-5577, fax 775-237-5155, 10200 Main St) has nine rooms for $30 to $57.

Ely
• population 4800 • elevation 6421 feet
Ely is the biggest town for miles around, the White Pine County seat and as good a place as any to stop for a night. Three highways converge on the town, and it's a convenient base for exploring Great Basin National Park.

Ely was established as a silver mining town in the 1860s, but large-scale copper mining brought the railroad in 1906 and was the local economic mainstay for over 70 years. A vast open-pit mine was opened at Ruth, just west of town, with railway tracks spiraling into the abyss and snaking 12 miles north to a smelter at McGill. The tracks ran another 90 miles north to join the Southern Pacific line at Cobre, east of Wells.

The mine closed down in 1979, and the population declined from its 1950s level of 12,000. Some new mining ventures have started, and tourism and a new state prison are also providing employment, but it's not exactly a boomtown at the moment.

Orientation & Information
Aultman St is the main drag, running east-west through town. Pick up visitor information at the White Pine Chamber of Commerce (☎ 775-289-8877, fax 775-289-6144), 636 Aultman, open 8 am to 5 pm weekdays. Just west of here are the Jailhouse Motel & Casino and the solid 1920s Hotel Nevada, the biggest commercial buildings in town.

Nevada Northern Railway Museum
Railroad transport was essential for moving huge quantities of material from the open-pit mine. The railway carried passengers from 1906 to 1941, but the vast majority of its work was hauling ore. For each ton of copper extracted, 100 tons of ore were hauled to the smelter and 420 tons of waste were taken to the tailings dumps. Railyards, a depot and a complete railway workshop supported this operation. After the mine closure, the Kennecott Corporation donated the whole shebang – locomotives, buildings, railyard and 32 miles of track – to the White Pine Historical Railroad Foundation, which now offers railway excursions on trains pulled by historic steam engines. The foundation also shows off the depot and workshops as a working museum.

The 'Ghost Train of Old Ely,' pulled by a coal-fired 1910 Baldwin locomotive, does a 1½-hour roundtrip ($14), passing downtown Ely and two ghost towns, going through a curved tunnel and up a scenic canyon. The Hiline Route, usually pulled by a 1952 Alco diesel, does a 1½-hour roundtrip ($10) through the Steptoe Valley and into the hills near McGill where the smelter used to be. You can do both trips for $18, $16 if over 65 or under 18, $8 children.

Walking tours of the depot and sheds let you see and touch a variety of old steam locomotives, carriages and freight cars. Special vehicles, like the rotary steam snowblower and the wrecking crane, are particularly interesting. Tours ($2.50) depart several times between 9:30 am and 4 pm daily, Memorial Day to Labor Day; call the museum (☎ 775-289-2085) for details.

White Pine Public Museum
This museum (☎ 775-289-4710), 2000 Aultman St, has the usual displays of stuff from the late 19th century, some mining and Indian artifacts, an impressively large doll collection and quirky oddities. It's worth a quick look and is open 8:30 am to 1 pm weekdays, 10 am to 4 pm weekends; donation requested.

Places to Stay
There are six motels on Aultman St and a couple more on High St, one block to the north. The ***Rustic Inn*** (☎ 775-289-4404, 1555 Aultman St) has adequate if basic facilities costing $25 to $50.

Hotel Nevada & Gambling Hall (☎ 775-289-6665, 800-406-3055, 501 Aultman) is one of the bigger places and comes with some old-fashioned appeal, if not charm. Rooms are $65. The *Four Sevens Motel* (☎ 775-289-4747, 500 High St) is nice and new and charges $37 to $52.

On 7th St, south of the center at Ave O, *Motel 6* (☎ 775-289-6671, 777 Ave O) is one of the few places with a pool. It has rooms for $28 to $42. Those requiring higher standards and more amenities should fall back on the *Holiday Inn* (☎ 775-289-8900, fax 775-289-4607, 1501 Avenue F) or the *Ramada Inn/Copper Queen Hotel & Casino* (☎ 775-289-4884, 800-851-9526, fax 775-289-1492), on 7th St at Ave I. Both have a casino, a pool and restaurant and charge between $50 and $80.

Steptoe Valley Inn (☎ 775-289-8687, 220 E 11th St) is a twee B&B, with heavily decorated rooms from $68 to $90. It's open only from June to September. There's also a *KOA Campground* (☎ 775-289-3413, 800-562-3413) on Pioche Hwy (Hwy 93) east of town, and several RV parks in the vicinity.

Places to Eat Casino-subsidized food at the *Hotel Nevada* is a pretty good value. *Señorita's*, on Aultman at 5th St, has tasty Mexican main courses starting at $8. For Chinese, try the *Good Friends Restaurant* (1455 Aultman St) with set dinners for around $7.

Around Ely

The huge open-pit mine at **Ruth**, a few miles west, may not be accessible, but you can't miss the mountainous tailings dumps. South of town, off Hwy 93, are the half-dozen well-preserved 1876 **Ward Charcoal Ovens**, 30-foot-tall beehive-shaped structures that are now part of a state historic park. To get there, catch a dirt road off Hwy 93, about 5 miles south of Ely, then head west for 11 miles. The park is open May through October only; $3. Nearby **Cave Lake State Park** (☎ 775-728-4467) has an artificial lake stocked with trout and several campgrounds. It's 15 miles southwest of Ely and reached via Hwys 50, 6, 93 and Success Summit Rd.

Great Basin National Park

This 120-sq-mile park is an absolute gem and worth a long detour and a visit of several days if you enjoy nature and the great outdoors. Mountains of over 11,000 feet rise abruptly from the desert, creating a full range of life zones and landscapes within a very compact area. In a few miles you climb from the desert to piñon pine to forests of fir and aspen and finally reach the tree line, where the hardiest bristlecone pines, the oldest living things on Earth, have lived for thousands of years. The highest peaks are snow-capped in winter and embroidered with wildflowers in spring and summer; there's even a small glacier. The whole range sits like a temperate island surrounded by a sea of sagebrush and is home to a rich variety of animals, including pronghorn antelope, mule deer, coyotes and blacktail jackrabbits. More than 207 bird species have been recorded here, most of them migratory birds like ducks, geese, grouse and cranes.

The wonders continue underground, where the Lehman Caves, lavishly decorated

Bristlecone pine

with limestone formations, are the main attraction.

History In prehistoric times, the area supported a lakeside culture on the shores of the ancient Lake Bonneville. Around 800 years ago, small villages on the eastern side of the Snake Range grew corn, beans and squash. From about 1300 AD, Shoshone and Paiute hunter-gatherers occupied the area, using piñon nuts as their staple food.

Explorers, miners and homesteaders arrived in the mid-1800s. Absalom Lehman

established a ranch in the 1860s and discovered the cave that bears his name around 1885. Much of the Snake Range became a national forest in 1909, and the caves were declared a national monument in 1922. As a result of obstructing efforts from mining and ranching interests, the area did not become a national park until 1986.

Information Coming from the little settlement of Baker, the access road leads straight to the visitor center (☎ 775-234-7331, www.nps.gov/grba), near the Lehman Caves.

GREAT BASIN NATIONAL PARK

1 Wheeler Peak Campground
2 Upper Lehman Creek Campground
3 Lower Lehman Creek Campground
4 Silver Jack Motel
5 Outlaw Family Restaurant
6 Baker Creek Campground
7 Shoshone Creek Primitive Campground
8 Snake Creek Primitive Campground

The center is open 7 am to 6 pm daily, 8 am to 5 pm in winter. It has an excellent selection of books and maps, and the helpful rangers can answer just about any question about the area or book a cave tour for you. Outside you'll find a short nature trail with labeled plants, a cafe and a gift shop, open May to October. Park entry is free. Gas, food and limited accommodations are available in Baker.

In winter, much of the park is covered in snow and, as the upper roads are not plowed, access will be limited unless you come prepared for backcountry skiing or snowshoeing. In summer, especially on weekends, the park can get quite crowded, though most people come just to see the caves and drive the Wheeler Peak Trail. The park rarely has that human zoo feeling that can detract from the enjoyment of better-known parks.

Lehman Caves A tour of the Lehman Caves is a highlight of any visit to the park. Though not particularly large, the caves brim with beautiful and enigmatic formations – stalactites, stalagmites, columns, curtains, flowstones – grouped in chambers with evocative names like Gothic Palace, Cypress Swamp and Grand Palace. Tours last 30, 60 or 90 minutes and cost $2/4/6 (free/$2/3 for children up to age 11). They leave continuously throughout the day, with the last tour departing around 4:30 pm.

Make a booking or buy your ticket at the visitor center as soon as you arrive, as there can be a wait for the next available tour. The temperature inside is a constant 50°F, so bring a sweater.

Wheeler Peak Scenic Drive Impressive Wheeler Peak is 13,063 feet high, the second-highest point in the state, and is dusted by snowdrifts even in the middle of summer. From the park entrance, a paved road winds up its northern slopes for about 12 miles, gaining 3400 feet in the process and culminating at 10,000 feet. En route, you'll have spectacular views of the Great Basin and a chance to experience the changes in temperature, landscape and vegetation. Stop at some of the scenic lookouts and take one of the short walks. Try to allow two hours at the top of the road, near Wheeler Peak Campground, to do the hiking circuit through superb country to Stella and Teresa lakes. Ideally, take more time and do some longer hikes.

Hiking There are a number of fine hikes that will take the better part of a day but do not entail backcountry camping. Keep on established trails whenever possible; the alpine ecosystem is more fragile than its rugged looks suggest. If you plan an overnight trip, there's a backcountry registration system; sign up where you leave your car or with the rangers at the station. Water in the streams and lakes may be unsafe to drink, so carry your own for any day hikes and purify any untreated water. The visitor center can advise you on current trail and weather conditions.

The trail to the summit of Wheeler Peak, from the trailhead on the scenic road, is about 10 miles roundtrip, with a climb of nearly 3000 feet. The most accessible group of gnarled and twisted bristlecone pines, a highlight of the park, is the grove about 2 miles from the Wheeler Peak Campground. Another mile away is the edge of the ice field. You can see both the bristlecone grove and the ice field on a 6-mile loop trail, with an elevation gain of 1400 feet. A longer walk is the 11-mile circuit around Baker Lake and Johnson Lake, with a total climb of 3200 feet.

Camping The park has four developed campgrounds with toilets, tables, fire rings and water (in summer). *Lower Lehman Creek*, *Upper Lehman Creek* and *Wheeler Peak* campgrounds are along Wheeler Peak Scenic Drive. *Baker Creek Campground* is by the visitor center. Fees are $7 per site, first-come, first-served. Two primitive campgrounds on Snake Creek have pit toilets but no water (free).

Getting There & Away Take Hwy 6/50 about 30 miles east from the junction with Hwy 93 and fork right at Hwy 487. Follow that for about 5 miles south to Baker, 5 miles west of the park visitor center.

Baker

• **population 50** • **elevation 5310 feet**

Don't expect too much – it's a tiny place – but you can stay at the *Silverjack Motel* (☎ 775-234-7323) on Main St, a friendly little place charging $32 to $60. The *Border Inn* (☎ 775-234-7300), right on the highway, is slightly cheaper. For food, the *Outlaw Family Restaurant* is a well-known institution, and for a drink, drop by the *Hitchin' Post*.

ALONG HWY 95

This is the main highway going vaguely north-south through the western part of the state, though it's hardly a direct route between Reno and Las Vegas. It zigzags to avoid mountain ranges and to pass through places that were once important mining centers but are now not much more than ghost towns. The area is very sparsely populated.

Hawthorne

• **population 4162** • **elevation 4320 feet**

Coming south from Fallon (see the Along Hwy 50 section earlier in this chapter), you pass Walker Lake and a village with gas, food and a motel. The first real town is Hawthorne, with about 4000 people, one casino and about a dozen motels. The **Mineral County Museum** (☎ 775-945-5142) has displays on mining and early pioneers and is open 11 am to 5 pm Tuesday to Saturday. The surrounding desert is dotted with concrete bunkers storing millions of tons of munitions and explosives from the army's Hawthorne Ammunition Depot.

Tonopah

• **population 3616** • **elevation 6030 feet**

The next town of any size, 104 miles on, Tonopah was once a major silver mining center. Huge mine headframes still loom above the town, which clings onto its population in a starkly beautiful desert setting. The **Central Nevada Museum** (☎ 775-482-9676) has a good collection of Shoshone baskets, early photographs, mining relics and mortician's instruments. Hours are 9 am to 5 pm daily in summer, 11 am to 5 pm, closed Sunday, in winter; free.

NEVADA GREAT BASIN

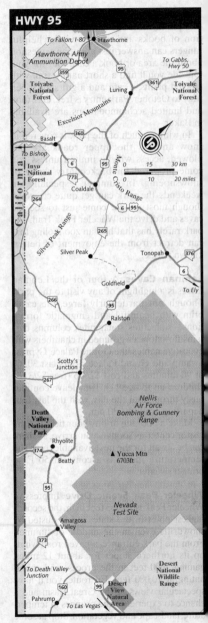

The restored **Mizpah Hotel** (☎ 775-482-6202, 800-646-4641, 100 Main St) dates from 1907 and is the most elegant place to stay. Rates range from $25 to $84, depending on the room and the season. The **Station House Hotel & Casino** (☎ 775-482-9777, 1100 Erie Main) has good, cheap food, 24 hours a day, and live entertainment most nights. Rooms are $33 to $80. At the **Best Western Hi-Desert Inn** (☎ 775-482-3511, 323 Main St), you'll pay about $40 to $69, and there's a pool.

Goldfield
• **population 400** • **elevation 5689 feet**

Another 25 miles south brings you to what once was the largest town in Nevada. It is now somewhat smaller, but it's still the seat of Esmeralda County (population 1340).

Gold was discovered here in 1902, and the growth was spectacular – a tent city by 1903, Goldfield had a post office and railway station a year later and more than 10,000 people by 1907. The population peaked in 1910 with 20,000, as did production, but then the decline was precipitous. The town flooded in 1913; the biggest mining company pulled out in 1919, and a fire in 1923 destroyed nearly all the buildings.

A few stone and brick structures survive, including the four-story Goldfield Hotel, once the most luxurious hotel between San Francisco and Kansas City. Also here are the old telephone exchange, high school and the still operating courthouse (note the brass and oak fixtures). Another survivor is the **Santa Fe Saloon & Motel** (☎ 775-485-3431), 900 N 5th Ave, an atmospheric stop for a drink and the town's only place to rest your head ($30 to $42).

Nevada Test Site & Yucca Mountain

Continuing on US 95 takes you past a 'boom' area of another kind. To the east is the Nellis Air Force Bombing and Gunnery Range, which abuts the Nevada Test Site on three sides. In the 1950s, some 120 nuclear weapons were exploded in the atmosphere over the test site, and another 600 underground explosions were detonated over the next 30 years. The tests have now been discontinued following the Nuclear Test Ban Treaty, but a high incidence of cancer still shows up in the areas of southern Utah that were downwind of the atmospheric tests.

On the western edge of the test site is **Yucca Mountain**, a long, low ridge of volcanic rock that the Department of Energy has selected as the location for a high-level nuclear waste repository. The DOE has developed a specific proposal that is currently the subject of a feasibility study due to be completed by 2001. If approved, the repository would start operation in 2010. Nevadans are divided on the proposal, a large project yielding jobs and revenue but also incalculable environmental risks. The government operates free monthly tours of Yucca Mountain. Reservations must be made at least two weeks in advance by calling ☎ 800-225-6972; non-US citizens must apply at least four weeks early. For dates and details, check www.ymp.gov.

Highway 95 continues through Beatty, with side roads going west to Death Valley (see the California Deserts chapter). Just west of Beatty is the **Rhyolite Historic Site** (☎ 775-553-2424), a true ghost town with photogenic stone ruins (including a mission-style railroad depot), as well as the interesting Bottle House – built of, yes, bottles – and the Sculpture Park created by a group of Belgian artists. It's open 7 am to 4 pm Tuesday through Saturday; free. Rhyolite became a ghost town in the '30s, but recently a Canadian company discovered significant amounts of microscopic gold and has developed a sizable mine near the old site.

Along the way to Las Vegas, the mountains to the east have some of the most distinct and beautiful rainbow rock strata you'll see anywhere. Maybe it's the radiation...

ALONG HWY 93

Highway 93 is the route you'd take from Las Vegas to Great Basin National Park, passing great scenery, ghost towns and few people. From the south, Hwy 93 crosses the wall of Hoover Dam, goes through Las Vegas and joins I-15 for the next 22 miles. Diverging north, Hwy 93 parallels the Desert National

Wildlife Range, where you might spot a bighorn sheep. After about 70 miles, the road enters the Pahranagat Valley and its national wildlife refuge, whose spring-fed lakes are a major stopover for migratory birds. The lakeside's tall cottonwoods make a good picnic spot. Passing Alamo and Ash Springs leads to a junction where you turn east and go through interesting countryside to Caliente.

Caliente
• **population 1100** • **elevation 4400 feet**

Caliente is named for the hot springs in the area, which made it a good location for a stop on the Las Vegas-to-Salt Lake City railroad in the early 1900s. The town still has stone buildings from 1905, but its architectural highlight is the 1923 **railroad depot**, a large, white, mission-style structure with a long colonnade. Inside are the city hall, library, chamber of commerce and a mural depicting the history of southern Nevada. Next to the depot is the new Boxcar Museum, open 10 am to 2 pm weekdays; $1. The chamber of commerce (☎ 775-726-3129) has a walking tour pamphlet of the town's old buildings.

You can stay at the *Hot Springs Motel* (☎ *775-726-3777, 800-726-3777, fax 775-726-3513*), just north of the railroad tracks, for $34 to $75, including use of hot spring pools. Other motels, like the tiny *Rainbow Canyon* (☎ *775-726-3291*), charge about the same or less.

Around Caliente

A little south of town, on Hwy 317, **Rainbow Canyon** is known for its petroglyphs and the colorful cliffs flanking Meadow Valley wash. You can follow it for about 40 miles to Carp or take a rough back road that reaches Hwy 93 near the Desert Wildlife Range.

East of Caliente, near the Utah border, **Beaver Dam State Park** is well off the beaten track. It has a campground, good fishing in the reservoir and hiking in the forests and canyons.

Panaca
• **population 800** • **elevation 4738 feet**

This little agricultural town was founded as a Mormon colony in 1864 and was the first Non-Indian settlement in southern Nevada. Panaca prospered supplying food to Pioche, which displayed all the sin and lawlessness that the Mormon leaders so feared in a mining town. Panaca is just east of Hwy 93, on Hwy 319. Continuing on Hwy 319 brings you to Cedar City, Utah, a good base for trips to nearby Zion and Bryce Canyon national parks (see Canyon Country earlier in this book) and Cedar Breaks National Monument. For detailed coverage of the area, see Lonely Planet's *Southwest USA*.

Cathedral Gorge State Park On the west side of Hwy 93, just north of the Panaca turnoff, this park is another one of Nevada's little-known scenic treasures, featuring rows of natural spires and buttresses like those of Gothic cathedrals. By the entrance is an information center (☎ 775-728-4460), and there are several easy hikes into narrow side canyons

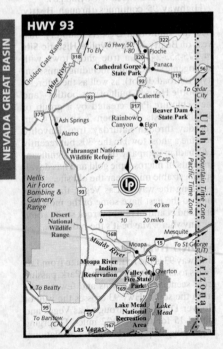

HWY 93

To Hwy 50,
I-80
To Ely
Golden Gate Range
Pioche
Cathedral Gorge State Park
Panaca
To Cedar City
Caliente
Beaver Dam State Park
Ash Springs
Rainbow Canyon
Elgin
Alamo
Pahranagat National Wildlife Refuge
Carp
Nellis Air Force Bombing & Gunnery Range
Desert National Wildlife Range
0   20   40 km
0   10   20 miles
Muddy River
Moapa
Mesquite
To St George (UT)
Moapa River Indian Reservation
Valley of Fire State Park
Overton
To Beatty
Lake Mead National Recreation Area
Lake Mead
To Barstow (CA)
Las Vegas
Utah
Arizona
Mountain Time Zone
Pacific Time Zone

The Extraterrestrial Highway

Never one to pass up a promotional moniker, the Nevada Tourism Commission has declared the 98 miles of Hwy 375 between Warm Springs and Ash Springs the state's 'Extraterrestrial Highway.' A specially designed highway sign even makes it official. The road's remoteness, desolation and proximity to Area 51 – a top secret section of Nellis Air Force Base, also known as 'Dreamland' – has spawned countless accounts of alleged UFO sightings: glimmering lights, hovering shapes, buzzing sounds and so on. The fact that the military only recently acknowledged the very existence of Area 51, which it uses to test planes like the stealth fighter and the SR-71, has only fueled further speculation. Some die-hard UFO fanatics suspect the government is really hiding aliens, maybe even test-piloting secretly landed alien spacecraft.

Be that as it may, those attempting to get to the truth of the matter should stop by the Little ÁLÉ Inn in the petite town of Rachel, population 100 – sort of the unofficial 'ET Hwy' HQ of UFOlogy. And bring those binoculars. You never know what's out there....

NEVADA GREAT BASIN

and a nice campground. Miller Point Overlook offers sweeping views of the canyon.

Pioche
• population 800 • elevation 6064 feet

Highway 93 actually bypasses this town; to get there take the Castleton loop (Hwy 320), which extends from Hwy 93 north and south of Pioche.

This old silver mining town was named after François Pioche, who in 1869 established the first successful mining and ore processing operation in the area. By 1873, according to one Nevada newspaper, Pioche was 'a synonym for murder and lawlessness throughout the state' and 'overrun with as desperate a class of scoundrels as probably ever afflicted any mining town.' These days the town is quiet, picturesque, not excessively prettied up and full of great stories about its wild past. There's a chamber of commerce (☎ 775-962-5544) on Main St.

The **Lincoln County Museum** (☎ 775-962-5207) on Main St has leaflets with some of the local legends and a brochure with a walking tour of the town. Exhibits include a portable dental surgery from the days when dentists made mine calls. The museum is open daily and deserves a donation.

Another attraction, which is a legend in itself, is the courthouse around the corner on Lacour St. Construction on the building was started in 1871 at an original price of $16,400. It was later subjected to outrageous cost increases, and financed with funny bond issues that ultimately cost the county $1 million. Inside the **Million-Dollar Courthouse** are old photos, documents and newspaper articles, as well as the courtroom, sheriff's office and jailhouse. It is open daily April to October; donation requested.

Hutchings Motel (☎ 775-962-5404) and *Motel Pioche* (☎ 775-962-5551) are the only games in town, with rooms costing about $35.

Places to eat include the **Silver Café** (☎ 775-962-5124) and the **Grub Steak** (☎ 775-962-5527), which is recommended. Both restaurants are reasonably priced and are within 150 feet of each other along Main St.

North of Pioche

Highway 93 follows a broad valley north for about 80 miles until it joins Hwy 50, where you can go east to the Great Basin National Park or west to Ely (see Along Hwy 50 earlier in this chapter). From Ely, Hwy 93 follows other valleys up to Wells (see Along I-80). North of Wells, Hwy 93 climbs into the mountains and crosses the Idaho border at **Jackpot**, a small town that thrives by providing casinos and gambling facilities for Idaho visitors.

Glossary

AAA – The American Automobile Association, also called the 'Auto Club' (see Useful Organizations in the Facts for the Visitor chapter). Northern California, Nevada and Southern California are in separate branches of the national organization.

adobe – A traditional Spanish-Mexican building material of sunbaked bricks of mud and straw; a structure built with this type of brick

alien – An official term for a non-US citizen, visiting or resident in the US (as in 'resident alien' or 'illegal alien')

Amtrak – The nation's federally sponsored railroad company

Angeleno – A resident of Los Angeles

antojito – (Spanish) An appetizer, snack or light meal

Arts & Crafts – A movement of architecture and design that gained popularity in America just after the turn of the 20th century; the style emphasizes simple craftsmanship and functional design and emerged as a reaction to the perceived shoddiness of machine-made goods; also called (American) craftsman

ATM – Automated teller machine, the place to obtain crisp $20 bills

ATV – All-terrain vehicle, used for off-road transportation, recreation and environmental destruction

back east – As seen from California, the East Coast is 'back east'

BLM – Bureau of Land Management, an agency of the US Department of the Interior that controls substantial portions of the public lands in the West

blue book – A guide that lists the average prices of used cars by year, make and model; available in libraries, bookstores and on the World Wide Web

boomtown – a town that has experienced rapid economic and population growth. Many areas experienced such a boom during the gold rush, then 'busted' when the gold ran out; many became ghost towns.

booster – A person who promotes the interests and growth of his or her town or city, usually with a view to advancing their own business interests at the same time. Historically, boosters in California have attempted to attract government facilities, private investments and especially railroads to their areas.

Californio – an early Spanish colonist in California

CCC – Civilian Conservation Corps, a depression-era federal program established in 1933 to employ unskilled young adults, mainly on projects aimed at the conservation of US wildlands

Chicano/Chicana – A Mexican-American man/woman

CHP – The California Highway Patrol

cirque – A circular depression, often containing a lake, created on a mountainside by glacial action

CNN – Cable News Network, a cable TV station based in Atlanta, Georgia, providing continuous bulletins of US and international news

country & western – An amalgamation of rock and folk music of the Southern and Western US; line dancing and the two-step are dances associated with this music

coyote – A small wild dog, native to the central and western North American lowlands; also, a person who assists illegal immigrants in crossing the border into the US

DEA – Drug Enforcement Administration, the government body responsible for enforcing the nation's drug laws

docent – A guide or attendant at a museum or gallery

El Camino Real – (Spanish) The Royal Road, the road that links the chain of California missions. Also known as the King's Highway, El Camino Real is distinguished by its commemorative bell-shaped green streetlamps.

entrée – The main course of a meal

forty-niners – Immigrants to California during the 1849 gold rush; also, the San Francisco professional football team

gated community – A walled residential area accessible only through security gates; common in conservative, affluent, suburban areas such as Orange County, Palm Springs

GOP – Grand Old Party, nickname of the Republican Party

HI-AYH – Hostelling International-American Youth Hostels, a term given to hostels affiliated with Hostelling International, a member group of the IYHF (International Youth Hostel Federation)

hookup – A facility at an RV camping site for connecting (hooking up) a vehicle to an electricity, water, sewer or cable TV system

IHOP – International House of Pancakes, a low-budget restaurant chain specializing in breakfast

INS – Immigration & Naturalization Service, the division of the US Department of Justice responsible for immigration and naturalization of people from foreign countries

IRS – Internal Revenue Service, a branch of the US Treasury Department responsible for administering and enforcing internal revenue laws; the tax collectors

Joshua tree – A tall, treelike type of yucca plant, common in the arid Southwest. The Joshua tree is said to have been named by a group of early Mormon settlers who likened its curving branches to the outstretched arms of Joshua, leading them out of the wilderness.

KOA – Kampgrounds of America, a private chain of campgrounds throughout the US, with extensive amenities and moderate- to high-priced sites for RVs and tents

laguna – (Spanish) lagoon

Latino/Latina – A man/woman of Latin-American descent

LDS – From the Church of Jesus Christ of Latter-Day Saints, the formal name of the Mormon Church

mariachi – (Spanish) Mexican street musicians, usually elaborately dressed, playing traditional folk songs on guitars and trumpets

marine layer – A coastal fog in Southern California that's sometimes mistaken for air pollution

morteros – Hollows in rocks used by Native Americans for grinding seeds; also called 'mortar holes'

NAACP – National Association for the Advancement of Colored People

National Guard – Each state's federally supported military reserves, used most often in civil emergencies. The National Guard can be called into action either by the state's governor or by Congress, for national service, at any time.

National Register of Historic Places – A listing of historic sites designated by the NPS, based on evidence supporting a structure's significance in the development of a community. Being listed on the National Register restricts property owners from making major structural changes to buildings, but also provides tax incentives for the buildings' preservation.

National Recreation Area – A term used to describe NPS units in areas of considerable scenic or ecological importance that have been modified by human activity, such as by major dam projects

nevada – (Spanish) snowy; snow-covered

NOW – National Organization for Women; strong proponents of women's issues, the group uses education, politics and legal action to improve the political and economic status of women in the US.

NPR – National Public Radio, a noncommercial, listener-supported broadcast organization, which produces and distributes news, public affairs and cultural programming via a network of loosely affiliated radio stations throughout the US

NPS – National Park Service, a division of the US Department of the Interior that administers national parks and national monuments

NRA – National Rifle Association, an influential lobbying body generally opposed to gun-control legislation of any kind

OHV or **ORV** – An off-highway vehicle or off-road vehicle

Parknet – A toll-free reservation service for state parks; previously known as Destinet
PBS – Public Broadcasting Service, a noncommercial television network known for nature shows, British imports and Pavarotti; the TV equivalent of NPR
PC – Politically correct; also means personal computer
PDT – Pacific Daylight Time, the time zone of the West Coast states and Nevada during the summer; one hour ahead of Pacific Standard Time
petroglyph – A work of rock art in which the design is pecked, chipped or abraded into the surface of the rock
PGA – Professional Golfers' Association.
pictograph – A work of rock art in which the design is painted on a rock surface with one or more colors
pound symbol – In the US, # is called the pound symbol (or pound key on a telephone), not £
PST – Pacific Standard Time, the normal time zone of the West Coast states and Nevada

RV – Recreational vehicle, also known as a 'motor home'

Santa Ana – A strong, dry, hot wind blowing from the California deserts toward the Pacific coast, usually in winter
sierra – (Spanish) Mountain range
So-Cal – Southern California
spot trip – Tour on which an outfitter carries your gear (and you, if you desire) to a chosen destination and either leaves you to hike out or picks you up days or weeks later
SSN – Social Security number, a nine-digit code required for employment and for receiving social security benefits

strip mall – a collection of retail businesses arranged along a parking lot, often in a tacky, neon-lit row or 'strip'

UC – University of California
USAF – United States Air Force
USFS – United States Forest Service, a division of the US Department of Agriculture; it manages federal forest lands, implementing policies based on the idea of 'multiple use,' including logging, wildlife management, and camping and recreation.
USGS – United States Geological Survey, an agency of the US Department of the Interior responsible for detailed topographic maps of the entire country. Widely available at outdoor-oriented businesses, USGS maps are popular with hikers and backpackers.
USMC – United States Marine Corps, a branch of the armed forces that enforces US policy abroad. Though reporting to the US Navy, the Marines have their own ships, artillery and aircraft and are usually the first forces dispatched to any foreign trouble spot.

wash – A watercourse in the desert, usually dry but subject to flash flooding
WPA – Works Progress (later, Work Projects) Administration, a depression-era program established under the Franklin D Roosevelt administration in 1935 as part of the New Deal to increase employment by funding public works projects. WPA projects included construction of roads and buildings, beautification of public structures (especially post offices) and the publication of a well-respected series of state and regional guidebooks.

zip code – A five- or nine-digit postal code, introduced in 1963 under the Zone Improvement Program to expedite the sorting and delivery of US mail

Toll-Free Numbers

Toll-free number information
☎ 800-555-1212

Accommodations

Best Western	☎ 800-528-1234
Budgetel	☎ 800-428-3438
Clarion	☎ 800-252-7466
Comfort Inn	☎ 800-228-5150
Courtyard by Marriott	☎ 800-321-2211
Days Inn	☎ 800-329-7466
Econo Lodge	☎ 800-424-4777
Embassy Suites Hotels	☎ 800-362-2779
Fairfield Inns	☎ 800-228-2800
Fairmont	☎ 800-527-4727
Four Seasons	☎ 800-332-3442
Hampton Inns	☎ 800-426-7866
HI-AYH	☎ 800-909-4776
Hilton	☎ 800-445-8667
Holiday Inn	☎ 800-465-4329
Howard Johnson	☎ 800-446-4656
Hyatt	☎ 800-233-1234
ITT Sheraton	☎ 800-325-3535
Inter-Continental Hotels	☎ 800-327-0200
La Quinta Motor Inns	☎ 800-531-5900
Loews	☎ 800-235-6397
Marriott	☎ 800-228-9290
Meridien	☎ 800-543-4300
Motel 6	☎ 800-466-8356
Omni	☎ 800-843-6664
Radisson	☎ 800-333-3333
Ramada	☎ 800-272-6232
Red Lion Inns	☎ 800-547-8010
Red Roof Inns	☎ 800-843-7663
Rodeway Inn	☎ 800-424-4777
Sheraton	☎ 800-325-3535
Sleep Inns	☎ 800-424-4777
Super 8	☎ 800-800-8000
Susse Chalet	☎ 800-524-2538
Travelodge	☎ 800-578-7878
Vagabond Hotels	☎ 800-522-1555
Westin	☎ 800-228-3000
Wyndham	☎ 800-822-4200

Airlines (Domestic)

Airtran	☎ 800-825-8538
Alaska	☎ 800-426-0333
American	☎ 800-433-7300
America West	☎ 800-235-9292
Aspen Mountain Air-Lone Star	☎ 800-877-3932
Big Sky	☎ 800-237-7788
Continental	☎ 800-525-0280
Delta	
(Domestic)	☎ 800-221-1212
(International)	☎ 800-241-4141
Hawaiian	☎ 800-367-5320
Northwest	
(Domestic)	☎ 800-225-2525
(International)	☎ 800-447-4747
Reno Air	☎ 800-736-6247
Skywest-	
Delta Connection	☎ 800-453-9417
Southwest	☎ 800-435-9792
Tower	☎ 800-348-6937
TWA	
(Domestic)	☎ 800-221-2000
(International)	☎ 800-892-4141
United	
(Domestic)	☎ 800-241-6522
(International)	☎ 800-538-2929
US Airways	☎ 800-428-4322

Airlines (International)

AeroLitoral	☎ 800-237-6639
Aeroméxico	☎ 800-237-6639
Air Canada	☎ 800-776-3000
Air France	☎ 800-237-2747
Air New Zealand	☎ 800-262-1234
Aviateca	☎ 800-327-9832
British Airways	☎ 800-247-9297
Canadian	☎ 800-426-7000
Grupo TACA	☎ 800-535-8780
Japan Air	☎ 800-525-3663
KLM	☎ 800-374-7747
Lufthansa	☎ 800-645-3880
Mexicana	☎ 800-531-7921
Qantas	☎ 800-227-4500
Virgin Atlantic	☎ 800-862-8621

TOLL-FREE NUMBERS

Car-Rental Agencies

Advantage	☎ 800-777-5500
Alamo	☎ 800-327-9633
Avis	☎ 800-831-2847
	800-331-1212
Budget	☎ 800-527-0700
	800-472-3325
CruiseAmerica (RV rental)	☎ 800-327-7799
Dollar	☎ 800-800-4000
Enterprise	☎ 800-325-8007
	800-736-8222
Hertz	☎ 800-654-3131
National	☎ 800-227-7368
	800-328-4567
	800-227-3876
National (TDD)	☎ 800-328-6323
Rent-a-Wreck	☎ 800-535-1391
Thrifty	☎ 800-367-2277

Money

Western Union	☎ 800-325-6000

State & Federal Agencies

California Department of Transportation	☎ 800-427-7623
California Division of Tourism	☎ 800-862-2543
National Park Service	☎ 800-365-2267
Parknet	☎ 800-444-7275
US Forest Service	☎ 800-280-2267
US Postal Service	☎ 800-275-8777

Transportation

AAA	☎ 800-272-2155
AAA road service & towing (members only)	☎ 800-222-4357
Amtrak	☎ 800-872-7245
Green Tortoise	☎ 800-227-4766
Greyhound	☎ 800-231-2222
Greyhound International	☎ 800-246-8572
SuperShuttle	☎ 800-258-3826

Travel Agencies

Council Travel	☎ 800-226-8624
STA	☎ 800-777-0112

Climate Charts

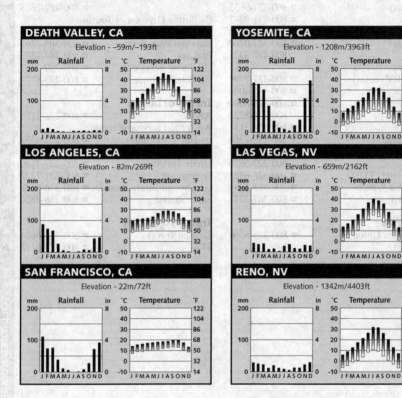

DEATH VALLEY, CA
Elevation - −59m/−193ft

LOS ANGELES, CA
Elevation - 82m/269ft

SAN FRANCISCO, CA
Elevation - 22m/72ft

YOSEMITE, CA
Elevation - 1208m/3963ft

LAS VEGAS, NV
Elevation - 659m/2162ft

RENO, NV
Elevation - 1342m/4403ft

Acknowledgments

THANKS

Thanks to the following travelers, who read the first edition of this book and wrote to us about their experiences in California and Nevada (apologies if we misspelled your name):

Jo Abbie, Elizabeth Abbott, Lars Anderson & Pernilla Siebenfreund, Magdalena Balcerek, Theodore C Bale, Sarah-Jane Bateman, Judith Beery, Caroline Bell, Stacy Benjamin, Bob Bergevin, Jo Billingham, Nicholas Burton, Regina Campbell, Camiel Camps, Robin Catto, Jacky Chalk, Brenda J Chapel, Darrin Charmley, Jennifer E Chase, RA Cherriman, Kate Chmiel, Henrik Stender Christensen, Lars Bruun Christensen & Krista Vanggaard, JE Collins, John Connell, Geoff Cook, Ray & Sena Copson, Kevin Cotter, Robert Crisp, Trisha Delbridge, Chris Delodder, Susan Derby, Pam Dickson, Michele DiNunzio & Veronica Cocco, Tim Dolta, Scott Donahue, Karina Duffy, Joanne Duggan, Monica Ehman, Lotta Emgard, Jenni Empson-Ridler, Marian Ferrari, Amy-Lynn Fischer, Jane Fitzpatrick & Bruce Wright, Andrea Foley, A Ford, Steve Fox, Nick Freeman, Vanessa Gajewska & Keith Greenfield, Jennifer Gaylord, C David Gibbons, Graham Gilpin, Erik Gothberg, Martin Green, JC Gwilliam, Claire Haddon, Jody Hansen, Shea Hardy, Sue Harvey, Brian Heeney, Kathleen Helgesen, Art & Barbara Hess, Del Hillger, Damien P Horigan, Faridah Iriani Tahir, Jude Isherwood, Asker Jeukendrup, Alan Jones, Romy Jouen, Heidi Kestnebaum, Jennifer Keys, Alan Kirsner & Frances Millane, Michael R Kluge, Vera Kramer, Peta & Pierre Kruse, Frances Kwok, Nathan Landau, Silviu Landman, Karin de Lauje, Stephen Andrew Lee, Elli Levy, Erin Lewis, Hope Liebersohn, Krista Lighthall, Keith A Liker, JD Lindsay, Anthony & Kristy Lombardo, Wendi Lunn, Christine Lutz, Annette McCormick, Jim McGillis, Jamie Mackenzie, Chris McLaughlin, JL Macomber, Jenny McRae, Andreas Mahn, Evan Malonai, Philippe Margaron, Sheryl Maring, Della Markey, P Marquis, Marti Matulis, Kristine Melby, Melina Mingari, Erik Moderegger, Nanelle Mulligan, Fiona & Claire Nash-Wortham, Julie Needham, Richard Nelson, Kenneth Newman, Leslie Newman, Tracey Nicholls, Juanita Nicholson, Hemming Nielsen, Marc Norman, Regina O'Connor, Miles Parker, Brett Paterson, Eliose de Paula Piva, Rachel J Pearcey, Grant Pearse, DJ Peterson, Jo Pilkington-Down, David Pinder, Peter Polednak, Monta Pooley, Mary Marcia Pope, Lindsay Pulliam, Christopher Race, Thomas Rau & Andrea Rogge, Theresa Rieder, Alex Ro, Jon Roberts, Kelly Roberts, Alan F Robilliard, Rodrigo Gouvea Rosique, Ryon Rosovold, Neil J Rubenking, Sally-Ann Ryder, S Sanderson, Mary & Martin Seed, Liz Seers & Andrew Britton, Sue Ellen Shaneyfelt, Sue Shepard, Elaine Simer, Simon Skerrit, Joyce Slaton, L Smith, Jeannette Stewart, Joe Suchman, Jean E Sunderland, Selvi Supramaniam, Melanie Thomas & David Wolfhart, Richard Thompson, Kerri Thomsen, Hannah Treworgy, Christa Van Schaardenburg, Paul von Wichert, A Weekes, Norman Weisser, Jodie Whan, Stephanie Wickersham, Monique Williamson, Adriaan Witjes, Allan Wong, Kenneth Woolley, Richard Yates, Donna Zalan, Sheila Zompa.

Guides by Region

Lonely Planet is known worldwide for publishing practical, reliable and no-nonsense travel information in our guides and on our Web site. The Lonely Planet list covers just about every accessible part of the world. Currently there are thirteen series: travel guides, shoestring guides, walking guides, city guides, phrasebooks, audio packs, city maps, travel atlases, diving and snorkeling guides, restaurant guides, first-time travel guides, healthy travel and travel literature.

AFRICA Africa – the South • Africa on a shoestring • Arabic (Egyptian) phrasebook • Arabic (Moroccan) phrasebook • Cairo • Cape Town • Cape Town city map • Central Africa • East Africa • Egypt • Egypt travel atlas • Ethiopian (Amharic) phrasebook • The Gambia & Senegal • Healthy Travel Africa • Kenya • Kenya travel atlas • Malawi, Mozambique & Zambia • Morocco • North Africa • South Africa, Lesotho & Swaziland • South Africa, Lesotho & Swaziland travel atlas • Swahili phrasebook • Tanzania, Zanzibar & Pemba • Trekking in East Africa • Tunisia • West Africa • Zimbabwe, Botswana & Namibia • Zimbabwe, Botswana & Namibia travel atlas
Travel Literature: The Rainbird: A Central African Journey • Songs to an African Sunset: A Zimbabwean Story • Mali Blues: Traveling to an African Beat

AUSTRALIA & THE PACIFIC Auckland • Australia • Australian phrasebook • Bushwalking in Australia • Bushwalking in Papua New Guinea • Fiji • Fijian phrasebook • Islands of Australia's Great Barrier Reef • Melbourne • Melbourne city map • Micronesia • New Caledonia • New South Wales & the ACT • New Zealand • Northern Territory • Outback Australia • Out To Eat – Melbourne • Papua New Guinea • Papua New Guinea (Pidgin) phrasebook • Queensland • Rarotonga & the Cook Islands • Samoa • Solomon Islands • South Australia • South Pacific Languages phrasebook • Sydney • Sydney city map • Tahiti & French Polynesia • Tasmania • Tonga • Tramping in New Zealand • Vanuatu • Victoria • Western Australia
Travel Literature: Islands in the Clouds • Kiwi Tracks • Sean & David's Long Drive

CENTRAL AMERICA & THE CARIBBEAN Bahamas and Turks & Caicos • Bermuda • Central America on a shoestring • Costa Rica • Cuba • Dominican Republic & Haiti • Eastern Caribbean • Guatemala, Belize & Yucatán: La Ruta Maya • Jamaica • Mexico • Mexico City • Panama • Puerto Rico
Travel Literature: Green Dreams: Travels in Central America

EUROPE Amsterdam • Amsterdam city map • Andalucía • Austria • Baltic States phrasebook • Barcelona • Berlin • Berlin city map • Britain • British phrasebook • Brussels, Bruges & Antwerp • Budapest city map • Canary Islands • Central Europe • Central Europe phrasebook • Corsica • Czech & Slovak Republics • Denmark • Dublin • Eastern Europe • Eastern Europe phrasebook • Edinburgh • Estonia, Latvia & Lithuania • Europe • Finland • France • French phrasebook • Germany • German phrasebook • Greece • Greek phrasebook • Hungary • Iceland, Greenland & the Faroe Islands • Ireland • Italian phrasebook • Italy • Lisbon • London • London city map • Mediterranean Europe • Mediterranean Europe phrasebook • Norway • Paris • Paris city map • Poland • Portugal • Portugal travel atlas • Prague • Prague city map • Provence & the Côte d'Azur • Romania & Moldova • Rome • Russia, Ukraine & Belarus • Russian phrasebook • Scandinavian & Baltic Europe • Scandinavian Europe phrasebook • Scotland • Slovenia • Spain • Spanish phrasebook • St Petersburg • Switzerland • Trekking in Spain • Ukrainian phrasebook • Vienna • Walking in Britain • Walking in Ireland • Walking in Italy • Walking in Switzerland • Western Europe • Western Europe phrasebook
Travel Literature: The Olive Grove: Travels in Greece

INDIAN SUBCONTINENT Bangladesh • Bengali phrasebook • Bhutan • Delhi • Goa • Hindi/Urdu phrasebook • India • India & Bangladesh travel atlas • Indian Himalaya • Karakoram Highway • Kerala • Mumbai • Nepal • Nepali phrasebook • Pakistan • Rajasthan • Read This First: Asia & India • South India • Sri Lanka • Sri Lanka phrasebook • Trekking in the Indian Himalaya • Trekking in the Karakoram & Hindukush • Trekking in the Nepal Himalaya
Travel Literature: In Rajasthan • Shopping for Buddhas

LONELY PLANET

Mail Order

onely Planet products are distributed worldwide. They are also available by mail order from Lonely Planet, so if you have difficulty finding a title please write to us. North and South American residents should write to 150 Linden St, Oakland, CA 94607, USA; European and African residents should write to 10a Spring Place, London NW5 3BH, UK; and residents of other countries to PO Box 617, Hawthorn, Victoria 3122, Australia.

ISLANDS OF THE INDIAN OCEAN Madagascar & Comoros • Maldives • Mauritius, Réunion & Seychelles

MIDDLE EAST & CENTRAL ASIA Arab Gulf States • Central Asia • Central Asia phrasebook • Hebrew phrasebook • Iran • Israel & the Palestinian Territories • Israel & the Palestinian Territories travel atlas • Istanbul • Istanbul city map • Istanbul to Cairo • Jerusalem • Jerusalem city map • Jordan & Syria • Jordan, Syria & Lebanon travel atlas • Lebanon • Middle East on a shoestring • Syria • Turkey • Turkish phrasebook • Turkey travel atlas • Yemen
Travel Literature: The Gates of Damascus • Kingdom of the Film Stars: Journey into Jordan

NORTH AMERICA Alaska • Backpacking in Alaska • Baja California • California & Nevada • Canada • Chicago • Chicago city map • Deep South • Florida • Hawaii • Honolulu • Las Vegas • Los Angeles • Miami • New England • New Orleans • New York City • New York city map • New York, New Jersey & Pennsylvania • Pacific Northwest USA • Puerto Rico • Rocky Mountain States • San Francisco • San Francisco city map • Seattle • Southwest USA • Texas • USA • USA phrasebook • Vancouver • Washington, DC & the Capital Region • Washington, DC city map
Travel Literature: Drive Thru America

NORTH-EAST ASIA Beijing • Cantonese phrasebook • China • Hong Kong • Hong Kong city map • Hong Kong, Macau & Guangzhou • Japan • Japanese phrasebook • Japanese audio pack • Korea • Korean phrasebook • Kyoto • Mandarin phrasebook • Mongolia • Mongolian phrasebook • North-East Asia on a shoestring • Seoul • South-West China • Taiwan • Tibet • Tibetan phrasebook • Tokyo
Travel Literature: Lost Japan

SOUTH AMERICA Argentina, Uruguay & Paraguay • Bolivia • Brazil • Brazilian phrasebook • Buenos Aires • Chile & Easter Island • Chile & Easter Island travel atlas • Colombia • Ecuador & the Galapagos Islands • Latin American Spanish phrasebook • Peru • Quechua phrasebook • Rio de Janeiro • Rio de Janeiro city map • South America on a shoestring • Trekking in the Patagonian Andes • Venezuela
Travel Literature: Full Circle: A South American Journey

SOUTH-EAST ASIA Bali & Lombok • Bangkok • Bangkok city map • Burmese phrasebook • Cambodia • Hanoi • Healthy Travel Asia & India • Hill Tribes phrasebook • Ho Chi Minh City • Indonesia • Indonesia's Eastern Islands • Indonesian phrasebook • Indonesian audio pack • Jakarta • Java • Laos • Lao phrasebook • Laos travel atlas • Malay phrasebook • Malaysia, Singapore & Brunei • Myanmar (Burma) • Philippines • Pilipino (Tagalog) phrasebook • Singapore • South-East Asia on a shoestring • South-East Asia phrasebook • Thailand • Thailand's Islands & Beaches • Thailand travel atlas • Thai phrasebook • Thai audio pack • Vietnam • Vietnamese phrasebook • Vietnam travel atlas

ALSO AVAILABLE: Antarctica • The Arctic • Brief Encounters: Stories of Love, Sex & Travel • Chasing Rickshaws • Lonely Planet Unpacked • Not the Only Planet: Travel Stories from Science Fiction • Sacred India • Travel with Children • Traveller's Tales

Index

Bold indicates maps.

Bold indicates maps.

Bold indicates maps.

Bold indicates maps.

Boxed Text

MAP LEGEND

BOUNDARIES

- International
- State
- County

HYDROGRAPHY

- Water
- Coastline
- Beach
- River, Waterfall
- Swamp, Spring

ROUTES & TRANSPORT

- Freeway
- Toll Freeway
- Primary Road
- Secondary Road
- Tertiary Road
- Unpaved Road
- Pedestrian Mall
- Trail
- Walking Tour
- Ferry Route
- Railway, Train Station
- Mass Transit Line & Station

ROUTE SHIELDS

80 Interstate Freeway	1	California State Highway
101 US Highway	375	Nevada State Highway
USFS F7 US Forest Service Road	95	State Highway
MEX 2 Mexico Highway	G4	County Road

AREA FEATURES

- Building
- Cemetery
- Forest
- Golf Course
- Park
- Plaza
- Reservation

MAP SYMBOLS

- ✪ NATIONAL CAPITAL
- ◉ State, Provincial Capital
- ● LARGE CITY
- ● Medium City
- ● Small City
- ● Town, Village
- ○ Point of Interest

- ■ Place to Stay
- ▲ Campground
- ⊞ RV Park

- ▼ Place to Eat
- ▯ Bar (Place to Drink)
- ☕ Café

- ✝ Airfield
- ✈ Airport
- ⁂ Archaeological Site, Ruins
- ⑨ Bank
- ⬠ Baseball Diamond
- ▷ Beach
- ⁑ Border Crossing
- ⚊ Buddhist Temple
- ● Bus Depot, Bus Stop
- ♜ Castle
- ⛪ Cathedral
- ⌂ Cave
- ✝ Church
- ◆ Dive Site
- ⋈ Footbridge
- ✿ Fish Hatchery
- ❀ Garden
- ✚ Hospital, Clinic
- ❶ Information
- ⛩ Lighthouse
- ☀ Lookout

- ⛏ Mine
- ⛪ Mission
- ⚐ Monument
- ⛰ Mountain
- ⛨ Museum
- ☉ Observatory
- ← One-Way Street
- ♣ Park
- Ⓟ Parking
-)(Pass
- ⛱ Picnic Area
- ▭ Pool
- ✉ Post Office
- ✧ Shopping Mall
- ⚡ Skiing (Alpine)
- ⚡ Skiing (Nordic)
- ⛫ Stately Home
- ⚑ Surfing
- ⚐ Trailhead
- ⚘ Winery
- 🐾 Zoo

Note: Not all symbols displayed above appear in this book.

LONELY PLANET OFFICES

Australia
PO Box 617, Hawthorn 3122, Victoria
☎ 03 9819 1877 fax 03 9819 6459
email talk2us@lonelyplanet.com.au

USA
150 Linden Street, Oakland, California 94607
☎ 510 893 8555, TOLL FREE 800 275 8555
fax 510 893 8572
email info@lonelyplanet.com

UK
10A Spring Place, London NW5 3BH
☎ 020 7428 4800 fax 020 7428 4828
email go@lonelyplanet.co.uk

France
1 rue du Dahomey, 75011 Paris
☎ 01 55 25 33 00 fax 01 55 25 33 01
email bip@lonelyplanet.fr
www.lonelyplanet.fr

World Wide Web: www.lonelyplanet.com *or* AOL keyword: lp
Lonely Planet Images: lpi@lonelyplanet.com.au